MANAGEMENT

THIRD EDITION

RICHARD L. DAFT

VANDERBILT UNIVERSITY

THE DRYDEN PRESS

𝒟

HARCOURT BRACE COLLEGE PUBLISHERS

FORT WORTH   PHILADELPHIA   SAN DIEGO   NEW YORK   ORLANDO   AUSTIN   SAN ANTONIO
TORONTO   MONTREAL   LONDON   SYDNEY   TOKYO

MANAGEMENT

THIRD EDITION

Publisher:	Liz Widdicombe
Director of Editing, Design, and Production:	Diane Southworth
Acquisitions Editor:	Ruth Rominger
Developmental Editor:	Jan Richardson
Project Editor:	Cheryl Hauser
Designer:	Linda Miller
Production Manager:	Kelly Cordes
Marketing Manager:	Lisé Johnson
Permissions Editor:	Doris Milligan
Photo Researcher:	Nancy Moudry
Copy Editor:	JaNoel Lowe
Indexer:	Leoni McVey
Compositor:	GTS Graphics, Inc.
Text Type:	10/12 Palatino

Address for orders:
The Dryden Press
6277 Sea Harbor Drive
Orlando, FL 32887
1-800-782-4479 or 1-800-433-0001 (in Florida)

Address for editorial correspondence:
The Dryden Press
301 Commerce Street, Suite 3700
Fort Worth, TX 76102

ISBN: 0-03-097688-X

Library of Congress Catalog Card Number: 93-70506

Photo Credits appear on pages P-1–P-2, which constitute a continuation of the copyright page.

Printed in the United States of America

3 4 5 6 7 8 9 0 1 2   048   9 8 7 6 5 4 3 2 1

The Dryden Press
Harcourt Brace College Publishers

● THE DRYDEN PRESS SERIES
IN MANAGEMENT

Anthony, Perrewe, and Kacmar
Strategic Human Resource Management

Bartlett
Cases in Strategic Management for Business

Bedeian
Management
Third Edition

Bedeian and Zammuto
Organizations: Theory and Design

Bereman and Lengnick-Hall
*Compensation Decision Making: A
Computer-Based Approach*

Boone and Kurtz
Contemporary Business
Seventh Edition

Bowman and Branchaw
Business Report Writing
Second Edition

Bracker, Montanari, and Morgan
Cases in Strategic Management

Calvasina and Barton
Chopstick Company: A Business Simulation

Costin
Readings in Total Quality Management

Czinkota, Ronkainen, and Moffett
International Business
Third Edition

Daft
Management
Third Edition

Eckert, Ryan, and Ray
Small Business: An Entrepreneur's Plan
Third Edition

Etienne-Hamilton
*Operations Strategies for Competitive
Advantage: Text and Cases*

Foegen
Business Planning Guide
Second Edition

Gaither
Production and Operations Management
Sixth Edition

Gatewood and Harris
Human Resource Selection
Third Edition

Gold
*Exploring Organizational Behavior: A
Management Challenge Readings, Cases,
Experiences*

Greenhaus
Career Management
Second Edition

Harris and DeSimone
Human Resource Development

Higgins and Vincze
Strategic Management: Text and Cases
Fifth Edition

Hills, Bergmann, and Scarpello
Compensation Decision Making
Second Edition

Hodgetts
Management: Theory, Process, and Practice

Hodgetts
Modern Human Relations at Work
Fifth Edition

Hodgetts and Kroeck
Personnel and Human Resource Management

Hodgetts and Kuratko
Effective Small Business Management
Fourth Edition

Hodgetts and Kuratko
Management
Third Edition

Holley and Jennings
The Labor Relations Process
Fifth Edition

Huseman, Lahiff, and Penrose
*Business Communication: Strategies and
Skills*
Fourth Edition

Jauch and Coltrin
*The Managerial Experience: Cases and
Exercises*
Sixth Edition

Kemper
Experiencing Strategic Management

Kuehl and Lambing
Small Business: Planning and Management
Third Edition

Kuratko and Hodgetts
*Entrepreneurship: A Contemporary
Approach*
Second Edition

Kuratko and Welsch
Entrepreneurial Strategies: Text and Cases

Lewis
Io Enterprises Simulation

Luthans and Hodgetts
Business
Second Edition

McMullen and Long
*Developing New Ventures: The Entrepreneur-
ial Option*

Matsuura
International Business: A New Era

Mauser
American Business: An Introduction
Sixth Edition

Montanari, Morgan, and Bracker
Strategic Management: A Choice Approach

Northcraft and Neale
*Organizational Behavior: A Management
Challenge*
Second Edition

Penderghast
Entrepreneurial Simulation Program

Sandburg
Career Design Software

Sawyer
*Business Policy and Strategic Management:
Planning, Strategy, and Action*

Schoderbek
Management
Second Edition

Schwartz
*Introduction to Management: Principles,
Practices, and Processes*
Second Edition

Varner
Contemporary Business Report Writing
Second Edition

Vecchio
Organizational Behavior
Second Edition

Walton
*Corporate Encounters: Law, Ethics, and the
Business Environment*

Wolford and Vanneman
Business Communication

Wolters and Holley
*Labor Relations: An Experiential and Case
Approach*

Zikmund
Business Research Methods
Fourth Edition

● THE HARCOURT BRACE COLLEGE
OUTLINE SERIES

Pentico
Management Science

Pierson
Introduction to Business Information Systems

Sigband
Business Communication

● PREFACE

SHAPING MANAGEMENT FOR THE 21ST CENTURY

My vision for the third edition of *Management* is to create the best management textbook available, a book that is interesting and valuable to students and from which instructors can be proud to teach. To achieve this vision I have included the most recent management thinking and research as well as the contemporary application of management ideas in organizations. As in the previous editions, The Dryden Press and I worked together to provide a textbook better than any other for capturing the excitement and adventure of organizational management.

Any textbook is limited as a medium for teaching management. A textbook about management is like a music video of the Boston Pops Orchestra—the listener isn't really there and much of the music's impact is lost. Most management textbooks present rather crude portrayals of the management symphony because so little of the change, excitement, adventure, and reality of management gets through to the reader. I revised *Management* to provide a visual recording of utmost quality that will create in students both respect for the field of management and confidence that they can understand and master it.

The "audio" or textual portion of this book has been enhanced through the easy-to-understand writing style and the many in-text examples and boxed items that make the concepts realistic and relevant to students. The "visual" or graphic component has been enhanced with a new set of photo essays that illustrate specific management concepts. The photo essays make the text more interesting, and significantly expand the amount of insight and understanding available to students. The well-chosen photographs provide vivid illustrations and intimate glimpses of management scenes, events, and people. The photos are combined with brief written essays that explain how a specific management concept looks and feels. Both the audio and visual portions of the textbook help students grasp the often abstract and distant world of management.

The third edition of *Management* is especially focused on shaping the future of management education by identifying and describing emerging management trends. Major new materials include the following:

- A new Chapter 3 provides an educational grounding in *international issues* and events relevant to management. In addition, material on *global competition* has been added to several chapters.

- Material on the new trends toward *employee participation, empowerment,* and *horizontal coordination* has been expanded.

- Substantial new material on *total quality management* has been added to Chapter 18 on quality control and productivity.

- A new Chapter 13 on *managing diverse employees* has been added to explain the value of having organizations embrace all types of employees.

- An *organizational behavior* appendix has been added to increase the coverage of OB and to show students how OB concepts apply to them personally.

- Boxed items that apply concepts to not-for-profit organizations have been added to several chapters.

- The most recent thinking on *network, modular,* and *team-based organization structures* has been included.

- The importance of *teamwork* in organizations at all levels has been emphasized, and material added that deals with how to resolve conflict both within and between organizational teams.

- New material has been included on *social responsibility* and on management and the *natural environment.*

- Information has been expanded on recent technical issues, such as the impact of new *information systems* and *production technologies* on business strategy, the importance of *designing products for simplicity* in assembly and use, and *time-based competition.*

- New concepts such as *chaos theory* and *paradigm shifts* have been noted because they represent potential significant trends in the future.

In addition, Dryden has provided the resources necessary to bring together a team of experts to create and coordinate color photographs, video cases, beautiful artwork, and supplementary materials for the best management textbook and package on the market. Dryden has also provided new supplements for this edition that include a management career-oriented interactive computer program tied to exercises in the textbook and a laser disk that will have maximum learning impact on students.

ORGANIZATION

The chapter sequence in *Management* is organized around the management functions of planning, organizing, leading, and controlling. These four functions effectively encompass both management research and characteristics of the manager's job.

Part I introduces the world of management, including the nature of the manager's job, historical perspectives on management, and the influence of the larger environment on organizations and management including ethics and social responsibility. A new Chapter 3, "Managing in a Global Environment," has been added to this section to provide students with a fundamental understanding of international issues relevant to the remaining chapters in the text.

Part II presents four chapters on planning. The first chapters describe ethics and corporate responsibility, which play increasingly important roles in today's complex business environment. Subsequent chapters describe orgnizational goal setting and planning, strategy formulation and implementation, and the decision-making process.

Part III focuses on organizing processes. These chapters describe the dimensions of structural design, the design alternatives managers can use to achieve strategic objectives, structural designs for promoting innovation and change, and the design and use of the human resource function. A new Chapter 13 has been added to this section to describe how managing diverse employees is significant to the organizing function.

Part IV is devoted to leadership. This section begins with a description of leadership and paves the way for the subsequent topics of employee motivation, communication, and management of teams.

Part V describes the controlling function of management, including basic principles of total quality management, the design of control systems, management information systems, and techniques for control of operations management.

Part VI describes two significant management issues—entrepreneurship and career management. The entrepreneurship chapter describes basic concepts for launching and managing a new business. The career management chapter describes both individual and organizational strategies for managing careers, and it includes a substantial section on managing individual stress and burnout. The Management Career Design Software gives students individual skills assessment and career advice.

The appendixes include supplementary material on organizational behavior and management science aids for decision making. Appendix A, "Insights into Individual Behavior," provides material for instructors who like to expand the amount of OB used in the management course. Moreover, Appendix A shows students how concepts apply specifically to them, giving them a more intimate feeling for the concepts. Appendix B, "Management Science Aids for Planning and Decision Making," contains the quantitative material that many instructors use to expand on the more qualitative decision approaches described in Chapter 8. The quantitative approaches of linear programming, breakeven analyses, forecasting, PERT charting, and decision tree analysis are all covered in Appendix B.

SPECIAL FEATURES

One major goal of this book is to offer better ways of using the textbook medium to convey management knowledge to the reader. To this end, the book includes several special features.

VIDEO CASES.   One innovation in this edition is the inclusion of 23 video cases. A written case follows each chapter and is accompanied by a video for students to view in class. The videos enhance class discussion because students can see the company and more directly apply management concepts. A detailed description of each video, classroom introductions, video assignments, and discussion questions and answers are provided in the *Video Instructor's Manual.*

PHOTO ESSAYS.   Another innovative feature of the book is the use of photographs accompanied by detailed captions that describe management events and how they relate to chapter material. The photo essays cover a rich assortment of organizations and management events. While many of the photos are beautiful to look at, all of them convey the vividness, immediacy, and concreteness of management events.

CHAPTER OUTLINE AND OBJECTIVES.   Each chapter begins with a clear statement of learning objectives and an outline of its contents. These devices provide an overview of what is to come and can also be used by students to see whether they understand and have retained important points.

MANAGEMENT PROBLEM/SOLUTION.   The text portion of each chapter begins with a real-life problem faced by organization managers. The problem pertains to the topic of the chapter and will heighten students' interest in chapter concepts. The problem is resolved at the end of the chapter, where chapter concepts guiding the management's actions are highlighted.

CONTEMPORARY EXAMPLES.   Every chapter of the text contains a large number of written examples of management incidents. These are placed at strategic points in the chapter and are designed to demonstrate the application of concepts to specific companies. The examples include well-known companies such as Citibank, IBM, Hewlett-Packard, Toyota, Motorola, Procter & Gamble, General Motors, Coca-Cola, and Marriott, as well as less well-known companies and not-for-profit organizations such as Huffy Corporation, Tacoma Park Police Department, Columbia Gas Systems, Crane Plastics, Parsons Pine Products, Trinity Computing Systems, and Whisler Manufacturing. They put students in immediate touch with the real world of organizations so that they can appreciate the value of management concepts.

WINNING MOVES.   This boxed feature explores how companies, when faced with new challenges, use innovative ideas to compete in both the domestic and global marketplace.

MANAGER'S SHOPTALK.   These boxed items contain issues of special interest to management students. They may describe a contemporary topic or problem that is relevant to chapter content or may contain a diagnostic questionnaire or a special example of how managers handle a problem. These boxes will heighten student interest in the subject matter and provide an auxiliary view of management issues not typically available in textbooks.

NEW HORIZONS BOXES.   These boxed items highlight topics such as diversity, quality, and the natural environment. The vignettes presented offer students a look at issues that will affect businesses into the 21st century.

FOCUS BOXES.   These boxed items pertain to ethics, global competition, and entrepreneurship. Their purpose is to help students integrate these topics with other concepts in the book. Too often such topics are presented in separate, discrete chapters that have no connection with other materials. Yet concepts in almost every chapter have implications for ethics, global competition, and entrepreneurship. The focus boxes are referenced in the chapter to help students understand the relevance of the chapter material for these important management topics.

GLOSSARIES.   Learning the management vocabulary is essential to understanding contemporary management. This process is facilitated in three ways. First, key concepts are boldfaced and completely defined where they first appear in the text. Second, brief definitions are set out in the margin for easy review and follow-up. Third, a glossary summarizing all key terms and definitions appears at the end of the book for handy reference.

EXHIBITS.   Many aspects of management are research based, and some concepts tend to be abstract and theoretical. To enhance students' awareness and understanding of these concepts, many exhibits have been included throughout the book. These exhibits consolidate key points, indicate relationships among variables, and visually illustrate concepts. They also make effective use of color to enhance their imagery and appeal.

MANAGEMENT IN PRACTICE EXERCISES.   End-of-chapter exercises called either "Management in Practice: Experiential Exercise" or "Management in Practice: Ethical Dilemma" provide a self-test for students and an opportunity to experience management issues in a personal way. Many exercises also provide an opportunity for students to work in teams.

CHAPTER SUMMARY AND DISCUSSION QUESTIONS.   Each chapter closes with a summary of key points that students should retain. The discussion questions are a complementary learning tool that will enable students to check their understanding of key issues, to think beyond basic concepts, and to determine areas that require further study. The summary and discussion questions help students discriminate between main and supporting points and provide mechanisms for self-teaching.

CASES FOR ANALYSIS.   Two brief but substantive end-of-chapter cases provide an opportunity for student analysis and class discussion. Approximately half the cases are about companies whose names students will recognize. The others are based on real management events but disguise the identities of the companies and managers. These cases provide an opportunity for students to apply concepts to real events and to sharpen their diagnostic skills for management problem solving.

SUPPLEMENTARY MATERIALS

Dryden has once again spared no expense to make *Management* the premier textbook in the market today. Many instructors face large classes with limited resources, and supplementary materials provide a way to expand and improve the students' learning experience. The learning package provided with *Management* was specifically designed to meet the needs of instructors facing a variety of teaching conditions and to enhance management students' experience of the subject.

TEST BANKS.   The most important part of the teaching package is the *Test Bank*, which is why Dryden is offering two full test banks with this edition. *Test Banks A* and *B* were given special attention during the preparation of the third edition because instructors desire test questions that accurately and fairly assess student competence in subject material. Prepared by Jackie Jankovich, Colorado State University—Fort Collins, and John Hall, University of Florida, *Test Bank A* provides 2,500 multiple-choice, true/false, matching, and essay test items. New multiple-choice questions based on self-contained mini-cases are a great time-saving substitute for essay questions, combining the comprehensive testing of concepts and applications with the ease of an objective test. *Test Bank B*, created by Ken Anderson, Gonzaga University, and Dan McAlister, University of Nevada—Las Vegas, contains an additional 2,000 multiple-choice, true/false, and essay test items.

The test items have been reviewed and class tested to ensure the highest quality. Each question is keyed to chapter learning objectives, has been rated for level of difficulty, and is designated either as factual or application so that instructors can provide a balanced set of questions for student exams.

COMPUTERIZED TEST BANKS.   Both *Computerized Test Banks* are available for IBM and Macintosh computers and are free to adopters. The *Computerized Test Banks* allow instructors to select and edit test items from the printed *Test Banks* as well as add an unlimited number of their own questions. Up to 99 versions of each test can be custom printed.

INSTRUCTOR'S MANUAL.   A completely reorganized *Instructor's Manual* has been prepared to provide fundamental support to new professors teaching the course and innovative new materials for experienced professors. The manual features detailed "Lecture Outlines" that include additional information and examples not found in the text. "International Perspectives" provide additional international examples and material for each chapter with suggestions on where to integrate the information. "Class Starter" suggestions are included for each chapter, as well as a "Lecture Example File" that includes three to five additional management examples to integrate into class lectures.

The manual also contains annotated learning objectives, changes to the third edition, answers to chapter discussion questions, and teaching notes for the end-of-chapter experiential exercises, ethical incidents, and cases. Answers for the end-of-chapter video cases are also provided.

The *Instructor's Manual* was prepared by a talented pair of authors: Cliff Barbee of Houston Baptist University and Tom Jones of Southern Oregon State University.

COMPUTERIZED INSTRUCTOR'S MANUAL.   A disk will be available to instructors that contains most elements of the *Instructor's Manual*. Teachers can electronically cut and paste together the parts of the manual they desire for customized lecture outlines.

VIDEO INSTRUCTOR'S MANUAL.   This completely new manual contains video cases and teaching notes for each chapter of the text. It lists the title, running time, teaching objectives, and a detailed outline for each video case. It also provides page references for chapter concepts to be observed in the videos, video warm-ups, answers to case questions, video recap discussion questions, and coordinated experiential exercises for the videos. A multiple-choice test is also available for each video.

STUDY GUIDE.   This guide is invaluable for helping students master management concepts. Prepared by Stephen Hiatt, Catawba College, the *Study Guide* provides a summary and completion exercise for each chapter; a chapter review with multiple-choice, true/false, and short-answer questions; and a mini-case with multiple-choice questions. Each chapter also contains management applications and an experiential exercise that can be assigned as homework or used in class.

TRANSPARENCY MASTERS AND ACETATES.   More than 150 transparency masters from text art and 100 all-new color acetates are available to adopters. Masters and acetates are accompanied by detailed teaching notes that include summaries of key concepts and discussion questions for in-class use. The transparencies and teaching notes were developed by Jan Feldbauer, Austin Community College.

COMPUTER SIMULATION.   This management simulation, written by Eugene Calvasina of Auburn University at Montgomery, places students in the manager's role and requires them to make decisions about key areas of the business. This is an interactive simulation designed to offer students the opportunity to learn how decisions affect an organization.

SUPPLEMENTAL MODULES.   Supplemental written modules in the areas of diversity, quality, and the natural environment are available to augment text coverage and to address the needs of schools whose management principles courses emphasize any of these areas. The natural environment module is accompanied by a video program featuring various business responses to a concern for the environment.

MANAGEMENT TEACHING TIPS.   Dryden has gathered various teaching tips, cases, exercises, supplemental lecture topics, and more from instructors throughout the country to inspire creative teaching of management. In response to requests from principles instructors who wanted new ideas and to learn what their colleagues are doing to enhance the presentation of management concepts in the classroom, we offer this new and innovative supplement. The contributors have offered their successful approaches, and we would like to hear from others with more teaching ideas to include in the next edition of this supplement.

EXPERIENTIAL EXERCISES AND CASES. Two separate supplements are available for those instructors looking for additional experiential exercises or cases to use in the classroom. *Management: A Case Approach* and *Management: An Experiential Approach* are both authored by Lawrence R. Jauch and Sally A. Coltrin, and each is supported by an instructor's manual.

MANAGEMENT CAREER DESIGN SOFTWARE. This excellent student software by Eric Sandburg provides students with interactive exercises coordinated with each part of the text. It includes modules on such topics as decision making, leadership, delegation, ethics, diversity, sexual harassment, budgeting, entrepreneurship, and career planning. Exercises to accompany the software are found in the text at the end of each part. After completing one or more questionnaires or activities, students can use the software program to help measure their current level of awareness and capabilities and then obtain personalized advice for improving various options and skills.

MANAGEMENT QUARTERLY REPORT. Adopters may subscribe to a quarterly video series new to this edition from The Dryden Press. The video series will include recent news from the world of business. These quarterly segments can be used in the classroom to provide current examples of management principles at work.

LASER DISK. The Dryden Press is once again shaping management education by being the first publisher to offer a management laser disk. The disk includes graphic and textual elements from the textbook and support materials integrated with video and animation sequences to provide a dynamic, easy-to-use multimedia presentation of the principles of management.

● ACKNOWLEDGMENTS

A gratifying experience for me was working with the Fort Worth team of dedicated professionals at The Dryden Press who were committed to the vision of producing the best management text ever. I am grateful to Butch Gemin, whose enthusiasm and ideas kept the book's spirit alive, and to his successor, Ruth Rominger, for her creative ideas, assistance, and vision for this text. Lisé Johnson provided keen market knowledge and innovative ideas for instructional support. Jan Richardson did an extraordinary job of critiquing the materials and chapter pedagogy. Linda Miller created a rich and elegant book design. Doris Milligan pursued permissions with her usual enthusiasm. JaNoel Lowe provided the right touch of copyediting. Nancy Moudry once again researched the photo essays, bringing her gift of finding the perfect photographs to illustrate conceptual materials in a way that significantly enhances student learning. Kelly Cordes coordinated the production team. Cheryl Hauser provided superb project coordination and made excellent suggestions to overcome obstacles and keep the project moving on schedule. These people brought enormous caring and commitment to this textbook, and I thank each of you very much.

Two other people who made a special contribution to this textbook are Susan Halfhill and Anne London. Susan Halfhill drafted materials for Appendix A, based on her teaching experience at California State University, Fresno. The expansion of organizational behavior concepts and application to individual students is a significant addition to this edition. Anne London cowrote the diversity module that accompanied the second edition of *Management*. Anne did a superb job, and that material became the foundation for Chapter 13, "Managing Diverse Employees," in this edition.

Here at Vanderbilt I want to extend special appreciation to Rita Carswell. Rita helped me make the transition to Vanderbilt, and we have worked together almost four years now. Without her typing, administrative assistance, and friendship this book could not have been completed. Donna Zavada, my research assistant, made one fast trip to the library after another to find an article or reference when I needed it most. I also want to acknowledge an intellectual debt to my colleagues, Bruce Barry and Tom Mahoney. Thanks also to Dean Marty Geisel who supported this project and maintained a positive scholarly atmosphere here at the Owen School.

Another group of people who made a major contribution to this textbook were the management experts who provided advice, reviews, answers to questions, and suggestions for changes, insertions, and clarifications. I want to thank each of these colleagues for their valuable feedback and suggestions:

Larry Aaronson
Catonsville Community College

Royce Abrahamson
Southwest Texas State University

Robert J. Ash
Rancho Santiago College

Hal Babson
Columbus State Community College

Robert W. Baker
Metro Community College

McRae C. Banks II
Mississippi State University

Allen Bluedorn
University of Missouri—Columbia

Peggy Brewer
Eastern Kentucky University

Eugene Calvasina
Auburn University at Montgomery

Thomas Carey
Western Michigan University

James Cashman
University of Alabama

Herchel Chait
Indiana State University

Sharon Clinebell
University of Northern Colorado

Daniel S. Cochran
Mississippi State University

Raymond L. Cook
University of Texas—Austin

Roy A. Cook
Fort Lewis College

Richard Cuba
University of Baltimore

Michael Czinkota
Georgetown University

Dr. Tammy Davis
Indiana State University

L. A. Digman
University of Nebraska

Vernon Dorweiler
Michigan Technological School of Business

John W. Eastman
Kent State University
Tom Edwards
York Technical College
Judson Faurer
Metro State College
Janice M. Feldbauer
Austin Community College
William Fitzpatrick
Villanova University
Charles Flaherty
University of Minnesota
Steven W. Floyd
University of Massachusetts
Patricia A. Greenfield
University of Massachusetts
Allen Gulezian
Central Washington University
Fred C. House
Northern Arizona University
Charles W. Hubbard
Southwest Texas State University
Edmund Hunter
Delaware County Community College
Robert Insley
University of North Texas
Jackie Lynn Jankovich
Colorado State University
William Jedlicka
*William Rainey Harper Community
College*

Bradley R. Johnson
University of Nebraska at Omaha
R. Sitk. Karahan
Montana State University
Alan Kardoff
University of Wisconsin—Superior
Ronald A. Klocke
Mankato State University
Dale Konicek
Houston Community College
Allan Levy
Macomb Community College
Don Lytle
University of Oregon
Albert H. Mahrer
Front Range Community College
Robert Marx
University of Massachusetts
Daniel McAllister
University of Nevada—Las Vegas
Bruce Meglino
University of South Carolina
Carolyn Patton Nickeson
Del Mar College
Leah R. Pietron
University of Nebraska at Omaha
Clinton H. Richards
University of Nevada—Las Vegas
Jane Preston Rose
Hiram College

Richard Saavedra
University of Minnesota
Nick Sarantakes
Austin Community College
Karen Schenkenfelder
Oak Park, Illinois
Jane Seibler
Oregon State University
S. R. Siegel
Drexel University
Ray Sifrit
Del Mar College
James O. Smith
East Carolina University
Leon L. Smith
University of North Alabama
William Soukup
University of San Diego
Martin St. John
Westmoreland City Community College
Richard L. Sutton
University of Nevada—Las Vegas
John Todd
University of Arkansas
Linda Trevino
Pennsylvania State University
Trudy Verser
Western Michigan University
Stephen I. Winter
Orange County Community College

The support package for the third edition benefited from the valuable input of management instructors throughout the country. I would like to especially thank those who responded to our questions about how they teach management:

Nadine P. Almasy
Eastern Nazarene College
Gail R. Athas
Notre Dame College
Dorman C. Batson
Montreat-Anderson
Ellis G. Buchanan
University of Texas at San Antonio
Richard T. Christoph
James Madison University
Timothy Donahue
Sioux Falls College
Patrick Gordon
Pratt Community College
R. Johe
Salem College

Randall S. Kingsbury
Augustana College
Peter Kirby
Our Lady of the Lake College
Ronald A. Klocke
Mankato State University
Rickey H. Madden
Erskine College
Paul D. Maxwell
Bridgewater State College
Gene Murkison
Georgia Southern University
John Murray
Massasoit Community College
Daniel McAllister
University of Nevada—Las Vegas

Tony Ortega
California State University, Bakersfield
Clinton Richards
University of Nevada—Las Vegas
Al Rosenbloom
Lewis University
Martin St. John
Westmoreland City Community College
Jiaqin Yang
University of North Dakota
John Zhuang Yang
Fordham University

I also want to acknowledge those people who contributed to the first edition, because their impact is still felt in the third edition.

Michael Abelson
Texas A&M University
Paul Babrowski
University of Oregon
Jay Barney
Texas A&M University
Gerald Bassford
Arizona State University
Bruce Blaylock
Eastern Kentucky University
Art Bell
University of Southern California
Van Clouse
University of Louisville
Richard Cuba
University of Baltimore
Barbara Deaux
Santa Fe State University
Fran Emory
Northern Virginia Community College—Woodbridge
J. E. Estes
University of South Carolina
Phyllis Fowler
Macomb Community College
Jeff Heyl
University of Colorado at Denver

Jim Higgins
Rollins College
Chuck Kuehl
University of Missouri at St. Louis
Peggy Lambing
University of Missouri at St. Louis
Janina Latack
Ohio State University
Marcia Miceli
Ohio State University
Thomas Miller
Memphis State University
Van Miller
Baylor University
Marilyn Morgan
University of Virginia
David Nagao
Georgia Tech University
Glen Oddou
San Jose State University
Nikki Paahana
DeVry Institute of Technology
Floyd Paulk
Central State University
Carole Saunders
Texas Christian University

Charles Shrader
Iowa State University
Susan Smith
Central Michigan University
William Smith
Hofstra University
Robert Sullivan
University of Texas—Austin
Eugene Szwajkowski
University of Illinois at Chicago
Mary Thibodeaux
University of North Texas
David Van Fleet
Texas A&M University
Jim Weekly
University of Toledo
Lewis Welshofer
Miami of Ohio University
Daniel Wren
University of Oklahoma
Marlin C. Young
Southwest Texas State University

I would like to extend a personal word of thanks to the many dedicated authors who contributed to the extensive supplement package for the third edition. John Hall, Jackie Jankovich, Ken Anderson, and Dan McAlister have written wonderful *Test Banks*. Cliff Barbee and Tom Jones have made the *Instructor's Manual* a valuable teaching tool with innovative new features. Stephen Hiatt has worked hard to ensure that the *Study Guide* reflects the chapter material in the textbook. Eric Sandburg has added tremendous career assessment opportunities for students with his *Management Career Software*. Jan Feldbauer enhanced the teachability of the *Teaching Acetates and Transparency Masters* with instructive notes.

I also want to acknowledge my daughters, Danielle and Amy, and their husbands, Brian and Gary, for their love and support this past year. We don't live in the same city, but we have developed a wonderful understanding and appreciation for one another, reached in part through the joy of skiing together. Thanks also to B. J. and Kaitlyn for their warmth, silliness and laughter that brightens my life during our days together.

Finally, I'd like to pay special tribute to my at-home assistants, Chris Atcher and DeeGee Lester. Chris came to work to see whether added structure and assistance could add quality time to my life. Because of her hard work, superb organization, and willingness to confront me on difficult issues, I gained personal and professional insights that provided both free time and enhanced quality of life. At Chris's recommendation, DeeGee was hired, who triggered another step forward for me. DeeGee brought her innate enthusiasm and sense of humor, along with a professor's eye and a student's ear, to the revision of this text. She provided ideas, dug out sources, drafted a variety of examples and boxed items, and provided enormous assistance in wading through the copyedited manuscript, galley proofs, and ancillary materials. I wouldn't have believed that one person could provide so much assistance and also invite me over for holiday meals. My friendships with Chris and DeeGee are an important part of my life, and I could not have achieved the high level of excellence in the third edition without them.

RICHARD L. DAFT
Nashville, Tennessee
August 1993

● ABOUT THE AUTHOR

Richard L. Daft, Ph.D., holds the Ralph Owen Chair in Management at Vanderbilt University, where he specializes in the study of organization theory and management. Dr. Daft is a Fellow of the Academy of Management and has served on the editorial boards of *Academy of Management Journal*, *Administrative Science Quarterly*, and *Journal of Management Education*. He is the Associate Editor-in-Chief of *Organization Science* and served for three years as associate editor of *Administrative Science Quarterly*.

Professor Daft has authored or co-authored six books including *Organization Theory and Design* (West Publishing, 1992) and *What to Study: Generating and Developing Research Questions* (Sage, 1982). He has also authored dozens of scholarly articles, papers, and chapters. His work has been published in *Administrative Science Quarterly*, *Academy of Management Journal*, *Academy of Management Review*, *Strategic Management Journal*, *Journal of Management*, *Accounting Organizations and Society*, *Management Science*, *MIS Quarterly*, *California Management Review*, and *Organizational Behavior Teaching Review*. Professor Daft has been awarded several government research grants to pursue studies of organization design, organizational innovation and change, strategy implementation, and organizational information processing.

Dr. Daft also is an active teacher and consultant. He has taught management, organizational change, organizational behavior, organizational theory, and leadership. He has been actively involved in management development and consulting for many companies and government organizations including the American Banking Association, Bell Canada, NL Baroid, Tenneco, and the United States Air Force.

BRIEF CONTENTS

CONTENTS

PART I
INTRODUCTION TO
MANAGEMENT   3

WINNING MOVES
Garth Brooks and the Grateful Dead

FOCUS ON DIVERSITY
Do Women Manage Differently?

NEW HORIZONS . . . ETHICS
"If It's Hootin', I'm Shootin'"

FOCUS ON GLOBAL COMPETITION
American Teachings for Japan

MANAGER'S SHOPTALK
*Ebbs and Flows of Management
Innovations, 1950–1992*

EXAMPLES
UNITED PARCEL SERVICE
SATURN CORPORATION
ALCAN ALUMINUM LTD.
PEPSICO, INC.

MANAGER'S SHOPTALK
Buy American!

NEW HORIZONS . . . DIVERSITY
Wanted: Global Managers

EXAMPLE
Citibank

FOCUS ON NOT-FOR-PROFIT
Unions on the Ropes?

MANAGER'S SHOPTALK
Keeping Culture Strong

EXAMPLES
Northern Telecom Ltd.
Wal-Mart

● CHAPTER 5
MANAGERIAL ETHICS AND CORPORATE SOCIAL
RESPONSIBILITY   148

● CHAPTER 6
ORGANIZATIONAL GOAL SETTING AND
PLANNING   182

PART II
PLANNING   147

FOCUS ON ETHICS
AIDS in the Workplace

MANAGER'S SHOPTALK
Guidelines for Ethical Decision Making

NEW HORIZONS . . . THE NATURAL ENVIRONMENT
The Global Green Movement

EXAMPLES
BROWN & WILLIAMSON
BEECH-NUT NUTRITION
   CORPORATION
CATERPILLAR, INC.

WINNING MOVES
Timex

FOCUS ON ETHICS
Sexual Harassment Policies

EXAMPLES
MADISON, WISCONSIN, CITY HALL
PRODUCERS GAS AND
   TRANSMISSION
TOYOTA
H. J. HEINZ COMPANY

NEW HORIZONS . . . GLOBAL COMPETITON
Partnership Strategies

WINNING MOVES
Goodbye, Goldome—Hello, Hanover

EXAMPLES
MORTON INTERNATIONAL, INC.
GILLETTE COMPANY
H. J. HEINZ COMPANY

FOCUS ON ENTREPRENEURSHIP
Risky Business, Big Rewards

MANAGER'S SHOPTALK
Decision Biases to Avoid

EXAMPLES
WARNER BROTHERS
CHRYSLER CORPORATION
COCA-COLA COMPANY
KO-REC-TYPE

PART III
ORGANIZING   287

MANAGER'S SHOPTALK
How to Delegate

FOCUS ON GLOBAL COMPETITION
The Global Matrix Manager

MANAGER'S SHOPTALK
The Modular Corporation

EXAMPLES
CRANE PLASTICS, INC.
AID ASSOCIATION FOR LUTHERANS

WINNING MOVES
Snap-on Tools Corporation

FOCUS ON NOT-FOR-PROFIT
Government That Means Business

MANAGER'S SHOPTALK
Restructuring by Downsizing

EXAMPLES
POLAROID
IBM
MARRIOTT CORPORATION

WINNING MOVES
Not-for-Profit Innovation in the Takoma Park Police Department

NEW HORIZONS . . . GLOBAL
COMPETITION
Motorola, Inc.

MANAGER'S SHOPTALK
The Virtual Corporation: Wave of the Future?

EXAMPLES
NAVISTAR INTERNATIONAL
HONEYWELL CORPORATION

MANAGER'S SHOPTALK
The Right Way to Interview a Job Applicant

FOCUS ON . . . ETHICS
Xerox Corporation

EXAMPLES
EDS
TOYOTA MOTOR CORPORATION

NEW HORIZONS . . . ETHICS
Office Romance

NEW HORIZONS . . . GLOBAL COMPETITION
Global Diversity

EXAMPLES
KINNEY SHOES
MONSANTO COMPANY

PART IV
LEADERSHIP 475

MANAGER'S SHOPTALK
Are You a Leader?

WINNING MOVES
H. Ross Perot, Charismatic Leader

EXAMPLES
CHICK-FIL-A, INC.
U.S. POSTAL SERVICE
McARTHUR-GLEN GROUP

FOCUS ON GLOBAL COMPETITION
Motivation in Russia

WINNING MOVES
Springfield Remanufacturing: Employees Are Owners Too

EXAMPLES
YSI, INC.
NUCOR CORPORATION
SOLAR PRESS, INC.
PARSONS PINE PRODUCTS
TRAVELER'S INSURANCE COMPANY

WINNING MOVES
Boise Cascade Managers Listen

EXAMPLES
ITT
HYATT HOTELS

MANAGER'S SHOPTALK
How to Run a Great Meeting

FOCUS ON ENTREPRENEURSHIP
Teamwork at Whole Foods Market

EXAMPLES
GM's SATURN PLANT
HONEYWELL
SALVO, INC.

**PART V
CONTROL   619**

FOCUS ON ETHICS
Is Your Boss "Bugging" You?

MANAGER'S SHOPTALK
*The Malcolm Baldrige National
Quality Award*

EXAMPLES
MARQUETTE ELECTRONICS
FLORIDA POWER & LIGHT
FRITO-LAY

● CHAPTER 19
MANAGEMENT CONTROL SYSTEMS   654

WINNING MOVES
No Taste for Waste

EXAMPLES
GRANITE ROCK COMPANY
INCOMNET
TRINITY COMPUTING SYSTEMS
THRIFTY SCOTT WAREHOUSE FOOD

● CHAPTER 20
INFORMATION SYSTEMS FOR
MANAGEMENT   682

NEW HORIZONS . . . DIVERSITY
Telecommuting and the Family

MANAGER'S SHOPTALK
An Information Revolution

EXAMPLES
GROMER SUPERMARKET, INC.
AMERICAN HOSPITAL SUPPLY
CORPORATION

● CHAPTER 21
OPERATIONS AND SERVICE
MANAGEMENT   712

MANAGER'S SHOPTALK
Simplify, Stupid!

MANAGER'S SHOPTALK
Productivity or Customer Service?

EXAMPLES
FORD MOTOR COMPANY
COLEMAN COMPANY

**PART VI
EMERGING
MANAGEMENT
ISSUES   751**

**NEW HORIZONS . . . NATURAL
ENVIRONMENT**
Opportunities for Entrepreneurs

WINNING MOVES
*Frieda's Finest Brings Exotic Fare to
U.S. Groceries*

MANAGER'S SHOPTALK
Hint's for Writing the Business Plan

● CHAPTER 22
ENTREPRENEURSHIP AND SMALL BUSINESS
MANAGEMENT   752

● CHAPTER 23
CAREER MANAGEMENT   784

● APPENDIX A
INSIGHTS INTO INDIVIDUAL BEHAVIOR   A-1

● APPENDIX B
MANAGEMENT SCIENCE AIDS FOR PLANNING
AND DECISION MAKING   A-21

MANAGEMENT

THIRD EDITION

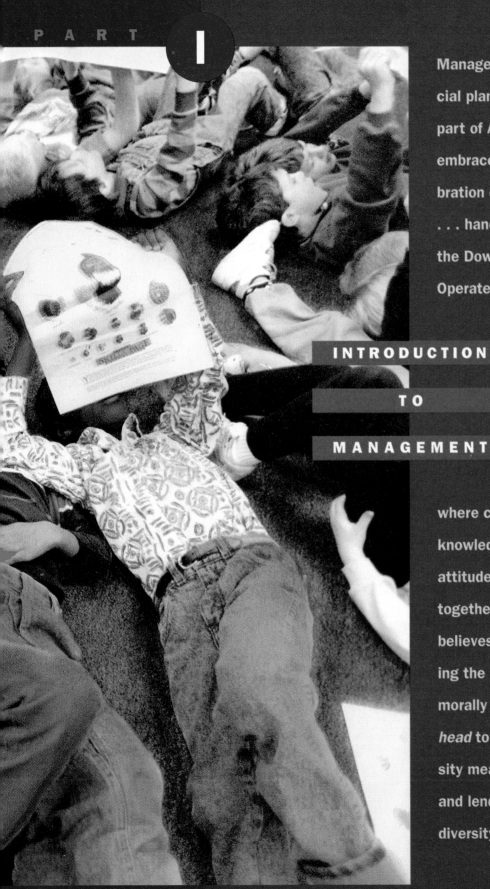

PART I

INTRODUCTION TO MANAGEMENT

Management at IDS, a financial planning company and part of American Express, embraces diversity as a celebration of "hearts . . . heads . . . hands." IDS co-sponsors the Downtown Open School. Operated by Minneapolis Public Schools, this child-centered, bilingual (English and Spanish) school offers free classes where children acquire the knowledge, skills, and positive attitudes to solve problems together. IDS management believes "Diversity means having the *heart* to do what's morally correct . . . using your *head* to recognize that diversity means good business . . . and lending a *hand* to make diversity happen."

THE NATURE OF MANAGEMENT

1 CHAPTER

No city slicker, Lucie Fjeldstad grew up milking cows and driving a tractor on a cattle ranch before establishing a management reputation in her rise up the corporate ranks at IBM. The first woman ever in charge of the 900-engineer development laboratory, she was later promoted to head *eight* development divisions. Fjeldstad made her mark by achieving development goals while cutting personnel by 25 percent. Facing her greatest challenge, Fjeldstad has now been promoted to general manager of IBM's multimedia business, a $100

million venture that represents the future marriage of PCs with home television and consumer electronics. A multimedia personal computer could order and store a range of movies, CD music, and periodicals. Rival

Sony, for example, has big film and record libraries to link up with home computers built by IBM's competitors. Starting from nothing, Fjeldstad's huge management challenge is to make multimedia the next major business at IBM. This management challenge involves shifting Big Blue away from business customers, developing new retail channels, and reducing IBM's traditional high-cost production. For these tasks, Fjeldstad will need enormous management skill.[1] ■ If you were in Fjeldstad's position, how would you proceed? What management techniques would you use to create a new business division for IBM?

M A N A G E M E N T   P R O B L E M

Few students have heard of Lucie Fjeldstad or IBM's multimedia division. Most are unfamiliar with the management actions needed to create a division that is thriving, inspired, and productive. The management problem at IBM represents a situation that is repeated daily for managers in hundreds of organizations. Successful departments and successful organizations do not just happen—they are managed to be that way. Every organization has problems and challenges, and every organization needs skilled management.

Managers like Lucie Fjeldstad have the opportunity to make a difference. Lee Iacocca made a difference at Chrysler Corporation when he rescued it from bankruptcy by reducing internal costs, developing new products, and gaining concessions from lenders, the union, and government. Iacocca transformed Chrysler again by implementing a strategy for developing a new generation of LH cars that appeared beginning 1993.[2] General William Creech made a difference to the huge Tactical Air Command of the U.S. Air Force when he reversed a sortie rate (number of flights flown with tactical aircraft) that had been declining 7.8 percent a year. Within a year of his appointment as TAC commander, the sortie rate increased 11.2 percent and continued to rise at that rate for five years with no additional

CEO Linda Wachner's enthusiastic management style has *made a difference* at Warnaco. This once quiet apparel maker is now a Fortune 500 company. Wachner's "Do It Now!" philosophy begins at the top and energizes the entire work force. The CEO seems to be everywhere—from stitchroom to showroom—giving Warnaco a competitive edge in the traditionally tough apparel markets.

people or resources. Kelly Johnson made a difference to an ailing satellite program at Lockheed. Launch effectiveness had been running 12.5 percent, was way behind schedule and over budget, and, as Johnson discovered, one subcontractor was using an astronomical 1,271 inspectors. Within a year, Johnson had the program back on schedule, improved launch effectiveness to 98 percent, and reduced the number of inspectors to 35.[3] On the international level, Nobuhiko Kawamoto, the new president of Honda, made a difference by shaking up the legendary Honda organization. His drastic reorganization included a move away from the traditional Japanese decision making by consensus. Early results indicate his changes have provided significant gains in efficiency via improved communications and speedier decision making throughout the company's 38-country manufacturing empire.[4]

These managers are not unusual. Every day managers solve difficult problems, turn organizations around, and achieve astonishing performances. Every organization needs skilled managers to be successful. And managers can make a difference in a negative direction too. Poor judgment, personal vanity, or greed can cause corporate disaster. For example, Harding Lawrence of Braniff Airlines was responsible for a misguided strategy of rapid national and international expansion, and he alienated executives and employees with his domineering, bullying behavior. His influence launched Braniff on a flight path to bankruptcy.[5] Robert Fomon gained absolute power at E. F. Hutton. Acting like a feudal lord, he banished traditional organization structure, budgets, and planning, thereby initiating the lingering death of an old-line brokerage firm.[6] In another case, Robert Schoellhorn guided Abbott Laboratories to unprecedented profits, and then became obsessed with rewarding himself for company success. He accumulated money and hefty perks, including pricey "his-and-her" corporate jets used only by Schoellhorn and his wife. His self-serving behavior had sufficient negative impact that the board of directors had to let him go.[7]

This book introduces and explains the process of management. By analyzing examples of successful and not-so-successful managers and reviewing studies of management techniques and styles, you will learn the fundamentals of management. The problems Fjeldstad faces with the multimedia division at IBM are not unusual for middle managers. By the end of this chapter, you will already understand the approach Fjeldstad must take to get her division on track. By the end of this book, you will understand fundamental management skills for planning, organization, leading, and controlling a department or an entire organization. In the remainder of this chapter, we will define management and look at the roles and activities of managers in today's organizations.

● THE DEFINITION OF MANAGEMENT

What do managers like Lee Iacocca, General Creech, and Lucie Fjeldstad have in common? They get things done through their organizations. One management scholar, Mary Parker Follett, described management as "the art of getting things done through people."[8]

Peter Drucker, a noted management theorist, explains that managers give direction to their organizations, provide leadership, and decide how to use organizational resources to accomplish goals.[9] Getting things done through people and other resources and providing direction and leadership are what managers do. These activities apply not only to top executives such as Lee Iacocca or General Creech, but also to a new lieutenant in charge of a TAC maintenance squadron, a supervisor in the Ontario plant that makes Plymouth minivans, and Lucie Fjeldstad as multimedia manager at IBM. Moreover, management often is considered universal because it uses organizational resources to accomplish goals and attain high performance in all types of profit and not-for-profit organizations. Thus, our definition of management is as follows:

management

The attainment of organizational goals in an effective and efficient manner through planning, organizing, leading, and controlling organizational resources.

> **Management** is the attainment of organizational goals in an effective and efficient manner through planning, organizing, leading, and controlling organizational resources.

There are two important ideas in this definition: (1) the four functions of planning, organizing, leading, and controlling and (2) the attainment of organizational goals in an effective and efficient manner. The management process of using resources to attain goals is illustrated in Exhibit 1.1. Although some management theorists identify additional management functions, such as staffing, communicating, or decision making, those additional functions will be discussed as subsets of the four primary functions in Exhibit 1.1. Chapters of this book are devoted to the multiple activities and skills associated with each function, as well as to the environment, global competitiveness, and ethics, which influence how managers perform these functions. The next section begins with a brief overview of the four functions.

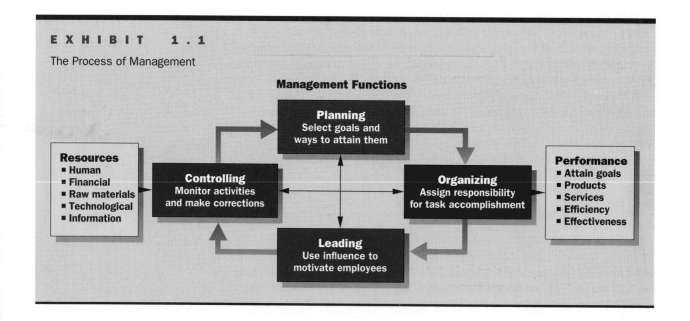

EXHIBIT 1.1

The Process of Management

Management Functions

Resources
- Human
- Financial
- Raw materials
- Technological
- Information

Planning
Select goals and ways to attain them

Organizing
Assign responsibility for task accomplishment

Leading
Use influence to motivate employees

Controlling
Monitor activities and make corrections

Performance
- Attain goals
- Products
- Services
- Efficiency
- Effectiveness

● THE FOUR MANAGEMENT FUNCTIONS

PLANNING

Planning defines where the organization wants to be in the future and how to get there. **Planning** means defining goals for future organizational performance and deciding on the tasks and use of resources needed to attain them. Senior managers at Bausch & Lomb defined a specific plan: to capture at least 50 percent of every segment of the contact lens market even if prices had to be cut and profits reduced to maintain market share. Senior managers at Chase Manhattan Bank decided to make it the number-one service-quality bank in the world and, through extensive planning, to develop a worldwide network of branch banks, implement a sophisticated foreign exchange system, and offer a state-of-the art electronic funds transfer system. General Creech successfully turned around the Tactical Air Command because he had a specific plan including targets for improved sortie rates and techniques for achieving the new rates.

A lack of planning—or poor planning—can hurt an organization's performance. For example, Ashton-Tate Corporation, a PC software giant ranked in the big three of the industry, tumbled sharply as a result of planning errors attributed to chief executive Edward Esber, Jr. Critics cite Esber's lack of vision in perceiving market direction and a weak planning effort that left too many bugs in the dBASEV software introduction along with failed efforts to develop other software products. Planning is a major reason for the sharp decline in Ashton-Tate's market share and revenue growth rate, producing the company's first net loss of $30 million.[10]

planning
The management function concerned with defining goals for future organizational performance and deciding on the tasks and resource use needed to attain them.

ORGANIZING

Organizing typically follows planning and reflects how the organization tries to accomplish the plan. **Organizing** involves the assignment of tasks, the grouping of tasks into departments, and the allocation of resources to departments. For example, Hewlett-Packard, Sears Roebuck, Xerox, and Digital Equipment have all undergone structural reorganizations to accommodate their changing plans. General Creech accomplished his plan for TAC's improved sortie rate largely through decentralization and the development of small, independent maintenance units—a drastic departure from the traditional structure that had encouraged centralization and consolidation of Air Force resources. Kelly Johnson used organizing wizardry at Lockheed to reduce the number of subcontractor inspectors from 1,271 to 35 and still achieve the objective of improved launch effectiveness. Indeed, his organizing was so good that the Air Force insisted that a competitor be allowed to visit Johnson's team. The competitor used 3,750 people to perform a similar task and was years behind and way over budget. Johnson's organization was on schedule and under budget—and with only 126 people.[11] Honeywell managers reorganized new product development into "tiger teams" consisting of marketing, engineering, and

organizing
The management function concerned with assigning tasks, grouping tasks into departments, and allocating resources to departments.

design employees. The new structural design reduced the time to produce a new thermostat from 4 years to 12 months.[12] Many companies today are following Honeywell's lead by using teams that have more responsibility for self-management. Indeed, reorganizing into teams is a major trend in North America.

Likewise, weak organizing facilitated the destruction of Braniff Airlines under Harding Lawrence. Braniff did not have enough departments and offices to handle passengers and airplanes for the new national and international routes Lawrence grabbed during deregulation of the airline industry. Braniff needed an enormous amount of money to set up a structure to fit its strategy. Even before its expansion Braniff lacked a strong internal structure with clearly defined roles for accomplishing tasks. The structure produced a group of "yes men" who deferred to Lawrence's every decision.[13]

LEADING

leading

The management function that involves the use of influence to motivate employees to achieve the organization's goals.

The third management function is to provide leadership for employees. **Leading** is the use of influence to motivate employees to achieve organizational goals. Leading means communicating goals to employees throughout the organization and infusing them with the desire to perform at a high level. Leading involves motivating entire departments and divisions as well as those individuals working immediately with the manager.

Managers such as Lee Iacocca are exceptional leaders. They are able to communicate their vision throughout the organization and energize employees into action. General Creech was a leader when he improved the motivation of aircraft maintenance technicians in hundreds of maintenance squadrons. Maintenance people previously had been neglected in favor of pilots. Creech set up highly visible bulletin boards displaying pictures of the maintenance crew chiefs, improved their living quarters, and established decent maintenance facilities, complete with paintings and wall murals. He introduced competition among the newly independent maintenance squadrons. He created trophy rooms to hold plaques and other prizes won in maintenance competitions. This prominent display of concern for maintenance specialists greatly increased their motivation to keep the planes flying.

When current Maryland governor William Donald Schaefer was mayor of Baltimore, he saw a city of dirty parks, housing violations, abandoned cars, dead trees, and uncollected trash. Schaefer involved citizens in a local ownership program that helped to pay for and maintain city services. More importantly, he motivated city workers to clean up the mess through a number of techniques including action memos that were blunt and direct: "Get the trash off East Lombard Street," "Broken pavement at 1700 Carey," "Abandoned car at 2900 Remington." One action memo said, "There is an abandoned car . . . but I'm not telling you where it is." City crews ran around for a week and towed several hundred cars.[14]

Leadership has a negative side, too. Again consider Harding Lawrence. His leadership of Braniff was said to contribute to employees' *demotivation.*

How do managers *lead* employees to go beyond the norm? One way is by acknowledging employee efforts. At Compaq Computer Corporation, manufacturing managers Doug Johns and Greg Petsch arranged a rousing parade throughout the plant, complete with bagpipe band and signs of personal thanks from Johns and Petsch, for a job well done.

Lawrence won notoriety on Braniff's Flight 6, which he took weekly to visit his wife, who worked in New York City:

> His tantrums on Flight 6 are legend. On one flight a stewardess served him an entire selection of condiments with his meal instead of asking him which one he preferred. He slammed his fist into the plate, splattering food on the surrounding seats of the first-class cabin. "Don't you ever assume what I want!" he screamed.
>
> "On several occasions flight attendants came to me in tears, fearful of losing their jobs," says Ed Clements, former director of flight attendant services at Braniff. "I was sickened by what he was doing to the employees."
>
> Lawrence's appearance on an aircraft was likely to arouse two emotions in the crew: fear and hatred.[15]

Inevitably, dissatisfied employees led to dissatisfied customers. Marketing surveys indicated that Braniff was unpopular with many of its passengers. Without a loyal customer base, successful expansion and high performance proved impossible.[16]

CONTROLLING

controlling

The management function concerned with monitoring employees' activities, keeping the organization on track toward its goals, and making corrections as needed.

Controlling is the fourth function in the management process. **Controlling means monitoring employees' activities, determining whether the organization is on target toward its goals, and making corrections as necessary.** Managers must ensure that the organization is moving toward its goals. Controlling often involves using an information system to advise managers on performance and a reward system for recognizing employees who make progress toward goals. For example, at Domino's Pizza Distribution Company over 1,200 franchises are measured weekly. A phone survey of customers determines the quality of service at each franchise, which is reported to management. Compensation for all employees is based on the results. Expected performance levels are reviewed every six months and set slightly higher for the next six months. The control system then monitors whether employees achieve the higher targets.

One reason for organization failure is that managers are not serious about control or lack control information. Robert Fomon, longtime autocratic chief executive of E. F. Hutton, refused to set up control systems because he wanted to supervise senior management personally. At one time he reviewed the salaries and bonuses of more than 1,000 employees, but Hutton grew too big for his personal supervision. To achieve profit goals managers got involved in an undetected check-kiting scheme, and the firm pleaded guilty to 2,000 counts of mail and wire fraud. Other undetected behaviors were the $900,000 in travel and entertainment expenses for one executive in one year and the listing of women from escort services as temporary secretarial help. The lack of control led to Fomon's demise. E. F. Hutton never fully recovered.[17]

● ORGANIZATIONAL PERFORMANCE

The other part of our definition of management is the attainment of organizational goals in an efficient and effective manner. One reason management is so important is that organizations are so important. In an industrialized society where complex technologies dominate, organizations bring together knowledge, people, and raw materials to perform tasks no individual could do alone. Without organizations how could 17,000 airline flights a day be accomplished without an accident, electricity produced from large dams or nuclear power generators, millions of automobiles manufactured, or hundreds of films, videos, and records made available for our entertainment? Organizations pervade our society. Most college students will work in an organization—perhaps Hospital Corporation of America, Federated Department Stores, Boise Cascade, or Standard Oil. College students already are members of several organizations, such as a university, junior college, YMCA, church, fraternity, or sorority. College students also deal with organizations every day: to renew a driver's license, be treated in a hospital emergency room, buy food from a supermarket, eat in a restaurant, or buy new clothes.

Efficiency, *effectiveness*, and a long tradition of *innovation* and *performance* are the hallmarks of management at Dole Food Company, Inc. These lettuce harvesters use a unique harvesting and packing system, which was the brain-child of Dole employees. The Precision Pack Harvester reduces labor costs and improves quality through minimal physical handling of the product.

Managers are responsible for these organizations and for seeing that resources are used wisely to attain organizational goals.

Our formal definition of an **organization** is a social entity that is goal directed and deliberately structured. *Social entity* means being made up of two or more people. *Goal directed* means designed to achieve some outcome, such as make a profit (Boeing, Mack Trucks), win pay increases for members (AFL-CIO), meet spiritual needs (Methodist church), or provide social satisfaction (college sorority). *Deliberately structured* means that tasks are divided and responsibility for their performance assigned to organization members. This definition applies to all organizations, including both profit and not-for-profit. Vickery Stoughton runs Toronto General Hospital and manages a $200 million budget. He endures intense public scrutiny, heavy government regulation, and daily crises of life and death. Hamilton Jordan, formerly President Carter's chief of staff, created a new organization called the Association of Tennis Professionals that will take control of the professional tennis circuit. John and Marie Bouchard launched a small business called Wild Things that sells goods for outdoor activities. Small, offbeat, and not-for-profit organizations are more numerous than large, visible corporations—and just as important to society.

Based on our definition of management, the manager's responsibility is to coordinate resources in an effective and efficient manner to accomplish

organization

A social entity that is goal directed and deliberately structured.

effectiveness

The degree to which the organization achieves a stated objective.

efficiency

The use of minimal resources—raw materials, money, and people—to produce a desired volume of output.

the organization's goals. Organizational **effectiveness** is the degree to which the organization achieves a stated objective. It means that the organization succeeds in accomplishing what it tries to do. Organizational effectiveness means providing a product or service that customers value. Organizational **efficiency** refers to the amount of resources used to achieve an organizational goal. It is based on how much raw materials, money, and people are necessary for producing a given volume of output. Efficiency can be calculated as the amount of resources used to produce a product or service.

Efficiency and effectiveness can both be high in the same organization. Consider the impact of Dick Dauch, vice-president of manufacturing at Chrysler. His leadership has allowed a startling increase in efficiency. Chrysler now can build 8,000 cars and trucks a day compared with 4,500 a few years ago. The number of worker-hours per vehicle has shrunk from 175 to 102. Resources are used more efficiently: Worker absenteeism is down sharply. New technology has transformed the assembly line.[18] Likewise, management efforts at Stanley Works, the 140-year-old toolmaker, to increase automation and employee training and to establish quality circles and decision-making worker teams led to a scrap rate reduction from 15 percent to 3 percent.[19] In addition to increasing efficiency, managers at Chrysler and Stanley Works improved effectiveness as revealed in product quality, revenues, and profits.

Managers in other organizations, especially service firms, are improving efficiency, too. Labor shortages in the Midwest and northeastern United States have prompted managers to find labor-saving tricks. Burger King and Taco Bell restaurants let customers serve themselves drinks. Sleep Inn hotels have a washer and dryer installed behind the desk so that clerks can launder sheets and towels while waiting on customers.[20] McDonald's is experimenting with a grill that cooks hamburgers on both sides at once to improve efficiency, and to improve effectiveness with respect to the environment, it is experimenting with new food waste controls, decomposable packaging, and expanded recycling.[21]

performance

The organization's ability to attain its goals by using resources in an efficient and effective manner.

The ultimate responsibility of managers, then, is to achieve high **performance**, which is the attainment of organizational goals by using resources in an efficient and effective manner. Two examples of extraordinary management performance in the entertainment industry—Garth Brooks and the Grateful Dead—are described in the Winning Moves box. Whether managers are responsible for the organization as a whole, such as Garth Brooks or the Grateful Dead, or for a single department or division, such as Lucie Fjeldstad at IBM, their ultimate responsibility is performance. Harold Geneen, a legendary manager who transformed ITT into one of the world's largest and best-run corporations, explained it this way:

> I think it is an immutable law in business that words are words, explanations are explanations, promises are promises—but only performance is reality. Performance alone is the best measure of your confidence, competence, and courage. Only performance gives you the freedom to grow as yourself.
> Just remember that: *performance is your reality.* Forget everything else. That is why my definition of a manager is what it is: one who turns in the performance.

GARTH BROOKS AND THE GRATEFUL DEAD

Garth Brooks and the Grateful Dead represent astonishing success stories during a recessionary period when record companies are not promoting new recordings, and stars such as Elton John and Hammer have reduced or cut their tours. Garth Brooks sits atop both country and pop charts with sales of 20 million albums, and the Grateful Dead is once again "Knocking on Heaven's Door," in the number-one position as touring's most popular act after nearly three decades of performances. These two organizations achieve startling efficiency and effectiveness.

Why so much success? One answer is management skills. Garth Brooks has been working on a master's degree in business and believes in human skills, employing a variation of MBWA (management by walking around). Brooks does in-store appearances to learn what customers want. He also has a knack for building support among employees. According to comanager Pam Lewis, "Garth was willing to go to the warehouses. He understands the importance of the people who are loading the trucks, the people shrink-wrapping the product, the truck drivers. He reaches these people and makes them a believer."

The Grateful Dead is another story of superb management. The group listens to customers. Most rock bands forbid tape-recording at concerts to prevent copyright infringement, yet the Dead ropes off a portion of the concert floor just for "tapeheads." The Dead's 50 employees are fully empowered, with large doses of job enrichment, few rules and procedures, and owner-ship of their jobs. Staff members earn large salaries and attractive benefits (life and medical insurance, trust funds for children), and they share in concert profits. Staff members feel part of the business, and turnover is low in an industry known for its instability.

Management counts. Garth Brooks and the Grateful Dead have organizations with powerful cultures, significant visions, and the moti-vation of human energy that set great organizations apart. ∎

SOURCE: David E. Bowen and Caren Siehl, "Sweet Music: Grateful Employees, Grateful Customers, 'Grate' Profits," *Journal of Management Inquiry* (June 1992), 154–156; Robert K. Oermann, "Marketing Breaks Brooks away from Competition," *The Tennessean*, July 15, 1992, E1, E4; and Janice C. Simpson, "The Bands of Summer," *Time*, August 3, 1992, 66–67.

No alibis to others or to one's self will change that. And when you have per-formed well, the world will remember it, when everything else is forgotten. And most importantly, so will you.[22]

● MANAGEMENT TYPES

The four management functions must be performed in all organizations. But not all managers' jobs are the same. Managers are responsible for different departments, work at different levels in the hier-archy, and meet different requirements for achieving high performance. For example, Mary Lee Bowen is a middle manager at Rubbermaid responsible for teams that create new home organization and bath acces-sories products. Phillip Knight is chief executive officer for Nike, world leader in sports shoe design and manufacturing.[23] Both are managers, and both must contribute to planning, organizing, leading, and controlling their organizations—but in different amounts and ways.

VERTICAL DIFFERENCES

top manager

A manager who is at the top of the organizational hierarchy and responsible for the entire organization.

middle manager

A manager who works at the middle levels of the organization and is responsible for major departments.

An important determinant of the manager's job is hierarchical level. Three levels in the hierarchy are illustrated in Exhibit 1.2. **Top managers** are at the top of the hierarchy and are responsible for the entire organization. They have such titles as president, chairperson, executive director, chief executive officer (CEO), and executive vice-president. Top managers are responsible for setting organizational goals, defining strategies for achieving them, monitoring and interpreting the external environment, and making decisions that affect the entire organization. They look to the long-term future and concern themselves with general environmental trends and the organization's overall success. They also influence internal corporate culture.

Middle managers work at middle levels of the organization and are responsible for business units and major departments. Examples of mid-

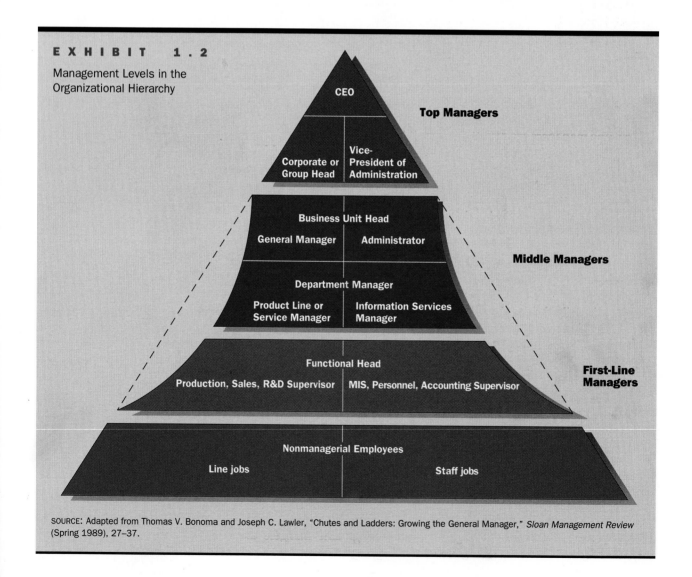

EXHIBIT 1.2

Management Levels in the Organizational Hierarchy

SOURCE: Adapted from Thomas V. Bonoma and Joseph C. Lawler, "Chutes and Ladders: Growing the General Manager," *Sloan Management Review* (Spring 1989), 27–37.

dle managers are department head, division head, manager of quality control, and director of the research lab. Middle managers typically have two or more management levels beneath them. They are responsible for implementing the overall strategies and policies defined by top managers. Middle managers are concerned with the near future, are expected to establish good relationships with peers around the organization, encourage teamwork, and resolve conflicts.

Recent trends in corporate restructuring and downsizing have made the middle manager's job difficult. Many companies have become lean and efficient by laying off middle managers, and by slashing middle management levels. Traditional pyramidal organization charts are flattening, allowing information to flow quickly from top to bottom and decisions to be made with the greater speed necessary in today's highly competitive global marketplace. The shrinking middle management is illustrated in Exhibit 1.2. For example, Eastman Kodak recently cut middle management by 30 percent and reduced its middle management levels from seven to three. The Medical Systems Group at General Electric cut middle management by 35 percent. These reductions increase the work load for remaining managers and contribute to job insecurity and a decline in opportunities for promotion. However, these cuts have improved the efficiency and performance of many corporations via improved responsiveness to customers, speed in new product development, and increased profits.[24]

First-line managers are directly responsible for the production of goods and services. They are the first or second level of management and have such titles as supervisor, line manager, section chief, and office manager. They are responsible for groups of nonmanagement employees. Their primary concern is the application of rules and procedures to achieve efficient production, provide technical assistance, and motivate subordinates. The time horizon at this level is short, with the emphasis on accomplishing day-to-day objectives.

An illustration of how the four functional activities differ for the three management levels is shown in Exhibit 1.3. Managers at all levels perform all four functions, but in different amounts. Planning and organizing the firm are primarily the province of top managers, with the time devoted to these tasks decreasing for middle managers and first-line managers. Leading, in contrast, is highest for first-time managers because more time is spent directing and supervising subordinates than at higher management levels. A primary concern of first-line managers is the leadership and motivation of technical employees. Controlling is similar for all three levels, with somewhat more time devoted by middle and top managers.

HORIZONTAL DIFFERENCES

The other major difference in management jobs occurs horizontally across the organization. **Functional managers** are responsible for departments that perform a single functional task and have employees with similar training and skills. Functional departments include advertising, sales, finance, personnel, manufacturing, and accounting. Line mangers are responsible for the manufacturing and marketing departments that make

first-line manager

A manager who is at the first or second management level and directly responsible for the production of goods and services.

functional manager

A manager who is responsible for a department that performs a single functional task and has employees with similar training and skills.

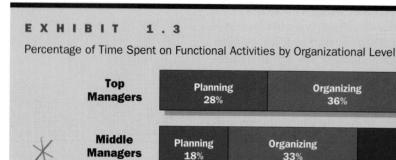

EXHIBIT 1.3

Percentage of Time Spent on Functional Activities by Organizational Level

| Top Managers | Planning 28% | Organizing 36% | Leading 22% | Controlling 14% |

| Middle Managers | Planning 18% | Organizing 33% | Leading 36% | Controlling 13% |

| First-Line Managers | Planning 15% | Organizing 24% | Leading 51% | Controlling 10% |

SOURCE: Based on T. A. Mahoney, T. H. Jerdee, and S. J. Carroll, "The Job(s) of Management," *Industrial Relations,* vol. 4 no. 2 (1965), 103. A similar pattern of activity was reported in Luis Gomez-Mejia, Joseph E. McCann, and Ronald C. Page, "The Structure of Managerial Behaviors and Rewards," *Industrial Relations* 24 (1985), 147–154.

general manager

A manager who is responsible for several departments that perform different functions.

project manager

A manager who coordinates people across several departments to accomplish a specific project.

or sell the product or service. Staff managers are in charge of departments such as finance and personnel that support line departments.

General managers are responsible for several departments that perform different functions. A general manager is responsible for a self-contained division, such as a Dillard's department store, and for all of the functional departments within it. **Project managers** also have general management responsibility, because they coordinate people across several departments to accomplish a specific project. Companies as diverse as consumer products and aerospace firms, for example, use project managers to coordinate people from marketing, manufacturing, finance, and production when a new product—breakfast cereal, guidance system—is developed. General and project managers require significant human skills, because they coordinate a variety of people to attain project or division goals.

● MANAGEMENT SKILLS

A manager's job is diverse and complex and, as we shall see throughout this book, requires a range of skills. Although some management theorists propose a long list of skills, the necessary skills for planning, organizing, leading, and controlling can be summarized in three categories that are especially important: conceptual, human, and technical.[25] As illustrated in Exhibit 1.4, all managers need each skill, but the amounts differ by hierarchical level.

CONCEPTUAL SKILLS

conceptual skill

The cognitive ability to see the organization as a whole and the relationship among its parts.

Conceptual skill is the cognitive ability to see the organization as a whole and the relationship among its parts. Conceptual skill involves the manager's thinking and planning abilities. It involves knowing where one's

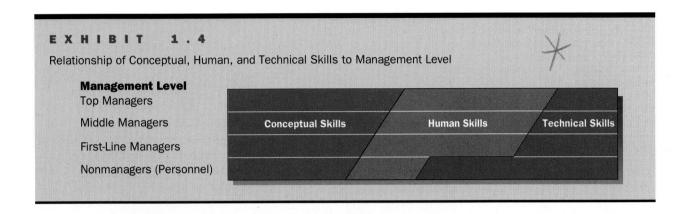

E X H I B I T   1 . 4

Relationship of Conceptual, Human, and Technical Skills to Management Level

department fits into the total organization and how the organization fits into the industry and the community. It means the ability to think "strategically"—to take the broad, long-term view.

Conceptual skills are needed by all managers, but are especially important for managers at the top. They must perceive significant elements in a situation and broad, conceptual patterns. For example, Microsoft Corporation, the giant software company, reflects the conceptual skills of its founder and chairman, Bill Gates. Overall business goals are clearly stated and effectively communicated throughout the company, contributing to Microsoft's leadership reputation and billion dollar revenues. While actively participating in and coordinating small units devoted to functional areas such as programming and marketing, Gates spreads his concept for Microsoft by delegating to a cadre of strong managers. As Scott Oki, senior vice-president for U.S. sales and marketing, pointed out, "Each part of the company has a life of its own now, but Bill [Gates] is the glue that holds it all together."[26]

As managers move up the hierarchy, they must develop conceptual skills or their promotability will be limited. A senior engineering manager who is mired in technical matters rather than thinking strategically will not perform well at the top of the organization. Many of the responsibilities of top managers, such as decision making, resource allocation, and innovation, require a broad view.

HUMAN SKILLS

Human skill is the manager's ability to work with and through other people and to work effectively as a group member. This skill is demonstrated in the way a manager relates to other people, including the ability to motivate, facilitate, coordinate, lead, communicate, and resolve conflicts. A manager with human skills allows subordinates to express themselves without fear of ridicule and encourages participation. A manager with human skills likes other people and is liked by them. Barry Merkin, chairman of Dresher, Inc., the largest U.S. manufacturer of brass beds, is a cheerleader for his employees. He visits the plant floor and uses humor and hoopla to motivate them. Employees may have buckets of fried chicken served to them by supervisors wearing chef's hats.

human skill

The ability to work with and through other people and to work effectively as a group member.

In exercising the *human skills* of management and leadership, Hewlett-Packard division general manager Bob Olson applies one guiding principle: "Always remember what it was like *before* you were a leader." Whether taking time to welcome new employees to the division, or dealing with myriad daily problems and personalities, Olson maintains an approachable, down-to-earth management style.

Managers who lack human skills often are abrupt, critical, and unsympathetic toward others. Harding Lawrence of Braniff, described earlier, did not excel in human skills. Another example is the executive who walked into a subordinate's office and insisted on talking to him. When the subordinate tried to explain that he was occupied, the manager snarled, "I don't give a damn. I said I wanted to see you now."[27] Managers without human skills are insensitive and arrogant. They often make other people feel stupid and resentful.

In recent years, the awareness of human skills has increased. Books such as *In Search of Excellence* and *A Passion for Excellence* stress the need for managers to take care of the human side of the organization. Excellent companies and excellent managers do not take people for granted. For example, former auto racer Roger Penske purchased struggling Detroit Diesel Corporation from General Motors and stressed the importance of a "team concept"—**t**eamwork, **e**ffort, **a**ttitude, and **m**anagement. Penske focused on people, answering questions from hundreds of employees and meeting regularly with union workers. Because of Penske's use of his people skills to motivate workers toward speedy and courteous response to customers, the Penske team's share of heavy truck engine sales rose 25 percent in its first year.[28] Effective managers are cheerleaders, facilitators, coaches, and nurturers. They build through people. Effective human skills enable managers to unleash subordinates' energy and help them grow as future managers.

TECHNICAL SKILLS

technical skill

The understanding of and proficiency in the performance of specific tasks.

<u>**Technical skill**</u> is the understanding of and proficiency in the performance <u>of specific tasks</u>. Technical skill includes mastery of the methods, techniques, and equipment involved in specific functions such as engineering,

manufacturing, or finance. Technical skill also includes specialized knowledge, analytical ability, and the competent use of tools and techniques to solve problems in that specific discipline. One reason Lucie Fjeldstad, described at the beginning of this chapter, was placed in charge of IBM's new multimedia division was her technological understanding of this dynamic new area, which she demonstrated in a two-hour presentation before IBM's management committee.

Technical skills are most important at lower organizational levels. Many managers get promoted into their first management jobs by having excellent technical skills. However, technical skills are less important than human and conceptual skills as managers move up the hierarchy.

MAKING THE TRANSITION

As illustrated in Exhibit 1.4, the major difference between nonmanagers and managers is the shift from reliance on technical skills to focus on human skills. This is a difficult transition, because high achievement in the technical area may have been the basis for promotion to a supervisory position. New managers often mistakenly continue to rely on technical skills rather than concentrate on working with others, motivating employees, and building a team. Indeed, some people fail to become managers at all because they let technical skills take precedence over human skills.

Consider Peter Martin, who has a bachelor's degree and has worked for five years as a computer programmer for an oil company. In four short years, he has more new software programs to his credit than anyone else in the department. He is highly creative and widely respected. However, Pete is impulsive and has little tolerance for those whose work is less creative. Pete does not offer to help coworkers, and they are reluctant to ask because he often "puts them down." Pete is also slow to cooperate with other departments in meeting their needs, because he works primarily to enhance his own software-writing ability. He spends evenings and weekends working on his programs. Pete is a hardworking technical employee, but he sees little need to worry about other people.

Pete received high merit raises but was passed over for promotion and does not understand why. His lack of interpersonal skills, inconsideration for coworkers, and failure to cooperate with other departments severely limit his potential as a supervisor. Pete has great technical skills, but his human skills simply are inadequate for making the transition from worker to supervisor. Until Pete is ready to work on human skills, he has little chance of being promoted.

● WHAT IS IT LIKE TO BE A MANAGER?

So far we have described how managers perform four basic functions that help ensure that organizational resources are used to attain high levels of performance. These tasks require conceptual, human, and technical skills. Unless someone has actually performed managerial work, it is hard to understand exactly what managers do on an hour-by-hour, day-to-day basis. The manager's job is so diverse that a number of studies have been undertaken in an attempt to describe exactly what happens. The question of what managers actually do to plan, organize, lead, and control was answered by Henry Mintzberg, who followed managers around and recorded all of their activities.[29] He developed a description of managerial work that included three general characteristics and ten roles. These characteristics and roles have been supported in subsequent research.[30]

MANAGER ACTIVITIES

One of the most interesting findings about managerial activities is how busy managers are and how hectic the average workday can be.

MANAGERIAL ACTIVITY IS CHARACTERIZED BY VARIETY, FRAGMENTATION, AND BREVITY.[31] The manager's involvements are so widespread and voluminous that there is little time for quiet reflection. The average time spent on any one activity is less than nine minutes. Managers shift gears quickly. Significant crises are interspersed with trivial events in no predictable sequence.[32] One example of the morning activities for a typical general manager, Janet Howard, follows. Note the frequent interruptions, brevity, and variety.

7:30 A.M.   Janet arrives at work, unpacks her briefcase, and begins to plan her day.

7:37 A.M.   A subordinate, Morgan Cook, arrives and stops in Janet's office to discuss a dinner party the previous night and to review the cost-benefit analysis her department is working up for a proposed microcomputer.

7:45 A.M.   Janet's secretary, Pat, motions for Janet to pick up the telephone. "Janet, they had serious water damage at the downtown office last night. A pipe broke, causing about $50,000 damage. Everything will be back in shape in three days. Thought you should know."

8:00 A.M.   Another subordinate, Tim Birdwell, stops by. They chat about the water damage. Tim tells a joke. Tim and Morgan both leave, laughing at the story.

8:10 A.M.   Pat brings in the mail. She also asks instructions for typing a report Janet gave her yesterday.

8:17 A.M.   The mail includes an unsolicited proposal for a microcomputer from a prospective vendor and a clipped *Fortune* article about strategic decision making from Janet's boss.

8:30 A.M.   Janet gets a phone call from the accounting manager, who is returning a call from the day before. They talk about an accounting report.

8:45 A.M.   Janet leaves early to attend a regular 9:00 A.M. meeting in her boss's office. She tours the office area and informally chats with people before the meeting starts.

9:45 A.M.   Janet arrives back at her office, and a Mr. Nance is ushered in. Mr. Nance complains that a sales manager mistreats his employees and something must be done. Janet rearranges her schedule to investigate this claim.

The recipe for successful management at Sizzler International, Inc., follows: Pick bright applicants, train two years, and add on-the-job fine tuning of people skills and a dash of personal flair. The results are top-notch managers like Rona Kay. As coach, cheerleader, director, facilitator, and boss, a Sizzler manager handles a *variety* of daily tasks, from creating a warm, friendly dining environment, or overseeing a hectic kitchen, to exercising quality control on meat deliveries.

10:05 A.M. Janet returns to the mail. One letter is from an irate customer who is unhappy with the product and feels the sales engineer was unresponsive. Janet dictates a helpful, restrained reply.

10:20 A.M. Pat brings in phone messages. Janet makes two phone calls and receives one. She goes back to the mail and papers on her desk.

10:35 A.M. Another subordinate stops by with a question about how to complete forms requesting a maternity leave.

10:45 A.M. Janet receives an urgent phone call from Larry Baldwin. They go back and forth talking about lost business, unhappy subordinates, a potential promotion, and what should be done. It is a long conversation, with much exchange of both official information and gossip.

11:15 A.M.   Janet decides to skip lunch, preferring to eat an apple in her office so she will have some time to plan divisional goals for the next six months.[33]

THE MANAGER PERFORMS A GREAT DEAL OF WORK AT AN UNRE-LENTING PACE.[34]   Managers' work is fast paced and requires great energy. The managers observed by Mintzberg processed 36 pieces of mail each day, attended 8 meetings, and took a tour through the building or plant. As soon as a manager's daily calendar is set, unexpected disturbances erupt. New meetings are required. During time away from the office, executives catch up on work-related reading and paperwork.

Sloan Wilson, author of *The Man in the Gray Flannel Suit*, had an opportunity to work with top managers from several companies. He tried to understand how these people had become so famous, rich and successful. They had no special advantages or influence, because each was a self-made person.

So what was the secret? As I attempted to work around the clock on the many projects they undertook in addition to their real jobs, one simple answer came to me: raw energy. Super-abundant, inexhaustible energy—that was the one thing all these very successful men had.

They were people who enthusiastically could undertake the fifth rewriting of a speech on education at three in the morning when they were up against a deadline, fly across the continent to deliver it and fly back again, working out of a briefcase on a plane all the time. And when they got to their offices, they were fresh and eager to see what their engagement calendar had to offer for the day and evening ahead. I never understood how they did it, and I was never able to keep up with them.[35]

MANAGER ROLES

Mintzberg's observations and subsequent research indicate that diverse manager activities can be organized into ten roles.[36] A **role** is a set of expectations for a manager's behavior. The ten roles are divided into three

role

A set of expectations for one's behavior.

Goodness, gracious, "Great Balls of Foil!" Reynolds Metals executives marvel at a portion of the 1,464 miles of recycled aluminum foil collected by school children in the Great Balls of Foil annual recycling contest. Executives enjoy the *figurehead role*, interacting with children, awarding prizes in categories such as the most creative entry. It's all fun and games with a message: "Wrap up a cleaner world."

Category	Role	Activity
Interpersonal	**Figurehead**	Perform ceremonial and symbolic duties such as greeting visitors, signing legal documents.
	Leader	Direct and motivate subordinates; train, counsel, and communicate with subordinates.
	Liaison	Maintain information links both inside and outside organization; use mail, phone calls, meetings. *NETWORKING*
Informational	**Monitor**	Seek and receive information, scan periodicals and reports, maintain personal contacts.
	Disseminator	Forward information to other organization members; send memos and reports, make phone calls.
	Spokesperson	Transmit information to outsiders through speeches, reports, memos.
Decisional	**Entrepreneur**	Initiate improvement projects; identify new ideas, delegate idea responsibility to others.
	Disturbance handler	Take corrective action during disputes or crises; resolve conflicts among subordinates; adapt to environmental crises.
	Resource allocator	Decide who gets resources; schedule, budget, set priorities.
	Negotiator	Represent department during negotiation of union contracts, sales, purchases, budgets; represent departmental interests.

EXHIBIT   1 . 5

Ten Manager Roles

BASED ON 5 CEO's

SOURCE: Adapted from Henry Mintzberg, The Nature of Managerial Work (New York: Harper & Row, 1973), 92–93, and Henry Mintzberg, "Managerial Work: Analysis from Observation," *Management Science* 18 (1971), B97–B110.

categories: interpersonal, information, and decisional. Each role represents activities that managers undertake to ultimately accomplish the functions of planning, organizing, leading, and controlling. The ten roles and brief examples are provided in Exhibit 1.5.

INTERPERSONAL ROLES.   Interpersonal roles pertain to relationships with others and are related to the human skills described earlier. The *figurehead* role involves handling ceremonial and symbolic activities for the department or organization. The manager represents the organization in his or her formal managerial capacity as the head of the unit. The presentation of employee awards by a division manager at Taco Bell is an example of the figurehead role. The *leader* role encompasses relationships with subordinates, including motivation, communication, and influence. The *liaison* role pertains to the development of information sources both inside and outside the organization. An example is a face-to-face discussion between a controller and plan supervisor to resolve a misunderstanding about the budget.

INFORMATIONAL ROLES.   Informational roles describe the activities used to maintain and develop an information network. General managers spend about 75 percent of their time talking to other people. The *monitor* role involves seeking current information from many sources. The manager acquires information from others and scans written materials to stay well informed. One manager at a Canadian insurance company takes a turn at the switchboard every 40 days, plugging directly into customer and employee satisfaction.[37] The *disseminator* role is just the opposite: The manager transmits current information to others, both inside and outside the organization, who can use it. Managers do not hoard information; they pass it around to others. The *spokesperson* role pertains to official statements to people outside the organization about company policies, actions, or plans. For example, Lod Cook, chairman of Atlantic Richfield Company, talked to environmentalists about his backing of a ten-year ban on drilling in certain areas off the California coast, spoke in favor of a gas tax hike, and helped Arco proudly trumpet its price freeze during the buildup for the war in the Persian Gulf. Cook's figurehead activities not only show Arco's enlightenment but contribute to increased gasoline sales as well.[38]

DECISIONAL ROLES.   Decisional roles pertain to those events about which the manager must make a choice. These roles often require conceptual as well as human skills. The *entrepreneur* role involves the initiation of change. Managers are constantly thinking about the future and how to get there.[39] Managers become aware of problems and search for improvement projects that will correct them. One manager studied by Mintzberg had 50 improvement projects going simultaneously. The *disturbance handler* role involves resolving conflicts among subordinates or between the manager's department and other departments. For example, the division manager for a large furniture manufacturer got involved in a personal dispute between two section heads. One section head was let go because he did not fit the team. The *resource allocator* role pertains to decisions about how to allocate people, time, equipment, budget, and other resources to attain desired outcomes. The manager must decide which projects receive budget allocations, which of several customer complaints receive priority, and even how to spend his or her own time. The *negotiator* role involves formal negotiations and bargaining to attain outcomes for the manager's unit of responsibility. For example, the manager meets and formally negotiates with others—a supplier about a late delivery, the controller about the need for additional budget resources, or the union about a worker grievance during the normal workday.

SMALL BUSINESS

One interesting finding is that managers in small businesses tend to emphasize different roles than managers in large corporations. In small firms, the most important role is spokesperson, because managers must promote the small, growing company to the outside world. The entrepreneur role is also very important in small businesses, because managers must be creative and help their organizations develop new ideas to be competitive. Small-business managers tend to rate lower on the leader role and on information-processing roles compared with counterparts in large corporations. In large firms, the most important role is resource allocator and the least important is entrepreneur.[40]

● MANAGING FOR THE FUTURE

One final question: How do you learn to be a manager for the year 2000 in an uncertain and rapidly changing world? More specifically, how does a course in management or a college degree in business prepare you to become a manager ready to face the challenges of the twenty-first century?

LEARNING MANAGEMENT SKILLS

Management is both an art and a science. It is an art because many skills cannot be learned from a textbook. Management takes practice, just like golf, tennis, or volleyball. Studying a book helps, but this is not enough. Many skills, especially the human and, to some extent, the conceptual skills, and roles such as leader, spokesperson, disturbance handler, and negotiator, take practice. These skills are learned through experience.

Management is also a science because a growing body of knowledge and objective facts describes management and how to attain organizational performance. The knowledge is acquired through systematic research and can be conveyed through teaching and textbooks. Systematic knowledge about planning, organizing, and control system design, for example, helps managers understand the skills they need, the types of roles they must perform, and the techniques needed to manage organizations. Harding Lawrence of Braniff and Robert Fomon of E. F. Hutton relied solely on their experience and intuition, and they made grave mistakes.

Becoming a successful manager requires a blend of formal learning and practice, of science and art. Practice alone used to be enough to learn how to manage, but no longer. Formal course work in management can help a

How do people at BANK ONE learn *management skills*? One way is through this workshop to stimulate innovation and creativity. At BANK ONE college, participants look at problem solving through the eyes of a judge, warrior, artist, and explorer, and then put on the hats of the characters as they role-play problem-solving scenarios. Other training sessions focus on leadership, collaboration, and communication, all adding to each manager's store of management knowledge and skill.

manager become more competent and be prepared for the challenges of the future. The study of management enables people to see and understand things about organizations that others cannot. Training that helps one acquire the conceptual, human, and technical skills necessary for management will be an asset.

MANAGEMENT SUCCESS AND FAILURE

A few clues about the importance of acquiring management skills were uncovered by the Center for Creative Leadership in Greensboro, North Carolina.[41] This study compared 21 derailed executives with 20 executives who had arrived at the top of the company. The derailed executives were successful people who had been expected to go far but reached a plateau, were fired, or were forced to retire early. Successful and derailed managers were similar in many ways. They were bright, worked hard, and excelled in a technical area such as accounting or engineering.

The most striking difference between the two groups was the ability to use human skills. Only 25 percent of the derailed group were described as having good ability with people, whereas 75 percent of those who had arrived at the top had such skill. The managers who arrived were sensitive to others and did not have negative qualities such as abrasiveness, aloofness, or arrogance. The successful managers also developed conceptual skills and were able to think strategically, that is, take a broad, long-term view. For example, one derailed manager was a superb engineer who got bogged down in details and tended to lose composure under stress. Another manager was known as cold and arrogant, but once he realized these limits to his career, he changed almost overnight. He made a genuine effort to develop better human skills—and succeeded.

PREPARING FOR THE YEAR 2000

Over the next few years, new forces are going to shape managerial careers. Managers will have to rely heavily on human skills and conceptual skills, but they will apply them in new ways. Major changes on the horizon for which managers must prepare include paradigm shifts, chaos theory, workplace diversity, and globalization.

paradigm

A mind-set that presents a fundamental way of thinking, perceiving, and understanding the world.

PARADIGM SHIFTS.   A **paradigm** is a mind-set that presents a fundamental way of thinking, perceiving, and understanding the world. Changing one's management paradigm is extremely difficult yet is becoming important in a world of rapidly changing products, technologies, and management techniques. Not too many years ago, Swiss companies made the best watches in the world, cornering 65 percent of sales and 80 percent of profits. A paradigm shift in the fundamental rules of watchmaking from mechanical to electronic dropped Swiss market share to 10 percent and profits to less than 20 percent. Another shift is in the speed with which work must be accomplished. Ford, Honda, and Chrysler have cut the time to develop a new car from five years to three, thus demanding new ways of thinking and organizing. The Limited retail chain rushes new fashions into its stores in less than 60 days, compared to six months for competitors.

Another fundamental management shift is toward the belief that companies can be managed best by underpowering people to manage themselves.[42]

CHAOS THEORY.   The new science of chaos theory reveals the existence of randomness and disorder within larger patterns of order. This means that day-to-day events for most organizations are random and unpredictable. Chaos theory will be associated with a paradigm shift away from the belief that managers can predict and control future events toward a management philosophy that organizations must become fluid, adaptable, and stay connected to customers and the environment on a day-to-day basis. Managers may become less concerned with detailed planning and control, orienting themselves instead toward facilitating teams and managing overall patterns, not day-to-day events.[43]

WORKPLACE DIVERSITY.   The increasing diversity of people within organizations is reflected in several ways. The number of male students going into business education has been stable since the mid-1970s. The increase of students has been accounted for by women, who now constitute 45 percent of all bachelor's degrees in business. By the year 2000, most new hires will be women or black, Hispanic, or Asian men. Organizations must learn to welcome diverse people into their upper ranks. Different people offer varying styles. Some research indicates, for example, that women have a different, and often superior, management style, as discussed in the Focus on Diversity box. Managers must learn to motivate and lead different types of people and to attract the best people from these groups. U.S.-born white males will make up only about 15 percent of the new entrants into the labor force.[44]

MERGERS AND ACQUISITIONS.   Mergers and acquisitions have a major impact on managerial careers and will continue through the 1990s. During the 1980s, more than 10,000 companies changed hands, and over 2 million people saw their jobs disappear. Mergers and reorganizations are seen as an opportunity for companies to become more efficient, but they require new management responses. Managers have to be flexible enough to work for different bosses within new corporate cultures. Lifetime loyalty to a single firm may be a thing of the past. Downsizing middle management ranks requires managers to produce in ways that are highly visible and guarantee job mobility.[45]

NOT-FOR-PROFIT ORGANIZATIONS.   Not-for-profit organizations represent a major source of management talent and innovation. The Salvation Army, Girl Scouts, universities, city governments, hospitals, public schools, symphonies, and art museums all require superb management. Many not-for-profit organizations have been leaders in creating a sense of purpose and mission that motivates employees, encouraging workers to innovate and try new ideas, using boards and committees drawn from community members, and trimming long vertical hierarchies.[46]

GLOBALIZATION.   Managers need to think globally because companies are enmeshed with foreign competitors, suppliers, and customers. By one

Strength through *diversity* is reflected in the faces of these Dow Chemical employees, and in Dow's vision of welcoming and valuing the contributions of each of its 61,000 employees around the world. These Los Angeles workers represent eleven countries, and each person brings a unique perspective and range of experience that benefits the entire organization.

DO WOMEN MANAGE DIFFERENTLY?

CEO Linda Wachner acquired Warnaco, Inc., in the mid-1980s, increasing sales to $563 million in 1991. Under her leadership, the lingerie company is achieving her vision of becoming the "Coca-Cola of the bra business." Despite her success, however, Wachner, like other women managers, cannot escape the "too soft or too strident" assessment trap. Her tough leadership style has drawn the complaint that she is "very, very difficult to work for." If she is not tough, she is perceived as too soft to run a large corporation.

Buoyed by reputations as nurturing, inclusive, and natural sharers of information, women managers are touted by many as being ideally suited to the flattened organization of the 1990s. Women are comfortable persuading, encouraging, and motivating, while men often want to issue orders and have them followed. Enthusiastic proponents of a female managerial style argue that early socialization and skills that grew from home and family experiences give women somewhat better human skills than men. Indeed, people often expect these skills, and when a woman manages aggressively she may be unfairly criticized as too tough.

"Feminine" qualities such as openness, encouragement, understanding, sensitivity, and consensus-building appear to fit the requirements of leaders who are facilitators and coaches rather than autocrats. Modern human-oriented techniques, such as MBWA (managing by walking around) easily combine with feminine qualities such as "stroking" people that enable top managers to achieve positive results from employees.

The traditional "male" command-and-control style is suited to hierarchical organizations of the past. "Masculine" qualities such as aggression, assertiveness, rational analysis, and competitiveness grew out of male-dominated military and sports traditions. Research by a number of people supports the argument that women's managerial styles, on average, differ from those of their male counterparts.

Other researchers question whether male and female stereotypes should apply to management. Masculine and feminine traits, including those needed for human skills, they say, can be developed in both sexes to manage modern corporations. As more women move into important management positons, they can be valued for assertiveness as well as nurturing. Indeed, women have already succeeded in many companies, including General Mills, Hewitt Associates, Neiman-Marcus, and PepsiCo.

Although women appear to manage somewhat differently on average, the final answer may be for companies to value the diversity of management styles held by both men and women to find the strength and flexibility to survive in a highly competitive global environment. ■

SOURCE: Sharon Nelton, "Men, Women and Leadership," *Nation's Business*, May 1991, 16–22; Laurie Kretchmar, "Do Women Manage Differently?" *Fortune*, December 17, 1990, 115–118; Judy B. Rosener, "Ways Women Lead," *Harvard Business Review* (November–December 1990), 119–125; and Gary N. Powell, "One More Time: Do Female and Male Managers Differ?" *Academy of Management Executive* 4 (August 1990), 68–75.

estimate, industrial countries on average import nearly 40 percent of the parts used in domestic manufacturing. Foreign companies have strong influence in the United States and Canada, with many citizens working for foreign employers. Some experts feel that globalization presents a management challenge because the United States is losing worldwide market share in important product areas.

The 12 nations of the European Community will reduce long-standing barriers to the transfer of goods, financing, and people across their borders. This true common market will be substantially larger than the United

States, allowing European companies to grow large and powerful and to become more competitive on the global stage. U.S. companies are trying to get a foothold in Europe now to avoid potential barriers in the future. In addition, the North American Free Trade Agreement reduces the trade barriers in North America, creating another common market. These rapid developments are changing the global picture, forcing managers to think internationally.[47]

Successful managers of tomorrow will be able to cross borders, will be good at languages, and will understand cultural differences. Right now executive recruiting organizations are searching worldwide for managers to take assignments in global organizations. Global experience is a prize asset of the managers of tomorrow.[48]

SUMMARY AND MANAGEMENT SOLUTION

This chapter introduced a number of important concepts about management. High performance requires the efficient and effective use of organizational resources through the four management functions of planning, organizing, leading, and controlling. Their importance differs somewhat by hierarchical level. Top and middle managers are most concerned with planning and place greater emphasis on organizing and controlling. First-line managers focus more on leading. To perform the four functions, managers need three skills—conceptual, human, and technical. Conceptual skills are more important at the top of the hierarchy; human skills are important at all levels; and technical skills are most important for first-line managers.

Lucie Fjeldstad, who recently took over the 1,000-employee multimedia division at IBM, is a perfect example of a top manager using conceptual skills. As senior manager in the division, she is planning to shake up IBM's traditional corporate culture so that the multimedia business can be a major player in the future of IBM and to get out of product lines that are not essential to IBM's future. Her concern with organizing is to make her business division an independent unit within IBM and to create independent structural units and teams within her division. Controlling is realized through Fjeldstad's creation of new incentive plans that grant bonuses to employees of successful units.[49]

Two characteristics of managerial work also were explained in the chapter: (1) Managerial activities involve variety, fragmentation, and brevity and (2) managers perform a great deal of work at an unrelenting pace. Managers also are expected to perform activities associated with ten roles: the interpersonal roles of figurehead, leader, and liaison; the informational roles of monitor, disseminator, and spokesperson; and the decisional roles of entrepreneur, disturbance handler, resource allocator, and negotiator.

Lucie Fjeldstad was selected for the important multimedia position at IBM because she had excellent interpersonal and decisional skills. She is superb with people and knows how to facilitate change, handle problems, and negotiate solutions. Fjeldstad, like most managers, learned these roles and skills through both formal training and actual management experience. Typically, managers who succeed have excellent human skills. In the future, managers will need even greater human skills as well as conceptual skills to deal with the pressing issues of paradigm shifts, chaos, workplace diversity, mergers, and globalization.

DISCUSSION QUESTIONS

1. Assume you are a research engineer at a petrochemical company, collaborating with a marketing manager on a major product modification. You notice that every memo you receive from her has been copied to senior management. At every company function, she spends time talking to the big shots. You are also aware that sometimes when you are slaving away over the project, she is playing golf with senior managers. What is your evaluation of her behavior?

2. What similarities do you see among the four management functions of planning, organizing, leading, and controlling? Do you think these functions are related—that is, is a manager who performs well in one function likely to perform well in the others?

3. Why did a top manager such as Harding Lawrence at Braniff fail while a top manager such as General Creech of Tactical Air Command succeed? Which of the four management functions best explains this difference? Discuss.

4. What is the difference between efficiency and effectiveness? Which is more important for performance? Can an organization succeed in both simultaneously?

5. What changes in management functions and skills occur as one is promoted from a nonmanagement to a management position? How can managers acquire the new skills?

6. If managerial work is characterized by variety, fragmentation, and brevity, how do managers perform basic management functions such as planning, which would seem to require reflection and analysis?

7. A college professor told her students, "The purpose of a management course is to teach students *about* management, not to teach them to be managers." Do you agree or disagree with this statement? Discuss.

8. What does it mean to say that management is both an art and a science? Discuss.

9. In the Center for Creative Leadership study, many managers made it to the middle and upper levels of the organization before derailing. How do you think managers got so far if they had flaws that prevented them from reaching the top?

10. How should the teaching of management change to prepare future managers to deal with work-force diversity? Do you think diversity will have a more substantial impact on organizations than globalization will?

MANAGEMENT IN PRACTICE: EXPERIENTIAL EXERCISE

● TEST YOUR HUMAN SKILLS

The 60 questions that follow will help you evaluate your human skills compared with those of current managers. Be honest in your responses. Your instructor will provide you with information about the meaning of your responses.

Circle the letter, as illustrated here, that represents your acceptance or rejection of the statements that follow.

Strongly disagree:	Ⓓ	d	?	a	A
Moderately disagree:	D	ⓓ	?	a	A
Sometimes yes/no:	D	d	⑦	a	A
Moderately agree:	D	d	?	ⓐ	A
Strongly agree:	D	d	?	a	Ⓐ

---

1. You have been elected or promoted to several leadership positions in your school/work/community/church involvements.	D	d	?	a	A
2. You have impeccably good manners, and people comment on your courteous behavior time and again.	D	d	?	a	A
3. You feel comfortable and at ease when others make you the center of attention.	D	d	?	a	A
4. It irritates you when others treat life as nothing more than a game.	D	d	?	a	A
5. You love old things, poetry, going out to the country, and being alone.	D	d	?	a	A
6. You would love to make a citizen's arrest of someone honking his or her horn needlessly or disturbing the peace.	D	d	?	a	A
7. You are good at praising others and give credit readily when credit is due.	D	d	?	a	A
8. When you deal with people, you tread softly and give them the "kid glove" treatment.	D	d	?	a	A
9. You allow people to manipulate and boss you around too much.	D	d	?	a	A
10. In the end, with every liaison established primarily for ambition's sake, you have to give away a bit of your "soul."	D	d	?	a	A
11. You have a knack for harmonizing the seemingly irreconcilable.	D	d	?	a	A
12. You believe that nothing gets done properly unless you do it yourself.	D	d	?	a	A
13. You seem to possess a natural charm and easily win people over.	D	d	?	a	A
14. In large or new social situations, you are poised, relaxed, and self-assured.	D	d	?	a	A
15. You have a real capacity for selling yourself to others.	D	d	?	a	A
16. You really dislike others teasing or making fun of you.	D	d	?	a	A
17. You feel a natural and real warmth toward all people.	D	d	?	a	A
18. You have little patience for human ignorance and incompetence.	D	d	?	a	A
19. You will usually give others the benefit of the doubt rather than argue openly with them.	D	d	?	a	A
20. You seldom (or never) say anything to others without considering how they may receive it.	D	d	?	a	A
21. When friends ask you out, you usually go, even when you would prefer your privacy.	D	d	?	a	A
22. You stay on the lookout for people who can promote your advancement.	D	d	?	a	A
23. You have a talent for diffusing tension and anger when situations are strained.	D	d	?	a	A
24. You usually end up doing other people's jobs in addition to your own.	D	d	?	a	A
25. You go out of your way to introduce yourself and start up conversation with strangers.	D	d	?	a	A

26. You have a special magnetism that attracts people to you.   D   d   ?   a   A

27. You go out of your way to make sure other people recognize your accomplishments.   D   d   ?   a   A

28. You have an ability to see humor in situations many people overlook.   D   d   ?   a   A

29. If people are not doing a good job, you believe they should be fired.   D   d   ?   a   A

30. There are a lot of things you would change about people if you had your way.   D   d   ?   a   A

31. Others find you very easy to get along with and easy to work with.   D   d   ?   a   A

32. You freely tell others what you think is wrong with them.   D   d   ?   a   A

33. You dislike having to deal with conflict situations requiring confrontation.   D   d   ?   a   A

34. You realize you have to compete for promotions as much on the basis of politics as on merit.   D   d   ?   a   A

35. If invited to venture an opinion around a hot issue, you usually seek a conciliatory or middle position.   D   d   ?   a   A

36. The average person avoids responsibilities and must be strongly directed to work effectively.   D   d   ?   a   A

37. You are an all-around type who can "hit it off" with just about anyone.   D   d   ?   a   A

38. You go out of your way to create a lasting first impression when meeting new people.   D   d   ?   a   A

39. You pretend to be shy or quiet to avoid attention.   D   d   ?   a   A

40. It is very hard to "ruffle your feathers" or "get your back up."   D   d   ?   a   A

41. Until you get to know people, you tend to act distant or aloof.   D   d   ?   a   A

42. You have little patience for people who ask irrelevant and elementary questions.   D   d   ?   a   A

43. You find it easy to seek the advice and counsel of others, as opposed to doing something all on your own.   D   d   ?   a   A

44. You are quick to criticize and discount the foolish opinions and actions of people you cannot stand.   D   d   ?   a   A

45. You will usually wait for someone else to complain about something that displeases you.   D   d   ?   a   A

46. You accept that cultivating your coworkers and bosses is often necessary in getting ahead.   D   d   ?   a   A

47. You are a masterful strategist at deftly maneuvering others toward your views.   D   d   ?   a   A

48. You prefer to make all the important decisions and then expect others to carry them out.   D   d   ?   a   A

49. You avoid superficial "cocktail" talk whenever possible.   D   d   ?   a   A

50. Others find you exciting and are swept along by your personal manner.   D   d   ?   a   A

51. You are really worried about making people jealous or envious of your accomplishments.   D   d   ?   a   A

52. You exude an optimistic appreciation of life that says "all is well."   D   d   ?   a   A

53. You have little sympathy for the "dumb messes" people get themselves into.   D   d   ?   a   A

54. When dealing with others, you have a very easygoing, "laid-back" style.   D   d   ?   a   A

55. You usually have no difficulty collaborating or going along with the majority opinion.   D   d   ?   a   A

56. Head-on, direct, "tell it as it is" confrontation is your style of relating to people.   D   d   ?   a   A

57. When a quarrel takes place between yourself and others, you usually give in first.	D	d	?	a	A
58. You are a person who is particularly adept at currying special favors when you want something.	D	d	?	a	A
59. You have a facility for altering your opinions and viewpoints and adopting new value standards.	D	d	?	a	A
60. If there are ten ways of correctly doing a job, you would press to have it done your way.	D	d	?	a	A

CASES FOR ANALYSIS

COMPUTER SPECIALISTS, INC.

Computer Specialist, Inc. (CSI), a real company, achieved sales of about $3 million by providing computer programmers and system designers under contract to clients. The major client is a well-known bank in western Pennsylvania for whom CSI writes programs for its MasterCard and VISA applications.

While on vacation, Warren Rodgers, CEO of CSI, learned that a star programmer entered the wrong set of instructions into the bank's computer. The mistake caused roughly 500,000 credit cards to be wrongly invalidated, and several thousand cards were quickly confiscated by automatic teller machines. Bank officers were furious, evicting the programmer from the premises and going to the press with the story. The story appeared on the evening news and in the morning newspaper, with the blame placed on CSI.

Two senior managers at CSI, the director of human resources and the marketing director, did not get involved in solving the problem because they had little technical grounding in the bank's data-processing system and no desire to step into this mess. The star programmer was sent home, where she was getting the cold shoulder from CSI managers and the bank. The bank blamed CSI for the fiasco and started demands for financial concessions. CSI's chief competitors were running CSI's name into the ground. They were telling other clients that CSI was totally responsible for the problem.

Before reading on, think for a moment about what you would do if you were Warren Rodgers returning from vacation. Rodgers' response went something like this: (1) Call the star employee at home to let her know that he was behind her 100 percent. This sent the right signal to other programmers and to the bank about her value. (2) Rectifying this problem was made the top management priority for the next few weeks. All available employees were at that bank making amends. Everyone—bank managers, secretaries—was taken to lunch. If any CSI employee was in the area, he or she walked through the bank to show a presence so that bank officials would know the problem was not being avoided. (3) Rodgers did not make a financial settlement with the bank. Instead, he offered a reduced rate for programmers, thereby increasing the number of CSI programmers at the bank. This effectively scuttled the rumor that CSI caused the problem. (4) The managers who failed to take immediate action are no longer with CSI. Managers are now promoted from within, and everyone must have some data-processing experience and be willing to get involved with customers in a proactive mode.

● **QUESTIONS**

1. How would you evaluate Rodgers' response to the crisis? Do you consider him a good manager?
2. How would you rate Rodgers on conceptual, human, and technical skills?
3. Do the managerial roles revealed in this case seem consistent with the small-business managers described in the text?

SOURCE: Based on Warren Rodgers, "My Terrible Vacation," *INC.*, February 1988, 116–117.

GENERAL PRODUCTS BRITAIN

Carl Mitchell was delighted to accept a job in the British branch office of General Products, Inc., a consumer products multinational. Two months later Mitchell was miserable. The problem was George Garrow, the general manager in charge of the British branch, to whom Mitchell reported.

Garrow had worked his way to the general manager position by keeping his nose clean. He kept from making mistakes by avoiding controversial and risky decisions.

As Mitchell complained to his wife, "Any time I ask him to make a decision, he just wants us to dig deeper and provide 30 more pages of data, most of which are irrelevant. I can't get any improvements started."

For example, Mitchell believed that the line of frozen breakfasts and dinners he was in charge of would be more successful if prices were lowered. He and his four product managers spent weeks preparing graphs and charts to justify a lower price. Garrow reviewed the data but kept waffling, asking for more information. His latest request for weather patterns that might affect shopping habits seemed absurd.

Garrow seemed terrified of departing from the status quo. The frozen breakfast and dinner lines still had 1960s-style packaging, even though reformulated for microwave ovens. Garrow wouldn't approve a coupon program in March because in previous years coupons had been run in April. Garrow measured progress not by new ideas or sales results but by hours spent in the office. He arrived early and shuffled memos and charts until late in the evening and expected the same from everyone else.

After four months on the job, Mitchell made a final effort to reason with Garrow. He argued that the branch was taking a big risk by avoiding decisions to improve things. Market share was slipping. New pricing and promotion strategies were essential. But Garrow just urged more patience and told Mitchell that he and his product managers would have to build a more solid case. Soon after, Mitchell's two best product managers quit, burned out by the marathon sessions analyzing pointless data without results.

● QUESTIONS

1. How would you evaluate Garrow as a manager? Evaluate his strengths and weaknesses based on the functions, skills, or roles described in the chapter.
2. If you were Mitchell, what would you do at this point?
3. If you were Garrow's boss and Mitchell came to see you, how would you handle this situation?

SOURCE: Based on Vaune Davis, "Coping with Indecision," *Canadian Business*, May 1990, 91–92.

REFERENCES

1. Evan I. Schwartz, "The Lucie Show: Shaking Up a Stodgy IBM," *Business Week*, April 6, 1992, 64–65.

2. Kathleen Kerwin and James B. Treece, "Detroit's Big Chance," *Business Week*, June 29, 1992, 82–90; Wendy Zellner, "Chrysler's Next Generation," *Business Week*, December 19, 1988, 52–55.

3. Tom Peters and Nancy Austin, *A Passion for Excellence: The Leadership Difference* (New York: Random House, 1985).

4. Alex Taylor III, "A U.S. Style Shakeup at Honda," *Fortune*, December 30, 1991, 115–120.

5. Byron Harris, "The Man Who Killed Braniff," *Texas Monthly*, July 1982, 116–120, 183–189.

6. Brett Duval Fromson, "The Slow Death of E. F. Hutton," *Fortune*, February 29, 1988, 82–88.

7. John A. Byrne, William C. Symonds, and Julia Flynn Syler, "CEO Disease: Egotism Can Breed Corporate Disaster—and the Malady Is Spreading," *Business Week*, April 1, 1991, 52–60.

8. James A. F. Stoner and R. Edward Freeman, *Management*, 4th ed. (Englewood Cliffs, N.J.: Prentice-Hall, 1989).

9. Peter F. Drucker, *Management Tasks, Responsibilities, Practices* (New York: Harper & Row, 1974).

10. G. Pascal Zachary, "How Ashton-Tate Lost Its Leadership in PC Software Arena," *The Wall Street Journal*, April 11, 1990, A1, A12.

11. Peters and Austin, *A Passion for Excellence*, 11–12.

12. John Bussey and Douglas R. Sease, "Manufacturers Strive to Slice Time Needed to Develop Products," *The Wall Street Journal*, February 23, 1988, 1, 13.

13. Harris, "The Man Who Killed Braniff."

14. Peters and Austin, *A Passion for Excellence*.

15. Harris, "The Man Who Killed Braniff," 118–120.

16. Ibid.

17. Fromson, "The Slow Death of E. F. Hutton."

18. Alex Taylor III, "Lee Iacocca's Production Whiz," *Fortune*, June 22, 1987, 36–44.

19. Eric Calonius, "Smart Moves by Quality Champs," *Fortune*, special 1991 issue—The New American Century, 24–28.

20. David Wessel, "With Labor Scarce, Service Firms Strive to Raise Productivity," *The Wall Street Journal*, June 1, 1989, A1, A8.

21. Frank Edward Allen, "McDonald's Launches Plan to Cut Waste," *The Wall Street Journal*, April 17, 1991, B1.

22. Harold Geneen and Alvin Moscow, *Managing* (Garden City, N.Y.,: Doubleday, 1984), 285.

23. Calonius, "Smart Moves by Quality Champs."

24. Carol Hymowitz, "When Firms Slash Middle Management, Those Spared Often Bear a Heavy Load," *The Wall Street Journal*, April 5, 1990, B1.

25. Robert L. Katz, "Skills of an Effective Administrator," *Harvard Business Review* 52 (September–October 1974), 90–102.

26. Brenton Schlender, "How Bill Gates Keeps the Magic Going," *Fortune*, June 18, 1990, 82–89.

27. Morgan W. McCall, Jr., and Michael M. Lombardo, "Off the Track: Why and How Successful Executives Get Derailed" (Technical Report No. 21, Center for Creative Leadership, Greensboro, N.C., January 1983).

28. Joseph B. White, "How Detroit Diesel, Out from under GM, Turned around Fast," *The Wall Street Journal*, August 16, 1991, A1, A8.

29. Henry Mintzberg, *The Nature of Managerial Work* (New York: Harper & Row, 1973).

30. Robert E. Kaplan, "Trade Routes: The Manager's Network of Relationships," *Organizational Dynamics* (Spring 1984), 37–52; Rosemary Stewart, "The Nature of Management: A Problem for Management Education," *Journal of Management Studies* 21 (1984) 323–330; John P. Kotter, "What Effective General Managers Really Do," *Harvard Business Review* (November–December 1982), 156–167; Morgan W. McCall, Jr., Ann M. Morrison, and Robert L. Hannan, "Studies of Managerial Work: Results and Methods" (Technical Report No. 9, Center for Creative Leadership, Greensboro, N.C., 1978).

31. Henry Mintzberg, "Managerial Work: Analysis from Observation," *Management Science* 18 (1971), B97–B110.

32. Alan Deutschman, "The CEO's Secret of Managing Time," *Fortune*, June 1, 1992, 135–146.

33. Based on Carol Saunders and Jack William Jones, "Temporal Sequences in Information Acquisition for Decision Making: A Focus on Source and Medium," *Academy of Management Review* 15 (1990), 29–46; and John P. Kotter, "What Effective General Managers Really Do," *Harvard Business Review* (November–December 1982), 156–167; Mintzberg, "Managerial Work."

34. Mintzberg, "Managerial Work."

35. Sloan Wilson, "What Do Successful Men Have in Common? Raw Energy," *Houston Chronicle*, March 30, 1980, section 6, 11.

36. Lance B. Kurke and Howard E. Aldrich, "Mintzberg Was Right!: A Replication and Extension of *The Nature of Managerial Work*," *Management Science* 29 (1983), 975–984; Cynthia M. Pavett and Alan W. Lau, "Managerial Work: The Influence of Hierarchical Level and Functional Specialty," *Academy of Management Journal* 26 (1983), 170–177; Colin P. Hales, "What Do Managers Do? A Critical Review of the Evidence," *Journal of Management Studies* 23 (1986), 88–115.

37. Wendy Trueman, "CEO Isolation and How to Fight It," *Canadian Business*, July 1991, 28–32.

38. Ronald Grover, "Lod Cook: Mixing Oil and PR," *Business Week*, October 8, 1990, 110–116.

39. Harry S. Jonas III, Ronald E. Fry, and Suresh Srivastva, "The Office of the CEO: Understanding the Executive Experience," *Academy of Management Executive* 4 (August 1990), 36–48.

40. Martha E. Mengelsdorf, "Big vs. Small," *INC.*, May 1989, 22; Joseph G. P. Paolillo, "The Manager's Self-Assessment of Managerial Roles: Small vs. Large Firms," *American Journal of Small Business* (January/March 1984), 61–62.

41. McCall and Lombardo, "Off the Track"; and Carol Hymowitz, "Five Main Reasons Why Managers Fail," *The Wall Street Journal*, May 2, 1988, 21.

42. Joel Arthur Barker, *Future Edge* (New York: William Morrow, 1992).

43. James Gleick, *Chaos: Making a New Science* (New York: Viking, 1987).

44. Janice Castro, "Get Set: Here They Come!" *Time*, Fall 1990 special issue, 50–51; Carol Hymowitz, "Day in the Life of Tomorrow's Manager," *The Wall Street Journal*, March 20, 1989, B1; and Amanda Troy Segal, "Corporate Women," *Business Week*, June 8, 1992, 74–78.

45. Brian Bremner, "The Age of Consolidation," *Business Week*, October 14, 1991, 86–94.

46. John A. Byrne, "Profiting from the Nonprofits," *Business Week*, March 26, 1990, 66–74; and Michael Ryval, "Born-Again Bureaucrats," *Canadian Business*, November 1991, 64–71.

47. "Readying for the Global Bazaar," *Management Review*, September 1989, 18–19.

48. Bob Hagerty, "Firms in Europe Try to Find Executives Who Can Cross Borders in a Single Bound," *The Wall Street Journal*, January 25, 1991, B1; and Shawn Tully, "The Hunt for the Global Manager," *Fortune*, May 21, 1990, 140–144.

49. Schwartz, "The Lucie Show: Shaking Up a Stodgy IBM."

Microsoft CEO William H. Gates has been called many things: whiz-kid, cut-throat salesman, computer cult figure, capitalist brigand, and the richest man in America. But while others have tried to pin down a label, Gates has worked hard and Microsoft has emerged as the single most important force in the computer industry.

Launched in 1978, Microsoft employed only 13 workers and sold $1 million worth of software. It now employs more than 11,800 people worldwide and sold $2.76 billion worth of software in 39 languages in fiscal 1992. In an industry of incredible dynamics, where Microsoft leads, others follow.

Gates amassed a personal fortune of more than $7 billion by foreseeing the pervasiveness of the personal computer. His first deep shot came when IBM decided to use Microsoft's MS-DOS operating system in 1980. Today the system is in 100 million PCs.

From this established pinnacle in operating systems, Microsoft hopes to move into a similarly commanding position in applications programs. Such a concentration of muscle has not been seen in the computer industry since the glory days of IBM in the 1970s.

Despite the company's phenomenal growth, Bill Gates remains the single most important influence in Microsoft's corporate culture. Gates strives to maintain a sense of connectedness among employees and to avoid big-company pitfalls. Whether in programming or marketing, group size is limited and may be divided into subgroups, ensuring task manageability and full participation. When new products are developed, Gates selects a team of approximately 10 people from engineering and marketing, sets goals, and divides up work. Gates willingly delegates authority, but can be persnickety about how it's used. He meets with the group every two weeks to review progress and iron out problems, and it is here that Gates can be incisive, sarcastic, and often intimidating.

Gates is not above employing competitors' successful techniques. He learned from IBM that large companies are better at keeping development projects on track, a rarity for most start-up companies. He emulated the IBM meeting schedules for new product teams and laid down strict parameters and deadlines.

Gates has followed another simple rule: hire smart people, challenge them to think, be committed, and work hard. The average worker puts in 60 to 80 hours a week, yet the company typically receives more than 120,000 résumés in a year, and many recruits turn down higher paying offers with other companies in favor of Microsoft's performance bonuses and stock ownership options.

Meanwhile Gates, who envisioned bringing computing power to the masses well before his time, is pressing relentlessly forward with Windows NT, the latest evolution in graphic interface software. His product strategy of determining where the future lies and betting the ranch on getting there first has been vindicated. He combines a rare blend of characteristics: business sense and intellectual depth, go-power and technical expertise. His excellent planning brings in the type of professional upper management he needs and entices the best young technical minds in the nation to jump on board. He exhibits phenomenal staying power in an industry known for high burnout.

Some of Microsoft's tactics have software rivals screaming foul and claiming Microsoft routinely engages in unfair trade practices. Among the charges, which the Federal Trade Commission has investigated, are allegations that Microsoft's licensing procedure for MS-DOS, and the accompanying Windows system that interfaces spreadsheet and word processing programs, amounts to a freeze out on competitive systems. Under the Microsoft contract, PC makers pay a fee to Microsoft for every unit shipped, whether or not it includes their software. The obvious result is a disinclination to install a competing system.

Microsoft also preempts rival products by allegedly announcing superior systems years before they even exist. Even if the competitors' in-hand product has the promised features of the Microsoft phantom, customers are hesitant, opting to wait for the so-called safe choice of Microsoft. Competitors describe the technique as "fudding," spreading fear, uncertainty, and doubt about rival products.

What is Gates' opinion of the FTC probe? "The worst that could come of this is I could fall down on the steps of the FTC [building], hit my head, and kill myself." And Bill Gates doesn't seem to care what people call him.

● QUESTIONS

1. What is Gates' method of implementing the four functions of management when launching a new product?

2. How does Microsoft reflect Gates' management skills, as described in this case?

3. Describe some of the roles Gates plays at Microsoft. Are they typical of managerial activities? Discuss.

4. What changes have occurred at Microsoft since this video was aired?

FOUNDATIONS OF MANAGEMENT UNDERSTANDING

2 CHAPTER

LEARNING OBJECTIVES

After studying this chapter, you should be able to

■ Understand how historical forces in society have influenced the practice of management.

■ Identify and explain major developments in the history of management thought.

■ Describe the major components of the classical management perspective.

■ Describe the major components of the human resource management perspective.

■ Discuss the quantitative management perspective.

■ Explain the major concepts of systems theory.

■ Discuss the basic concepts underlying contingency views.

■ Describe the recent influences of global competition on management in North America.

Mired in the problems of inflation and battered by government-subsidized foreign competition, the Aluminum Company of America (Alcoa) reassessed its position in the changing global market as it entered the 1990s. CEO Paul O'Neill analyzed the boom and bust cycles over Alcoa's 100-year history. He considered the huge military markets for aluminum created during World War II, the new civilian applications afterward, and the cycle of the increasing and then decreasing militancy of Alcoa's labor unions. He also explored the waxing and waning of Alcoa's scientific reputation over the years, Alcoa's poor performance during every serious recession, and recent stiff competition from newer materials such as plastics, ceramics, and composites. O'Neill's analysis led him to conclude that Alcoa  thrived when it developed new products such as the easy open aluminum tops, when it provided the lowest cost production in the industry, and when company marketing was aggressive. Now management must evaluate these historical lessons to determine which should be applied to the strategy and direction of Alcoa.[1]

■ During the deepening recession of 1990, Alcoa experienced a sharp profit decline. Do you feel that CEO O'Neill should use his historical analysis to explain away this decline and continue with current strategy or create a new strategy based on trying to increase profits despite the recession?

M A N A G E M E N T   P R O B L E M

Why should history matter to corporate managers like Paul O'Neill of Alcoa? Alcoa's success may well hinge on O'Neill's bets about historical trends and Alcoa's ability to capitalize on the cycles of economic growth and new product introductions that have persisted for 100 years. A historical perspective matters to executives, because it is a way of thinking, a way of searching for patterns and determining whether they recur across time periods. A historical perspective provides a context or environment in which to interpret problems. Only then does a major problem take on real meaning, reveal its severity, and point the way toward management actions.[2]

A study of the past contributes to understanding both the present and the future. It is a way of learning: learning from others' mistakes so as not to repeat them; learning from others' successes so as to repeat them in the appropriate situation; and, most of all, learning to understand why things happen to improve things in the future.

For example, such companies as Polaroid, AT&T, International Harvester, Consolidated Edison, and Wells Fargo Bank have all asked historians to research their pasts. Managers want to know their corporate roots. Polaroid's W-3 plant in Waltham, Massachusetts, started out as a model of efficiency, but over the years productivity dropped and relations with workers soured. A corporate historian was hired to interview employees and examine old records. He pieced together how managers had imposed ever tighter controls over the years that lowered workers' morale.[3] Or consider the signing of Randy Travis, now a country music superstar, by Warner Brothers. Country music had been invaded by pop music influence, and industry managers wanted more pop in the country sound to appeal to younger audiences. Martha Sharp, a vice-president for Warner Brothers, loved Travis's voice and used a cycle-of-history argument on her bosses. She argued that based on historical patterns, a traditional country sound would reemerge, and Travis would be in the forefront. Her argument won, Travis was signed, and he led a resurgence in country music.[4]

This chapter provides an overview of how managers' philosophies have changed over the years. This foundation of management understanding illustrates that the value of studying management lies not in learning current facts and research but in developing a perspective that will facilitate the broad, long-term view needed for management success.

History can benefit companies in a variety of ways. For example, historical images associated with company names can be an asset. The name, Wells Fargo & Co., evokes images of rugged, independent pioneers, as well as a historical period when a "man's word was his bond." True to its frontier legacy, Wells Fargo focuses on business and expansion of proven strengths, along familiar trails, while keeping a watchful eye on the horizon for innovations that will carry this legendary company into the 21st century.

● HISTORICAL FORCES SHAPING MANAGEMENT

Studying history does not mean merely arranging events in chronological order; it means developing an understanding of the impact of societal forces on organizations. Studying history is a way to achieve strategic thinking, see the big picture, and improve conceptual skills. We will start by examining how social, political, and economic forces have influenced organizations and the practice of management.[5]

Social forces refer to those aspects of a culture that guide and influence relationships among people. What do people value? What do people need? What are the standards of behavior among people? These forces shape what is known as the *social contract*, which refers to the unwritten, common rules and perceptions about relationships among people and between employees and management. Expressions such as "a man's as good as his word" and "a day's work for a day's pay" convey such perceptions.

Political forces refer to the influence of political and legal institutions on people and organizations. Political forces include basic assumptions underlying the political system, such as the desirability of self-government, property rights, contract rights, the definition of justice, and the determination of innocence or guilt of a crime. Further, political forces determine managers' rights relative to those of owners, customers, suppliers, and workers as well as other publics with whom the organization must interact. For example, deregulation is a political force that has influenced the way of doing business in the banking and airline industries. Managers can understand deregulation by studying the regulations' original impact on corporations and how new regulations changed the market.

social forces

The aspects of a culture that guide and influence relationships among people—their values, needs, and standards of behavior.

political forces

The influence of political and legal institutions on people and organizations.

Lewis Hine's famous 1911 "Breaker Boys" photograph helped promote passage of laws forbidding child labor. While bent in a back-breaking position and breathing coal dust, these boys picked impurities from coal 12 to 14 hours a day, six days a week, for $.75 a day. Public outcry became a strong *social force* against child labor. *Political forces* prompted Congress to outlaw the employment of children. *Economic forces* reallocated resources to materials-handling machinery, which reduced the need for child labor.

focus on ETHICS

"IF IT'S HOOTIN', I'M SHOOTIN'"

The historical clash between environmentalists and industry is being played out right now in the great Northwest. The spotted owl endangers the Northwest lumber industry, and vice versa.

Typical of the logging firms is Gregory Forest Products, purchased by William Gregory in Glendale, Oregon, so he could run his own business. Gregory invested heavily in new technology, enabling his lumber mill to recover 20 percent more from each log. Efficiency combined with increased prices produced healthy profits in 1989, yet Gregory is now investing in employee training to help workers find jobs elsewhere.

What's the problem? Powerful political and economic forces. Gregory's mill may be forced to close because of a court injunction against harvesting old-growth timber. The spotted owl nests in the tops of the 200-year-old trees. Environmentalists want to protect old-growth forests because they harbor thousands of animals and plants. Because of the injunction, Gregory has eliminated his swing shift, and other mills are cutting back as well. If current bans are made permanent, 25,000 jobs may be lost. Gloom has settled over the area. The local school district cancelled extracurricular activities because of reduced tax income. Yellow ribbons flutter from car antennas, and 1,100 logging trucks streamed through Grants Pass in protest. Bumper stickers sum up the feeling of unemployed residents

toward the owl: "If It's Hootin', I'm Shootin'."

Political decisions and the clash of social and economic forces have suspended logging in the old-growth forest, costing hundreds of jobs that will not be recovered. Environmentalists are winning at this point because federal courts have ruled that harvesting practices are in violation of environmental laws. But lumber industry people feel that harvesting the timber is a legitimate way to provide jobs. Without new legislation from Congress to protect the logging industry, even more people will be out of work. ■

SOURCE: Based on Charles McCoy, "Timber Town Is Bitter over Efforts to Save the Rare Spotted Owl," *The Wall Street Journal*, January 6, 1992, A1, A6; and Jonathan B. Levine, "The Spotted Owl Could Wipe Us Out," *Business Week*, September 18, 1989, 94–99.

The Focus on Ethics box gives an example of how social and political forces have affected the logging industry in Oregon and Washington. Economic forces are also involved in the struggle surrounding the spotted owl.

Economic forces pertain to the availability, production, and distribution of resources in a society. Governments, military agencies, churches, schools, and business organizations in every society require resources to achieve their objectives, and economic forces influence the allocation of scarce resources. Resources may be human or material, fabricated or natural, physical or conceptual, but over time they are scarce and must be allocated among competing users. Economic scarcity is often the stimulus for technological innovation with which to increase resource availability. The perfection of the moving assembly line at Ford in 1913 cut the number of worker-hours needed for assembling a Model T from 12 to 1.5. Ford doubled its daily pay rate to $5, shortened working hours, and cut the price of Model Ts until its market share reached 57 percent in 1923.

economic forces

Forces that affect the availability, production, and distribution of a society's resources among competing users.

● CLASSICAL PERSPECTIVE

The practice of management can be traced to 3000 B.C. to the first government organizations developed by the Sumerians and Egyptians, but the formal study of management is relatively recent.[6] The early study of management as we know it today began with what is now called the *classical perspective*.

The **classical perspective** on management emerged during the nineteenth and early twentieth centuries. It was grounded in management experiences from manufacturing, transportation, and communication industries, which were heavily staffed by engineers. Firms tended to be small or composed of departments or divisions consisting of small groups. Most organizations produced only one line of product or service. Further, major educational, social, and cultural differences existed among owners, managers, and workers.

The factory system that began to appear in the 1800s posed management challenges that earlier organizations had not encountered. Problems arose in tooling the plants, organizing managerial structure, training employees (many of them non-English-speaking immigrants), scheduling complex manufacturing operations, and dealing with increased labor dissatisfaction and resulting strikes. These problems offset the factory system's increased efficiency brought about by interchangeable parts, standardization of products, division of labor, and improved rail transportation.

Traditional small, family-owned industrial plants with an average work force of eight employees in 1870 found the rapid growth in the late nineteenth century to be overwhelming. For example, McCormick Harvester Works of Chicago began in the 1840s with 23 employees. By 1884 it had a monstrous 12-acre plant employing 1,300 workers. A nostalgic longing for the "old and pleasant relations" of the small family-owned business failed to deal effectively with mounting labor grievances. The unhappy results were strikes and, ultimately, the disastrous Hay Market strike and violent labor riot in Chicago in May 1886.[7]

In light of such events and in response to the myriad new problems facing management throughout industrial America, managers developed and tested solutions to the mounting challenges. The evolution of modern management, called the *classical perspective*, thus began. This perspective contains three subfields, each with a slightly different emphasis: scientific management, bureaucratic organization, and administrative principles.[8]

classical perspective

A management perspective that emerged during the nineteenth and early twentieth centuries that emphasized a rational, scientific approach to the study of management and sought to make organizations efficient operating machines.

Frederick Winslow Taylor (1856–1915)
Taylor's theory that labor productivity could be improved by scientifically determined management practices earned him the status of "father of scientific management."

SCIENTIFIC MANAGEMENT

Organizations' somewhat limited success in achieving improvements in labor productivity led a young engineer to suggest that the problem lay more in poor management practices than in labor. Frederick Winslow Taylor (1856–1915) insisted that management itself would have to change and, further, that the manner of change could be determined only

Frederick Taylor's *scientific management* techniques were expanded by automaker Henry Ford, who replaced workers with machines for heavy lifting and moving. One of the first applications of the moving assembly line was the Magneto assembly operation at Ford's Highland Park plant in 1913. Magnetos moved from one worker to the next, reducing production time by one-half. The same principle was applied to total-car assembly, improving efficiency and reducing worker hours required to produce a Model-T Ford to less than two. Under this system, a Ford rolled off the assembly line every ten seconds.

scientific management

A subfield of the classical management perspective that emphasized scientifically determined changes in management practices as the solution to improving labor productivity.

Lillian M. Gilbreth (1878–1972)
Frank B. Gilbreth (1868–1924)
This husband-and-wife team contributed to the principles of scientific management. His development of time and motion studies and her work in industrial psychology pioneered many of today's management and human resource techniques.

by scientific study; hence, the label **scientific management** emerged. Taylor suggested that decisions based on rules of thumb and tradition be replaced with precise procedures developed after careful study of individual situations.

While working at the Midvale Steel Company in Philadelphia, Taylor began experimenting with management methods, procedures, and practices. Taylor wrote frequently, had others write under his name, and consulted with businesses to encourage utilization of his ideas.[9] However, it was after the Eastern Railroad Rate Case hearings before the House of Representatives that his work really caught on. The attorney for the shippers, Louis D. Brandeis, used the term *scientific management* and successfully argued the shippers' side of the issue for using these techniques. The popular press picked up the term, and Taylor and his ideas became heralded as the way to prosperity for the United States.[10]

Taylor's approach is illustrated by the unloading of iron from rail cars and reloading finished steel for the Bethlehem Steel plant in 1898. Taylor calculated that with correct movements, tools, and sequencing, each man was capable of loading 47.5 tons per day instead of the typical 12.5 tons. He also worked out an incentive system that paid each man $1.85 a day for meeting the new standard, an increase from the previous rate of $1.15. Productivity at Bethlehem Steel shot up overnight.

Although known as the "father of scientific management," Taylor was not alone in this area. Henry Gantt, an associate of Taylor's, developed the *Gantt Chart*—a bar graph that measures planned and completed work along each stage of production by time elapsed. Two other important pioneers in this area were the husband-and-wife team of Frank B. and Lillian M. Gilbreth. Frank B. Gilbreth (1868–1924) pioneered time and motion study and arrived at many of his management techniques independently of Taylor. He stressed efficiency and was known for his quest for the "one best way" to do work. Although Gilbreth is known for his early work with bricklayers, his work had great impact on medical surgery by drastically reducing the time patients spent on the operating table. Surgeons were able to save countless lives through the application of time and motion study. Lillian M. Gilbreth (1878–1972) was more interested in the human aspect of work. When her husband died at the age of 56, she had 12 children ages 2 to 19. The undaunted "first lady of management" went right on with her work. She presented a paper in place of her late husband, continued their seminars and consulting, lectured, and eventually became a professor at Purdue University.[11] She pioneered in the field of industrial psychology and made substantial contributions to personnel management.

The basic ideas of scientific management are shown in Exhibit 2.1. To use this approach, managers should develop standard methods for doing each job, select workers with the appropriate abilities, train workers in the standard methods, support workers and eliminate interruptions, and provide wage incentives.

Although scientific management improved productivity, its failure to deal with the social context and workers' needs led to increased conflict between managers and employees. Under this system, workers often felt exploited. This was in sharp contrast to the harmony and cooperation that Taylor and his followers had envisioned.

BUREAUCRATIC ORGANIZATIONS

A systematic approach developed in Europe that looked at the organization as a whole is the **bureaucratic organizations** approach, a subfield within the classical perspective. Max Weber (1864–1920), a German theorist, introduced most of the concepts on bureaucratic organizations.[12]

During the late 1800s, many European organizations were managed on a "personal," family-like basis. Employees were loyal to a single individual rather than to the organization or its mission. The dysfunctional consequence of this management practice was that resources were used to realize individual desires rather than organizational goals. Employees in effect owned the organization and used resources for their own gain rather than to serve clients. Weber envisioned organizations that would

bureaucratic organizations

A subfield of the classical management perspective that emphasized management on an impersonal, rational basis through elements such as clearly defined authority and responsibility, formal recordkeeping, and separation of management and ownership.

General Approach
- Developed standard method for performing each job.
- Selected workers with appropriate abilities for each job.
- Trained workers in standard method.
- Supported workers by planning their work and eliminating interruptions.
- Provided wage incentives to workers for increased output.

Contributions
- Demonstrated the importance of compensation for performance.
- Initiated the careful study of tasks and jobs.
- Demonstrated the importance of personnel selection and training.

Criticisms
- Did not appreciate the social context of work and higher needs of workers.
- Did not acknowledge variance among individuals.
- Tended to regard workers as uninformed and ignored their ideas and suggestions.

E X H I B I T   2 . 1

Characteristics of Scientific Management

Max Weber
(1864–1920)
The German theorist's concepts on *bureaucratic organizations* have contributed to the efficiency of many of today's corporations.

be managed on an impersonal, rational basis. This form of organization was called a *bureaucracy*. Exhibit 2.2 summarizes the six characteristics of bureaucracy as specified by Weber.

Weber believed that an organization based on rational authority would be more efficient and adaptable to change because continuity is related to formal structure and positions rather than to a particular person, who may leave or die. To Weber, rationality in organizations meant employee selection and advancement based on competence rather than on "whom you know." The organization relies on rules and written records for continuity. The manager depends not on his or her personality for successfully giving orders but on the legal power invested in the managerial position.

The term *bureaucracy* has taken on a negative meaning in today's organizations and is associated with endless rules and red tape. We have all been frustrated by waiting in long lines or following seemingly silly procedures. On the other hand, rules and other bureaucratic procedures provide a standard way of dealing with employees. Everyone gets equal treatment, and everyone knows what the rules are. This has enabled many organizations to become extremely efficient. Consider United Parcel Service, also called the "Brown Giant" for the color of the packages it delivers.

 UNITED PARCEL SERVICE

United Parcel Service took on the U.S. Postal Service at its own game— and won. UPS specializes in the delivery of small packages. Why has the Brown Giant been so successful? One important reason is the concept of bureaucracy. UPS is bound up in rules and regulations. There are safety rules for drivers, loaders, clerks, and managers. Strict dress codes are enforced—no beards; hair cannot touch the collar; mustaches must be trimmed evenly; and no sideburns. Rules specify cleanliness standards for buildings and other properties. No eating or drinking is permitted at employee desks. Every manager is given bound copies of policy books and expected to use them regularly.

UPS also has a well-defined division of labor. Each plant consists of specialized drivers, loaders, clerks, washers, sorters, and maintenance personnel. UPS thrives on written records. Daily worksheets specify performance goals and work output. Daily employee quotas and achievements are recorded on a weekly and monthly basis.

Technical qualification is the criterion for hiring and promotion. The UPS policy book says the leader is expected to have the knowledge and capacity to justify the position of leadership. Favoritism is forbidden. The bureaucratic model works just fine at UPS, "the tightest ship in the shipping business."[13] ∎

administrative principles

A subfield of the classical management perspective that focused on the total organization rather than the individual worker, delineating the management functions of planning, organizing, commanding, coordinating, and controlling.

ADMINISTRATIVE PRINCIPLES

Another major subfield within the classical perspective is known as the **administrative principles** approach. Whereas scientific management focused on the productivity of the individual worker, the administrative

EXHIBIT   2 . 2

Characteristics of Weberian
Bureaucracy

SOURCE: Adapted from A. M. Henderson
and Talcott Parsons, eds. and trans.,
Max Weber, *The Theory of Social and
Economic Organizations* (New York:
Free Press, 1947), 328–337.

Elements of Bureaucracy

1. Labor is divided with clear definitions of authority and responsibility that are legitimized as official duties.
2. Positions are organized in a hierarchy of authority, with each position under the authority of a higher one.
3. All personnel are selected and promoted based on technical qualifications, which are assessed by examination or according to training and experience.
4. Administrative acts and decisions are recorded in writing. Recordkeeping provides organizational memory and continuity over time.
5. Management is separate from the ownership of the organization.
6. Managers are subject to rules and procedures that will ensure reliable, predictable behavior. Rules are impersonal and uniformly applied to all employees.

principles approach focused on the total organization. The contributors to this approach included Henri Fayol, Mary Parker Follett, and Chester I. Barnard.

Henri Fayol (1841–1925) was a French mining engineer who worked his way up to the head of a major mining group known as Comambault. Comambault survives today as part of Le Creusot-Loire, the largest mining and metallurgical group in central France. In his later years, Fayol wrote down his concepts on administration, based largely on his own management experiences.[14]

In his most significant work, *General and Industrial Management*, Fayol discussed 14 general principles of management, several of which are part of management philosophy today. For example:

- *Unit of command.* Each subordinate receives orders from one—and only one—superior.

- *Division of work.* Managerial and technical work are amenable to specialization to produce more and better work with the same amount of effort.

- *Unity of direction.* Similar activities in an organization should be grouped together under one manager.

- *Scalar chain.* A chain of authority extends from the top to the bottom of the organization and should include every employee.

Fayol felt that these principles could be applied in any organizational setting. He also identified five basic functions or elements of management: planning, organizing, commanding, coordinating, and controlling. These functions underlie much of the general approach to today's management theory.

Mary Parker Follett (1868–1933) was trained in philosophy and political science at what today is Radcliffe College. She applied herself in many fields, including social psychology and management. She wrote of the importance of common superordinate goals for reducing conflict in organizations.[15] Her work was popular with businesspeople of her day but was often overlooked by management scholars.[16] Follett's ideas served as a contrast to scientific management and are reemerging as

Mary Parker Follett
(1868–1933)
Follett was a major contributor to the *administrative principles* approach to management. Her emphasis on worker participation and shared goals among managers was embraced by many businesspeople of the day, and has been recently "rediscovered" by corporate America.

This 1914 photograph shows the initiation of a new arrival at a Nebraska planting camp. This initiation was not part of the formal rules and illustrates the significance of the *informal organization* described by Barnard. Social values and behaviors were powerful forces that could help or hurt the planting organization depending on how they were managed.

applicable for modern managers dealing with rapid changes in today's global environment. Her approach to leadership stressed the importance of people rather than engineering techniques. She offered the pithy admonition, "Don't Hug Your Blueprints," and analyzed the dynamics of management-organization interactions. Follett addressed issues that are timely in the 1990s, such as ethics, power, and how to lead in a way that encourages employees to give their best. The concepts of empowerment, facilitating rather than controlling employees, and allowing employees to act depending on the authority of the situation opened new areas for theoretical study by Chester Barnard and others.[17]

Chester I. Barnard (1886–1961) studied economics at Harvard but failed to receive a degree because he lacked a course in laboratory science. He went to work in the statistical department of AT&T and in 1927 became president of New Jersey Bell. One of Barnard's significant contributions was the concept of the informal organization. The *informal organization* occurs in all formal organizations and includes cliques and naturally occurring social groupings. Barnard argued that organizations are not machines and informal relationships are powerful forces that can help the organization if properly managed. Another significant contribution was the *acceptance theory of authority*, which states that people have free will and can choose whether to follow management orders. People typically follow orders because they perceive positive benefit to themselves, but they do have a choice. Managers should treat employees properly because their acceptance of authority may be critical to organization success in important situations.[18]

The overall classical perspective as an approach to management was very powerful and gave companies fundamental new skills for establishing high productivity and effective treatment of employees. Indeed, America surged ahead of the world in management techniques, and other countries, especially Japan, borrowed heavily from American ideas. One example of how the Japanese learned from early American managers is described in the Focus on Global Competition box.

● HUMAN RESOURCE PERSPECTIVE

America has always had a spirit of human equality. However, this spirit has not always been translated into practice when it comes to power sharing between managers and workers. The **human resource perspective** has recognized and directly responded to social pressures for enlightened treatment of employees. The early work on industrial psychology and personnel selection received little attention because of the prominence of scientific management. Then a series of studies at a Chicago electric company changed all that.

human resource perspective

A management perspective that emerged around the late nineteenth century that emphasized enlightened treatment of workers and power sharing between managers and employees.

THE HAWTHORNE STUDIES

Beginning about 1895, a struggle developed between manufacturers of gas and electric lighting fixtures for control of the residential and industrial market.[19] By 1909 electric lighting had begun to win, but the increas-

AMERICAN TEACHINGS FOR JAPAN

What the Japanese learned about management after World War II they learned from the Americans. And the Americans forgot their own lessons.

HOMER M. SARASOHN
First U.S. Consultant on Rebuilding Japan's Post-War Industry

In 1946, General Douglas MacArthur, commander of U.S. occupational forces in Japan, summoned Homer Sarasohn from the United States. The task for the young product development engineer was to assist the Japanese in the development of radio mass production that would allow speedy communications between occupation authorities and the villages scattered throughout the war-torn country. Sarasohn's immediate problems were to find materials, facilities, and a work force capable of manufacturing production. The Japanese work force was naive and saw no reason why vacuum tubes could not be assembled in dirt-floored shacks. To solve these problems, Sarasohn assumed temporary industrial power comparable to the authority of General MacArthur.

Western Electric engineer Charles Protzman joined Sarasohn in 1948. Together they analyzed the Japanese production methods and concluded that the major problems were managerial. In 1949, along with Frank Polkinghorn, they proposed and developed a basic management course. Other divisions of the occupational force objected strenuously and made counterpresentations to MacArthur. After hearing the objections, MacArthur turned to Sarasohn and snapped, "Go do it." MacArthur's three-word order changed the history of management in Japan.

Drawing heavily from Frederick Taylor's scientific management ideas and administrative principles, the management course stressed careful analysis of each organization part and design for maximum efficiency of the *entire* system. The foundation of a successful organization, course attendees learned on the first day, is the overall objective or social mission of the enterprise. The course drew heavily upon lessons from successful American companies, such as Newport News Shipbuilding, that stressed high quality: "We shall build good ships here: At a profit if we can, at a loss if we must, but always good ships."

The Japanese quickly embraced the American lessons. Management graduates included the ultimate heads of Matsushita Electric, Mitsubishi Electric, Fujitsu, Sumitomo Electric, and Sony. The lessons from that original management course were strongly reinforced by a second wave of Americans, including Total Quality prophets, W. Edwards Deming and J. M. Juran, and, together, these form the basis of management in Japan today. Japan's prestigious award for quality is named for Deming, and echoes of the first U.S. seminars still appear in interviews with top Japanese business leaders. For example, the chairman of Canon, Inc., recently spoke of the need for organizations to find a sense of mission and coherent philosophy that fits both the domestic and global community. The social mission of the enterprise should provide a "mutually rewarding coexistence" among companies worldwide. ■

SOURCE: Robert Chapman Wood, "A Lesson Learned and a Lesson Forgotten," *Forbes*, February 6, 1989, 70–78; and "Global Management in the 1990s," *Fortune*, global business advertising supplement, July 27, 1992, S–12.

ingly efficient electric fixtures used less total power. The electric companies began a campaign to convince industrial users that they needed more light to get more productivity. When advertising did not work, the industry began using experimental tests to demonstrate their argument. Managers were skeptical about the results, so the Committee on Industrial Lighting (CIL) was set up to run the tests. To further add to the tests' credibility, Thomas Edison was made honorary chairman of the

Hawthorne studies

A series of experiments on worker productivity begun in 1924 at the Hawthorne plant of Western Electric Company in Illinois; attributed employees' increased output to managers' better treatment of them during the study.

CIL. In one test location—the Hawthorne plant of the Western Electric Company—some interesting events occurred. These and subsequent experiments have come to be known as the **Hawthorne studies**.

The major part of this work involved four experimental and three control groups. In all, five different "tests" were conducted. These pointed to the importance of factors *other* than illumination in affecting productivity. To more carefully examine these factors, numerous other experiments were conducted.[20] These were the first Relay Assembly Test Room, the second Relay Assembly Group, the Mica Splitting Group, the Typewriting Group, and the Bank Wiring Observation Room. The results of the most famous study, the first Relay Assembly Test Room (RATR) experiment, were extremely controversial. Under the guidance of two Harvard professors, Elton Mayo and Fritz Roethlisberger, the RATR studies lasted nearly six years (May 10, 1927, to May 4, 1933) and involved 24 separate experimental periods. So many factors were changed and so many unforeseen factors uncontrolled that scholars disagree on the factors that truly contributed to the general increase in performance over that period. Most early interpretations, however, agreed on one thing: Money was not the cause of the increased output.[21] Recent analyses of the experiments, however, suggest that money may well have been the single most important factor.[22] An interview with one of the original participants revealed that just getting into the experimental group had meant a huge increase in income.[23]

These new data clearly show that money mattered a great deal at Hawthorne, but it was not recognized at the time of the experiments.

This is the Relay Room of the Western Electric Hawthorne, Illinois, plant in 1927. Six women worked in this *relay assembly test room* during the controversial experiments on employee productivity. Professors Mayo and Roethlisberger evaluated conditions such as rest breaks and workday length, physical health, amount of sleep, and diet. Experimental changes were fully discussed with the women and were abandoned if they disapproved. Gradually the researchers began to realize they had created a change in supervisory style and human relations, which they believed was the true cause of the increased productivity.

Then it was felt that the factor that best explained increased output was "human relations." Employees' output increased sharply when managers treated them in a positive manner. These findings were published and started a revolution in worker treatment for improving organizational productivity. To be historically accurate, money was probably the best explanation for increases in output, but at that time experimenters believed the explanation was human relations. Despite the inaccurate interpretation of the data, the findings provided the impetus for the human relations movement. That movement shaped management theory and practice for well over a quarter-century, and the belief that human relations is the best approach for increasing productivity persists today. See the Manager's Shoptalk box for a number of management innovations that have become popular over the years.

PEOPLE ASPECT

THE HUMAN RELATIONS MOVEMENT

One reason that "human relations" interpretation may have been so readily attached to the Hawthorne studies was the Great Depression. An unprecedented number of people were out of work. Emerging social forces supported people's humanitarian efforts to help one another. The **human relations movement** initially espoused a "dairy farm" view of management—contented cows give more milk, so satisfied workers will give more work. Gradually, views with deeper content began to emerge. Two of the best-known contributors to the human relations movement were Abraham Maslow and Douglas McGregor.

Abraham Maslow (1908–1970), a practicing psychologist, observed that his patients' problems usually stemmed from an inability to satisfy their needs. Thus, he generalized his work and suggested a hierarchy of needs. Maslow's hierarchy started with physiological needs and progressed to safety, belongingness, esteem, and, finally, self-actualization needs. Chapter 15 discusses his ideas in more detail.

Douglas McGregor (1906–1964) had become frustrated with the early simplistic human relations notions while president of Antioch College in Ohio. He challenged both the classical perspective and the early human relations assumptions about human behavior. Based on his experiences as a manager and consultant, his training as a psychologist, and the work of Maslow, McGregor formulated his Theory X and Theory Y, which are explained in Exhibit 2.3.[24] McGregor believed that the classical perspective was based on Theory X assumptions about workers. He also felt that a slightly modified version of Theory X fit early human relations ideas. In other words, human relations ideas did not go far enough. McGregor proposed Theory Y as a more realistic view of workers for guiding management thinking.

The point of Theory Y is that organizations can take advantage of the imagination and intellect of all their employees. Employees will exercise self-control and will contribute to organizational objectives when given the opportunity. A few companies today still use Theory X management, but many are trying Theory Y techniques. Saturn Corp., with one of the greatest success stories in the auto industry, has practiced Theory Y from its beginning.

human relations movement

A movement in management thinking and practice that emphasized satisfaction of employees' basic needs as the key to increased worker productivity.

EBBS AND FLOWS OF MANAGEMENT INNOVATIONS, 1950–1992

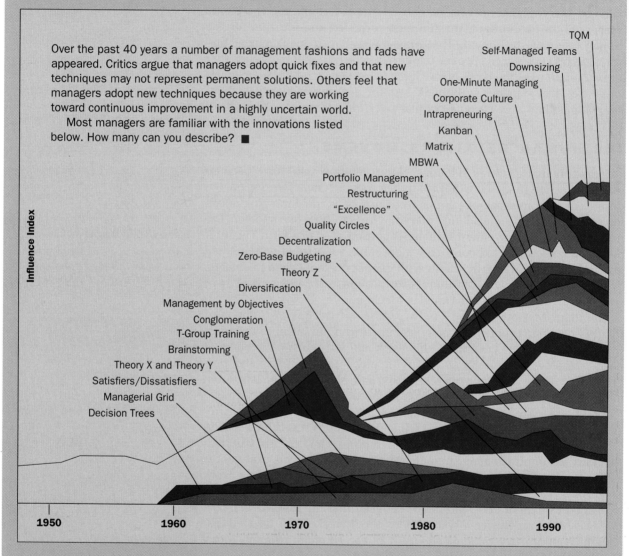

Over the past 40 years a number of management fashions and fads have appeared. Critics argue that managers adopt quick fixes and that new techniques may not represent permanent solutions. Others feel that managers adopt new techniques because they are working toward continuous improvement in a highly uncertain world.

Most managers are familiar with the innovations listed below. How many can you describe? ■

Influence Index

TQM
Self-Managed Teams
Downsizing
One-Minute Managing
Corporate Culture
Intrapreneuring
Kanban
Matrix
MBWA
Portfolio Management
Restructuring
"Excellence"
Quality Circles
Decentralization
Zero-Base Budgeting
Theory Z
Diversification
Management by Objectives
Conglomeration
T-Group Training
Brainstorming
Theory X and Theory Y
Satisfiers/Dissatisfiers
Managerial Grid
Decision Trees

1950   1960   1970   1980   1990

SOURCE: Adapted from Fig. 1.3, Richard Tanner Pascale, *Managing on the Edge* (New York: Touchstone/Simon & Schuster, 1990) 20. Copyright © 1990 by Richard Pascale. Reprinted by permission of Simon & Schuster, Inc.

 SATURN CORPORATION

For years, General Motors poured billions of dollars into the Spring Hill, Tennessee, Saturn plant while critics claimed GM would never be able to build a small car that would compete with the Japanese. The critics

Assumptions of Theory X

- The average human being has an inherent dislike of work and will avoid it if possible....
- Because of the human characteristic of dislike for work, most people must be coerced, controlled, directed, or threatened with punishment to get them to put forth adequate effort toward the achievement of organizational objectives....
- The average human being prefers to be directed, wishes to avoid responsibility, has relatively little ambition, wants security above all.

Assumptions of Theory Y

- The expenditure of physical and mental effort in work is as natural as play or rest. The average human being does not inherently dislike work....
- External control and the threat of punishment are not the only means for bringing about effort toward organizational objectives. A person will exercise self-direction and self-control in the service of objectives to which he or she is committed....
- The average human being learns, under proper conditions, not only to accept but to seek responsibility....
- The capacity to exercise a relatively high degree of imagination, ingenuity, and creativity in the solution of organizational problems is widely, not narrowly, distributed in the population.
- Under the conditions of modern industrial life, the intellectual potentialities of the average human being are only partially utilized.

E X H I B I T   2 . 3

Theory X and Theory Y

SOURCE: Douglas McGregor, *The Human Side of Enterprise* (New York: McGraw-Hill, 1960), 33–48.

---

didn't understand the extent to which Saturn Corp. would trust employees, engaging their hearts and minds in the production of a world-class automobile. Organized into teams, assembly line workers hire new employees, approve parts from suppliers, choose their own equipment, and handle administrative matters such as the budget. Worker teams keep costs down and pass the savings to customers. And the teams have the responsibility to achieve quality targets, which they will not compromise. Saturn's revolutionary labor agreement makes full partners of union members and managers, giving everyone the authority to solve quality problems. Line workers have the authority, for example, to telephone the supplier when defective parts are discovered to get them fixed. The 14-member door assembly team recently suggested rearranging machinery to improve quality and productivity, which meant using two fewer people. The two extra employees were transferred to another part of the plant, reflecting the trust employees have that they won't be worked out of a job.

Saturn has been so successful at taking advantage of the imagination, creativity, and ability of its employees that it has jumped to the top of the customer approval ratings, joining Lexus and Infiniti, which cost tens of thousands more. The cars also race out of dealer showrooms. Karen M. Tibus, a dealer in Michigan, recently had just four Saturns on hand instead of the usual 200. She had already sold the nine demonstration models her sales staff drove. More Saturns are on the way, but production won't be increased without the consent of employees and unless superb quality is maintained.[25] ■

BEHAVIORAL SCIENCES APPROACH

behavioral sciences approach

A subfield of the human resource management perspective that applied social science in an organizational context, drawing from economics, psychology, sociology, and other disciplines.

The word *science* is the keyword in the **behavioral sciences approach** (see Exhibit 2.4). Systematic research is the basis for theory development and testing, and its results form the basis for practical applications. The behavioral sciences approach can be seen in practically every organization. When General Electric conducts research to determine the best set of tests, interviews, and employee profiles to use when selecting new employees, it is employing behavioral science techniques. Emery Air Freight has utilized reinforcement theory to improve the incentives given to workers and increase the performance of many of its operations. When Westinghouse trains new managers in the techniques of employee motivation, most of the theories and findings are rooted in behavioral science research.

In the behavioral sciences, economics and sociology have significantly influenced the way today's managers approach organizational strategy and structure. Psychology has influenced management approaches to motivation, communication, leadership, and the overall field of personnel management. The conclusions from the tremendous body of behavioral science research are much like those derived from the natural sciences. Although we understand more, that understanding is not simple. Scholars have learned much about the behavior of people at work, but they have also learned that organizational processes are astonishingly complex.

All of the remaining chapters of this book contain research findings and applications that can be attributed to the behavioral sciences approach to the study of organizations and management. The Manager's Shoptalk box shows the trend of new management concepts from the behavioral sciences. Note the increase in concepts about 1970 and then again from 1980 until the present. The increasing intensity of global competition has produced great interest in improved behavioral approaches to management. The continued development of new management techniques can be expected in the future.

E X H I B I T   2 . 4

The Behavioral Sciences Approach

General Approach
- Applies social science in an organizational context.
- Draws from an interdisciplinary research base, including anthropology, economics, psychology, and sociology.

Contributions
- Has improved our understanding of and practical applications for organizational processes such as motivation, communication, leadership, and group processes.
- Regards members of organizations as full human beings, not as tools.

Criticisms
- Because findings are increasingly complex, practical applications often are tried incorrectly or not at all.
- Some concepts run counter to common sense, thus inviting managers' rejection.

● MANAGEMENT SCIENCE PERSPECTIVE

World War II caused many management changes. The massive and complicated problems associated with modern global warfare presented managerial decision makers with the need for more sophisticated tools than ever before. The **management science perspective** emerged to treat those problems. This view is distinguished for its application of mathematics, statistics, and other quantitative techniques to management decision making and problem solving. During World War II, groups of mathematicians, physicists, and other scientists were formed to solve military problems. Because those problems frequently involved moving massive amounts of materials and large numbers of people quickly and efficiently, the techniques had obvious applications to large-scale business firms.[26]

Operations research grew directly out of the World War II groups (called *operational research teams* in Great Britain and *operations research teams* in the United States).[27] It consists of mathematical model building and other applications of quantitative techniques to managerial problems.

Operations management refers to the field of management that specializes in the physical production of goods or services. Operations management specialists use quantitative techniques to solve manufacturing problems. Some of the commonly used methods are forecasting,

management science perspective

A management perspective that emerged after World War II and applied mathematics, statistics, and other quantitative techniques to managerial problems.

Management information systems, a subfield of the *management science perspective*, uses computers to assist managerial and technical decision making. Frank's Nursery & Crafts (a unit of General Host Corporation) is the nation's largest chain of specialty retail stores devoted to lawn and garden products, crafts, and Christmas merchandise. Management information systems in each of its 277 stores track daily sales and inventory. Such information gives Frank's management and sales staff up-to-the-minute information regarding customers' changing needs and habits, improves store response, and provides a competitive edge.

inventory modeling, linear and nonlinear programming, queuing theory, scheduling, simulation and breakeven analysis.

Management information systems (MIS) is the most recent subfield of the management science perspective. These systems are designed to provide relevant information to managers in a timely and cost-efficient manner. The advent of the high-speed digital computer opened up the full potential of this area for management.

Many of today's organizations have departments of management science specialists to help solve quantitatively based problems. When Sears used computer models to minimize its inventory costs, it was applying a quantitative approach to management. When AT&T performed network analysis to speed up and control the construction of new facilities and switching systems, it was employing management science tools.

One specific technique used in many organizations is queuing theory. *Queuing theory* uses mathematics to calculate how to provide services that will minimize the waiting time of customers. Queuing theory has been used to analyze the traffic flow through the Lincoln Tunnel and to determine the number of toll booths and traffic officers for a toll road. Queuing theory was used to develop the single waiting line for tellers used in many banks. Wesley Long Community Hospital in Greensboro, North Carolina, used queuing theory to analyze the telemetry system used in wireless cardiac monitors. The analysis helped the hospital acquire the precise number of telemetry units needed to safely monitor all patients without overspending scarce resources.[28]

● CONTEMPORARY EXTENSIONS

Each of the three major management perspectives is still in use today. The most prevalent is the human resource perspective, but even it has been undergoing change in recent years. Two major contemporary extensions of this perspective are systems theory and the contingency view. Examination of each will allow a fuller appreciation of the state of management thinking today.

SYSTEMS THEORY

system

A set of interrelated parts that function as a whole to achieve a common purpose.

systems theory

An extension of the human resources perspective that describes organizations as open systems that are characterized by entropy, synergy, and subsystem interdependence.

A **system** is a set of interrelated parts that function as a whole to achieve a common purpose.[29] A system functions by acquiring inputs from the external environment, transforming them in some way, and discharging outputs back to the environment. Exhibit 2.5 shows the basic **systems theory** of organizations. Here there are five components: inputs, a transformation process, outputs, feedback, and the environment. *Inputs* are the material, human, financial, or information resources used to produce goods or services. The *transformation process* is management's use of production technology to change the inputs into outputs. *Outputs* include the organization's products and services. *Feedback* is knowledge of the results that influence the selection of inputs during the next cycle of the process. The *environment* surrounding the organization includes the social, political, and economic forces noted earlier in this chapter.

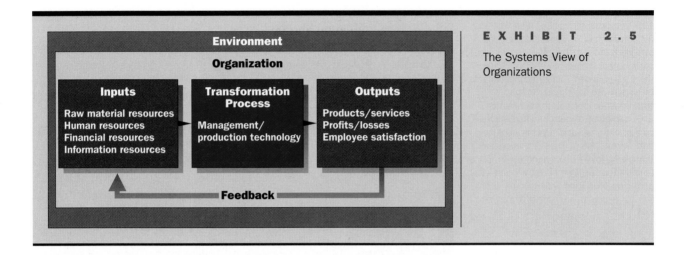

EXHIBIT 2.5

The Systems View of Organizations

Some ideas in systems theory have had substantial impact on management thinking. These include open and closed systems, entropy, synergy, and subsystem interdependencies.[30]

Open systems must interact with the environment to survive; **closed systems need not**. In the classical and management science perspectives, organizations were frequently thought of as closed systems. In the management science perspective, closed system assumptions—the absence of external disturbances—are sometimes used to simplify problems for quantitative analysis. In reality, however, all organizations are open systems and the cost of ignoring the environment may be failure. A prison tries to seal itself off from its environment; yet it must receive prisoners from the environment, obtain supplies from the environment, recruit employees from the environment, and ultimately release prisoners back to the environment.

Entropy is a universal property of systems and refers to their tendency to run down and die. If a system does not receive fresh inputs and energy from its environment, it will eventually cease to exist. Organizations must monitor their environments, adjust to changes, and continuously bring in new inputs in order to survive and prosper. Managers try to design the organization/environment interfaces to reduce entropy.

Synergy means that the whole is greater than the sum of its parts. When an organization is formed, something new comes into the world. Management, coordination, and production that did not exist before are now present. Organizational units working together can accomplish more than those same units working alone. The sales department depends on production, and vice versa.

Subsystems are parts of a system that depend on one another. Changes in one part of the organization affect other parts. The organization must be managed as a coordinated whole. Managers who understand subsystem interdependence are reluctant to make changes that do not recognize subsystem impact on the organization as a whole. Consider the management decision to remove time clocks from the Alcan Plant in Canada.

open system

A system that interacts with the external environment.

closed system

A system that does not interact with the external environment

entropy

The tendency for a system to run down and die.

synergy

The concept that the whole is greater than the sum of its parts.

subsystems

Parts of a system that depend on one another for their functioning.

To paraphrase the Genie in Disney's 1992 blockbuster movie, *Aladdin*: "You ain't never had a friend like . . . *synergy*." Indeed, The Walt Disney Company is the synergy champion. Since the 1930s, when Disney licensed rights to Mickey Mouse products, the company has perfected the creation and marketing of merchandise such as books, clothing, and toys, in conjunction with its films. These children riding Dumbo in Tokyo Disneyland have no doubt seen the *Dumbo* movie, and may persuade Mom and Dad to drop a few yen for a plush Dumbo toy by day's end.

 ALCAN ALUMINUM LTD.

A personnel specialist proposed that time clocks be removed from the shop floor. The shop managers agreed but after a few months, several problems emerged. A few workers began to show up late, or leave early, or stay away too long at lunch.

Supervisors had new demands placed on them to observe and record when workers came and left. They were responsible for reprimanding workers, which led to antagonistic relationships between supervisors and employees. As a consequence, the plant manager found it necessary to reduce the supervisors' span of control. Supervisors were unable to manage as many people because of the additional responsibility.

As Alcan managers discovered, the simple time clock was interdependent with many other parts of the organization system. The time clock influenced worker tardiness and absenteeism, closeness of supervision, the quality of the relationship between supervisors and workers, and span of management. The organization system was more complex than the personnel specialist had realized when he proposed the idea of removing time clocks.[31] ∎

CONTINGENCY VIEW

The second contemporary extension to management thinking is the contingency view. The classical perspective assumed a *universalist* view. Management concepts were thought to be universal, that is, whatever worked—leader style, bureaucratic structure—in one organization would work in another. It proposed the discovery of "one-best-way" management principles that applied the same techniques to every organization. In business education, however, an alternative view exists. This is the *case* view, in which each situation is believed to be unique. There are no universal principles to be found, and one learns about management by experiencing a large number of case problem situations. Managers face the task of determining what methods will work in every new situation.

To integrate these views the **contingency view** has emerged, as illustrated in Exhibit 2.6.[32] Here neither of the above views is seen as entirely correct. Instead, certain contingencies, or variables, exist for helping management identify and understand situations. The contingency view means that a manager's response depends on identifying key contingencies in an organizational situation. For example, a consultant may mistakenly recommend the same management-by-objectives (MBO) system for a manufacturing firm that was successful in a school system. A central government agency may impose the same rules on a welfare agency that it did in a worker's compensation office. A large corporation may take over a chain of restaurants and impose the same organizational charts and financial systems that are used in a banking division. The contingency view tells us that what works in one setting may not work in another. Management's job is to search for important contingencies. When managers learn to identify important patterns and characteristics of their organizations, they can then fit solutions to those characteristics.

Industry is one important contingency. Management practice in a rapidly changing industry will be very different from that in a stable one. Other important contingencies that managers must understand are manufacturing technology and international cultures. For example, several major banks, such as Manufacturers Hanover Corporation, misunderstood the nature of making loans to developing countries. As these big banks raised loan-loss reserves to cope with the prospect of bad international loans, their balance sheet was weakened to the extent that they had to stop expansion into new regions and new business activities. Having been through this experience, managers in the future will know how to handle this contingency in the international financial environment.[33]

contingency view

An extension of the human resource perspective in which the successful resolution of organizational problems is thought to depend on managers' identification of key variables in the situation at hand.

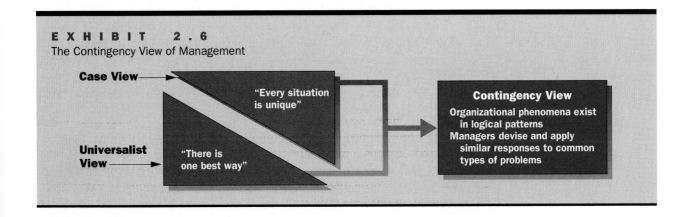

E X H I B I T   2 . 6
The Contingency View of Management

Case View → "Every situation is unique"

Universalist View → "There is one best way"

Contingency View
Organizational phenomena exist in logical patterns
Managers devise and apply similar responses to common types of problems

● RECENT HISTORICAL TRENDS

The historical forces that influence management perspective continue to change and influence the practice of management. The most striking change now affecting management is international competition. This important trend has social, political, and economic consequences for organizations.

INDUSTRIAL GLOBALIZATION

The domain of business now covers the entire planet, where Reeboks, stock markets, fax machines, television, personal computers, and T-shirts intermingle across national boundaries. The world of commerce is becoming wired like an integrated circuit, with no nation left out of the loop.

The impact on firms in the United States and Canada has been severe. International competition has raised the standard of performance in quality, cost, productivity, and response times.[34] As a result, the United States and Canada have seen a decline in worldwide market share in traditional products. Moreover, as recently as 1975, the U.S. balance of payments was close to zero. In recent years it has been hundreds of billions of dollars in the red.[35] Likewise, the business world is reeling under the impact of recent historical events—the breakup of the Soviet Union and the opening of markets among its former republics and throughout the former Eastern block; the long-awaited arrival of Europe '92 with its lowering of internal trade boundaries; and the rush to the formation of a North American trade alliance. All of this means a new set of opportunities and upheavals for companies that strive to meet global competitive standards.

Globalization causes the need for innovation and new levels of customer service. Companies must shorten the time for developing new products, and new products must account for a larger percentage of total income because international competitors are relentless innovators.[36] Winning companies in the 1990s must provide extraordinary service. The CEO of one home electronics retailer is gearing up to provide international service through computerized files. If someone has a problem, he or she just calls the company and a computer screen shows the product's serial number, warranty information, whether parts are in stock, and when it can be repaired.[37]

Although managers have tried many techniques and ideas in recent years, two management trends that seem significant in response to international competition are the adoption of Japanese management practices and the renewed efforts to achieve excellence in product and service quality.

JAPANESE MANAGEMENT PRACTICES

In recent years, Japanese management practices have been thought to create more efficient and more effective companies, while American efficiency has been criticized and the American worker described as "lazy"

Believing its people to be the key to excellence, The Stanley Works adapts well to *Japanese-style management practices*, which emphasize teamwork, trust, and empowerment. Team leaders, like those pictured here at Stanley's Richmond, Virginia, consumer hardware facility, are elected on a 9-month rotation, and meet daily to set schedules and sequence production. The results of effective teamwork are quality, improved service, new products, and expanded "reach" for Stanley into the 135 countries in which its products are sold.

by Japanese Diet leader Yosio Sakurauchi. Japanese products—whether motorcycles, automobiles, or VCRs—garner praise as the world's standard in high quality and low price. The problem for U.S. companies was dramatized a few years ago by the visit of American executives of General Motors' Buick division who had visited a Buick car dealership in Japan:

> The operation appeared to be a massive repair facility, so they asked how he had built up such a large service business. He explained with some embarrassment that this was not a repair facility at all but rather a reassembly operation where newly delivered cars were disassembled and rebuilt to Japanese standards. While many Japanese admire the American automobile, they would never accept the low quality with which they are put together.[38]

How was American management expected to compete with NEC, Nissan, Sanyo, Sony, Toyota, and Kawasaki? Answers have been suggested in William Ouchi's *Theory Z* and Richard Pascale and Anthony Athos' *The Art of Japanese Management*.[39] The success of Japanese firms is often attributed to their group orientation. The Japanese culture focuses on trust and intimacy within the group and family. In North America, in contrast, the basic cultural orientation is toward individual rights and achievements. These differences in the two societies are reflected in how companies are managed.

Exhibit 2.7 illustrates differences in the management approaches used in America and Japan. American organizations are characterized as Type

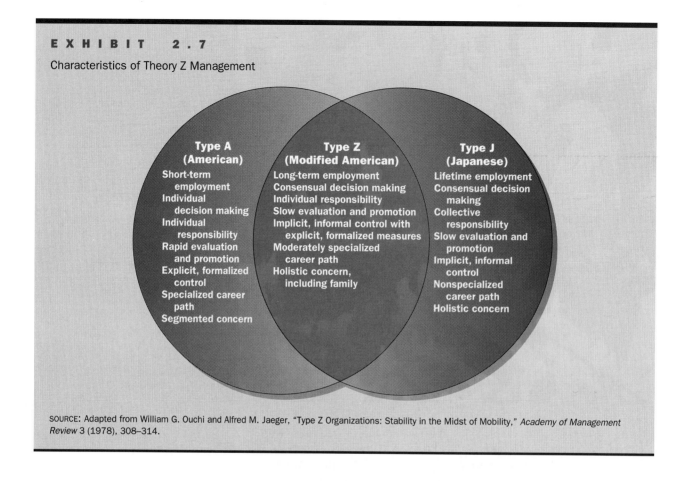

EXHIBIT 2.7

Characteristics of Theory Z Management

Type A (American)
Short-term employment
Individual decision making
Individual responsibility
Rapid evaluation and promotion
Explicit, formalized control
Specialized career path
Segmented concern

Type Z (Modified American)
Long-term employment
Consensual decision making
Individual responsibility
Slow evaluation and promotion
Implicit, informal control with explicit, formalized measures
Moderately specialized career path
Holistic concern, including family

Type J (Japanese)
Lifetime employment
Consensual decision making
Collective responsibility
Slow evaluation and promotion
Implicit, informal control
Nonspecialized career path
Holistic concern

SOURCE: Adapted from William G. Ouchi and Alfred M. Jaeger, "Type Z Organizations: Stability in the Midst of Mobility," *Academy of Management Review* 3 (1978), 308–314.

Theory Z

A management perspective that incorporates techniques from both Japanese and North American management practices.

A and Japanese organizations Type J. However, it is impractical to take a management approach based on the culture of one country and apply it directly to that of another country. **Theory Z** proposes a hybrid form of management that incorporates techniques from both Japanese and North American management practices. Type Z is a blend of American and Japanese characteristics that can be used to revitalize and strengthen corporate cultures in North America.[40]

As illustrated in Exhibit 2.7, the Type Z organization uses the Japanese characteristic of long-term employment, which means that employees become familiar with the organization and are committed to and fully integrated into it. The Theory Z hybrid also adopts the Japanese approach of slow evaluation and promotion for employees. Likewise, the highly specialized American convention of a narrow career path is modified to reflect career training in multiple departments and functions.

In the Theory Z approach, control over employees combines the U.S. preference for explicit and precise performance measures and the Japanese approach to control based on social values. The Theory Z hybrid also encourages the Japanese characteristic of consensual decision making—that is, managers discuss among themselves and with subordinates until everyone is in agreement. Responsibility for outcomes, however, is based on the American approach of rewarding individuals. Finally, Theory Z adopts the Japanese holistic concern for employees' total personal lives.[41]

ACHIEVING EXCELLENCE

Spurred by ideas from Japanese management and global competition, American managers have reawakened an interest in attaining high-quality products through human resource management. The most notable publication in this area is *In Search of Excellence* by Peters and Waterman.[42] The book reported a study of U.S. companies, including Digital Equipment, 3M, Bechtel, Dow, Johnson & Johnson, Disney, Fluor, Caterpillar, Procter & Gamble, and McDonald's. These companies showed above-average performance for several years, and Peters and Waterman's research sought to uncover why. The findings revealed eight **excellence characteristics** that reflected these companies' management values and corporate culture.

excellence characteristics

A group of eight features found to typify the highest-performing U.S. companies.

1 **Bias toward Action.** Successful companies value action, doing, and implementation. They do not talk problems to death or spend all their time creating exotic solutions. The CEO of a computer peripherals company put it this way: "We tell our people to make at least 10 mistakes a day. If you are not making 10 mistakes a day, you are not trying hard enough."[43] H. Ross Perot, after selling his company, EDS, to General Motors and serving on GM's board, remarked on the action differences between the two companies: "The first EDSer to see a snake kills it. At GM, the first thing you do is organize a committee on snakes. Then you bring in a consultant who knows a lot about snakes. The third thing you do is talk about it for a year."[44]

2 **Closeness to the Customer.** Successful companies are customer driven. A dominant value is customer need satisfaction, whether through excellent service or through product innovation. Managers often call customers directly and learn their needs. Successful companies value sales and service overkill. J. Willard Marriott, Sr., read every single customer complaint card—raw and unsummarized.

3 **Autonomy and Entrepreneurship.** Organization structure in excellent corporations is designed to encourage innovation and change. Technical people are located near marketing people so that they can lunch together. Organizational units are kept small to create a sense of belonging and adaptability. W. L. Gore & Associates will not let a plant grow larger than about 150 employees. Companies such as IBM, 3M, and Hewlett-Packard give freedom to idea champions and venture groups to generate creative new products.

4 **Productivity through People.** Rank-and-file employees are considered the roots of quality and productivity. People are encouraged to participate in production, marketing, and new-product decisions. Conflicting ideas are encouraged rather than suppressed. The ability to move ahead by consensus preserves trust and a sense of family, increases motivation, and facilitates both innovation and efficiency.

5 **Hands On, Value Driven.** Excellent companies are clear about their value system. Managers and employees alike know what the company stands for. Leaders provide a vision of what can be accomplished and give employees a sense of purpose and meaning. Leaders are willing to roll up their sleeves and become involved in problems at all levels.

6 **Sticking to the Knitting.** Successful firms stay close to the business they know and understand. Successful firms are highly focused. For example, Boeing, Intel, and Genentech confine themselves to a single product line of commercial aircraft, integrated circuits, and genetic engineering, respectively. Successful companies do what they know best.

7 **Simple Form, Lean Staff.** The underlying structural form and systems of excellent companies are elegantly simple, and few personnel are employed in staff positions. Large companies are subdivided into small divisions that allow each to do its job. For example, when Jack Reichert took over Brunswick Corporation, the headquarters' staff was reduced from 560 to 230 people. The vertical hierarchy was reduced to only five layers of management.[45]

8 **Simultaneous Loose-Tight Properties.** This may seem like a paradox, but excellent companies use tight controls in some areas and

Achieving excellence at Gerber Products Co. is reflected in the company motto: "Babies are our business . . . our only business." By "sticking to the knitting," Gerber Superbrands products capture 72.6 percent of the U.S. baby food market and lead in providing clothing and other care products for children from birth through age three. Gerber's priority on excellence is pursued through open communication with customers to encourage feedback (toll-free numbers, surveys, and coupon redemptions), and product innovation (including Gerber Graduates, a selection of main dishes for toddlers). Such highly focused strategies keep Gerber a favorite among the parents of babies like those pictured here.

loose controls in others. Tight, centralized control is used for the firm's core values. At McDonald's, no exceptions are made to the core values of quality, service, cleanliness, and value. At IBM, top management will tolerate no disagreement with the cultural value of respect for the individual. Yet in other areas employees are free to experiment, to be flexible, to innovate, and to take risks in ways that will help the organization achieve its goals.

In Peters and Waterman's original study and subsequent research, not every company scored high on all eight values, but a preponderance of these values was often part of their management culture. One company that displays many characteristics of excellence is PepsiCo, Inc.

 ### P E P S I C O ,   I N C .

PepsiCo is on a roll. Pepsi-Cola is now the best-selling soft drink in supermarkets, and it just launched its new Crystal Pepsi, a drink for clear soda pop enthusiasts. A recent reorganization eliminated layers of supervision, creating teams that better link together customers, front line employees, and headquarters.

What makes Pepsi excel is a fast-moving, risk-oriented management philosophy. As president D. Wayne Calloway puts it, the underlying philosophy is "ready, fire, aim." Pepsi is biased toward action rather than toward studying things to death.

Decentralization and autonomy create a highly charged atmosphere that pressures people to perform. High performers are well compensated. Low performers are fired. Calloway also believes that senior managers must look, listen, and learn. "Walk through the hallway at Pepsi, and you hear a lot of conversations about what's going on at the supermarket, what the competition is doing," which reflects the customer orientation.

Pepsi rewards autonomy and risk taking. It made a quick decision to purchase 7-Up Company in order to compete with Coca-Cola's Sprite brand, but the merger was not approved. Pepsi got the jump on Coca-Cola by being the first to introduce a 100 percent Nutrasweet formula in 1984. To avoid tipping off Coca-Cola, Pepsi didn't test the product in advance. Diet Pepsi's sales volume soared 25 percent to $1.2 billion. As one manager says, "We believe it's more important to do something than sit around and worry about it."[46] ■

Excellence guidelines and Japanese management practices are not a panacea for all companies. Indeed, some of the high-performance companies originally studied are no longer performing well.[47] But the general approach seems more than a passing fad. These ideas reflect management's response to international competitive forces that have increased the need to fully utilize all employees. They represent a major new trend in the international environment.

SUMMARY AND MANAGEMENT SOLUTION

The practice of management has changed in response to historical conditions. The importance of this chapter is to outline the evolution of management so that present and future managers can understand where we are now and continue to progress toward better management. The evolution of management perspectives is summarized in Exhibit 2.8.

Three major forces that affect management are social, political, and economic. These forces have influenced management from ancient times to the present. These forces also shape individual companies, as CEO Paul O'Neill found as he analyzed the 100-year history of Alcoa. Social and political forces that influenced union strength and economic forces such as recession had direct impact on Alcoa's performance.

The three major perspectives on management that have evolved since the late 1800s are the classical perspective, the human resource perspective, and the management science perspective. Each perspective has several specialized subfields. Two recent extensions of management perspectives are systems theory and contingency views. The most recent historical force affecting management is industrial globalization. The higher standards of quality, productivity, and responsiveness have caused a renewed concern for the full participation of people within organizations. The most recent trend in management has been to adopt Japanese management practices and to create the widespread desire for achieving excellence in North American organizations.

EXHIBIT 2.8

Management Perspectives over Time

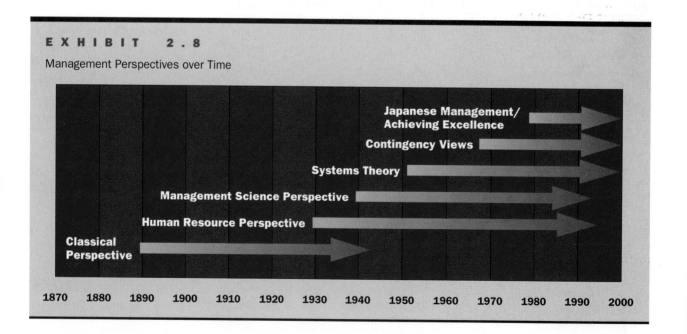

The analysis of historical forces at Alcoa indicated that success was typically associated with healthy economic times, strong research and development within the company, cost efficiency, and effective sales and marketing. Appreciating the importance of these patterns, CEO O'Neill developed a strategy to revitalize and improve Alcoa's aluminum business. First was a billion-dollar program to modernize Alcoa's plants, making them the most efficient in the industry. Next he increased the R&D budget dramatically, paving the way for new product developments and new markets in the future. The sales and marketing departments at Alcoa were already strong. This strategic direction produced back-to-back years of record profits to close the 1980s. However, there was profit decline in the early 1990s because of the deepening recession, historically the company's greatest adversary. Based on historical trends, O'Neill knows the profit decline is expected and will not prematurely depart from the successful corporate strategy of plant revitalization and upgraded R&D.[48]

DISCUSSION QUESTIONS

1. Why is it important to understand the different perspectives and approaches to management theory that have evolved throughout the history of organizations?
2. A recent article in *Fortune* magazine commented about the death of socialism around the world and the resurgence of capitalist economies. What impact will the trend away from socialism in other countries have on management in North America?
3. How do societal forces influence the practice and theory of management? Do you think management techniques are a response to these forces?
4. What change in management emphasis has been illustrated by the interest in "Japanese management" and "achieving excellence"?
5. What is the behavioral science approach? How does it differ from earlier approaches to management?
6. Explain the basic idea underlying the contingency view and provide an example.
7. Contrast open and closed systems. Can you give an example of each? Can a closed system survive?
8. Why can an event such as the Hawthorne studies be a major turning point in the history of management even if the idea is later shown to be in error? Discuss.
9. Identify the major components of systems theory. Is this perspective primarily internal or external?
10. Which approach to management thought is most appealing to you? Why?
11. Do you think management theory will ever be as precise as theories in the fields of physics, chemistry, or experimental psychology? Why or why not?

MANAGEMENT IN PRACTICE: EXPERIENTIAL EXERCISE

● ARE YOU COSMOPOLITAN?

One historical shift occurring in employee attitudes is the extent to which their allegiance is to their organization or to their profession. In recent years, salaried professionals, such as engineers, accountants, and lawyers, work within organizations, but express more loyalty to professional standards than to organizational rules and norms. To identify your own work orientation, answer the eight questions below. Use a scale 1 to 5, with 1 representing "strongly disagree"; 2, "somewhat disagree"; 3, "neutral"; 4, "somewhat agree"; and 5, "strongly agree."

_____ 1. You believe it is the right of the professional to make his or her own decisions about what is to be done on the job.

_____ 2. You believe a professional should stay in an individual staff role regardless of the income sacrifice.

_____ 3. You have no interest in moving up to a top administrative post.

_____ 4. You believe that professionals are better evaluated by professional colleagues than by management.

_____ 5. Your friends tend to be members of your profession.

_____ 6. You would rather be known or get credit for your work outside rather than inside the company.

_____ 7. You would feel better making a contribution to society than to your organization.

_____ 8. Managers have no right to place time and cost schedules on professional contributors.

This scale indicates the extent to which your work orientation is that of a "cosmopolitan" or a "local." A cosmopolitan identifies with the career profession, and a local identifies with the employing organization. A score between 30 and 40 indicates a cosmopolitan work orientation, between 10 and 20 is a local orientation, and between 20 and 30 represents a mixed orientation.

Discuss the pros and cons of each orientation for organizations and employees. What conflicts are likely to occur when "cosmopolitan" professionals work for a company?

SOURCE: Joseph A. Raelin, *The Clash of Cultures, Managers and Professionals* (Harvard Business School Press, 1986).

CASES FOR ANALYSIS

TRANS WORLD AIRLINES, INC.

Once TWA ruled the international skies; now it's become the fallen emperor of the air. Will TWA survive? In January 1992, TWA filed for Chapter 11 bankruptcy, joining a group of seven airlines that have filed since March 1989. Although a few of these seven airlines are still flying, none have yet emerged from reorganization.

TWA's chairman Carl Icahn has no doubt the carrier will emerge from reorganization, stating "We have a 90–10 chance to make it." But many, including TWA's pilots union, feel the airline is doomed.

TWA first soared to prominence by carrying mail. Formed in the 1930 merger of Transcontinental Air Transport and Western Air, it became America's first coast-to-coast airline. TWA expanded rapidly under flying mogul Howard Hughes, who acquired the airline in 1939. Hughes was considered an erratic businessman who delayed key decisions. As a result, TWA was the last large carrier to enter the jet age.

TWA encountered stiff competition overseas and found itself in the red during the 1973 oil embargo and recession. This prompted top management to diversify and spend more by taking over companies such as Hardee's restaurant chain and Century 21 realty, which it placed under a holding company. When the diversification failed, the holding company spun off TWA to shareowners in 1984.

In the midst of takeover fever in 1986, Carl Icahn acquired control of TWA for $435 million. In 1988, the carrier reported a record $250 million profit, partly due to Icahn's cost cutting and his refusal to invest in TWA's aging fleet. But TWA lost $287 million the next year, after Icahn took it private in a leveraged buyout and loaded it with over $2 billion of debt. A TWA collapse wouldn't seem to hurt Icahn very much; the 1988 privatization helped him recoup his initial investment plus a reported $33 million dollar profit.

Icahn's strategy for the aging airline is difficult to define. Many claim he was distracted in the late 1980s by his takeover battles for Texaco, Inc., and USX Corporation. Increased fuel costs, slow passenger growth, and expansion by other airlines hurt too. In 1989, Icahn had to be prodded by the airline's unions to place a $3 billion order for new airplanes that won't be delivered until 1994. In the meantime, TWA has sold $1.49 billion in assets, including its London routes to American Airlines for $676.6 million. Despite these sales, TWA is going through cash quickly. Just one month after its Chapter 11 reorganization, TWA had about $200 million in cash and $100 million in cash equivalents and was experiencing losses at a rate of $750,000 a day.

Adding to TWA's problems are competition and higher-than-average fuel costs for its aging fleet. Its market share is falling, and with it, its service quality. TWA had the highest number of complaints per 100,000 passengers (2.55) in November 1991. Some observers wonder whether Icahn has a master plan to help TWA surface from reorganization or whether he is just waiting for the once great airline's ultimate grounding.

● QUESTIONS

1. If Carl Icahn had carefully examined the historical forces influencing TWA, could he have predicted TWA's gradual demise?
2. Which management perspective described in the chapter would best describe Icahn's approach at TWA?
3. What historical forces are affecting U.S. airlines today? What management approaches should be used in response to these forces?

SOURCE: Asra Q. Nomani, "TWA's Emergence from Chapter 11 Hinges on Icahn's Ability to Slash Debt," *The Wall Street Journal*, February 3, 1992, A3, A4; John Greenwald, "Fallen Emperors of the Air," *Time*, January 7, 1991; and Agis Salpukas, "Airlines' Big Gamble on Expansion," *The New York Times*, February 20, 1990, D1, D6.

SOCIAL SERVICE AGENCY

Charlotte Hines had been employed for 17 years in a social service agency in a mid-sized city in Illinois. In 1984, she had a rare opportunity to become a supervising clerk in charge of about 20 employees in the typing room, mail room, and security areas. She worked hard at being a good supervisor, paid attention to the human aspects of employee problems, and introduced modern management techniques.

In 1988, the state Civil Service Board required that a promotional exam be taken to find a permanent placement for the supervising clerk position. For the sake of fairness, the exam was an open competition—that is, anyone, even a new employee, could sign up and take it. The person with the highest score would get the job.

More than 50 candidates took the test. Charlotte was devastated. "After I accepted the provisional opening and proved myself on the job, the entire clerical force was deemed qualified to take the same test. My experience counted for nothing."

Charlotte placed twelfth in the field of candidates, and one of her clerks placed first. Now she must forfeit her job to a virtual beginner with no on-the-job supervisory experience.

● QUESTIONS

1. What management perspective is reflected in the way the Civil Service Board selected people for supervisory jobs? Would another perspective be better for this type of organization?
2. Why did the Civil Service Board pick a permanent supervisor strictly by test results? Is this fair to employees who have supervisory experience? Is it fair to select a supervisor based only on job experience?
3. If you were Charlotte Hines, what would you do? What options would you explore in order to make the best of the situation?

SOURCE: Based on Betty Harrigan, "Career Advice," *Working Woman*, July 1986, 22–24.

REFERENCES

1. Dan Cordtz, "Alcoa, the Microcosm," *Financial World*, June 25, 1991, 76–80.

2. Alan M. Kantro, ed., "Why History Matters to Managers," *Harvard Business Review* 64 (January–February 1986), 81–88.

3. Susan Dentzer, "Profiting from the Past," *Newsweek*, May 10, 1982, 73–74.

4. Kim Heron, "Randy Travis: Making Country Music Hot Again," *The New York Times Magazine*, June 25, 1989, 28–58.

5. Daniel A. Wren, *The Evolution of Management Thought*, 2d ed. (New York: Wiley, 1979), 6–8. Much of the discussion of these forces comes from Arthur M. Schlesinger, *Political and Social History of the United States, 1829–1925* (New York: Macmillan, 1925), and Homer C. Hockett, *Political and Social History of the United States, 1492–1828* (New York: Macmillan, 1925).

6. Daniel A. Wren, "Management History: Issues and Ideas for Teaching and Research," *Journal of Management* 13 (1987), 339–350.

7. R. J. Wilson, J. Gilbert, S. Nissenbaum, K. O. Cupperman, and D. Scott, "The Climax of the Industrial Revolution: The Haymarket: Strike and Violence in Chicago," *The Pursuit of Liberty*, vol. II, 2nd ed. (Belmont, Calif.: Wadsworth, 1990), 607–609.

8. The following is based on Wren, *Evolution of Management Thought*, Chapters 4, 5; and Claude S. George, Jr., *The History of Management Thought* (Englewood Cliffs, N.J.: Prentice-Hall, 1968), Chapter 4.

9. Charles D. Wrege and Ann Marie Stoka, "Cooke Creates a Classic: The Story behind F. W. Taylor's Principles of Scientific Management," *Academy of Management Review* (October 1978), 736–749.

10. John F. Mee, "Pioneers of Management," *Advanced Management—Office Executive* (October 1962), 26–29; and W. J. Arnold and the editors of *Business Week*, *Milestones in Management* (New York: McGraw-Hill, vol. I, 1965; vol. II, 1966).

11. Wren, *Evolution of Management Thought*, 171; and George, *History of Management Thought*, 103–104.

12. Max Weber, *General Economic History*, trans. Frank H. Knight (London: Allen & Unwin, 1927); Max Weber, *The Protestant Ethic and the Spirit of Capitalism*, trans. Talcott Parsons (New York: Scribner, 1930); and Max Weber, *The Theory of Social and Economic Organizations*, ed. and trans. A. M. Henderson and Talcott Parsons (New York: Free Press, 1947).

13. "UPS," *The Atlanta Journal and Constitution*, April 26, 1992, H1; Richard L. Daft, *Organization Theory and Design*, 3d ed. (St. Paul, Minn.: West, 1989), 181–182; and Kathy Goode, Betty Hahn, and Cindy Seibert, "United Parcel Service: The Brown Giant" (Unpublished manuscript, Texas A&M University, 1981).

14 Henri Fayol, *Industrial and General Administration*, trans. J. A. Coubrough (Geneva: International Management Institute, 1930); Henri Fayol, *General and Industrial Management*, trans. Constance Storrs (London: Pitman and Sons, 1949); and Arnold, "Milestones in Management."

15. Mary Parker Follett, *The New State: Group Organization: The Solution of Popular Government* (London: Longmans, Green, 1918); and Mary Parker Follett, *Creative Experience* (London: Longmans, Green, 1924).

16. Henry C. Metcalf and Lyndall Urwick, eds., *Dynamic Administration: The Collected Papers of Mary Parker Follett* (New York: Harper & Row, 1940), and Arnold, "Milestones in Management."

17. Mary Parker Follett, *The New State* (London: Longmans, Green, 1924), and *Dymanic Administration* (London: Sir Isaac Pitman, 1941).

18. William B. Wolf, *How to Understand Management: An Introduction to Chester I. Barnard* (Los Angeles: Lucas Brothers, 1968); and David D. Van Fleet, "The Need-Hierarchy and Theories of Authority," *Human Relations* 9 (Spring 1982), 111–118.

19. Charles D. Wrege, "Solving Mayo's Mystery: The First Complete Account of the Origin of the Hawthorne Studies—The Forgotten Contributions of Charles E. Snow and Homer Hibarger" (Paper presented to the Management History Division of the Academy of Management, August 1976).

20. Ronald G. Greenwood, Alfred A. Bolton, and Regina A. Greenwood, "Hawthorne a Half Century Later: Relay Assembly Participants Remember," *Journal of Management* 9 (Fall/Winter 1983), 217–231.

21. F. J. Roethlisberger, W. J. Dickson, and H. A. Wright, *Management and the Worker* (Cambridge, Mass.: Harvard University Press, 1939).

22. H. M. Parson, "What Happened at Hawthorne?" *Science* 183 (1974), 922–932.

23. Greenwood, Bolton, and Greenwood, "Hawthorne a Half Century Later," 219–221.

24. Douglas McGregor, *The Human Side of Enterprise* (New York: McGraw-Hill, 1960), 16–18.

25. Leah Nathans Spiro and Michele Galen, "Saturn," *Business Week*, August 17, 1992, 86–91.

26. Mansel G. Blackford and K. Austin Kerr, *Business Enterprise in American History* (Boston: Houghton Mifflin, 1986), Chapters 10, 11; and Alex Groner and the editors of *American Heritage* and *Business Week*, *The American Heritage History of American Business and Industry* (New York: American Heritage Publishing, 1972), Chapter 9.

27. Larry M. Austin and James R. Burns, *Management Science* (New York: Macmillan, 1985).

28. Tom Scott and William A. Hailey, "Queue Modeling Aids Economic Analysis at Health Center," *Industrial Engineering* (February 1981), 56–61.

29. Ludwig von Bertalanffy, Carl G. Hempel, Robert E. Bass, and Hans Jonas, "General Systems Theory: A New Approach to Unity of Science," *Human Biology* 23 (December 1951), 302–361; and Kenneth E. Boulding, "General Systems Theory—The Skeleton of Science," *Management Science* 2 (April 1956), 197–208.

30. Fremont E. Kast and James E. Rosenzweig, "General Systems Theory: Applications for Organization and Management," *Academy of Management Journal* (December 1972), 447–465.

31. Daft, *Organization Theory*, 16–17.

32. Fred Luthans, "The Contingency Theory of Management: A Path out of the Jungle," *Business Horizons* 16 (June 1973), 62–72; and Fremont E. Kast and James E. Rosenzweig, *Contingency Views of Organization and Management* (Chicago: Science Research Associates, 1973).

33. Robert Gunther, "Major Banks' Increases in Loan-Loss Reserves May Cramp Expansion," *The Wall Street Journal*, July 29, 1987, 1, 10.

34. Koh Sera, "Corporate Globalization: A New Trend," *Academy of Management Executive* 6 no. 1 (1992), 89–96; and B. Joseph White, "The Internationalization of Business: One Company's Response," *Academy of Management Executive* 2 (1988), 29–32.

35. Arnoldo C. Hax, "Building the Firm of the Future," *Sloan Management Review* (Spring 1989), 75–82.

36. Tom Peters, "Prometheus Barely Unbound," *Academy of Management Executive* 4 (November 1990), 70–84.

37. Brian Dumaine, "What the Leaders of Tomorrow See," *Fortune*, July 3, 1989, 48–62.

38. William Ouchi, *Theory Z: How American Business Can Meet the Japanese Challenge* (Reading, Mass.: Addison-Wesley, 1981).

39. Ouchi, *Theory Z*; and R. Pascale and A. Athos, *The Art of Japanese Management: Applications for American Executives* (New York: Simon and Schuster, 1981).

40. William G. Ouchi and Alfred M. Jaeger, "Type Z Organizations: Stability in the Midst of Mobility," *Academy of Management Review* 3 (1978), 305–314.

41. Ibid.

42. Thomas J. Peters and Robert H. Waterman, Jr., *In Search of Excellence: Lessons from America's Best-Run Companies* (New York: Harper & Row, 1982); Tom Peters and Nancy Austin, *A Passion for Excellence: The Leadership Difference* (New York: Random House, 1985); and Tom Peters, "Putting Excellence into Management," *Business Week*, July 21, 1980, 196–201.

43. Tom Peters, "An Excellent Question," *INC.*, December 1984, 155–162.

44. "Ross Perot's Crusade," *Business Week*, October 6, 1986, 60–65.

45. "A Slimmed-Down Brunswick Is Proving Wall Street Wrong," *Business Week*, May 28, 1984, 90–98.

46. Michael J. McCarthy, "PepsiCo Promotes Barnes and Novak to Reorganize, Tighten Pepsi-Cola Unit," *The Wall Street Journal*, September 22, 1992, D18; and "Pepsi's Marketing Magic: Why Nobody Does It Better," *Business Week*, February 10, 1986, 52–57.

47. "Who's Excellent Now?" *Business Week*, November 5, 1984, 76+; Daniel T. Carroll, "A Disappointing Search for Excellence," *Harvard Business Review* 61 (November–December 1983), 78–79+; Jeremiah J. Sullivan, "A Critique of Theory Z," *Academy of Management Review* (January 1983), 132–142; and William Bowen, "Lessons from behind the Kimono," *Fortune*, June 15, 1981, 247–250.

48. Dan Cordtz, "Alcoa, the Microcosm."

International Business Machines Corporation's announcement that it was slashing its work force by 25,000 people marked the end of an era in American business. The job cuts were only the latest in a string of downsizing moves at IBM. For the first time in its 78-year history, the world's largest computer company abandoned its no-layoff policy.

A few weeks later, IBM again made history when it announced a net 1992 loss of $5 billion—the largest ever reported by a U.S. corporation. The numbers on Wall Street were nearly as shocking. The price of IBM stock fell from $175 a share in 1987 to $100 in 1992 to around $46 by early 1993. The company's once untouchable dividend was cut by more than half.

John Akers' decision to step down as chief executive officer in January 1993 marked the final scene in a long and troubled story. During Akers' eight-year tenure, Big Blue, once the most profitable company in the world joined the ranks of fallen giants like General Motors, Sears, and American Express.

The company's fall was so swift and staggering that it left many people asking where it went wrong. The answer was that IBM had become complacent. Instead of focusing on future plans and the innovations of IBM scientists, the company basked in past successes and stubbornly held on to its mainframe business, which still accounts for more than half of its profits. Meanwhile, the computer industry was racing ahead. Where IBM once dominated every aspect of the business, it increasingly had to make way for companies like Microsoft and Compaq that didn't even exist 20 years ago. These smaller and more dynamic rivals were pushing sales of powerful and inexpensive personal computers and workstations, which cut into IBM's core business of minicomputers and mainframes. "The problem has never been technology," says Richard Shaffer, publisher of *The Computer Letter*. "It's been lethargy and bureaucracy."

Like the other corporations that ruled for most of this century, IBM was big, centralized, and hierarchical. Employees complied with strict rules in exchange for a guarantee of lifetime employment. The old corporate philosophy was so deeply entrenched that Akers even had his two predecessors looking over his shoulder during his entire reign. By 1991, Akers decided to shake up the bureaucracy by allowing more room for independence and creativity. He divided the company into 13 autonomous units called Baby Blues. Though good in theory, critics contend the units were never given enough independence.

In his efforts to streamline the company, Akers initially could not bring himself to drop IBM's no-layoffs policy and offered round after round of expensive early-retirement packages. Employees who once enjoyed the comfort of life-time employment now labored under the pressure of pay for performance and new evaluation procedures.

Akers' 1992 decision to cut research and development spending of mainframe development and concentrate on the workstation and personal computer arena proved to be too little, too late. IBM found itself behind its competitors. Charles Ferguson, co-author with Charles Morris of *Computer Wars*, charges that "even if its managers started running the company perfectly tomorrow, for the next five years they would face very serious problems that have been locked in by the past decade's bad management."

Assessments like that may have prompted the board of directors to do what once would have been unthinkable: bring in an outsider to fill the company's top job. Unlike Akers who had worked his way up during 24 years with IBM, his replacement, Louis Gerstner, Jr., had no experience in running a computer company.

While Gerstner admits his computer experience is limited to having an IBM in his office during his tenure as CEO at RJR Nabisco Holdings Corp., he brings new perspective to the position as IBM CEO. In addition, Gerstner is no stranger to leading a major corporate turnaround. While some suggest Gerstner is taking on the most difficult management challenge in America, Gerstner said the same thing when he took the reins at RJR in 1989. The food and tobacco giant was mired in $26 billion in debt stemming from its record-setting leveraged buyout. In four years, Gerstner slashed the debt to $14 billion and cut jobs.

Similar leadership will be needed at IBM where many analysts believe another 500,000 jobs must be trimmed. Although Gerstrer's appointment initially caused low morale among some IBM rank and file. IBM's remaining 300,000 employees are now looking to Gerstner to lead the company into a new era. But they also know a good deal of pain still lies ahead.

● QUESTIONS

1. How have historical forces shaped management practices at IBM?

2. Which elements of bureaucracy prevail at IBM?

3. Are any of IBM's management practices typical of those used by the Japanese? How could the company improve its management practices? Describe.

4. What changes have occurred at IBM since this video case aired?

MANAGING IN A GLOBAL ENVIRONMENT ③

LEARNING OBJECTIVES

After studying this chapter, you should be able to

■ Describe the emerging borderless world.

■ Define international management and explain how it differs from the management of domestic business operations.

■ Indicate how dissimilarities in the economic, sociocultural, and legal-political environments throughout the world can affect business operations.

■ Describe market entry strategies that businesses use to develop foreign markets.

■ Describe the characteristics of a multinational corporation and the generic strategies available to them.

■ Explain the strategic approaches used by multinational corporations.

Frederick W. Smith created an "overnight" sensation when he founded Federal Express, which quickly established itself as the giant in America's fledgling express mail service. Smith's bold attempt to duplicate that success overseas, however, has foundered on the rocks of reality. FEDEX's North American system of centralized controls and hub-and-spoke delivery was a disaster overseas and by the time it began its global strategy, competitors had already established loyal followings throughout Europe and Asia. Attempts at tight control ran headlong into problems caused by various cultures, such as late office hours in Spain and the penchant  among Russian workers to take home the soap used for daily truck cleaning because of consumer shortages. FEDEX, suffering under $1.2 billion in losses, shut down operations in over 100 European cities in 1992. As one competitor glibly noted, "Federal Express is one of the finest examples that the rest of the world is not the United States of America."[1] ■ Why do you think Federal Express had such difficulty duplicating its U.S. success overseas? What would you recommend Fred Smith do before FEDEX launches another global expansion?

Federal Express is a well-established company facing enormous challenges developing a successful international business. Companies such as McDonald's, IBM, Coca-Cola, Kellogg's, Boeing, General Motors, and Caterpillar Tractor all rely on international business for a substantial portion of sales and profits. These companies face special problems in trying to tailor their products and business management to the unique needs of foreign countries—but if they succeed, the whole world is their marketplace.

How important is international business to the study of management? *If you are not thinking international, you are not thinking business management.* It's that serious. As you read this page, ideas, takeover plans, capital investments, business strategies, Reeboks, services, and T-shirts are traveling around the planet by telephone, fax, and overnight mail. As Federal Express considers its future in both domestic and international arenas, it will evaluate the risk of continued global involvement. And, even more important, FEDEX must carefully evaluate the risk of abandoning or limiting global participation.

If you think you are isolated from global influence, think again. Even if you will not budge from your hometown, your company may be purchased by the English, Japanese, or Germans tomorrow. People who work for Standard Oil, any of the Federated Department Stores, Pillsbury, Shell Oil, Chesebrough-Pond's, Carnation, Celanese, Firestone, or CBS Records are already working for foreign bosses. In addition, the Japanese alone can be expected to purchase about 200 small- and medium-size American companies each year while also hiring additional American workers in expanding U.S.-owned plants.

Or consider this: You arrive at work tomorrow and your CEO puts globalization in the company's mission statement and orders promotion of employees who have international experience and foreign-language ability. Or worse yet, a foreign competitor may be launching a competitive assault on your industry. A few years ago, U.S. firms made 85 percent of the world's memory chips and were unassailable, or so they thought. Soon Japan had a 75 percent share of the world market, with the U.S. share shrunk to 15 percent. No one is immune. A small entrepreneurial company, Florod Corporation, made a laser eraser that had a small market of no more than 40 companies. Giant NEC from Japan pushed its way in with a better product, practically destroying Florod, which had to find other products to survive. With this kind of competition, is it any surprise that foreign-born people with international experience have been appointed to run such companies as DuPont, Coca-Cola, Revlon, Gerber, NCR, and Heinz?[2]

This chapter introduces basic concepts about the global environment and international management. First, we consider the difficulty managers have operating in an increasingly borderless world. We will address challenges—economic, legal-political, and sociocultural—facing companies within the global business environment. Then we will discuss multinational corporations and touch upon the various types of strategies and techniques needed for entering and succeeding in foreign markets.

● A BORDERLESS WORLD

Why would FEDEX CEO Fred Smith want to pursue a global strategy despite previous failures and losses? Conventional wisdom is that companies involved in global industries must play the global game. If a company doesn't think globally, someone else will. Companies failing to keep up will be swallowed up. As FEDEX competitors rush toward globalization with acquisitions, mergers, and alliances, FEDEX risks significant losses in its domestic market share unless it has the capacity to meet the expanding global express mail needs of clients.

International companies increasingly find that globalization provides a competitive edge at all stages of developing, manufacturing, and marketing products. A global approach to development enabled Otis Elevator, Inc., to use research centers in five countries during development of its customized Elevonic 411, saving an estimated $10 million in design costs and cutting in half the normal elevator development time.[3] The

NIKE, Inc., of Eugene, Oregon, a front-runner in sports and fitness innovation, epitomizes rapid growth in a *borderless world* where Chinese students recently ranked basketball player and NIKE spokesperson Michael Jordan with former Chinese leader Chou En Lai as the world's greatest men. NIKE's global reach is reflected in its annual report's five-language message to shareholders and in the rapid growth of its international division, which will outsell its U.S. divisions by 1996. Superior quality, product innovation, and the continued endorsement of the world's top athletes break down cultural barriers and propel this $3.4 billion company toward the 21st century.

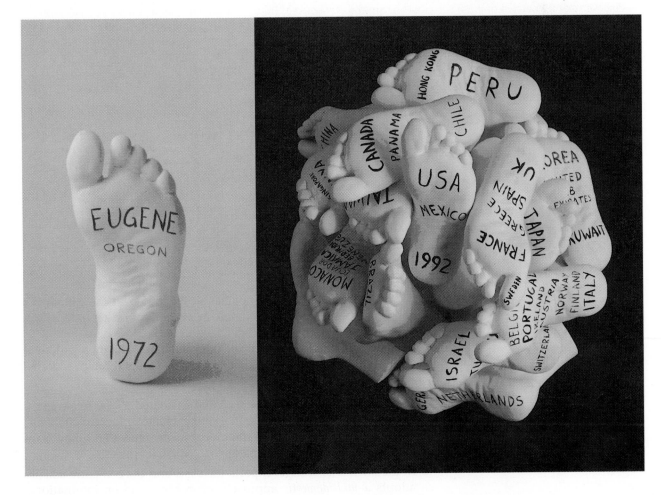

BUY AMERICAN!

Under vocal pressure to "Buy American!" the town council of Greece, New York, voted in January 1992 to reject the purchase of a Japanese Komatsu excavator in favor of a John Deere model that cost $15,000 more. The council supported the patriotic principle of supporting American jobs. Only later did council members discover that 95 percent of the Komatsu models were made in the United States through a Japanese-American joint venture headquartered in Illinois. Meanwhile, only the engine of the John Deere was built in the United States. The excavator itself was made in Japan through Deere's joint venture with Hitachi. Today's consumers must face the complexity of a seemingly border-less international market.

The 1980s marked a pivotal period during which national boundaries began blurring with regard to the development, manufacture, and marketing of products. Industries such as chemicals, tires, steel, and building supplies have been reshaped by international dynamics. As Robert Reich of Harvard noted, "Every industrialized country is moving in the same direction, toward an industrial base that is global in ownership and orientation."

Americans find it increasingly difficult to buy purely American products. The Mercury Tracer parked outside may come from Mexico, while a neighbor's Nissan may have been built in Smyrna, Tennessee. By 1990, approximately 40 percent of Japanese cars sold in the United States were built in America by American workers. In the clothing industry, American consumers are likely to find their Van Heusen shirts with a "Made in Thailand" label and their Nike warmup suits made in Malaysia. As the production and marketing of goods become more global, consumers around the world will struggle with questions of quality and value for their money versus patriotic support for the home team.

For the town council of Greece, New York, the question of how to benefit America is difficult—buy the product with an American name or the product built by American workers? "We would like to purchase American-made equipment and keep Americans on the job," said Roger Boily, a supervisor for Greece. "But it becomes a very complicated issue." His town council eventually canceled the John Deere order and decided to rent the Komatsu excavator to clear a creek and prevent the flooding of a man's home. That grateful man didn't stop to ask whether the machine was American or Japanese. ∎

SOURCE: James S. Hirsch and Dana Milbank, "'Buy American' Is Easier Said Than Done," *The Wall Street Journal*, January 28, 1992, B1, B5; Bradley A. Stertz, "New York Car Dealers Hope to Put Some Drive into 'Too Lazy' Workers," *The Wall Street Journal*, January 28, 1992, B1, B5; and Hillary Appleman, "Buying 'Made in USA' Not So Easy," *Nashville Tennessean*, January 26, 1992, 1E.

reality of today's borderless companies is illustrated in the Manager's Shoptalk box. Consumers cannot tell in which country products are made.

Corporations can participate in the international arena on a variety of levels, and the process of globalization typically passes through four distinct stages.

1 In the *domestic stage*, market potential is limited to the home country with all production and marketing facilities located at home. Managers may be aware of the global environment and may want to consider foreign involvement.

2 In the *international stage*, exports increase, and the company usually adopts a *multidomestic* approach, probably using an international

division to deal with the marketing of products in several countries individually.

3 In the *multinational stage*, the company has marketing and production facilities located in many countries, with more than one-third of its sales outside the home country. Companies typically have a single home country, although they may opt for a *binational* approach, whereby two parent companies in separate countries maintain ownership and control. Examples are Unilever and the Royal Dutch/Shell Group, both of which are based in the United Kingdom and the Netherlands.

4 Finally, the *global* (or *stateless*) *stage* of corporate international development transcends any single home country. These corporations operate in true global fashion, making sales and acquiring resources in whatever country offers the best opportunities and lowest cost. At this stage, ownership, control, and top management tend to be dispersed among several nationalities.[4]

As the number of "stateless" corporations increases, so too the awareness of national borders decreases, as reflected by the frequency of foreign participation at the management level. Rising managers are expected to know a second or third language and to have international experience. The need for global managers is intense, as discussed in the Focus on Diversity box. Consider the makeup of global companies in today's environment. Nestlé (Switzerland) personifies the stateless corporation with 98 percent of sales and 96 percent of employees outside the home country. Nestlé's CEO is German and half of the company's general managers are non-Swiss. U.S. firms also show a growing international flavor. At CRC International, one-third of the officers are foreign nationals, while Heinz has an Irish citizen as CEO and a mixed board. At a British firm, ICI, 40 percent of the top 170 executives are non-British. Meanwhile, German companies such as Hoechst and BASF rely on local managers to run foreign operations.[5]

In recent years, a major player in the global game has been ABB (Asea Brown Boveri). This company generates over $25 billion in revenues and employs 240,000 in Europe, North and South America, Asia, and India. CEO Percy Barnevik points out that ABB has no geographical center. With a Swedish CEO, a Zurich headquarters, a multinational board, and posting financial results in American dollars, ABB is "a company with many homes."[6]

● THE INTERNATIONAL BUSINESS ENVIRONMENT

International management is the management of business operations conducted in more than one country. The fundamental tasks of business management, including the financing, production, and distribution of products and services, do not change in any substantive way when a firm is transacting business across international borders. The basic management functions of planning, organizing, leading, and

international management
The management of business operations conducted in more than one country.

WANTED: GLOBAL MANAGERS

A new minority is in demand in corporate America and overseas. Colgate-Palmolive Co. calls these people *globalites*. In Europe, they are known as *Euromanagers*. Regardless of the name, corporations around the world are scrambling to locate and nab the brightest and best candidates for global management.

Competition is intense. Colgate-Palmolive's program, introduced in 1987, attracts 15,000 applicants for 15 slots. The need for global managers has spawned several successful executive search firms. Top international headhunters such as Korn/Ferry, Egon Zehnder International, and Russell Reynolds Associates, Inc., recruit multilingual executives with wide experience and the ability to deal with other cultures.

Could you qualify? Do you have enough international knowledge to answer these questions? A smiling fish is (1) a term used in the Middle East or (b) a dish served in China. During meals in Belgium, you should (a) keep your hands off the table or (b) keep your hands on the table. Eye contact and gestures of openness are important when discussing business in (a) Mexico or (b) Saudi Arabia. Americans stand closer when talking than do South Americans or Africans: (a) true or (b) false. In England, to table an issue means to (a) put it aside or (b) bring it up for discussion. (The correct answer for each question is b.)

Global corporations have initiated and promoted management programs to overcome cultural blinders. A program at General Electric's aircraft engine unit encourages foreign language and cross-cultural training for mid-level managers and engineers. American Express regularly transfers junior managers to overseas units. PepsiCo, Raychem, Honda of America, and GM are among the growing number of companies with global management training programs. As one international human resource manager pointed out, "Knowing how to conduct business in foreign cultures and to grasp global customers' different needs is the key to global business."

But multilingual skills are not enough. Corporations seek candidates with highly developed human skills. "We tend to look for people who can work in teams and understand the value of cooperation and consensus," said the chairman of Unilever. Successful globalization requires teamwork and overcoming national, racial, and religious prejudice. That minority of managers who quickly grasp global skills will increasingly find themselves on the fast track to success. ■

SOURCE: Joann S. Lublin, "Companies Use Cross-Cultural Training to Help Their Employees Adjust Abroad," *The Wall Street Journal*, August 4, 1992, B1, B9, and "Younger Managers Learn Global Skills," *The Wall Street Journal*, March 31, 1992, B1; Shawn Tully, "The Hunt for the Global Manager," *Fortune*, May 21, 1990, 140–144; Bob Hagerty, "Firms in Europe Try to Find Executives Who Can Cross Borders in a Single Bound," *The Wall Street Journal*, January 25, 1991, B1, B2; and William A. Nowlin, "What's Your Cross-Cultural IQ?" *Spirit*, May 1990, 33–36.

controlling are the same whether a company operates domestically or internationally. However, managers will experience greater difficulties and risks when performing these management functions on an international scale. For example:

- Managers at one American company were shaken when they discovered that the brand name of the cooking oil they had introduced in Latin America translated into Spanish as "jackass oil."

- Still another company tried to sell its toothpaste in Southeast Asia by stressing that it whitens teeth. Managers were chagrined to discover that local people chew betel nut to blacken their teeth because they find the result attractive.[7]

- One company stamped "OK" on each page of its catalog. In many parts of South America, OK is a vulgar gesture. Six months were lost because the company had to reprint the catalogs.

The complexities of global management are further demonstrated in the Focus on Diversity box. What should managers of emerging global companies look for to avoid obvious international mistakes? When comparing one country with another, the economic, legal-political, and sociocultural sectors present the greatest difficulties. Key factors to understand in the international environment are summarized in Exhibit 3.1.

● THE ECONOMIC ENVIRONMENT

The economic environment represents the economic conditions in the country where the international organization operates. This part of the environment includes such factors as economic development; resource and product markets; infrastructure; exchange rates; and inflation, interest rates, and economic growth.

ECONOMIC DEVELOPMENT. Economic development differs widely among the countries and regions of the world. Countries can be categorized as either "developing" or "developed." The developing countries are referred to as *less-developed countries (LDCs)*. The criterion

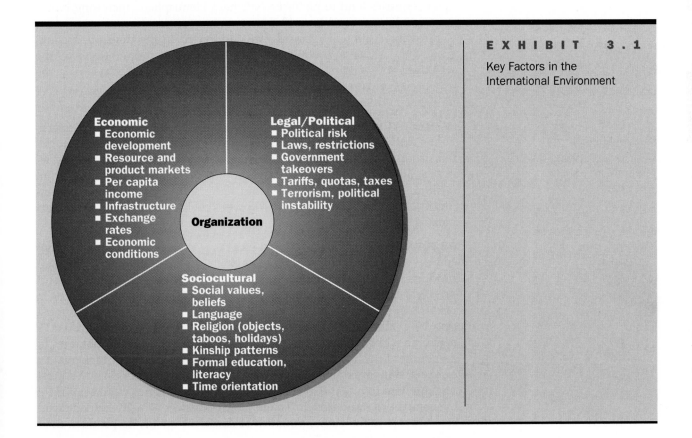

EXHIBIT 3.1

Key Factors in the International Environment

The vast global enterprise of Archer Daniels Midland Company (ADM) reflects its commitment to be the "supermarket of the world." Creating and sustaining a powerful and efficient transportation infrastructure within the *economic environment* is essential to ADM goals. Recent developments, such as European economic collaboration, the opening of markets in Eastern Europe and Russia, and completion of the Main-Danube Canal (pictured here) that provides unrestricted waterway access to the Black Sea, all improve ADM's transportation opportunities. The company, meanwhile, adds to its own infrastructure by expanding its giant Europort facility in the Netherlands.

traditionally used to classify countries as developed or developing is *per capita income*, which is the income generated by the nation's production of goods and services divided by total population. The developing countries have low per capita incomes. LDCs generally are in the Southern Hemisphere, including Africa, Asia, and South America, whereas developed countries tend to be in the Northern Hemisphere, including North America, Europe, and Japan.[8]

Most international business firms are based in the developed countries. They show a preference for confining their operations to the wealthier and economically advanced nations. However, based on the number of prospective customers, developing countries constitute an immense and largely untapped market.

infrastructure

A country's physical facilities that support economic activities.

INFRASTRUCTURE.   A country's physical facilities that support economic activities make up its **infrastructure,** which includes transportation facilities such as airports, highways, and railroads; energy-producing facilities such as utilities and power plants; and communication facilities such as telephone lines and radio stations. Companies operating in LDCs must contend with lower levels of technology and perplexing logistical, distribution, and communication problems.

RESOURCE AND PRODUCT MARKETS.   When operating in another country, company managers must evaluate the market demand for their products. If market demand is high, managers may choose to export products to that country. To develop manufacturing plants, however, resource markets for providing needed raw materials and labor must also be available. For example, the greatest challenge for McDonald's restaurants overseas is to obtain supplies of everything from potatoes to hamburger buns to plastic straws. Often supplies that meet McDonald's exacting standards are unavailable. The hamburger bun was the most difficult item to procure in Britain because local bakeries would not meet the company's standards. In Thailand, McDonald's actually helped farmers cultivate Idaho russet potatoes of sufficient quality to produce their golden french fries.[9]

EXCHANGE RATES.   *Exchange rates* are the rate at which one country's currency is exchanged for another country's. Changes in the exchange rate can have major implications for the profitability of international operations.[10] For example, assume that the American dollar is exchanged for 8 French francs. If the dollar increases in value to 10 francs, U.S. goods will be more expensive in France because it will take more francs to buy a dollar's worth of U.S. goods. It will be more difficult to export American goods to France, and profits will be slim. If the dollar drops to a value of 6 francs, on the other hand, U.S. goods will be cheaper in France and can be exported at a profit.

● THE LEGAL-POLITICAL ENVIRONMENT

Businesses must deal with unfamiliar political systems when they go international, as well as with more government supervision and regulation. Government officials and the general public often view foreign companies as outsiders or even intruders and are suspicious of their impact on economic independence and political sovereignty. Some of the major legal-political concerns affecting international business are political risk, political instability, and laws and restrictions.

POLITICAL RISK.   A company's **political risk** is defined as its risk of loss of assets, earning power, or managerial control due to politically based events or actions by host governments.[11] Political risk includes government takeovers of property and acts of violence directed against a firm's properties or employees. Because such acts are not uncommon, companies must formulate special plans and programs to guard against unexpected losses. For example, Hercules, Inc., a large chemical company, has increased the number of security guards at several of its European

political risk

A company's risk of loss of assets, earning power, or managerial control due to politically motivated events or actions by host governments.

As the world's premier producer, distributor, and marketer of bananas, Chiquita Brands International's continued growth and success are strongly influenced by the *legal-political environment*. The EC's single-market economy, the opening of Eastern Europe, and the lifting of a government ban in Korea offer Chiquita access to previously restricted markets. Meanwhile, heavy dependence on products grown in Central and South American countries means daily risks of expropriation, increased taxes, currency restrictions, and other legal-political problems. Chiquita's international expertise assures consumers that quality products reach diverse retail outlets from American supermarkets to the Eastern European street vendors pictured here.

plants. Because of a rumored protest, Monsanto Corporation canceled a ceremony to celebrate the opening of a new plant in England.[12]

POLITICAL INSTABILITY.   Another frequently cited problem for international companies is political instability, which includes riots, revolutions, civil disorders, and frequent changes in government. Political instability increases uncertainty. Companies moving into former Soviet republics face continued instability because of changing government personnel and political philosophies. For example, Czechoslovakian hero and playwright Vaclav Havel, initially selected president by voters in a celebration of freedom, had already been replaced by mid-1992. The Czech government has peacefully coped with nationalist tensions in Slovakia and in 1993 separated into two countries. The former Yugoslavia, by contrast, has been beset by a shooting war among ethnic groups.

For global companies, the threat of violence is strongest among those nations with political, ethnic, or religious upheaval. In the first seven months of 1991, BRI (Business Risk International), a security consulting firm, reported 1,236 bombings, 382 assassinations, and 103 kidnappings. Western businesses are often targeted to gain publicity for the "cause" and to damage the local economy. In recent years, Peruvian insurgents targeted companies such as Kentucky Fried Chicken and Pizza Hut. BRI compiles an annual list of the ten riskiest countries for business. Peru (with over 500 incidents in 1990) topped the 1991 listing, which included El Salvador, India, Turkey, Colombia, the Philippines, Sri Lanka, and Nicaragua, as well as two European countries—Spain and Northern Ireland.[13]

LAWS AND REGULATIONS.   Government laws and regulations differ from country to country and make manufacturing and sales a true challenge for international firms. Host governments have myriad laws concerning libel statutes, consumer protection, information and labeling, employment and safety, and wages. International companies must learn these rules and regulations and abide by them. After years of Communist mismanagement, markets in Eastern Europe with 100 million consumer households have been opened, creating both potential payoffs and pitfalls for global managers. Within months of the fall of communism, companies such as Volkswagen (Germany), Suzuki (Japan), Pilkington (Britain), General Electric (United States), and Sanofi (France) entered a variety of partnerships and acquisitions with companies in Poland, Czechoslovakia, and Hungary. However, there are still questions about emerging laws and regulations. Despite western money and know-how, factory closures, shortages, and rising unemployment attest to the difficulty of movement toward free market economies.[14]

The most visible changes in legal-political factors grow out of the emerging international trade alliance system. Consider, for example, the impact of the European Community (EC) and the North American Free Trade Agreement (NAFTA).

EUROPEAN COMMUNITY

Formed in 1958 to improve the economic and social conditions among its members, the European Community has since expanded to a 12-

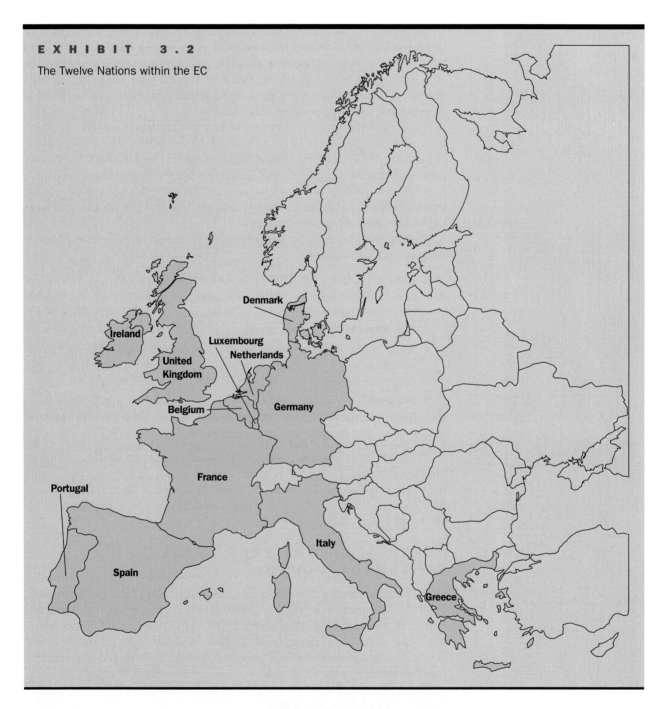

EXHIBIT   3 . 2

The Twelve Nations within the EC

nation alliance illustrated in Exhibit 3.2. In the early 1980s, Europeans initiated steps to create a powerful single market system, called *Europe '92*. The initiative called for creation of open markets for Europe's 340 million consumers. Europe '92 consisted of 282 directives, most scheduled for implementation by January 1, 1993, proposing dramatic reform and deregulation in areas such as banking, insurance, health, safety standards, airlines, telecommunications, auto sales, social policy, and monetary union.

Initially opposed and later embraced by European industry, the increased competition and economies of scale within Europe will enable companies to grow large and efficient, becoming more competitive in U.S. and other world markets. Some observers fear that the EC will become a trade barrier, creating a "fortress Europe" that will be difficult to penetrate by companies in other nations.

Implementation of directives regarding the elimination of border controls and deregulations have proceeded on schedule. The deregulation of banking (1993) and insurance (1994) expect to be followed by investment services between 1995 and 1999. New open competition in telecommunications (1993) will lead to deregulation on cross-border calling by mid-decade. The airlines now enjoy free pricing and the licensing of new carriers as a result of deregulation.

Despite the successes, other directives languish amid stiff opposition from member countries:

- *Monetary union*, calling for the establishment of a European central bank and a single currency, met defeat on June 2, 1992, by Danish voters. If approved by other EC members, the issue may force a second referendum in Denmark.

- *Social policy,* calling for increased regulations for worker's rights, working hours, subcontracting, and equal benefits for full-time and part-time employees, has been blocked by the British.

- *Automobile legislation* seeks to end the gridlock of antitrust exemptions, exclusive dealer territories, and quotas that force Europeans to pay 25 percent more for automobiles.[15]

These facets of the proposal show the difficulty of building alliances among countries. However, solutions are expected, and the verdict is still out regarding the success of the Europe '92 agenda. Meanwhile, Canada, Mexico, and the United States have established what is expected to be an equally powerful trading alliance.

NORTH AMERICAN FREE TRADE AGREEMENT (NAFTA)

Upon ratification by the Canadian, Mexican, and U.S. governments, NAFTA will open a $6 trillion megamarket to 363 million consumers. Supporters expect NAFTA to break down as many as 20,000 separate tariffs over a 10 to 15 year period. The treaty builds upon the 1989 U.S.–Canada agreement and is expected to spur growth and investment, increase exports, and expand jobs in all three nations.[16]

The 14-month negotiations climaxed August 12, 1992, with agreements in a number of key areas.

- *Agriculture.* Immediate removal on tariffs on half of U.S. farm exports to Mexico with phasing out of remaining tariffs over 15 years.

- *Autos.* Immediate 50 percent cut of Mexican tariffs on autos, reaching zero in 10 years. Mandatory 62.5 percent North American content on cars and trucks to qualify for duty-free status.

J. B. Hunt, a diversified transportation company, is poised to reap the benefits of *NAFTA*, which extends the U.S.–Canadian free trade agreement to Mexico. The largest U.S. carrier in Canada, Hunt recently expanded service into Mexico, joining Transportacion Maritima Mexicana to provide truckline service throughout Mexico and ocean shipping container services from all Mexican ports. Hunt's expanded railway service agreement with Union Pacific will offer eventual interline service to FNM, the Mexican national railroad. Taking advantage of international opportunities such as NAFTA will enable J. B. Hunt to reach its goal of being the premier North American container carrier.

- *Transport.* U.S. trucking of international cargo allowed in Mexican border area by mid-1990s and throughout Mexico by the end of the decade.

- *Intellectual property.* Mexico's protection for pharmaceutical patents boosted to international standards and North American copyrights safeguarded.

Many groups in the United States oppose the agreement, warning of job loss to Mexico and the potential for industrial "ghost towns." Some environmentalists fear weakened pollution standards and the potential for toxic dumping. Treaty advocates admit there may be short-term problems but stress the long-term benefits in job creation and heightened standard of living within all three trading partners.[17]

TRADE ALLIANCES: PROMISE OR PITFALL?

The future will probably see the approval of NAFTA, full implementation of most EC agreements, and possible new trade alliances in Central and South America, Southeast Asia, and Eastern Europe. These developments will provide cheaper Mexican watermelons in the United States, more Israeli shoes in Central Europe, and more Colombian roses in Venezuela. These agreements entail a new future for international companies and pose a range of new questions for international managers.

- Will the creation of multiple trade blocs lead to economic warfare among them?

- Will trade blocs gradually evolve into three powerful trading blocs composed of the American hemisphere, Europe (from Ireland across the former Soviet Union), and the "yen bloc" encompassing the Pacific Rim?

■ Will the expansion of global, stateless corporations bypass trading zones and provide economic balance among them?[18]

Only the future will provide answers to these questions. International managers and global corporations will both shape and be shaped by these important trends.

● THE SOCIOCULTURAL ENVIRONMENT

culture

The shared knowledge, beliefs, values, behaviors, and ways of thinking among members of a society.

A nation's **culture** includes the shared knowledge, beliefs, and values, as well as the common modes of behavior and ways of thinking, among members of a society. Cultural factors are more perplexing than political and economic factors in foreign countries. Culture is intangible, pervasive, and difficult to learn. It is absolutely imperative that international businesses comprehend the significance of local cultures and deal with them effectively.

SOCIAL VALUES.   Research done by Geert Hofstede on 116,000 IBM employees in 40 countries identified four dimensions of national value systems that influence organizational and employee working relationships.[19]

power distance

The degree to which people accept inequality in power among institutions, organizations, and people.

1 *Power distance.* High **power distance** means that people accept inequality in power among institutions, organizations, and people. Low power distance means that people expect equality in power. Countries that value high power distance are Malaysia, the Philippines, and Panama. Countries that value low power distance are Denmark, Austria, and Israel.

uncertainty avoidance

A value characterized by people's intolerance for uncertainty and ambiguity and resulting support for beliefs that promise certainty and conformity.

2 *Uncertainty avoidance.* High **uncertainty avoidance** means that members of a society feel uncomfortable with uncertainty and ambiguity and thus support beliefs that promise certainty and conformity. Low uncertainty avoidance means that people have high tolerance for the unstructured, the unclear, and the unpredictable. High uncertainty avoidance countries include Greece, Portugal, and Uruguay. Countries with low uncertainty avoidance values are Singapore and Jamaica.

individualism

A preference for a loosely knit social framework in which individuals are expected to take care of themselves.

collectivism

A preference for a tightly knit social framework in which individuals look after one another and organizations protect their members' interests.

3 *Individualism and collectivism.* **Individualism** reflects a value for a loosely knit social framework in which individuals are expected to take care of themselves. **Collectivism** means a preference for a tightly knit social framework in which individuals look after one another and organizations protect their members' interests. Countries with individualist values include the United States, Canada, Great Britain, and Australia. Countries with collectivist values are Guatemala, Ecuador, and Panama.

masculinity

A cultural preference for achievement, heroism, assertiveness, and material success.

femininity

A cultural preference for modesty, caring for the weak, and quality of life.

4 *Masculinity/femininity.* **Masculinity** stands for preference for achievement, heroism, assertiveness, and material success. **Femininity** reflects the values of relationships, modesty, caring for the weak, and quality of life. Societies with strong masculine values are Japan, Austria, Mexico, and Germany. Countries with feminine values are Sweden, Norway, Denmark, and Yugoslavia. Both men and women subscribe to the dominant value in masculine and feminine cultures.

Social values influence organizational functioning and management styles. For example, organizations in France and Latin and Mediterranean countries tend to be hierarchical bureaucracies. Germany and other central European countries have organizations that strive to be impersonal, well-oiled machines. In India, Asia, and Africa, organizations are viewed as large families. Effective management styles differ in each country, depending on cultural characteristics.[20]

OTHER CULTURAL CHARACTERISTICS.　Other cultural characteristics that influence international organizations are language, religion, attitudes, social organization, and education. Some countries, such as India, are characterized by *linguistic pluralism*, meaning that several languages exist there. Other countries rely heavily on spoken versus written language. Religion includes sacred objects, philosophical attitudes toward life, taboos, and rituals. Attitudes toward achievement, work, and time can all affect organizational productivity. An attitude called **ethnocentrism** means that people have a tendency to regard their own culture as superior and to downgrade other cultures. Ethnocentrism within a country makes it difficult for foreign firms to operate there. Social organization includes status systems, kinship and families, social institutions, and

ethnocentrism

A cultural attitude marked by the tendency to regard one's own culture as superior to others.

Global companies such as LSI Logic Corporation, a leading manufacturer of high-performance semiconductors, appreciate the diverse elements in the *sociocultural environment*. Here, LSI company executives participate in an ancient Korean ritual for luck, wealth, and fortune. By placing cash in the pig's mouth on the traditional Korean *Gosa* table, these executives please the spirits and ensure prosperity for the company's expanded Korean design center. Participation in cultural ceremonies offers special insight for managers and plays an integral part in intercultural understanding.

opportunities for social mobility. Education influences the literacy level, the availability of qualified employees, and the predominance of primary or secondary degrees.

Managers in international companies have found that cultural differences cannot be ignored if international operations are to succeed. For example, Procter & Gamble ran into unanticipated cultural barriers when marketing its Cheer laundry soap in Japan. Cheer initially prospered by discounting its price, but that alienated wholesalers who were not used to having reduced margins.[21] Coke withdrew its 2-liter bottle from the Spanish market after discovering that compartments of Spanish refrigerators were too small for it.[22] Even the powerful Disney organization seriously misjudged per person food and souvenir spending and accommodation needs at EuroDisney in France, forcing the temporary seasonal closing of its 1,100-room Newport Bay Club in the winter of 1992.[23]

On the other hand, organizations that manage cultural differences report major successes. Kellogg introduced breakfast cereals into Brazil, where the traditional breakfast is coffee and a roll. Through carefully chosen advertising, many Brazilians were won over to the American breakfast. Many families now start the day with Kellogg's Sucrilhos (Frosted Flakes) and Crokinhos (Cocoa Krispies).[24]

SUMMARY OF THE INTERNATIONAL ENVIRONMENT

Some of the complexities of operating in diverse countries are illustrated in Exhibit 3.3. The upper portion of the exhibit shows a firm operating in its domestic market and native culture. The lower portion shows how complicated business operations can become when operating in several countries simultaneously. Through its foreign affiliates, the organization must carry on the same basic types of relationships in other countries, but to do so, it must adapt to their cultures and legal-political systems. Moreover, the organization must transcend the boundaries of separate cultures to transfer resources and products between the firm and foreign affiliates. The organization must also coordinate technological know-how, advertising, and managerial directives across cultural boundaries.

One company that is successfully crossing cultural boundaries throughout Asia is Citibank.

 CITIBANK

While other U.S. and foreign banks shy away from the potential cultural problems and uncertainty of Asian markets, Citibank has openly courted these booming economies and a generation of Asian yuppies. Citi's modern banks and high-tech approach appeal to the region's newly affluent entrepreneurs. Services such as consumer credit, 24-hour banking-by-phone, automated tellers, and credit cards are redefining the region's retail banking.

While Citibank has struggled at home to overcome losses, annual growth within its Asian division is averaging 25 percent to 30 percent, with 3-year growth in Taiwan, India, and Thailand soaring 56 percent, 57 percent, and 75 percent, respectively. In reaction to fears regarding the average Asian's lack of experience with personal debt, several Asian governments have raised minimal income qualification levels for credit cards and credit lines. Citi officials are confident, however, pointing to Asian customers' stellar credit records thus far. As it pioneers a new path across Asia, Citibank is pleased with its intercultural experience.[25] ■

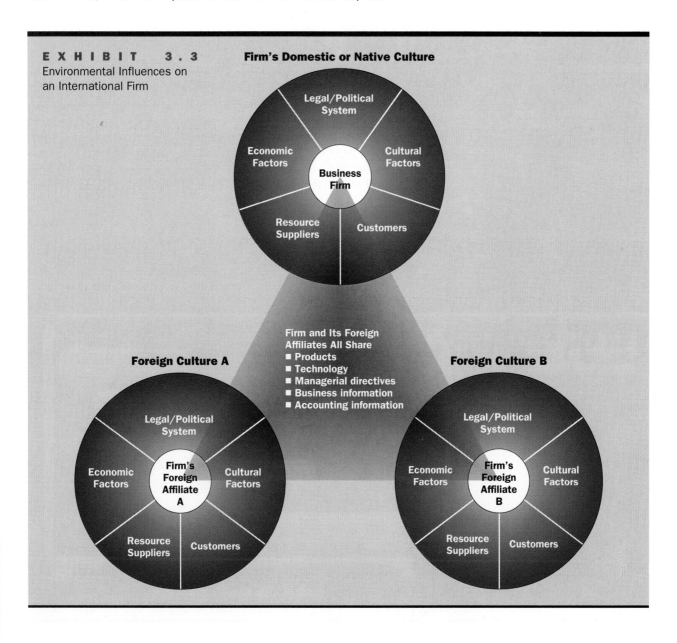

EXHIBIT   3.3
Environmental Influences on an International Firm

Firm's Domestic or Native Culture

Legal/Political System
Economic Factors
Cultural Factors
Business Firm
Resource Suppliers
Customers

Firm and Its Foreign Affiliates All Share
■ Products
■ Technology
■ Managerial directives
■ Business information
■ Accounting information

Foreign Culture A

Legal/Political System
Economic Factors
Cultural Factors
Firm's Foreign Affiliate A
Resource Suppliers
Customers

Foreign Culture B

Legal/Political System
Economic Factors
Cultural Factors
Firm's Foreign Affiliate B
Resource Suppliers
Customers

GETTING STARTED INTERNATIONALLY

Small- and medium-size companies have a couple of ways to become involved internationally. One is to seek cheaper sources of supply offshore, which is called *outsourcing*. Another is to develop markets for finished products outside their home country, which may include exporting, licensing, and direct investing. These are called **market entry strategies**, because they represent alternative ways to sell products and services in foreign markets. Most firms begin with exporting and work up to direct investment. Exhibit 3.4 shows the strategies companies can use to enter foreign markets.

■
market entry strategy
An organizational strategy for entering a foreign market.

OUTSOURCING

■
global outsourcing
Engaging in the international division of labor so as to obtain the cheapest sources of labor and supplies regardless of country; also called *global sourcing*.

Global outsourcing, sometimes called *global sourcing*, means engaging in the international division of labor so that manufacturing can be done in countries with the cheapest sources of labor and supplies. A company may take away a contract from a domestic supplier and place it with a company in the Far East, 8,000 miles away. For example, Seagate Technology sells low-cost hard disk drives for personal computers. Its enormous success has been based on using low-cost Asian labor to crank out products cheaply. These products are then finished off and sold in the United States.[26]

A unique variation is the *Maquiladora* industry along the Texas-Mexico border. In the beginning, twin plants were set up with the U.S. plant manufacturing components with sophisticated machinery and the Mexican plant assembling components using cheap labor. With increas-

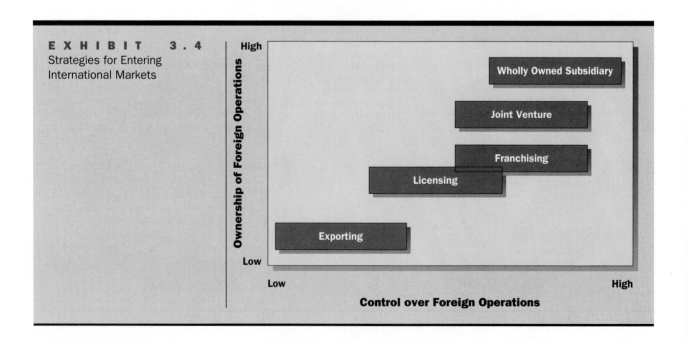

E X H I B I T   3 . 4
Strategies for Entering International Markets

ing sophistication in Mexico, new factories with sophisticated equipment are being built further south of the border, with assembled products imported into the United States at highly competitive prices.[27] The auto industry took advantage of the Maquiladora industry throughout the 1980s to combat the Japanese price challenge. By 1992, over 100,000 Mexicans were employed by U.S. auto companies in towns such as Hermosillo, giving the area the nickname "Detroit South." The low-cost, high-quality Mexican work force has also attracted manufacturers from other countries, such as Nissan, Renault, and Volkswagen.[28]

EXPORTING

With **exporting**, the corporation maintains its production facilities within the home nation and transfers its products for sale in foreign countries.[29] Exporting enables a country to market its products in other countries at small resource cost and with limited risk. Exporting does entail numerous problems based on physical distances, government regulations, foreign currencies, and cultural differences, but it is less expensive than committing the firm's own capital to building plants in host countries. For example, a high-tech equipment supplier called Gerber Scientific Inc. prefers not to get involved directly in foreign country operations. Because machinery and machine tools are hot areas of export, executives are happy to ship overseas. Indeed, more and more small businesses are experiencing great success in international markets.[30]

A form of exporting to less-developed countries is called **countertrade**, which is the barter of products for products rather than the sale of products for currency. Many less-developed countries have products to exchange but have no foreign currency. An estimated 20 percent of world trade is countertrade.

exporting

An entry strategy in which the organization maintains its production facilities within its home country and transfers its products for sale in foreign markets.

countertrade

The barter of products for other products rather than their sale for currency.

Freedom is catching worldwide, and the appeal of a borderless world beckons independent spirits to the open road, many aboard a Harley-Davidson motorcycle. To meet the growing international demand for motorcycles, which outstrips supply, Harley-Davidson, Inc., developed *market entry strategies*, including the reorganization of motorcycle sales and marketing. One step was unification of its domestic and international divisions, creating a global, single-market view. Joint ventures with Tomen and ASIC and investment in new equipment and employee training overseas reflect the increased importance of Harley's 30-nation export trade, roughly one-third of total sales.

licensing

An entry strategy in which an organization in one country makes certain resources available to companies in another in order to participate in the production and sale of its products abroad.

franchising

A form of licensing in which an organization provides its foreign franchisees with a complete assortment of materials and services.

direct investing

An entry strategy in which the organization is involved in managing its production facilities in a foreign country.

joint venture

A variation of direct investment in which an organization shares costs and risks with another firm to build a manufacturing facility, develop new products, or set up a sales and distribution network.

wholly owned foreign affiliate

A foreign subsidiary over which an organization has complete control.

LICENSING

With **licensing**, a corporation (the licensor) in one country makes certain resources available to companies in another country (the licensee). These resources include technology, managerial skills, and/or patent and trademark rights. They enable the licensee to produce and market a product similar to what the licensor has been producing. This arrangement gives the licensor an opportunity to participate in the production and sale of products outside its home country. Hasbro has licensing agreements with companies in several Latin American countries and Japan. Hasbro builds brand identity and consumer awareness by contracting with toy companies to manufacture products locally. Glidden has licensing arrangements for its paint manufacturing technology with manufacturers in over 25 countries.

Franchising is a form of licensing in which the franchisor provides foreign franchisees with a complete package of material and services, including equipment, products, product ingredients, trademark and trade name rights, managerial advice, and a standardized operating system. Some of the best known international franchisers are the fast-food chains. Kentucky Fried Chicken, Burger King, Wendy's and McDonald's outlets are found in almost every large city in the world. The story is often told of the Japanese child visiting Los Angeles who excitedly pointed out to his parents, "They have McDonald's in America."

Licensing and franchising offer a business firm relatively easy access to international markets, but they limit its participation in and control over the development of those markets.

DIRECT INVESTING

A higher level of involvement in international trade is direct investment in manufacturing facilities in a foreign country. **Direct investing** means that the company is involved in managing the productive assets, which distinguishes it from other entry strategies that permit less managerial control.

Currently, the most popular type of direct investment is to engage in strategic alliances and partnerships. In a **joint venture**, a company shares costs and risks with another firm, typically in the host country, to develop new products, build a manufacturing facility, or set up a sales and distribution network.[31] A partnership is often the fastest, cheapest, and least risky way to get into the global game. Entrepreneurial companies such as Molex, a manufacturer of connectors, and Nypro, a maker of industrial components, both used partnerships to gain overseas access to several countries. Giants such as AT&T and Japan's NEC Corporation joined forces to share design technology and microchip manufacturing. Other giant partnerships include Texas Instruments with Kobe Steel (Japan), Mitsubishi of Japan with Daimler-Benz AG of Germany, and Ford with Volkswagen (in South America) and with Mazda of Japan.[32] International joint ventures are expected to be the hallmark of business in the 1990s.

The other choice is to have a **wholly owned foreign affiliate**, over which the company has complete control. Direct investment provides cost savings over exporting by shortening distribution channels and reducing storage and transportation costs. Local managers also have heightened awareness of economic, cultural, and political conditions. The company must expend capital funds and human resources to acquire productive assets that will be exposed to risks from the host country's economic, legal-political, and sociocultural environments.

For example, companies in the advertising industry have recently become involved in direct investment by buying agencies around the globe to provide advertising services for global companies. Foote Cone & Belding acquired advertising agencies in Europe, South America, and Asia. Saatchi & Saatchi, based in London, has taken over 12 agencies in Europe and the United States. Such mergers create wholly owned subsidiaries that enable advertising agencies to coordinate the advertising for multinational clients. Direct investment gives them complete control over agencies in host countries.[33]

● THE MULTINATIONAL CORPORATION

The size and volume of international business are so large that they are hard to comprehend. The revenue of General Motors ($124 billion) is comparable to the gross domestic product (GDP) of Finland, that of General Electric ($60 billion) is comparable in size to Israel's GDP, Toyota revenues ($78 billion) to Hong Kong's GDP, and those of the Royal Dutch/Shell Group ($104 billion) to the GDP of Norway.[34]

As discussed earlier in this chapter, a large volume of international business is being carried out in a seemingly borderless world by very large international businesses that can be thought of as *global corporations, stateless corporations,* or *transnational corporations.* In the business world, these large international firms typically are called *multinational corporations (MNCs),* which have been the subject of enormous attention and concern. MNCs can move a wealth of assets from country to country and influence national economies, politics, and cultures.

CHARACTERISTICS OF MULTINATIONAL CORPORATIONS

Although there is no precise definition, a **multinational corporation (MNC)** typically receives more than 25 percent of its total sales revenues from operations outside the parent's home country. MNCs also have the following distinctive managerial characteristics:

1 An MNC is managed as an integrated worldwide business system. This means that foreign affiliates act in close alliance and cooperation with one another. Capital, technology, and people are transferred among country affiliates. The MNC can acquire materials and manufacture parts wherever in the world it is most advantageous to do so.

2 An MNC is ultimately controlled by a single management authority that makes key, strategic decisions relating to the parent and all

multinational corporation (MNC)

An organization that receives more than 25 percent of its total sales revenues from operations outside the parent company's home country; also called *global corporation* or *transnational corporation.*

affiliates. Although some headquarters are binational, such as the Royal Dutch/Shell Group, some centralization of management is required to maintain worldwide integration and profit maximization for the enterprise as a whole.

3 MNC top managers are presumed to exercise a global perspective. They regard the entire world as one market for strategic decisions, resource acquisition, location of production, advertising, and marketing efficiency.

In few cases, the MNC management philosophy may differ from that described above. For example, some researchers have distinguished among *ethnocentric companies*, which place emphasis on their home countries, *polycentric companies*, which are oriented toward the markets of individual foreign host countries, and *geocentric companies*, which are truly world oriented and favor no specific country.[35] In general, a multinational corporation can be thought of as a business enterprise that is composed of affiliates located in different countries and whose top managers make decisions primarily on the basis of global business opportunities and objectives.

The Upjohn Company has learned to tailor *management style* to local culture as it expands its pharmaceutical business worldwide. Employees in Upjohn manufacturing plants increased productivity 20 percent when Upjohn went from a six- to a five-day week, fitting the local culture. Since 70 percent of Korean patients get their medical advice from pharmacists, highly trained company representatives increase respect for Upjohn in the Korean health-care industry. Here, a representative provides information to a pharmacist in Seoul. Drawers in the background contain traditional (herbal) medicine.

● TAILORING MANAGEMENT STYLE TO INTERNATIONAL CULTURES

Managers in MNCs deal with employees from different cultures. What one culture sees as participative management another sees as incompetence. Before undertaking an assignment in a foreign country, managers must understand the subtleties of culture and how to provide proper leadership, decision making, motivation, and control.[36]

LEADERSHIP

In relationship-oriented societies, leaders should take a strong personal interest in employees. In Asia, the Arab world, and Latin America, managers should use a warm, personalized approach, appearing at soccer games and birthday parties. In Latin America and China, managers should have periodic social visits with workers, inquiring about morale and health.

Leaders should be especially careful about criticizing others. To Asians, Africans, Arabs, and Latin Americans, the loss of self-respect brings dishonor to themselves and their families. Public criticism is intolerable. In a moment of exasperation, an American supervisor on an oil rig in Indonesia shouted at his timekeeper to take the next boat to shore. A mob of outraged Indonesians grabbed fire axes and went after the supervisor. He escaped and barricaded himself in his quarters. The moral: One simply never berates an Indonesian in public.

DECISION MAKING

European managers frequently use centralized decision making. American employees might discuss a problem and give the boss a recommendation, but German managers expect the boss to issue specific instructions. East Indian and Latin American employees typically do not understand participatory decision making. Deeply ingrained social customs suggest that a supervisor's effort toward participation signifies ignorance and weakness.

In Arab and African nations, managers are expected to use consultative decision making in the extreme. Arabs prefer one-on-one consultation and make decisions in an informal and unstructured manner.

The Japanese prefer a bottom-up style of decision making, which is consistent with Far Eastern cultures that emphasize group harmony. In Taiwan, Hong Kong, and South Korea, managers are paternalistic figures who guide and help employees.

MOTIVATION

Motivation must fit the incentives within the culture. In Japan, employees are motivated to satisfy the company. A financial bonus for star performance would be humiliating to employees from Japan, China, or the former Yugoslavia. An American executive in Japan offered a holiday trip to the top salesperson, but employees were not interested. After he realized that Japanese are motivated in groups, he changed the reward to a trip for everyone if together they achieved the sales target. They did.

In Latin America, employees work for an individual rather than for a company. Among Turks and Arabs the individual is supreme, and employees are evaluated on their loyalties to superiors more than on job performance.

CONTROL

When things go wrong, managers in foreign countries often are unable to get rid of employees who do not work out. In Europe, Mexico, and Indonesia, to hire and fire on performance seems unnaturally brutal. Workers are protected by strong labor laws and union rules. In Mexico, employees are considered permanent after a 30-day work period. British and Belgian labor laws dramatically favor employees. Managers must find creative ways of dealing with unproductive employees.

In foreign cultures, managers also should not control the wrong things. A Sears manager in Hong Kong insisted that employees come to work on time instead of 15 minutes late. The employees did exactly as they were told, but they also left on time instead of working into the evening as they had previously. A lot of work was left unfinished. The manager eventually told the employees to go back to their old ways. His attempt at control had a negative effect.

In another case a Japanese manager was told to criticize an American employee's performance. It took the manager five tries before he could be direct enough to confront the American on his poor performance. Japanese managers are unused to confrontations.

SUMMARY AND MANAGEMENT SOLUTION

This chapter has stressed the growing importance of an international perspective on management. Successful companies are preparing to expand their business overseas and to withstand domestic competition from foreign competitors. Business in the global arena involves special risks and difficulties because of complicated economic, legal-political, and sociocultural forces. Moreover, the global environment changes rapidly, as illustrated by the emergence of the European Community, the North American Free Trade Agreement, and the shift in Eastern Europe to democratic forms of government.

International markets provide many opportunities but are fraught with difficulty, as Federal Express, described at the beginning of this chapter, discovered. Major alternatives for serving foreign markets are exporting, licensing, franchising, and direct investing through joint ventures or wholly owned subsidiaries. Federal Express attempted to shortcut local regulations from freight weight to landing rights in European and Asian countries through a series of acquisitions. The purchase of Flying Tigers opened unrestricted cargo routes to several European and Japanese cities. But international competitors such as TNT and DHL had already established loyal followings and negotiated new deals with Lufthansa and Japan Airlines. UPS purchased Seaborne European Express Parcels and laid plans for a European trucking business. When FEDEX's system of controls and management methods did not work in foreign cultures, the intense competition took its toll, causing FEDEX to fall back and regroup.[37]

Much of the growth in international business has been carried out by large businesses called *MNCs*. These large companies exist in an almost borderless world, encouraging the free flow of ideas, products, manufacturing, and marketing among countries to achieve the greatest efficiencies. Products sold in any one country may contain parts manufactured and assembled in several countries. Managers in MNCs deal with employees from various countries and can learn to tailor their management style to cultural differences.

DISCUSSION QUESTIONS

1. Why do you think international businesses traditionally prefer to operate in industrialized countries? Discuss.
2. What considerations in recent years have led international businesses to expand their activities into less-developed countries?
3. What policies or actions would you recommend to an entrepreneurial business wanting to do business in Europe?
4. What steps could a company take to avoid making product design and marketing mistakes when introducing new products into a foreign country?

5. Compare the advantages associated with the foreign market entry strategies of exporting, licensing, and wholly owned subsidiaries.

6. Should a multinational corporation operate as an integrated, worldwide business system, or would it be more effective to let each subsidiary operate autonomously?

7. What does it mean to say that the world is becoming "borderless"? That large companies are "stateless"?

8. What might managers do to avoid making mistakes concerning control and decision making when operating in a foreign culture?

9. What is meant by the cultural values of individualism and masculinity/femininity? How might these values affect organization design and management processes?

MANAGEMENT IN PRACTICE: EXPERIENTIAL EXERCISE

A global environment requires that American managers learn to deal effectively with people in other countries. The assumption that foreign business leaders behave and negotiate in the same manner as Americans is false. How well prepared are you to live with globalization? Consider the following.

Are you guilty of:	Definitely No				Definitely Yes
1. Impatience? Do you think "Time is money" or "Let's get straight to the point"?	1	2	3	4	5
2. Having a short attention span, bad listening habits, or being uncomfortable with silence?	1	2	3	4	5
3. Being somewhat argumentative, sometimes to the point of belligerence?	1	2	3	4	5
4. Ignorance about the world beyond your borders?	1	2	3	4	5
5. Weakness in foreign languages?	1	2	3	4	5
6. Placing emphasis on short-term success?	1	2	3	4	5
7. Believing that advance preparations are less important than negotiations themselves?	1	2	3	4	5
8. Being legalistic? Of believing "A deal is a deal," regardless of changing circumstances?	1	2	3	4	5
9. Having little interest in seminars on the subject of globalization, failing to browse through libraries or magazines on international topics, not interacting with foreign students or employees?	1	2	3	4	5

Total Score _____

If you scored less than 27, congratulations. You have the temperament and interest to do well in a global company. If you scored more than 27, it's time to consider a change. Regardless of your score, go back over each item and make a plan of action to correct deficiencies indicated by answers to any question of 4 or 5.

SOURCE: Reprinted by permission of the publisher from Cynthia Barmun and Netasha Wolninsky, "Why Americans Fail at Overseas Negotiations," *Management Review* (October 1989), 55–57, © 1989 American Management Association, New York. All rights reserved.

CASES FOR ANALYSIS

NESTLÉ

A few years ago, the outlook for Nestlé, the lethargic Swiss chocolate maker, was not favorable. Unprofitable, bloated by corporate staff, and fighting a storm of controversy about marketing infant formula to Third World mothers, it was time for a change. Chief executive Helmut Maucher has since turned Nestlé into a powerhouse. How? Great strategy. He ended the boycott of infant formula by meeting with church leaders, halting Third World consumer advertising, and creating a commission to monitor Nestlé compliance. Then he drastically cut staff at headquarters and gave authority to operating units.

Maucher also emphasized marketing Nestlé's food lines—ranging from Friskies pet food to Kit Kat candy bars—around the world. The food business is capital intensive. Developing new prepared foods requires expensive research and development. To get maximum mileage from the investment, selling similar brands worldwide is the key.

Here is an example of how the strategy works. Lean Cuisine is a hit in the U.S. market. At great expense, this product was exported to Britain, where it was a success despite high shipping costs and customs duties. Manufacturing plants then were built in Britain, and Nestlé now holds 33 percent of the British market for frozen dinners. Another component of strategy is to acquire related companies, such as Carnation in the United States, the chocolate maker Rowntree in Britain, and the Italian pasta maker Buitoni. These companies provide marketing and distribution systems for foods manufactured in Nestlé's 60 plants around the globe. The acquisition of the British and Italian companies also provides a wedge to the unified market created by Europe 1992. Nestlé is using Carnation to break into the huge infant formula market in the United States with products developed elsewhere.

What's next? The Third World and the food of tomorrow, pasta. Chairman Maucher does not believe the world can be fed on beefsteak, so noodles are the pathway into less-developed countries. With his success so far, observers believe he can do it, further solidifying Nestlé as the number-one food company in the world.

● QUESTIONS

1. Evaluate Nestlé's overall international strategy. Would you characterize it as primarily a globalization strategy or a multidomestic strategy? Discuss.
2. In what stage of globalization would you classify Nestlé? Why?

SOURCE: Based on Shawn Tully, "Nestlé Shows How to Gobble Markets," *Fortune*, January 16, 1989, 74–78.

OK TEDI MINING LTD.

Ok Tedi (pronounced "owk teddy") is a joint venture headed by Standard Oil Company of Indiana and Broken Hill Proprietary Company of Australia that was formed in the early 1980s to mine gold and copper in Papua New Guinea. Papua New Guinea is a newly independent "developing" country that needed advanced foreign technology for extracting its mineral ores. The Ok Tedi mine was expected to help develop a remote and poor region of the country that is rich in natural resources. The minerals were expected to be easily mined, since all that Ok Tedi had to do was bulldoze Mount Fublian, a 6,000-foot mountain of copper ore capped by a crown of gold-bearing ore. The joint venture was put together quickly during a period of rapidly rising metal prices. There was no time to conduct detailed engineering studies or to purchase insurance against political risk.

Local tribes believe that Mount Fublian is the haunt of evil spirits, and the western engineers working on the project no longer laugh at this belief. The region surrounding the mine is one of the wettest on earth; yet as soon as Ok

Tedi began bringing heavy equipment upriver by barge, the rains stopped for five months and equipment had to be airlifted to the mine site. When the rains returned they did so with a vengeance, washing away roads and equipment. Just after work on a tailings dam was started, 50 million tons of soft, black mud slid down the mountainside and covered the dam site. The estimated cost of building the dam jumped from $50 million to $350 million. To start mining gold, Ok Tedi tried a chemical method of neutralizing wastes. Two accidents released untreated cyanide into nearby streams. Alarmed villagers found dead fish and crocodiles, and the government became concerned about the villagers' health.

Ok Tedi managers believe that local unhappiness has caused additional problems with the government. Because of simultaneous cost overruns and falling metal prices, the company decided to concentrate on producing gold, which has higher profit potential. The government of Papua New Guinea regarded this as a violation of its agreement with Ok Tedi, which called for both copper and gold production. The government insisted that Ok Tedi build processing lines for copper ore, hydroelectric facilities, and a permanent dam to contain the mine tailings, despite an additional cost of $800 million, which managers could not afford.

In February 1985, the government ordered the mine closed. The company can resume gold production if it agrees to proceed with the construction of the waste dam and one copper processing line.

● **QUESTIONS**

1. Did senior managers at Ok Tedi fail to provide sufficient strategic planning, or can the project's problems be attributed to uncontrollable circumstances?
2. Discuss the interplay among economic, political, and cultural factors in this situation. Do you think that unanticipated problems such as these could occur in any less-developed country?
3. What do you think Ok Tedi's managers should do now?

SOURCE: "Ok Tedi Can Stay Open If Foreign Owners Guarantee Completion of Copper-Gold Mine," *The Wall Street Journal*, February 13, 1985, 34; "Government of Papua New Guinea Orders Ok Tedi Mine Closed," *The Asian Wall Street Journal*, February 4, 1985, 2; "Ok Tedi Will Start Up Its Gold and Copper Mine in Papua New Guinea in May, 1984," *American Metal Markets*, January 1, 1984, 2; and "Papua New Guinea Goes for the Gold," *Business Asia*, February 10, 1984, 46.

REFERENCES

1. Chuck Hawkins, "FEDEX: Europe Nearly Killed the Messenger," *Business Week*, May 25, 1992, 124–126; Daniel Pearl, "Innocence Abroad: Federal Express Finds Its Pioneering Formula Falls Flat Overseas," *The Wall Street Journal*, April 15, 1991, A1, A8; and Erik Calonius, "Federal Express's Battle Overseas," Fortune, December 3, 1990, 137–140.

2. Yao-Su Yu, "Global or Stateless Corporations Are National Firms with International Operations," *California Management Review* 34 (Winter), 107–126; Jonathan P. Hicks, "Foreign Owners Are Shaking Up the Competition," *The New York Times*, May 28, 1989, sec. 3, 9; and Ira C. Magaziner and Mark Patinkin, *The Silent War* (New York: Random House, 1989).

3. William Holstein, Stanley Reed, Jonathan Kapstein, Todd Vogel, and Joseph Weber, "The Stateless Corporation," *Business Week*, May 14, 1990, 98–105.

4. Nancy J. Adler, *International Dimensions of Organizational Behavior* (Boston: PWS-Kent, 1991), 7–8; Holstein et al., "The Stateless Corporation"; and Richard Daft, *Organization Theory and Design* (St Paul, Minn.: West, 1992).

5. Holstein et al., "The Stateless Corporation."

6. William Taylor, "The Logic of Global Business: An Interview with ABB's Percy Barnevik," *Harvard Business Review* (March–April 1991), 91–105; and Holstein et al., "The Stateless Corporation."

7. John S. Hill and Richard R. Still, "Adapting Products to LDC Tastes," *Harvard Business Review* 62 (March–April 1984), 92–101; and David A. Ricks, *Big Business Blunders: Mistakes in Multinational Marketing* (Homewood, Ill.: Dow Jones-Irwin, 1983).

8. Karen Paul and Robert Barbarto, "The Multinational Corporation in the Less Developed Country: The Economic Development Model versus the North-South Model," *Academy of Management Review* 10 (1985), 8–14.

9. Kathleen Deveny, "McWorld?" *Business Week*, October 13, 1986, 78–86.

10. Bruce Kogut, "Designing Global Strategies: Profiting from Operational Flexibility," *Sloan Management Review* 27 (Fall 1985), 27–38.

11. Mark Fitzpatrick, "The Definition and Assessment of Political Risk in International Business: A Review of the Literature," *Academy of Management Review* 8 (1983), 249–254.

12. "Multinational Firms Act to Protect Overseas Workers from Terrorism," *The Wall Street Journal*, April 29, 1986, 31.

13. Patricia Sellers, "Where Killers and Kidnappers Roam," *Fortune*, September 23, 1991, 8.

14. John Templeton, Ken Olsen, David Greising, Jonathan Kapstein, and William Glasgall, "Eastward Ho! The Pioneers Plunge In," *Business Week,* April 15, 1991, 51–53.

15. Shawn Tully, "Europe '92: More Unity Than You Think," *Fortune*, August 24, 1992, 136–142.

16. Barbara Rudolph, "Megamarket," *Time*, August 10, 1992, 43–44.

17. Amy Borrus, "A Free-Trade Milestone, with Many More Miles to Go," *Business Week*, August 24, 1992, 30–31.

18. Keith Bradsher, "As Global Talks Stall, Regional Trade Pacts Multiply," *The New York Times*, August 23, 1992, F5.

19. Geert Hofstede, "The Interaction between National and Organizational Value Systems," *Journal of Management Studies* 22 (1985), 347–357; and Geert Hofstede, "The Cultural Relativity of the Quality of Life Concept," *Academy of Management Review* 9 (1984), 389–398.

20. Ellen F. Jackofsky, John W. Slocum, Jr., and Sara J. McQuaid, "Cultural Values and the CEO: Alluring Companions?" *Academy of Management Executive* 2 (1988), 39–49.

21. Jeffrey A. Trachtenberg, "They Didn't Listen to Anybody," *Forbes*, December 15, 1986, 168–169.

22. Orla Sheehan, "Managing a Multinational Corporation: Tomorrow's Decision Makers Speak Out," *Fortune*, August 24, 1992, 233.

23. Stewart Toy, Patricia Oster, and Ronald Grover, "The Mouse Isn't Roaring," *Business Week*, August 24, 1992, 38.

24. Kenneth Labich, "America's International Winners," *Fortune*, April 14, 1986, 34–46.

25. Pete Engardio and Bruce Einhorn, "For Citibank, There's No Place Like Asia," *Business Week,* March 30, 1992, 66–69.

26. Frank T. Curtin, "Global Sourcing: Is It Right for Your Company?" *Management Review* (August 1987), 47–49; and Richard Brandt, "Seagate Goes East—and Comes Back a Winner," *Business Week*, March 16, 1987, 94.

27. Gary Jacobson, "The Boom on Mexico's Border," *Management Review* (July 1988), 21–25.

28. Stephen Baker, David Woodruff, and Elizabeth Weiner, "Detroit South," *Business Week*, March 16, 1992, 98–103.

29. Jen Kerr, "Export Strategies," *Small Business Reports* (May 1989), 20–25.

30. William J. Holstein and Brian Bremmer, "The Little Guys Are Making It Big Overseas," *Business Week*, February 27, 1989, 94–96; and Iris Lorenz-Fife, "Resource Guide: Small-Business Help from the Government," *Entrepreneur*, December 1989, 168–174.

31. Kathryn Rudie Harrigan, "Managing Joint Ventures," *Management Review* (February 1987), 24–41; and Therese R. Revesz and Mimi Cauley de Da La Sierra, "Competitive Alliances: Forging Ties Abroad," *Management Review* (March 1987), 57–59.

32. Bernard Wysocki, Jr., "Cross-Border Alliances Become Favorite Way to Crack New Markets," *The Wall Street Journal*, March 26, 1990, A1, A12; and Andrew Kupfer, "How to Be a Global Manager," *Fortune*, March 14, 1988, 52–58.

33. Janice Castro, "Heavy-Duty Mergers," *Time*, May 12, 1986, 72–73.

34. "How Revenues of the Top Ten Global Companies Compare with Some National Economies," *Fortune*, July 27, 1992, 16.

35. Howard V. Perlmutter, "The Tortuous Evolution of the Multinational Corporation," *Columbia Journal of World Business* (January/February 1969), 9–18; and Youram Wind, Susan P. Douglas, and Howard V. Perlmutter, "Guidelines for Developing International Marketing Strategies," *Journal of Marketing* (April 1973), 14–23.

36. The following discussion is based on Lennie Copeland and Lewis Gregg, "Getting the Best from Foreign Employees," *Management Review* (June 1986), 19–26.

37. Hawkins, "FEDEX: Europe Nearly Killed the Messenger."

Free and fair trade is at best a subjective call and opinions usually depend on whose side is currently running the trade surplus. But charges and countercharges regarding the levelness of the playing field become less significant in a world where trade barriers are fast disappearing and billion dollar markets are emerging. The question for the remainder of the decade won't be who can enter multinational markets abroad, but who can target effectively, produce efficiently, decipher the political tea leaves, and do it all competitively.

In Europe, the prevailing trend has been toward consolidation: the opening of borders and lowering of barriers. The six-country European Free Trade Association—Austria, Finland, Iceland, Norway, Sweden, and Switzerland—has already been virtually integrated into the 12-member European Community (EC). Czechoslovakia, Hungary, and Poland have agreed to open markets before the end of the decade. The consensus for the 1990s is that Central Europe—previously an anemic consumer of Western goods—is expected to be one of the ripest growth markets for the EC, as well as for the United States and Japan. The EC, along with a number of established U.S. and Japanese multinationals, are poised to move into the former Eastern Bloc countries. But the expansion is not without serious pitfalls.

Civil unrest, the inability to adjust to a free market, and rising poverty in the former Eastern Bloc countries could lead to the rollback of reform, possibly setting in motion a torrent of destitute refugees. Also looming on the horizon is the imploded hulk of the former Soviet Union, where the political picture is even murkier and unpredictable. By 1993, the German government, already allocating $10 billion a year to settle new immigrants, was considering steps to stem the tide of East European and Russian refugees into that nation.

Another impediment to viable expansion will be the pool of available capital, and here again it is Germany that must lead the way. Unfortunately, the cost of reunification led to a rise in taxes and a large budget deficit, while at the same time the government tamped down inflation by tightening credit. The result was higher interest rates, which spilled across Europe and stifled other EC economies.

Under the most optimistic scenario, the nations of Central Europe would pay for their own development through tax surpluses, domestic savings, and export income. Tapping those savings would be sufficient to buy a good portion of required capital equipment, with no more than $30 billion a year in foreign capital investment needed to close the gap. Some argue that approach could generate as much as $150 billion a year, which would buy a lot of widgets indeed.

Another less rosy view postulates that the capital investment required to transform 125 million East Europeans into eager consumers will be more like $200 billion a year, for at least ten years, with the majority coming from Germany. A capital outlay of that magnitude would almost certainly raise interest rates and throttle growth throughout Europe.

When Western Europe does decide to forge ahead into Central Europe it would do well to follow the lead of the Japanese, who have prospered mightily in the world trade arena by not only embracing the latest technologies and perfecting the techniques of "lean manufacturing," which have made traditional methods of mass production obsolete.

The broadly defined field of consumer, computer, and microchip electronics is projected to grow faster than any other segment in Europe over the next decade. However, it is also the largest single industry in Japan. Where Europeans get high marks for the latest innovations, Japan scores once again in the area of lean manufacturing and getting products into stores quickly. This is particularly critical with products such as CDs, camcorders, and VCRs, which are constantly replaced by updated models.

Multinational expansion requires careful planning, fast feet and courage throughout, and a big enough R&D budget to come up with the market's next great product. The pace of change is ever increasing while product cycles are diminishing. The emphasis is on quality products designed for global customers who demand and expect the highest standards, while keeping manufacturing methods flexible enough to turn on a dime. In a shrinking world where borders are disappearing, global expansion is becoming a necessity. "If we hadn't entered the Japanese and American markets," British-based Glaxo's Chairman Sir Paul Girolami said, "we wouldn't be independent now, and we wouldn't deserve to be."

● QUESTIONS

1. How has the potential for free trade increased since the fall of the Berlin Wall? What barriers to free trade still remain?

2. Describe the strategic approaches used by Japanese corporations. How do they differ from those of the Europeans?

3. How has the European Community failed in its bid to unify? What obstacles remain?

4. What changes have occurred since this video case aired?

THE ENVIRONMENT AND CORPORATE CULTURE

4

LEARNING OBJECTIVES

After studying this chapter, you should be able to

■ Describe the task and general environments and the dimensions of each.

■ Explain how organizations adapt to an uncertain environment and identify techniques managers use to influence and control the external environment.

■ Define corporate culture and give organizational examples.

■ Explain organizational symbols, stories, heroes, slogans, and ceremonies and how they relate to corporate culture.

■ Describe how corporate culture relates to the environment.

■ Define a symbolic manager and explain the tools a symbolic manager uses to change corporate culture.

Throughout the 1980s, thousands of women—breast cancer patients, as well as healthy women—received Dow Corning's silicone breast implants. Dow Corning dominated this field in 1991 with 600,000 implant recipients. Its managers took pride in the assessment of physicians and consumers regarding the product's ease of implantation and natural feel and appearance. ■ By 1992, however, everything had changed. Faulty implants were reported. Severe health problems resulting from leaking silicone had developed in some implant recipients, leading to widespread fear, a barrage of lawsuits, and a ban on cosmetic silicone breast implants. Dow

Corning faced the prospect that damages paid to implant recipients could exceed $500 million. In addition, the company faced suits from stockholders and possible criminal charges against company executives. Some observers suggested that Dow Corning seek Chapter 11 bankruptcy protection.[1] ■ Do you feel that Dow Corning executives could have anticipated and avoided the problems with the silicone implants? If you were Keith R. McKennon, new Dow Corning CEO, how would you respond to these problems from the environment?

M A N A G E M E N T   P R O B L E M

Dow Corning faced a crisis brought on by seemingly unpredictable events within both the internal and external environment. The environment surprises many companies. Union Carbide faced a crisis when a gas leak killed more than 2,000 people in Bhopal, India. That disaster damaged Carbide's ability to compete for international contracts and by 1992 had reduced the company to half its prior size.[2]

Organizations may be affected by a variety of environmental forces such as strikes, technological advances in the industry, or competitive price wars. Government actions, regulations and red tape can also affect an organization's environment and foment a crisis. Passage of the Americans with Disabilities Act forced companies to evaluate existing conditions that required compliance and make adjustments in a number of areas—from promotion practices to parking and restroom access. Changes in Medicare payments may force many rural hospitals to close.

Although few companies experience a crisis as serious as the one resulting from a gas leak, unexpected events that can seriously harm performance occur in the environment of every organization. During the lingering recession in the early 1990s, companies such as H. J. Heinz, Sears, TRW, and General Electric underwent major internal changes—restructuring, discarding product lines, and trimming work forces. Without these major changes, the companies would no longer fit the reality of the changing external environment.

The study of management traditionally has focused on factors within the organization—a closed systems view—such as leading, motivating, and controlling employees. The classical, behavioral, and management science schools described in Chapter 2 focused on internal aspects of organizations over which managers have direct control. These views are accurate but incomplete. As discussed in Chapter 3, globalization and the trend toward a borderless world affects companies in new ways. Even for those companies that try to operate solely on the domestic stage, events that have greatest impact typically originate in the external environment. To be effective, managers must monitor and respond to the environment—an open systems view.

This chapter explores in detail components of the external environment and how they affect the organization. We will also examine a major part of the organization's internal environment—corporate culture. Corporate culture is shaped by the external environment and is an important part of the context within which managers do their jobs.

● THE EXTERNAL ENVIRONMENT

The world as we know it is undergoing tremendous and far-reaching change. This change can be understood by defining and examining components of the external environment.

organizational environment

All elements existing outside the organization's boundaries that have the potential to affect the organization.

The external **organizational environment** includes all elements existing outside the boundary of the organization that have the potential to affect the organization.[3] The environment includes competitors, resources, technology, and economic conditions that influence the organization. It does not include those events so far removed from the organization that their impact is not perceived.

The organization's external environment can be further conceptualized as having two layers: general and task environments as illustrated in Exhibit 4.1.[4]

The **general environment** is the outer layer that is widely dispersed and affects organizations indirectly. It includes social, demographic, and economic factors that influence all organizations about equally. Increases in the inflation rate or the percentage of dual-career couples in the work force are part of the organization's general environment. These events do not directly change day-to-day operations, but they do affect all organizations eventually. The **task environment** is closer to the organization and includes the sectors that conduct day-to-day transactions with the organization and directly influence its basic operations and performance. It is generally considered to include competitors, suppliers, and customers.

The organization also has an **internal environment,** which includes the elements within the organization's boundaries. The internal environment is composed of current employees, management, and especially corporate culture, which defines employee behavior in the internal environment and how well the organization will adapt to the external environment.

general environment

The layer of the external environment that affects the organization indirectly.

task environment

The layer of the external environment that directly influences the organization's operations and performance.

internal environment

The environment within the organization's boundaries.

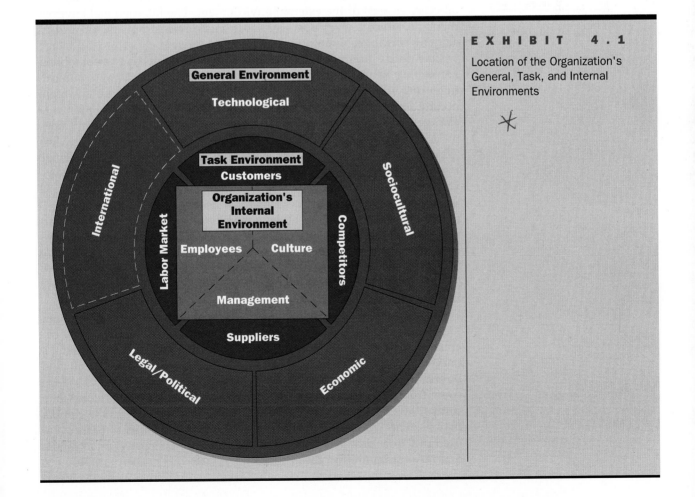

E X H I B I T   4 . 1

Location of the Organization's General, Task, and Internal Environments

Exhibit 4.1 illustrates the relationship among the general, task, and internal environments. As an open system, the organization draws resources from the external environment and releases goods and services back to it. We will now discuss the two layers of the external environment in more detail. Then we will discuss corporate culture, the key element in the internal environment. Other aspects of the internal environment such as structure and technology will be covered in Parts III and IV of this book.

GENERAL ENVIRONMENT

The general environment represents the outer layer of the environment. These dimensions influence the organization over time but often are not involved in day-to-day transactions with it. The dimensions of the general environment include international, technological, sociocultural, economic, and legal-political.

international dimension

Portion of the external environment that represents events originating in foreign countries as well as opportunities for American companies in other countries.

INTERNATIONAL.   The **international dimension** of the external environment represents events originating in foreign countries as well as opportunities for American companies in other countries. Note in Exhibit 4.1 that the international dimension represents a context that influences all other aspects of the external environment. The international environment provides new competitors, customers, and suppliers, as well as shaping social, technological, and economic trends.

One study identified 136 U.S. industries—including automobiles, accounting services, entertainment, consumer electronics, and publishing—that will have to compete on a global basis or disappear. The high-quality, low-priced automobiles from Japan and Korea have permanently changed the American automobile industry. As we discussed in Chapter 3, many companies have parts supplied from countries such as Mexico because of low-priced labor. A drop in the dollar's foreign exchange rate lowers the price of U.S. products overseas, increasing export competitiveness.

One example of fierce foreign competition is Toyo Toki, Japan's leading maker of toilets and bathtubs, which has now targeted the U.S. market. Toyo Toki plans to offer initially products not produced by American manufacturers, such as an electronically controlled toilet and bidet combined in one unit. American companies are worried about the competition. The chief executive of American Standard said, "I would rank them as our number-one threat in the future. We have to hurry."[5]

Managers used to working and thinking about the domestic environment must learn new rules to cope with goods, services, and ideas circulating around the globe. For example, products and services exist in a one-world market. A better machine built in Oklahoma City will find buyers from Europe and Asia. Moreover, competitors in a global village come from all over. A company that does not export will still run into competitors in its own marketplace, including some from developing nations. The world is also a source of supply as well as a market. For example, new products such as liquid Tide are composed of materials and ideas from around the world.

Perhaps the hardest lesson for managers in the United States to learn is that they do not know best. U.S. decision makers know little about issues and competition in foreign countries. U.S. arrogance is a shortcut to failure. To counter this, Pall Corporation keeps a team of Ph.D.s traveling around the world gathering current information on markets and issues.[6]

The global environment represents an ever-changing and uneven playing field compared with the domestic environment. Changes in the international domain can abruptly turn the domestic environment upside down. Consider, for example, the "peace dividend" brought on by the end of the Cold War, and the fall of communism. Despite the need for periodic military action in areas such as the Persian Gulf or Somalia, the peace dividend has increased demand for military cuts, pushing smaller defense contractors out of business and forcing large companies such as McDonnell Douglas, General Dynamics, and Martin Marietta to convert a significant portion of their operations into nonmilitary production.[7] Top industry scientists and engineers are switching to civilian developments such as high-definition television and new areas of transportation such as electric cars.[8]

TECHNOLOGICAL. The **technological dimension** includes scientific and technological advancements in a specific industry as well as in society at large. In recent years, the most striking advances have been in the computer industry. Supercomputers have astonishing power, and many companies are utilizing computerized systems such as automated offices, robotics, and computer-controlled machines. High-definition television promises to revolutionize the worldwide electronics industry. Revolutionary discoveries in biomimetics (the use of nature as models) and atomscompics (molecular architecture) are leading to high-performance materials that are lighter, stronger, and more resistant to temperature extremes. Smart composite materials, embedded with sensors that enable

technological dimension

The dimension of the general environment that includes scientific and technological advancements in the industry and society at large.

The *technological dimension* of the *general environment* plays a major role in Ford Motor Company's push for quality. A vast array of modern technologies in assembly, safety testing, quality assurance, manufacturing, environmental controls, and design keeps Ford on the technological cutting edge. Here, Ford's Emeline King uses an electronic pen to design a new car, which is then projected on a life-size, high-definition screen for evaluation and modification. New technology will keep quality high and Ford competitive in the 1990s.

them to think for themselves, promise new strides for the space program and the aircraft industry.[9] Aircraft surface materials can be embedded with fiber-optic sensors that can feel the weight of ice or the "touch" of enemy radar.[10] These and other technological advances can change the rules of the game; thus, every organization must be ready to respond.

SOCIOCULTURAL.   The **sociocultural dimension** of the general environment represents the demographic characteristics as well as the norms, customs, and values of the general population. Important sociocultural characteristics are geographical distribution and population density, age, and education levels. Today's demographic profiles are the foundation of tomorrow's work force and consumers. Forecasters see increased globalization of both consumer markets and the labor supply, with increasing diversity both within organizations and consumer markets.[11] For example, the 1990 U.S. census reports the following key demographic trends:

sociocultural dimension

The dimension of the general environment representing the demographic characteristics, norms, customs, and values of the population within which the organization operates.

1 African Americans are the largest ethnic group with a median age in the 18–35 range.

2 Aging baby-boomers (born between 1946 and 1964) make up 31 percent of the population.

3 In 1990, the 4.2 million births were the most since 1963, giving credence to the prediction of a "baby-boomlet" as career women race to beat their biological clocks.

4 The United States will continue to receive a flood of immigrants, largely from Asia (35.2 percent) and Mexico (23.7 percent).[12]

Demography also shapes society's norms and values. Recent sociocultural trends that are affecting many companies include the trend toward no smoking, the anti-cholesterol ferver, the greater purchasing power of young children, and the increased diversity of consumers, with specialized markets for groups such as Hispanics and women over 30.

economic dimension

The dimension of the general environment representing the overall economic health of the country or region in which the organization functions.

ECONOMIC.   The **economic dimension** represents the general economic health of the country or region in which the organization operates. Consumer purchasing power, unemployment rate, and interest rates are part of an organization's economic environment. Not-for-profit organizations such as the Red Cross and the Salvation Army find a greater demand for their services during economic decline but receive smaller contributions. They must adapt to these changes in economic conditions. One significant recent trend in the economic environment is the frequency of mergers and acquisitions. The corporate economic landscape is being altered. One of the hottest deals was the merger of Time, the nation's biggest publisher, with Warner Communications, an entertainment conglomerate. In the media industry alone, Sony purchased CBS Records to guarantee control over a supply of music for its Walkman customers. News Corporation acquired both Fox TV and Triangle, publisher of *TV Guide*. Bertelsmann acquired both Doubleday Publishers and RCA Records. The impact of these deals on employees can be overwhelming, creating uncertainty about future job security. The deal is just the beginning of employee uncertainty, because about half of the acquired companies are resold.[13]

LEGAL-POLITICAL.   The **legal-political dimension** includes government regulations at the local, state, and federal levels as well as political activities designed to influence company behavior. The U.S. political system encourages capitalism, and the government tries not to overregulate business. However, government laws do specify rules of the game. The federal government influences organizations through the Occupational Safety and Health Administration (OSHA), Environmental Protection Agency (EPA), fair trade practices, libel statutes allowing lawsuits against business, consumer protection legislation, product safety requirements, import and export restrictions, and information and labeling requirements. Although designed to solve problems, the influx of regulations often creates problems for organizations. For example, OSHA's 1992 mandatory regulations for exposure to blood-born diseases require a detailed list of all exposed workers, free vaccinations, creation of a detailed exposure-controlled plan, free employee exposure-reduction training, provision of protective garments, and maintenance records for OSHA review. Employers agree to the need for stronger safety measures, but many view the new regulations as "overkill" and a costly intrusion on companies.[14]

TASK ENVIRONMENT

As described above, the task environment includes those sectors that have a direct working relationship with the organization, among them customers, competitors, suppliers, and the labor market.

CUSTOMERS.   Those people and organizations in the environment who acquire goods or services from the organization are **customers.** As recipients of the organization's output, customers are important because they determine the organization's success. Patients are the customers of hospitals, students the customers of schools, and travelers the customers of airlines. Companies such as AT&T, General Foods, and Beecham Products have all designed special programs and advertising campaigns to court their older customers, who are, with the aging of baby boomers, becoming a larger percentage of their market.[15] Overbuilding in the hotel industry forced companies such as Hyatt and Marriott to spend additional money on advertising, direct mail, giveaways, and expansion into new markets to improve customer demand.

COMPETITORS.   Other organizations in the same industry or type of business that provide goods or services to the same set of customers are referred to as **competitors.** Each industry is characterized by specific competitive issues. The recording industry differs from the steel industry and the pharmaceutical industry. Competition in the steel industry, especially from international producers, caused some companies to go bankrupt. Companies in the pharmaceutical industry are highly profitable because it is difficult for new firms to enter it. Within some industries, competitors must unite to achieve common objectives. By the 1990s, Apple, IBM, and Compaq were locked in a titanic power struggle

legal-political dimension

The dimension of the general environment that includes federal, state, and local government regulations and political activities designed to control company behavior.

The Intermodal Surface Transportation Act of 1991 is an example of changes in the *legal-political environment*. This landmark legislation will provide billions of dollars for improvement of the nation's *infrastructure*. It provides opportunities for firms such as Morrison Knudsen Corporation, which designs, constructs, and manages construction of complex projects such as Baltimore's new light-rail commuter system shown here. MK stands poised to benefit from its reputation for excellence and its ability to design, construct, operate, and finance complex infrastructure projects.

customers

People and organizations in the environment who acquire goods or services from the organization.

competitors

Other organizations in the same industry or type of business that provide goods or services to the same set of customers.

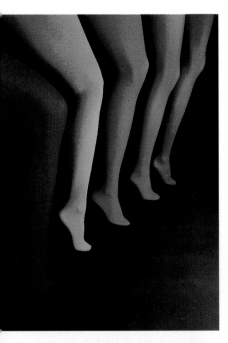

Crompton & Knowles Corporation's dye business has a "leg up" on the competition as *supplier* to a number of industries, including the hosiery and apparel markets. C&K is a leader in producing and marketing dyes in North America, and has expanded its global markets in the Far East and Europe. As part of the supplier environment for customers, C&K's success has reached record levels during a time marked by general industry decline.

suppliers

People and organizations who provide the raw materials the organization uses to produce its output.

labor market

The people available for hire by the organization.

to dominate the personal computer hardware industry as well as to break Microsoft Corporation's domination of the software industry. In a flanking action against Microsoft, Apple and IBM entered a joint venture called Taligent, Inc., for the development of new operating systems software.[16]

SUPPLIERS.   The raw materials the organization uses to produce its output are provided by **suppliers.** A steel mill requires iron ore, machines, and financial resources. A small, private university may utilize hundreds of suppliers for paper, pencils, cafeteria food, computers, trucks, fuel, electricity, and textbooks. Large companies such as General Motors, Westinghouse, and Exxon depend on as many as 5,000 suppliers. The Big Three automakers now acquire a larger share of parts from fewer suppliers. They are trying to build a good relationship with these suppliers so that they will receive high-quality parts as well as low prices. With just a few suppliers, a company becomes vulnerable to supplier problems. For example, a UAW walkout at a fabrication plant in Lordstown, Ohio, idled GM's Saturn plant in Tennessee. Organizations also depend on banks for capital with which to finance new equipment and buildings.

LABOR MARKET.   The **labor market** represents people in the environment who can be hired to work for the organization. Every organization needs a supply of trained, qualified personnel. Unions, employee associations, and the availability of certain classes of employees can influence the organization's labor market. Two labor market factors having an impact on organizations right now are (1) the necessity for continuous investment through education and training in human resources to meet the competitive demands of the borderless world and (2) the effects of international trading blocs, automation, and shifting plant location upon labor dislocations, creating unused labor pools in some areas and labor shortages in others.[17] These factors have an impact on unions too, as discussed in the Focus on Not-for-Profits box.

Northern Telecom, a Canadian company with U.S. headquarters in Nashville, Tennessee, is an example of a complex environment.

 NORTHERN TELECOM LTD.

The external environment for Northern Telecom Ltd. is illustrated in Exhibit 4.2 on page 118. Once considered only an appendage of powerful AT&T, the Canadian company now challenges the U.S. giant by securing top global accounts such as supplying digital switching equipment for the White House. Most problems from the external environment come from competitors and changes in technology. European rivals such as Siemens and Alcatel attempt to block entry of Northern to European Community public phone contracts, arguing that European companies have no supply access to the lucrative North American markets. At the same time, Northern is attempting to crack the Japanese market dominated by Fujitsu, Oki, NEC, and Hitachi. Northern's efforts to resolve these competitive problems include establishing a $1 billion R&D budget. The company is playing catch-up in both cellular and wireless markets and is pioneering fiber-optic technology for transmission equipment. Globally, Northern may slip past EC problems by purchasing Britain's STC PLC, forming an alliance with France's Matra, and launching joint ventures in Spain and Poland.

Northern Telecom's 57,000 employees also have a strong internal environment, developing the "no-excuses" culture necessary to compete in the tough telecommunications industry. Northern's "Vision 2,000 Leadership" campaign uses rallies, banners, and slogans to reinforce its goal of "one team, one vision." Under a strong team concept, the company's switch factory in North Carolina has been heralded as one of the top manufacturing operations in the world, with workers setting their own pace and charting their own production. Northern Telecom is Canada's most successful multinational and under CEO Paul Stern is clearly headed toward a major role on the world stage.[18] ■

focus on NOT-FOR-PROFIT   UNIONS ON THE ROPES?

Where are unions heading? Some believe today's industrial unions are going the route of the dinosaur, citing a 15-year drop in union membership from 22.6 percent of the work force to 16.1 percent. Others believe that unions, like corporations, are undergoing dramatic change and will emerge in a strong leadership position.

Unions must deal with a rapidly changing environment. Employees in a growing number of companies, such as California Steel Industries, Inc., and Nissan, have rejected union membership. Because of the recession, thousands of unemployed workers crossed picket lines to replace strikers. Powerful unions more often cave in to company demands and threats of plant closures and foreign wage

competition. Workers think twice about the security of their jobs when companies use global competition as an excuse to lower wages.

Labor leaders fear that company tactics hurt both their ability to organize and their bargaining clout. Taking advantage of a more diverse work force that includes more women and minorities, some companies support the emergence of worker associations such as 9 to 5, the Association of Working Women, or Xerox Corporation's Black Caucus. Many companies also implemented a "team" concept that has managers and workers meeting together to resolve grievances.

Established unions are fighting back. The team concept used by companies such as Motorola and over 60 percent of the Fortune 500 has come under fire as a violation of the 1935 amendment to the National Labor Relations Act, which outlawed company-dominated

"sham unions." Other tactics, such as banding together several unions in a coalition and organizing "associate members" among Hispanics, are being tested in areas such as West Virginia and California.

On the eve of the twenty-first century, unions may find ways to thrive on employee diversity. And, like business and industry, unions must adjust to rapid environmental changes to survive. ■

SOURCE: Dani Milbank, "On the Ropes: Union's Woes Suggest How the Labor Force in U.S. Is Shifting," *The Wall Street Journal*, May 5, 1992, A1, A14; Ron Suskind, "Tough Vote: Threat of Cheap Labor Abroad Complicates Decisions to Unionize," *The Wall Street Journal*, July 28, 1992, A1, A8; and Larry Reynolds, "An Old NLRB Rule Threatens Quality Circles," *Management Review*, January 1992, 53–55.

EXHIBIT   4.2

The External Environment of Northern Telecom (NT)

Economic
- Sales over $102 billion
- 11 straight quarters of record earnings
- Sales to exceed $200 billion by 2000 with 1/2 outside North America
- Focus is low-cost manufacturing
- Recession in North America

Legal/Political
- Canadian ownership
- Breakup of AT&T in 1984
- Tough EC regulations
- Canada & U.S. trade agreement
- New tax laws
- Protectionist legislation abroad

Competitors
- AT&T, U.S.
- Siemens, Germany
- Alcatel, France
- Ericson, Sweden
- NEC, Japan
- Focus on low-cost manufacturing

Customers
- Want low price and high quality
- Businesses, not-for-profit organizations
- New cellular and wireless markets

Technological
- Pioneer digital switch
- $1.2 billion R&D budget
- Catching up in cellular and wireless developments
- Seeking new telecommunications applications
- Developing fiber optics for transmission equipment

NT

Suppliers
- Components from subcontractors
- Banks, bondholders provide capital
- Obtain quality parts from suppliers worldwide

Labor Market
- U.S.: Texas, North Carolina, Tennessee, and California
- Treat employees well
- Not unionized
- Hire college graduates

Sociocultural
- New telecommunications applications
- Opening of new markets worldwide
- Cellular phone life-styles

International
- Headquarters in Toronto & McLean, Virginia
- Bought Britain's STC PLC
- Won business in China, Turkey, Australia, and Russia
- Largest supplier of telecommunications gear to Japanese market

- Joint ventures in Spain and Poland
- Alliance with Alcatel of France for digital mobile phone equipment
- Hire nationals in host countries

SOURCE: W. C. Symonds, J. B. Levine, N. Gross, and P. Coy, "High-Tech Star: Northern Telecom Is Challenging Even AT&T," *Business Week,* July 27, 1992, 54–58.

● THE ORGANIZATION-ENVIRONMENT RELATIONSHIP

Why do organizations care so much about factors in the external environment? The reason is that the environment creates uncertainty for organization managers, and they must respond by designing the organization to adapt to the environment or to influence the environment.

ENVIRONMENTAL UNCERTAINTY

Organizations must manage environmental uncertainty to be effective. *Uncertainty* means that managers do not have sufficient information about environmental factors to understand and predict environmental needs and changes.[19] As indicated in Exhibit 4.3, environmental characteristics that influence uncertainty are the number of factors that affect the organization and the extent to which those factors change. A large multinational like Northern Telecom has thousands of factors in the external environment creating uncertainty for managers. When external factors change rapidly, the organization experiences very high uncertainty; examples are the electronics and aerospace industries. Firms must make efforts to adapt to these changes. When an organization deals with only a few external factors and these factors are relatively stable, such as for soft-drink bottlers or food processors, managers experience low uncertainty and can devote less attention to external issues.

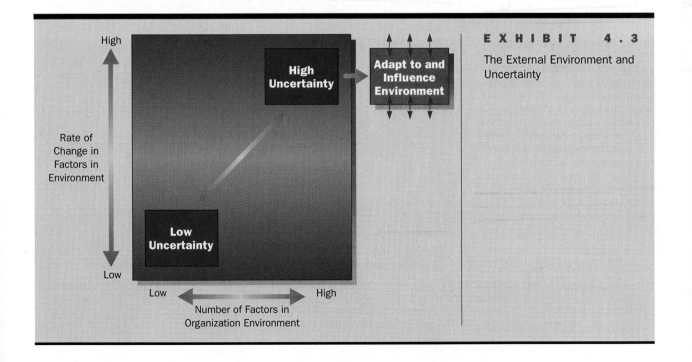

EXHIBIT 4.3

The External Environment and Uncertainty

Two basic strategies for coping with high environmental uncertainty are to adapt the organization to changes in the environment and to influence the environment to make it more compatible with organizational needs.

ADAPTING TO THE ENVIRONMENT

If the organization faces increased uncertainty with respect to competition, customers, suppliers, or government regulation, managers can use several strategies to adapt to these changes, including boundary-spanning roles, increased planning and forecasting, a flexible structure, and mergers or joint ventures.

BOUNDARY-SPANNING ROLES.   Departments and **boundary-spanning roles** link and coordinate the organization with key elements in the external environment. Boundary spanners serve two purposes for the organization: They detect and process information about changes in the environment, and they represent the organization's interest to the environment.[20] People in departments such as marketing and purchasing span the boundary to work with customers and suppliers, both face to face and through market research. Perhaps the largest growth area in boundary spanning is competitive intelligence, also known as snooping and spying. McDonnell Douglas used competitive intelligence to get the jump on Boeing with its new prop-fan airliner. Coors used competitive intelligence to avoid getting behind in wine coolers. Mary Kay executives cried "foul" after discovering rival Avon had hired Dallas private detectives to dig through its trash.[21] Xerox buys rival copiers for its engineers, who take them apart and design a better product component by component. Eighty percent of the Fortune 1000 companies maintain in-

■
boundary-spanning roles

Roles assumed by people and/or departments that link and coordinate the organization with key elements in the external environment.

Stanley Hardware Vice-President of Marketing Scott Bannell (seated center) carefully notes responses from a consumer focus group about the Stanley Closet Organizer. Bannell and market researcher Larry Dostal (standing) act as *boundary spanners* to test reactions to a new product and assess whether it meets customer needs. Boundary spanning to potential customers provided competitive intelligence that the closet organizer was clearly preferred over other products for its design and sturdy construction.

house snoops, also known as *competitor intelligence professionals.* Most of their work is strictly legal, relying on commercial data bases, news clippings, help-wanted advertisements, trade publications, product literature, and personal contacts.[22]

FORECASTING AND PLANNING. Forecasting and planning for environmental changes are major activities in many corporations. Planning departments often are created when uncertainty is high.[23] Forecasting is an effort to spot trends that enable managers to predict future events. Forecasting techniques range from quantitative economic models of environmental business activity to newspaper clipping services. One of these services, called Burrelle's Information Services, Inc., monitors 16,000 newspapers and magazines and predicts future trends. Chase investors used information about rapidly multiplying television channels in Western Europe to invest in MCA, Inc., which had a valuable film library.

Control Data, Heinz, United Airlines, and Waste Management Inc. have devised specific management plans for handling crises. Whether the crisis is a hostile takeover attempt or product tampering, an organization that does not have a plan will make mistakes. Planning can soften the adverse effect of rapid shifts in the environment.

FLEXIBLE STRUCTURE. An organization's structure should enable it to effectively respond to external shifts. Research has found that a loose, flexible structure works best in an uncertain environment and a tight structure is most effective in a certain environment.[24] The term **organic structure** characterizes an organization that is free flowing, has few rules and regulations, encourages teamwork among employees, and decentralizes decision making to employees doing the job. This type of structure works best when the environment changes rapidly. Dow Chemical and Star-Kist Foods set up "SWAT" teams that can swing into action if an unexpected disaster strikes. These teams include members from multiple departments who can provide the expertise needed for solving an immediate problem, such as a plant explosion. Organic organizations create many teams to handle changes in raw materials, new products, government regulations, or marketing. A **mechanistic structure** is just the opposite, characterized by rigidly defined tasks, many rules and regulations, little teamwork, and centralization of decision making. This is fine for a stable environment.

organic structure

An organizational structure that is free flowing, has few rules and regulations, encourages employee teamwork, and decentralizes decision making to employees doing the job.

mechanistic structure

An organizational structure characterized by rigidly defined tasks, many rules and regulations, little teamwork, and centralized decision making.

MERGERS AND JOINT VENTURES. As we discussed, mergers are a major factor in a company's external environment. A merger is also a way to reduce uncertainty. A **merger** occurs when two or more organizations combine to become one. For example, General Host acquired Hickory Farms, a retail chain, to become an outlet for General Host's meat products, thereby reducing uncertainty in the customer sector.

A **joint venture** involves a strategic alliance or program by two or more organizations. This typically occurs when the project is too complex, expensive, or uncertain for one firm to do alone. Oil companies have used joint ventures to explore for oil on the continental shelf or in

merger

The combination of two or more organizations into one.

joint venture

A strategic alliance or program by two or more organizations.

inaccessible regions of Alaska and Canada. Many small businesses are turning to joint ventures with large firms or with international partners.[25] A larger partner can provide sales staff, distribution channels, financial resources, or a research staff. Small businesses seldom have the expertise to deal internationally, so a company such as Nypro, Inc., a plastic injection-molding manufacturer in Clinton, Massachusetts, joins with overseas experts who are familiar with the local rules. Nypro now does business in four countries.

INFLUENCING THE ENVIRONMENT

The other major strategy for handling environmental uncertainty is to reach out and change those elements causing problems. Widely used techniques for changing the environment include advertising and public relations, political activity, and trade associations. Exhibit 4.4. summarizes the techniques organizations can use to adapt to and influence the external environment.

ADVERTISING AND PUBLIC RELATIONS.   Advertising has become a highly successful way to manage demand for a company's products. Companies spend large amounts of money to influence consumer tastes. Hospitals have begun to advertise through billboards, newspapers, and radio commercials to promote special services. Increased competitiveness among CPA firms and law firms has caused them to start advertising for clients, a practice unheard of a few years ago. Advertising is an important way to reduce uncertainty about clients.

Public relations is similar to advertising except that its goal is to influence public opinion about the company itself. Most companies care a great deal about their public image. Each year *Fortune* rates over 300 companies to see which are the most and least admired in each of 32 industries. Public relations and a good public image are accomplished through advertising as well as speeches and press reports. In the 1960s and 1970s, Dow Chemical became infamous for supplying napalm and Agent Orange to the military for use in Vietnam. Even when it stopped

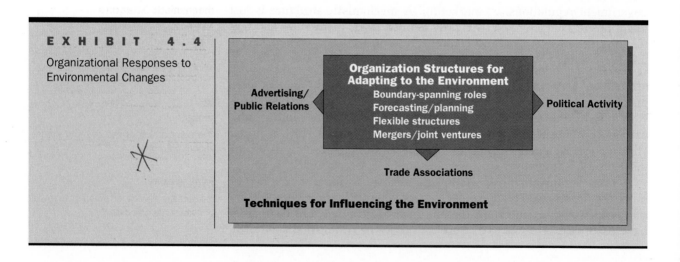

EXHIBIT   4.4

Organizational Responses to Environmental Changes

Advertising/Public Relations

Organization Structures for Adapting to the Environment
Boundary-spanning roles
Forecasting/planning
Flexible structures
Mergers/joint ventures

Political Activity

Trade Associations

Techniques for Influencing the Environment

making these products, the image persisted. Dow Chemical attempts to change this view with an upbeat advertising campaign—"Dow Lets You Do Great Things"—and other external communications emphasizing Dow Chemical research and the humanitarian use of its products. Dow Chemical also has a strong in-house ethics program, a model for the industry.[26]

POLITICAL ACTIVITY. **Political activity** represents organizational attempts to influence government legislation and regulation. Corporations pay lobbyists to express their views to federal and state legislators. Foreign companies are becoming increasingly savvy in U.S. political maneuvering. For example, Japanese companies have placed former key U.S. political insiders on their payrolls as Washington lobbyists and advisers. Canada's Northern Telecom benefited from its relationship with a Spanish minister in landing a Spanish joint venture. Under pressure from U.S. companies about government-business collaboration in foreign countries, Washington has warmed to a technology policy that provides government policy support to critical technologies and industry study groups.[27]

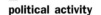

political activity

Organizational attempts, such as lobbying, to influence government legislation and regulation.

TRADE ASSOCIATIONS. Most organizations join with others having similar interests; the result is a **trade association**. In this way, organizations work together to influence the environment, including federal legislation and regulation. Most manufacturing companies are part of the National Association of Manufacturers. The National Rifle Association has thousands of individual and corporate members whose interests are served by the freedom to use guns. One of the most influential trade associations in past years was the U.S. League of Savings Institutions, which virtually controlled government regulations pertaining to the savings and loan industry. Federal Home Loan Bank Board officials admit they took many actions and changed regulations to suit the League. That kind of influence over the years may have contributed to problems during the early 1990s within the savings and loan industry, which were partially caused by lack of close and effective regulation.[28]

trade association

An association made up of organizations with similar interests for the purpose of influencing the environment.

During the 1992 election year, employees of McDonnell Douglas tried to influence the environment through *political activity*. At this mass rally at MCAIR in St. Louis, 35,000 people, including contractors, workers, suppliers, and unions, united in an effort to convince Washington to build and sell F-15s to Saudi Arabia. A 20-foot banner proclaiming "U.S. JOBS NOW" reinforced the call to save the 40,000 jobs that would be lost to foreign competition if the United States nixed the Saudi deal.

THE INTERNAL ENVIRONMENT: CORPORATE CULTURE

The internal environment within which managers work includes corporate culture, production technology, organization structure, and physical facilities. Of these, corporate culture has surfaced as extremely important to competitive advantage. The internal culture must fit the needs of the external environment and company strategy. When this fit occurs, highly committed employees create a high-performance organization that is tough to beat.[29]

<u>Culture</u> can be defined as the set of key values, beliefs, understandings, and norms shared by members of an organization.[30] Culture represents the unwritten, informal norms that bind organization members together. Culture can be analyzed at two organizational levels, as illustrated in Exhibit 4.5.[31] At the surface level are visible artifacts, which include manners of dress, stories, physical symbols, organizational ceremonies, and office layout. The surface level represents the cultural patterns observable within an organization. At a deeper level are the values and norms that govern behavior. Values cannot be observed directly, but they can be interpreted from the stories, language, and symbols that represent them. These values are held by organization members who jointly understand their importance. The giant retailer Wal-Mart is an example of how the elements of culture give competitive advantage.

culture

The set of key values, beliefs, understandings, and norms that members of an organization share.

◈ WAL-MART

One organization with a strong culture is Wal-Mart, where folksy values continue to reflect its small-town beginnings and the personality and principles of its late founder, Sam Walton. Walton and other senior managers

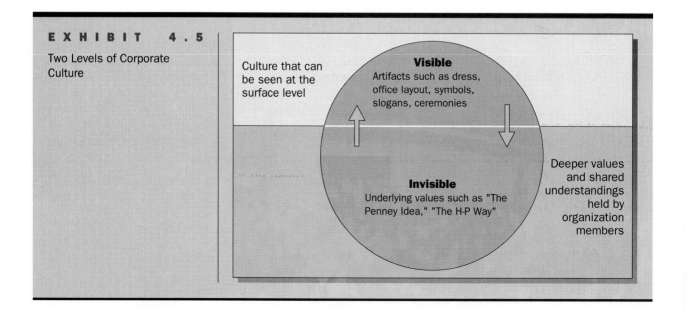

EXHIBIT 4.5

Two Levels of Corporate Culture

Culture that can be seen at the surface level

Visible
Artifacts such as dress, office layout, symbols, slogans, ceremonies

Invisible
Underlying values such as "The Penney Idea," "The H-P Way"

Deeper values and shared understandings held by organization members used fun-loving motivational tactics that included hog calls, songs, hulas, and the Wal-Mart cheer, "W-A-L-M-A-R-T." These antics, merged with Walton's "break-the-rules" philosophy, formed the cultural core of this unbelievable company. The culture stresses the personal touch, and associates are urged to provide community involvement and individual attention. Department buyers are urged to "get their noses in it" by working with customers on the sales floor once a week. CEO David Glass continues the policy of daily experimentation and change. Individual empowerment, continuous improvement, and profit sharing contribute to that small-town culture of "belonging" that is so easily picked up by Wal-Mart's loyal customers.[32] ■

Some companies put underlying values in writing so they can be passed on to new generations of employees. James Cash Penney believed in the golden rule: Treat employees and customers as you would like to be treated. He wrote down the underlying values in seven guiding principles called "The Penney Idea" that guide employee behavior. One J. C. Penney store manager was reprimanded for making too much profit at customers' expense.[33] Hewlett-Packard created a list of cultural concepts called "The H-P Way." At 3M Company, two fundamental values are the 25 percent rule, which requires that a quarter of sales come from products introduced within the past five years, and the 15 percent rule, which allows any employee to spend up to 15 percent of the workweek on anything he or she prefers, so long as it is product related.[34]

The fundamental underlying values that characterize cultures at J. C. Penney, Wal-Mart, and Hewlett-Packard can be understood through the visible manifestations of symbols, stories, heroes, slogans, and ceremonies. Any company's culture can be interpreted by observing these factors.

SYMBOLS

A **symbol** is an object, act, or event that conveys meaning to others. Symbols associated with corporate culture convey the organization's important values. For example, John Thomas, CEO of a mechanical contractor in Andover, Massachusetts, wanted to imprint the value of allowing mistakes and risk taking. He pulled a $450 mistake out of the dumpster, mounted it on a plaque, and named it the "No-Nuts Award," for the missing parts. The award is presented annually and symbolizes the freedom to make mistakes but not to make the same mistake twice.[35] Symbolizing his commitment to a true open-door policy, Bill Arnold, president of Nashville's Centennial Medical Center, ripped his office door from its hinges and suspended it from the lobby ceiling for all employees to see.[36] Sequint Computer Systems, Inc., developed the symbol of red buttons worn by people who performed tasks critical to the production of hardware that was behind schedule yet essential to company survival. The red buttons symbolized the gravity of the situation, and all Sequint employees were expected to pitch in and help anybody wearing one.[37]

■
symbol

An object, act, or event that conveys meaning to others.

Standing in the snow, these First Security Corporation employees serve as living *symbols* of company values and employee commitment to giving 110 percent. This Salt Lake City, Utah-based financial services company is focused on superior customer service and has invested thousands of hours in the training of employees. The result: giving 110 percent is a way of life, and surveys of 60,000 customers rated First Security performance an astonishing 6.2 overall (on a 7-point scale) in 30 categories. Whether going the extra mile, or standing in the snow, First Security employees pride themselves on a culture in which more is expected.

story

A narrative based on true events that is repeated frequently and shared by organizational employees.

STORIES

A **story** is a narrative based on true events that is repeated frequently and shared among organizational employees. Stories are told to new employees to keep the organization's primary values alive. At Nordstrom, Inc., management does not deny the story about a customer who got his money back on a tire. Nordstrom does not sell tires. The story reinforces the store's no-questions-asked return policy. A story at Dayton Hudson about Ken Macke, CEO, tells how he gave a woman a new washing machine because she complained about wanting a broken belt replaced. The story still serves to improve complaint handling at the lowest company levels. A popular story at Hewlett-Packard communicates the values of the founders, David Packard and Bill Hewlett. Bill Hewlett is said to have gone to a plant one Saturday and found a lab stockroom door locked. He cut the padlock and left a note saying, "Don't ever lock this door again. Thanks, Bill." Hewlett wanted engineers to have free access to components—even take them home—to stimulate the creativity that was part of "The H-P Way." Stories in these companies are widely told; every employee knows them and the values they represent.[38]

hero

A figure who exemplifies the deeds, character, and attributes of a corporate culture.

HEROES

A **hero** is a figure who exemplifies the deeds, character, and attributes of a strong culture. Heroes are role models for employees to follow. Sometimes heroes are real, such as Lee Iacocca, and sometimes they are symbolic, such as the mythical sales representative at Robinson Jewelers who delivered a wedding ring directly to the church because the ring had been ordered late. The deeds of heroes are out of the ordinary but not so far out as to be unattainable by other employees. Heroes show how to do the right thing in the organization. Companies with strong cultures take advantage of achievements to define heroes who uphold key values.

At Minnesota Mining and Manufacturing (3M), top managers keep alive the heroes who developed projects that were killed by top management. One hero was a vice-president who was fired earlier in his career for persisting with a new product even after his boss had told him, "That's a stupid idea. Stop!" After the worker was fired, he would not leave. He stayed in an unused office, working without a salary on the new product idea. Eventually he was rehired, the idea succeeded, and he was promoted to vice-president. The lesson of this hero as a major element in 3M's culture is persist at what you believe in.[39]

SLOGANS

A **slogan** is a phrase or sentence that succinctly expresses a key corporate value. Many companies use a slogan or saying to convey special meaning to employees. H. Ross Perot of Electronic Data Systems established the philosophy of hiring the best people he could find and noted how difficult it was to find them. His motto was "Eagles don't flock. You gather them one at a time." A variation used at PepsiCo to describe the value of turning bright young people into strong managers is "We take eagles and teach them to fly in formation." The slogan chiseled into a 6,000-pound granite slab next to the front door of Stew Leonard's dairy store is "Rule 1—The customer is always right! Rule 2—If the customer is ever wrong, reread Rule 1."[40]

CEREMONIES

A **ceremony** is a planned activity that makes up a special event and is conducted for the benefit of an audience. Managers hold ceremonies to provide dramatic examples of company values. Ceremonies are special occasions that reinforce valued accomplishments, create a bond among people by allowing them to share an important event, and anoint and celebrate heroes.[41]

The value of a ceremony can be illustrated by the presentation of a major award. For example, Quaker State Minit-Lube, Inc., uses an annual contest and winner's ceremony to signal the importance of speed and quality service for customers. Fourteen jobs associated with an oil change must be performed perfectly in 8 minutes. The award ceremony includes contestants arriving in a white stretch limo, walking on a red carpet through a cheering crowd, and being entertained by a jazz band. This ceremony is consistent with Quaker State's Big Q symbol that stands for quality. An award can also be bestowed secretly by mailing it to the employee's home or, if a check, by depositing it in a bank. But such procedures would not make the bestowal of rewards a significant organizational event and would be less meaningful to the employee.

slogan
A phrase or sentence that succinctly expresses a key corporate value.

ceremony
A planned activity that makes up a special event and is conducted for the benefit of an audience.

The "New Company Employee Ceremony" has special importance in Japan. Minoru Murofushi, president of Japan's ITOCHU Corporation, is aware of the significance of ceremony in selecting April 1st (a traditional time of beginnings in Japanese industry and academia) to welcome new employees to the 134-year-old company. The timing and the company-wide broadcasting of the event reinforce corporate culture, and the significance of beginning a career with ITOCHU. President Murofushi recognizes the significance of the day for new company employees as a "milestone in their lives." The ceremony incorporates both the vigor of youth and the heritage of predecessors in meeting the challenges of the age.

In summary, organizational culture represents the values and understandings that employees share, and these values are signified by symbols, stories, heroes, slogans, and ceremonies. Managers help define important symbols, stories, and heroes to shape the culture.

● ENVIRONMENT AND CULTURE

A big influence on internal corporate culture is the external environment. Corporate culture should embody what it takes to succeed in the environment. If the external environment requires extraordinary customer service, the culture should encourage good service; if it calls for careful technical decision making, cultural values should reinforce managerial decision making.

ADAPTIVE CULTURES

Research at Harvard on 207 U.S. firms illustrated the critical relationship between corporate culture and the external environment. The study found that a strong corporate culture alone did not ensure business success unless the culture encouraged healthy adaptation to the external environment. As illustrated in Exhibit 4.6, adaptive corporate cultures have different values and behavior from unadaptive corporate cultures. In adaptive cultures, managers were concerned about customers and those internal people and processes that brought about useful change. In the unadaptive corporate cultures, managers were concerned about themselves, and their values tended to discourage risk taking and change. Thus a strong culture alone is not enough, because an unhealthy culture may encourage the organization to march resolutely in the wrong direction. Healthy cultures help companies adapt to the environment.[42]

	Adaptive Corporate Cultures	Unadaptive Corporate Cultures	
Core Values	Managers care deeply about customers, stockholders, and employees. They also strongly value people and processes that can create useful change (e.g., leadership initiatives up and down the management hierarchy).	Managers care mainly about themselves, their immediate work group, or some product (or technology) associated with that work group. They value the orderly and risk-reducing management process much more highly than leadership initiatives.	**EXHIBIT 4.6** Environmentally Adaptive versus Unadaptive Corporate Cultures
Common Behavior	Managers pay close attention to all their constituencies, especially customers, and initiate change when needed to serve their legitimate interests, even if it that entails taking some risks.	Managers tend to behave somewhat insularly, politically, and bureaucratically. As a result, they do not change their strategies quickly to adjust to or take advantage of changes in their business environments.	SOURCE: John P. Kotter and James L. Heskett, *Corporate Culture and Performance* (New York: The Free Press, 1992) 51.

TYPES OF CULTURES

One way to think about corporate cultures was suggested by Jeffrey Sonnenfeld and included four types of culture—baseball team, club, academy, and fortress. Each culture has somewhat different potential for supporting a healthy, successful company and has a different impact on the satisfaction and careers of employees.[43]

The *baseball team culture* emerges in an environmental situation with high-risk decision making and fast feedback from the environment. Decision makers quickly learn whether their choice was right or wrong. Talent, innovation, and performance are valued and rewarded. Top performers see themselves as "free agents," and companies scramble for their services. Performers with "low batting averages" are quickly dropped from the line-up. Baseball team cultures are found in fast-paced, high-risk companies involved in areas such as movie production, advertising, and software development where futures are bet on a new product or project.

The *club culture* is characterized by loyalty, commitment, and fitting into the group. This stable, secure environment values age and experience and rewards seniority. As in the case of career military personnel, individuals start young and stay. Club cultures promote from within, and members are expected to progress slowly, proving competence at each level. Individuals tend to be generalists and may have vast experience in a number of organizational functions. Top executives in commercial banks, for example, frequently began as tellers. While many club qualities contribute to flexibility within the organization, they can also contribute to the perception of a closed company, reluctant to change.

The *academy culture* also hires young recruits interested in a long-term association and a slow, steady climb up the organization. Unlike the club culture, however, employees rarely cross from one division to another. Each person enters a specific "track" and gains a high level of expertise in that area. Job and technical mastery are the bases for reward and advancement. Many long-established organizations such as universities, Coca-Cola, Ford, and GM maintain strong academy cultures. While specialization provides job security, this culture may limit broad individual development and interdepartmental collaboration, although it works very well in a stable environment.

The *fortress culture* may emerge in an environmental survival situation. Textile firms and savings and loan organizations are examples of former dominant industries that are now retrenching for survival. The fortress culture offers little job security or opportunity for professional growth while companies restructure and downsize to fit the new environment. This culture is perilous for employees but also offers tremendous turnaround opportunities for individual managers with confidence and love of challenge. Those who succeed, such as Lee Iaccoca (Chrysler) or William Crouse (president of Ortho Diagnostic Systems, Inc.) earn recognition nationally or within their industry.[44] The Manager's Shoptalk box shows how companies create strong corporate cultures.

(handwritten margin note: SURVIVAL / LITTLE SECURITY / No professional growth)

MANAGER'S shop talk

KEEPING CULTURE STRONG

A strong corporate culture enables people to feel good about what they do. They are committed to a higher purpose and are likely to work harder. Being able to say "I'm with Morgan Guaranty Trust" rather than "I work at a bank" is important. An often overlooked way to strengthen corporate culture is through the selection and socialization of new employees. Recruits need to understand what makes their company's culture tick. Great American companies that pass a strong culture from one generation to the next include Delta Air Lines, Procter & Gamble, and Morgan Guaranty Trust.

Seven steps for cultural socialization are as follows:

1. Subject employment candidates to a selection process so rigorous that it seems designed to discourage rather than encourage individuals to take the job. Recruits should not be oversold. They should be grilled and told the bad as well as the good side of the job. Andersen Consulting subjects thousands of raw recruits to a rugged three-week indoctrination at its 150-acre training center in St. Charles, Illinois. Andersen offers only two career tracks—up or out. Recruits are told in advance that only 5 percent will make partner but that even then the rigorous travel and work schedules continue.

2. Subject newly hired individuals to experiences calculated to *induce humility and to make them question prior behavior, beliefs, and values.* New recruits get little glory and work long hours at mundane tasks. Associates at Morgan Stanley New York investment house work 12- to 14-hour days and most weekends, and lunches are 30 minutes long in a very unplush cafeteria.

3. Send newly humbled recruits into the trenches, pushing them to master one of the core disciplines of the company's business. It takes 6 years to become an IBM marketing representative, 12 years to become a controller. There is no quick way to jump ranks and reach the top. Progress is slow and based on performance.

4. At every stage of new managers' careers, measure the operating

● CHANGING AND MERGING CORPORATE CULTURES

A corporation's culture may not always be in alignment with its needs and environment. Cultural values may reflect what worked in the past. The difference between desired cultural norms and values and actual norms and values is called the **culture gap**.[45]

Culture gaps can be immense, especially in mergers and acquisitions.[46] Despite the popularity of mergers and acquisitions as a corporate strategy, many fail. Almost one-half of acquired companies are sold within five years, and some experts claim that 90 percent of mergers never live up to expectations.[47] One reason for failure is that although managers are able to integrate the acquired firm's financial systems and production technologies, they typically are unable to integrate the unwritten norms and values that have an even greater impact on a company's success.[48] These problems increase in scope and frequency with global companies and cross-cultural mergers and acquisitions. A merger or acquisition exacts an enormous toll in employee anxiety, fear, and tension. After all, most mergers produce some redefinition of pay, benefits,

culture gap

The difference between an organization's desired cultural norms and values and actual norms and values.

(handwritten marginal note: Mergers & acquisitions don't do well because of diverse culture)

---

results they have achieved and reward them accordingly. Procter & Gamble Co. instituted a 3- to 4-day "combat" training program for new recruits, designed to "imprint people as they enter the system." Additional courses and feedback results are provided to them at each stage of their career. At IBM, managers track adherence to the core value of respecting the decency of the individual. Climate surveys and open-door procedures let IBM management know whether new employees are on the right track.

5. Repeatedly promote adherence to the company's transcendent values—those overarching purposes that rise above the day-to-day imperative to make a buck. The important thing at Delta is the "Delta family feeling." New employees hear about the sacrifices required. Managers take a pay cut during lean times, and senior flight attendants and pilots voluntarily work fewer hours to avoid laying off junior people. Before AT&T's

divestiture, new employees learned about the transcendent value of guaranteeing phone service through any emergency.

6. Constantly harp on watershed events in the organization's history that reaffirm the importance of your firm's culture. Folklore and stories reinforce key values and the code of conduct for "how we do things around here." Stories have morals that teach employees about key values. The Wal-Mart phrase "get their noses in it" arose when Sam Walton informed two buyers they should work on the sales floor each week to learn what was going on. The phrase reinforced the Wal-Mart value of putting the customer first and that there are no big-shots in the Wal-Mart family.

7. Supply role models. Exemplary individuals—the heroes—convey the traits the culture values most. Role models can be current employees, recognized as winners, whom the new employees can imitate. McDonald's has an

obsessive concern for quality control, IBM for customer service, and Bell Atlantic for innovation. Bell's "Champion" program provides employees who have new ideas with full pay, training, and funding for the idea being championed. In the program's first two years, 2 patents were granted and 11 more were pending, with the champions serving as role models for the strong innovation values. Role models are the most powerful culture training program available. ■

SOURCE: Richard Pascale, "The Paradox of 'Corporate Culture': Reconciling Ourselves to Socialization," *California Management Review* 27 (Winter 1985), 26–41; Glenn Rifkin, "Andersen Consultant's Culture of Clones," *The New York Times*, September 6, 1992, Section 3, 1, 6; Zachary Schiller, "Ready, Aim, Market: Combat Training at P&G College," *Business Week*, February 3, 1992, 56; and Brian Dumaine, "Closing the Innovation Gap," *Fortune*, December 2, 1991, 56, 62.

tasks, and other forms of employee security. Approximately one-third of mergers and acquisitions result in layoffs.[49] These factors create a breakdown in communication, reduced commitment, attempts at self-preservation, and resistance to change. Corporate culture becomes a negative force in which norms and values impede success.

What can managers do to change norms and values toward what is needed for the external environment or for smooth cultural integration during a merger? The answer is symbolic management.

SYMBOLIC MANAGEMENT

To change corporate culture, managers can use cultural artifacts of symbols, stories, slogans, and ceremonies. Managers literally must overcommunicate to ensure that employees understand the new cultural values, and they must signal these values in actions as well as words. A **symbolic manager** defines and uses signals and symbols to influence corporate culture. Symbolic managers influence culture in the following manner:

symbolic manager

A manager who defines and uses signals and symbols to influence corporate culture.

1 *The symbolic manager articulates a vision for the organizational change that generates excitement and that employees can believe in.* This means the manager defines and communicates central values that employees believe in and will rally around.

2 *The symbolic manager heeds the day-to-day activities that reinforce the vision.* The symbolic manager makes sure that symbols, ceremonies, and slogans match the new values. Even more important, actions speak louder than words. Symbolic managers "walk their talk."[50]

Magma Copper Company uses *symbolic management* to demonstrate a new day in corporate culture. Gone are the days of adversarial union-management relationships. These miners look forward to a new partnership marked by shared goals. A visible symbol of commitment to the future was distribution by CEO Burgess Winter and a local union president of a Joint Union-Management Cooperation Commitment at the mine entrance during shift changes. Other steps, such as team-building, development of "Breakthrough Business Projects," and implementation of "gainsharing" pay based on productivity and efficiency are positive signs of genuine change.

The reason symbolic management works is that executives are watched by employees. Employees attempt to read signals from what executives do, not just from what they say. For example, a senior manager told a story of how employees always knew in advance when someone was to be laid off in his company. He finally picked up the pattern. Employees noticed that he always dressed in his favorite pink shirt and matching tie when layoffs were to be announced.

When Les Tiffany, director of production at Physio-Control, Inc., saw falling production and rising employee tension, he developed a vision to increase production levels and to celebrate the achievement of each $500,000 level. Upon attainment of each level, a manager, beginning with Tiffany himself, donned a clown costume and pedaled a tricycle through the plant, towing a siren-screaming red wagon with a banner proclaiming the accomplishment. Employees loved it. A "parade route" developed over the three-month period of the celebrations, and although production was interrupted for several minutes each day, motivation ran high to reach the next level and witness the "clowning" of yet another manager.[51]

Jack Welch transformed General Electric—a huge corporation—by defining a new type of senior manager. His demand was for symbolic managers, which he described as follows: "Somebody who can develop a vision of what he or she wants their . . . activity to do and be. Somebody who is able to articulate what the business is, and gain through a sharing of the discussion—listening and talking—an acceptance of the vision. And someone who then can relentlessly drive implementation of that vision to a successful conclusion."[52]

Even well-established companies with strong cultures may implement changes through symbolic management. In December 1991, then IBM chairman John Akers announced massive reforms to update the structure and culture of "Big Blue." Awakened by a $2.8 billion loss and a surge of innovative technology and increased competition from the environment, Akers divided Big Blue into 13 autonomous divisions ("Baby Blues") to symbolize the need for autonomy and flexibility. Divisional managers relished their liberation and set new goals in the areas of quality, customer satisfaction, and employee morale.[53]

Symbolic managers search for opportunities. They make public statements, including both oral and written communications, to the organization as a whole. After articulating a vision, managers change corporate culture through hundreds of small deeds, actions, statements, and ceremonies. A strong leader who articulated a clear vision accounted for the extraordinary success of Dana, Wal-Mart, Disney, McDonald's, and Levi Strauss. Harold Geneen, former CEO of ITT captured his corporate value in a few words, "Search for the unshakeable facts."

Scott Kohno, managing director of Chaix & Johnson, shocked and revitalized his 30 employees by hauling his desk from a comfortable executive office with 18-foot ceilings to the middle of the work floor. Kohno compared the move to the "difference between being on the basketball floor instead of the bleachers." The increased contact with staff was soon matched by a supercharged employee energy level.[54]

Another story involving a desk illustrates Mars executives' concern for employees and began when Mr. Mars made a mid-summer visit to a chocolate factory:

> He went up to the third floor, where the biggest chocolate machines were placed. It was hotter than the hinges of hell. He asked the factory manager, "How come you don't have air conditioning up here?" The factory manager replied that it wasn't in his budget, and he darn well had to make the budget. While Mr. Mars allowed that was a fact, he nonetheless went over to the nearby phone and dialed the maintenance people downstairs and asked them to come up immediately. He said, "While we (he and the factory manager) stand here, would you please go downstairs and get all (the factory manager's) furniture and other things from his office and bring them up here? Sit them down next to the big chocolate machine up here, if you don't mind." Mr. Mars told him that once the factory had been air conditioned, he could move back to his office any time he wanted.[55]

Stories such as these can be found in most companies and used to enhance the desired culture. The value of stories depends not on whether they are precisely true but whether they are repeated frequently and convey the correct values.

To summarize, symbolic managers can bring about cultural change through the use of public statements, ceremonies, stories, heroes, symbols, and slogans. To change culture, executives must learn ceremonial skills and how to use speech, symbols, and stories to influence company values. Executives do not drive trucks or run machines. To change culture, they must act like evangelists rather than accountants.[56] Symbolic activities provide information about what counts in the company.

SUMMARY AND MANAGEMENT SOLUTION

This chapter discussed several important ideas about internal and external organizational environments. Events in the external environment are considered important influences on organizational behavior and performance. The external environment consists of two layers: the task environment and the general environment. The task environment includes customers, competitors, suppliers, and labor market. The general environment includes technological, sociocultural, economic, legal-political, and international dimensions. Management techniques for helping the organization adapt to the environment include boundary-spanning roles, forecasting and planning, a flexible structure, and mergers and joint ventures. Techniques managers can use to influence the external environment include advertising and public relations, political activities, and trade associations.

Dow Corning, described in the chapter opening case, probably did not have sufficient boundary-spanning capacity to head off the problems with silicone breast implants. Sometimes environmental problems cannot be anticipated. Now Dow Corning is relying heavily on techniques to influence the external environment. The CEO associated with the breast implants was replaced by Keith R. McKennon, who rehabilitated Dow Chemical's image regarding napalm bombs during the Vietnam War. In addition, McKennon has signaled his desire to tell the complete truth and face the public and the facts, which will be a strong public relations effort. By winning public opinion, Dow Corning can move forward and get through this problem. Other moves to influence the environment will be to set up an information center where women and their doctors can obtain information and settle claims, and to set up a fund for research on silicone effects and to pay the medical bills of poor women.[57]

Corporate culture, a major element of the internal environment, includes the key values, beliefs, understandings, and norms that organization members share. Organizational activities that illustrate corporate culture include symbols, stories, heroes, slogans, and ceremonies. For the organization to be effective, corporate culture should be aligned with the needs of the external environment.

Four types of culture are baseball team, club, academy, and fortress, each of which suits a specific environment. Dow Corning currently has something of a fortress mentality as it attempts to retrench and turn around from this difficult implant controversy. Strong cultures are effective when they enable the organization to adapt to changes in the external environment.

Symbolic managers can change corporate culture by (1) communicating a vision to employees and (2) reinforcing the vision with day-to-day public statements, ceremonies, slogans, symbols, and stories.

DISCUSSION QUESTIONS

1. Some scientists predict major changes in the earth's climate, including a temperature rise of 8°F over the next 60 years. Should any companies be paying attention to this long-range environmental trend? Explain.
2. Would the task environment for a bank contain the same elements as that for a government welfare agency? Discuss.
3. What forces influence organizational uncertainty? Would such forces typically originate in the task environment or the general environment?
4. *In Search of Excellence*, described in Chapter 2, argued that customers were the most important element in the external environment. Are there company situations for which this may not be true?
5. Caterpillar Corporation was thriving until the mid-1980s, when low oil prices, high interest rates, a worldwide recession, a soaring U.S. dollar, and Japanese competition stunned the giant equipment builder. Discuss the type of response Caterpillar's management might take.
6. Define corporate culture and explain its importance for managers.
7. Why are symbols important to a corporate culture? Do stories, heroes, slogans, and ceremonies also have symbolic value? Discuss.

8. Describe the cultural values of a company for which you have worked. Did those values fit the needs of the external environment? Of employees?
9. What type of environmental situation is associated with a baseball team culture? How does this culture differ from the academy culture?
10. Do you think a corporate culture with strong values is better for organizational effectiveness than a culture with weak values? Are there times when a strong culture might reduce effectiveness?

MANAGEMENT IN PRACTICE: ETHICAL DILEMMA

● THE $10,000 LUNCH

Rich has decision responsibility for a $5 million, five-year budget to install a communications network in his company's headquarters building. Suppliers are competitively vying to win contracts for providing the necessary hardware and systems equipment.

Rich is having lunch with his favorite salesperson, Scott. Near the end of lunch, Scott says, "Rich, listen. The end of the quarter is next week, and I am about $100,000 in sales short to get a big $10,000 bonus. If you could sign the purchase agreement on that computer network now instead of in three months, I've got tickets to the Super Bowl. How about it?"

Rich responded, "I've got to think about this. I'll call you tomorrow." Rich wanted desperately to attend the Super Bowl because his favorite team was playing, and his wife wanted to visit family in Pasadena. Back at the office, Rich

thought about the company tradition of purchasing agents and others accepting small favors from suppliers. He also knew that Scott put a lot of effort into bidding for the contract, and his company's bid looked better than any other. Rich also remembered that a newly issued company policy states, "Program managers are prohibited from accepting gifts of any size or form from vendors."

● WHAT DO YOU DO?

1. Sign the contract and accept the tickets. After all, Scott deserved it and would have won the bidding anyway.
2. Ask the support of coworkers. After all, company tradition and cultural values are more important for defining behavior than are written policies.
3. Do not sign the contract or accept the tickets. Breaking company policy is inappropriate.

CASES FOR ANALYSIS

NORTHROP CORPORATION

Industry skeptics doubt the ability of Northrop Corporation to successfully restructure and change corporate culture in response to its environment. New chairman Kent Kresa inherited a shopping list of woes, headed by a disastrous ethical and legal record. A court in Seoul, Korea, accused the company of influence peddling in an attempt to sell its F-20 fighter jets to South Korea. Northrop pleaded guilty to falsifying test results on several U.S. weapon systems, including a nuclear missile. In 1992, the FBI began an investigation into charges that Northrop ordered employees to hide or destroy incriminating documents. Rival companies in the defense industry such as Lockheed have lost no time moving in on Northrop's territory, with Northrop losing several key contracts to rivals.

Other environmental problems also threaten the company. The fall of communism and the outbreak of peace hurt Northrop as the Pentagon slashed budgets and competition stiffened throughout the defense industry. Moreover, some lawmakers won't vote for Northrop's best-known project, the B-2 stealth bomber, because of the company's poor reputation. Although Northrop had sales of over $5 billion in 1990, company morale continued to drop and a sense of urgency set in.

Chairman Kresa's strategy has been a two-pronged attack. First, he addressed past sins with apologies to Congress, agreements to repair defective weapons, and settlements in a number of lawsuits. He has also addressed corporate culture, which some see as the greater challenge.

Kresa began with a mission statement, the first ever for Northrop, that emphasized six values. *Integrity* topped the list. Customer satisfaction, respect for colleagues, team building with suppliers, responsibility for quality, and leadership round out the new message.

Kresa's leadership style is to lead by example, providing symbols and stories that reinforce the new culture values. After investing in a rigorous new training program, Kresa and top executives were the first to march off to "boot camp." Under a new feedback system, the chairman himself often handwrites replies to employees in response to their ideas and concerns. Under the new system, subordinates regularly evaluate their supervisors, and the first to undergo evaluation was the chairman. Kresa also encourages employees to come forward with problems, in stark contrast to the tradition of scolding employees who spoke up with bad news (called Northrop's "kill-the-briefer" style).

Skeptics see the situation as already out of hand, with major problems on every front. Chairman Kresa looks to the future and insists Northrop will learn from past mistakes and march back into the fray.

● QUESTIONS

1. What aspects of the external environment are having the greatest impact on Northrop?
2. What approaches—adapting to or influencing the environment—seem appropriate for Northrop?
3. Chairman Ken Kresa seems to be working on the external environment and internal environment at the same time. Does this seem feasible for a chief executive? Discuss.

SOURCE: Rick Watzman, "On the Defensive: Pentagon Budget Cuts, Past Ethical Lapses Haunt Northrop Corporation," *The Wall Street Journal* (January 2, 1992), 1, I-E.

SOCIETY OF EQUALS

Ted Shelby doesn't make very many mistakes, but . . .

"Hey, Stanley," says Ted Shelby, leaning in through the door, "you got a minute? I've just restructured my office. Come on and take a look. I've been implementing some great new concepts!"

Stanley is always interested in Ted Shelby's new ideas, for if there is anyone Stanley wants to do as well as, it is Edward W. Shelby IV. Stanley follows Ted back to his office and stops, nonplussed.

Restructured is right! Gone are Ted's size B (Junior Exec.) walnut veneer desk and furniture, and his telephone table. In fact, the room is practically empty save for a large, round, stark white cafeteria table and the half-dozen padded vinyl swivel chairs that surround it.

"Isn't it a beauty! As far as I know, I'm the first executive in the plant to innovate this. The shape is the crucial factor here—no front or rear, no status problems. We can all sit there and communicate more effectively."

We? Communicate? Effectively? Well, it seems that Ted has been attending a series of Executive Development Seminars given by Dr. Faust. The theme of the seminars was—you guessed it—"participative management." Edward W. Shelby IV has always liked to think of himself as a truly democratic person.

"You see, Stanley," says Ted, managing his best sincere/intense attitude, "the main thing wrong with current mainstream management practice is that the principal communication channel is down-the-line oriented. We on the top send our messages down to you people, but we ne-

glect the feedback potential. But just because we have more status and responsibility doesn't mean that we are necessarily (Stanley duly noted the word, "necessarily") better than the people below us. So, as I see the situation, what is needed is a two-way communication network: down-the-line and up-the-line."

"That's what the cafeteria table is for?" Stanley says.

"Yes!" says Ted. "We management people don't have all the answers, and I don't know why I never realized it before that seminar. Why . . . let's take an extreme example . . . the folks who run those machines out there. I'll bet that any one of them knows a thing or two that I've never thought of. So I've transformed my office into a full-feedback communication net."

"That certainly is an innovation around here," says Stanley.

A few days later Stanley passed by Ted Shelby's office and was surprised that Ted's desk, furniture, and telephone table were back where they used to be.

Stanley, curious about the unrestructuring, went to Bonnie for enlightenment. "What," he asked "happened to Shelby's round table?"

"That table we were supposed to sit around and input things?" she said. "All I know is, about two days after he had it put in, Mr. Drake came walking through here. He looked in that office, and then he sort of stopped and went back—and he looked in there for a long time. Then he came over to me, and you know how his face sort of gets red when he's really mad? Well, this time he was so mad that his face was absolutely white. And when he talked to me, I don't think he actually opened his mouth; and I could barely hear him, he was talking so low. And he said, 'Have that removed. Now. Have Mr. Shelby's furniture put back in his office. Have Mr. Shelby see me.'"

My, my. You would think Ted would have known better, wouldn't you? But then, by now you should have a pretty firm idea of just why it is those offices are set up as they are.

● **Q U E S T I O N S**

1. How would you characterize the culture in this company? What are the dominant values?

2. Why did Ted Shelby's change experiment fail? To what extent did Ted use the appropriate change tools to increase employee communication and participation?

3. What would you recommend Ted do to change his relationship with subordinates? Is it possible for a manager to change cultural values if the rest of the organization, especially top management, does not agree?

SOURCE: R. Richard Ritti and G. Ray Funkhouser, *The Ropes to Skip & The Ropes to Know*, 3d. ed. (New York: Wiley, 1987), 176–177. Reprinted by permission of John Wiley & Sons, Inc.

REFERENCES

1. Michele Galen, John A. Byrne, Tim Smart, and David Woodruff, "Debacle at Dow Corning: How Bad Will It Get?" *Business Week,* March 2, 1992, 36–38; and Tim Smart, "Breast Implants: What Did the Industry Know, and When?" *Business Week,* June 10, 1991, 94–98.

2. Scott McMurray, "Wounded Giant: Union Carbide Offers Some Sober Lessons in Crisis Management," *The Wall Street Journal,* January 28, 1991, A1, A9.

3. Richard L. Daft, *Organization, Theory and Design,* 4th ed. (St. Paul, Minn.: West, 1992).

4. L. J. Bourgeois, "Strategy and Environment: A Conceptual Integration," *Academy of Management Review* 5 (1980), 25–39.

5. Based on Marc Beauchamp, "Toilets with Chips," *Forbes,* January 22, 1990, 100–104.

6. Richard I. Kirkland, Jr., "Entering a New Age of Boundless Competition," *Fortune,* March 14, 1988, 40–48; and Kenichin Ohmae, "Managing in a Borderless World," *Harvard Business Review* (May–June 1989), 152–161.

7. Nancy J. Perry, "The Arms Makers' Next Battle," *Fortune,* August 27, 1990, 84–88.

8. Eric Shine, Amy Borrus, John Carey, and Geoffery Smith, "The Defense Whizzies Making It in Civvies," *Business Week,* September 7, 1992, 88–90.

9. Naomi Frundlich, Neil Gross, John Carey, and Robert D. Hof, "The New Alchemy: How Science Is Molding Molecules into Miracle Materials," *Business Week,* July 29, 1991, 48–52.

10. Otis Port, "Materials That Think for Themselves," *Business Week,* December 5, 1988, 166–167.

11. William B. Johnston, "Global Work Force 2000: The New World Labor Market," *Harvard Business Review* (March–April 1991), 115–127.

12. Maria Malloryn and Stephanie Anderson Forest, "Waking Up to a Major Market," *Business Week,* March 23, 1992, 70–73; William Dunn, "Survival by Numbers," *Nation's Business,* August 1991, 14–21; Joseph Spiers, "The Baby Boomlet Is for Real," *Fortune,* February 10, 1992, 101–104; and Michael Mandel, Christopher Farrell, Dori Jones Yang, Gloria Lau, Christina Del Valle, and S. Lynne Walker, "The Immigrants: How They're Helping to Revitalize the U.S. Economy," *Business Week,* July 13, 1992, 114–122.

13. David Lieverman, "Keeping Up with the Murdochs," *Business Week*, March 20, 1989, 32–34; and Don Lee Bohl, ed., *Tying the Corporate Knot* (New York: American Management Association, 1989).

14. Victoria Reid, "Businesses Upset with OSHA Rules," *The Tennessean*, July 7, 1992, 4E.

15. Walecia Konrad and Gail DeGeorge, "U.S. Companies Go for the Gray," *Business Week*, April 3, 1989, 64–67.

16. Peter H. Lewis, "Apple–IBM Venture, with New Leaders, Searchers for a Soul," *The New York Times*, March 8, 1992, F8; and Mark Ivey and Geoff Lewis, "Compaq vs. IBM: Peace Comes to Shove," *Business Week*, May 1, 1989, 132.

17. Michael R. Czinkota and Ilkka A. Ronkines, "Global Marketing 2000: A Marketing Survival Guide," *Marketing Management* (Winter 1992), 37–42.

18. William C. Symonds, Jonathan B. Levine, Neil Gross, and Peter Coy, "High-Tech Star: Northern Telecom Is Challenging Even AT&T," *Business Week*, July 27, 1992, 54–58.

19. Robert B. Duncan, "Characteristics of Organizational Environment and Perceived Environmental Uncertainty," *Administrative Science Quarterly* 17 (1972), 313–327; and Daft, *Organization Theory and Design*.

20. David B. Jemison, "The Importance of Boundary Spanning Roles in Strategic Decision-Making," *Journal of Management Studies* 21 (1984), 131–152; and Marc J. Dollinger, "Environmental Boundary Spanning and Information Processing Effects on Organizational Performance," *Academy of Management Journal* 27 (1984), 351–368.

21. Wendy Zellner and Bruce Hager, "Dumpster Raids? That's Not Very Ladylike, Avon," *Business Week*, April 1, 1991, 32.

22. Brian Dumaine, "Corporate Spies Snoop to Conquer," *Fortune*, November 7, 1988, 68–76; Dodui Tsiantar and John Schwartz, "George Smiley Joins the Firm," *Newsweek*, May 2, 1988, 46–47; and James E. Svatko, "Analyzing the Competition," *Small Business Reports*, January 1989, 21–28.

23. R. T. Lenz and Jack L. Engledow, "Environmental Analysis Units and Strategic Decision-Making: A Field Study of Selected 'Leading Edge' Corporations," *Strategic Management Journal* 7 (1986), 69–89; and Mansour Javidan, "The Impact of Environmental Uncertainty on Long-Range Planning Practices of the U.S. Savings and Loan Industry," *Strategic Management Journal* 5 (1984), 381–392.

24. Tom Burns and G. M. Stalker, *The Management of Innovation* (London: Tavistock, 1961).

25. James E. Svatko, "Joint Ventures," *Small Business Reports*, December 1988, 65–70; and Joshua Hyatt, "The Partnership Route," *INC.*, December 1988, 145–148.

26. John A. Byrne, "The Best-Laid Ethics Program . . . ," *Business Week*, March 9, 1992, 67–69; and "Dow Chemical: From Napalm to Nice Guy," *Fortune*, May 12, 1986, 75–78.

27. Edmund Faltermayer, "The Thaw in Washington," *Fortune* (The New American Century), 1991, 46–51; David B. Yoffie, "How an Industry Builds Political Advantage," *Harvard Business Review* (May–June 1988), 82–89; and Douglas Harbrecht, "How to Win Friends and Influence Lawmakers," *Business Week*, November 7, 1988, 36.

28. Monica Langley, "Thrifts' Trade Group and Their Regulators Get Along Just Fine," *The Wall Street Journal*, July 16, 1986, 1, 14.

29. Yoash Wiener, "Forms of Value Systems: A Focus on Organizational Effectiveness and Culture Change and Maintenance," *Academy of Management Review* 13 (1988), 534–545; V. Lynne Meek, "Organizational Culture: Origins and Weaknesses," *Organization Studies* 9 (1988), 453–473; and John J. Sherwood, "Creating Work Cultures with Competitive Advantage," *Organizational Dynamics* (Winter 1988), 5–27.

30. Ralph H. Kilmann, Mary J. Saxton, and Roy Serpa, "Issues in Understanding and Changing Culture," *California Management Review* 28 (Winter 1986), 87–94; and Linda Smircich, "Concepts of Culture and Organizational Analysis," *Administrative Science Quarterly* 28 (1983), 339–358.

31. Edgar H. Schein, "Coming to a New Awareness of Organizational Culture," *Sloan Management Review* (Winter 1984), 3–16; and Vijay Sathe, "Implications of Corporate Culture: A Manager's Guide to Actions," *Organizational Dynamics* (Autumn 1983), 5–23.

32. Wendy Zellner, "Mr. Sam's Experiment Is Alive and Well," *Business Week*, April 20, 1992, 39; Sam Walton (with John Huey), *Sam Walton: Made in America* (New York: Doubleday, 1992); and John Huey, "America's Most Successful Merchant," *Fortune*, September 23, 1991, 46–59.

33. William Taylor, "The Gray Area," *Harvard Business Review* (May–June 1988), 178–182, and "Corporate Culture," *Business Week*, October 27, 1980, 148–160.

34. Russell Mitchell, "Masters of Innovation," *Business Week*, April 10, 1989, 58–63.

35. "Make No Mistake," *INC.*, June 1989, 115.

36. Nancy K. Austin, "Wacky Management Ideas That Work," *Working Woman*, November 1991, 42–44.

37. Susan Benner, "Culture Shock," *INC.*, August 1985, 73–82.

38. Joan O'C. Hamilton, "Why Rivals Are Quaking as Nordstrom Heads East," *Busines Week*, June 15, 1987, 99–100; and Charlotte B. Sutton, "Richness Hierarchy of the Cultural Network: The Communication of Corporate Values" (Unpublished manuscript, Texas A&M University, 1985).

39. Terrence E. Deal and Allan A. Kennedy, *Corporate Cultures: The Rites and Rituals of Corporate Life* (Reading, Mass.: Addison-Wesley, 1982).

40. Brian Dumaine, "Those Highflying PepsiCo Managers," *Fortune*, April 10, 1989, 78–86; and Stew Leonard, "Love that Customer!" *Management Review* (October 1987), 36–39.

41. Harrison M. Trice and Janice M. Beyer, "Studying Organizational Cultures through Rites and Ceremonials," *Academy of Management Review* 9 (1984), 653–669.

42. John P. Kotter and James L. Heskett, *Corporate Culture and Performance* (New York: The Free Press, 1992).

43. Jeffrey Sonnenfeld, *The Hero's Farewell: What Happens When CEO's Retire* (New York: Oxford University Press, 1988).

44. William A. Schiermann, "Organizational Change: Lessons from a Turnaround," *Management Review*, April 1992, 34–37.

45. Ralph H. Kilmann, Mary J. Saxton, Roy Serpa, and Associates, *Gaining Control of the Corporate Culture* (San Francisco: Jossey-Bass, 1985).

46. Ralph Kilmann, "Corporate Culture," *Psychology Today*, April 1985, 62–68.

47. Morty Lefkoe, "Why So Many Mergers Fail," *Fortune*, June 20, 1987, 113–114.

48. Ibid.; and Afsaneh Nahavandi and Ali R. Malekzadeh, "Acculturation in Mergers and Acquisitions," *Academy of Management Review* 13 (1988), 79–90.

49. Bohl, *Tying the Corporate Knot.*

50. Thomas J. Peters and Robert H. Waterman, Jr., *In Search of Excellence* (New York: Warner, 1988).

51. Charles A. Jaffe, "Management by Fun," *Nation's Business*, January 1990, 58–60.

52. Russell Mitchell, "Jack Welch: How Good a Manager?" *Business Week*, December 14, 1987, 92–103.

53. David Kirkpatrick, "Breaking Up IBM," *Fortune*, July 27, 1992, 44–53.

54. Ellyn E. Spragins, "Motivation: Out of the Frying Pan," *INC.*, December 1991, 157.

55. Tom Peters and Nancy Austin, *A Passion for Excellence: The Leadership Difference* (New York: Random House, 1985), 278.

56. Karl E. Weick, "Cognitive Processes in Organizations," in *Research in Organizations*, vol. 1, ed. B. M. Staw (Greenwich, Conn.: JAI Press, 1979).

57. John A. Byrne, "Here's What to Do Next, Dow Corning," *Business Week*, February 24, 1992, 33; and Galen et al., "Debacle at Dow Corning."

DOW CORNING

For the two million women who received silicone-gel breast implants during the nearly 30 years they were on the market, the news came as a hard blow. Some experts were linking the implants with health problems, ranging from fatigue and mild muscle and joint pain to arthritis-like diseases of the immune system and cancer.

For Dow Corning Corporation, the world's largest manufacturer of the implants, the news was nearly as devastating. Although the company contended there was no known medical evidence to prove that fluid leaking from the implants caused disease, it still faced the prospect of years of litigation and millions of dollars in court costs.

Many plastic surgeons sided with Dow Corning. "The overwhelming majority of American women who have gel-filled implants and have not been scared to death by all this publicity are in good health and are generally happy with their results," said breast surgeon Dr. Boyd Berkhard.

The Food and Drug Administration reacted to the controversy by imposing a voluntary moratorium on silicone-gel breast implants until their safety could be ensured. "These implants are intended to be a part of women's bodies for a lifetime. We must, therefore, understand better how long these devices last and be satisfied that they will not be harmful in the years to come," says FDA commissioner Dr. David Kessle.

Soon after the moratorium was announced in January 1992, Dow Corning opted to stop making and selling the implants. Three months later, the company said it was pulling out of the business for good. "I believe that the future use of this product will be curtailed to a considerable extent," Dow Corning Chairman Keith McKennon said at a news conference announcing the decision. The company closed its implant factories in Arlington, Tennessee, and Hemlock, Michigan, and laid off or reassigned about 100 employees.

But far from being the end of the story, in some ways it was only the beginning for Dow Corning, a joint venture of Dow Chemical Company and Corning, Inc. Sales of silicone breast implants accounted for just 1 percent of the company's 1.8 billion in 1991 sales, but the business had suddenly turned high profile. What's worse, it had become a public relations nightmare.

Dow Corning immediately took steps to limit the damage and improve its image in the eyes of a wary public. While continuing to deny knowledge of any link between the implants and disease, it agreed with the FDA that more studies were needed. The company said it would even set up a $10 million fund to pay for breast implant research. "We are committed to fund additional research to provide an expanded scientific base to answer these ques-

tions," McKennon said. "We will ensure that results of these studies be made available to all interested parties."

To soothe the concerns of anxious customers, Dow Corning promised to help defray the cost of removing the implants for women who could not afford to pay for the surgery themselves. The company pledged to pay as much as $1,200 to such patients as long as the implant had been made by Dow Coring and a physician believed removal was medically necessary.

Dow Corning's concessions were not enough to apease women who believed the implants were responsible for their health problems. More than 3,000 lawsuits were filed in courts across the nation by women who said the company failed to tell the public of safety concerns. Some estimates put the potential cost of the product liability at more than $2 billion. The company rejected those claims, contending that its $250 million in liability insurance would probably suffice, based on other cases where products had been shown to cause injury.

In one case, a California jury ordered the company to pay $7.14 million in damages to a woman who claimed her silicone implants had ruptured and leaked, leaving her unable to work. She also alleged Dow Corning covered up evidence that raised questions about the safety of its implants. The company appealed the ruling but later released hundreds of pages of internal documents, which showed that concerns about the implants spanned decades. Many of the documents had been sealed by protective court orders issued at the company's request.

The disclosures touched off a storm of controversy, generated both because of the information contained in the documents and the methods the company had used to keep it out of public hands. Russ Herman, who opposed the use of protective orders during his stint as president of the Association of Trial Lawyers of America, said the documents showed Dow Corning had a pattern of releasing only "partial information . . . and half-truths." Herman contended that secrecy orders and agreements should only be used in very narrow cases. "If these scoundrels are forced to disclose early on the problems with their product, either consumers will not buy them or manufacturers will have to conduct the research necessary to make them safe," he said.

Others jumped to Dow Corning's defense, saying that many of the documents were used in a public trial that ended with a jury verdict. "The plaintiffs' lawyers want to publicize all the information they possibly can so they can bring more and more cases," said Alfred Cortese of Lawyers for Civil Justice, an organization made up of defense attorneys who oppose limits on protective orders. "They're not interested in protecting the public, they're interested in creating hysteria so they get more cases."

Recently, Dow Corning became the target of a federal grand jury investigation and received a subpoena for more documents pertaining to its implants. The subpoena included requests for details of an in-house study conducted by former U.S. Attorney General Griffin Bell in 1992. A federal district judge previously ruled the study was privileged attorney-client information. "We will be complying and providing all of the information that isn't either privileged or otherwise protected," said Barbara Carmichael, a spokesperson for Midland, Michigan–based Dow Corning.

With so many questions still unanswered about the safety of breast implants, there are only two companies left in the business, and neither uses silicone gel anymore. Both Mentor Corporation and McGhan Medical Corporation make implants using salt water, which are also under a safety review. How have Mentor and McGhan Medical reacted to the uproar? Both companies raised their prices to pay for increased litigation and the cost of preparing research to comply with regulators' demands.

● QUESTIONS

1. Describe how changes in Dow Corning's external environment affected the company. Were the changes in the company's general environment or task environment? Which dimensions of those environments were most important?

2. How could Dow Corning have better managed the uncertainty of environmental factors? Discuss.

3. What steps should Dow Corning take to overcome its problems?

4. What changes have taken place at Dow Corning since this video case was aired?

■ BUSINESS ETHICS

Chapter 5, "Managerial Ethics and Corporate Social Responsibility," explained that ethics represents a code of moral principles and values that govern the behaviors of a person or group with respect to what is right or wrong. When all the choices you face may have a potentially harmful effect on one or more parties, including coworkers, the organization, customers, the general public, and you personally, it may not be clear what choice is right. This situation is called an ethical dilemma.

In this exercise, you will be presented with different ethical dilemmas and asked to make choices. Then, the software program will provide some personal feedback about your decisions.

THIS EXERCISE WILL HELP YOU TO:

- Clarify your code of business ethics.
- Consider the consequences of your decisions before making them.

HOW TO LOCATE THE EXERCISE

When you see the main menu for Career Design, select "Other Management Topics." Then select "Business Ethics."

PART II

PLANNING

In meeting its strategic goals for diversity, IDS took a cooking tip from Trinidad and Tobago. There, the national dish, Callaloo, is a metaphor for ethnic diversity in the area, mixing together a wild assortment of ingredients. IDS's corporate version of Callaloo has been developed through a four-point strategic plan for diversity, called LEAD. This recipe includes Leadership from managers, creating an Environment that is open to diversity, Acquiring new and diverse employees, planners, and clients, and Delivering measurable results. IDS has already seen significant increases in work-force diversity. IDS Callaloo has arrived.

MANAGERIAL ETHICS AND CORPORATE SOCIAL RESPONSIBILITY

5 CHAPTER

LEARNING OBJECTIVES

After studying this chapter, you should be able to

- Define ethics and explain how ethical behavior relates to behavior governed by law and free choice.

- Explain the utilitarian, individualism, moral-rights, and justice approaches for evaluating ethical behavior.

- Describe how both individual and organizational factors shape ethical decision making.

- Define corporate social responsibility and how to evaluate it along economic, legal, ethical, and discretionary criteria.

- Describe four corporate responses to social demands.

- Explain the concept of stakeholder and identify important stakeholders for organizations.

- Describe structures managers can use to improve their organizations' ethics and social responsiveness.

Nynex Corporation, a New York–based "Baby Bell" telephone company, entered the 1990s under a cloud of scandal. FCC charges of questionable financial transactions and rate hikes due to overbilling resulted in stiff penalties of over $35 million. Reeling from the embarrassment, Nynex faced additional damaging publicity with revelations that employees from the purchasing department attended sleazy parties in a Florida hotel, hosted by vendors and prostitutes.

Although no laws were broken, Nynex responded to the newest scandal with strong disciplinary action and the firing of two employees. "I'm sick and tired of this stuff," said chairman William C. Ferguson.[1] ■ How do you think Nynex got into this situation? If you were Ferguson, how would you respond to this mess, and how would you implement a higher ethical standard within Nynex?

M A N A G E M E N T   P R O B L E M

Everyone associated with the Nynex scandals was surprised—surprised by the lapse in values, surprised that basically honest people would deceive the public, surprised at the loss of respect for the company and its management. The outcry against Nynex symbolizes the rising importance of the need to discuss ethics and social responsibility. In the 1990s ethics and social responsibility issues are in the forefront of corporate concerns. Corporations are rushing to adopt codes of ethics. Ethics consultants are doing a land-office business. Unfortunately, the trend is necessary.[2]

The state of California charged that 72 Sears Roebuck tire and auto centers defrauded customers with unnecessary repairs. The findings followed a two-year undercover investigation and resulted in a public apology by Sears chairman Edward Brennan and abandonment of commission sales for auto service departments. In an even farther-reaching scandal, the federal government charged the Bank of Credit and Commerce International (BCCI) with a number of criminal counts, including the laundering of drug money and influence peddling. Exxon faced public anger, enormous fines, and a massive cleanup effort following the *Valdez* oil spill. These instances of fraud, criminal activity, and pollution illustrate the negative side of ethics issues.[3]

There is also positive news to report. In the wake of the 1992 Los Angeles riots, McDonald's fed burned-out citizens, fire fighters, police, and national guard troops and delivered free lunches to 300 students at a nearby school. Anita Roddick's retail chain of Bodyshops supports a variety of environmental and social causes, such as Amnesty International. H. J. Heinz funded infant nutrition studies in China and Thailand

Florida Progress Corporation's efforts to preserve the environment and conserve resources show its commitment to a *social responsibility approach* to the environment. Florida Progress employees cleaned beaches and waterways and opened a fish hatchery. Concerned employees constructed elevated platforms to encourage birds, such as this osprey, to locate nests away from power line poles. These efforts add to the company's reputation as a socially responsible industry leader.

through its Institute of Nutritional Sciences. Companies such as Northrop and Manville, embarrassed by scandals, are working overtime to prevent future ethical problems. Among Northrop's reforms, as discussed in the case at the end of Chapter 4, managers are rated by peers and subordinates through anonymous questionnaires. Manville is overcoming its asbestos-tainted past with a trust fund to compensate asbestos victims, regular audits by an independent health committee, and the installation of scrubbers on its smokestacks.[4]

This chapter expands on the ideas about environment and culture discussed in Chapter 4. We will first focus on specific ethical values that build on the idea of corporate culture. Then we will examine corporate relationships to the external environment as reflected in social responsibility. The topic of ethics is hot in corporate America, but it should be approached as more than a fad. We will discuss fundamental approaches that help managers think through ethical issues. Understanding ethical approaches helps managers build a solid foundation on which to base future decision making.

● WHAT IS MANAGERIAL ETHICS?

Ethics is difficult to define in a precise way. In a general sense, **ethics** is the code of moral principles and values that govern the behaviors of a person or group with respect to what is right or wrong. Ethics sets standards as to what is good or bad in conduct and decision making.[5] Ethics deals with internal values that are a part of corporate culture and shapes decisions concerning social responsibility with respect to the external environment. An ethical issue is present in a situation when the actions of a person or organization may harm or benefit others.[6]

Ethics can be more clearly understood when compared with behaviors governed by laws and by free choice. Exhibit 5.1 illustrates that human behavior falls into three categories. The first is codified law, in which values and standards are written into the legal system and enforceable in the courts. In this area, lawmakers have ruled that people and corporations must behave in a certain way, such as obtaining licenses for cars or paying corporate taxes. The domain of free choice is at the opposite end of the scale and pertains to behavior about which

ethics

The code of moral principles and values that govern the behaviors of a person or group with respect to what is right or wrong.

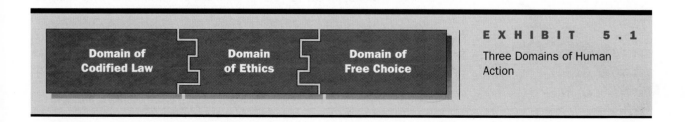

| Domain of Codified Law | Domain of Ethics | Domain of Free Choice |

E X H I B I T   5 . 1

Three Domains of Human Action

law has no say and for which an individual or organization enjoys complete freedom. An individual's choice of a marriage partner or religion or a corporation's choice of the number of dishwashers to manufacture are examples of free choice.

Between these domains lies the area of ethics. This domain has no specific laws, yet it does have standards of conduct based on shared principles and values about moral conduct that guide an individual or company. In the domain of free choice, obedience is strictly to oneself. In the domain of codified law, obedience is to laws prescribed by the legal system. In the domain of ethical behavior, obedience is to unenforceable norms and standards about which the individual or company is aware. An ethically acceptable decision is both legally and morally acceptable to the larger community.

Many companies and individuals get into trouble with the simplified view that choices are governed by either law or free choice. It leads people to mistakenly assume that "If it's not illegal, it must be ethical," as if there were no third domain.[7] A better option is to recognize the domain of ethics and accept moral values as a powerful force for good that can regulate behaviors both inside and outside corporations. As principles of ethics and social responsibility are more widely recognized, companies can use codes of ethics and their corporate cultures to govern behavior, thereby eliminating the need for additional laws and avoiding the problems of unfettered choice.

Because ethical standards are not codified, disagreements and dilemmas about proper behavior often occur. An **ethical dilemma** arises in a situation when each alternative choice or behavior is undesirable because of potentially harmful ethical consequences. Right or wrong cannot be clearly identified.

The individual who must make an ethical choice in an organization is the *moral agent*.[8] Consider the dilemmas facing a moral agent in the following situations:

> Shareholders demand that your company pull out of China as a result of the continued repression following the massacre in Tiananmen Square. If you pull out, you withdraw any influence your company may have for change and your Chinese employees will be hurt. If you stay, your company will be indirectly supporting an oppressive government.
>
> You have been asked to fire a marketing supervisor for cheating the company out of $500 on an inflated expense account. You are aware that a manufacturing supervisor allows thousands of dollars of waste because of poor work habits.
>
> Your company has been asked to pay a gratuity in India to speed the processing of an import permit. This is standard procedure, and your company will suffer if you do not pay the gratuity. Is this different from tipping a maitre d' in a nice restaurant?
>
> You are the accounting manager of a division that is $15,000 below profit targets. Approximately $20,000 of office supplies were delivered on December 21. The accounting rule is to pay expenses when incurred. The division general manager asks you not to record the invoice until February.
>
> Your boss says he cannot give you a raise this year because of budget constraints, but he will look the other way if your expense accounts come in a little high because of your good work this past year.

ethical dilemma

A situation that arises when all alternative choices or behaviors have been deemed undesirable because of potentially negative ethical consequences, making it difficult to distinguish right from wrong.

AIDS IN THE WORKPLACE

As division manager, you take great pride in the accomplishments of your employees. One day, the brightest and best of your employees stops you in the hall and whispers, "Can we talk?" You usher him into your office, close the door, and offer a chair. "What's on your mind?" The division wonder kid closes his eyes, takes a deep breath, and blurts out, "I need some time off. I have a problem. I have AIDS."

This scenario is every employer's nightmare. Unfortunately, it is a scenario being repeated daily in companies around the world, as increasing numbers of employees are infected with the deadly virus. As the disease reaches epidemic proportions, the federal Centers for Disease Control estimate "one in every 250 Americans may be infected by HIV, the virus that causes acquired immune deficiency syndrome." For corporate America, these gloomy statistics mean mounting pressure for implementation of sound AIDS policies, including ongoing education and support.

Efforts of corporate America to deal with the problems surrounding the virus are thus far inadequate.

Many companies can point to a non-discriminatory corporate policy toward victims, including a continuation of benefits. However, the greatest challenges in dealing with AIDS involve carefully honed people skills in the most difficult areas—"dealing with fear, discrimination, and dying in the workplace."

Although the disease cannot be transmitted through casual contact, fear stalks the workplace as non-infected employees cope with irrational worries about using the same restroom facilities or drinking fountain or try to insulate themselves from the pain and suffering of their coworker. Even initial sympathy for the coworker with AIDS can turn to resentment as other employees must increasingly take up the slack caused by the coworker's deteriorating health. In today's team-oriented work environment performance and morale of the entire group may suffer.

Company efforts to deal with the problems of AIDS must be pursued along three fronts. First, the company must develop a policy that protects the right to privacy for all employees and guarantees full benefits for employees with AIDS. The policy must have the full support of the top executives, and allow employees with AIDS to lead a productive work life as long as possible, without fear of isolation.

Second, the company should provide training for management, union officials, supervisors, and all employees. At the management level, training should include professional guidance in addressing worker fears. The company policy should be explained to all employees and include procedures to follow when an employee reports being HIV-positive or having AIDS. All employees should learn the facts about AIDS and should be encouraged through workshops, open discussion, or role-playing exercises, to develop empathy for those who suffer from AIDS.

Third, companies should assist employees with AIDS in coping with the disease, through ongoing counseling, and by helping managers and employees to deal with the special problems and issues involved with AIDS.

By dispelling myths, sensitizing employees, and creating a supportive atmosphere, corporate America will deal more effectively with this tragic disease. ∎

SOURCE: Ron Stodghill II, Russell Mitchell, Karen Thurston, and Christina Del Valle, "Why AIDS Policy Must Be a Special Policy," *Business Week* (February 1, 1993), 53–54; and Ron Stodghill II, "Managing AIDS: How One Boss Struggled to Cope," *Business Week* (February 1, 1993), 48–52.

These are the kinds of dilemmas and issues with which managers must deal that fall squarely in the domain of ethics. For a dilemma that really hits home, read the Focus on Ethics box. Now let's turn to approaches to ethical decision making that provide criteria for understanding and resolving these difficult issues.

● CRITERIA FOR ETHICAL DECISION MAKING

Werner Enterprises, Inc., a leading truckload carrier throughout the United States and Canada, takes both *utilitarian and moral-rights approaches* in establishing its mandatory drug-testing program. Here, Dr. Leo Weiler completes drug screening paperwork. Werner sees this program as securing the greatest good for the greatest number as well as securing the right to life and safety for its drivers and other motorists. Drug screening is only one aspect of the program, which includes intense training, on-the-road operating and safety performance monitoring, rewards for safety, and bonuses for mileage and fuel efficiency.

Most ethical dilemmas involve a conflict between the needs of the part and the whole—the individual versus the organization, or the organization versus society as a whole. For example, should a company install mandatory alcohol and drug testing for employees, which may benefit the organization as a whole but reduce the individual freedom of employees? Or should products that fail to meet tough FDA standards be exported to other countries where government standards are lower, benefiting the company but being potentially harmful to world citizens? Sometimes ethical decisions entail a conflict between two groups. For example, should the potential for local health problems resulting from a company's effluents take precedence over the jobs it creates as the town's leading employer?

Managers faced with these kinds of tough ethical choices often benefit from a normative approach—one based on norms and values—to guide their decision making. Normative ethics uses several approaches to describe values for guiding ethical decision making. Four of these that are relevant to managers are the utilitarian approach, individualism approach, moral-rights approach, and justice approach.[9]

UTILITARIAN APPROACH

■ **utilitarian approach**

The ethical concept that moral behaviors produce the greatest good for the greatest number.

The **utilitarian approach,** espoused by the nineteenth century philosophers Jeremy Bentham and John Stuart Mill, holds that moral behavior produces the greatest good for the greatest number. Under this approach, a decision maker is expected to consider the effect of each decision alternative on all parties and select the one that optimizes the satisfaction for the greatest number of people. Because actual computations can be very complex, simplifying them is considered appropriate. For example, a simple economic frame of reference could be used by calculating dollar costs and dollar benefits. Also, a decision could be made that considers only the people who are directly affected by the decision, not those who are indirectly affected. When GM chose to continue operations at its Arlington, Texas, plant while shutting down its Ypsilanti, Michigan, plant, managers justified the decision as producing the greater good for the corporation as a whole. The utilitarian ethic is cited as the basis for the recent trend among companies to police employee personal habits such as alcohol and tobacco consumption on the job, and in some cases after hours as well, because such behavior affects the entire workplace.[10]

The utilitarian ethic was the basis for the state of Oregon's decision to extend Medicaid to 400,000 previously ineligible recipients by refusing to pay for high-cost, high-risk procedures such as liver transplants and bone-marrow transplants. Although a few people needing these procedures have died because the state would not pay, many people have benefited from medical services they would otherwise have had to go without.[11] Critics of the utilitarian ethic fear a developing tendency toward a "Big Brother" approach and question whether the common good is squeezing the life out of the individual. Critics also claim that the Oregon decision does not fully take into account the concept of justice toward the unfortunate victims of life-threatening diseases.[12]

INDIVIDUALISM APPROACH

The **individualism approach** contends that acts are moral when they promote the individual's best long-term interests. Individual self-direction is paramount, and external forces that restrict self-direction should be severely limited.[13] Individuals calculate the best long-term advantage to themselves as a measure of a decision's goodness. The action that is intended to produce a greater ratio of good to bad for the individual compared with other alternatives is the right one to perform. With everyone pursuing self-direction, the greater good is ultimately served because people learn to accommodate each other in their own long-term interest. Individualism is believed to lead to honesty and integrity because that works best in the long run. Lying and cheating for immediate self-interest just causes business associates to lie and cheat in return. Thus, individualism ultimately leads to behavior toward others that fits standards of behavior people want toward themselves.[14] One value of understanding this approach is to recognize short-term variations if they are proposed. People might argue for short-term self-interest based on individualism, but that misses the point. Because individualism is easily misinterpreted to support immediate self-gain, it is not popular in the highly organized and group-oriented society of today. Individualism is closest to the domain of free choice described in Exhibit 5.1.

individualism approach

The ethical concept that acts are moral when they promote the individual's best long-term interests, which ultimately leads to the greater good.

MORAL-RIGHTS APPROACH

The **moral-rights approach** asserts that human beings have fundamental rights and liberties that cannot be taken away by an individual's decision. Thus an ethically correct decision is one that best maintains the rights of those people affected by it.

Moral rights that could be considered during decision making are

moral-rights approach

The ethical concept that moral decisions are those that best maintain the rights of those people affected by them.

1 The right of free consent—individuals are to be treated only as they knowingly and freely consent to be treated.

2 The right to privacy—individuals can choose to do as they please away from work and have control of information about their private life.

3 The right of freedom of conscience—individuals may refrain from carrying out any order that violates their moral or religious norms.

4 The right of free speech—individuals may criticize truthfully the ethics or legality of actions of others.

5 The right to due process—individuals have a right to an impartial hearing and fair treatment.

6 The right to life and safety—individuals have a right to live without endangerment or violation of their health and safety.

To make ethical decisions, managers need to avoid interfering with the fundamental rights of others. Thus a decision to eavesdrop on employees violates the right to privacy. Sexual harassment is unethical because it violates the right to freedom of conscience. The right of free speech would support whistle-blowers who call attention to illegal or inappropriate action within a company.

JUSTICE APPROACH

justice approach

The ethical concept that moral decisions must be based on standards of equity, fairness, and impartiality.

distributive justice

The concept that different treatment of people should not be based on arbitrary characteristics. In the case of substantive differences, people should be treated differently in proportion to the differences between them.

procedural justice

The concept that rules should be clearly stated and consistently and impartially enforced.

compensatory justice

The concept that individuals should be compensated for the cost of their injuries by the party responsible and also that individuals should not be held responsible for matters over which they have no control.

The **justice approach** holds that moral decisions must be based on standards of equity, fairness, and impartiality. Three types of justice are of concern to managers. **Distributive justice** requires that different treatment of people not be based on arbitrary characteristics. Individuals who are similar in respects relevant to a decision should be treated similarly. Thus men and women should not receive different salaries if they are performing the same job. However, people who differ in a substantive way, such as job skills or job responsibility, can be treated differently in proportion to the differences in skills or responsibility between them. This difference should have a clear relationship to organizational goals and tasks.

  Procedural justice requires that rules be administered fairly. Rules should be clearly stated and be consistently and impartially enforced. **Compensatory justice** argues that individuals should be compensated for the cost of their injuries by the party responsible. Moreover, individuals should not be held responsible for matters over which they have no control.

  The justice approach is closest to the thinking underlying the domain of law in Exhibit 5.1, because it assumes that justice is applied through rules and regulations. This theory does not require complex calculations such as those demanded by a utilitarian approach, nor does it justify self-interest as the individualism approach does. Managers are expected to define attributes on which different treatment of employees is acceptable. Questions such as how minority workers should be compensated for

The *distributive justice* approach is exemplified by Gannett Company's leadership in hiring and promoting women and minorities such as KVUE-TV (Austin, Texas) reporter Deborah Duncan and photographer Lalo Garcia pictured here. In addition to its recruiting and advancement practices, Gannett's Partners in Progress program illustrates the company's commitment to active solicitation of minority and women suppliers. Gannett's efforts have been recognized and rewarded by *Black Enterprise* magazine and Women in Communications, Inc. The number of women and minorities at Gannett continues to rise.

past discrimination are extremely difficult. However, this approach does justify as ethical behavior efforts to correct past wrongs, playing fair under the rules, and insisting on job-relevant differences as the basis for different levels of pay or promotion opportunities. Most of the laws guiding human resource management (Chapter 13) are based on the justice approach.

The challenge of applying these ethical approaches is illustrated by decisions facing companies in the tobacco industry.

BROWN & WILLIAMSON

Brown & Williamson, RJR Nabisco, and other tobacco companies are working hard to increase cigarette exports. Japan, Taiwan, and South Korea are lucrative markets because many people there are heavy smokers. U.S. trade representatives negotiated freer access to foreign markets on behalf of U.S. companies.

Former U.S. Surgeon General Koop thinks U.S. cigarette exports are like Latin American cocaine. He believes it is the height of hypocrisy to export tobacco. Tobacco companies respond that their brands are actually beneficial. For example, Taiwan's most successful brand with 90 percent of the market has double the nicotine and tar of Marlboro. Because Asians are heavy smokers, they are better off with American cigarettes than with the brands they smoke now.[15] ∎

Consider for a moment how you think the ethics approaches support and refute cigarette companies' actions.

⬤ FACTORS AFFECTING ETHICAL CHOICES

When managers are accused of lying, cheating, or stealing, the blame is usually placed on the individual or on the company situation. Most people believe that individuals make ethical choices because of individual integrity, which is true, but it is not the whole story. The values held in the larger organization also shape ethical behavior.[16] Let's examine how both the manager and the organization shape ethical decision making.

THE MANAGER

Managers bring specific personality and behavioral traits to the job. Personal needs, family influence, and religious background all shape a manager's value system. Specific personality characteristics, such as ego strength, self-confidence, and a strong sense of independence may enable managers to make ethical decisions.

One important personal trait is the stage of moral development.[17] A simplified version of one model of personal moral development is shown in Exhibit 5.2. At the *preconventional level,* a manager is concerned with

EXHIBIT 5.2	Stage	What Is Considered to Be Right
Three Levels of Personal Moral Development	Level one: Preconventional	Follows rules to avoid physical punishment. Acts in one's immediate interest. Obedience for its own sake.
SOURCE: Based on L. Kohlberg, "Moral Stages and Moralization: The Cognitive–Developmental Approach," in *Moral Development and Behavior: Theory, Research, and Social Issues*, ed. T. Lickona (New York: Holt, Rhinehart, and Winston, 1976).	Level two: Conventional	Good behavior is living up to what is expected by others. Fulfills duties and obligations of social system. Upholds laws.
	Level three: Principled	Aware that people hold different values. Upholds values and rights regardless of majority opinion. Follows self-chosen ethical principles of justice and right.

At ServiceMaster, *corporate culture* exerts a powerful force for ethical behavior. These are the four official goals displayed at the company's headquarters in Illinois. Employees honor these values while performing jobs as mundane as polishing floors and cleaning carpets for customers. ServiceMaster achieves extraordinary responsiveness and quality because every manager worries not only about ServiceMaster employees, but about its customer's employees too. Not surprisingly, ServiceMaster is one of the most admired companies in the United States.

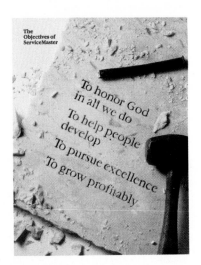

the external rewards and punishment and the concrete personal consequences. At level two, called the *conventional level*, people learn to conform to the expectations of good behavior as defined by colleagues, friends, family, and society. People at the conventional level respect external expectations. At level three, called the *principled level*, individuals develop an internal set of standards and values. The individual will even disobey laws that violate these principles. Internal values are more important than expectations of significant others.

The great majority of managers operate at level two. A few have not advanced beyond level one. Only about 20 percent of American adults reach the level three stage of moral development. People at level three are able to act in an independent, ethical manner regardless of expectations from others inside or outside the organization. Managers at level three of moral development will make ethical decisions whatever the organizational consequences for them. The Manager's Shoptalk box lists some general guidelines to follow for making ethical decisions.

Higher levels of ethical conduct, especially the principled level, are important because of the impact of globalization upon organizational ethics and corporate culture. American managers need to develop sensitivity and openness to other systems. Cross-cultural alliances and mergers create the need to work out differences where ethical values differ. For example, bribery is an accepted way of conducting business in many developing countries. "Grease" payments to customs officials are considered part of their living wage. Failure to play the game could result in loss of outlets, suppliers, and foreign revenues. On the other hand, foreign bribery is illegal under the U.S. Foreign Corrupt Practices Act. Managers must use mature ethical judgment in resolving these difficult international issues.[18]

THE ORGANIZATION

The values adopted within the organization are important, especially when we understand that most people are at the level two stage of moral development, which means they believe their duty is to fulfill obligations and expectations of others. As discussed in Chapter 4, corporate culture can exert a powerful influence on behavior in organizations. For example, an investigation of thefts and kickbacks in the oil business

GUIDELINES FOR ETHICAL DECISION MAKING

A list of guidelines follows that you, the future manager, can apply to difficult social problems and ethical dilemmas you almost surely will face one day. The guidelines will not tell you exactly what to do, but taken in the context of the text discussion, they will help you evaluate the situation more clearly by examining your own values and those of your organization. The answers to these questions will force you to think hard about the social and ethical consequences of your behavior.

1. Is the problem/dilemma really what it appears to be? If you are not sure, *find out*.
2. Is the action you are considering legal? Ethical? If you are not sure, *find out*.
3. Do you understand the position of those who oppose the action you are considering? Is it reasonable?
4. Whom does the action benefit? Harm? How much? How long?
5. Would you be willing to allow everyone to do what you are considering doing?
6. Have you sought the opinion of others who are knowledgeable on the subject and who would be objective?
7. Would your action be embarrassing to you if it were made known to your family, friends, coworkers, or superiors? Would you be comfortable defending your actions to an investigative reporter on the evening news?

There are no correct answers to these questions in an absolute sense. Yet, if you determine that an action is potentially harmful to someone, would be embarrassing to you, or if you do not know the ethical or legal consequences, these guidelines will help you clarify whether the action is socially responsible. ■

SOURCE: Anthony M. Pagano and Jo Ann Verdin, *The External Environment of Business* (New York: Wiley, 1988), Chapter 5.

found that the cause was the historical acceptance of thefts and kickbacks. Employees were socialized into those values and adopted them as appropriate. In most companies, employees believe that if they do not go along with the ethical values expressed, their jobs will be in jeopardy or they will not fit in.[19]

Culture can be examined to see the kinds of ethical signals given to employees. Exhibit 5.3 indicates questions to ask to understand the cultural system. Heroes provide role models that can either support or refute ethical decision making. Founder Tom Watson stood for integrity at IBM and his values are still very much alive. With respect to company rituals, high ethical standards are affirmed and communicated through public awards and ceremonies. Myths and stories can reinforce heroic ethical behavior. For example, a story at Johnson & Johnson describes its reaction to the cyanide poisoning of Tylenol capsule users. After seven people in Chicago died, the capsules were removed from the market voluntarily, costing the company over $100 million. This action was taken against the advice of external agencies—FBI and FDA—but was necessary because of Johnson & Johnson's ethical standards.

Culture is not the only aspect of an organization that influences ethics, but it is a major force because it defines company values. Other aspects of the organization such as explicit rules and policies, the reward system, the extent to which the company cares for its people, the selection system, emphasis on legal and professional standards, and leadership

E X H I B I T 5 . 3	1.	Identify the organization's heroes. What values do they represent? Given an ambiguous ethical dilemma, what decision would they make and why?
Questions for Analyzing a Company's Cultural Impact on Ethics	2.	What are some important organizational rituals? How do they encourage or discourage ethical behavior? Who gets the awards, people of integrity or individuals who use unethical methods to attain success?
	3.	What are the ethical messages sent to new entrants into the organization—must they obey authority at all costs, or is questioning authority acceptable or even desirable?
SOURCE: Linda Klebe Trevino, "A Cultural Perspective on Changing and Developing Organizational Ethics," in *Research in Organizational Change and Development*, eds. R. Woodman and W. Pasmore (Greenwich, Conn.: JAI Press, 1990), 4.	4.	Does analysis of organizational stories and myths reveal individuals who stand up for what's right, or is conformity the valued characteristic? Do people get fired or promoted in these stories?
	5.	Does language exist for discussing ethical concerns? Is this language routinely incorporated and encouraged in business decision making?
	6.	What informal socialization processes exist and what norms for ethical/unethical behavior do they promote?

and decision processes can also all have an impact on ethical values and manager decision making.[20]

WHAT IS SOCIAL RESPONSIBILITY?

social responsibility

The obligation of organization management to make decisions and take actions that will enhance the welfare and interests of society as well as the organization.

Now let's turn to the issue of social responsibility. In one sense, the concept of corporate social responsibility, like ethics, is easy to understand: it means distinguishing right from wrong and doing right. It means being a good corporate citizen. The formal definition of **social responsibility** is management's obligation to make choices and take actions that will contribute to the welfare and interests of society as well as to the organization's.[21]

As straightforward as this definition seems, social responsibility can be a difficult concept to grasp, because different people have different beliefs as to which actions improve society's welfare.[22] To make matters worse, social responsibility covers a range of issues, many of which are ambiguous with respect to right or wrong. For example, if a bank deposits the money from a trust fund into a low-interest account for 90 days, from which it makes a substantial profit, has it been unethical? How about two companies' engaging in intense competition, such as that between Cleveland Electric Illuminating Co. and Cleveland Public Power? Is it socially responsible for the stronger corporation to drive the weaker one into bankruptcy? Or consider companies such as A. H. Robins, maker of the Dalkon shield, Manville Corporation, maker of asbestos, Eastern Airlines, or Texaco, the oil company, all of which declared bankruptcy—which is perfectly legal—to avoid mounting financial obligations to suppliers, labor unions, or competitors. These examples contain moral, legal, and economic considerations that make socially responsible behavior hard to define. A company's environmental impact must also be taken into consideration, as illustrated in the Focus on the Natural Environment box.

THE GLOBAL GREEN MOVEMENT

A company obsessed with "the Green" these days is probably concerned with more than money. In worldwide response to environmental problems, the Green Movement increasingly affects the way companies operate. Hand in hand with international free trade goals are the demands for a cleaner environment and increased social responsibility.

The increased emphasis upon environmental concerns was highlighted by the 1992 Earth Summit in Rio de Janeiro. Billed as the largest such meeting in history, the Earth Summit focused on issues such as emissions control, global warming,

deforestation, and the extinction of plant and animal life. With global population expected to double by 2050, 90 percent in underdeveloped countries, the need for clean air and water, preservation of rain forests, and other environmental concerns intensifies.

Governments and corporations are responding. The 1992 Earth Summit is just one example of government cooperation to address the problems. In the United States, President George Bush pledged expenditures of $1.2 trillion for environmental protection through the year 2002. Fueled by consumer demand for ecologically safe products, the European Community has increased government restrictions on products such as plastic bottling.

Corporations are showing

increased ethical awareness too. 3M has been a leader in waste-reduction efforts with its "3 P's" program (Pollution Prevention Pays). McDonald's responded quickly to consumer demands to replace styrene packaging with paper. Internationally, Volkswagon and BMW are making efforts to create recyclable automobiles. These ongoing efforts illustrate corporate commitment to a healthy natural environment. ∎

SOURCE: Art Kleiner, "What Does It Mean to Be Green?" *Harvard Business Review* (July-August 1991), 38–47; Eugene Robinson, "At Earth Summit, South Aims to Send Bill North," *Washington Post*, June 1, 1992, A1, A14; Shawn Tully, "What the 'Greens' Mean for Business," *Fortune*, October 23, 1989, 159–164; and *U.S. News & World Report*, "Bush's Bumpy Road to Rio," June 22, 1992, 20.

● ORGANIZATIONAL STAKEHOLDERS

One reason for the difficulty understanding social responsibility is that managers must confront the question "responsibility to whom?" Recall from Chapter 3 that the organization's environment consists of several sectors in both the task and general environment. From a social responsibility perspective, enlightened organizations view the internal and external environment as a variety of stakeholders.

A **stakeholder** is any group within or outside the organization that has a stake in the organization's performance. Each stakeholder has a different criterion of responsiveness, because it has a different interest in the organization.[23]

Exhibit 5.4 illustrates important stakeholders, including employees, customers, owners, creditors, suppliers, and investors. Investors', owners', and suppliers' interests are served by managerial efficiency, that is, use of resources to achieve profits. Employees expect work satisfaction, pay, and good supervision. Customers are concerned with decisions about the quality and availability of goods and services.

stakeholder

Any group within or outside the organization that has a stake in the organization's performance.

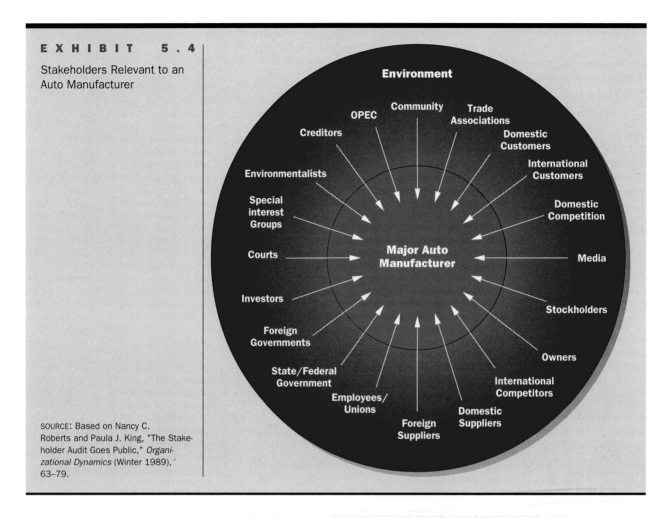

EXHIBIT 5.4

Stakeholders Relevant to an Auto Manufacturer

SOURCE: Based on Nancy C. Roberts and Paula J. King, "The Stakeholder Audit Goes Public," *Organizational Dynamics* (Winter 1989), 63–79.

Other important stakeholders are the government and the community. Most corporations exist only under the proper charter and licenses and operate within the limits of safety laws, environmental protection requirements, and other laws and regulations in the government sector. The community includes local government, the natural and physical environments, and the quality of life provided for residents. Special-interest groups, still another stakeholder, may include trade associations, political action committees, professional associations, and consumerists. Socially responsible organizations consider the effects of their actions upon all stakeholders. Today, special-interest groups continue to be one of the largest stakeholder concerns that companies face.

Enlightened corporations invest in a number of philanthropic and in-house causes that benefit stakeholders. Cray Research, Inc., invests heavily in science and math education, providing both funding and employee expertise.[24] In New York, Alexander's Department Stores, American Express, Citibank, and IBM are all involved with high schools, either offering courses, providing realistic previews of job demands, or simply taking teenagers to Yankee Stadium if they have good school attendance records.[25] DuPont executive Faith Wohl is a corporate pioneer in the area of work-family coordination—attempting to meet the personal and social needs of employees. Wohl's division established child care centers, job sharing for working mothers, and workshops addressing issues such as rape prevention, racial bias, and sexual harassment.[26]

Well-meaning companies sometimes run afoul of stakeholders anyway. For example, Fina, Inc., established an oil refinery in Port Arthur, Texas, in 1937. Over the years, subdivisions of attractive ranch-style homes grew up in the shadow of the Fina plant. Homeowners became unhappy with the plant in their midst because of its noise and odor. Residents expected the company to purchase their homes at top market price. Fina made several good faith efforts to resolve problems and then agreed to purchase the homes because the residents had legitimate gripes.[27] Companies such as Fina and DuPont are acting in a socially responsible way by helping stakeholders.

● EVALUATING CORPORATE SOCIAL PERFORMANCE

Once a company is aware of its stakeholders, what criteria can be used to evaluate social performance? One model for evaluating corporate social performance is presented in Exhibit 5.5. The model indicates that total corporate social responsibility can be subdivided into four criteria—economic, legal, ethical, and discretionary responsibilities.[28] The responsibilities are ordered from bottom to top based on their relative magnitude and the frequency with which managers deal with each issue.

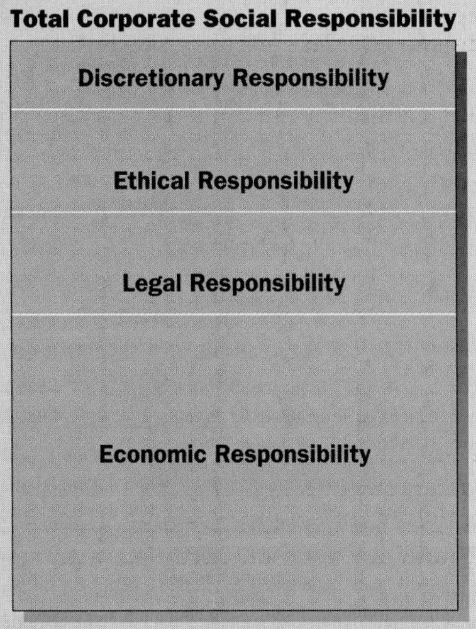

Total Corporate Social Responsibility

Discretionary Responsibility

Ethical Responsibility

Legal Responsibility

Economic Responsibility

EXHIBIT 5.5

Criteria of Corporate Social Performance

SOURCE: Archie B. Carroll, "A Three-Dimensional Conceptual Model of Corporate Performance," *Academy of Management Review* 4 (1979), 499.

Note the similarity between the categories in Exhibit 5.5 and those in Exhibit 5.1. In both cases, ethical issues are located between the areas of legal and freely discretionary responsibilities. Exhibit 5.5 also has an economic category, because profits are a major reason for corporations' existence.

ECONOMIC RESPONSIBILITIES

The first criterion of social responsibility is *economic responsibility*. The business institution is, above all, the basic economic unit of society. Its responsibility is to produce the goods and services that society wants and to maximize profits for its owners and shareholders. Economic responsibility, carried to the extreme, is called the *profit-maximizing view*, advocated by Nobel economist Milton Friedman. This view argues that the corporation should be operated on a profit-oriented basis, with its sole mission to increase its profits so long as it stays within the rules of the game.[29]

The purely profit-maximizing view is no longer considered an adequate criterion of performance in Canada, the United States, and Europe. This approach means that economic gain is the only social responsibility and can lead companies into trouble. A notorious example was Salomon Brothers' attempt to corner the Treasury securities market. Corporate greed, fostered by former chairman John Gutfreund's "win-at-all-costs" culture, resulted in mistakes that led to record penalties of $280 million.[30]

LEGAL RESPONSIBILITIES

All modern societies lay down ground rules, laws, and regulations that businesses are expected to follow. *Legal responsibility* defines what society deems as important with respect to appropriate corporate behavior.[31] Businesses are expected to fulfill their economic goals within the legal framework. Legal requirements are imposed by local town councils, state legislators, and federal regulatory agencies.

Organizations that knowingly break the law are poor performers in this category. Intentionally manufacturing defective goods or billing a client for work not done is illegal. An example of the punishment given to one company that broke the law is shown in Exhibit 5.6.

ETHICAL RESPONSIBILITIES

Ethical responsibility includes behaviors that are not necessarily codified into law and may not serve the corporation's direct economic interests. As described earlier in this chapter, to be *ethical*, organization decision makers should act with equity, fairness, and impartiality, respect the rights of individuals, and provide different treatment of individuals only when relevant to the organization's goals and tasks.[32] *Unethical* behavior occurs when decisions enable an individual or company to gain at the expense of society.

When Control Data took a chance by building a plant in Minneapolis' inner city, it performed an ethical act because top management

February 12, 1985

American Caster Corporation

Dear Businesses & Residents of the City & County of Los Angeles

Pollution of our environment has become a crisis.

Intentional clandestine acts of illegal disposal of hazardous waste, or "midnight dumping" are violent crimes against the community.

Over the past 2 years almost a dozen Chief Executive Officers of both large and small corporations have been sent to jail by the L.A. Toxic Waste Strike Force.

They have also been required to pay huge fines; pay for clean-ups; speak in public about their misdeeds; and in some cases place ads publicizing their crime and punishment.

THE RISKS OF BEING CAUGHT ARE TOO HIGH—
AND THE CONSEQUENCES IF CAUGHT ARE NOT WORTH IT!

We are paying the price. *TODAY*, while you read this ad our President and Vice President are serving time in *JAIL* and we were forced to place this ad.

PLEASE TAKE THE LEGAL ALTERNATIVE AND PROTECT OUR ENVIRONMENT.

Very Truly Yours,

American Caster Corporation
141 WEST AVENUE 34
LOS ANGELES, CA 90031

EXHIBIT 5.6

One Company's Punishment for Breaking the Law

SOURCE: Barry C. Groveman and John L. Segal, "Pollution Police Pursue Chemical Criminals," *Business and Society Review* 55 (Fall 1985), 41.

wanted to provide equal opportunity for the disadvantaged. Other businesses had built in the ghetto and failed. Chairman Norris insisted that the plant attempt to be profitable, but the company also wanted to provide jobs to inner-city residents. In this case, the ethical goals were compatible with the economic goals, and the company achieved both.[33]

DISCRETIONARY RESPONSIBILITIES

<u>Discretionary responsibility</u> is purely voluntary and guided by a company's desire to make social contributions not mandated by economics, law, or ethics. Discretionary activities include generous philanthropic contributions that offer no payback to the company and are not expected. An example of discretionary behavior occurred when Pittsburgh Brewing Company helped laid-off steelworkers by establishing and contributing to food banks in the Pittsburgh area. It also started a fund-raising program in which people could drink beer with members of the Pittsburgh Steelers for a $5 contribution to their local food bank. Discretionary responsibility is the highest criterion of social responsibility, because it goes beyond societal expectations to contribute to the community's welfare.

discretionary responsibility

Organizational responsibility that is voluntary and guided by the organization's desire to make social contributions not mandated by economics, law, or ethics.

"The Vietnam Wall Experience," a project launched in 1990 by Service Corporation International (SCI), is an example of *discretionary responsibility*. SCI is the largest owner and operator of funeral homes and cemeteries in North America. The 100-city tour of the 240 foot replica of the Vietnam Veteran Memorial expands SCI's grief-counseling program by assisting thousands of Americans in the national grief and healing process following the Vietnam War. The girl pictured here might never have the opportunity to travel to Washington, D.C. SCI uses its discretionary responsibility to meet the needs of these people.

● CORPORATE ACTIONS TOWARD SOCIAL DEMANDS

Confronted with a specific social demand, how might a corporation respond? If a stakeholder such as the local government places a demand on the company, what types of corporate action might be taken? Management scholars have developed a scale of response actions that companies use when a social issue confronts them.[34] These actions are obstructive, defensive, accommodative, and proactive and are illustrated on the continuum in Exhibit 5.7.

obstructive response

A response to social demands in which the organization denies responsibility, claims that evidence of misconduct is misleading or distorted, and attempts to obstruct investigation.

OBSTRUCTIVE.   Companies that adopt **obstructive responses** deny all responsibility, claim that evidence of wrongdoing is misleading or distorted, and place obstacles to delay investigation. During the Watergate years, such obstruction was labeled *stonewalling*. A. H. Robins Company reportedly used obstructive actions when it received warnings about its Dalkon shield, an intrauterine device. The company built a wall around itself. It stood against all evidence and insisted to the public that the product was safe and effective. The company spared no effort to resist investigation. As word about injuries caused by the Dalkon shield kept pouring in, one attorney was told to search the files and destroy all papers pertaining to the product.[35]

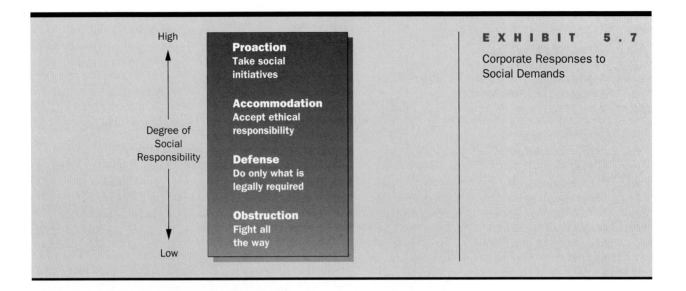

EXHIBIT 5.7

Corporate Responses to
Social Demands

DEFENSIVE. The **defensive response** means that the company admits to some errors of omission or commission. The company cuts its losses by defending itself but is not obstructive. Defensive managers generally believe that "these things happen, but they are nobody's fault." Goodyear adopted a defensive strategy by deciding to keep its South Africa plants open and provided an intelligent argument for why that was the proper action.

ACCOMMODATIVE. An **accommodative response** means that the company accepts social responsibility for its actions, although it may do so in response to external pressure. Firms that adopt this action try to meet economic, legal, and ethical responsibilities. If outside forces apply pressure, managers agree to curtail ethically questionable activities. Exxon's decision to clean up the oil spill in Prince William Sound was an accommodative decision based largely on the public's outcry.

PROACTIVE. The **proactive response** means that firms take the lead in social issues. They seek to learn what is in the public interest and respond without coaxing or pressure from stakeholders. One example of proactive behavior is the Potlatch Corporation. Potlatch makes milk cartons and came up with the idea of printing photographs of missing children on them. The company reported that within days after the Alta-Dena Dairy of Los Angeles placed a missing-kids carton in grocery stores, one of the youngsters returned home.[36] Another proactive response is corporate philanthropy. Many companies, including Miller Brewing, Coca-Cola, and Westinghouse, make generous donations to universities, United Way, and other charitable groups as a way of reaching out and improving society.

These four categories of action are similar to the scale of social performance described in Exhibit 5.5. Obstructiveness tends to occur in firms whose actions are based solely on economic considerations. Defensive organizations are willing to work within the letter of the law.

defensive response

A response to social demands in which the organization admits to some errors of commission or omission but does not act obstructively.

accommodative response

A response to social demands in which the organization accepts—often under pressure—social responsibility for its actions to comply with the public interest.

proactive response

A response to social demands in which the organization seeks to learn what is in its constituencies' interest and to respond without pressure from them.

Corporate *proactive responses* toward *social demands* recognize and meet both employee and community needs. At The Stride Rite Corporation, the "bottom line" is its investment in people. The company has taken the lead in meeting its social responsibilities. Stride Rite was the first company to offer on-site day care and one of the first to offer a smoke-free workplace policy. In 1990, Stride Rite opened the first Intergenerational Day Care Center (pictured here). These unique day care facilities bring together elderly people and children in a loving environment. The reading, play, and conversation bring special joy to all participants.

Accommodative organizations respond to ethical pressures. Proactive organizations use discretionary responsibilities to enhance community welfare.

Beech-Nut Nutrition Corporation was accused of unethical and socially irresponsible behavior. How would you evaluate its response?

 ## BEECH-NUT NUTRITION CORPORATION

To Beech-Nut, feeding babies is a sacred trust. Bottles of fruit juice say, "100% fruit juice." Yet Beech-Nut was found to have adulterated its best-selling line of apple juice products. Gerome LiCari became suspicious that the concentrate acquired from suppliers was diluted and alerted management, who resisted this information. The top managers were not hardened criminals trying to swindle customers. They were honest and well respected, but under great financial pressure. The cheap concentrate from the new supplier saved millions of dollars and managers simply did not want to recognize that they were receiving a poor product. Beech-Nut was running on a shoestring, and enormous financial pressure forced managers to stay with the low-cost supplier.

As suspicions began to circulate, state and federal agencies started investigating. Had Beech-Nut admitted its error, payment of a fine would have closed the issue. But management stonewalled, and this became the issue. The case changed from civil to criminal, and it became a nightmare. Beech-Nut's strategy was to stall investigations and avoid publicity until it could unload its diluted apple juice products. The case ended with Beech-Nut's two top executives and its concentrate supplier indicted for conspiring to defraud the public. The two executives were each sentenced to one year and a day in prison and charged a $100,000 fine. Beech-Nut paid almost $10 million in settlements and fines.[37] ■

● MANAGING COMPANY ETHICS AND SOCIAL RESPONSIBILITY

Many managers are concerned with improving the ethical climate and social responsiveness of their companies. They do not want to be surprised or be forced into an obstructionist or defensive position. As one expert on the topic of ethics said, "Management is responsible for creating and sustaining conditions in which people are likely to behave themselves."[38] Managers must take active steps to ensure that the company stays on an ethical footing. Management methods for helping organizations be more responsible include leadership by example, codes of ethics, ethical structures, and supporting whistle-blowers.

LEADERSHIP BY EXAMPLE.   The Business Roundtable, an association of chief executives from 250 large corporations, issued a report on ethics policy and practice in companies such as Boeing, Chemical Bank, General Mills, GTE, Xerox, Johnson & Johnson, and Hewlett-Packard.[39] The report concluded that no point emerged more clearly than the crucial role of top management. The chief executive officer and senior managers need to be openly and strongly committed to ethical conduct. They must give constant leadership in renewing the ethical values of the organization. They must be active in communicating that commitment in speeches, directives, company publications, and especially in actions. Top managers must set the tone of the organization by the example of their behavior.

CODE OF ETHICS.   A **code of ethics** is a formal statement of the company's values concerning ethics and social issues; it communicates to employees what the company stands for. Codes of ethics tend to exist in two types: principle-based statements and policy-based statements. *Principle-based statements* are designed to affect corporate culture, define fundamental values, and contain general language about company responsibilities, quality of products, and treatment of employees. General statements of principle are often called *corporate credos*. Examples are GTE's "Vision and Values," Johnson & Johnson's "The Credo," and Hewlett-Packard's "The HP Way."[40]

Policy-based statements generally outline the procedures to be used in specific ethical situations. These situations include marketing practice, conflicts of interest, observance of laws, proprietary information, political gifts, and equal opportunities. Examples of policy-based statements are Boeing's "Business Conduct Guidelines," Chemical Bank's "Code of Ethics," GTE's "Code of Business Ethics" and "Anti-Trust and Conflict of Interest Guidelines," and Norton's "Norton Policy on Business Ethics."[41]

code of ethics
A formal statement of the organization's values regarding ethics and social issues.

A strong example of *principle-based statements* is Rockwell International's "What We Believe" credo, which focuses, among other things, on recognition of the company's corporate citizenship in the community. Ethical structures such as ethics awareness training, corporate Ombudsmen, and a Business Standards Compliance Committee show Rockwell's commitment to ethics. Encouraged by the corporate structure, Rockwell employees work to improve their communities. Here Rockwell volunteers in Dallas make repairs to the home of a senior citizen.

Codes of ethics state the values or behaviors that are expected and those that will not be tolerated, backed up by management's action. Without top management support, there is little insurance that the code will be followed. Caterpillar's code of ethics covers worldwide business conduct.

 ## CATERPILLAR, INC.

Caterpillar, Inc., published "A Code of Worldwide Business Conduct and Operating Principles" that begins with a clear statement of corporate values. The code is 14 pages long and covers human relationships, disposal of waste, privacy of information about employees, product quality, sharing of technology, public responsibility, observance of local laws, and inside information. The initial statement of "Business Ethics," quoted below, indicates that Caterpillar expects its employees to display ethical behavior well above that required by law.

> The law is a floor. Ethical business conduct should normally exist at a level well above the minimum required by law.
>
> One of a company's most valuable assets is a reputation for integrity. If that be tarnished, customers, investors, suppliers, employees, and those who sell our products will seek affiliation with other, more attractive companies. We intend to hold a single high standard of integrity everywhere. We will keep our word. We won't promise more than we can reasonably expect to deliver; nor will we make commitments we don't intend to keep.
>
> The goal of corporate communication is the truth—well and persuasively told. In our advertising and other public communications, we will avoid not only untruths, but also exaggeration and overstatement. Caterpillar employees shall not accept costly entertainment or gifts (excepting mementos and nov-

elties of nominal value) from dealers, suppliers, and others with whom we do business. And we don't tolerate circumstances that produce, or reasonably appear to produce, conflict between personal interests of an employee and interests of the company.

We seek long-lasting relationships—based on integrity—with all whose activities touch upon our own.

The ethical performance of the enterprise is the sum of the ethics of the men and women who work here. Thus, we are all expected to adhere to high standards of personal integrity. For example, perjury or any other illegal act ostensibly taken to 'protect' the company is wrong. A sale made because of deception is wrong. A production quota achieved through questionable means or figures is wrong. The end doesn't justify the means.[42] ■

ETHICAL STRUCTURES.   Ethical structures represent the various systems, positions, and programs a company can undertake to implement ethical behavior. An **ethics committee** is a group of executives appointed to oversee company ethics. The committee provides rulings on questionable ethical issues. The ethics committee assumes responsibility for disciplining wrongdoers, which is essential if the organization is to directly influence employee behavior. For example, Boeing has an ethics committee of senior managers that reports directly to the board of directors. An **ethics ombudsman** is an official given the responsibility of corporate conscience who hears and investigates ethical complaints and points out potential ethics failures to top management. Pitney Bowes has an ethics ombudsman and offers training seminars and a conduct guide on ethics for employees.

Other structures are ethics training programs and hot lines. For example, Chemical Bank has extensive education programs. All new employees attend an orientation session at which they read and sign off on Chemical's code of ethics. Another part of the program provides vice-presidents with training in ethical decision making.[43] The bank has several other seminars, and the CEO is personally involved by stating his commitment to ethical behavior. A hot line is a toll-free number to which employees can report questionable behavior as well as possible fraud, waste, or abuse. For example, Boeing has a toll-free number for employees to report any kind of ethical violation. LTV Corporation uses a hot line to supplement existing procedures for reporting violations. No reprisals will be taken against anyone using it.

A strong ethics program is important, but it is no guarantee against lapses. Recall Dow Corning, the opening case for Chapter 4, whose faulty silicone breast implants shocked the business community. Dow Corning pioneered an ethics program that was looked upon as a model. Established in the mid-1970s, Dow's ambitious ethics program included the Business Conduct committee, training programs, regular reviews and audits to monitor compliance, and reports to the Audit and Social Responsibility committee. What went wrong? The ethics program dealt with the overall environment, but specific programs such as product safety were handled through normal channels—in this case the Medical Device Business Board, which wanted further safety studies.[44] Dow Corning's problems sent a warning to other industries. It is not enough to *have* an impressive ethics program. The ethics program must be

ethics committee

A group of executives assigned to oversee the organization's ethics by ruling on questionable issues and disciplining violators.

ethics ombudsman

An official given the responsibility of corporate conscience who hears and investigates ethics complaints and points out potential ethical failures to top management.

merged with day-to-day operations, encouraging ethical decisions to be made throughout the company.

WHISTLE-BLOWING.   Employee disclosure of illegal, immoral, or illegitimate practices on the employer's part is called **whistle-blowing**.[45] Anyone in the organization can blow the whistle if he or she detects illegal or immoral organizational activities. Whistle-blowers often report wrongdoings to outsiders, such as regulatory agencies, senators, representatives, or newspaper reporters. In enlightened companies, whistle-blowers can also report to an ethics advocate or ethics committee.

Whistle-blowers must be protected if this is to be an effective ethical safeguard; otherwise, they will suffer and the company may continue its unethical or illegal activity. Helen Guercil noticed something peculiar when she went to work as a secretary to the bankruptcy court of Detroit. The multimillion-dollar cases seemed to be heard by the same judge and handled by the same attorneys. She discovered that one lawyer had been awarded $400,000 in bankruptcy fees from this judge. She blew the whistle when she discovered evidence of special favors bought with lavish trips, expensive gifts, and on-the-job sex. An investigation led to the retirement of two judges, the indictment of the chief clerk, and the conviction of the attorney who had been awarded all the money. However, Helen Guercil received a lot of pressure on the job and was eventually fired.[46]

■
whistle-blowing

The disclosure by an employee of illegal, immoral, or illegitimate practices by the organization.

"Do Good Citizens Finish First?" Rohm & Haas Company believes success can be measured in many categories that do not show up in financial statements. An example is the smile on the face of this child—one of over 800 participants in the company-sponsored Houston Handicapped Kids Day program. The annual event brings together disabled children and their families for a day of supervised play and activities, generating long-lasting positive impact.

● DO GOOD CITIZENS FINISH FIRST?

The relationship of a corporation's social responsibility to its financial performance concerns both managers and management scholars and has generated a lively debate.[47] One concern of managers is whether good citizenship will hurt performance—after all, ethics programs cost money. A number of studies have been undertaken to determine whether heightened ethical and social responsiveness increases or decreases financial performance. Studies have provided varying results but generally have found that there is a small positive relationship between social responsibility and financial performance.[48] These findings are very encouraging, because they mean that use of resources for the social good does not hurt the company.

A related finding is that firms founded on spiritual values usually perform very well. These firms succeed because they have a clear mission, employees seldom have alcohol and drug problems, and a strong family orientation exists. One of the largest and most successful companies is Chick-fil-A, Inc., which refuses to open on Sunday. The Sunday closing costs some sales and has gotten the chain frozen out of some shopping malls, but the policy helps attract excellent workers, and this offsets any disadvantages.[49]

The important point is that being ethical and socially responsible does not hurt a firm. Enlightened firms can use their discretion to contribute to society's welfare and, in so doing, improve performance.

SUMMARY AND MANAGEMENT SOLUTION

Ethics and social responsibility are hot topics for managers in the 1990s. One study reported that 45 percent of America's 1,000 largest companies entered the 1990s with established ethics programs or workshops, and the percentage was expected to increase.[50] The ethical domain of behavior pertains to values of right and wrong. Ethical decisions and behavior are typically guided by a value system. Four value-based approaches that serve as criteria for ethical decision making are utilitarian, individualism, moral rights, and justice. For an individual manager, the ability to make correct ethical choices will depend on both individual and organizational characteristics. An important individual characteristic is level of moral development. Corporate culture is an organizational characteristic that influences ethical behavior.

Corporate social responsibility concerns a company's values toward society. How can organizations be good corporate citizens? The model for evaluating social performance uses four criteria: economic, legal, ethical, and discretionary. Organizations may use four types of response to specific social pressures: obstructive, defensive, accommodative, and proactive. Evaluating corporate social behavior often requires assessing its impact on organizational stakeholders. Techniques for improving social responsiveness include leadership, codes of ethics, ethical structures, and whistle-blowing. Companies that are socially responsible perform as well as—and often better than—companies that are not socially responsible.

Nynex's ethics crisis surrounding overbilling and sleazy parties led to a complete reappraisal of its approach to ethics and social responsibility. In 1990, Nynex launched a massive ethics program. The first step was to establish a full-time ethics office with a vice-president for ethics and business conduct. A code of ethics was issued that stressed core values of quality, ethics, and caring. A massive training program included day-long seminars for all top managers. Nynex also established methods for reporting misconduct. Corporate surveys and a whistle-blower's hot line provided employees with new avenues for relaying concerns. Nynex has implemented excellent techniques in its goal to prevent further ethical lapses.[51]

DISCUSSION QUESTIONS

1. Dr. Martin Luther King, Jr., said, "As long as there is poverty in the world, I can never be rich. . . . As long as diseases are rampant, I can never be healthy. . . . I can never be what I ought to be until you are what you ought to be." Discuss this quote with respect to the material in this chapter. Would this be true for corporations, too?

2. Environmentalists are trying to pass laws for oil spills that would remove all liability limits for the oil companies. This would punish

corporations financially. Is this the best way to influence companies to be socially responsible?

3. Compare and contrast the utilitarian approach with the moral-rights approach to ethical decision making. Which do you believe is the best for managers to follow? Why?

4. Imagine yourself in a situation of being encouraged to inflate your expense account. Do you think your choice would be most affected by your individual moral development or by the cultural values of the company for which you worked? Explain.

5. Is it socially responsible for organizations to undertake political activity or join with others in a trade association to influence the government? Discuss.

6. The criteria of corporate social responsibility suggest that economic responsibilities are of the greatest magnitude, followed by legal, ethical, and discretionary responsibilities. How do these four types of responsibility relate to corporate responses to social demands? Discuss.

7. From where do managers derive ethical values? What can managers do to help define ethical standards for the corporation?

8. Have you ever experienced an ethical dilemma? Evaluate the dilemma with respect to its impact on other people.

9. Lincoln Electric considers customers and employees to be more important stakeholders than shareholders. Is it appropriate for management to define some stakeholders as more important than others? Should all stakeholders be considered equal?

10. Do you think a code of ethics combined with an ethics committee would be more effective than leadership for implementing ethical behavior? Discuss.

MANAGEMENT IN PRACTICE: EXPERIENTIAL EXERCISE

● ETHICAL WORK CLIMATES

Answer the following questions by circling the number that best describes an organization for which you have worked.

	Disagree				Agree
1. What is the best for everyone in the company is the major consideration here.	1	2	3	4	5
2. Our major concern is always what is best for the other person.	1	2	3	4	5
3. People are expected to comply with the law and professional standards over and above other considerations.	1	2	3	4	5
4. In this company, the first consideration is whether a decision violates any law.	1	2	3	4	5
5. It is very important to follow the company's rules and procedures here.	1	2	3	4	5

	Disagree				Agree
6. People in this company strictly obey the company policies.	1	2	3	4	5
7. In this company, people are mostly out for themselves.	1	2	3	4	5
8. People are expected to do anything to further the company's interests, regardless of the consequences.	1	2	3	4	5
9. In this company, people are guided by their own personal ethics.	1	2	3	4	5
10. Each person in this company decides for himself or herself what is right and wrong.	1	2	3	4	5

Total Score _____

Add up your score. These questions measure the dimensions of an organization's ethical climate. Questions 1 and 2 measure caring for people, questions 3 and 4 measure lawfulness, questions 5 and 6 measure rules adherence, questions 7 and 8 measure emphasis on financial and company performance, and questions 9 and 10 measure individual independence. Questions 7 and 8 are reverse scored. A total score above 40 indicates a very positive ethical climate. A score from 30 to 40 indicates above-average ethical climate. A score from 20 to 30 indicates a below-average ethical climate, and a score below 20 indicates a very poor ethical climate.

Go back over the questions and think about changes that you could have made to improve the ethical climate in the organization. Discuss with other students what you could do as a manager to improve ethics in future companies you work for.

SOURCE: Based on Bart Victor and John B. Cullen, "The Organizational Bases of Ethical Work Climates," *Administrative Science Quarterly* 33 (1988), 101–125.

CASES FOR ANALYSIS

PHILIP MORRIS

The people attending the opening night gala for the Alvin Ailey American Dance Theatre in Washington's Kennedy Center did not breathe a word about smoking. They mingled through the invitations-only crowd consisting of politicians, art lovers, and the media, munching on strawberries and salmon, listening to the steel band, and enjoying the show. Except for the free packs of cigarettes being offered, an unknowing observer would never guess that the bash was funded entirely by Philip Morris, the maker of Virginia Slims, Merit, Marlboro, and other cigarette brands.

Philip Morris spends about $13 million a year on art events. It is widely praised for its contributions to smaller arts organizations, often without publicity. It supports institutions such as Carnegie Hall and the Joffrey Ballet.

Those who accept invitations to these events politely refrain from using the occasion to debate smoking. The object is not the promotion of smoking. Philip Morris is selling itself. Philip Morris achieves access to presidents, prime ministers, and the rich and powerful for "the calculated business of portraying themselves as good citizens—and indeed they are not killers," says Charles Simon, a Whitney Museum trustee.

Arts sponsorship by Philip Morris has sparked debate, however. Some people cannot ignore 300,000 deaths in the United States each year attributed to smoking. Nor can they ignore Philip Morris' proclivity toward strong ad campaigns in low-income areas where smoking levels are high. But a money-hungry art world appears to have few qualms. It does not care where the cash comes from, so long as it keeps flowing. Some claim the art community is prostituting itself with cigarette sponsorship. Others respond by arguing that Philip Morris sells products other than cigarettes. It owns Miller Brewing Company and General Foods Corporation. However, 80 percent of Philip Morris' profits are from cigarette sales. Peter Brown of the Alvin Ailey American Dance Theatre, which received more than $420,000 from Philip Morris in two years, does not seem to mind. He said, "We would accept money from the Mafia if they offered it."

● **QUESTIONS**

1. Is Philip Morris acting in a socially responsible way? What criteria of social responsibility is it following?
2. Are art organizations acting in a socially responsible way by accepting this money? Should they take a symbolic stand against cigarette smoking?

3. Do you think this money is well spent by Philip Morris? Does its image improve sufficiently to justify the cost?

SOURCE: Based on Alix M. Freedman, "Tobacco Firms, Pariahs to Many People, Still Are Angels to the Arts," *The Wall Street Journal*, June 8, 1988, 112.

WHAT IS RIGHT?

It is often hard for a manager to determine what is "right" and even more difficult to put ethical behavior into practice. A manager's ethical orientation often brings him or her into conflict with people, policies, customers, or bosses. Consider the following dilemmas. How would you handle them?

1. A well-liked member of your staff with an excellent record confides to you that he has Acquired Immune Deficiency Syndrome (AIDS). Although his illness has not affected his performance, you're concerned about his future health and about the reactions of his coworkers. You
   a. tell him to keep you informed about his health and say nothing to his coworkers.
   b. arrange for him to transfer to an area of the organization where he can work alone.
   c. hold a staff meeting to inform his coworkers and ask them how they feel about his continued presence on your team.
   d. consult your human resources officer on how to proceed.

2. During a reorganization, you're told to reduce staff in the department you manage. After analyzing staffing requirements, you realize the job would be a lot easier if two professionals, who are both over 60, would retire. You
   a. say nothing and determine layoffs based purely on performance and length of service.
   b. schedule a meeting with both employees and ask if they'd consider early retirement.
   c. schedule a meeting with all staff and ask if anyone is interested in severance or early retirement.
   d. lay off the older workers.

3. One of your colleagues has recently experienced two personal tragedies—her husband filed for divorce and her mother died. Although you feel genuine sympathy for her, her work is suffering. A report you completed, based on inaccurate data she provided, has been criticized by your management. Your manager asks you for an explanation. You
   a. apologize for the inaccuracies and correct the data.

   b. tell your manager that the data supplied by your colleague was the source of the problem.
   c. say your colleague has a problem and needs support.
   d. tell your manager that because of your work load, you didn't have time to check the figures in the report.

4. Your firm recently hired a new manager who is at the same level you are. You do not like the man personally and consider him a rival professionally. You run into a friend who knows your rival well. You discover this man did not attend Harvard as he stated on his resume and in fact has not graduated from any college. You know his supposed Harvard background was instrumental in getting him hired. You
   a. expose the lie to your superiors.
   b. without naming names, consult your human resources officer on how to proceed.
   c. say nothing. The company obviously failed to check him out, and the lie will probably surface on its own.
   d. confront the man with the information and let him decide what to do.

5. During a changeover in the accounting department, you discover your company has been routinely overcharging members of the public for services provided to them. Your superiors say repayment of charges would wreak havoc on company profits. Your company is federally regulated, and the oversight commission has not noticed the mistake. Your bosses say the problem will never come to light and they will take steps to correct the problem so it never happens again. You
   a. contact the oversight commission.
   b. take the matter public, anonymously or otherwise.
   c. say nothing. It is now in the hands of the bosses.
   d. work with the bosses on a plan to recognize the company's error and set up a schedule of rebates that would not unduly penalize the company.

6. In this morning's mail, you received plans and samples for a promising new product from a competitor's disgruntled employee. You
   a. throw the plans away.

b. send the samples to your research department for analysis.

c. notify your competitor about what is going on.

d. call the FBI.

● QUESTIONS

1. Use the guidelines described in Manager's Shoptalk: Guidelines for Ethical Decision Making to determine the appropriate behavior in these cases. Do you have all the information you need to make an ethical decision?

How would family or friends react to each alternative if you were in these situations?

2. Which approach to ethical decision making—utilitarian, individualism, justice, or moral rights—seems most appropriate for handling these situations?

SOURCE: Game developed by Katherine Nelson, "Board Games," *Owen Manager,* Spring 1990, 14–16; Craig Dreilinger and Dan Rice, "Office Ethics," *Working Woman,* December 1991, 35–39; and Kevin Kelly and Joseph Weber, "When a Rival's Trade Secret Crosses Your Desk . . . ," *Business Week,* May 20, 1991, 48.

REFERENCES

1. Barnaby J. Feder, "Helping Corporate America Hew to the Straight and Narrow," *The New York Times,* September 3, 1991, F5; and Bruce Hager, "What's Behind Business' Sudden Fervor for Ethics?" *Business Week,* September 23, 1991, 65.

2. Gregory Stricharchuk, "Bolar Recalls Antibiotic after U.S. Says It Switched Drugs to Get FDA Approval," *The Wall Street Journal,* October 10, 1989, A4; and John A. Byrne, "Businesses Are Signing Up for Ethics 101," *Business Week,* February 15, 1988, 56–57.

3. Kevin Kelly and Eric Schine, "How Did Sears Blow This Gasket?" *Business Week,* June 29, 1992, 38; and David Dishneau, "Use of Sales Commissions under Scrutiny," *The State,* Columbia, S.C., July 17, 1992, 12B.

4. Edwin M. Raingold, "America's Hamburger Helper," *Time,* June 29, 1992, 66–67; Laura Zinn, "Whales, Human Rights, Rainforest—and the Heady Smell of Profits," *Business Week,* July 15, 1991, 114–115; Michael Schrofer and Jonathan Kapstein, "Charity Doesn't Begin at Home Anymore," *Business Week,* February 25, 1991, 91; Kenneth Labich, "The New Crisis in Business Ethics," *Fortune,* April 20, 1992, 167–176; and Marge Marjcharlier, "Life after Asbestos: Manville Tries to Build New Identity as a Firm Keen on Environment," *The Wall Street Journal,* May 31, 1990, A1, A9.

5. Gordon F. Shea, *Practical Ethics* (New York: American Management Association, 1988); and Linda K. Trevino, "Ethical Decision Making in Organizations; A Person-Situation Interactionist Model," *Academy of Management Review* 11 (1986), 601–617.

6. Thomas M. Jones, "Ethical Decision Making by Individuals in Organizations: An Issue-Contingent Model," *Academy of Management Review* 16 (1991), 366–395.

7. Rushworth M. Kidder, "The Three Great Domains of Human Action," *Christian Science Monitor,* January 30, 1990.

8. Jones, "Ethical Decision Making."

9. This discussion is based on Gerald F. Cavanagh, Dennis J. Moberg, and Manuel Velasquez, "The Ethics of Organizational Politics," *Academy of Management Review* 6 (1981), 363–374; and Justin G. Longenecker, Joseph A. McKinney, and Carlos W. Moore, "Egoism and Independence: Entrepreneurial Ethics," *Organizational Dynamics* (Winter 1988), 64–72.

10. Zachary Schiller, Walecia Conrad, and Stephanie Anderson Forest, "If You Light Up on Sunday Don't Come in on Monday," *Business Week,* August 26, 1992, 68–72.

11. Ron Winslow, "Rationing Care," *The Wall Street Journal,* November 13, 1989, R24.

12. Alan Wong and Eugene Beckman, "An Applied Ethical Analysis System in Business," *Journal of Business Ethics* 11 (1992), 173–178.

13. John Kekes, "Self-Direction: The Core of Ethical Individualism," *Organizations and Ethical Individualism,* ed. Konstanian Kolenda (New York: Praeger, 1988), 1–18.

14. Tad Tulega, *Beyond the Bottom Line* (New York: Penguin Books, 1987).

15. James Drummond, "Hazardous to Who's Health?" *Forbes,* December 11, 1989, 89–92.

16. This discussion is based on Trevino, "Ethical Decision Making in Organizations."

17. L. Kohlberg, "Moral Stages and Moralization: The Cognitive-Developmental Approach," in *Moral Development and Behavior: Theory, Research, and Social Issues,* ed. T. Lickona (New York: Holt, Rinehart & Winston, 1976); and L. Kohlberg, "Stage and Sequence: The Cognitive-Developmental Approach to Socialization," in *Handbook of Socialization Theory and Research,* ed. D. A. Goslin (Chicago: Rand McNally, 1969).

18. Alan Wong and Eugene Beckman, "An Applied Ethical Analysis System in Business," *Journal of Business Ethics* 11 (1992), 173–178; and Kent Hodgson, "Adapting Ethical Decisions to a Global Marketplace," *Management Review,* May 1992, 53–57.

19. This discussion is based on Linda Klebe Trevino, "A Cultural Perspective on Changing and Developing Organizational Ethics," in *Research and Organizational Change and Development,* ed. R. Woodman and W. Pasmore (Greenwich, Conn.: JAI Press, 1990), 4.

20. Ibid.; John B. Cullen, Bart Victor, and Carroll Stephens, "An Ethical Weather Report: Assessing the Organization's Ethical Climate," *Organizational Dynamics* (Autumn 1989), 50–62; and Bart Victor and John B. Cullen, "The Organizational Bases of Ethical Work Climates," *Administrative Science Quarterly* 33 (1988), 101–125.

21. Eugene W. Szwajkowski, "The Myths and Realities of Research on Organizational Misconduct," in *Research in Corporate Social Performance and Policy,* ed. James E. Post (Greenwich, Conn.: JAI Press, 1986), 9:103–122; and Keith Davis, William C. Frederick, and Robert L. Blostrom, *Business and Society: Concepts and Policy Issues* (New York: McGraw-Hill, 1979).

22. Douglas S. Sherwin, "The Ethical Roots of the Business System," *Harvard Business Review* 61 (November–December 1983), 183–192.

23. Nancy C. Roberts and Paul J. King, "The Stakeholder Audit Goes Public," *Organizational Dynamics* (Winter 1989), 63–79.

24. Minda Zetlin, "Companies Find Profit in Corporate Giving," *Management Review* (December 1990), 10–15.

25. Jane Salodof, "Public Schools and the Business Community: An Uneasy Marriage," *Management Review* (January 1989), 31–37.

26. Joseph Weber, "Meet DuPont's 'In-house' Conscience," *Business Week,* June 29, 1991, 62–65.

27. Caleb Solomon, "Big Payoff: How a Neighborhood Talked Fina Refinery into Buying It Out," *The Wall Street Journal,* January 10, 1991, A1, A8.

28. Archie B. Carroll, "A Three-Dimensional Conceptual Model of Corporate Performance," *Academy of Management Review* 4 (1979), 497–505.

29. Milton Friedman, *Capitalism and Freedom* (Chicago: University of Chicago Press, 1962), 133; and Milton Friedman and Rose Friedman, *Free to Choose* (New York: Harcourt Brace Jovanovich, 1979).

30. Hager, "What's behind Business."

31. Eugene W. Szwajkowski, "Organizational Illegality: Theoretical Integration and Illustrative Application," *Academy of Management Review* 10 (1985), 558–567.

32. David J. Fritzsche and Helmut Becker, "Linking Management Behavior to Ethical Philosophy—An Empirical Investigation," *Academy of Management Journal* 27 (1984), 165–175.

33. James J. Chrisman and Archie B. Carroll, "Corporate Responsibility—Reconciling Economic and Social Goals," *Sloan Management Review* 25 (Winter 1984), 59–65.

34. Elizabeth Gatewood and Archie B. Carroll, "The Anatomy of Corporate Social Response: The Rely, Firestone 500, and Pinto Cases," *Business Horizons* 24 (September–October 1981), 9–16.

35. John Kenneth Galbraith, "Behind the Wall," *New York Review of Books,* April 10, 1986, 11–13.

36. Milton R. Moskowitz, "Company Performance Roundup," *Business and Society Review* 53 (Spring 1985), 74–77.

37. Chris Welles, "What Led Beech-Nut Down the Road to Disgrace," *Business Week,* February 22, 1988. 124–128; and Joe Queenan, "Juicemen: Ethics and the Beech-Nut Sentences," *Barron's,* June 20, 1988, 37–38.

38. Saul W. Gellerman, "Managing Ethics from the Top Down," *Sloan Management Review* (Winter 1989), 73–79.

39. "Corporate Ethics: A Prime Business Asset," The Business Roundtable, 200 Park Avenue, Suite 2222, New York, New York, 10166, February 1988.

40. Ibid.

41. Ibid.

42. "A Code of Worldwide Business Conduct and Operating Principles," Caterpillar Inc. Revised May 1, 1985. Used by permission.

43. Patrick E. Murphy, "Creating Ethical Corporate Structure," *Sloan Management Review* (Winter 1989), 81–87.

44. John A. Byrne, "The Best Laid Ethics Programs . . . ," *Business Week,* March 9, 1992, 67–69.

45. Marcia Parmarlee Miceli and Janet P. Near, "The Relationship among Beliefs, Organizational Positions, and Whistle-Blowing Status: A Discriminant Analysis," *Academy of Management Journal* 27 (1984), 687–705.

46. Clair Safran, "Women Who Blew the Whistle," *Good Housekeeping,* April 1985, 25, 216–219.

47. Philip L. Cochran and Robert A. Wood, "Corporate Social Responsibility and Financial Performance," *Academy of Management Journal* 27 (1984), 42–56.

48. Jean B. McGuire, Alison Sundgren, and Thomas Schneeweis, "Corporate

Social Responsibility and Firm Financial Performance," *Academy of Management Journal* 31 (1988), 854–872.

49. Roger Ricklefs, "Christian-Based Firms Find Following Principles Pays," *The Wall Street Journal*, December 8, 1989, B1; and Jo David and Karen File, "Saintly Companies That Make Heavenly Profits," *Working Woman*, October 1989, 122–126, 169–175.

50. Hager, "What's behind Business," and Feder, "Helping Corporate America."

51. Ibid.

GENERAL MOTORS

General Motors Corporation's decision to choose between its plants in Ypsilanti, Michigan, and Arlington, Texas, was a tug of war from the very beginning. GM announced in 1991 that it was consolidating the two facilities, which made the same cars. But the moment the giant automaker announced it would be closing one assembly line and leaving the other open, each side launched a campaign to convince GM that it should be the one to keep producing automobiles.

Proponents of the Michigan side pointed to the Willow Run plant's efficiency, saying it ranked third in shipping with the fewest defects. The Texas autoworkers made concessions, offering to work three shifts to keep the plant operating around the clock, a proposal the Michigan workers had rejected. When all was said and done, it may have been the politicians who wielded the most influence. State leaders in Texas offered GM incentives to stay. It also didn't hurt that President George Bush called Texas home, as did 30 congressional representatives, 14 more than represented Michigan.

The final decision came in early 1992. GM said it would close the Ypsilanti plant, lay off 90 percent of its 4,000 workers, and shift production of the Chevrolet Caprice to an expanded Arlington plant. But as it turned out, GM's decision was far from final.

Nearly a year later, a Michigan circuit-court judge issued an injunction barring GM from shutting the Willow Run plant. The reason? The Ypsilanti township had filed a lawsuit claiming that GM had implied it would keep the plant open when it accepted $13.5 million worth of local tax breaks from the community. The judge ruled that even though the township has no written contract associated with the tax abatements, the common law theory of "promissory estoppel" prevented GM from closing the plant. One labor consultant said the court decision sent a message to all of corporate America. "It says that corporations can't just invest, take tax breaks, take abatement, take government subsidies and then when they see fit, shut their plant down and leave," he said.

GM said it would appeal the injunction, countering that it had done nothing different than any other company. In a brief filed with the Michigan Court of Appeals, GM said the ruling was a "dramatic, unprecedented, and unwarranted departure" from established legal precedents.

The court ruling sent ripples of shock through the 300 Michigan workers who had already uprooted their lives and moved to Texas. It also cast a pall of uncertainty over the 100 who were getting ready to leave their jobs in Ypsilanti to move to Arlington.

In seeking to convince the court of appeals to reverse the circuit-court judge's ruling, GM cited the repercussions the decision was having on its workers. "While ostensibly designed to benefit GM's employees, the decision in fact does workers no favor," the company said. "It subjects thousands . . . to uncertainty about their employment prospects and inevitably will lead to reduced . . . employment within the state." The financial health of GM also was at stake, the automaker said. The injunction would cause "irrevocable injury" to the company because it would have to spend $5.5 million to buy duplicate equipment to produce 1994 model vehicles at Willow Run.

Undoubtedly, the decision to close the Willow Run factory presented serious ethical, legal, and financial dilemmas for GM. But it was only one of many similar problems the company was likely to face over the next several years. In its efforts to slim down and return to profitability, the automaker said it would close 21 plants in all and eliminate 74,000 jobs before 1995. The plant closings would cut GM's capacity by 1 million to 5.4 million cars and trucks.

The first round of casualties was unveiled in February 1992 and included the Willow Run plant and an engine plant in Flint, Michigan. GM also announced 10 other closings that would cut a total of 16,000 jobs from the payroll.

Analysts say GM will have to figure out how to make fewer car models using fewer parts with fewer employees. It also will have to sell, spin off, or close many of its parts operations, which are unprofitable or redundant. Avoiding labor unrest also is essential if GM is to overcome inefficient manufacturing, another of its major weaknesses. The company's labor costs are $2,358 per car, compared to $1,872 for Chrysler and $1,563 for Ford, according to one estimate. But cutting labor costs means cutting jobs. And that's something no GM worker will like.

● QUESTIONS

1. Which approach to ethical decision making would you use to justify GM's decision to close the Willow Run factory? Why?

2. What stakeholders would have been considered in this decision?

3. What criterion of corporate social responsibility (e.g., economic, legal) is at work in this case, and what is GM's social response (e.g., accommodation, defense)?

ORGANIZATIONAL GOAL SETTING AND PLANNING

LEARNING OBJECTIVES

After studying this chapter, you should be able to

■ Define goals and plans and explain the relationship between them.

■ Explain the concept of organizational mission and how it influences goal setting and planning.

■ Describe the types of goals an organization should have and why they resemble a hierarchy.

■ Define the characteristics of effective goals.

■ Describe the four essential steps in the MBO process.

■ Explain the difference between single-use plans and standing plans.

■ Describe how responsibility can be allocated to accomplish planning and goal setting.

■ Examine the barriers to the organization's planning process.

A few years ago, when the price of oil was $28 a barrel and rising, the planning group for the Royal Dutch/Shell Group proposed planning for tough times ahead if oil hit $15 per barrel. None of Shell's managers believed that oil prices could fall that sharply, nor did they want to spend time considering negative scenarios. After all, Shell's business was booming. The planning group persisted, feeling a responsibility to help managers adopt a war games mentality that would consider "What would we do if it happens?" for both high and low oil prices. The

planning group believed senior managers should start learning about a world of $15 oil as well as one of $30 oil. Planning for each possibility would help Shell quickly adapt to new environmental conditions.[1] ■ If you were a member of the planning group at Shell, how would you engage senior executives in the planning process? How would you get them to anticipate and plan responses to a world of $15 oil?

M A N A G E M E N T   P R O B L E M

The senior managers at Shell are not unusual. They do not want to spend time contemplating unlikely future events and developing responses to them. Yet one of the responsibilities of management is to decide where they want the organization to be in the future and how to get it there.

In some organizations, typically small ones, planning is informal. In others, managers follow a well-defined planning framework. The company establishes a basic mission and develops formal goals and strategic plans for carrying it out. Shell, IBM, Royal LaPaige, Mazda, and United Way undertake a strategic planning exercise each year—reviewing their missions, goals, and plans to meet environmental changes or the expectations of important stakeholders such as the community, owners, or stockholders.

Of the four management functions—planning, organizing, leading, and controlling—described in Chapter 1, planning is considered the most important. Everything else stems from planning. Yet planning is also the most controversial management function. Planning cannot read an uncertain future. Planning cannot tame a turbulent environment. Consider the following comment by a noted authority on planning:

> Most corporate planning is like a ritual rain dance; it has no effect on the weather that follows, but it makes those who engage in it feel that they are in control. Most discussions of the role of models in planning are directed at improving the dancing, not the weather.[2]

In this chapter, we are going to explore the process of planning and whether it can help bring needed rain.

Special attention is given to goals and goal setting, for that is where planning starts. Then the types of plans organizations can use to achieve those goals are discussed. In Chapter 7, we examine a special type of planning—strategic planning—and a number of strategic options managers can use in a competitive environment. In Chapter 8 we look at management decision making. Proper decision-making techniques are crucial to selecting the organization's goals, plans, and strategic options.

● OVERVIEW OF GOALS AND PLANS

goal

A desired future state that the organization attempts to realize.

plan

A blueprint specifying the resource allocations, schedules, and other actions necessary for attaining goals.

planning

The act of determining the organization's goals and the means for achieving them.

Goals and plans have become general concepts in our society. A **goal** is a desired future state that the organization attempts to realize.[3] Goals are important because organizations exist for a purpose and goals define and state that purpose. A **plan** is a blueprint for goal achievement and specifies the necessary resource allocations, schedules, tasks, and other actions. Goals specify future ends; plans specify today's means. The word **planning** usually incorporates both ideas; it means determining the organization's goals and defining the means for achieving them. Consider Levi Strauss. Shortly after his appointment as its CEO, Robert Haas set the 140-year-old company on course toward a new goal—being a marketing company at the center of mutual responsibility and collaboration with retailers and suppliers. To achieve this outcome in the highly uncertain environment of the early 1990s, Levi's plan included both organization and technology components.[4]

Levi's flattened its organization, redefined its values, and reduced the work force. Levi's advanced technology, meanwhile, focuses on production, communication with retailers, and delivery. Installation of sewing station computer terminals improves production control. Levi's Advanced Business System tracks products from conception to delivery, while LeviLink, a data interchange system, speeds communication between the company and its retailers. By investing now in both new organization and new technology, Levi's management should succeed in achieving its long-term goal.

Exhibit 6.1 illustrates the levels of goals and plans in an organization. The planning process starts with a formal mission that defines the basic purpose of the organization, especially for external audiences. The mission is the basis for the strategic (company) level of goals and plans, which in turn shapes the tactical (divisional) level and the operational (department) level.[5] Planning at each level supports the other levels.

THE IMPORTANCE OF GOALS AND PLANS[6]

Developing explicit goals and plans at each level illustrated in Exhibit 6.1 is important because of the external and internal messages they send. These messages go to both external and internal audiences and provide important benefits for the organization

LEGITIMACY.   An organization's mission describes what the organization stands for and its reason for existence. It symbolizes legitimacy to

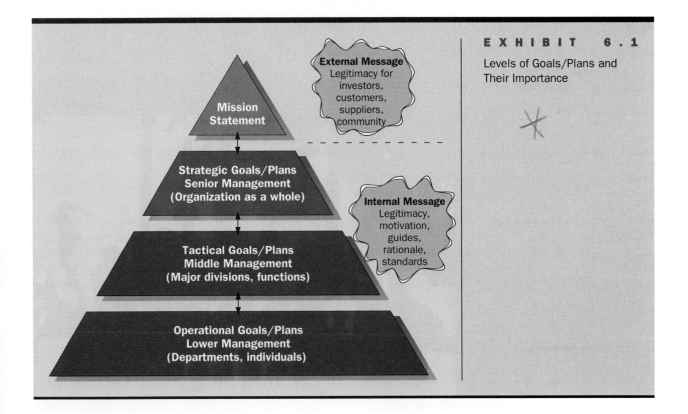

E X H I B I T   6 . 1

Levels of Goals/Plans and Their Importance

external audiences such as investors, customers, and suppliers. The mission helps them and the local community look on the company in a favorable light and, hence, accept its existence. A strong mission also has an impact on employees, enabling them to become committed to the organization because they can identify with its overall purpose and reason for existence. For example, McCaw Cellular Communications, Inc., has a mission to become the premier convenience communications company in the world, to emphasize long-term growth, and to take advantage of industry leadership opportunities and the continued loyalty of customers. McCaw's mission is written and provided to investors, customers, and suppliers as well as to employees.

SOURCE OF MOTIVATION AND COMMITMENT.   A goal statement describes the purpose of the organization or subunit to employees. A goal provides the "why" of an organization's or subunit's existence. A plan tells employees what actions to undertake. A plan tells "how" to achieve the goal. Goals and plans facilitate employees' identification with the organization and help motivate them by reducing uncertainty and clarifying what they should accomplish.

GUIDES TO ACTION.   Goals and plans provide a sense of direction. They focus attention on specific targets and direct employee efforts toward important outcomes.

RATIONALE FOR DECISIONS.   Through goal setting and planning, managers learn what the organization is trying to accomplish. They can make decisions to ensure that internal policies, roles, performance, structure, products, and expenditures will be made in accordance with desired outcomes. Decisions throughout the organization will be in alignment with the plan.

"Leadership through Exceptional Customer Service"—the *mission statement* for Lennox International, Inc.—tells the world what the company stands for and symbolizes its *legitimacy*—the reason for its existence. It also serves as a *motivational* tool for employees, each of whom carries an embossed card bearing the mission statement as a reminder of the goal. Lennox knows effective service to the external environment is the result of an effective, confident, goal-oriented work force such as the employees pictured here.

STANDARD OF PERFORMANCE.   Because goals define desired out-comes for the organization, they also serve as performance criteria. They provide a standard of assessment. If an organization wishes to grow by 15 percent, and actual growth is 17 percent, managers will have exceeded their prescribed standard. PPG (formerly Pittsburgh Plate Glass Company) set goals for 1994 of $10 billion in sales and an 18 percent return on equity. If the company achieves sales of $9 billion and return on equity of 17 percent, the standard will not be met.

The overall planning process prevents managers from thinking merely in terms of day-to-day activities. When organizations drift away from goals and plans, they typically get into trouble. This occurred at the Madison, Wisconsin City Hall. A new mayor was able to implement a strong planning system, illustrating the power of planning to improve organizational performance.

 MADISON, WISCONSIN, CITY HALL

When Joseph Sensenbrenner was elected mayor of Madison, Wisconsin, in the early 1980s, the city was plagued by shrinking revenues, poor city services, an increased service area, and irate citizens who refused to pay any additional taxes. From the city garage with its nine-day vehicle repair time, to on-the-job injuries among trash-collection workers, to low morale among city office workers, Madison was adrift and in desperate need of strong goals and planning.

Sensenbrenner's initial step was to define key goals. The mayor identified his mission after attending a presentation by quality guru W. Edwards Deming. Sensenbrenner charted a course for Madison city government in terms of two goals:

1 Increase city revenues.

2 Increase employee and citizen participation in improving the city government.

The mayor made plans that addressed specific problems in various departments. For example, the mayor along with an assistant and the local union president formed a team to investigate problems at the First Street Garage. After gathering information and listening to complaints from workers, they developed a plan to reduce repair costs and down-time for city vehicles. After addressing such initial problems, Sensenbrenner focused his plan on teamwork and improved front-line employee problem-solving efforts. For instance, trash-collection workers developed a plan to make their workplace safer and reduce lost-time injuries.

Sensenbrenner used similar planning procedures to make other city improvements. Madison hired the nation's first full-time municipal quality-improvement coordinator and established advisor networks, which included experts from local businesses and the University of Wisconsin at Madison, for city managers. Special programs—such as Tool Kit, which allows workers to determine and select cost-efficient materials for their departments—improved city services and created tax-dollar savings that eliminated or reduced program costs. Such special programs testify to the success of Madison's planning program.[7]   ■

● GOALS IN ORGANIZATIONS

Setting goals starts with top managers. The overall planning process begins with a mission statement and strategic goals for the organization as a whole.

ORGANIZATIONAL MISSION

mission

The organization's reason for existence.

mission statement

A broadly stated definition of the organization's basic business scope and operations that distinguish it from similar types of organizations.

At the top of the goal hierarchy is the **mission**—the organization's reason for existence. The mission describes the organization's values, aspirations, and reason for being. The formal **mission statement** is a broadly stated definition of basic business scope and operations that distinguishes the organization from others of a similar type.[8] The content of a mission statement often focuses on the market and customers and identifies desired fields of endeavor. Some mission statements describe company characteristics such as corporate values, product quality, location of facilities, and attitude toward employees. Mission statements often reveal the company's philosophy as well as purpose. The mission statement for a Vermont-based construction company is presented in Exhibit 6.2. Bread Loaf Construction Company devised its three-sentence mission statement as a way to spur continued growth and to close the communication gap between management and employees. A group of 20 employees—hourly and salaried—was given responsibility for devising the mission statement. Each group member interviewed three coworkers. Armed with this information, the team joined company founders on a weekend retreat. The group envisioned the company's future, its potential as a global player, and members' own personal futures. The simple statement relays to both employees and customers Bread Loaf's

EXHIBIT   6.2

Mission Statement for Bread Loaf Construction Co.

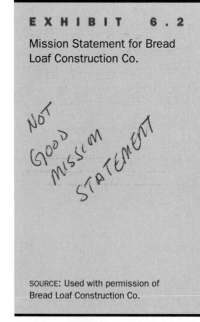

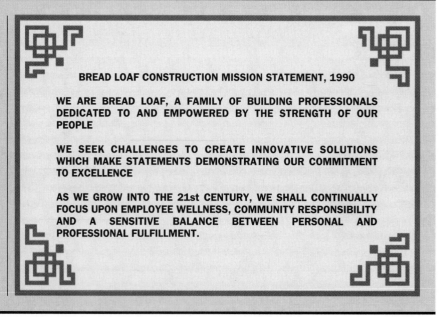

BREAD LOAF CONSTRUCTION MISSION STATEMENT, 1990

WE ARE BREAD LOAF, A FAMILY OF BUILDING PROFESSIONALS DEDICATED TO AND EMPOWERED BY THE STRENGTH OF OUR PEOPLE

WE SEEK CHALLENGES TO CREATE INNOVATIVE SOLUTIONS WHICH MAKE STATEMENTS DEMONSTRATING OUR COMMITMENT TO EXCELLENCE

AS WE GROW INTO THE 21st CENTURY, WE SHALL CONTINUALLY FOCUS UPON EMPLOYEE WELLNESS, COMMUNITY RESPONSIBILITY AND A SENSITIVE BALANCE BETWEEN PERSONAL AND PROFESSIONAL FULFILLMENT.

vision of who it is. The mission statement challenges the status quo, demonstrates a commitment to excellence, focuses on day-to-day priorities, reinforces values, and balances priorities.[9]

Such short, straightforward mission statements describe basic business activities and purposes. Another example of this type of mission statement is that of Columbia Gas System, a large gas transmission and distribution company:

> Columbia Gas System, through its subsidiaries, is active in pursuing opportunities in all segments of the natural gas industry and in related energy resource development. Exemplified by Columbia's three-star symbol, the separately managed companies work to benefit: *system stockholders*—through competitive return on their investment; *customers*—through efficient, safe, reliable service; and *employees*—through challenging and rewarding careers.[10]

PRODUCTS, SERVICES
CUSTOMERS
Function

Because of mission statements such as Bread Loaf's and Columbia's, employees, as well as customers, suppliers, and stockholders, know the company's stated purpose.

GOALS AND PLANS

Broad statements describing where the organization wants to be in the future are called **strategic goals**. They pertain to the organization as a whole rather than to specific divisions or departments. Strategic goals are often called *official* goals, because they are the stated intentions of what the organization wants to achieve. Peter Drucker suggests that business organizations' goals encompass more than profits. He suggests that organizations focus on eight content areas: market standing, innovation, productivity, physical and financial resources, profitability, managerial performance and development, worker performance and attitude, and public responsibility.[11]

strategic goals

Broad statements of where the organization wants to be in the future; pertain to the organization as a whole rather than to specific divisions or departments.

PETER DRUCKER

The lush, green lawn pictured here epitomizes the *goals* set forth in the *mission statement* of the TORO company: "To beautify and preserve the outdoor environment—make the landscapes green, healthy, and safe—with superior quality, innovative and environmentally sound products, services, and systems." TORO's turf-maintenance equipment, such as this greens mower which features an oil-leak detector, keeps TORO number one in golf sales and addresses environmental and safety concerns.

strategic plans

The action steps by which an organization intends to attain its strategic goals.

tactical goals

Objectives that define the outcomes that major divisions and departments must achieve in order for the organization to reach its overall goals.

tactical plans

Plans designed to help execute major strategic plans and to accomplish a specific part of the company's strategy.

operational goals

Specific, measurable results expected from departments, work groups, and individuals within the organization.

operational plans

Plans developed at the organization's lower levels that specify action steps toward achieving operational goals and support tactical planning activities.

Strategic plans define the action steps by which the company intends to attain strategic goals. The strategic plan is the blueprint that defines the organizational activities and resource allocations—in the form of cash, personnel, space, and facilities—required for meeting these targets. Strategic planning tends to be long-term and may define organizational action steps from two to five years in the future. The purpose of strategic plans is to turn organizational goals into realities within that time period.

As an example, a small company wanted to improve its market share from 15 to 20 percent over the next three years. This strategic goal was pursued through the following strategic plans: (1) allocate resources for the development of new, competitive products with high growth potential; (2) improve production methods to achieve higher output at lower costs; and (3) conduct research to develop alternative uses for current products and services.[12]

The results that major divisions and departments within the organization intend to achieve are defined as **tactical goals**. These objectives apply to middle management and describe what major subunits must do in order for the organization to achieve its overall goals. For example, one tactical goal for Columbia Gas was to "regain a long-term debt rating by the end of 1988." This tactical goal pertains to strategic goal 2 regarding access to reasonable amounts of capital. Achieving this goal will increase the organization's ability to borrow money at a reasonable rate. The Winning Moves box tells how Timex used strategic and tactical goals to reassert itself in the wristwatch market.

Tactical plans are designed to help execute major strategic plans and to accomplish a specific part of the company's strategy.[13] Tactical plans typically have a shorter time horizon than strategic plans—over the next year or so. The word *tactical* comes from the military. For example, strategic weapon systems, such as intercontinental ballistic missiles or the B-2 Stealth Bomber, are designed to deliver major blows to the enemy. These weapon systems reflect the country's overall strategic plan. Tactical weapon systems, such as fighter airplanes, are used to achieve just one part of the overall strategic plan. Tactical plans define what the major departments and organizational subunits will do to implement the overall strategic plan. Normally, it is the middle manager's job to take the broad strategic plan and identify specific tactical actions.

The specific results expected from departments, work groups, and individuals are the **operational goals**. They are precise and measurable. "Process 150 sales applications each week," "achieve 90 percent of deliveries on time," "reduce overtime by 10 percent next month," and "develop two new elective courses in accounting" are examples of operational objectives.

Operational plans are developed at the lower levels of the organization to specify action steps toward achieving operational goals and to support tactical plans. The operational plan is the department manager's tool for daily and weekly operations. Objectives are stated in quantitative terms, and the department plan describes how objectives will be achieved. Operational planning specifies plans for supervisors, department managers, and individual employees. For example, DuPont has a program called Individual Career Management that involves a series of discussions that define what each manager's new goals should be and whether last year's operational goals were met. At DuPont the goals are set as high as possible to stretch the employee to ensure continued improvement. These year-end discussions also provide the basis for rewards to those who have excelled.[14]

Schedules are an important component of operational planning. Schedules define precise time frames for the completion of each objective required for the organization's tactical and strategic goals. Operational planning also must be coordinated with the budget, because resources must be allocated for desired activities. For example, Apogee Enterprises, a window and glass fabricator with 150 small divisions, is fanatical about operational planning and budgeting. Committees are set up that require inter- as well as intra-divisional review and challenge of budgets, profit plans, and proposed capital expenditures. Assigning the dollars makes the operational plan work for everything from hiring new salespeople to increasing travel expenses.

HIERARCHY OF OBJECTIVES

Effectively designed organizational goals and objectives fit into a hierarchy; that is, the achievement of objectives at lower levels permits the

WINNING moves   TIMEX

In the late 1970s Timex was running down. Timex pushed durability in cheap watches, but consumers became more interested in style. Timex's claim that its watches "take a lickin' and keep on tickin'" did not mean much to consumers in 1990.

Then Timex defined a bold strategic plan. Its strategic goal was to recapture lost market share. Its strategic plan was to appeal to young customers, many of whom were health nuts and who purchased zippy watches from competitors that had hot colors and striking designs.

Timex's tactical objective was to target amateur athletes. Says the marketing vice-president, "We asked athletes exactly what they wanted on a watch, and then we gave it to them." The operational plan was to bring out the Triathlon watch that could clock swimming, bicycle riding, and running. The watch sold 400,000 units its first year. That was exciting because there are only some 300,000 triathletes in the United States. Without realizing it, Timex had caught the wave of sports chic. Most people cannot do a triathlon, but they want to look as if they can by sporting the triathlon watch.

Timex lost no time exploiting this idea. It developed a watch for skiers that measures temperature, a watch

for aerobics fanatics that takes the wearer's pulse rate, and a Victory watch aimed at sailors.

Timex's advertising is as chic as its watches. An ad for *Ski* magazine shows a polar bear's wrist sporting the ski watch, illustrating how it will fit over any sleeve. Timex's remarkably successful goal achievement can be traced directly to its clear mission and planning. Timex is not selling a timepiece; it is selling fun and fitness, which is what consumers want. ■

SOURCE: Based on Christie Brown, "Sweat Chic," *Forbes*, September 5, 1988, 96–101.

OPERATIONAL goals
TACTICAL Goals
STRATEGIC goals ✗

attainment of higher-level goals. This is called a *means-ends chain* because lower-level goals lead to accomplishment of higher-level goals. Operational goals lead to the achievement of tactical goals, which in turn lead to the attainment of strategic goals. Strategic goals typically are the responsibility of top management, tactical goals that of middle management, and operational goals that of first-line supervisors and workers.

An example of a goal hierarchy is illustrated in Exhibit 6.3. Note how the strategic goal of "excellent service to customers" translates into "open one new sales office" and "respond to customer inquiries within 2 hours" at lower management levels.

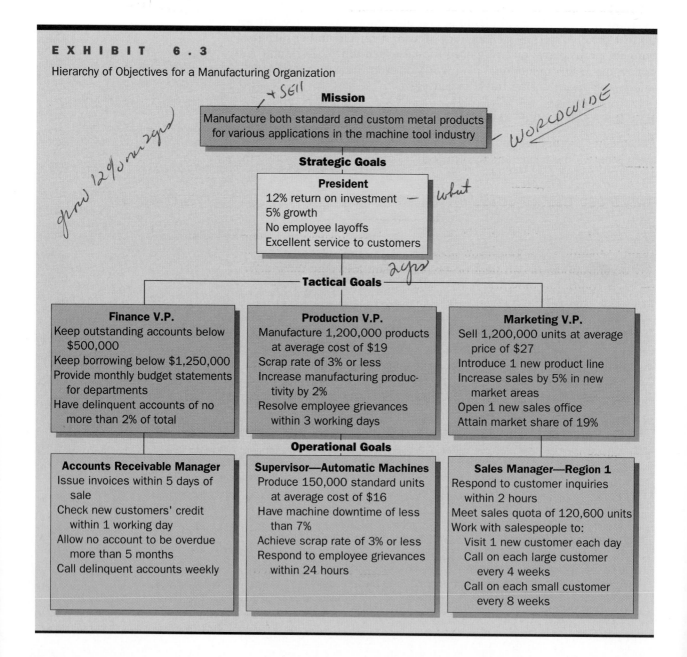

EXHIBIT   6.3

Hierarchy of Objectives for a Manufacturing Organization

+ Sell

Mission

Manufacture both standard and custom metal products for various applications in the machine tool industry

WORLDWIDE

Strategic Goals

grow 12% or more/year

President
12% return on investment — *what*
5% growth
No employee layoffs
Excellent service to customers

Tactical Goals *2yrs*

Finance V.P.
Keep outstanding accounts below $500,000
Keep borrowing below $1,250,000
Provide monthly budget statements for departments
Have delinquent accounts of no more than 2% of total

Production V.P.
Manufacture 1,200,000 products at average cost of $19
Scrap rate of 3% or less
Increase manufacturing productivity by 2%
Resolve employee grievances within 3 working days

Marketing V.P.
Sell 1,200,000 units at average price of $27
Introduce 1 new product line
Increase sales by 5% in new market areas
Open 1 new sales office
Attain market share of 19%

Operational Goals

Accounts Receivable Manager
Issue invoices within 5 days of sale
Check new customers' credit within 1 working day
Allow no account to be overdue more than 5 months
Call delinquent accounts weekly

Supervisor—Automatic Machines
Produce 150,000 standard units at average cost of $16
Have machine downtime of less than 7%
Achieve scrap rate of 3% or less
Respond to employee grievances within 24 hours

Sales Manager—Region 1
Respond to customer inquiries within 2 hours
Meet sales quota of 120,600 units
Work with salespeople to:
Visit 1 new customer each day
Call on each large customer every 4 weeks
Call on each small customer every 8 weeks

● CRITERIA FOR EFFECTIVE GOALS

To ensure goal-setting benefits for the organization, certain characteristics and guidelines should be adopted. The characteristics of both goals and the goal-setting process are listed in Exhibit 6.4.

GOAL CHARACTERISTICS

The following characteristics pertain to organizational goals at the strategic, tactical, and operational levels.

SPECIFIC AND MEASURABLE. When possible, goals should be expressed in quantitative terms, such as increasing profits by 2 percent, decreasing scrap by 1 percent, or increasing average teacher effectiveness ratings from 3.5 to 3.7. Not all goals can be expressed in numerical terms, but vague goals and objectives have little motivating power for employees. At the top of the organization, goals often are qualitative as well as quantitative. In July 1992, H. Laurance Fuller, chief executive of Amoco, defined both quantitative and qualitative goals for his organization, including trimming the work force by 8,500, decentralizing into smaller units, targeting proven energy reserves while cutting wildcatting and developing and marketing products, such as Amoco's Crystal Clear Ultimate (a cleaner gasoline).[15] Each goal is precisely defined and allows for measurable progress.

COVER KEY RESULT AREAS. Goals cannot be set for every aspect of employee behavior or organizational performance; if they were, their sheer number would render them meaningless. Instead, managers should identify a few key result areas—perhaps up to four or five for any organizational department or job. Key result areas are those activities that contribute most to company performance.[16] For example, the marketing department at ALLTEL, a telephone company covering several regions in the United States, identified the following key result areas for which goals were specified: identify emerging areas of service opportunities, assist regions with meaningful information to support current marketing programs, improve marketing of existing products, and develop a strategic market plan based on customer needs, competitive studies, and market trends.[17]

CHALLENGING BUT REALISTIC. Goals should be challenging but not unreasonably difficult. One value of limiting operational goals to key result areas is that these offer important challenges to employees. If a goal is too difficult, employees may give up; if too easy, employees may not feel motivated.[18] Managers should also ensure that goals are set within the existing resource base, not beyond departments' time, equipment, and financial resources.

DEFINED TIME PERIOD. Goals and objectives should specify the time period over which they will be achieved. A time period is a deadline specifying the date on which goal attainment will be measured. A goal of revising a company's job classification system could have a deadline such as June 30, 1994. If a strategic goal involves a two-to-three-year time horizon, specific dates for achieving parts of it can be set up. For example, strategic sales goals could be established on a three-year time

EXHIBIT 6.4

Characteristics of Effective Goal Setting

Goal Characteristics
- Specific and measurable
- Cover key result areas
- Challenging but realistic
- Defined time period
- Linked to rewards

The distinctive blue and yellow cards and enthusiastic cardholders pictured here are the keys to continued success for Blockbuster Entertainment Corporation. Five-year goals established by Blockbuster include a 20 percent share of the domestic home video market by 1995 with 3,000 stores operating in North America and full implementation of a store manager's incentive compensation program. These stated goals meet all *five goal characteristics*: (1) specific and measurable, (2) covering key areas, (3) challenging but realistic, (4) defined time period, and (5) linked to rewards.

horizon, with a $100 million target in year 1, a $129 million target in year 2, and a $165 million target in year 3.

LINKED TO REWARDS.   The ultimate impact of goals depends on the extent to which salary increases, promotions, and awards are based on goal achievement. People who attain goals should be rewarded. Rewards give meaning and significance to goals and help commit employees to achieving goals. Failure to attain goals often is due to factors outside employees' control. Failure to achieve a financial goal may be associated with a drop in market demand due to industry recession; thus, an employee could not be expected to reach it. Nevertheless, a positive reward may be appropriate if the employee partially achieved goals under difficult circumstances.[19]

● PLANNING TYPES AND MODELS

Once strategic, tactical, and operational goals have been determined, managers may select a planning approach most appropriate for their situation. Critical to successful planning are *flexibility* and *adaptability* to changing environments. Managers have a number of planning approaches from which to choose. Among the most popular are management by objectives, single-use plans, standing plans, and contingency (or scenario) plans.

MANAGEMENT BY OBJECTIVES

management by objectives

A method of management whereby managers and employees define objectives for every department, project, and person and use them to control subsequent performance.

Management by objectives (MBO) is a method whereby managers and employees define objectives for every department, project, and person and use them to control subsequent performance.[20] A model of the essential steps of the MBO process is presented in Exhibit 6.5. Four major activities must occur in order for MBO to be successful:[21]

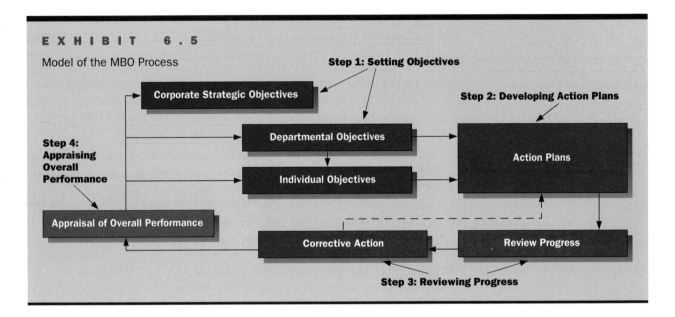

E X H I B I T   6 . 5

Model of the MBO Process

Step 1: Setting Objectives

Corporate Strategic Objectives

Step 2: Developing Action Plans

Step 4: Appraising Overall Performance

Departmental Objectives

Action Plans

Individual Objectives

Appraisal of Overall Performance

Corrective Action

Review Progress

Step 3: Reviewing Progress

1 **Setting objectives.** This is the most difficult step in MBO. Setting objectives involves employees at all levels and looks beyond day-to-day activities to answer the question "What are we trying to accomplish?" A good objective should be concrete and realistic, provide a specific target and time frame, and assign responsibility. Objectives may be quantitative or qualitative, depending on whether outcomes are measurable. Quantitative objectives are described in numerical terms, such as "Salesperson Jones will obtain 16 new accounts in December." Qualitative objectives use statements such as "Marketing will improve customer service by reducing complaints next year." Objectives should be jointly derived. Mutual agreement between employee and supervisor creates the strongest commitment to achieving objectives. In the case of teams, all team members may participate in setting objectives.

2 **Developing action plans.** An *action plan* defines the course of action needed to achieve the stated objectives. Action plans are made for both individuals and departments.

3 **Reviewing progress.** A periodic progress review is important to ensure that action plans are working. These reviews can occur informally between managers and subordinates, where the organization may wish to conduct three-, six-, or nine-month reviews during the year. This periodic checkup allows managers and employees to see whether they are on target or whether corrective action is necessary. Managers and employees should not be locked into predefined behavior and must be willing to take whatever steps are necessary to produce meaningful results. The point of MBO is to achieve objectives. The action plan can be changed whenever objectives are not being met.

4 **Appraising overall performance.** The final step in MBO is to carefully evaluate whether annual objectives have been achieved for

"How are we doing?" The four long-term objectives of Tenneco Gas, the natural gas transmission and marketing subsidiary of Tenneco, Inc., are to be financially strong, the pipeline of choice, the employer of choice, and a good corporate citizen, which are supported by specific and measurable goals. This *management-by-objectives* type system, along with strategies and measurements of achievement, enables employees to see the company's overall direction and to better understand how they fit into that direction.

both individuals and departments. Success or failure to achieve objectives can become part of the performance appraisal system and the designation of salary increases and other rewards. The appraisal of departmental and overall corporate performance shapes objectives for the next year. The MBO cycle repeats itself on an annual basis. The specific application of MBO must fit the needs of each company. An example of how one company used MBO to solve safety problems follows.

 ## PRODUCERS GAS AND TRANSMISSION

Producers Gas and Transmission Company is a medium-size refinery and distributor of gasoline and other refinery products. A major concern of top management was an unusually high employee accident rate during the previous year. Ten employees had minor injuries, four were severely injured, and one was killed. The company lost 112 employee days of work due to accidents. Top management discussed the accident rate with department heads and decided on a corporate objective of a 50 percent reduction in all accidents for 1991.

Middle managers developed an action plan that included (1) the establishment of an employee safety training program, (2) the creation of a company-wide safety committee, and (3) a new system of safety recognition. Also, (4) line supervisors were asked to develop safety training sessions for their departments within 60 days, and (5) middle managers were given 30 days to nominate supervisors to the safety committee. Finally, (6) the safety committee had 30 days in which to design a safety recognition program, including awards.

Progress was reviewed through the compilation of quarterly safety reports measuring percentage of accidents compared to the previous year. The action plan could be revised if obstacles were discovered. The safety committee appraised the safety performance of each department every 90 days and posted the results for all employees to see. Letters of commendation were given to departments that met or exceeded the 50 percent reduction objective.

At the end of the year, an overall performance appraisal was held for individuals, departments, and the corporation as a whole. Departments that had successfully reduced accidents by 50 percent were given awards (wall plaques). Information about safety procedures and accident rates was used to set a new safety objective for 1992. Delinquent departments were given stringent objectives. Most important, the company achieved its 1991 objective of reducing accidents by 50 percent. The MBO system energized employee actions companywide toward a goal deemed critical by top management. MBO got all employees working toward the same end.[22] ■

BENEFITS AND PROBLEMS WITH MBO.   Many companies such as Intel, Tenneco, Black & Decker, and DuPont have adopted MBO, and most managers believe that MBO is an effective management tool.[23] Managers believe they are better oriented toward goal achievement when MBO is used. Like any system, MBO achieves benefits when used properly but results in problems when used improperly. Benefits and problems are summarized in Exhibit 6.6.

The benefits of the MBO process can be many. Corporate objectives are more likely to be achieved when they focus manager and employee efforts. Performance is improved because employees are committed to attaining the objective, are motivated because they help decide what is expected, and are free to be resourceful. Objectives at lower levels are aligned with and enable the attainment of objectives at top management levels.

Problems with MBO occur when the company faces rapid change. The environment and internal activities must have some stability for performance to be measured and compared against goals. If new objectives are defined every few months, there is no time for action plans and appraisal to take effect. Also, poor employer-employee relations reduce effectiveness because managers lack confidence in subordinates. If managers discourage participation, employees will lack the training and values to jointly set objectives with employers. Finally, if MBO becomes a process of filling out annual paperwork rather than energizing employees to achieve goals, it becomes an empty exercise. Once the paperwork is completed, employees forget about the objectives, perhaps even resenting the paperwork in the first place.

SINGLE-USE PLANS

Single-use plans are developed to achieve a set of objectives that are not likely to be repeated in the future. Single-use plans typically include both programs and projects.

A **program** is a complex set of objectives and plans for attaining an important, one-time organizational goal. The program is designed to carry out a major course of action for the organization. Examples of such a program are the development of the space shuttle for NASA, the 767 aircraft by Boeing, and the System 360 computer by IBM. Programs are major undertakings, may take several years to complete, and often require the creation of a separate organization. Programs are large in scope and may be associated with several projects.

single-use plans

Plans that are developed to achieve a set of objectives that are unlikely to be repeated in the future.

program

A complex set of objectives and plans for achieving an important, one-time organizational goal.

Benefits of MBO	Problems with MBO	
1. Manager and employee efforts are focused on activities that will lead to goal attainment.	1. Constant change prevents MBO from taking hold.	**E X H I B I T 6 . 6** MBO Benefits and Problems
2. Performance can be improved at all company levels.	2. An environment of poor employer-employee relations reduces MBO effectiveness.	
3. Employees are motivated.	3. Organizational values that discourage participation can harm the MBO process.	
4. Departmental and individual objectives are aligned with company objectives.	4. Too much paperwork saps MBO energy.	

project

A set of relatively short-term, narrow objectives and plans for achieving a major, one-time organizational goal.

A **project** is also a set of objectives and plans designed to achieve a one-time goal but generally is smaller in scope and complexity than a program. It normally has a shorter time horizon and requires fewer resources. A project is often one part of a program. Thus, when NASA works to complete its space station program, it will have one project for a rocket booster, one for the environment inside the space station, and one for the station's external shell. A specific project is defined for each major component of the overall program. Within business corporations, projects often are undertaken to perform a specific activity that is not part of the normal production process. For example, the name change from U.S. Steel to USX Corporation was a project. Hundreds of worker-hours and millions of dollars were spent researching a name that would characterize the corporation's new mission. USX also used a project team to make the decision to close some of its steel plants. Toyota also used a program and projects for its organization.

 TOYOTA

An example of a major program is Toyota's 1993 reorganization under new president Tatsuro Toyoda. While other companies are adopting Toyota's legendary "lean production" methods, the automaker is again at the forefront of innovation and change. Some of the program's objectives follow:

1 Increase sales to 6 million cars and trucks by the year 2000.

2 Expand facilities and increase automation.

3 Improve efficiency.

These objectives are being followed up with specific projects to help make the program a success. Despite tight profits and "global overcapacity," within the auto industry, Toyota is avoiding layoffs by focusing one project on building or expanding six plants and improving automation. Meanwhile, the cost-cutting project focuses on areas such as travel, white-collar overtime, expense-account budgets, and product development. In another project, the company's 26 model variations, each developed under a powerful leader called a "shusa," are to be gradually reduced into three groups—front-wheel drive, rear-wheel drive, and trucks—each controlled by a chief engineer. Under the new groupings, shusas are expected to coordinate their efforts with a goal of 30 percent reduction in model variants.

Toyota's capacity for adaptability and its historically successful response to challenges have contributed to its reputation as the world's most efficient automaker. Competitors are again keeping a wary eye on Toyota's latest effort to play a more vigorous role on the industry's world stage.[24] ■

standing plans

Ongoing plans that are used as guidance for tasks performed repeatedly within the organization.

STANDING PLANS

Standing plans are ongoing plans that are used to provide guidance for tasks performed repeatedly within the organization. The major standing plans are organizational policies, rules, and procedures. These plans pertain to matters such as employee illness, absences, smoking, discipline, hiring, and dismissal.

A **policy** is a general guide to action. It is a general statement based on the organization's overall goals and strategic plans that provides directions for people within the organization. It may define boundaries within which to make decisions. For example, the graduate program of a business school may adopt the goal of increasing the quality of students admitted. It may issue a policy statement requiring applicants to have a minimum general aptitude test score of 500. Many companies have adopted smoking policies. These may include prohibiting smoking in meeting rooms, reception areas, office areas, or cafeterias or even dismissing employees unless they stop smoking totally, which is the case at USG Acoustical Products Company. The Focus on Ethics box describes policy formulation regarding sexual harassment.

A **rule** describes how a specific action is to be performed. Rules often apply to specific settings, such as a no-smoking rule in areas of the plant where hazardous materials are stored. Universities often have rules pertaining to incomplete grades. Such rules may specify the condition under which a student can be given an incomplete and require that the grade be removed within one semester or it will be changed to an F.

A **procedure,** sometimes called a *standard operating procedure,* defines a precise series of steps to be used in achieving certain objectives for a specific job. Rules and procedures play a similar role. Both are narrow in scope and describe desired activities. The key difference is that procedures normally describe a series of steps or activities, but rules pertain to one specific action.

Total quality management (TQM) is an example of a standing plan manufacturing companies use in striving to improve quality and production. Under TQM, employees are encouraged to participate in the improvement of product and service quality, which will be described in more detail in Chapter 18. One company using TQM as a standing plan is Heinz.

policy

A general statement based on the organization's overall goals and strategic plans that provides directions for individuals within the company.

rule

A guideline for how a specific action is to be performed.

procedure

A precise series of steps to be used in achieving certain objectives for a specific job.

total quality management (TQM)

A standing plan that manufacturing companies use in striving to improve quality and production.

Single-use plans enabled these Norwest Corporation employees to achieve their goal of the smooth conversion of 500,000 new customer accounts following the acquisition of First Minnesota Savings Bank in 1990. A conversion team of 225 employees coordinated computer programming, marketing, systems conversion, and delivery support, and managed to make it all look easy.

 H. J. HEINZ COMPANY

In 1987, Heinz chairman Anthony J. F. O'Reilly warned his top executives of a looming crisis. Several of Heinz's big brands were losing market share. After a stem-to-stern review of the company, Heinz decided to redirect standing plans away from cost cutting in the 1980s to a quality focus in the 1990s.

Quality consultants helped Heinz implement a TQM plan. Heinz focused on quality improvement with the belief that this would also improve productivity. At the Ore-Ida division, for example, training budgets were tripled, and quality teams of hourly and salaried employees brainstormed for solutions to product problems. They actually slowed production to restore the chunky texture and crispy flavor of Tater-Tots. This quality improvement was immediately reflected in sales, which jumped 18 percent. At Star-Kist Tuna, adding more workers actually saved money. Because cleaning tuna is a labor-intensive hand process, overworked employees were inadvertently throwing away choice meat. Heinz has learned that the cheapest way to do business is to have a standing plan to produce top-quality products from manufacturing operations.[25] ∎

CONTINGENCY PLANS

contingency plans

Plans that define company responses to specific situations such as emergencies or setbacks.

Contingency plans, also referred to as *scenarios*, define company responses to be taken in the case of emergencies or setbacks. To develop contingency plans, planners identify uncontrollable factors, such as recession, inflation, technological developments, or safety accidents. To

focus on ETHICS   **SEXUAL HARASSMENT POLICIES**

In the fall of 1991, sexual harassment charges against U.S. Supreme Court nominee Clarence Thomas by his former assistant, Anita Hill, catapulted the issue of on-the-job sexual harassment to the forefront of the corporate, as well as the government, agenda. Months later, the nation again reeled under a sexual harassment controversy in the Navy's "Tailhook" scandal and botched investigation. These events provided corporate America with models of what *not* to do when dealing with sexual harassment. In both cases, ineffective organizational policies compounded the alleged violation of the victim's civil rights.

Today any physical or verbal conduct that demeans or demoralizes an employee on the basis of sex and creates a hostile work environment falls under the area of sexual harassment. Research indicates that many men see sexual harassment as limited to touching. However, sexual harassment charges may arise from

requests for sexual favors, unwelcome sexual advances, or physical or verbal contact of a sexual nature.

Companies are getting the message and are scrambling to create policies that relay the word to employees. At the height of the Thomas/Hill senate hearings, for example, CEO Robert Allen inserted the full text of AT&T's sexual harassment policy into all employee computers.

Realistically, the creation and distribution of a corporate policy is only the first step. Management must periodically reinforce these policies. CBS employees are reminded of their sexual harassment policy through annual memos from the CEO. At Honeywell, management reinforces handbook policy with posters and work area inspections. Training also helps. Corning provides diversity workshops that include a segment on sexual harassment. Digital hires outside consultants to hold one-day workshops for managers. At DuPont, 65,000 employees have attended sexual harassment workshops.

What does an effective policy include? It should provide an avenue of complaint that allows

employees to bypass normal grievance channels and their immediate supervisors. DuPont and Corning, for example, provide 24-hour hotlines offering advice and confidentiality to employees. Moreover, the policy should provide for immediate investigation of charges and protection of complainants. DuPont offers security guards, if necessary, to prevent retaliation against an employee.

As companies implement sound harassment policies and as employees are increasingly aware of the problem, corporate culture and acceptable behavior will change, and employee morale and productivity can be expected to improve. ∎

SOURCE: Stephanie Strom, "Many Companies Assailed on Sex Harassment Rules," *The New York Times*, October 20, 1991, F1, F15; Susan B. Garland and Troy Segal, "Thomas vs. Hill: The Lessons for Corporate America," *Business Week*, October 21, 1991, 32; Alan Deutschman, "Dealing with Sexual Harassment," *Fortune*, November 4, 1991, 145–148; and Michele Galen, Zachary Schiller, Joan O'C. Hamilton, and Keith H. Hammonds, "Ending Sexual Harassment: Business Is Getting the Message," *Business Week*, March 18, 1991, 98–100.

minimize the impact of these potential factors, a planning team can forecast the worst-case scenarios. For example, if sales fall 20 percent and prices drop 8 percent, what will the company do? Contingency plans can then be defined for possible layoffs, emergency budgets, and sales efforts.[26] As mentioned at the beginning of this chapter, contingency planning was used at Shell for dealing with a potential drop in oil prices that could be catastrophic.

The Exploration and Development Division of Statoil, a Norwegian oil and gas producer, discovered a number of benefits from scenario planning. Managers were confronted with scenarios such as a market drop in oil prices, a depressed world economy, and a national restructuring that reduced oil dependence. Scenario planning enabled Statoil managers to assess and understand trends, deal more openly with acknowledged uncertainty, learn critical lessons about the need for flexibility and adaptability, and react quickly to obtain a competitive advantage.[27]

Contingency planning enables crews from British Telecommunications to react quickly to customer needs in times of crisis. A 1992 IRA blast in London affected 200 businesses in 30 buildings. Through BT's business recovery program, 400 BT employees, such as the man pictured here, quickly restored service, installing 500 new lines, 420 telephones, and 60 private circuits. In addition to coordinating recovery, BT assists companies in drawing up contingency plans before disaster strikes. Effective planning is the key to quick recovery.

● PLANNING TIME HORIZON

Organizational goals and plans are associated with specific time horizons. The time horizons are long term, intermediate term, and short term, as illustrated in Exhibit 6.7. *Long-term planning* includes strategic goals and plans and may extend as far as five years into the future. *Intermediate-term planning* includes tactical objectives and has a time horizon of from one to two years. *Short-term planning* includes operational objectives for specific departments and individuals and has a time horizon of one year or less.

One of the major problems in companies today is the emphasis on *short-term results.* Long-term planning is difficult because the world is so uncertain. Moreover, the financial community, including stock analysts and mutual funds managers, push companies for strong financial results in the short term. This pressure fits the natural inclination of many result-oriented managers, who are concerned with outcomes for today and next week, not next year and for sure not five years out. These pressures tend to reward short-term performance and undercut long-range

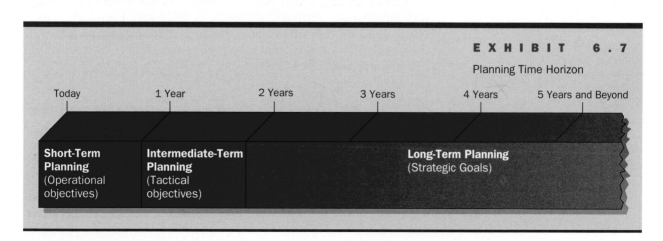

EXHIBIT 6.7

Planning Time Horizon

| Today | 1 Year | 2 Years | 3 Years | 4 Years | 5 Years and Beyond |

Short-Term Planning (Operational objectives)

Intermediate-Term Planning (Tactical objectives)

Long-Term Planning (Strategic Goals)

Tomen Corporation excels at *long-term planning*. The 10-year business plan, called ACT-21st (Aggressive Challenge to the 21st Century), focuses on diversification and allocation of business resources in high-growth areas, including flowers and greenery. Tomen, a Japanese general trading company active in over 60 countries, increased growth potential in its bulbs and cut flowers business through acquisition of Bloomers Growers & Exporters, Ltd., a New Zealand supplier. Such moves assure Tomen's high profile in high growth areas into the long-term future.

planning. For example, a Tennessee manufacturer of temperature control devices badly needed new plants and facilities that required massive expenditures. The managers' bonuses were calculated on profits for a one-year period. In this case, the pressures for short-term results took precedence, and the managers did not invest money in new facilities because short-term profits would suffer.

Many well-managed companies, however, resist short-term pressures. Matsushita Electric of Japan, the world's leading producer of consumer electronics, VCRs, color televisions, and video cameras, has succeeded by taking a long-term view. Sixty years ago, Konosuke Matsushita foresaw the day when the United States would provide both major markets and manufacturing centers for his company's small appliances. In 1932 he announced an ambitious 250-year plan for the company, perhaps an all-time record for long-range planning.[28] Long-term planning need not resort to such extremes. Today, senior executives are redirecting Matsushita into four areas where future growth is expected: semiconductors, factory automation, office automation, and audiovisual products. These products generate only 13 percent of sales but are expected to do well in the twenty-first century and so today are receiving 70 percent of the company's research expenditures.[29]

● ORGANIZATIONAL RESPONSIBILITY FOR PLANNING

Who should do organizational planning? Chief executive officers and other line managers have primary responsibility for planning. Line managers are responsible for setting goals and objectives and devising plans for achieving them. However, not all line managers have the expertise or skills for doing the analysis required for detailed planning. Thus, three different approaches are used to structure the planning function: central planning departments, decentralized planning staff, and planning task forces.

CENTRAL PLANNING DEPARTMENT

The traditional approach to corporate planning was to have a **central planning department** report to the president or chief executive officer, as illustrated in Exhibit 6.8. This approach was popular during the 1970s. Planning specialists were hired to gather data and develop detailed strategic plans for the corporation as a whole. This planning approach was top down because objectives and plans were assigned to major divisions and departments from the planning department after approval by the president.

central planning department

A group of planning specialists who develop plans for the organization as a whole and its major divisions and departments and typically report to the president or CEO.

This approach works well in many applications. For example, the Columbia Gas System, described earlier in this chapter, has a Corporate Planning Department with eight full-time specialists. The department has two sections. The Operations Analysis Section is responsible for acquiring and analyzing economic and other data for use in the strategic planning process. The Planning Section successfully prepares the strategic plan for the system and also provides guidance to subsidiary companies for strategic planning activities.[30]

The central planning department has run into trouble in some companies. Conflicts have arisen because centralized planning people did not have detailed knowledge of the major operating units' activities. At GE's Major Appliance Business Group, the planners made mistakes because they relied on abstract data. In one case, GE's corporate planners analyzed data showing that houses and families were shrinking and concluded that small appliances were the wave of the future. But the planners did not realize that working women wanted *big* refrigerators in order to cut down on trips to the supermarket. GE wasted a lot of time designing smaller appliances because the planning group had failed to

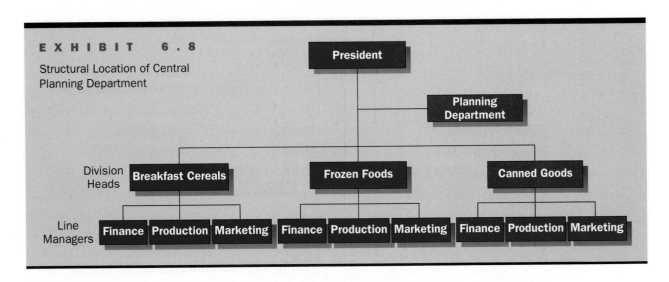

EXHIBIT 6.8

Structural Location of Central Planning Department

have contact with customers.[31] Problems such as these have caused many companies to decentralize planning to divisional managers.

DECENTRALIZED PLANNING STAFF

decentralized planning staff

A group of planning specialists assigned to major departments and divisions to help managers develop their own strategic plans.

The **decentralized planning staff** evolved when planning experts were assigned to major departments and divisions to help managers develop their own strategic plans, as indicated in Exhibit 6.9. Corporate planners no longer wrote the plans themselves. This change helped resolve some of the conflicts between planners and staff, as did the improved strategic planning training of line managers. By the 1980s, business school graduates understood the basics of strategic planning and were able to take on more planning responsibility.

At Sonat, Inc., headquarters staff members have been assigned to the operating units to provide a support function for line managers. A centralized strategic staff was introduced at General Motors in 1971. Several years later, the planners were assigned to each business unit to support line managers. At Borg-Warner, the central planning staff has been reduced from ten to three people; they now serve as consultants to business divisions, giving advice and helping managers write their own plans.[32]

PLANNING TASK FORCE

planning task force

A temporary group consisting of line managers responsible for developing strategic plans.

The third approach to strategic planning has been the use of planning task forces. A **planning task force** is a temporary group of line managers who have the responsibility of developing a strategic plan. A group of line managers thus takes over responsibility for planning. In one study of corporate planning practices, approximately one-third of the companies used an interdepartmental task force to make plans for achieving strategic goals. Each team identified and analyzed alternatives for reaching a specific objective and then outlined the major action steps necessary for achieving it.[33]

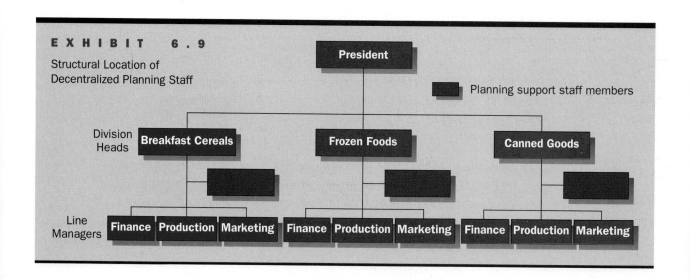

EXHIBIT 6.9

Structural Location of Decentralized Planning Staff

Millipore Corporation, a maker of high-tech filtration systems, fired its planning staff of six, which was replaced by task forces of operating managers. They meet every 18 months to brainstorm; they pool ideas on current market events and those likely to occur over the next five years. They set long-term and intermediate-term objectives and hammer out action plans for meeting them. Millipore executives claim this approach has helped make the company a leader in the industry because its plans are based on market realities and operational-level activities.[34]

● BARRIERS TO ORGANIZATIONAL PLANNING

Although planning is the primary management function, it does not happen automatically. Planning is difficult because it deals with complex environments and must look toward an uncertain future.

SPECIFIC BARRIERS

Several barriers can interfere with the organizational planning process. Managers can try to remove these barriers to facilitate planning.

DELEGATION TO STAFF SPECIALISTS. Line managers must be involved in planning. When the goal-setting and planning functions are assigned to planning specialists, negative things can happen. First, strategic planning may put too much emphasis on numbers. Strategic planners collect large amounts of data, conduct statistical analyses, and create a paper plan that may lie unused in line managers' bottom drawers. Second, lack of involvement by line managers may mean that the strategic plan is too abstract and inapplicable to the organization's operational and market needs. Third, this approach may result in overemphasis on planning techniques. Although the latest statistical methods may be used, the substance of the plan may not be what the organization needs.

LITTLE TOP MANAGEMENT SUPPORT. Top-level managers must provide the direction, scope, and statement of purpose for the strategic plan. They must support the idea of strategic planning, become involved themselves, and encourage the involvement of line managers at middle and lower levels. Sometimes top managers disagree about strategic objectives. They must build a coalition around a specific set of objectives toward which the organization will move. Without top management support, middle management will not allocate time and energy to planning activities.

LIMITED LINE MANAGEMENT EXPERTISE. Strategic planning requires knowledge of markets and other sectors in the external environment and a thorough understanding of internal operations. Many managers have little expertise in interpreting complex, changing environments or gathering and analyzing data. Managers may feel intimidated by the skills and education associated with planning techniques. Line managers must collaborate with corporate planning specialists who are good with techniques but do not understand the substance of the company.

OVERCOMING BARRIERS

The above barriers are not insurmountable. The following techniques can be used to overcome them.

START PLANNING AT THE TOP. Effective planning must have the explicit support and involvement of top managers. If top managers take the time to plan and involve other line managers in the planning process, many of the barriers will be overcome. Top managers can remove emphasis on short-term results, help increase middle management's faith in planning, and even provide training opportunities for line managers.

USE PLANNING SUPPORT STAFF. Planning experts who work in an advisory or consulting capacity can help overcome line managers' lack of expertise. Support staff can gather data, perform statistical analyses, use sophisticated scheduling systems, and do other specialized tasks. However, these people perform a support role and do not decide on the substance of goals or plans. Support staff in a consulting role can facilitate line management planning.

ENCOURAGE LINE MANAGEMENT PARTICIPATION. Many companies are realizing that planning comes alive for the organization when line managers participate. Managers can have scheduled training sessions—perhaps a two-to-three-day retreat—to discuss the future or create a task force to define goals and plans. Line management participation in planning deemphasizes techniques such as data analysis and increases the importance of substantive planning issues. It also increases management's faith in planning outcomes.

"We're facilitators," says Glenn Rogers, manager of strategic planning for Public Service Enterprise Group Incorporated. "We work closely with the other business units to advise and counsel them with their planning and development efforts." The Strategic Planning Group acts as a *planning support staff* to overcome planning barriers by analyzing key competitive issues and providing financial analyses, thereby helping managers make difficult financial decisions necessary to produce excellent results.

SUMMARY AND MANAGEMENT SOLUTION

This chapter described several important ideas about organizational planning. Organizational planning involves defining goals/objectives and developing a plan with which to achieve them. An organization exists for a single, overriding purpose known as its *mission*—the basis for strategic goals and plans. Goals within the organization are defined in a hierarchical fashion, beginning with strategic goals followed by tactical and operational goals. Plans are defined similarly, with strategic, tactical, and operational plans used to achieve the objectives. Other goal concepts include characteristics of effective goals and goal-setting behavior.

Several types of plans were described, including strategic, tactical, operational, single-use, standing, and contingency plans, and management by objectives. Long-term, intermediate-term, and short-term plans have time horizons of from five years down to six months. Organizational responsibility for planning typically includes one of three options: a centralized planning department, a decentralized planning staff, or an inter-departmental task force composed of line managers.

The planning group at Shell was faced with the task of planning for a sudden drop in oil prices when the likelihood seemed small. No one can read the future, so the planning group developed a written case—called a *scenario*—showing one of many ways by which the price of oil could fall. Executives agreed to explore the question, "What will we do if it happens?" This involved contingency planning for the intermediate term. Managers took the work seriously and began to consider responses to the possibility of lower-priced oil. As it happened, the price of oil fell from $28 to $15 a few months later, and Shell executives were ready.[35]

After preparing Shell management for the oil crisis, the planning team pursued other "war games" in preparation for the unexpected. Tanker fleet crews and local operating companies now face simulated accidents or supply disruptions so that employees may confidently face the real thing when it occurs. Global instability is likewise addressed in contingency planning. When an event such as the Persian Gulf war occurred, Shell quickly implemented new procedures that had been thoroughly studied and debated, keeping Shell well ahead of competitors.[36]

DISCUSSION QUESTIONS

1. What types of planning would have helped Exxon respond more quickly to the oil spill from the *Exxon Valdez* near Alaska?
2. Write a brief mission statement for a local business. Can the purpose and values of a small organization be captured in a written statement?
3. What strategies could the college or university at which you are taking this management course adopt to compete for students in the marketplace? Would these strategies depend on the school's goals?
4. If you were a top manager of a medium-size real estate sales agency, would you use MBO? If so, give examples of objectives you might set for managers and sales agents.
5. A new business venture has to develop a comprehensive business plan to borrow money to get started. Companies such as Federal Express, Nike, and Rolm Corporation say they did not follow the original plan very closely. Does that mean that developing the plan was a waste of time for these eventually successful companies?
6. A famous management theorist proposed that the time horizons for all strategic plans are becoming shorter because of the rapid changes in organizations' external environments. Do you agree? Would the planning time horizon for IBM or Ford Motor Company be shorter than it was 20 years ago?
7. What are the characteristics of effective goals? Would it be better to have no goals at all than to have goals that do not meet these criteria?
8. What do you think are the advantages and disadvantages of having a central planning department to do an organization's planning

compared with having decentralized planning groups provide planning support to line managers?

9. Assume Southern University decides to (1) raise its admission standards and (2) initiate a business fair to which local townspeople will be invited. What types of plans would it use to carry out these two activities?

MANAGEMENT IN PRACTICE: EXPERIENTIAL EXERCISE

● COMPANY CRIME WAVE

Senior managers in your organization are concerned about internal theft. Your department has been assigned the task of writing an ethics policy that defines employee theft and prescribes penalties. Stealing goods is easily classified as theft, but other activities are more ambiguous. Before writing the policy, go through the following list and decide which behaviors should be defined as stealing and whether penalties should apply. Discuss the items with your department members until agreement is reached. Classify each item as an example of (1) theft, (2) acceptable behavior, or (3) in between with respect to written policy. Is it theft when an employee

- Gets paid for overtime not worked?
- Takes a longer lunch or coffee break than authorized?
- Punches a time card for another?
- Comes in late or leaves early?

- Fakes injury to receive workers' compensation?
- Takes care of personal business on company time?
- Occasionally uses company copying machines or makes long-distance telephone calls for personal purposes?
- Takes a few stamps, pens, or other supplies for personal use?
- Takes money from the petty cash drawer?
- Uses company vehicles or tools for own purposes, but returns them?
- Damages merchandise so a cohort can purchase it at a discount?
- Accepts a gift from a supplier?

Now consider those items rated "in between." Do these items represent ethical issues as defined in Chapter 4? How should these items be handled in the company's written policy?

CASES FOR ANALYSIS

WEYERHAEUSER COMPANY

Weyerhaeuser's personal products division launched UltraSoft diapers amid a hail of hype and promotions. Touted as the "world's best diaper," the product's cloth-like outer covering and superabsorbent pad made from a special pulp material promised to separate UltraSoft from its major competitors, Pampers and Huggies.

The company tried to take all the right steps for introducing a new product, including consumer testing and testimonials. Planners also devised a unique marketing plan tying UltraSoft to popular local retail chains. For example, in Rochester, New York, Weyerhaeuser provided 50,000 area shoppers with samples and $1-off coupons for purchasing UltraSoft at Wegman's Food Market. This marketing plan allowed a 10 percent lower price compared to Pampers and Huggies.

The UltraSoft line got off to a great start, but ten months later, UltraSoft sales were languishing. Market share had dropped by one-third, and Weyerhaeuser decided there was no chance of going national with the product.

Weyerhaeuser had concentrated on the unique product design and marketing strategy, but the fledgling product had suffered from poor planning in Weyerhaeuser's lessglamorous manufacturing division and a serious miscalculation of production cost. The manufacturing plant faced major mechanical problems, because systems spraying the superabsorbent material clogged and corroded production lines. Poor scheduling resulted in frequently running out of stock. These problems forced a price increase of 22 percent. Meanwhile, planners miscalculated competitor reaction. Procter & Gamble and Kimberly Clark moved quickly to preserve shelf space and customer loyalty, sending discount coupons to thousands of customers and promoting their own improved products—including new blue and pink boy/girl diapers.

As Weyerhaeuser prepares to close down UltraSoft production completely, planners are analyzing where they went wrong and are considering future options such as utilizing diaper technology in other product lines.

● QUESTIONS

1. Can the types of problems faced by the UltraSoft line be anticipated and avoided with sufficient planning?

2. What types of goal setting and planning took place at Weyerhaeuser? Why do you think they failed?

3. What types of goal setting and planning would you recommend for Weyerhaeuser managers if they were to reintroduce the UltraSoft line? How should they plan for contingencies such as strong competitor responses?

SOURCE: Alecia Swasy, "Diaper's Failure Shows How Poor Plans, Unexpected Woes Can Kill New Products," *The Wall Street Journal*, October 9, 1990, B1, B4.

H.I.D.

Dave Collins, president of H.I.D., sat down at the conference table with his management team members, Karen Setz, Tony Briggs, Dave King, and Art Johnson. H.I.D. owns ten Holiday Inns in Georgia, eight hotels of different types in Canada, and one property in the Caribbean. It also owns two Quality Inns in Georgia. Dave Collins and his managers got together to define their mission, goals, and objectives and to set strategic plans. As they began their strategic planning session, the consultant they had hired suggested that each describe what he or she wanted for the company's domestic operations in the next ten years—how many hotels it should own, where to locate them, and who the target market was. Another question he asked them to consider was what the driving force of the company should be—that is, the single characteristic that would separate H.I.D. from other companies.

The team members wrote their answers on flip-charts, and the consultant summarized the results. Dave Collins' goal included 50 hotels in ten years, with the number increasing to 26 or 27 in five years. All the other members saw no more than 20 hotels in ten years and a maximum of 15 or 16 within five years. Clearly there was disagreement among the top managers about long-term goals and desirable growth rate.

With the consultant's direction, the team members began to critique their growth objectives. Dave King, director of operations and development, observed, "We just can't build that many hotels in that time period, certainly not given our current staffing, or any reasonable staffing we could afford. I don't see how we could achieve that goal." Art Johnson, the accountant, agreed. Karen Setz then asked, "Could we build them all in Georgia? You know we've centered on the medium-priced hotel in smaller towns. Do we need to move to bigger towns now, such as Jacksonville, or add another to the one we have in Atlanta?" Dave Collins responded, "We have an opportunity out in California, we may have one in New Jersey, and we are looking at the possibility of going to Jacksonville."

The consultant attempted to refocus the discussion: "Well, how does this all fit with your mission? Where are you willing to locate geographically? Most of your operation is in Georgia. Can you adequately support a national building effort?"

Tony Briggs responded, "Well, you know we have always looked at the smaller-town hotels as being our niche, although we deviated from that for the hotel in Atlanta. But we generally stay in smaller towns where we don't have much competition. Now we are talking about an expensive hotel in California."

Dave Collins suggested, "Maybe it's time we changed our target market, changed our pricing strategy, and went for larger hotels in urban areas across the whole country. Maybe we need to change a lot of factors about our company."

● QUESTIONS

1. What is H.I.D.'s mission at the present time? How may this mission change?

2. What do you think H.I.D.'s mission, strategic goals, and strategic plans are likely to be at the end of this planning session? Why?

3. What goal-setting behavior is being used here to reach agreement among H.I.D.'s managers? Do managers typically disagree about the direction of their organization?

SOURCE: This case was provided by James Higgins.

REFERENCES

1. Christopher Knowlton, "Shell Gets Rich by Beating Risk," *Fortune*, August 26, 1991, 79–82; and Arie P. de Geus, "Planning as Learning," *Harvard Business Review* (March–April 1988), 70–74.

2. Russell L. Ackoff, "On the Use of Models in Corporate Planning," *Strategic Management Journal* 2 (1981), 353–359.

3. Amitai Etzioni, *Modern Organizations* (Englewood Cliffs, N.J.: Prentice-Hall, 1984), 6.

4. Robert Howard, "Values Make the Company: An Interview with Robert Haas," *Harvard Business Review* (September–October 1990), 133–144.

5. Max D. Richards, *Setting Strategic Goals and Objectives*, 2d ed. (St. Paul, Minn.: West, 1986).

6. This discussion is based on Richard L. Daft and Richard M. Steers, *Organizations: A Micro/Macro Approach* (Glenview, Ill.: Scott, Foresman, 1986), 319–321; Herbert A. Simon, "On the Concept of Organizational Goals," *Administrative Science Quarterly* 9 (1964), 1–22; and Charles B. Saunders and Francis D. Tuggel, "Corporate Goals," *Journal of General Management* 5 (1980), 3–13.

7. Joseph Sensenbrenner, "Quality for Cities," *Nation's Business*, October 1991, 60–62, and "Quality Comes to City Hall," *Harvard Business Review* (March–April 1991), 64–75.

8. Mary Klemm, Stuart Sanderson, and George Luffman, "Mission Statements: Selling Corporate Values to Employees," *Long-Range Planning* 24, no. 3 (1991), 73–78; John A. Pearce II and Fred David, "Corporate Mission Statements: The Bottom Line," *Academy of Management Executive* (1987) 109–116; and Jerome H. Want, "Corporate Mission: The Intangible Contributor to Performance," *Management Review* (August 1986), 46–50.

9. Teri Lammers, "The Effective and Indispensable Mission Statement," *INC.*, August 1992, 75–77.

10. "Preparing for the Unexpected," *Columbia Today* (Winter 1985/1986), 2–4.

11. Peter F. Drucker, *The Practice of Management* (New York: Harper & Brothers, 1954), 65–83.

12. "Strategic Planning: Part 2," *Small Business Report* (March 1983), 28–32.

13. Paul Meising and Joseph Wolfe, "The Art and Science of Planning at the Business Unit Level," *Management Science* 31 (1985), 773–781.

14. Kenneth Libich, "Making Over Middle Managers," *Fortune*, May 8, 1989, 58–64.

15. Lois Therrien, "AMOCO: Running Smoother on Less Gas," *Business Week*, February 15, 1993, 110–112.

16. John O. Alexander, "Toward Real Performance: The Circuit-Breaker Technique," *Supervisory Management* (April 1989), 5–12.

17. "Positioning for the 1990s," *Intercom: A Monthly Publication for ALLTEL Employees and Friends*, September 1988, 1–2.

18. Edwin A. Locke, Garp P. Latham, and Miriam Erez, "The Determinants of Goal Commitment," *Academy of Management Review* 13 (1988), 23–39; and Carl R. Anderson, *Management* (Dubuque, Iowa: Wm. C. Brown, 1984), 262.

19. Locke, Latham, and Erez, "The Determinants of Goal Commitment."

20. George S. Odiorne, "MBO: A Backward Glance," *Business Horizons* 21 (October 1978), 14–24.

21. Jan P. Muczyk and Bernard C. Reimann, "MBO as a Complement to Effective Leadership," *The Academy of Management Executive* 3 (1989), 131–138; and W. Giegold, *Objective Setting and the MBO Process*, vol. 2 (New York: McGraw-Hill, 1978).

22. "Delegation," *Small Business Reports* (July 1986), 71–75, and R. Henry Migliore, Constance A. Pogue, and Jeffrey S. Horvath, "Planning for the Future," *Small Business Reports* (July 1991), 53–63.

23. John Ivancevich, J. Timothy McMahon, J. William Streidl, and Andrew D. Szilagyi, "Goal Setting: The Tenneco Approach to Personnel Development and Management Effectiveness," *Organizational Dynamics* (Winter 1978), 48–80.

24. Alex Taylor III, "How Toyota Copes with Hard Times," *Fortune*, January 25, 1993, 78–81.

25. Gregory L. Miles, "Heinz Ain't Broke, But It's Doing a Lot of Fixing," *Business Week*, December 11, 1989, 84–88.

26. "Corporate Planning: Drafting a Blueprint for Success," *Small Business Report* (August 1987), 40–44.

27. P. R. Stokke, W. K. Ralston, T. A. Boyce, and I. H. Wilson, "Scenario Planning for Norwegian Oil and Gas," *Long-Range Planning* 23 (April 1990), 17–26.

28. Anne B. Fisher, "Is Long-Range Planning Worth It?" *Fortune*, April 23, 1990, 281–284.

29. Andrew Tanzer, "We Do Not Take a Short-Term View," *Forbes*, July 13, 1987, 372–374.

30. "Preparing for the Unexpected," 2–4.

31. "The New Breed of Strategic Planner," *Business Week*, September 17, 1984, 62–68.

32. Ibid.

33. Daniel H. Gray, "Uses and Misuses of Strategic Planning," *Harvard Business Review* 64 (January–February 1986), 89–97.

34. "The New Breed."

35. de Geus, "Planning as Learning."

36. Christopher Knowlton, "Shell Gets Rich by Beating Risk," *Fortune,* August 26, 1991, 79–82.

FORD

VIDEO CASE

For decades American automakers reigned supreme. By the dawn of the 1990s there was concern about their very survival. Reasons for the decline range from unfair trade practices by the Japanese to currency differences that translated to price advantages, and the list went on.

"Some of the American products in the 1970s weren't as good as they should have been," Allan Gilmour, president of Ford Motor Company's Automotive Group, said. "But I think we are into this decade ready for action."

How did Ford battle back from the perception that American products were inferior, and red ink that culminated with a $2.3 billion loss in 1992? By setting goals and objectives for everyone from top management to service-department mechanics and following up to quantify and evaluate results. "We are much more competitive than we were 10 or 15 years ago, in quality and efficiency. We are working extremely hard to be the best that there is," Gilmour said.

To combat the perception that foreign competitors produce a mechanically superior product, Ford launched the "Quality Care" advertising campaign from their parts and service division. The objective: emphasizing owner satisfaction as the basis for building a sustainable competitive advantage. With active participation from dealers, Ford implemented enhanced technician education and training, and introduced high technology service support equipment, such as the Service Bay Diagnostic System. An improved process for evaluating customer service needs was introduced as well as an extended service plan, and next day parts delivery.

Ford went all out to implement a quality control and customer satisfaction plan at their Avon Lake, Ohio, plant, where the Mercury Villager is co-produced through a joint venture with Nissan. To anticipate and fine tune consumer needs and desires, the company conducted six customer encounter sessions. Participants gave input about likes and dislikes in competitor minivans, as well as a wish list of additional features.

Said Pat Lynch, regional sales manager for Ford's Dallas division, "We've had 10 years to study the others [minivan manufacturers] to decide what we wanted to do. So we took the best, refined it, and dropped the worst. Now, I think we've got the best minivan on the market."

They may well have. No U.S. automaker has ever undertaken such all-encompassing quality control measures. While the first shift at the Mercury plant manufactures the minivan, the task of the second shift is solely to inspect and test the finished product, which can include driving vehicles as far as 60 miles. After a Villager comes off the line it rolls into what amounts to an aquarium where quality assurance personnel conduct more than 125 assurance tests.

The first 2,000 Villagers were shipped to dealers in July 1992 and the company followed up with queries to tabulate customer satisfaction. Ford received overwhelmingly positive response, with only a handful of minor complaints.

The Villager has a sales goal of 70,000 units for 1993. According to Carolyn Brown of Lincoln Mercury's corporate sales information department, through the first quarter of 1993, 29,452 units have been sold, far exceeding expectations.

Ford will seek to enhance product quality through plant modernization as well. Substantial modernization of Ford plants is planned in conjunction with the introduction of new products, as was done in Louisville, Kentucky, when the Explorer was introduced.

New approaches to doing things at Ford have not been limited to their automaking operations. In an effort to make slower-growing advertising budgets work more effectively, the company announced a print media plan with a sharpened focus. The automaker's $150-million budget will be allocated among fewer periodicals, with primary emphasis placed on magazine quality and price.

The road back to profitability for Ford will not be easy or quick, but the company is looking to the future and decided that it will not be German or Japanese, but American. Carefully formulated management plans that target goals and motivate personnel will ensure that the future is brighter than the past. "If you can get all the resources at Ford Motor Company aimed in the right direction, I think we'll do a good job," Allan Gilmour said.

● **QUESTIONS**

1. Describe how Ford set its goals and then set about making plans to achieve those goals.

2. Describe how Ford's new strategies reflect management by objective.

3. Were the actions taken by Ford in the 1990s as revolutionary as those taken by the company's founder, Henry Ford? Discuss.

4. What barriers does Ford still face in today's car market?

STRATEGY FORMULATION AND IMPLEMENTATION

LEARNING OBJECTIVES

After studying this chapter, you should be able to

■ Define the components of strategic management.

■ Describe the strategic planning process and SWOT analysis.

■ Understand Grand Strategies for Domestic and International Operations.

■ Define corporate-level strategies and explain the portfolio approach.

■ Describe business-level strategies, including competitive strategies and product life cycle.

■ Explain the major considerations in formulating functional strategies.

■ Enumerate the organizational dimensions used for implementing strategy.

When ex-cabinet secretary Elizabeth Dole was named president of the American Red Cross in 1991, she found the humanitarian organization pummeled by criticism. The Red Cross faced the AIDS scare and concerns about "tainted" blood supplies, government charges of poor record keeping, and criticism of its preparedness for major disasters such as Hurricane Hugo, specifically regarding its inadequate services and poor distribution of funds. Moreover, a deepening national recession created the potential for fund-raising problems. Dole's mission was to develop an overall strategy within which to establish priorities, address fund-raising and distribution problems, and implement new directions for blood operations and disaster relief while maintaining quality programs such as personal disaster relief (to victims of house fires, for example) and health-safety training.[1]

If you were Elizabeth Dole, where would you start to formulate and implement new strategies for the Red Cross? What strategies would you adopt to ensure quality services for an organization so crucial to America?

M A N A G E M E N T P R O B L E M

The American Red Cross was suddenly confronted with new events that created the urgent need for strategic planning. Previous strategies could not cope with the AIDS scare or the strain of unexpectedly huge national disasters. Dole and other Red Cross executives must carefully analyze the situation to formulate a strategy that will suit the organization's strengths as well as fit changing economic times and rapidly changing world events.

Every organization is concerned with strategy. Hershey developed a new strategy after losing its number-one candy bar status to Mars. Hershey's new strategy in the bar wars was to be a fierce product innovator. New products included Take Five, Symphony, and the Big Block line of Hershey's standard chocolate bars.[2] The Roman Catholic church in the United States is faced with the need to reevaluate strategy. Its 115,000 nuns, now with a median age of over 60, have no satisfactory retirement benefits and a depressing medical situation. Sherwin-Williams' CEO, John G. Breen, anticipated the recession of the 1990s and successfully adjusted company strategy to meet the slow-growth period by targeting brands to specific markets.[3] Many large corporations engaged in acquisitions or divestments as part of a strategic plan. AT&T purchased NCR for $7.5 million. Two large southern banks, C&S/Sovran and NCNB merged to become NationsBank. Electronic Data Systems, a General Motors subsidiary, nabbed the CAD/CAM unit of McDonnell Douglas. Going in the other direction, Canada's Seagram distiller sold seven of its brands to American Brands (maker of Jim Beam). Georgia-Pacific sold 80 percent of two paper and pulp mills, 2 million acres of timberland, a hydroelectric power facility to Bowater and a corrugated container facility and additional timberland to Tenneco.[4]

All of these organizations are involved in strategic management. They are finding ways to respond to competitors, cope with difficult environmental changes, and effectively use available resources. In this chapter, we focus on the topic of strategic management. First we define components of strategic management and then discuss a model of the strategic management process. Next we examine several models of strategy formulation. Finally, we discuss the tools managers use to implement their strategic plans.

● THINKING STRATEGICALLY

Chapter 6 provided an overview of the types of goals and plans that organizations use. In this chapter, we will explore strategic management, which is considered one specific type of planning. Strategic planning in for-profit business organizations typically pertains to competitive actions in the marketplace. In not-for-profit organizations like the Red Cross, strategic planning pertains to events in the external environment. Although some companies hire strategic planning experts, the final responsibility for strategic planning rests with line managers. Senior executives at companies such as General Electric, Westinghouse, and Delta want middle- and lower-level line managers to think strategically. Strategic thinking means to take the long-term view and to see

the big picture, including the organization and the competitive environment, and how they fit together. Understanding the strategy concept, the
levels of strategy, and strategy formulation versus implementation is an
important start toward strategic thinking.

WHAT IS STRATEGIC MANAGEMENT?

Strategic management is the set of decisions and actions used to formulate and implement strategies that will provide a competitively superior fit between the organization and its environment so as to achieve
organizational objectives.[5] Strategic management is a process used to
help managers answer strategic questions such as "Where is the organization now? Where does the organization want to be? What changes and
trends are occurring in the competitive environment? What courses of
action will help us achieve our goals?" Through strategic management,
executives define an overall direction for the organization, which is the
firm's grand strategy.

GRAND STRATEGY

Grand strategy is the general plan of major action by which a firm
intends to achieve its long-term objectives.[6] Grand strategies fall into
three general categories: growth, stability, and retrenchment. A separate
grand strategy can also be defined for global operations.

GROWTH.   *Growth* can be promoted internally by investing in expansion or externally by acquiring additional business divisions. Internal
growth can include development of new or changed products, such as
Goodyear's development of the Eagle tire, or expansion of current products into new markets, such as Coors' expansion into the Northeast.
External growth typically involves *diversification*, which means the acquisition of businesses that are related to current product lines or that take
the corporation into new areas. Sometimes expansion involves acquiring
competitors, such as Northwest Airlines' acquisition of Republic, or suppliers or distributors, such as Alcan's acquisition of bauxite mines. One
strategy for international growth is the formation of a joint venture, as
described in the Focus on Global Competition box.

STABILITY.   *Stability,* sometimes called a *pause strategy,* means that the
organization wants to remain the same size or grow slowly and in a controlled fashion. The corporation wants to stay in its current business,
such as Allied Tire Stores, whose motto is "We just sell tires." After organizations have undergone a turbulent period of rapid growth, executives
often focus on a stability strategy to integrate strategic business units and
ensure that the organization is working efficiently.

RETRENCHMENT.   *Retrenchment* means that the organization goes
through a period of forced decline by either shrinking current business
units or selling off or liquidating entire businesses. The organization may
have experienced a precipitous drop in demand for its products, prompt-
ing managers to order across-the-board cuts in personnel and expenditures. Borden Inc. did so in 1992, closing ten plants and cutting four food

strategic management

The set of decisions and actions used
to formulate and implement strategies
that will provide a competitively superior fit between the organization and its
environment so as to achieve organizational objectives.

grand strategy

The general plan of major action by
which an organization intends to
achieve its long-term objectives.

Turner Broadcasting System, Inc.,
proved itself "smarter than the average bear" with the purchase of "Yogi
Bear" and other American cartoon
classics acquired as part of the
Hanna-Barbera library. The acquisition
fits TBS' *grand strategy* for growth.
The addition of over 3,000 half-hour
cartoon segments to the cable
company's entertainment repertoire
enabled TBS to launch a cable
cartoon network in 1992, and
assures Turner will remain "Top Cat"
in the cartoon cable industry.

PARTNERSHIP STRATEGIES

How do companies—big and small—strategically position themselves to compete internationally? Without experience, an international strategy may turn into disaster. Why not team up with companies abroad?

Consider the strategy employed by Whirlpool Corporation, the huge appliance manufacturer. Senior executives realized they could not simply defend domestic boundaries and continue to prosper. Brainstorming new strategies pointed to globalization. Unfortunately, big American refrigerators do not fit into small Japanese kitchens. Europeans tend not to buy dishwashers.

A Whirlpool strength was a strong position in Canada and Mexico. Europe seemed like the next big market so Whirlpool acquired a ready-made distribution system and manufacturing operation by purchasing 53 percent of Holland's Philips N. V.'s $2 billion appliance business.

Philips and Whirlpool streamlined the two companies, giving them enormous buying clout that will lower cost for materials and components. This streamlining puts Whirlpool in a position of being a low-cost producer in both North America and Europe, a powerful strategic advantage. Whirlpool also achieves an international synergy by using its worldwide distribution network to market products from both American and European plants.

At Nypro, Inc., a small plastic injection-molding and industrial components manufacturer in Clinton, Massachusetts, President Gordon Lankton found the local rules and customs of other countries too complex to fathom from the United States. So he found partners in Ireland, France, and Hong Kong. His initial efforts failed because he did not understand the other companies or their goals. Finally, though, Nypro hit it off with partner companies in Switzerland and Singapore. Trial and error worked, and sharing technology has been a big plus, helping both sides.

Nypro has a presence in six countries now and four joint venture plants in the United States. Disputes over quality, management techniques, and strategy still occur, but joint ventures account for 25 percent of revenues. More important, Nypro overcame limitations on markets, technology, knowledge, and people. The expanded horizon was possible only with partners. And employees love it—they cannot wait for the next foreign adventure. Like marriage partners, the best alliances focus on long-term commitment, flexibility in resolving differences when dealing with the unexpected, establishment of trust, and an autonomy combined with a spirit of cooperation by both parties. ■

SOURCES: Stratford Sherman, "Are Strategic Alliances Working?" *Fortune*, September 21, 1992, 77–78; Claudia H. Deutsch, "Whirlpool Is Gathering a Global Momentum," *The New York Times*, April 23, 1989, sec. 3, 10; and Joshua Hyatt, "The Partnership Route," *INC.*, December 1988, 145–148.

divisions and 3,000 jobs. *Liquidation* means selling off a business unit for the cash value of the assets, thus terminating its existence. An example is the liquidation of Minnie Pearl Fried Chicken. *Divestiture* involves the selling off of businesses that no longer seem central to the corporation. When ITT sold 115 of 200 business divisions and when General Electric sold its family financial services and housewares divisions, both corporations were going through periods of retrenchment, also called *downsizing*.

GLOBAL STRATEGY

In addition to the three alternatives above—growth, stability, and retrenchment—companies may pursue a fourth grand strategy as the focus of global business. In today's global corporations, senior executives try to formulate coherent strategies to provide synergy among world-wide operations for the purpose of fulfilling common objectives. A systematic strategic planning process for deciding on the appropriate strategic alternative should be used. The grand strategy of growth is a major motivation for both small and large businesses going international. Each country or region represents a new market with the promise of increased sales and profits.

In the international arena, companies face a strategic dilemma between global integration and national responsiveness. Organizations must decide whether they want each global affiliate to act autonomously or whether activities should be standardized and centralized across countries. This choice leads managers to select a basic grand strategy alternative such as globalization versus multidomestic strategy.

GLOBALIZATION.   When an organization chooses a strategy of globalization, it means that its product design and advertising strategies are standardized throughout the world.[7] This approach is based on the assumption that a single global market exists for most consumer and industrial products. The theory is that people everywhere want to buy the same products and live the same way. People everywhere want to drink Coca-Cola and wear Levi blue jeans.[8] For example, the dropping of European customs barriers in 1992 helped make Europe one unified market for standardized manufacturing, packaging, and ads. Ford Motor Company treats the world as one market by selling the same Escort in all markets. Assembly plants around the world all use standard products, saving millions of dollars compared with designing a unique car for each country or region.

Globalization enables marketing departments alone to save millions of dollars. For example, Colgate-Palmolive Company sells Colgate toothpaste in over 40 countries. For every country where the same commercial runs, it saves $1 to $2 million in production costs alone. More

globalization

The standardization of product design and advertising strategies throughout the world.

Creating new products for the world is a major part of Colgate-Palmolive Company's ongoing *globalization* strategy. Its 1990 five-year plan included an aggressive new products program, along with plans for geographical expansion and strategic acquisitions. Here, new Palmolive Optims products are tested on various hair types by Distinguished Research Fellow Dr. Clarence Robbins. Launched in the Philippines and Australia in 1991 before going worldwide, the patented Optims shampoo and conditioner are among Colgate-Palmolive's new product lines that contribute $1.2 billion to its annual worldwide sales.

millions have been saved by standardizing the look and packaging of brands.[9] International Playtex developed a single advertising campaign for selling its Wow bra in 12 countries. It avoided the more expensive approach of assigning ad agencies in each country the job of developing a marketing campaign.[10]

MULTIDOMESTIC STRATEGY.   When an organization chooses a **multidomestic strategy,** it means that competition in each country is handled independently of industry competition in other countries. Thus, a multinational company is present in many countries, but it encourages marketing, advertising, and product design to be modified and adapted to the specific needs of each country.[11] Many companies reject the idea of a single global market. They have found that the French do not drink orange juice for breakfast, that laundry detergent is used to wash dishes in parts of Mexico, and that people in the Middle East prefer toothpaste that tastes spicy. Parker Pen launched a single international ad campaign and reduced pen styles from 500 to 100, causing a strategic disaster. New pens and advertising campaigns have now been developed for each market.[12] DuPont produces customized herbicides for problems with weeds that are unique to countries such as Brazil and Japan. Avon found that its door-to-door sales strategy would not work in Japan and thus customized a soft-sell approach.[13]

PURPOSE OF STRATEGY

Within the overall grand strategy of an organization, executives define an explicit **strategy,** which is the plan of action that describes resource allocation and activities for dealing with the environment and attaining the organization's goals. Through this strategy, executives try to develop within the organization a core competence and synergy.

CORE COMPETENCE.   A company's **core competence** is something the organization does especially well in comparison to its competitors. A core competence represents a competitive advantage because the company acquires expertise that competitors do not have. A core competence may be in the area of superior research and development, mastery of a technology, manufacturing efficiency, or customer service.[14] For example, James River Corporation invested in state-of-the-art automation that has given it the core competence of being able to produce paper towels and tissues more cheaply than Scott Paper Company and Procter & Gamble. Perdue Farms has achieved a competitive advantage by investing resources to guarantee the highest-quality chickens available in supermarkets. This core competence allows Perdue to charge a higher price for its chickens. Briggs & Stratton enjoys a core competence by keeping its costs lower than the Japanese and thus is producing more small motors than anyone else.

SYNERGY.   When organizational parts interact to produce a joint effect that is greater than the sum of the parts acting alone, **synergy** occurs. The organization may attain a special advantage with respect to cost, market power, technology, or management skill. For example, AT&T is attempting to develop synergy between communication services and

multidomestic strategy

The modification of product design and advertising strategies to suit the specific needs of individual countries.

strategy

The plan of action that prescribes resource allocation and other activities for dealing with the environment and helping the organization attain its goals.

core competence

A business activity that an organization does particularly well in comparison to competitors.

synergy

The condition that exists when the organization's parts interact to produce a joint effect that is greater than the sum of the parts acting alone.

hardware. Sparked by its 1991 acquisition of NCR, AT&T hopes to fuse voice and data capabilities with sophisticated equipment, enabling corporations to "one-stop shop" for communication services and hardware needed for globalization.[15] Synergy can also be obtained by good relations between suppliers and customers and by strong alliances between large and small companies. Hammond Enterprises, a seven-employee firm in Marietta, Georgia, designs and produces promotional caps, mugs, and T-shirts for major corporations such as Coca-Cola and Lockheed. Synergy develops because Hammond relieves the corporate giants of the hassle of research, paperwork, and design of logo-bearing promotional items, enabling them to obtain the items at less cost than if they produced the items themselves.[16]

LEVELS OF STRATEGY

Another aspect of strategic management concerns the organizational level to which strategic issues apply. Strategic managers normally think in terms of three levels of strategy—corporate, business, and functional—as illustrated in Exhibit 7.1.[17]

CORPORATE-LEVEL STRATEGY. The question *What business are we in?* concerns **corporate-level strategy.** Corporate-level strategy pertains to the organization as a whole and the combination of business units and product lines that make up the corporate entity. Strategic actions at this level usually relate to the acquisition of new businesses; additions or divestments of business units, plants, or product lines; and joint ventures with other corporations in new areas. An example of corporate-level strategy was Sears, Roebuck's 1992 decision to drop its "socks and

corporate-level strategy

The level of strategy concerned with the question: "What business are we in?" Pertains to the organization as a whole and the combination of business units and product lines that make it up.

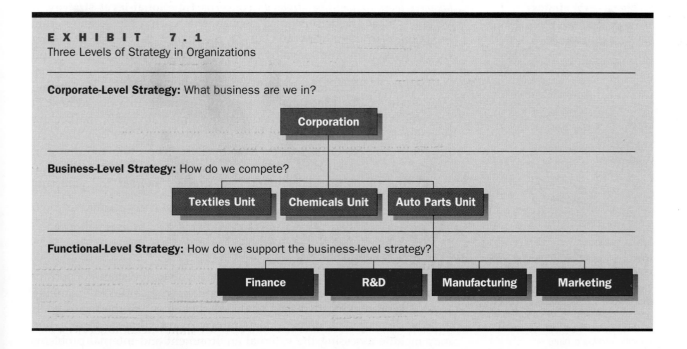

EXHIBIT 7.1
Three Levels of Strategy in Organizations

Corporate-Level Strategy: What business are we in?

Corporation

Business-Level Strategy: How do we compete?

Textiles Unit   Chemicals Unit   Auto Parts Unit

Functional-Level Strategy: How do we support the business-level strategy?

Finance   R&D   Manufacturing   Marketing

stocks" image and focus again on retailing. This decision reversed a decade-long corporate strategy that saw acquisitions in service areas such as real estate (Coldwell Banker), insurance (Allstate), financial services (Dean Witter), and credit cards (Discover Card). In an attempt to reduce billions in debt and rebound from its number-three industry position behind Wal-Mart and K mart, Sears is selling much of its financial services divisions to refocus on its core—the retail store.[18] Using the opposite corporate-level strategy, Black & Decker's acquisition of GE's housewares division and then Emhart Corporation redefined it from a power tools producer to a company that also provides household appliances and products for home improvement.[19]

business-level strategy

The level of strategy concerned with the question: "How do we compete?" Pertains to each business unit or product line within the organization.

BUSINESS-LEVEL STRATEGY.   The question *How do we compete?* concerns **business-level strategy**. Business-level strategy pertains to each business unit or product line. It focuses on how the business unit competes within its industry for customers. Strategic decisions at the business level concern amount of advertising, direction and extent of research and development, product changes, new-product development, equipment and facilities, and expansion or contraction of product lines. For example, Food Lion, Inc., one of the fastest-growing grocery chains in the nation, has a business-level strategy of cost reduction. Food Lion's economizing allows it to sell more cheaply than rivals yet maintain a higher profit margin. Jostens, Inc., a Minneapolis producer of high-school rings, has a business-level strategy of competing through product innovation. Although students have become less interested in buying class rings over the years, Jostens now offers 23 different stones and 16,000 ring permutations to fit every student's needs. Salespeople visit high schools personally to beat competitors to the student's door.[20]

functional-level strategy

The level of strategy concerned with the question: "How do we support the business-level strategy?" Pertains to all of the organization's major departments.

FUNCTIONAL-LEVEL STRATEGY.   The question *How do we support the business-level competitive strategy?* concerns **functional-level strategy**. It pertains to the major functional departments within the business unit. Functional strategies involve all of the major functions, including finance, research and development, marketing, manufacturing, and finance. For Hershey to compete on the basis of new-product innovation, its research department adopted a functional strategy for developing new products. The functional strategy for the marketing department of Sherwin-Williams is to develop advertising aimed at specific markets for its paint. For example, its Dutch Boy paint, touted as "the look that gets the looks," is advertised to do-it-yourselfers who shop the discount chains. The "Ask Sherwin-Williams" advertisements target the professional line of paints. This marketing strategy helped the company increase sales when total industry sales fell.[21]

STRATEGY FORMULATION VERSUS IMPLEMENTATION

strategy formulation

The stage of strategic management that involves the planning and decision making that lead to the establishment of the organization's goals and of a specific strategic plan.

The final aspect of strategic management involves the stages of formulation and implementation. **Strategy formulation** includes the planning and decision making that lead to the establishment of the firm's goals and the development of a specific strategic plan.[22] Strategy formulation may include assessing the external environment and internal problems and integrating the results into goals and strategy. This is in contrast to **strategy implementation,** which is the use of managerial and organizational tools to direct resources toward accomplishing strategic results.[23] Strategy implementation is the administration and execution of the strategic plan. Managers may use persuasion, new equipment, changes in organization structure, or a reward system to ensure that employees and resources are used to make formulated strategy a reality.

strategy implementation

The stage of strategic management that involves the use of managerial and organizational tools to direct resources toward achieving strategic outcomes.

THE STRATEGIC MANAGEMENT PROCESS

The overall strategic management process is illustrated in Exhibit 7.2. It begins when executives evaluate their current position with respect to mission, goals, and strategies. They then scan the organization's internal and external environments and identify strategic factors that may require change. Internal or external events may indicate a need to redefine the mission or goals or to formulate a new strategy at either the corporate, business, or functional level. Once a new strategy is selected, it is implemented through changes in leadership, structure, human resources, or information and control systems.

SITUATION ANALYSIS

Situation analysis typically includes a search for SWOT—strengths, weaknesses, opportunities, and threats that affect organizational performance. Situational analysis is important to all companies but is crucial

situation analysis

Analysis of the strengths, weaknesses, opportunities, and threats (SWOT) that affect organizational performance.

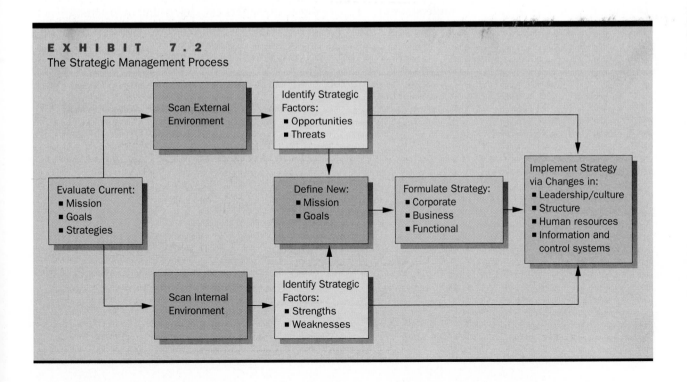

E X H I B I T   7 . 2
The Strategic Management Process

to those considering globalization because of the diverse environments in which they will operate. External information about opportunities and threats may be obtained from a variety of sources, including customers, government reports, professional journals, suppliers, bankers, friends in other organizations, consultants, or association meetings. Many firms hire special scanning organizations to provide them with newspaper clippings and analyses of relevant domestic and global trends. Some firms use more subtle techniques to learn about competitors, such as asking potential recruits about their visits to other companies, hiring people away from competitors, debriefing former employees or customers of competitors, taking plant tours posing as "innocent" visitors, and even buying competitors' garbage.[24]

Executives acquire information about internal strengths and weaknesses from a variety of reports, including budgets, financial ratios, profit and loss statements, and surveys of employee attitudes and satisfaction. Managers spend 80 percent of their time giving and receiving information from others. Through frequent face-to-face discussions and meetings with people at all levels of the hierarchy, executives build an understanding of the company's internal strengths and weaknesses.

INTERNAL STRENGTHS AND WEAKNESSES. *Strengths* are positive internal characteristics that the organization can exploit to achieve its strategic performance goals. *Weaknesses* are internal characteristics that may inhibit or restrict the organization's performance. Some examples of what executives evaluate to interpret strengths and weaknesses are given in Exhibit 7.3. The information sought typically pertains to specific functions such as marketing, finance, production, and R&D. Internal analysis also examines overall organization structure, management competence and quality, and human resource characteristics. Based on their understanding of these areas, managers can determine their strengths or weaknesses vis-à-vis other companies. For example, Marriott Corpora-

---

E X H I B I T   7 . 3

Checklist for Analyzing Organizational Strengths and Weaknesses

SOURCE: Based on Howard H. Stevenson, "Defining Corporate Strengths and Weaknesses," *Sloan Management Review* 17 (Spring 1976), 51–68, and M. L. Kastens, *Long-Range Planning for Your Business* (New York: American Management Association, 1976).

Management and Organization	Marketing	Human Resources
Management quality	Distribution channels	Employee age, education
Staff quality	Market share	Union status
Degree of centralization	Advertising efficiency	Turnover, absenteeism
Organization charts	Customer satisfaction	Work satisfaction
Planning, information, control systems	Product quality	Grievances
	Service reputation	
	Sales force turnover	

Finance	Production	Research and Development
Profit margin	Plant location	Basic applied research
Debt-equity ratio	Machinery obsolescence	Laboratory capabilities
Inventory ratio	Purchasing system	Research programs
Return on investment	Quality control	New-product innovations
Credit rating	Productivity/efficiency	Technology innovations

tion has been able to grow rapidly because of its financial strength. It has a strong financial base, enjoys an excellent reputation with creditors, and has always been able to acquire financing needed to support its strategy of constructing hotels in new locations.[25]

EXTERNAL OPPORTUNITIES AND THREATS.   *Threats* are characteristics of the external environment that may prevent the organization from achieving its strategic goals. *Opportunities* are characteristics of the external environment that have the potential to help the organization achieve or exceed its strategic goals. Executives evaluate the external environment with information about the nine sectors described in Chapter 4. The task environment sectors are the most relevant to strategic behavior and include the behavior of competitors, customers, suppliers, and the labor supply. The general environment contains those sectors that have an indirect influence on the organization but nevertheless must be understood and incorporated into strategic behavior. The general environment includes technological developments, the economy, legal-political and international events, and sociocultural changes. Additional areas that might reveal opportunities or threats include pressure groups,

Mobil Corporation cites environmental excellence as one of five core *strengths* and areas of *opportunity* for the 1990s. The high priority given to environmental protection is evidenced by Mobil's billion dollar budgets and the deployment of over 700 professionals to environmental projects. Mobil's pledge to reduce chemical emissions 50 percent by 1995, establishing the industry's first coast-to-coast used oil collection program, and efforts to attract and shelter marine life near producing rigs in the Gulf of Mexico (shown here) illustrate the company's commitment to analysis of its environment and development of programs to meet the world's environmental needs.

interest groups, creditors, natural resources, and potentially competitive industries.

An example of how external analysis can uncover a threat occurred in the Post cereal business of General Foods. Scanning the environment indicated that Kellogg had increased its market share from 38 to 40 percent while Post's share had dropped from 16 to 14 percent. Information from the competitor and customer sectors indicated that Kellogg had stepped up advertising and new-product introductions. This threat to Post was the basis for a strategic response. The first step was to throw additional dollars into cents-off coupons and discounts to grocery stores. The next step was to develop new cereals, such as the successful Fruit & Fibre.[26]

The value of situation analysis in helping executives formulate the correct strategy is illustrated by Morton International, Inc.

 # MORTON INTERNATIONAL, INC.

Do you remember Morton Thiokol, whose production of a faulty booster rocket sparked the 1986 explosion of the *Challenger* space shuttle? That tragedy, resulting in the deaths of all seven crew members, including schoolteacher Christa McAuliffe, forced the company to consider a new strategic direction, including a new company name—Morton International—that can be explained with SWOT analysis.

Following the *Challenger* tragedy, Morton continued to have enormous *strengths*, including a well-trained high-tech work force. Its rocket-propulsion and technological know-how had potential for application in other areas. In addition, Morton forged into a leadership position in the design and production of air bags for automobiles. Achieving 55 percent of the global market, air bag production is a major strength for the company's future.

In light of the *Challenger* disaster, Morton had visible *weaknesses* and took the major steps of axing the Thiokol name and its aeronautics division. The specialty chemicals division was negatively affected by the recession and downturns in both housing and auto industries. By 1992, Morton faced a weak financial outlook.

Opportunities in the external environment arose from Morton's strength in air bags. Although the field is one of slow growth and major investment, Morton has achieved an excellent reputation. It is the sole supplier for Chrysler and likewise grabbed the Ford market. Globally, Morton teamed with Germany's Robert Bosch for joint development of air bags for the European market, giving Morton an inside track at auto manufacturers worldwide.

The biggest *threat* facing Morton is the increased competition in the air bag industry from TRW (United States), Siemens (Germany), Electrolux Autoliv (Sweden), and Takata Corporation (Japan). Global competition is especially stiff where the battlefield is suddenly crowded. The threat is that the air bag focus may not pay off because of the huge investment required.

What does SWOT analysis suggest for Morton's future strategy? It should capitalize on its strengths and opportunities with continued technology improvement in the expanding air bag industry and strengthen the Morton-Bosch alliance and other joint ventures to take advantage of global trade opportunities.[27] ■

● FORMULATING CORPORATE-LEVEL STRATEGY

PORTFOLIO STRATEGY

Portfolio strategy pertains to the mix of business units and product lines that fit together in a logical way to provide synergy and competitive advantage for the corporation. For example, an individual may wish to diversify in an investment portfolio with some high-risk stocks, some low-risk stocks, some growth stocks, and perhaps a few income bonds. In much the same way, corporations like to have a balanced mix of business divisions called **strategic business units (SBUs)**. An SBU has a unique business mission, product line, competitors, and markets relative to other SBUs in the corporation.[28] Executives in charge of the entire corporation generally define the grand strategy and then bring together a portfolio of strategic business units to carry it out. The BCG matrix is a useful way to think about portfolio strategy.

THE BCG MATRIX.   The BCG (for Boston Consulting Group) matrix is illustrated in Exhibit 7.4. The **BCG matrix** organizes businesses along two dimensions—business growth rate and market share.[29] *Business growth rate* pertains to how rapidly the entire industry is increasing. *Market share* defines whether a business unit has a larger or smaller share than competitors. The combinations of high and low market share and high and low business growth provide four categories for a corporate portfolio.

The *star* has a large market share in a rapidly growing industry. The star is important because it has additional growth potential, and profits should be plowed into this business as investment for future growth and profits. The star is visible and attractive and will generate profits and a positive cash flow even as the industry matures and market growth slows.

The *cash cow* exists in a mature, slow-growth industry but is a dominant business in the industry, with a large market share. Because heavy investments in advertising and plant expansion are no longer required, the corporation earns a positive cash flow. It can milk the cash cow to invest in other, riskier businesses.

The *question mark* exists in a new, rapidly growing industry but has only a small market share. The question mark business is risky: It could become a star, but it could also fail. The corporation can invest the cash earned from cash cows in question marks with the goal of nurturing them into future stars.

The *dog* is a poor performer. It has only a small share of a slow-growth market. The dog provides little profit for the corporation and may be targeted for divestment or liquidation if turnaround is not possible.

Hasbro, Inc., has adopted a portfolio strategy for its many product lines, which include Milton Bradley board games and puzzles, Playskool infant and preschool products, and Hasbro's traditional toys such as G.I. Joe, Cabbage Patch Kids, and My Little Pony. Hasbro's diversified portfolio includes products that cover the full spectrum of toy users from infants to adults, as well as products in different stages of the product life cycle. For example, games for older children such as Chutes & Ladders are balanced with innovations such as Playskool's Sandwich-Board Aprons for toddlers shown here.

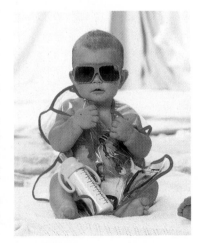

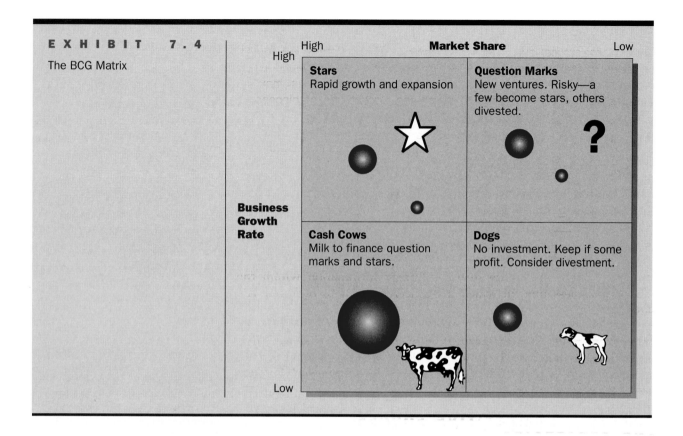

EXHIBIT 7.4

The BCG Matrix

The circles in Exhibit 7.4 represent the business portfolio for a hypothetical corporation. Circle size represents the relative size of each business in the company's portfolio. Most organizations, like Gillette, have businesses in more than one quadrant, thereby representing different market shares and growth rates.

 GILLETTE COMPANY

Gillette has several cash cows in its corporate portfolio. The most famous is the shaving division, which accounts for two-thirds of the company's total profits and holds a large share of a stable market. This division sells Atra, Trac II, the Sensor shaving system, Good News disposables, and a new Sensor razor for women. In 1992 the company captured major control of the largest razor blade company in China and access to that nation's vast population pool. The Oral-B laboratories division is also a cash cow with its steady sales of toothbrushes and other dental hygiene products. The stationery products division has star status. With a $561 million purchase of Parker Pen Holdings Limited, this division has become the world's largest marketer of writing instruments, which also includes Paper Mate, Flair, Erasermate, and Waterman, and it shows potential for rapid growth overseas. Gillette's question marks are in the personal care division. A line of women's toiletries aimed at the European market failed, and Gillette's success with other lines—for example, men's Right Guard deodorant and Foamy shaving cream—have enjoyed only cyclical success. A new line of men's toiletries featuring a gel-based deodorant and a gel shaving cream was recently launched. If this new line fails to generate sales and market share, it may be assigned to the dog category, to which the Cricket line of disposable lighters was relegated. Bic disposable lighters dominated the Cricket line so completely that Cricket became a dog and was eventually put out of its misery through liquidation. Gillette continues to experiment with new products and question marks to ensure that its portfolio will include stars and cash cows in the future.[30] ■

● FORMULATING BUSINESS-LEVEL STRATEGY

Now we turn to strategy formulation within the strategic business unit, in which the concern is how to compete. The same three generic strategies—growth, stability, and retrenchment—apply at the business level, but they are accomplished through competitive actions rather than the acquisition or divestment of business divisions. Two models for formulating strategy are Porter's competitive strategies and the product life cycle. Each provides a framework for business unit competitive action.

PORTER'S COMPETITIVE FORCES AND STRATEGIES

Michael E. Porter studied a number of business organizations and proposed that business-level strategies are the result of five competitive forces in the company's environment.[31]

FIVE COMPETITIVE FORCES.   Exhibit 7.5 illustrates the competitive forces that exist in a company's environment. These forces help determine a company's position vis-à-vis competitors in the industry environment.

1. *Potential new entrants.* Capital requirements and economies of scale are examples of two potential barriers to entry that can keep out new competitors. It is far more costly to enter the automobile industry, for example, than to start a specialized mail-order business.

2. *Bargaining power of buyers.* Informed customers become empowered customers. As advertising and buyer information educates customers about the full range of price and product options available in the marketplace, their influence over a company increases. This is especially true when a company relies on one or two large, powerful customers for the majority of its sales.

3. *Bargaining power of suppliers.* The concentration of suppliers and the availability of substitute suppliers are significant factors in determining supplier power. The sole supplier of engines to a manufacturer of small airplanes will have great power. Other factors include

E X H I B I T   7 . 5

The Five Forces Affecting Industry Competition

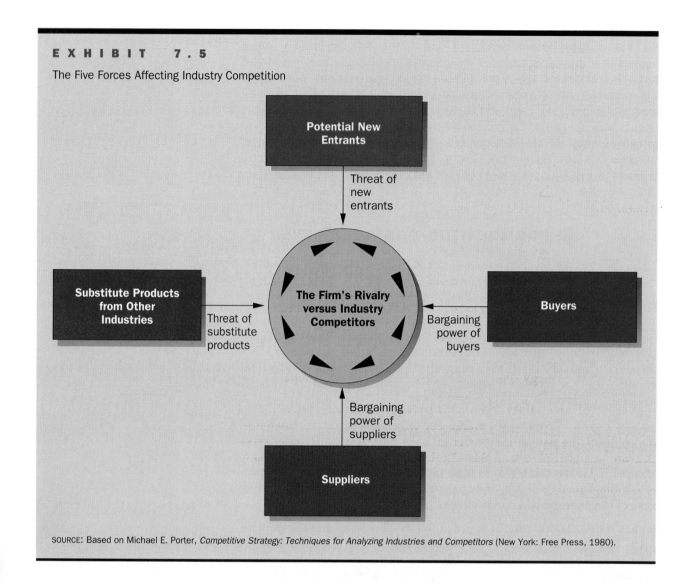

SOURCE: Based on Michael E. Porter, *Competitive Strategy: Techniques for Analyzing Industries and Competitors* (New York: Free Press, 1980).

whether a supplier can survive without a particular purchaser, or whether the purchaser can threaten to self-manufacture the needed supplies.

4 *Threat of substitute products.* The power of alternatives and substitutes for a company's product may be affected by cost changes or trends such as increased health consciousness that will deflect buyer loyalty to companies. Companies in the sugar industry suffered from the growth of sugar substitutes; manufacturers of aerosol spray cans lost business as environmentally conscious consumers chose other products.

5 *Rivalry among competitors.* The scrambling and jockeying for position is often exemplified by what Porter called the "advertising slugfest." As illustrated in Exhibit 7.5, these rivalries are influenced by the preceding four forces as well as cost and product differentiation. A famous example of competitive rivalry is the battle between Pepsi and Coke. In the fountain war, for example, Pepsi used a three-page ad in a 1991 trade journal to report that Coke's pricing policies allowed price breaks to McDonald's, requiring other fast-food chain purchasers of Coke to subsidize the operations of their largest competitor.[32]

COMPETITIVE STRATEGIES. In finding its competitive edge within these five forces, Porter suggests that a company can adopt one of three strategies: differentiation, cost leadership, and focus. The organizational characteristics typically associated with each strategy are summarized in Exhibit 7.6.

1. Differentiation. The **differentiation** strategy involves an attempt to distinguish the firm's products or services from others in the industry. The organization may use advertising, distinctive product features, exceptional service, or new technology to achieve a product perceived as unique. The differentiation strategy can be profitable because customers are loyal and will pay high prices for the product. Examples of products that have benefited from a differentiation strategy include Mercedes-Benz automobiles, Maytag appliances, and Tylenol, all of which are perceived as distinctive in their markets. Companies that pursue a differentiation strategy typically need strong marketing abilities, a creative flair, and a reputation for leadership.[33]

A differentiation strategy can reduce rivalry with competitors if buyers are loyal to a company's brand. For example, successful differentiation reduces the bargaining power of large buyers because other products are less attractive, and this also helps the firm fight off threats of substitute products. Differentiation also erects entry barriers in the form of customer loyalty that a new entrant into the market would have difficulty overcoming.

differentiation

A type of competitive strategy with which the organization seeks to distinguish its products or services from competitors'.

Strategy	Commonly Required Skills and Resources
Differentiation	Strong marketing abilities
	Strong coordination among functional departments
	Creative flair
	Strong capability in basic research
	Corporate reputation for quality or technological leadership
Overall cost leadership	Tight cost control
	Process engineering skills
	Intense supervision of labor
	Products designed for ease in manufacture
	Frequent, detailed control reports
Focus	Combination of the above policies directed at the particular strategic target

E X H I B I T   7 . 6

Organizational Characteristics for Porter's Competitive Strategies

SOURCE: Reprinted with permission of The Free Press, a Division of Macmillan, Inc., from *Competitive Strategy: Techniques for Analyzing Industries and Competitors* by Michael E. Porter. Copyright © 1980 by The Free Press.

A *focus* and *differentiation* strategy gives Dreyer's Grand Ice Cream a competitive edge among premium ice creams. Modern distribution facilities and a second-to-none direct-store delivery system contributed to record sales and earnings despite recession, as well as attracting distribution of "partner brands" such as Ben & Jerry's, Dove brands, and Mars' Snickers and Milky Way ice cream bars. Dreyer's continues to focus on its own premium recipe using the old-fashioned batch method while meeting the changing needs of consumers with a new sugar free ice cream.

cost leadership

A type of competitive strategy with which the organization aggressively seeks efficient facilities, cuts costs, and employs tight cost controls to be more efficient than competitors.

focus

A type of competitive strategy that emphasizes concentration on a specific regional market or buyer group.

2. Cost Leadership. With a **cost leadership** strategy, the organization aggressively seeks efficient facilities, pursues cost reductions, and uses tight cost controls to produce products more efficiently than competitors. A low-cost position means that the company can undercut competitors' prices and still offer comparable quality and earn a reasonable profit. Scottish Inns and Motel 6 are low-priced alternatives to Holiday Inn and Ramada Inn. The Food Lion, Inc., grocery chain is a superb example of cost leadership. The company's credo is to do "1,000 things 100% better." Food Lion builds distribution warehouses close to its stores, recycles banana crates as bins for cosmetics, and even uses waste heat from refrigerator units to warm the store. With the lowest costs and lowest prices in the industry, Food Lion is still highly profitable.[34]

Being a low-cost producer provides a successful strategy to defend against the five competitive forces in Exhibit 7.5. For example, the most efficient, low-cost company is in the best position to succeed in a price war while still making a profit. Likewise, the low-cost producer is protected from powerful customers and suppliers, because customers cannot find lower prices elsewhere, and other buyers would have less slack for price negotiation with suppliers. If substitute products or potential new entrants occur, the low-cost producer is better positioned than higher-cost rivals to prevent loss of market share. The low price acts as a barrier against new entrants and substitute products.[35]

3. Focus. With a **focus** strategy, the organization concentrates its strategy on a specific regional market or buyer group. The company will use either a differentiation or low-cost approach, but only for a narrow target market. One example of focus strategy is the brokerage firm of Edward D. Jones & Company. It focused on the investment needs of rural America, moving into small towns where Merrill Lynch representatives would not even stop for gas. In this ignored market niche, Jones has opened 1,300 offices and now serves over 1 million customers with its conservative investment philosophy.[36]

Porter found that some businesses did not consciously adopt one of these three strategies and were stuck with no strategic advantage. Without a strategic advantage, businesses earned below-average profits compared with those that used differentiation, cost leadership, or focus strategies.

PRODUCT LIFE CYCLE

The **product life cycle** is a series of stages that a product goes through in its market acceptance, as illustrated in Exhibit 7.7. First, a product is developed within the laboratories of selected companies and then is introduced into the marketplace. If the product succeeds, it enjoys rapid growth as consumers accept it. Next is the maturity stage, in which widespread product acceptance occurs but growth peaks. Gradually the product grows out of favor or fashion and enters the decline stage.[37]

The life cycle concept also applies to services, as the banking example in Exhibit 7.7 shows. In-home banking is a new product, and discount broker services is in the rapid growth stage. Money market accounts have been around for a while and are approaching maturity, which is where drive-in tellers are. Passbook savings accounts are in decline, being replaced by money market accounts and certificates of deposit. The Christmas Club accounts are in serious decline and are available at only a few banks.

product life cycle

The stages through which a product or service goes: (1) development and introduction into the marketplace, (2) growth, (3) maturity, and (4) decline.

INTRODUCTION
GROWTH
MATURITY
DECLINE

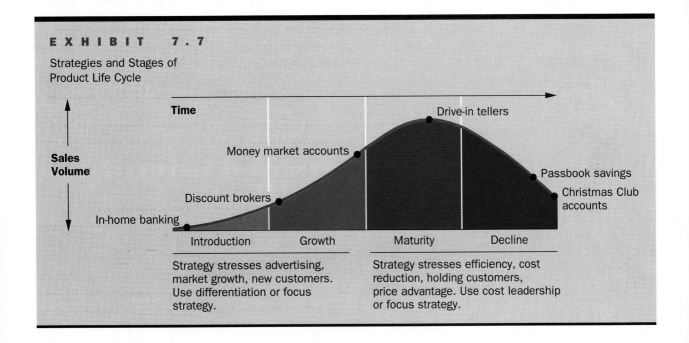

EXHIBIT 7.7

Strategies and Stages of Product Life Cycle

Time

Sales Volume

Drive-in tellers
Money market accounts
Discount brokers
In-home banking
Passbook savings
Christmas Club accounts

Introduction | Growth | Maturity | Decline

Strategy stresses advertising, market growth, new customers. Use differentiation or focus strategy.

Strategy stresses efficiency, cost reduction, holding customers, price advantage. Use cost leadership or focus strategy.

Banks and other organizations can tailor strategy to product life cycle stages.[38] During the introduction and growth stages, differentiation strategy is appropriate, because it stresses advertising, attracting new customers, and market growth. After the product reaches maturity, a low-cost strategy is important, because competitors will have developed products that look and perform similarly. Company strategy for a mature product or service should stress efficiency, reduce overhead costs, and seek a price advantage over competitors.

To summarize, the two models that describe business-level strategies contain similarities. One company that uses these strategies is H. J. Heinz Company.

 H. J. HEINZ COMPANY

Heinz produces a number of mature products in the consumer food industry, and attempted during the 1980s to become the low-cost producer in ketchup, french fries, cat food, tuna, baby food, and soup. At a management get-together, called the Low-Cost Operator Conference, chief executive Tony O'Reilly admonished managers to cut costs even further. One technique was to procure cheap raw materials. Another was to hold down manufacturing costs. In five years, Heinz eliminated $4 million in expenses each year with such ideas as removing the back label from large bottles. Consolidation of factories and renegotiation of work rules eliminated 2,000 jobs. Heinz reduced advertising costs by using 15- versus 30-second television commercials. The next step was an automated facility. To keep managers on their toes, O'Reilly planned to eliminate one layer of management if costs could not be cut in other ways.

But Heinz also worked to introduce new products. The Weight Watchers frozen entree and dessert lines are doing well, as is a new line of dried instant baby food. Heinz used the cost savings made in mature product areas to increase advertising and development to differentiate the new product lines.[39]

Heinz used a low-cost strategy for mature product lines, and it worked. Market share and profits increased. Products in the early stages of the life cycle were differentiated in the marketplace with heavy advertising and promotion, which is appropriate during the growth stage in order to gain market share. ■

● FORMULATING FUNCTIONAL-LEVEL STRATEGY

Functional-level strategies are the action plans adopted by major departments to support the execution of business-level strategy. Major organizational functions include marketing, production, finance, personnel, and research and development. Senior managers in these departments adopt strategies that are coordinated with the business-level strategy to achieve the organization's strategic goals.[40]

A child's fantasy is wall-to-wall, ceiling-to-floor toy selection. In any language that translates into Toys "Я" Us. In order to satisfy global demand for Barbies, Nintendos, or Legos, the world's largest children's retail chain formulated a *functional-level marketing strategy* that increased the international appeal of toys through advertising (pictured here), high-tech distribution, and price selection.

For example, consider a company that has adopted a differentiation strategy and is introducing new products that are expected to experience rapid growth in the early stages of the life cycle. The personnel department should adopt a strategy appropriate for growth, which would mean recruiting additional personnel and training middle managers for movement into new positions. The marketing department should undertake test marketing, aggressive advertising campaigns, and consumer product trials. The finance department should adopt plans to borrow money, handle large cash investments, and authorize construction of new production facilities.

A company with mature products or a low-cost strategy will have different functional strategies. The personnel department should develop strategies for retaining and developing a stable work force, including transfers, advancements, and incentives for efficiency and safety. Marketing should stress brand loyalty and the development of established, reliable distribution channels. Production should maintain long production runs, routinization, and cost reduction. Finance should focus on net cash flows and positive cash balances.

● PUTTING STRATEGY INTO ACTION

The final step in the strategic management process is implementation—which is how strategy is put into action. Some people argue that strategy implementation is the most difficult and important part of strategic management.[41] No matter how creative the formulated strategy, the organization will not benefit if it is incorrectly implemented. Implementation involves several tools—parts of the firm that can be changed—as illustrated in Exhibit 7.8. It requires changes in the organization's behavior, which can be brought about by changing management's leadership approach, structural design, information and control systems, and human resources.[42]

LEADERSHIP

Leadership is the ability to influence organization members to adopt the behaviors needed for strategy implementation. Leadership includes persuasion, motivation, and changes in corporate values and culture. Managers seeking to implement a new strategy may make speeches to employees, issue edicts, build coalitions, and persuade middle managers

EXHIBIT 7.8

Tools for Putting Strategy into Action

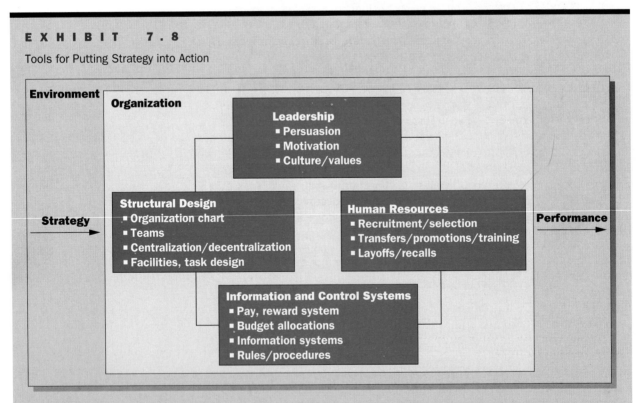

SOURCE: Adapted from Jay R. Galbraith and Robert K. Kazanjian, *Strategy Implementation: Structure, Systems and Process*, 2d ed. (St. Paul, Minn.: West, 1986), 115. Used with permission.

to go along with their vision for the corporation. If leaders let other managers participate during strategy formulation, implementation will be easier because managers and employees will already understand and be committed to the new strategy. In essence, leadership is used to motivate employees to adopt new behaviors and, for some strategies, to infuse new values and attitudes.

For example, Linda Koslow, manager of Marshall Field's department store in Oak Brook, Illinois, uses leadership to meet holiday sales targets by pumping up morale, encouraging aggressive selling, and being accessible to employees.[43] As another example, Q. T. Wiles purchases failing electronics manufacturers and turns them around. His emphasis is on strategy implementation. He uses an almost autocratic leadership style to reinforce a new way of thinking and new values within a firm. To this end, each manager must memorize a 12-item list of "Q. T. disciplines" and the organization's official charter.[44]

STRUCTURAL DESIGN

Structural design typically begins with the organization chart. It pertains to managers' responsibilities, their degree of authority, and the consolidation of facilities, departments, and divisions. Structure also pertains to the degree of decentralization, task design, and production technology. (Structure will be described in Chapter 10.)

Q. T. Wiles used structural changes to implement strategy in electronic companies. At MiniScribe Corporation, he reorganized the work force into small groups, each responsible for a single product, a single customer, or some other narrowly defined target. Each group was an autonomous structural unit with skills and functions necessary to achieve its goals.[45] However, the strategy of merging Uniroyal and Goodrich was unprofitable for the first two years because of implementation problems concerning structural design. Such simple things as the incompatibility of tire molds in the two companies' plants prevented consolidation of equipment and facilities. Blending the marketing and the accounting departments of the two companies proved difficult because of different philosophies and cost accounting systems.[46] By contrast, an almost perfect merging of departments occurred when Manufacturers Hanover took over Goldome Bank as described in the Winning Moves box.

INFORMATION AND CONTROL SYSTEMS

Information and control systems include reward systems, pay incentives, budgets for allocating resources, information systems, and the organization's rules, policies, and procedures. Changes in these systems represent major tools for putting strategy into action. For example, resources can be reassigned from research and development to marketing if a new strategy requires increased advertising but no product innovations. Managers and employees must be rewarded for adhering to the new strategy and making it a success.[47]

Jim Bernstein, CEO of General Health, Inc., set the strategy of sales growth of 50 percent in one year. He used a pay incentive by promising

WINNING moves

GOODBYE, GOLDOME— HELLO, HANOVER

Presto. Change-o. When a strategy is carefully formulated and successfully implemented, it looks like the work of a master magician. When Manufacturers Hanover Trust Company took over the ten-branch Goldome Bank, the carefully designed implementation created a perfect "now-you-see-it, now-you-don't" conversion. Over a Memorial Day weekend, Goldome simply disappeared.

How did Manufacturers Hanover pull off this magic feat? Leonard E. Malkin, managing director (and, in this case, the star magician), points to focus groups and strategic planning that involved 280 people

headed by 40 conversion team leaders (magician's assistants) and a ten-month preparation (practicing the sleight-of-hand). The goal of conversion weekend: getting the former Goldome branches open and fully assimilated into Hanover on Tuesday morning without a hitch.

Each of the 40 conversion team leaders was responsible for a specific function, such as making sure that Goldome account programs were compatible with Hanover computers. Each team met weekly to break down assignments into small, manageable parts and to delegate work. Schedules were established for each task, and crucial events were red flagged. Using contingency or scenario planning, team members crafted plans for every conceivable problem. "What ifs" covered every possible

disruption—computer breakdown, airport closure, lost delivery truck, Memorial Day parade route, equipment delivery to a wrong branch or floor. Every piece of information from color-coded floor plans and branch-to-branch maps to Memorial Day weekend phone numbers was entered into a loose-leaf conversion notebook given to team members. Training sessions were set up for Goldome employees.

With the closing of the banks on Friday, the carefully laid plans kicked in, and on Tuesday morning presto, change-o! Goldome was instantly Manufacturers Hanover. ∎

SOURCE: Claudia H. Deutsch, "Breaking Chaos into Constituent Parts," *The New York Times*, June 2, 1991, F23.

every employee an extra month's pay if the company hit the sales target. The strategy worked almost too well, creating a greater increase in sales than the company could handle, which shows the impact of pay incentives for strategy implementation. As another example, John Hancock Mutual Life Insurance Company sold whole-life policies that were out of fashion in the wave of new financial instruments and insurance policies that occurred during the 1980s. President John McElwee's strategy was to change Hancock into a financial supermarket, offering banking and investment opportunities along with insurance products. But because insurance agents received bigger commissions from the traditional insurance policies, McElwee had to increase the commissions for selling noninsurance products. Implementing McElwee's strategy also required changes in information systems, because new reports had to be developed showing whether agents were meeting their goals in new-product areas.[48]

HUMAN RESOURCES

The organization's *human resources* are its employees. The human resource function recruits, selects, trains, transfers, promotes, and lays

Motors Insurance Corporation, a subsidiary of General Motors Acceptance Corporation, is *putting strategy into action* through human resources with a game plan of total customer satisfaction. Employees and team captains suggested they could improve service if all employees were trained to handle all department functions. So MIC set up classes and a six-month curriculum to cross-train all employees. These grads celebrate completing the course and bringing to their jobs new skills and confidence that raise the level of their service and the satisfaction of their customers.

off employees to achieve strategic goals. For example, training employees can help them understand the purpose and importance of a new strategy or help them develop the necessary specific skills and behaviors. Sometimes employees may have to be let go and replaced with new people. One newspaper shifted its strategy from an evening to a morning paper to compete with a large newspaper from a nearby city. The new strategy fostered resentment and resistance among department heads. In order to implement it, 80 percent of the department heads had to be let go because they refused to cooperate. New people were recruited and placed in those positions, and the morning newspaper strategy was a resounding success.[49]

Since the poison gas disaster at a Union Carbide plant in Bhopal, India, many chemical companies have implemented a strategy of increased safety. American Cyanamid requires workers to attend safety classes. The company had four safety incidents and wants no more. The training consists of 40 hours in the classroom, including courses in basic chemistry to help workers understand plant processes and how to cope with chemical reactions.[50]

IMPLEMENTING GLOBAL STRATEGIES

The difficulty of implementing strategy is greater when a company goes global. In the international arena, flexibility and superb communication emerge as mandatory leadership skills. Likewise, structural design must merge successfully with foreign cultures as well as link foreign operations to the home country. Information and control systems must fit the needs and incentives within local cultures. In a country such as Japan or China, financial bonuses for star performance would be humiliating to an individual, whereas group motivation and reward are acceptable. As in North America, control is typically created through timetables and budgets and by monitoring progress toward desired goals. Finally, the recruitment, training, transfer, promotion, and layoff of international human resources face an array of problems not confronted in North America. Labor laws, guaranteed jobs, and cultural traditions of keeping unproductive employees on the job provide special problems for strategy implementation. Strategy implementation must receive even more attention in the international domain than the domestic realm.

In summary, strategy implementation is essential for effective strategic management. Managers implement strategy through the tools of leadership, structural design, information and control systems, and human resources. Without effective implementation, even the most creative strategy will fail.

SUMMARY AND MANAGEMENT SOLUTION

This chapter described important concepts of strategic management. Strategic management begins with an evaluation of the organization's current mission, goals, and strategy. This evaluation is followed by situation analysis (called SWOT analysis), which examines opportunities and threats in the external environment as well as strengths and weaknesses within the organization. Situation analysis leads to the formulation of explicit strategic plans, which then must be implemented.

Strategy formulation takes place at three levels: corporate, business, and functional. Corporate grand strategies include growth, stability, retrenchment, and global. Frameworks for accomplishing them include the BCG matrix. Business-level strategies include Porter's competitive strategies and the product life cycle. Once business strategies have been formulated, functional strategies for supporting them can be developed.

Even the most creative strategies have no value if they cannot be translated into action. Four organizational tools used for strategy implementation are leadership, structural design, information and control systems, and human resources.

When Elizabeth Dole took over the presidency of the American Red Cross in 1991, the organization's most visible programs—blood supplies and disaster relief—were feeling intense scrutiny and were the subjects of increased criticism. Dole formulated a new business-level strategy to improve disaster response, anchored by a computerized disaster command headquarters in Alexandria, Virginia. The strategy was implemented via the new information and control system. The computer could track material and transportation requirements, as well as the coordination of local officials and volunteers. In addition, human resources were increased with the number of paid disaster workers doubling since 1989. A training program for "cultural diversity" was implemented.

The Red Cross also formulated a major rule change to allow disaster relief monies to be earmarked by donors for specific use. This was implemented by a new information system that provided a detailed accounting of disaster fund-raising and spending.

In an effort to overhaul the blood operations, Dole launched a new strategy, with computerization once again the key to implementation and improved recordkeeping. Other steps implemented for better blood control include increased training of employees, blood testing in regional labs, and frequent inspections.[51]

DISCUSSION QUESTIONS

1. Assume you are the general manager of a large hotel and have formulated a strategy of renting banquet facilities to corporations for big events. At a monthly management meeting, your sales manager informed the head of food operations that a big reception in one week will require converting a large hall from a meeting room to a banquet facility in only 60 minutes—a difficult but doable operation that will require precise planning and extra help. The food operations manager is furious about not being informed earlier. What is wrong here?

2. Which is more important—strategy formulation or strategy implementation? Do they depend on each other? Is it possible for strategy implementation to occur first?

3. If an organization has hired strategic management professionals to help top managers, during which part of the strategic management process would they play the largest role?

4. Perform a situation (SWOT) analysis for the university you attend. Do you think university administrators consider these factors when devising their strategy?

5. What is meant by the core competence and synergy components of strategy? Give examples.

6. Using Porter's competitive strategies, how would you describe the strategies of Wal-Mart, Bloomingdale's, and K mart?

7. Walt Disney Company has four major strategic business units: movies (Touchstone), theme parks, consumer products, and television (primarily cable). Place each of these SBUs on the BCG matrix based on your knowledge of them.

8. As administrator for a medium-sized hospital, you and the board of directors have decided to change to a drug dependency hospital from a short-term, acute-care facility. Which organizational dimensions would you use to implement this strategy?

9. How would functional strategies in marketing, research and development, and production departments differ if a business changed from a differentiation to a low-cost strategy?

MANAGEMENT IN PRACTICE: EXPERIENTIAL EXERCISE

● **DEVELOPING STRATEGY FOR A SMALL BUSINESS**

Instructions: Your instructor may ask you to do this exercise individually or as part of a group. Select a local business with which you (or group members) are familiar. Complete the following activities.

Activity 1   Perform a SWOT analysis for the business.

Strengths: _____

_____

_____

_____

_____

Opportunities: _____

_____

_____

_____

_____

Weaknesses:

_____

_____

_____

_____

Threats: _____

_____

_____

_____

_____

Activity 2   Write a statement of the business's current strategy.

Activity 3   Decide on a goal you would like the business to achieve in two years, and write a statement of proposed strategy for achieving that goal.

Activity 4   Write a statement describing how the proposed strategy will be implemented.

Activity 5   What have you learned from this exercise?

CASES FOR ANALYSIS

DIGITAL EQUIPMENT COMPANY

In 1987 Digital Equipment Company (DEC) was riding high and challenging number-one IBM. Its nine-day DEC-world technology carnival at Boston's World Trade Center showcased both the company's confidence and its hardware, such as the highly touted VAX minicomputer. In a festive "damn-the-cost" atmosphere, customers enjoyed day-long seminars, were wined and dined, and then retired to Boston's top hotels or cabins aboard the luxury liner *Queen Elizabeth II*—all at DEC's expense.

By 1992 DEC's confident days of fun and games were over. Corporate customers were shifting away from minicomputers to smaller, high-powered alternatives. DEC-world's attendance and budgets were scaled back dramatically, and sales quotas for the show's visitors were imposed. Within months, Robert Palmer replaced company founder and legend CEO Kenneth Olsen, following a dismal $3.4 billion loss over two years.

Palmer faces a major turnaround challenge. Olsen's legacy is a strong engineering-centered company stuck in a slow-growth minicomputer technology, characterized by a plodding, almost anarchical decision-making style that delayed market response and missed numerous industry trends, such as "open systems." DEC's recent history is haunted by failure to secure an alliance with Apple Computer and by frequent reorganizations and management changes that confused both employees and customers.

As new CEO, Palmer initiated a number of changes, including consolidation of business units, reduction of engineering control over budgets and new product decisions, establishing commissions for sales-force productivity, and slashing costs through job eliminations and product-line reduction. Skeptics of Palmer's turnaround strategy insist that investment in major new technology would do more for DEC's fortune

● QUESTIONS

1. How would you rate DEC on Porter's five competitive forces? Does this suggest to you that DEC should adopt a differentiation or low-cost leader strategy?
2. What techniques has Palmer used for implementation? How would implementation differ if the strategy were to emphasize new technology?
3. To what extent are corporate-level, business-level, and functional-level strategies used at Digital?

SOURCE: Gary McWilliams, "Crunch Time at DEC," *Business Week*, May 4, 1992, 30–33; John R. Wilke, "On the Spot: At Digital Equipment Ken Olsen Is Feeling Pressure to Produce," *The New York Times*, May 13, 1992, A1, A6; and Gary McWilliams, "Punching a Whole New Set of Commands at DEC," *Business Week*, October 12, 1992, 160.

EASTMAN KODAK

Eastman Kodak is a giant in what Wall Street labels a "mature industry." Its U.S. amateur film sales stagnated by the mid-1980s—victim of the new camcorder craze, the sluggish national economy, and inroads by archrival Fuji Photo and cheaper brands.

Kodak's great strength is its technological and research capabilities. Its strategy is to maintain market share in amateur film while developing a new generation of equipment that merges photography and compact discs. Its new photo CD system, heralded by the company as the "future of photography," allows snapshots to be displayed on a television or high-resolution personal computer screen. The photo CD may combat Kodak's reputation for bringing new products to market too late to take advantage of opportunities. Kodak expects this product line to compete successfully

with electronic photography from rivals such as Sony. Electronic photography, still in its infancy, must overcome price gaps and fuzzy quality before it can compete successfully with traditional photography. Kodak must work quickly to promote its high-resolution photo CD and has sharply increased its advertising budget to promote the product's quality, ease of manipulation, storage, and transmission before electronic photography becomes widely used.

In the meantime, Kodak retains excellent visibility and a reputation for top-quality film. It has a powerful distribution network and huge financial resources, allowing it to undertake the basic research necessary for new products. The new values in innovation and fast reaction to market opportunities are taking precedence over the strategy of simply protecting its core film line.

● QUESTIONS

1. What strengths, weaknesses, opportunities, and threats characterize Kodak? What are its current mission and strategy?
2. What strategy would you recommend for Kodak? Why?

SOURCE: Mark Maremont, "Smile You're on Compact Disk," *Business Week*, August 10, 1992, 26; Leslie Helm, "Has Kodak Set Itself up for a Fall?" *Business Week*, February 22, 1988, 134–138; Leslie Helm, "Why Kodak Is Starting to Click Again," *Business Week*, February 23, 1987; and Subrata N. Chakravarty and Ruth Simon, "Has the World Passed Kodak By?" *Forbes*, November 5, 1984, 184–192.

REFERENCES

1. Pamela Sebastian, "Tough Times: Red Cross Is Strained by Disasters Even As It Revamps Its Programs," *The Wall Street Journal*, September 15, 1992, A1, A10.

2. Steve Lawrence, "Bar Wars: Hershey Bites Mars," *Fortune*, July 8, 1985, 52–57.

3. Kathleen Madigan, Julia Flynn, and Joseph Walker, "Masters of the Game," *Business Week*, October 12, 1992, 110–118.

4. Fred F. Jespersen, "The Top 100 Deals," *Business Week 1000*, 1992, 67–72.

5. John E. Prescott, "Environments as Moderators of the Relationship between Strategy and Performance," *Academy of Management Journal* 29 (1986), 329–346; John A. Pearce II and Richard B. Robinson, Jr., *Strategic Management: Strategy, Formulation, and Implementation*, 2d ed. (Homewood, Ill.: Irwin, 1985); and David J. Teece, "Economic Analysis and Strategic Management," *California Management Review* 26 (Spring 1984), 87–110.

6. Kotha Suresh and Daniel Orna, "Generic Manufacturing Strategies: A Conceptual Synthesis," *Strategic Management Journal* 10 (1989), 211–231; and John A. Pearce II, "Selecting among Alternative Grand Strategies," *California Management Review* (Spring 1982), 23–31.

7. Kenichi Ohmae, "Managing in a Borderless World," *Harvard Business Review* (May–June 1990), 152–161.

8. Theodore Levitt, "The Globalization of Markets," *Harvard Business Review* (May–June 1983), 92–102.

9. Joanne Lipman, "Marketers Turn Sour on Global Sales Pitch Harvard Guru Makes," *The Wall Street Journal*, May 12, 1988, 1, 8.

10. Christine Dugas, "Playtex Kicks Off a One-Ad-Fits-All Campaign," *Business Week*, December 16, 1985, 48–49.

11. Michael E. Porter, "Changing Patterns of International Competition," *California Management Review* 28 (Winter 1986), 40.

12. Lipman, "Marketers Turn Sour on Global Sales Pitch."

13. Kenneth Labich, "America's International Winners," *Fortune*, April 14, 1986, 34–46.

14. Arthur A. Thompson, Jr., and A. J. Strickland III, *Strategic Management: Concepts and Cases*, 6th ed. (Homewood, Ill.: Irwin, 1992.)

15. Peter Coy, "Twin Engines: Can Bob Allen Blend Computers and Telecommunications at AT&T?" *Business Week*, January 20, 1992, 56–63.

16. Bradford McKee, "Ties That Bind Large and Small," *Nation's Business*, February 1992, 24–26.

17. Milton Leontiades, *Strategies for Diversification and Change* (Boston: Little, Brown, 1980), 63; and Dan E. Schendel and Charles W. Hofer, eds., *Strategic Management: A New View of Business Policy and Planning* (Boston: Little, Brown, 1979), 11–14.

18. Gregory A. Patterson and Francine Schwadel, "Back in Time: Sears Suddenly Undoes Years of Diversifying beyond Retailing Field," *The Wall Street Journal*, September 30, 1992, A1, A16; and Julia Flynn, David Greising, Kevin Kelly, and Leah Nathans Spiro, "Smaller but Wiser," *Business Week*, October 12, 1992, 28–29.

19. Joseph Weber, "Black & Decker Cuts a Neat Dovetail Joint," *Business Week*, July 31, 1989, 52–53.

20. Richard W. Anderson, "That Roar You Hear Is Food Lion," *Business Week*, August 24, 1987, 65–66; and Jaclyn Fierman, "How to Make Money in Mature Markets," *Fortune*, November 25, 1985, 47–53.

21. Madigan, Flynn, and Weber, "Master of the Game."

22. Milton Leontiades, "The Confusing Words of Business Policy," *Academy of Management Review* 7 (1982), 45–48.

23. Lawrence G. Hrebiniak and William F. Joyce, *Implementing Strategy* (New York: Macmillan, 1984).

24. James E. Svatko, "Analyzing the Competition," *Small Business Reports* (January 1989), 21–28; and Brian Dumaine, "Corporate Spies Snoop to Conquer," *Fortune*, November 7, 1988, 68–76.

25. Steve Swartz, "Basic Bedrooms: How Marriott Changes Hotel Design to Tap Mid-Priced Market," *The Wall Street Journal*, September 18, 1985, 1.

26. Pamela Sherrid, "Fighting Back at Breakfast," *Forbes*, October 7, 1985, 126–130.

27. David Greising, "Will Air Bags Cushion the New Morton?" *Business Week*, July 8, 1992, 82–83.

28. Frederick W. Gluck, "A Fresh Look at Strategic Management," *Journal of Business Strategy* 6 (Fall 1985), 4–19.

29. Thompson and Strickland, *Strategic Management;* and William L. Shanklin and John K. Ryans, Jr., "Is the International Cash Cow Really a Prize Heifer?" *Business Horizons* 24 (1981), 10–16.

30. Mark Maremont and Paula Sawyer, "How Gillette Is Honing Its Edge," *Business Week*, September 28, 1992, 60–65; Keith H. Hammonds, "At Gillette, Disposable Is a Dirty Word," *Business Week*, May 29, 1989, 54–58; and Bobbie Holbrook, Sondra Rodgers, and Greg Lock, "Gillette Company" (Unpublished manuscript, Texas A&M University, 1986).

31. Michael E. Porter, *Competitive Strategy* (New York: Free Press, 1980), 36–46; Danny Miller, "Relating Porter's Business Strategies to Environment and Structure: Analysis and Performance Implementations," *Academy of Management Journal* 31 (1988), 280–308; and Michael E. Porter, "From Competitive Advantage to Corporate Strategy," *Harvard Business Review* (May–June 1987), 43–59.

32. Walecia Konrad and Gail DeGeorge, "Sorry, No Pepsi. How 'Bout a Coke?" *Business Week*, May 27, 1991, 71–72.

33. Thomas L. Wheelen and J. David Hunger, *Strategic Management and Business Policy* (Reading, Mass.: Addison-Wesley, 1989).

34. Anderson, "That Roar You Hear Is Food Lion."

35. Thompson and Strickland, *Strategic Management*.

36. Nathaniel Gilbert, "John W. Bachmann: Securities Well in Hand," *Management Review* (January 1988), 17–19.

37. George W. Potts, "Exploit Your Product's Service Life Cycle," *Harvard Business Review* (September–October 1988), 32–36; and C. R. Wasson, *Dynamic Competitive Strategy and Product Life Cycles*, 3d ed. (Austin, Tex.: Austin Press, 1978).

38. Carl R. Anderson and Carl P. Zeithaml, "Stage of the Product Life Cycle, Business Strategy, and Business Performance," *Academy of Management Journal* 27 (1984), 5–24.

39. Walter G. Schmid, "Heinz Covers the Globe," *The Journal of Business Strategy* (March/April 1989), 17–20; and Bill Saporito, "Heinz Pushes to Be the Low-Cost Producer," *Fortune*, June 24, 1985, 44–54.

40. Harold W. Fox, "A Framework for Functional Coordination," *Atlanta Economic Review* (now *Business Magazine*) (November/December 1973).

41. L. J. Bourgeois III and David R. Brodwin, "Strategic Implementation: Five Approaches to an Elusive Phenomenon," *Strategic Management Journal* 5 (1984), 241–264; and Anil K. Gupta and V. Govindarajan, "Business Unit Strategy, Managerial Characteristics, and Business Unit Effectiveness at Strategy Implementation," *Academy of Management Journal* (1984), 25–41.

42. Jay R. Galbraith and Robert K. Kazanjian, *Strategy Implementation: Structure, Systems and Process*, 2d ed. (St. Paul, Minn.: West, 1986); and Paul C. Nutt, "Selecting Tactics to Implement Strategic Plans," *Strategic Management Journal* 10 (1989), 145–161.

43. Francine Schwadel, "Christmas Sales' Lack of Momentum Tests Store Managers' Mettle," *The Wall Street Journal*, December 16, 1987, 1, 13.

44. "Company Doctor: Q. T. Wiles," *INC.*, February 1988, 27–38; and Michael W. Miller, "Q. T. Wiles Revives Sick High-Tech Firms with Strong Medicine," *The Wall Street Journal*, June 23, 1986, 1, 12.

45. Miller, "Q. T. Wiles."

46. Zachary Schiller, "What's Deflating Uniroyal Goodrich," *Business Week*, November 30, 1987, 35.

47. Gupta and Govindarajan, "Business Unit Strategy," and Bourgeois and Brodwin, "Strategic Implementation."

48. Alex Beam, "Can the Boston Brahmin of Insurance Shake Off the Cobwebs?" *Business Week*, August 26, 1985, 51.

49. James E. Skivington and Richard L. Daft, "A Study of Organizational 'Framework' and 'Process' Modalities for the Implementation of Business-Level Strategies" (Unpublished manuscript, Texas A&M University, 1987).

50. Barry Meier, "Under Public Pressure, Chemical Firms Push Plant Safety Programs," *The Wall Street Journal*, November 11, 1985, 1, 17.

51. Sebastian, "Red Cross Is Strained by Disasters."

When was the last time you ordered anything out of a Sears catalog? If the answer is never, maybe you can understand why the Chicago-based retailing giant decided the book's 97th year would be its last. Sears announced in January 1993 that it was scrapping its catalog division to concentrate more of its efforts on new strategies that could give the company an edge over powerful competitors like Wal-Mart and Kmart.

To be sure, the catalog had occupied a cherished place in American homes. When it first came out in 1896, it was a guidebook to the middle-class way of life, chock-full of nearly everything anybody could ever want or need, from buggy whips and barbering aids to tires and perfume.

For today's younger generation, whose idea of home shopping is flipping on the cable television and ordering up merchandise through the Home Shopping Network, the catalog's legendary past was something for the history books. Inexpensive durable goods hardly have the same allure as specialty shops and high-fashion designer labels.

It took some time, but Sears finally decided to make some changes. On the same day the company announced it was retiring its trademark catalog, it also said it would close 113 unprofitable stores and cut 50,000 full- and part-time jobs. The move followed a 1992 decision to sell off many of its financial services divisions and focus instead on what it had always done best: retailing.

Driving the changes that are aimed at bringing Sears into the 1990s is Arthur Martinez, the new head of the company's flagship merchandise group. The former vice-chairman of upscale Saks Fifth Avenue was brought in to spruce up the nation's third largest retailer, and develop a business strategy for taking on competitors. For a company whose CEOs had previously worked their way up by way of store management, the decision to pick an outsider for the job was a radical move.

Martinez could see what executives inside the company had missed. The stores were dull, their apparel was even duller, and the service was indifferent at best. It was no wonder that some formerly loyal customers had not walked into a Sears store in years. Business had fallen a long way since the 1960s when it had sold more merchandise than its next four rivals combined.

The reversal of fortune at Sears could be traced to the advent of discount stores like Kmart and Wal-Mart. Instead of seeing the warning signs that pointed to a change in customer preferences, Sears management continued to consider themselves caretakers of a greatness they thought was unassailable.

Even as Sears' growth was slowing in the 1970s, the company was building a monument to its success—the opulent Sears Tower in Chicago. Soon after, the company started taking its eye off retailing to venture into stocks, bonds, and real estate. It added Dean Witter and Coldwell Banker to its existing Allstate insurance business.

In the meantime, Sears continued to dismiss the importance of the discount retailers long after it was apparent the company was past its heyday. Well into the 1980s, Sears was putting out position papers that made no mention of Wal-Mart in their discussion of competitors.

By 1992, Sears could no longer afford to ignore its competitors. It lost $3.9 billion dollars that year, with the majority of the red ink coming from its merchandising group, which had sales of $32 billion. During the same period, Kmart had $38 billion in sales and posted profits of $940 million. Wal-Mart had a whopping $55 billion in sales and earned $2 billion.

Major problems called for new strategy. Shortly after Martinez was tapped to head the Sears merchandising group in September 1992, he moved to cut jobs, dispose of losing businesses, and when necessary, part with tradition. He also set plans in motion to improve the company's sagging image. One priority was to remodel many of the chain's 746 stores, using wider aisles, brighter lighting and classier decor. "No matter whether you're selling lettuce or lawn mowers, retailing is theater," Martinez said.

He also made plans to upgrade the store's fashion departments and stock a wider selection. The changes were made with a specific target in mind: households with incomes of $18,000 to $48,000.

Whether Sears will succeed in winning back the hearts of consumers is still unclear. It has rolled out new retailing strategies in the past, to no avail. But Martinez believes this time will be different.

● QUESTIONS

1. How would you describe Sears' grand strategy? How does it differ from the company's strategy during the 1980s?

2. What is Sears' business level strategy and what steps is it taking to support it?

3. Describe Sears' strengths and weaknesses, opportunities, and threats. Which of the five competitive forces, as defined by Porter, represent the greatest threat to Sears?

4. Do you believe Sears can ever achieve the kind of dominant position it once enjoyed? Why or why not?

5. What changes have taken place since this videocase was aired?

LEARNING OBJECTIVES

After studying this chapter, you should be able to

■ Explain why decision making is an important component of good management.

■ Explain the difference between programmed and nonprogrammed decisions and the decision characteristics of risk, uncertainty, and ambiguity.

■ Describe the classical and administrative models of decision making and their applications.

■ Identify the six steps used in managerial decision making.

■ Discuss the advantages and disadvantages of using groups to make decisions.

■ Identify guidelines for improving decision-making effectiveness in organizations.

he challenge facing Peter Coors, CEO of the Adolph Coors Company, is how to move the brewer up from the number-three position in the industry. Since its early days, Coors has made decisions to invest in a number of businesses, including food and vitamins for pets, auto parts, and packaging. Suddenly, its core business is falling further behind number-one Anheuser-Busch and number-two Miller Brewing. Even Coors' popular Coors Light is being bypassed by the competition. Despite universal agreement

that Coors makes exceptionally fine beer, unit sales for 1991 squeaked by with a 1.2 percent increase while overall earnings fell by 34 percent. Clearly, decisions have to be made before the situation worsens.[1] ■ If you were Peter Coors, what decisions would you consider to increase market share for your core business? What alternatives would you consider, and what course of action would you select?

Coors is not in trouble yet, but Peter Coors and other top executives need to harness their skills to make important decisions that will affect the future of their business. Every organization grows, prospers, or fails as a result of decisions by its managers.

Managers often are referred to as *decision makers.* Although many of their important decisions are strategic, managers also make decisions about every other aspect of an organization, including structure, control systems, responses to the environment, and human resources. Managers scout for problems, make decisions for solving them, and monitor the consequences to see whether additional decisions are required. Good decision making is a vital part of good management, because decisions determine how the organization solves its problems, allocates resources, and accomplishes its objectives.

Decision making is not easy. It must be done amid ever-changing factors, unclear information, and conflicting points of view. For example, when Chairman Patrick Hayes of Waterford Glass tried to cut costs by offering early retirement to the highly paid work force that made Waterford crystal, too many experienced glassblowers opted for retirement. The remaining workers were not able to achieve enough output; hence, crystal operations lost money for two years straight. John Sculley, chairman of Apple Computer, bet on a shortage of memory chips, the personal computer's most common component. Apple acquired a big inventory of high-priced chips, and when the shortage was alleviated a few months later, Apple was forced to lower the price of its expensive Apple products.

Kay Koplovitz worked her way up to CEO of the successful USA Network and recently launched a Sci-Fi network. This is a nail-biting gamble as Washington stalks the cable industry with new regulations to cap charges to the public, and an FCC ruling allows phone companies, such as Bell Atlantic, to experiment with "video dial tones," which would bring video movies and other materials into homes by phone rather than cable. Still, Koplovitz and many corporate sponsors believe there are enough fans of ghouls and monsters and Martians to risk the plunge into an area where no network has gone before.[2]

Chapters 6 and 7 described strategic planning. This chapter explores the decision process that underlies strategic planning. Plans and strategies are arrived at through decision making; the better the decision making, the better the strategic planning. First we will examine decision characteristics. Then we will look at decision-making models and the steps executives should take when making important decisions. We will also examine how groups of managers make decisions. Finally, we will discuss techniques for improving decision making in organizations.

● TYPES OF DECISIONS AND PROBLEMS

decision

A choice made from available alternatives.

A **decision** is a choice made from available alternatives. For example, an accounting manager's selection among Bill, Nancy, and Joan for the position of junior auditor is a decision. Many people assume that making a choice is the major part of decision making, but it is only a part.

Decision making is the process of identifying problems and opportunities and then resolving them.[3] Decision making involves effort both prior to and after the actual choice. Thus, the decision as to whether to select Bill, Nancy, or Joan requires the accounting manager to ascertain whether a new junior auditor is needed, determine the availability of potential job candidates, interview candidates to acquire necessary information, select one candidate, and follow up with the socialization of the new employee into the organization to ensure the decision's success.

PROGRAMMED AND NONPROGRAMMED DECISIONS

Management decisions typically fall into one of two categories: programmed and nonprogrammed. **Programmed decisions** involve situations that have occurred often enough to enable decision rules to be developed and applied in the future.[4] Programmed decisions are made in response to recurring organizational problems. The decision to reorder paper and other office supplies when inventories drop to a certain level is a programmed decision. Other programmed decisions concern the types of skills required to fill certain jobs, the reorder point for manufacturing inventory, exception reporting for expenditures 10 percent or more over budget, and selection of freight routes for product deliveries. Once managers formulate decision rules, subordinates and others can make the decision, freeing managers for other tasks.

decision making

The process of identifying problems and opportunities and then resolving them.

programmed decision

A decision made in response to a situation that has occurred often enough to enable decision rules to be developed and applied in the future.

Entering new businesses or joint ventures is an example of *nonprogrammed decision making.* Toshiba prefers to enter new businesses with strong venture partners. But joint venture decisions are uncertain and complex because of changes in technology and difficulty knowing what the future holds. Toshiba's 1989 joint venture with IBM Japan Ltd., called Display Technologies, Inc., enabled the partners to share costs in production of a 10.4-inch color liquid crystal display (LCD), shown here, that is considered the wave of the future in computer hardware.

nonprogrammed decision

A decision made in response to a situation that is unique, is poorly defined and largely unstructured, and has important consequences for the organization.

Nonprogrammed decisions are made in response to situations that are unique, are poorly defined and largely unstructured, and have important consequences for the organization. Nonprogrammed decisions often involve strategic planning, because uncertainty is great and decisions are complex. Nonprogrammed decisions would include decisions to build a new factory, develop a new product or service, enter a new geographical market, or relocate headquarters to a new city. The decision facing Coors's CEO Peter Coors described at the beginning of this chapter is an example of a nonprogrammed decision. Routine decision rules or techniques for solving this problem do not exist. Peter Coors will spend long hours analyzing the problems, developing alternatives, and making a choice about how to increase market share.

CERTAINTY, RISK, UNCERTAINTY, AND AMBIGUITY

In a perfect world, managers would have all the information necessary for making decisions. In reality, however, some things are unknowable; thus, some decisions will fail to solve the problem or attain the desired outcome. Managers try to obtain information about decision alternatives that will reduce decision uncertainty. Every decision situation can be organized on a scale according to the availability of information and the possibility of failure. The four positions on the scale are certainty, risk, uncertainty, and ambiguity, as illustrated in Exhibit 8.1.

certainty

All the information the decision maker needs is fully available.

CERTAINTY.   Certainty means that all the information the decision maker needs is fully available.[5] Managers have information on operating conditions, resource costs or constraints, and each course of action and possible outcome. For example, if a company considers a $10,000 investment in new equipment that it knows for certain will yield $4,000 in cost savings per year over the next five years, managers can calculate a before-tax rate of return of about 40 percent. If managers compare this

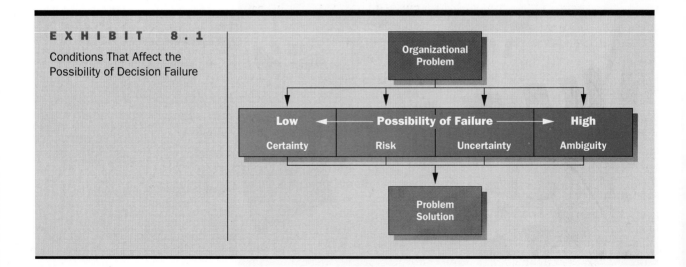

EXHIBIT 8.1

Conditions That Affect the Possibility of Decision Failure

investment with one that will yield only $3,000 per year in cost savings, they can confidently select the 40 percent return. However, few decisions are certain in the real world. Most contain risk or uncertainty.

RISK.   Risk means that a decision has clear-cut objectives and that good information is available, but the future outcomes associated with each alternative are subject to chance. However, enough information is available to allow the probability of a successful outcome for each alternative to be estimated.[6] Statistical analysis might be used to calculate the probabilities of success or failure. The measure of risk captures the possibility that future events will render the alternative unsuccessful. For example, a petroleum executive may bid to sell 10,000 barrels of a petroleum distillate, knowing that there is an 80 percent chance of success with a $5 per barrel price and a 50 percent chance with a $4.20 price. McDonald's took a calculated risk by encouraging franchise experimentation in menus and formats to meet the changing demands of a health-conscious public and increased competition, but with the possible downside risk of harming McDonald's reputation for speed and consistency.[7]

UNCERTAINTY.   Uncertainty means that managers know which objectives they wish to achieve but information about alternatives and future events is incomplete.[8] Managers do not have enough information to be clear about alternatives or to estimate their risk. Factors that may affect a decision, such as price, production costs, volume, or future interest rates, are difficult to analyze and predict. Managers may have to make assumptions from which to forge the decision even though it will be wrong if the assumptions are incorrect. Managers may have to come up with creative approaches to alternatives and use personal judgment to determine which alternative is best.

For example, Boeing faces great uncertainty in the decision to build the twenty-first century airplane. Bypassing the traditional design route of building mock-ups, Boeing will build the new 777 plane, making the radical jump directly from computer image to finished product. Despite the collapse of air carriers such as Eastern and Pan Am, Boeing is gambling that its 777 will secure its future by filling the gap between the 218-passenger 767 and the 419-passenger 747.[9]

Many decisions made under uncertainty do not work out as desired, but sometimes managers must be risk takers. Risk taking is especially important when starting a new business, as illustrated in the Focus on Entrepreneurship box.

AMBIGUITY.   Ambiguity is by far the most difficult decision situation. Ambiguity means that the objectives to be achieved or the problem to be solved is unclear, alternatives are difficult to define, and information about outcomes is unavailable.[10] Ambiguity is what students would feel if an instructor created student groups, told each group to write a paper, but gave the groups no topic, direction, or guidelines whatsoever. Ambiguity has been called a "wicked" decision problem. Managers have a difficult time coming to grips with the issues. Wicked problems are associated with manager conflicts over objectives and decision alternatives, rapidly changing circumstances, fuzzy information, and unclear linkages

risk

A decision has clear-cut objectives, and good information is available, but the future outcomes associated with each alternative are subject to chance.

uncertainty

Managers know what objective they wish to achieve but information about alternatives and future events is incomplete.

ambiguity

The objectives to be achieved or the problem to be solved is unclear, alternatives are difficult to define, and information about outcomes is unavailable.

RISKY BUSINESS, BIG REWARDS

Welcoming risk and uncertainty is part of small business decision making. David Paschal, president of the highly successful Paschal Petroleum, Inc., describes his attitude toward risk taking.

"People looked at me quizzically when I started an oil company in Texas in 1983. . . . Despite the oil industry's downturn, I believed big profits could still be made from Texas' black gold. Since I had only a rudimentary education in the oil business, I decided to learn the industry from the bottom, with a job as a landman—a title researcher—and all-purpose gofer.

"It was 1980, and there I was—26, no job, a mortgage, a wife, and a child. I called every oil company in the Dallas Yellow Pages. I even called Bunker Hunt, the Texas oil millionaire, at home; I had found his number in the White Pages. I told him I wanted to get into the oil business and asked him for five minutes of his time; he had me come to his office, and he gave me maybe 10 or 15 minutes. Meeting Bunker Hunt at this point in my life really gave me fire. He sent me to a company geologist, which led to my next job, as a landman at Spindletop Oil & Gas Co. For three years I got my hands dirty learning every aspect of the oil business. In 1983, I was ready to go out on my own, ready to generate profits for myself as owner of Paschal Petroleum, Inc.

"I cajoled my banker into giving me a $10,000 signature loan to buy an oil lease in an unproven area in Knox County, Texas. I personally raised $70,000, enough to drill the well. It blew in 1984, spewing sizable profits for me and my investors. We have drilled many more wells, whose in-ground reserves total about $35 million.

"I attribute my success to two things. I'm not afraid of taking risks—big risks. In fact, I prefer to take big risks because that's the only way to score big returns. And I'm not afraid of failure. I know that if I make the wrong decision and lose everything in some venture, I still could find another opportunity and become just as successful as I have been in the oil business.

"One reason I enjoy risk is that I believe in my instincts. They are based on detailed observation of the marketplace, which is my second secret of success . . . I read many periodicals and get an overview of developments and directions in business. I can spot brewing trends and devise plans to take advantage of the opportunities they present.

"Season that with a lot of hard work, and you have the formula for my success." ■

SOURCE: David Paschal, "Risky Business, Big Rewards," *Nation's Business*, March 1990, 6. Reprinted by permission. Copyright 1990, U.S. Chamber of Commerce.

among decision elements.[11] Fortunately, most decisions are not characterized by ambiguity. But when they are, managers must conjure up objectives and develop reasonable scenarios for decision alternatives in the absence of information. One example of an ambiguous decision was the marketing department assignment to develop an advertising campaign for a birth control device. Managers were unclear about advertising norms, to whom the ad should be targeted (men, women, marrieds, singles), ad content, or media. The entire approach had to be worked out without precedent.

Another example is the movie industry—one of the most difficult in which to make decisions, because so many new movies are flops. Studio decision makers, however, are seeking new ways to reduce risk and uncertainty.

WARNER BROTHERS

Warner Brothers had a megahit in *Batman*, and it is no accident that it led the industry in market share with 45 percent of the box office in 1989. Warner Brothers' executives reduce risk by maintaining a special relationship with stars who have drawing power. Studio executives build personal relationships with these stars so they will want to do pictures with Warner. Warner Brothers also spends lavishly to ensure the comfort of top stars, providing them with jets and making them feel appreciated.

Another approach to reduce risk of huge losses is to provide stars with a percentage of gross revenues rather than a huge salary. For *Batman*, Jack Nicholson received up to 15 percent of the studio take, and Michael Keaton 8 percent. Nicholson and Keaton made millions because *Batman* was so successful, but they would have made little if it failed. This arrangement may be risky for the studio, but a small profit is better than a huge loss. Senior studio executives have learned to manage risks.[12] ■

The approach of Warner Brothers is becoming more common because the movie industry is so uncertain and volatile. By getting the commitment of stars and sharing the profit, movies have a higher probability of succeeding and less chance of financial losses.

● DECISION-MAKING MODELS

The approach managers use to make decisions usually falls into one of two types—the classical model or the administrative model. The choice of model depends on the manager's personal preference, whether the decision is programmed or nonprogrammed, and the extent to which the decision is characterized by risk, uncertainty, or ambiguity.

CLASSICAL MODEL

The **classical model** of decision making is based on economic assumptions. This model has arisen within the management literature because managers are expected to make decisions that are economically sensible and in the organization's best economic interests. The assumptions underlying this model are as follows:

1 The decision maker operates to accomplish objectives that are known and agreed upon. Problems are precisely formulated and defined.

2 The decision maker strives for conditions of certainty, gathering complete information. All alternatives and the potential results of each are calculated.

3 Criteria for evaluating alternatives are known. The decision maker selects the alternative that will maximize the economic return to the organization.

classical model

A decision-making model based on the assumption that managers should make logical decisions that will be in the organization's best economic interests.

4 The decision maker is rational and uses logic to assign values, order preferences, evaluate alternatives, and make the decision that will maximize the attainment of organizational objectives.

normative

An approach that defines how a decision maker should make decisions and provides guidelines for reaching an ideal outcome for the organization.

The classical model of decision making is considered to be **normative,** which means it defines how a decision maker *should* make decisions. It does not describe how managers actually make decisions so much as it provides guidelines on how to reach an ideal outcome for the organization. The value of the classical model has been its ability to help decision makers be more rational. For example, many senior managers rely solely on intuition and personal preferences for making decisions.[13] In recent years, the classical approach has been given wider application because of the growth of quantitative decision techniques that use computers. Quantitative techniques (discussed in detail in the appendix) include such things as decision trees, pay-off matrices, breakeven analysis, linear programming, forecasting, and operations research models. The use of computerized information systems and data bases has increased the power of the classical approach.

In many respects, the classical model represents an "ideal" model of decision making that is often unattainable by real people in real organizations. It is most valuable when applied to programmed decisions and to decisions characterized by certainty or risk, because relevant infor-

Terra Industries, Inc., uses the classical model of decision making to help agribusiness customers make economically and environmentally sound decisions. Terra Industries utilizes Crop-Master, a unique computer-aided crop input recommendation program, to help growers analyze soil fertility, chemical, seed, and financial data to make decisions for planting each field. These decision applications increase the productivity and profitability of Terra's grower-customers.

mation is available and probabilities can be calculated. One example of the classical approach is the decision model developed by Weyerhaeuser Company for converting a timber harvest into end products. It starts with the description of a tree—size and shape—and evaluates such factors as harvesting costs, hauling, mill location, facility operations, expected end products (plywood, dried trim, fiber, lumber), and customer demand. The model helps managers evaluate hundreds of possibilities for moving lumber through the production process to the consumer and choose the most economically efficient alternatives.[14]

ADMINISTRATIVE MODEL

The **administrative model** of decision making describes how managers actually make decisions in difficult situations, such as those characterized by nonprogrammed decisions, uncertainty, and ambiguity. Many management decisions are not sufficiently programmable to lend themselves to any degree of quantification. Managers are unable to make economically rational decisions even if they want to.[15]

BOUNDED RATIONALITY AND SATISFICING.   The administrative model of decision making is based on the work of Herbert A. Simon. Simon proposed two concepts that were instrumental in shaping the administrative model: bounded rationality and satisficing. **Bounded rationality** means that people have limits, or boundaries, on how rational they can be. The organization is incredibly complex, and managers have the time and ability to process only a limited amount of information with which to make decisions.[16] Because managers do not have the time or cognitive ability to process complete information about complex decisions, they must satisfice. **Satisficing** means that decision makers choose the first solution alternative that satisfies minimal decision criteria. Rather than pursuing all alternatives to identify the single solution that will maximize economic returns, managers will opt for the first solution that appears to solve the problem, even if better solutions are presumed to exist. The decision maker cannot justify the time and expense of obtaining complete information.[17]

An example of both bounded rationality and satisficing occurs when a junior executive on a business trip stains her blouse just prior to an important meeting. She will run to a nearby clothing store and buy the first satisfactory replacement she finds. Having neither the time nor the opportunity to explore all the blouses in town, she satisfices by choosing a blouse that will solve the immediate problem. In a similar fashion, managers generate alternatives for complex problems only until they find one they believe will work. For example, several years ago then-Disney chairman Ray Watson and chief operating officer Ron Miller attempted to thwart takeover attempts, but they had limited options. They satisficed with a quick decision to acquire Arivda Realty and Gibson Court Company. The acquisition of these companies had the potential to solve the problem at hand; thus, they looked no further for possibly better alternatives.[18]

The administrative model relies on assumptions different from those of the classical model and focuses on organizational factors that influence individual decisions. It is more realistic than the classical model for

administrative model

A decision-making model that describes how managers actually make decisions in situations characterized by nonprogrammed decisions, uncertainty, and ambiguity.

bounded rationality

The concept that people have the time and cognitive ability to process only a limited amount of information on which to base decisions.

satisfice

To choose the first solution alternative that satisfies minimal decision criteria regardless of whether better solutions are presumed to exist.

descriptive

An approach that describes how managers actually make decisions rather than how they should.

intuition

The immediate comprehension of a decision situation based on past experience but without conscious thought.

coalition

An informal alliance among managers who support a specific goal.

Intuition or "hunchmanship" enabled Harry V. Quadracci to pursue a dream, armed with only a handful of employees and one printing press. Today, Quad/Graphics enters its third decade, employs 5,000 people, and is one of the nation's fastest growing printers, serving magazines such as *Time*, *INC.*, and *Business Month*. The key to its success is "active risk taking," which demands flexibility, risk taking, information, and no formal plans. Quad's "act now, think later" culture avoids budgets and other traditional management techniques that can stifle flexibility. Intuition is right on target at Quad, which recently topped $500 million in sales.

complex, nonprogrammed decisions. According to the administrative model,

1. Decision objectives often are vague, conflicting, and lack consensus among managers. Managers often are unaware of problems or opportunities that exist in the organization.

2. Rational procedures are not always used, and when they are, they are confined to a simplistic view of the problem that does not capture the complexity of real organizational events.

3. Managers' search for alternatives is limited because of human, information, and resource constraints.

4. Most managers settle for a satisficing rather than a maximizing solution. This is partly because they have limited information and partly because they have only vague criteria for what constitutes a maximizing solution.

The administrative model is considered to be **descriptive,** meaning that it describes how managers actually make decisions in complex situations rather than dictating how they *should* make decisions according to a theoretical ideal. The administrative model recognizes the human and environmental limitations that affect the degree to which managers can pursue a rational decision-making process.

INTUITION.   Another aspect of administrative decision making is intuition. **Intuition** represents a quick apprehension of a decision situation based on past experience but without conscious thought.[19] Intuitive decision making is not arbitrary or irrational, because it is based on years of practice and hands-on experience that enable managers to quickly identify solutions without going through painstaking computations. Managers rely on intuition to determine when a problem exists and to synthesize isolated bits of data and experience into an integrated picture. They also use their intuitive understanding to check the results of rational analysis. If the rational analysis does not agree with their intuition, managers may dig further before accepting a proposed alternative.[20]

Intuition helps managers understand situations characterized by uncertainty and ambiguity that have proven impervious to rational analysis. For example, virtually every major studio in Hollywood turned down the *Star Wars* concept except 20th Century Fox. George Lucas, the creator of *Star Wars*, had attempted to sell the concept to 12 major studios before going to Fox. In each case, the concept had been rejected. All 13 studios saw the same numbers, but only Alan Ladd and his associates at Fox had the right "feel" for the decision. Their intuition told them that *Star Wars* would be a success. In addition, George Lucas was told by many experts that the title *Star Wars* would turn away crowds at the box office. His intuition said the title would work. The rest is history.[21]

COALITION BUILDING.   The uncertainty of administrative decision making often requires coalition building. A **coalition** is an informal alliance among managers who support a specific goal. *Coalition building* is the process of forming alliances among managers. In other words, a manager who supports a specific alternative, such as increasing the cor-

Classical Model	Administrative Model	EXHIBIT 8.2
Clear-cut problem and objectives	Vague problem and objectives	Characteristics of Classical and Administrative Decision-Making Models
Condition of certainty	Condition of uncertainty	
Full information about alternatives and their outcomes	Limited information about alternatives and their outcomes	
Rational choice by individual for maximizing outcomes	Satisficing choice for resolving problem using intuition and coalitions	

poration's growth by acquiring another company, talks informally to other executives and tries to persuade them to support the decision. When the outcomes are not predictable, managers gain support through discussion, negotiation, and bargaining. Without a coalition, a powerful individual or group could derail the decision-making process. Coalition building gives several managers an opportunity to contribute to decision making, enhancing their commitment to the alternative that is ultimately adopted.[22]

The successful coalition building of President George Bush in response to Sadam Hussein's invasion of Kuwait in 1990 was an example for both business and political decision makers. Bush successfully built a coalition among the heads of several countries by first having a clear understanding of the need for a coalition, then targeting his message to each coalition member by explaining why Hussein's action threatened each nation's future, and finally by constant communication with the head of each country in the coalition, Congress, and the American public.[23]

The key dimensions of the classical and administrative models are listed in Exhibit 8.2. Recent research into decision-making procedures has found rational, classical procedures to be associated with high performance for organizations in stable environments. However, administrative decision-making procedures and intuition have been associated with high performance in unstable environments in which decisions must be made rapidly and under more difficult conditions.[24]

● DECISION-MAKING STEPS

Whether a decision is programmed or nonprogrammed and regardless of managers' choice of the classical or administrative model of decision making, six steps typically are associated with effective decision processes. These are summarized in Exhibit 8.3.

RECOGNITION OF DECISION REQUIREMENT

Managers confront a decision requirement in the form of either a problem or an opportunity. A **problem** occurs when organizational accomplishment is less than established objectives. Some aspect of performance is unsatisfactory. An **opportunity** exists when managers see potential

problem

A situation in which organizational accomplishments have failed to meet established objectives.

opportunity

A situation in which managers see potential organizational accomplishments that exceed current objectives.

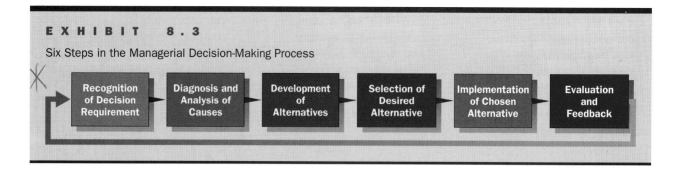

EXHIBIT 8.3

Six Steps in the Managerial Decision-Making Process

| Recognition of Decision Requirement | Diagnosis and Analysis of Causes | Development of Alternatives | Selection of Desired Alternative | Implementation of Chosen Alternative | Evaluation and Feedback |

diagnosis

The step in the decision-making process in which managers analyze underlying causal factors associated with the decision situation.

Seizing *opportunity*, this bunny (a symbol of rapid growth) is hopping off to conquer the world for PepsiCo, Inc. In identifying opportunities for the soft drink industry, PepsiCo recognizes that the international market represents 95 percent of the population and only 25 percent of sales. PepsiCo has now targeted international expansion as the long-term growth opportunity for the future. Global plans include introduction of vending machines, expansion of diet products, and encouragement of bigger package purchases such as cartons over the traditional single bottle.

accomplishment that exceeds specified current objectives. Managers see the possibility of enhancing performance beyond current levels.

Awareness of a problem or opportunity is the first step in the decision sequence and requires surveillance of the internal and external environment for issues that merit executive attention.[25] This resembles the military concept of gathering intelligence. Managers scan the world around them to determine whether the organization is satisfactorily progressing toward its goals. For example, managers at Wells Fargo & Company in San Francisco survey employees to detect potential human resource problems. The survey covers effectiveness of company advertising, product quality, and responsibility to the community, as well as employee satisfaction and organizational climate.[26]

Some information comes from periodic accounting reports, MIS reports, and other sources that are designed to discover problems before they become too serious. Managers also take advantage of informal sources. They talk to other managers, gather opinions on how things are going, and seek advice on which problems should be tackled or which opportunities embraced.[27]

Recognizing decision requirements is difficult, because it often means integrating bits and pieces of information in novel ways. For example, Worlds of Wonder, Inc., developed the first animated talking toy, called Teddy Ruxpin, and Lazer Tag. The astonishing success of these products was due to the pulse taking of customers. Worlds of Wonder works regularly with 1,000 families chosen at random to learn about problems and opportunities in the marketplace for toys. This early recognition contributed directly to the success of Lazer Tag, a toy geared for the young-adult market.[28]

DIAGNOSIS AND ANALYSIS OF CAUSES

Once a problem or opportunity has come to a manager's attention, the understanding of the situation should be refined. **Diagnosis** is the step in the decision-making process in which managers analyze underlying causal factors associated with the decision situation. Managers make a mistake here if they jump right into generating alternatives without first exploring the cause of the problem more deeply.

Kepner and Tregoe, who have conducted extensive studies of manager decision making, recommend that managers ask a series of questions to specify underlying causes, including the following:

- What is the state of disequilibrium affecting us?
- When did it occur?
- Where did it occur?
- How did it occur?
- To whom did it occur?
- What is the urgency of the problem?
- What is the interconnectedness of events?
- What result came from which activity?[29]

Such questions help specify what actually happened and why. Toyota asked questions like these when diagnosing the need for a new luxury car.

TOYOTA

Toyota's most popular car in North America is the inexpensive Camry, the car targeted at the lower end of the market. Based on informal information from sales records and competitor sales, Toyota executives, especially Chairman Toyoda, perceived a need to move into the luxury car market. The people who for years bought Camrys were moving up in life and wanting more expensive cars, such as the BMW, Mercedes, Porsche, and Cadillac.

To define fully the decision requirements, Toyota dispatched 20 designers to the United States to study what customers wanted. They visited dealers, buttonholed car buyers, and organized focus groups. They learned that the need was for a luxury car that would suit younger buyers who wanted to buy European cars but could not yet afford them. Because the United States was the major market, a small team stayed in California designing clay models. In the meantime, the U.S. subsidiary, Toyota Motor Sales USA, Inc., staged expensive consumer research and discovered that the average sales prospect was a 43-year-old male with a household income of $100,000. A separate dealer network to handle the luxury car was also recommended.

After all this information was pulled together, the Lexus was born. Proper problem diagnosis by Toyota resulted in the tremendously successful automobile line.[30]   ■

Built at the turn of the century, Chevron Corporation's Port Arthur Refinery ranked low in profitability and high in cost of maintenance. To meet the standards of the 1990 Clean Air Act, investment of $1 billion would be required to modernize and save the aging refinery. The following *alternative* plans of action were considered: find a buyer, find a joint venture partner, shut the plant down, keep only the chemical operation, or reduce to a single-train from a double-train operation. The single-train alternative emerged as the most attractive and workable, eliminating 247 storage tanks and duplicate older equipment, and saving only the newest and most efficient.

DEVELOPMENT OF ALTERNATIVES

Once the problem or opportunity has been recognized and analyzed, decision makers begin to consider taking action. The next stage is to generate possible alternative solutions that will respond to the needs of the situation and correct the underlying causes.

For a programmed decision, feasible alternatives are easy to identify and in fact usually are already available within the organization's rules and procedures. Nonprogrammed decisions, however, require developing new courses of action that will meet the company's needs. For decisions made under conditions of high uncertainty, managers may develop only one or two custom solutions that will satisfice for handling the problem.

Decision alternatives can be thought of as the tools for reducing the difference between the organization's current and desired performance. Consider how Chrysler Corporation handled a problem of too little production capacity.

 CHRYSLER CORPORATION

After the turnaround led by Lee Iacocca, Chrysler found itself with greater demand for cars in both American and European markets than it could provide. Chrysler executives considered three alternatives, including building new plants, having employees work nights and weekends in existing plants, or obtaining additional production capacity. If Chrysler built new plants, it might get stuck with high overhead and excess capacity, and because current plants were working full tilt, additional labor hours would not produce many additional cars. The third alternative represented a creative and potentially risky solution. Chrysler then bought out troubled American Motors, maker of Jeep. The acquisition gave Chrysler access to manufacturing plants in Kenosha, Wisconsin and Toledo, Ohio. AMC workers avoided layoffs and Chrysler fulfilled its requirement of greater short-run production capacity. Developing decision alternatives led to a creative idea that helped Chrysler stay efficient and at the same time sell more cars.[31] ∎

SELECTION OF DESIRED ALTERNATIVE

Once feasible alternatives have been developed, one must be selected. The decision choice is the selection of the most promising of several alternative courses of action. The manager's goal is to make the choice with the least amount of risk and uncertainty. Because some risk is inherent for most nonprogrammed decisions, managers try to gauge prospects for success. Under conditions of uncertainty, they may have to rely on their intuition and experience to estimate whether a given course of action is likely to succeed.

Making choices depends on managers' personality factors and willingness to accept risk and uncertainty. For example, **risk propensity** is the willingness to undertake risk with the opportunity of gaining an increased payoff. The level of risk a manager is willing to accept will influence the analysis of cost and benefits to be derived from any decision. Consider the situations in Exhibit 8.4. In each situation, which alternative would you choose? A person with a low risk propensity would tend to take assured moderate returns by going for a tie score, building a domestic plant, or pursuing a career as a physician. A risk taker would go for the victory, build a plant in a foreign country, or embark on an acting career. The Manager's Shoptalk box on pages 264–265 describes biases to avoid when selecting the desired alternative.

■
risk propensity
The willingness to undertake risk with the opportunity of gaining an increased payoff.

E X H I B I T   8 . 4

Decision Alternatives with
Different Levels of Risk

For each of the following decisions, which alternative would you choose?

1. In the final seconds of a game with the college's traditional rival, the coach of a college football team may choose a play that has a 95 percent chance of producing a tie score or one with a 30 percent chance of leading to victory or to sure defeat if it fails.

2. The president of a Canadian company must decide whether to build a new plant within Canada that has a 90 percent chance of producing a modest return on investment or to build it in a foreign country with an unstable political history. The latter alternative has a 40 percent chance of failing, but the returns would be enormous if it succeeded.

3. A college senior with considerable acting talent must choose a career. She has the opportunity to go on to medical school and become a physician, a career in which she is 80 percent likely to succeed. She would rather be an actress but realizes that the opportunity for success is only 20 percent.

IMPLEMENTATION OF CHOSEN ALTERNATIVE

The **implementation** stage involves the use of managerial, administrative, and persuasive abilities to ensure that the chosen alternative is carried out. This is similar to the idea of strategic implementation described in Chapter 7. The ultimate success of the chosen alternative depends on whether it can be translated into action. Sometimes an alternative never becomes reality because managers lack the resources or energy needed to make things happen. Implementation may require discussion with people affected by the decision. Communication, motivation, and leadership skills must be used to see that the decision is carried out.

One reason Lee Iacocca succeeded in turning Chrysler around was his ability to implement decisions. Iacocca personally hired people from Ford to develop new auto models. He hired people who shared his vision and were eager to carry out his decisions. By contrast, Tandy Corporation's decision to become a major supplier to businesses by setting up 386 computer centers to support a new direct sales force foundered. Tandy has great success selling to consumers through its Radio Shack stores but simply did not know how to sell computers to businesses. The results were disappointing, and many of the computer centers had to be closed. Tandy lacked the ability to implement the decision to go after business customers.[32]

implementation

The step in the decision-making process that involves the employment of managerial, administrative, and persuasive abilities to translate the chosen alternative into action.

EVALUATION AND FEEDBACK

In the evaluation stage of the decision process, decision makers gather information that tells them how well the decision was implemented and whether it was effective in achieving its objectives. For example, Tandy executives' evaluation of and feedback on the decision to open computer centers revealed poor sales performance. Feedback indicated that implementation was unsuccessful, so computer centers were closed and another approach was tried.

Feedback is important because decision making is a continuous, never-ending process. Decision making is not completed when an executive or board of directors votes yes or no. Feedback provides decision

DECISION BIASES TO AVOID

At a time when decision making is so important, many corporate executives do not know how to make a good choice among alternatives. They may rely on computer analyses or personal intuition without realizing that their own cognitive biases affect their judgment. The complexities of modern corporate life make good judgment more critical than ever. Many errors in judgment originate in the human mind's limited capacity and in the natural biases most executives display during decision making. Awareness of the six biases below can help managers make more enlightened choices:

1. Ignoring the laws of randomness. Randomness means that the outcome of one event has nothing to do with the outcome of another.

Managers often ignore this principle in making business decisions. For example, even though retail sales should be expected to fluctuate each month, a businessperson decides that a slight sales dip is the beginning of a downward trend and takes significant action, such as increasing the advertising budget. If sales rise the following month—which would be expected even without a change in advertising—the executive attributes it to the new advertising strategy. Trends should not be interpreted from a single, random event.

2. Hindsight bias. Hindsight bias means that people tend to overestimate after the fact the degree to which they could have predicted an event. This is sometimes called the "I-knew-it-all-along effect." One example occurs when you are traveling in an unfamiliar area with your spouse behind the wheel. You reach an unmarked fork in the road,

and your spouse decides to turn left. Twenty minutes later you are hopelessly lost, and you exclaim, "I knew you should have turned right at the fork!" Research on hindsight demonstrates that people are not very good at recalling or reconstructing how an uncertain situation appeared beforehand. Managers should be cautious about evaluating decision errors made by themselves and subordinates, because uncertainty may have been greater before the decision than they recall.

3. Giving too much weight to readily available information. Decisions often are based on information that is easily available to certain executives, which precludes their digging for additional information that may provide a more balanced view. For example, geologists at a major oil company were asked to estimate the potential yield at several drilling sites. To do so, they relied on

makers with information that can precipitate a new decision cycle. The decision may fail, thus generating a new analysis of the problem, evaluation of alternatives, and selection of a new alternative. Many big problems are solved by trying several alternatives in sequence, each providing modest improvement. Feedback is the part of monitoring that assesses whether a new decision needs to be made.

An illustration of the overall decision-making process, including evaluation and feedback, was Coca-Cola's decision to introduce a "new" Coke flavor.

 COCA-COLA COMPANY

"Dear Chief Dodo: What ignoramus decided to change the formula of Coke?" This was one of thousands of letters sent to Coca-Cola chairman Roberto Goizueta after the introduction of the new Coke flavor in 1985. Coca-Cola had made its decision via a cautious, rational decision

geological features similar to those of existing oil fields. The results were probably flawed because the geologists failed to consider un-productive fields that had features similar to those of the new sites.

4. Being influenced by problem framing. The decision response of a manager can be influenced by the mere wording of a problem. For example, consider whether a new product decision is framed to emphasize job savings or job losses. If managers are given the option of approving (A) a modified product that will mean a 100 percent chance of saving 200 manufacturing jobs or (B) a new product that has a one-third chance of saving 600 positions and a two-thirds chance of saving zero posi-tions, most managers choose option A. The same problem with a negative frame would give managers the choice of selecting (C) a modified product that had a 100 percent chance of losing 400 jobs, or (D) a totally new product that had a one-third chance of losing 600 jobs and a two-thirds chance of losing zero jobs. With this negative frame, most managers choose D.

Because both problems are identical, the difference in decision choice is accountable strictly by how the problem is framed.

5. Misconception of chance. When a series of similar events occurs, managers may incorrectly gauge the probability of their future recurrence. For example, a manager who is hiring the fifth sales director in two years may feel that the person should work out well. After all, the first four did not work out, and the odds against five failures is small. In truth, the four people who failed have no bearing on the potential performance of the fifth. Each failure was a random event, and the chance of success on the fifth try should not be overestimated.

6. Overconfidence. One of the interesting research findings on decision-making biases is that most people overestimate their ability to predict uncertain outcomes. Before making a decision, managers have unrealistic expectations of their ability to understand the risk and make the right choice. Overconfi-dence is greatest when answering questions of moderate to extreme difficulty. For example, when a group

of people were asked to define quantities about which they had little direct knowledge ("What was the dollar value of Canadian lumber exports in 1977?" "What was the amount of taxes collected by the U.S. Internal Revenue Service in 1970?"), they overestimated their accuracy. Evidence of overconfi-dence is illustrated in cases where subjects were so certain of an answer that they assigned odds of 1,000 to 1 of being correct but in fact were correct only about 85 percent of the time. These findings are especially important for strategic decision making, in which uncertainty is high because managers may unrealistically expect that they can successfully predict outcomes and hence select the wrong alternative. ■

SOURCE: Based on David E. Vell, Howard Raiffa, and Amos Tversky, *Decision Making* (Cambridge University Press, 1988); John McCormick, "The Wisdom of Solomon," *Newsweek*, August 17, 1987, 62–63; and Max H. Bazerman, *Judgment in Managerial Decision Making* (New York: Wiley, 1990).

process. The problem leading to the decision was clear: Pepsi was increasing market share at Coke's expense through supermarket sales. Pepsi was slightly sweeter and tended to beat Coke in blind taste tests. And the enormous success of Diet Coke—sweeter than regular Coke—reinforced the idea of changing the Coke formula.

The problem led to diagnosis and the development of several alter-natives. Coca-Cola spent $4 million to taste-test the new flavor on nearly 200,000 consumers in 30 cities. Coca-Cola identified the flavor people most preferred: 35 percent chose the new Coke over the old, and 52 percent chose it over Pepsi.

Yet within three months after the decision was implemented, old Coke was back in the supermarkets. Why? Because feedback revealed that brand loyalty is an elusive quality that cannot be measured. People had an emotional attachment to the original Coca-Cola from childhood. Mil-lions of advertising dollars could not swing enough people to the new Coke flavor.

Why did the decision fail? It was a bold decision—and bold decisions are inherently risky. Coca-Cola could not measure intangible emotional attachments. On the other hand, thanks to evaluation and feedback, the decision should not be considered a total failure. Coke's near fiasco rejuvenated sagging product loyalty as customers contemplated the loss of their old favorite. After the old Coke was reintroduced under the name "Coca-Cola Classic," there were two Coke brands with which to battle Pepsi. As chairman Goizueta commented, "Had I known in April what I know today, I definitely would have introduced the new Coke. Then I would have said I planned the whole thing."[33] ■

Coca-Cola's decision to introduce a new flavor illustrates all the decision steps, and the process ultimately ended in success. Strategic decisions always contain some risk. In this case, feedback and follow-up decisions got Coke back on track with two brands instead of one.

● GROUP APPROACHES TO DECISION MAKING

Decision making is something that individual managers often do, but decision makers in the business world also operate as part of a group. Decisions may be made through a committee, a task group, departmental participation, or informal coalitions. Beginning with the Vroom-Jago model, here are some ideas for including groups in decision making.

VROOM-JAGO MODEL

Some situations call for group rather than individual decision making. Vroom and Jago developed a model of participation in decision making that provides guidance for practicing managers.[34] The **Vroom-Jago model** helps the manager gauge the appropriate amount of participation for subordinates. It has three major components: leader participation styles, a set of diagnostic questions with which to analyze a decision situation, and a series of decision rules.

LEADER PARTICIPATION STYLES.   The model employs five levels of subordinate participation in decision making ranging from highly autocratic to highly democratic, as illustrated in Exhibit 8.5. Autocratic leadership styles are represented by AI and AII, consulting style by CI and CII, and a group decision by G. The five styles fall along a continuum, and the manager should select one depending on the situation. If the situation warrants, the manager could make the decision alone (AI), share the problem with subordinates individually (CI), or let group members make the decision (G).

DIAGNOSTIC QUESTIONS.   How does a manager decide which of the five decision styles to use? The appropriate degree of decision participation depends on the responses to eight diagnostic questions. These questions deal with the problem, the required level of decision quality, and the importance of having subordinates commit to the decision.

Vroom-Jago model

A model designed to help managers gauge the amount of subordinate participation in decision making.

EXHIBIT 8.5

Five Leader Decision Styles

	Decision Style	**Description**
Highly Autocratic ↑	AI	You solve the problem or make the decision yourself using information available to you at that time.
	AII	You obtain the necessary information from your subordinates and then decide on the solution to the problem yourself.
	CI	You share the problem with relevant subordinates individually, getting their ideas and suggestions without bringing them together as a group. Then you make the decision.
	CII	You share the problem with your subordinates as a group, collectively obtaining their ideas and suggestions. Then you make the decision.
↓ **Highly Democratic**	G	You share a problem with your subordinates as a group. Your role is much like that of chairman. You do not try to influence the group to adopt "your" solution, and you are willing to accept and implement any solution that has the support of the entire group.

Note: A = autocratic; C = consultative; G = group.

SOURCE: Reprinted from *The New Leadership: Managing Participation in Organizations* by Victor H. Vroom and Arthur G. Jago, Englewood Cliffs, NJ: Prentice-Hall, 1988. Copyright 1987 by V. H. Vroom and A. G. Jago. Used with permission of the authors.

1 *Quality Requirement* (**QR**): *How important is the quality of this decision?* If a high-quality decision is important for group performance, the leader has to be actively involved.

2 *Commitment Requirement* (**CR**): *How important is subordinate commitment to the decision?* If implementation requires that subordinates commit to the decision, leaders should involve the subordinates in the decision process.

3 *Leader's Information* (**LI**): *Do I have sufficient information to make a high-quality decision?* If the leader does not have sufficient information or expertise, the leader should involve subordinates to obtain that information.

4 *Problem Structure* (**ST**): *Is the decision problem well structured?* If the problem is ambiguous and poorly structured, the leader will need to interact with subordinates to clarify the problem and identify possible solutions.

5 *Commitment Probability* (**CP**): *If I were to make the decision by myself, is it reasonably certain that my subordinates would be committed to the decision?* If subordinates typically go along with whatever the leader decides, their involvement in the decision process will be less important.

6 *Goal Congruence* (**GC**): *Do subordinates share the organizational goals to be attained in solving this problem?* If subordinates do not share the goals of the organization, the leader should not allow the group to make the decision alone.

7 *Subordinate Conflict* (**CO**): *Is conflict over preferred solutions likely to occur among subordinates?* Disagreement among subordinates can be resolved by allowing their participation and discussion.

8 *Subordinate Information* (**SI**): *Do subordinates have enough information to make a high-quality decision?* If subordinates have good information, then more responsibility for the decision can be delegated to them.

These questions seem detailed, but they quickly narrow the options available to managers and point to the appropriate level of group participation in the decision.

SELECTING A DECISION STYLE. The decision flowchart in Exhibit 8.6 allows a leader to adopt a participation style by answering the questions in sequence. The leader begins at the left side of the chart with question QR: How important is the quality of the decision? If the answer is high, then the leader proceeds to question CR: How important is subordinate commitment to the decision? If the answer is high, the next question is LI: Do I have sufficient information to make a high-quality

EXHIBIT 8.6

Vroom-Jago Decision Tree for Determining an Appropriate Decision-Making Method—Group Problems

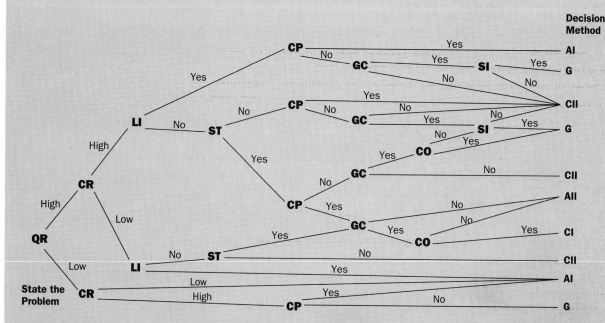

QR How important is the quality of this decision?

CR How important is subordinate commitment to the decision?

LI Do you have sufficient information to make a high-quality decision?

ST Is the problem well structured?

CP If you were to make the decision by yourself, is it reasonably certain that your subordinates would be committed to it?

GC Do subordinates share the organization goals to be attained in solving this problem?

CO Is conflict among subordinates over preferred solutions likely?

SI Do subordinates have sufficient information to make a high-quality decision?

SOURCE: Reprinted from *The New Leadership: Managing Participation in Organizations* by Victor H. Vroom and Arthur G. Jago, Englewood Cliffs, NJ: Prentice-Hall, 1988. Copyright 1987 by V. H. Vroom and A. G. Jago. Used with permission of the authors.

decision? If the answer is yes, the leader proceeds to answer question CP because question ST is irrelevant if the leader has sufficient information to make a high-quality decision. Managers can quickly learn to use the basic model to adapt their leadership styles to fit their decision problem and the situation.

Several decision styles are equally acceptable in many situations. When this happens, Vroom and Jago recommend using the most autocratic style because this will save time without reducing decision quality or acceptance.

Although the decision tree model has been criticized as being less than perfect,[35] it is useful to decision makers, and the body of supportive research is growing.[36] Managers make timely, high-quality decisions when following the model. One application of the model occurred at Barouh-Eaton Allen Corporation.

 ## K·O·R·E·C·T·Y·P·E

Barouh-Eaton Allen started prospering when owner Vic Barouh noticed that a typist kept a piece of white chalk by her machine. To erase an error, she would lightly rub over it with the chalk. It took several passes, but the correction was neatly made. Barouh's company already made carbon paper, so he tried rubbing chalk on one side of a sheet of paper, putting the paper between the error and typewriter, and striking the same key. Most of the error disappeared under a thin coating of chalk dust. Thus, Ko-Rec-Type was born. Demand for the product was enormous, and the company prospered.

Then IBM invented the self-correcting typewriter. Within two days after IBM's announcement, nearly 40 people told Barouh that the company was in trouble. Nobody was going to buy Ko-Rec-Type again.

Barouh bought a self-correcting typewriter, took it to the plant, called everybody together, and told them what they had to do. To survive, the company had to learn to make this ribbon. They also had to learn to make the cartridge that held the ribbon, because cartridges could not be purchased on the market. They also had to learn to make the spools that held the tape. They had to learn to make the ink, the machine that puts on ink, injection-molding to make the spools, and so on. It was an enormous challenge. Barouh got everyone involved regardless of position or education.

To everyone's astonishment, Ko-Rec-Type produced the first self-correcting ribbon in only six months. Moreover, it was the only company in the world to produce that product. Barouh later learned that it took IBM six years to make its self-correcting ribbon. With the new product, Ko-Rec-Type's sales remained high and the company avoided disaster.[37] ∎

The Vroom-Jago model shows that Vic Barouh used the correct decision style. Moving from left to right in Exhibit 8.6, the questions and answers are as follows. (QR) *How important is the quality of this decision?* Definitely high. (CR) *How important is subordinate commitment to the decision?* Importance of commitment is probably low, because subordinates had a great deal of respect for Barouh and would do whatever he asked. (LI) *Did Barouh have sufficient information to make a high-quality decision?* Definitely no. (ST) *Is the problem well structured?* Definitely no. The remaining questions are not relevant because at this point the decision tree leads directly to the CII decision style. Barouh should have used a consultative decision style by having subordinates participate in problem discussions as a group—which he did.

GROUP DECISION FORMATS

The Vroom-Jago model illustrates that managers can select the amount of group participation in decision making. They can also select decision format. Three formats generally can be used: the interactive group, the nominal group, and the Delphi group. Each format has unique characteristics that make it more suitable for certain decisions. Most task forces, committees, and work groups fall into the category of interactive groups. Nominal and Delphi groups normally are convened for the purpose of increasing creativity during group decision making.

INTERACTIVE GROUPS.   Research on the Vroom-Jago model indicates that having subordinates meet as an interactive group leads to more effective decisions than having the group leader meet with each member individually.[38] An **interactive group** simply means that members are brought together face to face and have a specific agenda and decision objectives. Interactive groups typically begin with a group leader stating a problem and asking for inputs from members. Discussion is unorganized. The group may meander through problem identification and may require some problem redefinition. Alternatives are generated and evaluated. Eventually, participants will vote or perhaps discuss alternatives until they reach a consensus on a desired solution. A staff meeting or departmental meeting formed to discuss next year's goals is a good example of interactive group decision making. Interactive groups will be described in more detail in Chapter 16.

NOMINAL GROUPS.   Because some participants may talk more and dominate group discussions in interactive groups, the **nominal group** technique was developed to ensure that every group participant has equal input in the decision-making process.[39] The nominal group is structured in a series of steps to equalize participation:

1 Each participant writes down his or her ideas on the problem to be discussed. These ideas usually are suggestions for a solution.

2 A round robin in which each group member presents his or her ideas to the group is set up. The ideas are written down on a blackboard for all members to see. No discussion of the ideas occurs until every person's ideas have been presented and written down for general viewing.

3 After all ideas have been presented, there is an open discussion of the ideas for the purpose of clarification and evaluation. This part of the discussion tends to be spontaneous and unstructured.

---

interactive group

A group decision-making format in which group members are brought together face to face and have a specific agenda and decision objectives.

nominal group

A group decision-making format that emphasizes equal participation in the decision process by all group members.

In three days a *group decision* by this CSX Corporation Western Network Team successfully plotted turnaround strategy for the company's domestic cargo-carrying container program. The Western Network Team is one of six multidisciplinary teams that manage CSX. Faced with a downturn in business, excessive equipment turnaround time, and too many empty eastbound containers, the Western Network Team debated and scuttled a plan for additional containers. The group opted for limiting new container investment, launching a West Coast sales blitz, and greater control of westbound loadings. Within two months empty container and equipment turnaround costs declined sharply.

4 After the discussion, a secret ballot is taken in which each group member votes for preferred solutions. The adopted decision is the one that receives the most votes.

DELPHI GROUPS.   Developed by the Rand Corporation, the **Delphi group** technique is used to combine expert opinions from different perspectives about an ambiguous problem.[40] Unlike interactive and nominal groups, Delphi group participants do not meet face to face—in fact, they never see one another. This technique calls for a group leader to solicit and collate written, expert opinions on a topic through the use of questionnaires. After the answers are received, a summary of the opinions is developed and distributed to participants. Then a new questionnaire on the same problem is circulated. In this second round, participants have the benefit of knowing other people's opinions and can change their suggested answers to reflect this new information. The process of sending out questionnaires and then sharing the results continues until a consensus is reached.

ADVANTAGES AND DISADVANTAGES OF GROUP DECISION MAKING

Whatever group techniques managers use for decision making, there are clear advantages and disadvantages compared with individual decision making.[41] Because managers often have a choice between making a decision by themselves or including others, they should understand the advantages and disadvantages of group decision making, which are summarized in Exhibit 8.7.

Delphi group

A group decision-making format that involves the circulation among participants of questionnaires on the selected problem, sharing of answers, and continuous recirculation/refinement of questionnaires until a consensus has been obtained.

EXHIBIT 8.7

Advantages and Disadvantages of Group Decision Making

Advantages

1. Broader perspective for problem definition and analysis.
2. More knowledge, facts, and alternatives can be evaluated.
3. Discussion clarifies ambiguous problems and reduces uncertainty about alternatives.
4. Participation fosters member satisfaction and support for decision.

Disadvantages

1. Time-consuming.
2. Compromise decisions may satisfy no one.
3. Groupthink: Group norms may reduce dissent and opinion diversity.
4. Knowledge overkill and wasted resources if used for programmed decisions.
5. No clear focus for decision responsibility.

groupthink

A phenomenon in which group members are so committed to the group that they are reluctant to express contrary opinions.

ADVANTAGES.   Groups have an advantage over individuals because they bring together a broader perspective for defining the problem and diagnosing underlying causes and effects. In addition to enriching problem diagnosis, groups offer more knowledge and facts with which to identify potential solutions and produce more decision alternatives. Moreover, people who participate in decision making are more satisfied with the decision and more likely to support it, thereby facilitating implementation. Group discussion also can help reduce uncertainty for decision makers who may be unwilling to undertake a big risk by themselves. Finally, group discussion enhances member satisfaction and produces support for a possibly risky decision.

DISADVANTAGES.   Group decisions tend to be time-consuming. People must be consulted, and they jointly diagnose problems and discuss solutions. Moreover, groups may reach a compromise solution that is less than optimal for the organization. Another problem is groupthink. **Groupthink** is a "mode of thinking that people engage in when they are deeply involved in a cohesive in-group, and when the members' strivings for unanimity override their motivation to realistically appraise alternative courses of action."[42] Groupthink means that people are so committed to the group that they are reluctant to disagree with one another; thus, the group loses the diversity of opinions essential to effective decision making. Another problem—particularly when groups are used for programmed decisions—is decision overkill due to the task's lack of challenge for group members. Finally, there is no clear focus of decision responsibility, because the group rather than any single individual makes the decision.

One example of the disadvantage of group decision making occurred when a coalition at Citibank refused to change the practice of "parking"—the bogus transfer of foreign exchange deposits to shift bank profits to countries with low tax rates. The line between illegal and legal activities was hazy, and groupthink appeared so people were unwilling to disagree with the current practice because group norms supported high profits and reduced taxes. Group members were willing to com-

Kimball International, Inc., pursues the *advantages of group decision making* through a variety of programs that encourage employee thinking and leadership. Its National Office Furniture Manufacturing business unit, pictured here, uses empowerment, individual initiative, and teamwork to achieve its goals. Management encouraged group participation, and employees took responsibility for reaching unit goals. Kimball teams contributed to the company mission statement and guiding principles, and they contribute to and support management's decisions for running the business.

promise their values, groupthink reduced dissent, and there was no clear focus of responsibility because everyone had agreed to the potentially illegal practice.[43]

● IMPROVING DECISION-MAKING EFFECTIVENESS

How can managers overcome groupthink and other disadvantages to avoid costly mistakes? A number of techniques have been developed to help individual managers and groups arrive at better decisions.

A **devil's advocate** is assigned the role of challenging the assumptions and assertions made by the group.[44] The devil's advocate forces the group to rethink its approach to the problem and to avoid reaching premature consensus or making unreasonable assumptions before proceeding with problem solutions.

Multiple advocacy is similar to a devil's advocate except that more advocates and points of view are presented. Minority opinions and unpopular viewpoints are assigned to forceful representatives, who then debate before the decision makers. President Bush was renowned for using multiple advocacy in his decision making. The proposal for clean-air legislation in 1989 was a textbook case, because White House aides staged debates they called "Scheduled Train Wrecks" to help Bush think

devil's advocate

A decision-making technique in which an individual is assigned the role of challenging the assumptions and assertions made by the group to prevent premature consensus.

multiple advocacy

A decision-making technique that involves several advocates and presentation of multiple points of view, including minority and unpopular opinions.

■
brainstorming

A decision-making technique in which group members present spontaneous suggestions for problem solution, regardless of their likelihood of implementation, in order to promote freer, more creative thinking within the group.

through the issue. These were live scrimmages with Bush asking questions back and forth during the debate. The result was a decision based on solid argument and understanding of all perspectives.[45]

Brainstorming uses a face-to-face, interactive group to spontaneously suggest ideas for problem solution.[46] Brainstorming is perhaps the best-known decision aid; its primary role is to supply additional, creative solutions. Group members are invited to suggest alternatives regardless of their likelihood of being implemented. No critical comments of any kind are allowed until all suggestions have been listed. Members are encouraged to brainstorm possible solutions out loud, and freewheeling is welcomed. The more novel and unusual the idea, the better. The object of brainstorming is to promote freer, more flexible thinking and to enable group members to build on one another's creativity. The typical session begins with a warmup wherein definitional issues are settled, proceeds through the freewheeling idea-generation stage, and concludes with an evaluation of feasible ideas.[47]

SUMMARY AND MANAGEMENT SOLUTION

This chapter made several important points about the process of organizational decision making. The study of decision making is important because it describes how managers make successful strategic and operational decisions. Managers must confront many types of decisions, including programmed and nonprogrammed, and decisions differ according to the amount of risk, uncertainty, and ambiguity in the environment.

Two decision-making approaches were described: the classical model and the administrative model. The classical model explains how managers should make decisions so as to maximize economic efficiency. The administrative model describes how managers actually make nonprogrammed, uncertain decisions with skills that include intuition and coalition building.

Decision making should involve six basic steps: problem recognition, diagnosis of causes, development of alternatives, choice of an alternative, implementation of alternative, and feedback and evaluation.

Peter Coors used the administrative model to make a decision about how to solve the problem of declining earnings and market share. Further delay would make things worse, because in the past Coors had been known to delay entry into new markets, such as dry beer, and was slow to initiate new advertising. Coors's top managers built a coalition to "sharpen our spears" and double market share (now only 10.3 percent). After considering several alternatives, Coors decided to spin off nonbrewing businesses and refocus on the brewery. Cutting distractions will enable Coors to focus on its new Keystone line as well as on a line of new fruit-flavored beer coolers.[48]

The chapter also described how decisions can be made within organizational groups. The Vroom-Jago model specifies decision characteristics that indicate when groups should participate in decision making. The types of groups managers may use include interactive groups, nominal groups, and Delphi groups. Groups offer a number of advantages and disadvantages compared with individuals. Techniques for improving decision-making quality include devil's advocate, multiple advocacy, and brainstorming. These techniques help managers define problems and develop more creative solutions.

DISCUSSION QUESTIONS

1. You are a busy partner in a legal firm, and an experienced secretary complains of continued headaches, drowsiness, dry throat, and occasional spells of fatigue and flu. She tells you she believes air quality in the building is bad and would like something done. How would you respond?
2. Why is decision making considered a fundamental part of management effectiveness?
3. Explain the difference between risk and ambiguity. How might decision making differ for each situation?
4. Analyze three decisions you made over the last six months. Which of these are programmed and which are nonprogrammed?
5. Why are many decisions made by groups rather than by individuals?
6. The Vroom-Yetton model describes five decision styles. How should a manager go about choosing which style to use?
7. What are three types of decision-making groups? How might each be used to help managers make a decision to market a product in a new geographical territory?
8. What is meant by *satisficing* and *bounded rationality*? Why do managers not strive to find the economically best solution for many organizational decisions?
9. What techniques could you use to improve your own creativity and effectiveness in decision making?
10. Which of the six steps in the decision-making process do you think is most likely to be ignored by a manager? Explain.

MANAGEMENT IN PRACTICE: EXPERIENTIAL EXERCISE

● **THE DESERT SURVIVAL SITUATION**

The situation described in this exercise is based on over 2,000 actual cases in which men and women lived or died depending on the survival decisions they made. Your "life" or "death" will depend on how well your group can share its present knowledge of a relatively unfamiliar problem so that the team can make decisions that will lead to your survival.

This exercise will challenge your ability to take advantage of a group approach to decision making and to apply decision steps such as developing alternatives and selecting the correct alternative. When instructed, read about the situation and do Step 1 without discussing it with the rest of the group.

The Situation It is approximately 10:00 A.M. in mid-August, and you have just crash landed in the Sonora Desert in the southwestern United States. The light twin-engine plane, containing the bodies of the pilot and the copilot, has completely burned. Only the air frame remains. None of the rest of you has been injured.

The pilot was unable to notify anyone of your position before the crash. However, he had indicated before impact that you were 70 miles south-southwest from a mining camp that is the nearest known habitation and that you were approximately 65 miles off the course that was filed in your VFR Flight Plan.

The immediate area is quite flat and, except for occasional barrel and saguaro cacti, appears to be rather barren. The last weather report indicated the temperature would reach 110° that day, which means that the temperature at ground level will be 130°. You are dressed in lightweight clothing: short-sleeved shirts, pants, socks, and street shoes. Everyone has a handkerchief. Collectively, your pockets contain $2.83 in change, $85.00 in bills, a pack of cigarettes, and a ballpoint pen.

Your Task Before the plane caught fire, your group was able to salvage the 15 items listed in the following table.

Your task is to rank these items according to their importance to your survival, starting with "1," the most important, to "15," the least important.

You may assume the following:

1. The number of survivors is the same as the number on your team.
2. You are the actual people in the situation.
3. The team has agreed to stick together.
4. All items are in good condition.

Step 1 Each member of the team is to individually rank each item. Do not discuss the situation or problem until each member has finished the individual ranking.

Step 2 After everyone has finished the individual ranking, rank order the 15 items as a team. Once discussion begins, do not change your individual ranking. Your instructor will inform you how much time you have to complete this step.

Items	Step 1: Your Individual Ranking	Step 2: The Team's Ranking	Step 3: Survival Expert's Ranking	Step 4: Difference between Step 1 and Step 3	Step 5: Difference between Step 2 and Step 3
Flashlight (4-battery size)	_____	_____	_____	_____	_____
Jackknife	_____	_____	_____	_____	_____
Sectional air map of the area	_____	_____	_____	_____	_____
Plastic raincoat (large size)	_____	_____	_____	_____	_____
Magnetic compass	_____	_____	_____	_____	_____
Compress kit with gauze	_____	_____	_____	_____	_____
.45 caliber pistol (loaded)	_____	_____	_____	_____	_____
Parachute (red and white)	_____	_____	_____	_____	_____
Bottle of salt tablets (1,000 tablets)	_____	_____	_____	_____	_____
1 quart of water per person	_____	_____	_____	_____	_____
A book entitled *Edible Animals of the Desert*	_____	_____	_____	_____	_____
A pair of sunglasses per person	_____	_____	_____	_____	_____
2 quarts of 180 proof vodka	_____	_____	_____	_____	_____
1 topcoat per person	_____	_____	_____	_____	_____
A cosmetic mirror	_____	_____	_____	_____	_____
Totals (the lower the score, the better)				_____ Your Score, Step 4	_____ Team Score, Step 5

Please complete the following steps and insert the scores under your team's number.	Team Number					
	1	**2**	**3**	**4**	**5**	**6**
Step 6: Average Individual Score Add up all the individual scores (Step 4) on the team and divide by the number on the team.						
Step 7: Team Score						
Step 8: Gain Score The difference between the Team Score and the Average Individual Score. If the Team Score is lower than Average Individual Score, then gain is "+." If Team Score is higher than Average Individual Score, then gain is "−."						
Step 9: Lowest Individual Score on the Team						
Step 10: Number of Individual Scores Lower Than the Team Score						

SOURCE: J. Clayton Lafferty, Patrick M. Eady, and Alonzo W. Pond, "The Desert Survival Situation: A Group Decision Making Experience for Examining and Increasing Individual and Team Effectiveness," 8th ed. Copyright © 1974 by Experiential Learning Methods, Inc., 15200 E. Jefferson, Suite 107, Grosse Pointe Park, MI 48230, (313)823-4400.

CASES FOR ANALYSIS

NBC, INC.

Olympic athletes can tell you: When "going for the gold," there are no guaranteed winners. NBC executives and their Cablevision allies learned that lesson as they attempted to marry the top sports event of 1992 (the Barcelona Olympics) and the successful pay-per-view trend. NBC's much ballyhooed TripleCast, offering three-channel, commercial-free, around-the-clock Olympic coverage, flopped. Experts estimated NBC's loss could reach $60 to $70 million; Cablevision estimates its own losses at $20 million.

The TripleCast concept appeared to be low risk in light of cable television's pay-per-view success with sports enthusiasts. Network and cable executives based their decision on this trend as well as the expressed desire in recent years for expanded Olympic coverage. Yet only 250,000 homes participated in TripleCast. What went wrong?

Executives overlooked a number of important factors. Although they estimated 60 million households with cable access, only about 40 million have pay-per-view technology, and only 20 million can receive pay-per-view on demand. Such figures cut deeply into projected viewer numbers. In addition, the $125 price tag for TripleCast was too high for many traditional sports viewers.

The refusal on the part of affiliates, both network and cable, to play ball also hurt TripleCast. A large number of affiliates refused to advertise pay-per-view, fearing cuts into their own viewership. Many cable operators refused to free three channels for the pay-per-view telecast.

Cablevision's chairman Charles F. Dolan believes the Barcelona experience taught executives a valuable lesson in pay-per-view. With the 1996 Atlanta Games looming on the horizon, the question is whether broadcasters should take another shot at TripleCast.

● QUESTIONS

1. Which decision-making steps are evident in the Triple-Cast decision? Explain.
2. What was the role of evaluation and feedback in this case? Should broadcasters try TripleCast again in 1996? Why?
3. Was the TripleCast decision characterized by risk, uncertainty, or ambiguity? Explain.

SOURCE: Peter Coy, "Why NBC's 'TripleCast' Never Made a Run at the Gold," *Business Week*, August 17, 1992, 34–38.

GUARDIAN ENGINEERING

Lew Calderone, engineering manager, was beside himself. The problem he faced was complex and highly personal in nature. Joey Stark had been an employee of Guardian Engineering for 15 years and had a record of reliable, consistent work. Joey had reported to Lew for two years. However, his performance recently had become so poor that Lew felt Joey must be fired. For one thing, Joey was frequently absent on Mondays despite the company's policy against excessive absences. Once or twice Lew had smelled alcohol on Joey's breath while at work, and he suspected that alcohol was the problem. A couple of other employees had commented on Joey's drinking, but Lew had never personally witnessed Joey drinking excessively.

Lew had talked with Joey twice about his absences and declining performance. He had asked Joey about his family life, personal life, and working conditions to learn whether any of these were causing the problem. Joey had simply said everything was all right. After the second conversation, Lew wrote a short memorandum specifying his concerns, and the memo went into Joey's personnel file. Joey improved his performance for a couple of weeks, but nothing seemed to have changed permanently.

If alcoholism was Joey's problem, Lew was thinking about alternative solutions. One would be to fire Joey, because Lew had read that alcoholics lose their jobs and their families before they become motivated to change their behavior. Another would be to confront Joey and accuse him

of alcoholism to let him know the company was aware of his drinking problem. A third would be to refer Joey to a private counselor or physician for possible rehabilitation. A fourth would be to give Joey one more warning, making it clear that the next absence or lapse in performance would cost him his job.

Complicating the problem was Lew's feeling that Joey was a friend as well as a senior employee. However, Lew felt he had to proceed with whatever was best for the company. The company had no clearly defined policy on alcoholism, which made choosing a solution somewhat more difficult. Lew wondered whether he should talk to other senior managers about the problem and seek their guidance and agreement. He also wondered if there were some way he could gather more information about the true nature of the problem before deciding on a solution. Frankly, Lew realized he needed to take action, but he just was not sure what to do

● **QUESTIONS**

1. Is the decision facing Lew Calderone considered programmed or nonprogrammed?
2. How should Lew proceed to make the decision? Should he investigate the nature of the problem? Should he make a decision among the available alternatives?
3. What would you do in this situation? Why?

REFERENCES

1. Ronald Grover, "Coors Is Thinking Suds 'R' Us," *Business Week,* June 8, 1992, 34.

2. Mark Maremont, "Waterford Is Showing a Few Cracks," *Business Week,* February 20, 1989, 60–65; John Markoff, "John Sculley's Biggest Test," *The New York Times,* February 26, 1989, sec. 3, 1, 26; Mark Landler, "People of Earth, We Are a Friendly Channel," *Business Week,* October 5, 1992, 50; and Joseph Weber and Peter Coy, "Look Ma, No Cable: It's Video-By-Phone," *Business Week,* November 14, 1992, 86.

3. Ronald A. Howard, "Decision Analysis: Practice and Promise," *Management Science* 34 (1988), 679–695.

4. Herbert A. Simon, *The New Science of Management* (Englewood Cliffs, N.J.: Prentice-Hall, 1977), 47.

5. Samuel Eilon, "Structuring Unstructured Decisions," *Omega* 13 (1985), 369–377; and Max H. Bazerman, *Judgment in Managerial Decision Making* (New York: Wiley, 1986).

6. James G. March and Zur Shapira, "Managerial Perspectives on Risk and Risk Taking," *Management Science* 33 (1987), 1404–1418; and Inga Skromme Baird

and Howard Thomas, "Toward a Contingency Model of Strategic Risk Taking," *Academy of Management Review* 10 (1985), 230–243.

7. Lois Therrian, "McRisky," *Business Week*, October 21, 1991, 114–122.

8. Eilon, "Structuring Unstructured Decisions," and Philip A. Roussel, "Cutting Down the Guesswork in R&D," *Harvard Business Review* 61 (September–October 1983), 154–160.

9. Jeremy Main, "Betting on the 21st Century," *Fortune*, April 20, 1992, 102–117.

10. Michael Masuch and Perry LaPotin, "Beyond Garbage Cans: An AI Model of Organizational Choice," *Administrative Science Quarterly* 34 (1989), 38–67; and Richard L. Daft and Robert H. Lengel, "Organizational Information Requirements, Media Richness and Structural Design," *Management Science* 32 (1986), 554–571.

11. David M. Schweiger, William R. Sandberg, and James W. Ragan, "Group Approaches for Improving Strategic Decision Making: A Comparative Analysis of Dialectical Inquiry, Devil's Advocacy, and Consensus," *Academy of Management Journal* 29 (1986), 51–71; and Richard O. Mason and Ian I. Mitroff, *Challenging Strategic Planning Assumptions* (New York: Wiley Interscience, 1981).

12. Ronald Grover, "Fat Times for Studios, Fatter Times for Stars," *Business Week*, July 24, 1989, 48.

13. Boris Blai, Jr., "Eight Steps to Successful Problem Solving," *Supervisory Management* (January 1986), 7–9; and Earnest R. Acher, "How to Make a Business Decision: An Analysis of Theory and Practice," *Management Review* 69 (February 1980), 54–61.

14. Douglas A. Hay and Paul N. Dahl, "Strategic and Midterm Planning of Forest-to-Product Flows," *Interfaces* 14 (September/October 1984), 33–43.

15. Herbert A. Simon, *The New Science of Management Decision* (New York: Harper & Row, 1960), 5–6; and Amitai Etzioni, "Humble Decision Making," *Harvard Business Review* (July–August 1989), 122–126.

16. James G. March and Herbert A. Simon, *Organizations* (New York: Wiley, 1958).

17. Herbert A. Simon, *Models of Man* (New York: Wiley, 1957), 196–205; and Herbert A. Simon, *Administrative Behavior*, 2d ed. (New York: Free Press, 1957).

18. John Taylor, "Project Fantasy: A Behind-the-Scenes Account of Disney's Desperate Battle against the Raiders," *Manhattan* (November 1984).

19. Weston H. Agor, "The Logic of Intuition: How Top Executives Make Important Decisions," *Organizational Dynamics* 14 (Winter 1986), 5–18; and Herbert A. Simon, "Making Management Decisions: The Role of Intuition and Emotion," *Academy of Management Executive* 1 (1987), 57–64.

20. Daniel J. Isenberg, "How Senior Managers Think," *Harvard Business Review* 62 (November–December 1984), 80–90.

21. Annetta Miller and Dody Tsiantar, "A Test for Market Research," *Newsweek*, December 28, 1987, 32–33; and David Frost and Michael Deakin, *David Frost's Book of the World's Worst Decisions* (New York: Crown, 1983), 60–61.

22. William B. Stevenson, Jon L. Pierce, and Lyman W. Porter, "The Concept of 'Coalition' in Organization Theory and Research," *Academy of Management Review*, 10 (1985), 256–268.

23. Ann Reilly Dowd, "George Bush as Crisis Manager," *Fortune*, September 10, 1990, 55–56, and "How Bush Decided," *Fortune*, February 11, 1991, 45–46.

24. James W. Fredrickson, "Effects of Decision Motive and Organizational Performance Level on Strategic Decision Processes," *Academy of Management*

Journal 28 (1985), 821–843; and James W. Fredrickson, "The Comprehensiveness of Strategic Decision Processes: Extension, Observations, Future Directions," *Academy of Management Journal* 27 (1984), 445–466.

25. Marjorie A. Lyles and Howard Thomas, "Strategic Problem Formulation: Biases and Assumptions Embedded in Alternative Decision-Making Models," *Journal of Management Studies* 25 (1988), 131–145; and Susan E. Jackson and Jane E. Dutton, "Discerning Threats and Opportunities," *Administrative Science Quarterly* 33 (1988), 370–387.

26. Larry Reibstein, "A Finger on the Pulse: Companies Expand Use of Employee Surveys," *The Wall Street Journal,* October 27, 1986, 27.

27. Richard L. Daft, Juhani Sormumen, and Don Parks, "Chief Executive Scanning, Environmental Characteristics, and Company Performance: An Empirical Study" (Unpublished manuscript, Texas A&M University, 1988).

28. Jerry Jakuvovics, "Rising Stars in Toys and Togs," *Management Review* (May 1987), 19–20.

29. C. Kepner and B. Tregoe, *The Rational Manager* (New York: McGraw-Hill, 1965).

30. Alex Taylor III, "Here Come Japan's New Luxury Cars," *Fortune,* August 14, 1989, 62–66.

31. Alex Taylor III, "U.S. Cars Come Back," *Fortune,* November 16, 1992, 52–85; and William J. Hampton, "The Next Act at Chrysler," *Business Week,* November 3, 1986, 66.

32. Todd Mason, "Tandy Finds a Cold, Hard World Outside the Radio Shack," *Business Week,* August 31, 1987, 68–70.

33. Glen Whyte, "Decision Failures: Why They Occur and How to Prevent Them," *Academy of Management Executive* 5, no. 3 (1991), 23–31; and Betsy D. Gelb and Gabriel M. Gelb, "New Coke's Fizzle—Lessons for the Rest of Us," *Sloan Management Review* (Fall 1986), 71–76.

34. V. H. Vroom and Arthur G. Jago, *The New Leadership: Managing Participation in Organizations* (Englewood Cliffs, N.J.: Prentice-Hall, 1988).

35. R. H. G. Field, "A Test of the Vroom-Yetton Normative Model of Leadership," *Journal of Applied Psychology* (October 1982), 523–532; and R. H. G. Field, "A Critique of the Vroom-Yetton Contingency Model of Leadership Behavior," *Academy of Management Review* 4 (1979), 249–257.

36. Jennifer T. Ettling and Arthur G. Jago, "Participation under Conditions of Conflict: More on the Validity of the Vroom-Yetton Model," *Journal of Management Studies* 25 (1988), 73–83; Madeline E. Heilman, Harvey A. Hornstein, Jack H. Cage, and Judith K. Herschlag, "Reactions to Prescribed Leader Behavior as a Function of Role Perspective: The Case of the Vroom-Yetton Model," *Journal of Applied Psychology* (February 1984), 50–60; and Arthur G. Jago and Victor H. Vroom, "Some Differences in the Incidence and Evaluation of Participative Leader Behavior," *Journal of Applied Psychology* (December 1982), 776–783.

37. Tom Richman, "One Man's Family," *INC.,* November 1983, 151–156.

38. Ettling and Jago, "Participation under Conditions of Conflict."

39. Andre Delbecq, Andrew Van de Ven, and D. Gustafson, *Group Techniques for Program Planning* (Glenview, Ill.: Scott, Foresman, 1975); and William M. Fox, "Anonymity and Other Keys to Successful Problem-Solving Meetings," *National Productivity Review* 8 (Spring 1989), 145–156.

40. "Group Decision Making: Approaches to Problem Solving," *Small Business Reports* (July 1988), 30–33; and N. Delkey, *The Delphi Method: An Experimental Study of Group Opinion* (Santa Monica, Cal.: Rand Corporation, 1969).

41. John L. Cotton, David A. Vollarth, Kirk L. Froggatt, Mark L. Lengnick-Hall, and Kenneth R. Jennings, "Employee Participation: Diverse Forms and Different Outcomes," *Academy of Management Review* 13 (1988), 8–22; and Walter C. Swap, "Destructive Effects of Groups on Individuals" in *Group Decision Making*, ed. Walter C. Swap and Associates (Beverly Hills, Cal.: Sage, 1984).

42. Irving L. Janis, *Group Think*, 2d ed. (Boston: Houghton Mifflin, 1982), 9; and Glen Whyte, "Groupthink Reconsidered," *Academy of Management Review* 14 (1989), 40–56.

43. Roy Rowan, "The Maverick Who Yelled Foul at Citibank," *Fortune*, January 10, 1983, 46–56.

44. David M. Schweiger and William R. Sandberg, "The Utilization of Individual Capabilities in Group Approaches to Strategic Decision-Making," *Strategic Management Journal* 10 (1989), 31–43, and "The Devil's Advocate," *Small Business Report* (December 1987), 38–41.

45. Michael Duffy, "Mr. Consensus," *Time*, August 21, 1989, 16–22.

46. "Group Decision-Making," *Small Business Report* (July 1988), 30–33.

47. A. Osborn, *Applied Imagination* (New York: Scribner, 1957).

48. Grover, "Coors Is Thinking Suds 'R' Us."

AMERICAN AIRLINES

In the heady days between February and March 1989, American Airlines made a commitment to grow bigger and faster than any competitor. It ordered 370 new jetliners with a tab of $15.3 billion and that was only a portion of a late 1980s spending orgy that totaled $24 billion.

Since June 1990 the airline has lost $1.4 billion, and in February 1993 AMR Corporation chairman and the airline president Robert L. Crandall announced a so-called Transition Plan that could ultimately lead to the unthinkable: the break-up and piecemeal sell-off of the world's largest air carrier. The factors that led to the possible grounding of American stem from strategy begun 15 years ago.

With the advent of deregulation in 1978, American had to either cut labor costs or risk being run out of the business by low-cost, nonunion competitors. Instead of seeking wage cuts with existing personnel, the airline negotiated union contracts allowing the hiring of new workers at wages half the previous level. This innovative approach meant that American could only lower its unit labor costs by growing, and it undertook to do just that in a hurry. Since deregulation the company has invested $26 billion, principally in new aircraft and facilities and added more than 80,000 new people to the payroll. From 1986 to 1989, it established five new hubs: Nashville and San Juan in the first year, Raleigh-Durham in 1987 and San Jose a year later, and finally Miami in 1989. AMR set an earnings record of $477 million in 1988, before the portents of profit doom had topped the horizon.

"This is not a case of the industry doing poor planning, but of being caught up in the very fundamental pressures that force them to produce too much capacity and leave them vulnerable," said former American executive Mel Brenner.

The chief executive of bankrupt Continental Airlines held a different view of American's aggressive expansion. He charged that American, along with the other two largest domestic carriers United and Delta, engaged in predatory pricing in an effort to eliminate competition and fill seats on their own planes.

The capital expenditures for new jets and costs of adding five hubs sent unit costs through the roof, while external variables were conspiring to flatten revenues. The economy went into a tailspin, while the Persian Gulf War led to a spike in fuel costs. In 1988, it cost American about 7.6 cents to fly one seat one mile. Revenue at that time was 8.4 cents per available seat mile. In 1992, revenue had increased only nominally to 8.75 cents, but the cost to fly one seat was 8.8 cents.

In an effort to boost average fare prices, American introduced its four-tiered Value Plan fare structure in April 1992.

The hope was that business travel would be stimulated with slightly reduced, unrestricted fares, while the wide availability of discounted fares was cut back. Competitors, with still simmering memories of American's fare-slashing tactics of the past, undercut the plan and plunged the industry into a ruinous fare war that led to record losses for American and several other carriers.

With the backdrop of an expansion strategy that inflated costs and moved the carrier into routes and markets where profits were impossible, to a tiered fare strategy that backfired and exacerbated losses, American's Crandall announced the Transition Plan. It may be his biggest gamble—or bluff.

On February 18, 1993, Robert Crandall, architect of the Growth Plan Strategy of the 1980s, stated his belief that AMR would eventually break up and sell its principal subsidiary, American Airlines. He said that over an unspecified number of years the assets would be made available to people who could operate them more profitably. "The core problems of the industry are structural and not economic," Crandall said. "There are simply too many flights to too many places too often. As a consequence, at every time except at those peak times of demand, the industry suffers a great deal of excess capacity. There are simply more seats than there are passengers."

In an industry long accustomed to suicidal fare wars, bankruptcies, and turmoil, the announcement was nothing short of a bombshell, and conflicting speculation began immediately. Could he be serious, and if so, how far would he take the dismantling? Or was the radical proposal merely a tactic to force labor representatives to the table with the Damoclesian specter of 120,000 lost jobs dangling overhead?

"We have embarked on a proposition predicated on our understanding of this long-term truth: The low-cost producer always prevails," Crandall said.

Insiders agree that the Transition Plan is more of a varied options approach than a set of edicts chiseled in stone. Crandall sought to emphasize publicly the worst scenario. And few doubted his seriousness about abandoning the industry if he couldn't bring about changes he thought necessary for American to produce an adequate return to shareholders. But that was a huge "if" from a company that had been doing business since 1926.

The less drastic alternative to a complete shutdown was a phased scale back, with the grounding of airplanes and the sell-off of divisions built around the nationwide hubs.

Shrinking American began with the grounding of 25 wide-body McDonnell Douglas DC-10s. As many as 75 Boeing 727s may also be grounded over four years. The wide-body DC-10s come in four versions and have from

227 to 290 seats. They make up about 3.5 percent of the airplanes in American's fleet, and 6 percent of total seats. Crandall no longer believes they can continue to provide cost-efficient service. The narrow-bodied Boeings, which have from 118 to 150 seats, could be returned to lessors as terms expire. The wide-body jets could be replaced without diminishing flights by using narrow bodies on routes that larger planes had previously serviced, and replacing the narrow bodies with turbo-prop aircraft. American also plans to expand into markets where it can earn a profit and downsize and pull out of markets where it loses money.

Decisions regarding the possible closing of some of the nationwide hubs established in the late 1980s will not be easy or painless either. As early as 1991 American served notice to airport officials in Nashville, Raleigh-Durham, and San Jose that they might take steps to stop the bleeding. American can abandon San Jose with a 30-day notice and not incur further obligation; however, they must cease all operations. If they operate a single flight, almost all current rents and charges are still payable. At Raleigh-Durham and Nashville, leases obligate American for better than 20 years, whether it shuts down operations or not. If American decides to punch out at all three airports, the cost could run into tens of millions of dollars over the next two decades.

Besides possible hub shutdowns and elimination of unprofitable routes, the company plans to undertake aggressive expansion in profitable nonairline sectors of AMR's business such as reservation services, data processing, telecommunications, and money management. The 1992 revenues from these operations, $1.2 billion, are dwarfed by the $13.2 billion generated the same year by American, but the airline industry is a historically low-return enterprise. At its financial pinnacle in 1988, when it became the world's largest carrier, AMR earned $447 million on revenues of $8.8 billion, a miserly net profit margin of 5.4 percent. Conversely, pre-tax profits for Amris Information Services, Sabre reservations systems, and the other service, technology, and money or consulting services are estimated in the 15 to 25 percent range.

AMR management, from a sea of red ink, has publicly sought to lay blame for rising costs at the door of labor. Comparison of the numbers suggests the onus may instead belong in the boardroom. From 1988 to 1992, unit labor costs escalated 10.87 percent. The four other major cost areas—facilities and fees, aircraft ownership, agent commissions, and fuel—exploded. Increased spending on facilities—like new and better airports, headquarters, and training and maintenance centers—topped 56 percent. Crandall has repeatedly pledged that he will not seek concessions from labor unions while maintaining that the only solution to the crisis is to lower American's labor costs.

Even if American can regain control of costs and limit operations to profitable routes, the ability to raise average fare prices remains beyond its control. Even a robust economic recovery is not expected to ameliorate the company's financial problems. The coming decade is expected to be one of retrenchment for both individuals and businesses, with emphasis on saving and debt reduction. The translation is less available money to spend on travel.

Despite the current bleak state of affairs for American, few airline company veterans expect that a team that took such pride in leading the industry for the past 15 years will simply walk away.

● QUESTIONS

1. Describe the various strategies implemented at American since deregulation. What have been the results of each to date?

2. State specific goals in the Growth Plan Strategy, the four-tiered Value Plan, and the Transition Plan.

3. Analyze American's strengths and weaknesses, opportunities and threats.

4. If you were the chairperson, would you break up AMR? Why or why not?

5. Which of the 6 steps in the decision making process do you think AMR management has ignored?

6. What changes have occurred at AMR since this video case aired?

■ MAKING DECISIONS

Chapter 8, "Managerial Decision Making," described the classical model for making decisions. One of the key steps in this model is to review the criteria for evaluating the alternatives before making a choice. For example, a retailer is trying to decide where to locate new stores. To help in making this decision, criteria are listed, such as no more than two direct competitors within 3 miles and a neighborhood with an average annual household income of $35,000–$50,000.

The same approach may be used in making job or career decisions. In this exercise, you will explore your decision-making process by listing your criteria for the kind of career or job you want. Later, you can refer to your list in evaluating the alternatives you have listed.

THIS EXERCISE WILL HELP YOU

- Gain a better perspective about the importance of preparation before making important decisions.
- Develop criteria for the kind of work you want upon graduation.

HOW TO LOCATE THE EXERCISE:

When you see the main menu for Career Design, select "Planning." Then select "Making Decisions."

■ CHECK YOUR DECISION-MAKING SKILLS

Chapter 8, "Managerial Decision Making," explored ways organizations can arrive at the best decisions. Individual versus group decision making was analyzed. Specific methods for bringing out the opinions of participants in the decision-making process were discussed, including brainstorming and interactive groups.

Ultimately, the quality and timeliness of an organization's decisions depend on the capacity and willingness of its employees to make the choices expected of them. If employees are uncomfortable with the responsibilities of decision making, the results will be diminished.

THIS EXERCISE WILL HELP YOU

- Identify how comfortable you feel about making decisions.
- Learn some techniques for improving your decision-making skills.

HOW TO LOCATE THE EXERCISE:

When you see the main menu for Career Design, select "Planning." Then select "Check Your Decision-Making Skills."

PART **III**

ORGANIZING

Reaching across cultural boundaries, the international languages of music and dance illustrate the creative contributions of diversity. This Korean National Flower Dance Group was sponsored by IDS' East-West Exchange, highlighting the company's Asian-Pacific heritage Month. IDS is organized to provide a half-dozen minority employee networks that bring diversity to corporate and community life. These networks develop strong bonds among members and assist management by identifying group issues, opening lines of communication, contributing to diversity awareness, and tapping into the strengths of diverse cultures and experience.

FUNDAMENTALS OF ORGANIZING

9

LEARNING OBJECTIVES

After studying this chapter, you should be able to

- Explain the fundamental characteristics of organizing, including such concepts as work specialization, chain of command, line and staff, and task forces.

- Explain when specific structural characteristics such as centralization, span of management, and formalization should be used within organizations.

- Explain the functional approach to structure.

- Explain the divisional approach to structure.

- Explain the matrix approach to structure and its application to both domestic and international organizations.

- Explain the contemporary team and network structures and why they are being adopted by organizations.

CHAPTER OUTLINE

Organizing the Vertical Structure

Work Specialization
Chain of Command
Authority, Responsibility, and
    Delegation
Span of Management
Centralization and
    Decentralization
Administrative Overhead
Formalization

Departmentalization

Functional Approach
Divisional Approach
Matrix Approach
Team Approach
Network Approach

CEO Paul A. Allaire is initiating a major restructuring of Xerox Corporation. The company's functional structure worked well, enabling advances in manufacturing processes and customer service that helped it capture the Malcolm Baldrige National Quality Award in 1989. Yet Allaire is aware that Xerox is too slow getting new technologies to market and is falling behind other companies in areas such as laser printers. Allaire wants Xerox to run more like a small, high-tech start-up than a lumbering

behemoth. He appointed a team of six Xerox managers to examine the type of structure needed and to make recommendations for a new structural design.[1] ■ If you were on the team examining Xerox's structure, what advice would you give CEO Allaire about structural design? What structural changes would allow Xerox to move quickly to launch new products?

M A N A G E M E N T   P R O B L E M

The problem confronting Xerox is one of structural design. CEO Paul Allaire wants to use structure to help the company be more competitive and to launch new products faster.

Every firm wrestles with the problem of how to organize. Reorganization often is necessary to reflect a new strategy, changing market conditions, or innovative production technology. Many companies are restructuring to become leaner, more efficient, and more nimble in a highly competitive global environment.

IBM has decentralized many top-management functions to newly independent divisions.[2] Greyhound Lines, Inc., restructured itself from one large company into four independent regional divisions.[3] International firms such as Unilever have taken steps to decentralize decision making and give middle managers more authority.[4] Brunswick Corporation chopped out many of its headquarters' staff departments and one layer of management to reduce administrative overhead.[5]

Each of these organizations is using fundamental concepts of organizing. **Organizing** is the deployment of organizational resources to achieve strategic objectives. The deployment of resources is reflected in the organization's division of labor into specific departments and jobs, formal lines of authority, and mechanisms for coordinating diverse organization tasks.

Organizing is important because it follows from strategy—the topic of Part 2. Strategy defines *what* to do; organizing defines *how* to do it. Organization structure is a tool that managers use to harness resources for getting things done. Part 3 explains the variety of organizing principles and concepts used by managers. This chapter covers fundamental concepts that apply to all organizations and departments. These ideas are extended in Chapter 10, where we look at how structural designs are tailored to the organization's situation. Chapter 11 discusses how organizations can be structured to facilitate innovation and change. Chapters

organizing

The deployment of organizational resources to achieve strategic objectives.

Organizing enables Kellogg's to take advantage of a rapidly expanding global market as worldwide consumption of ready-to-eat cereal surpasses 5 billion pounds per year. In 1992, Kellogg's restructured into four divisions: Kellogg North America, Kellogg Europe, Kellogg Australasia, and Kellogg Latin America. An Asian operations team was formed within the Australasia division to *coordinate* development of emerging markets in Thailand, Indonesia, the Philippines, Taiwan, Pakistan, Sri Lanka, and Bangladesh.

12 and 13 examine how to utilize human resources to the best advantage within the organization's structure.

● ORGANIZING THE VERTICAL STRUCTURE

The organizing process leads to the creation of organization structure, which defines how tasks are divided and resources deployed. **Organization structure** is defined as (1) the set of formal tasks assigned to individuals and departments; (2) formal reporting relationships, including lines of authority, decision responsibility, number of hierarchical levels, and span of managers' control; and (3) the design of systems to ensure effective coordination of employees across departments.[6]

The set of formal tasks and formal reporting relationships provides a framework for vertical control of the organization. The characteristics of vertical structure are portrayed in the **organization chart**, which is the visual representation of an organization's structure.

A sample organization chart for a textile mill is illustrated in Exhibit 9.1. The mill has five major departments—accounting, personnel, manufacturing, marketing, and research and development. The organization chart delineates the chain of command, indicates departmental tasks and how they fit together, and provides order and logic for the organization. Every employee has an appointed task, line of authority, and decision responsibility. The following sections discuss several important features of vertical structure in more detail.

organization structure
The framework in which the organization defines how tasks are divided, resources are deployed, and departments are coordinated.

organization chart
The visual representation of an organization's structure.

WORK SPECIALIZATION

Organizations perform a wide variety of tasks. A fundamental principle is that work can be performed more efficiently if employees are allowed to specialize.[7] **Work specialization,** sometimes called *division of labor,* is the degree to which organizational tasks are subdivided into separate jobs. Work specialization in Exhibit 9.1 is illustrated by the separation of manufacturing tasks into weaving, yarn, finishing, and needling. Employees within each department perform only the tasks relevant to their specialized function. When work specialization is extensive, employees specialize in a single task. Jobs tend to be small, but they can be performed efficiently. Work specialization is readily visible on an automobile assembly line where each employee performs the same task over and over again. It would not be efficient to have a single employee build the entire automobile or even perform a large number of unrelated jobs.

Despite the apparent advantages of specialization, many organizations are moving away from this principle. With too much specialization, employees are isolated and do only a single, tiny, boring job. Many companies are enlarging jobs to provide greater challenges and are even

work specialization
The degree to which organizational tasks are subdivided into individual jobs; also called *division of labor.*

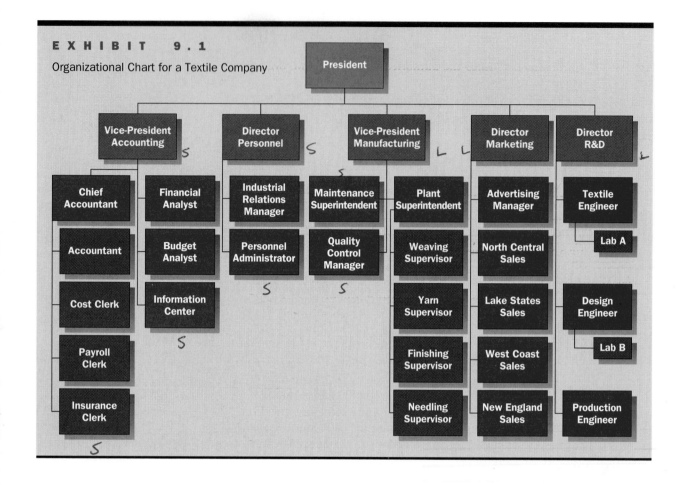

EXHIBIT 9.1

Organizational Chart for a Textile Company

assigning teams to tasks so that employees can rotate among the several jobs performed by the team. The team approach to organization design will be discussed later in this chapter, and approaches to designing jobs to fit employee needs are described in Chapters 15 and 17.

CHAIN OF COMMAND

chain of command

An unbroken line of authority that links all individuals in the organization and specifies who reports to whom.

The **chain of command** is an unbroken line of authority that links all persons in an organization and shows who reports to whom. It is associated with two underlying principles. *Unity of command* means that each employee is held accountable to only one supervisor. The *scalar principle* refers to a clearly defined line of authority in the organization that includes all employees. Authority and responsibility for different tasks should be distinct. All persons in the organization should know to whom they report as well as the successive management levels all the way to the top. In Exhibit 9.1, the payroll clerk reports to the chief accountant, who in turn reports to the vice-president, who in turn reports to the company president.

AUTHORITY, RESPONSIBILITY, AND DELEGATION

The chain of command illustrates the authority structure of the organization. **Authority** is the formal and legitimate right of a manager to make decisions, issue orders, and allocate resources to achieve organizationally desired outcomes. Authority is distinguished by three characteristics:[8]

1 *Authority is vested in organizational positions, not people.* Managers have authority because of the positions they hold, and other people in the same positions would have the same authority.

2 *Authority is accepted by subordinates.* Although authority flows top down through the organization's hierarchy, subordinates comply because they believe that managers have a legitimate right to issue orders. The acceptance theory of authority argues that a manager has authority only if subordinates choose to accept his or her commands. If subordinates refuse to obey because the order is outside their zone of acceptance, a manager's authority disappears.[9] For example, Richard Ferris, the former chairman of United Airlines, resigned because few people accepted his strategy of acquiring hotels, a car rental company, and other organizations to build a

authority

The formal and legitimate right of a manager to make decisions, issue orders, and allocate resources to achieve organizationally desired outcomes.

A new arrangement of *authority*, *responsibility*, and *delegation* is the hallmark of Sara Lee Corporation's Farmington Road Knit Products plant in Mocksville, North Carolina. Development of a team sewing concept eliminated the fifty-year-old piece-rate-by-bundle method. Team members diagrammed a configuration plan and set daily production quotas, with each team responsible for its own productivity, quality, and safety. Facilitators replaced supervisors. Within a four-year period, the new structural arrangement enabled Farmington Road employees to show a 70 percent increase in productivity, cost reduction of 15 percent, and reduced through-put time from 2.5 days to 2.5 hours.

travel empire. When key people refused to accept his direction, his authority was lost, and he resigned.

3 *Authority flows down the vertical hierarchy.* Positions at the top of the hierarchy are vested with more formal authority than are positions at the bottom.

responsibility

The duty to perform the task or activity an employee has been assigned.

Responsibility is the flip side of the authority coin. **Responsibility** is the duty to perform the task or activity an employee has been assigned. Typically, managers are assigned authority commensurate with responsibility. When managers have responsibility for task outcomes, but little authority, the job is possible but difficult. They rely on persuasion and luck. When managers have authority exceeding responsibility, they may become tyrants, using authority toward frivolous outcomes.[10]

accountability

The fact that the people with authority and responsibility are subject to reporting and justifying task outcomes to those above them in the chain of command.

Accountability is the mechanism through which authority and responsibility are brought into alignment. **Accountability** means that the people with authority and responsibility are subject to reporting and justifying task outcomes to those above them in the chain of command.[11] Subordinates must be aware that they are accountable for a task and accept the responsibility and authority for performing it. Accountability can be built into the organization structure. For example, at Whirlpool incentive programs provide strict accountability. Performance of all managers is monitored and bonus payments are tied to successful outcomes.

delegation

The process managers use to transfer authority and responsibility to positions below them in the hierarchy.

Another concept related to authority is delegation.[12] **Delegation** is the process managers use to transfer authority and responsibility to positions below them in the hierarchy. Most organizations today encourage managers to delegate authority to the lowest possible level to provide maximum flexibility to meet customer needs and adapt to the environment. Managers are encouraged to delegate authority, although they often find it difficult. Techniques for delegation are discussed in the Manager's Shoptalk box. The trend toward increased delegation begins in the chief executive's office in companies such as USX, PPG Industries, Johnsonville Foods, Ford, and General Electric. At Johnsonville, a committee of employees from the shop floor has been delegated authority to formulate the manufacturing budget.

LINE AND STAFF AUTHORITY. An important distinction in many organizations is between line authority and staff authority, reflecting whether managers work in line or staff departments in the organization's structure. *Line departments* perform tasks that reflect the organization's primary goal and mission. In a manufacturing organization, line departments make and sell the product. *Staff departments* include all those that provide specialized skills in support of line departments. Staff departments have an advisory relationship with line departments and typically include strategic planning, labor relations, research, accounting, and personnel. Exhibit 9.2 shows a partial organization chart for an international manufacturing company such as Eaton Corporation or Borg-Warner. The line departments follow the line of authority from the office of the chief executive down to the manufacturing plants. Staff departments exist at the corporate level and assist company managers in discharging their line responsibilities.

HOW TO DELEGATE

The attempt by top management to decentralize decision making often gets bogged down because middle managers are unable to delegate. Managers may cling tightly to their decision-making and task responsibilities. Failure to delegate occurs for a number of reasons: Managers are most comfortable making familiar decisions; they feel they will lose personal status by delegating tasks; they believe they can do a better job themselves; or they have an aversion to risk—they will not take a chance on delegating because performance responsibility ultimately rests with them.

Yet decentralization offers an organization many advantages. Decisions are made at the right level, lower-level employees are motivated, and employees have the opportunity to develop decision-making skills. Overcoming barriers to delegation in order to gain these advantages is a major challenge. The following approach can help each manager delegate more effectively:

1. *Delegate the whole task.* A manager should delegate an entire task to one person rather than dividing it among several people. This gives the individual complete responsibility and increases his or her initiative while giving the manager some control over the results.

2. *Select the right person.* Not all employees have the same capabilities and degree of motivation. Managers must match talent to task if delegation is to be effective. They should identify subordinates who have made independent decisions in the past and have shown a desire for more responsibility.

3. *Delegate responsibility and authority.* Merely assigning a task is not effective delegation. The individual must have the responsibility for completing the task and the authority to perform the task as he or she thinks best.

4. *Give thorough instruction.* Successful delegation includes information on what, when, why, where, who, and how. The subordinate must clearly understand the task and the expected results. It is a good idea to write down all provisions discussed, including required resources and when and how the results will be reported.

5. *Maintain feedback.* Feedback means keeping open lines of communication with the subordinate to answer questions and provide advice, but without exerting too much control. Open lines of communication make it easier to trust subordinates. Feedback keeps the subordinate on the right track.

6. *Evaluate and reward performance.* Once the task is completed, the manager should evaluate results, not methods. When results do not meet expectations, the manager must assess the consequences. When they do meet expectations, the manager should reward employees for a job well done with praise, financial rewards when appropriate, and delegation of future assignments.

ARE YOU A POSITIVE DELEGATOR?

Positive delegation is the way an organization implements decentralization. Do you help or hinder the decentralization process? If you answer yes to more than three of the following questions, you may have a problem delegating:

■ I tend to be a perfectionist.
■ My boss expects me to know all the details of my job.
■ I don't have the time to explain clearly and concisely how a task should be accomplished.
■ I often end up doing tasks myself.
■ My subordinates typically are not as committed as I am.
■ I get upset when other people don't do the task right.
■ I really enjoy doing the details of my job to the best of my ability.
■ I like to be in control of task outcomes. ■

SOURCE: Thomas R. Horton, "Delegation and Team Building: No Solo Acts Please," *Management Review*, September 1992, 58–61; Andrew E. Schwartz, "The Why, What, and to Whom of Delegation," *Management Solutions* (June 1987), 31–38; and "Delegation," *Small Business Report* (June 1986), 38–43.

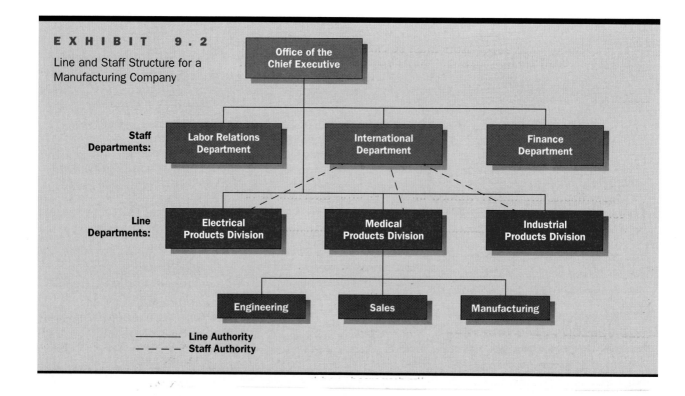

EXHIBIT 9.2

Line and Staff Structure for a Manufacturing Company

Office of the Chief Executive

Staff Departments:
Labor Relations Department | International Department | Finance Department

Line Departments:
Electrical Products Division | Medical Products Division | Industrial Products Division

Engineering | Sales | Manufacturing

———— Line Authority
– – – – Staff Authority

line authority

A form of authority in which individuals in management positions have the formal power to direct and control immediate subordinates.

staff authority

A form of authority granted to staff specialists in their areas of expertise.

Line authority means that people in management positions have formal authority to direct and control immediate subordinates. **Staff authority** is narrower and includes the right to advise, recommend, and counsel in the staff specialists' area of expertise. Staff authority is a communication relationship; staff specialists advise managers in technical areas. Thus, a manager in the international department in Exhibit 9.2 has authority to advise managers in the line divisions about the procedures for selling their products abroad. Likewise, the finance department has staff authority to coordinate with the line divisions about which accounting forms to use to facilitate purchases of new equipment and standard payroll services. Staff authority is confined to the area of staff expertise and can be represented by dashed lines as illustrated in Exhibit 9.2. Dashed lines drawn on an organizational chart imply that corporate staff members communicate with and advise line managers.

SPAN OF MANAGEMENT

span of management

The number of employees who report to a supervisor; also called *span of control*.

The **span of management** is the number of employees reporting to a supervisor. Sometimes called the *span of control*, this characteristic of structure determines how closely a supervisor can monitor subordinates. Traditional views of organization design recommend a span of management of from four to seven subordinates per manager. However, many organizations have been observed to have larger spans of management and a few smaller. Research on the Lockheed Missile and Space Company and other manufacturing companies has suggested that span of management can vary widely and that several factors influence the span.[13] Generally, when supervisors must be closely involved with subordinates, the span should be small, and when supervisors need little involvement with subordinates, it can be large. The following factors are associated with less supervisor involvement and thus larger spans of control:

1 Work performed by subordinates is stable and routine.

2 Subordinates perform similar work tasks.

3 Subordinates are concentrated in a single location.

4 Subordinates are highly trained and need little direction in performing tasks.

5 Rules and procedures defining task activities are available.

6 Support systems and personnel are available for the manager.

7 Little time is required in nonsupervisory activities such as coordination with other departments or planning.

8 Managers' personal preferences and styles favor a large span.

TALL VERSUS FLAT STRUCTURE.   The average span of control used in an organization determines whether the structure is tall or flat. A **tall structure** has an overall narrow span and more hierarchical levels. A **flat structure** has a wide span, is horizontally dispersed, and has fewer hierarchical levels.

The trend in the 1980s and 1990s has been toward wider spans of control as a way to facilitate delegation.[14] Exhibit 9.3 illustrates how an

tall structure

A management structure characterized by an overall narrow span of management and a relatively large number of hierarchical levels.

flat structure

A management structure characterized by an overall broad span of control and relatively few hierarchical levels.

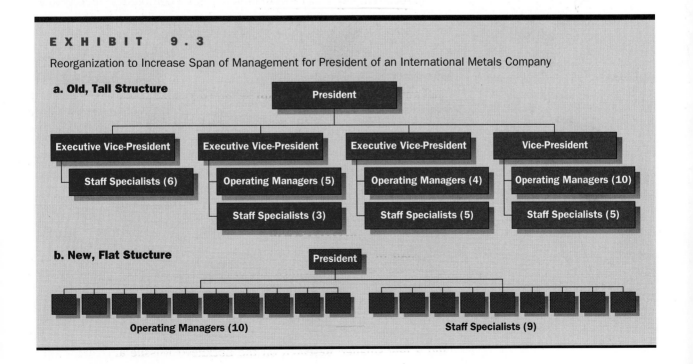

E X H I B I T   9 . 3

Reorganization to Increase Span of Management for President of an International Metals Company

international metals company was reorganized. The multilevel set of managers shown in panel (a) was replaced with ten operating managers and nine staff specialists reporting directly to the CEO, as shown in panel (b). The CEO welcomed this wide span of 19 management subordinates because it fit his style, his management team was top quality and needed little supervision, and they were all located on the same floor of an office building.

CENTRALIZATION AND DECENTRALIZATION

centralization

The location of decision authority near top organizational levels.

decentralization

The location of decision authority near lower organizational levels.

Centralization and decentralization pertain to the hierarchical level at which decisions are made. **Centralization** means that decision authority is located near the top of the organization. With **decentralization,** decision authority is pushed downward to lower organization levels. Organizations may have to experiment to find the correct hierarchical level at which to make decisions.

In the United States and Canada, the trend over the last 30 years has been toward greater decentralization of organizations. Decentralization is believed to make greater use of human resources, unburden top managers, ensure that decisions are made close to the action by well-informed people, and permit more rapid response to external changes.

However, this trend does not mean that every organization should decentralize all decisions. Managers should diagnose the organizational situation and select the decision-making level that will best meet the organization's needs. Factors that typically influence centralization versus decentralization are as follows:

1 Greater change and uncertainty in the environment are usually associated with decentralization. Most companies feel greater

Coca-Cola Enterprises, the world's largest Coca-Cola bottler, has adopted an operating strategy of *decentralization* of its organizational structure into 10 regions. Each regional manager takes responsibility for production, warehousing, sales, and distribution. The use of double-bottom trailers, such as these at the Portsmouth, Ohio, distribution center, improves efficiency and controls costs.

uncertainty today because of intense global competition; hence, many have decentralized.

2 Corporate history and culture socialize managers into a decision approach, although the approach can be changed. When Alcoa decentralized authority to division managers, it took a long time for them to use their new freedom fully and not expect monitoring from headquarters.

3 In times of crisis or risk of company failure, authority may be centralized at the top. When Honda could not get agreement among divisions about new car models, President Kawamoto made the decision himself.

4 The amount of centralization or decentralization should fit the firm's strategy. For example, Johnson & Johnson gives almost complete authority to its 166 operating companies to develop and market their own products. This decentralization fits the corporate strategy of empowerment that gets each division close to customers so it can speedily adapt to their needs.[15] Decentralization at Alcoa fit the strategy of faster response to customer needs by individual divisions; Honda's move toward centralization achieved standardized decisions for the entire company.[16]

ADMINISTRATIVE OVERHEAD

Because organization structure is the deployment of resources so as to accomplish organizational goals, one characteristic of interest to many managers pertains to the percentage of resources deployed for line activities versus that for administrative and support activities. Two elements of **administrative overhead** can be measured by the following ratios:

1 *Indirect-to-direct-labor ratio.* Direct labor includes line employees who work directly on the organization's product or service. Indirect employees include all other employees—accountants, engineers, clerks—in the organization. This ratio is similar to a line-staff ratio.

2 *Top administrator ratio.* This ratio measures the percentage of total employment made up by top management. For a wide span of control in a flat organization, this percentage would be low.

administrative overhead

The resources allocated to administrative and support activities.

In the highly competitive global environment that managers face today, reducing administrative overhead is often a priority. For example, in 1993 Sears announced cuts of 50,000 employees and elimination of the catalog division to reduce its high administrative cost, which runs 29.9 percent of sales compared with Wal-Mart's 15.3 percent. This difference amounts to millions of dollars in overhead. Many companies have made a religion of staying lean at the top. Frito Lay factories cut management 40 percent by 1992. Most of the 11,000 employees cut at Merrill Lynch came from management and support staff. International corporations are likewise trimming off the top. Daimler Benz slashed two of five management levels at both Mercedes and Daimler and reduced staff at its AEG appliance subsidiary headquarters in Frankfurt from 940 employees to less than 2.[17]

FORMALIZATION

formalization

The written documentation used to direct and control employees.

Formalization is the written documentation used to direct and control employees. Written documentation includes rule books, policies, procedures, job descriptions, and regulations. These documents complement the organization chart by providing descriptions of tasks, resonsibilities, and decision authority. The use of rules, regulations, and written records of decisions is part of the bureaucratic model of organizations described in Chapter 2. As proposed by Max Weber, the bureaucratic model defines the basic organizational characteristics that enable the organization to operate in a logical and rational manner.

Although written documentation is intended to be rational and helpful to the organization, it often creates "red tape" that causes more problems than it solves. If an organization tries to do everything through the written word, rules and procedures become burdensome. As a practical matter, many organizations today are becoming less formal in order to be flexible and responsive to a changing global environment.

● DEPARTMENTALIZATION

departmentalization

The basis on which individuals are grouped into departments and departments into total organizations.

Another fundamental characteristic of organization structure is **departmentalization,** which is the basis for grouping positions into departments and departments into the total organization. Managers make choices about how to use the chain of command to group people together to perform their work. There are five approaches to structural design that reflect different uses of the chain of command in departmentalization. The functional, divisional, and matrix are traditional approaches that rely on the chain of command to define departmental groupings and reporting relationships along the hierarchy. Two contemporary approaches are the use of teams and networks. These newer approaches have emerged to meet organizational needs in a highly competitive global environment. A brief illustration of the five structural alternatives is in Exhibit 9.4 on pages 302–303.

1 *Functional approach.* People are grouped together in departments by common skills and work activities, such as in an engineering department and an accounting department.

2 *Divisional approach.* Departments are grouped together into separate, self-contained divisions based on a common product, program, or geographical region. Diverse skills rather than similar skills are the basis of departmentalization.

3 *Matrix approach.* Functional and divisional chains of command are implemented simultaneously and overlay one another in the same departments. Two chains of command exist, and some employees report to two bosses.

4 *Team approach.* The organization creates a series of teams to accomplish specific tasks and to coordinate major departments. Teams can exist from the office of the president all the way down to the shop floor.

5 *Network approach.* The organization becomes a small, central broker electronically connected to other organizations that perform vital functions. Departments are independent contracting services to the broker for a profit. Departments can be located anywhere in the world.[18]

Each approach to structure serves a distinct purpose for the organization, and each has advantages and disadvantages. The basic difference among structures is the way in which employees are departmentalized and to whom they report. The differences in structure illustrated in Exhibit 9.4 have major consequences for employee goals and motivation. Let us now turn to each of the five structural designs and examine their implications for managers.[19]

FUNCTIONAL APPROACH

Functional structure is the grouping of positions into departments based on similar skills, expertise, and resource use. A functional structure can be thought of as departmentalization by organizational resources, because each type of functional activity—personnel, engineering, manufacturing—represents specific resources for performing the organization's task. People and facilities representing a common organizational resource are grouped together into a single department.

An example of a functional structure for American Airlines is presented in Exhibit 9.5 (on page 303). The major departments under the chairman are groupings of similar expertise and resources, such as employee relations, government affairs, operations, information systems, and marketing. Each of the functional departments at American Airlines is concerned with the airline as a whole. The employee relations vice-president is concerned with personnel issues for the entire airline, and the marketing department is responsible for all sales and marketing.

ADVANTAGES AND DISADVANTAGES. Grouping employees into departments based on similar skills has many advantages for an organization. Employees who perform a common task are grouped together so as to permit economies of scale and efficient resource use. At American Airlines, as illustrated in Exhibit 9.5, all information systems people work in the same department. They have the expertise for handling almost any problem within a single, large department. The large functional departments enhance the development of in-depth skills because people work on a variety of problems and are associated with other experts. Career progress is based on functional expertise; thus, employees are motivated to develop their skills. Managers and employees are compatible because of similar training and expertise.

The functional structure also offers a way to centralize decision making and provide unified direction from the top, because the chain of command converges at the top of the organization. Sometimes the functional structure is also associated with wider spans of control because of large departments and common expertise. Communication and coordination among employees within each department are excellent. Finally, functional structure promotes high-quality technical problem solving. Having a pool of well-trained experts, especially those that work with

functional structure

An organization structure in which positions are grouped into departments based on similar skills, expertise, and resource use.

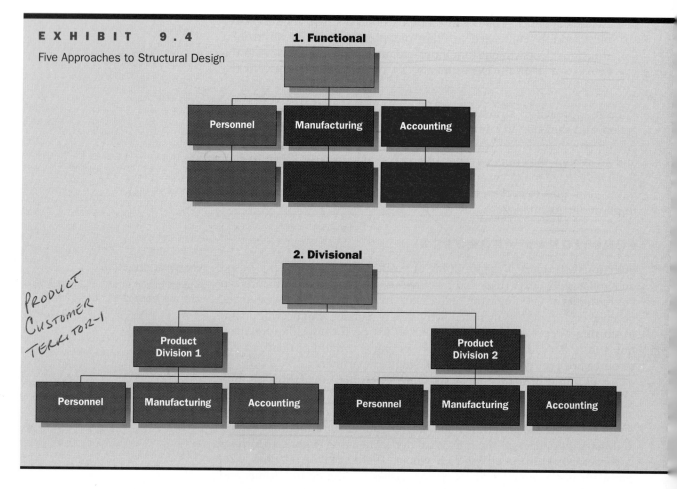

EXHIBIT 9.4

Five Approaches to Structural Design

[handwritten: PRODUCT CUSTOMER TERRITORY]

sophisticated technology, motivated toward functional expertise, gives the company an important resource.

The disadvantages of functional structure reflect the barriers that exist across departments and a slow response to environmental changes. Because people are separated into distinct departments, communication and coordination across functions are often poor. Poor coordination means a slow response to environmental changes, because innovation and change require involvement of several departments. Because the chains of command are separate beneath the top of the organization, decisions involving more than one department may pile up at the top of the organization and be delayed. The functional structure also stresses work specialization and division of labor, which may produce routine, nonmotivating employee tasks.

The functional structure also creates management problems, such as difficulty in pinpointing problems within departments. In the case of an insurance company, for example, each function works on all products and performs only a part of the task for any product line. Hence, if one life insurance product is not performing well, there is no specific department or group that bears responsibility. In addition, employees tend to focus on the attainment of departmental goals, often to the exclusion of organizational goals. They see only their respective tasks, not the big pic-

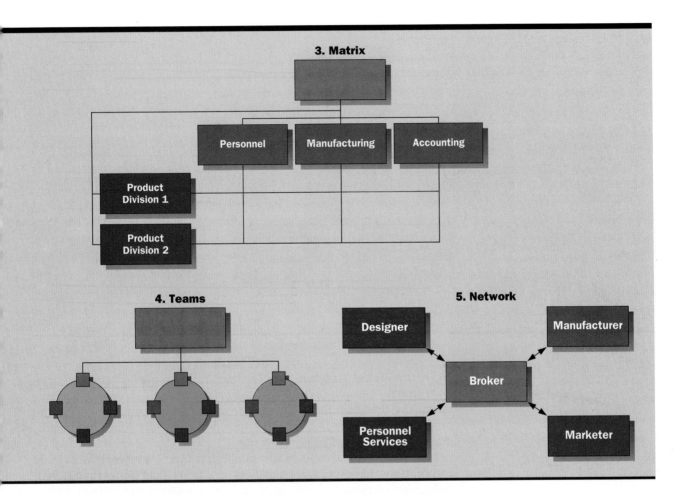

ture. Because of this narrow task specialization, employees are trained to become experts in their fields, not to manage and coordinate diverse departments. Thus, they fail to become groomed for top management and general management positions.

The advantages and disadvantages of functional structure are summarized in Exhibit 9.6.

DIVISIONAL APPROACH

In contrast to the functional approach, in which people are grouped by common skills and resources, the **divisional structure** occurs when departments are grouped together based on organizational outputs. Functional and divisional structures are illustrated in Exhibit 9.7. In the divisional structure, divisions are created as self-contained units for producing a single product. Each functional department resource needed to produce the product is assigned to one division. For example, in a functional structure, all engineers are grouped together and work on all products. In a divisional structure, separate engineering departments are established within each division. Each department is smaller and focuses on a single product line. Departments are duplicated across product lines.

divisional structure

An organization structure in which departments are grouped based on similar organizational outputs.

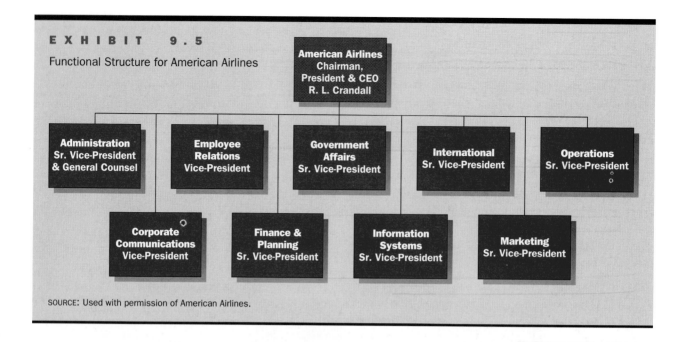

EXHIBIT 9.5

Functional Structure for American Airlines

SOURCE: Used with permission of American Airlines.

The divisional structure is sometimes called a *product structure, program structure*, or *self-contained unit structure*. Each of these terms means essentially the same thing: Diverse departments are brought together to produce a single organizational output, whether it be a product, a program, or service to a single customer.

In very large companies, a divisional structure is essential. Most large corporations have separate business divisions that perform different tasks, serve different clients, or use different technologies. When a huge organization produces products for different markets, the divisional structure works because each division is an autonomous business. For example, PepsiCo uses a divisional structure. Frito-Lay, Pizza Hut, Taco Bell, North American Van Lines, and Wilson's Sporting Goods are stand-alone divisions within PepsiCo. Tenneco, Inc., also uses a divisional structure. Divisions include J. I. Case, a manufacturer of farm imple-

EXHIBIT 9.6

Advantages and Disadvantages of Functional Structure

Advantages

- Efficient use of resources, economies of scale
- In-depth skill specialization and development
- Career progress within functional departments
- Top manager direction and control
- Excellent coordination within functions
- High-quality technical problem solving

Disadvantages

- Poor communication across functional departments
- Slow response to external changes, lagging innovation
- Decisions concentrated at top of hierarchy, creating delay
- Responsibility for problems is difficult to pinpoint
- Limited view of organizational goals by employees
- Limited general management training for employees

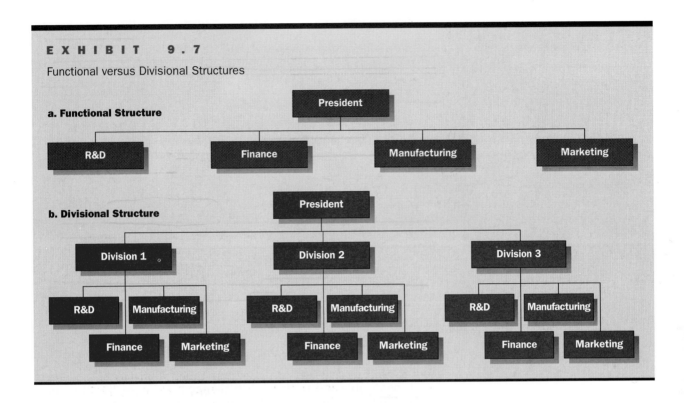

EXHIBIT   9.7

Functional versus Divisional Structures

a. Functional Structure

President

R&D   Finance   Manufacturing   Marketing

b. Divisional Structure

President

Division 1   Division 2   Division 3

R&D   Manufacturing   R&D   Manufacturing   R&D   Manufacturing

Finance   Marketing   Finance   Marketing   Finance   Marketing

ments, and Newport News Shipbuilding, which builds submarines and other ships for the Navy. Each of these companies is run as a separate division under the guidance of Tenneco corporate headquarters.

A major difference between divisional and functional structures is that the chain of command from each function converges lower in the hierarchy. In an organization such as the one in Exhibit 9.7, differences of opinion among research and development, marketing, manufacturing, and finance would be resolved at the divisional level rather than by the president. Thus, the divisional structure encourages decentralization. Decision making is pushed down at least one level in the hierarchy, freeing up the president and other top managers for strategic planning.

GEOGRAPHIC-BASED DIVISIONS.   An alternative for assigning divisional responsibility is to group company activities by geographic region, as illustrated in Exhibit 9.8. In this structure, all functions in a specific country or region report to the same division manager. This structure focuses company activities on local market conditions. For example, competitive advantage may come from the production or sale of a product adapted to a given country. For example, at LSI Logic Corporation, management's strategy is to divide the world into three geographic markets—Japan, the United States, and Europe. This way each division has all the resources to focus on the fierce competition in its part of the world.[20] In North America, Sears, Roebuck is organized into five regions, each with its own warehousing, inventory control, distribution system, and stores. This geographic structure enables close coordination of activities to meet the needs of customers within each region.

EXHIBIT 9.8

Geographic-Based Global Organization Structure

ADVANTAGES AND DISADVANTAGES. For medium-size companies, the choice between functional and divisional structure is difficult because each represents different strengths and weaknesses. The advantages and disadvantages of the divisional structure are listed in Exhibit 9.9. By dividing employees and resources along divisional lines, the organization will be flexible and responsive to change because each unit is small and tuned in to its environment. By having employees working on a single product line, the concern for customers' needs is high. Coordination across functional departments is better because employees are grouped together in a single location and committed to one product line. Great coordination exists within divisions. The divisional structure also enables top management to pinpoint responsibility for performance problems in product lines. Because each division is a self-contained unit, poor performance can be assigned directly to the manager of that unit. Finally, employees' goals typically are directed toward product success rather than toward their own functional departments. Employees develop a broader goal orientation that can help them develop into general managers.

EXHIBIT 9.9

Advantages and Disadvantages of Divisional Structure

Advantages

- Fast response, flexibility in an unstable environment
- Fosters concern for customers' needs
- Excellent coordination across functional departments
- Easy pinpointing of responsibility for product problems
- Emphasis on overall product and division goals
- Development of general management skills

Disadvantages

- Duplication of resources across divisions
- Less technical depth and specialization in divisions
- Poor coordination across divisions
- Less top management control
- Competition for corporate resources

Gaylord Entertainment Company utilizes the *divisional approach* in entertainment, cable networks, broadcasting, and cable television systems. Gaylord successfully achieves synergy among its various divisions that focus on country music and country life-style. The entertainment division includes Nashville-based properties such as Opryland U.S.A., the Grand Ole Opry (pictured here), the Opryland Hotel, and the General Jackson Showboat. The cable networks division includes the Nashville Network, one of the nation's largest cable networks with over 54,000,000 subscribers.

The product structure also has well-defined disadvantages. The major disadvantage is duplication of resources and the high cost of running separate divisions. Instead of a single research department in which all research people use a single facility, there may be several. The organization loses efficiency and economies of scale. Because departments within each division are small, there is a lack of technical specialization, expertise, and training. The divisional structure fosters excellent coordination *within* divisions, but coordination *across* divisions is often poor. Companies such as Hewlett-Packard and Digital Equipment prided themselves on the divisional structure that gave autonomy to many small divisions. Problems occurred, however, when these divisions went in opposite directions. The software produced in one division did not fit the hardware produced in another. Thus, divisional structures were realigned to establish adequate coordination across divisions. Moreover, divisions may feel themselves in competition with one another, especially for resources from corporate headquarters. This can lead to political behavior that is unhealthy for the company as a whole. Because top management control is somewhat weaker under the divisional structure, top managers must assert themselves in order to get divisions to work together.

Many companies must carefully decide whether the divisional or functional structure better suits their needs. It is not uncommon for a company to try one structure and then switch to another as its needs change. One example is Apple Computer, which went to a divisional structure to ensure excellent cooperation within divisions and a rapid response to the external environment. However, a declining market for personal computers made efficiency more important, and Apple reorganized back into a functional structure. Then in 1992 Apple reorganized into a product structure, with each division reporting to the CEO, John Sculley.[21]

Airborne Express uses the *matrix approach* to solve specific problems through task-oriented work teams that cut across disciplines and departments to coordinate and focus all assigned people on a single problem. Project APEX (Airborne's Program for Excellence) used the matrix approach to dramatically improve how Airborne handles paperwork, how it tracks shipments, and how it provides customers with timely information about their shipments.

matrix approach

An organization structure that utilizes functional and divisional chains of command simultaneously in the same part of the organization.

two-boss employee

An employee who reports to two supervisors simultaneously.

matrix boss

A product or functional boss, responsible for one side of the matrix.

MATRIX APPROACH

The **matrix approach** utilizes functional and divisional chains of command simultaneously in the same part of the organization.[22] The matrix actually has dual lines of authority. In Exhibit 9.10, the functional hierarchy of authority runs vertically and the divisional hierarchy of authority runs laterally. The lateral chain of command formalizes the divisional relationships. Thus, the lateral structure provides coordination across functional departments while the vertical structure provides traditional control within functional departments. The matrix approach to structure therefore provides a formal chain of command for both the functional and divisional relationships.

The matrix structure often is used by global corporations such as Dow Corning or Asea Brown Boveri. The problem for global companies is to achieve simultaneous coordination of various products within each country or region and for each product line. An example of a global matrix structure is illustrated in Exhibit 9.11. The two lines of authority are geographic and product. Managers of local affiliate companies within a country such as Germany report to two superiors. As noted in Exhibit 9.11, for example, the general manager of a plant producing plastic containers in Germany reports to both the head of the plastics products division and the head of German operations. The German boss coordinates all the affiliates within Germany, and the plastics products boss coordinates the manufacturing and sale of plastics products around the world. The dual authority structure causes confusion, but after managers learn to use it, the matrix provides excellent coordination simultaneously for each geographic region and product line.

KEY RELATIONSHIPS. The success of the matrix structure depends on the abilities of people in key matrix roles. Exhibit 9.12 provides a close-up of the reporting relationships in the dual chain of command for a domestic company. The senior engineer in the medical products division reports to both the medical products vice-president and the engineering director. This violates the unity of command concept described earlier in this chapter but is necessary to give equal emphasis to both functional and divisional lines of authority. Confusion is reduced by separating responsibilities for each chain of command. The functional boss is responsible for technical and personnel issues, such as quality standards, providing technical training, and assigning technical personnel to projects. The divisional boss is responsible for programwide issues, such as overall design decisions, schedule deadlines, and coordinating technical specialists from several functions.

The senior engineer is called a **two-boss employee** because he or she reports to two supervisors simultaneously. Two-boss employees must resolve conflicting demands from the matrix bosses. They must confront senior managers and reach joint decisions. They need excellent human relations skills with which to confront managers and resolve conflicts. The **matrix boss** is the product or functional boss, who in Exhibit 9.12 is the engineering director and the medical products vice-president. The matrix boss is responsible for one side of the matrix. The top leader

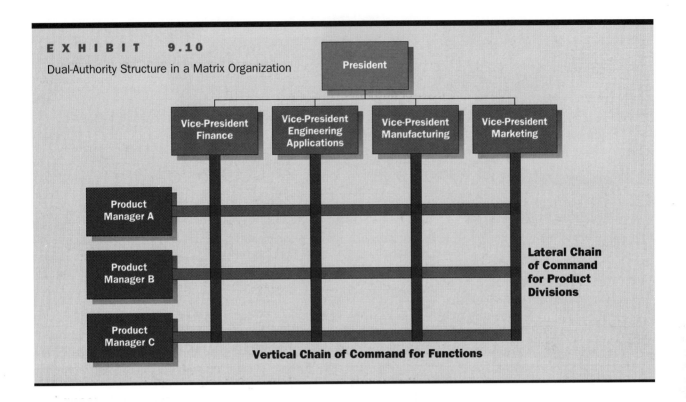

E X H I B I T   9.10

Dual-Authority Structure in a Matrix Organization

is responsible for the entire matrix. The **top leader** oversees both the product and functional chains of command. His or her responsibility is to maintain a power balance between the two sides of the matrix. If disputes arise between them, the problem will be kicked upstairs to the top leader.[23] The Focus on Global Competition box explains how matrix managers can be successful in a global matrix organization.

top leader

The overseer of both the product and the functional chains of command, responsible for the entire matrix.

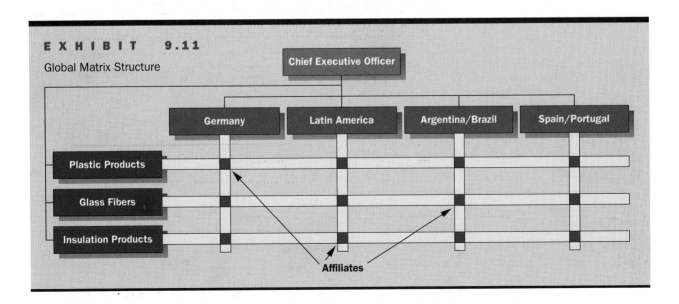

E X H I B I T   9.11

Global Matrix Structure

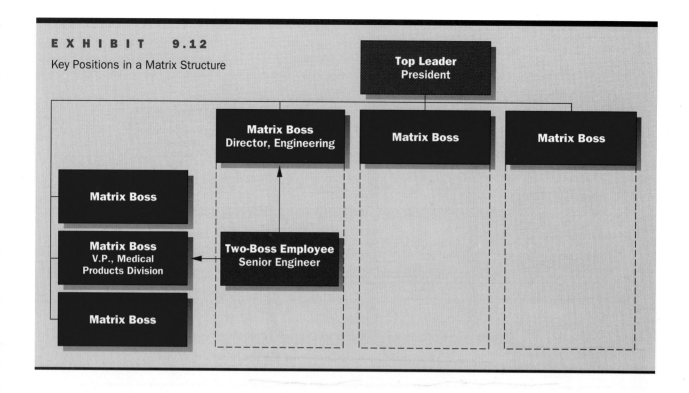

EXHIBIT 9.12

Key Positions in a Matrix Structure

Matrix bosses and two-boss employees often find it difficult to adapt to the matrix. The matrix boss has only half of each employee. Without complete control over employees, bosses must consult with their counterparts on the other side of the matrix. This necessitates frequent meetings and discussions to coordinate matrix activities. The two-boss employee experiences problems of conflicting demands and expectations from the two supervisors.

ADVANTAGES AND DISADVANTAGES. The matrix structure is controversial because of the dual chain of command. However, it has been used successfully in companies such as Unilever. Most important, it makes efficient use of human resources because specialists can be transferred from one division to another. Moreover, the matrix structure works well in a shifting environment, wherein the organization is expected to be adaptable and innovative. The conflict and frequent meetings generated by the matrix enable new issues to be raised and resolved. The matrix also provides training for both specialist and general management skills. People within a functional department or within a specific country in a global matrix have access to in-depth training and specialization. At the same time, they coordinate with other programs or divisions, which helps employees develop a general management perspective. Finally, the matrix structure engages the participation of employees in team meetings and in the achievement of divisional goals. Thus, it challenges and motivates employees, giving them a larger task than would be possible in a functional structure.

THE GLOBAL MATRIX MANAGER

When a company, such as Corning Glass, begins a drive toward global expansion, managers have to learn new skills. The successful global firm needs highly specialized national businesses *and* businesses that are closely linked despite country differences. Through a flexible management process, matrix managers can work to build (1) efficiency and competitiveness on a global scale and (2) flexibility and responsiveness within each nation. These responsibilities become the focus of matrix bosses and corporate leadership in a global matrix corporation.

The matrix business manager responsible for a worldwide product line must be both coordinator and strategist. This person's job is to coordinate transactions across national borders and to serve as global strategist for the product. For example, Electrolux has a manager responsible for developing strategy for the high prestige Zanussi brand. This manager coordinates manu-

facture and distribution across several countries. As businesses grow and products proliferate, the need for coordination increases and product-line managers develop a repertoire of management tools to refine strategy and keep communication channels open.

The country matrix manager has a different responsibility—that of sensing and interpreting issues and threats within the country, building national capabilities and resources for several product lines, and contributing knowledge and ideas to the company's global strategy. The country matrix manager is "king of the country," gathers and sifts information, and has the sometimes difficult task of communicating the importance of this intelligence to people higher up. For example, NEC, a Japanese company, assigned a single manager to be responsible for its digital-switch design and promotion in the United States. His time was spent tailoring the product to U.S. needs and feeding strategic information back to Tokyo.

At the top of the matrix are corporate managers, who define overall global strategy and become both talent scouts and developers

of managers. Corporate leaders identify and develop talented business and country managers and facilitate coordination and negotiations among them. At a company like Unilever, developing managers who can function effectively in diverse global situations is an absolute top priority. Locating top people is difficult, but success of the global corporation depends on its management resources.

The matrix is a powerful structure for global business, but managers must be trained to take advantage of the dual hierarchy to achieve efficiency on a global scale and at the same time achieve flexibility and responsiveness within each country. Business and country matrix managers take primary responsibility for these capabilities. Top corporate managers are responsible for finding and developing matrix managers, and providing the leadership to enable the global corporation to prosper. ■

SOURCE: Based on Christopher A. Bartlett and Sumantra Ghoshal, "What Is a Global Manager?" *Harvard Business Review*, September–October 1992, 124–132.

The matrix structure also has several disadvantages. The major problem is the confusion and frustration caused by the dual chain of command. Matrix bosses and two-boss employees have difficulty with the dual reporting relationships. The matrix structure also can generate high conflict because it pits divisional against functional goals in a domestic structure, or product line versus country goals in a global structure. This leads to the third disadvantage: time lost to meetings and discussions devoted to resolving this conflict. Often the matrix structure leads to more discussion than action because different goals and points of view

---

E X H I B I T   9 . 1 3

Advantages and Disadvantages of Matrix Structure

Advantages	**Disadvantages**
▪ More efficient use of resources than single hierarchy	▪ Frustration and confusion from dual chain of command
▪ Flexibility, adaptability to changing environment	▪ High conflict between two sides of matrix
▪ Development of both general and specialist management skills	▪ Many meetings, more discussion than action
▪ Interdisciplinary cooperation, expertise available to all divisions	▪ Human relations training needed
▪ Enlarged tasks for employees	▪ Power dominance by one side of matrix

---

are being addressed. To survive and perform well in a matrix, employees need human relations training to learn to deal with two bosses, to get by with only "half" of each employee, and to confront and manage conflict. Finally, many organizations find it difficult to maintain the power balances essential for matrix success. The functional and divisional sides of the matrix must have equal power. If one side acquires greater formal authority, the advantages of the matrix structure are lost. The organization then operates like a functional structure with informal lateral relationships.

The advantages and disadvantages of the matrix structure are summarized in Exhibit 9.13.

One company in which the matrix structure works very well is Crane Plastics, Inc., in Columbus, Ohio. There is only one matrix boss on the divisional side, but the approach has succeeded because of the skills of Howard Bennett.

 C R A N E   P L A S T I C S ,   I N C .

Gary Fulmer, executive vice-president of Crane Plastics, had not even heard of the matrix structure until he ran across some published articles. The matrix seemed a solution to the intense cooperation needed among departments during a product changeover. "Making the conversion in our large-volume custom products was driving me up a wall," said Fulmer. "Rarely had we done anything that cut across so many departments. It took compounding experts, toolmakers, extrusion people, quality control people—in all, it took about five different disciplines to make this thing work. . . . But it wasn't working." He continued, "People would have a meeting. They'd come back after two or three weeks with all good intentions, but they just didn't get it done, because they had more important things to do in their own functional areas."

Managers resisted the matrix, because team members work for two bosses—product team and function—at the same time. Crane Plastics implemented the matrix with one team boss, and it really began to click when Howard Bennett took that position. Bennett understood lateral relationships. He guarded against interdepartmental friction by having functional department heads sign an agreement allowing their subordinates participation in a product team. His style encouraged cooperation. But Bennett admits it took some practice: "When I assumed this position, I was totally engrossed in manufacturing. . . . I had no sympathy for marketing, accounting, or most of the other functions. This job gave me a broader outlook." Said one team member, "With other companies, matrix management is reduced to shouting matches. . . . It's inevitable any time you have two bosses." But thanks to Howard Bennett, this did not happen at Crane Plastics.[24] ■

TEAM APPROACH

Probably the most widespread trend in departmentalization has been the effort by companies to implement team concepts. The vertical chain of command is a powerful means of control, but passing all decisions up the hierarchy takes too long and keeps responsibility at the top. Companies in the 1990s are trying to find ways to delegate authority, push responsibility to low levels, and create participative teams that engage the commitment of workers. This approach enables organizations to be more flexible and responsive in the competitive global environment.

Cross-functional teams consist of employees from various functional departments who are responsible to meet as a team and resolve mutual problems. Team members typically still report to their functional departments, but they also report to the team, one member of whom may be the leader. Computer-based companies such as Lanier Technology Corporation, Compaq Computer Corporation, Quantum Corporation, and AST Research are obsessed with creating a team atmosphere using cross-functional teams.[25] At Compaq, lateral groups are called "smart teams," which represent an interdisciplinary approach to management. This structural approach assumes that people from the treasurer's office and engineering have ideas to contribute to decisions about marketing and manufacturing. The Deskpro 286 was created by a smart team in response to IBM's super PC. Kevin Ellington, who was in charge of the project, created his own smart team, drawing members from every department in the company. Team members communicated constantly. Within six months, Compaq was shipping its first models—indeed, it beat IBM to the punch, because IBM was still suffering production problems.[26]

Permanent teams are brought together as a formal department in the organization. Instead of just working together, employees are placed in the same location and report to the same supervisor. In some organizations, such as Ford, permanent teams start at the top with what is called the Office of the Chairman or the Office of the President, in which the two or three top executives work as a team.

At lower organization levels, the permanent-team approach resembles the divisional approach described earlier, except that teams are much smaller. Teams may consist of only 20 to 30 members, each bringing a

cross-functional team

A group of employees assigned to a functional department that meets as a team to resolve mutual problems.

permanent team

A group of participants from several functions who are permanently assigned to solve ongoing problems of common interest.

Permanent teams are an important ingredient in the continued success of Chrysler Corporation. In January 1991, Chrysler reorganized into four "platform" teams focusing on the areas of large car, small car, Jeep/truck, and minivan. Each team had the same goal: to develop world-class vehicles that met the demands and needs of customers. Each platform team operates like a small company. Members of the large car development team shown here represent marketing, manufacturing, design, engineering, procurement, supply, planning, and finance. Working together, team members slashed months from the traditional development time for Chrysler's successful new line of mid-size cars—the Chrysler Concorde, Dodge Intrepid, and Eagle Vision.

functional specialty to the team. For example, Kollmorgen Corporation, a manufacturer of electronic circuitry and other goods, divided its organization into teams that average 75 employees.[27] Even at this size, employees think of themselves as a team. Performance jumped dramatically after Kollmorgen shifted to this concept.

Kodak has adopted teams for specific products, such as black and white film. Team members—called Zebras—coordinate activities of all departments necessary to produce the film. Hallmark Cards created teams to develop new cards. Previously, artists, designers, and printers were located as much as a block apart although working on the same card. Now they work face-to-face, producing better cards faster.[28]

One dramatic example of reorganizing into permanent teams occurred at an old-line insurance company called Aid Association for Lutherans (AAL).

 AID ASSOCIATION FOR LUTHERANS

AAL's traditional organization structure consisted of three functional departments with employees specialized to handle health insurance, life insurance, or support services as illustrated in part (a) of Exhibit 9.14. This structure seemed efficient, but policyholder inquiries often were passed among several departments and then back again. For example, a request to use the cash value of a life policy to pay the premiums for health insurance would bounce through all sections, taking at least 21 days. Coordination across sections took additional time when misunderstandings arose.

Top managers decided to risk everything on a team approach. At precisely 12 noon, nearly 500 clerks, technicians, and managers wheeled their chairs to new locations, becoming part of 25-person teams. The new structure is illustrated in part (b) of Exhibit 9.14. Each section consists of three to four teams that serve a region of the country. Each team has specialists who can do any of the 167 tasks required for policyholder sales and service. The request to pay health insurance premiums with life insurance cash value now is handled in five days. Productivity is up 20 percent and case-processing time has been reduced by as much as 75 percent. Administrative overhead is way down, because teams need little supervision. A total of 55 middle management jobs was eliminated as the teams took over self-management responsibility. AAL now handles 10 percent more transactions of all kinds, with 10 percent fewer employees, thanks to the team concept.[29] ∎

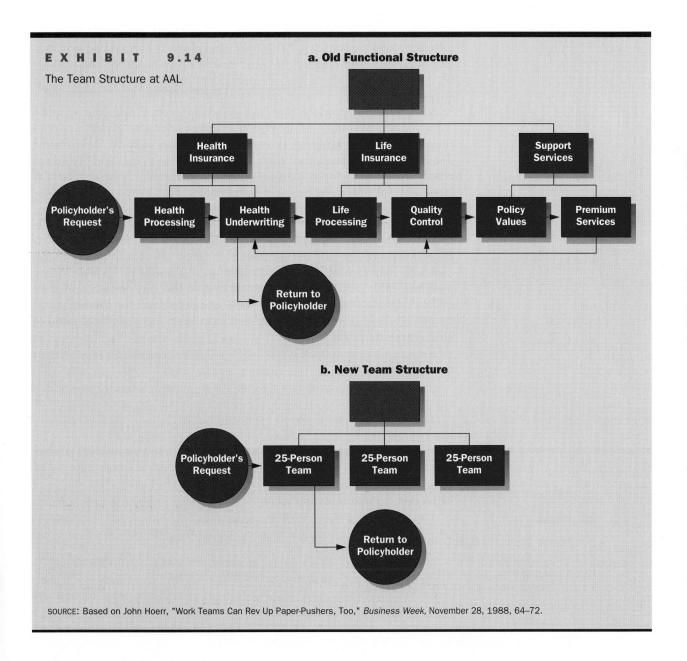

E X H I B I T   9 . 1 4

The Team Structure at AAL

a. Old Functional Structure

b. New Team Structure

SOURCE: Based on John Hoerr, "Work Teams Can Rev Up Paper-Pushers, Too," *Business Week,* November 28, 1988, 64–72.

ADVANTAGES AND DISADVANTAGES. Designing team relationships often helps overcome shortcomings in a functional top-down approach to organizing. With cross-functional teams, the organization is able to retain some advantages of a functional structure, such as economies of scale and in-depth training while gaining the benefits of team relationships. The team concept breaks down barriers across departments. Team members know one another's problems and compromise rather than blindly pursue their own goals. The team concept also allows the organization to more quickly adapt to customer requests and environmental changes and speeds decision making because decisions need not go to the top of the hierarchy for approval. Another big advantage is the morale boost. Employees are enthusiastic about their involvement in bigger projects rather than narrow departmental tasks. Jobs are enriched. The final advantage is reduced administrative overhead. The creation of teams enables responsibility and authority to be pushed down the hierarchy, requiring fewer managers for supervision.

But the team approach also has disadvantages. Employees may be enthusiastic about team participation, but they may also experience conflicts and dual loyalties. A cross-functional team may make different demands on members than their department managers, and members who participate in more than one team must resolve these conflicts. A large amount of time is devoted to meetings, thus increasing coordination time. Unless the organization truly needs teams to coordinate complex projects and adapt to the environment, it will lose production efficiency with them. Finally, the team approach may cause too much decentralization. Senior department managers who traditionally made decisions may feel left out when a team moves ahead on its own. Team members often do not see the big picture of the corporation and may make decisions that are good for their group but bad for the organization as a whole. Top management can help keep the team in alignment with corporate goals.

The advantages and disadvantages of the team structure are summarized in Exhibit 9.15.

EXHIBIT   9.15

Advantages and Disadvantages of Team Structure

Advantages	Disadvantages
■ Some advantages of functional structure	■ Dual loyalties and conflict
■ Reduced barriers among departments, increased compromise	■ Time and resources spent on meetings
■ Less response time, quicker decisions	■ Unplanned decentralization
■ Better morale, enthusiasm from employee involvement	
■ Reduced administrative overhead	

NETWORK APPROACH

The newest approach to departmentalization has been called a "dynamic network" organization.[30] The **network structure** means that the organization disaggregates major functions into separate companies that are brokered by a small headquarters organization. Rather than manufacturing, engineering, sales, and accounting being housed under one roof, these services are provided by separate organizations working under contract and connected electronically to the central office.[31] An illustration of a hypothetical network organization is shown in Exhibit 9.16.

The network approach is revolutionary, because it is difficult to answer the question, "Where is the organization?" in traditional terms. For example, a firm may contract for expensive services such as training, transportation, legal, and engineering, so these functions are no longer part of the organization. Or consider a piece of ice hockey equipment that is designed in Scandinavia, engineered in the United States, manufactured in Korea, and distributed in Canada by a Japanese sales organization. These pieces are drawn together contractually and coordinated electronically, creating a new form of organization.

This organizational approach is especially powerful for international operations. For example, Schwinn Bicycle Company went to a network structure, importing bicycles manufactured in Asia and distributing them through independent dealers who are coordinated electronically. Cigna Corporation took over an unused factory in Ireland and hired workers to process medical claims more cheaply and efficiently than could be done in the United States. McGraw-Hill has people working at computer terminals in Ireland also, maintaining worldwide circulation files for its magazines. These departments are tied electronically to the home offices in the United States.[32] High-tech firms such as IBM and Digital Equipment previously did all manufacturing in-house but now are contracting with suppliers around the world.[33] Lewis Galoob Toys,

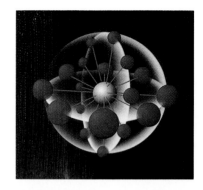

Safeguard Scientifics, Inc., distributes microcomputer hardware and develops and sells telecommunications equipment and software systems. The company uses a *network structure* in which Safeguard acts as controlling shareholder and is linked closely with its partnership companies. The network that includes Safeguard and its partners is based on open communication, teamwork, selective risk taking, and creativity and is united to achieve a common objective.

network structure

An organization structure that disaggregates major functions into separate companies that are brokered by a small headquarters organization.

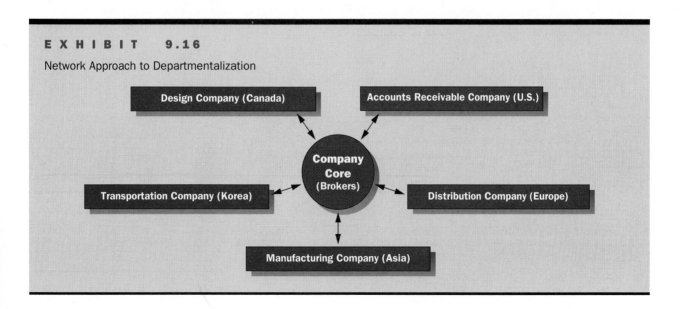

EXHIBIT 9.16

Network Approach to Departmentalization

Design Company (Canada)

Accounts Receivable Company (U.S.)

Company Core (Brokers)

Transportation Company (Korea)

Distribution Company (Europe)

Manufacturing Company (Asia)

Inc., sold $58 million worth of toys with only 115 employees. Galoob farmed out manufacturing and packaging to contractors in Hong Kong, toy design to independent inventors, and sales to independent distribution representatives. Another name for the network organization is the modular corporation, which is described in the Manager's Shoptalk box.

ADVANTAGES AND DISADVANTAGES.   The network approach to organizing is still new, but the biggest advantage to date seems to be competitiveness on a global scale. Network organizations, even small ones, can be truly global. A network organization can draw on resources worldwide to achieve the best quality and price and can sell its products and services worldwide. A second advantage is work-force flexibility and challenge. Flexibility comes from the ability to hire whatever services are needed, such as engineering design or maintenance, and to change a few months later without constraints from owning plant,

MANAGER'S shop talk

THE MODULAR CORPORATION

In the past, companies took great pride in creating a huge, self-sufficient enterprise that did everything for itself from making its own supplies to trucking them to manufacturing facilities sprawled nationwide. As we rush toward the 21st century, these monoliths are being replaced by lean structures called the modular corporation. Two industries, apparel and electronics, have championed the modular model with companies such as Nike pioneering the system. But other industries are also catching the modular wave.

The flexible modular structure enables companies to react quickly to the rapidly changing needs of today's marketplace by focusing its personnel, technology, and money on a few core activities while purchasing other activities, such as deliveries, accounting, and even manufacturing, from outside specialists. The modular company is a hub surrounded by a flexible network of top suppliers whose modules can be expanded or cut out in response to changing needs.

The modular system offers two advantages: (1) cost reduction and (2) the opportunity to direct capital to core areas where the company has its greatest competitive edge. Nike and Chrysler offer examples of these advantages.

Nike's corporate offices in Beaverton, Oregon, focus investment on research, design, and technology to meet the changing needs and demands of athletic and fashion-conscious consumers. By outsourcing manufacturing to suppliers in Asia, Nike avoids a huge investment in fixed assets, thereby showing a high return on shareholder equity.

Chrysler Corporation was the first U.S. automaker to adopt the modular approach. Outside suppliers provide 70 percent of Chrysler parts. Cars are built in modules, saving production costs. Four separate interior units, for example, arrive from suppliers in various locations, ready to install on the auto frame.

The keys to success for the modular company are focusing company efforts on the right core specialty, and carefully selecting loyal, dependable suppliers capable of guarding trade secrets and changing and retooling to meet new demands. Strong networks provide a competitive edge, and modular companies may indeed be the wave of the future . ■

SOURCE: Shawn Tully, "The Modular Corporation," *Fortune*, February 8, 1993, 106–116.

EXHIBIT 9.17

Advantages and Disadvantages of Network Structure

Advantages	Disadvantages
■ Global competitiveness	■ No hands-on control
■ Work-force flexibility/challenge	■ Can lose organizational part
■ Reduced administrative overhead	■ Employee loyalty weakened

equipment, and facilities. The organization can continually redefine itself to fit new products and market opportunities. For those employees who are a permanent part of the organization, the challenge comes from greater job variety and job satisfaction from working within the lean structure. Finally, this structure is perhaps the leanest of all organization forms. Administrative overhead is small because little supervision is required. Large teams of staff specialists and administrators are not needed. A network organization may have only two or three levels of hierarchy compared with ten or more in traditional organizations.[34] These advantages of a network structure, along with the disadvantages, are summarized in Exhibit 9.17.

One of the major disadvantages is lack of hands-on control. Managers do not have all operations under one roof and must rely on contracts, coordination, negotiation, and electronic messages to hold things together. A problem of equal importance is the possibility of losing an organizational part. If a subcontractor fails to deliver, goes out of business, or has a plant burn down, the headquarters organization can be put out of business. Uncertainty is higher because necessary services are not under one roof and under direct management control. Finally, in this type of organization, employee loyalty can weaken. Employees may feel they can be replaced by contract services. A cohesive corporate culture is less likely to develop, and turnover tends to be higher because emotional commitment between organization and employee is weak. With changing products and markets, the organization may need to reshuffle employees at any time to acquire the correct mix of skills.

SUMMARY AND MANAGEMENT SOLUTION

This chapter introduced a number of important organizing concepts. Fundamental characteristics of organization structure include work specialization, chain of command, authority and responsibility, span of management, centralization and decentralization, and administrative overhead. These dimensions of organization represent the vertical hierarchy and indicate how authority and responsibility are distributed along the hierarchy.

The other major concept is departmentalization, which describes how organization employees are grouped. Three traditional approaches are functional, divisional, and matrix; contemporary approaches are team and network structures. The functional approach groups employees by common skills and tasks. The opposite structure is divisional, which groups people by organizational output such that each division has a mix of functional skills and tasks. The matrix structure uses two chains of command simultaneously, and some employees have two bosses. The two chains of command in a domestic organization typically are functional and product division, and for international firms, the two chains of command typically are product and geographic regions. The team approach uses permanent teams and cross-functional teams to achieve better coordination and employee commitment than is possible with a pure functional structure. The network approach, including the modular organization, represents the newest form of organization structure. Departmental tasks are subcontracted to other organizations, so the central organization is simply a broker that coordinates several independent organizations to accomplish its goal. Each organization form has advantages and disadvantages and can be used by managers to meet the needs of the competitive situation.

The structural changes championed by CEO Paul Allaire at Xerox illustrate these structural principles. Xerox had attained high quality with its functional structure, but coordination was insufficient to provide rapid response to market changes. Allaire's decision was to reorganize the company into nine product divisions. Thus, Xerox traded the old functional hierarchy for independent business divisions such as printing systems, office document products, and the XSoft Division, which provides software packages for desktop computers. This new structure allows collaboration within each division that provides fast transition of new technology into products for the marketplace. The same philosophy permeates down within the divisions. XSoft divided its 450 employees into small teams that have successfully launched software such as PaperWorks and Rooms in record time. The team approach also reduces the number of managers and keeps the divisions linked to customer needs.[35]

DISCUSSION QUESTIONS

1. Sonny Holt, manager of Electronics Assembly, asked Hector Cruz, his senior technician, to handle things in the department while Sonny worked on the budget. Sonny needed peace and quiet for at least a week to complete his figures. After ten days, Sonny discovered that Hector had hired a senior secretary, not realizing that Sonny had promised interviews to two other people. Evaluate Sonny's approach to delegation.

2. Many experts note that organizations have been making greater use of teams in recent years. What factors might account for this trend?
3. Contrast centralization with span of management. Would you expect these characteristics to affect each other in organizations? Why?
4. An organizational consultant was heard to say, "Some aspect of functional structure appears in every organization." Do you agree? Explain.
5. The divisional structure is often considered almost the opposite of a functional structure. Do you agree? Briefly explain the major differences in these two approaches to departmentalization.
6. What are important skills for matrix bosses and two-boss employees in a matrix organization?
7. Some people argue that the matrix structure should be adopted only as a last resort because the dual chains of command can create more problems than they solve. Do you agree or disagree? Why?
8. What is the network approach to structure? Is the use of authority and responsibility different compared with other forms of departmentalization? Explain.
9. Why are divisional structures frequently used in large corporations? Does it make sense for a huge corporation such as American Airlines to stay in a functional structure?
10. An international matrix structure tends to be organized by product divisions and geographic regions. Why would these two chains of command be used rather than product and function as in domestic companies? Explain.

MANAGEMENT IN PRACTICE: ETHICAL DILEMMA

● QUALITY CONTROL SUPERVISION

Jane was an engineer in the quality control department of a new manufacturing plant. She used to work under Ed, the head of quality control, who in turn reported to the vice-president of manufacturing. Jane is a college graduate and learned a lot from Ed, who has worked in manufacturing for 32 years.

One of Jane's responsibilities was to measure the chemical concentrations in the plant's waste water and sign the monthly reports sent to city officials certifying that the concentrations are below dangerous levels. She recently decided to switch to a newer test that is more reliable and less expensive and discovered that the actual concentrations of pollutants are above mandated levels.

Jane showed the new results to Ed, who agreed the situation was serious. However, the vice-president of manufacturing did not agree. After many arguments between Ed and the vice-president, Ed was found overqualified for his job and was transferred to another plant. The vice-president of manufacturing reinstated the old test.

Jane is now head of quality control. The plant just received an exclusive contract that will cause production to double in two years. The chemical concentrations keep rising. The vice-president of manufacturing tells Jane that when concentrations become too high as measured by the old test, they will add more water to dilute the waste.

● WHAT DO YOU DO?

1. Obey the vice-president of manufacturing. He has ultimate authority and responsibility for this task.
2. Confront the vice-president of manufacturing and argue the case for better control of pollutants, being prepared to lose your job if necessary.
3. Blow the whistle on the company by taking test results to city officials and the press. This will protect you and force the company to adhere to the tests.

CASES FOR ANALYSIS

TENNESSEE MANUFACTURING

Norma Franklin has been with Tennessee Manufacturing for eight years. Norma is a graphics technician in the engineering drafting department, developing slides and other visual aids for company presentations. Tennessee Manufacturing is expanding at a rapid rate, and its new emphasis is on innovation. With the introduction of a matrix structure, Norma found herself working for two managers. In addition to working for Tim Hendricks, manager of drafting, she now also works for Rick Wilson, who is responsible for the development of a new line of plastic products. Norma is part of a plastic products team that meets twice weekly with Rick.

Norma noticed an immediate increase in her work load. Her new boss gave her frequent assignments at the last minute, needing excellent graphics for presentations about the new plastics line to senior management and potential customers. Meanwhile, Tim Hendricks took it for granted that Norma would be able to complete her normal work load in the graphics department. After two months, the heavy work load began to wear on Norma. Her performance review was due, during which Tim explained he was giving her an average rating. "Your attitude has been poor, and you are not turning out the work the way you used to," he said.

Norma exploded. "You don't seem to realize my work load has doubled since this matrix structure thing started. Between you and Rick, I have been run ragged, and you have the nerve to tell me I am doing only average work. I'm doing the work of two people. You seem to think the work I do for Rick shouldn't affect the work I do for you, but I've had to stay late almost every night for the past month."

"Norma," Tim said, "I'm sorry, but the work needs to go out, and we can't get another graphics technician. Your work has not been as good as before, and I have to rate you strictly on your performance."

● QUESTIONS

1. Did Tim Hendricks handle this situation correctly? As a matrix boss, what is his responsibility toward Norma?
2. What should Norma do in this situation to manage her work load?
3. How would you evaluate the implementation of this matrix structure?

SOURCE: Based on Grace Lander, "Double Duty," *Supervisory Management* (February 1989), 44–45.

TUCKER COMPANY

In 1978 the Tucker Company underwent an extensive reorganization that divided the company into three major divisions. These new divisions represented Tucker's three principal product lines. Mr. Harnett, Tucker's president, explained the basis for the new organization in a memo to the board of directors as follows:

> The diversity of our products requires that we reorganize along our major product lines. Toward this end I have established three new divisions: commercial jet engines, military jet engines, and utility turbines. Each division will be headed by a new vice-president who will report directly to me. I believe that this new approach will enhance our performance through the commitment of individual managers. It should also help us to identify unprofitable areas where the special attention of management may be required.
>
> For the most part, each division will be able to operate independently. That is, each will have its own engineering, manufacturing, accounting departments, etc. In some

cases, however, it will be necessary for a division to utilize the services of other divisions or departments. This is necessary because the complete servicing with individual divisional staffs would result in unjustifiable additional staffing and facilities.

The old companywide laboratory was one such service department. Functionally, it continued to support all of the major divisions. Administratively, however, the manager of the laboratory reported to the manager of manufacturing in the military jet engine division.

From the time the new organization was initiated until February of 1988, when the laboratory manager Mr. Garfield retired, there was little evidence of interdepartmental or interdivisional conflict. His replacement, Mr. Hodge, unlike Mr. Garfield, was always eager to gain the attention of management. Many of Hodge's peers perceived him as an empire builder who was interested in his own advancement rather than the company's well-being. After about six months in the new position, Hodge became involved in several interdepartmental conflicts over work that was being conducted in his laboratory.

Historically, the engineering departments had used the laboratory as a testing facility to determine the properties of materials selected by the design engineers. Hodge felt that the laboratory should be more involved in the selection of these materials and in the design of experiments and subsequent evaluations of the experimental data. Hodge discussed this with Mr. Franklin of the engineering department of the utility turbine division. Franklin offered to consult with Hodge but stated that the final responsibility for the selection of materials was charged to his department.

In the months that followed, Hodge and Franklin had several disagreements over the implementation of the results. Franklin told Hodge that, because of his position at the testing lab, he was unable to appreciate the detailed design considerations that affected the final decision on materials selection. Hodge claimed that Franklin lacked the materials expertise that he, as a metallurgist, had.

Franklin also noted that the handling of his requests, which had been prompt under Garfield's management, was taking longer and longer under Hodge's management. Hodge explained that military jet engine divisional problems had to be assigned first priority because of his administrative reporting structure. He also said that if he were more involved in Franklin's problems, he could perhaps appreciate when a true sense of urgency existed and could revise priorities.

The tensions between Franklin and Hodge reached a peak when one of Franklin's critical projects failed to receive the scheduling that he considered necessary. Franklin phoned Hodge to discuss the need for a schedule change. Hodge suggested that they have a meeting to review the need for the work. Franklin then told Hodge that this was not a matter of his concern and that his function was merely to perform the tests as requested. He further stated that he was not satisfied with the low priority rating that his division's work received. Hodge reminded Franklin that when Hodge had suggested a means for resolving this problem, Franklin was not receptive. At this point, Franklin lost his temper and hung up on Hodge.

● QUESTIONS

1. Sketch out a simple organization chart showing Tucker Company's three divisions, including the location of the laboratory. Why would the laboratory be located in the military jet engine division?

2. Analyze the conflict between Mr. Hodge and Mr. Franklin. Do you think the conflict is based on personalities or on the way in which the organization is structured?

3. Sketch out a new organization chart showing how you would restructure Tucker Company so that the laboratory would provide equal services to all divisions. What advantages and disadvantages do you see in the new structure compared with the previous one?

SOURCE: Reprinted with permission of Macmillan Publishing Company from "The Laboratory," *Organizational Behavior: Readings and Cases*, 2d ed., pp. 385–387, by L. Katz, prepared under the supervision of Theodore T. Herbert. Copyright 1981 by Theodore T. Herbert.

REFERENCES

1. Lisa Driscoll, "The New, New Thinking at Xerox," *Business Week*, June 22, 1992, 120–121, and Robert Howard, "The CEO as Organizational Architect: An Interview with Xerox's Paul Allaire," *Harvard Business Review* (September–October 1992), 107–121.

2. Robert M. Tomasko, "Restructuring: Getting It Right," *Management Review* (April 1992), 10–15.

3. "Greyhound Splitting into Four to Go after Short-Haul Trade," *Chicago Tribune*, April 30, 1986, sec. 3, 8.

4. Andrew C. Brown, "Unilever Fights Back in the U.S.," *Fortune*, May 26, 1986, 32–38, and "The Toughest Job in Business: How They're Remaking U.S. Steel," *Business Week*, February 25, 1985, 50–55.

5. "A Slimmed-Down Brunswick Is Proving Wall Street Wrong," *Business Week*, May 28, 1984, 90–98, and J. Vettner, "Bowling for Dollars," *Forbes*, September 12, 1983, 138.

6. John Child, *Organization: A Guide to Problems and Practice*, 2d ed. (London: Harper & Row, 1984).

7. Adam Smith, *The Wealth of Nations* (New York: Modern Library, 1937).

8. This discussion is based on Richard L. Daft, *Organization Theory and Design*, 4th ed. (St. Paul, Minn.: West, 1992), 387–388.

9. C. I. Barnard, *The Functions of the Executive* (Cambridge, Mass.: Harvard University Press, 1938).

10. Thomas A. Stewart, "CEOs See Clout Shifting," *Fortune*, November 6, 1989, 66.

11. Michael G. O'Loughlin, "What Is Bureaucratic Accountability and How Can We Measure It?" *Administration & Society* 22, 3 (November 1990), 275–302.

12. Carrie R. Leana, "Predictors and Consequences of Delegation," *Academy of Management Journal* 29 (1986), 754–774.

13. Paul D. Collins and Frank Hull, "Technology and Span of Control: Woodward Revisited," *Journal of Management Studies* 23 (March 1986), 143–164; David D. Van Fleet and Arthur G. Bedeian, "A History of the Span of Management," *Academy of Management Review* 2 (1977), 356–372; and C. W. Barkdull, "Span of Control—A Method of Evaluation," *Michigan Business Review* 15 (May 1963), 25–32.

14. Brian Dumaire, "What the Leaders of Tomorrow See," *Fortune*, July 3, 1989, 48–62.

15. Joseph Weber, "A Big Company That Works," *Business Week*, May 4, 1992, 124–132.

16. Dana Milbank, "Changes at Alcoa Point Up Challenges and Benefits of Decentralized Authority," *The Wall Street Journal*, November 7, 1991, B1; and Clay Chandler and Paul Ingrassia, "Just as U.S. Firms Try Japanese Management, Honda Is Centralizing," *The Wall Street Journal*, April 11, 1991, A1, A10.

17. Patricia Sellers, "If It Ain't Broke, Fix It Anyway," *Fortune*, December 28, 1992, 49–50; Leah Nathans Spiro, "Raging Bull: The Trimmer New Look of Merrill Lynch," *Business Week*, November 25, 1991, 218–221; and John Templeman, David Woodruff, Stanley Reed, "Downshift at Daimler," *Business Week*, November 16, 1992, 88–90.

18. Raymond E. Miles, "Adapting to Technology and Competition: A New Industrial Relation System for the 21st Century," *California Management Review* (Winter 1989), 9–28.

19. The following discussion of structural alternatives draws heavily on Jay R. Galbraith, *Designing Complex Organizations* (Reading, Mass.: Addison-Wesley, 1973); Jay R. Galbraith, *Organization Design* (Reading, Mass.: Addison-Wesley, 1977); Robert Duncan, "What Is the Right Organization Structure?" *Organizational Dynamics* (Winter 1979), 59–80; and J. McCann and Jay R. Galbraith, "Interdepartmental Relations," in *Handbook of Organizational Design*, ed. P. Nystrom and W. Starbuck (New York: Oxford University Press, 1981), 60–84.

20. Mike Tharp, "LSI Logic Corp. Does as the Japanese Do," *The Wall Street Journal*, April 17, 1986, 6.

21. Kathy Rebello, "Apple's Daring Leap into the All-Digital Future," *Business Week*, May 25, 1992, 120–122.

22. Lawton R. Burns, "Matrix Management in Hospitals: Testing Theories of Matrix Structure and Development," *Administrative Science Quarterly* 34 (1989), 349–368.

23. Stanley M. Davis and Paul R. Lawrence, *Matrix* (Reading, Mass.: Addison-Wesley, 1977).

24. Ellen Kolton, "Team Players," *INC.*, September 1984, 140–144; and personal communication from Howard Bennett, matrix vice-president.

25. Joel Kotkin, "The `Smart-Team' at Compaq Computer," *INC.*, February 1986, 48–56.

26. Ibid., 56.

27. Lucien Rhodes, "The Passion of Robert Swiggett," *INC.*, April 1984, 121–140.

28. Thomas A. Stewart, "The Search for the Organization of Tomorrow," *Fortune*, May 18, 1992, 92–98.

29. John Hoerr, "Work Teams Can Rev Up Paper-Pushers, Too," *Business Week*, November 28, 1988, 64–72.

30. Charles C. Snow, Raymond E. Miles, and Henry J. Coleman, Jr., "Managing 21st Century Network Organizations," *Organizational Dynamics* 20 (Winter 1992), 5–20, and Miles, "Adapting to Technology and Competition."

31. Raymond E. Miles and Charles C. Snow, "Organizations: New Concepts for New Forms," *California Management Review* 28 (Spring 1986), 62–73, and "Now, The Post-Industrial Corporation," *Business Week*, March 3, 1986, 64–74.

32. Bernard Wysocki, Jr., "American Firms Send Office Work Abroad to Use Cheaper Labor," *The Wall Street Journal*, August 14, 1991, A1, A4.

33. G. Pascal Zachary, "High-Tech Firms Find It's Good to Line Up Outside Contractors," *The Wall Street Journal*, July 29, 1992, A1, A5.

34. Miles, "Adapting to Technology and Competition."

35. Driscoll, "The New, New Thinking at Xerox."

A little more than 10 years ago 34.5 million people annually left the driving to Greyhound. Then regional air carriers started siphoning off passengers with bargain-basement fares. By the late 1980s ridership had declined by more than half. The company had become inefficient and debt-ridden, and the worst was yet to come.

In early March 1990, Greyhound drivers began a bitter and protracted strike against the carrier. Management's decision to hire replacement drivers increased tensions. The depth of sentiment was evident early on when several sniper attacks occurred and at least 40 buses were fired upon. The prospect of hopping onto a rolling shooting gallery did not improve passenger loads. Almost three months to the day after the strike was called, Greyhound sought protection under Chapter 11 bankruptcy.

Despite the level of emotions involved, the fight at Greyhound had far more to do with market changes than the typical management versus labor dispute. The company was being forced to respond to fundamental social and economic shifts that made service to small communities economically unfeasible. At the time it entered bankruptcy, Greyhound serviced 3,800 routes and had a work force of 5,800 people. The company also had debt of $100 million left over from a leveraged buyout in 1987. Costs so far outstripped revenues that a downsizing of the existing organization, followed by more efficient operation of what was left, was the only solution.

The company eliminated over 72 million miles of chronically unprofitable service. It trimmed the aging bus fleet by more than 900 and axed high-dollar leases on 474 others. It purchased more than 151 newer buses, models that can travel 150,000 to 200,000 miles a year at a 70 percent reduction in maintenance, as replacements. Greyhound expects the savings on fuel efficiency to run into the millions. Greyhound also upgraded its image for both terminals and buses. In the past inspectors routinely signed off on stations that met 85 percent of the company checklist, and that was after the terminal chief was given a week's notice of the visit. Prior warning is no longer given, and the terminals must meet 100 percent of the requirements.

The company has placed new emphasis on customer service. An additional 250 staffers were added to assist travelers at the company's busiest terminals, and employees at every level were drilled on the importance of treating bus passengers as valued customers. Greyhound cut the advance time on its cheapest tickets, and reduced the four-level advance-purchase fare structure to three levels. The new sliding plan allowed passengers to get as much as a 50 percent discount on tickets bought 14 days before the departure date, down to a 15 percent discount on tickets purchased 3 days in advance. Although the revamped fare structure was designed for summer travel, it generated $129.9 million in passenger revenue in the first three months of 1992.

Greyhound buses now carry on-board radar systems in the hope that collisions can be minimized. The company also added a yield-management program to match available seats with demand and better mix discount- and full-fare riders. The program is used in conjunction with a new computerized reservations system, called TRIPS, which is similar to those airlines use. The company also adopted a hub-and-spoke system to route passengers into one terminal and increase passenger loads on each trip.

The changes seem to be working. President CEO Frank Schmieder said Greyhound's operating margin—operating income divided by total revenue—should hit 10 percent in 1993, an increase of 8.1 percent over 1992 and 1.5 percent in 1991. Net income per share should approach $1.40 for 1993, he said, up from $1.10 per share in 1992.

Healing the wounds of the strike may be as difficult as trying to return Greyhound to profitability. A 6-year agreement between the company and the Amalgamated Transit Union was reached in May 1993. The deal calls for the distribution of $22 million in back pay, amnesty and reinstatement of most of the 200 strikers dismissed for alleged misconduct, a recall of 550 drivers who were replaced, and annual wage increases of almost 20 percent over the life of the contract. Despite approval by the union, many former drivers and mechanics were far from satisfied.

If Greyhound can heal the rifts among its rank-and-file and continue to implement cost-cutting measures, both analysts and industry experts agree that the future looks optimistic. "There are only two kinds of companies," Schmieder said, "those coming and those going. And we're on the come."

● QUESTIONS

1. What were the endemic problems at Greyhound, and what external factors were the primary motivations for change?

2. Contrast the changes necessary at Greyhound with the changes that might have been beneficial at the Amalgamated Transit Union. What sorts of compromises might have either averted the strike, or have shortened its duration?

3. What are Greyhound's chances of success? What variables outside the control of any manager could derail the comeback? How could these variables be anticipated and what contingency plans formulated to cope with them?

USING STRUCTURAL DESIGN TO ACHIEVE STRATEGIC OBJECTIVES

10 CHAPTER

Executives at Cincinnati Milacron rarely saw a competitive foreign-built plastics machine until the early 1980s. Within five years, however, foreign suppliers had seized 50 percent of the market, driving two-thirds of the 15 U.S. companies making injection molding machines out of business. Milacron was the largest domestic manufacturer, and Harold Faig, a product manager, saw the problem. Milacron's price was 40 percent higher than foreign competitors', and delivery took months. Foreign machines would arrive the day

after the order was placed, and quality was superior. Faig realized that Milacron, to be competitive, had to reduce costs 40 percent, increase machinery speed and operating times 40 percent, and cut the two-year development time for a new machine in half.[1] ■ If you were Harold Faig, how would you develop a competitive injection molding machine? What advice would you give him about using organization structure to achieve this goal?

Managers in companies like Cincinnati Milacron frequently must rethink structure and may reorganize to meet new competitive conditions in the environment. In Chapter 9, we examined the fundamentals of structure that apply to all organizations. In this chapter, we focus more precisely on structure as a tool, especially on how managers can use such concepts as departmentalization and chain of command to achieve specific goals. In recent years, many corporations, including American Express, Apple, IBM, Amex Corporation, and Bausch & Lomb, have realigned departmental groupings, chains of command, and teams and task forces to attain new strategic goals. Structure is a powerful tool for reaching strategic goals, and a strategy's success often is determined by its fit with organization structure. By the end of this chapter, the problem at Milacron will be easily identified as a mismatch of Milacron's structure and competitive situation. Milacron's solution to achieve better coordination called for a new structural approach.

● COORDINATION

As organizations grow and evolve, two things happen. First, new positions and departments are added to deal with factors in the external environment or with new strategic needs.[2] For example, Raytheon established a new-products center to facilitate innovation in its various divisions. Korbel Champagne Cellars created a Department of Romance, Weddings, and Entertaining to enhance the linkage between romance and champagne consumption among potential customers. Exhibit 10.1 shows an ad for Korbel's Director of Romance that generated more than 800 applications.[3] Comerica created a position of corporate quality manager to form a department that would be responsible for Comerica's Managing Total Quality program. Employees in this new department help people understand and implement the quality process within their area. As companies add positions and departments to meet changing needs, they grow more complex, with hundreds of positions and departments performing incredibly diverse activities.

Second, senior managers have to find a way to tie all of these departments together. The formal chain of command and the supervision it provides is effective, but it is not enough. The organization needs systems to process information and enable communication among people in different departments and at different levels. **Coordination** refers to the quality of collaboration across departments. Without coordination, a company's left hand will not act in concert with the right hand, causing problems and conflicts. Coordination is required regardless of whether the organization has a functional, divisional, or team structure. Employees identify with their immediate department or team, taking its interest to heart, and may not want to compromise with other units for the good of the organization as a whole.

Without a major effort at coordination, an organization may be like Chrysler Corporation when Lee Iacocca took over:

coordination

The quality of collaboration across departments.

DIRECTOR OF ROMANCE

Korbel Champagne Cellars, California-based producer of America's best-selling premium champagne, seeks dynamic individual for one-of-a-kind corporate position as Director of Romance for the winery's Department of Romance, Weddings & Entertaining. Position involves:
- reporting to media on lighthearted romance surveys commissioned by Korbel
- researching the latest news and information on the romance front
- writing articles on romance-related subjects
- appearing on television and radio programs to discuss the subject of romance

Ideal candidate will have published books or articles on the subject of romance, possess a degree in a related field such as psychology and/or personify romance in some highly visible or glamorous way. Previous media experience preferred. Individuals and spokesperson search firm applicants welcome. No phone calls please. An equal opportunity employer. Send resume to:

FRANK DE FALCO
KORBEL CHAMPAGNE CELLARS
13250 RIVER ROAD
GUERNEVILLE, CA 95446

E X H I B I T   10.1

Example of a Position Created to Deal with Environment and Strategy

SOURCE: Courtesy of Korbel Champagne Cellars.

What I found at Chrysler were 35 vice presidents, each with his own turf.... I couldn't believe, for example, that the guy running engineering departments wasn't in constant touch with his counterpart in manufacturing. But that's how it was. Everybody worked independently. I took one look at that system and I almost threw up. That's when I knew I was in really deep trouble.

I'd call in a guy from engineering, and he'd stand there dumbfounded when I'd explain to him that we had a design problem or some other hitch in the engineering-manufacturing relationship. He might have the ability to invent a brilliant piece of engineering that would save us a lot of money. He might come up with a terrific new design. There was only one problem: he didn't know that the manufacturing people couldn't build it. Why? Because he had never talked to them about it. Nobody at Chrysler seemed to understand that interaction among the different functions in a company is absolutely critical. People in engineering and manufacturing almost have to be sleeping together. These guys weren't even flirting![4]

If one thing changed at Chrysler in the years before Iacocca retired, it was improved coordination. Cooperation among engineering, marketing, and manufacturing enabled the design and production of the stunning line of new LH automobiles in only three years, compared with the five years of development previously required.

In the international arena, coordination is especially important. How can managers ensure that needed coordination will take place in their company? Both domestically and globally? Coordination is the outcome of information and cooperation. Managers can design systems and structures to promote communication. The most important methods for achieving coordination are information systems, task forces and teams, and integrating managers.

information system

A written or electronic internal system for processing data and information among employees.

INFORMATION SYSTEMS

Information systems are the written and electronically based internal systems for processing data and information among employees. Information systems include memos, bulletins, and written reports, as well as technological systems such as computers, electronic mail, electronic bulletin boards, and teleconferences. Electronic systems have the capacity to process enormous volumes of data across hierarchical levels and departments, thereby enabling greater coordination.

An effective use of information systems for vertical coordination is the customer attitude survey, which Ford and other auto manufacturers use. All car buyers are surveyed about a month after purchase, and again a year later, to find out how they were treated by dealers. The compiled data provide information that helps the manufacturer and dealers pinpoint problems and ultimately win steady customers.[5] Another application of information systems for coordination was used in the Air Force. A base commander used a portable radio network to link all senior officers. Each officer could overhear conversations among other officers and thus was kept informed of ongoing events.

These specialists monitor Compaq Computer Corporation's vast *information systems* from the Network Control Center in Houston. Data from 12,000 employee PCs and hundreds of Compaq Systempro computers are processed to allow smooth coordination between Compaq departments, offices, manufacturing plants, and service facilities throughout the United States and twenty other countries.

TASK FORCES AND TEAMS

A **task force** is a temporary team or committee designed to solve a short-term problem involving several departments.[6] Task force members represent their departments and share information that enables coordination.

For example, the Shawmut National Corporation created two task forces in the human resources department to consolidate all employment services into a single area. The task force looked at job banks, referral programs, employment procedures, and applicant tracking systems; found ways to perform these functions for all Shawmut's divisions in one human resource department; and then disbanded.[7] General Motors uses task forces to solve temporary problems in its manufacturing plants. When a shipment of car doors arrived from a fabricating plant with surface imperfections, the plant manager immediately created a task force to solve the problem: "I got the vice president of manufacturing—who is my boss—the plant manager of the stamping plant, the die engineers, the quality engineers, the United Auto Workers representatives from both plants, the Olds guy from Lansing, a Cadillac guy, and the Fisher Body guy from the Tech Center. So I had everybody right out there on the floor looking at the exact part that is giving us the problem, and the problem was resolved in about two hours."[8]

In addition to creating task forces, companies also set up teams. As used for coordination, a **team** is a group of participants from several departments who meet regularly to solve ongoing problems of common interest.[9] The permanent team is similar to a task force except that it works with continuing rather than temporary problems and may exist for several years. Teams used for coordination are like the cross-functional teams described in Chapter 9. For example, PLY GEM, a national manufacturer of home improvement products, has eight operating divisions. To coordinate technology, marketing, and operations skills, an Executive Management Committee consisting of each division president was created. Chemical Bank created a team of consumer banking specialists to devise a unified management system for all of Chemical's suburban branches. The team cuts across departments to develop and implement management techniques that involve customer flow management and teller scheduling that make all branches more efficient.[10] Teams also gave a competitive edge to Snap-on Tools, described in the Winning Moves box.

INTEGRATING MANAGERS

An **integrating manager** is a person in a full-time position created for the purpose of coordinating the activities of several departments.[11] The distinctive feature of the integrating position is that the person is not a member of one of the departments being coordinated. These positions often have titles such as product manager, project manager, program manager, or branch manager. The coordinator is assigned to coordinate departments on a full-time basis to achieve desired project or product outcomes.

---

task force

A temporary team or committee formed to solve a specific short-term problem involving several departments.

team

A group of participants from several departments who meet regularly to solve ongoing problems of common interest.

integrating manager

An individual responsible for coordinating the activities of several departments on a full-time basis to achieve specific project or product outcomes.

WINNING moves   **SNAP-ON TOOLS CORPORATION**

For a long time, Snap-on Tools Corp. customers would buy everything it could produce. Suddenly, the market was swamped with competitive products that were clones of Snap-on's popular designs. To keep its lead, Snap-on Tools had to become more aggressive in developing new concepts and products, which called for innovative reorganization. Snap-on's desire was to eliminate the functional department structure, wherein each department performed its task in isolation, "throwing the project over the wall" to the next department when finished.

The first step was to restructure the Research and Engineering Division into four product groups—traditional hand tools, air tools, sheet-metal goods, and electronic products. Each was a self-contained unit with its own engineering function. Next, engineering teams were created to work with marketing and customer focus groups to discuss ideas and define new products. Cross-divisional teams solve potential problems before they arise. Thanks to team cooperation, new-product projects now sail smoothly through the various phases of the new-product design cycle.

Thanks largely to an innovative use of team concepts, Snap-on Tools Corp. has regained its momentum with a higher percentage of sales coming from new products. ■

SOURCE: Joyce Hoffman, editor, *Reflections*, vol. 10, 1989, 12–15.

General Mills, Procter & Gamble, and General Foods all use product managers to coordinate their product lines. A manager is assigned to each line, such as Cheerios, Bisquick, and Hamburger Helper. Product managers set budget goals, marketing targets, and strategies and obtain the cooperation from advertising, production, and sales personnel needed for implementing product strategy.

In some organizations, project managers are included on the organization chart, as illustrated in Exhibit 10.2. The project manager is drawn to one side of the chart to indicate authority over the project but not over the people assigned to it. Dashed lines to the project manager indicate responsibility for coordination and communication with assigned team members, but department managers retain line authority over functional employees.

An interesting variation of the integrator role was developed at Florida Power & Light Company. To keep the construction of a nuclear power plant on schedule, several project managers were assigned the role of "Mothers." The philosophy of the person in charge was "If you want something to happen, it has to have a mother." The Mothers could nurture their projects to timely completion. This unusual label worked. Although departmental employees did not report directly to a Mother, the Mothers had a great deal of responsibility, which encouraged departmental managers to listen and cooperate.[12]

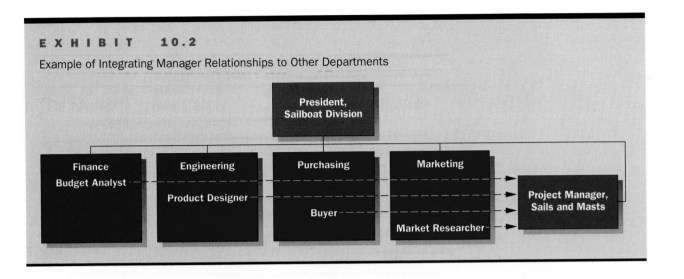

EXHIBIT 10.2

Example of Integrating Manager Relationships to Other Departments

LOOSE VERSUS TIGHT ORGANIZATION STRUCTURE

Recall that the purpose of structure is to organize resources to accomplish organizational goals. Elements of structure such as chain of command, centralization/decentralization, formal authority, teams, and coordination devices fit together to form an overall structural approach. In some organizations, the formal, vertical hierarchy is emphasized as the way to achieve control and coordination. In other organizations, decision making is decentralized, cross-functional teams are implemented, and employees are given great freedom to pursue their tasks as they see fit. In many organizations, a trade-off occurs, because an emphasis on vertical structure means less opportunity for horizontal coordination and vice versa.

The balance between vertical and horizontal structure reflects the trend toward greater employee empowerment and is similar to the concepts of mechanistic and organic organizations introduced in Chapter 4.[13] When the vertical structure is very tight, as in traditionally designed organizations, the structure is *mechanistic*. The organization emphasizes vertical control. Tasks are broken into routine jobs and are rigidly defined. Voluminous rules exist, and the hierarchy of authority is the major form of control. Decision making is centralized, and communication is vertical.

When horizontal structures dominate, as in contemporary empowered companies, the structure is *organic*.[14] Tasks are frequently redefined to fit employee and environmental needs. There are few rules, and authority is based on expertise rather than hierarchy. Decision making is decentralized. Communication is horizontal and is facilitated through the use of task forces, teams, and integrators. An organic organization may not

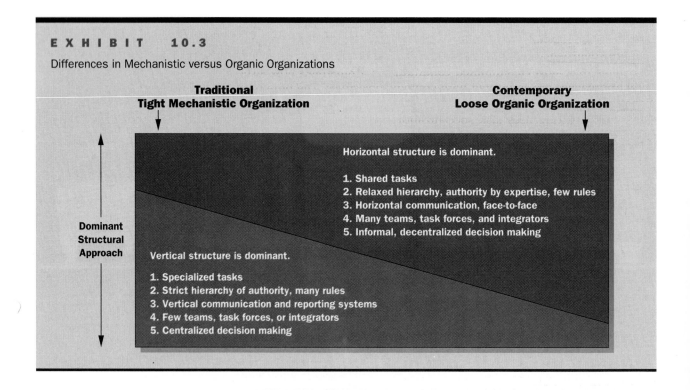

EXHIBIT 10.3

Differences in Mechanistic versus Organic Organizations

Traditional
Tight Mechanistic Organization

Contemporary
Loose Organic Organization

Dominant
Structural
Approach

Horizontal structure is dominant.

1. Shared tasks
2. Relaxed hierarchy, authority by expertise, few rules
3. Horizontal communication, face-to-face
4. Many teams, task forces, and integrators
5. Informal, decentralized decision making

Vertical structure is dominant.

1. Specialized tasks
2. Strict hierarchy of authority, many rules
3. Vertical communication and reporting systems
4. Few teams, task forces, or integrators
5. Centralized decision making

have job descriptions or even an organization chart. A comparison of mechanistic versus organic organizations is presented in Exhibit 10.3.

FACTORS AFFECTING STRUCTURE

How do managers know whether to design a tight or loose structure? The answer lies in the contingency factors that influence organization structure. Recall from Chapter 2 that *contingency* pertains to those factors on which structure depends. Research on organization structure shows that the emphasis given to loose or tight structure depends on the contingency factors of strategy, environment, size/life cycle, production technology, and departmental interdependence. The right structure is designed to "fit" the contingency factors as illustrated in Exhibit 10.4. Let us look at the relationship between each contingency factor and organization structure in more detail to see how structure should be designed.

CONTINGENCY FACTOR: STRATEGIC OBJECTIVES

In Chapter 7, we discussed several strategies that business firms can adopt. Two strategies proposed by Porter are differentiation and cost leadership.[15] With a differentiation strategy, the organization attempts to develop innovative products unique to the market. With a cost leadership strategy, the organization strives for internal efficiency. The strategies of cost leadership versus differentiation typically require different structural approaches, so managers try to pick strategies and structures that are congruent.

Exhibit 10.5 shows a simplified continuum that illustrates how structural approaches are associated with strategic objectives. The pure functional structure is appropriate for achieving internal efficiency goals. The functional structure uses task specialization and a strict chain of command to gain efficient use of scarce resources, but it does not enable the organization to be flexible or innovative. In contrast, the team structure described in Chapter 9 is appropriate when the primary goal is innovation and flexibility. Each team is small, able to be responsive, and has the people and resources necessary for performing its task. Team structure enables organizations to differentiate themselves and respond quickly to the demands of a shifting environment but at the expense of efficient resource use. Changing strategy and environmental conditions also shape structure in government organizations, as described in the Focus on Not-for-Profit Organizations box.

Exhibit 10.5 also illustrates how the other forms of structure described in Chapter 9—decentralized with lateral coordination, matrix, and divisional—represent intermediate steps on the organization's path to efficiency and/or innovation. The functional structure with lateral teams and integrating managers provides greater coordination and flexibility than the pure functional structure. The matrix structure uses two chains of command, a functional hierarchy to promote efficiency and a product hierarchy to promote innovation and coordination. The divisional structure promotes differentiation because each division can focus on specific products and customers, although divisions tend to be larger and less flexible than small teams. Exhibit 10.5 does not include all possible structures, but it illustrates how structures can be used to facilitate the strategic objectives of cost leadership or differentiation. For example, Polaroid changed its structure as it changed its strategy.

 POLAROID

Polaroid president I. M. Booth used a scale similar to the one in Exhibit 10.5 to describe his efforts to tear down internal barriers, decentralize decisions, and achieve coordination across functional departments. He defined a structural scale of 1 to 10. A 10 is a structure made up of autonomous teams, each with its own marketing, engineering, and management people. A 1 is a totally functional structure, with a single manufacturing division for the whole company, a single marketing division, and so on. Booth claims that Polaroid was a 1 for many years. Its departments were uncoordinated, and little things were being neglected. Booth's goal was to break up Polaroid's functional structure by creating separate divisions for three businesses: magnetics, consumer products, and industrial photography products. Booth felt that the right amount of flexibility and innovation would put Polaroid at a 6 or 7 on the structural scale, and he planned to continue pushing until it neared the high end of the scale.[16] ■

The vertical alignment of these Marines symbolizes the *mechanistic structure* that typifies military organizations. Military organizations emphasize vertical control. Tasks are broken into narrow, clearly defined jobs. Many rules exist, and the hierarchy of authority is a major form of control. Military organizations need a mechanistic structure because their mission is relatively stable, and they must have employee compliance when called into action.

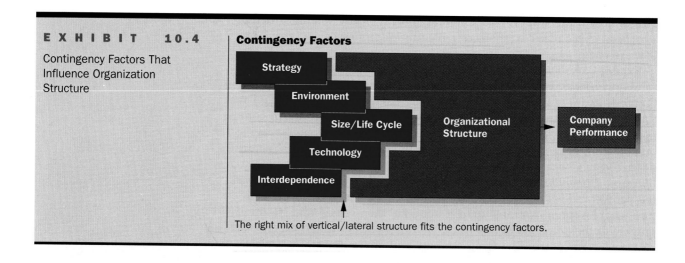

EXHIBIT 10.4

Contingency Factors That Influence Organization Structure

Contingency Factors

Strategy

Environment

Size/Life Cycle

Technology

Interdependence

Organizational Structure → Company Performance

The right mix of vertical/lateral structure fits the contingency factors.

CONTINGENCY FACTOR: THE ENVIRONMENT

In Chapter 4, we discussed the nature of environmental uncertainty. Environmental uncertainty means that decision makers have difficulty acquiring good information and predicting external changes. Uncertainty occurs when the external environment is rapidly changing and complex. An uncertain environment causes three things to happen within an organization.

1 *Increased differences occur among departments.* In an uncertain environment, each major department—marketing, manufacturing, research and development—focuses on the task and environmental sectors for which it is responsible and hence distinguishes itself from the others with respect to goals, task orientation, and time

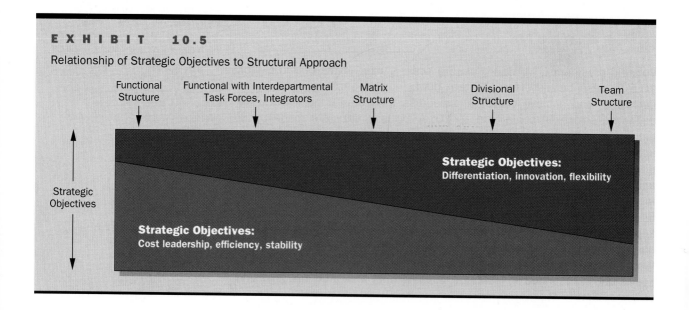

EXHIBIT 10.5

Relationship of Strategic Objectives to Structural Approach

Functional Structure

Functional with Interdepartmental Task Forces, Integrators

Matrix Structure

Divisional Structure

Team Structure

Strategic Objectives

Strategic Objectives:
Differentiation, innovation, flexibility

Strategic Objectives:
Cost leadership, efficiency, stability

The ongoing fiscal crisis facing most state and local governments has created urgency to do more with less. Politicians are desperate for ways to save money without eliminating vital services.

One solution gaining attention is to reorganize government to make it more like a business. Championed by David Osborne, coauthor of *Reinventing Government*, the new message is that centralized, bureaucratic government is failing. Only through wrenching reorganization can government be more responsive to citizens.

The first step is to decentralize. Rather than having all health employees in one hospital, or all public works employees in one building, as in a traditional functional structure, decentralization enables the creation of small divisions to provide services to local areas. Florida is planning to break up that state's health agency into 15 districts, reducing headquarters staff as the budget and workers are dispersed locally.

Next, link the organization to the environment and design structure to fit strategy. Schools can be linked to the environment by letting teachers and parents run their own schools and even letting schools compete for students. That will signal which structure and programs are most effective.

The third step is to clarify the strategy and mission and to pay attention to outcomes. Rather than financing schools, welfare departments, and police departments based on personnel estimates that continue to provide money when organizations do poorly, budgets can be allocated based on service levels. A public works organization can develop the strategy to fix 80 percent of deteriorated road surface or achieve 90 percent customer satisfaction. Schools can be financed based on parental satisfaction and graduation rates. Linking employee activity to strategy generates tremendous productivity.

Finally, let independent divisions drive government so that government divisions compete with private companies. The city of Phoenix requires its Public Works Department to bid against private waste removal firms. At first the department lost business, but after trimming its staff and developing a structure to fit a changing competitive environment, it won back the business and Phoenix's waste removal costs have dropped sharply. Massachusetts is privatizing big chunks of state government in the hope of achieving similar gains.

The gospel of effective structural design is being heard in city and state governments all around the United States. Although the federal government may seem immune to these improvements, it may yet yield to new structural efficiencies that mean good business. ∎

SOURCE: Paula Dwyer, "The New Gospel of Good Government," *Business Week*, January 20, 1992, 66–70; and David Osborne, "Government That Means Business," *The New York Times Magazine*, March 1, 1992, 20–28.

horizon.[17] Departments work autonomously. These factors create barriers among departments.

2 *The organization needs increased coordination to keep departments working together.* Additional differences require more emphasis on lateral coordination to link departments together and overcome differences in departmental goals and orientations.

3 *The organization must adapt to change.* The organization must maintain a flexible, responsive posture toward the environment. Changes in products and technology require cooperation among departments, which means additional emphasis on coordination through the use of teams, task forces, and lateral information processing.[18]

The contingency relationship between environmental uncertainty and structural approach is illustrated in Exhibit 10.6. When the external environment is more stable, the organization should have a mechanistic structure that emphasizes vertical control. There is little need for change, flexibility, or intense coordination. The structure can emphasize specialization, centralized decision making, wide spans of control, and low administrative overhead. When environmental uncertainty is high, an organic structure that emphasizes lateral relationships such as teams and task forces is appropriate. Vertical structure characteristics such as specialization, centralization, and formalized procedures should be downplayed. In an uncertain environment, the organization figures things out as it goes along, departments must cooperate, and decisions should be decentralized to the teams and task forces working on specific problems.

When managers use the wrong structure for the environment, reduced performance results. A rigid, mechanistic structure in an uncertain environment prevents the organization from adapting to change. Likewise, a loose, organic structure in a stable environment is inefficient. Too many resources are devoted to meetings and discussions when employees could be more productive focusing on specialized tasks.

Many companies are forced to alter their structures as the environment changes. Consider recent reorganizations at IBM.

 I B M

In the past few years, IBM repeatedly introduced structural changes in an attempt to get back on course. Why? Because IBM, one of the most complex companies in the world, lost sight of customers' changing tastes. Computer users are shifting from big mainframe machines to powerful desktop models, which IBM was late to develop. New technologies eroded IBM's near-monopoly of the 1980s, while its sluggish bureaucracy fell behind in software and microcomputers. The now-famous 1991 tirade

---

E X H I B I T   10.6

Relationship between Environment and Structure

	STRUCTURE	
	Mechanistic	Organic
ENVIRONMENT		
Uncertain (Unstable)	**Incorrect Fit:** Mechanistic structure in uncertain environment Structure too tight	**Correct Fit:** Organic structure in uncertain environment
Certain (Stable)	**Correct Fit:** Mechanistic structure in certain environment	**Incorrect Fit:** Organic structure in certain environment Structure too loose

by CEO John Akers, urging increased sales, flew in the face of market-place reality as mainframe sales continued to slide. A bold move in late 1991 broke the giant into 13 independent units and plans followed in 1992 to further empower the units. Some critics saw these moves as mere window-dressing and claimed Akers' own management appointments proved his continued devotion to mainframes. By January 1993, IBM posted nearly $5 billion in losses, John Akers was on his way out, and Big Blue prepared for yet another structural change. The change came sooner than many expected. On January 25, 1993, Akers announced his resignation.

The highly publicized job of CEO went to Louis Gerstner, Jr., chairman of RJR Nabisco. One of Gerstner's first tasks is to decide what business IBM is in. IBM has watched continued decline of the mainframe, but Gerstner enters the game with no devotion to Big Blue tradition or to the mainframe business. Gerstner must also decide whether to pursue Akers' 1991 structure that included the 13 "Baby Blues." Gerstner, a real "roll-up-his-sleeves kind of guy," shuns centralization in preference to calling the play (strategic direction) and handing off the ball (delegation) to division chiefs.[19] ∎

CONTINGENCY FACTOR: SIZE AND LIFE CYCLE

The organization's **size** is its scope or magnitude and frequently is measured by number of employees. A considerable body of research findings has shown that large organizations are structured differently than small ones. Small organizations are informal, have little division of labor, few rules and regulations, ad hoc budgeting and performance systems, and small professional and clerical support staffs. Large organizations such as IBM necessarily have an extensive division of labor, large professional staffs, numerous rules and regulations, and internal systems for control, rewards, and innovation.[20]

Organizations evolve from small to large by going through stages of a life cycle. Within the **organization life cycle,** organizations follow predictable patterns through major developmental stages that are sequential in nature. This is similar to the product life cycle described in Chapter 7 except that it applies to the organization as a whole. Each stage involves changes in the range of organization activities and overall structure.[21] Every organization progresses through the life cycle at its own pace, but most encounter the four stages defined in Exhibit 10.7: birth, youth, midlife, and maturity.

BIRTH STAGE. In the **birth stage,** the organization is created. The founder is an entrepreneur, who alone or with a handful of employees performs all tasks. The organization is very informal, and tasks are overlapping. There are no professional staff, no rules and regulations, and no internal systems for planning, rewards, or coordination. Decision authority is centralized with the owner. Apple Computer was in the birth stage when it was created by Steven Jobs and Stephen Wozniak in Wozniak's parents' garage. Jobs and Wozniak sold their own belongings to raise money to personally build 200 Apple computers. Kentucky Fried

size

The organization's scope or magnitude, typically measured by number of employees.

organization life cycle

The organization's evolution through major developmental stages.

birth stage

The phase of the organization life cycle in which the company is created.

EXHIBIT   10.7

Structural Characteristics during Organization Life Cycle Stages

	Birth Stage	Youth Stage	Midlife Stage	Maturity Stage
Size	Small	Medium	Large	Very large
Bureaucracy	Nonbureaucratic	Prebureaucratic	Bureaucratic	Very bureaucratic
Division of labor	Overlapping tasks	Some departments	Many departments, well-defined tasks, organization chart	Extensive—small jobs, written job descriptions
Centralization	One-person rule	Top leaders rule	Decentralization to department heads	Enforced decentralization, top management overloaded
Formalization	No written rules	Few rules	Policy and procedures manuals	Extensive—most activities covered by written manuals
Administrative intensity	Secretary, no professional staff	Increasing clerical and maintenance, little professional staff	Increasing professional support staff	Large—multiple professional and clerical staff departments
Internal systems (information, budget, planning, performance)	Nonexistent	Crude budget and information system	Control systems in place—budget, performance, operational reports	Extensive—planning, financial, and personnel systems added
Lateral teams, task forces for coordination	None	Top leaders only	Some use of integrators and task forces	Frequent at lower levels to break down barriers of bureaucracy

SOURCE: Based on Robert E. Quinn and Kim Cameron, "Organizational Life Cycles and Some Shifting Criteria of Effectiveness: Some Preliminary Evidence," *Management Science* 29 (1983), 31–51; Richard L. Daft and Richard M. Steers, *Organizations: A Micro/Macro Approach* (Glenview, Ill.: Scott, Foresman, 1986).

Chicken was in the birth stage when Colonel Harlan Sanders was running a combination gas station/restaurant in Corbin, Kentucky, before the popularity of his restaurant began to spread.

youth stage

The phase of the organization life cycle in which the organization is growing rapidly and has a product enjoying some marketplace success.

YOUTH STAGE.   In the **youth stage,** the organization has more employees and a product that is succeeding in the marketplace. The organization is growing rapidly. The owner no longer has sole possession. A few trusted colleagues share in the decision making, although control is still relatively centralized. A division of labor is emerging, with some designation of task responsibility to newly created departments. Internal systems remain informal. A few formal rules and policies appear, and there are few professional and administrative personnel. Apple Computer was in the youth stage during the years of rapid growth from 1978 to 1981, when the major product line was established and over 2,000 dealers signed on to sell Apple computers. Kentucky Fried Chicken was in the youth stage when Colonel Sanders convinced over 400 franchises in the United States and Canada to use his original recipe. Although both organizations were growing rapidly, they were still being run in a very informal fashion.

MIDLIFE STAGE. By the **midlife stage,** the organization has prospered and grown quite large. At this point, the organization begins to look like a more formalized bureaucracy. An extensive division of labor appears, with statements of policies and responsibilities. Rules, regulations, and job descriptions are used to direct employee activities. Professional and clerical staff are hired to undertake specialized activities in support of manufacturing and marketing. Reward, budget, and accounting control systems are put in place. Top management decentralizes many responsibilities to functional departments, but flexibility and innovation may decline. Apple Computer is now well into the midlife stage because it has adopted a host of procedures, internal systems, and staff departments to provide greater control over the organization. Kentucky Fried Chicken moved into the midlife stage when Colonel Sanders sold his company to John Y. Brown, who took the company through a national promotion and building campaign.

> **midlife stage**
> The phase of the organization life cycle in which the firm has reached prosperity and grown substantially large.

MATURITY STAGE. In the **maturity stage,** the organization is large and mechanistic—indeed, the vertical structure often becomes too strong. Budgets, control systems, rules, policies, large staffs of engineering, accounting, and finance specialists, and a refined division of labor are in place. Decision making is centralized. At this point, the organization is in danger of stagnation. To offset the rigid vertical hierarchy, inspire innovation, and shrink barriers among departments, the organization may reorganize, as IBM did. To regain flexibility and innovation, managers may decentralize and create teams, task forces, and integrator positions. This is especially true for such mature organizations as Procter & Gamble, Sears, Westinghouse, Deere, and General Motors, which have experienced major changes in the external environment and found that the mature vertical structure inhibited flexible responses. Some companies decide to downsize as a way to revitalize, as described in the Manager's Shoptalk box.

> **maturity stage**
> The phase of the organization life cycle in which the organization has become exceedingly large and mechanistic.

MOVING THROUGH THE LIFE CYCLE. Organizations do not progress through the four life cycle stages in a logical, orderly fashion. Stages may lead or lag in a given organization. The transition from one stage to the next is difficult and often promotes crises. Employees who were present at the organization's birth often long for the informal atmosphere and resist the formalized procedures, departmentalization, and staff departments required in maturing organizations. Organizations that prematurely emphasize a rigid vertical structure or that stay informal during later stages of the life cycle have the wrong structure for their situation. Performance suffers. The failure of People's Express airline occurred because the firm never grew up. Despite its being the fifth largest airline, top management ran it informally without a strong vertical structure. The structure fit neither People's Express' size nor life cycle stage.

RESTRUCTURING BY DOWNSIZING

When the corporate heat is on, the white collar crowd begins to sweat and to listen for the "D" word—downsizing. Defined as the planned elimination of positions (the headcount), jobs (groups of positions), functions, hierarchical levels, or units, downsizing in the 1990s has proven to be especially targeted toward middle management. Although middle management comprises only five to eight percent of the work force, it suffered a whopping seventeen percent of dismissals between 1989 and 1991. Thirty-six percent of unemployed Americans in 1992 were formerly white collar workers.

Generally viewed as a sure-fire remedy to mounting debt and declining earnings, downsizing spread rapidly. By 1992, elimination of workers began sounding like battlefield casualty lists—IBM, 40,000; General Motors, 75,000; the U.S. Postal Service, 30,000; TRW, Inc., 10,000. Similar statistics poured in from foreign competitors—France's Group Bull, 8,000 and Siemens Nixdorf, 6,000.

Benefits of the "get lean and mean" strategy include reduced overhead, increased productivity, reduced bureaucracy, and improved communications and decision making. However, the down side of downsizing is that it tends to become a never-ending pattern, weaving its way into the corporate culture and negatively affecting worker morale, as companies such as IBM, Kodak, and Xerox undertake repeated restructuring measures. Even workers who escape the job cuts often distrust management and suffer increased job stress and a malady known as "survivors' syndrome."

In order to succeed, downsizing must be viewed as an aggressive strategy with both short-term and long-term goals. Although implemented from the top, management should solicit the recommendations of lower-level employees in job and task analysis and identifying areas of redundancy, inefficiency, and excess cost, in order to make informed decisions. Management should also pay attention to the transition of employees who lose their jobs (through retraining, assistance with job searches, and family counseling), as well as to the survivors (through increased information and training).

By viewing downsizing as a process of continuous improvement, corporations can avoid the "quick fix" merry-go-round. ■

SOURCE: Wayne F. Cascio, "Downsizing: What Do We Know? What Have We Learned?" *Academy of Management Executive*, 1993, vol. 7, no. 1, 95–103; and John W. Verity, "Deconstructing the Computer Industry," *Business Week*, November 23, 1992, 90–100.

CONTINGENCY FACTOR: MANUFACTURING AND SERVICE TECHNOLOGIES

technology

The knowledge, tools, techniques, and activities used to transform the organization's inputs into outputs.

Technology includes the knowledge, tools, techniques, and activities used to transform organizational inputs into outputs.[22] Technology includes machinery, employee skills, and work procedures. A useful way to think about technology is as "work flow." The production work flow may be to produce steel castings, television programs, or computer software.

Production technology is significant because it has direct influence on the organization structure. Structure must be designed to fit the technology as well as to accommodate the external environment and organization size. Technologies vary between manufacturing and service organizations. In the following paragraphs, we discuss each characteristic of technology and the structure that best fits it.

WOODWARD'S MANUFACTURING TECHNOLOGY.   The most influential research into the relationship between manufacturing technology

Century-old General Electric is an example of a company that has reached the *maturity stage* in both size and life cycle. In its efforts to stay young, flexible, and efficient, GE implemented a transformation of the company through a program called Work-Out. The new strategy calls for a reduction in management layers and horizontal barriers as well as functional boundaries. The goal is to mine GE's mother lode of human resources as a vast laboratory of ideas, innovation, experience, and technological know-how. Employees in GE Medical Systems, pictured here, are developing global methods of compressing cycle time and advancing technology as part of the Work-Out revitalization process.

and organization structure was conducted by Joan Woodward, a British industrial sociologist.[23] She gathered data from 100 British firms to determine whether basic structural characteristics, such as administrative overhead, span of control, centralization, and formalization, were different across firms. She found that manufacturing firms could be categorized according to three basic types of work flow technology:

1 *Small batch and unit production.* **Small batch production** firms produce goods in batches of one or a few products designed to customer specification. Each customer orders a unique product. This technology also is used to make large, one-of-a-kind products, such as computer-controlled machines. Small batch manufacturing is close to traditional skilled-craft work, because human beings are a large part of the process; they run machines to make the product. Examples of items produced through small batch manufacturing include custom clothing, special-order machine tools, space capsules, satellites, and submarines.

small batch production

A type of technology that involves the production of goods in batches of one or a few products designed to customer specifications.

2 *Large batch and mass production.* **Mass production** technology is distinguished by standardized production runs. A large volume of products is produced, and all customers receive the same product. Standard products go into inventory for sale as customers need them. This technology makes greater use of machines than does small batch production. Machines are designed to do most of the physical work, and employees complement the machinery. Examples of mass production are automobile assembly lines and the large batch techniques used to produce Macintosh computers, tobacco products, and textiles.

mass production

A type of technology characterized by the production of a large volume of products with the same specifications.

3 *Continuous process production.* In **continuous process production,** the entire work flow is mechanized. This is the most sophisticated and complex form of production technology. Because the process runs continuously, there is no starting and stopping. Human operators are not part of actual production because machinery does all of the

continuous process production

A type of technology involving mechanization of the entire work flow and nonstop production.

work. Human operators simply read dials, fix machines that break down, and manage the production process. Examples of continuous process technologies are chemical plants, distilleries, petroleum refineries, and nuclear power plants.

The difference among the three manufacturing technologies is called technical complexity. **Technical complexity** means the degree to which machinery is involved in the production to the exclusion of people. With a complex technology, employees are hardly needed except to monitor the machines.

technical complexity

The degree to which complex machinery is involved in the production process to the exclusion of people.

The structural characteristics associated with each type of manufacturing technology are illustrated in Exhibit 10.8. Note that formalization and centralization are high for mass production technology and low for continuous process. Unlike small batch and continuous process, standardized mass production machinery requires centralized decision making and well-defined rules and procedures. The administrative ratio and the percentage of indirect labor required also increase with technological complexity. Because the production process is nonroutine, closer supervision is needed. More indirect labor in the form of maintenance people is required because of the machinery's complexity; thus, the indirect–direct labor ratio is high. Span of control for first-line supervisors is greatest for mass production. On an assembly line, jobs are so routinized that a supervisor can handle an average of 48 employees. The number of employees per supervisor in small batch and continuous process production is lower because closer supervision is needed. Overall, small batch and continuous process firms have organic structures, and mass production firms have mechanistic structures.

The important conclusion about manufacturing technology was described by Woodward as follows: "Different technologies impose different kinds of demands on individuals and organizations, and these demands have to be met through an appropriate structure."[24] Woodward found that the relationship between structure and technology was directly related to company performance. Low-performing firms tended

---

EXHIBIT   10.8

Relationship between Manufacturing Technology and Organization Structure

SOURCE: Based on Joan Woodward, *Industrial Organizations: Theory and Practice* (London: Oxford University Press, 1965).

	Manufacturing Technology		
	Small Batch	Mass Production	Continuous Process
Technical complexity of production technology	Low	Medium	High
Organization structure:			
Formalization	Low	High	Low
Centralization	Low	High	Low
Top administrator ratio	Low	Medium	High
Indirect–direct labor ratio	1/9	1/4	1/1
Supervisor span of control	23	48	15
Communication:			
Written (vertical)	Low	High	Low
Verbal (lateral)	High	Low	High
Overall structure	Organic	Mechanistic	Organic

The *flexible manufacturing system* (FMS) at Toshiba enables employees to synchronize production to meet changing customer demands. For example, these workers run laptop and desktop computers on one line. Production-line screens link the factory to offices and to engineering to provide just-in-time inventory information and manufacturing instructions for the various products. This technology is typically associated with a team-oriented, organic approach to structure.

to deviate from the preferred structural form, often adopting a structure appropriate for another type of technology. High-performing organizations had characteristics very similar to those listed in Exhibit 10.8.

FLEXIBLE MANUFACTURING.   The most recent development in manufacturing technology is called **flexible manufacturing,** which uses computers to automate and integrate manufacturing such components as robots, machines, product design, and engineering analysis. Companies such as Deere, General Motors, Intel, and Illinois Tool Works use flexible manufacturing in a single manufacturing plant to do small batch and mass production operations *at the same time.* Bar codes enable machines to make instantaneous changes—such as putting a larger screw in a different location—as different batches flow down the automated assembly line. Flexible manufacturing is considered to be at a higher level of technical complexity than the three manufacturing technologies studied by Woodward. The structures associated with the new technology tend to have few rules, decentralization, a small ratio of administrators to workers, face-to-face lateral communication, and a team-oriented, organic approach.[25]

flexible manufacturing

A manufacturing technology using computers to automate and integrate manufacturing components such as robots, machines, product design, and engineering analysis.

SERVICE TECHNOLOGY.   Service organizations are becoming increasingly important in North America. Since 1982, more employees have been employed in service organizations than in manufacturing organizations. Thus, new research has been undertaken to understand the structural characteristics of service organizations. **Service technology** can be defined as follows:

service technology

Technology characterized by intangible outputs and direct contact between employees and customers.

1 *Intangible output.* The output of a service firm is intangible. Services are perishable and, unlike physical products, cannot be stored in inventory. The service is either consumed immediately or lost forever. Manufactured products are produced at one point in time and can be stored until sold at another time.

2 *Direct contact with customers.* Customers and employees interact directly to provide and purchase the service. Production and consumption are simultaneous. Service firm employees have direct contact with customers. In a manufacturing firm, technical employees are separated from customers, and hence no direct interactions occur.[26]

The output of service organizations is frequently intangible; that of manufacturing organizations is tangible. Examples of service firms include consulting companies, law firms, brokerage houses, airlines, hotels, advertising firms, public relations firms, amusement parks, and educational organizations. Service technology also characterizes many departments in large corporations, even manufacturing firms. In a manufacturing organization such as Ford Motor Company, the legal, personnel, finance, and market research departments provide service. Thus, the structure and design of each of these departments reflect its own service technology rather than the manufacturing plant's technology. Service technology concepts therefore can be used to structure both service organizations and the many large service departments within manufacturing organizations.

A useful way of characterizing service technology is the extent to which it is routine versus nonroutine.[27] The routine-nonroutine distinction can be used to describe differences across organizational technologies as well as those among various departments within a single organization. A **routine service technology** means that the work can be reduced to a series of explicit steps and employees can follow an objective procedure for serving customers and solving problems. The number of problems is low. There is little task variety, because the service is provided in a repetitive manner. Day-to-day job requirements are similar, such as those for sales clerks in a discount store. In service organizations, routine technologies are used when services are not labor intensive because physical facilities standardize the services. Examples of providers of routine services are sanitation firms, hotels, airlines, and ferry boats.

A **nonroutine service technology** means that new problems are encountered every day and variety is high. Moreover, when problems arise there is no specific procedure for telling people what to do. Solutions depend on the individual's education, experience, and trial-and-error processes. An example is a lawyer for the defense in a trial. Nonroutine services typically are labor intensive and provided entirely by individuals. For example, a tax accountant provides a complete tax service for a customer. Nonroutine services are provided by doctors, lawyers, architects, and accountants.[28]

Selected characteristics of organization structure for service technologies are illustrated in Exhibit 10.9. The nonroutine, people-intensive services tend to be more organic.[29] They are informal and decentralized. These services are also dispersed; hence, each firm is typically small, as in the case of local video stores or doctors' offices. Services must be located close to geographically dispersed customers. Routine services, in comparison, involve a more mechanistic structure and fewer people.

routine service technology

Service technology in which work can be broken down into explicit steps and employees can follow objective procedures for serving customers and solving problems.

nonroutine service technology

Service technology in which there are no specific procedures for directing employees, problem situations are varied, and employees must rely on personal resources for problem solving.

	Service Technology		EXHIBIT 10.9
	Routine	**Nonroutine**	Relationship between Service Technology and Organization Structure
Labor intensity and complexity of service	Low	High	
Structural characteristics:			
Division of labor	High	Low	
Formalization	High	Low	
Centralization	High	Low	
Administrative ratio	Low	Moderate	
Span of control	High	Moderate	
Employee skill and training	Low	High	
Geographical dispersion	High	Moderate	
Overall structure	Mechanistic	Organic	

Examples include hotels, banks, and auto repair facilities. Formalization and division of labor are greater, and decision making can be centralized. As a general pattern, however, even routine service firms have greater variety in the production process than do assembly line manufacturing technologies, and structures tend to be more organic.

An example of how structure should fit technology in a more routine service firm is Marriott Corporation.

MARRIOTT CORPORATION

Marriott Corporation is now the nation's largest hotel operator, and the president, Bill Marriott, plans to make it even larger. Marriott's success has come from two strategies: Put hotels where the customers are and provide excellent service. Putting hotels where the customers are means building hotels downtown and at airports. Convention centers, such as Atlantic City, are another target. Marriott also searches for new niches. The Courtyard is a new type of garden apartment hotel aimed at the moderate-priced segment of the market. Courtyards are scattered around major metropolitan areas.

At Marriott, the hotel itself is the main service, and a mind-boggling system is used to make the right impression every time. Top managers make no apologies for the tightly centralized system of policies, procedures, and controls for operational details. Room attendants have 66 things to do in cleaning a room, from dusting the tops of pictures (number 7) to keeping the telephone book and Bibles in a neat condition (number 37). Bill Marriott says, "The more the system works like the Army, the better." The cooks have 6,000 recipes available to them, and they are not allowed to deviate. One rule for chefs says, "Deviations from the standard written specifications may not be made without prior approval and written consent of the vice president of food and beverages."

Marriott Corporation plans to add new hotels each year. It routinizes the service and builds luxury into the physical structure to ensure that guests are treated the same way every time. The most recent program

International Technology Corporation (IT), a turnkey environmental services company, provides *nonroutine service technology*. On a project-by-project basis, teams of IT engineers, scientists, technicians, and support personnel provide innovative solutions to complex environmental problems involving hazardous and toxic, chemical, and radioactive materials. Nonroutine services include the predesign field investigation pictured here where samples are collected to provide data that will help form the basis for remedial design work. Through regional offices and laboratories, IT serves a geographically dispersed clientele. Nonroutine service firms like IT typically are decentralized.

is First 10, which focuses on making a lasting impression of great service on customers during the first 10 minutes of their hotel stay. Marriott was rated as one of the five best-managed companies, and Bill Marriott and four executive vice-presidents spend half the year on the road visiting company facilities. The close, personal supervision and careful reading of customer suggestions help Bill Marriott give business travelers the service they expect and deserve.[30] ■

The managers at Marriott designed the structure and procedures to reflect a routine service technology. The many rules and procedures, centralized decision making, and refined division of labor provide a mechanistic structure that is suited to the underlying technology.

CONTINGENCY FACTOR: DEPARTMENTAL INTERDEPENDENCE

interdependence

The extent to which departments depend on each other for resources or materials to accomplish their tasks.

The final characteristic of the organization's situation that influences structure is called interdependence. **Interdependence** means the extent to which departments depend on each other for resources or materials to accomplish their tasks. A low level of interdependence means that departments do their work independently and have little need for interaction, coordination, or exchange of materials. A high level of interdependence means that departments must constantly exchange information and resources. Three types of interdependence that influence organization structure are illustrated in Exhibit 10.10.[31]

POOLED INTERDEPENDENCE. *Pooled interdependence* means that each department is part of the organization and contributes to the common good, but each department is relatively independent because work does not flow between units. Citibank branch banks or Wendy's restaurants are examples of pooled interdependence. They share financial resources from a common pool but do not interact with each other.

SEQUENTIAL INTERDEPENDENCE. *Sequential interdependence* means that parts or outputs of one department become inputs to another department in serial fashion. The first department must perform correctly so that the second department can perform correctly. An example is assembly line technology, such as in the automobile industry. This is greater interdependence than with the pooled type, because departments exchange resources and depend on others to perform well.

RECIPROCAL INTERDEPENDENCE. The highest level is *reciprocal interdependence*, which means that the output of operation A is the input to operation B, and the output of operation B is the input back again to operation A. Departmental outputs influence other departments in reciprocal fashion. For example, hospitals must coordinate services to patients, such as when a patient moves back and forth between the surgery, physical therapy, and X-ray departments.

STRUCTURAL IMPLICATIONS. When interdependence among departments is pooled, coordination is relatively easy. Managers can develop standardized procedures, rules, and regulations that ensure sim-

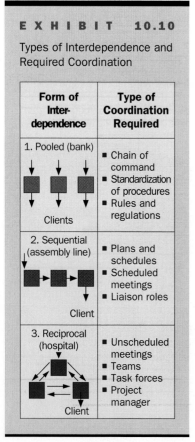

E X H I B I T   10.10

Types of Interdependence and Required Coordination

Form of Inter-dependence	Type of Coordination Required
1. Pooled (bank)	■ Chain of command ■ Standardization of procedures ■ Rules and regulations
2. Sequential (assembly line)	■ Plans and schedules ■ Scheduled meetings ■ Liaison roles
3. Reciprocal (hospital)	■ Unscheduled meetings ■ Teams ■ Task forces ■ Project manager

ilar performance in all branches. For sequential interdependence, coordination is somewhat more difficult, requiring future planning and scheduling so that the flow of outputs and resources is coordinated to the benefit of all departments. Moreover, scheduled meetings and face-to-face discussions are used for day-to-day coordination between departments. Reciprocal interdependence is the most difficult. These departments should be located physically close together in the organization so that communication is facilitated. Structural mechanisms for coordination include teams, task forces, unscheduled meetings, and perhaps an integrating manager to ensure that departments are working out coordination problems on a daily basis.[32]

Within most organizations, interdependence will be high (reciprocal) for some departmental activities and low (pooled) for others. For example, Exhibit 10.11 illustrates how reciprocal interdependence among sets of departments exists for the tasks of product development, product delivery, and customer service. The design and purchasing departments can work independently on many tasks, but for product development, they must be coordinated, perhaps with a team or task force. Purchasing must be coordinated with distribution for the delivery of products. Suppliers and customers are also a part of the interdependence and in some organizations may be included as part of a team.

When consultants analyzed NCR (formerly National Cash Register Company) to learn why new products were so slow in being developed,

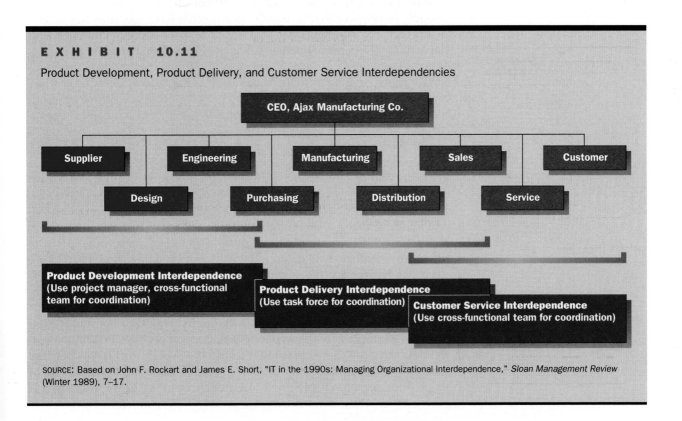

EXHIBIT 10.11

Product Development, Product Delivery, and Customer Service Interdependencies

SOURCE: Based on John F. Rockart and James E. Short, "IT in the 1990s: Managing Organizational Interdependence," *Sloan Management Review* (Winter 1989), 7–17.

they found that the development and marketing of products took place in separate divisions with little communication. NCR broke up its traditional functional structure and created several stand-alone units of about 500 people each. Locating together all the people needed to develop a new product made coordination easier. When an organization has sufficient personnel, stand-alone units may be created; otherwise, coordination is achieved through teams, task forces, and project managers.

SUMMARY AND MANAGEMENT SOLUTION

This chapter introduced a number of important organizing concepts. As organizations grow, they add new departments, functions, and hierarchical levels. A major problem confronting management is how to tie the whole organization together. Structural characteristics such as chain of command, work specialization, and departmentalization are valuable organization concepts but often are not sufficient to coordinate far-flung departments. Lateral coordination mechanisms provide coordination across departments and include information systems, task forces, teams, and integrating managers.

Managers can design organizations to be organic or mechanistic. Mechanistic organizations rely heavily on vertical structure and are characterized by tight control, whereas organic organizations are loosely structured and rely heavily on lateral coordination mechanisms. Contingency factors of strategy, environment, size and life cycle, production technology, and departmental interdependence influence the correct structural approach. When a firm's strategy is to differentiate the firm's product from competitors, a more organic structural approach using teams, decentralization, and perhaps a divisional matrix structure is appropriate. When environmental uncertainty is high, lateral coordination is important and the organization should have an organic structure.

Cincinnati Milacron needed a strategy of innovation in a changing environment. Foreign competitors were producing better plastics machinery faster and at a lower cost. Harold Faig's response was to create a team with people from several departments to facilitate development of a new machine. Employees from purchasing, marketing, inventory, engineering, and manufacturing were brought together and given only nine months to create a machine superior to those of Milacron's foreign competitors. The nine team members broke down the walls between departments, making decisions to produce the best product even when it meant changing old habits. For one thing, the machine was developed using metric measurements to allow globalization. The team built relations with only a few suppliers in return for top-quality parts and delivery schedules, and it even shared design plans with suppliers to help lower costs. In nine months to the day, the president was invited to flip the switch to turn on the new machine, and only a few months later, it was selling at 2.5 times the rate of its predecessor. Now Cincinnati Milacron is breaking down walls everywhere by creating cross-functional teams to develop new machines to replace its current line. The structural changes to enable greater horizontal coordination have made Cincinnati Milacron an industry leader.[33]

Other factors that influence structure are technology, size, and interdependence. For manufacturing firms, small batch, continuous process, and flexible manufacturing technologies tend to be structured organically, whereas a mechanistic structure is appropriate for mass production. Service technologies are people oriented, but services such as those offered by hotels and the transportation industry are considered routine and can be controlled with a mechanistic structure. Nonroutine, people-intensive services tend to be organically structured.

As organizations increase in size, they require greater vertical control. Organizations in the birth and youth stages typically are loosely structured. In the midlife stage, a strong vertical structure emerges. In a mature organization, the vertical structure may be too strong, necessitating the installation of teams, task forces, and other horizontal devices to achieve greater cooperation across departments. Finally, departmental interdependence also determines the form of structure. An organization with a low level of interdependence, such as the pooled type, can be controlled mainly with the vertical chain of command and standardization of procedures, rules, and regulations. When interdependence is high, such as for new-product introductions, then horizontal coordination mechanisms such as unscheduled meetings, teams, and project managers are required, or the organization may place the interdependent groups into separate, self-contained units.

DISCUSSION QUESTIONS

1. Carnival Cruise Lines provides pleasure cruises to the masses. Carnival has several ships and works on high volume/low price rather than offering luxury cruises. Would this be a routine or nonroutine service technology, and what would you predict about the organization structure of a Carnival Cruise ship?

2. Why is structure different depending on whether a firm's strategy is low cost or differentiation?

3. The chapter suggested that structure should be designed to fit strategy. Some theorists argue that strategy should be designed to fit the organization's structure. With which theory do you agree? Explain.

4. Explain the three levels of departmental interdependence and give an example of each.

5. Some experts argue that interdependence within organizations is greater now than 15 years ago because of rapid changes in the global environment. If so, what does this mean for the present structure of organizations compared with that of 15 years ago?

6. What is the difference between a task force and an integrating manager? Which would be more effective in achieving coordination?

7. Discuss why an organization in an uncertain environment requires more horizontal relationships than one in a certain environment.

8. Explain the difference between assembly line and continuous process production. How do these two technologies influence structural characteristics such as indirect–direct labor ratio and span of control?
9. What is the difference between manufacturing and service technology? How would you classify a university, a local discount store, a nursery school? How would you expect the structure of a service organization to differ from that of a manufacturing organization?
10. Flexible manufacturing systems combine elements of both small batch and mass production. What effect might this new form of technology have on organization structure? Explain.

MANAGEMENT IN PRACTICE: EXPERIENTIAL EXERCISE

● **FAMILY BUSINESS**

You are the parent of ten children and have just used your inheritance to acquire a medium-sized pharmaceutical company. Last year's sales were down 18 percent from the previous year. In fact, the last three years have been real losers. You want to clean house of current managers over the next ten years and bring your children into the business. Being a loving parent, you agree to send your children to college to educate each of them in one functional specialty. The ten children are actually five sets of twins exactly one year apart. The first set will begin college this fall, followed by the remaining sets the next four years. The big decision is which specialty each child should study. You want to have the most important functions taken over by your children as soon as possible, so you will ask the older children to study the most important areas.

Your task right now is to rank in order of priority the functions to which your children will be assigned and develop reasons for your ranking.

The ten functions follow:

_____ Distribution
_____ Manufacturing
_____ Market Research
_____ New-Product Development
_____ Personnel
_____ Product Promotion
_____ Quality Assurance
_____ Sales
_____ Legal and Governmental Affairs
_____ Office of the Controller

Analyze your reasons for how functional priority relates to the company's environmental/strategic needs. Now rank the functions as part of a group. Discuss the problem until group members agree on a single ranking. How does the group's reasoning and ranking differ from your original thinking?

CASES FOR ANALYSIS

REPUBLIC NATIONAL BANK

Republic National Bank was located in a well-to-do suburb in southern California. The population grew rapidly to 250,000, and growth stabilized by the late 1980s.

Under the guidance of its founder and president, Richard Johnson, the bank's deposits grew to $15 million during its first 5 years paralleling the rapid growth of the community. The bank's organization structure was informal and included no organizational chart despite having some 30 employees and two branches. Richard Johnson believed in keeping things informal so that employees could enjoy a family atmosphere.

A few years later, the bank was purchased by Ted White. White immediately imposed a traditional management structure. He asked the personnel director to write job descriptions for all positions and to develop an up-to-date organization chart. He stressed centralized decision making and standard procedures. The two branches and the main bank were urged to offer the same services despite their proximity to different customer groups. One branch was in an ethnic community, the other was near a junior college, and the main branch was in a residential area. Vertical communication and "following the rules" were deemed safe, responsible management approaches for a community bank.

This approach worked successfully for 15 years, but major changes in the 1980s caused problems within the bank. The bank's assets had grown to over $500 million. Management trainees had been hired from universities and promoted to managerial positions. The new managers began to propose changes. One manager suggested that the bank establish an advisory board to involve residents in bank decisions and provide bank officials with good information about community needs. Another manager urged the creation of several committees to study the effects of government regulation. One committee could study asset/liability management to help the bank make the transition to variable-rate loans and to explore new investment opportunities. Another could work on cost control and the use of new electronic technology to reduce the cost of fund transfers. Yet another could investigate service pricing and the generation of noninterest income, including fees for returned checks, overdrafts, and checking account services.

Ted White resisted these changes. He did not want to create task forces that would decentralize decision making to a lower level. White believed that banks had to have tight control to ensure depositors' safety. Within a year, three of the new managers quit in frustration. White also noticed that the bank was not growing and even had lost market share to competitors, some of which were newly created banks run in an informal fashion.

● QUESTIONS

1. Was it appropriate to develop a stronger vertical structure as the bank grew larger?
2. What are the advantages and disadvantages of implementing horizontal relationships in the form of task forces? Do you feel the bank should place greater emphasis on horizontal relationships? Why or why not?
3. Would you characterize Republic National Bank's structure as organic or mechanistic? What is the correct structure for the bank's contingency factors of technology, environment, and size/life cycle?

SOURCE: Based on Richard L. Daft and Richard M. Steers, *Organizations: A Micro/Macro Approach* (Glenview, Ill.: Scott, Foresman and Company, 1986), 314–316.

MALARD MANUFACTURING COMPANY

Malard Manufacturing Company produces control valves that regulate flows through natural gas pipelines. Malard has approximately 1,400 employees and has successfully produced a standard line of control valves that are price competitive in the industry. However, whenever the production of a new control valve is required, problems arise. Developments in electronics, metallurgy, and flow control theory require the introduction of new products every year or two. These new products have been associated with interdepartmental conflict and disagreement.

Consider the CV305, which is in process. As usual, the research and development group developed the basic design, and the engineering department converted it into a prototype control valve. Now the materials department must acquire parts for the prototype and make plans for obtaining parts needed for production runs. The production department is to manufacture and assemble the product, and marketing is responsible for sales.

Department heads believe that future work on the CV305 should be done simultaneously instead of sequentially. Marketing wants to provide input to research and development so that the design will meet customer needs. Production insists that the design fit machine limitations and be cost efficient to manufacture—indeed, it wants to speed up development of the final plans so that it can acquire tooling and be ready for standard production. Engineering, on the other hand, wants to slow down development to ensure that specifications are correct and have been thoroughly tested.

All of these controversies with the CV305 exist right now. Department managers are frustrated and becoming uncommunicative. The research and development and engineering departments are keeping their developmental plans secret, causing frustration for the other departments. Moreover, several department managers are new and inexperienced in new-product development. Ms. Crandell, the executive vice-president, likes to keep tight control over the organization. Department managers must check with her before making major decisions. However, with the CV305, she has been unable to keep things running smoothly. The span of control is so large that Crandell has no time to personally shepherd the CV305 through the system.

On November 1, Crandell received a memo from the marketing department head. It said, in part,

The CV305 must go to market immediately. This is urgent. It is needed now because it provides the precision control our competitors' products already have. Three of our salespeople reported that loyal customers are about to place orders with competitors. We can keep this business if we have the CV305 ready for production in 30 days.

● QUESTIONS

1. What is the balance between vertical and horizontal structure in Malard Manufacturing? Is it appropriate that department managers always turn to the executive vice-president for help rather than to one another?
2. If you were Ms. Crandell, how would you resolve this problem? What could you do to facilitate production of the CV305 over the next 30 days?
3. What structural changes would you recommend to prevent these problems in future new-product developments? Would a smaller span of control help? An integrating manager with responsibility for coordinating the CV305? A task force?

REFERENCES

1. Peter Nulty, "The Soul of an Old Machine," *Fortune*, May 21, 1990, 67–72.
2. Richard L. Daft, *Organization Theory and Design*, 4th ed. (St. Paul, Minn.: West, 1992).
3. Bruce Buursma, "Wanted: Romance Executive," *Chicago Tribune*, July 19, 1989.
4. Lee Iacocca with William Novak, *Iacocca: An Autobiography* (New York: Phantom Books, 1984), 152–153.
5. Thomas Moore, "Would You Buy a Car from This Man?" *Fortune*, April 11, 1988, 72–74.
6. William J. Altier, "Task Forces: An Effective Management Tool," *Management Review* (February 1987), 52–57.
7. "Task Forces Tackle Consolidation of Employment Services," *Shawmut News*, Shawmut National Corporation, May 3, 1989, 2.
8. Michael Brody, "Can GM Manage It All?" *Fortune*, July 8, 1985, 22–28.
9. Henry Mintzberg, *The Structure of Organizations* (Englewood Cliffs, N.J.: Prentice-Hall, 1979).
10. Vicki Moss, "BUMP: The Consumer Bank's New Program Helps the Branches Run More Efficiently and Effectively," *Chemical Chronicle*, Chemical Banking Corporation, June–July 1989, 14–15.
11. Paul R. Lawrence and Jay W. Lorsch, "New Managerial Job: The Integrator," *Harvard Business Review* (November–December 1967), 142–151.
12. Ron Winslow, "Utility Cuts Red Tape, Builds Nuclear Plant Almost on Schedule," *The Wall Street Journal*, February 22, 1984, 1, 18.
13. Tom Burns and G. M. Stalker, *The Management of Innovation* (London: Tavistock, 1961).
14. Frank Shipper and Charles C. Manz, "An Alternative Road to Empowerment," *Organizational Dynamics* 20 (Winter 1992), 48–61.
15. Michael E. Porter, *Competitive Strategy* (New York: Free Press, 1980), 36–46.
16. Clem Morgello, "Booth: Creating a New Polaroid," *Dun's Business Month*, August 1985, 51–52.
17. Paul R. Lawrence and Jay W. Lorsch, *Organization and Environment* (Homewood, Ill.: Irwin, 1969).
18. Robert B. Duncan, "Characteristics of Organizational Environments and Perceived Environmental Uncertainty," *Administrative Science Quarterly* 17 (1972), 313–327; W. Alan Randolph and Gregory G. Dess, "The Congruence Perspective of Organization Design: A Conceptual Model and Multivariate

Research Approach," *Academy of Management Review* 9 (1984), 114–127; and Masoud Yasai-Ardekani, "Structural Adaptations to Environments," *Academy of Management Review* 11 (1986) 9–21.

19. David Kirkpatrick, "Breaking Up IBM," *Fortune*, July 27, 1992, 44–55; Catherine Arnst and Joseph Weber, "IBM after Akers," *Business Week*, February 8, 1993, 22–24; Judith H. Dobrzynski, "Commentary: IBM's Board Should Clean Out the Corner Office," *Business Week*, February 1, 1993, 27; and Catherine Arnst, Judith Dobrzynski, and Bart Ziegler, "Faith in a Stranger," *Business Week*, April 5, 1993, 18–21.

20. W. Graham Astley, "Organization Size and Bureaucratic Structure," *Organization Studies* 6 (1985), 201–228; John B. Cullen, Kenneth S. Anderson, and Douglas D. Baker, "Blau's Theory of Structural Differentiation Revisited: A Theory of Structural Change or Scale?" *Academy of Management Journal* 29 (1986), 203–229; and Daft, *Organization Theory and Design*.

21. Robert E. Quinn and Kim Cameron, "Organizational Life Cycles and Shifting Criteria of Effectiveness: Some Preliminary Evidence," *Management Science* 29 (1983) 33–51, and John R. Kimberly, Robert H. Miles, and associates, *The Organizational Life Cycle* (San Francisco: Jossey-Bass, 1980).

22. Denise M. Rousseau and Robert A. Cooke, "Technology and Structure: The Concrete, Abstract, and Activity Systems of Organizations," *Journal of Management* 10 (1984), 345–361; Charles Perrow, "A Framework for the Comparative Analysis of Organizations," *American Sociological Review* 32 (1967), 194–208; and Denise M. Rousseau, "Assessment of Technology in Organizations: Closed versus Open Systems Approaches," *Academy of Management Review* 4 (1979), 531–542.

23. Joan Woodward, *Industrial Organizations: Theory and Practice* (London: Oxford University Press, 1965), and Joan Woodward, *Management and Technology* (London: Her Majesty's Stationery Office, 1958).

24. Woodward, *Industrial Organizations*, vi.

25. Raghavan Parthasarthy and S. Brakash Sethi, "The Impact of Flexible Automation on Business Strategy and Organizational Structure," *Academy of Management Review* 17 (1992), 86–111; Patricia L. Nemetz and Louis W. Fry, "Flexible Manufacturing Organizations: Implementation for Strategy Formulation and Organization Design," *Academy of Management Review* 13 (1988), 627–638; and Paul S. Adler, "Managing Flexible Automation," *California Management Review* (Spring 1988), 34–56.

26. Peter K. Mills and Thomas Kurk, "A Preliminary Investigation into the Influence of Customer-Firm Interface on Information Processing and Task Activity in Service Organizations," *Journal of Management* 12 (1986), 91–104; Peter K. Mills and Dennis J. Moberg, "Perspectives on the Technology of Service Operations," *Academy of Management Review* 7 (1982), 467–478; and Roger W. Schmenner, "How Can Service Businesses Survive and Prosper?" *Sloan Management Review* 27 (Spring 1986), 21–32.

27. Michael Withey, Richard L. Daft, and William C. Cooper, "Measures of Perrow's Work Unit Technology: An Empirical Assessment and a New Scale," *Academy of Management Journal* 25 (1983), 45–63.

28. Schmenner, "How Can Service Businesses Survive?"

29. Richard B. Chase and David A. Tansik, "The Customer Contact Model for Organization Design," *Management Science* 29 (1983), 1037–1050, and Gregory B. Northcraft and Richard B. Chase, "Managing Service Demand at the Point of Delivery," *Academy of Management Review* 10 (1985), 66–75.

30. Maryfran Johnson, "Marriott Rests on RS/6000," *Computerworld*, October 5, 1992, 6, and Thomas Moore, "Marriott Grabs for More Rooms," *Fortune*, October 31, 1983, 107–122.

31. James Thompson, *Organizations in Action* (New York: McGraw-Hill, 1967).

32. Jack K. Ito and Richard B. Peterson, "Effects of Task Difficulty and Interdependence on Information Processing Systems," *Academy of Management Journal* 29 (1986), 139–149, and Andrew H. Van de Ven, Andre Delbecq, and Richard Koenig, "Determinants of Coordination Modes within Organizations," *American Sociological Review* 41 (1976), 322–338.

33. Nulty, "The Soul of an Old Machine."

The wake of Hurricane Andrew was only a prelude to a storm of criticism leveled at the Red Cross, the nation's premiere disaster relief agency. The still unanswered question: could anyone have done better?

Andrew came ashore in south Florida on August 24, 1992, leaving 41 people dead, 250,000 homeless, and $20 billion in property damage. Three days before the storm made landfall, all 42 of Florida's Red Cross chapters were placed on alert and told to be prepared to open shelters and provide services. But no one was certain where the hurricane would hit. "We were as prepared for this as we've ever been," Red Cross disaster specialist Jim Toole said. "The magnitude [was] just ungodly."

Two of the Red Cross' primary missions after a disaster are providing food and shelter for victims. The day the storm struck the agency had 25 mobile feeding units and 1,436 volunteers and paid staff working. By week's end, the number of feeding units had climbed to 69, and staff and volunteers numbered more than 3,100. "We had those 10 kitchens up and serving food within the first 24 hours," Don Jones, Red Cross general manager of disaster services, said. "I certainly don't think our response was slow."

Dade County director of emergency management Kate Hale disagreed, "It was well into the second week before the Red Cross was really providing measurable services to this community."

Critics also charged that the Red Cross mishandled operations at the large supply depot that had been set up at the Palm Beach County Fairgrounds. State emergency managers established the center to receive donated food, clothing, and medicine from around the country, and then coordinate dispersal. There weren't enough people on hand to do the job. "They were literally overwhelmed," said B. T. Kennedy, Palm Beach director of emergency management.

In addition to dealing with pressing emergencies, Red Cross personnel were busy distributing 42,448 comfort kits and making 9,031 disaster welfare inquiries for people in search of relatives or friends, all in an area almost totally lacking phone service. They also issued financial assistance vouchers and provided victim counseling.

Some volunteers from IBM's Boca Raton mobile data systems group lent the Red Cross a big hand in improving communication. Normal phone coverage was erratic and limited; cellular service was slow because so many people were using it. Five days after the storm the IBM team donated 30 IBM PCRadios and the rights to the Ardis network, allowing users to transmit messages and make short file transfers. The network could be left open all day without having to sign on and off, and relief officials could relay information about available supplies directly to their counterparts throughout the disaster area.

Besides the destructive magnitude of Andrew, it's doubtful the timing could have been worse. Two other disasters, Hurricane Hugo and the San Francisco earthquake, dispersed volunteer ranks around the country and depleted resources. Red Cross disaster services, which rely almost entirely on donations, faced a $40 million overrun. Many have blamed bureaucratic inertia for slowing the response to the emergency.

Plans for future catastrophic relief operations will no doubt incorporate lessons learned from the south Florida effort. Red Cross director Elizabeth Dole undertook an overhaul of disaster services when she became president of the agency in 1991. This $12 million revitalization increased volunteer strength twofold. A college for training workers in disaster relief was created, along with yearly exercises conducted nationwide to test plans and systems. A 24-hour operations center to direct Red Cross units was also set up. Perhaps implementation procedures broke down during Andrew; perhaps they were beyond human capability.

After picking up most of the pieces, Florida officials from the affected areas generally agreed that only the military has sufficient resources to cope with a natural disaster like Andrew.

The last of the south Florida Red Cross service centers closed in early January 1993. In all, they helped 60,000 families and spent upwards of $63 million. The agency demonstrated the ability to perform innumerable services well, but perhaps not in as timely a manner as some would like.

● QUESTIONS

1. Evaluate vertical hierarchical delegation and communication by Red Cross management, and critique implementation by staff and volunteers in south Florida. What key shortfalls occurred?

2. What contingencies could have been better anticipated? How could services have been better coordinated? Was departmental interdependence what it should have been?

3. To what degree did the inherent uncertainties contribute to breakdowns in providing relief services?

4. Are disaster relief operations simply beyond the pale with respect to structuring an organization capable of coping?

5. What would you have done differently had you been in charge of the Red Cross agency during Hurricane Andrew?

INNOVATION AND CHANGE  CHAPTER

LEARNING OBJECTIVES

After studying this chapter, you should be able to

■ Define organizational change and explain the forces for change.

■ Describe the sequence of four change activities that must be performed in order for change to be successful.

■ Explain the techniques managers can use to facilitate the initiation of change in organizations, including idea champions and new-venture teams.

■ Define sources of resistance to change.

■ Explain force field analysis and other implementation tactics that can be used to overcome resistance to change.

■ Explain the difference among technology, product, structure, and culture/people changes.

■ Explain the change process—bottom up, top down, horizontal—associated with each type of change.

■ Define organizational development and organizational revitalization.

Several years ago, top managers at Maryland-based Preston Trucking Company started to fear for the future of their organization. Deregulation was making the trucking industry more competitive, and a survey of employees uncovered 40 negative comments for every positive comment about the company. Rather than help the company become more efficient, employees were unhappy and often hostile. One  truck driver stayed parked on a customer's lot for two hours to show Preston managers who ran the company. Top managers at Preston were frustrated, because creating a culture that fostered innovation and commitment seemed so difficult.[1] ■ If you were a manager at Preston Trucking Company, how would you engage employees in innovative behavior to help the company be more efficient? How would you improve employee attitudes?

Managers at Preston are not alone. Every organization experiences stress and difficulty in coping with change. Innovation from within is widely recognized as one of the critical problems facing business today in the United States and Canada. To be successful, organizations must embrace many types of change. Businesses must develop improved production technologies, create new products desired in the marketplace, implement new administrative systems, and upgrade employees' skills. Companies such as Westinghouse, Intel, Black & Decker, Herman Miller, and Merck implement all of these changes and more.

How important is organizational change? Consider this: The parents of today's college students grew up without cable television, voice mail, stain-resistant carpet, personal computers, VCRs, electronic games, CDs, cellular phones, video stores, or laser checkout systems in supermarkets. Companies that produce the new products have prospered, but many companies caught with outdated products and technologies have failed. Organizations that change and innovate successfully, such as General Electric, Hewlett-Packard, Raychem, 3M, and Frito-Lay, are both profitable and admired.

organizational change

The adoption of a new idea or behavior by an organization.

Organizational change is defined as the adoption of a new idea or behavior by an organization.[2] In this chapter, we will look at how organizations can be designed to respond to the environment through internal innovation and change. First we will examine the basic forces for organizational change. Then we will look closely at how managers facilitate two change requirements: initiation and implementation. Finally, we will discuss the four major types of change—technology, new product, structure, and culture/people—and how the organization can be designed to facilitate each.

● MANAGING ORGANIZATIONAL CHANGE

Change can be managed. By observing external trends, patterns, and needs, managers use planned change to help the organization adapt to external problems and opportunities.[3] When organizations are caught flat-footed, failing to anticipate or respond to new needs, management is at fault.

An overall model for planned change is presented in Exhibit 11.1. Four events make up the change sequence: (1) internal and external forces for change exist; (2) organization managers monitor these forces and become aware of a need for change; (3) the perceived need triggers the initiation of change, which (4) is then implemented. How each of these activities is handled depends on the organization and managers' styles.

We now turn to a brief discussion of the specific activities associated with the first two events—forces for change and the perceived need for the organization to respond.

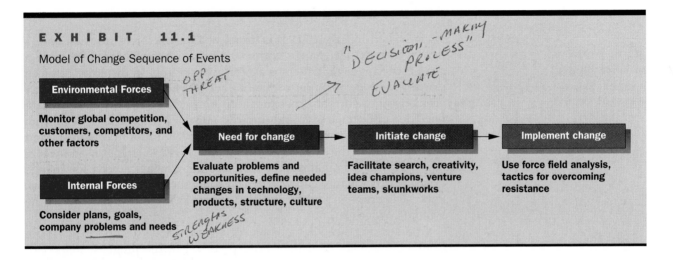

EXHIBIT 11.1

Model of Change Sequence of Events

[handwritten annotations: "DECISION-MAKING PROCESS", "EVALUATE", "OPP? THREAT"]

Environmental Forces

Monitor global competition, customers, competitors, and other factors

Internal Forces

Consider plans, goals, company problems and needs *[handwritten: STRENGTHS, WEAKNESS]*

Need for change

Evaluate problems and opportunities, define needed changes in technology, products, structure, culture

Initiate change

Facilitate search, creativity, idea champions, venture teams, skunkworks

Implement change

Use force field analysis, tactics for overcoming resistance

FORCES FOR CHANGE

Forces for organizational change exist both in the external environment and within the organization.

ENVIRONMENTAL FORCES. As described in Chapters 3 and 4, external forces originate in all environmental sectors, including customers, competitors, technology, economic forces, and the international arena. For example, many North American companies have been blindsided by global competition. Consider General Electric, which built a new factory to produce microwave ovens. As GE's plans were being made, Yun Soo Chu was working 80 hours per week for Samsung in Korea to perfect a microwave oven. About the time the GE plant came on stream, Samsung started exporting thousands of microwaves to the United States at one-third the cost of GE microwaves. Today, Samsung has 25 percent of the U.S. market, and GE is one of its best customers. GE closed its microwave plant, preferring to buy the cheaper Samsung ovens to sell under the GE label.[4] After three engineers started Ensoniq Corporation to produce home computers, they experienced an external force of low consumer demand and switched product lines to electronic keyboards. Using innovative technologies, Ensoniq's founders produced an affordable Mirage keyboard, enabling people with various musical talents as well as the untalented to make music. Ensoniq responded to other environmental needs by producing the Sound Selector hearing aid, which is programmable to meet the particular needs of each individual.[5]

INTERNAL FORCES. Internal forces for change arise from internal activities and decisions. If top managers select a goal of rapid company growth, internal actions will have to be changed to meet that growth. New departments or technologies will be created. General Motors' senior management, frustrated by poor internal efficiency, designed the Saturn manufacturing plant to solve this internal need. Demands by employees, labor unions, and production inefficiencies can all generate a force to which management must respond with change.

As it entered the 1990s, James River Corporation, a marketer and manufacturer of consumer products, food and consumer packaging, and communications paper products, responded to both external and internal *forces for change*. Economic conditions led James River to reduce cost and energy requirements while improving product quality. James River also renewed its commitment to the growing concern for the nation's solid waste volume. In response to the environment, James River implemented a program of recycling, waste and raw materials reduction, and the reduction of product volume and weight. Its much-heralded QUILT-RAP™ sandwich wrap, shown here, replaces fast-food foam clamshell packages with environmentally sound packaging of low weight, volume, and cost.

NEED FOR CHANGE

As indicated in Exhibit 11.1, external or internal forces translate into a perceived need for change within the organization.[6] Managers sense a need for change when there is a **performance gap**—a disparity between existing and desired performance levels. The performance gap may occur because current procedures are not up to standard or because a new idea or technology could improve current performance. Recall from Chapter 7 that management's responsibility is to monitor threats and opportunities in the external environment as well as strengths and weaknesses within the organization to determine whether a need for change exists. A performance gap was perceived by the chief of the Takoma Park Police Department, and he initiated many changes as described in the Winning Moves box.

One striking need for change occurred when executives at Apple Computer realized that they needed to sell in the toughest market of

performance gap

A disparity between existing and desired performance levels.

WINNING moves   **NOT-FOR-PROFIT INNOVATION IN THE TAKOMA PARK POLICE DEPARTMENT**

When the mostly white, middle-class suburb of Takoma Park, Maryland, named A. Tony Fisher, a black man, as police chief, the community considered the appointment itself a dramatic change. It quickly became clear that dramatic change within the police force was just beginning, because Chief Fisher proved a master of innovation.

Abandoning the traditional "us versus them" paramilitary style so often associated with police-community relations, Fisher initiated COP—community oriented policing. Based on the belief that both officers and citizens must respond to each other as individuals, the program establishes police-community partnerships to deal with complex problems. As Chief Fisher

sees it, cold, impersonal "slap on the cuffs, book 'em, and write a report" methods foster only negative relationships. Fisher's critics question the implementation of a "touchy-feely" police style. Is it necessary, they ask, that citizens "like" the officers?

Fisher remains committed to his program, although he makes frequent adjustments and is willing to abandon anything that doesn't work. His programs stress innovative community relations. For example, officer continuing-education programs stress "soft skills" such as persuasion and reasoning in addition to traditional police techniques. Crime prevention programs, press accessibility, and police meetings with neighbor-hood groups and merchants contribute to a climate of cooperation.

Officers are encouraged to leave their vehicles and use foot patrols. The use of unarmed traffic enforce-

ment assistants relieves the officers of tedious, time-consuming chores. In a much-appreciated program, crime victims are no longer ignored but receive regular reports on the status of investigations.

The jury on COP and similar community-based programs is still out. However, in reaction to the failed policies spotlighted by recent violence in Los Angeles, Miami, and other U.S. cities, more and more police departments are innovating with some form of community-based action.

The days of "Dragnet's" Joe Friday may soon give way to the days of Takoma Park's Tony Fisher. ∎

SOURCE: Joseph N. Boyce, "New Attitude: Softer Style of Policing Takes Hold in Cities Like Takoma Park, Maryland," *The Wall Street Journal*, August 5, 1992, A1, A6.

all—Japan's consumer-electronics fortress. In response to this need, Apple has innovated new methods (hiring local management, listing itself on the Japanese stock market), product lines (CD-ROM players and personal digital assistants), and community activism (sponsoring the 1990 Janet Jackson Tokyo concert and the 1992 Japanese Ladies Pro Golf Tournament). Apple not only has penetrated the Japanese fortress but also has achieved a major foothold to become one of the best-selling brands in Japan.[7]

Managers in every company must be alert to problems and opportunities, because the perceived need for change is what sets the stage for subsequent actions that create a new product or technology. Big problems are easy to spot. Sensitive monitoring systems are needed to detect gradual changes that can fool managers into thinking their company is doing fine. An organization may be in greater danger when the environment changes slowly, because managers may fail to trigger an organizational response. Failing to use planned change to meet small needs can place the organization in hot water, as illustrated in the following passage:

> When frogs are placed in a boiling pail of water, they jump out—they don't want to boil to death. However, when frogs are placed in a cold pail of water, and the pail is placed on a stove with the heat turned very low, over time the frogs will boil to death.[8]

● INITIATING CHANGE

After the need for change has been perceived, the next part of the change process is initiating change, a truly critical aspect of change management. This is where the ideas that solve perceived needs are developed. Responses that an organization can make are to search for or create a change to adopt.

SEARCH

Search is the process of learning about current developments inside or outside the organization that can be used to meet the perceived need for change. Search typically uncovers existing knowledge that can be applied or adopted within the organization. Managers talk to friends and colleagues, read professional reports, or hire consultants to learn about ideas used elsewhere. For example, an internal consulting program was developed for the Office of Employee Relations for New York State, creating teams of 10 to 20 managers from a cross section of agencies to provide information to managers experiencing problems. The consulting team provided a quick way for managers to search out new ideas used in other departments.

Many needs, however, cannot be resolved through existing knowledge but require that the organization develop a new response. Initiating a new response means that managers must design the organization so as to facilitate creativity of both individuals and departments, encourage innovative people to initiate new ideas, or create new-venture

search

The process of learning about current developments inside or outside the organization that can be used to meet a perceived need for change.

departments. These techniques have been adopted by such corporations as GE and Apple with great success.

CREATIVITY

creativity

The development of novel solutions to perceived organizational problems.

Creativity is the development of novel solutions to perceived problems.[9] Creative individuals develop ideas that can be adopted by the organization. People noted for their creativity include Edwin Land, who invented the Polaroid camera; Frederick Smith, who came up with the idea for Federal Express's overnight delivery service during an undergraduate class at Yale; and Swiss engineer George de Mestral, who created Velcro after noticing the tiny hooks on the burrs caught on his wool socks. Each of these people saw unique and creative opportunities in a familiar situation.

One test of creativity is to imagine a block of ice sitting on your desk. What use could you make of it? A creative person might see that it could be used to quench someone's thirst, reduce a patient's fever, crack a victim's skull, or produce steam by boiling.[10] Or consider the person interviewing college graduates for job openings. "Show me a new use for this stapler," the interviewer said. Calmly picking up the scissors on the desk, one creative woman cut the interviewer's tie in half and then stapled it back together. Smiling, she asked, "Now that I've demonstrated my instant mender, how many will you take?"

Each of us has the capacity to be creative. Characteristics of highly creative people are illustrated in the left-hand column of Exhibit 11.2. Creative people often are known for originality, open-mindedness, curiosity, a focused approach to problem solving, persistence, a relaxed and playful attitude, and receptivity to new ideas.[11]

Creativity can also be designed into organizations. Companies or departments within companies can be organized to be creative and ini-

EXHIBIT 11.2	The Creative Individual	The Creative Organization or Department
Characteristics of Creative People and Organizations	1. Conceptual fluency Openmindedness	1. Open channels of communication Contact with outside sources Overlapping territories Suggestion systems, brainstorming, nominal group techniques
	2. Originality	2. Assignment of nonspecialists to problems Eccentricity allowed Use of teams
SOURCE: Based on Gary A. Steiner, ed., *The Creative Organization* (Chicago: University of Chicago Press, 1965), 16–18; Rosabeth Moss Kanter, "The Middle Manager as Innovator," *Harvard Business Review* (July–August 1982), 104–105; James Brian Quinn, "Managing Innovation: Controlled Chaos," *Harvard Business Review* 63 (May–June 1985), 73–84.	3. Less authority Independence	3. Decentralization, loosely defined positions, loose control Acceptance of mistakes Risk-taking norms
	4. Playfulness Undisciplined exploration Curiosity	4. Freedom to choose and pursue problems Not a tight ship, playful culture Freedom to discuss ideas, long time horizon
	5. Persistence Commitment Focused approach	5. Resources allocated to creative personnel and projects without immediate payoff Reward system encourages innovation Absolution of peripheral responsibilities

tiate changes. The characteristics of creative organizations correspond to those of individuals, as illustrated in the right-hand column of Exhibit 11.2. Creative organizations are loosely structured. People find themselves in a situation of ambiguity, assignments are vague, territories overlap, tasks are poorly defined, and much work is done through teams.[12] Creative organizations have an internal culture of playfulness, freedom, challenge, and grass-roots participation.[13] They harness all potential sources of new ideas from within. Many participative management programs are born out of the desire to enhance creativity for initiating changes. People are not stuck in the rhythm of routine jobs. Managers in an insurance company that had been tightly controlled from the top remarked on the changes that enabled them to be more creative:

> We used to run by the book and now I don't even know where the book is.

> Yesterday's procedures are outdated today.

> If you don't like the organization chart, just wait until next week, we'll have a new one.[14]

The most creative companies encourage employees to make mistakes. Jim Read, president of the Read Corporation, says, "When my employees make mistakes trying to improve something, I give them a round of applause. No mistakes mean no new products. If they ever become afraid to make one, my company is doomed."[15] Ross Perot, who founded EDS, said creative managers could not keep their noses clean: "We teach people that mistakes are like skinned knees for little children. ... My people are covered with the scars of their mistakes. By the time they get to the top, their noses are pretty well broken."[16]

Open channels of communication, overlapping jobs, discretionary resources, decentralization, and employees' freedom to choose problems and make mistakes can generate unexpected benefits for companies. Creative organizational conditions such as those described in Exhibit 11.2 enable more than 200 new products a year to bubble up from 3M's research labs.

The same creative conditions enabled the solution to the following problem: How do you pack many potato chips into a small space without crushing them? A small company used the analogy in nature of stacking dry leaves and wet leaves. Through the use of such creative thinking, the obvious solution emerged: Mold the chips into uniform, stackable shapes *before* they dry. Armed with this innovation, the company sold its idea to Procter & Gamble, and the canned chip Pringles was born.[17]

IDEA CHAMPIONS

If creative conditions are successful, new ideas will be generated that must be carried forward for acceptance and implementation. This is where idea champions come in. The formal definition of an **idea champion** is a person who sees the need for and champions productive change within the organization. For example, Bonnie McKeever of Federal Express championed the idea of a coalition of companies to combat

Creativity is one of two strategic goals in Takashimaya Company, Ltd.'s 21st century vision. Japan's industry leader in interior design, Takashimaya is dedicated to the creation of livable spaces. For example, the Takashimaya Relaxation System created by Tetsuya Takano (pictured here) is designed for improvement of office environments. The system, which includes a body-sonic chair, LCD screens, and brain-wave controllers, can be used by office personnel in 15–30 minute sessions to reduce stress and open creative channels through increased brain production of alpha waves.

idea champion

A person who sees the need for and champions productive change within the organization.

mounting medical fees. The Memphis Business Group on Health was created, saving its members an estimated tens of millions of dollars through competitive bidding and discounts.[18] Wendy Black of Best Western International championed the idea of coordinating the corporate mailings to the company's 2,800 hoteliers into a single packet every two weeks. Some hotels were receiving three special mailings a day from different departments. Her idea saved $600,000 a year for five years in postage alone.[19]

Remember: Change does not occur by itself. Personal energy and effort are required to successfully promote a new idea. Often a new idea is rejected by management. Champions are passionately committed to a new product or idea despite rejection by others.

Championing an idea successfully requires roles in organizations, as illustrated in Exhibit 11.3. Sometimes a single person may play two or more of these roles, but successful innovation in most companies involves an interplay of different people, each adopting one role. The *inventor* develops a new idea and understands its technical value but has neither the ability nor the interest to promote it for acceptance within the organization. The *champion* believes in the idea, confronts the organizational realities of costs and benefits, and gains the political and financial support needed to bring it to reality. The *sponsor* is a high-level manager who approves the idea, protects the idea, and removes major organizational barriers to acceptance. The *critic* counterbalances the zeal of the champion by challenging the concept and providing a reality test against hard-nosed criteria. The critic prevents people in the other roles from adopting a bad idea.[20]

Al Marzocchi was both an inventor and a champion at Owens-Corning Fiberglass. He invented ways to strengthen fiberglass, developed the fiberglass-belted tire in conjunction with Armstrong Tire, and pioneered

---

EXHIBIT 11.3

Four Roles in Organizational Change

Inventor	Champion	Sponsor	Critic
Develops and understands technical aspects of idea	Believes in idea	High-level manager who removes organizational barriers	Provides reality test
Does not know how to win support for the idea or make a business of it	Visualizes benefits	Approves and protects idea within organization	Looks for shortcomings
	Confronts organizational realities of cost, benefits		Defines hard-nosed criteria that idea must pass
	Obtains financial and political support		
	Overcomes obstacles		

SOURCE: Based on Harold L. Angle and Andrew H. Van De Ven, "Suggestions for Managing the Innovation Journey," in *Research in the Management of Innovation: The Minnesota Studies*, ed. A. H. Van De Ven, H. L. Angle, and M. S. Poole (Cambridge, Mass.: Ballinger/Harper & Row, 1989), and Jay R. Galbraith, "Designing the Innovating Organization," *Organizational Dynamics* (Winter 1982), 5–25.

new ways of using asphalt. One reason Marzocchi thrived was that Owens-Corning's president, Harold Boeschenstein, sponsored his activities and held critics at bay. Once Marzocchi violated company rules by going directly to a potential customer, but the president protected him and his idea.[21]

Managers can directly influence whether champions will flourish. When Texas Instruments studied 50 of its new-product introductions, a surprising fact emerged: Without exception, every new product that had failed had lacked a zealous champion. In contrast, most of the new products that succeeded had a champion. Texas Instruments' managers made an immediate decision: No new product would be approved unless someone championed it.

NEW-VENTURE TEAMS

A recent idea for facilitating corporate innovation is known as a new-venture team. A **new-venture team** is a unit separate from the rest of the organization and is responsible for developing and initiating a major innovation.[22] New-venture teams give free reign to members' creativity because their separate facilities and location free them from organizational rules and procedures. These teams typically are small, loosely structured, and organic, reflecting the characteristics of creative organizations described in Exhibit 11.2. Peter Drucker advises organizations that wish to innovate to use a separate team or department:

new-venture team

A unit separate from the mainstream of the organization that is responsible for developing and initiating innovations.

For the existing business to be capable of innovation, it has to create a structure that allows people to be entrepreneurial. . . . This means, first, that the entrepreneurial, the new, has to be organized separately from the old and the existing. Whenever we have tried to make an existing unit the carrier of the entrepreneurial project, we have failed.[23]

The new-venture team is quite different from the horizontal relationships or the matrix structure described in Chapter 9. In those structures, employees remain members of their everyday departments and simply work on a project part-time while reporting to their regular boss. Under the new-venture team concept, employees no longer report through the normal structure.[24] The team exists as a separate departmental entity, as illustrated in Exhibit 11.4. New-venture teams are kept small and separate to ensure that no bureaucracy will intrude.

For a giant corporation such as IBM, new-venture teams free people from the constraints of the large organization. IBM's biggest success—the personal computer—was built by a new-venture group. The PC new-venture team was so appealing that 5,000 employees applied for the initial 50 positions.[25] The most recent successful new-venture team at IBM is a small group that built the Power Visualization System, a graphics supercomputer introduced after a mere two years in development. The supercomputer lets scientists and engineers literally "see" the billions of pieces of data their experiments generate.[26]

Other companies that have created new-venture units are Monsanto, Levi Strauss, Exxon, DuPont, Dow, and Motorola. 3M utilizes action teams to create new products. The action team concept allows individuals with new product ideas to recruit team members from throughout the company. These people may end up running the newly created division if the idea is successful.[27]

skunkworks

Small, informal, and sometimes unauthorized groups that create innovations.

One variation of venture teams used by some companies is called *skunkworks*.[28] **Skunkworks** are small, informal, and sometimes unauthorized groups that create innovations. Companies such as Kollmorgen, IBM, Merck, Philip Morris, and Macy encourage employees to form informal groups, often working nights and weekends, to develop a new idea. If the new venture is successful, group members are rewarded and encouraged to run the new business.

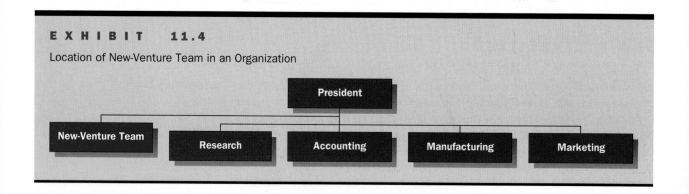

E X H I B I T   11.4

Location of New-Venture Team in an Organization

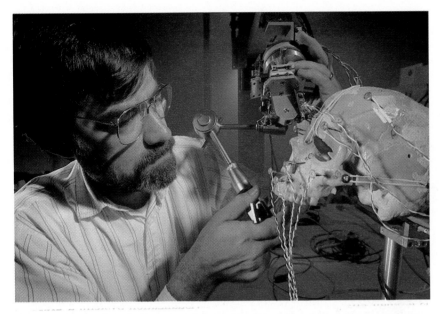

Robosurgeon is an innovative and highly successful surgical device developed through a *new-venture fund*. Acting as a partner and venture capitalist for the project, IBM worked with robotics specialists at the University of California, Davis, to develop the system and set up a separate company, Integrated Surgical Systems, to market the technology. New venture teamwork moves innovative products from idea to market. Robosurgeon has proven successful in hip replacement surgery and will next be targeted on facial reconstruction, an area requiring enormous surgical precision.

Another variation of new-venture teams is the **new-venture fund**, which provides resources from which individuals and groups can draw to develop new ideas, products, or businesses. For example, Teleflex, a producer of many technical and consumer products, allocates one-half of 1 percent of sales to a new-venture fund. More than $1 million dollars was allocated to employees in one year to explore new ideas.[29]

new-venture fund

A fund providing resources from which individuals and groups draw to develop new ideas, products, or businesses.

● IMPLEMENTING CHANGE

Creative culture, idea champions, and new-venture teams are ways to facilitate the initiation of new ideas. The other step to be managed in the change process is implementation. A new, creative idea will not benefit the organization until it is in place and being fully utilized. One frustration for managers is that employees often seem to resist change for no apparent reason. To effectively manage the implementation process, managers should be aware of the reasons for employee resistance and be prepared to use techniques for obtaining employee cooperation.

RESISTANCE TO CHANGE

Idea champions often discover that other employees are unenthusiastic about their new ideas. Members of a new-venture group may be surprised when managers in the regular organization do not support or approve their innovations. Managers and employees not involved in an innovation often seem to prefer the status quo. Employees appear to resist change for several reasons, and understanding them helps managers implement change more effectively.

SELF-INTEREST.   Employees typically resist a change they believe will take away something of value. A proposed change in job design, structure, or technology may lead to a perceived loss of power, prestige, pay, or company benefits. The fear of personal loss is perhaps the biggest obstacle to organizational change.[30] When Mesa Oil Corporation tried to buy Phillips Petroleum, Phillips employees started a campaign to prevent the takeover. Employees believed that Mesa would not treat them well and that they would lose financial benefits. Their resistance to change was so effective that the merger failed to take place.

LACK OF UNDERSTANDING AND TRUST.   Employees often do not understand the intended purpose of a change or distrust the intentions behind it. If previous working relationships with an idea champion have been negative, resistance may occur. One manager had a habit of initiating a change in the financial reporting system about every 12 months and then losing interest and not following through. After the third time, employees no longer went along with the change because they did not trust the manager's intention to follow through to their benefit.

UNCERTAINTY.   *Uncertainty* is the lack of information about future events. It represents a fear of the unknown. Uncertainty is especially threatening for employees who have a low tolerance for change and fear the novel and unusual. They do not know how a change will affect them and worry about whether they will be able to meet the demands of a new procedure or technology.[31] Union leaders at General Motors' Steering Gear Division in Saginaw, Michigan, resisted the introduction of employee participation programs. They were uncertain about how the program would affect their status and thus initially opposed it.

DIFFERENT ASSESSMENTS AND GOALS.   Another reason for resistance to change is that people who will be affected by innovation may assess the situation differently than an idea champion or new-venture group. Often critics voice legitimate disagreements over the proposed benefits of a change. Managers in each department pursue different goals, and an innovation may detract from performance and goal achievement for some departments. For example, if marketing gets the new product it wants for its customers, the cost of manufacturing may increase and the manufacturing superintendent thus will resist. Resistance may call attention to problems with the innovation. At a consumer products company in Racine, Wisconsin, middle managers resisted the introduction of a new employee program that turned out to be a bad idea. The managers truly believed that the program would do more harm than good. One manager bluntly told his boss, "I've been here longer than you, and I'll be here after you've gone, so don't tell me what really counts at this company."[32]

These reasons for resistance are legitimate in the eyes of employees affected by the change. The best procedure for managers is not to ignore resistance but to diagnose the reasons and design strategies to gain acceptance by users.[33] Strategies for overcoming resistance to change typically involve two approaches: the analysis of resistance through the force field technique and the use of selective implementation tactics to overcome resistance.

FORCE FIELD ANALYSIS

Force field analysis grew from the work of Kurt Lewin, who proposed that change was a result of the competition between *driving* and *restraining forces.*[34] When a change is introduced, some forces drive it and other forces resist it. To implement a change, management should analyze the change forces. By selectively removing forces that restrain change, the driving forces will be strong enough to enable implementation, as illustrated by the move from A to B in Exhibit 11.5. As restraining forces are reduced or removed, behavior will shift to incorporate the desired changes.

Just-in-time (JIT) inventory control systems schedule materials to arrive at a company just as they are needed on the production line. In an Ohio manufacturing company, management's analysis showed that the driving forces associated with the implementation of JIT were (1) the large cost savings from reduced inventories, (2) savings from needing fewer workers to handle the inventory, and (3) a quicker, more competitive market response for the company. Restraining forces discovered by managers were (1) a freight system that was too slow to deliver inventory on time, (2) a facility layout that emphasized inventory maintenance over new deliveries, (3) worker skills inappropriate for handling rapid inventory deployment, and (4) union resistance to loss of jobs. The driving forces were not sufficient to overcome the restraining forces.

To shift the behavior to JIT, managers attacked the restraining forces. An analysis of the freight system showed that delivery by truck provided the flexibility and quickness needed to schedule inventory arrival at a specific time each day. The problem with facility layout was met by adding four new loading docks. Inappropriate worker skills were

force field analysis

The process of determining which forces drive and which resist a proposed change.

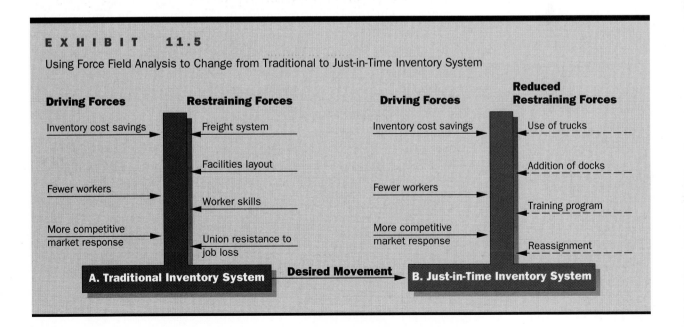

EXHIBIT 11.5

Using Force Field Analysis to Change from Traditional to Just-in-Time Inventory System

Driving Forces	Restraining Forces	Driving Forces	Reduced Restraining Forces
Inventory cost savings	Freight system	Inventory cost savings	Use of trucks
	Facilities layout		Addition of docks
Fewer workers	Worker skills	Fewer workers	Training program
More competitive market response	Union resistance to job loss	More competitive market response	Reassignment

A. Traditional Inventory System → **Desired Movement** → **B. Just-in-Time Inventory System**

attacked with a training program to instruct workers in JIT methods and in assembling products with uninspected parts. Union resistance was overcome by agreeing to reassign workers no longer needed for maintaining inventory to jobs in another plant. With the restraining forces removed, the driving forces were sufficient to allow the JIT system to be implemented.

IMPLEMENTATION TACTICS

The other approach to managing implementation is to adopt specific tactics to overcome employee resistance. For example, resistance to change may be overcome by educating employees or inviting them to participate in implementing the change. Methods for dealing with resistance to change have been studied by researchers. The following five tactics, summarized in Exhibit 11.6, have proven successful.[35]

COMMUNICATION AND EDUCATION. Communication and education are used when solid information about the change is needed by users and others who may resist implementation. Education is especially important when the change involves new technical knowledge or users are unfamiliar with the idea. Florida Power & Light Company instituted a change in company procedures that initially confused managers. Realizing it had implemented the change too quickly, the company tailored special training sessions to educate managers. The training program resolved the difficulty, and implementation was a success.[36]

PARTICIPATION. *Participation* involves users and potential resisters in designing the change. This approach is time-consuming, but it pays off because users understand and become committed to the change. When General Motors tried to implement a new management appraisal system for supervisors in its Adrian, Michigan, plant, it met with immediate resistance. Rebuffed by the lack of cooperation, top managers proceeded more slowly, involving supervisors in the design of the new appraisal

E X H I B I T 11.6	**Approach**	**When to Use**
Tactics for Overcoming Resistance to Change	Communication, education	■ Change is technical. ■ Users need accurate information and analysis to understand change.
	Participation	■ Users need to feel involved. ■ Design requires information from others. ■ Users have power to resist.
	Negotiation	■ Group has power over implementation. ■ Group will lose out in the change.
	Coercion	■ A crisis exists. ■ Initiators clearly have power. ■ Other implementation techniques have failed.
SOURCE: Based on J. P. Kotter and L. A. Schlesinger, "Choosing Strategies for Change," *Harvard Business Review* 57 (March–April 1979), 106–114.	Top management support	■ Change involves multiple departments or reallocation of resources. ■ Users doubt legitimacy of change.

In its new thrust toward customer satisfaction, Consolidated Rail Corporation (Conrail) utilized the *implementation tactics* of communication, education, and participation. Conrail began by communicating goals to employees and encouraging their participation in all levels of decision making. As centerpiece of its customer service strategy, Conrail consolidated 10 small service centers into a large state-of-the-art National Customer Service Center in Pittsburgh. Here, customer service employees receive an intensive eight-week course in problem solving and professional handling of customer telephone inquiries.

system. Through participation in system design, managers understood what the new approach was all about and dropped their resistance to it.

NEGOTIATION.   Negotiation is a more formal means of achieving cooperation. *Negotiation* uses formal bargaining to win acceptance and approval of a desired change. For example, if the marketing department fears losing power if a new management structure is implemented, top managers may negotiate with marketing to reach a resolution. General Motors, General Electric, and other companies that have strong unions frequently must formally negotiate change with the unions. The change may become part of the union contract reflecting the agreement of both parties.

COERCION.   *Coercion* means that managers use formal power to force employees to change. Resisters are told to accept the change or lose rewards or even their jobs. Coercion is necessary in crisis situations when a rapid response is urgent. When middle managers at TRW, Inc.'s Valve Division in Cleveland refused to go along with a new employee involvement program, top management reassigned several first-line supervisors and managers. The new jobs did not involve supervisory responsibility. Further, other TRW managers were told that future pay increases depended on their adoption of the new procedures. The coercive techniques were used as a last resort because managers refused to go along with the change any other way.[37]

TOP MANAGEMENT SUPPORT.   The visible support of top management also helps overcome resistance to change. Top management support symbolizes to all employees that the change is important for the organization. Top management support is especially important when a change involves multiple departments or when resources are being reallocated among departments. Without top management support, these changes can get bogged down in squabbling among departments. Moreover, when top managers fail to support a project, they can inadvertently undercut it by issuing contradictory orders. This happened at Flying

Tiger Lines before it was acquired by Federal Express. The airborne freight hauler came up with a plan to eliminate excessive paperwork by changing the layout of offices so that two agents rather than four could handle each shipment. No sooner had part of the change been implemented than top management ordered another system; thus, the office layout was changed again. The new layout was not as efficient, but it was the one that top management supported. Had middle managers informed top managers and obtained their support earlier, the initial change would not have been defeated by a new priority.[38]

In another example, Navistar managers saved a good deal of money for the company by adopting smart implementation techniques.

 NAVISTAR INTERNATIONAL

Managers at Navistar International—formerly International Harvester—successfully introduced a maintenance, repair, and operating (MRO) buying program. Purchasing costs were far too high, buyers were buried under an avalanche of 14,000 requisitions per year, hundreds of suppliers were used, inventory turnover was slow, and there was little coordination between warehousing and purchasing.

James Hall and Pierre Bodeau of the Construction Equipment Group in Melrose Park, Illinois, proposed a redesigned requisition process, including a computerized inventory control system and a new procedure for analyzing vendor capability. They also devised a plan for successful implementation.

Implementation involved several steps: Survey 120 industrial suppliers for accurate information, involve Navistar employees in discussions to further refine and improve the buying program, undertake internal training to teach employees the new procedures, and analyze other forces for resistance. After the program was fully developed, key employees were already on board because they had participated in program design. Training for other employees went smoothly. The program was launched in June, and by April of the next year, 90 percent of the purchases had gone through the MRO system. Cost savings through price reductions amounted to $78,000 the first year, and MRO inventories dropped $1 million in eight months.[39] ∎

 TYPES OF PLANNED CHANGE

Now that we have explored how the initiation and implementation of change can be carried out, let us look at the different types of change that occur in organizations. We will address two issues: what parts of the organization can be changed and how managers can apply the initiation and implementation ideas to each type of change.

The four types of organizational change are technology, products, structure, and culture/people, as illustrated in Exhibit 11.7. Organizations may innovate in one or more areas, depending on internal and external forces for change. In the rapidly changing toy industry, a man-

TECHNOLOGY
PRODUCTS
STRUCTURE
CULTURE/PEOPLE

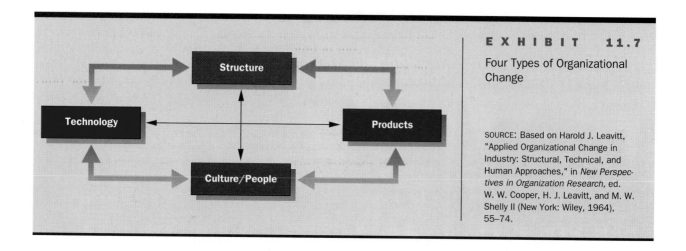

EXHIBIT   11.7

Four Types of Organizational Change

SOURCE: Based on Harold J. Leavitt, "Applied Organizational Change in Industry: Structural, Technical, and Human Approaches," in *New Perspectives in Organization Research*, ed. W. W. Cooper, H. J. Leavitt, and M. W. Shelly II (New York: Wiley, 1964), 55–74.

ufacturer has to introduce new products frequently. In a mature, competitive industry, production technology changes are adopted to improve efficiency. The arrows connecting the four types of change in Exhibit 11.7 show that a change in one part may affect other parts of the organization: A new product may require changes in technology, and a new technology may require new people skills or a new structure. For example, when Shenandoah Life Insurance Company computerized processing and claims operations, the structure had to be decentralized, employees required intensive training, and a more participative culture was needed. Related changes were required for the new technology to increase efficiency. Motorola, discussed in the Focus on Global Competition box, underwent several types of changes to become competitive again.

TECHNOLOGY CHANGES

A **technology change** is related to the organization's production process—how the organization does its work. Technology changes are designed to make the production of a product or service more efficient. For example, the adoption of robotics to improve production efficiency at General Motors and Chrysler is an example of a technology change, as is the adoption of laser-scanning checkout systems at supermarkets. At IBM's manufacturing plant in Charlotte, North Carolina, an automated miniload storage and retrieval system was installed to handle production parts. This change provided an efficient method for handling small-parts inventory and changed the technology of the IBM plant.

How can managers encourage technology change? The general rule is that technology change is bottom up.[40] The *bottom-up approach* means that ideas are initiated at lower organization levels and channeled upward for approval. Lower-level technical experts act as idea champions—they invent and champion technological changes. Employees at lower levels understand the technology and have the expertise needed to propose changes. For example, at Kraft General Foods, employees have proposed several hundred cost-saving projects. One that can save $3.5 million a year is simply to improve the accuracy of machines that weigh product portions.[41]

technology change

A change that pertains to the organization's production process.

new HORIZONS . . . . . . global competition   MOTOROLA, INC.

In the early and mid-1980s, foreign competitors—mostly Japanese—deluged the world with extremely high-quality cellular phones, pagers, and memory chips. Because of this, Motorola temporarily withdrew from selected U.S. and foreign markets. But Motorola refused to be counted out. Under the leadership of Chairman Robert Galvin, the company decided to get in shape for a return bout. Innovation was to be the key.

Motorola spent, and continues to spend, billions of dollars in research and development. It invested ten years of R&D—an unheard-of length of time for a U.S. company—in the MicroTac cellular phone (one-third lighter than the nearest foreign competitor). The MicroTac allowed Motorola to flex its muscles, regaining market share in the United States and foreign markets with this innovative cellular telephone.

Next Motorola came out with the first Dick Tracy–type wristwatch pager. Motorola also introduced a new signal-processing chip capable of storing and transmitting images, sounds, and other analog signals. Motorola is increasing market share in both products in Europe, Southeast Asia, and Japan in the face of withering competition.

How is Motorola pulling off all these innovations? By emphasizing R&D; adding American flair; changing culture, technology, and products at the same time; and applying Japanese-style management improvements. The new emphasis on quality has enabled Motorola to reach Six Sigma quality manufacturing, or a mere 3.4 defects per million, on products like calculators.

Another tactic has been to knock down barriers wherever they can be found. People from departments such as design, manufacturing, and marketing work together in the early stages of new projects. This also means that Motorola divisions are expected to collaborate with one another, with new products coming on stream that involve two, three, or four divisions. Horizontal linkages are even in place between Motorola

and other companies. Motorola supports R&D consortiums through which companies develop and share new technology together.

These changes cannot be made without investments in overhauling culture and upgrading people. All 105,000 employees are being trained in topics such as decision making, global competitiveness, and statistical quality control to the tune of $60 million a year.

What's next? Cellular phones are the wave of the future, so expect more innovations here. Also expect innovation in new technologies and products such as new electronic ballasts to run fluorescent lighting systems. Focusing on anticipating customer needs and having solutions ready, Motorola again is one of the best in the global marketplace, thanks to the management of innovation. ■

SOURCE: Based on Lois Therrien, "The Rival Japan Respects," *Business Week*, November 13, 1989, 108–118; Kevin Kelly, "Motorola Wants to Light Up Another Market," *Business Week*, October 14, 1991, 50; and John Carey, Neil Gross, Mark Maremont, and Gary McWilliams, "Innovation," *Business Week* (Special issue: Reinventing America), 1992, 161–171.

Managers can facilitate the bottom-up approach by designing creative departments as described earlier in this chapter. A loose, flexible, decentralized structure provides employees with the freedom and opportunity to initiate continuous improvements. A rigid, centralized, standardized structure stifles technology innovation. Anything managers can do to involve the grass roots of the organization—the people who are experts in their parts of the production process—will increase technology change.

A *top-down approach* to technology change usually does not work.[42] Top managers are not close to the production process and lack expertise in technological developments. Mandating technology change from the

Top Down Doesn't Work

top produces fewer rather than more technology innovations. The spark for a creative new idea comes from people close to the technology. The rationale behind Motorola's "participative management program," Data General's "pride teams," and Honeywell's "positive action teams" is to encourage new technology ideas from people at lower levels of the organization.

NEW-PRODUCT CHANGES

A **product change** is a change in the organization's product or service output. New-product innovations have major implications for an organization, because they often are an outcome of a new strategy and may define a new market.[43] Examples of new products are Frito-Lay's introduction of O'Grady's potato chips, Hewlett-Packard's introduction of a professional computer, and GE's development at its Medical Division of a device for monitoring patients' heart cycles.

The introduction of a new product is difficult, because it not only involves a new technology but also must meet customers' needs. In most industries, only about one in eight new-product ideas is successful.[44] Companies that successfully develop new products usually have the following characteristics:

1 People in marketing have a good understanding of customer needs.

2 Technical specialists are aware of recent technological developments and make effective use of new technology.

3 Members from key departments—research, manufacturing, marketing—cooperate in the development of the new product.[45]

These findings mean that the ideas for new products typically originate at the lower levels of the organization just as they do for technology changes. The difference is that new-product ideas flow horizontally among departments. Product innovation requires expertise from several departments simultaneously. A new-product failure is often the result of failed cooperation.[46]

One approach to successful new-product innovation is called the **horizontal linkage model,** which is illustrated in Exhibit 11.8[47] The model shows that research, manufacturing, and marketing must simultaneously develop new products. People from these departments meet frequently in teams and task forces to share ideas and solve problems. Research

Technology changes in computers and aircraft design allow Boeing Company aircraft designers to skip the paper drawings and work in teams with input from the airlines, mechanics, and marketers. These Boeing designers working on the new 777 widebody, twin-jet program can use the new technology to reduce errors through digital design and preassembly. A three-dimensional digital mechanic can crawl through on-screen aircraft images to locate defects. This technology allows designers to test innovative ideas without the cost of building a full mock-up.

product change

A change in the organization's product or service output.

horizontal linkage model

An approach to product change that emphasizes shared development of innovations among several departments.

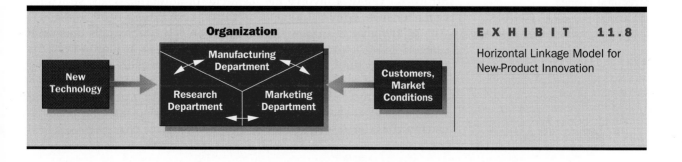

EXHIBIT   11.8

Horizontal Linkage Model for New-Product Innovation

Ocean Spray Ruby Red Grapefruit Juice Drink™, a new grapefruit drink by Ocean Spray Cranberries, Inc., was developed and on store shelves in a record nine months compared to the usual two-year development time. This feat was accomplished through *horizontal linkage*. A Technology Transfer Team including management representatives from Food Technology, Flavor Development & Manufacturing, Research, Production Planning & Control, Quality Assurance, and the Business Unit, combined their expertise, and through teamwork, communication, and constant monitoring of the process created a successful addition to the Ocean Spray family of products.

time-based competition

A strategy of competition based on the ability to deliver products and services faster than competitors.

structural change

Any change in the way in which the organization is designed and managed.

people inform marketing of new technical developments to learn whether they will be useful to customers. Marketing people pass customer complaints to research to use in the design of new products. Manufacturing informs other departments whether a product idea can be manufactured within cost limits. When the horizontal linkage model is used, the decision to develop a new product is a joint one.

Horizontal linkages are being adopted in the computer industry to overcome new-product problems. For example, at Convergent Technologies, Workslate, a portable computer, received accolades when it was introduced. One year later, Workslate was dead. Production problems with the new product had not been worked out. Marketing people had not fully analyzed customer needs. The idea had been pushed through without sufficient consultation among research, manufacturing, and marketing. At Lotus Development Corporation, the delays in new software ran on for months and years, earning the name "vaporware" because they never appeared. New senior vice-president Frank King enforced a regime of daily and weekly meetings involving programmers and code writers, and monthly gatherings of all employees to update one another. These enforced linkages gradually reduced product development time.[48]

Innovation is becoming a major strategic weapon in the global marketplace. One example of innovation is the use of **time-based competition,** which means delivering products and services faster than competitors, giving companies a significant strategic advantage. For example, Hewlett-Packard reduced the time to develop a new printer from 4.5 years to 22 months. Lenscrafters jumped from 3 to 300 stores based on its ability to provide quality eyeglasses in one hour. Dillard's department stores went to an automatic reorder system that replenishes stocks in 12 days rather than 30, providing retail goods to customers more quickly.[49] Sprinting to market with a new product requires a *parallel approach*, or *simultaneous linkage* among departments. This is similar to a rugby match wherein players run together, passing the ball back and forth as they move downfield together. The teamwork required for the horizontal linkage model is a major component of using rapid innovation to beat the competition with speed.[50] The latest approach to horizontal coordination and rapid innovation, called the Virtual Corporation, is discussed in the Manager's Shoptalk box.

STRUCTURAL CHANGES

Structural changes involve the hierarchy of authority, goals, structural characteristics, administrative procedures, and management systems.[51] Almost any change in how the organization is managed falls under the category of structural change. At General Telephone & Electronics Corporation, structural changes included a structural reorganization, new pay incentives, a revised performance appraisal system, and affirmative action programs. IBM's change from a functional to a product structure was a structural change. The implementation of a no-smoking policy is usually considered a structural or an administrative change.

THE VIRTUAL CORPORATION: WAVE OF THE FUTURE?

How can a company move beyond its limited resources to embrace new product opportunities in today's fast-paced, competitive, global environment? One answer may be a new model called The Virtual Corporation, which is the ultimate in horizontal coordination for rapid innovation. Coined by DEC executive Jan Hopland, and espoused by authors William Davidow and Michael Malone, The Virtual Corporation is "a temporary network of companies that share costs, skills, and access to global markets" to exploit market opportunities.

Partnership and technology are the keys to successful development of the virtual organization. Here's how it works: When computer veteran Ron Oklewicz wanted to launch TelePad (a hand-held, pen-based computer), his small company of 14 employees had no manufacturing plant and only limited design and engineering capabilities. Oklewicz established more than two dozen collaborations. For example, GVO, Inc., designed and co-developed the computer, while an Intel swat team refined the details. Automatic Data Processing, Inc., handled payroll, and an IBM plant in North Carolina made available its spare capacity manufacturing facilities. The result is a world-class partnership, speeding an innovative product to market in record time.

Benefits to small companies are obvious, but larger corporations are also embracing the virtual concept. Apple Computer entered a one-year alliance with Sony Corp. in 1991 for the manufacture of the least-expensive model of its Powerbook notebooks. MCI, Applied Materials, Inc., and AT&T are enthusiastic about their own separate alliance efforts. Corning, Inc.'s nineteen partnerships allow speedy development and launching of new products. Chairman James Houghton insists "more companies are waking up to the fact that alliances are critical to the future."

Virtual Corporations allow each partner to contribute its "core competence" to the united effort. Technology and information sharing allows companies to work together across regional, international, and industrial boundaries. Shared information means development of trust among participants united in a sense of "co-destiny." Most important, companies create short-term partnerships that take advantage of brief windows of opportunity and meet changing market needs by quickly getting entry-level products to world markets.

The special skills needed by managers in this innovative organization include the ability to locate and select the right partners, to negotiate "win-win" solutions benefitting all parties, and to collaborate horizontally rather than rely on a vertical hierarchy. ∎

SOURCE: John A. Byrne, Richard Brandt, and Otis Port, "The Virtual Corporation," *Business Week*, February 8, 1993, 98–102, and William H. Davidow and Michael S. Malone, *The Virtual Corporation: Customization and Instantaneous Response in Manufacturing and Service: Lessons from the World's Most Advanced Companies* (New York: Harper Business, 1992).

Successful structural change is accomplished through a top-down approach, which is distinct from technology change (bottom up) and new products (horizontal).[52] Structural change is top down because the expertise for administrative improvements originates at the middle and upper levels of the organization. The champions for structural change are middle and top managers. Lower-level technical specialists have little interest or expertise in administrative procedures. If organization structure causes negative consequences for lower-level employees, complaints and dissatisfaction alert managers to a problem. Employee dissatisfaction is an internal force for change. The need for change is

Weirton Steel Corporation is breaking away from the traditional mind-set in the tough steel industry. Four hundred employee-owners created Weirton's "Vision for Success" that encourages empowerment and employee participation in problem solving and decision making. This change in *culture and people values* empowers employees to respond quickly to changes in automation and market demand. The 120 Employee Participation Groups eagerly take advantage of the cross-functional workshops such as the one pictured here and free computer skills courses offered by West Virginia Community College.

■

culture/people change

A change in employees' values, norms, attitudes, beliefs, and behavior.

perceived by higher managers, who then take the initiative to propose and implement it.

The top-down process does not mean that coercion is the best implementation tactic. Implementation tactics include education, participation, and negotiation with employees. Unless there is an emergency, managers should not force structural change on employees. They may hit a resistance wall, and the change will fail. This is exactly what happened at the company for which Mary Kay Ash worked before she started her own cosmetics business. The owner learned that even a top-down change in commission rate needs to incorporate education and participation to succeed:

> I worked for a company whose owner decided to revise the commission schedule paid to his sales managers. All brochures and company literature were changed accordingly. He then made plans for personally announcing the changes during a series of regional sales conferences. I accompanied him to the first conference. I'll never forget it.
>
> To an audience of 50 sales managers he announced that the 2 percent override they were presently earning on their units' sales production was to be reduced to 1 percent. "However," he said, "in lieu of that 1 percent, you will receive a very nice gift for each new person you recruit and train."
>
> At that point a sales manager stood up and let him have it with both barrels. She was absolutely furious. "How dare you do this to us? Why, even 2 percent wasn't enough. But cutting our overrides in half and offering us a crummy gift for appeasement insults our intelligence." With that she stormed out of the room. And every other sales manager for that state followed her—all 50 of them. In one fell swoop the owner had lost his entire sales organization in that region—the best in the country. I had never seen such an overwhelming rejection of a change of this kind in my entire life![53]

Top-down change means that initiation of the idea occurs at upper levels and is implemented downward. It does not mean that lower-level employees are not educated about the change or allowed to participate in it.

CULTURE/PEOPLE CHANGES

A **culture/people change** refers to a change in employees' values, norms, attitudes, beliefs, and behavior. Changes in culture and people pertain to how employees think; these are changes in mindset rather than technology, structure, or products. People change pertains to just a few employees, such as when a handful of middle managers is sent to a training course to improve their leadership skills. Culture change pertains to the organization as a whole, such as when Union Pacific Railroad changed its basic mindset by becoming less bureaucratic and focusing employees on customer service and quality through teamwork and employee participation.[54] Training is the most frequently used tool for changing the organization's mindset. A company may offer training programs to large blocks of employees on subjects such as teamwork, listening skills, quality circles, and participative management. Training programs will be discussed further in Chapter 12 on human resource management.

Another major approach to changing people and culture is organizational development. This has evolved as a separate field that is devoted to large-scale organizational change.

● ORGANIZATIONAL DEVELOPMENT

Organizational development (OD) is the application of behavioral science knowledge to improve an organization's health and effectiveness through its ability to cope with environmental changes, improve internal relationships, and increase problem-solving capabilities.[55] Organizational development improves working relationships among employees.

The following are three types of current problems that OD can help managers address.[56]

1 *Mergers/Acquisitions*. The disappointing financial results of many mergers and acquisitions are caused by the failure of executives to determine whether the administrative style and corporate culture of the two companies "fit." Executives may concentrate on potential synergies in technology, products, marketing, and control systems but fail to recognize that two firms may have widely different values, beliefs, and practices. These differences create stress and anxiety for employees, and these negative emotions affect future performance. Cultural differences should be evaluated during the acquisition process, and OD experts can be used to smooth the integration of two firms.

2 *Organizational Decline/Revitalization*. Organizations undergoing a period of decline and revitalization experience a variety of problems, including a low level of trust, lack of innovation, high turnover, and high levels of conflict and stress. The period of transition requires opposite behaviors, including confronting stress, creating open communication, and fostering creative innovation to emerge with high levels of productivity. OD techniques can contribute greatly to cultural revitalization by managing conflicts, fostering commitment, and facilitating communication.

3 *Conflict Management.* Conflict can occur at any time and place within a healthy organization. For example, a product team for the introduction of a new software package was formed at a computer company. Made up of strong-willed individuals, the team made little progress because members would not agree on project goals. At a manufacturing firm, salespeople promised delivery dates to customers that were in conflict with shop supervisor priorities for assembling customer orders. In a publishing company, two managers disliked each other intensely. They argued at meetings, lobbied politically against each other, and hurt the achievement of both departments. Organizational development efforts can help solve these kinds of conflicts.

organizational development (OD)

The application of behavioral science techniques to improve an organization's health and effectiveness through its ability to cope with environmental changes, improve internal relationships, and increase problem-solving capabilities.

Organizational development can be used to solve the types of problems described above and many others. Specialized OD techniques have been developed for these applications.

OD ACTIVITIES

A number of OD activities have emerged in recent years. Some of the most popular and effective are as follows.

team building

A type of OD intervention that enhances the cohesiveness of departments by helping members to learn to function as a team.

1 *Team-Building Activities.* **Team building** enhances the cohesiveness and success of organizational groups and teams. For example, a series of OD exercises can be used with members of cross-departmental teams to help them learn to act and function as a team. An OD expert can work with team members to increase their communication skills, facilitate their ability to confront one another, and accept common goals.

survey feedback

A type of OD intervention in which questionnaires on organizational climate and other factors are distributed among employees and the results reported back to them by a change agent.

2 *Survey-Feedback Activities.* **Survey feedback** begins with a questionnaire distributed to employees on values, climate, participation, leadership, and group cohesion within their organization.[57] After the survey is completed, an OD consultant meets with groups of employees to provide feedback about their responses and the problems identified.[58] Employees are engaged in problem solving based on the data.

3 *Intergroup Activities.* These activities include retreats and workshops to improve the effectiveness of groups or departments that must work together. The focus is on helping employees develop the skills to resolve conflicts, increase coordination, and develop better ways of working together.

When he took the reins of Goodyear Tire & Rubber, CEO Stanley Gault used *symbolic leadership* to reduce debt by attacking costs at all levels, starting in the executive suite. In a dramatic "do as I do" gesture, Gault removed 25 light bulbs in his own office, replaced executive limousines with economical family sedans, and sold five corporate jets. Gault's open management style includes production workers, suppliers, and distributors in the slashing of debt as well as promoting new tire products such as Aquatred. Gault's symbolic leadership enabled Goodyear to reverse earnings losses.

4 *Process-Consultation Activities.* Organizational development consultants help managers understand the human processes within their organization and how to manage them. Managers learn to think in terms of cultural values, leadership, communication, and intergroup cooperation.

5 *Symbolic Leadership Activities.* This approach helps managers learn to use the techniques for cultural change described in Chapter 4, including public statements, symbols, ceremonies, and slogans. For example, public statements that define a pathfinding vision and cultural values account for the success of such companies as Disney, Dana, and Wal-Mart. Managers can signal appropriate behavior through symbols and ceremonies, such as when Roy Ash had several of AM International's copying machines removed to signal the need for less paperwork. Harold Geneen, president of ITT, captured the new value for his corporation with the slogan: "Search for the Unshakeable Facts," which helped do away with smoke screens and political games.

OD STEPS

Consider the cultural change at Westinghouse Canada's manufacturing facility at Airdrie, Alberta. Cycle time for made-to-order motor-controlled devices was reduced from 17 weeks to 1 week. One major requirement for reducing the time was to change the mindset of both managers and workers to give workers more discretion. Instead of waiting for approval from superiors, production employees now talk directly with customers and suppliers to solve their problems.[59]

Organizational development experts acknowledge that corporate culture and human behavior are relatively stable and that companywide changes, such as those at Westinghouse Canada, require major effort. The theory underlying organizational development proposes three distinct steps for achieving behavioral and attitudinal change: (1) unfreezing, (2) changing, and (3) refreezing.[60]

In the first step, **unfreezing,** participants must be made aware of problems and be willing to change. This step is often associated with *diagnosis,* which uses an outside expert called a *change agent.* The **change agent** is an OD specialist who performs a systematic diagnosis of the organization and identifies work-related problems. He or she gathers and analyzes data through personal interviews, questionnaires, and observations of meetings. The diagnosis helps determine the extent of organizational problems and helps unfreeze managers by making them aware of problems in their behavior.

The second step, **changing,** occurs when individuals experiment with new behavior and learn new skills to be used in the workplace. This is sometimes known as *intervention,* during which the change agent implements a specific plan for training managers and employees. This plan may include team-building, intergroup, process-consultation, and symbolic leadership activities as described above.

The Direct Response Group (DRG) of Capital Holding Corp. is undergoing a culture change from mass marketers of insurance products to a customer-driven target marketer. DRG's Lifetime Learning Center helps employees learn new behaviors and skills—the *intervention* step in OD. Videotaped role play, pictured here, allows employees to simulate real-life customer situations in a team-oriented environment.

unfreezing / DIAGNOSING

A step in the diagnosis stage of organizational development in which participants are made aware of problems in order to increase their willingness to change their behavior.

change agent

An OD specialist who contracts with an organization to facilitate change.

changing

A step in the intervention stage of organizational development in which individuals experiment with new workplace behavior.

refreezing

A step in the reinforcement stage of organizational development in which individuals acquire a desired new skill or attitude and are rewarded for it by the organization.

The third step, **refreezing,** occurs when individuals acquire new attitudes or values and are rewarded for them by the organization. The impact of new behaviors is evaluated and reinforced. The change agent supplies new data that show positive changes in performance. Senior executives can reward positive behavioral changes by employees. Managers and employees also participate in refresher courses to maintain and reinforce the new behaviors.

The spirit of what OD tries to accomplish with culture/people change was illustrated in Honeywell's use of OD to change the corporate culture from an autocratic to a participative mindset.

 HONEYWELL CORPORATION

For many years, a Honeywell division had been an authoritarian entity. Then top managers believed that individuals could contribute to effectiveness if middle- and lower-level managers would allow them to participate more fully:

> Many organizations today want to break out of the beat-'em-up school of management and move toward a more participative management style. But like abused children who grow up to become abusive parents, managers raised in a less enlightened manner may have difficulty operating under a new set of rules.
>
> At Honeywell, we have been working to change from what I call the Patton style of management to a more collaborative way of operating. The way we manage people is still less than perfect. But now our employees can have a real share of the action rather than feeling blocked or frustrated by a rigid bureaucracy.[61]

The implementation of this new way of thinking was not easy. Managers and employees alike had to think in a different way and approach one another with respect and a desire for a positive working relationship. The new values that Honeywell wished to inculcate included the following management principles, published and circulated among all of its employees:

1 Productivity is a responsibility shared by both management and employees.

2 Broadened employee participation in the decision-making process will be fostered.

3 Teamwork, mutual respect, and a sense of ownership will be promoted at all divisional levels.

4 A positive climate for career growth will be supported throughout the division.

5 Work life and personal life have interacting requirements that will be recognized.

Through OD, Honeywell created a higher level of participation for employees. Managers learned to think of employees as whole people, not as instruments of production. ■

SUMMARY AND MANAGEMENT SOLUTION

Change is inevitable in organizations. This chapter discussed the techniques available for managing the change process. Managers should think of change as having four elements—the forces for change, the perceived need for change, the initiation of change, and the implementation of change. Forces for change can originate either within or outside the firm, and managers are responsible for monitoring events that may require a planned organizational response. Techniques for initiating changes include designing the organization for creativity, encouraging change agents, and establishing new-venture teams or skunkworks. The final step is implementation. Force field analysis is one technique for diagnosing restraining forces, which often can be removed. Managers also should draw on the implementation tactics of communication, participation, negotiation, coercion, or top management support.

This chapter also discussed specific types of change. Technology changes are accomplished through a bottom-up approach that utilizes experts close to the technology. Successful new-product introduction requires horizontal linkage among marketing, research and development, manufacturing, and perhaps other departments. Structural changes tend to be initiated in a top-down fashion, because upper managers are the administrative experts and champion these ideas for approval and implementation. Culture/people change pertains to the skills, behaviors, and attitudes of employees. Organizational development is an important approach to changes in people's mindset and corporate culture. The OD process entails three steps—unfreezing (diagnosis of the problem), the actual change (intervention), and refreezing (reinforcement of new attitudes and behaviors). Popular OD techniques include team building, survey feedback, intergroup skills, and process consultation.

These concepts apply to the Preston Trucking Company discussed in the chapter opening problem. Preston, hammered by deregulation and unhappy employees, decided to revise its corporate culture and encourage bottom-up change in its production process. The survey results indicating how bad things were unfroze management. Consultants were brought in, and meetings were held to determine the best way to proceed and to gain employee participation. A new mindset was introduced that made employees equal partners in the trucking business. Improved production efficiency occurred through weekly idea meetings from which suggestions flowed from lower-level employees. In one year, over 4,000 money-making ideas were proposed, worth about $1.5 million. One idea helped decrease truck service maintenance from 23 hours to 11 hours. With both a new corporate culture and a steady bottom-up flow of modifications in production technology, Preston has become the darling of the trucking industry. Growth is rapid, sales and profits are up, and grievances are way down. Preston is a model for how to change effectively.[62]

DISCUSSION QUESTIONS

1. A manager of an international chemical company said that very few new products in her company were successful. What would you advise the manager to do to help increase the company's success rate?

2. What are internal and external forces for change? Which force do you think is the major cause of organizational change?

3. Carefully planned change often is assumed to be effective. Do you think unplanned change can sometimes be beneficial to an organization? Discuss.

4. Why do organizations experience resistance to change? What techniques can managers use to overcome resistance?

5. Explain force field analysis. Analyze the driving and restraining forces for a change with which you have been associated.

6. Define the roles associated with an idea champion. Why are idea champions so essential to the initiation of change?

7. To what extent would changes in technology affect products, and vice versa? Compare the process for changing technology and that for product change.

8. Given that structure change is often made top down, should coercive implementation techniques be used?

9. Do the underlying values of organizational development differ from assumptions associated with other types of change? Discuss.

10. Compare and contrast team-building and survey-feedback techniques for OD intervention.

MANAGEMENT IN PRACTICE: EXPERIENTIAL EXERCISE

● IS YOUR COMPANY CREATIVE?

An effective way to assess the creative climate of an organization for which you have worked is to fill out the questionnaire below. Answer each question based on your work experience in that firm. Discuss the results with members of your group and talk about whether changing the firm along the dimensions in the questions would make it more creative.

Instructions: Answer each of the following questions using the five-point scale. (*Note there is no rating of 4:* 0, we never do this; 1, we rarely do this; 2, we sometimes do this; 3, we frequently do this; 5, we always do this.)

_____ We are encouraged to seek help anywhere inside or outside the organization with new ideas for our work unit.

_____ Assistance is provided to develop ideas into proposals for management review.

_____ Our performance reviews encourage risky, creative efforts, ideas, and actions.

_____ We are encouraged to fill our minds with new information by attending professional meetings, trade fairs, visiting customers, and so on.

_____ Our meetings are designed to allow people to freewheel, brainstorm, and generate ideas.

_____ All members contribute ideas during meetings.

_____ During meetings, there is much spontaneity and humor.

_____ We discuss how company structure and our actions help or spoil creativity within our work unit.

_____ During meetings, the chair is rotated among members.

_____ Everyone in the work unit receives training in creativity techniques and maintaining a creative climate.

To measure how effectively your organization fosters creativity, use the following scale:

SOURCE: Adapted from Edward Glassman, *Creativity Handbook: Idea Triggers and Sparks That Work* (Chapel Hill, N.C.: LCS Press, 1990). Used by permission. (919/967-2015)

Highly effective:	15–20
Moderately effective:	10–14
Moderately ineffective:	5–9
Ineffective:	0–4

CASES FOR ANALYSIS

DELL IMAGING SYSTEMS, INC.

Monica was angry and frustrated. "How do *they* expect me to run my department if I don't know what's going on?" she asked herself. The "they" she was angry with were Rudy Levine, her immediate supervisor, and Andy Shoreham, the vice-president of the division.

Monica's department was responsible for the production and assembly of high-performance computer terminals. Her team was experienced and knowledgeable about all phases of production. Production for the last quarter was down, the number of rejects was up, and the number of complaint calls for delayed deliveries was well above normal. But Monica did not blame her staffers. The problem was with upper management, namely Rudy and Andy.

For weeks, Rudy and Andy had discussed producing a newer, better type of terminal. Much research had been done on the new design, and an outside contractor had been hired to produce a dozen prototypes. These were tested and found to be superior to the former model. So Rudy and Andy decided to start production as soon as the new equipment had been ordered, delivered, and installed. Then Rudy told Monica about their plans. Monica was so flabbergasted that she at first couldn't speak.

"The new equipment will be coming in a couple of weeks," he said, "and we'd like you to start production as soon as everything is set up."

"This is a fine time to tell me about your plans," Monica finally said. "How am I supposed to have my staff ready for the new operation?"

"Well, there'll be a training period, of course," Rudy said, "but your team of experts should have no trouble picking up a new routine. The equipment isn't so different from what they're using now. We expect production to be up to your usual standards by the end of the quarter."

"That's not very much time, Rudy."

"Well, I'm sure your staff can handle it."

"I'm glad you're so sure," Monica said just before she left his office.

When Monica told her staffers the news, they were shocked. They wanted to know all about the change: why they weren't told about it sooner, what the new equipment was like, how much training would be needed, how much time they had to master the new procedures. Monica answered their questions as best she could, but Rudy hadn't given her much information during their meeting.

By the end of the quarter, Monica was not surprised that some of her staff had not mastered the equipment. She had attended the training sessions with them and had helped out wherever she could. But production was slow going, and Rudy was asking what the problems were with output.

● QUESTIONS

1. What type of innovation is the new terminal, and what process was used for its introduction?
2. How could Rudy and Andy have better handled this situation?
3. What might Monica do to ease the situation for her staffers?

SOURCE: Grace Lander, "Terminal Trouble," *Supervisory Management* (September 1989), 3–5. Reprinted by permission of publisher from Supervisory Management, September 1989, © 1989 American Management Association, New York. All rights reserved.

UNITED ELECTRIC CONTROLS COMPANY

Maker of industrial temperature and pressure controls, United Electric Controls Company was a conservative, 60-year-old, family-run company. United Electric's autocratic management style and old manufacturing methods seemed adequate to meet market needs. But in 1987, the company suffered its worst-ever sales loss, shaking everyone up.

How did United Electric respond? Chairman Robert Reis and President David Reis launched a massive cultural revamping. The first step was to abandon the old manufacturing approach and give new emphasis to Japanese methods of *pakayoke* (mistake proofing) and *kanban* (inventory control). As the centerpiece of their new program, the Reis brothers launched a program to encourage employees to champion their own ideas. Vice-President Bruce Hamilton admitted, "We had developed a structure, over time, that was designed to resist employee participation." The new structure was based on the concept that employees are the company's best resource and was designed to empower those employees.

Management devised a program that actively sought, supported, and rewarded employee ideas. The idea-harvesting plans included (1) a value-ideas program that offers a $100 cash bonus for each usable idea and for unused suggestions awards chances in a drawing; (2) action centers involving employee-initiated formation of short-term groups that meet during work hours in conference rooms to find solutions to specific problems; and (3) CEDAC (cause and effect diagram with the addition of cards), a problem-solving method using long-term teams to analyze and determine causes of major problems that affect several departments. All possible causes were charted and subjected to rigorous study over a period of months.

The results of these efforts were astonishing. The innovative culture is working, as indicated by a tidal wave of innovative ideas. In 1990 alone, 90 percent of the Watertown, Massachusetts, employees submitted ideas, compared to a mere 20 employee suggestions in the entire 20 years prior to the program. By 1991 United Electric's sales had risen by $8 million over 1987 sales. The experience of United Electric illustrates the power of management-facilitated innovation.

● QUESTIONS

1. Did the changes taking place at United Electric follow the four stages of forces, need, initiation, and implementation? Explain.

2. What was the major type of change—technology, product, structure, or culture/people—in this case? To what extent does the primary change have secondary effects on other types of change at United Electric?

3. What techniques were used for change implementation? Would you recommend additional techniques to implement the new culture and philosophy at United Electric?

SOURCE: Based on Joshua Hyatt, "Ideas at Work," *INC.*, May 1991, 59–66.

REFERENCES

1. Patty Watts, "Preston and the Teamsters Keep On Trucking," *Management Review* (March 1988), 22–24, and Alan Farnham, "The Trust Gap," *Fortune*, December 4, 1989, 56–78.

2. Richard L. Daft, "Bureaucratic vs. Nonbureaucratic Structure in the Process of Innovation and Change," in *Perspectives in Organizational Sociology: Theory and Research*, ed. Samuel B. Bacharach (Greenwich, Conn.: JAI Press, 1982), 129–166.

3. Andre L. Delbecq and Peter K. Mills, "Managerial Practices That Enhance Innovation," *Organizational Dynamics* 14 (Summer 1985), 24–34.

4. Ira Magaziner and Mark Tatinkin, *The Silent War: Inside the Global Business Battles Shaping America's Future* (New York: Random House, 1989).

5. Sharon Nelton, "How a Pennsylvania Company Makes the Sweet Sounds of Innovation," *Nation's Business*, December 1991, 16.

6. Andrew H. Van de Ven, Harold Angle, and Marshall Scott Poole, *Research on the Management of Innovation* (Cambridge, Mass.: Ballinger, 1989).

7. Edward W. Desmond, "Byting Japan," *Time*, October 5, 1992, 68–69.

8. Attributed to Gregory Bateson in Andrew H. Van de Ven, "Central Problems in the Management of Innovation," *Management Science* 32 (1986), 595.

9. Charles Pearlman, "A Theoretical Model for Creativity," *Education* 103 (1983), 294–305, and Robert R. Godfrey, "Tapping Employees' Creativity," *Supervisory Management* (February 1986), 16–20.

10. Craig R. Hickman and Michael A. Silva, "How to Tap Your Creative Powers," *Working Woman*, September 1985, 26–30.

11. Gordon Vessels, "The Creative Process: An Open-Systems Conceptualization," *Journal of Creative Behavior* 16 (1982), 185–196, and Pearlman, "A Theoretical Model."

12. James Brian Quinn, "Managing Innovation: Controlled Chaos," *Harvard Business Review* 63 (May–June 1985), 73–84; Howard H. Stevenson and David E. Gumpert, "The Heart of Entrepreneurship," *Harvard Business Review* 63 (March–April 1985), 85–94; and Marsha Sinetar, "Entrepreneurs, Chaos, and Creativity—Can Creative People Really Survive Large Company Structure?" *Sloan Management Review* 6 (Winter 1985), 57–62.

13. Cynthia Browne, "Jest for Success," *Moonbeams,* August 1989, 3–5, and Rosabeth Moss Kanter, *The Change Masters* (New York: Simon and Schuster, 1983).

14. Kanter, *The Change Masters.*

15. "Hands On: A Manager's Notebook," *INC.,* January 1989, 106.

16. Bo Burlingham and Curtis Hartman, "Cowboy Capitalist," *INC.,* January 1989, 60.

17. Magaly Olivero, "Some Wacko Ideas That Worked," *Working Woman,* September 1990, 147–148.

18. Bonnie McKeever, "How I Did It: Teaming Up to Cut Medical Costs," *Working Woman,* July 1992, 23–24.

19. Katy Koontz, "How to Stand Out from the Crowd," *Working Woman,* January 1988, 74–76.

20. Harold L. Angle and Andrew H. Van de Ven, "Suggestions for Managing the Innovation Journey," in *Research in the Management of Innovation: The Minnesota Studies,* ed. A. H. Van de Ven, H. L. Angle, and Mabel S. Poole (Cambridge, Mass.: Ballinger/Harper & Row, 1989).

21. Gifford Pinchot III, *Intrapreneuring* (New York: Harper & Row, 1985).

22. Christopher K. Bart, "New Venture Units: Use Them Wisely to Manage Innovation," *Sloan Management Review* (Summer 1988), 35–43.

23. Peter F. Drucker, *Innovation and Entrepreneurship* (New York: Harper & Row, 1985).

24. Michael Tushman and David Nadler, "Organizing for Innovation," *California Management Review* 28 (Spring 1986), 74–92.

25. Carl E. Larson and Frank M. J. LaFasto, *TeamWork* (Newbury Park, Calif.: Sage, 1989), and "How the PC Changed the Way IBM Thinks," *Business Week,* October 3, 1983, 86–90.

26. John Markoff, "Abe Peled's Secret Start-Up at IBM," *The New York Times,* December 8, 1991, 3–1, 6.

27. Russell Mitchell, "Masters of Innovation: How 3M Keeps Its New Products Coming," *Business Week,* April 10, 1989, 58–63.

28. Tom Peters and Nancy Austin, *A Passion for Excellence: The Leadership Difference* (New York: Random House, 1985).

29. "Teleflex Incorporated Annual Report," 1988, Limerick, Penn.

30. John P. Kotter and Leonard A. Schlesinger, "Choosing Strategies for Change," *Harvard Business Review* 57 (March–April 1979), 106–114.

31. G. Zaltman and R. Duncan, *Strategies for Planned Change* (New York: Wiley Interscience, 1977).

32. Leonard M. Apcar, "Middle Managers and Supervisors Resist Moves to More Participatory Management," *The Wall Street Journal,* September 16, 1985, 25.

33. Dorothy Leonard-Barton and Isabelle Deschamps, "Managerial Influence in the Implementation of New Technology," *Management Science* 34 (1988), 1252–1265.

34. Kurt Lewin, *Field Theory in Social Science: Selected Theoretical Papers* (New York: Harper & Brothers, 1951).

35. Paul C. Nutt, "Tactics of Implementation," *Academy of Management Journal* 29 (1986), 230–261; Kotter and Schlesinger, "Choosing Strategies"; Richard L. Daft and Selwyn Becker, *Innovation in Organizations: Innovation Adoption in School Organizations* (New York: Elsevier, 1978); and Richard Beckhard, *Organization Development: Strategies and Models* (Reading, Mass.: Addison-Wesley, 1969).

36. Patricia J. Paden-Bost, "Making Money Control a Management Issue," *Management Accounting* (November 1982), 48–56, and Apcar, "Middle Managers."

37. Apcar, "Middle Managers."

38. Jeremy Main, "The Trouble with Managing Japanese-Style," *Fortune,* April 2, 1984, 50–56.

39. Jabby Lowe, Greg Millsap, and Bill Breedlove, "International Harvester" (Unpublished manuscript, Texas A&M University, 1982), and Barbara Marsh, *A Corporate Tragedy: The Agony of International Harvester Company* (Garden City, N.Y.: Doubleday, 1985).

40. Richard L. Daft, *Organization Theory and Design* (St. Paul, Minn.: West, 1989), and Tom Burns and G. M. Stalker, *The Management of Innovation* (London: Tavistock Publications, 1961).

41. Stratford P. Sherman, "How Philip Morris Diversified Right," *Fortune,* October 23, 1989, 120–129.

42. Richard L. Daft, "A Dual-Core Model of Organizational Innovation," *Academy of Management Journal* 21 (1978), 193–210, and Kanter, *The Change Masters.*

43. Harold J. Leavitt, "Applied Organizational Change in Industry: Structural, Technical, and Human Approaches," in *New Perspectives in Organization Research,* ed. W. W. Cooper, H. J. Leavitt, and M. W. Shelly II (New York: Wiley, 1964), 55–74.

44. Edwin Mansfield, J. Rapoport, J. Schnee, S. Wagner, and M. Hamburger, *Research and Innovation in Modern Corporations* (New York: Norton, 1971).

45. Andrew H. Van de Ven, "Central Problems in the Management of Innovation," *Management Science* 32 (1986), 590–607; Daft, *Organization Theory;* and Science Policy Research Unit, University of Sussex, *Success and Failure in Industrial Innovation* (London: Centre for the Study of Industrial Innovation, 1972).

46. William L. Shanklin and John K. Ryans, Jr., "Organizing for High-Tech Marketing," *Harvard Business Review* 62 (November–December 1984), 164–171; and Arnold O. Putnam, "A Redesign for Engineering," *Harvard Business Review* 63 (May–June 1985), 139–144.

47. Daft, *Organization Theory.*

48. Keith H. Hammonds, "Teaching Discipline to Six-Year-Old Lotus," *Business Week,* July 4, 1988, 100–102.

49. Susan Caminiti, "A Quiet Superstar Rises in Retailing," *Fortune,* October 23, 1989, 167–74.

50. Brian Dumaine, "How Managers Can Succeed through Speed," *Fortune,* February 13, 1989, 54–59, and George Stalk, Jr., "Time—The Next Source of Competitive Advantage," *Harvard Business Review* (July–August 1988), 41–51.

51. Fariborz Damanpour, "The Adoption of Technological, Administrative, and Ancillary Innovations: Impact of Organizational Factors," *Journal of Management* 13 (1987), 675–688.

52. Daft, "Bureaucratic vs. Nonbureaucratic Structure."

53. Mary Kay Ash, *Mary Kay on People Management* (New York: Warner, 1984), 75.

54. Edgar H. Schein, "Organizational Culture," *American Psychologist* 45 (February 1990), 109–119, and Andrew Kupfer, "An Outsider Fires Up a Railroad," *Fortune*, December 18, 1989, 133–146.

55. Marshall Sashkin and W. Warner Burke, "Organization Development in the 1980s," *General Management* 13 (1987), 393–417, and Edgar F. Huse and Thomas G. Cummings, *Organization Development and Change*, 3d ed. (St. Paul, Minn.: West, 1985).

56. Paul F. Buller, "For Successful Strategic Change: Blend OD Practices with Strategic Management," *Organizational Dynamics* (Winter 1988), 42–55, and Robert M. Fulmer and Roderick Gilkey, "Blending Corporate Families: Management and Organization Development in a Postmerger Environment," *The Academy of Management Executive* 2 (1988), 275–283.

57. David A. Nadler, *Feedback and Organizational Development: Using Data-Based Methods* (Reading, Mass.: Addison-Wesley, 1977).

58. Wendell L. French and Cecil H. Bell, Jr., *Organization Development: Behavioral Science Interventions for Organization Improvement*, 3d ed. (Englewood Cliffs, N.J.: Prentice-Hall, 1984).

59. Buller, "For Successful Strategic Change."

60. Kurt Lewin, "Frontiers in Group Dynamics: Concepts, Method, and Reality in Social Science," *Human Relations* 1 (1947), 5–41, and Huse and Cummings, *Organization Development*.

61. Richard J. Boyle, "Wrestling with Jelly Fish," *Harvard Business Review* (January–February 1984), 74–83.

62. Farnham, "The Trust Gap," and Watts, "Preston and the Teamsters Keep On Trucking."

APPLE COMPUTER

As the curtain fell on the decade of the 1980s, Apple Computer, Inc., faced some formidable hurdles: a paltry customer base, an unwieldy portable computer, poor avenues of distribution, and overpriced computers. New product development had slowed and Apple's market share had dipped below 10 percent.

Chairman and CEO John Sculley, who had generated enmity when he ousted the company's legendary founder Steve Jobs in 1985, responded by purging Apple's upper management and naming himself chief technology officer. Sculley again received a great deal of criticism, but he had decided that Apple's only option to remain a viable player in the computer industry was to branch out and invest in the innovative, high-growth sectors of the future. Such a shift in direction was not without risk.

After a little over three years Sculley's gamble seems to be paying off. The Mac Classic, Mac LC, and PowerBook families are selling briskly, and Apple now also offers the high-end 68040-based Quadras. The company has allied with IBM on the production of Taligent, a modular operating system and a set of class libraries. Apple also has made a move into the higher-end professional publishing systems, putting high priority on color for desktop publishers. Its future plans include adding imaging servers—imaging-centric data bases with storage and retrieval that can be based on content—to the product line. It will market five lucrative new software foundation technologies through the next decade as well.

Sculley has also realized his goal of becoming competitive in the sophisticated Japanese consumer electronics market. Apple developed a Japanese language software package, then recruited some prominent Japanese executives. Apple sold just a few thousand Macintoshes in 1988; in 1992 sales were around 180,000 units, or about 6 percent of the $7 billion Japanese market. Sculley personally travels to Japan about every six weeks.

Sculley has been one of the boldest to embrace another exciting innovation as well. He views the move from analog to digital technology as probably the biggest trend in the industry. Analog technology—modulated, continuous wave—is what television, radio, and stereo systems use. Digital technology compresses more capacity, as much as 10,000 times more, enabling networks to multiply information flow astronomically. The translation: In a wireless world, products that are small enough to carry around have the capability of sending and receiving enormous amounts of data.

Enter Newton, Apple's pint-sized offering that is touted as a portable office that goes anywhere. The personal digital assistant (PDA) integrates the functions of a laptop or pen-based computer, electronic-mail messenger, fax machine, and cellular phone. The scratch-command device could ultimately permit people to conduct business anywhere from the eighteenth fairway to a ski chalet in the Rockies.

Another of Sculley's goals has been the desire to make technology accessible, and if possible, invisible to computer users. Bringing what he calls a "human-centric" view would enable people to use computers without mastering all of the expert jargon now required. He says putting a human-centric passion together with the revolution in digital communication is the vision he's striving for at Apple.

Makers of powerful, fast, miniaturized components that can be produced inexpensively will also see big opportunities in the future. But Sculley believes that PDAs will also need exceptional human interface and great software technologies for spontaneous connection, disconnection, and reconnection, as well as for interactive media.

The latest technological leaps may actually force corporate America to revamp the way companies are now run. A host of top executives have expressed the view that moving into the computer age has not lead to productivity gains sufficient to justify the costs. The Apple chairman counters that the problem lies in many executives' failure to adapt to or embrace the advances. He believes that in the future, reorganizing how work is done within the corporate structure will be the key to determining which companies prosper in the 1990s.

John Sculley clearly has his hands full. He moved Apple from high-centered inertia out to the cutting edge of several sectors of the industry. Regardless of what the future holds, his operational philosophy will be to anticipate where technology is headed, and then drive his business in that direction. He perhaps best represents the emerging breed of CEOs who formulate corporate plans and strategies around where the innovations of the future are leading, instead of looking backward to the way decisions were made in the past.

● QUESTIONS

1. Describe the organizational changes John Sculley implemented, and analyze the motivations for each.

2. To what degree does Sculley's attitude and approach to technological advances apply to corporate management challenges and problems in the 1990s?

3. How did Sculley modify the Apple organization in Japan to better accommodate market needs?

4. What has changed since this video aired?

HUMAN RESOURCE MANAGEMENT 12

LEARNING OBJECTIVES

After studying this chapter, you should be able to

■ Explain the role of human resource management in organizational strategic planning

■ Describe federal legislation and societal trends that influence human resource management.

■ Describe how human resource professionals work with line managers to attract, develop, and maintain human resources in the organization.

■ Explain how organizations determine their future staffing needs through human resource planning.

■ Describe the tools managers use to recruit and select employees.

■ Describe how organizations develop an effective work force through training and performance appraisal.

■ Explain how organizations maintain a work force through the administration of wages and salaries, benefits, and terminations.

When Thomas Melohn acquired North American Tool & Die, Inc., the company was in trouble. The metal-stamping and subassembly small business used older, labor-intensive machines, whereas its well-heeled, offshore competitors used highly automated technology to achieve efficiency and quality. Other domestic job-shops were going out of business left and right, so Melohn needed a strategy to regain his company's competitiveness. North American's profits were marginal, its work force unenthusiastic,

and its prospects dim. Employee turnover was 27 percent annually. A full 7 percent of production output was rejected. CEO Melohn agonized over his top priority—how to find and keep good people.[1] ■ What should Thomas Melohn do to meet the need for high-quality employees? Can human resources be part of the strategy to restore North American's competitiveness?

M A N A G E M E N T   P R O B L E M

human resource management (HRM)

Activities undertaken to attract, develop, and maintain an effective work force within an organization.

North American Tool & Die's past performance illustrates the need for managing human resources. Thomas Melohn and his management team must develop the company's ability to recruit, train, and keep first-quality employees; otherwise, company growth will be restricted and performance will continue to suffer. The term **human resource management (HRM)** refers to activities undertaken to attract, develop, and maintain an effective work force within an organization. Companies such as General Electric and Hewlett-Packard have become famous for their philosophy about human resource management, which is the foundation of their success. HRM is equally important for not-for-profit organizations. For example, the Catholic church must address the crisis of the sharply declining number of priests. Unless the church can find ways to attract and keep priests, a mere 17,000 priests will be serving 75 million U.S. Catholics by the year 2005.[2]

Over the past decade, human resource management has shed its old "personnel" image and gained recognition as a vital player in corporate strategy. Despite its importance, company employees often do not understand HRM functions. For example, at Transamerica surveys indicated employees were not aware of the full range of human resource services or their access to those services. Effective education about HRM functions is essential.[3]

Human resource management consists of three parts. First, all managers are human resource managers. For example, at IBM every manager is expected to pay attention to the development and satisfaction of subordinates. Line managers use surveys, career planning, performance appraisal, and compensation to encourage commitment to IBM.[4] Second,

As a vital player in corporate strategy, *HRM activities* include developing and maintaining an effective work force. At MagneTek's Blytheville, Arkansas, plant, these employees enjoy a daily aerobic class as part of a Total Excellence at MagneTek (TEAM) program. This program stresses promotion of health and stress reduction as part of overall human resource improvement. Fitness is only one of the HR "tools" available to MagneTek associates to stimulate action, creative thinking, and overall improvement.

employees are viewed as assets. Employees, not buildings and machinery, give a company a competitive advantage, such as Tom Melohn is trying to accomplish with North American Tool & Die. Third, human resource management is a matching process, integrating the organization's goals with employees' needs. Employees should receive satisfaction equal to that of the company.

● GOALS OF HRM

       In this chapter, we will examine the three primary goals of HRM as illustrated in Exhibit 12.1. These goals, which take place within the organizational environment, include competitive strategy, federal legislation, and societal trends. The three goals are to attract an effective work force to the organization, develop the work force to its potential, and maintain the work force over the long term.[5] Achieving these goals requires skills in planning, forecasting, training, performance appraisal, wage and salary administration, benefit programs, and even termination. Each of the activities in Exhibit 12.1 will be discussed in this chapter. Most organizations employ human resource professionals to perform these functions. *Human resource specialists* focus on one of the HRM areas, such as recruitment of employees or administration of wage or benefit programs. *Human resource generalists* have responsibility in more than one HRM area.

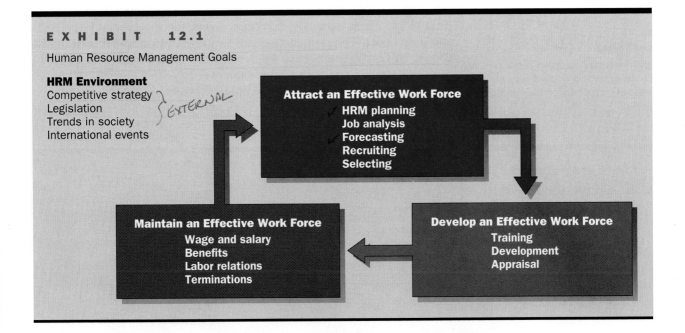

E X H I B I T   1 2 . 1

Human Resource Management Goals

HRM Environment
Competitive strategy
Legislation
Trends in society
International events

Attract an Effective Work Force
   HRM planning
   Job analysis
   Forecasting
   Recruiting
   Selecting

Maintain an Effective Work Force
   Wage and salary
   Benefits
   Labor relations
   Terminations

Develop an Effective Work Force
   Training
   Development
   Appraisal

● ENVIRONMENTAL INFLUENCES ON HRM

"Our strength is the quality of our people."

"Our people are our most important resource."

These often-repeated statements by executives emphasize the importance of HRM. Human resource managers must find, recruit, train, nurture, and retain the best people. Human resource programs are designed to fit organizational needs, core values, and strategic goals. Without the proper personnel, the brightest idea or management fad—whether teams, quality circles, or flexible compensation—is doomed to failure. For these reasons, it is important that human resource executives be involved in competitive strategy. Human resource executives also interpret federal legislation and help detect issues and trends both in society and internationally.[6]

COMPETITIVE STRATEGY

The human resource management function has changed enormously over the years. In the 1920s, HRM was a low-level position charged with ensuring that procedures were developed for hiring and firing employees and with implementing benefit plans. By the 1950s unions were a major force, and the HRM manager was elevated to a senior position as chief negotiator. During the 1980s, unions began to decline, and top HRM managers became directly involved in corporate strategic management.[7]

Exhibit 12.2 illustrates the interdependence between company and human resource strategy. The organization's competitive strategy may include mergers and acquisitions, downsizing to increase efficiency, international operations, or the acquisition of automated production technology. These strategic decisions determine the demand for skills and employees. The human resource strategy, in turn, must include the correct employee makeup to implement the organization's strategy. In the 1990s strategic decisions more than ever have to be based on human resource considerations. For example, **downsizing** is the systematic reduction in the number of managers and employees to make a com-

downsizing

The systematic reduction in the number of managers and employees to make a company more cost efficient and competitive.

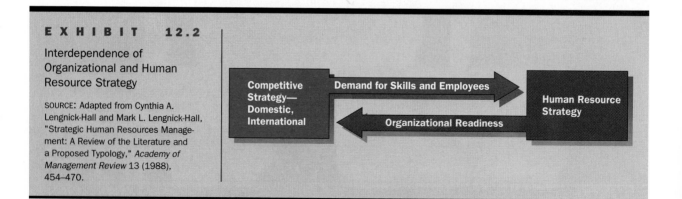

E X H I B I T   12.2

Interdependence of Organizational and Human Resource Strategy

SOURCE: Adapted from Cynthia A. Lengnick-Hall and Mark L. Lengnick-Hall, "Strategic Human Resources Management: A Review of the Literature and a Proposed Typology," *Academy of Management Review* 13 (1988), 454–470.

pany more cost efficient and competitive.[8] When Boeing CEO Frank Shrontz predicted 1993 price wars and increased competition, the company targeted 25 to 30 percent cost reduction goals. Shrontz focused on the Defense & Space Group, eliminating 16,000 of 53,000 workers through attrition and transfers to other units, making effective use of human resource strategy.[9]

As another example, the introduction of flexible manufacturing systems such as those described in Chapter 10 have dramatically changed the need for work-force skill. These new machines require a highly skilled work force, including interpersonal skills and the ability to work as a team. To make the strategic change to automated technology, the HRM department must upgrade the skills of shop machine operators and recruit new employees who have human skills as well as technical skills.[10]

FEDERAL LEGISLATION

Over the last 30 years, several federal laws have been passed to ensure equal employment opportunity (EEO). Key legislation and executive orders are summarized in Exhibit 12.3. The point of the laws is to stop discriminatory practices that are unfair to specific groups and to define enforcement agencies for these laws. EEO legislation attempts to balance the pay given to men and women; provide employment opportunities without regard to race, religion, national origin, and sex; ensure fair treatment for employees of all ages; and avoid discrimination against handicapped individuals. More recent legislation pertains to illegal aliens and people with disabilities.

The Equal Employment Opportunity Commission (EEOC) created by the Civil Rights Act of 1964 initiates investigations in response to complaints concerning discrimination. The EEOC is the major agency

As a winner of the Katherine G. Peden award for corporate excellence in the promotion of women, Louisville Gas & Electric Company prides itself on its strong *affirmative action* program. LG&E's Career Woman of the '90s seminars help women balance their personal and professional lives. These women gain the confidence necessary for advancement. AT LG&E, women held 17 percent of management positions in 1992, which is testimony that the company's affirmative action vision is becoming a reality.

EXHIBIT 12.3	Federal Law	Year	Provisions
Major Federal Laws Related to Human Resource Management	Equal Pay Act	1963	Prohibits sex differences in pay for substantially equal work.
	Civil Rights Act, Title VII	1964 1967	Prohibits discrimination in employment on basis of race, religion, color, sex, or national origin.
	Executive Orders 11246 and 11375	1965	Requires federal contractors to eliminate employment discrimination through affirmative actions.
	Age Discrimination in Employment Act (amended 1978 and 1986)	1967	Prohibits age discrimination against those between the ages of 40 and 65 years and restricts mandatory retirement.
	Executive Order 11478	1969	Prohibits discrimination in the U.S. Postal Service and various government agencies.
	Occupational Safety and Health Act (OSHA)	1970	Establishes mandatory safety and health standards in organizations.
	Vocational Rehabilitation Act	1973	Prohibits discrimination based on physical or mental handicap and requires that employees be informed about affirmative action plans.
	Vietnam-Era Veterans Readjustment Act	1974	Prohibits discrimination against disabled veterans and Vietnam-era veterans and requires affirmative action.
	Pregnancy Discrimination Act	1978	Requires that women affected by pregnancy, childbirth, or related medical conditions be treated as all other employees for employment-related purposes, including benefits.
	Immigration Reform and Control Act	1986	Prohibits employers from knowingly hiring illegal aliens and prohibits employment on the basis of national origin or citizenship.
	Americans with Disabilities Act	1990	Prohibits discrimination of qualified individuals by employers on the basis of disability, and demands that "reasonable accommodations" be provided for the disabled to allow performance of duties.
	Civil Rights Act	1991	Provides for possible compensatory and punitive damages plus traditional back pay for cases of intentional discrimination brought under Title VII of the 1964 Civil Rights Act. Shifts the burden of proof to the employer.

discrimination

The hiring or promoting of applicants based on criteria that are not job relevant.

involved with employment discrimination. **Discrimination** occurs when some applicants are hired or promoted based on criteria that are not job relevant. For example, refusing to hire black people for jobs they could readily handle or paying a woman a lower wage than a man for the same work are discriminatory acts. When discrimination is found, remedies include providing back pay and taking affirmative action. **Affirmative**

action requires that an employer take positive steps to guarantee equal employment opportunities for people within protected groups. An affirmative action plan is a formal document that can be reviewed by employees and enforcement agencies. Organizational affirmative action reduces or eliminates internal inequities among affected employee groups.

affirmative action

A policy requiring employers to take positive steps to guarantee equal employment opportunities for people within protected groups.

Failure to comply with equal employment opportunity legislation can result in substantial fines and penalties for employers. For example, Shoney's was accused of discrimination against black employees and job applicants. The class-action suit charged that company policy conspired to limit the number of black employees working in public areas of the restaurant. In 1992 the company agreed to pay $105 million to victims of its hiring, promotion, and firing policies, dating back to 1985.[11] AT&T agreed to pay over $15 million in back wages to women and other minority groups whose pay was deemed to be arbitrarily low because of discriminatory practices. In another case, a policewoman was found to have been sexually harassed and then retaliated against by management for filing a discrimination complaint. She was awarded over $22,000 in back pay and $24,000 in lieu of being reinstated as a police officer.[12]

One thing concerning human resource legislation is clear: The scope of equal employment opportunity legislation is increasing at federal, state, and municipal levels. The working rights and conditions of women, minorities, older employees, and the handicapped will receive increasing legislative attention in the future. Also, most cases in the past have concerned lower-level jobs, but the 1990s will see more attention given to equal employment opportunity in upper-level management positions.

TRENDS IN SOCIETY

The complexity of demands on human resource executives often seems overwhelming. Just as human resource managers learn to insert themselves into corporate strategy making and learn the subtleties of such federal regulations as the Americans with Disabilities Act, other trends that surface raise new problems for staffing the firm. These trends include everything from court decisions that rule against companies that fire employees to dramatic changes in the makeup of the labor force. A few of the important current trends are as follows.

WORK-FORCE DIVERSITY.   The ethnic and gender makeup of the people filling jobs in the year 2000 will be different than that of current employees. The implications of this trend are so important that Chapter 13 is devoted to them.

LABOR SUPPLY FLUCTUATIONS.   Changing demographics and economic conditions affect labor supply. In the late 1980s, predictions of severe labor shortages proved untrue because of the persistent recession in the early 1990s and the end of the Cold War. The massive reduction in the nation's defense needs and widespread corporate downsizing reversed the labor "shortage" as millions of white-collar and blue-collar Americans joined the ranks of the unemployed. The future labor supply may fluctuate further between shortage and oversupply as economic or demographic conditions change, such as the beginning of baby-boomer retirement in the year 2000.

EMPLOYMENT AT WILL.   Employers no longer enjoy the undisputed right to fire employees. Many discharged employees are filing lawsuits with almost 80 percent of the verdicts favoring the employee and damage awards exceeding $100,000. The *employment-at-will* rule traditionally permitted an employer to fire an employee for just cause, or even no cause. Now 40 states have written employment laws to severely limit the "at will" doctrine and to protect against wrongful firing of employees who refuse to violate a law or expose an illegal action by their employers. Although termination is generally accepted by the courts when employers can show employee incompetence or changing business requirements, many employers remain confused about their rights regarding termination. Employers now avoid terms such as *permanent employment,* and many employers are now spelling out their termination policy to employees, asking them to acknowledge that the employment agreement can be terminated at any time, thereby avoiding an implied long-term employment contract.[13]

EMPLOYEE FLEXIBILITY.   One of the clearest trends is the increased effort to obtain quality employees and at the same time reduce excess employee costs so that firms can remain competitive in the global marketplace. This means that employers will be making greater use of part-time employees, work schedules that allow employees to work other than the traditional hours during the day, employee leasing and temporary employees, and employees who work under contract only for specific hours and tasks, thereby allowing employers to get exactly what they need and avoiding the necessity of providing offices and benefits on a full-time basis. Companies such as Bowater, Digital Equipment, Hallmark, Pacific Bell, and Worthington Industries have turned to employee flexibility to reduce costs without having to lay off valued employees.

UNIONIZATION.   The general trend in North America is away from unionization, but many employees belong to unions, and labor continues to unionize new companies. The National Labor Relations Act of 1935 provides that employees may elect to be represented by unions in negotiations with employers over wages, hours, and other terms and conditions of employment. Currently, about one-fourth of all workers are covered by collective bargaining agreements. In companies where unions represent workers, union officials research the needs of members, the elements of the pay package, and the employers' financial condition. When a contract expires, union officials negotiate on behalf of the members of the bargaining unit for desired pay components and other issues relevant to workers.[14]

Some companies find unionization a benefit; others try to avoid unionization. Indeed, just the threat of a union may cause an employer to adjust pay and benefits. At Cannon Mills Company, three mills had to be closed and as a result, some employees tried to unionize. Cannon's

One of the recent *trends in society* is the new responsiveness of unions to changes in competition. At Federal-Mogul Corporation's Lititz, Pennsylvania, plant, unions and management joined hands to successfully launch production of green rings, a component previously outsourced to suppliers. Here, union-management cooperation is celebrated and recognized by state government officials.

management responded by persuading workers that the union would not improve benefits and would simply take part of the employees' paychecks in the form of union dues. The most promising trend in recent years has been the responsiveness of unions to new competitive conditions. The need for cross-training, employee participation, and new compensation systems to meet global competition have brought unions into closer collaboration with management.

Within this context of trends in society, human resource managers must achieve the three primary goals described earlier in this chapter: <u>attracting</u>, <u>developing</u>, and <u>maintaining</u> an effective work force for the organization. Let us now review some of the established techniques for accomplishing these goals.

● ATTRACTING AN EFFECTIVE WORK FORCE

The first goal of HRM is to attract individuals who show signs of becoming valued, productive, and satisfied employees. The first step in attracting an effective work force involves human resource planning, in which managers or HRM professionals predict the need for new employees based on the types of vacancies that exist, as illustrated in Exhibit 12.4. The second step is to use recruiting procedures to communicate with potential applicants. The third step is to select from

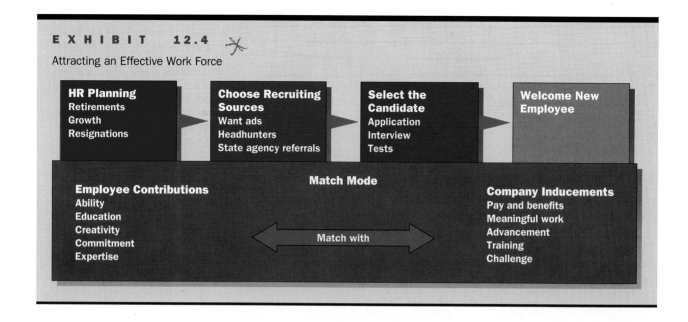

EXHIBIT 12.4

Attracting an Effective Work Force

HR Planning
Retirements
Growth
Resignations

Choose Recruiting Sources
Want ads
Headhunters
State agency referrals

Select the Candidate
Application
Interview
Tests

Welcome New Employee

Match Mode

Employee Contributions
Ability
Education
Creativity
Commitment
Expertise

Match with

Company Inducements
Pay and benefits
Meaningful work
Advancement
Training
Challenge

the applicants those persons believed to be the best potential contributors to the organization. Finally, the new employee is welcomed into the organization.

Underlying the organization's effort to attract employees is a matching model. With the **matching model,** the organization and the individual attempt to match the needs, interests, and values that they offer each other. The organization offers "inducements," and the employee offers "contributions."[15] HRM professionals attempt to identify a correct match. For example, a small software developer may require long hours from creative, technically skilled employees. In return, it can offer freedom from bureaucracy, tolerance of idiosyncrasies, and potentially high pay. A large manufacturer can offer employment security and stability, but it may have more rules and regulations and require greater skills for "getting approval from the higher-ups." The individual who would thrive working for the software developer might feel stymied and unhappy working for a large manufacturer. Both the company and the employee are interested in finding a good match.

HUMAN RESOURCE PLANNING

Human resource planning is the forecasting of human resource needs and the projected matching of individuals with expected vacancies. Human resource planning begins with several questions:

- What new technologies are emerging, and how will these affect the work system?
- What is the volume of the business likely to be in the next five to ten years?
- What is the turnover rate, and how much, if any, is avoidable?

matching model

An employee selection approach in which the organization and the applicant attempt to match each other's needs, interests, and values.

human resource planning

The forecasting of human resource needs and the projected matching of individuals with expected job vacancies.

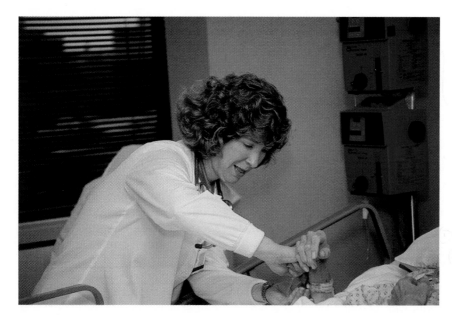

Human resource planning enables Galen Health Care, Inc., to respond effectively to a variety of health-care service needs, from recruitment and training programs to mobile nursing programs that supplement staffing for Galen hospitals during times of vacancy or patient surges. Short- and long-range planning, utilizing focus groups and task forces, enables Galen to deal effectively with the complex issues of nursing supply and demand. Here, a member of Galen's mobile nursing team adjusts a patient's intra-venous feeding tubes.

The responses to these questions are used to formulate specific questions pertaining to HRM activities, such as the following:

- How many senior managers will we need during this time period?
- What types of engineers will we need, and how many?
- Are persons with adequate computer skills available for meeting our projected needs?
- How many administrative personnel—technicians, secretaries—will we need to support the additional managers and engineers?[16]

Answers to these questions help define the direction for the organization's HRM strategy. For example, if forecasting suggests that there will be a strong need for more technically trained individuals, the organization can (1) define the jobs and skills needed in some detail, (2) hire and train recruiters to look for the specified skills, and/or (3) provide new training for existing employees. By anticipating future HRM needs, the organization can prepare itself to meet competitive challenges more effectively than organizations that react to problems only as they arise.

One of the most successful applications of human resource planning occurred at EDS (Electronic Data Systems), now a division of General Motors.

 E D S

EDS's mission is to assume responsibility for customers' computer infor-mation processing needs. Following the merger of EDS into General Motors, EDS's work force grew in one year from 14,000 to 40,000. The integration into General Motors more than doubled the demand for EDS services, because EDS took over the reshaping of all GM information systems. Specific projects included a computer-aided telemarketing center, a toll-free customer assistance network, and integration of computers, robots, and other information technologies to improve information efficiencies.

The impact on human resources was dramatic. EDS had to recruit and hire more than 16,000 new employees and assimilate 9,000 of General Motors' information services employees. EDS's human resources nearly tripled in one year.

HRM professionals responded. EDS defined 7,000 new technical development positions and sought applications, which totaled 225,000. The HRM staff increased the number of full-time recruiters from 70 to over 220. EDS line managers provided backup support and shared the interviewing and selection tasks. One source of pride was that EDS standards were not lowered to meet the enormous hiring goals. Test results showed the new recruits to be among the best qualified ever. Without excellent human resource planning, EDS could not have hired and assimilated this large number of new employees. Human resource management was perhaps the year's single greatest achievement for EDS.[17] ■

HRM FORECASTING TECHNIQUES.   A variety of HRM forecasting techniques is in use today. These can be classified as short range and long range.

Short-range forecasting frequently uses the following steps:

- The demand for the organization's product or service is predicted. Major expected external changes (such as increased demand for a new line of products) are accounted for in this estimation.

- The overall sales forecast is estimated; anticipated internal changes (for example, the conversion to word processors from typewriters) are considered.

- Working budgets to reflect the expected work loads of every department are estimated.

- Personnel requirements are determined through conversion of dollars or units into numbers of people.

- Forecasts of labor market conditions or internal organization factors (such as turnover rate) that may affect the future labor supply are considered.

An example of short-range forecasting is USAir's introduction of the first Boeing 737-300 into scheduled service. Introducing a new aircraft into an airline operation required careful planning and coordination, beginning with a forecast of the number of pilots needed. Then 737-300 flight simulators had to be obtained and set up in a classroom. Pilots had to be trained before the new aircraft was introduced. New pilots with qualifications fitting the 737-300 also had to be hired.

Long-range forecasting ranges from the intuitive to the sophisticated. As described in Chapter 8, some forecasting techniques are based on mathematical extrapolation from past trends. Others involve group decision-making techniques, such as the Delphi method, wherein groups of top managers or other experts use their judgment to make forecasts. Statistical data are also used to project the impact of future employment levels, sales activity, employee turnover, and other variables on the organization's future labor needs.

The need for long-range planning was illustrated by General Electric when top executives realized that corporate human resources did not fit new products and technologies. General Electric's chairman said, "We were a company with 30,000 electromechanical engineers becoming a company that needed electronics engineers. We didn't plan for this change . . . and it caused us big problems. . . ." Without planning, a company such as GE could be forced to drain engineers and managers from a stable division to support a growing division, which would propel people into positions above their competence and necessitate a costly rapid-hiring effort.[18]

RECRUITING

Recruiting is defined as "activities or practices that define the characteristics of applicants to whom selection procedures are ultimately applied."[19] Although we frequently think of campus recruiting as a typical recruiting activity, many organizations use *internal recruiting*, or "promote-from-within" policies, to fill their higher-level positions.[20] At Mellon Bank, for example, current employees are given preference when a position opens. Open positions are listed in Mellon's career opportunity bulletins, which are distributed to employees. Internal recruiting has several advantages: It is less costly than an external search, and it generates higher employee commitment, development, and satisfaction, because it offers opportunities for career advancement to employees rather than outsiders.

recruiting
The activities or practices that define the desired characteristics of applicants for specific jobs.

These crowded corporate hallways reflect the rapid growth at Franklin Resources, Inc. In 1990, while many companies were downsizing, Franklin's staffing increased 8.9 percent between September 1989 and September 1990 (from 1,850 to 2,014 employees). In a competitive job market, Franklin has implemented a vigorous *recruiting* program. In external recruiting, Franklin's Management Training Program prepares college graduates for supervisory and managerial positions. As complement to the external applicant search, Franklin offers rewards for employee referrals.

Frequently, however, *external recruiting*—recruiting newcomers from outside the organization—is advantageous. Applicants are provided by a variety of outside sources including newspaper advertising, state employment services, private employment agencies ("headhunters"), job fairs, and employee referrals. Some employers even provide cash awards for employees who submit names of people who subsequently accept employment, because referral is one of the cheapest and most reliable methods for external recruiting.[21]

REALISTIC JOB PREVIEWS.   One approach to enhancing recruiting effectiveness is called a *realistic job preview*. A **realistic job preview (RJP)** gives applicants all pertinent and realistic information—positive and negative—about the job and the organization.[22] RJPs enhance employee satisfaction and reduce turnover, because they facilitate matching individuals, jobs, and organizations. Individuals have a better basis on which to determine their suitability to the organization and "self-select" into or out of positions based on full information. When employees choose positions without RJPs, unmet expectations may cause initial job dissatisfaction and increased turnover. For example, Linda McDermott left a good position in an accounting firm to become an executive vice-president of a new management consulting company. She was told she would have a major role in helping the business grow. As it turned out, her boss relegated her to administrative duties so she quit after a few months, causing the company to initiate another lengthy search and sidetracking her career for a year or two.[23]

LEGAL CONSIDERATIONS.   Organizations must ensure that their recruiting practices conform to the law. As discussed earlier in this chapter, equal employment opportunity (EEO) laws stipulate that recruiting and hiring decisions cannot discriminate on the basis of race, national origin, religion, or sex. *Affirmative action* refers to the use of goals, timetables, or other methods in recruiting to promote the hiring, development, and retention of "protected groups"—persons historically underrepresented in the workplace. For example, companies adopting an affirmative action policy may recruit at colleges with large enrollments of black students. A city may establish a goal of recruiting one black firefighter for every white firefighter until the proportion of black firefighters is commensurate with that in the community.

Most large companies try to comply with affirmative action and EEO guidelines. Prudential Insurance Company's policy is presented in Exhibit 12.5. Prudential actively recruits employees and takes affirmative action steps to recruit individuals from all walks of life.

SELECTING

The next step for managers is to select desired employees from the pool of recruited applicants. In the **selection** process, employers attempt to determine the skills, abilities, and other attributes a person needs to perform a particular job. Then they assess applicants' characteristics in an attempt to determine the "fit" between the job and applicant characteristics.

---

realistic job preview (RJP)

A recruiting approach that gives applicants all pertinent and realistic information about the job and the organization.

---

selection

The process of determining the skills, abilities, and other attributes a person needs to perform a particular job.

EXHIBIT 12.5

Prudential's Corporate Recruiting Policy

An Equal Opportunity Employer

Prudential recruits, hires, trains, promotes, and compensates individuals without regard to race, color, religion or creed, age, sex, marital status, national origin, ancestry, liability for service in the armed forces of the United States, status as a special disabled veteran or veteran of the Vietnam era, or physical or mental handicap.

This is official company policy because:
- we believe it is right
- it makes good business sense
- it is the law

We are also committed to an ongoing program of affirmative action in which members of under-represented groups are actively sought out and employed for opportunities in all parts and at all levels of the company. In employing people from all walks of life, Prudential gains access to the full experience of our diverse society.

SOURCE: Prudential Insurance Company.

JOB DESCRIPTIONS. A good place to start in making a selection decision is the job description. Human resource professionals or line managers who make selection decisions may have little direct experience with the job to be filled. If these persons are to make a good match between job and candidate, they should read the job description before they review applications.

A **job description** typically lists job duties as well as desirable qualifications for a particular job. An example of a job description for American Airlines appears in Exhibit 12.6.

SELECTION DEVICES. Several devices are used for assessing applicant qualifications. The most frequently used are the application form, interview, paper-and-pencil test, and assessment center. Human resource professionals may use a combination of these devices to obtain a valid prediction of employee job performance. **Validity** refers to the relationship between one's score on a selection device and one's future job performance. A valid selection procedure will provide high scores that correspond to subsequent high job performance.

Application Form. The **application form** is used to collect information about the applicant's education, previous job experience, and other background characteristics. Research in the life insurance industry shows that biographical information inventories can validly predict future job success.[24]

One pitfall to be avoided is the inclusion of questions that are irrelevant to job success. In line with affirmative action, the application form should not ask questions that will create an adverse impact on "protected groups" unless the questions are clearly related to the job.[25] For example, employers should not ask whether the applicant rents or owns his or her own home because (1) an applicant's response might adversely affect his or her chances at the job, (2) minorities and women may be less likely to own a home, and (3) homeownership is probably unrelated to job performance. On the other hand, the CPA exam is relevant to job performance in a CPA firm; thus, it is appropriate to ask whether an applicant for employment has passed the CPA exam even if only one-

job description

A listing of duties as well as desirable qualifications for a particular job.

validity

The relationship between an applicant's score on a selection device and his or her future job performance.

application form

A device for collecting information about an applicant's education, previous job experience, and other background characteristics.

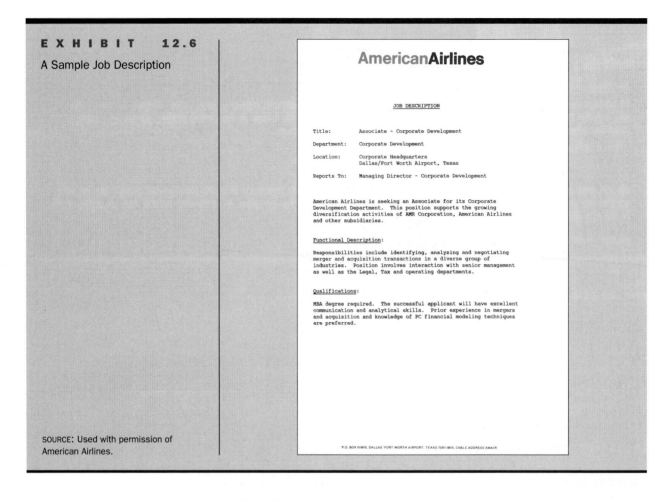

EXHIBIT 12.6

A Sample Job Description

AmericanAirlines

JOB DESCRIPTION

Title: Associate - Corporate Development

Department: Corporate Development

Location: Corporate Headquarters
                 Dallas/Fort Worth Airport, Texas

Reports To: Managing Director - Corporate Development

American Airlines is seeking an Associate for its Corporate
Development Department. This position supports the growing
diversification activities of AMR Corporation, American Airlines
and other subsidiaries.

Functional Description:

Responsibilities include identifying, analyzing and negotiating
merger and acquisition transactions in a diverse group of
industries. Position involves interaction with senior management
as well as the Legal, Tax and operating departments.

Qualifications:

MBA degree required. The successful applicant will have excellent
communication and analytical skills. Prior experience in mergers
and acquisition and knowledge of PC financial modeling techniques
are preferred.

P.O. BOX 619616, DALLAS/FORT WORTH AIRPORT, TEXAS 75261-9616, CABLE ADDRESS AMAIR

half of all women or minority applicants have done so versus nine-tenths of men applicants.

Interview.[26]   The interview is used in the hiring process in almost every job category in virtually every organization. The *interview* serves as a two-way communication channel that allows both the organization and the applicant to collect information that would otherwise be difficult to obtain.

Although widely used, the interview as generally practiced is not a valid predictor of later job performance. Researchers have identified many reasons for this. Interviewers frequently are unfamiliar with the job. They tend to make decisions in the first few minutes of the interview before all relevant information has been gathered. They also may base decisions on personal biases (such as against minority groups or physically unattractive persons and in favor of those similar to themselves). The interviewer may talk too much and spend time discussing matters irrelevant to the job.[27]

Organizations will continue to use interviews in spite of the pitfalls. Thus, researchers have identified methods for increasing their validity. Advice for effective interviewing—as well as some unusual interview experiences—is summarized in the Manager's Shoptalk box.

THE RIGHT WAY TO INTERVIEW A JOB APPLICANT

A so-so interview usually nets a so-so employee. Many hiring mistakes can be prevented during the interview. The following techniques will ensure a successful interview:

1. Know what you want. Before the interview, prepare questions based on your knowledge of the job to be filled. If you do not have a thorough knowledge of the job, read a job description. If possible, call one or more jobholders and ask them about the job duties and what is required to succeed. Another idea is to make up a list of traits and qualifications for the ideal candidate. Be specific about what it will take to get the job done.

2. Prepare a road map. Develop questions that will reveal whether the candidate has the correct background and qualifications. The questions should focus on previous experiences that are relevant to the current job. If the job requires creativity and innovation, ask a question such as "What do you do differently from other sales reps?"

3. Use open-ended questions in which the right answer is not obvious. Ask the applicant to give specific examples of previous work experiences. For example, don't ask, "Are you a hard worker?" or "Tell me about yourself." Instead ask, "Can you give me examples from your previous work history that reflect your level of motivation?" or "How did you go about getting your current job?"

4. Do not ask questions that are *irrelevant to the job.* This is particularly important when the irrelevant questions might adversely affect minorities or women. Questions that are considered objectionable are the same as those considered objectionable on application forms.

5. Listen, don't talk. You should spend most of the interview listening. If you talk too much, the focus will shift to you and you may miss important cues. Listen carefully to tone of voice as well as content. Body language also can be revealing; for example, failure to make eye contact is a danger signal.

6. Allow enough time so that the interview will not be rushed. Leave time for the candidate to ask questions about the job. The types of questions the candidate asks can be an important clue to his or her interest in the job. Try to delay forming an opinion about the applicant until after the entire interview has been completed.

7. Avoid reliance on your memory. Request the applicant's permission to take notes; then do so unobtrusively during the interview or immediately after. If several applicants are interviewed, notes are essential for remembering what they said and the impressions they made.

Even a well-planned interview may be disrupted by the unexpected. Robert Half asked vice-presidents and personnel directors at 100 major American corporations to describe the most unusual thing that they were aware of ever happening during a job interview. Various applicants reportedly:

- "Wore a Walkman and said she could listen to me and the music at the same time."
- "Announced she hadn't had lunch and proceeded to eat a hamburger and french fries in the interviewer's office."
- "Wore a jogging suit to interview for a position as a vice-president."
- "He said he was so well-qualified that if he didn't get the job, it would prove that the company's management was incompetent."
- "A balding candidate abruptly excused himself. He returned to the office a few minutes later wearing a hairpiece."
- "Not only did he ignore the 'No Smoking' sign in my office, he lit up the wrong ends of several filter-tip cigarettes."
- "She chewed bubble gum and constantly blew bubbles."
- "Job applicant challenged the interviewer to arm wrestle."
- "He stretched out on the floor to fill out the job application."
- "He interrupted to telephone his therapist for advice on answering specific interview questions."
- "He dozed off and started snoring during the interview."
- "He said that if he were hired, he would demonstrate his loyalty by having the corporate logo tattooed on his forearm." ∎

SOURCE: James M. Jenks and Brian L. P. Zevnik, "ABCs of Job Interviewing," *Harvard Business Review* (July–August 1989), 38–42, and Martha H. Peak, "What Color Is Your Bumbershoot?" Reprinted by permission of publisher from *Management Review* (October 1989), 63, © 1989. American Management Association, New York. All rights reserved.

paper-and-pencil test

A written test designed to measure a particular attribute such as intelligence or aptitude.

assessment center

A technique for selecting individuals with high managerial potential based on their performance on a series of simulated managerial tasks.

Paper-and-Pencil Test. Many companies use **paper-and-pencil tests** such as intelligence tests, aptitude and ability tests, and personality inventories, particularly those shown to be valid predictors.[28] For example, a 109-question personality test has been used by independent insurance agents to hire clerical and customer service employees. The test is designed to measure such traits as "motivation to please others" and "people orientation." The insurance agencies believe they need something to accurately gauge applicants' strengths and weaknesses. The test has been successful, because candidates hired have displayed strong tendencies to provide service to customers.[29]

Assessment Center. First developed by psychologists at AT&T, assessment centers are used to select individuals with high potential for managerial careers by such organizations as AT&T, IBM, General Electric, and JCPenney.[30] **Assessment centers** present a series of managerial situations to groups of applicants over, say, a two- or three-day period. One technique is the "in-basket" simulation, which requires the applicant to play the role of a manager who must decide how to respond to ten memos in his or her in-basket within a two-hour period. Panels of two or three trained judges observe the applicant's decisions and assess the extent to which they reflect interpersonal, communication, and problem-solving skills.

Assessment centers have proven to be valid predictors of managerial success,[31] and some organizations now use them for hiring technical workers. At Kimberly-Clark's newest plants, for example, applicants for machine operator jobs are put through a simulation in which they are asked to play the role of a supervisor. The idea is to see whether candidates have sufficient "people skills" to fit into the participative work atmosphere. Assessment centers are important because they provide a more valid measure of interpersonal skills than do paper-and-pencil tests.

Companies such as Toyota rely heavily on a combination of selection techniques to fill jobs at a higher than 90 percent success rate.

 TOYOTA MOTOR CORPORATION

To land a production job at a North American Toyota plant takes at least 18 hours. First, prospective employees must pass a literacy and general knowledge exam as well as a test of their attitudes toward work. Applicants go in groups of 12 to an assessment center where they must demonstrate skills in areas such as communication, mental flexibility, problem solving, and teamwork. Applicants may go through a manufacturing exercise in which they are expected to improve the method of assembling plastic pipes. Or they may be told that a lawn mower manufacturer has production problems to see which applicants ask the right questions and can work cooperatively to find a solution. Finally, intense interviews help weed out those who appear to have bad attitudes. Only 10 percent of applicants make it through the tests for reading, math, manual dexterity, job fitness, technical knowledge, hypothetical production problems, interpersonal skills, and attitude. The resulting Toyota team members are a spirited elite who love their jobs and are devoted to Toyota.[32] ■

● DEVELOPING AN EFFECTIVE WORK FORCE

Following selection, the major goal of HRM is to develop employees into an effective work force. Development includes training and performance appraisal.

TRAINING AND DEVELOPMENT

Training and development represent a planned effort by an organization to facilitate employees' learning of job-related behaviors.[33] Some authors distinguish the two forms of intervention by noting that the term *training* usually refers to teaching lower-level or technical employees how to do their present jobs, whereas *development* refers to teaching managers and professionals the skills needed for both present and future jobs. For simplicity, we will refer to both interventions as *training.*

Organizations spend nearly $100 billion each year on training. In 1987 IBM reported spending more than $750 million a year on corporate schooling, more than the entire budget of Harvard University.[34] Training may occur in a variety of forms. The most common method is on-the-job training. In **on-the-job training (OJT),** an experienced employee is asked to take a new employee "under his or her wing" and show the newcomer how to perform job duties. OJT has many advantages, such as few out-of-pocket costs for training facilities, materials, or instructor fees and easy transfer of learning back to the job. The learning site is the work site.

Other frequently used training methods include

- *Orientation training,* in which newcomers are introduced to the organization's "culture," its standards, and goals.
- *Classroom training,* including lectures, films, audiovisual techniques, and simulations.
- *Programmed and computer-assisted instruction,* in which the employee works at his or her own pace to learn material from a text that includes exercises and quizzes to enhance learning
- *Conference and case discussion groups,* in which participants analyze cases or discuss topics assisted by a training leader.

Companies such as Toyota that spend heavily on selection also invest in employee training. The 10 percent of employees selected undergo several weeks of training for their specific jobs, often at the employees' own expense. At General Motors' truck plant, each assembly line worker received 400 to 500 hours of paid training. Each skilled worker got training of 1,000 hours—the equivalent to almost six months. Motorola, Macy's, and Texas Instruments are examples of companies that appreciate the importance of thorough training to remain competitive in the global marketplace.

Not only are companies increasing training budgets but also they are experimenting with a variety of new training methods. The popularity of manufacturing teams, for example, has led to new ideas in training. "Cross-discipline" training enables employees to understand the rela-

on-the-job training (OJT)

A type of training in which an experienced employee "adopts" a new employee to teach him or her how to perform job duties.

Global companies face special challenges in *training and developing* an effective work force. Dow Corning's European Graduate Recruitment Program skips American-style campus presentations and job fairs in favor of innovative programs such as The New Graduate Induction Weekend in Belgium. Combining mountain bikes and orientation, the program (pictured here) stresses teamwork, strategy, and stamina in attainment of goals within specific time limits.

tionship of their job to others so that everyone works toward the common corporate goal. "Integrative learning" uses team exercises to establish and reinforce effective teamwork habits.[35]

PROMOTION FROM WITHIN.   Promotion from within helps companies retain and develop productive employees. It provides challenging assignments, prescribes new responsibilities, and helps employees grow by developing their abilities.

One approach to promotion from within is *job posting*, which means that positions are announced on bulletin boards or in company publications as openings occur. Interested employees notify the human resource department, which then helps make the fit between employees and positions.

Another approach is the *employee resource chart*, which is designed to identify likely successors for each management position. The chart looks like a typical organization chart with every employee listed. Every key position includes the names of top candidates to move into that position when it becomes vacant. Candidates are rated on a five-point scale reflecting whether they are ready for immediate promotion or need additional experience. These charts show the potential flow of employees up through the hierarchy and provide motivation to employees who have an opportunity for promotion.

PERFORMANCE APPRAISAL

performance appraisal

The process of observing and evaluating an employee's performance, recording the assessment, and providing feedback to the employee.

Performance appraisal is another important technique for developing an effective work force. **Performance appraisal** comprises the steps of observing and assessing employee performance, recording the assessment, and providing feedback to the employee. Managers use performance appraisal to describe and evaluate the employees' performances. During performance appraisal, skillful managers give feedback and praise concerning the acceptable elements of the employee's performance. They also describe performance areas that need improvement. Employees can use this information to change their job performance. Performance appraisal can also reward high performers with merit pay, recognition, and other rewards.

For example, PepsiCo uses performance appraisal to weed out the weak and nurture the strong. First, each boss is required to sit down with subordinates once a year and discuss performance. This appraisal pertains to what the manager did to make a big difference in the business, not whether he or she is a nice person. Second, managers then are divided into four categories. Those at the top are promoted. Those in the second group get challenging jobs. Those in the third category continue to be evaluated and rotated. Those in the bottom category are out.[36]

Generally, HRM professionals concentrate on two things to make performance appraisal a positive force in their organization: (1) the accurate assessment of performance through the development and application of assessment systems such as rating scales and (2) training managers to effectively use the performance appraisal interview so managers can provide feedback that will reinforce good performance and motivate employee development.

ASSESSING PERFORMANCE ACCURATELY.   To obtain an accurate performance rating, managers must acknowledge that jobs are multidimensional and performance thus may be multidimensional as well. For example, a sports broadcaster may perform well on the job-knowledge dimension; that is, she or he may be able to report facts and figures about the players and describe which rule applies when there is a questionable play on the field. But the same sports broadcaster may not perform as well on another dimension, such as communication. She or he may be unable to express the information in a colorful way that interests the audience or may interrupt the other broadcasters.

If performance is to be rated accurately, the performance appraisal form should require the rater—usually the supervisor—to assess each relevant performance dimension. A multidimensional form increases the usefulness of the performance appraisal for giving rewards and facilitates employee growth and development.

Although we would like to believe that every manager carefully assesses employees' performances, researchers have identified several rating problems.[37] For example, **halo error** occurs when an employee receives the same rating on all dimensions even if his or her performance is good on some dimensions and poor on others. **Homogeneity** occurs when a rater gives all employees a similar rating even if their performances are not equally good.

One approach to overcome management performance evaluation errors is to use a behavior-based rating technique, such as the behaviorally anchored rating scale. The **behaviorally anchored rating scale (BARS)** is developed from critical incidents pertaining to job performance. Each job performance scale is anchored with specific behavioral statements that describe varying degrees of performance. By relating employee performance to specific incidents, raters can more accurately evaluate an employee's performance.[38]

Exhibit 12.7 illustrates the BARS method for evaluating a production line supervisor. The production supervisor's job can be broken down into several dimensions, such as equipment maintenance, employee training, or work scheduling. A behaviorally anchored rating scale should be developed for each dimension. The dimension in Exhibit 12.7 is work scheduling. Good performance is represented by a 7, 8, or 9 on the scale and unacceptable performance as a 1, 2, or 3. If a production supervisor's job has eight dimensions, the total performance evaluation will be the sum of the scores for each of eight scales.[39]

PERFORMANCE APPRAISAL INTERVIEW.   Most corporations provide formal feedback in the form of an annual **performance appraisal interview** with the employee. Too often, however, this meeting between boss and subordinate does not stimulate better job performance.[40] Managers may be unaware of the true causes of performance problems, because they have not carefully observed employee job activities. They may have a number of useful ideas for subordinates but present them in a threatening manner. As a result, employees may feel defensive and reject suggestions for improvement.

Research into the performance appraisal interview suggests a number of steps that will increase its effectiveness.[41]

halo error

A type of rating error that occurs when an employee receives the same rating on all dimensions regardless of his or her performance on individual ones.

homogeneity

A type of rating error that occurs when a rater gives all employees a similar rating regardless of their individual performances.

behaviorally anchored rating scale (BARS)

A rating technique that relates an employee's performance to specific job-related incidents.

performance appraisal interview

A formal review of an employee's performance conducted between the superior and the subordinate.

EXHIBIT 12.7

Example of a Behaviorally Anchored Rating Scale

Job: Production Line Supervisor
Work Dimension: Work Scheduling

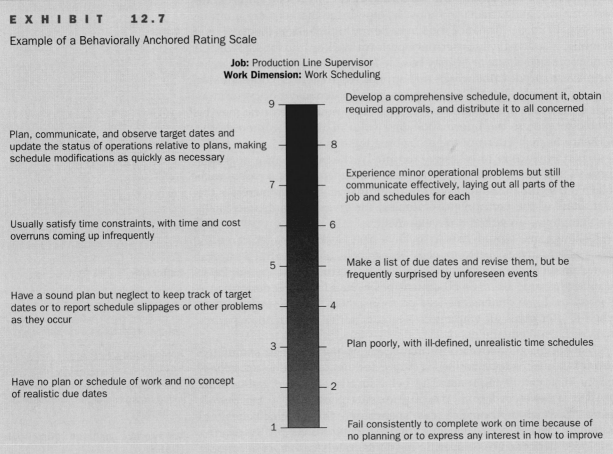

Develop a comprehensive schedule, document it, obtain required approvals, and distribute it to all concerned

Plan, communicate, and observe target dates and update the status of operations relative to plans, making schedule modifications as quickly as necessary

Experience minor operational problems but still communicate effectively, laying out all parts of the job and schedules for each

Usually satisfy time constraints, with time and cost overruns coming up infrequently

Make a list of due dates and revise them, but be frequently surprised by unforeseen events

Have a sound plan but neglect to keep track of target dates or to report schedule slippages or other problems as they occur

Plan poorly, with ill-defined, unrealistic time schedules

Have no plan or schedule of work and no concept of realistic due dates

Fail consistently to complete work on time because of no planning or to express any interest in how to improve

SOURCE: Based on J. P. Campbell, M. D. Dunnette, R. D. Arvey, and L. V. Hellervik, "The Development and Evaluation of Behaviorally Based Rating Scales," *Journal of Applied Psychology* 57 (1973), 15–22, and Francine Alexander, "Performance Appraisals," *Small Business Reports* (March 1989), 20–29.

1 Raters (usually supervisors) should be knowledgeable about the subordinates' jobs and performance levels.

2 Raters should welcome employee participation during the interview rather than "tell and sell" their views by lecturing to subordinates. This is particularly true when the employee is knowledgeable and accustomed to participating with the supervisor.

3 A flexible approach to feedback based on the characteristics of the subordinate, the job, and his or her performance level is useful. For example, newer employees need more frequent feedback than other employees do.

4 Training is used to help supervisors devise interview strategies for different situations. Role-playing that involves practice appraisal interviews is helpful for this purpose.

Performance feedback is more effective when it includes specific examples of good and bad performance. For example, "Your attendance

Performance appraisal is an excellent opportunity for communication between managers and employees. However, some managers find it difficult to provide negative feedback during a performance appraisal interview. In this role-play sequence designed to build supervisory skills for employees of Varian Associates, Inc., managers practice performance appraisal interviewing. Employees take turns in roles of manager and subordinate. Managers learn to assess performance accurately and give the positive and negative feedback necessary for their subordinates' continued development.

record shows that you were here on time nearly every day this month, and this is a great improvement over last month" is more specific and helpful than "You seem to have a much better attitude these days about your work." Some experts suggest that managers keep diaries of employee performance so they will not have to rely on their memories to generate specific examples.

One of the most recent appraisal innovations is to involve peers in performance review. Companies such as General Electric, Eastman Kodak, Public Service of New Mexico, and Raritan Steel have found that this *peer review* process dramatically increases openness, commitment, and trust within the organization and prevents problems that sometimes occur with a one-on-one interview. Managers learn that employees have good opinions about performance, and soliciting opinions from other employees provides a group approach to problem solving around important performance issues.[42] A few forward-looking companies are even experimenting with a bottom-up performance appraisal process in which subordinates provide a performance appraisal of their boss.

● MAINTAINING AN EFFECTIVE WORK FORCE

Now we turn to the topic of how managers and HRM professionals maintain a work force that has been recruited and developed. Maintenance of the current work force involves compensation, wage and salary structure, benefits, and occasional terminations.

COMPENSATION

The term **compensation** refers to (1) all monetary payments and (2) all goods or commodities used in lieu of money to reward employees.[43] An organization's compensation structure includes wages and/or salaries

compensation

Monetary payments (wages, salaries) and nonmonetary goods/commodities (fringe benefits, vacations) used to reward employees.

and fringe benefits such as health insurance, paid vacations, or employee fitness centers. A company's compensation structure does not just happen. It is designed to fit company strategy and to provide compensation equity.

COMPENSATION STRATEGY.   Ideally, management's strategy for the organization should be a critical determinant of the features and operations of the pay system.[44] For example, managers may have the goal of maintaining or improving profitability or market share by stimulating employee performance. Thus, they should design and use a merit pay system rather than a system based on other criteria such as seniority. As another example, managers may have the goal of attracting and retaining desirable employees. Here they can use a pay survey to determine competitive wages in comparable companies and adjust pay rates to meet or exceed the going rates.

Pay-for-performance systems are becoming extremely popular in both large and small businesses, including Caterpillar, Aluminum Company of America, and au Bon Pain. These systems are usually designed as a form of profit sharing to reward employees when profitability goals are met. At Alcoa, payouts to employees equal 7 percent of each worker's salary. Caterpillar employees each received an $800 bonus, and Ford employees received an average $3,700 per employee. Employees have an incentive to make the company more efficient and profitable, because if goals are not met, no bonuses are paid. Jim Bernstein, CEO of General Health, Inc., a small business, promised all 30 employees they would get an extra month's pay if the company hit the sales target. Sales shot up, going far beyond the target, showing how powerful the correct incentive can be.[45]

An effective compensation strategy is a major component in *maintaining an effective work force*. As part of a strategy of employee empowerment, MDU Resources Group, Inc., initiated BETA (Bonus Earned Through Achievement) in 1990. Goal-oriented bonus incentives encourage employees to enhance overall company competitiveness by working toward five common marketing and efficiency goals that stress cost control and marketing.

COMPENSATION EQUITY.　　Managers often wish to maintain a sense of fairness and equity within the pay structure and thereby fortify employee morale. **Job evaluation** refers to the process of determining the value or worth of jobs within an organization through an examination of job content. Job evaluation techniques enable managers to compare similar and dissimilar jobs and to determine internally equitable pay rates—that is, pay rates that employees believe are fair compared with those for other jobs in the organization. Managers also may want to provide income security so that their employees need not be overly concerned with the financial consequences of disability or retirement.

WAGE AND SALARY STRUCTURE

Large organizations typically employ HRM compensation specialists to establish and maintain a pay structure. They may also hire outside consultants, such as the Hay Group or PAQ (Position Analysis Questionnaire) Associates, whose pay systems have been adopted by many companies and government organizations. The majority of large public- and private-sector U.S. employers use some formal process of job evaluation.[46]

The most commonly used job evaluation system is the **point system.**[47] First, compensation specialists must ensure that job descriptions are complete, up to date, and accurate. Next, top managers select compensable job factors (such as skill, effort, and responsibility) and decide how each factor will be weighed in establishing job worth. These factors are described in a point manual, which is used to assign point values to each job. For example, the characteristic of "responsibility" could receive from 0 to 5 points depending on whether job responsibility is "routine work performed under close supervision" (0 points) or "complete discretion with errors having extreme consequences to the organization and public safety" (5 points).

The compensation specialist then compares each job factor in a given job description to that specified in the point manual. This process is repeated until the job has been evaluated on all factors. Then the compensation specialist evaluates a second job and repeats the process until all jobs have been evaluated.

The job evaluation process can establish an internal hierarchy of job worth. However, to determine competitive market pay rates, most organizations obtain one or more pay surveys. **Pay surveys** show what other organizations pay incumbents in jobs that match a sample of "key" jobs selected by the organization. Pay surveys are available from many sources, including consulting firms and the U.S. Bureau of Labor Statistics.

The compensation specialist then compares the survey pay rates for key jobs with their job evaluation points by plotting them on a graph as illustrated in Exhibit 12.8. The **pay-trend line** shows the relationship between pay and total point values. The compensation specialist can use the pay-trend line to determine the pay values of all jobs for which point values have been calculated. Ranges of pay for each job class are established, enabling a newcomer or lower performer to be paid less than

job evaluation

The process of determining the values of jobs within an organization through an examination of job content.

point system

A job evaluation system that assigns a predetermined point value to each compensable job factor in order to determine the worth of a given job.

pay survey

A study of what other companies pay employees in jobs that correspond to a sample of key positions selected by the organization.

pay-trend line

A graph that shows the relationship between pay and total job point values for determining the worth of a given job.

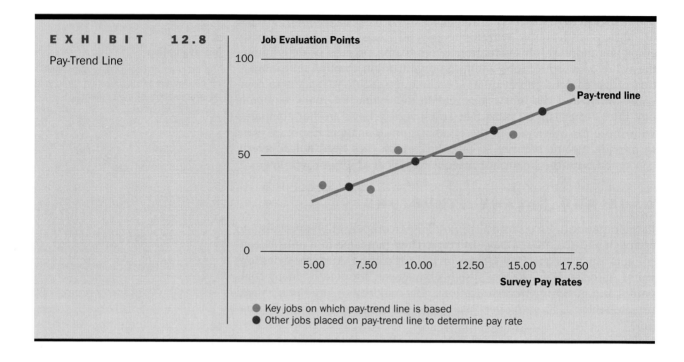

EXHIBIT   12.8

Pay-Trend Line

Job Evaluation Points

Key jobs on which pay-trend line is based
Other jobs placed on pay-trend line to determine pay rate

other people in the same job class. The organization must then specify how individuals in the same job class can advance from the low to the high end of the range. For example, the organization can reward merit, seniority, or a combination of both.

BENEFITS

The wage and salary structure is an important part of the compensation package that maintains a productive work force, but equally important are the benefits offered by the organization. Benefits were once called "fringe" benefits, but this term is no longer accurate because they are now a central rather than peripheral part of the pay structure. A U.S. Chamber of Commerce survey has revealed that benefits in general compose more than one-third of labor costs and in some industries, nearly two-thirds.[48]

A major reason that benefits make up such a large portion of the compensation package is that health care costs have been increasing so quickly. Because employers frequently provide health care insurance as an employee benefit, these costs are important in the management of benefits. Between 1983 and 1993, annual corporate spending on health care tripled, to $225 billion.[49] Health benefit packages may change again during health care reform under President Clinton. As a result, many companies are reviewing health plans.

Organizations that want to provide cost-effective benefits should be sensitive to changes in employee life-styles. Several years ago, benefits were based on the assumption that the typical worker was a married man with a dependent wife and two school-age children. The benefits

NationsBank is an example of a company offering *benefits* that fit the complex work-family needs of today's diverse work force. Programs such as parental leave, child-care subsidies based on income, assistance in finding child-care providers, and adjustments to working hours for employees caring for family members ease the burdens of caring for children or aging parents. These benefits increase overall productivity and assist NationsBank in recruiting and retaining top people such as commercial loan officer Stephanie Kerr, pictured here with twin daughters Reagan and Erin.

packages provided life insurance coverage for the worker, health insurance coverage for all family members, and no assistance with child care expenses. But today fewer than 10 percent of American workers fit the description of the so-called typical worker.[50] Increased work-force diversity means that far more workers are single; in addition, both spouses in most families are working. These workers are not likely to value the traditional benefits package. In response, some companies are establishing *cafeteria-plan benefits packages* that allow employees to select the benefits of greatest value to them.[51] Other companies use surveys to determine which combination of fixed benefits is most desirable. The benefits packages provided by large companies attempt to meet the needs of all employees. One of the newest types of benefits is allowing employees paid leaves of absence to perform social service work, as illustrated in the Focus on Ethics box.

TERMINATION

Despite the best efforts of line managers and HRM professionals, the organization will lose employees. Some will retire, others will depart voluntarily for other jobs, and still others will be forced out through mergers and cutbacks or for poor performance. The value of termination for maintaining an effective work force is twofold. First, employees who are poor performers can be dismissed. Productive employees often resent

XEROX CORPORATION

One day in 1988, Sarah Lampard carried paper bags full of bread, cereal, and vegetables up the steps into Denver's inner-city Agape Christian Church. That day, she was helping deliver a truckload of food to churches that would help feed over 1,200 poverty-stricken families for the next week. In days past, she has harvested spinach under the August sun, negotiated with food company executives to acquire surplus food, and unloaded thousands of pounds of potatoes from a semitrailer. No matter what the task, it's all in a day's work for this Xerox employee: She's a Social Service Leavetaker.

In 1988, through the Social Service Leave Program, Sarah took a six-month, fully paid leave of absence from her job as a Xerox account manager in Denver, Colorado, to work for a nonprofit food bank cooperative called COMPA. COMPA acquires and purchases surplus food from supermarkets, restaurants, and farmers and gives it to 33 local churches that feed hundreds of Denver people who just cannot afford to eat every day.

Now back at her regular Xerox job, Sarah says: "Social Service Leave changed my personal values. Before, material things were important; now I use my money to help others. I also learned how to listen to people's problems and help them find solutions. This helps

with my Xerox customers. They're very impressed that Xerox would invest so much money, time, and talent in such worthwhile community projects. In fact, some of my customers are thinking about modeling programs of their own after Xerox's program."

Since the program began in 1971, nearly 350 employees have taken sabbaticals of a month to a year from their Xerox jobs to pursue social-action projects of their own choosing within their communities. Leavetakers continue to receive full pay and benefits, and on their return to Xerox they get their old jobs back or new positions of equal responsibility. ■

SOURCE: Xerox, 1988 Annual Report. Used by permission.

■

exit interview

An interview conducted with departing employees to determine the reasons for their termination.

disruptive, low-performing employees who are allowed to stay with the company and receive pay and benefits comparable to theirs. Second, employers can use exit interviews. An **exit interview** is an interview conducted with departing employees to determine why they are leaving.[52] The value of the exit interview is to provide an excellent and inexpensive tool for learning about pockets of dissatisfaction within the organization and hence for reducing future turnover.

With so many companies experiencing downsizing through mergers or because of global competition, often a large number of managers and workers are terminated at the same time. In these cases, enlightened companies try to find a smooth transition for departing employees. For example, General Electric laid off 900 employees in three gradual steps. It also set up a reemployment center to assist employees in finding new jobs or in learning new skills. It provided counseling in how to write a resume and conduct a job search. An additional step General Electric took was to place an advertisement in local newspapers saying that these employees were available. By showing genuine concern in helping place laid-off employees, a company communicates the value of human resources and helps maintain a positive corporate culture.[53]

SUMMARY AND MANAGEMENT SOLUTION

This chapter described several important points about human resource management in organizations. All managers are responsible for human resources, and most organizations have a human resource department that works with line managers to ensure a productive work force. The human resource department is responsible for interpreting and responding to the large human resource environment. The HR department must be part of the organization's competitive strategy, implement procedures to reflect federal and state legislation, and respond to trends in society. Within this context, the HR department tries to achieve three goals for the organization. The first goal of the human resource department is to attract an effective work force through human resource planning, recruiting, and employee selection. The second is to develop an effective work force. Newcomers are introduced to the organization and to their jobs through orientation and training programs. Moreover, employees are appraised through performance appraisal programs. The third goal is to maintain an effective work force. Human resource managers retain employees with wage and salary systems, benefits packages, and termination procedures.

Thomas Melohn, president of North American Tool & Die, used these ideas when he was faced with low profits, an unenthusiastic work force, a 7 percent customer reject rate of production, and 27 percent employee turnover. He attacked this problem by setting up systems to recruit and hire the best possible employees. First, he got the word out to generate a large pool of applicants, only 10 percent of whom made it to a formal interview. The interviews focused on finding people with the right values who could do quality work and fit the culture and strategy of North American. References were carefully checked, and a trial work period was used to see if the employee was compatible. These procedures took a great deal of time, but acquiring the right human resources has produced impressive results: employee turnover plummeted to less than 4 percent, the customer reject rate dropped below 0.1 percent, employees became enthusiastic, and profits increased 100 percent a year for seven years. Human resources have enabled this small company to beat well-heeled foreign competitors at price, quality, and delivery.[54]

DISCUSSION QUESTIONS

1. It is the year 2010. In your company, central planning has given way to front-line decision making and bureaucracy has given way to teamwork. Shop floor workers use computers and robots. There is a labor shortage for many job openings, and the few applicants lack skills to work in teams, make decisions, or use sophisticated technology. As vice-president of human resource management since 1990, what did you do to prepare for this problem?

2. If you were asked to advise a private company about its equal employment opportunity responsibilities, what two points would you emphasize as most important?

3. How can the human resource activities of planning, recruiting, performance appraisal, and compensation be related to corporate strategy?

4. Think back to your own job experience. What human resource management activities described in this chapter were performed for the job you filled? Which ones were absent?

5. Why are planning and forecasting necessary for human resource management? Discuss.

6. How "valid" do you think the information obtained from a personal interview versus a paper-and-pencil test versus an assessment center would be for predicting effective job performance for a college professor? An assembly-line worker in a team-oriented plant? Discuss.

7. What techniques can managers adopt to improve their recruiting and interviewing practices?

8. How does affirmative action differ from equal employment opportunity in recruiting and selection?

9. How can exit interviews be used to maintain an effective work force?

10. Describe the procedure used to build a wage and salary structure for an organization.

MANAGEMENT IN PRACTICE: ETHICAL DILEMMA

● FRATERNIZATION POLICY

Previous complications prompted Aeronautical Associates to write a human resource policy prohibiting married couples from working in the company, even in different departments.

Tom and Ginny were secretly married two years after Ginny was hired by the company. Although they worked in separate departments, cross-functional projects sometimes required professional cooperation between them. Tom and Ginny always maintained a professional relationship at work, making sure their performance was not hampered by their personal life.

After completion of an especially important project, Tom and Ginny's departments met informally to celebrate at a local restaurant. During the gathering, one of Tom and Ginny's friends from outside the company entered the restaurant by chance and unknowingly revealed their secret in front of several coworkers.

Monday morning, Tom came to see you, his supervisor, about an appropriate course of action.

● WHAT DO YOU DO?

1. Do nothing. Things have worked out okay, so do not make an issue of it.

2. Work toward keeping Tom and Ginny with the company but also seek mild punishment for them. Unpunished disregard of company policy would send a negative message to other employees.

3. Insist one of them leave the company. Tom and Ginny caused the problem by not being forthright.

4. Fight the policy. Champion Tom and Ginny's cause with upper management, because the company has no right to limit personal relationships.

CASES FOR ANALYSIS

MONY

Senior executives at Mutual of New York (MONY) decided to relocate its operations division from Manhattan to nearby Westchester County. Although MONY's headquarters remained in New York City, many economies could be achieved by moving the operations division to another location.

The human resource environment in Westchester County was different from that in Manhattan, and Sue Garbey, director of Human Resources, had her work cut out for her. More than 50 percent of the needed 1,000 employees would relocate from Manhattan, thanks to a generous relocation package. However, as the corporate newcomer in the area, MONY was a small competitor compared with neighbors IBM, General Foods, PepsiCo, and Reader's Digest, and would have to be innovative to recruit and retain quality employees. Members of the human resource department realized that they were facing a labor shortage due to the baby bust, made even more difficult by recruiting competition from MONY's corporate neighbors. Moreover, the pool of potential workers was affluent, had many choices, and was considered selective about employers.

In response, MONY's HR department decided to experiment with nontraditional programs such as flexible hours, summer hours, job sharing, variable work sites, and child care assistance. Flexible hours mean that each department must have coverage during the core business hours of 8:30 A.M. to 4:30 P.M., but individual staff members can work any time from 7:30 A.M. to 9:00 P.M. Some 25 employees are involved in job sharing, which means that the position is filled by two people, each working less than 40 hours. Part-time employees receive prorated benefits. Variable work sites allow many people to work at home at least part of the time. These employees do computer work and can log on anytime of the day or night. Child care assistance includes six months of unpaid leave and guaranteed same job upon return. MONY also offers flexible spending accounts as part of the benefit package that can help reimburse for dependent care.

MONY's philosophy is "What's good for the individual is also good for business." Top management and HR professionals believe the use of innovative means to recruit and retain people will enable high productivity and a successful division.

● QUESTIONS

1. Evaluate the extent to which the recruiting and retention policies reflect the environment within which the human resource department works.
2. Would you like to work for MONY's operations division? Why?
3. What suggestions would you make about additional programs MONY might undertake to recruit and retain employees in this environment?

SOURCE: Based on Marlene C. Piturro, "HR Policies Give Companies New Direction," *Management Review* (April 1989), 16–18.

TRIANGLE EQUIPMENT

In 1989, Jane Foster joined Triangle Equipment, a Kansas manufacturer of farm equipment located in a rural area. Triangle employed 1,700 people, most of whom were welders, machine operators, and assemblers in the plant. The company was successful because of a loyal clientele, committed employees, and efficient production methods.

Jane was in charge of administrative services, but she had a problem. She had reviewed her first-level managers for merit pay. She had worked hard on the performance appraisal and kept records about employee performance. She believed in rewarding those who contributed the most to the organization. However, before holding the appraisal interview with each employee, and implementing the promised raises, she was required to get approval from her boss, Frank Galloway.

Frank was a vice-president, a close personal friend of the president, and was well liked by many employees. Unfortunately, he wanted to change the recommended merit pay increases for each of Jane's managers. He told Jane that this year's performance was not as important as the individual's potential, attitude, years to retirement, age, and family situation. Because Jane was still new, Frank believed that his evaluations more clearly reflected company policy and decided to overrule her in each case.

The following information reflects Jane's notes about the performance of three employees as well as Frank's response.

David Thompson had 18 years with Triangle but had never been an outstanding performer. His recent poor effort had held up the assembly operation, and Jane had sent several memos requesting improvement. David was a close personal friend of Frank Galloway and had several children, two of whom were in college. Jane recommended a salary increase from $30,000 to $31,000, but Frank believed David's salary should be increased to $35,000.

Dolores Rodriguez had shown remarkable improvement over the last year. She was a hard worker and had been coming to work early and staying late. She had spent many hours untangling problems created by others and had clearly found her position in the organization. Jane could always rely on Dolores to do whatever was needed and do it in an efficient manner. Dolores was unmarried and a high-school graduate. Jane's salary increase recommendation was from $22,000 to $26,500. Frank would approve only a $1,500 increase.

Ray Sanders had always been an outstanding employee. However, during the last year Ray had experienced family problems, including a divorce, following which his former wife and children moved out of state. His performance had declined markedly; his misspecified equipment drawings had cost the company time and money. Jane recommended a small salary increase from $41,000 to $42,500. Frank believed that Ray's salary should be increased to $46,000.

● QUESTIONS

1. Frank believed his recommended raises reflected the company's goals. Do you agree?
2. Do any of Frank's recommendations violate laws concerning equitable pay for employees?
3. If you were a personnel specialist consulting with Jane, what would you recommend that she do?

REFERENCES

1. Thomas Melohn, "Screening for the Best Employees," *INC.*, January 1987, 104–106.

2. R. Gustav Niebuhr, "Mass Shortage: Catholic Church Faces Crisis as Priests Quit and Recruiting Falls," *The Wall Street Journal*, November 13, 1990, A1, A13.

3. David E. Bowen and Edward E. Lawler III, "Total Quality-Oriented Human Resource Management," *Organizational Dynamics* (Spring 1992), 29–41.

4. D. Kneale, "Working at IBM: Intense Loyalty in a Rigid Culture," *The Wall Street Journal*, April 7, 1986, 17.

5. Cynthia D. Fisher, "Current and Recurrent Challenges in HRM," *Journal of Management* 15 (1989), 157–180.

6. Lloyd Baird and Iian Meshoulam, "Getting Payoff from Investment in Human Resource Management," *Business Horizons* (January–February 1992), 60–75, and Donna Brown, "HR: Survival Tool for the 1990s," *Management Review* (March 1991), 10–14.

7. Cynthia A. Lengnick-Hall and Mark L. Lengnick-Hall, "Strategic Human Resources Management: A Review of the Literature and a Proposed Typology," *Academy of Management Review* 13 (1988), 454–470, and "Human Resources Managers Aren't Corporate Nobodies Any More," *Business Week*, December 2, 1985, 58–59.

8. Steven H. Appelbaun, Roger Simpson, and Barbara T. Shapiro, "The Tough Test of Downsizing," *Organizational Dynamics* (Autumn 1987), 68–79.

9. Shawn Tully, "Can Boeing Reinvent Itself?" *Fortune*, March 8, 1993, 66–73.

10. Richard E. Walton and Gerald I. Susman, "People Policies for the New Machines," *Harvard Business Review* 87 (March–April 1987), 98–106, and Randall S. Schuler and Susan E. Jackson, "Linking Competitive Strategies with Human Resource Management Practices," *The Academy of Management Executive* 1 (1987), 207–219.

11. Deidre A. Depke, "Picking Up the Tab for Bias at Shoney's," *Business Week,* November 6, 1992, 50.

12. Robert L. Mathis and John H. Jackson, *Personnel/Human Resource Management* (St. Paul, Minn.: West, 1988), and Terry L. Leap and Michael D. Crino, *Personnel/Human Resource Management* (New York: Macmillan, 1989).

13. William E. Fulmer and Ann Wallace Casey, "Employment at Will: Options for Managers," *Academy of Management Executive* 4 (May 1990), 102–107; Aaron Bernstein, "More Dismissed Workers Are Telling It to the Judge," *Business Week,* October 17, 1988, 68–69; and Michael Goldblatt, "Preserving the Right to Fire," *Small Business Report* (December 1986), 87.

14. Rod Willis, "Can American Unions Transform Themselves?" *Management Review* (February 1988), 12–21.

15. James G. March and Herbert A. Simon, *Organizations* (New York: Wiley, 1958).

16. Dennis J. Kravetz, *The Human Resources Revolution* (San Francisco, Calif.: Jossey-Bass, 1989).

17. Electronic Data Systems Corporation, *1985 Annual Report,* 4–12.

18. D. Quinn Mills, "Planning with People in Mind," *Harvard Business Review* 63 (July–August 1985), 97–105, and USAir, *1985 Annual Report,* 5.

19. J. W. Boudreau and S. L. Rynes, "Role of Recruitment in Staffing Utility Analysis," *Journal of Applied Psychology* 70 (1985), 354–366.

20. Brian Dumaine, "The New Art of Hiring Smart," *Fortune,* August 17, 1987, 78–81.

21. P. Farish, "HRM Update: Referral Results," *Personnel Administrator* 31 (1986), 22.

22. J. P. Wanous, *Organizational Entry* (Reading, Mass.: Addison-Wesley, 1980).

23. Larry Reibstein, "Crushed Hopes: When a New Job Proves to Be Something Different," *The Wall Street Journal,* June 10, 1987, 25.

24. P. W. Thayer, "Somethings Old, Somethings New," *Personnel Psychology* 30 (1977), 513–524.

25. J. Ledvinka, *Federal Regulation of Personnel and Human Resource Management* (Boston: Kent, 1982); and Civil Rights Act, Title VII, 42 U.S.C. Section 2000e *et seq.* (1964).

26. The material in this section is largely drawn from R. D. Arvey and J. E. Campion, "The Employment Interview: A Summary and Review of Recent Research," *Personnel Psychology* 35 (1982), 281–322.

27. James M. Jenks and Brian L. B. Zevnik, "ABCs of Job Interviewing," *Harvard Business Review* (July–August 1989), 38–42.

28. A. Brown, "Employment Tests: Issues without Clear Answers," *Personnel Administrator* 30 (1985), 43–56.

29. Larry Reibstein, "More Firms Use Personality Tests for Entry-Level, Blue-Collar Jobs," *The Wall Street Journal,* January 16, 1986, 25.

30. "Assessment Centers: Identifying Leadership through Testing," *Small Business Report* (June 1987), 22–24, and W. C. Byham, "Assessment Centers for Spotting Future Managers," *Harvard Business Review* (July–August 1970), 150–167.

31. G. F. Dreher and P. R. Sackett, "Commentary: A Critical Look at Some Beliefs about Assessment Centers," in *Perspectives on Employee Staffing and Selection,* ed. G. F. Dreher and P. R. Sackett (Homewood, Ill.: Irwin, 1983), 258–265.

32. Bruce McDougall, "The Thinking Man's Assembly Line," *Canadian Business,* November 1991, 40–44; Louis Kraar, "Japan's Gun-Ho U.S. Car Plants," *Fortune,* January 30, 1989, 98–108; and Richard Koenig, "Toyota Takes Pains, and Time, Filling Jobs at Its Kentucky Plant," *The Wall Street Journal,* December 1, 1987, 129.

33. Bernard Keys and Joseph Wolfe, "Management Education and Development: Current Issues and Emerging Trends," *Journal of Management* 14 (1988), 205–229.

34. Michael Brody, "Helping Workers to Work Smarter," *Fortune,* June 8, 1987, 86–88.

35. Max Messmar, "Cross-Discipline Training: A Strategic Method to Do More with Less," *Management Review* (May 1992), 26–28; Robert Cournoyer, "Integrative Learning Speeds Teamwork," *Management Review* (December 1991), 43–44; and Christopher Power, "Coffee, Tea, and the Power of Positive Thinking," *Business Week,* July 31, 1989, 36.

36. Brian Dumaine, "Those Highflying PepsiCo Managers," *Fortune,* April 10, 1989, 78–86.

37. V. R. Buzzotta, "Improve Your Performance Appraisals," *Management Review* (August 1988), 40–43, and H. J. Bernardin and R. W. Beatty, *Performance Appraisal: Assessing Human Behavior at Work* (Boston: Kent, 1984).

38. Ibid.

39. Francine Alexander, "Performance Appraisals," *Small Business Reports* (March 1989), 20–29.

40. D. Cederblom, "The Performance Appraisal Interview: A Review, Implications, and Suggestions," *Academy of Management Review* 7 (1982), 219–227.

41. Buzzotta, "Improve Your Performance Appraisals," and Alexander, "Performance Appraisals."

42. Andrea Gabor, "Take This Job and Love It," *The New York Times,* January 26, 1992, F1, F6 and Steve Ventura and Eric Harvey, "Peer Review: Trusting Employees to Solve Problems," *Management Review* (January 1988), 48–51.

43. Henderson, *Compensation Management.*

44. Renée F. Broderick and George T. Milkovich, "Pay Planning, Organization Strategy, Structure and 'Fit': A Prescriptive Model of Pay" (Paper presented at the 45th Annual Meeting of the Academy of Management, San Diego, August 1985).

45. Michael Schroeder, "Watching the Bottom Line Instead of the Clock," *Business Week,* November 7, 1988, 134–136, and Bruce G. Posner, "You Get What You Pay For," *INC.,* September 1988, 91–92.

46. L. R. Burgess, *Wage and Salary Administration* (Columbus, Ohio: Merrill, 1984), and E. J. McCormick, *Job Analysis: Methods and Applications* (New York: AMACOM, 1979).

47. B. M. Bass and G. V. Barrett, *People, Work, and Organizations: An Introduction to Industrial and Organizational Psychology,* 2d ed. (Boston: Allyn & Bacon, 1981), and D. Doverspike, A. M. Carlisi, G. V. Barrett, and R. A. Alexander, "Generalizability Analysis of a Point-Method Job Evaluation Instrument," *Journal of Applied Psychology* 68 (1983), 476–483.

48. U.S. Chamber of Commerce, *Employee Benefits 1983* (Washington, D.C.: U.S. Chamber of Commerce, 1984).

49. Christopher Farrell, Paul Magnusson, and Wendy Zellner, "The Scary Math of New Hires," *Business Week,* February 22, 1993, 70–71.

50. J. A. Haslinger, "Flexible Compensation: Getting a Return on Benefit Dollars," *Personnel Administrator* 30 (1985), 39–46, 224.

51. Robert S. Catapano-Friedman, "Cafeteria Plans: New Menu for the '90s," *Management Review* (November 1991), 25–29.

52. "Exit Interviews: An Overlooked Information Source," *Small Business Report* (July 1986), 52–55.

53. Rod Willis, "What's Happening to America's Middle Managers," *Management Review* (January 1987), 23–26, and Yvette Debow, "GE: Easing the Pain of Layoffs," *Management Review* (September 1987), 15–18.

54. Melohn, "Screening for the Best Employees."

CEO COMPENSATION

In 1960 the American worker dreamed of a new house, having children, and a better life-style, while fitting those dreams into an average yearly salary of $4,665. That same year the average CEO could dream a little longer; the average annual compensation was $109,383. Just over three decades later, the average worker has to pare down options and priorities based on a typical yearly salary of $24,411, or a little over 5 times the 1960 average. But now the average CEO can dream like Rip van Winkle. The annual compensation in 1992 was $3,842,247, greater than 20 times the 1960 average.

A CEO's compensation used to be determined by a chummy get-together between the chief executive and the top human resource officer. They would select an outside consultant to conduct a study—usually a survey of what competitors paid their top executives—and a summary report would be presented to the compensation committee to justify the boss's paycheck. The CEO was often present while directors debated what was appropriate, and the predictable result was a rubber stamp approval.

Not any more. Ionospheric compensation packages and the sometimes close-to-the-vest manner in which they are doled out have raised hackles from Washington to the Securities and Exchange Commission to common shareholders. The result: many boards are picking the outside consultants themselves and are scrutinizing details and asking questions about competitor pay packages. They quite often are taking the tack that executives be paid based on performance.

To put the issue in perspective, a quick look at the spiralling CEO compensation numbers is helpful. The $3.842 million dollar 1992 average pay was 56 percent higher than the previous year. In 1993 a chief executive will need to ring up almost $23 million to even crack the top 10. The figures keep getting bigger and there is general agreement that the driving force behind the increase is the exercising of stock options. For example, Michael D. Eisner of Walt Disney hauled in a staggering $197 million from stock options.

Bill Clinton's vow to increase future personal and corporate income taxes may have accelerated the exercising of stock options in 1992. It certainly contributed to the widening of the gap between boardroom and factory floor worker salary levels. By 1992, the CEO was knocking down 157 times the pay of the rank and file. In contrast, the average Japanese chief makes only 32 times that of the ordinary worker.

Since the vast majority of these monumental compensation packages comes in the form of stock options, the Financial Accounting Standards Board recently handed down a decision that would require companies to charge options against earnings. The change, however, is not scheduled to take effect for three years.

CEOs say that viewing lump sum gains from exercising options in the same light as yearly salary compensation is misleading. Reaping a windfall from options that may have accrued over five or ten years is a one-time payoff for years of work and is realized only if the stock has appreciated and shareholders benefit as well. Critics disagree, charging that too many executives move from company to company, benefiting from well-timed stock sales rather than personal or company performance.

Companies such as AT&T and Colgate-Palmolive Company have sought to address the excessive compensation through options issue by adjusting the exercise prices well above the share's current trading price. Such an approach ensures stockholders will realize pre-established gains well before the CEO can cash in. Some pay experts are promoting an even more stringent step. They believe the strike price of options should fluctuate in either direction, commensurate with a rise or fall in the stock market. The establishment of CEO compensation packages is no longer the rubber stamp process it once was.

Committees are also beginning to reevaluate whether stock options are the best method of linking pay with performance. "We're spending more time reviewing the CEO's goals at the beginning of a year and measuring his progress at the end."

Perhaps American CEOs should consider the opinion of one of their counterparts and chief competitors across the Pacific. "American top executives give themselves very high salaries and then blame us by saying that our prices are too low," Akio Morita, chairman of Sony Corporation said. "American top management must adjust and restrain themselves."

● QUESTIONS

1. Discuss the issue of executive compensation vis-à-vis rank-and-file attitudes and the necessity of salaries sufficient to attract top management personnel.

2. Is the exercising of company options tantamount to insider trading? What restrictions should apply to executives who effectively sell their own company stock short?

3. Name and discuss areas that could be used to measure executive performance. Should a predetermined, across-the-board venue of results be required before bonus or stock options are granted?

4. Explain the disparity between executive pay for Japanese and Americans. Are American executives overpaid, or are Japanese executives undercompensated? Why?

MANAGING DIVERSE EMPLOYEES **13** CHAPTER

The Kentucky Fried Chicken unit of PepsiCo, Inc., established its Designate program to attract seasoned executives from other companies, with special attention given to attracting and keeping female and minority-group members. The Designate philosophy is to bring in the best people but to choose diversity when two people are equally qualified. One such executive is Larry Drake, recruited from archrival Coca-Cola Co. While being recruited, Drake had genuine reservations about the program. He did not want to be hired as a "token." He did not want to generate resentment among white colleagues who

wanted the job, and he did not want the affirmative action stigma of being hired because of race rather than talent. KFC executives had similar concerns and wanted to prevent a backlash from white employees seeking promotions for themselves.[1] ■ How do you feel about KFC's Designate program for recruiting minorities? Do you agree with Drake's concerns about accepting a job through the program? If you were a senior manager at KFC, how would you resolve the concerns of Drake and KFC executives?

KFC's Designate program represents the type of program many companies are undertaking to promote diversity in the workplace, including top management ranks. While KFC actively recruits women and minorities, backlash among white workers seeking promotions is reduced by hiring candidates who already have established solid careers and have a positive chemistry with the company. Drake, for example, was interviewed by many people at KFC to head off any problems.

The management of employee diversity entails recruiting, training, and fully utilizing workers who reflect the broad spectrum of society in all areas—gender, race, age, ethnicity, religion, disability, sexual orientation, education, and economic level.

Companies such as Hewlett-Packard, Honeywell, Procter & Gamble, Avon, Xerox, and Mobil Oil all have established programs for increasing diversity. These programs teach current employees to value ethnic, racial, and gender differences, direct their recruiting efforts, and provide development training for females and minorities. These companies value diversity and are enforcing this value in day-to-day recruitment and promotion decisions.

Companies are beginning to reflect the U.S. image as a melting pot, but with a difference. In the past, the United States was a place where people of different national origins, ethnicities, races, and religions came together and blended to resemble one another. The U.S. melting pot attracted immigrants from Ireland following the famine in the mid-1800s, and immigrants came later from Poland, Russia, and Italy to work in railroads, mines, and factories. Opportunities for advancement were limited to those workers who fit easily into the mainstream of the larger culture. Some immigrants chose desperate measures to fit in, such as abandoning their native language, changing their last name, and sacrificing their own unique cultures. In essence, everyone in workplace organizations was encouraged to share similar beliefs, values, and life-styles despite differences in gender, race, and ethnicity.[2]

Now organizations such as KFC recognize that everyone is not the same and that the differences people bring to the workplace are valuable.[3] Rather than expecting all employees to adopt similar attitudes and values, companies are learning that these differences enable them to compete globally and to acquire rich sources of new talent. Although diversity in North America has been a reality for many years, genuine efforts to accept and *manage* diverse people are a phenomenon of the 1990s.

This chapter introduces the topic of diversity, its causes and consequences. Ways to deal with work-force diversity are discussed, and organizational responses to diversity are explored. The negative consequences of ignoring diversity in today's world are identified, and the benefits of successfully maintaining a diverse work force are discussed.

● VALUING DIVERSITY

A Digital Equipment Corporation factory near Boston produces keyboards for Digital's computers. The factory employs 350 people, who come from 44 countries and speak 19 languages. When

Consumers Gas, Canada's largest natural gas distribution utility, is one example of a company that *values diversity*. CG's commitment to diversity is evidenced by a long-term program, including in-house surveys to determine cultural diversity, efforts to attract a diverse work force through an aggressive ad campaign, and participation in BRIDGES, a City of Toronto sponsored program to increase skills for women in nontraditional careers. Here, some of the CG employees representing 22 countries celebrate cultural diversity at CG's 1992 Consumers Caravan.

plant managers issue written announcements, they are printed in English, French, Spanish, Chinese, Portuguese, Vietnamese, and Haitian Creole.[4] This astonishing diversity is becoming typical in many companies.

Most managers, from any ethnic background, are ill-prepared to handle these multicultural differences. Many Americans attended segregated schools, lived in racially unmixed neighborhoods, and were unexposed to people substantially different from themselves.[5] A typical manager, schooled in traditional management training, easily could make the following mistakes.[6]

- Delighted with the new technique developed by a Native American employee, a manager rewarded her with great fanfare and congratulations in front of her peers. The employee was humiliated and didn't return to work for three weeks.

- A manager, having learned that a friendly pat on the arm or back would make workers feel good, took every chance to touch his subordinates. His Asian employees hated being touched, and thus started avoiding him, and several asked for transfers.

- A manager declined a gift offered by a new employee, an immigrant who wanted to show gratitude for her job. He was concerned about ethics and explained the company's policy about not accepting gifts. The employee was so insulted she quit.

- Hoping to head off problems with new equipment, a production supervisor asked his Filipino staff to alert him to difficulties with new equipment. They responded by using masking tape and other makeshift remedies to get the machines working without telling him.

These issues related to cultural diversity are difficult and real. But before discussing how companies handle them, let's define *diversity* and explore people's attitudes toward it.

DIMENSIONS OF DIVERSITY

work-force diversity

Hiring people with different human qualities who belong to various cultural groups.

Work-force diversity means the hiring and inclusion of people with different human qualities or who belong to various cultural groups. From the perspective of individuals, diversity means including people different from themselves along dimensions such as age, ethnicity, gender, or race.

Several important dimensions of diversity are illustrated in Exhibit 13.1. The inner circle represents primary dimensions of diversity, which include inborn differences or differences that have ongoing impact throughout one's life.[7] These are age, ethnicity, gender, physical abilities, race, and sexual orientation. These dimensions are core elements through which people shape their self-image and world view.

Secondary dimensions of diversity, illustrated in the outer ring of Exhibit 13.1, can be acquired or changed throughout one's lifetime. These dimensions tend to have less impact than those of the core but nevertheless have impact on a person's self-definition and world view. For example, Vietnam veterans may be perceived differently from other people and may have been profoundly affected by their military experience.

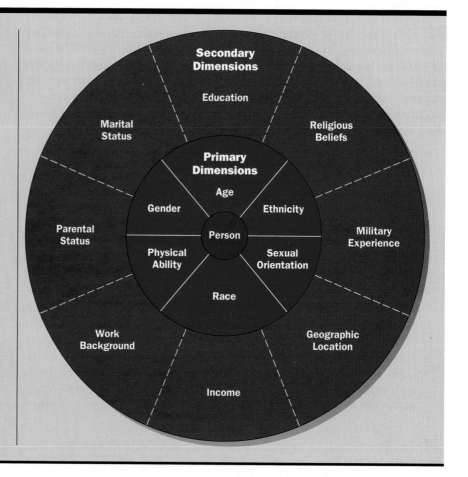

EXHIBIT 13.1

Primary and Secondary Dimensions of Diversity

SOURCE: Adapted from Marilyn Loden and Judy B. Rosener, *Workforce America!* (Homewood, Ill: Business One Irwin, 1991), 20. Used with permission.

Married people may be perceived differently and have somewhat different attitudes from people who are single. Likewise, work experience, education, and geographic location add dimensions to the way people define themselves and are defined by others.

A 55-year-old white male, an M.B.A. from Harvard and the father of two grown children, who is vice-president of a Fortune 500 company, may be perceived very differently from a female clerical worker, age 25, who is a single mother of two children and is attending evening classes to earn a college degree. Based on this information, can you predict the personal priorities and career expectations each person may have of the organization? The challenge for companies today is to recognize these differences and to value and use the unique strengths each person brings to the workplace.[8]

ATTITUDES TOWARD DIVERSITY

Valuing diversity by welcoming, recognizing, and cultivating differences among people so they can develop their unique talents and be effective organizational members is difficult to achieve. **Ethnocentrism** is the belief that one's own group and subculture are inherently superior to other groups and cultures. Ethnocentrism makes it difficult to value diversity. Viewing one's own culture as the best culture is a natural tendency among most people.[9] Moreover, the business world tends to reflect the values, behaviors, and assumptions based on the experiences of a rather homogeneous, white, middle-class, male work force.[10] Indeed, most theories of management presume that workers share similar values, beliefs, motivations, and attitudes about work and life in general. These theories presume there is one set of behaviors that best help an organization to be productive and effective and therefore should be adopted by all employees.[11] This one-best-way approach explains why a male manager may cause a problem by touching Asian employees or not knowing how to handle a gift from an immigrant.

Ethnocentric viewpoints and a standard set of cultural practices produce a **monoculture,** a culture that accepts only one way of doing things and one set of values and beliefs. Exhibit 13.2 illustrates the assumptions that produce a monoculture and the type of monoculture that exists in many U.S. organizations. The assumption that people who are different are somehow deficient hampers efforts to take advantage of unique talents and abilities. Assumptions that diversity threatens smooth organizational functioning, that people who complain are oversensitive, or that people should not call attention to differences all support the status quo. These assumptions discourage analysis of organizational subcultures and allow managers to ignore the changes occurring in the workplace. These assumptions create a dilemma for women, blacks, gays, immigrants, physically disabled, and other culturally diverse people who are expected to behave like members of the dominant group.

These assumptions of equality as sameness typically produce an "ideal" employee, qualities of which are listed in the center of Exhibit 13.2. When qualities such as being married, competitive, and Protestant become the norm for everyone, many people feel as if they do not fit

ethnocentrism

The belief that one's own group or subculture is inherently superior to other groups or cultures.

monoculture

A culture that accepts only one way of doing things and one set of values and beliefs.

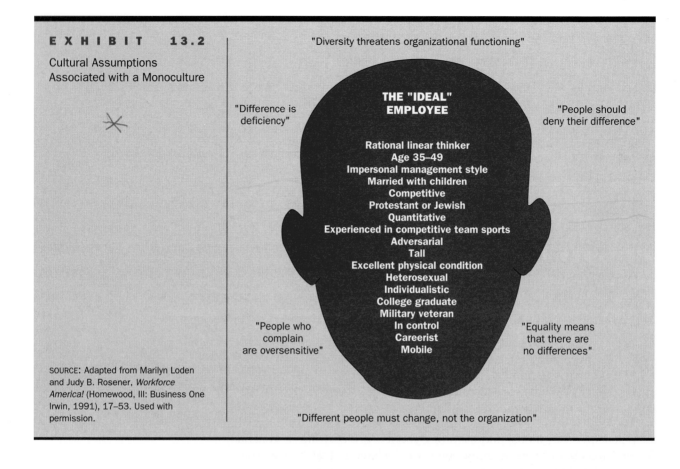

EXHIBIT   13.2

Cultural Assumptions
Associated with a Monoculture

"Diversity threatens organizational functioning"

"Difference is
deficiency"

**THE "IDEAL"
EMPLOYEE**

"People should
deny their difference"

**Rational linear thinker
Age 35–49
Impersonal management style
Married with children
Competitive
Protestant or Jewish
Quantitative
Experienced in competitive team sports
Adversarial
Tall
Excellent physical condition
Heterosexual
Individualistic
College graduate
Military veteran
In control
Careerist
Mobile**

"People who
complain
are oversensitive"

"Equality means
that there are
no differences"

SOURCE: Adapted from Marilyn Loden
and Judy B. Rosener, *Workforce
America!* (Homewood, Ill: Business One
Irwin, 1991), 17–53. Used with
permission.

"Different people must change, not the organization"

ethnorelativism

The belief that groups and subcultures
are inherently equal.

pluralism

The organization accommodates several
subcultures, including employees who
would otherwise feel isolated and
ignored.

into the organization. Diverse employees may feel undue pressure to conform, may be the victims of stereotyping attitudes, and may be presumed guilty because they are deficient. White males who typically fit the notions of an ideal employee often see themselves as quite diverse but are perceived by others to be homogeneous; such stereotyped ideas leave little room for people of color, gay men, women, the elderly, and others who do not fit the image of the ideal employee.

The goal for organizations seeking cultural diversity is pluralism rather than a monoculture, ethnorelativism rather than ethnocentrism. **Ethnorelativism** is the belief that groups and subcultures are inherently equal. **Pluralism** means that an organization accommodates several subcultures. Movement toward pluralism seeks to fully integrate into the organization the employees who otherwise would feel isolated and ignored. As the work force changes, organizations will come to resemble a global village.

Most organizations must undertake conscious efforts to shift from a monoculture perspective to one of pluralism. Employees in a monoculture may not be aware of culture differences, or they may have acquired negative stereotypes toward other cultural values and assume that their own culture is superior. Through effective training, employees can be helped to accept different ways of thinking and behaving, the first step

When the "mix" is just right, you have a winner—in the kitchen and in the work force. Umanoff & Parsons, a New York bakery and catering firm, illustrates *ethnorelativism and pluralism*. By going beyond the traditional job pool of white male candidates, and embracing women, minorities, and immigrants, Umanoff & Parsons has created a diverse management team of loyal, dedicated workers such as the group pictured here.

away from narrow, ethnocentric thinking. Ultimately, employees are able to integrate diverse cultures, which means that judgments of appropriateness, goodness, badness, and morality are no longer applied to cultural differences. Cultural differences are experienced as essential, natural, and joyful, enabling an organization to enjoy true pluralism and take advantage of diverse human resources.[12]

For example, Avon has the expressed goal of breaking out of its monoculture thinking about appropriate salespeople and customers in order to accept employees from multiple cultures. Avon has implemented training courses through which top management and other employees learn how to make this transition. By helping employees develop greater sensitivity and acceptance of cultural difference, Avon moves away from an ethnocentric attitude and is able to accept and integrate people from diverse cultural backgrounds.

● THE CHANGING WORKPLACE

The importance of cultural diversity and employee attitudes that welcome cultural differences will result from the inevitable changes taking place in the workplace, in our society, and in the economic environment. These changes include globalization and the changing work force.[13] Earlier chapters described the impact of global competition on business in North America. Competition is intense. About 70 percent of all U.S. businesses are engaged directly in competition with companies overseas. Companies that succeed in this environment need to adopt radical new ways of doing business, with sensitivity toward the needs of different cultural practices. For example, approximately 18 car companies, especially those from Japan and Germany, have established design centers in Los Angeles. Southern California is viewed as a melting pot, an Anglo-Afro-Latino-Asian ethnic mix. Companies that need to sell cars all over the world love the diverse values in this multicultural proving ground.[14]

Other companies such as 3M and Hewlett-Packard built plants overseas in places such as Bangalore, India, or Guadalajara, Mexico, not only to obtain inexpensive labor but also to develop a presence in rapidly growing markets. The international diversity must be integrated into the overall company to allow it to work effectively.[15]

The single biggest challenge facing companies is the changing composition of the work force. The average worker is older now, and many more women, people of color, and immigrants are entering the work force. Indeed, white males, the majority of workers in the past, compose less than half of the work force, and white, native-born males are expected to contribute only 15 percent of new entrants to the work force through the year 2000.[16]

Exhibit 13.3 illustrates the management activities required for dealing with a culturally diverse work force. For example, consider the increased career involvement of women. By the year 2000, it is estimated that 61 percent of the women in the United States will be employed, constituting 47 percent of the work force, almost equaling the percentage of male workers.[17] This change represents an enormous opportunity to organizations, but it also means that organizations must deal with issues such as work-family conflicts, dual-career couples, and sexual harassment. Since seven of ten women in the labor force have children, organizations should prepare to take more of the responsibility for child care.

Moreover, can human resource management systems operate bias free, dropping the perception of a middle-age white male as the ideal employee? People of African, Asian, and Hispanic descent make up 21 percent of the American population today, and that figure will grow to 25 percent in ten years. Already more than 30 percent of New York City's residents are foreign born. Miami is two-thirds Hispanic-American; Detroit is two-thirds African-American; San Francisco is one-third Asian-American.[18] Organizations must face the issues of dealing with race, ethnicity, and nationality without bias in order to provide a prejudice-free workplace.

Top managers can help shape organizational values and employee mindsets about cultural differences. Moreover, educational programs can promote knowledge and acceptance of diverse cultures and educate management on valuing these differences. As yet another example of the urgent need for valuing and managing diversity, an increasing number of immigrants are entering North America. In previous generations, most foreign-born immigrants came from Western Europe. Now more than 84 percent come from Asia and Latin America.[19] Immigrants come to the United States with a wide range of backgrounds, often without adequate skill in using English. They need sufficient educational programs to acquire the technical and customer service skills required in a service economy. Much of this training will be provided by corporations.

Companies that recognize these management requirements not only are accepting diversity but also are teaching employees to value it. Kinney Shoes is one leader in this area.

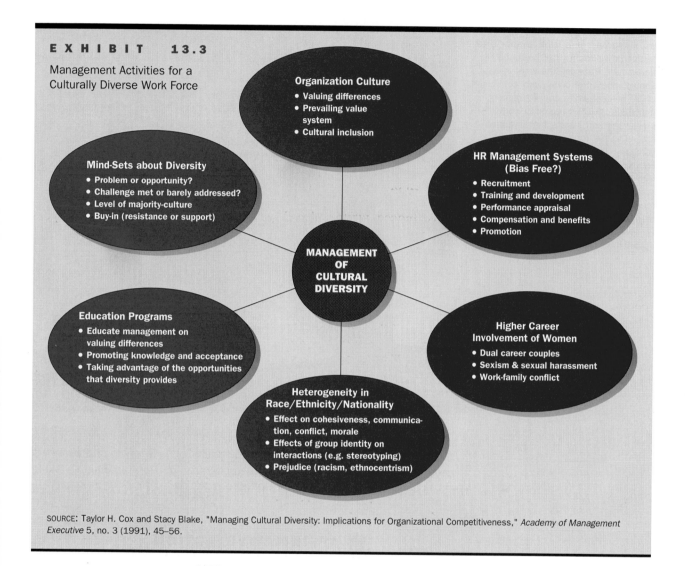

EXHIBIT 13.3

Management Activities for a
Culturally Diverse Work Force

Organization Culture
- Valuing differences
- Prevailing value system
- Cultural inclusion

Mind-Sets about Diversity
- Problem or opportunity?
- Challenge met or barely addressed?
- Level of majority-culture
- Buy-in (resistance or support)

HR Management Systems (Bias Free?)
- Recruitment
- Training and development
- Performance appraisal
- Compensation and benefits
- Promotion

MANAGEMENT OF CULTURAL DIVERSITY

Education Programs
- Educate management on valuing differences
- Promoting knowledge and acceptance
- Taking advantage of the opportunities that diversity provides

Higher Career Involvement of Women
- Dual career couples
- Sexism & sexual harassment
- Work-family conflict

Heterogeneity in Race/Ethnicity/Nationality
- Effect on cohesiveness, communication, conflict, morale
- Effects of group identity on interactions (e.g. stereotyping)
- Prejudice (racism, ethnocentrism)

SOURCE: Taylor H. Cox and Stacy Blake, "Managing Cultural Diversity: Implications for Organizational Competitiveness," *Academy of Management Executive* 5, no. 3 (1991), 45–56.

 KINNEY SHOES

Top managers at Kinney Shoes recognize that the company's customer base is diverse and that its retail employees should reflect that diversity. An education program has been implemented to ensure that the hiring practices of store managers will enable women and minorities to enter the corporation in numbers that reflect the customer base. John Kozlouski, senior vice-president of human resources, says this is not a question of numbers but of teaching people to value ethnic, racial, and gender differences as the right thing to do. Executives and store managers attend a diversity training program that encourages people to face their own stereotypes and prejudices and to recognize that many assumptions they make about groups of people are erroneous.

As one example, some store managers mistakenly interpreted an accent, in particular a Spanish accent, as evidence of low intelligence.

Stockton Record president Orage Quarles III (second from right) *shaped organizational values* for the California newspaper. Believing the work force should reflect the community composed of 57 percent white and 43 percent minorities, Quarles recruits diverse employees and insists that diversity extend to the top leadership of the company. The executive committee composition reflects that commitment with two black members, two white female members, one Hispanic male member, and three white male members. Quarles' leadership serves as an example to the entire community.

Indeed, accents are not reflections of ability or lack of it, and Kinney's program helped store managers to recognize that limited English skills do not mean a person cannot sell shoes.[20] ∎

● AFFIRMATIVE ACTION

Since 1964, civil legislation has prohibited discrimination in hiring based on race, religion, sex, or national origin. As described in Chapter 12 of the text, these policies were designed to facilitate recruitment, retention, and promotion of minorities and women. To some extent, these policies have been successful, opening organization doors to women and minorities. However, despite the job opportunities, women and minorities have not succeeded in getting into top management posts. The reasons are associated with shortcomings in the affirmative action approach.

AFFIRMATIVE ACTION—LIMITED SUCCESS

Affirmative action was developed in response to conditions 30 years ago. Adult white males dominated the work force, and economic conditions were stable and improving. Because of widespread prejudice and discrimination, legal and social coercion were necessary to allow women, people of color, immigrants, and other minorities to become part of the economic system.[21]

Today, the situation has changed. More than half the U.S. work force consists of women and minorities; the economic situation is changing rapidly, as a result of international competition.

Within this fluid situation, many companies actively recruited women and minorities to comply with affirmative action guidelines. Companies often succeeded in identifying a few select individuals who were recruited, trained, and given special consideration. These people carried great expectations and pressure. They were highly visible role models for the newly recruited groups. It was generally expected that these individuals would march right to the top of the corporate ladder.

Within a few years, it became clear that few of these people would reach the top. Management typically was frustrated and upset because of the money poured into the affirmative action programs. The individuals were disillusioned about how difficult it was to achieve and felt frustrated and alienated. Managers were unhappy with the program failures and may have doubted the qualifications of people they recruited. Did they deserve the jobs at all? Were women and minority candidates to blame for the failure of the affirmative action program?

The cycle may begin again with additional women, people of color, and immigrants brought into the system dominated by white, male, native-born individuals who compose a homogeneous culture. The burden of adaptation once again is placed on the candidates coming through the system rather than on the organization itself. The affirmative action cycle may fail repeatedly, with part of the reason attributed to what is called the *glass ceiling*.

THE GLASS CEILING

The **glass ceiling** is an invisible barrier that separates women and minorities from top management positions. They can look up through the ceiling and see top management, but prevailing attitudes are invisible obstacles to their own advancement. A recent study suggested the additional existence of "glass walls," which serve as invisible barriers to important lateral movement within the organization. Glass walls bar experience in areas such as line supervisor positions that would enable women and minorities to advance vertically.[22]

Evidence of the glass ceiling is the distribution of women and minorities where they are clustered at the bottom levels of the corporate hierarchy. Only 2 percent of top executives in the United States are women, and only 9 percent of all managers are minorities.[23] Women and minorities also earn substantially less. Black employees earn only 10 to 26 percent of what their white counterparts earn, even when educational backgrounds are similar. Women earn considerably less than their male peers, and the gap widens as they move up the corporate hierarchy. At the level of vice-president, a woman's average salary is 42 percent less than her male counterpart.

Why does the glass ceiling persist? The monoculture at top levels is the most frequent explanation. Top-level corporate culture evolves

glass ceiling

Invisible barrier that separates women and minorities from top management positions.

PREVAILING
ATTITUDES

A survey of British Petroleum showed dissatisfaction among the company's women employees. Why? Dissatisfaction with career prospects (the same reason given by men, incidentally) was the reason. They had crashed into the *glass ceiling*. Career prospects suddenly dropped off, and bright, promising employees were leaving the company. In a new commitment to break the barrier, BP Exploration started Worldwide Initiative—72 recommendations on the recruiting, retention, and development of women in the company, with a target of 7 percent women in senior grade positions by 1995. In addition, Women in BP is a network offering advice and support to women across all grades, businesses, and national boundaries. By following intentions with effective action, BP is helping more women rise to the top.

around white American males, who tend to hire and promote people who look, act, and think like them. Compatibility in thought and behavior plays an important role at higher levels of organizations.[24] Of the people moving up the corporate ladder, white men tend to be more compatible with those already at the top.

Another reason for the persistent glass ceiling is the relegation of women and minorities to less visible positions and projects so that their work fails to come to the attention of top executives. Stereotyping by male middle managers may lead to the assumption that a woman's family life will interfere with her work or that minorities lack competence for important assignments. Women and minorities often believe that they must work harder and perform at higher levels than their white male counterparts in order to be noticed, recognized, fully accepted, and promoted. Women and minorities also may believe that they, not the culture of the organization, carry the burden of change.

CURRENT DEBATES ABOUT AFFIRMATIVE ACTION

In recent years, Washington has sent mixed messages to women and minorities. President Bush's firm "no quotas" position stood in sharp contrast to the passage of the 1990 Americans with Disabilities Act, or the 1991 Civil Rights Act. Each issue stirred debate about cultural bias versus increasing government interference with business.

A hotly debated diversity issue at present is homosexuals in the work-place. Recent debate has focused upon the inclusion of gays in the military. The Supreme Court ordered return of an admitted gay naval petty officer to his military duties, and President Clinton voiced support for a policy that would allow gays to serve in the military. Incidents of "gay bashing" have been reported, indicating the extreme responses of some people to this issue.[25]

Most gay men and lesbians believe that they are asked to check their private lives at the door of their company. Thus, they feel isolated and afraid, believing they will be victims of hostility and discrimination on the basis of sexual orientation. Many gays fabricate heterosexual identities. One man, a successful manager at a direct-marketing company, lost his mentor when his own homosexuality was revealed. Another man, who makes several hundred thousand dollars a year buying and selling commodities, says that his fellow traders would destroy him if they knew he is gay. Apple and Digital Equipment were among the first companies to encourage gay employee groups to form support networks. Homosexual employees at AT&T, Boeing, Coors, DuPont, and Sun Microsystems have formed groups to lobby top management on issues important to them. Slowly these companies are learning to accept diversity that includes sexual orientation.[26]

Ultimately, the problem with affirmative action boils down to an unspoken and often unintended sexism and racism in organizations. Top managers find it hard to understand just how white and male their corporate culture is, and how forbidding it seems to those who obviously are different.[27] Racism and sexism often take the form of subtle exclusiveness whereby women and minorities are not able to establish relationships that enable them to learn, move up, and succeed in an organization. Their ideas may not be taken as seriously as those of a white man. A typical situation is that of a committee meeting, with several white male managers and one white woman manager sitting around a conference table. The woman offers a suggestion that is ignored. Ten minutes later a man makes the same suggestion and it readily is discussed and accepted. Typically, the men are not even aware that they have discriminated.

● NEW RESPONSES TO CULTURAL DIVERSITY

Affirmative action opened the doors of organizations in this country to women and minorities. However, the path toward promotion to top ranks has remained closed for the most part, with many women and minorities hitting the glass ceiling.[28] Recognizing this, the federal government responded with the Civil Rights Act of 1991 to amend and strengthen the Civil Rights Act of 1964 and to strengthen and improve federal civil rights laws. In particular, the 1991 act is designed "to provide appropriate remedies for intentional discrimination and unlawful harassment in the workplace," and "to expand the scope of relevant civil rights statutes in order to provide adequate protection of victims of discrimination." Affirmative action helps, but it is not enough. Companies are finding new ways to deal with the obstacles that prevent women and minorities from advancing to senior management positions in the future.

How can managers prepare their organizations to accommodate diversity in the future? One approach involves evaluating the value of diversity to an organization.[29] Questions such as those in Exhibit 13.4 can be used to examine beliefs and values about a diverse work force and should clarify a vision of the new workplace. Organization leaders and managers must come to terms with their own definitions of diversity and should be encouraged to think beyond race and gender issues to consider factors such as education, background, and personality differences.

EXHIBIT 13.4

Organizational Steps to Valuing Diversity

SOURCE: Adapted from Roosevelt Thomas, Jr., "From Affirmative Action to Affirming Diversity," *Harvard Business Review* 68, no. 2 (1990), 107–117.

Why is valuing diversity good for this organization?

Compliance with the law
Community relations, social/ethical responsibility
Valuing diversity=competitive edge

What is my vision of a diverse work force?

Values women and minorities at all levels
Keeps people's identities intact
Is diverse and offers opportunity

What is my definition of diversity?

Race, gender, religion, ethnicity, age
Sexual orientation, background, education
"Differences" among people

What is the corporate culture in my organization?

Values (Who is important here?)
Myths (Who are the "heroes"?)
Norms (How should one act to get ahead?)
Can differences be accommodated?

What modifications do we make?

Change recruitment and promotion patterns
Develop new systems (mentoring, sponsorship, promotion)
Change the models of acceptable managerial behavior

What kind of support will people need?

Recognition that people are "pioneers"
Dealing constructively with conflict
Training and helping as people change

What can we do to help us value diversity?

Keep affirmative action programs, but move beyond
Keep the doors of the organization open
Open doors at higher levels in the organization

Once a vision for a diverse workplace has been created and defined, the organization can analyze and assess the current culture and systems within the organization. This assessment is followed by a willingness to change the status quo in order to modify current systems and ways of thinking. Throughout this process, people need support in dealing with the many challenges and inevitable conflicts they will face. Training and support are important for the people in pioneering roles. Finally, managers should not de-emphasize affirmative action programs, because these are critical for giving minorities and women access to jobs in the organization.

Once managers truly accept the need for a program to develop a truly diverse workplace, action can begin. A program to implement such a change involves three major steps: (1) building a corporate culture that values diversity; (2) changing structures, policies, and systems to support diversity; and (3) providing diversity awareness training. For each of these efforts to succeed, top management support is critical, as well as holding all managerial ranks accountable for increasing diversity.

CHANGING THE CORPORATE CULTURE

For the most part, today's corporate cultures reflect the white male model of doing business. These cultures are not conducive to including women and minorities in important decision-making processes or enabling them to go high in the corporate hierarchy. The end result of this mismatch between the dominant culture and the growing employee population of minorities and women is that many employees' talents will be underutilized, and the corporation will be less competitive.

Chapters 4 and 11 describe approaches for changing corporate culture. Managers can start by actively using symbols for the new values, such

Changing corporate culture to accommodate work-force diversity includes devising programs for disabled employees that will meet their physical challenges as well as confront work-force insensitivity. McDonnell Douglas leads the way in providing special services, working conditions, and equipment to physically disabled people. Rick Caldwell's readjustment following an automobile accident was made easier by raising his desk level and providing a PC and a lightweight phone with easy-dial numbers. Such corporate concern goes beyond compliance with the Americans with Disabilities Act by encouraging employees to adopt a positive attitude toward disabled coworkers.

as encouraging and celebrating the promotion of minorities. To promote positive change, executives must change their own assumptions and recognize that employee diversity is real, is good, and must be valued. Executives must lead the way in changing from a white male monoculture to a multiculture in which differences among people are valued.

To accomplish this, managers must be willing to examine the unwritten rules and assumptions. What are the myths about minorities? What are the values that exemplify the existing culture? Are unwritten rules communicated from one person to another in a way that excludes women and minorities? For example, many men may not discuss unwritten rules with women and minorities because they assume everyone is aware of them and they do not want to seem patronizing.[30]

Companies are addressing the issue of changing culture in a variety of ways. Some are using surveys, interviews, and focus groups to identify how the cultural values affect minorities and women. Others have set up structured networks of people of color, women, and other minority groups to explore the issues they face in the workplace, and to recommend changes to senior management. Monsanto is an excellent example of using new programs to deal with high turnover among women and minority employees.

 MONSANTO COMPANY

At Monsanto's Chocolate Bayou chemical complex in southeast Texas, the human resource department actively recruits women and minorities, with minority hires accounting for 17 percent and female recruits 29 percent of new hires in 1990. Although the plant was very good at hiring women and minorities, they were quitting at a high rate. Reasons given were that they were not getting enough job responsibility, they experienced difficulty dealing with supervisors, and they were treated arbitrarily or unfairly concerning pay and promotion opportunities. Managers knew the plant could not lose these employees and remain competitive. Changes had to be made.

The Chocolate Bayou plant conducted surveys of departing women and minorities to identify their exact perceptions of problems. Top managers were surprised to learn that minorities felt left out of things. Results provided eye-opening information that prompted systematic changes in the plant's culture, beginning with a series of diversity programs. Participants identified unspoken biases and stereotypes about race and gender. One exercise required small groups of employees to write down the characteristics they associated with different racial, ethnic, and gender groups. These lists sparked discussion that clarified cultural misconceptions. Other programs were undertaken to push both employees and managers to talk about race, gender, and age differences so their assumptions were made explicit. Once people learned to talk about these issues, they learned to handle them, increasing the satisfaction of minorities with their opportunities at Monsanto.[31] ■

Many companies have discovered, as did Monsanto, that people will choose companies that are accepting, inviting, friendly, and that help them meet personal goals.[32] Successful companies, like Monsanto, carefully assess their cultures and make changes from the top down because the key to productivity is a loyal, trained, capable work force. New cultural values mean that the exclusionary practices of the past must come to an end.

CHANGING STRUCTURES AND POLICIES

Many policies within organizations originally were designed to fit the stereotypical male employee. Now leading companies are changing structures and policies to facilitate the recruitment and career advancement of diverse employee groups.

RECRUITMENT. A good way to revitalize the recruiting process is for the company to examine employee demographics, the composition of the labor pool in the area, and the composition of the customer base. Managers then can work toward a work force composition that reflects the labor pool and the customer base. Moreover, the company can look at dimensions of diversity other than race and gender, including age, ethnicity, physical abilities, and sexual orientation.[33]

For many organizations, a new approach to recruitment will mean recruiting more effectively than today. This could mean making better use of formal recruiting strategies, internship programs to give people opportunities, and developing creative ways to draw upon previously unused labor markets.

CAREER ADVANCEMENT. The successful advancement of diverse group members means that the organizations must find ways to eliminate the glass ceiling. One of the most successful structures to accomplish this is the mentoring relationship. A mentor is a higher ranking, senior organizational member who is committed to providing upward mobility and support to a protégé's professional career.[34] Mentoring provides minorities and women with direct training and inside information on the norms and expectations of the organization. A mentor also acts as a friend or counselor, enabling the employee to feel more confident and capable.

Research indicates that women and minorities are less likely than men to develop mentoring relationships.[35] In the workplace where people's backgrounds are diverse, forging these relationships may be more difficult. Women often do not seek mentors because they feel job competency is enough to succeed, or they may fear that initiating a mentoring relationship could be misunderstood as a romantic overture. Male mentors may feel uncomfortable with minority male protégés. Their backgrounds and interests may differ, leaving them with nothing but work in common. Male mentors may stereotype women as mothers, wives, or sisters rather than as executive material. The few minorities and women who have reached the upper ranks often are overwhelmed with mentoring requests from people like themselves, and they may feel uncomfortable in highly visible minority-minority or female-female mentoring relationships, which isolate them from the white male status quo.

The solution is for organizations to overcome some of the barriers to mentor relationships between white males and minorities. When organizations can institutionalize the value of white males actively seeking women and minority protégés, the benefits will mean that women and minorities will be steered into pivotal jobs and positions critical to advancement. Mentoring programs also are consistent with the Civil Rights Act of 1991 that requires the diversification of middle and upper management.

ACCOMMODATING SPECIAL NEEDS.   Many people have special needs of which male top managers are unaware. For example, if a number of people entering the organization at the lower level are single parents, the company can reassess job scheduling and opportunities for child care. If a substantial labor pool is non-English-speaking, training materials and information packets can be provided in another language.

In many families today, both parents work, which means that the company may provide structures to deal with child care, maternity or paternity leave, flexible work schedules, home-based employment, and perhaps part-time employment or seasonal hours that reflect the school year. The key to attracting and keeping elderly or disabled workers may include long-term-care insurance and special health or life benefits. Alternative work scheduling also may be important for these groups of workers.

In the United States, racioethnic minorities and immigrants have fewer educational opportunities than most other groups. Many companies have started working with high schools to provide fundamental skills in literacy and arithmetic, or they provide these skills within the company to upgrade employees to appropriate educational levels. The movement toward increasing educational services for employees can be expected to increase for immigrants and the economically disadvantaged in the years to come.

DIVERSITY AWARENESS TRAINING

diversity awareness training

Special training designed to make people aware of their own prejudices and stereotypes.

Many organizations, including Monsanto, Xerox, and Mobil Oil, provide special training, called **diversity awareness training,** to help people become aware of their own cultural boundaries, their prejudices and stereotypes, so they can learn to work and live together. Working or living within a multicultural context requires a person to use interaction skills that transcend the skills typically effective when dealing with others from one's own in-group.[36] Diversity awareness programs help people learn how to handle conflict in a constructive manner, which tends to reduce stress and negative energy in diverse work teams.

A basic aim of awareness training is to help people recognize that hidden and overt biases direct their thinking about specific individuals and groups. If people can come away from a training session recognizing that they prejudge people and that this needs to be consciously addressed in communications with and treatment of others, an important goal of diversity awareness training has been reached.

Many diversity awareness programs used today are designed to help people of varying backgrounds communicate effectively with one another and to understand the language and context used in dealing with people from other groups. The point of this training is to help people be more flexible in their communications with others, to treat each person as an individual, and not to rely on stereotypes. Effective programs move people toward being open in their relationships with others. For example, if you were a part of such a program, it would help you develop an explicit awareness of your own cultural values, your own cultural boundaries, and your own cultural behaviors. Then you would be provided the same information about other groups, and you would be given the opportunity to learn about and communicate with people from other groups. One of the most important elements in diversity training is to bring together people of differing perspectives so that they can engage in learning new interpersonal communication skills with one another.

Communication

● DEFINING NEW RELATIONSHIPS IN ORGANIZATIONS

Men, women, people of color, whites, older people, younger people, the physically able, the physically disabled, and others are all struggling to define new ways of relating in the workplace. In the past, ways of relating to other groups were defined outside the workplace, in the family or community. The stereotypes and role expectations that define traditional ways of relating often did not allow these groups to develop their unique strengths at work. Diverse organizations have the potential to meet the wants of all groups, including "invisible" minorities, while fostering balanced priorities and psychological intimacy, and preventing sexual harassment.

WHAT PEOPLE WANT

People in all groups are struggling to identify how to relate to people who are different from themselves. Most employees genuinely want to learn how to handle work relationships without being affected by stereotypes and prejudices, and they are becoming more sensitive to what others need and want in work relationships.

Questions for understanding what people want and for avoiding stereotypes are illustrated in Exhibit 13.5. Men have needs as well as women, whites as well as blacks.[37] Exhibit 13.5 illustrates factors that would increase comfort levels in organizations and decrease tension among people of diverse backgrounds. Understanding what people want enables them to relate to one another with authenticity and acceptance. Understanding these needs helps managers to respect and accept others on their own terms. Everyone, not just minorities, has needs and wants that can be met in a workplace that acknowledges and values diversity.

EXHIBIT   13.5

Building a Multiculture:
What Do People Want?

Younger and Older Employees Want

To have more respect for their life experiences
To be taken seriously
To be challenged by their organizations, not patronized

Women Want

To be recognized as equal contributors
To have active support of male colleagues
To have work and family issues actively addressed by organizations

Men Want

To have the same freedom to grow/feel that women have
To be perceived as allies, not the enemy
To bridge the gap with women at home and at work

People of Color Want

To be valued as unique individuals, as members of ethnically
    diverse groups, as people of different races, and as equal contributors
To establish more open, honest, working relationships with people of other races and
    ethnic groups
To have the active support of white people in fighting racism

White People Want

To have their ethnicity acknowledged
To reduce discomfort, confusion, and dishonesty in dealing with people of color
To build relationships with people of color based on common goals, concerns, and
    mutual respect for differences

Disabled People Want

To have greater acknowledgment of and focus on abilities, rather than on disabilities
To be challenged by colleagues and organizations to be the best
To be included, not isolated

Able-Bodied People Want

To develop more ease in dealing with physically disabled people
To give honest feedback and appropriate support without being patronizing or
    overprotective

Gay Men and Lesbians Want

To be recognized as whole human beings, not just sexual beings
To have equal employment protection
To have increased awareness among people regarding the impact of heterosexism in the
    workplace

Heterosexuals Want

To become more aware of lesbian and gay issues
To have a better understanding of the legal consequences of being gay in America
To increase dialogue about heterosexist issues with lesbians and gay men

SOURCE: Adapted from Marilyn
Loden and Judy B. Rosener,
Workforce America! (Homewood,
Ill: Business One Irwin, 1991),
76–78. Used with permission.

INVISIBLE MINORITIES

Considerable focus has been placed on the problems, rights, and working conditions of visible minorities—women, blacks, Asians, Hispanics,
the aged, the disabled—but members of "invisible minorities" continue

suffering prejudice, alienation, and isolation. **Invisible minorities** include individuals who share a social stigma that is not visibly recognizable.[38] Concerns about unmasking the stigma so that it becomes visible become the major social dynamic for these groups. We all have so-called skeletons in our closets, but the potential social stigma toward invisible minorities dominates their working and social relationships. For example, gays and lesbians, unwed parents, atheists, children of gays, family members of people with AIDS, and members of 12-step recovery programs for alcohol, drugs, or eating disorders often feel they must carefully guard their "real" lives. Members of invisible minorities wonder: "Should I tell?" "Whom should I tell?" "Will they find out?" "How will they react?"

As companies increasingly focus on diversity issues and establish programs dealing with various groups and subcultures, management can also develop an awareness of, and sensitivity to, the experiences of people in less visible minority groups.

BALANCING FAMILY PRIORITIES

With 8.7 million single moms and 1.4 million single dads in the work force, managers are discovering that family programs are no longer a luxury, but a necessity, for competitive companies. Many companies have come to believe that successful family policies will increasingly attract and retain the most talented workers.[39]

Family-friendly companies such as Johnson & Johnson, IBM, Aetna, Corning, and AT&T have established a variety of programs—family-care leave, on-site day-care centers, health care for part-timers, flexible schedules, job-sharing, subsidies and grants for child care, work at home, and children's after-school or summer programs—to meet changing family needs and values. Despite the programs and policies of some companies, however, business in general has not been able to respond to family needs or to assist employees trying to balance work and family responsibilities. Family issues have become a topical corporate issue, but only a small percentage of businesses actually have strong family programs to address them. The pressure for developing these programs is mounting, but companies attempting to implement them should avoid acting precipitously. They must carefully analyze employee needs as well as company resources in responding to this pressure. One expert on work and family issues states that to be successful, family programs must be seen as a central part of the company's business mission.[40]

EMOTIONAL INTIMACY

Another outcome of diversity is a greater incidence of close friendships between men and women in the workplace. Close relationships between men and women often have been discouraged in companies for fear that they would disrupt the balance of power and threaten organizational stability.[41] This opinion grew out of the assumption that organizations are designed for rationality and efficiency, which were best achieved in a nonemotional environment. Close relationships between men and women could become romantic or sexual in nature, upsetting the stable

invisible minorities

Individuals who share a social stigma that is not visibly recognizable.

working relationships. The Focus on Ethics box discusses some ethical problems with office romances.

A recent study of friendships in organizations sheds interesting light on this issue.[42] Managers and workers responded to a survey about emotionally intimate relationships with both male and female coworkers. Many men and women reported having close relationships with an opposite-sex coworker. Called "nonromantic love relationships," the friendships resulted in trust, respect, constructive feedback, and support in achieving work goals. Intimate friendships did not necessarily become

focus on ETHICS   OFFICE ROMANCE

These days when Cupid strikes a pose, arrow at the ready, many office workers run for cover. Whether it's a reaction to memories of the Clarence Thomas confirmation hearings, or lessons learned from infamous office liaisons reported in the press, many employees are thinking twice about answering love's call, and management is especially "arrow-shy."

Why? Office romance is an increasingly risky business. Although most companies have no policy forbidding employee dating, in today's changing business environment there is increased concern about conflicts of interest, sexual harassment, employee morale, and public perception. These concerns mean that while the majority of companies accept coworker dating among peers, an increasing number are reevaluating and formulating policies regarding boss-subordinate romantic relationships.

How should supervisor-subordinate affairs be handled? The romance seldom escapes the suspicions and gossip of other employees. More important, knowledge of an affair often undermines the business environment, monopolizes conversations, invites controversy and potential embarrassment, and damages company morale. Employees scrutinize the behavior and judgment of the supervisor, whose leadership and credibility may suffer irreparable damage. In today's business climate, a supervisor is more likely than in previous eras to suffer the consequences of an office affair.

An example is Standley H. Hoch, CEO of General Public Utilities Corp. of New Jersey. G.P.U. board members received an anonymous letter charging Hoch with conflict of interest, resulting from a long affair with Susan Schepman, G.P.U.'s recently hired vice-president of communications. The letter claimed Hoch awarded Schepman's previous employer, Fleishman-Hillard, Inc., a public relations contract without competitive bidding, and later hired Schepman and awarded her with a vice-presidency based on their relationship. A confrontation between Hoch and the board resulted in the CEO's resignation.

While such scenarios involving the supervisor are becoming more frequent, the subordinate generally suffers most from office affairs. The reasons vary, but the main reason stems from the fact that women are still more likely to be the subordinate in a supervisor-subordinate relationship. The bottom line is that women face a social double standard that more often punishes the woman involved in an affair. In addition, women who are attempting to break through the glass ceiling find that if they get involved in an office romance they face the age-old inference of office romance as a contributing factor in their success.

In addressing the issue of employee dating, only a few companies, such as Apple Computer and DuPont, have rules pertaining to boss-subordinate relationships. When such relationships develop, the typical solution is to transfer one of the parties involved. But as ethics issues take on greater significance in the corporate world, new policies can be expected to evolve. ■

SOURCE: Ellen Rapp, "Dangerous Liaisons," *Working Woman*, February 1992, 56–61, and Marilyn Moats Kennedy, "Romance in the Office," *Across the Board*, March 1992, 23–27.

romantic, and they affected each person's job and career in a positive way. Rather than causing problems, nonromantic love relationships, according to the study, affected work teams in a positive manner because conflict was reduced. Indeed, men reported somewhat greater benefit than women from these relationships, perhaps because the men had fewer close relationships outside the workplace upon which to depend.

In any event, the evidence suggests that close psychological and emotional relationships between men and women at work are healthy and helpful. The challenge is for people to learn to cultivate these relationships and thus benefit themselves and their organizations.

SEXUAL HARASSMENT

While psychological closeness between men and women in the workplace may be a positive experience, sexual harassment is not. Sexual harassment is illegal. As a form of sexual discrimination, sexual harassment in the workplace is a violation of Title VII of the 1964 Civil Rights Act. Sexual harassment in the classroom is a violation of Title VIII of the Education Amendment of 1972. The following categorize various forms of sexual harassment:

- *Generalized*. This form involves sexual remarks and actions that are not intended to lead to sexual activity but that are directed toward a coworker based solely on gender and reflect on the entire group.

- *Inappropriate/Offensive*. Though not sexually threatening, it causes discomfort in a coworker, whose reaction in avoiding the harasser may limit his or her freedom and ability to function in the workplace.

- *Solicitation with Promise of Reward*. This action treads a fine line as an attempt to "purchase" sex, with the potential for criminal prosecution.

- *Coercion with Threat of Punishment*. The harasser coerces a coworker into sexual activity by using the threat of power (through recommendations, grades, promotions and so on) to jeopardize the victim's career.

- *Sexual Crimes and Misdemeanors*. The highest level of sexual harassment, these acts would, if reported to the police, be considered felony crimes and misdemeanors.[43]

The Anita Hill–Clarence Thomas hearings focused national attention on the problem of sexual harassment. Sexual harassment claims increased 50 percent in the months following the 1991 hearings.[44] Perhaps this focus on sexual harassment is responsible for the recent court cases that shifted the focus away from the harasser's *intentions* toward the *feelings* of the alleged victim.[45]

Women who are moving up the corporate hierarchy by entering male-dominated industries report a high frequency of harassment. Surveys report an increase in sexual harassment programs, but female employees also report a lack of prompt and just action by executives to incidents of sexual harassment. However, companies are discovering that

Companies such as Safeway, Inc., recognize that *sexual harassment* exists and takes various forms (verbal, visual, and physical). Safeway's long-standing policy against sexual harassment is communicated to employees through bulletin board postings (pictured here), as well as orientation workshops, and distribution of its employee handbook that includes definitions, complaint procedures, company responsibility for investigation, and steps for corrective action. Such aggressive company policies reflect management concern and help create a positive, harassment-free work environment.

"an ounce of prevention really is worth a pound of cure." Top executives are seeking to address problems of harassment through company diversity programs, revised complaint systems and grievance procedures, written policy statements, workshops, lectures, and role-playing exercises to increase employee sensitivity and awareness to the issue.[46]

● GLOBAL DIVERSITY

One of the most rapidly increasing sources of diversity in North American companies is globalization, which means hiring employees in many countries. Some estimate that by the year 2000, half of the world's assets will be controlled by multinational corporations.[47] Globalization means that companies must apply diversity management across a broader stage than North America. This means that managers must develop new skills and awareness to handle the unique challenges of global diversity: cross-cultural understanding, the ability to build networks, and the understanding of geopolitical forces. The rapid change in global work-force diversity is explained in the New Horizons Global Competition box. Two significant aspects of global diversity programs involve employee selection and training and the understanding of the communication context.

GLOBAL DIVERSITY

Work-force diversity extends beyond the shop floor and office partitions of American business. Work-force diversity and the migration of jobs is a worldwide phenomenon. The U.S. "labor shortage" described by academics only a few years ago has given way to a labor surplus as corporations take advantage of newly industrialized markets and increasingly sophisticated labor pools throughout Asia, Eastern Europe, and Mexico.

The shift is not simply a search for low-wage workers. Employers are competing for sophisticated, skilled, efficient labor pools, and countries are competing to attract top corporations, promoting advantages

such as lower operating costs, tax incentives, and, in many cases, an abundance of well-educated and underemployed workers.

As the 21st century approaches, countries find it increasingly difficult to restrict job flow or to "protect" jobs at home. Companies must compete globally, and a major component in global competition is the location of manufacturing and service facilities for greatest efficiency and economic advantage. GE's 1990 purchase of Tungstram, the Hungarian light bulb manufacturer, opened new markets *and* provided a supply of skilled engineers recognized as world leaders in the design and manufacturing of bulbs and lighting fixtures.

Likewise, Metropolitan Life's 150 medical claims analysts in Ireland have provided that company with a

skilled, dedicated work force with operating costs 30–35 percent less than typical U.S. costs. And the turnover rate? "About 1 percent," according to Met Life executive Frank Verminski. "We've lost three people in three years."

Corporate leaders such as Percy Barnevik, CEO of global giant ABB (Asea Brown Boveri), predict further changes in global work flow, comparing changes to the agricultural changes that occurred during industrialization at the beginning of the 20th century. Corporations must embrace change and adopt new skills and organization designs that reflect these new dynamics, rather than cling to old, familiar patterns. ■

SOURCE: Brian O'Reilly, "Your New Global Work Force," *Fortune*, December 14, 1992, 52–66.

SELECTION AND TRAINING

Expatriates are employees who live and work in a country other than their own. Careful screening, selection, and training of employees to serve overseas increase the potential for corporate global success. Human resource managers consider global skills in the selection process. In addition, expatriates receive cross-cultural training that develops language skills and cultural and historical orientation. Career-path counseling is often available.[48]

Equally important, however, is honest self-analysis by overseas candidates and their families. Before seeking or accepting an assignment in another country, a candidate should ask himself or herself questions such as the following:

■ Is your spouse interrupting his or her own career path to support your career? Is that acceptable to both of you?

■ Is family separation for long periods involved?

expatriates

Employees who live and work in a country other than their own.

The children in this Avezzano, Italy, school share cultures and learn firsthand the dynamics of *global diversity*. The school was established by Texas Instruments for the families of U.S. and Japanese employees involved in T.I.'s six-nation team that is building Europe's largest semiconductor. Such efforts, along with Minority Procurement programs demonstrate T.I.'s commitment to a diverse, multinational corporate environment.

- Can you initiate social contacts in a foreign culture?
- Can you adjust well to different environments and changes in personal comfort or quality of living, such as the lack of television, gasoline at $5 per gallon, limited hot water, varied cuisine, national phone strikes, and *warm* beer?
- Can you manage your future reentry into the job market by networking and maintaining contacts in your home country?[49]

Employees working overseas must adjust to all of these conditions. Managers going global may find that their own management "style" needs adjustment to succeed in a foreign country. One aspect of this adjustment is learning the communication context of a foreign location.

COMMUNICATION CONTEXT

People from some cultures tend to pay more attention to the social context (social setting, nonverbal behavior, social status) of their verbal communication than Americans do. For example, General Norman Schwarzkopf soon realized that social context was of considerable importance to leaders of Saudi Arabia. During the initial buildup for the Persian Gulf War, he suppressed his own tendency toward impatience and devoted hours to "philosophizing" with members of the Saudi royal family. Schwarzkopf realized it was *their* way of making decisions.[50]

Exhibit 13.6 indicates how the emphasis on social context varies among countries. In a **high-context culture**, people are sensitive to circumstances surrounding social exchanges. People use communication primarily to build personal social relationships; meaning is derived from context—setting, status, nonverbal behavior—more than from explicit words; relationships and trust are more important than business; and the

high-context culture

A culture in which communication is used to enhance personal relationships.

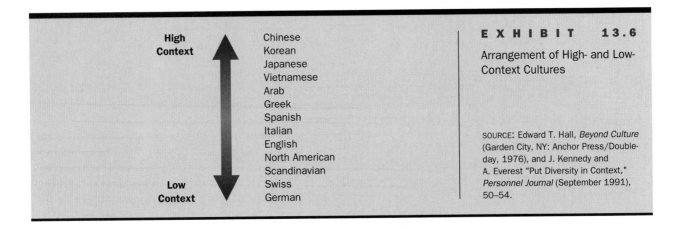

High Context		Chinese Korean Japanese Vietnamese Arab Greek Spanish Italian English North American Scandinavian
Low Context		Swiss German

E X H I B I T   13.6

Arrangement of High- and Low-Context Cultures

SOURCE: Edward T. Hall, *Beyond Culture* (Garden City, NY: Anchor Press/Double-day, 1976), and J. Kennedy and A. Everest "Put Diversity in Context," *Personnel Journal* (September 1991), 50–54.

welfare and harmony of the group are valued. In a **low-context culture,** people use communication primarily to exchange facts and information, meaning is derived primarily from words, business transactions are more important than building relationships and trust, and individual welfare and achievement are more important than the group.[51]

To understand how differences in cultural context affect communications, consider the U.S. expression, "The squeaky wheel gets the oil." It means that the loudest person will get the most attention, and attention is assumed to be favorable. Equivalent sayings in China and Japan are "Quacking ducks get shot" and "The nail that sticks up gets hammered down," respectively. Standing out as an individual in these cultures clearly merits unfavorable attention.

High-context cultures include Asian and Arab countries. Low-context cultures tend to be American and Northern European. Even within North America, cultural subgroups vary in the extent to which context counts, explaining why differences between groups make successful communication difficult. White females, Native Americans, and African-Americans all tend to prefer higher context communication than do white males. A high-context interaction requires more time because a relationship has to be developed, and trust and friendship must be established. Furthermore, most male managers and most people doing the hiring in organizations are from low-context cultures, which conflicts with people entering the organization from a background in a higher context culture. Overcoming these differences in communication is a major goal of diversity awareness training.

low-context culture

A culture in which communication is used to exchange facts and information.

● BENEFITS AND COSTS OF DIVERSITY

As a general rule, organizations have not been highly successful in managing women and minorities, as evidenced by higher turnover rates, higher absenteeism, lower job satisfaction, and general frustration over career development for these groups. Moreover, the fact that women and minorities are clustered at lower organization levels indicates they are not progressing as far as they might and are not developing their full potential.[52] Thus, valuing diversity provides distinct benefits to organizations and ignoring diversity has specific costs, which are summarized in Exhibit 13.7.

BENEFITS OF VALUING DIVERSITY

Hal Burlingham, AT&T senior vice-president for human resources, said, "Valuing diversity is not only the right thing to do, it's the right business thing to do. Companies that do a good job of valuing and effectively managing diversity in the 1990s will have a competitive advantage over the ones that don't."[53] Paying attention to the diverse work force has become an economic imperative. There is no question that the work force is changing and that U.S. organizations have to change to reflect the new work force composition.

The first benefit of valuing diversity is the opportunity to develop employee and organizational potential. This means higher morale, because people feel valued for what they bring to the organization. It also produces better relationships at work, because people acquire the skills to recognize, understand, and accept cultural differences. Developing employee skills and valuing diversity have become a bottom-line business issue. If organizations do not welcome people who look and act differently from white males, then the organizations will not have enough people to do the job. As David Charms, president of Xerox Corporation, said, "American business will not be able to survive if we do not have a large, diverse work force, because those are the demographics, no choice. The company that gets out in front of managing diversity, in my opinion, will have a competitive edge."[54]

Second, companies that treat women and racioethnic minorities well will be able to recruit the best employees, both those new to the work force and experienced employees from other organizations. Retaining these employees means a qualified, trained work force for the future. Demographics tell us that the labor market is slowly tightening, and those organizations that boast a healthy environment for women and minorities will be in the best competitive position to attract and retain scarce employees.

EXHIBIT 13.7 Benefits and Costs from Diversity Issues	BENEFITS of Valuing Diversity	COSTS of Ignoring Diversity
	1. Increased opportunity to develop employee and organizational potential	1. Reduced individual and organizational productivity
	2. Enhanced recruiting and retention	2. Tarnished corporate image
	3. Successful interaction with clients/marketplace	3. Substantial monetary cost
	4. Increased creativity and adaptation	

"Just like home." These "Tianguis" supermarkets were designed by The Vons Companies, Inc., to look and feel like a modern Mexican marketplace in order to cater to Southern California's growing Hispanic population. The benefits of *valuing diversity* are reflected in the interaction between clients, such as those pictured here, and the store. Product selection, marketing and merchandising, and use of bilingual employees are targeted toward this important segment of the population. Attention to such details fosters consumer loyalty in a competitive business.

Successful interaction between the client and the marketplace is the third benefit from diversity. A representational work force enables a company to understand better the needs of its clients. Culture plays an important part in determining the goods, entertainment, social services, and household products that people buy and use. Understanding how people live and what they need will help organizations adapt to changing consumer populations. This understanding comes in part from including representatives from that population in the work force.

Finally, organizations can expect enhanced creativity and adaptability from a diverse work force. Research has shown that diverse groups tend to be more creative than homogeneous groups, in part because people with diverse backgrounds bring different perspectives to problem solving. The presence of cultural and gender diversity in a group reduces the risk of "groupthink" when people contribute freely to a discussion.

Research also indicates that women and racioethnic minorities tend to have more flexible cognitive styles, thereby helping establish norms of flexible thinking. Moreover, the simple act of learning about other cultural practices enables organizations to expand their thinking about the world. Once employees increase flexibility in cultural thinking, it becomes easier for them to be flexible in their thinking about other things as well.

COSTS OF IGNORING DIVERSITY

The costs associated with high turnover and absenteeism are well understood. When organizations can adapt to the needs of a diverse work force, rather than expect the work force to adapt to the organization, absenteeism and turnover can be turned around and satisfaction increased.[55] The consequences of not valuing diversity include loss of productivity, a poor image for the organization, and the monetary cost of unhappy employees.

Reduced individual and organizational productivity occurs when women and minorities experience prejudice and nonacceptance. They feel unappreciated, do not expect to advance, and feel resentment that saps energy and productivity for the organization. People who feel excluded do not take risks for the organization, are less innovative, and are less aggressive in pressing their ideas or in assuming leadership. They will not voice disagreement, because they want to be accepted and included.

Second, a less obvious cost is the tarnished corporate image and reputation developed around employee dissatisfaction. If a corporation becomes known as one that alienates nontraditional employees, that corporation will have a hard time finding qualified workers and managers in a period of limited labor supply. Organizational reputation spreads quickly through informal networks in minority and female groups. Networks even can cause students to avoid certain organizations in campus interviews.

The third important cost is financial. A company loses all the money invested in recruiting and training when a dissatisfied employee leaves. One formula to help compute how much money is wasted when minorities and females are dissatisfied includes the fees for Equal Employment Opportunity disputes, costs of recruiting replacement employees, the wasted training for those who left, and the cost of additional training for those who stay.[56] The sum of these items indicates the amount of money a company wastes each year when diversity is not valued. For example, legal experts estimate that $25,000 is the minimum cost to open an EEO case, increasing to $100,000 if the case goes to trial, before damages or rewards. Or consider an organization with 10,000 employees, 35 percent of whom are likely to be women and minorities. If the turnover rate for these employees is double that of white males, and it costs $25,000 to recruit and train each person, an average annual savings of $3.5 million accrues from reducing their turnover rates to that of white males.

With the anticipated tight job market, corporations that want to be successful must embrace diversity. A number of innovative companies are already responding. Apple Computer appointed a multicultural and affirmative action manager, Avon established a cultural network, and Corning provides minority job rotation for expanded job experience and better promotion opportunities. DuPont and Hewlett-Packard provide diversity awareness workshops, seminars, and training, and Honeywell, Procter & Gamble, and Security Pacific Bank have established mentoring programs, adversary counsels, and minority networks.[57]

As one senior executive said, "In a country seeking competitive advantage in a global economy, the goal of managing diversity is to develop our capacity to accept, incorporate, and empower the diverse human talents of the most diverse nation on earth. It is our reality. We need to make it our strength."[58]

SUMMARY AND MANAGEMENT SOLUTION

Several important ideas pertain to work-force diversity, which is the inclusion of people with different human qualities and from different cultural groups. Dimensions of diversity are both primary, such as age, gender, and race, and secondary, such as education, marital status, and income. Ethnocentric attitudes generally produce a monoculture that accepts only one way of doing things and one set of values and beliefs, thereby excluding nontraditional employees from full participation.

Acceptance of work-force diversity is becoming especially important because of sociocultural changes and the changing work force. Diversity in the workplace reflects diversity in the larger environment. Innovative companies are initiating a variety of programs to take advantage of the diverse work force.

Consider Larry Drake at KFC, who was described in the chapter opening management problem. Upon entering KFC's Designate program, his anticipation of a new challenge was tempered by genuine concerns that he and other minority participants might become mere "tokens" in another high-sounding program with good intentions but little substance. These fears seemed legitimate during his first months with KFC as he breaded onion rings and scrubbed floors in the middle of the night. However, during its first two years, KFC's Designate program raised the number of KFC women and minority top-level managers from zero to seven. Among them, Drake has now risen to the position of vice-president and general manager in charge of more than 1,000 KFC restaurants, making him the most senior black executive. This diversity program works.[59]

Affirmative action programs have been successful in gaining employment for women and minorities, but the glass ceiling has kept many women and minorities from obtaining top management positions. The Civil Rights Act of 1991 amends and strengthens the Civil Rights Act of 1964.

Breaking down the glass ceiling ultimately means changing the corporate culture within organizations, changing internal structures and policies toward employees, including accommodating special needs, and providing diversity awareness training to help people become aware of their own cultural boundaries and prejudices. This training also helps employees learn to communicate with people from other cultural contexts.

The increased diversity in organizations has produced unexpected benefits, such as enabling all groups to define what they want from the company; it has enabled women who use an interactive leadership style to succeed and has provided opportunities for emotional intimacy and friendship between men and women that are beneficial to all parties. Increasing diversity also means that organizations must develop programs to deal with global as well as domestic diversity and with potential conflicts, such as sexual harassment, that arise.

Valuing diversity has many benefits, such as developing employees to their full potential and allowing successful interaction with diverse clients in the marketplace. Organizations that ignore diversity reduce productivity, suffer tarnished corporate images, and suffer substantial financial costs associated with turnover, training, and EEO disputes.

DISCUSSION QUESTIONS

1. If you were a senior manager at a company such as KFC, how would you resolve the concerns of everyone involved when female or minority senior managers are hired from outside?
2. Some people argue that social class is a major source of cultural differences, yet social class is not listed as a primary or secondary dimension in Exhibit 13.1. Discuss reasons for this.
3. Have you been associated with an organization that made assumptions associated with a monoculture? Describe the culture.
4. Do you think any organization successfully can resist diversity today? Discuss.
5. What is the glass ceiling, and why do you think it has proved to be such a barrier to women and minorities?
6. In preparing an organization to accept diversity, do you think it is more important to change the corporate culture or to change structures and policies? Explain.
7. If a North American corporation could choose either high-context or low-context communications, which do you think would be best for the company's long-term health? Discuss.
8. What do you think the impact on an organization would be for diversity within its own country versus international diversity? Discuss.
9. Many single people meet and date people from their work organization because the organization provides a context within which to know and trust another person. How do you think this practice affects the potential for emotional intimacy? Sexual harassment?

MANAGEMENT IN PRACTICE: ETHICAL DILEMMA

● PROMOTION OR NOT?

You are the president of CrownCutters, Inc. You have worked closely with Bill Smith for several years now. In many situations, he has served as your *de facto* right-hand person.

Due to a retirement, you have an opening in the position of executive vice-president. Bill is the natural choice—and this is obvious to the other mid- and senior-level managers at CrownCutters. Bill is popular with most of the managers in the company. Of course, he also has his share of detractors.

Prior to announcing the appointment of Bill Smith, you receive a memo from Jane Jones, your controller. Jane's memo indicates that she was subjected to sporadic sexual harassment by Bill starting ten years ago when she first joined the company and was working for him. Her memo indicates that the harassment essentially stopped six years ago when she moved to a position in which Bill was no longer her superior. She requests that this information be kept totally confidential.

You have never heard of any allegations like this about Bill before.

● **W H A T   D O   Y O U   D O ?**

1. Move ahead with the promotion because even if true, this is an isolated incident that is a part of Bill's past and is not his current behavior.
2. Stop the promotion because Bill is not the type of person who should help lead the company and shape its values.
3. Put the promotion on hold until you can discuss the situation extensively with Bill and Jane, although this means the accusation probably will become public knowledge.

SOURCE: This case was provided by Professor David Scheffman, Owen Graduate School of Management, Vanderbilt University, Nashville, Tennessee.

CASES FOR ANALYSIS

LOOK ME IN THE EYE

In a mid-size corporation in the Midwest, a department manager was faced with a touchy situation. On two occasions, money and office supplies had disappeared from her secretary's desk. The manager wondered what she should do. Her decision was to deal openly with the employees in the office. One by one, she called them into her office and asked if they knew or had heard anything about the missing materials. She explained that if they reported anything at all, confidentiality would be maintained and there would be no serious repercussions.

Several talks with employees produced no information about the missing money and office supplies. The manager then called in one of the newer employees, a young Asian. She asked him the same questions she had asked everyone else. "Are you aware of the problem in our office? Have you heard anyone talking about the thefts? Do you have any personal knowledge of the thefts?"

A few minutes into the conversation the manager began to feel very uncomfortable. She realized the reason was that the young man would not look at her. She began to feel suspicious. Why would he not look at her when answering questions? The manager asked even more direct questions about his possible involvement. Still, there was no direct response and no eye contact.

The manager started to get angry. She said, "Look, can you honestly tell me you did not do this?" The man replied,

"Of course I did not steal the money or the office supplies." The manager became even more uncomfortable and suspicious. The employee seemed evasive and looked at the floor as he talked. She said, "Look me in the eye and tell me you did not steal the money." Again, the young man looked at the floor and said, "I am sorry. I did not steal those items."

In frustration, the manager ended the interview, assuming that this man had stolen the money. She was angry with him for refusing to face up to his wrongdoing and admit his guilt. She made a recommendation that he be terminated.

● **Q U E S T I O N S**

1. Was this manager being ethnocentric or ethnorelative? Explain. *He should react to question*
2. This manager learned later that the Asian subculture, of which the employee was part, believes that looking an authority figure in the eye is a sign of disrespect. Upon learning this, what should the supervisor do next? *Apologize*
3. Would diversity awareness training be a positive thing in this company? Explain how it could be applied.

Explain other cultural varieties + beliefs
Yes.

SOURCE: This case was provided by Anne London, University of Hartford, Hartford, Connecticut.

NORDSTROM, INC.

Nordstrom, Inc., is one of the nation's leading retailers. It made diversity a corporate goal after several minority employees at its downtown Seattle store filed discrimination complaints with the Equal Employment Opportunity Commission.

A consultant who helps companies deal with multicultural workplaces created the following composite in 1987

that represented the Nordstrom look: "She was young, blond and light-skinned. She had a slim, athletic build. She came from a middle- to upper-class background, and she projected an image of sorority-girl enthusiasm." This composite emerged after asking employees to describe Nordstrom's shoppers, corporate culture, and personal traits required to rise in the employee ranks.

Top managers were stunned by the narrowness of the composite and suddenly understood why they had failed to hire outstanding minority candidates. Nordstrom was sending a subliminal culture message that a person of color wouldn't fit in the organization.

Since that finding, Nordstrom has created a new human resource department charged with the hiring and promotion of people of color. Nordstrom has begun to use models from various ethnic backgrounds in its catalogs and to advertise in publications such as *Ebony* and *Jet* that target minority groups. Nordstrom has solicited minority-owned companies as its suppliers.

Today, nearly one-third of its employees, including 17 percent of its department managers, are people of color. Three of its vice-presidents are people of color, and the president is female. This is a good record in an industry largely dominated by white men. As Nordstrom opens new stores, its human resource directors make sure employees hired reflect a range of races and ethnic backgrounds. Although a few minority people still complain about discrim-

ination, Nordstrom believes that it has come a long way in four years.

Consultants tell Nordstrom that minorities are shopping there more frequently and feel more identification with the chain.

● **QUESTIONS**

1. Do you believe the changes made by Nordstrom were necessary, considering the work force and marketplace? Explain.
2. Was Nordstrom's change primarily that of corporate culture or structures and policies? Should the focus of change be redirected? Why?
3. Do you believe Nordstrom has successfully shattered the glass ceiling? Discuss.

SOURCE: From Himanee Gupta, "Nordstrom Retools Image for More Inclusive Market," *Dallas Morning News*, February 2, 1992, Section H, 1, 18. Reprinted with permission of The Dallas Morning News.

REFERENCES

1. Joan E. Rigdon, "PepsiCo's KFC Scouts for Blacks and Women for Its Top Echelons," *The Wall Street Journal*, November 13, 1991, A1, A5.
2. M. Fine, F. Johnson, and M. S. Ryan, "Cultural Diversity in the Workforce," *Public Personnel Management* 19 (1990), 305–319.
3. Taylor Cox, Jr., "Managing Cultural Diversity: Implications for Organizational Competitiveness," *Academy of Management Executive* 5, no. 3 (1991), 45–56.
4. Joel Dreyfuss, "Get Ready for the New Workforce," *Fortune*, April 29, 1990, 165–181.
5. Lennie Copeland, "Valuing Diversity, Part I: Making the Most of Cultural Differences at the Workplace," *Personnel*, June 1988, 52–60.
6. Lennie Copeland, "Learning to Manage a Multicultural Workforce," *Training*, May 25, 1988, 48–56.
7. Marilyn Loden and Judy B. Rosener, *Workforce America!* (Homewood, Ill.: Business One Irwin, 1991).
8. N. Songer, "Workforce Diversity," *B & E Review*, April–June 1991, 3–6.
9. G. Haight, "Managing Diversity," *Across the Board* 27, no. 3 (1990), 22–29.
10. Songer, "Workforce Diversity."
11. Robert Doktor, Rosalie Tung, and Maryann Von Glinow, "Future Directions for Management Theory Development," *Academy of Management Review* 16 (1991), 362–365.
12. M. Bennett, "A Developmental Approach to Training for Intercultural Sensitivity," *International Journal of Intercultural Relations* 10 (1986), 179–196.
13. C. Keen, "Human Resource Management Issues in the '90s," *Vital Speeches* 56, no. 24 (1990), 752–754.

14. Kurt Anderson, "California Dreamin'," *Time,* September 23, 1991, 38–42.

15. Brian O'Reilly, "Your New Global Workforce," *Fortune,* December 14, 1992, 52–66.

16. W. B. Johnston and A. H. Packer, *Workforce 2000* (Indianapolis, Ind.: Hudson Institute, 1987).

17. United States Department of Labor, *Opportunity 2000: Creative Affirmative Action Strategies for a Changing Workforce* (Indianapolis, Ind.: Hudson Institute, 1988).

18. Copeland, "Valuing Diversity, Part I: Making the Most of Cultural Differences at the Workplace."

19. S. Hutchins, Jr., "Preparing for Diversity: The Year 2000," *Quality Process* 22, no. 10 (1989), 66–68.

20. J. Santoro, "Kinney Shoes Steps into Diversity," *Personnel Journal* 70, no. 9 (1991), 72–77.

21. Roosevelt Thomas, Jr., "From Affirmative Action to Affirming Diversity," *Harvard Business Review* (March–April 1990), 107–117.

22. Julie Amparano Lopez, "Study Says Women Face Glass Walls as Well as Ceilings," *The Wall Street Journal,* March 3, 1992, B1, B2.

23. C. Soloman, "Careers under Glass," *Personnel Journal* 69, no. 4 (1990), 96–105.

24. Ibid.

25. William A. Henry III, "A Mind-set Under Siege," *Time,* November 30, 1992, 40–42.

26. Thomas A. Stewart, "Gay in Corporate America," *Fortune,* December 16, 1991, 42–56.

27. B. Geber, "Managing Diversity," *Training* 27, no. 7 (1990), 23–30.

28. Anne B. Fisher, "When Will Women Get to the Top?" *Fortune,* September 21, 1992, 44–56.

29. Thomas, "From Affirmative Action to Affirming Diversity."

30. Copeland, "Learning to Manage a Multicultural Workforce."

31. James E. Ellis, "Monsanto's New Challenge: Keeping Minority Workers," *Business Week,* July 8, 1991, 60–61.

32. Geber, "Managing Diversity."

33. Loden and Rosener, *Workforce America!*

34. B. Ragins, "Barriers to Mentoring: The Female Manager's Dilemma," *Human Relations* 42, no. 1 (1989), 1–22.

35. Mary Zey, "A Mentor for All," *Personnel Journal,* January 1988, 46–51.

36. J. Black and M. Mendenhall, "Cross-Cultural Training Effectiveness: A Review and a Theoretical Framework for Future Research," *Academy of Management Review* 15 (1990), 113–136.

37. Loden and Rosener, *Workforce America!*

38. David Shallenberger, "Invisible Minorities: Coming out of the Classroom Closet," *Journal of Management Education* (August 1991), 325–334.

39. Aaron Bernstein, "When the Only Parent Is Daddy," *Business Week,* November 23, 1992, 122–127; Keith H. Hammonds and William C. Symonds, "Taking Baby Steps toward a Daddy Track," *Business Week,* April 15, 1991, 90–92; and Sue Shellenbarger, "More Job Seekers Put Family Needs First," *The Wall Street Journal,* November 15, 1991, B1, B12.

40. Aaron Bernstein, Joseph Weber, Lisa Driscoll, and Alice Cuneo, "Corporate America Is Still No Place for Kids," *Business Week,* November 21, 1991, 234–238.

41. E. G. Collins, "Managers and Lovers," *Harvard Business Review* 61 (1983), 142–153.

42. S. A. Lobel, R. E. Quinn, and A. Warfield, "Between Men and Women: An Exploration of Psychological Intimacy in Relationships at Work." Working paper, University of Michigan, 1991.

43. "Sexual Harassment: Vanderbilt University Policy" (Nashville: Vanderbilt University, 1993).

44. Troy Segal, Kevin Kelly, and Alisa Solomon, "Getting Serious about Sexual Harassment," *Business Week,* November 9, 1992, 78–82.

45. "The *INC.* FaxPoll: What Are You Doing about Sexual Harassment?" *INC.,* August 1992, 16.

46. Segal et al., "Getting Serious"; "The *INC.* FaxPoll"; and Gary Baseman, "Sexual Harassment: The Inside Story," *Working Woman,* June 1992, 47–51, 78.

47. Joel Dreyfuss, "Get Ready for the New Work Force," *Fortune,* April 23, 1990, 165–181; and Ronald E. Dulek, John S. Fielden, and John S. Hill, "International Communication: An Executive Primer," *Business Horizons,* January–February 1991, 20–25.

48. Joanne S. Lublin, "Companies Use Cross-Cultural Training to Help Their Employees Adjust Abroad," *The Wall Street Journal,* August 4, 1992, B1, B9.

49. Gilbert Fuchsberg, "As Costs of Overseas Assignments Climb, Firms Select Expatriates More Carefully," *The Wall Street Journal,* January 9, 1992, B3, B4.

50. Brian Dumaine, "Management Lessons from the General," *Fortune,* November 2, 1992, 143.

51. J. Kennedy and A. Everest, "Put Diversity in Context," *Personnel Journal,* September 1991, 50–54.

52. Cox, "Managing Cultural Diversity."

53. J. Castelli, "Education Forms Common Bond," *HRMagazine* 35, no. 6 (1990), 46–49.

54. Copeland, "Valuing Diversity, Part 1: Making the Most of Cultural Differences at the Workplace."

55. Cox, "Managing Cultural Diversity."

56. S. Caudron, "Monsanto Response to Diversity," *Personnel Journal* 69, no. 11 (1990), 72–80.

57. Suzanne B. Laporte, "12 Companies That Do the Right Thing," *Working Woman,* January 1991, 57–59.

58. Thomas, "From Affirmative Action to Affirming Diversity."

59. Rigdon, "PepsiCo's KFC Scouts."

In April 1992, Charles H. Wessel was diagnosed with a terminal brain tumor and told he had less than a year to live. Three months later, he was fired from his job as executive director of AIC Security Investigations Ltd., a Chicago-based company with 300 employees. "At the time I was terminated, I was working on the job descriptions for the company's Americans with Disabilities Act policies," the 59-year-old executive explained later in a videotaped deposition submitted in connection with his lawsuit against the company.

The Americans with Disabilities Act (ADA) was passed in 1990 to make public buildings accessible and bar workplace discrimination against disabled people. The employment provisions, which went into effect in July 1992, were designed to protect some 43 million people like Wessel across the United States. But while the new law bans employment discrimination against "any qualified individual with a disability," it does not specify exactly who falls into that category.

Based on past court cases and legislation, a disability could mean anything from former drug use, alcoholism, or depression to HIV infection, dyslexia, or unusual sensitivity to tobacco smoke. The Equal Employment Opportunity Commission warns that other problems, such as obesity, might be added to the list if future court rulings dictate it. In fact, the law is so broad that Congress had to go out of its way to specify what was not included on the list of disabilities.

In the lawsuit against his former employer, Wessel contended that his dismissal violated provisions of the ADA because he was fired even though he was still capable of doing his job. After reviewing the evidence, a federal court jury sided with Wessel, awarding him $572,000 in back pay, compensatory, and punitive damages for job discrimination. Since the award exceeded the limits set by law, the judge was expected to reduce the amount to $200,000 in damages, and add about $22,000 in back pay. Still, the case set a legal precedent.

One of the key points of ADA lawsuits is the employee's ability to do the job. "It doesn't matter what disability you may have—it's how well you do your job," said Linda Baker Oberst, program director at Paraquad, a nonprofit group that helps place disabled workers in mainstream jobs. "A person with a terminal illness can go on working for 10, 12, 15 years."

Scores of other disabled employees may soon be joining Wessel in court. The EEOC estimates it has received an average of 1,000 complaints a month since the employment provisions of the ADA went into effect. The numbers indicate that many companies have not figured out how to comply with the law, which applies to any business with 25 or more employees. Beginning in 1994, the law will extend to businesses with as few as 15 workers.

The main employment provisions of the ADA require businesses to make any "reasonable accommodations," that do not pose an "undue hardship" on the company, and would allow any qualified individual with a disability to perform the essential functions of a job. Looks simple on the surface, but the law could impose a tremendous financial burden on businesses, especially since employers have no way of knowing what is considered "reasonable."

The National Federation of Independent Business says the government has done a bad job of spreading the word about the law's requirements. "I would give the government an F on the effort to get information out so far," says Wendy Lechner, head of research and policy for the group, which represents more than 500,000 small companies nationwide. "We're constantly speaking to companies that had never heard of ADA until someone from our organization told them about it.

Many employers are beginning to see the benefits of hiring disabled employees. "Gone are the days when somebody will say, 'How are we going to hire a person in a wheelchair or a person who is hearing impaired?' That's nonsense," says Jim Frangos, corporate vice-president of UJB Financial Corporation. "We're way past that hurdle. I can't say, regrettably, that it's that way across corporate America."

Many are optimistic that the ADA will bring even more positive changes with time. "I think it parallels the Civil Rights Act of 1964," says Gregory Mizanin, editor of *People with Disabilities* magazine. "Things didn't change overnight for people of color, and things won't change immediately for people with disabilities."

● QUESTIONS

1. Why have businesses resisted the changes brought about by the ADA? What implementation tactics, as described in Chapter 11, can companies use?

2. How will companies have to change their recruiting tactics to bring them into compliance with the ADA?

3. Compare the ADA with other major federal laws as described in Chapter 12.

4. Describe in what way the ADA will help diversify the workplace. List some of the benefits and costs of that diversification.

5. Name a few key points that a manager should keep in mind when dealing with a diverse work force.

6. Describe the changes that have occurred since this video case aired.

■HOW WELL DO YOU DELEGATE?

Chapter 9, "Fundamentals of Organizing," emphasized that most organizations today encourage their managers to delegate much of their authority and responsibilities to those below them. That way, employees can respond quickly and flexibly to customers, competitors, changes in technology, and other factors that require an organization to be adaptable.

However, many managers have difficulty depending on others, especially when they still retain the final responsibility. They may not believe that anyone else can do the job besides themselves or they may not want to accept the risk that employees will not complete their assigned tasks correctly or on time.

THIS EXERCISE WILL HELP YOU

- Rate your ability to delegate effectively.
- Learn proven methods for improving your delegation skills.

HOW TO LOCATE THE EXERCISE:

When you see the main menu for Career Design, select "Organizing." Then select "How Well Do You Delegate."

■SEXUAL HARASSMENT ISSUES

One of the many subjects covered in Chapter 13, "Managing Diverse Employees," was sexual harassment in the workplace. You learned that sexual harassment can take many forms. Even if the perpetrator doesn't direct sexual remarks or actions toward a specific person, sexual harassment may be taking place. For example, a comment demeaning one gender, such as, "The only way women on the sales force can compete with the men is to use their sex appeal to entice customers to do business with them," would fall into the category of sexual harassment.

Although many offenders know they are sexually harassing someone, others violate a person's rights out of ignorance of what constitutes appropriate behavior with the opposite sex at work. Furthermore, victims of sexual harassment may not know how to handle it.

THIS EXERCISE WILL HELP YOU

- Measure your understanding about what words and actions may be defined as sexual harassment.
- Improve your sensitivity about sexual harassment issues.
- Take appropriate actions if you become a victim of sexual harassment.

HOW TO LOCATE THE EXERCISE:

When you see the main menu for Career Design, select "Organizing." Then select "Sexual Harassment Issues."

■MANAGING CULTURAL DIVERSITY

Chapter 13, "Managing Diverse Employees," explored how organizations can effectively recruit, train, and utilize the talents and experience of workers from all areas of society. Our ability to manage people depends on how well we understand their perspectives and motivations. All too often, we make assumptions about how people different from ourselves want to be treated. Our ignorance and biases may inadvertently cause offense.

In this exercise, you'll be presented with a series of work situations where the differences between people could lead to conflict or misunderstanding. You'll be asked to choose the best course of action in each scenario.

THIS EXERCISE WILL HELP YOU

- Measure your awareness of how people different from yourself prefer to interact in a work setting.
- Improve your interpersonal effectiveness in motivating and communicating with people in a multicultural workplace.

HOW TO LOCATE THE EXERCISE:

When you see the main menu for Career Design, select "Organizing." Then select "Managing Cultural Diversity."

PART **IV**

LEADERSHIP

Rollerblades? Safari hat? Crazy T-shirts? Who are these guys racing through the corporate hallways of downtown Minneapolis? It's part of IDS' approach to leadership, motivation, and teamwork. President and CEO Jeff Stiefler (center) and Gary Lumpkin from the TV show "Good Company" recognize winners of the annual Premier Performers Award. This prestigious award recognizes employees who personify IDS values, provide superior customer service, contribute to team spirit, and appreciate the diversity of other employees. The winners, such as Anne Green of TransAction Services (second from left), are proven leaders who reflect the values of senior management.

LEADERSHIP IN ORGANIZATIONS

14

LEARNING OBJECTIVES

After studying this chapter, you should be able to

■ Define leadership and explain its importance for organizations.

■ Identify personal characteristics associated with effective leaders.

■ Explain the five sources of leader influence and how each causes different subordinate behavior.

■ Describe the leader behaviors of initiating structure and consideration and when they should be used.

■ Describe Hersey and Blanchard's situational theory and its application to subordinate participation.

■ Explain the path-goal model of leadership.

■ Explain how leadership fits the organizational situation and how organizational characteristics can substitute for leadership behaviors.

■ Describe leadership and when it should be used.

When it was time to replace the head of United Technologies Corporation, Robert F. Daniell seemed an unlikely choice. He had rescued United Technologies' Sikorsky helicopter division but had little headquarters experience and a style opposite that of his predecessor, Harry Gray. Gray ruled the conglomerate with an iron grip, creating an autocratic, impersonal, compartmental-ized organization. Daniell's

strength had been to inspire cooperation, see the big picture, and listen to problems from all levels. At Sikorsky he was known as a shop floor president, and some questioned whether this style would work to run a huge conglomerate.[1]

■ Will Robert Daniell's people-oriented style be a good thing for United Technologies? What leadership style would you recommend that he adopt for this company?

M A N A G E M E N T   P R O B L E M

Fred Cain and his "Bull Gang" of maintenance workers at Asarco's Tennessee mines have accumulated 350,000 hours over a 15-year period without a single lost-time injury, earning them Tennessee's 1990 Excellence at Work Award. Cain's position as foreman is a source of *legitimate power* through which he leads the department. The skills he has developed over 30 years in maintenance is *expert power*. And Cain's own 30-year record without lost time serves as example and inspiration to his crew, which is a *referent power source*.

leadership

The ability to influence people toward the attainment of organizational goals.

power

The potential ability to influence others' behavior.

Robert Daniell is the leader of a giant corporation, and his style is different from that of the previous CEO. Many styles of leadership can be successful in organizations depending on the leader and the situation. For example, Compaq Computer Corporation recently lapsed into recession doldrums, but the aggressive, "can-do" leadership style of new president Eckhard Pfeiffer fired up the company's vision for producing lower-priced computers. Under this leadership style, Compaq turned around in a year and is now going after the competition with a vengeance. In another case, Steve Chen inspired 40 people to leave Cray Research with him because of his dream to build a super computer that Cray decided not to build. Consider the leadership style of Irish pop star Bob Geldof, who mobilized aid for Ethiopia's famine-stricken population in the 1980s. Geldof threaded together diverse international forces to create historical music events, Band Aid and Live Aid. Alternatively stroking, coaxing, and prodding, Geldof successfully coordinated communication technology and delicate star egos into a "collective individualism." Today, executives for global companies study Geldof's multinational coordination techniques.[2]

This chapter explores one of the most widely discussed and researched topics in management—leadership. Here we will define leadership and explore the sources of leadership influence. We will discuss trait, behavioral, and contingency theories of leadership effectiveness. We will also explore the *charismatic leader*, who creates a vision, inspires loyalty, and leads corporate transformation. Chapters 15 through 17 deal with many of the functions of leadership, including employee motivation, communication, and leading groups.

● THE NATURE OF LEADERSHIP

Among all the ideas and writings about leadership, three aspects stand out—people, influence, and goals. Leadership occurs between people, involves the use of influence, and is used to attain goals.[3] *Influence* means that the relationship among people is not passive. Moreover, influence is designed to achieve some end or goal. Thus, **leadership** as defined here is the ability to influence people toward the attainment of goals. This definition captures the idea that leaders are involved with other people in the achievement of objectives.

Leadership is reciprocal, occurring *between* people.[4] Leadership is a "people" activity, distinct from administrative paper shuffling or problem-solving activities. Leadership is dynamic and involves the use of power. Power is important for influencing others, because it determines whether a leader is able to command compliance from followers.

SOURCES OF LEADER INFLUENCE

Power is the potential ability to influence the behavior of others.[5] Power represents the resources with which a leader effects changes in employee behavior. Leadership is the actual use of that power. Within organizations, leaders typically have five sources of power: legitimate, reward, coercive, expert, and referent.[6]

LEGITIMATE POWER. Power coming from a formal management position in an organization and the authority granted to it is called **legitimate power.** For example, once a person has been selected as a supervisor, most workers understand that they are obligated to follow his or her direction with respect to work activities. Subordinates accept this source of power as legitimate, which is why they comply.

REWARD POWER. Another kind of power, **reward power,** stems from the leader's authority to bestow rewards on other people. Leaders may have access to formal rewards, such as pay increases or promotions. They also have at their disposal rewards such as praise, attention, and recognition. Leaders can use rewards to influence subordinates' behavior.

COERCIVE POWER. The opposite of reward power is **coercive power:** It refers to the leader's authority to punish or recommend punishment. Leaders have coercive power when they have the right to fire or demote employees, criticize, or withdraw pay increases. For example, if Paul, a salesman, does not perform as expected, his supervisor has the coercive power to criticize him, reprimand him, put a negative letter in his file, and hurt his chance for a raise.

EXPERT POWER. Power resulting from a leader's special knowledge or skill regarding the tasks performed by followers is referred to as **expert power.** When the leader is a true expert, subordinates go along with recommendations because of his or her superior knowledge. Leaders at supervisory levels often have experience in the production process that gains them promotion. At top management levels, however, leaders may lack expert power because subordinates know more about technical details than they do.

REFERENT POWER. The last kind of power, **referent power,** comes from leader personality characteristics that command subordinates' identification, respect, and admiration so they wish to emulate the leader. When workers admire a supervisor because of the way she deals with them, the influence is based on referent power. Referent power depends on the leader's personal characteristics rather than formal title or position and is most visible in the area of charismatic leadership, which will be discussed later in this chapter.

THE USE OF POWER

Leaders use the above five sources of power to affect the behavior and performance of followers. But how do followers react to each source? Three reactions that have been studied are commitment, compliance, and resistance by followers.[7] *Commitment* means that workers will share the leader's point of view and enthusiastically carry out instructions. Expert power and referent power are the sources most likely to generate follower commitment. *Compliance* means that workers will obey orders and carry out instructions, although they may personally disagree with the instructions and will not necessarily be enthusiastic. Legitimate power and reward power are most likely to generate follower compliance.

legitimate power

Power that stems from a formal management position in an organization and the authority granted to it.

reward power

Power that results from the leader's authority to reward others.

coercive power

Power that stems from the leader's authority to punish or recommend punishment.

expert power

Power that stems from the leader's special knowledge of or skill in the tasks performed by subordinates.

referent power

Power that results from leader characteristics that command subordinates' identification with, respect and admiration for, and desire to emulate the leader.

Resistance
coercive

Resistance means that workers will deliberately try to avoid carrying out instructions and attempt to disobey orders. Coercive power most often generates resistance.

For example, Glenn Van Pelt, production supervisor at a steel fabrication plant, was respected by everyone for his knowledge of production and for his pleasant attitude. Glenn asked John Simmons, one of his line managers, to reassign one of his people to help finish a project under way in another department. Although John's own people were stretched to the max, he appreciated his boss's good judgment and trusted his expertise. John agreed to lend an employee to Glenn, and thus committed himself to the success of the project. If Glenn's leadership style had been more coercive, John would likely have resisted and found a reason why he could not spare an employee. Glenn's referent and expert leadership style inspired support and cooperation.

A significant recent trend in corporate America is for top executives to *empower* lower employees. Fully 74 percent of executives in a survey claimed that they are more participatory, more concerned with consensus building, and rely more on communication than on command compared with the past. Executives no longer hoard power. For example, at Johnsonville Foods, the real power of top executives comes from giving it up to others who are in a better position to get things done. Empowering employees works because total power in the organization seems to increase. Everyone has more say and hence contributes more to organizational goals. The goal of senior executives in many corporations today is not simply to wield power but also to give it away to people who can get jobs done.[8]

Clorox's Cindy Ransom avoids the word "manager," preferring the term "sponsor." And Ransom walks her talk. When she decided as factory manager to revamp operations at the Fairfield, California, plant, Ransom *empowered* her employees. A team was given responsibility for establishing everything from training programs to work rules. The result was a plant reorganization into five business unit teams centered on customer service. Since the teams took over much of management's responsibility, Ransom focused her attention on supplier and customer needs. In 1992, Ransom and her 100 employees were recognized by Clorox as the most improved plant.

● LEADERSHIP TRAITS

Early efforts to understand leadership success focused on the leader's personal characteristics or traits. **Traits are the** distinguishing personal characteristics of a leader, such as intelligence, values, and appearance. The early research focused on leaders who had achieved a level of greatness and hence was referred to as the *great man* approach. The idea was relatively simple: Find out what made these people great and select future leaders who already exhibited the same traits or could be trained to develop them. Generally, research found only a weak relationship between personal traits and leader success.[9] For example, three football coaches—Tom Osborne at Nebraska, Lou Holtz at Notre Dame, and Joe Paterno at Penn State—have different personality traits, but all are successful leaders of their football programs.

In addition to personality traits, physical, social, and work-related characteristics of leaders have been studied. Exhibit 14.1 summarizes the physical, social, and personal leadership characteristics that have received the greatest research support.[10] However, these characteristics do not stand alone. The appropriateness of a trait or set of traits depends on the leadership situation. The same traits do not apply to every organization.

For example, Sarah Brown is the manager of Far Eastern imports for a major steel corporation. There is an opening for a subordinate manager in her department who will supervise the field sales personnel. For this position, the personal characteristic of intelligence and a working knowledge of steel product marketing are important, as are desire for responsibility, a task orientation, and supervisory skills. Sarah Brown's ability to understand the situation and the type of leader who will succeed in it will help her select the appropriate person for the job.

traits

The distinguishing personal characteristics of a leader, such as intelligence, values, and appearance.

EXHIBIT   14.1

Personal Characteristics of Leaders

Physical characteristics	**Personality**	**Social characteristics**
Activity	Alertness	Ability to enlist cooperation
Energy	Originality, creativity	Cooperativeness
	Personal integrity, ethical conduct	Popularity, prestige
Social background	Self-confidence	Sociability, interpersonal skills
Mobility		Social participation
	Work-related characteristics	Tact, diplomacy
Intelligence and ability	Achievement drive, desire to excel	
Judgment, decisiveness	Drive for responsibility	
Knowledge	Responsibility in pursuit of objectives	
Fluency of speech	Task orientation	

SOURCE: Adapted from Bernard M. Bass, *Stogdill's Handbook of Leadership*, rev. ed. (New York: Free Press, 1981), 75–76. This adaptation appeared in R. Albanese and D. D. Van Fleet, *Organizational Behavior: A Managerial Viewpoint* (Hinsdale, Ill.: The Dryden Press, 1983).

AUTOCRATIC VERSUS DEMOCRATIC LEADERS

autocratic leader

A leader who tends to centralize authority and rely on legitimate, reward, and coercive power to manage subordinates.

democratic leader

A leader who delegates authority to others, encourages participation, and relies on expert and referent power to manage subordinates.

One way to approach leader characteristics is to examine autocratic and democratic leaders. An **autocratic leader** is one who tends to centralize authority and rely on legitimate, reward, and coercive power. A **democratic leader** delegates authority to others, encourages participation, and relies on expert and referent power to influence subordinates.

The first studies on these leadership characteristics were conducted at Iowa State University by Kurt Lewin and his associates.[11] These studies compared autocratic and democratic leaders and produced some interesting findings. The groups with autocratic leaders performed highly so long as the leader was present to supervise them. However, group members were displeased with the close, autocratic style of leadership, and feelings of hostility frequently arose. The performance of groups who were assigned democratic leaders was almost as good, and these were characterized by positive feelings rather than hostility. In addition, under the democratic style of leadership, group members performed well even when the leader was absent and left the group on its own.[12] The participative techniques and majority rule decision making used by the democratic leader trained and involved group members such that they performed well with or without the leader present. These characteristics of democratic leadership explain why the empowerment of lower employees is a popular trend in companies today.

This early work suggested that leaders were either autocratic or democratic in their approach. However, further work by Tannenbaum

These recruits in the U.S. Army learn about *autocratic leadership*. The military has a well-defined authority structure, and leaders are able to use legitimate, reward, and coercive power on subordinates. Drill sergeants insist that each soldier maintain army standards, and they can bestow rewards or punishments to help recruits learn to perform.

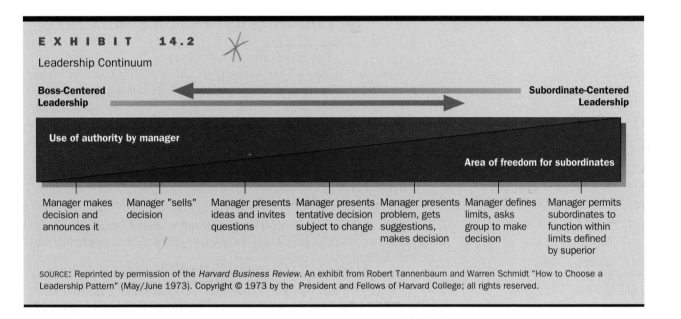

EXHIBIT   14.2

Leadership Continuum

| Boss-Centered Leadership | | | | | | | Subordinate-Centered Leadership |

Use of authority by manager

Area of freedom for subordinates

| Manager makes decision and announces it | Manager "sells" decision | Manager presents ideas and invites questions | Manager presents tentative decision subject to change | Manager presents problem, gets suggestions, makes decision | Manager defines limits, asks group to make decision | Manager permits subordinates to function within limits defined by superior |

SOURCE: Reprinted by permission of the *Harvard Business Review*. An exhibit from Robert Tannenbaum and Warren Schmidt "How to Choose a Leadership Pattern" (May/June 1973). Copyright © 1973 by the President and Fellows of Harvard College; all rights reserved.

and Schmidt indicated that leadership could be a continuum reflecting different amounts of employee participation.[13] Thus, one leader might be autocratic (boss centered), another democratic (subordinate centered), and a third a mix of the two styles. The leadership continuum is illustrated in Exhibit 14.2.

Tannenbaum and Schmidt suggested that the extent to which leadership is boss centered or subordinate centered depends on organizational circumstances. For example, if there is time pressure on a leader or if it takes too long for subordinates to learn how to make decisions, the leader will tend to use an autocratic style. When subordinates are able to learn decision-making skills readily, a participative style can be used. Another situational factor is the skill difference between subordinates and leader. The greater the skill difference, the more autocratic the leader approach, because it is difficult to bring subordinates up to the leader's expertise level.[14]

For example, Stephen Fleming uses an autocratic style as a marketing manager in an oil products company. He is being groomed for a higher position because his marketing department has performed so well. However, this has meant time spent at meetings away from his group, and their performance has declined because the subordinates have not learned to function independently. In contrast, Dorothy Roberts, CEO of Echo Scarves, believes that people are managed best by showing them respect and courtesy. Decision making is shared by representatives of design, sales, marketing, and operations. In the traditionally tough fashion industry, her nice-guy leadership style permeates the entire company, creating a unique corporate culture that is open, honest, and supportive of employees. Company prosperity is centered on treating people well. Roberts' leadership style creates satisfied employees who in turn create satisfied customers, which may be more difficult with an autocratic leadership style.[15]

● TWO-DIMENSIONAL APPROACHES

The autocratic and democratic styles suggest that it is the "behavior" of the leader rather than a personality trait that determines leadership effectiveness. Perhaps any leader can adopt the correct behavior with appropriate training. The focus of recent research has shifted from leader personality traits toward the behaviors successful leaders display. Important research programs on leadership behavior were conducted at Ohio State University, the University of Michigan, and the University of Texas.

OHIO STATE STUDIES

Researchers at Ohio State University surveyed leaders to study hundreds of dimensions of leader behavior.[16] They identified two major behaviors, called *consideration* and *initiating structure*.

Consideration is the extent to which the leader is mindful of subordinates, respects their ideas and feelings, and establishes mutual trust. Considerate leaders are friendly, provide open communication, develop teamwork, and are oriented toward their subordinates' welfare.

Initiating structure is the extent to which the leader is task oriented and directs subordinate work activities toward goal attainment. Leaders with this style typically give instructions, spend time planning, emphasize deadlines, and provide explicit schedules of work activities.

Consideration and initiating structure are independent of each other, which means that a leader with a high degree of consideration may be either high or low on initiating structure. A leader may have any of four styles: high initiating structure–low consideration, high initiating structure–high consideration, low initiating structure–low consideration, or low initiating structure–high consideration. The Ohio State research

consideration

A type of leader behavior that describes the extent to which a leader is sensitive to subordinates, respects their ideas and feelings, and establishes mutual trust.

initiating structure

A type of leader behavior that describes the extent to which a leader is task oriented and directs subordinates' work activities toward goal achievement.

Joyce Meskis, owner of Denver's Tattered Cover Book Store, exemplifies the leadership quality of *consideration*. Despite the store's enormous size—500,000 volumes in a five-story building—Meskis creates a comfortable, unpressured atmosphere so sacred to book browsers. Meskis' consideration also extends to her workers. She takes new workers under her wing on their first day of employment to explain the history, philosophy, and customer service tradition of Tattered Cover Books. Her up-front, honest attitude and employee sensitivity provide a leadership example for the book-selling industry.

found that the high consideration–high initiating structure style achieved better performance and greater satisfaction than the other leader styles. However, new research has found that effective leaders may be high on consideration and low on initiating structure or low on consideration and high on initiating structure, depending on the situation. Thus, the "high-high" style is not always the best.[17]

MICHIGAN STUDIES

Studies at the University of Michigan at about the same time took a different approach by comparing the behavior of effective and ineffective supervisors.[18] The most effective supervisors were those who focused on the subordinates' human needs in order to "build effective work groups with high performance goals." The Michigan researchers used the term *employee-centered leaders* for leaders who established high performance goals and displayed supportive behavior toward subordinates. The less effective leaders were called *job-centered leaders*; these tended to be less concerned with goal achievement and human needs in favor of meeting schedules, keeping costs low, and achieving production efficiency.

THE LEADERSHIP GRID

Blake and Mouton of the University of Texas proposed a three-dimensional leadership theory called **leadership grid** that builds on the work of the Ohio State and Michigan studies.[19] The three-dimensional model and five of its seven major management styles are depicted in Exhibit 14.3. Each axis on the grid is a 9-point scale, with 1 meaning low concern and 9 high concern.

leadership grid

A three-dimensional leadership theory that measures a leader's concern for people and concern for production.

Team management (9,9) often is considered the most effective style and is recommended for managers because organization members work together to accomplish tasks. *Country club management* (1,9) occurs when primary emphasis is given to people rather than to work outputs. *Authority-obedience management* (9,1) occurs when efficiency in operations is the dominant orientation. *Organization Man management* (5,5) reflects a moderate amount of concern for both people and production. *Impoverished management* (1,1) means the absence of a management philosophy; managers exert little effort toward interpersonal relationships or work accomplishment. Consider these examples.

 CHICK-FIL-A, INC.

Samuel Truett Cathy is founder and president of Chick-fil-A, Inc. Cathy has been remarkably successful, and one of the keys is his people orientation. "Truett Cathy is probably the most person-oriented individual I've ever known," says a close friend. "He honestly believes his highest obligation is to help people reach their highest potential. . . . He's one of the most tolerant persons I've known." The executive vice-president of Chick-fil-A calls his boss "the most patient man I've ever encountered, and one totally committed to individual development. He delegates easily, lets people grow by trusting them."

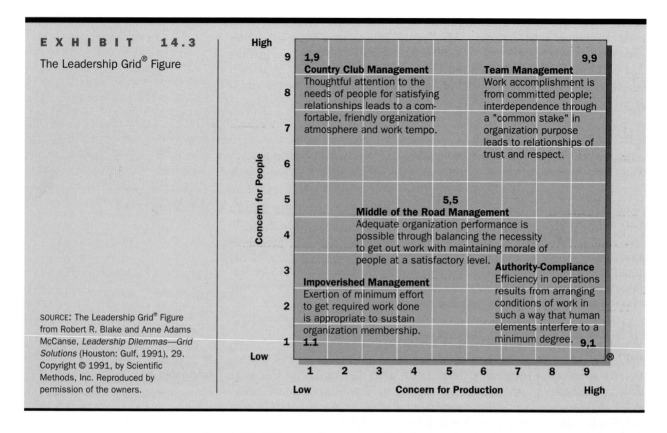

EXHIBIT 14.3

The Leadership Grid® Figure

SOURCE: The Leadership Grid® Figure from Robert R. Blake and Anne Adams McCanse, *Leadership Dilemmas—Grid Solutions* (Houston: Gulf, 1991), 29. Copyright © 1991, by Scientific Methods, Inc. Reproduced by permission of the owners.

Of course, to be successful, Cathy also had to set goals and provide direction for his company. But the reason he succeeded was that he was an outstanding encourager of other people.[20]

Compare Cathy's leadership style with that of the "Smiling Barracuda," Thomas Graham. The former president of U.S. Steel Group, Graham has taken the reins of the ailing Washington Steel Corporation. Stressing discipline, cost cutting, and high productivity, the Barracuda whips companies into action. Wall Street investors applaud him. Bureaucrats, unions, and paper shufflers loathe him. Middle managers dread the grillings at his weekly "prayer meetings." Graham points gleefully to a union magazine cartoon showing pallbearers hauling his coffin as he sits up and barks, "If you'd put this thing on wheels, we could get rid of six jobs!"[21] ∎

Truett Cathy's leadership style is characterized by high people concern and moderate concern for production. Thomas Graham, in contrast, is high on concern for production and low on concern for people. However, both managers are successful because of their situations.

contingency approach

A model of leadership that describes the relationship between leadership styles and specific organizational situations.

 CONTINGENCY APPROACHES

Several models of leadership that explain the relationship between leadership styles and specific situations have been developed. These are termed **contingency approaches** and include the leadership model developed by Fiedler and his associates, the situational theory of Hersey and Blanchard, the path-goal theory presented by Evans and House, and the substitutes-for-leadership concept.

FIEDLER'S CONTINGENCY THEORY

An early, extensive effort to combine leadership style and organizational situation into a comprehensive theory of leadership was made by Fiedler and his associates.[22] The basic idea is simple: Match the leader's style with the situation most favorable for his or her success. By diagnosing leadership style and the organizational situation, the correct fit can be arranged.

LEADERSHIP STYLE. The cornerstone of Fiedler's contingency theory is the extent to which the leader's style is relationship oriented or task oriented. A *relationship-oriented leader* is concerned with people, as in the consideration style described earlier. A *task-oriented leader* is primarily motivated by task accomplishment, which is similar to the initiating structure style described earlier.

Leadership style was measured with a questionnaire known as the least preferred coworker (LPC) scale. The **LPC scale** has a set of 16 bipolar adjectives along an 8-point scale. Examples of the bipolar adjectives used by Fiedler on the LPC scale are as follows:

open	—	—	—	—	—	—	—	—	guarded
quarrelsome	—	—	—	—	—	—	—	—	harmonious
efficient	—	—	—	—	—	—	—	—	inefficient
self-assured	—	—	—	—	—	—	—	—	hesitant
gloomy	—	—	—	—	—	—	—	—	cheerful

[handwritten margin notes: "consideration style", "initiating style"]

LPC scale

A questionnaire designed to measure relationship-oriented versus task-oriented leadership style according to the leader's choice of adjectives for describing the "least preferred coworker."

Millard S. Drexler has transformed The Gap into the most popular and profitable specialty clothing chain in the United States. When Drexler took over in 1983, he illustrated *Fiedler's contingency theory* by being a tough, *task-oriented leader* in an unfavorable situation. He pushed new designs, tight controls, and customer service. Now that The Gap is so successful, Drexler also stresses a people-oriented culture while planning for more growth and success.

If the leader describes the least preferred coworker using positive concepts, he or she is considered relationship oriented, that is, cares about and is sensitive to other people's feelings. Conversely, if a leader uses negative concepts to describe the least preferred coworker, he or she is considered task oriented, that is, sees other people in negative terms and places greater value on task activities than on people.

SITUATION.   Leadership situations can be analyzed in terms of three elements: the quality of leader-member relationships, task structure, and position power.[23] Each of these elements can be described as either favorable or unfavorable for the leader.

1 *Leader-member relations* refers to group atmosphere and members' attitude toward and acceptance of the leader. When subordinates trust, respect, and have confidence in the leader, leader-member relations are considered good. When subordinates distrust, do not respect, and have little confidence in the leader, leader-member relations are poor.

2 *Task structure* refers to the extent to which tasks performed by the group are defined, involve specific procedures, and have clear, explicit goals. Routine, well-defined tasks, such as those of assembly-line workers, have a high degree of structure. Creative, ill-defined tasks, such as research and development or strategic planning, have a low degree of task structure. When task structure is high, the situation is considered favorable to the leader; when low, the situation is less favorable.

3 *Position power* is the extent to which the leader has formal authority over subordinates. Position power is high when the leader has the power to plan and direct the work of subordinates, evaluate it, and reward or punish them. Position power is low when the leader has little authority over subordinates and cannot evaluate their work or reward them. When position power is high, the situation is considered favorable for the leader; when low, the situation is unfavorable.

Combining the three situational characteristics yields a list of eight leadership situations, which are illustrated in Exhibit 14.4. Situation I is most favorable to the leader because leader-member relations are good, task structure is high, and leader position power is strong. Situation VIII is most unfavorable to the leader because leader-member relations are poor, task structure is low, and leader position power is weak. All other octants represent intermediate degrees of favorableness for the leader.

CONTINGENCY THEORY.   When Fiedler examined the relationships among leadership style, situational favorability, and group task performance, he found the pattern shown in Exhibit 14.5. Task-oriented leaders are more effective when the situation is either highly favorable or highly unfavorable. Relationship-oriented leaders are more effective in situations of moderate favorability.

The reason the task-oriented leader excels in the favorable situation is that when everyone gets along, the task is clear and the leader has

E X H I B I T   14.4

Fiedler's Classification of Situation Favorableness

	Very Favorable		Intermediate				Very Unfavorable	
Leader-Member Relations	Good	Good	Good	Good	Poor	Poor	Poor	Poor
Task Structure	High		Low		High		Low	
Leader Position Power	Strong	Weak	Strong	Weak	Strong	Weak	Strong	Weak
Situations	I	II	III	IV	V	VI	VII	VIII

SOURCE: Fred E. Fiedler, "The Effects of Leadership Training and Experience: A Contingency Model Interpretation," *Administrative Science Quarterly* 17 (1972), 455. Reprinted by permission of *Administrative Science Quarterly*.

power; all that is needed is for someone to take charge and provide direction. Similarly, if the situation is highly unfavorable to the leader, a great deal of structure and task direction is needed. A strong leader defines task structure and can establish authority over subordinates. Because leader-member relations are poor anyway, a strong task orientation will make no difference in the leader's popularity.

The reason the relationship-oriented leader performs better in situations of intermediate favorability is that human relations skills are important in achieving high group performance. In these situations, the leader may be moderately well liked, have some power, and supervise jobs that contain some ambiguity. A leader with good interpersonal skills

E X H I B I T   14.5

How Leader Style Fits the Situation

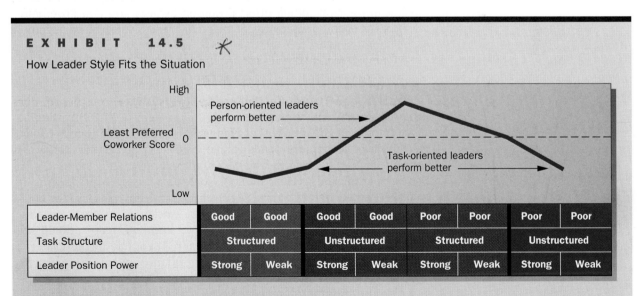

	Good	Good	Good	Good	Poor	Poor	Poor	Poor
Leader-Member Relations	Good	Good	Good	Good	Poor	Poor	Poor	Poor
Task Structure	Structured		Unstructured		Structured		Unstructured	
Leader Position Power	Strong	Weak	Strong	Weak	Strong	Weak	Strong	Weak

SOURCE: Fred E. Fiedler, "The Effects of Leadership Training and Experience: A Contingency Model Interpretation," *Administrative Science Quarterly* 17 (1972), 455. Reprinted by permission of *Administrative Science Quarterly*.

can create a positive group atmosphere that will improve relationships, clarify task structure, and establish position power.

A leader, then, needs to know two things in order to use Fiedler's contingency theory. First, the leader should know whether he or she has a relationship- or task-oriented style. Second, the leader should diagnose the situation and determine whether leader-member relations, task structure, and position power are favorable or unfavorable.

Fitting leader style to the situation can yield big dividends in profits and efficiency.[24] Consider the situation at the U.S. Postal Service.

U.S. POSTAL SERVICE

In 1992, Marvin Runyon became the nation's 70th postmaster general, a situation that fits his leadership style. "Carvin' Marvin," so named because of the cost-cutting reputation he earned as chairman of Tennessee Valley Authority, relished the opportunity to take on yet another bloated bureaucracy. Runyon considers the job of postmaster general second only to the U.S. presidency as "the most challenging management job in the country," with employees and payrolls equaling those of IBM and GM combined. Runyon faces rising costs, angry customers, cantankerous unions, and increased competition from electronic mail, faxes, and overnight delivery services.

Runyon's major focus is management reduction. His initial moves to reduce the number of managers outraged postal supervisors, whose union president said, "We knew we needed some surgery, but instead of Dr. Kildare, we got Freddy Kruger." The "carvin'" during the first six months extended beyond jobs as Runyon cut paperwork and job perks, including free postage for the department's own newspaper. In 1992, as a result of his cost-cutting efforts, Runyon became the first government official to be named Executive of the Year by the National Management Association.[25] ■

Marvin Runyon's experience at the U.S. Postal Service illustrates Fiedler's model; a task-oriented leadership style was correct for a difficult, unfavorable situation.

An important contribution of Fiedler's research is that it goes beyond the notion of leadership styles to show how styles fit the situation to improve organizational effectiveness. On the other hand, the model has also been criticized.[26] Using the LPC score as a measure of relationship- or task-oriented behavior seems simplistic, and how the model works over time is unclear. For example, if a task-oriented leader is matched with an unfavorable situation and is successful, the organizational situation is likely to improve and become more favorable to the leader. In other words, as the Postal Service's performance improves, the formal position power, leader-member relations, and task structure also improve and become more positive for the leader, and the hard-nosed style of Marvin Runyon might no longer be appropriate. Runyon might want to change his style or go to a new situation to find the same challenge for his task-oriented leader style.

HERSEY AND BLANCHARD'S SITUATIONAL THEORY

The **situational theory** of leadership is an interesting extension of the two-dimensional theories described earlier and summarized in the managerial grid (Exhibit 14.3). The point of Hersey and Blanchard is that subordinates vary in maturity level. People low in task maturity, because of little ability or training, or insecurity, need a different leadership style than those who are highly mature and have good ability, skills, confidence, and willingness to work.[27]

The relationships between leader style and task maturity are summarized in Exhibit 14.6. The upper part of the exhibit indicates style of leader, which is based on a combination of relationship behavior and task behavior. The bell-shaped curve is called a prescriptive curve, because it indicates when each leader style should be used. The four styles—telling (S1), selling (S2), participating (S3), and delegating (S4)—depend on the maturity of followers, indicated in the lower part of Exhibit 14.6. M1 is low maturity and M4 represents high maturity. The telling style is for low-maturity subordinates, because people are unable

situational theory

A contingency approach to leadership that links the leader's two-dimensional style with the task maturity of subordinates.

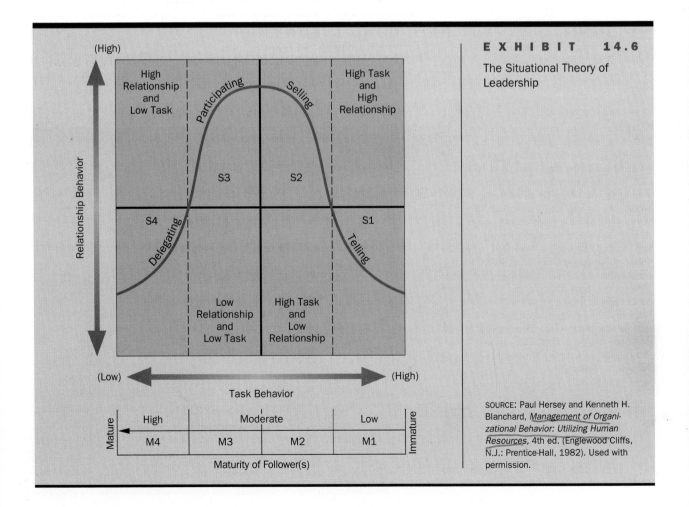

EXHIBIT 14.6

The Situational Theory of Leadership

SOURCE: Paul Hersey and Kenneth H. Blanchard, *Management of Organizational Behavior: Utilizing Human Resources*, 4th ed. (Englewood Cliffs, N.J.: Prentice-Hall, 1982). Used with permission.

and unwilling to take responsibility for their own task behavior. The selling and participating styles work for followers with moderate maturity, and delegating is appropriate for employees with high maturity.

This contingency model is easier to understand than Fiedler's model, but it incorporates only the characteristics of followers, not those of the situation. The leader should evaluate subordinates and adopt whichever style is needed. If one or more followers are immature, the leader must be very specific, telling them exactly what to do, how to do it, and when. For followers high in maturity, the leader provides a general goal and sufficient authority to do the task as they see fit. Leaders must carefully diagnose the maturity level of followers and then tell, sell, participate, or delegate.

A public example of the wrong leadership style occurred at the Department of Housing and Urban Development (HUD). Samuel Pierce, Jr., the secretary of HUD during the Reagan administration, used a hands-off, delegating style. Yet employees within HUD were not mature, reportedly using their positions to provide favors and contracts to friends and political supporters. The net result has been a charge of mismanagement against the leader of HUD, because the leadership style did not fit the situation.[28]

PATH-GOAL THEORY

Another contingency approach to leadership is called the path-goal theory.[29] According to the **path-goal theory**, the leader's responsibility is to

path-goal theory

A contingency approach to leadership specifying that the leader's responsibility is to increase subordinates' motivation by clarifying the behaviors necessary for task accomplishment and rewards.

Southwest Airlines, the champion of no-frills flying, continues to make healthy profits while other airlines lose money. How? Much of the credit can go to CEO Herb Kelleher's innovative leadership style and his ability to motivate employees by clarifying the path to success, which is consistent with the *path-goal theory*. While keeping costs at rock bottom, Kelleher, a folksy Texan known to employees as "Uncle Herb," encourages creation of a fun-loving atmosphere, both at corporate headquarters and in flight. The company-wide, gung-ho spirit that results appeals to customers, boosts employee morale and productivity, and steers employees along Southwest's successful flightpath.

increase subordinates' motivation to attain personal and organizational goals. As illustrated in Exhibit 14.7, the leader increases their motivation by either (1) clarifying the subordinates' path to the rewards that are available or (2) increasing the rewards that they value and desire. Path clarification means that the leader works with subordinates to help them identify and learn the behaviors that will lead to successful task accomplishment and organizational rewards. Increasing rewards means that the leader talks with subordinates to learn which rewards are important to them—that is, whether they desire intrinsic rewards from the work itself or extrinsic rewards such as raises or promotions. The leader's job is to increase personal payoffs to subordinates for goal attainment and to make the paths to these payoffs clear and easy to travel.[30]

This model is called a contingency theory because it consists of three sets of contingencies—leader behavior and style, situational contingencies, and the use of rewards to meet subordinates' needs.[31]

LEADER BEHAVIOR.   The path-goal theory suggests a fourfold classification of leader behaviors.[32] These classifications are the types of leader behavior the leader can adopt and include supportive, directive, achievement-oriented, and participative styles.

Supportive leadership involves leader behavior that shows concern for subordinates' well-being and personal needs. Leadership behavior is

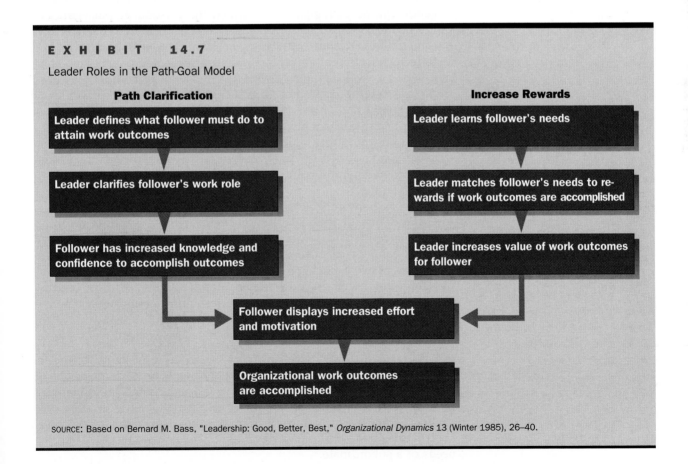

EXHIBIT   14.7

Leader Roles in the Path-Goal Model

Path Clarification

Leader defines what follower must do to attain work outcomes

Leader clarifies follower's work role

Follower has increased knowledge and confidence to accomplish outcomes

Increase Rewards

Leader learns follower's needs

Leader matches follower's needs to rewards if work outcomes are accomplished

Leader increases value of work outcomes for follower

Follower displays increased effort and motivation

Organizational work outcomes are accomplished

SOURCE: Based on Bernard M. Bass, "Leadership: Good, Better, Best," *Organizational Dynamics* 13 (Winter 1985), 26–40.

open, friendly, and approachable, and the leader creates a team climate and treats subordinates as equals. Supportive leadership is similar to the consideration leadership described earlier.

Directive leadership occurs when the leader tells subordinates exactly what they are supposed to do. Leader behavior includes planning, making schedules, setting performance goals and behavior standards, and stressing adherence to rules and regulations. Directive leadership behavior is similar to the initiating structure leadership style described earlier.

Participative leadership means that the leader consults with his or her subordinates about decisions. Leader behavior includes asking for opinions and suggestions, encouraging participation in decision making, and meeting with subordinates in their workplaces. The participative leader encourages group discussion and written suggestions.

Achievement-oriented leadership occurs when the leader sets clear and challenging objectives for subordinates. Leader behavior stresses high-quality performance and improvement over current performance. Achievement-oriented leaders also show confidence in subordinates and assist them in learning how to achieve high goals.

The four types of leader behavior are not considered ingrained personality traits; rather, they reflect types of behavior that every leader is able to adopt, depending on the situation.

SITUATIONAL CONTINGENCIES. The two important situational contingencies in the path-goal theory are (1) the personal characteristics of group members and (2) the work environment. Personal characteristics of subordinates are similar to Hersey and Blanchard's maturity level and include such factors as ability, skills, needs, and motivations. For example, if an employee has a low level of ability or skill, the leader may need to provide additional training or coaching in order for the worker to improve performance. If a subordinate is self-centered, the leader must manipulate rewards to motivate him or her. Subordinates who want clear direction and authority require a directive leader who will tell them exactly what to do. Craftworkers and professionals, however, may want more freedom and autonomy and work best under a participative leadership style.

The work environment contingencies include the degree of task structure, the nature of the formal authority system, and the work group itself. The task structure is similar to the same concept described in Fiedler's contingency theory; it includes the extent to which tasks are defined and have explicit job descriptions and work procedures. The formal authority system includes the amount of legitimate power used by managers and the extent to which policies and rules constrain employees' behavior. Work group characteristics are the educational level of subordinates and the quality of relationships among them.

USE OF REWARDS. Recall that the leader's responsibility is to clarify the path to rewards for subordinates or to increase the amount of rewards to enhance satisfaction and job performance. In some situations, the leader works with subordinates to help them acquire the skills and confidence needed to perform tasks and achieve rewards already available. In others, the leader may develop new rewards to meet the specific needs of a subordinate.

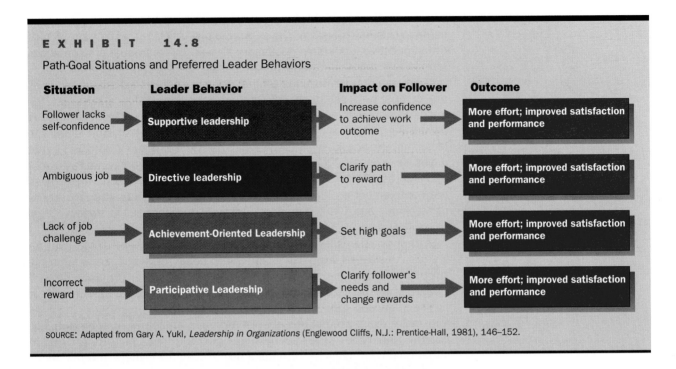

EXHIBIT 14.8

Path-Goal Situations and Preferred Leader Behaviors

Situation	Leader Behavior	Impact on Follower	Outcome
Follower lacks self-confidence	Supportive leadership	Increase confidence to achieve work outcome	More effort; improved satisfaction and performance
Ambiguous job	Directive leadership	Clarify path to reward	More effort; improved satisfaction and performance
Lack of job challenge	Achievement-Oriented Leadership	Set high goals	More effort; improved satisfaction and performance
Incorrect reward	Participative Leadership	Clarify follower's needs and change rewards	More effort; improved satisfaction and performance

SOURCE: Adapted from Gary A. Yukl, *Leadership in Organizations* (Englewood Cliffs, N.J.: Prentice-Hall, 1981), 146–152.

Exhibit 14.8 illustrates four examples of how leadership behavior is tailored to the situation. In situation 1, the subordinate lacks confidence; thus, the supportive leadership style provides the social support with which to encourage the subordinate to undertake the behavior needed to do the work and receive the rewards. In situation 2, the job is ambiguous and the employee is not performing effectively. Directive leadership behavior is used to give instructions and clarify the task so that the follower will know how to accomplish it and receive rewards. In situation 3, the subordinate is unchallenged by the task; thus, an achievement-oriented behavior is used to set higher goals. This clarifies the path to rewards for the employee. In situation 4, an incorrect reward is given to a subordinate and the participative leadership style is used to change this. By discussing the subordinate's needs, the leader is able to identify the correct reward for task accomplishment. In all four cases, the outcome of fitting the leadership behavior to the situation produces greater employee effort by either clarifying how subordinates can receive rewards or changing the rewards to fit their needs.

In some organizations, such as McArthur/Glen Group, leaders display complementary leadership styles to meet subordinates' needs.

 McARTHUR-GLEN GROUP

The leadership of Cheryl McArthur and Alan Glen, cofounders of a company that developed and manages 13 outlet malls, illustrates the strengths that differing leadership styles can bring to an organization.

McArthur's management style stresses interactive characteristics often displayed by women managers. Empowerment is a priority and McArthur willingly shares information and strives to keep the lines of communication open. McArthur's people skills enable her to convey the company vision to each of the 125 employees, clarify tasks, and provide the supportive leadership necessary to help the individual employee perform effectively under deadline pressure.

Glen, by contrast, focuses on the creative end. His experience enables the company to set deadlines and realistic timetables and to get the malls up and running with the minimum of hassle. Glen prefers to focus on the big picture and leave the daily organizational and staff details to McArthur. However, Glen credits his partner with the "ambition" that drives the company forward and makes his vision a reality. Each partner appreciates the strengths of the other, and the two contrasting styles are complementary. Employees, too, appreciate these leadership styles of McArthur and Glen, remarking, "they fit together like a zipper."[33] ∎

Although Glen's leadership style is achievement oriented, McArthur's style is considered supportive leadership behavior, which gives Glen the support to overcome obstacles and achieve higher performance.

Path-goal theorizing can be complex, but much of the research on it has been encouraging.[34] Using the model to specify precise relationships and make exact predictions about employee outcomes may be difficult, but the four types of leader behavior and the ideas for fitting them to situational contingencies provide a useful way for leaders to think about motivating subordinates.

SUBSTITUTES FOR LEADERSHIP

The contingency leadership approaches considered so far have focused on the leaders' style, the subordinates' nature, and the situation's characteristics. The final contingency approach suggests that situational variables can be so powerful that they actually substitute for or neutralize the need for leadership.[35] This approach outlines those organizational settings in which a leadership style is unimportant or unnecessary.

Exhibit 14.9 shows the situational variables that tend to substitute for or neutralize leadership characteristics. A **substitute** for leadership makes the leadership style unnecessary or redundant. For example, highly professional subordinates who know how to do their tasks do not need a leader who initiates structure for them and tells them what to do. A **neutralizer** counteracts the leadership style and prevents the leader from displaying certain behaviors. For example, if a leader has absolutely no position power or is physically removed from subordinates, the leader's ability to give directions to subordinates is greatly reduced.

Situational variables in Exhibit 14.9 include characteristics of the group, the task, and the organization itself. For example, when subordinates are highly professional and experienced, both leadership styles are less important. The employees do not need much direction or consideration. With respect to task characteristics, highly structured tasks substitute for a task-oriented style and a satisfying task substitutes for a people-oriented style. With respect to the organization itself, group cohesiveness substitutes for both leader styles. Formalized rules and procedures substitute for leader task orientation. Physical separation of leader and subordinate neutralizes both leadership styles.

substitute

A situational variable that makes a leadership style redundant or unnecessary.

neutralizer

A situational variable that counteracts a leadership style and prevents the leader from displaying certain behaviors.

EXHIBIT 14.9

Substitutes and Neutralizers for Leadership

Variable		Task-Oriented Leadership	People-Oriented Leadership
Organizational variables:	Group cohesiveness	Substitutes for	Substitutes for
	Formalization	Substitutes for	No effect on
	Inflexibility	Neutralizes	No effect on
	Low positional power	Neutralizes	Neutralizes
	Physical separation	Neutralizes	Neutralizes
Task characteristics:	Highly structured task	Substitutes for	No effect on
	Automatic feedback	Substitutes for	No effect on
	Intrinsic satisfaction	No effect on	Substitutes for
Group characteristics:	Professionalism	Substitutes for	Substitutes for
	Training/Experience	Substitutes for	No effect on
	Low value of rewards	Neutralizes	Neutralizes

The value of the situations described in Exhibit 14.9 is that they help leaders avoid leadership overkill. Leaders should adopt a style with which to complement the organizational situation. For example, the work situation for bank tellers provides a high level of formalization, little flexibility, and a highly structured task. The head teller should not adopt a task-oriented style, because the organization already provides structure and direction. The head teller should concentrate on a people-oriented style. In other organizations, if group cohesiveness or previous training meet employees' social needs, the leader is free to concentrate on task-oriented behaviors. The leader can adopt a style complementary to the organizational situation to ensure that both task needs and people needs of the work group will be met.

● CHARISMATIC LEADERSHIP

In Chapter 1, we defined management to include the management functions of leading, planning, organizing, and controlling. But recent work on leadership has begun to distinguish leadership as something more: a quality that inspires and motivates people beyond their normal levels of performance.

TRANSACTIONAL LEADERS

The traditional management function of leading has been called *transactional leadership*.[36] **Transactional leaders** clarify the role and task requirements of subordinates, initiate structure, provide appropriate rewards, and try to be considerate to and meet the social needs of subordinates. The transactional leader's ability to satisfy subordinates may improve productivity. Transactional leaders excel at management functions. They are hardworking, tolerant, and fair minded. They take pride in keeping things running smoothly and efficiently. Transactional leaders often

■
transactional leader
A leader who clarifies subordinates' role and task requirements, initiates structure, provides rewards, and displays consideration for subordinates.

stress the impersonal aspects of performance, such as plans, schedules, and budgets. They have a sense of commitment to the organization and conform to organizational norms and values.

CHARISMATIC LEADERS

charismatic leader

A leader who has the ability to motivate subordinates to transcend their expected performance.

Charismatic leadership goes beyond transactional leadership techniques. The **charismatic leader** has the capacity to motivate people to do more than normally expected. The impact of charismatic leaders is normally from (1) stating a lofty vision of an imagined future that employees identify with, (2) shaping a corporate value system for which everyone stands, and (3) trusting subordinates and earning their complete trust in return.[37] Charismatic leaders raise subordinates' consciousness about new outcomes and motivate them to transcend their own interests for the sake of the department or organization. Charismatic leaders tend to be less predictable than transactional leaders. They create an atmosphere of change, and they may be obsessed by visionary ideas that excite, stimulate, and drive other people to work hard. Charismatic leaders have an emotional impact on subordinates. They stand for something, have a vision of the future, are able to communicate that vision to subordinates, and motivate them to realize it.[38] The Manager's Shoptalk box provides a short quiz to help you determine whether you have the potential to be a charismatic leader.

Charismatic leaders include Mother Theresa; Martin Luther King, Jr.; and Adolf Hitler. The true charismatic leader often does not fit within a traditional organization and may lead a social movement rather than a formal organization. The Winning Moves box on H. Ross Perot shows how charismatic leadership can provide the foundation for a successful business, or a political movement.

Disney CEO Michael Eisner is considered a *charismatic leader*. Disney's uniqueness stems from having a creative executive in charge rather than a financier or lawyer. He shapes the corporate value system by inducing creativity in others and calls himself the "head cheerleader." Freewheeling and wildly creative brainstorming sessions are typical of what Eisner will do to get creative energy flowing. His vision of creativity extends the corporate culture founded by Walt Disney and fuels Disney's current growth and competitiveness.

ARE YOU A LEADER?

If you were the head of a major department in a corporation, how important would each of the following activities be to you? Answer yes or no to indicate whether you would strive to perform each activity.

1. Help subordinates clarify goals and how to reach them.
2. Give people a sense of mission and overall purpose.
3. Help get jobs out on time.
4. Look for the new product or service opportunities.
5. Use policies and procedures as guides for problem solving.
6. Promote unconventional beliefs and values.
7. Give monetary rewards in exchange for high performance from subordinates.
8. Command respect from everyone in the department.
9. Work alone to accomplish important tasks.
10. Suggest new and unique ways of doing things.
11. Give credit to people who do their jobs well.
12. Inspire loyalty to yourself and to the organization.
13. Establish procedures to help the department operate smoothly.
14. Use ideas to motivate others.
15. Set reasonable limits on new approaches.
16. Demonstrate social nonconformity.

The even-numbered items represent behaviors and activities of charismatic leaders. Charismatic leaders are personally involved in shaping ideas, goals, and direction of change. They use an intuitive approach to develop fresh ideas for old problems and seek new directions for the department or organization. The odd-numbered items are considered more traditional management activities, or what would be called *transactional leadership*. Managers respond to organizational problems in an impersonal way, make rational decisions, and coordinate and facilitate the work of others. If you answered yes to more even-numbered than odd-numbered items, you may be a potential charismatic leader. ■

SOURCE: Based on Bernard M. Bass, *Leadership and Performance beyond Expectations* (New York: Free Press, 1985), and Lawton R. Burns and Selwyn W. Becker, "Leadership and Managership," in *Health Care Management*, ed. S. Shortell and A. Kaluzny (New York: Wiley, 1986).

Charismatic leaders like Perot would applaud the corporate viewpoint expressed in Exhibit 14.10, and agree with critics who charge that today's typical U.S. company has a tendency to be "overmanaged and underled." Managers cope with "organizational complexity"; leaders initiate "productive change."[39] Transformational leaders balance the demands of both. **Transformational leaders** are similar to charismatic leaders but are distinguished by their special ability to bring about innovation and change.[40]

Transformational leaders emerge to take an organization through a major strategic change, such as revitalization. They have the ability to make the necessary changes in the organization's mission, structure, and human resource management. Employees are persuaded to go along. In recent years, a number of firms, such as Compaq Computer, Campbell Soup, and Tenneco, have undergone transformation after appointing a new chief to act in the leadership role. Eckhard Pfeiffer of Compaq, David Johnson of Campbell Soup, and Mike Walsh of Tenneco helped invigorate and revitalize their firms.

■

transformational leader

A leader distinguished by a special ability to bring about innovation and change.

H. Ross Perot is a charismatic leader. The Texas billionaire rallied voters who felt alienated and dissatisfied during the 1992 presidential campaign, creating a powerful political third force and becoming the most successful third-party presidential candidate since 1924. Fired by a desire to "help his country" and demanding government accountability, Perot's campaign reflected his can-do cowboy capitalist reputation.

As with many high-profile personalities, Perot has many loyal supporters and vocal critics. As founder of EDS (Electronic Data Systems), Perot created and nurtured a climate of loyalty and unity. Employees insist "the Boss"

was always a leader rather than a manager. He selected the best people and gave them the necessary tools to reach their potential. He had a clear vision and demanded much. Taking risks and making mistakes were not grounds for punishment but stepping stones to greater achievement. Indeed, for this superpatriot, each of the troops carried equal weight. The flexibility of EDS has been compared to shifting bands of guerrillas, able to adjust quickly to a changing environment and to completely restructure in a few days. Some view Perot's leadership as one command: "Ready, aim, fire, fire, fire, fire, fire, fire!" Others see a brilliant tactician who clearly understands both the terrain and the rapidly changing world order.

Perot's anticipation of changing business needs led to the creation

of EDS and the systems-integrated industry. Likewise, Perot was able to tap into the changing political climate in 1992, and connect with the mounting fears and dissatisfaction of a large portion of American voters. The dialogue he initiated and the questions he raised about government responsibility and government bureaucracy continued into the Clinton administration. That ability to keep an eye on the future and to express the thoughts and beliefs of a large number of people characterizes the charismatic leader. ■

SOURCE: Wendy Zellner, "Ross Perot, Plain as Day," *Business Week*, November 9, 1992, 40; Douglas Harbrecht and Wendy Zellner, "Now, Who Will Harness Perot's Third Force?" *Business Week*, November 16, 1992, 33; and Bo Burlinghamn and Curtis Hartman, "Cowboy Capitalist," *INC.*, January 1989, 54–69.

● FEMALE LEADERSHIP

As women move into higher positions in organizations, changes in management style and corporate culture can be expected. One of the first changes to be perceived is that women bring a different leadership style to organizations, a style that is very effective in today's turbulent corporate environment.

Leadership qualities for white American males have included aggressiveness, initiative, individual assertiveness, and presenting oneself as a take-charge kind of person. Men tend to be competitive, individualistic, and like working in a vertical hierarchy. Many men describe their leadership behavior as transactional, that is, as a series of transactions with subordinates. Employees do things for the manager in exchange for rewards. When engaging in transactional leadership, white males are likely to use legitimate power, reward power, and formal authority.

EXHIBIT 14.10

Leaders versus Managers

Let's Get Rid of Management

People don't want to be managed. They want to be led. Whoever heard of a world manager? World leader, yes. Educational leader. Political leader. Religious leader. Scout leader. Community leader. Labor leader. Business leader. They lead. They don't manage. The carrot always wins over the stick. Ask your horse. You can *lead* your horse to water, but you can't *manage* him to drink. If you want to manage somebody, manage yourself. Do that well and you'll be ready to stop managing. And start leading.

SOURCE: Courtesy of United Technologies Corporation, Hartford, CT 06101.

Although women also possess assertiveness, initiative, and aggressiveness, they tend to stress and engage in leadership behaviors that can be called *interactive*. An **interactive leader** is concerned with consensus building, is open and inclusive, encourages participation by others, and is more caring than the leadership style of many males.[41] Interactive leadership helps subordinates see that their self-interest and the organization's interest are the same—striving to reach organizational goals enables employees to reach personal goals. Female leaders such as Anita Roddick of the Body Shop, or Linda Wachner or Warnaco, are often more willing to empower people, enhance people's self-worth, and to share power and information.

The interactive leadership style is not limited to women. Anyone can develop these qualities, and both men and women engage in this style of leadership if they so choose. Interactive leadership is consistent with the recent trend toward participation and empowerment taking place in our society, and it is especially appropriate in fast-changing organizations. Many male managers are learning to develop an interactive leadership style that includes empathy, attention to nonverbal behavior, cooperation, collaboration, and listening.[42]

interactive leader

A leader who is concerned with consensus building, is open and inclusive, and encourages participation.

SUMMARY AND MANAGEMENT SOLUTION

This chapter covered several important ideas about leadership. The early research on leadership focused on personal traits such as intelligence, energy, and appearance. Later, research attention shifted to leadership behaviors that are appropriate to the organizational situation. Two-dimensional approaches dominated the early work in this area; consideration and initiating structure were suggested as behaviors that lead work groups toward high performance. The Ohio State and Michigan approaches and the managerial grid are in this category. Contingency approaches include Fiedler's theory, Hersey and Blanchard's situational theory, the path-goal model, and the substitutes-for-leadership concept.

Recent leadership concepts include charismatic leadership and interactive leadership. Charismatic leadership is the ability to articulate a vision and motivate employees to make it a reality. Charismatic leaders are especially important during organizational transformation. Interactive leadership is typical of many females; it involves consensus building, empowerment, and information and power sharing. Interactive leadership fits today's turbulent environment and trend toward empowerment. Robert Daniell's style at United Technologies reflects both charismatic and interaction qualities.

When Robert Daniell took over as CEO of United Technologies, the conglomerate had been used to a heavy-handed, autocratic leadership style. Daniell's approach was to promote teamwork and cooperation and to treat employees as family. His vision was to put the "United" back in United Technologies. He started Saturday morning meetings of managers from various divisions to share experiences. He confronted the operating managers with "What are the bureaucratic issues that bother you . . .?" "Let's cut the crap and get it right on the table." Things changed after that. At the Carrier division, for example, air-conditioning fans were too noisy. Five engineers from Hamilton's propeller operations were dispatched to the Carrier division, and a quieter fan was designed within a month. Later, when profits eroded and times got tough, Daniell became more demanding and task oriented. Daniell's change in style agrees with the Fiedler and Hersey and Blanchard theories. His original vision inspired teamwork and commitment. A people-oriented leadership style worked in a moderately favorable situation, and a telling or selling leadership style was best when United Technologies hit a rough spot and had to be turned around.[43]

DISCUSSION QUESTIONS

1. Rob Martin became manager of a forklift assembly plant and believed in participative management, even when one supervisor used Rob's delegation to replace two competent line managers with his own

friends. What would you say to Rob about his leadership style in this situation?

2. Suggest some personal traits that you believe would be useful to a leader. Are these traits more valuable in some situations than in others?

3. What is the difference between trait theories and behavioral theories of leadership?

4. Suggest the sources of power that would be available to a leader of a student government organization. To be effective, should student leaders keep power to themselves or delegate power to other students?

5. Would you prefer working for a leader who has a consideration or an initiating structure leadership style? Discuss the reasons for your answer.

6. What similarities do you see among the following contingency leadership theories: Hersey-Blanchard, Fiedler, and path-goal?

7. What is charismatic leadership? Differentiate between charismatic leadership and transactional leadership. Give an example of each.

8. One critic argued that women should not be stereotyped as having a leadership style different from that of men. Do you agree? Do you think that women, on average, have a more interactive style of leadership than men? Discuss.

9. Do you think leadership style is fixed and unchangeable for a leader or flexible and adaptable? Discuss.

10. Consider the leadership position of a senior partner in a law firm. What task, subordinate, and organizational factors might serve as substitutes for leadership in this situation?

MANAGEMENT IN PRACTICE: EXPERIENTIAL EXERCISE

● **T – P LEADERSHIP QUESTIONNAIRE: AN ASSESSMENT OF STYLE**

Some leaders deal with general directions, leaving details to subordinates. Other leaders focus on specific details with the expectation that subordinates will carry out orders. Depending on the situation, both approaches may be effective. The important issue is the ability to identify relevant dimensions of the situation and behave accordingly. Through this questionnaire, you can identify your relative emphasis on two dimensions of leadership: task orientation and people orientation. These are not opposite approaches, and an individual can rate high or low on either or both.

Directions: The following items describe aspects of leadership behavior. Respond to each item according to the way you would most likely act if you were the leader of a work group. Circle whether you would most likely behave in the

described way: always (A), frequently (F), occasionally (O), seldom (S), or never (N).

A F O S N   1. I would most likely act as the spokesperson of the group.

A F O S N   2. I would encourage overtime work.

A F O S N   3. I would allow members complete freedom in their work.

A F O S N   4. I would encourage the use of uniform procedures.

A F O S N   5. I would permit members to use their own judgment in solving problems.

A F O S N   6. I would stress being ahead of competing groups.

A F O S N   7. I would speak as a representative of the group.

A F O S N ( ) 8. I would needle members for greater effort.

A F O S N | 9. I would try out my ideas in the group.

A F O S N ( ) 10. I would let members do their work the way they think best.

A F O S N | 11. I would be working hard for a promotion.

A F O S N | 12. I would tolerate postponement and uncertainty.

A F O S N 13. I would speak for the group if there were visitors present.

A F O S N | 14. I would keep the work moving at a rapid pace.

A F O S N ( ) 15. I would turn the members loose on a job and let them go to it.

A F O S N 16. I would settle conflicts when they occur in the group.

A F O S N | 17. I would get swamped by details.

A F O S N ( ) 18. I would represent the group at outside meetings.

A F O S N 19. I would be reluctant to allow the members any freedom of action.

A F O S N 20. I would decide what should be done and how it should be done.

A F O S N | 21. I would push for increased production.

A F O S N 22. I would let some members have authority which I could keep.

A F O S N | 23. Things would usually turn out as I had predicted.

A F O S N ( ) 24. I would allow the group a high degree of initiative.

A F O S N | 25. I would assign group members to particular tasks.

A F O S N ( ) 26. I would be willing to make changes.

A F O S N | 27. I would ask the members to work harder.

A F O S N ( ) 28. I would trust the group members to exercise good judgment.

A F O S N 29. I would schedule the work to be done.

A F O S N ( ) 30. I would refuse to explain my actions.

A F O S N | 31. I would persuade others that my ideas are to their advantage.

A F O S N ( ) 32. I would permit the group to set its own pace.

A F O S N | 33. I would urge the group to beat its previous record.

A F O S N ( ) 34. I would act without consulting the group.

A F O S N ( ) 35. I would ask that group members follow standard rules and regulations.

T 14 P 12

SOURCE: The T–P Leadership Questionnaire was adapted by J. B. Ritchie and P. Thompson in *Organization and People* (New York: West, 1984). Copyright 1969 by the American Educational Research Association. Adapted by permission of the publisher.

The T–P Leadership Questionnaire is scored as follows:

a. Circle the item number for items 8, 12, 17, 18, 19, 30, 34, and 35.

b. Write the number 1 in front of a *circled item number* if you responded S (seldom) or N (never) to that item.

c. Also write a number 1 in front of *item numbers not circled* if you responded A (always) or F (frequently).

d. Circle the number 1s that you have written in front of the following items: 3, 5, 8, 10, 15, 18, 19, 22, 24, 26, 28, 30, 32, 34, and 35.

e. *Count the circled number 1s.* This is your score for concern for people. Record the score in the blank following the letter P at the end of the questionnaire.

f. *Count uncircled number 1s.* This is your score for concern for task. Record this number in the blank following the letter T.

CASES FOR ANALYSIS

SOUTHWEST AIRLINES

The zaniness of Herbert D. Kelleher, chairman and CEO of Southwest Airlines Company, permeates the airline. He loves people and wants employees' work to be fun filled. On a flight to Austin, Texas, flight attendants once dressed as reindeer and elves, and the pilot sang Christmas carols over the loudspeaker while gently rocking the plane. New employees watch a rap-music video that describes departmental functions. Kelleher has been described as "crazy," and "a real maniac." But these people underestimate his impact on Southwest. Kelleher's vision is to use fun to create the most efficient airline, and Southwest's operating costs per passenger-mile are the industry's lowest. His vision also includes aggressive expansion, opening new routes in California and the Midwest that will put him up against big carriers such as American Airlines and USAir. He plans to double the number of airplanes over the next ten years, expanding services while keeping costs low.

Kelleher's unique style did not emerge until he took over the CEO's job in 1981. He had set up a law firm in San Antonio and then founded Southwest with a group of investors, owning only a small stake himself. Kelleher is the airline's most visible property, and many of his 7,000 plus employees call him "Uncle Herb" or "Herbie." He publicly claims to "love" his employees, and his approach is working. During the early 1990s, as many other carriers suffered losses or fell into bankruptcy, Southwest posted hefty profits.

Under Kelleher, Southwest is paying attention to the customer. The company has an executive vice-president serving as an advocate for the public. It also places frequent flyers in special focus groups that solicit new ideas and gauge responses from customers. Letters to the airline are answered promptly—often by Kelleher himself. Some-

times his sense of humor intrudes, as when one passenger nit-picked that the lavatory's toilet paper was inserted the wrong way. Kelleher fired off an answer: "What the hell were you doing upside-down in our lavatory?"

Kelleher admits to having made a few mistakes, but his expanding route structure reflects controlled growth rather than reckless pursuit of a dream. So far, Kelleher's style has been good medicine for Southwest Airlines.

● QUESTIONS

1. How would you characterize Kelleher's leadership style using the models from this chapter? Include at least three models or concepts in your discussion.
2. What sources of power does Kelleher seem to rely on, and is the reaction of followers what you would predict? Explain.
3. If Kelleher were replaced tomorrow, what leadership style would you recommend for his successor?

SOURCE: Based on Richard S. Teitelbaum, "Southwest Airlines: Where Service Flies Right," *Fortune*, August 24, 1992, 115–116, and Kevin Kelly, "Southwest Airlines: Flying High with 'Uncle Herb,' " *Business Week*, July 3, 1989, 53–55.

TECHNICAL SERVICES DIVISION

When DGL International, a manufacturer of refinery equipment, brought in John Terrill to manage its Technical Services division, company executives informed him of the urgent situation. Technical Services, with 20 engineers, was the highest-paid, best-educated, and least-productive division in the company. Terrill's instructions: Turn it around. Terrill called a meeting of the engineers. He showed great concern for their personal welfare and asked point blank: "What's the problem? Why can't we produce? Why does this division have such turnover?"

Without hesitation, employees launched a hail of complaints. "I was hired as an engineer, not a pencil pusher." "We spend over half our time writing asinine reports in triplicate for top management, and no one reads the reports."

After a two-hour discussion, Terrill concluded he had to get top management off the engineers' backs. He promised the engineers, "My job is to stay out of your way so you can do your work, and I'll try to keep top management off your backs too." He called for the day's reports and issued an order effective immediately that the originals be turned in daily to his office rather than mailed to headquarters. For three weeks, technical reports piled up on his desk. By month's end, the stack was nearly 3 feet high. During that time no one called for the reports. When other managers entered his office and saw the stack, they usually asked,

"What's all this?" Terrill answered, "Technical reports." No one asked to read them.

Finally, at month's end, a secretary from finance called and asked for the monthly travel and expense report. Terrill responded, "Meet me in the president's office tomorrow morning."

The next morning the engineers cheered as Terrill walked through the department pushing a cart loaded with the enormous stack of reports. They knew the showdown had come.

Terrill entered the president's office and placed the stack of reports on his desk. The president and the other senior executives looked bewildered.

"This," Terrill announced, "is the reason for the lack of productivity in the Technical Services division. These are the reports you people require every month. The fact that they sat on my desk all month shows that no one reads this material. I suggest that the engineers' time could be used in a more productive manner, and that one brief monthly report from my office will satisfy the needs of other departments."

● QUESTIONS

1. What leadership style did John Terrill use? What do you think was his primary source of power?

2. Based on the Hersey-Blanchard theory, should Terrill have been less participative? Should he have initiated more task structure for the engineers? Explain.

3. What leadership approach would you have taken in this situation?

REFERENCES

1. Russell Mitchell, "After Harry Gray: Reshaping United Technologies," *Business Week,* January 18, 1988, 46–48.

2. Catherine Arnst and Stephanie Anderson Forest, "Compaq: How It Made Its Impressive Move out of the Doldrums," *Business Week,* November 2, 1992, 146–151; "The Newsmakers," *Business Week,* April 18, 1986, 194; and David C. Limerick, "Managers of Meaning: From Bob Geldof's Band Aid to Australian CEOs," *Organizational Dynamics,* Spring 1990, 22–23.

3. Gary Yukl, "Managerial Leadership: A Review of Theory and Research," *Journal of Management* 15 (1989), 251–289.

4. James M. Kouzes and Barry Z. Posner, "The Credibility Factor: What Followers Expect from Their Leaders," *Management Review,* January 1990, 29–33.

5. Henry Mintzberg, *Power in and around Organizations* (Englewood Cliffs, N.J.: Prentice-Hall, 1983), and Jeffrey Pfeffer, *Power in Organizations* (Marshfield, Mass.: Pitman, 1981).

6. J. R. P. French, Jr., and B. Raven, "The Bases of Social Power," in *Group Dynamics,* ed. D. Cartwright and A. F. Zander (Evanston, Ill.: Row, Peterson, 1960), 607–623.

7. G. A. Yukl and T. Taber, "The Effective Use of Managerial Power," *Personnel* (March–April 1983), 37–44.

8. Ralph Stayer, "How I Learned to Let My Workers Lead," *Harvard Business Review* (November–December 1990), 66–83; Thomas A. Stewart, "New Ways to Exercise Power," *Fortune,* November 6, 1989, 52–64; and Thomas A. Stewart, "CEOs See Clout Shifting," *Fortune,* November 6, 1989, 66.

9. G. A. Yukl, *Leadership in Organizations* (Englewood Cliffs, N.J.: Prentice-Hall, 1981), and S. C. Kohs and K. W. Irle, "Prophesying Army Promotion," *Journal of Applied Psychology* 4 (1920), 73–87.

10. R. Albanese and D. D. Van Fleet, *Organizational Behavior: A Managerial Viewpoint* (Hinsdale, Ill.: Dryden Press, 1983).

11. K. Lewin, "Field Theory and Experiment in Social Psychology: Concepts and Methods," *American Journal of Sociology* 44 (1939), 868–896; K. Lewin and R. Lippitt, "An Experimental Approach to the Study of Autocracy and Democracy: A Preliminary Note," *Sociometry* 1 (1938), 292–300; K. Lewin, R. Lippitt, and R. K. White, "Patterns of Aggressive Behavior in Experimentally Created Social Climates," *Journal of Social Psychology* 10 (1939), 271–301.

12. R. K. White and R. Lippitt, *Autocracy and Democracy: An Experimental Inquiry* (New York: Harper, 1960).

13. R. Tannenbaum and W. H. Schmidt, "How to Choose a Leadership Pattern," *Harvard Business Review* 36 (1958), 95–101.

14. F. A. Heller and G. A. Yukl, "Participation, Managerial Decision-Making and Situational Variables," *Organizational Behavior and Human Performance* 4 (1969), 227–241.

15. Patricia O'Toole, "How Do You Build a $44 Million Company? By Saying 'Please,'" *Working Woman*, April 1990, 88–92.

16. C. A. Schriesheim and B. J. Bird, "Contributions of the Ohio State Studies to the Field of Leadership," *Journal of Management* 5 (1979), 135–145, and C. L. Shartle, "Early Years of the Ohio State University Leadership Studies," *Journal of Management* 5 (1979), 126–134.

17. P. C. Nystrom, "Managers and the High-High Leader Myth," *Academy of Management Journal* 21 (1978), 325–331, and L. L. Larson, J. G. Hunt, and R. N. Osborn, "The Great High-High Leader Behavior Myth: A Lesson from Occam's Razor," *Academy of Management Journal* 19 (1976), 628–641.

18. R. Likert, "From Production- and Employee-Centeredness to Systems 1–4," *Journal of Management* 5 (1979), 147–156.

19. Robert R. Blake and Jane S. Mouton, *The Managerial Grid III* (Houston: Gulf, 1985).

20. Jasper Dorsey, "S. Truett Cathy," *SKY*, February 1985, 45–50.

21. Michael Schroeder, "This 'Barracuda' Is Still on the Attack," *Business Week*, January 20, 1992, 96–97.

22. F. E. Fiedler, "Assumed Similarity Measures as Predictors of Team Effectiveness," *Journal of Abnormal and Social Psychology* 49 (1954), 381–388; F. E. Fiedler, *Leader Attitudes and Group Effectiveness* (Urbana, Ill.: University of Illinois Press, 1958), and F. E. Fiedler, *A Theory of Leadership Effectiveness* (New York: McGraw-Hill, 1967).

23. F. E. Fiedler and M. M. Chemers, *Leadership and Effective Management* (Glenview, Ill.: Scott, Foresman, 1974).

24. F. E. Fiedler, "Engineer the Job to Fit the Manager," *Harvard Business Review* 43 (1965), 115–122, and F. E. Fiedler, M. M. Chemers, and L. Mahar, *Improving Leadership Effectiveness: The Leader Match Concept* (New York: Wiley, 1976).

25. Steve Lohr, "730,000 Employees and a Challenge," *The New York Times*, November 15, 1992, F8; Mark Lewyn, "Exodus at the Post Office," *Business Week*, October 12, 1992, 33, and "Thrifty Runyon Post Master Today," *The Tennessean*, July 6, 1992, E1.

26. R. Singh, "Leadership Style and Reward Allocation: Does Least Preferred Coworker Scale Measure Tasks and Relation Orientation?" *Organizational Behavior and Human Performance* 27 (1983), 178–197; and D. Hosking, "A Critical Evaluation of Fiedler's Contingency Hypotheses," *Progress in Applied Psychology* 1 (1981), 103–154.

27. Paul Hersey and Kenneth H. Blanchard, *Management of Organizational Behavior: Utilizing Human Resources*, 4th ed. (Englewood Cliffs, N.J.: Prentice-Hall, 1982).

28. E. J. Dionne, Jr., "Pierce at H.U.D.: Eight Years of Hands-Off Management," *The New York Times*, June 18, 1989, 1.

29. M. G. Evans, "The Effects of Supervisory Behavior on the Path-Goal Relationship," *Organizational Behavior and Human Performance* 5 (1970), 277–298; M. G. Evans, "Leadership and Motivation: A Core Concept," *Academy of Management Journal* 13 (1970), 91–102, and B. S. Georgopoulos, G. M. Mahoney, and N. W. Jones, "A Path-Goal Approach to Productivity," *Journal of Applied Psychology* 41 (1957), 345–353.

30. Robert J. House, "A Path-Goal Theory of Leader Effectiveness," *Administrative Science Quarterly* 16 (1971), 321–338.

31. M. G. Evans, "Leadership," in *Organizational Behavior,* ed. S. Kerr (Columbus, Ohio: Grid, 1974), 230–233.

32. Robert J. House and Terrence R. Mitchell, "Path-Goal Theory of Leadership," *Journal of Contemporary Business* (Autumn 1974), 81–97.

33. Sharon Nelton, "Men, Women, & Leadership," *Nation's Business,* May 1991, 16–22.

34. Charles Greene, "Questions of Causation in the Path-Goal Theory of Leadership," *Academy of Management Journal* 22 (March 1979), 22–41, and C. A. Schriesheim and M. A. von Glinow, "The Path-Goal Theory of Leadership: A Theoretical and Empirical Analysis," *Academy of Management Journal* 20 (1977), 398–405.

35. S. Kerr and J. M. Jermier, "Substitutes for Leadership: Their Meaning and Measurement," *Organizational Behavior and Human Performance* 22 (1978), 375–403, and Jon P. Howell and Peter W. Dorfman, "Leadership and Substitutes for Leadership among Professional and Nonprofessional Workers," *Journal of Applied Behavioral Science* 22 (1986), 29–46.

36. The terms *transactional* and *transformational* come from James M. Burns, *Leadership* (New York: Harper & Row, 1978), and Bernard M. Bass, "Leadership: Good, Better, Best," *Organizational Dynamics* 13 (Winter 1985), 26–40.

37. Jay A. Conger and Rabindra N. Kanungo, "Toward a Behavioral Theory of Charismatic Leadership in Organizational Settings," *Academy of Management Review* 12 (1987), 637–647; Walter Kiechel III, "A Hard Look at Executive Vision," *Fortune,* October 23, 1989, 207–211; and Allan Cox, "Focus on Teamwork, Vision, and Values," *The New York Times,* February 26, 1989, F3.

38. Robert J. House, "Research Contrasting the Behavior and Effects of Reputed Charismatic vs. Reputed Non-Charismatic Leaders" (Paper presented as part of a symposium, "Charismatic Leadership: Theory and Evidence," Academy of Management, San Diego, 1985).

39. John P. Kotter, "What Leaders Really Do," *Harvard Business Review* (May–June 1990), 103–111.

40. Noel M. Tichy and David O. Ulrich, "The Leadership Challenge—A Call for the Transformational Leader," *Sloan Management Review* 26 (Fall 1984), 59–68.

41. Judy Rosener, "Ways Women Lead," *Harvard Business Review* (November–December 1990), 119–125, and Nelton, "Men, Women, & Leadership."

42. M. Fine, F. Johnson, and M. S. Ryan, "Cultural Diversity in the Workforce," *Public Personnel Management* 19 (1990), 305–319.

43. Mitchell, "After Harry Gray: Reshaping United Technologies," and Todd Vogel, "United Technologies Goes in for a Little Engine Work," *Business Week,* October 21, 1991, 108–110.

LEE IACCOCA

An anxious young man did his best to coax the beat-up 60 horsepower '38 Ford up a hilly Allentown avenue before the cluster gear went and he and his friends were rolling back the way they came. "Those guys [at Ford] need me. Anybody who builds a car this bad can use some help."

Maybe it was preordained. Ford did need the help. And the young man, Lido Anthony Iacocca, had always wanted to work in the auto industry. Lee Iacocca's rise at Ford was nothing short of meteoric. Beginning there as a student engineer, he spent nine months realizing he was better suited to sell cars than build them. "I've been selling cars ever since," he says.

The young sales trainee shot through the ranks and became one of Ford's youngest executives ever when he was named vice-president and general manager of the Ford Division in 1960. In 1964, he led the team that launched the super-successful Mustang on a meager $75 million budget. He was named president of the automaker on December 10, 1970. Just short of eight years later he was fired, and in a sense, that was where the story really began.

"It was gut-wrenching," he said. "There are times in everyone's life when something constructive is born out of adversity. That's what happened to me. Instead of getting mad, I got even. I went to work at Chrysler, which at the time was going bankrupt. But with help from a lot of good people, we brought Chrysler back."

Few executives would have attempted or even thought about trying to sell the U.S. government on the notion that guaranteeing Chrysler's loans would save taxpayers money. Iacocca did, to the tune of $1.5 billion. Not many would have had the brass to face the rank-and-file with the hard nostrum of across the board pay cuts. He did that too. And he went public and so successfully personalized the message about his car company that the names Chrysler and Iacocca became almost interchangeable. Here was an unabashed car salesman and plain-spoken advocate of all things American that for once everyone could trust.

Printable descriptions of Iacocca include brutally honest, authoritative, inspirational, caustic, charismatic, arrogant, and extremely shy. Many who worked with him over the years have also called him a genius. Flabbergasted was the appropriate adjective for Washington bureaucrats on July 13, 1983, when Chrysler repaid the government loan—seven years early. Five years after being sacked at Ford, Iacocca had resurrected a shattered car company and returned a $350 million profit to the U.S. Treasury.

It was far from smooth sailing at Chrysler after Iacocca paid off the government loans and became a household name. As profitability returned he diversified into financial operations and purchased American Motors Corporation, and with it Jeep, as well as Gulfstream Aerospace Corpora-tion. By his own admission diversification didn't work, and in the late 1980s Chrysler was again in the red. Iacocca launched a major cost-cutting campaign in 1989, severing 11,000 salaried workers and saving $4 billion, while getting a 5-year $6.5 billion new vehicle program under way. Chrysler stock more than tripled and earnings for 1992 exceeded $310 billion.

Despite the setbacks, the 1980s were the decade during which Iacocca erased Chrysler's image as a producer of lusterless, outsized dinosaurs. The minivan was introduced in 1984 and has rolled on successfully ever since, with the company claiming a technological lead on competitors who scrambled to emulate it. Sales were better than 500,000 in 1992, and an all new minivan that Iacocca described as "revolutionary" is slated to debut in 1995. The Jeep Grand Cherokee, the first designed and engineered by Chrysler, was launched in 1991 and has carved out an enviable niche in the sport utility market with sales of almost 100,000. The new mid-sized LH cars—Dodge Intrepid, Chrysler Concorde, and Eagle Vision—represent a departure from what was produced in the past. Another departure is the introduction of the first line of full-size pickups Chrysler has produced in 20 years. The T-300 series features an optional V-10 engine and styling similar to an 18-wheeler. Iacocca has described it as a "junior Peterbuilt." Chrysler's U.S. truck market share rose above 22 percent in 1992, nearly 3 percentage points ahead of the previous year.

After 46 years in the automobile industry, Lee Iacocca retired on December 31, 1992. He selected former General Motors of Europe AG President Robert J. Eaton as his successor. Iacocca's ongoing role at Chrysler, as he puts it, will be as "counselor and consultant," but quickly added that he didn't think he would be needed in any way.

Whatever the outcome, it will likely be some time before another chief executive becomes as synonymous with his company as the name Lee Iacocca is with Chrysler.

● **Q U E S T I O N S**

1. Identify some of the personal characteristics that make Iacocca an effective leader. Name characteristics that detract.

2. Would you say Iacocca is more of a leader or a manager? Why? How do you think the inspirational leadership of Iacocca might have influenced Chrysler?

3. Which of the four classifications under the path-goal theory best represent Iacocca's leadership style? Discuss.

4. How has Chrysler fared since Iacocca's retirement? Have there been any radical departures from his style of leadership?

MOTIVATION IN ORGANIZATIONS

15 CHAPTER

At 30, Gary Aronson was frustrated, bored, and wondering why he was in the gourmet fast-food business. As manager of an Au Bon Pain store, he made a meager $26,000 a year and was known as a whiner and complainer. His heart was not in what he considered a dead-end job, and many of his employees seemed to feel  the same. The best he could hope for after five more years was another $3,000 in annual income, so he put in his time trying to figure out what he was going to do next. Unfortunately, Gary Aronson was typical of managers in all 40 Au Bon Pain stores.[1] ■ If you were the president of Au Bon Pain, how would you motivate managers like Gary Aronson to give their all to the company? Is high motivation even possible in this kind of service business?

The problem for Au Bon Pain is that unmotivated managers mean unmotivated employees, all doing minimum work and causing the chain to lose its competitive edge. One secret of success for small- and medium-size businesses is motivated and enthusiastic employees. The challenge facing Au Bon Pain and other companies is to keep employee motivation consistent with organizational objectives. Motivation is a challenge for managers because motivation arises from within employees and typically differs for each employee. For example, Janice Rennie makes a staggering $350,000 a year selling residential real estate in Toronto; she attributes her success to the fact that she likes to listen carefully to clients and then find a house to meet their needs. Greg Storey is a skilled machinist who is challenged by writing programs for numerically controlled machines. After dropping out of college, he swept floors in a machine shop and was motivated to learn to run the machines. Frances Blais sells *World Book Encyclopedia*. She is a top salesperson, but she does not care about the $50,000-plus commissions: "I'm not even thinking money when I'm selling. I'm really on a crusade to help children read well." In stark contrast, Rob Michaels gets sick to his stomach before he goes to work. Rob is a telephone salesperson who spends all day trying to get people to buy products they do not need, and the rejections are painful. His motivation is money; he earned $120,000 in the past year and cannot make nearly that much doing anything else.[2]

Rob is motivated by money, Janice by her love of listening and problem solving, Frances by the desire to help children read, and Greg by the challenge of mastering numerically controlled machinery. Each person is motivated to perform, yet each has different reasons for performing. With such diverse motivations, it is a challenge for managers to motivate employees toward common organizational goals.

This chapter reviews theories and models of employee motivation. First we will review traditional approaches to motivation. Then we will cover models that describe the employee needs and processes associated with motivation. Finally, we will discuss the designing of jobs to increase employee motivation.

● THE CONCEPT OF MOTIVATION

Most of us get up in the morning, go to school or work, and behave in ways that are predictably our own. We respond to our environment and the people in it with little thought as to why we work hard, enjoy certain classes, or find some recreational activities so much fun. Yet all of these behaviors are motivated by something. **Motivation** generally is defined as the arousal, direction, and persistence of behavior.[3] The study of motivation concerns what prompts people to initiate action, what influences their choice of action, and why they persist in that action over time.

A simple model of human motivation is illustrated in Exhibit 15.1. People have basic *needs*, such as for food, achievement, or monetary gain, that translate into an internal tension that motivates specific behaviors with which to fulfill the need. To the extent that the behavior is suc-

motivation

The arousal, direction, and persistence of behavior.

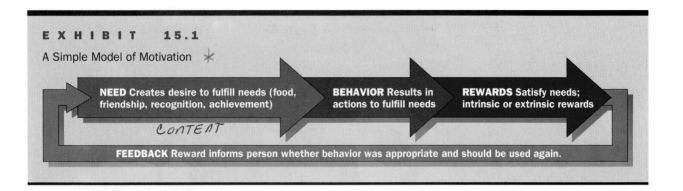

EXHIBIT   15.1

A Simple Model of Motivation ✶

NEED Creates desire to fulfill needs (food, friendship, recognition, achievement)

CONTENT

BEHAVIOR Results in actions to fulfill needs

REWARDS Satisfy needs; intrinsic or extrinsic rewards

FEEDBACK Reward informs person whether behavior was appropriate and should be used again.

cessful, the person is rewarded in the sense that the need is satisfied. The reward also informs the person that the behavior was appropriate and can be used again in the future.

Rewards are of two types: intrinsic and extrinsic. **Intrinsic rewards** ✶ are received as a direct consequence of a person's actions. The completion of a complex task may bestow a pleasant feeling of accomplishment. **Extrinsic rewards** are given by another person, typically a manager, and ✶ include promotions and pay increases. For example, Frances Blais sells encyclopedias for the intrinsic reward of helping children read well. Rob Michaels, who hates his sales job, nevertheless is motivated by the extrinsic reward of high pay.

The importance of motivation as illustrated in Exhibit 15.1 is that it can lead to behaviors that reflect high performance within organizations.[4] Managers can use motivation theory to help satisfy employees' needs and simultaneously encourage high work performance.

intrinsic reward

A reward received as a direct consequence of a person's actions.

extrinsic reward

A reward given by another person.

⬤ FOUNDATIONS OF MOTIVATION

A manager's assumptions about employee motivation and use of rewards depend on his or her perspective on motivation. Three distinct perspectives on employee motivation that have evolved are the traditional approach, the human relations approach, and the human resources approach.[5] The most recent theories about motivation represent a fourth perspective called *contemporary approaches*.

TRADITIONAL APPROACH

The study of employee motivation really began with the work of Frederick W. Taylor on scientific management. Recall from Chapter 2 that scientific management pertains to the systematic analysis of an employee's job for the purpose of increasing efficiency. Economic rewards are pro- ✶ vided to employees for high performance. The emphasis on pay evolved into the perception of workers as *economic people*—people who would work harder for higher pay. This approach led to the development of incentive pay systems, in which people were paid strictly on the quantity and quality of their work outputs.

The "Lend a Helping Hand" contest sponsored by GMAC Albany's Quality Council provided these employees with both *intrinsic and extrinsic rewards*. The winners were judged for helpfulness to other employees during the five-week contest. These smiles reflect not only the extrinsic reward of gift certificates, but the intrinsic reward that comes with the good feeling of helping others.

HUMAN RELATIONS APPROACH

The economic man was gradually replaced by a more sociable employee in managers' minds. Beginning with the landmark Hawthorne studies at a Western Electric plant, noneconomic rewards, such as congenial work groups who met social needs, seemed more important than money as a motivator of work behavior.[6] For the first time, workers were studied as people, and the concept of *social man* was born. Further study led researchers to conclude that simply paying attention to workers could change their behavior for the better, this was called the *Hawthorne effect*.

HUMAN RESOURCE APPROACH

The human resource approach carries the concepts of economic man and social man further to introduce the concept of the *whole person*. Human resource theory suggests that employees are complex and motivated by many factors. For example, the work by McGregor on Theory X and Theory Y described in Chapter 2 argued that people want to do a good job and that work is as natural and healthy as play. Proponents of the human resource approach believed that earlier approaches had tried to manipulate employees through economic or social rewards. By assuming that employees are competent and able to make major contributions, managers can enhance organizational performance. The human resource approach laid the groundwork for contemporary perspectives on employee motivation.

CONTEMPORARY APPROACHES

Contemporary approaches to employee motivation are dominated by three types of theories, each of which will be discussed in the remaining sections of this chapter. The first are *content theories,* which stress the analysis of underlying human needs. Content theories provide insight (2) into the needs of people in organizations and help managers understand how needs can be satisfied in the workplace. *Process theories* concern the (3) thought processes that influence behavior. They focus on how employees seek rewards in work circumstances. *Reinforcement theories* focus on (4) employee learning of desired work behaviors. In Exhibit 15.1, content theories focus on the concepts in the first box, process theories on those in the second, and reinforcement theories on those in the third.

● CONTENT PERSPECTIVES ON MOTIVATION

Content theories emphasize the needs that motivate people. At any point in time, people have basic needs such as those for food, achievement, or monetary reward. These needs translate into an internal drive that motivates specific behaviors in an attempt to fulfill the needs. An individual's needs are like a hidden catalog of the things he or she wants and will work to get. To the extent that managers understand worker needs, the organization's reward systems can be designed to meet them and reinforce employees for directing energies and priorities toward attainment of organizational goals.

content theories

A group of theories that emphasize the needs that motivate people.

HIERARCHY OF NEEDS THEORY

Probably the most famous content theory was developed by Abraham Maslow.[7] Maslow's **hierarchy of needs theory** proposes that humans are motivated by multiple needs and that these needs exist in a hierarchical order as illustrated in Exhibit 15.2. Maslow identified five general types of motivating needs in order of ascendance:

hierarchy of needs theory

A content theory that proposes that people are motivated by five categories of needs—physiological, safety, belongingness, esteem, and self-actualization—that exist in a hierarchical order.

1 *Physiological needs*. These are the most basic human physical needs, including food, water, and sex. In the organizational setting, these are reflected in the needs for adequate heat, air, and base salary to ensure survival.

2 *Safety needs*. These are the needs for a safe and secure physical and emotional environment and freedom from threats, that is, for freedom from violence and for an orderly society. In an organizational workplace, safety needs reflect the needs for safe jobs, fringe benefits, and job security.

3 *Belongingness needs*. These needs reflect the desire to be accepted by one's peers, have friendships, be part of a group, and be loved. In the organization, these needs influence the desire for good relationships with coworkers, participation in a work group, and a positive relationship with supervisors.

4 *Esteem needs*. These needs relate to the desire for a positive self-image and to receive attention, recognition, and appreciation from others. Within organizations, esteem needs reflect a motivation for recognition, an increase in responsibility, high status, and credit for contributions to the organization.

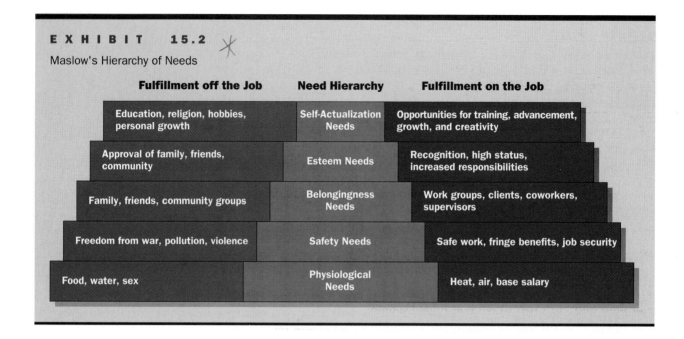

EXHIBIT 15.2

Maslow's Hierarchy of Needs

Fulfillment off the Job	Need Hierarchy	Fulfillment on the Job
Education, religion, hobbies, personal growth	Self-Actualization Needs	Opportunities for training, advancement, growth, and creativity
Approval of family, friends, community	Esteem Needs	Recognition, high status, increased responsibilities
Family, friends, community groups	Belongingness Needs	Work groups, clients, coworkers, supervisors
Freedom from war, pollution, violence	Safety Needs	Safe work, fringe benefits, job security
Food, water, sex	Physiological Needs	Heat, air, base salary

5 *Self-actualization needs.* These represent the need for self-fulfillment, which is the highest need category. They concern developing one's full potential, increasing one's competence, and becoming a better person. Self-actualization needs can be met in the organization by providing people with opportunities to grow, be creative, and acquire training for challenging assignments and advancement.

According to Maslow's theory, lower-order needs take priority—they must be satisfied before higher-order needs are activated. The needs are satisfied in sequence: Physiological needs come before safety needs, safety needs before social needs, and so on. A person desiring physical safety will devote his or her efforts to securing a safer environment and will not be concerned with esteem needs or self-actualization needs. Once a need is satisfied, it declines in importance and the next higher need is activated. When a union wins good pay and working conditions for its members, basic needs are met; union members may then desire to have belongingness and esteem needs met in the workplace.

ERG THEORY. Clayton Alderfer proposed a modification of Maslow's theory in an effort to simplify it and respond to criticisms of its lack of empirical verification.[8] His **ERG theory** identified three categories of needs:

1 *Existence needs.* These are the needs for physical well-being.

2 *Relatedness needs.* These pertain to the need for satisfactory relationships with others.

3 *Growth needs.* These focus on the development of human potential and the desire for personal growth and increased competence.

ERG theory

A modification of the needs hierarchy theory that proposes three categories of needs: existence, relatedness, and growth.

The ERG model and Maslow's need hierarchy are similar because both are in hierarchical form and presume that individuals move up the hierarchy one step at a time. However, Alderfer reduced the number of need categories to three and proposed that movement up the hierarchy is more complex, reflecting a **frustration-regression principle,** namely, that failure to meet a higher-order need may trigger a regression to an already fulfilled lower-order need. Thus, a worker who cannot fulfill a need for personal growth may revert to a lower-order social need and redirect his or her efforts toward making a lot of money. The ERG model therefore is less rigid than Maslow's need hierarchy, suggesting that individuals may move down as well as up the hierarchy, depending on their ability to satisfy needs.

Need hierarchy theory helps explain why organizations find ways to recognize employees and encourage their participation in decision making. Employees at Federal Express receive "Bravo Zulu" awards for outstanding performance, and the recognition letter is more important to recipients than the money. The importance of filling higher-level belongingness and esteem needs on the job was illustrated by a young manager who said, "If I had to tell you in one sentence why I am motivated by my job, it is because when I know what is going on and how I fit into the overall picture, it makes me feel important." Many companies are finding that "fun" is also a great, high-level motivator. A regular infusion of silliness, such as the antics of the "Joy Gang" at Ben and Jerry's Ice Cream who initiate fun activities, lightens up the daily routine and creates a feeling of belonging.[9]

TWO-FACTOR THEORY

Frederick Herzberg developed another popular theory of motivation called the *two-factor theory*.[10] Herzberg interviewed hundreds of workers

> **frustration-regression principle**
> The idea that failure to meet a higher-order need may cause a regression to an already satisfied lower-order need.

In an effort to meet the needs of its work force, Tyson Foods, Inc., works to satisfy employee needs in all three categories of the *ERG Theory*. These team members are part of Tyson's regular ergonomic exercise program that strengthens muscles and satisfies *existence needs* for physical well-being. Roundtable suggestion programs and luncheons between management and employees encourage participation to fulfill *relatedness needs*. Educational programs and the Tyson Improvement Program give team members opportunities to grow, improve skills, and reach their potential, satisfying individual *growth needs*.

about times when they were highly motivated to work and other times when they were dissatisfied and unmotivated at work. His findings suggested that the work characteristics associated with dissatisfaction were quite different from those pertaining to satisfaction, which prompted the notion that two factors influence work motivation.

The two-factor theory is illustrated in Exhibit 15.3. The center of the scale is neutral, meaning that workers are neither satisfied nor dissatisfied. Herzberg believed that two entirely separate dimensions contribute to an employee's behavior at work. The first, called **hygiene factors,** involves the presence or absence of job dissatisfiers, such as working conditions, pay, company policies, and interpersonal relationships. When hygiene factors are poor, work is dissatisfying. However, good hygiene factors simply remove the dissatisfaction; they do not in themselves cause people to become highly satisfied and motivated in their work.

The second set of factors does influence job satisfaction. **Motivators** are higher-level needs and include achievement, recognition, responsibility, and opportunity for growth. Herzberg believed that when motivators are absent, workers are neutral toward work, but when motivators are present, workers are highly motivated and satisfied. Thus, hygiene factors and motivators represent two distinct factors that influence motivation. Hygiene factors work only in the area of dissatisfaction. Unsafe working conditions or a noisy work environment will cause peo-

hygiene factors

Factors that involve the presence or absence of job dissatisfiers, including working conditions, pay, company policies, and interpersonal relationships.

motivators

Factors that influence job satisfaction based on fulfillment of higher-level needs such as achievement, recognition, responsibility, and opportunity for growth.

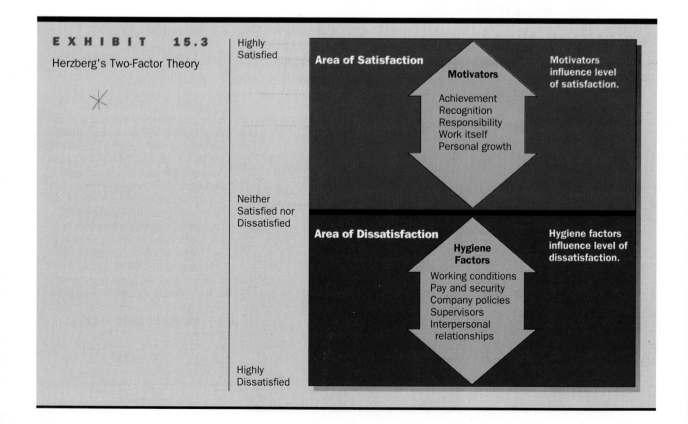

EXHIBIT   15.3

Herzberg's Two-Factor Theory

ple to be dissatisfied; their correction will not lead to a high level of motivation and satisfaction. Motivators such as challenge, responsibility, and recognition must be in place before employees will be highly motivated to excel at their work.

The implication of the two-factor theory for managers is clear. Providing hygiene factors will eliminate employee dissatisfaction but will not motivate workers to high achievement levels. On the other hand, recognition, challenge, and opportunities for personal growth are powerful motivators and will promote high satisfaction and performance. The manager's role is to remove dissatisfiers—that is, provide hygiene factors sufficient to meet basic needs—and then use motivators to meet higher-level needs and propel employees toward greater achievement and satisfaction. Consider the manager's role at YSI, Inc.

 ## YSI, INC.

Malte Von Matthiessen, president of YSI, Inc., knows about motivation. When he took the reins of YSI, the company was overstaffed, quality was low, and both growth and profits were stagnant. Relations between management and workers were good, but Matthiessen could ill afford to fail either to provide adequate hygiene factors or to meet higher-level needs of employees as he attempted to turn around YSI.

Matthiessen solved the overstaffing situation by allowing employee reduction through natural attrition rather than firings, and he placed new emphasis on higher-quality and new, advanced product lines. Perhaps his greatest change involved the use of a motivational tool: empowerment of employees. Shop-floor units were reorganized into work centers, each responsible for its own hiring, problem solving, and quality. Increased employee training and employee access to management information about customer needs, inventories, budgets, and manufacturing procedures motivated employees to think creatively and use their new-found authority to improve the company.

Has Matthiessen's motivational approach worked? Within its first two years, YSI, Inc., saved roughly $1 million in manufacturing costs. YSI employees have renewed pride in company profitability and in their own increased knowledge as they discuss yield rates, new methods of problem solving, or performance-to-schedule ratios.[11] ■

ACQUIRED NEEDS THEORY

The final content theory was developed by David McClelland. The *acquired needs theory* proposes that certain types of needs are acquired during the individual's lifetime. In other words, people are not born with these needs but may learn them through their life experiences.[12] The three needs most frequently studied are these:

1 *Need for achievement:* the desire to accomplish something difficult, attain a high standard of success, master complex tasks, and surpass others.

Tammy Ackers, Taco Bell store manager in Ashland, Kentucky, enjoys her new Trans Am, first prize in Taco Bell's World Series of Speed, a contest among store teams. Tammy possesses both *need for achievement* and *affiliation*, which account for her store's astonishing success, with 45 percent real growth in an area with 30 percent unemployment, an outstanding store quality rating, and increases of over 30 percent in profitability. Ackers loves high achievement and is uncompromising about store standards, but at the same time loves to develop people and interact with them.

2 *Need for affiliation:* the desire to form close personal relationships, avoid conflict, and establish warm friendships.

3 *Need for power:* the desire to influence or control others, be responsible for others, and have authority over others.

Early life experiences determine whether people acquire these needs. If children are encouraged to do things for themselves and receive reinforcement, they will acquire a need to achieve. If they are reinforced for forming warm human relationships, they will develop a need for affiliation. If they get satisfaction from controlling others, they will acquire a need for power.

For over 20 years, McClelland studied human needs and their implication for management. People with a high need for achievement tend to be entrepreneurs. They like to do something better than competitors and take sensible business risks. On the other hand, people who have a high need for affiliation are successful "integrators," whose job is to coordinate the work of several departments in an organization.[13] Integrators include brand managers and project managers who must have excellent people skills. People high in need for affiliation are able to establish positive working relationships with others.

A high need for power often is associated with successful attainment of top levels in the organizational hierarchy. For example, McClelland studied managers at AT&T for 16 years and found that those with a high need for power were more likely to follow a path of continued promotion over time. Over half of the employees at the top levels had a high need for power. In contrast, managers with a high need for achievement but a low need for power tended to peak earlier in their careers and at a lower level. The reason is that achievement needs can be met through the task itself, but power needs can be met only by ascending to a level at which a person has power over others.

In summary, content theories focus on people's underlying needs and label those that motivate people to behave. The hierarchy of needs theory, the ERG theory, the two-factor theory, and the acquired needs theory all help managers understand what motivates people. In this way, managers can design work to meet needs and hence elicit appropriate and successful work behaviors.

● PROCESS PERSPECTIVES ON MOTIVATION

Process theories explain how workers select behavioral actions to meet their needs and determine whether their choices were successful. There are two basic process theories: equity theory and expectancy theory.

EQUITY THEORY

Equity theory focuses on individuals' perceptions of how fairly they are treated compared with others. Developed by J. Stacy Adams, equity theory proposes that people are motivated to seek social equity in the rewards they expect for performance.[14]

According to equity theory, if people perceive their compensation as equal to what others receive for similar contributions, they will believe that their treatment is fair and equitable. People evaluate equity by a ratio of inputs to outcomes. Inputs to a job include education, experience, effort, and ability. Outcomes from a job include pay, recognition, benefits, and promotions. The input to outcome ratio may be compared to another person in the work group or to a perceived group average. A state of **equity** exists whenever the ratio of one person's outcomes to inputs equals the ratio of another's outcomes to inputs.

Inequity occurs when the input-outcome ratios are out of balance, such as when a person with a high level of education or experience

process theories

A group of theories that explain how employees select behaviors with which to meet their needs and determine whether their choices were successful.

equity theory

A process theory that focuses on individuals' perceptions of how fairly they are treated relative to others's.

 → INPuTs.

→ OuTcomEs

equity

A situation that exists when the ratio of one person's outcomes to inputs equals that of another's.

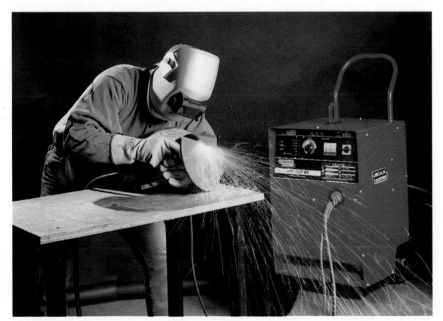

Lincoln Electric values its employees and is committed to developing a work environment in which workers feel secure, challenged, responsive to common goals, and treated fairly in line with *equity theory*. Under Lincoln's Incentive Management system, the worker pictured here and every worker is considered a manager, and every manager is considered a worker. Rules apply equally to both management and labor. Individual achievement is recognized and rewarded through "pay for performance" incentives that pay workers a bonus based on the amount of work they produce.

receives the same salary as a new, less educated employee. Perceived inequity also occurs in the other direction. Thus, if an employee discovers she is making more money than other people who contribute the same inputs to the company, she may feel the need to correct the inequity by working harder, getting more education, or considering lower pay. Perceived inequity creates tensions within individuals that motivate them to bring equity into balance.[15]

The most common methods for reducing a perceived inequity are these:

- *Change inputs.* A person may choose to increase or decrease his or her inputs to the organization. For example, underpaid individuals may reduce their level of effort or increase their absenteeism. Overpaid people may increase effort on the job.

- *Change outcomes.* A person may change his or her outcomes. An underpaid person may request a salary increase or a bigger office. A union may try to improve wages and working conditions in order to be consistent with a comparable union whose members make more money.

- *Distort perceptions.* Research suggests that people may distort perceptions of equity if they are unable to change inputs or outcomes. They may artificially increase the status attached to their jobs or distort others' perceived rewards to bring equity into balance.

- *Leave the job.* People who feel inequitably treated may decide to leave their jobs rather than suffer the inequity of being under- or overpaid. In their new jobs, they expect to find a more favorable balance of rewards.

The implication of equity theory for managers is that employees indeed evaluate the perceived equity of their rewards compared to others'. An increase in salary or a promotion will have no motivational effect if it is perceived as inequitable relative to that of other employees. Some organizations, for example, have created a two-tier wage system to reduce wage rates. New employees make far less than experienced ones, which creates a basis for inequity. Flight attendants at American Airlines are determined to topple the two-tier structure under which they are paid. Chris Boschert, who sorts packages for United Parcel Service, was hired after the two-tier wage system took effect. "It makes me mad," Boschert said. "I get $9.68 an hour, and the guy working next to me makes $13.99 doing exactly the same job."[16] Inequitable pay puts pressure on employees that is sometimes almost too great to bear. They attempt to change their work habits, try to change the system, or leave the job.[17]

Smart managers try to keep feelings of equity in balance in order to keep their work forces motivated. Consider Nucor Corporation.

 NUCOR CORPORATION

Ken Iverson, CEO at Nucor Corporation, goes one step beyond apparent equity to get the results he wants. During good times, some 75 bonus groups get extra pay based solely on level of production. Because of his commitment not to lay people off during hard times, everyone at Nucor Minimills shares the pain during bad times so that everyone can stay employed. In Iverson's "share-the-pain" program, the cuts get stiffer as they go *up* the corporate ladder. In order for everyone to remain employed, a worker might lose 25 percent of his or her salary; however, the worker's department head could lose 35 to 40 percent. The officers, whose compensation is tied to return on stockholders' equity, might lose 60 or 70 percent. These cuts are severe, but they are perceived as more than equitable by the work force. Iverson claims he heard no complaints from the production floor when workers were forced to go to a three-and-a-half-day week in order to avoid layoffs. Iverson correctly anticipated the workers' perception of relative inputs and outputs. As he puts it, "Management should take the biggest drop in pay because they have the most responsibility."[18] ■

EXPECTANCY THEORY

Expectancy theory suggests that motivation depends on individuals' expectations about their ability to perform tasks and receive desired rewards. Expectancy theory is associated with the work of Victor Vroom, although a number of scholars have made contributions in this area.[19] Expectancy theory is concerned not with identifying types of needs but with the thinking process that individuals use to achieve rewards. Consider Bill Bradley, a university student with a strong desire for a B in his accounting course. Bill has a C+ average and one more exam to take. Bill's motivation to study for that last exam will be influenced by (1) the expectation that hard study will lead to an A on the exam and (2) the expectation that an A on the exam will result in a B for the course. If Bill believes he cannot get an A on the exam or that receiving an A will not lead to a B for the course, he will not be motivated to study exceptionally hard.

Expectancy theory is based on the relationship among the individual's *effort*, the individual's *performance*, and the desirability of *outcomes* associated with high performance. These elements and the relationships among them are illustrated in Exhibit 15.4. The keys to expectancy theory are the expectancies for the relationships among effort, performance, and outcomes with the value of the outcomes to the individual.

E → P expectancy involves whether putting effort into a task will lead to high performance. For this expectancy to be high, the individual must have the ability, previous experience, and necessary machinery, tools, and opportunity to perform. For Bill Bradley to get a B in the accounting course, the E → P expectancy is high if Bill truly believes that with hard work, he can get an A on the final exam. If Bill believes he has neither the ability nor the opportunity to achieve high performance, the expectancy will be low, and so will be his motivation.

P → O expectancy involves whether successful performance will lead to the desired outcome. In the case of a person who is motivated to win a job-related award, this expectancy concerns the belief that high performance will truly lead to the award. If the P → O expectancy is high, the individual will be more highly motivated. If the expectancy is that high performance will not produce the desired outcome, motivation will

expectancy theory

A process theory that proposes that motivation depends on individuals' expectations about their ability to perform tasks and receive desired rewards.

Vroom

E → P expectancy

Expectancy that putting effort into a given task will lead to high performance.

P → O expectancy

Expectancy that successful performance of a task will lead to the desired outcome.

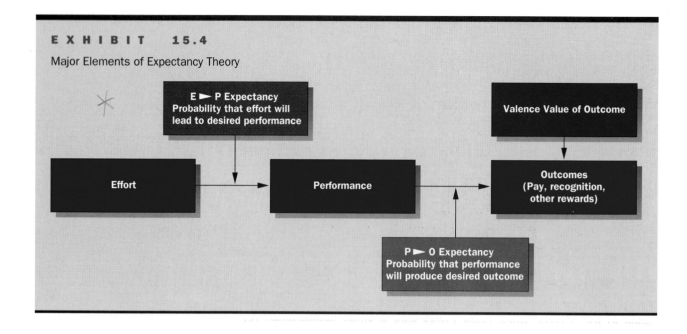

E X H I B I T   15.4

Major Elements of Expectancy Theory

E ▶ P Expectancy
Probability that effort will
lead to desired performance

Valence Value of Outcome

Effort

Performance

Outcomes
(Pay, recognition,
other rewards)

P ▶ O Expectancy
Probability that performance
will produce desired outcome

valence

The value or attraction an individual
has for an outcome.

be lower. If an A on the final exam is likely to produce a B in the accounting course, Bill Bradley's P → O expectancy will be high. Bill may talk to the professor to see whether an A will be sufficient to earn him the B in the course. If not, he will be less motivated to study hard for the final exam.

Valence is the value of outcomes, or attraction for outcomes, for the individual. If the outcomes that are available from high effort and good performance are not valued by employees, motivation will be low. Likewise, if outcomes have a high value, motivation will be higher.

Expectancy theory attempts not to define specific types of needs or rewards but only to establish that they exist and may be different for every individual. One employee may want to be promoted to a position of increased responsibility, and another may have high valence for good relationships with peers. Consequently, the first person will be motivated to work hard for a promotion and the second for the opportunity for a team position that will keep him or her associated with a group.

A simple sales department example will explain how the expectancy model in Exhibit 15.4 works. If Jane Anderson, a salesperson at the Diamond Gift Shop, believes that increased selling effort will lead to higher personal sales, we can say that she has a high E → P expectancy. Moreover, if Jane also believes that higher personal sales will lead to a bonus or pay raise, we can say that she has a high P → O expectancy. Finally, if Jane places a high value on the bonus or pay raise, valence is high and Jane will have a high motivational force. On the other hand, if either the E → P or P → O expectancy is low, or if the money or promotion has low valence for Jane, the overall motivational force will be low. For an employee to be highly motivated, all three factors in the expectancy model must be high.[20]

IMPLICATIONS FOR MANAGERS.   The expectancy theory of motivation is similar to the path-goal theory of leadership described in Chapter 14. Both theories are personalized to subordinates' needs and goals.
Managers' responsibility is to help subordinates meet their needs and at
the same time attain organizational goals. Managers must try to find a
match between a subordinate's skills and abilities and the job demands.
To increase motivation, managers can clarify individuals' needs, define
the outcomes available from the organization, and ensure that each individual has the ability and support (namely, time and equipment) needed
to attain outcomes.

Some companies use expectancy theory principles by designing incentive systems that identify desired organizational outcomes and give
everyone the same shot at getting the rewards. The trick is to design a
system that fits with employees' abilities and needs. Consider the
changes made by Solar Press, Inc.

SOLAR PRESS, INC.

Back in the 1970s, when Solar Press was a small family-owned business, owner John Hudetz passed out checks most months for $20 to
$60. Everybody got the same amount, but no one understood why they
received it.

To tie bonuses more clearly to productivity, this direct-mail company
next divided employees into teams, giving each team a bonus based on
whether it produced more than other teams. Production immediately
jumped, but teams started competing with one another in an unhealthy
way. Teams would not perform regular maintenance on equipment, for
example, and hoarded ideas from fellow employees for fear of not winning their bonus. This competitiveness within Solar Press caused more
problems than it solved.

In 1987 Solar Press adopted another system. When individual employees did a good job, they were given a pay increase. Moreover, all employees were given bonuses from a pool based on company profits. Thus
employees cooperated to help the company make more money. When the
company did well, employees got a share.

In 1989, management went one step further by increasing employee
participation in yearly planning. In a one-day planning session called
"brain day," employees reviewed sales, production goals, equipment
needs, and so on for the next year. The sessions allowed workers to see
where they fit in the overall plan and how their contribution affected overall performance. The system now in place works well. By 1990 sales
had increased 18 percent and the company had added 100 workers and
opened another plant.[21] ■

In the initial system at Solar Press, the connections among effort, performance, and outcomes were unclear. In the group system, employees
had the ability to keep the E → P expectancy high, and the P → O
expectancy was also high, although it threw groups into competition.
Expectancies under the most recent system are also high, and to achieve

desired outcomes, employees are motivated to cooperate for the benefit of the company.

REINFORCEMENT PERSPECTIVE ON MOTIVATION

The reinforcement approach to employee motivation sidesteps the issues of employee needs and thinking processes described in the content and process theories. **Reinforcement theory** simply looks at the relationship between behavior and its consequences. It focuses on changing or modifying the employees' on-the-job behavior through the appropriate use of immediate rewards and punishments.

REINFORCEMENT TOOLS

Behavior modification is the name given to the set of techniques by which reinforcement theory is used to modify human behavior. The basic assumption underlying behavior modification is the **law of effect,** which states that behavior that is positively reinforced tends to be repeated, and behavior that is not reinforced tends not to be repeated. **Reinforcement** is defined as anything that causes a certain behavior to be repeated or inhibited. The four reinforcement tools are positive reinforcement, avoidance learning, punishment, and extinction.[22] Each type of reinforcement is a consequence of either a pleasant or unpleasant event being applied or withdrawn following a person's behavior. The four types of reinforcement are summarized in Exhibit 15.5.

---

reinforcement theory

A motivation theory based on the relationship between a given behavior and its consequences.

behavior modification

The set of techniques by which reinforcement theory is used to modify human behavior.

law of effect

The assumption that positively reinforced behavior tends to be repeated and unreinforced or negatively reinforced behavior tends to be inhibited.

reinforcement

Anything that causes a given behavior to be repeated or inhibited.

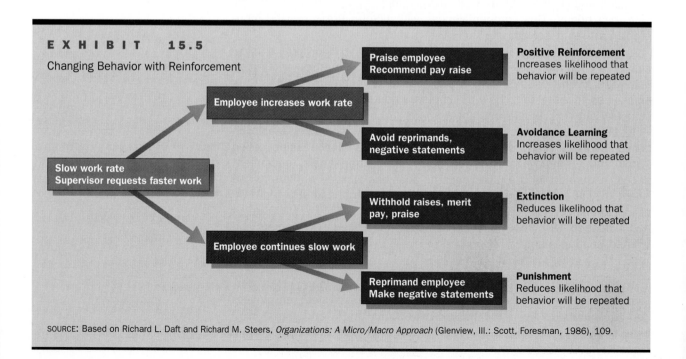

E X H I B I T   15.5

Changing Behavior with Reinforcement

SOURCE: Based on Richard L. Daft and Richard M. Steers, *Organizations: A Micro/Macro Approach* (Glenview, Ill.: Scott, Foresman, 1986), 109.

POSITIVE REINFORCEMENT.   *Positive reinforcement* is the administration of a pleasant and rewarding consequence following a desired behavior. A good example of positive reinforcement is immediate praise for an employee who arrives on time or does a little extra in his or her work. The pleasant consequence will increase the likelihood of the excellent work behavior occurring again.

AVOIDANCE LEARNING.   *Avoidance learning* is the removal of an unpleasant consequence following a desired behavior. Avoidance learning is sometimes called *negative reinforcement*. Employees learn to do the right thing by avoiding unpleasant situations. Avoidance learning occurs when a supervisor stops harassing or reprimanding an employee once the incorrect behavior has stopped.

PUNISHMENT.   *Punishment* is the imposition of unpleasant outcomes on an employee. Punishment typically occurs following undesirable behavior. For example, a supervisor may berate an employee for performing a task incorrectly. The supervisor expects that the negative outcome will serve as a punishment and reduce the likelihood of the behavior recurring. The use of punishment in organizations is controversial and often criticized because it fails to indicate the correct behavior.

EXTINCTION.   *Extinction* is the withdrawal of a positive reward, meaning that behavior is no longer reinforced and hence is less likely to occur in the future. If a perpetually tardy employee fails to receive praise and pay raises, he or she will begin to realize that the behavior is not producing desired outcomes. The behavior will gradually disappear if it is continually nonreinforced.

Some executives use reinforcement theory very effectively to shape employees' behavior. Jack Welch, chairman of General Electric, always made it a point to reinforce behavior. As an up-and-coming group executive, Welch reinforced purchasing agents by having someone telephone him whenever an agent got a price concession from a vendor. Welch would stop whatever he was doing and call the agent to say, "That's wonderful news; you just knocked a nickel a ton off the price of steel." He would also sit down and scribble out a congratulatory note to the agent. The effective use of positive reinforcement and the heightened motivation of purchasing employees marked Jack Welch as executive material in the organization.[23]

SCHEDULES OF REINFORCEMENT

A great deal of research into reinforcement theory suggests that the timing of reinforcement has an impact on the speed of employee learning. **Schedules of reinforcement** pertain to the frequency with and intervals over which reinforcement occurs. A reinforcement schedule can be selected to have maximum impact on employees' job behavior. There are five basic types of reinforcement schedules, which include continuous and four types of partial reinforcement.

CONTINUOUS REINFORCEMENT.   With a **continuous reinforcement schedule,** every occurrence of the desired behavior is reinforced. This

schedule of reinforcement

The frequency with and intervals over which reinforcement occurs.

continuous reinforcement schedule

A schedule in which every occurrence of the desired behavior is reinforced.

schedule can be very effective in the early stages of learning new types of behavior, because every attempt has a pleasant consequence.

PARTIAL REINFORCEMENT.   However, in the real world of organizations, it is often impossible to reinforce every correct behavior. With a **partial reinforcement schedule,** the reinforcement is administered only after some occurrences of the correct behavior. There are four types of partial reinforcement schedules: fixed interval, fixed ratio, variable interval, and variable ratio.

Fixed-Interval Schedule.   The *fixed-interval schedule* rewards employees at specified time intervals. If an employee displays the correct behavior each day, reinforcement may occur every week. Regular paychecks or quarterly bonuses are examples of a fixed-interval reinforcement.

Fixed-Ratio Schedule.   With a *fixed-ratio schedule,* reinforcement occurs after a specified number of desired responses, say, after every fifth. For example, paying a field hand $1.50 for picking 10 pounds of peppers is a fixed-ratio schedule. Most piece-rate pay systems are considered fixed-ratio schedules.

Variable-Interval Schedule.   With a *variable-interval schedule,* reinforcement is administered at random times that cannot be predicted by the employee. An example would be a random inspection by the manufacturing superintendent of the production floor, at which time he or she commends employees on their good behavior.

Variable-Ratio Schedule.   The *variable-ratio schedule* is based on a random number of desired behaviors rather than on variable time periods. Reinforcement may occur sometimes after 5, 10, 15, or 20 displays of behavior. One example is the attraction of slot machines for gamblers. People anticipate that the machine will pay a jackpot after a certain number of plays, but the exact number of plays is variable.

The schedules of reinforcement available to managers are illustrated in Exhibit 15.6. Continuous reinforcement is most effective for establishing new learning, but behavior is vulnerable to extinction. Partial reinforcement schedules are more effective for maintaining behavior over extended time periods. The most powerful is the variable-ratio schedule, because employee behavior will persist for a long time due to the administration of reinforcement only after a long interval.[24]

One example of a small business that successfully uses reinforcement theory is Parsons Pine Products.

 PARSONS PINE PRODUCTS

Parsons Pine Products has only 75 employees, but it is the world's largest manufacturer of slats for louvered doors and shutters. Managers have developed a positive reinforcement scheme for motivating and rewarding workers. The plan includes the following:

1 *Safety pay.* Every employee who goes for a month without a lost-time accident receives a bonus equal to four hours' pay.

EXHIBIT   15.6

Schedules of Reinforcement

Schedule of Reinforcement	Nature of Reinforcement	Effect on Behavior When Applied	Effect on Behavior When Withdrawn	Example
Continuous	Reward given after each desired behavior	Leads to fast learning of new bahavior	Rapid extinction	Praise
Fixed-interval	Reward given at fixed time intervals	Leads to average and irregular performance	Rapid extinction	Weekly paycheck
Fixed-ratio	Reward given at fixed amounts of output	Quickly leads to very high and stable performance	Rapid extinction	Piece-rate pay system
Variable-interval	Reward given at variable times	Leads to moderately high and stable performance	Slow extinction	Performance appraisal and awards given at random times each month
Variable-ratio	Reward given at variable amounts of output	Leads to very high performance	Slow extinction	Sales bonus tied to number of sales calls, with random checks

2 *Retro pay.* If the company saves money when its worker's compensation premiums go down because of a lower accident rate, the savings are distributed among employees.

3 *Well pay.* Employees receive monthly well pay equal to eight hours' wages if they have been neither absent nor tardy.

4 *Profit pay.* All company earnings above 4 percent after taxes go into a bonus pool, which is shared among employees.

The plan for reinforcing correct behaviors has been extraordinarily effective. Parsons's previous accident rate had been 86 percent above the state average; today it is 32 percent below it. Turnover and tardiness are minimal, and absenteeism has dropped to almost nothing. The plan works because the reinforcement schedules are strictly applied, with no exceptions. Owner James Parsons has said, "One woman called to say that a tree had fallen, and she couldn't get her car out. She wanted me to make an exception. If I did that, I'd be doing it all the time."[25] ■

Reinforcement also works at such organizations as Campbell Soup Co., Emery Air Freight, Michigan Bell, and General Electric, because managers reward appropriate behavior. They tell employees what they can do to receive reinforcement, tell them what they are doing wrong, distribute rewards equitably, tailor rewards to behaviors, and keep in mind that failure to reward deserving behavior has an equally powerful impact on employees.

Indeed, reinforcement as well as the content and process perspectives of motivation described earlier are now being adopted in Eastern European countries as well as in Russia and China. The Focus on Global

focus on GLOBAL COMPETITION   MOTIVATION IN RUSSIA

Following the fall of communism, Russia is experimenting with market competition and individual incentives. Psychologists claim that human motivation is similar the world over; hence similar incentives should work in various countries. Many Western companies see motivational problems in Russia, however, and criticize workers' lack of experience, as well as their laziness, alcoholism, and sloppy work habits.

Polaroid, by contrast, sees opportunities in Russia. By addressing worker needs and providing incentives, Polaroid dispels Russia's "lazy worker" myth. "The word is the Russians don't know how to work and can't make quality products," says George Marquart,

head of Polaroid's operations in Russia. "The reason is they haven't been in a position to work for something meaningful."

Polaroid followed a wise plan, starting small, developing a reputation for quality products, establishing a strong market demand, and laying groundwork for future expansion.

As part of this plan, Polaroid has motivated workers in a number of ways. In contrast to the drab work surroundings in typical Russian factories, Polaroid's small Obnisk facility is housed in five cheerful, freshly painted rooms filled with modern U.S.–made equipment. The 70 workers have an abundant supply of parts to keep busy. Financial incentives include high wages and a system of pay based on production. The company also provides training in areas such as teamwork and quality control, with

dozens of employees traveling to the United States or Scotland for advanced training.

Perhaps the most important motivational factor is Polaroid's approach to meeting the most basic needs of workers. Employees at Polaroid can avoid long consumer lines and foraging for daily necessities. The company provides an intermediator who negotiates deals with collective farms for essentials such as meat and eggs.

Workers see proof of Polaroid's commitment as profits are reinvested for future expansion.

Polaroid still faces problems, but productivity is high, reinforcing the notion that offering motivational incentives is a key to effective management in all cultures. ∎

SOURCE: Steven Greenhouse, "Polaroid's Russian Success Story," *The New York Times,* November 24, 1991, F1, F6.

Competition box tells about the implementation of incentives in Polaroid's Russian factory.

JOB DESIGN FOR MOTIVATION

A *job* in an organization is a unit of work that a single employee is responsible for performing. A job could include writing tickets for parking violators in New York City or doing long-range planning for ABC television. Jobs are important because performance of their components may provide rewards that meet employees' needs. An assembly line worker may install the same bolt over and over, whereas an emergency room physician may provide each trauma victim with a unique treatment package. Managers need to know what aspects of a job provide motivation as well as how to compensate for routine tasks that have little inherent satisfaction. **Job design** is the application of motivational theories to the structure of work for improving productivity and satisfaction. Approaches to job design are generally classified as job simplification, job rotation, job enlargement, and job enrichment.

job design

The application of motivational theories to the structure of work for improving productivity and satisfaction.

JOB SIMPLIFICATION

Job simplification pursues task efficiency by reducing the number of tasks one person must do. Job simplification is based on principles drawn from scientific management and industrial engineering. Tasks are designed to be simple, repetitive, and standardized. As complexity is stripped from a job, the worker has more time to concentrate on doing more of the same routine task. Workers with low skill requirements can perform the job, and the organization achieves a high level of efficiency. Indeed, workers are interchangeable, because they need little training or skill and exercise little judgment. As a motivational technique, however, job simplification has failed. People dislike routine and boring jobs and react in a number of negative ways, including sabotage, absenteeism, and unionization. Job simplification is compared with job rotation and job enlargement in Exhibit 15.7.

job simplification

A job design whose purpose is to improve task efficiency by reducing the number of tasks a single person must perform.

scientific managment

nat mot watery.
routine + boring

JOB ROTATION

Job rotation systematically moves employees from one job to another, thereby increasing the number of different tasks an employee performs without increasing the complexity of any one job. For example, an autoworker may install windshields one week and front bumpers the next. Job rotation still takes advantage of engineering efficiencies, but it provides variety and stimulation for employees. Although employees may find the new job interesting at first, the novelty soon wears off as the repetitive work is mastered.

Companies such as National Steel, Motorola, and Dayton Hudson have built on the notion of job rotation to train a flexible work force. As companies break away from ossified job categories, workers can perform several jobs, thereby reducing labor costs. One employee might shift between the jobs of drill operator, punch operator, and assembler, depending on the company's need at the moment. Some unions have resisted the idea, but many now go along, realizing that it helps the company be more competitive.[26]

job rotation

A job design that systematically moves employees from one job to another to provide them with variety and stimulation.

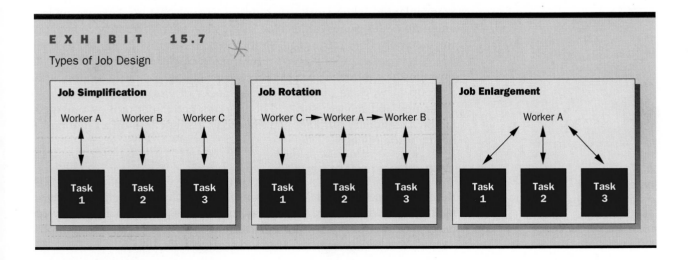

EXHIBIT 15.7

Types of Job Design

Job Simplification	Job Rotation	Job Enlargement
Worker A Worker B Worker C	Worker C → Worker A → Worker B	Worker A
Task 1 Task 2 Task 3	Task 1 Task 2 Task 3	Task 1 Task 2 Task 3

These GE workers in the Bayamon, Puerto Rico, plant enjoy the benefits of *job rotation* and *job enrichment* through self-managed teams and a pay plan that rewards learning and performance. Hourly workers, called "advisors," are divided into teams with each team "owning" part of the work—assembly, shipping, and so on. Hourly workers change jobs every six months, rotating through the factory's four areas and breaking the traditional monotony of factory jobs. They also take responsibility for managing the team. The result is a 20 percent improvement in productivity and a happy work force.

JOB ENLARGEMENT

job enlargement

A job design that combines a series of tasks into one new, broader job to give employees variety and challenge.

Job enlargement combines a series of tasks into one new, broader job. This is a response to the dissatisfaction of employees with oversimplified jobs. Instead of only one job, an employee may be responsible for three or four and will have more time to do them. Job enlargement provides job variety and a greater challenge for employees. At Maytag, jobs were enlarged when work was redesigned such that workers assembled an entire water pump rather than doing each part as it reached them on the assembly line. In General Motors' new assembly plants, the assembly line is gone. In its place is a motorized carrier that transports a car through the assembly process. The carrier allows a vehicle to stop, and a group of workers performs logical blocks of work, such as installing an engine and its accessories. The workers get to perform an enlarged job on a stationary automobile rather than a single task on a large number of automobiles.

JOB ENRICHMENT

job enrichment

A job design that incorporates achievement, recognition, and other high-level motivators into the work.

Recall the discussion of Maslow's need hierarchy and Herzberg's two-factor theory. Rather than just changing the number and frequency of tasks a worker performs, **job enrichment** incorporates high-level motivators into the work, including job responsibility, recognition, and opportunities for growth, learning, and achievement. In an enriched job, employees have control over the resources necessary for performing it, make decisions on how to do the work, experience personal growth, and set their own work pace. Many companies, including AT&T, IBM, and General Foods, have undertaken job enrichment programs to increase employees' motivation and job satisfaction.

JOB CHARACTERISTICS MODEL

The most recent work on job design is the job characteristics model developed by Richard Hackman and Greg Oldham.[27] Hackman and Oldham's research concerned **work redesign,** which is defined as altering jobs to increase both the quality of employees' work experience and their productivity. Hackman and Oldham's research into the design of hundreds of jobs yielded the **job characteristics model,** which is illustrated in Exhibit 15.8. The model consists of three major parts: core job dimensions, critical psychological states, and employee growth-need strength.

CORE JOB DIMENSIONS.   Hackman and Oldham identified five dimensions that determine a job's motivational potential:

1 *Skill variety* is the number of diverse activities that compose a job and the number of skills used to perform it. A routine, repetitious assembly line job is low in variety, whereas an applied research

work redesign

The altering of jobs to increase both the quality of employees' work experience and their productivity.

job characteristics model

A model of job design that comprises core job dimensions, critical psychological states, and employee growth-need strength.

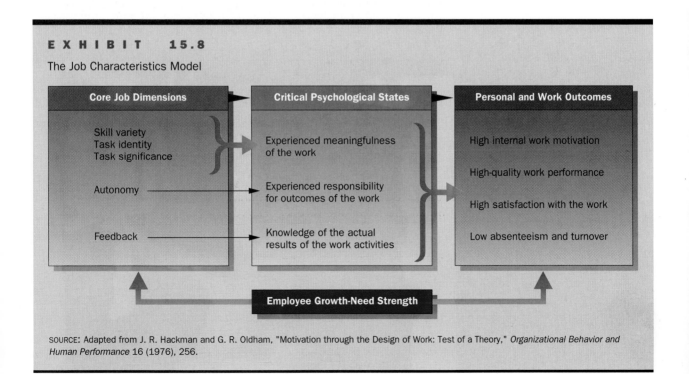

EXHIBIT   15.8

The Job Characteristics Model

Core Job Dimensions	Critical Psychological States	Personal and Work Outcomes
Skill variety Task identity Task significance	Experienced meaningfulness of the work	High internal work motivation
Autonomy	Experienced responsibility for outcomes of the work	High-quality work performance
Feedback	Knowledge of the actual results of the work activities	High satisfaction with the work
		Low absenteeism and turnover

Employee Growth-Need Strength

SOURCE: Adapted from J. R. Hackman and G. R. Oldham, "Motivation through the Design of Work: Test of a Theory," *Organizational Behavior and Human Performance* 16 (1976), 256.

position that entails working on new problems every day is high in variety.

2 *Task identity* is the degree to which an employee performs a total job with a recognizable beginning and ending. A chef who prepares an entire meal has more task identity than a worker on a cafeteria line who ladles mashed potatoes.

3 *Task significance* is the degree to which the job is perceived as important and having impact on the company or consumers. People who distribute penicillin and other medical supplies during times of emergencies would feel they have significant jobs.

4 *Autonomy* is the degree to which the worker has freedom, discretion, and self-determination in planning and carrying out tasks. A house painter can determine how to paint the house; a paint sprayer on an assembly line has little autonomy.

5 *Feedback* is the extent to which doing the job provides information back to the employee about his or her performance. Jobs vary in their ability to let workers see the outcomes of their efforts. A football coach knows whether the team won or lost, but a basic research scientist may have to wait years to learn whether a research project was successful.

The job characteristics model says that the more these five core characteristics can be designed into the job, the more the employees will be motivated and the higher will be performance quality and satisfaction.

CRITICAL PSYCHOLOGICAL STATES.   The model posits that core job dimensions are more rewarding when individuals experience three psychological states in response to job design. In Exhibit 15.8, skill variety,

Autonomy, or the freedom to act, is paramount among core *job dimensions* at Chaparral Steel. By creating a classless organization, universal education, and freedom to act, CEO Gordon Forward has empowered employees to steer the company to new heights as one of the world's lowest-cost steel producers. Workers such as the one pictured here are also motivated by task identity, skill variety, and task significance by utilizing knowledge gained through ongoing education and cross-training opportunities. "Real motivation," Forward says, "comes from within."

task identity, and task significance tend to influence the employee's psychological state of *experienced meaningfulness of work*. The work itself is satisfying and provides intrinsic rewards for the worker. The job characteristic of autonomy influences the worker's *experienced responsibility*. The job characteristic of feedback provides the worker with *knowledge of actual results*. The employee thus knows how he or she is doing and can change work performance to increase desired outcomes.

PERSONAL AND WORK OUTCOMES.   The impact of the five job characteristics on the psychological states of experienced meaningfulness, responsibility, and knowledge of actual results leads to the personal and work outcomes of high work motivation, high work performance, high satisfaction, and low absenteeism and turnover.

EMPLOYEE GROWTH-NEED STRENGTH.   The final component of the job characteristics model is called *employee growth-need strength*, which means that people have different needs for growth and development. If a person wants to satisfy lower-level needs, such as safety and belongingness, the job characteristics model has less effect. When a person has a high need for growth and development, including the desire for personal challenge, achievement, and challenging work, the model is especially effective. People with a high need to grow and expand their abilities respond very favorably to the application of the model and to improvements in core job dimensions.

One application of the job characteristics model that worked extremely well took place at Traveler's Insurance Company.

TRAVELER'S INSURANCE COMPANY

Traveler's Insurance Company executives wanted to increase the motivation and job satisfaction of keypunch operators. The company was experiencing absenteeism and turnover and believed that employees' needs were not being met. The keypunch operator's job consisted of a single skill—the ability to accurately punch data onto cards. Employees punched cards continuously and did not have identifiable, whole jobs. Once a batch was completed, it disappeared and the workers received no feedback on performance quality. Operators were isolated from the rest of the company and had little knowledge about how their work was used.

Researchers investigated the job and recommended several changes. First, instead of being assigned a random set of cards, each operator was given responsibility for a computer user account. In addition, each was given the opportunity for direct contact with clients when problems arose. The operators also were allowed to do planning and control in addition to keypunching. They were asked to correct obvious errors on their own and to set their own daily work schedules. Finally, all incorrectly punched cards were returned to operators for correction, along with weekly printouts of error rates.

These changes dramatically increased the motivating potential of the keypunch operator's job. The job now had greater variety, task identity, and perceived significance. Autonomy and task feedback also were increased.

What were the consequences of the work redesign? Productivity increased 39.6 percent. The error rate dropped from 1.53 to 0.99 percent. Absenteeism declined 24.1 percent. Reported job satisfaction increased 16.5 percent. Moreover, because operators had greater responsibility, supervision was reduced, providing more freedom for keypunch operators and even greater savings for Traveler's.[28] ■

● NEW MOTIVATIONAL PROGRAMS

Organizations have adopted a number of new programs in recent years that apply motivational theory to improve employees' satisfaction and performance. These new forms of incentive pay and employee involvement include pay for performance, gain sharing, ESOPs, lump-sum bonuses, pay for knowledge, and flexible work schedules. Companies can combine these ideas with other ideas from this chapter to create their own motivational program.

PAY FOR PERFORMANCE

pay for performance

A motivational compensation program that rewards employees in proportion to their performance contributions.

Pay for performance means that employees are rewarded in proportion to their performance contributions. Typically called *merit pay*, this is a logical outgrowth of such motivational concepts as expectancy theory and reinforcement theory because pay raises are tied to work behavior. In many organizations, pay raises had become automatic and merit pay had no meaning.

This trend is illustrated at General Motors, which dropped annual cost-of-living raises for salaried employees and established a pay-for-performance system. A merit increase is something employees have to earn. Bosses have to pick the top 10 percent of performers, the next 25 percent, the next 55 percent, and the bottom 10 percent and enforce pay differences among the groups.[29]

GAIN SHARING

gain sharing

A motivational compensation program that rewards employees and managers when predetermined performance targets are met.

Gain sharing is an incentive program in which employees and managers within a designated unit receive bonuses when unit performance beats a predetermined performance target. These targets may specify productivity, costs, quality, customer service, or profits. Unlike pay for performance, gain sharing encourages coordination and teamwork because all employees are contributing to the benefit of the business unit. Most companies develop a precise formula that is calculated for, say, a six-month period, after which bonuses may be paid.[30]

An example of successful gain sharing is the experience of Carrier, a subsidiary of United Technologies. Carrier's six plants in Syracuse, New York, adopted a gain-sharing program called *Improshare*. Under the program, the savings in labor cost resulting from increased productivity and quality are split 50-50 between the company and all employees (from management to line workers). Carrier workers enthusiastically embraced the new program. When a water main broke, flooding one shop floor, all employees pitched in, making repairs throughout the day and night, so that production could be met and no one would miss the weekly bonus. In the first year, Carrier employees in Syracuse shared in a total of $3 million in bonuses from savings due to increased productivity and quality.[31]

ESOPs

Employee stock ownership plans (ESOPs) give employees partial ownership of the business, thereby allowing them to share in improved profit performance. ESOPs have been popular with small businesses, although a few large businesses such as Avis, Procter & Gamble, and JC Penney have also adopted ESOPs. The ESOP allows a company to boost productivity at the cost of ownership, which most business executives are

employee stock ownership plan (ESOP)

A motivational compensation program that gives employees part ownership of the organization.

Science Applications International Corporation (SAIC), a high-tech research and engineering firm, believes the people who build the company should share in its success. SAIC's *employee stock ownership plan (ESOP)* and other stock programs allow employees to buy stock directly and acquire stock through bonuses and options given as recognition for achievements. SAIC has become one of the nation's largest employee-owned companies with almost 9,500 of its 15,000 employees owning stock in 1993. The potential for financial reward is great—*Fortune* magazine cited one production technician, a 14-year veteran, retiring with $300,000 in stock. Now, that's motivation.

finding to be a good trade. Employees work harder because they are owners and share in gains and losses. For ESOPs to work, managers must provide complete financial information to employees, give employees the right to participate in major decisions, and give employees voting rights, which include voting for the board of directors.

At Avis, employees take their ownership seriously. Each class of line worker, from mechanics to rental agents, meets in employee participation groups in which they suggest ways of improving customer service and running the business more efficiently. Since start of the ESOP, Avis has recorded higher profit-sales ratios than Hertz and now aims to overtake Hertz in market share.[32] The Winning Moves box on Springfield Remanufacturing shows how an ESOP plan, in combination with job enrichment, helped initiate a dramatic turnaround in the firm's success.

LUMP-SUM BONUSES

lump-sum bonus

A motivational compensation program that rewards employees with a one-time cash payment based on performance.

Often salary increases do not seem very large when spread over an entire year. **Lump-sum bonuses** are one-time cash payments based on performance. The single payment is designed to increase motivational value of a pay increase. For example, a 10 percent raise for an employee earning $20,000 would be a one-time $2,000 payment. This plan works when employees have a sense that their bonus truly mirrors the company's prosperity. It also lets the company control wage costs by not building increases into the permanent wage structure unless company performance is good.

PAY FOR KNOWLEDGE

pay for knowledge

A motivational compensation program that links employee's salary with the number of tasks performed.

Pay for knowledge means that an employee's salary is increased with the number of tasks he or she can do. This is linked to the ideas of job rotation and job enrichment, because employees learn the skills for many jobs. Pay for knowledge increases company flexibility and efficiency, because fewer employees are needed to perform all tasks. Workers achieve a broader perspective, making them more adept at problem solving. To implement this plan, a company must have a well-developed employee-assessment procedure, and jobs must be well identified so that pay can be increased as new job skills are acquired.

FLEXIBLE WORK SCHEDULES

Flexible work schedules drop the restriction that employees work the normal eight-hour workday from 8 A.M. to 5 P.M. These modifications include the four-day workweek, flex time, and job sharing.

With the *four-day workweek* employees work four days for ten hours each instead of five days for eight hours. The motivational factor is that of meeting the needs of workers who want more leisure time.

Flex time allows employees to determine their workday schedules. People can choose starting and quitting times. For example, a company may have core hours during which employees must be present, perhaps from 9 A.M. to 4 P.M. Employees then are free to start work anywhere from 7 A.M. to 9 A.M. and to finish anywhere from 4 P.M. to 6 P.M., depending on their own needs and desires. A number of companies, including DuPont, IBM, and Avon have implemented flexible scheduling.

WINNING moves

SPRINGFIELD REMANUFACTURING EMPLOYEES ARE OWNERS TOO

In 1983, Springfield Remanufacturing Corporation was a poorly performing division of International Harvester. By 1990, it was a phenomenally successful independent corporation that serviced clients such as Mercedes Benz and General Motors. With sales of over $58 million a year, SRC grew 35 to 40 percent annually during the seven years since its management team bought it. When asked about this remarkable turnaround, the corporation's director of human resources says, "It's pretty simple. We make sure every employee understands how their work adds to or subtracts from every line on the financial statement. . . . " Through strong job enrichment programs, as well as an ESOP plan, Springfield Remanufacturing motivates its workers to be full participants.

CEO Jack Stack credits his approach to problems he saw at International Harvester. "There was a tremendous distinction between the working class and management. The only way we communicated was through a contract." So when he took over SRC, Stack was determined to make a strong investment in human capital. Motivating employees was his first priority. The foundation of his approach is perhaps best expressed by director of human resources, Gary Brown: "We're trying to create a working environment that involves ordinary, blue-collar workers in more than just day-to-day routines. We firmly believe employees are capable of more than coming to work just to grind crankcases."

The most important part of Stack's program is the employee stock ownership plan. Like many ESOPs, it is designed to reinforce full participation and instill a sense of pride in the corporation's success. SRC wants its employees to feel like business partners who will see increased financial benefits from improving performance.

In fact, when an SRC employee is first hired, he or she is told that 70 percent of the job is rebuilding engines and 30 percent is learning how to make profits. As part of their basic training, all employees must learn how to evaluate weekly income statements, cash flow projections, debt-to-equity ratios, balance sheets, after-tax profits, and net earnings. Everyone is expected to understand the bottom line effect of his or her job and to help SRC achieve maximum profitability.

This involvement in the corporation's financial standing is carried out through information meetings held twice each month. Senior managers and supervisors begin each meeting with a status discussion that leads to a revised financial forecast. Supervisors then hold meetings on the shop floor. They pass out the revised forecast and conduct a question-and-answer session. In this way the entire work force, from telephone operators to top management, knows exactly how the company is doing.

As part of SRC's job enrichment policy, the company also offers regularly scheduled courses in topics such as accounting, warehousing, and remedial reading for those who need it. Many well-prepared employees go on to manage one of SRC's many branches and have the opportunity to buy out a large percent of the particular company they run.

Stack claims the difference that makes SRC so successful is that employees "understand performance and productivity as equity." SRC has given its people the tools to improve their careers and a piece of the profits that their efforts build. Given the fact that the stock has gone from 10 cents to $13.80 a share, this is some of the best motivation possible. ■

SOURCE: Based on Frank T. Adams, "Motivation and the Bottom Line," *Human Capital*, July 1990, 19–26.

Job sharing involves two or more persons jointly covering one job over a 40-hour week. Job sharing allows part-time workers, such as a mother with small children, to work only part of a day without having to create a special job. Job sharing also relieves job fatigue if work is routine or monotonous.

SUMMARY AND MANAGEMENT SOLUTION

This chapter introduced a number of important ideas about the motivation of people in organizations. The content theories of motivation focus on the nature of underlying employee needs. Maslow's hierarchy of needs, Alderfer's ERG theory, Herzberg's two-factory theory, and McClelland's acquired needs theory all suggest that people are motivated to meet a range of needs. Process theories examine how people go about selecting rewards with which to meet needs. Equity theory says that people compare their contributions and outcomes with others' and are motivated to maintain a feeling of equity. Expectancy theory suggests that people calculate the probability of achieving certain outcomes. Managers can increase motivation by treating employees fairly and by clarifying employee paths toward meeting their needs. Still another motivational approach is reinforcement theory, which says that employees learn to behave in certain ways based on the availability of reinforcements.

The application of motivational ideas is illustrated in job design and other motivational programs. Job design approaches include job enrichment and work redesign, which provide an opportunity for employees to meet higher-level needs. Other motivational programs include pay for performance, gain sharing, ESOPs, lump-sum bonuses, pay for knowledge, and flexible work schedules. A highly successful application of motivational ideas occurred for store managers at Au Bon Pain.

Recall from the chapter opening case that Gary Aronson was an unmotivated store manager at Au Bon Pain, making a mere $26,000 a year. Thanks to a new incentive system, Aronson will make at least $80,000 this year, and he throws his heart and soul into his work, putting in a minimum of 65 hours a week and loving it. The dramatic motivation began when top executives devised a plan to split controllable profits on a 50-50 basis with store managers. Controllable profits are ones store managers can do something about. Aronson got rid of one assistant manager to save on overhead, reorganized the store to increase seating capacity, and motivated his own staff more effectively to ensure prompt service. Aronson and other store managers solved problems they had previously dumped on the company. Under the new system, stores ran 40 percent ahead of their profit goals, showing that incentives and a sense of ownership work.[33] Perhaps the best explanation for the sharply improved performance is expectancy theory, because managers saw how to link effort and performance to the outcomes they desired. They also received positive reinforcement, and their job responsibilities were enriched, thereby satisfying higher-level needs.

DISCUSSION QUESTIONS

1. Low-paid service workers represent a motivational problem for many companies. Consider the ill-trained and poorly motivated X-ray machine operators trying to detect weapons in airports. How might

these people be motivated to reduce boredom and increase their vigilance?

2. One small company recognizes an employee of the month, who is given a parking spot next to the president's space near the front door. What theories would explain the positive motivation associated with this policy?

3. Campbell Soup Company reduces accidents with a lottery. Each worker who works 30 days or more without losing a day for a job-related accident is eligible to win prizes in a raffle drawing. Why has this program been successful?

4. One executive argues that managers have too much safety because of benefit and retirement plans. He rewards his managers for taking risks and has removed many guaranteed benefits. Would this approach motivate managers? Why?

5. If an experienced secretary discovered that she made less money than a newly hired janitor, how would she react? What inputs and outcomes might she evaluate to make this comparison?

6. Would you rather work for a supervisor high in need for achievement, need for affiliation, or need for power? Why? What are the advantages and disadvantages of each?

7. A survey of teachers found that two of the most important rewards were the belief that their work was important and a feeling of accomplishment. Is this consistent with Hackman and Oldham's job characteristics model?

8. The teachers in question 7 also reported that pay and fringe benefits were poor; yet they continued to teach. Use Herzberg's two-factor theory to explain this finding.

9. Many organizations use sales contests and motivational speakers to motivate salespeople to overcome frequent rejections and turndowns. How would these devices help motivate salespeople?

10. What characteristics of individuals determine the extent to which work redesign will have a positive impact on work satisfaction and work effectiveness?

11. Which of the new motivational programs would you be most comfortable with as a manager? Why?

MANAGEMENT IN PRACTICE: EXPERIENTIAL EXERCISE

● **MOTIVATION QUESTIONNAIRE**

You are to indicate how important each characteristic is to you. Answer according to your feelings about the most recent job you had or about the job you currently hold. Circle the number on the scale that represents your feeling—1 (very unimportant) to 7 (very important).

When you have completed the questionnaire, score it as follows:

Rating for question 5 = ___ . Divide by 1 = ___ security.
Rating for questions 9 and 13 = ___ . Divide by 2 = ___ social.

Rating for questions 1, 3, and 7 = ___ . Divide by 3 = ___ esteem.
Rating for questions 4, 10, 11, and 12 = ___ . Divide by 4 = ___ autonomy.
Rating for questions 2, 6, and 8 = ___ . Divide by 3 = self-actualization.

The instructor has national norm scores for presidents, vice-presidents, and upper middle-level, lower middle-level, and lower-level managers with which you can compare your *mean* importance scores. How do your scores compare with the scores of managers working in organizations?

1. The feeling of self-esteem a person gets from being in that job	1	2	3	4	5	6	7
2. The opportunity for personal growth and development in that job	1	2	3	4	5	6	7
3. The prestige of the job inside the company (that is, regard received from others in the company)	1	2	3	4	5	6	7
4. The opportunity for independent thought and action in that job	1	2	3	4	5	6	7
5. The feeling of security in that job	1	2	3	4	5	6	7
6. The feeling of self-fulfillment a person gets from being in that position (that is, the feeling of being able to use one's own unique capabilities, realizing one's potential)	1	2	3	4	5	6	7
7. The prestige of the job outside the company (that is, the regard received from others not in the company)	1	2	3	4	5	6	7
8. The feeling of worthwhile accomplishment in that job	1	2	3	4	5	6	7
9. The opportunity in that job to give help to other people	1	2	3	4	5	6	7
10. The opportunity in that job for participation in the setting of goals	1	2	3	4	5	6	7
11. The opportunity in that job for participation in the determination of methods and procedures	1	2	3	4	5	6	7
12. The authority connected with the job	1	2	3	4	5	6	7
13. The opportunity to develop close friendships in the job	1	2	3	4	5	6	7

SOURCE: Lyman W. Porter, *Organizational Patterns of Managerial Job Attitudes* (New York: American Foundation for Management Research, 1964), 17, 19.

CASES FOR ANALYSIS

BLOOMINGDALE'S

Bloomingdale's is at the forefront of a quiet revolution sweeping department store retailing. Thousands of hourly sales employees are being converted to commission pay. Bloomingdale's hopes to use commissions to motivate employees to work harder, to attract better salespeople, and to enable them to earn more money. For example, under the old plan, a Bloomingdale's salesclerk in women's wear would earn about $16,000 a year, based on $7 per hour and 0.5 percent commission on $500,000 sales. Under the new plan, the annual pay would be $25,000 based on 5 percent commission on $500,000 sales.

John Palmerio, who works in the men's shoe salon, is enthusiastic about the changeover. His pay has increased an average of $175 per week. But in women's lingerie, employees are less enthusiastic. A target of $1,600 in sales per week is difficult to achieve but is necessary for salespeople to earn previous salary and even to keep their jobs. In previous years, the practice of commission pay was limited to big-ticket items such as furniture, appliances, and men's suits, where extra sales skill pays off. The move into small-item purchases may not work as well, but Bloomingdale's and other stores are trying anyway.

One question is whether Bloomingdale's can create more customer-oriented salespeople when they work on commission. They may be reluctant to handle complaints, make returns, and clean shelves, preferring instead to chase customers. Moreover, it cost Bloomingdale's about $1 million per store to install the commission system because of training programs, computer changes, and increased pay in many departments. If the overall impact on service is negative, the increased efficiency may not seem worthwhile.

● QUESTIONS

1. What theories about motivation underlie the switch from salary to commission pay?
2. Are higher-level needs met under the commission system?
3. As a customer, would you prefer to shop where employees are motivated to make commissions?

SOURCE: Based on Francis Schwadel, "Chain Finds Incentives a Hard Sell," *The Wall Street Journal*, July 5, 1990, B4, and Amy Dunkin, "Now Salespeople Really Must Sell for Their Supper," *Business Week*, July 31, 1989, 50–52.

A FAIR DAY'S PAY

Richard manages a large hotel in a well-known chain. His staff consists of four department managers, a secretary, and the maintenance housekeeping supervisor, Marge. Marge has worked in the hotel for almost 25 years and supervises custodians.

Richard believes that the custodians are overworked and underpaid. But instead of formally changing their pay through a battle with the human resource department at headquarters, he deals with the problem in his own way. When Marge disciplined a custodian or decided who was to work overtime, Richard often countermanded her authority. Sometimes a custodian would not even bother to protest being assigned an overtime schedule and would merely stay home, believing that Richard would see that she wasn't penalized.

Richard also signed the time sheets and would sometimes allow custodians to claim hours they didn't work. Sometimes the number of hours worked was correct, but Richard would arrange for a custodian to be paid at the overtime rate for regular hours. Many custodians came from near-poverty households and desperately needed the extra money.

Christopher, one of the department managers, found out about the time sheet discrepancies from a custodian who was paid for an entire weekend that she didn't work. Sue, another department manager, also found out from a conversation with Marge. Marge said she would like to do something about Richard's interference in the custodians' pay but was afraid to speak up. She didn't have the required educational level for her job, and no other hotel would hire her for an equal position.

One day Christopher and Sue got together to talk about this problem. Sue was angry but decided she was powerless to do anything. Christopher wasn't so sure. He wanted to take action, even though he was not the direct supervisor for custodians and technically it wasn't his problem.

● QUESTIONS

1. Is Richard successfully motivating hotel employees? What mistakes is he making?
2. Use equity theory or expectancy theory to analyze the potential motivation of housekeepers and other employees. For example, what are the E → P and P → O expectancies?
3. If you were Sue or Christopher, what would you do now? What would be the ethical thing to do?

REFERENCES

1. Bruce G. Posner, "May the Force Be with You," *INC.*, July 1987, 70–75; and Carolyn Walkup, "Commissary, New Outlets Boost Au Bon Pain's Net," *Nation's Restaurant News,* December 2, 1991, 14.

2. David Silburt, "Secrets of the Super Sellers," *Canadian Business,* January 1987, 54–59; "Meet the Savvy Supersalesmen," *Fortune,* February 4, 1985, 56–62; Michael Brody, "Meet Today's Young American Worker," *Fortune,* November 11, 1985, 90–98; and Tom Richman, "Meet the Masters. They Could Sell You Anything . . . ," *INC.,* March 1985, 79–86.

3. Richard M. Steers and Lyman W. Porter, eds., *Motivation and Work Behavior,* 3d ed. (New York: McGraw-Hill, 1983).

4. Kenneth A. Kovach, "What Motivates Employees? Workers and Supervisors Give Different Answers," *Business Horizon* 30 (September-October), 58–65.

5. Steers and Porter, *Motivation.*

6. J. F. Rothlisberger and W. J. Dickson, *Management and the Worker* (Cambridge, Mass.: Harvard University Press, 1939).

7. Abraham F. Maslow, "A Theory of Human Motivation," *Psychological Review* 50 (1943), 370–396.

8. Clayton Alderfer, *Existence, Relatedness and Growth* (New York: Free Press, 1972).

9. Julia Lawlor, "Employees Encouraged to Lighten Up," *USA Today,* September 23, 1991, A1, B1; and Everett T. Suters, "Show and Tell," *INC.,* April 1987, 111–112.

10. Frederick Herzberg, "One More Time: How Do You Motivate Employees?" *Harvard Business Review* (January–February 1968), 53–62.

11. John Case, "The Open-Book Managers," *INC.,* September 1990, 104–113.

12. David C. McClelland, *Human Motivation* (Glenview, Ill.: Scott, Foresman, 1985).

13. David C. McClelland, "The Two Faces of Power," in *Organizational Psychology,* ed. D. A. Colb, I. M. Rubin, and J. M. McIntyre (Englewood Cliffs, N.J.: Prentice-Hall, 1971), 73–86.

14. J. Stacy Adams, "Injustice in Social Exchange," in *Advances in Experimental Social Psychology,* 2d ed., ed. L. Berkowitz (New York: Academic Press, 1965), and J. Stacy Adams, "Toward an Understanding of Inequity," *Journal of Abnormal and Social Psychology* (November 1963), 422–436.

15. Ray V. Montagno, "The Effects of Comparison to Others and Primary Experience on Responses to Task Design," *Academy of Management Journal* 28 (1985), 491–498, and Robert P. Vecchio, "Predicting Worker Performance in Inequitable Settings," *Academy of Management Review* 7 (1982), 103–110.

16. "The Double Standard That's Setting Worker Against Worker," *Business Week,* April 8, 1985, 70–71.

17. James E. Martin and Melanie M. Peterson, "Two-Tier Wage Structures: Implications for Equity Theory," *Academy of Management Journal* 30 (1987), 297–315.

18. George Gendron, "Steel Man Ken Iverson," *INC.,* April 1986, 41–48.

19. Victor H. Vroom, *Work and Motivation* (New York: Wiley, 1964); B. S. Gorgopoulos, G. M. Mahoney, and N. Jones, "A Path-Goal Approach to Productivity," *Journal of Applied Psychology* 41 (1957), 345–353; and E. E. Lawler III, *Pay and Organizational Effectiveness: A Psychological View* (New York: McGraw-Hill, 1981).

20. Richard L. Daft and Richard M. Steers, *Organizations: A Micro/Macro Approach* (Glenview, Ill.: Scott, Foresman, 1986).

21. Anne Murphy, "Outline for an Open-Book Company," *INC.,* September 1990, 112–113, and Bruce G. Posner, "If at First You Don't Succeed," *INC.,* May 1989, 132–184.

22. H. Richlin, *Modern Behaviorism* (San Francisco: Freeman, 1970), and B. F. Skinner, *Science and Human Behavior* (New York: Macmillan, 1953).

23. Tom Peters and Nancy Austin, *A Passion for Excellence: The Leadership Difference* (New York: Random House, 1985), 267.

24. L. M. Sarri and G. P. Latham, "Employee Reaction to Continuous and Variable Ratio Reinforcement Schedules Involving a Monetary Incentive," *Journal of Applied Psychology* 67 (1982), 506–508, and R. D. Pritchard, J. Hollenback, and P. J. DeLeo, "The Effects of Continuous and Partial Schedules of Reinforcement on Effort, Performance, and Satisfaction," *Organizational Behavior and Human Performance* 25 (1980), 336–353.

25. "Creating Incentives for Hourly Workers," *INC.,* July 1986, 89–90.

26. Norm Alster, "What Flexible Workers Can Do," *Fortune,* February 13, 1989, 62–66.

27. J. Richard Hackman and Greg R. Oldham, *Work Redesign* (Reading, Mass.: Addison-Wesley, 1980), and J. Richard Hackman and Greg Oldham, "Moti-

vation through the Design of Work: Test of a Theory," *Organizational Behavior and Human Performance* 16 (1976), 250–279.

28. J. Richard Hackman, Greg R. Oldham, R. Janson, and K. Purdy, "A New Strategy for Job Enrichment," *California Management Review* 17 (1975), 57–71, and Daft and Steers, *Organizations*, 173–174.

29. Jacob M. Schleslinger, "GM's New Compensation Plan Reflects General Trend Tying Pay to Performance," *The Wall Street Journal*, January 26, 1988, 31.

30. Timothy L. Ross, Larry Hatcher, and Ruth Ann Ross, "From Piecework to Companywide Gainsharing," *Management Review* (May 1989), 22–26, and Nancy J. Perry, "Here Come Richer, Riskier Pay Plans," *Fortune*, December 19, 1988, 50–58.

31. Perry, "Here Come Richer, Riskier Pay Plans."

32. Christopher Farrell and John Hoerr, "ESOPs: Are They Good for You?" *Business Week*, May 15, 1989, 116–123, and John Case, "ESOPs: Dead or Alive?" *INC.*, June 1988, 94–100.

33. "Expansion Boosts Au Bon Pain," *Nation's Restaurant News*, August 3, 1991, 14, and Posner, "May the Force Be with You."

ROSS PEROT: UNITED WE STAND AMERICA

During the 1992 presidential race, Ross Perot's frontal assaults on the Bush Administration helped speed the one-term incumbent into retirement and Bill Clinton into the White House. The Texas billionaire received 19 percent of the popular vote, and with that kind of political clout, he did not remain on the sidelines for long.

Early in 1993, Perot announced plans to transform his organization of volunteers into a permanent political force: United We Stand America. The purpose of the group is to apply pressure to both the president and Congress to reduce the $4 trillion federal debt, eliminate foreign political influence, and create jobs. He said the group might also endorse candidates in state and local races, starting with a special Senate race in Texas for the seat vacated by Lloyd Bentsen. Perot characterized the group's primary goals as political and economic reform.

"What are our priorities?" he asked rhetorically. "We want to re-create a government that comes from the people, not at the people. We can't leave it up to the special interests roaming around in their alligator shoes and their blow-dried hair."

Perot solicited members with a succession of national television appearances. Less than a week after the media blitz organizers said they had received nearly 30,000 pieces of mail, most containing the $15 annual membership fee. They also had logged half a million telephone calls.

One of the unprecedented ways the group hopes to enlighten voters and turn up the heat on business-as-usual politics is through discussion of major issues using the "electronic town-hall meeting" forum. Through the use of interactive television, viewers would make local calls to vote on specific issues, with the computer-tabulated results being forwarded to members of Congress.

Critics fear that forums of that sort, improperly moderated, could be subject to manipulation, and the effect they might have on the Clinton Administration is far from certain.

Ross Perot has never lacked detractors, and it has been charged that United We Stand America, founded to give voters a voice, could be the instrument used to give the overriding voice to Perot himself. "His vision seems to be Bonapartist—one leader, one people," Michael Schudson wrote in the fall issue of *The American Prospect.* "Would different parties present different alternatives? Apparently not, not in the view of a man who scoffs at political parties and thinks governing is just a matter of getting down to business."

So far the sometimes acerbic Texan is not impressed with how Bill Clinton has gotten down to business. When informed that the president's budget proposals, which combine tax increases and spending programs, would lead to an additional $1 trillion in red ink over four years, Perot said: "If that's true, that is not an acceptable plan." He has urged the government to set up a bookkeeping system to monitor progress on debt reduction and approve a consitutional amendment mandating a balanced budget. And he told supporters they should demand these changes before getting on board any economic plan that includes higher taxes. "I think we need to make it very clear that if Washington wants more tax money from us, this is what we want them committed to do," Perot said.

Perot's seeming ability to sway voters has brought political heavyweights from both sides of the aisle calling. Representatives who routinely come up $2 billion wide of the mark in budget calculations can manage simpler calculations: Clinton 43 percent, Bush 38 percent, Perot 19 percent. Since most state and district elections are two-person races, it becomes obvious that a lot of motivated Perot supporters can tip the balance.

The long-term impact of United We Stand America, and Ross Perot, will likely have an inverse relationship with how the economy performs. Committed activists might stay on the warpath, harassing Congress to reduce their pay, scale back pensions and perks, and rein in foreign special-interest lobbyists, but it's expected that an economic upswing would placate many voters.

In many ways United We Stand America represents American politics the best that it can be. Disaffected voters have coalesced behind a maverick leader too wealthy to be bought and seemingly too irascible to be swayed from the high-minded agenda he espouses.

But Perot is a dichotomy. His populist approach stirs hope that power can indeed be returned to the people and office holders held accountable to their constituency. On the other hand, the group's champion is often given to secrecy and behind-the-scene dealings that harken back to the old smoke-filled room.

● QUESTIONS

1. Explain the motivational factors that led to the formation of United We Stand America.

2. As head of United We Stand America, what type of motivational reinforcement does Ross Perot employ?

3. In your opinion, what are Ross Perot's motivations behind organizing United We Stand America? Are they more personal, or more altruistic?

4. How has United We Stand America evolved since this video was aired? Has the group become a force in the body politic? Do you think it will eventually become a third political party?

COMMUNICATING IN ORGANIZATIONS ⬤16

LEARNING OBJECTIVES

After studying this chapter, you should be able to

■ Explain why communication is essential for effective management.

■ Define the basic elements of the communication process.

■ Describe how perception, nonverbal behavior, and listening affect communication among people.

■ Describe the concept of channel richness and explain how communication channels influence the quality of communication among managers.

■ Explain the difference between formal and informal organizational communications and the importance of each for organization management.

■ Describe team communications and how structure influences communication outcomes.

■ Describe barriers to organizational communications and suggest ways to avoid or overcome them.

CHAPTER OUTLINE

Communication and the Manager's Job

What Is Communication?
The Communication Process

Communicating among People

Perception and Communication
Communication Channels
Nonverbal Communication
Listening

Organizational Communication

Formal Communication
  Channels
Informal Communication
  Channels

Communicating in Teams

Managing Organizational Communication

Barriers to Communication
Overcoming Communication
  Barriers

Optimism was high when Bernard Marcus and Arthur Blank opened their first Home Depot home-improvement center. Shelves bulged with an assortment of 18,000 items, and the owners' children manned the entrances, armed with 700 $1 bills as tokens of appreciation to the anticipated crowd of shoppers. The crowd never came. Blank recalls, "By 5 or 6 in the evening, our kids were out in the parking lot, stopping people, and giving them money to come into the store." The launching of store number two across town fared no better. During those first weeks, customer numbers remained low, mer-  chandise scarcely moved, and suppliers were paid directly from the cash registers. The duo had to find a way to reach customers and improve profitability and to reassure employees and suppliers. This meant improving communications in all directions.[1] ■ If you were Bernard Marcus and Arthur Blank, how would you improve communications at Home Depot? What steps do you think the founders made to enhance the communications to pull people together?

MANAGEMENT PROBLEM

The founders of Home Depot believed in communication but faced problems in breaking down communication barriers. In today's intensely competitive environment, senior executives at most companies are trying to improve communication. The president of Syntex Corporation, a pharmaceuticals maker, eats breakfast at 7:30 each morning in the employee cafeteria exchanging information with workers. The president and CEO of Windham Hill Records holds weekly one-hour meetings with rank-and-file employees, giving each the opportunity to discuss the week ahead. This formula keeps all employees informed about activities and problems in other departments. John Scully, CEO of Apple Computer, insists that top executives listen to customer complaints on the toll-free number. Although Apple executives often lack the technical expertise to solve customers' problems, they quickly learn customers' concerns about Apple computers.[2]

These executives are interested in staying connected with employees and customers and with shaping company direction. To do so, they must be in touch; hence they excel at personal communications. Nonmanagers often are amazed at how much energy successful executives put into communication. Consider the comment about Robert Strauss, former chairman of the Democratic National Committee and former ambassador to Russia:

> One of his friends says, "His network is everywhere. It ranges from bookies to bank presidents. . . ."
> He seems to find time to make innumerable phone calls to "keep in touch"; he cultivates secretaries as well as senators; he will befriend a middle-level White House aide whom other important officials won't bother with. Every few months, he sends candy to the White House switchboard operators.[3]

This chapter explains why executives such as Robert Strauss, John Scully, and the presidents of Windham Hill Records and Syntex Corporation are effective communicators. First we will see how managers' jobs require communication. Next, we will define *communication* and describe a model of the communication process. Then we will consider the interpersonal aspects of communication, including perception, channels, and listening skills, that affect managers' ability to communicate. Next, we will look at the organization as a whole and consider formal upward and downward communications as well as informal communications. Finally, we will examine barriers to communication and how managers can overcome them.

● COMMUNICATION AND THE MANAGER'S JOB

How important is communication? Consider this: Managers spend at least 80 percent of every working day in direct communication with others. In other words, 48 minutes of every hour is spent in meetings, on the telephone, or talking informally while walking around. The other 20 percent of a typical manager's time is spent doing desk work, most of which is also communication in the form of reading and writing.[4]

Communication permeates every management function described in Chapter 1.[5] For example, when managers perform the planning function, they gather information; write letters, memos, and reports; and then meet with other managers to explain the plan. When managers lead, they communicate with subordinates to motivate them. When managers organize, they gather information about the state of the organization and communicate a new structure to others. Communication skills are a fundamental part of every managerial activity.

WHAT IS COMMUNICATION?

Before going further, let us determine what communication is. A professor at Harvard once asked a class to define communication by drawing pictures. Most students drew a manager speaking or writing. Some placed "speech balloons" next to their characters; others showed pages flying from a typewriter. "No," the professor told the class, "none of you have captured the essence of communication." He went on to explain that communication means to "share"—not "to speak" or "to write."

Communication thus can be defined as the process by which information is exchanged and understood by two or more people, usually with the intent to motivate or influence behavior. Communication is not just sending information. This distinction between *sharing* and *proclaiming* is crucial for successful management. A manager who does not listen is like a used-car salesperson who claims, "I sold a car—they just did not buy it." Management communication is a two-way street that includes listening and other forms of feedback. Effective communication, in the words of one expert, is as follows:

> When two people interact, they put themselves into each other's shoes, try to perceive the world as the other person perceives it, try to predict how the other will respond. Interaction involves reciprocal role-taking, the mutual employment of empathetic skills. The goal of interaction is the merger of self and other, a complete ability to anticipate, predict, and behave in accordance with the joint needs of self and other.[6]

It is the desire to share understanding that motivates executives to visit employees on the shop floor or eat breakfast with them. The things managers learn from direct communication with employees shape their understanding of the corporation.

THE COMMUNICATION PROCESS

Many people think communication is simple because they communicate without conscious thought or effort. However, communication is usually complex, and the opportunities for sending or receiving the wrong messages are innumerable. How often have you heard someone say, "But that's not what I meant"? Have you ever received directions you thought were clear and yet still got lost? How often have you wasted time on misunderstood instructions?

communication

The process by which information is exchanged and understood by two or more people, usually with the intent to motivate or influence behavior.

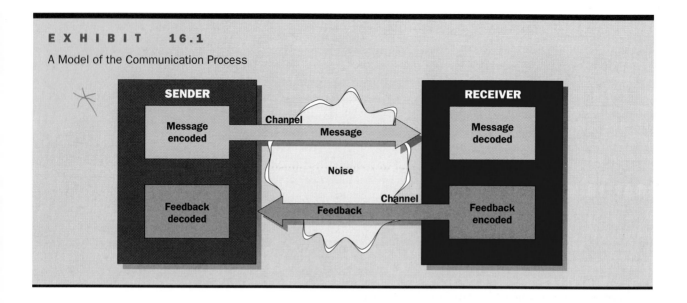

EXHIBIT   16.1

A Model of the Communication Process

encode

To select symbols with which to compose a message.

message

The tangible formulation of an idea to be sent to a receiver.

channel

The carrier of a communication.

decode

To translate the symbols used in a message for the purpose of interpreting its meaning.

feedback

A response by the receiver to the sender's communication.

To more fully understand the complexity of the communication process, note the key elements outlined in Exhibit 16.1. Two common elements in every communication situation are the sender and the receiver. The *sender* is anyone who wishes to convey an idea or concept to others, to seek information, or to express a thought or emotion. The *receiver* is the person to whom the message is sent. The sender **encodes** the idea by selecting symbols with which to compose a message. The **message** is the tangible formulation of the idea that is sent to the receiver. The message is sent through a **channel,** which is the communication carrier. The channel can be a formal report, a telephone call, or a face-to-face meeting. The receiver **decodes** the symbols to interpret the meaning of the message. Encoding and decoding are potential sources for communication errors, because knowledge, attitudes, and background act as filters and create "noise" when translating from symbols to meaning. Finally, **feedback** occurs when the receiver responds to the sender's communication with a return message. Without feedback, the communication is *one-way;* with feedback, it is *two-way.* Feedback is a powerful aid to communication effectiveness, because it enables the sender to determine whether the receiver correctly interpreted the message.

Managers who are effective communicators understand and use the circular nature of communication. For example, James Treybig of Tandem Computers, Inc., widened the open-door policy in order to communicate with employees. Treybig appears on a monthly television program broadcast over the company's in-house television station. Employees around the world watch the show and call in their questions and comments. The television is the channel through which Treybig sends his encoded message. Employees decode and interpret the message and encode their feedback, which is sent through the channel of the telephone hookup. The communication circuit is complete. Similarly,

Tom Monaghan, president of Domino's Pizza, maintains communication channels with employees when he fields complaints for two hours during a monthly "call-in." Monaghan also maintains toll-free numbers on which employees call him directly. Treybig and Monaghan understand the elements of communication and have developed systems that work.[7]

● COMMUNICATING AMONG PEOPLE

The communication model in Exhibit 16.1 illustrates the components that must be mastered for effective communication. Communications can break down if sender and receiver do not encode or decode language in the same way.[8] The selection of communication channels can determine whether the message is distorted by noise and interference. The listening skills of both parties can determine whether a message is truly shared. Thus, for managers to be effective communicators, they must understand how interpersonal factors such as perception, communication channels, nonverbal behavior, and listening all work to enhance or detract from communication.

PERCEPTION AND COMMUNICATION

The way we perceive people is the starting point for how we communicate. When one person wishes to share an idea with another, the message is formulated based on references constructed from past events, experiences, expectations, and current motivations. When a receiver hears a message, he or she relies on a particular frame of reference for decoding and understanding it. The more similar the frames of reference between people, the more easily they can communicate.

Perception is the process people use to make sense out of the environment. However, perception in itself does not always lead to an accurate picture of the environment.[9] **Perceptual selectivity** is the process by which individuals screen and select the various objects and stimuli that vie for their attention. Certain stimuli catch their attention, and others do not. Once a stimulus is recognized, individuals organize or categorize it according to their frame of reference, that is, **perceptual organization.** Only a partial cue is needed to enable perceptual organization to take place. For example, all of us have spotted an old friend from a long distance and, without seeing the face or other features, recognized the person from the body movement.

The most common form of perceptual organization is stereotyping. A **stereotype** is a widely held generalization about a group of people that assigns attributes to them solely on the basis of one or a few categories, such as age, race, or occupation. For example, young people may assume that older people are old-fashioned or conservative. Students may stereotype professors as absent-minded or as political liberals.

How do perceptual selectivity and organization affect manager behavior? Consider the following comment from Joe, a staff supervisor, on his expectations about the annual budget meeting with his boss, Charlie:

perception

The process of making sense out of one's environment.

perceptual selectivity

The screening and selection of objects and stimuli that compete for one's attention.

perceptual organization

The categorization of an object or stimulus according to one's frame of reference.

stereotype

A widely held generalization about a group of people that assigns attributes to them solely on the basis of a limited number of categories.

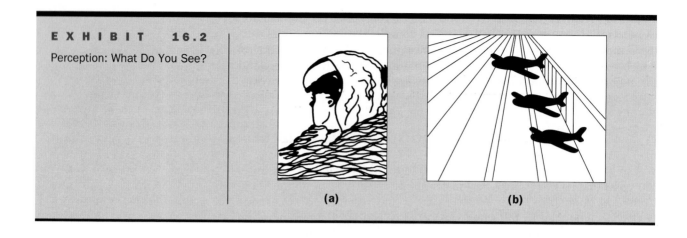

EXHIBIT   16.2

Perception: What Do You See?

(a)   (b)

Direct, *face-to-face communication* is the key to unity within the Ito-Yokado Co., Ltd., culture. In an era of computers, faxes, and voice-mail, management at Ito-Yokado spends money and time on personal communications for understanding and consensus. Here, a weekly meeting of management and store personnel provides face-to-face communication regarding marketing strategies, innovative ideas, and improved retail knowledge. In addition, biannual meetings between junior and senior level managers provide an opportunity for strategic planning and reform.

About a month before the meetings are to begin, I find myself waking up around 4:00 A.M., thinking about Charlie and the arguments I'm going to have with him. I know he'll accuse me of trying to "pad" my requests and, in turn, I'll accuse him of failing to understand the nature of my department's needs. I'll be trying to anticipate every little snide remark he can generate and every argument that he's likely to propose, and I'll be getting ready with snide remarks and arguments of my own. This year, as always, I've got to be sure to get him before he gets me.[10]

Joe's selective perception will cause him to immediately recognize any cues that resemble snide remarks. He will also organize these remarks to fit his belief that Charlie's motivation is to reduce his budget. No matter what frame of mind Charlie brings to the communication, Joe is set to perceive in his own way, which will surely prevent open and honest communication.

Perceptual differences and perceptual mistakes also occur when people perceive simple objects in dissimilar ways. Typical examples are illustrated in Exhibit 16.2. In panel (a), many people see a sad old woman, but others see a beautiful young lady with a large head covering. In panel (b), the top airplane looks larger to most people because of perceptual organization. The background lines provide a frame of reference that distorts the actual size of the airplanes.

An important point for managers to understand is that perceptual differences are natural but can distort messages and create noise and interference for communications. Each person has a distinct personality and perceptual style; hence each interprets messages in a personal way. Managers should remember that words can mean different things to different people and should not assume that they already know what the other person or the communication is about.

COMMUNICATION CHANNELS

Managers have a choice of many channels through which to communicate to other managers or employees. A manager may discuss a problem face-to-face, use the telephone, write a memo or letter, or put an item in a newsletter, depending on the nature of the message. Recent research has attempted to explain how managers select communication channels to enhance communication effectiveness.[11] The research has found that channels differ in their capacity to convey information. Just as a pipeline's physical characteristics limit the kind and amount of liquid that can be pumped through it, a communication channel's physical characteristics limit the kind and amount of information that can be conveyed among managers. The channels available to managers can be classified into a hierarchy based on information richness. **Channel richness** is the amount of information that can be transmitted during a communication episode. The hierarchy of channel richness is illustrated in Exhibit 16.3.

The capacity of an information channel is influenced by three characteristics: (1) the ability to handle multiple cues simultaneously; (2) the ability to facilitate rapid, two-way feedback; and (3) the ability to establish a personal focus for the communication. Face-to-face discussion is the richest medium, because it permits direct experience, multiple information cues, immediate feedback, and personal focus. Face-to-face discussions facilitate the assimilation of broad cues and deep, emotional understanding of the situation. For example, Tony Burns, CEO of Rider Systems, Inc., likes to handle things face-to-face: "You can look someone in the eyes, and you can tell by the look in his eyes or the inflection in his voice what the real problem or question or answer is."[12] Telephone conversations and interactive electronic media, such as video conferencing and electronic mail, lack the element of "being there." Eye contact, gaze, blush, posture, and body language cues are eliminated. Written media that are personalized, such as memos, notes, and letters, can be personally focused, but they convey only the cues written on paper and are slow to provide feedback. Impersonal written media, including fliers, bulletins, and standard computer reports, are the lowest in richness. These channels are not focused on a single receiver, use limited information cues, and do not permit feedback.

channel richness

The amount of information that can be transmitted during a communication episode.

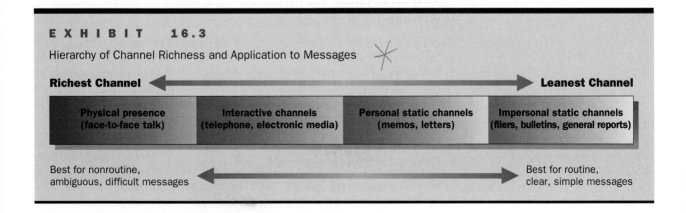

EXHIBIT 16.3

Hierarchy of Channel Richness and Application to Messages

Richest Channel ⟵―――――――――――――――⟶ **Leanest Channel**

| Physical presence (face-to-face talk) | Interactive channels (telephone, electronic media) | Personal static channels (memos, letters) | Impersonal static channels (fliers, bulletins, general reports) |

Best for nonroutine, ambiguous, difficult messages ⟵―――――――――⟶ Best for routine, clear, simple messages

Channel selection depends on whether the message is routine or nonroutine. *Nonroutine messages* typically are ambiguous, concern novel events, and impose great potential for misunderstanding. Nonroutine messages often are characterized by time pressure and surprise. Managers can communicate nonroutine messages effectively only by selecting rich channels. On the other hand, routine communications are simple and straightforward. *Routine messages* convey data or statistics or simply put into words what managers already agree on and understand. Routine messages can be efficiently communicated through a channel lower in richness. Written communications also should be used when the audience is widely dispersed or when the communication is "official" and a permanent record is required.[13]

Consider a CEO trying to work out a press release with public relations people about a plant explosion that injured 15 employees. If the press release must be ready in three hours, the communication is truly nonroutine and forces a rich information exchange. The group will meet face to face, brainstorm ideas, and provide rapid feedback to resolve disagreement and convey the correct information. If the CEO has three days to prepare the release, less information capacity is needed. The CEO and public relations people might begin developing the press release with an exchange of memos and telephone calls.

The key is to select a channel to fit the message. One successful manager who understood channel selection was Harold Geneen of ITT.

 I T T

Harold Geneen was at the helm of ITT for 18 years. He strove to make ITT a unified organization despite its huge size. One of his first decisions was to create ITT-Europe, which would serve as headquarters for European operations. ITT's strategy was to grow by acquisition, eventually increasing to more than 200 subsidiary companies around the world. One of Geneen's most difficult problems was how to get French, German, Italian, and American managers to go along with central decisions. Initial executive sessions sounded like a United Nations meeting. Gradually, Geneen solved the communication problem by relying on face-to-face channels:

> One of the first things I learned in those early days was that when I responded to a question or request from Europe while sitting in New York, my decision was often different from what it would have been had I been in Europe. In New York, I might read a request and say no. But in Europe, I could see the man's face, hear his voice, understand the intensity of his conviction, and the answer to the same question might be yes. So, early on, I decided that if I and my headquarters' team intended to monitor and oversee the European operations, I owed it to the European managers to be there on the spot. . . . It became our policy to deal with problems on the spot, face-to-face.[14]

Geneen discovered that the face-to-face channel was needed for handling difficult communications among managers from different countries.

Thus, for 17 years, Geneen and his senior staff went to Europe for one week every month to deal personally with the European managers' requests and needs. It worked: ITT went on to become one of the best-managed companies in the world. ■

NONVERBAL COMMUNICATION

Nonverbal communication refers to messages sent through human actions and behaviors rather than through words.[15] Although most non-verbal communication is unconscious or subconscious on our part, it represents a major portion of the messages we send and receive. Most managers are astonished to learn that words themselves carry little meaning. Major parts of the shared understanding from communication come from the nonverbal messages of facial expression, voice, mannerisms, posture, and dress.

Nonverbal communication occurs mostly face-to-face. One researcher found three sources of communication cues during face-to-face communication: the verbal, which are the actual spoken words; the vocal, which include the pitch, tone, and timber of a person's voice; and facial expressions. According to this study, the relative weights of these three factors in message interpretation are as follows: verbal impact, 7 percent; vocal impact, 38 percent; and facial impact, 55 percent.[16]

This research strongly implies that "it's not what you say, but how you say it." Nonverbal messages convey thoughts and feelings with greater force than do our most carefully selected words. Body language often communicates our real feelings eloquently. Thus, while the conscious mind may be formulating vocal messages such as "I'm happy" or "Congratulations on your promotion," the body language may be signaling true feelings through blushing, perspiring, glancing, crying, or avoiding eye contact. When the verbal and nonverbal messages are contradictory, the receiver may be confused and usually will give more weight to behavioral actions than to verbal messages.[17]

A manager's office also sends powerful nonverbal cues. For example, what do the following seating arrangements mean if used by your supervisor: (1) She stays behind her desk and you sit in a straight chair on the opposite side. (2) The two of you sit in straight chairs away from her desk, perhaps at a table. (3) The two of you sit in a seating arrangement consisting of a sofa and easy chair. To most people, the first arrangement indicates "I'm the boss here" or "I'm in authority." The second arrangement indicates "This is serious business." The third indicates a more casual and friendly, "Let's get to know each other."[18] Nonverbal messages can be a powerful asset to communication if they complement and support verbal messages. Managers should pay close attention to non-verbal behavior when communicating. They must learn to coordinate their verbal and nonverbal messages and at the same time be sensitive to what their peers, subordinates, and supervisors are saying nonverbally.

nonverbal communication

A communication transmitted through actions and behaviors rather than through words.

LISTENING

Managers who believe that giving orders is the important communication requirement are in for a surprise. The new skill is *listening,* both to customers and to employees. Most executives now believe that important information flows from the bottom up, not the top down, and managers had better be tuned in.[19] In the communication model in Exhibit 16.1, the listener is responsible for message reception, which is a vital link in the communication process. **Listening** involves the skill of receiving messages to accurately grasp facts and feelings to interpret the message's genuine meaning. Only then can the receiver provide the feedback with which to complete the communication circuit. Listening requires attention, energy, and skill.

Many people do not listen effectively. They concentrate on formulating what they are going to say next rather than on what is being said to them. Our listening efficiency, as measured by the amount of material understood and remembered by subjects 48 hours after listening to a 10-minute message, is, on average, no better than 25 percent.[20]

What constitutes good listening? Exhibit 16.4 gives ten keys to effective listening and illustrates a number of ways to distinguish a bad from a good listener. A good listener finds areas of interest, is flexible, works hard at listening, and uses thought speed to mentally summarize, weigh, and anticipate what the speaker says.

Norman Brinker, chairman of Chili's, Inc., has a bedrock belief in listening. He says it is important to hear what employees have to say. They

listening

The skill of receiving messages to accurately grasp facts and feelings to interpret the genuine meaning.

EXHIBIT   16.4

Ten Keys to Effective Listening

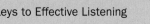

Keys	Poor Listener	Good Listener
1. Listen actively	Is passive, laid back	Asks questions, paraphrases what is said
2. Find areas of interest	Tunes out dry subjects	Looks for opportunities, new learning
3. Resist distractions	Is easily distracted	Fights or avoids distractions; tolerates bad habits; knows how to concentrate
4. Capitalize on the fact that thought is faster than speech	Tends to daydream with slow speakers	Challenges, anticipates, mentally summarizes; weighs the evidence; listens between the lines to tone of voice
5. Be responsive	Is minimally involved	Nods; shows interest, give and take, positive feedback
6. Judge content, not delivery	Tunes out if delivery is poor	Judges content; skips over delivery errors
7. Hold one's fire	Has preconceptions, starts to argue	Does not judge until comprehension is complete
8. Listen for ideas	Listens for facts	Listens to central themes
9. Work at listening	Shows no energy output; faked attention	Works hard, exhibits active body state, eye contact
10. Exercise one's mind	Resists difficult material in favor of light, recreational material	Uses heavier material as exercise for the mind

SOURCE: Adapted from Sherman K. Okum, "How to Be a Better Listener," *Nation's Business* (August 1975), 62, and Philip Morgan and Kent Baker, "Building a Professional Image: Improving Listening Behavior," *Supervisory Management* (November 1985), 34–38.

BOISE CASCADE MANAGERS LISTEN

In the southwestern Louisiana community of DeRidder, a Boise Cascade paper mill has transformed itself. Once a marginal operation, the DeRidder mill is now a jewel in the crown of Boise's network. By mid-1988, in just four years, a group of dedicated managers and staff had improved quality by 32 percent, increased productivity by 22 percent, and lowered costs by 22 percent. The mill also had won two awards for exceptional safety performance. The cornerstone of the DeRidder revitalization program has been good communication between management and staff.

Says Paul Parker, a veteran employee of the shipping department, "I used to hate to come to work, not because I didn't like my job but because of all the trouble we had here." Common problems included tension and infighting among departments, mistrust of management, minimal communication about key aspects of the mill's operation, and inconsistent management practices.

Worst of all were supervisor–employee relations. Milton Cole, a supervisor since 1977, remembers, "In those days we were message carriers. A decision was made and we were told to carry the message. Employees asked a question and I had to tell them I'd get an answer from my boss." This style created an atmosphere of mistrust and low morale. Employees did what was required of them and no more.

Then, in 1982, Boise decided to bring in an entirely new management team. Headed by Dave Spence, they introduced a plan for managing that most employees today recognize as the key factor in the turnaround. The plan put emphasis on safety, listening, training, and employee involvement. Says Cole, "Spence and his team began to push decisions down in the organization. Instead of carrying messages, I make the decisions I ought to be making and I allow my folks to make the decisions they ought to be making." For the first time, supervisors listened to employee ideas and worked with them to determine how their ideas could be implemented.

How did Spence accomplish this? One of the first things he did was to get DeRidder employees at all levels involved in listening sessions. "In those meetings," Spence says, "we talk about what employees want to talk about." Most important, he notes, "if you tell people you want to hear what they have to say you'd better be ready to respond; you'd better be ready to do something about what they tell you." Since these meetings began in 1984, the focus on listening has spread throughout the mill. "Now," says supervisor Peter Pugh, "instead of fighting among ourselves, employees are working as a team to make a quality product in a safe manner."

The DeRidder management group believes that the actions that have grown out of people listening more to each other have driven the dramatic results in safety, quality, productivity, and costs. While many factors certainly play a role in any turnaround situation, the DeRidder story shows how healthy communication practices are essential to overall success. ■

SOURCE: Andrew Drysdale, "Turnaround Time in the South," *Boise Cascade Insight*, November 1988, 1–4.

are not to be bullied. Tom Peters, the famous management author and consultant, says that executives can become good listeners by observing the following: Effective listening is engaged listening; ask dumb questions, break down barriers by participating with employees in casual get-togethers, force yourself to get out and about, provide listening forums, take notes, promise feedback—and deliver.[21] The Winning Moves box shows how Boise Cascade used listening as the foundation for a successful turnaround.

Employees at Mobil Oil Singapore have fine-tuned their *listening skills* in a program called EARS that encourages every employee to open his or her ears to what customers think of Mobil products and services. Employees attend training sessions to show them what to expect when they leave their office to meet customers. The results have improved total quality management because of greater customer loyalty and employees who learn about the ultimate results of their work.

● ORGANIZATIONAL COMMUNICATION

Another aspect of management communication concerns the organization as a whole. Organizationwide communications typically flow in three directions—downward, upward, and horizontally. Managers are responsible for establishing and maintaining formal channels of communication in these three directions. Managers also use informal channels, which means they get out of their offices and mingle with employees.

FORMAL COMMUNICATION CHANNELS

■ **formal communication channel**

A communication channel that flows within the chain of command or task responsibility defined by the organization.

Formal communication channels are those that flow within the chain of command or task responsibility defined by the organization. The three formal channels and the types of information conveyed in each are illustrated in Exhibit 16.5.[22]

■ **downward communication**

Messages sent from top management down to subordinates.

DOWNWARD COMMUNICATION. The most familiar and obvious flow of formal communication, **downward communication,** refers to the messages and information sent from top management to subordinates in a downward direction. For example, management at Trans-Matic (makers of stamped metal parts) distributes monthly reports to all employees, detailing financial data and performance analyses. The honest, up-front approach provides employees advance warning of potential downturns and keeps employees abreast of management strategies for cost cutting, retooling, and other necessary changes. The communication builds empathy for management and creates a climate of working *together* for solutions during tough times.[23]

Managers can communicate downward to employees through speeches, messages in company publications, electronic mail, information leaflets tucked into pay envelopes, material on bulletin boards, and policy and procedure manuals. When Gerald M. Lieberman, senior human resources officer at Citicorp, launched the company's Choices '91 flexible benefits plan, he communicated options to 56,000 employees using several information channels: workbooks, videos, seminars, software, and a hot line. Lieberman understands that different employees are responsive to different kinds of communication. A computer whiz likes information software better than reading a benefits booklet. A secretary may enjoy the give-and-take of an information seminar. Lieberman's communication strategy enabled individual employees to study their options and make wise choices.[24]

Downward communication in an organization usually encompasses the following topics:

1 *Implementation of goals, strategies, and objectives.* Communicating new strategies and goals provides information about specific targets and

Different people respond to different types of communications

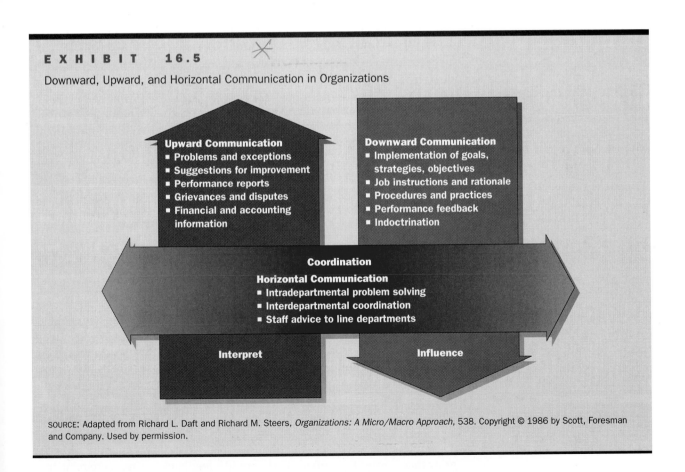

EXHIBIT 16.5

Downward, Upward, and Horizontal Communication in Organizations

Upward Communication
- Problems and exceptions
- Suggestions for improvement
- Performance reports
- Grievances and disputes
- Financial and accounting information

Downward Communication
- Implementation of goals, strategies, objectives
- Job instructions and rationale
- Procedures and practices
- Performance feedback
- Indoctrination

Coordination
Horizontal Communication
- Intradepartmental problem solving
- Interdepartmental coordination
- Staff advice to line departments

Interpret

Influence

SOURCE: Adapted from Richard L. Daft and Richard M. Steers, *Organizations: A Micro/Macro Approach*, 538. Copyright © 1986 by Scott, Foresman and Company. Used by permission.

Northwest Pipeline Corporation (NWP), operator of a 3,500-mile natural gas pipeline, publishes *Discovery* for its employees. This magazine is an important *downward communication* that conveys information about current pipeline projects, future plans, and NWP's commitment to environmental and archaeological concerns. This life-size replica of a dinosaur is from NWP's Vernal, Utah, district, one of the richest paleonto-logical areas in the world.

expected behaviors. It gives direction for lower levels of the organization. Example: "The new quality campaign is for real. We must improve product quality if we are to survive."

2 *Job instructions and rationale.* These are directives on how to do a specific task and how the job relates to other organizational activities. Example: "Purchasing should order the bricks now so the work crew can begin construction of the building in two weeks."

3 *Procedures and practices.* These are messages defining the organization's policies, rules, regulations, benefits, and structural arrangements. Example: "After your first 90 days of employment, you are eligible to enroll in our company-sponsored savings plan."

4 *Performance feedback.* These messages appraise how well individuals and departments are doing their jobs. Example: "Joe, your work on the computer network has greatly improved the efficiency of our ordering process."

5 *Indoctrination.* These messages are designed to motivate employees to adopt the company's mission and cultural values and to participate in special ceremonies, such as picnics and United Way campaigns. Example: "The company thinks of its employees as family and would like to invite everyone to attend the annual picnic and fair on March 3."

The major problem with downward communication is *drop off,* the distortion or loss of message content. Although formal communications are a powerful way to reach all employees, much information gets lost—25 percent or so each time a message is passed from one person to the next. In addition, the message can be distorted if it travels a great distance from its originating source to the ultimate receiver. A tragic example is the following:

> A reporter was present at a hamlet burned down by the U.S. Army 1st Air Cavalry Division in 1967. Investigations showed that the order from the Division headquarters to the brigade was: "On no occasion must hamlets be burned down."
>
> The brigade radioed the battalion: "Do not burn down any hamlets unless you are absolutely convinced that the Viet Cong are in them."
>
> The battalion radioed the infantry company at the scene: "If you think there are any Viet Cong in the hamlet, burn it down."
>
> The company commander ordered his troops: "Burn down that hamlet."[25]

Information drop off cannot be completely avoided, but the techniques described in the previous sections can reduce it substantially. Using the right communication channel, consistency between verbal and nonverbal messages, active listening, and aligning messages with the perception of users can maintain communication accuracy as it moves down the organization.

UPWARD COMMUNICATION. Formal **upward communication** includes messages that flow from the lower to the higher levels in the organization's hierarchy. Most organizations take pains to build in healthy channels for upward communication. Employees need to air grievances, report progress, and provide feedback on management ini-

upward communication

Messages transmitted from the lower to the higher level in the organization's hierarchy.

tiatives. Coupling a healthy flow of upward and downward communication ensures that the communication circuit between managers and employees is complete.[26] Five types of information communicated upward are the following:

1 *Problems and exceptions.* These messages describe serious problems with and exceptions to routine performance in order to make senior managers aware of difficulties. Example: "The printer has been out of operation for two days, and it will be at least a week before a new one arrives."

2 *Suggestions for improvement.* These messages are ideas for improving task-related procedures to increase quality or efficiency. Example: "I think we should eliminate step 2 in the audit procedure because it takes a lot of time and produces no results."

3 *Performance reports.* These messages include periodic reports that inform management how individuals and departments are performing. Example: "We completed the audit report for Smith & Smith on schedule but are one week behind on the Jackson report."

4 *Grievances and disputes.* These messages are employee complaints and conflicts that travel up the hierarchy for a hearing and possible resolution. Example: "The manager of operations research cannot get the cooperation of the Lincoln plant for the study of machine utilization."

5 *Financial and accounting information.* These messages pertain to costs, accounts receivable, sales volume, anticipated profits, return on investment, and other matters of interest to senior managers. Example: "Costs are 2 percent over budget, but sales are 10 percent ahead of target, so the profit picture for the third quarter is excellent."

"Speak up, we're listening." Northrop Corporation values *upward communication*, especially in a changing political environment that means huge cuts in defense spending. Here, members of the B-2 bomber team speak out to management with suggestions for reducing B-2 production hours. Communications like this enabled Northrop to resolve a number of program issues and showed the ability of employees to contribute innovative ideas and solutions. Upward communication emphasizes the importance of all employees in Northrop's success.

Many organizations make a great effort to facilitate upward communication. Mechanisms include suggestion boxes, employee surveys, open-door policies, management information system reports, and face-to-face conversations between workers and executives.

William J. O'Brien, CEO of Hanover Insurance Company, points out: "The fundamental movement in business in the next 25 years will be in the dispersing of power, to give meaning and fulfillment to employees in a way that avoids chaos and disorder." Power sharing means inviting upward communication. At Pacific Gas & Electric, CEO Richard A. Clark keeps employee communication lines open with employee surveys, biannual video presentations, and monthly brown-bag lunches to hear questions and complaints.[27]

Despite these efforts, however, barriers to accurate upward communication exist. Managers may resist hearing about employee problems, or employees may not trust managers sufficiently to push information upward.[28] One of the most innovative programs ensuring that information gets to top managers without distortion was developed by Hyatt Hotels.

 HYATT HOTELS

Honest communication is so important that Hyatt Hotels developed unique ways to keep information flowing upward from employees. Myrna Hellerman, vice-president of human resources, developed a communication strategy that includes several programs:

1 *Confidential surveys* allow employees to comment freely and confidentially on any aspect of Hyatt.

2 *Employee forums* provide an annual opportunity for employees to drop by and talk to their general manager in the relaxed atmosphere of a hotel suite. Discussions can be about anything during this personal-level communication.

3 *Hyattalks* are monthly gab sessions between managers and a select group of employees, focusing on employee needs and methods of improving service.

4 *In-Touch Day* is the most innovative of the programs. In-Touch Day gives management an opportunity to spend time in the trenches—folding napkins, making pastry, cleaning tubs and toilets—to better understand both employees and customers. As top executives acquaint themselves with the daily routines and problems of bellhops, waiters, housekeepers, and chefs, they increase their own awareness of how management actions affect others.

Hellerman sees Hyatt's many communication efforts as a bonding experience between management and employees. These innovative upward-communication techniques put the responsibility for the company's success with lower-level employees, and managers act on what they hear.[29] ∎

HORIZONTAL COMMUNICATION.   Horizontal communication is the lateral or diagonal exchange of messages among peers or coworkers. It may occur within or across departments. The purpose of horizontal communication is not only to inform but also to request support and coordinate activities. Horizontal communication falls into one of three categories:

1 *Intradepartmental problem solving.* These messages take place between members of the same department and concern task accomplishment. Example: "Betty, can you help us figure out how to complete this medical expense report form?"

2 *Interdepartmental coordination.* Interdepartmental messages facilitate the accomplishment of joint projects or tasks. Example: "Bob, please contact marketing and production and arrange a meeting to discuss the specifications for the new subassembly. It looks like we may not be able to meet their requirements."

3 *Staff advice to line departments.* These messages often go from specialists in operations research, finance, or computer services to line managers seeking help in these areas. Example: "Let's go talk to the manufacturing supervisor about the problem he's having interpreting the computer reports."

Recall from Chapters 9 and 10 that many organizations build in horizontal communications in the form of task forces, committees, or even a matrix structure to encourage coordination. For example, Carol Taber, publisher of *Working Woman*, was bothered by the separation of departments at her magazine. She instituted frequent meetings among department heads and a monthly report to keep everyone informed and involved on a horizontal basis.[30]

horizontal communication
The lateral or diagonal exchange of messages among peers or coworkers.

Hewlett-Packard relies heavily on communication systems such as the in-house video teleconferencing facilities pictured here to meet the challenge of doing business on several continents. This *horizontal communication* lets employees worldwide reach mutual understanding about issues such as new product designs, research lab activities, engineering modifications, and strategic plans.

INFORMAL COMMUNICATION CHANNELS

informal communication channel

A communication channel that exists outside formally authorized channels without regard for the organization's hierarchy of authority.

Informal communication channels exist outside the formally authorized channels and do not adhere to the organization's hierarchy of authority. Informal communications coexist with formal communications but may skip hierarchical levels, cutting across vertical chains of command to connect virtually anyone in the organization. For example, Jim Treybig of Tandem Computer uses informal channels by letting any employee reach him through his computer terminal. Treybig also holds a Friday afternoon beer bust at each of Tandem's 132 offices worldwide. The idea is to create an informal communication channel for employees. Treybig says, "Over beer and popcorn, employees are more willing to talk openly." [31] An illustration of both formal and informal communications is given in Exhibit 16.6. Note how formal communications can be vertical or horizontal, depending on task assignments and coordination responsibilities.

Two types of informal channels used in many organizations are "management by wandering around" and the "grapevine."

management by wandering around (MBWA)

A communication technique in which managers interact directly with workers to exchange information.

MANAGEMENT BY WANDERING AROUND. The communication technique known as **management by wandering around (MBWA)** was made famous by the books *In Search of Excellence* and *A Passion for Excellence*.[32] These books describe executives who talk directly with employees to learn what is going on. MBWA works for managers at all levels. They mingle and develop positive relationships with employees, and learn directly from them about their department, division, or organization. For example, the president of ARCO had a habit of visiting a district field office. Rather than schedule a big strategic meeting with the district supervisor, he would come in unannounced and chat with the lowest-level employees. Andy Pearson of PepsiCo started his tours from the bottom up: He went directly to a junior assistant brand manager and asked, "What's up?" In any organization, both upward and downward

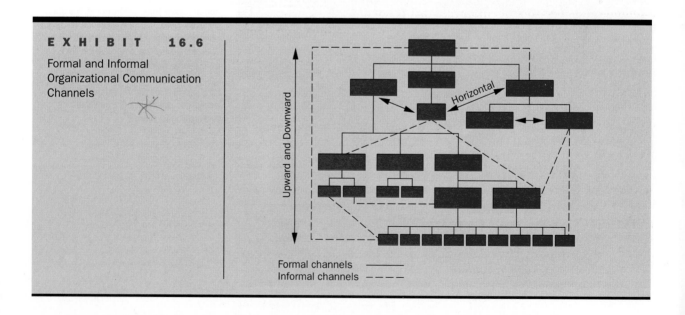

E X H I B I T   16.6

Formal and Informal Organizational Communication Channels

Upward and Downward

Horizontal

Formal channels ————
Informal channels − − − −

At Flowers Industries, Inc., a leader in the baked foods industry, Chairman Amos McMullian (left) encourages *information communication channels* to address the concerns of employees and the community. Flowers' employees are committed to a better society and seek involvement with government through the Chairman's Council for Better Government, a voluntary, non-profit organization. Council members study issues, review voting records of candidates, and vote. Employees also follow issues and voice opinions by contacting legislators. Over 1,500 Flowers employees participate in this unique program.

communication are enhanced with MBWA. Managers have a chance to describe key ideas and values to employees and in turn learn about the problems and issues confronting employees.

When managers fail to take advantage of MBWA, they become aloof and isolated from employees. For example, Peter Anderson, president of Ztel, Inc., a maker of television switching systems, preferred not to personally communicate with employees. He managed at arm's length. As one manager said, "I don't know how many times I asked Peter to come to the lab, but he stayed in his office. He wasn't that visible to the troops." This formal management style contributed to Ztel's troubles and eventual bankruptcy.[33]

THE GRAPEVINE. The **grapevine** is an informal, person-to-person communication network of employees that is not officially sanctioned by the organization.[34] The grapevine links employees in all directions, ranging from the president through middle management, support staff, and line employees. The grapevine will always exist in an organization, but it can become a dominant force when formal channels are closed. In such cases, the grapevine is actually a service because the information it provides helps makes sense of an unclear or uncertain situation. Employees use grapevine rumors to fill in information gaps and clarify management decisions. The grapevine tends to be more active during periods of change, excitement, anxiety, and sagging economic conditions. For example, when Jel, Inc., an auto supply firm, was under great pressure from Ford and GM to increase quality, rumors circulated on the shop floor about the company's possible demise. Management changes to improve quality—learning statistical process control, introducing a new compensation system, buying a fancy new screw machine from Germany—all started out as rumors, circulating days ahead of the actual announcements, and were generally accurate.[35]

Research suggests that a few people are primarily responsible for the grapevine's success. Exhibit 16.7 illustrates the two most typical

grapevine

An informal, person-to-person communication network of employees that is not officially sanctioned by the organization.

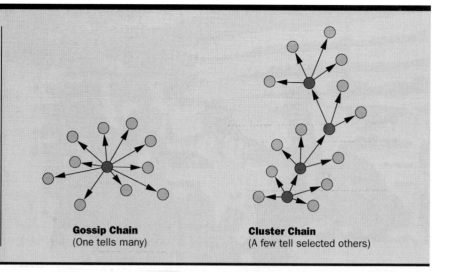

EXHIBIT 16.7

Two Grapevine Chains in Organizations

SOURCE: Based on Keith Davis and John W. Newstrom, *Human Behavior at Work: Organizational Behavior*, 7th ed. (New York: McGraw-Hill, 1985).

Gossip Chain
(One tells many)

Cluster Chain
(A few tell selected others)

grapevines.[36] In the *gossip chain*, a single individual conveys a piece of news to many other people. In a *cluster chain,* a few individuals each convey information to several others. Having only a few people conveying information may account for the accuracy of grapevines. If every person told one other person in sequence, distortions would be greater.

Surprising aspects of the grapevine are its accuracy and its relevance to the organization. About 80 percent of grapevine communications pertain to business-related topics rather than personal, vicious gossip. Moreover, from 70 to 90 percent of the details passed through a grapevine are accurate.[37] Many managers would like the grapevine to be destroyed because they consider its rumors to be untrue, malicious, and harmful to personnel. Typically this is not the case; however, managers should be aware that almost five of every six important messages are carried to some extent by the grapevine rather than through official channels. When official communication channels are closed, destructive rumors can occur.

● COMMUNICATING IN TEAMS

The importance of teamwork in organizations, discussed in more detail in Chapter 17, emphasizes the need for team communication. Team members work together to accomplish tasks, and the team's communication structure influences both team performance and employee satisfaction. Research into team communication has focused on two characteristics: the extent to which team communications are centralized and the nature of the team's task.[38] The relationship between these characteristics is illustrated in Exhibit 16.8. In a **centralized network,** team members must communicate through one individual to solve problems or make decisions. In a **decentralized network,** individuals can communicate freely with other team members. Members process information equally among themselves until all agree on a decision.[39]

centralized network

A team communication structure in which team members communicate through a single individual to solve problems or make decisions.

decentralized network

A team communication structure in which team members freely communicate with one another and arrive at decisions together.

In laboratory experiments, centralized communication networks achieved faster solutions for simple problems. Members could simply pass relevant information to a central person for a decision. Decentralized communications were slower for simple problems because information was passed among individuals until someone finally put the pieces together and solved the problem. However, for more complex problems, the decentralized communication network was faster. Because all necessary information was not restricted to one person, a pooling of information through widespread communications provided greater input into the decision. Similarly, the accuracy of problem solving was related to problem complexity. The centralized networks made fewer errors on simple problems but more errors on complex ones. Decentralized networks were less accurate for simple problems but more accurate for complex ones.[40]

The implication for organizations is as follows: In a highly competitive global environment, organizations use groups and teams to deal with complex problems. When team activities are complex and difficult, all members should share information in a decentralized structure to solve problems. Teams need a free flow of communication in all directions.[41] Members should be encouraged to discuss problems with one another, and a large percentage of employee time should be devoted to information processing. However, groups who perform routine tasks spend less time processing information, and thus communications can be centralized. Data can be channeled to a supervisor for decisions, freeing workers to spend a greater percentage of time on task activities.

● MANAGING ORGANIZATIONAL COMMUNICATION

Many of the ideas described in this chapter pertain to barriers to communication and how to overcome them. Barriers can be categorized as those that exist at the individual level and those that

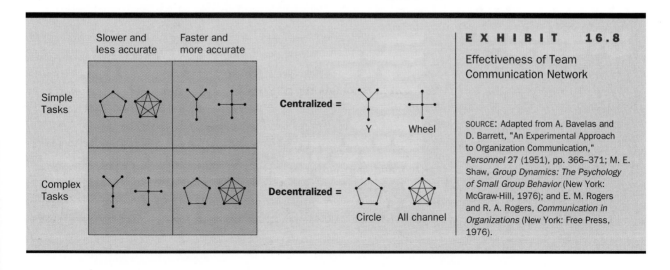

	Slower and less accurate	Faster and more accurate
Simple Tasks		
Complex Tasks		

Centralized = Y   Wheel

Decentralized = Circle   All channel

EXHIBIT   16.8

Effectiveness of Team Communication Network

SOURCE: Adapted from A. Bavelas and D. Barrett, "An Experimental Approach to Organization Communication," *Personnel* 27 (1951), pp. 366–371; M. E. Shaw, *Group Dynamics: The Psychology of Small Group Behavior* (New York: McGraw-Hill, 1976); and E. M. Rogers and R. A. Rogers, *Communication in Organizations* (New York: Free Press, 1976).

exist at the organizational level. First we will examine communication barriers; then we will look at techniques for overcoming them. These barriers and techniques are summarized in Exhibit 16.9.

BARRIERS TO COMMUNICATION

Barriers to communication can exist within the individual or as part of the organization.

INDIVIDUAL BARRIERS.   First, there are interpersonal barriers; these include problems with emotions and perceptions held by employees. For example, rigid perceptual labeling or categorizing of others prevents modification or alteration of opinions. If a person's mind is made up before the communication starts, communication will fail. Moreover, people with different backgrounds or knowledge may interpret a communication in different ways.

Second, selecting the wrong channel or medium for sending a communication can be a problem. For example, when a message is emotional, it is better to transmit it face-to-face rather than in writing. On the other hand, writing works best for routine messages but lacks the capacity for rapid feedback and multiple cues needed for difficult messages.

Third, semantics often causes communication problems. **Semantics** pertains to the meaning of words and the way they are used. A word such as "effectiveness" may mean achieving high production to a factory superintendent and employee satisfaction to a personnel staff specialist. Many common words have an average of 28 definitions; thus, communicators must take care to select the words that will accurately encode ideas.[42]

Fourth, sending inconsistent cues between verbal and nonverbal communications will confuse the receiver. If one's facial expression does not match one's words, the communication will contain noise and uncer-

semantics

The meaning of words and the way they are used.

E X H I B I T   16.9

Communication Barriers and Ways to Overcome Them

Barriers	How to Overcome
Individual	
Interpersonal dynamics	Active listening
Channels and media	Selection of appropriate channel
Semantics	Knowledge of other's perspective
Inconsistent cues	MBWA
Organizational	
Status and power differences	Climate of trust
Departmental needs and goals	Development and use of formal channels
Communication network unsuited to task	Changing organization or group structure to fit communication needs
Lack of formal channels	Encouragement of multiple channels, formal and informal

tainty. The tone of voice and body language should be consistent with the words, and actions should not contradict words.

ORGANIZATIONAL BARRIERS.   Organizational barriers pertain to factors for the organization as a whole. First is the problem of status and power differences. Low-power people may be reluctant to pass bad news up the hierarchy, thus giving the wrong impression to upper levels.[43] High-power people may not pay attention or may feel that low-status people have little to contribute.

Second, differences across departments in terms of needs and goals interfere with communications. Each department perceives problems in its own terms. The production department is concerned with production efficiency and may not fully understand the marketing department's need to get the product to the customer in a hurry.

Third, the communication flow may not fit the group's or organization's task. If a centralized communication structure is used for nonroutine tasks, there will not be enough information circulated to solve problems. The organization, department, or group is most efficient when the amount of communication flowing among employees fits the task.

Fourth, the absence of formal channels reduces communication effectiveness. Organizations must provide adequate upward, downward, and horizontal communication in the form of employee surveys, open-door policies, newsletters, memos, task forces, and liaison personnel. Without these formal channels, the organization cannot communicate as a whole.

OVERCOMING COMMUNICATION BARRIERS

Managers can design the organization so as to encourage positive, effective communication. Designing involves both individual skills and organizational actions.

INDIVIDUAL SKILLS.   Perhaps the most important individual skill is active listening. Active listening means asking questions, showing interest, and occasionally paraphrasing what the speaker has said to ensure that one is interpreting accurately. Active listening also means providing feedback to the sender to complete the communication loop.

Second, individuals should select the appropriate channel for the message. A complicated message should be sent through a rich channel, such as face-to-face discussion or telephone. Routine messages and data can be sent through memos, letters, or electronic mail, because there is little chance of misunderstanding.

Third, senders and receivers should make a special effort to understand each other's perspective. Managers can sensitize themselves to the information receiver so that they will be better able to target the message, detect bias, and clarify missed interpretations. By understanding others' perspectives, semantics can be clarified, perceptions understood, and objectivity maintained.

The fourth individual skill is management by wandering around. Managers must be willing to get out of the office and check communications with others. For example, John McDonnell of McDonnell

Stephen Frank, president and COO of Florida Power & Light Company, seeks to *overcome communication barriers* through a new program called "executive visits." The program is a series of meetings with small groups of FPL employees to obtain feedback about their jobs and their ideas for the direction of FPL. The initial meetings have proven so successful that the program is being expanded as part of a total communications program that also gives employees a better understanding of the issues facing the company.

Douglas always eats in the employee cafeteria when he visits far-flung facilities. Through direct observation and face-to-face meetings, managers develop an understanding of the organization and are able to communicate important ideas and values directly to others.

ORGANIZATIONAL ACTIONS.   Perhaps the most important thing managers can do for the organization is to create a climate of trust and openness. This will encourage people to communicate honestly with one another. Subordinates will feel free to transmit negative as well as positive messages without fear of retribution. Efforts to develop interpersonal skills among employees can be made to foster openness, honesty, and trust.

Second, managers should develop and use formal information channels in all directions. Scandinavian Design uses two newsletters to reach employees. GM's Packard Electric plant is designed to share all pertinent information—financial, future plans, quality, performance—with employees. Bank of America uses programs called Innovate and Idea Tap to get ideas and feedback from employees. Other techniques include direct mail, bulletin boards, and employee surveys.

Third, managers should encourage the use of multiple channels, including both formal and informal communications. Multiple communication channels include written directives, face-to-face discussions, MBWA, and the grapevine. For example, managers at GM's Packard Electric plant use multimedia, including a monthly newspaper, frequent meetings of employee teams, and an electronic news display in the cafeteria. Sending messages through multiple channels increases the likelihood that they will be properly received.

Fourth, the structure should fit communication needs. For example, Harrah's created the Communication Team as part of its structure at the

Casino/Holiday Inn in Las Vegas. The team includes one member from each department. It deals with urgent company problems and helps people think beyond the scope of their own departments to communicate with anyone and everyone to solve those problems. An organization can be designed to use teams, task forces, integrating managers, or a matrix structure as needed to facilitate the horizontal flow of information for coordination and problem solving. Structure should also reflect group information needs. When group tasks are difficult, a decentralized structure should be implemented to encourage discussion and participation.

SUMMARY AND MANAGEMENT SOLUTION

This chapter described several important points about communicating in organizations. Communication takes up 80 percent of a manager's time. Communication is a process of encoding an idea into a message, which is sent through a channel and decoded by a receiver. Communication among people can be affected by perceptions, communication channels, nonverbal communication, and listening skills.

At the organizational level, managers are concerned with managing formal communications in a downward, upward, and horizontal direction. Informal communications also are important, especially management by wandering around and the grapevine. Moreover, research shows that communication structures in groups and departments should reflect the underlying tasks.

Finally, several barriers to communication were described. These barriers can be overcome by active listening, selecting appropriate channels, engaging in MBWA, developing a climate of trust, using formal channels, and designing the correct structure to fit communication needs.

A remarkable example of overcoming barriers to communication occurred after Bernard Marcus and Arthur Blank opened the doors of the first Home Depot store, as described in the chapter opening Management Problem. They quickly realized the necessity of communicating their principles to employees, customers, and suppliers. They then developed what is regarded as state-of-the-art corporate communication. Listening was the key. The owners sought feedback at all levels. A favorite communication is the popular "Breakfast with Bernie and Arthur" television show for the company's 30,000 employees. The owners know that the special chemistry between employees and customers begins with a feeling of management trust toward employees. Tapping the talent and energy of employees requires open communication lines. Marcus and Blank still work on the sales floor periodically to listen to customers and understand both employee and customer needs. No one can argue with Home Depot's $5 billion formula for success. Sales are expected to reach a whopping $25 billion by the year 2000. It pays to LISTEN.[44]

DISCUSSION QUESTIONS

1. ATI Medical, Inc., has a "no-memo" policy. The 300 employees must interact directly for all communications. What impact do you think this policy would have on the organization?

2. Describe the elements of the communication process. Give an example of each part of the model as it exists in the classroom during communication between teacher and students.

3. How might perception influence communication accuracy? Is perception more important for ambiguous or unambiguous messages? Explain.

4. Should the grapevine be eliminated? How might managers control information that is processed through the grapevine?

5. What do you think are the major barriers to upward communication in organizations? Discuss.

6. What is the relationship between group communication and group task? For example, how should communications differ in a strategic planning group and a group of employees who stack shelves in a grocery store?

7. Some senior managers believe they should rely on written information and computer reports because these yield more accurate data than do face-to-face communications. Do you agree?

8. Why is management by wandering around considered effective communication? Consider channel richness and nonverbal communications in formulating your answer.

9. Is speaking accurately or listening actively the more important communication skill for managers? Discuss.

10. Assume that you have been asked to design a training program to help managers become better communicators. What would you include in the program?

MANAGEMENT IN PRACTICE: EXPERIENTIAL EXERCISE

● **LISTENING SELF-INVENTORY**

Instructions: Go through the following questions, checking yes or no next to each question. Mark it as truthfully as you can in the light of your behavior in the last few meetings or gatherings you attended.

	Yes	No
1. I frequently attempt to listen to several conversations at the same time.		✓
2. I like people to give me only the facts, then let me make my own interpretation.	✓	

	Yes	No
3. I sometimes pretend to pay attention to people.	✓	
4. I consider myself a good judge of nonverbal communications.	✓	
5. I usually know what another person is going to say before he or she says it.		✓
6. I usually end conversations that don't interest me by diverting my attention from the speaker.		✓
7. I frequently nod, frown, or whatever to let the speaker know how I feel about what he or she is saying.	✓	

	Yes	No
8. I usually respond immediately when someone has finished talking.		✓
9. I evaluate what is being said while it is being said.		✓
10. I usually formulate a response while the other person is still talking.		✓
11. The speaker's "delivery" style frequently keeps me from listening to content.	✓	
12. I usually ask people to clarify what they have said rather than guess at the meaning.	✓	
13. I make a concerted effort to understand other people's points of view.	✓	
14. I frequently hear what I expect to hear rather than what is said.		✓
15. Most people feel that I have understood their point of view when we disagree.	✓	

The correct answers according to communication theory are as follows: No for questions 1, 2, 3, 5, 6, 7, 8, 9, 10, 11, 14. Yes for questions 4, 12, 13, 15. If you missed only one or two questions, you strongly approve of your own listening habits, and you are on the right track to becoming an effective listener in your role as manager. If you missed three or four questions, you have uncovered some doubts about your listening effectiveness, and your knowledge of how to listen has some gaps. If you missed five or more questions, you probably are not satisfied with the way you listen, and your friends and coworkers may not feel you are a good listener either. Work on improving your active listening skills.

SOURCE: Ethel C. Glenn and Elliott A. Pood, "Listening Self-Inventory." Reprinted by permission of the publisher from *Supervisory Management* (January 1989), 12–15, © 1989. American Management Association, New York. All rights reserved.

CASES FOR ANALYSIS

ATLANTA TOOL AND DIE, INC.

The president of Atlanta Tool and Die, Inc., Rich Langston, wanted to facilitate upward communication. He believed an open-door policy was a good place to start. He announced that his own door was open to all employees and encouraged senior managers to do the same. He felt this would give him a way to get early warning signals that would not be filtered or redirected through the formal chain of command. Langston found that many employees who used the open-door policy had been with the company for years and were comfortable talking to the president. Sometimes messages came through about inadequate policies and procedures. Langston would raise these issues and explain any changes at the next senior managers' meeting.

The most difficult complaints to handle were those from people who were not getting along with their bosses. One employee, Leroy, complained bitterly that his manager had overcommitted the department and put everyone under too much pressure. Leroy argued that long hours and low morale were major problems. But he would not allow Rich Langston to bring the manager into the discussion nor to seek out other employees to confirm the complaint. Although Langston suspected that Leroy might be right, he could not let the matter sit and blurted out, "Have you considered leaving the company?" This made Leroy realize that a meeting with his immediate boss was unavoidable.

Before the three-party meeting, Langston contacted Leroy's manager and explained what was going on. He insisted that the manager come to the meeting willing to listen and without hostility toward Leroy. During the meeting, Leroy's manager listened actively and displayed no ill will. He learned the problem from Leroy's perspective and realized he was over his head in his new job. After the meeting, the manager said he was relieved. He had been promoted into the job from a technical position just a few months earlier and had no management or planning experience. He welcomed Rich Langston's offer to help him do a better job of planning.

● **QUESTIONS**

1. What techniques increased Rich Langston's communication effectiveness? Discuss.
2. Do you think that an open-door policy was the right way to improve upward communications? What other techniques would you suggest?
3. What problems do you think an open-door policy creates? Do you think many employees are reluctant to use it? Why?

SOURCE: Based on Everett T. Suters, "Hazards of an Open-Door Policy," *INC.*, January 1987, 99–102.

SENTRY MACHINE TOOLS, INC.

Michael Wesley had been with Sentry Machine Tools for 22 years, the last five working as a senior planner in the corporate strategy department. Over the years, he had dealt with every aspect of Sentry, from product development to manufacturing to overseas operations.

One of his friends in employee relations, April Faulk, called and asked Mike to speak at a new middle management training program on the current and future company strategy. After hearing a bit more about the program, Mike decided it would be a productive use of his time to clarify the company's position to those who were making important decisions at the plant level. Speaking to middle managers was also consistent with the company's stated policy of employee empowerment and pushing information down the hierarchy.

In planning his talk, Mike ran into a dilemma. Exactly how much information should he release? Middle managers are company employees, but information concerning sensitive areas such as product development and possible corporate acquisitions is tightly controlled to keep it from getting into the wrong hands. Mike knew the managers also would be interested in the rumors of a failed acquisition attempt, especially the effect that this would have on their profit-sharing checks. However, union contract negotiations were to begin in a few months, and Mike believed management wanted to keep the profit-sharing information quiet.

Mike sent a memo to his boss, with a copy to the company president, indicating that he would be talking to middle management trainees and that he wanted to share as much information as possible, in line with the company policy of information sharing. Mike understood the reasons behind the corporate strategy department's unwillingness to share certain data, but he still felt pressure to be open

with middle management. He believed openness was symbolically important and that middle managers who had been with the company 10 to 20 years could be trusted. For example, information about corporate strategy and finances would help the managers understand what sometimes seemed like unreasonable demands or changes in policy from top management. The last thing Mike wanted to say to a question was, "That's an important question and relevant to your job, but I'm not supposed to tell you the answer."

Mike did not hear back from his memo about sharing information, so he assumed it was okay. At the training session, he talked about the failed acquisition attempt and other planning matters. He also answered questions bluntly, and he let the managers know in a subtle manner that the information he provided was sensitive and he was putting himself at risk for the disclosures. The managers were grateful, giving him a long round of applause at the end of his talk. April thanked him profusely for his honesty, and after the session middle managers told him they valued the new policy of corporate openness with information.

● **QUESTIONS**

1. What mistakes did Mike Wesley make with respect to his communications?
2. Do you think it was correct for Mike to decide on his own to share sensitive information? Do you agree that corporate openness to stifle rumors and trust employees represents a higher purpose than the reasons for keeping information secret?
3. What would you do in this case if you were Mike's boss? Discuss.

REFERENCES

1. Roger Thompson, "There's No Place Like Home Depot," *Nation's Business,* February 1992, 30–33.
2. "Hands On: Tell Us about It," *INC.,* June 1990, 101, and Thomas F. O'Boyle and Carol Hymowitz, "More Corporate Chiefs Seek Direct Contact with Staff, Customers," *The Wall Street Journal,* February 27, 1985, 1, 12.
3. Elizabeth B. Drew, "Profile: Robert Strauss," *The New Yorker,* May 7, 1979, 55–70.
4. Henry Mintzberg, *The Nature of Managerial Work* (New York: Harper & Row, 1973).

5. Fred Luthans and Janet K. Larsen, "How Managers Really Communicate," *Human Relations* 39 (1986), 161–178, and Larry E. Penley and Brian Hawkins, "Studying Interpersonal Communication in Organizations: A Leadership Application," *Academy of Management Journal* 28 (1985), 309–326.

6. D. K. Berlo, *The Process of Communication* (New York: Holt, Rinehart and Winston, 1960), 24.

7. Nelson W. Aldrich, Jr., "Lines of Communication," *INC.*, June 1986, 140–144.

8. Bruce K. Blaylock, "Cognitive Style and the Usefulness of Information," *Decision Sciences* 15 (Winter 1984), 74–91.

9. Richard L. Daft and Richard M. Steers, *Organizations: A Micro/Macro Approach* (Glenview, Ill.: Scott, Foresman, 1986).

10. James R. Wilcox, Ethel M. Wilcox, and Karen M. Cowan, "Communicating Creatively in Conflict Situations," *Management Solutions* (October 1986), 18–24.

11. Robert H. Lengel and Richard L. Daft, "The Selection of Communication Media as an Executive Skill," *Academy of Management Executive* 2 (August 1988), 225–232, and Richard L. Daft and Robert H. Lengel, "Organizational Information Requirements, Media Richness and Structural Design," *Managerial Science* 32 (May 1986), 554–572.

12. Ford S. Worthy, "How CEOs Manage Their Time," *Fortune,* January 18, 1988, 88–97.

13. Richard L. Daft, Robert H. Lengel, and Linda Klebe Trevino, "Message Equivocality, Media Selection and Manager Performance: Implication for Information Systems," *MIS Quarterly* 11 (1987), 355–368.

14. Harold Geneen with Alvin Moscow, *Managing* (New York: Doubleday, 1984), 46–47.

15. I. Thomas Sheppard, "Silent Signals," *Supervisory Management* (March 1986), 31–33.

16. Albert Mehrabian, *Silent Messages* (Belmont, Calif.: Wadsworth, 1971), and Albert Mehrabian, "Communicating without Words," *Psychology Today,* September 1968, 53–55.

17. Sheppard, "Silent Signals."

18. Arthur H. Bell, *The Complete Manager's Guide to Interviewing* (Homewood, Ill.: Richard D. Irwin, 1989).

19. C. Glenn Pearce, "Doing Something about Your Listening Ability," *Supervisory Management* (March 1989), 29–34, and Tom Peters, "Learning to Listen," *Hyatt Magazine* (Spring 1988), 16–21.

20. Gerald M. Goldhaber, *Organizational Communication,* 4th ed. (Dubuque, Iowa: Wm. C. Brown, 1980), 189.

21. Peters, "Learning to Listen."

22. Daft and Steers, *Organizations,* and Daniel Katz and Robert Kahn, *The Social Psychology of Organizations,* 2d ed. (New York: Wiley, 1978).

23. Edward O. Welles, "Bad News," *INC.*, April 1991, 45–49.

24. Claudia H. Deutsch, "Managing: The Multimedia Benefits Kit," *The New York Times,* October 14, 1990, Sec. 3, 25.

25. J. G. Miller, "Living Systems: The Organization," *Behavioral Science* 17 (1972), 69.

26. Michael J. Glauser, "Upward Information Flow in Organizations: Review and Conceptual Analysis," *Human Relations* 37 (1984), 613–643, and

"Upward/Downward Communication: Critical Information Channels," *Small Business Report* (October 1985), 85–88.

27. Anne B. Fisher, "CEO's Think That Morale Is Dandy," *Fortune*, November 18, 1991, 83–84.

28. Mary P. Rowe and Michael Baker, "Are You Hearing Enough Employee Concerns?" *Harvard Business Review* 62 (May–June 1984), 127–135; W. H. Read, "Upward Communication in Industrial Hierarchies," *Human Relations* 15 (February 1962), 3–15; and Daft and Steers, *Organizations*.

29. Myrna Hellerman, "How I Did It: Giving Executives a Field Day," *Working Woman*, March 1992, 37–40.

30. Jacqueline Kaufman, "Carol Taber, Working Woman," *Management Review* (October 1986), 60–61.

31. O'Boyle and Hymowitz, "More Corporate Chiefs Seek Direct Contact with Staff, Customers."

32. Thomas J. Peters and Robert H. Waterman, *In Search of Excellence* (New York: Harper & Row, 1982); and Tom Peters and Nancy Austin, *A Passion for Excellence: The Leadership Difference* (New York: Random House, 1985).

33. Lois Therrien, "How Ztel Went from Riches to Rags," *Business Week*, June 17, 1985, 97–100.

34. Keith Davis and John W. Newstrom, *Human Behavior at Work: Organizational Behavior*, 7th ed. (New York: McGraw-Hill, 1985).

35. Joshua Hyatt, "The Last Shift," *INC.*, February 1989, 74–80.

36. Goldhaber, *Organizational Communication*; and Philip V. Louis, *Organizational Communication*, 3d ed. (New York: Wiley, 1987).

37. Donald B. Simmons, "The Nature of the Organizational Grapevine," *Supervisory Management* (November 1985), 39–42, and Davis and Newstrom, *Human Behavior*.

38. E. M. Rogers and R. A. Rogers, *Communication in Organizations* (New York: Free Press, 1976), and A. Bavelas and D. Barrett, "An Experimental Approach to Organization Communication," *Personnel* 27 (1951), 366–371.

39. This discussion is based on Daft and Steers, *Organizations*.

40. Bavelas and Barrett, "An Experimental Approach"; and M. E. Shaw, *Group Dynamics: The Psychology of Small Group Behavior* (New York: McGraw-Hill, 1976).

41. Richard L. Daft and Norman B. Macintosh, "A Tentative Exploration into the Amount and Equivocality of Information Processing in Organizational Work Units," *Administrative Science Quarterly* 26 (1981), 207–224.

42. James A. F. Stoner and R. Edward Freeman, *Management*, 4th ed. (Englewood Cliffs, N.J.: Prentice-Hall, 1989).

43. Janet Fulk and Sirish Mani, "Distortion of Communication in Hierarchical Relationships," in *Communication Yearbook*, vol. 9, ed. M. L. McLaughlin (Beverly Hills, Calif.: Sage, 1986), 483–510.

44. Thompson, "There's No Place Like Home Depot."

EURO DISNEY

From the first announcement in March 1987, the Euro Disneyland theme park built outside Paris was either an eagerly anticipated milestone or a hideous affront to French culture. It has been a roller coaster ride for Walt Disney Company officials, too.

The 2,000-acre mega-project was beset with expected weather and construction delays. In addition, the French press charged that local subcontractors were largely pushed aside because the Americans doubted their ability to meet specifications. Some that did work said they were not paid. CGT, the largest trade union in the country, complained often about working conditions and bristled at dress codes. Disney faced worker allegations that as many as 60 people had been killed on the project since 1988 but responded that only two workers had lost their lives and that accident rates were half the national average.

With labor in a mild uproar and Disney well into a budget that exceeded $4 billion, intellectuals of every stripe weighed in with scathing, sometimes even violent opinions of Euro Disney. Outspoken criticism ranged from dislike of American pop culture to accusations that the French government was too conciliatory to Disney, making cheap land available on favorable terms and agreeing to finance rail service to a special terminal adjacent to the park.

Despite a well-known reputation for intransigence, Disney officials reacted to the discord and sought to compromise without deviating from the Disney formula. Sleeping Beauty's Castle is known as Le Chateau de la Belle au Bois Dormant, and Mickey, Minnie, and Donald Duck all have French accents. Disney agreed that English and French should be the "official" languages at the park but vetoed the idea that French names be put on the attractions.

In deference to the sophisticated French palate, Disney officials upgraded food quality, but stood firm on their worldwide company policy of no alcohol in Disney parks.

Over four years, it is estimated that the Disney corporation and sponsors poured $220 million into various promotions prior to the two-hour, star-studded opening day ceremonies. However, the actual opening of the park was not without incident. Citizens from the nearby village of Meaux staged a demonstration against fireworks noise. A communist-led transport union strike protesting the increased rail volume shut down the line that connects Paris 20 miles to the west. And in an apparent effort to black out the park, two bombs damaged electric high-line towers, but there was no disruption of service.

In the end it appeared curiosity won out. Despite surrounding adversities, an excited, multilingual throng began gathering outside the park's 95 ticket booths well before dawn. Eisner awarded the traditional "lifetime passport" to the first family in line as doves flew, trumpets blared, and a chorus of children warbled "It's a Small World" in several languages.

Since the opening, operations at the park have continuously evolved as the needs and desires of European patrons are communicated. Almost 40 percent of the 16,000-member "cast" are from countries other than France. Despite the much publicized "borderless" Europe, very few companies have attracted personnel from across national boundaries the way Disney has. "We wanted to be able to greet them in their own language," Eisner said.

Weather realities have also led to alterations at Euro Disney. Severe wet winters in northern France led to a decline in visitors, so the company responded by adjusting admission prices during cold months. The park streamlined entry procedures to cope with the fact that only about 50 percent of Europeans carry credit cards. It introduced cut-rate evening tickets. Euro Disney now also features special seasonal attractions such as the German Oktoberfest, Scandinavia's St. Lucia's Day, French Bastille Day, and the Netherlands' celebration of Queen Beatrix's birthday.

Disney marketing specialists discovered that most visitors wanted authentic American entertainment. Cheap, cheerful trinkets, Mickey Mouse hats, Minnie Mouse mugs, and helium balloons pushed the more expensive merchandise off the shelves. Europeans also wanted cheaper meals, especially for children, and easier access to take-out food.

In April 1993, Euro Disney S.C.A. Chairman Robert Fitzpatrick stepped aside and was replaced by Frenchman Philippe Bourguignon. It was hoped the replacement of Fitzpatrick with a European manager would be of some public relations benefit, and might boost attendance by Parisians, who have generally stayed away. Bourguignon maintains that after the rocky start Disney now has a much better picture of what its customers actually want.

● **QUESTIONS**

1. Discuss the organizational aspects of a U.S. Disney theme park that were useful in the planning and development of Euro Disney, and those that proved to be a hindrance.

2. How did structural aspects of the park have to be augmented for the particular market environment in which Euro Disney was located?

3. Did Disney react appropriately to nationalistic sentiments of the French? What early steps might have allayed fears of "cultural imperialism"?

4. Discuss the pluses and minuses of employee recruitment for the park.

5. Evaluate Disney officials' reaction to consumer input. Could consumer preferences have been better anticipated?

TEAMWORK IN ORGANIZATIONS ⬤17 C H A P T E R

Tom Huber, president of Hearing Technology, Inc., founded his hearing-aid company to provide a flexible response to dealers. His six employees could provide a rapid three-day response to dealers for custom hearing aids. The sales, production, and credit people had the right attitude to make things happen. But when the company quickly grew to 80 employees, response times for orders stretched to eight days, enough to cause dealers to try other manufacturers. Moreover, the dealers complained about the sluggish credit department, its poor coordination with production and sales, and the slowness

with which suggestions were implemented. Huber tried to refocus everyone's efforts by one-on-one sessions and speeches, but sluggishness remained. Huber started to wonder if his company, at 80 employees, had grown so inflexible and unresponsive that it could not be competitive.[1] ■ What would you recommend to Tom Huber to recapture flexibility and responsiveness in his growing company? How might the formation of teams help solve this problem?

The problems facing a small business like Hearing Technology also confront large companies. How can they be more flexible and responsive in an increasingly competitive global environment? A quiet revolution is taking place in corporate America as more companies try using teams as a solution. The notion of teamwork is changing the look of organizations. Teams are replacing individuals as the basic building block of organizations. The significance of teamwork is reflected by the results of a *Wall Street Journal* survey of 200 Fortune 500 companies that found that teamwork was the most frequent topic to be taught in company training programs.[2] In an article called "The Team as Hero," the authors argue that

> If we are to compete in today's world, we must begin to celebrate collective entrepreneurship, endeavors in which the whole of the effort is greater than the sum of individual contributions. We need to honor our teams more, our aggressive leaders and maverick geniuses less.[3]

Teams are popping up in the most unexpected places. At AT&T, teams rather than individuals are used to create new telephones. Volvo uses teams of hourly workers to assemble a complete car, abandoning the assembly line. Hecla Mining Company uses teams for company goal setting; a major telecommunications company uses teams of salespeople to

Teams are emerging as a *powerful management tool* and are popping up in the most unexpected places. The Zoological Society of San Diego is using a new team concept to remodel animal displays according to bioclimatic zones. Under the new system, team members from various departments join forces to create and manage a display area, such as Gorilla Tropics or Tiger River. Team members cross-train in each other's skill areas. A horticulturist may learn fund-raising techniques or acquire skill in handling mammals or birds. The new team concept replaces 50 functional departments and focuses group attention on quality and goal achievement.

deal with big customers with complex purchasing requirements; and Lassiter Middle School in Jefferson County, Kentucky, uses teams of teachers to prepare daily schedules and handle student discipline problems. Multinational corporations are now using international teams composed of managers from different countries. Ford uses teams to spot quality problems and improve efficiency, and other manufacturers use teams to master sophisticated new production technologies.[4] And as we saw in Chapter 8, teams are often used to make important decisions, and many organizations are now run by top management teams under the title of Office of the CEO.

As we will see in this chapter, teams have emerged as a powerful management tool, because they involve and empower employees. Teams can cut across organizations in unusual ways. Hence workers are more satisfied, and higher productivity and product quality typically result. Moreover, managers discover a more flexible organization in which workers are not stuck in narrow jobs.

This chapter focuses on teams and their new applications within organizations. We will define various types of teams, explore their stages of development, and examine such characteristics as size, cohesiveness, and norms. We will discuss how individuals can make contributions to teams and review the benefits and costs associated with teamwork. Teams are an important aspect of organizational life, and the ability to manage them is an important component of manager and organization success.

● TEAMS AT WORK

In this section, we will first define teams and then discuss a model of team effectiveness that summarizes the important concepts.

WHAT IS A TEAM?

A **team** is a unit of two or more people who interact and coordinate their work to accomplish a specific objective.[5] This definition has three components. First, two or more people are required. Teams can be quite large, running to as many as 75 people, although most have fewer than 15 people. Second, people in a team have regular interaction. People who do not interact, such as when standing in line at a lunch counter or riding in an elevator, do not compose a team. Third, people in a team share a performance objective, whether it be to design a new type of hand calculator or write a textbook. Students often are assigned to teams to do classwork assignments, in which case the purpose is to perform the assignment and receive an acceptable grade. A "team" is similar to what is usually called a "group" in organizations, but "team" has become the popular word in the business community. The team concept implies a greater sense of mission and contest, although the words can be used interchangeably.

team

A unit of two or more people who interact and coordinate their work to accomplish a specific objective.

MODEL OF WORK TEAM EFFECTIVENESS

Some of the factors associated with team effectiveness are illustrated in Exhibit 17.1. Work team effectiveness is based on two outcomes—productive output and personal satisfaction.[6] *Satisfaction* pertains to the team's ability to meet the personal needs of its members and hence maintain their membership and commitment. *Productive output* pertains to the quality and quantity of task outputs as defined by team goals.

The factors that influence team effectiveness begin with the organizational context.[7] The organizational context in which the group operates is described in other chapters and includes such factors as structure, strategy, environment, culture, and reward systems. Within that context, managers define teams. Important team characteristics are the type of team, the team structure, and team composition. Managers must decide when to create permanent teams within the formal structure and when to use a temporary task team. Team size and roles also are important. Managers must also consider whether a team is the best way to do a task. If costs outweigh benefits, managers may wish to assign an individual employee to the task.

These team characteristics influence processes internal to the team, which in turn affect output and satisfaction. Leaders must understand and manage stages of development, cohesiveness, norms, and conflict in order to establish an effective team. These processes are influenced by team and organizational characteristics and by the ability of members and leaders to direct these processes in a positive manner.

The model of team performance in Exhibit 17.1 is the basis for this chapter. In the following sections, we will examine types of organizational teams, team structure, internal processes, and team benefits and costs.

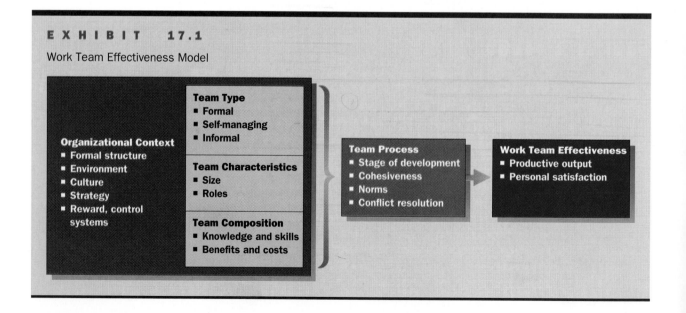

EXHIBIT 17.1

Work Team Effectiveness Model

● TYPES OF TEAMS

Many types of teams can exist within organizations. The easiest way to classify teams is in terms of those created as part of the organization's formal structure and those created to increase employee participation.

FORMAL TEAMS

Formal teams are created by the organization as part of the formal organization structure. Two common types of formal teams are vertical and horizontal, which typically represent vertical and horizontal structural relationships, as described in Chapters 9 and 10. These two types of teams are illustrated in Exhibit 17.2 A third type of formal team is the special-purpose team.

VERTICAL TEAM. A **vertical team** is composed of a manager and his or her subordinates in the formal chain of command. Sometimes called a *functional team* or a *command team*, the vertical team may in some cases include three or four levels of hierarchy within a functional department. Typically, the vertical team includes a single department in an organization. The third-shift nursing team on the second floor of St. Luke's Hospital is a vertical team that includes nurses and a supervisor. A financial analysis department, a quality control department, an accounting department, and a human resource department are all command teams. Each

formal team

A team created by the organization as part of the formal organization structure.

vertical team

A formal team composed of a manager and his or her subordinates in the organization's formal chain of command.

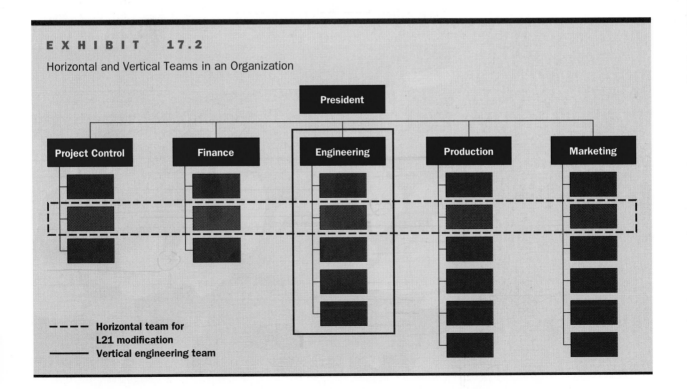

EXHIBIT 17.2

Horizontal and Vertical Teams in an Organization

- – – – Horizontal team for L21 modification
- ——— Vertical engineering team

is created by the organization to attain specific goals through members' joint activities and interactions.

HORIZONTAL TEAM.   A **horizontal team** is composed of employees from about the same hierarchical level but from different areas of expertise.[8] A horizontal team is drawn from several departments, is given a specific task, and may be disbanded after the task is completed. The two most common types of horizontal teams are task forces and committees.

As described in Chapter 10, a *task force* is a group of employees from different departments formed to deal with a specific activity and existing only until the task is completed. Sometimes called a *cross-functional team*, the task force might be used to create a new product in a manufacturing organization or a new history curriculum in a university. Several departments are involved and many views have to be considered, so these tasks are best served with a horizontal team. IBM used a large task force to develop the System 360. Contact among team members was intense, and principal players met every day.

A **committee** is generally long-lived and may be a permanent part of the organization's structure. Membership on a committee is usually decided by a person's title or position rather than by personal expertise. A committee often needs official representation, compared with selection for a task force, which is based on personal qualifications for solving a problem. Committees typically are formed to deal with tasks that recur regularly. For example, a grievance committee handles employee grievances; an advisory committee makes recommendations in the areas of employee compensation and work practices; a worker-management committee may be concerned with work rules, job design changes, and suggestions for work improvement.[9]

horizontal team

A formal team composed of employees from about the same hierarchical level but from different areas of expertise.

committee

A long-lasting, sometimes permanent team in the organization structure created to deal with tasks that recur regularly.

JWP is a worldwide leader in mechanical and electrical construction and maintenance services. JWP's Productivity Task Force, shown here, is a *horizontal team* composed of management and labor and focuses on finding methods for increased productivity and efficiency through reduction of downtime. This task force developed an employee training seminar that teaches modern efficiency methods and adapts them to specific jobs and areas of expertise.

As part of the horizontal structure of the organization, task forces and committees offer several advantages: (1) They allow organization members to exchange information; (2) they generate suggestions for coordinating the organizational units that are represented; (3) they develop new ideas and solutions for existing organizational problems; and (4) they assist in the development of new organizational practices and policies.

SPECIAL PURPOSE TEAM. Special-purpose teams are created outside the formal organization structure to undertake a project of special importance or creativity. McDonald's created a special team to create the Chicken McNugget. E. J. (Bud) Sweeney was asked to head up a team to bring bits of batter-covered chicken to the marketplace. The McNugget team needed breathing room and was separated from the formal corporate structure to give it the autonomy to perform successfully. A special-purpose team is still part of the formal organization and has its own reporting structure, but members perceive themselves as a separate entity.[10]

The formal teams described above must be skillfully managed to accomplish their purpose. One important skill, knowing how to run a team meeting, is described in the Manager's Shoptalk box.

SELF-MANAGING TEAMS

Employee involvement through teams is designed to increase the participation of lower-level workers in decision making and the conduct of their jobs, with the goal of improving performance. Employee involvement represents a revolution in business prompted by the success of teamwork in Japanese companies. Hundreds of companies, large and small, are jumping aboard the bandwagon, including Boeing, Caterpillar, LTV Steel, Cummins Engine, and Tektronix. Employee involvement started out simply with techniques such as information sharing with employees or asking employees for suggestions about improving the work. Gradually, companies moved toward greater autonomy for employees, which led first to problem-solving teams and then to self-managing teams.[11]

Problem-solving teams typically consist of 5 to 12 hourly employees from the same department who voluntarily meet two hours a week to discuss ways of improving quality, efficiency, and the work environment. Recommendations are proposed to management for approval. Problem-solving teams are usually the first step in a company's move toward greater employee participation. The most widely known application is quality circles, initiated by the Japanese, in which employees focus on ways to improve quality in the production process. USX has adopted this approach in several of its steel mills, recognizing that quality takes a team effort. Under the title All Product Excellence program (APEX), USX has set up 40 APEX teams of up to 12 employees at its plant in West Mifflin, Pennsylvania. These teams meet several times a month to solve quality problems. The APEX teams have since spread to mills in Indiana, Ohio, and California.[12]

special-purpose team

A team created outside the formal organization to undertake a project of special importance or creativity.

problem-solving team

Typically 5 to 12 hourly employees from the same department who meet to discuss ways of improving quality, efficiency, and the work environment.

Carolina Telephone & Telegraph is an example of a company using *problem-solving teams*. The company's POW (People Organizing Work) team investigated the feasibility of recycling corrugated cardboard boxes. The team conducted surveys to determine the number of boxes received, reused, or discarded. Team members then prepared a cause-and-effect analysis and cost-benefit charts and presented recommendations to management that included a cardboard "fashion show." The team's hard work and unique presentation sold management, and CT&T implemented the recycling plan.

HOW TO RUN A GREAT MEETING

Many executives believe that meetings are a waste of time. Busy executives may spend up to 70 percent of their time in meetings at which participants doodle, drink coffee, and think about what they could be doing back in their offices.

Meetings need not be unproductive. Most meetings are called to process important information or to solve a problem. The key to success is what the chairperson does. Most of the chairperson's contributions are made before the meeting begins. He or she should make sure discussion flows freely and follow up the meeting with agreed-upon actions. The success of a meeting depends on what is done in advance of, during, and after it.

Prepare in Advance. Advance preparation is the single most important tool for running an efficient, productive meeting. Advance preparation should include the following:

1. Define the objective. Is the objective to communicate critical information? To discuss a difficult problem? To reach a final decision? If the purpose of the meeting is to "discuss the reduction of the 1994 research and development budget," then say so explicitly in the memo sent out to members.

2. Circulate background papers. Any reading materials relevant to the discussion should be given to each member in advance. These can be circulated with the agenda or with the minutes of the previous meeting. Members as well as the chairperson must be prepared, so make sure members know their assignments and have background materials.

3. Prepare an agenda. The agenda is a simple list of the topics to be discussed. It is important because it keeps the meeting on track. The agenda provides order and logic and gives the chairperson a means of control during the meeting if the discussion starts to wander.

4. Issue invitations selectively. If the group gets too big, the meeting will not be productive. If members with little to learn or contribute are invited, they will be bored. If everyone is expected to participate, membership between four and seven is ideal. Twelve is the outside limit; above 12, many people will just sit and listen.

5. Set a time limit. A formal meeting should have a specified amount of time. The ending time should be announced in advance, and the agenda should require the meeting to move along at a reasonable pace. Unexpected issues can be handled if they will take little time; otherwise, they should be postponed until another meeting.

During the Meeting. If the chairperson is prepared in advance, the meeting will go smoothly. Moreover, certain techniques will bring out the

---

self-managing team

A team consisting of 5 to 20 multiskilled workers who rotate jobs to produce an entire product or service, often supervised by an elected member.

As a company matures, problem-solving teams can gradually evolve into self-managing teams, which represent a fundamental change in how employee work is organized. **Self-managing teams** consist of 5 to 20 multiskilled workers who rotate jobs and produce an entire product or service. Self-managing teams are permanent teams that typically include the following elements:

- The team includes employees with several skills and functions, and the combined skills are sufficient to perform a major organizational task. A team may include members from the foundry, machining, grinding, fabrication, and sales departments, with each member cross-trained to perform one another's jobs. The team eliminates barriers between departments, enabling excellent coordination to produce a product or service.

best in people and make the meeting even more productive:

6. *Start on time.* This sounds obvious—but do not keep busy people waiting. Some companies have a norm of waiting five minutes for everyone to arrive and then beginning the meeting even if some people are absent. Starting on time also has symbolic value, because it tells people that the topic is important.

7. *State the purpose.* The chairperson should start the meeting by stating the explicit purpose and clarifying what should be accomplished by the time the meeting is over. Members should already know the purpose, but this restatement helps refocus everyone's attention on the matter at hand.

8. *Encourage participation.* Good meetings contain lots of discussion. If the chairperson merely wants to present one-way information to members, he or she should send a memo. A few subtle techniques go a long way toward increasing participation:

a. *Draw out the silent.* This means saying "Bob, what do you think of Nancy's idea?"

b. *Control the talkative.* Some people overdo it and dominate the discussion. The chairperson's job is to redirect the discussion toward other people. This is more effectively done by drawing other people into the discussion than by trying to quiet the talkative people.

c. *Encourage the clash of ideas.* A good meeting is not a series of dialogues but a cross-current of discussion and debate. The chairperson guides, mediates, stimulates, and summarizes this discussion. Many effective chairpeople refuse to participate in the debate, preferring to orchestrate it instead.

d. *Call on the most senior people last.* Sometimes junior people are reluctant to disagree with senior people, so it is best to get the junior people's ideas on the table first. This will provide wider views and ideas.

e. *Give credit.* Make sure that people who suggest ideas get the credit, because people often make someone else's ideas their own. Giving due credit encourages continued participation.

f. *Listen.* The chairperson should not preach or engage in one-on-one dialogue with group members. The point is to listen and to facilitate discussion. If the chairperson really listens, he or she will be able to lead the meeting to a timely conclusion and summarize what has been accomplished.

After the meeting. The actions following the meeting are designed to summarize and implement agreed-upon points. Postmeeting activities are set in motion by a call to action.

9. *End with a call to action.* The last item of the meeting's agenda is to summarize the main points and make sure everyone understands his or her assignments. Deadlines should be prescribed. The chairperson should also commit to sending out minutes, organizing the next meeting, and mailing other materials that participants may need.

10. *Follow-up.* Mail minutes of the meeting to members. Use this memorandum to summarize the key accomplishments of the meeting, suggest schedules for agreed-upon activities, and start the ball rolling in preparation for the next meeting. ■

SOURCE: Based on Edward Michaels, "Business Meetings," *Small Business Reports* (February 1989), 82–88; Daniel Stoffman, "Waking Up to Great Meetings," *Canadian Business*, November 1986, 75–79; and Antoney Jay, "How to Run a Meeting," *Harvard Business Review* (March–April 1976), 120–134.

- The team is given access to resources such as information, equipment, machinery, and supplies needed to perform the complete task.
- The team is empowered with decision-making authority, which means that members have the freedom to select new members, solve problems, spend money, monitor results, and plan for the future.[13]

In a self-managing team, team members take over managerial duties such as scheduling work or vacations or ordering materials. They work with minimum supervision, perhaps electing one of their own as supervisor, who may change each year. Volvo uses self-managing teams of seven to ten hourly workers to assemble four cars per shift. At a General Mills cereal plant, manufacturing teams of hourly workers purchased the shop-floor machinery, and they now schedule, operate, and maintain the machinery. They do it so well that the factory runs without managers during the night shift.[14] The Focus on Entrepreneurship box provides an example of a small company, Whole Foods Market, that successfully uses self-managing teams.

AT&T Credit Corporation set up teams of 10 to 15 workers that are responsible for dealing with all customer requests. The credit teams establish a personal relationship with AT&T salespeople and customers and take responsibility for solving customers' problems. The teams are largely self-managing, making their own decisions about how to deal

focus on ENTREPRENEURSHIP

TEAMWORK AT WHOLE FOODS MARKET

Why would a wealthy Houston lawyer and his wife drive out of their way on a Sunday morning to shop at John Mackey's Whole Foods Market? Like many people, they have discovered that despite the higher prices, they prefer the quality and healthfulness of the foods his store offers. They recognize that the service is outstanding too. Mackey's first store started with a mission to get people to eat in a more healthy way. By 1992 Mackey's health-food chain stretched from coast to coast, continuing a policy of adding new regions and stores each year. Sales in 1992 doubled the 1989 figures to reach nearly $100 million.

A typical Whole Foods Market can be 20,000 square feet and carry over 10,000 items. Although many customers start out shopping at Whole Foods for gourmet products such as balsamic vinegar or radicchio, Mackey believes that they return because they become interested in healthier eating. In

fact, the stores are geared toward providing educational information about the products. Organic produce is clearly marked, as are high fiber, low sodium, and low fat items. Each store has an information booth and clerks frequently lead shoppers on a tour of the store. A monthly newsletter keeps patrons up to date on new products. Mackey attributes a large measure of his success to the spirit of teamwork that is found throughout the organization.

John Mackey compares his Austin-based company to the United Federation of Planets in "Star Trek." He uses this analogy because the key to his management style is teams. Each store department such as dairy, meats, or produce, has its own team of workers. Unlike the centralized buying of big food chains, each team at Whole Foods makes its own purchasing decisions. Mackey's belief is that team members will know their own customers best. He awards the team a bonus based on their gross margin so they have an incentive to purchase exactly the right amount of stock. To boost productivity, he sets a labor budget for each team but

allows members to keep any savings as an additional bonus. While this scheme does not save wages, it does save on benefits that would be paid to additional workers and encourages strong team unity. Teams are even responsible for voting on whether a new employee may stay on the job after a six-week probation period.

Mackey's team system motivates employees to feel good about their work, serve their customers well, and help bring in profits. Compared to the average supermarket chain's operating margin of 2.6 percent, Whole Foods maintains an impressive 3.7 percent.

Some may balk when Mackey says, "We're trying to build a company on trust and love," but as a successful entrepreneur with plans to keep growing, he has created the organization to do it. ∎

SOURCE: Based on Wendy Zellner, "Moving Tofu into the Mainstream," *Business Week*, May 25, 1992, 94, and Toni March, "Good Food, Great Margins," *Forbes*, October 17, 1988, 112–115.

with customers, schedule their time off, reassign work when people are absent, and interview prospective employees. The result is that teams process up to 800 credit applications a day versus 400 previously, and they often reach a final answer within 24 hours, compared with several days previously.[15]

Giant corporations such as General Motors are trying to integrate team approaches into their production plants. When designing the Saturn automobile, General Motors had a blank slate on which to design the plant structure as it wished and gave high priority to teams.

 ## GM'S SATURN PLANT

At GM's Saturn facility in Tennessee, work teams are trained to operate without bosses. GM reduced the traditional six levels of authority to four. Work Unit Teams (6–15 employees) are each led by an elected counselor. Team members hire workers, assign jobs, maintain equipment, order supplies, and keep tabs on everything from budgets and production schedules to freight deliveries and auto quality. At the top level of the plant, decisions are also made in teams that include top managers and UAW representatives.

Saturn's methods are seen as the wave of the future, and have been studied and copied by others.[16] Saturn quality is luring U.S. consumers away from foreign brands, and dealer sales for July 1992 topped 22,000, an average of 115 car sales per dealer—twice that of the closest competitor (Toyota). However, Saturn's success breeds new problems. As demand outstrips supply, parts suppliers repeatedly hold the popular auto "hostage" with labor strikes that halt or slow Saturn production. The team concept at Saturn faces new challenges in responding to these problems.[17] ∎

● WORK TEAM CHARACTERISTICS

Teams in organizations take on characteristics that are important to internal processes and team performance. Two characteristics of concern to managers are team size and member roles.

SIZE

The ideal size of work teams is often thought to be 7, although variations of from 5 to 12 are typically associated with good team performance. These teams are large enough to take advantage of diverse skills, enable members to express good and bad feelings, and aggressively solve problems. They are also small enough to permit members to feel an intimate part of the group.

In general, as a team increases in size, it becomes harder for each member to interact with and influence the others. A summary of research on group size suggests the following:

1 Small teams (two to four members) show more agreement, ask more questions, and exchange more opinions. Members want to get along with one another. Small teams report more satisfaction and enter into more personal discussions. They tend to be informal and make few demands on team leaders.

2 Large teams (12 or more) tend to have more disagreements and differences of opinion. Subgroups often form, and conflicts among them occur. Demands on leaders are greater because there is more centralized decision making and less member participation. Large teams also tend to be less friendly. Turnover and absenteeism are higher in a large team, especially for blue-collar workers. Because less satisfaction is associated with specialized tasks and poor communication, team members have fewer opportunities to participate and feel an intimate part of the group.[18]

As a general rule, large teams make need satisfaction for individuals more difficult; thus, there is less reason for people to remain committed to their goals. Teams of from 5 to 12 seem to work best. If a team grows larger than 20, managers should divide it into subgroups, each with its own members and goals.

MEMBER ROLES

For a team to be successful over the long run, it must be structured so as to both maintain its members' social well-being and accomplish its task. In successful teams, the requirements for task performance and social satisfaction are met by the emergence of two types of roles: task specialist and socioemotional.[19]

People who play the **task specialist role** spend time and energy helping the team reach its goal. They often display the following behaviors:

- *Initiation:* Propose new solutions to team problems.
- *Give opinions:* Offer opinions on task solutions; give candid feedback on others' suggestions.
- *Seek information:* Ask for task-relevant facts.
- *Summarize:* Relate various ideas to the problem at hand; pull ideas together into a summary perspective.
- *Energize:* Stimulate the team into action when interest drops.[20]

People who adopt a **socioemotional role** support team members' emotional needs and help strengthen the social entity. They display the following behaviors:

- *Encourage:* Are warm and receptive to others' ideas; praise and encourage others to draw forth their contributions.
- *Harmonize:* Reconcile group conflicts; help disagreeing parties reach agreement.
- *Reduce tension:* May tell jokes or in other ways draw off emotions when group atmosphere is tense.
- *Follow:* Go along with the team; agree to other team members' ideas.
- *Compromise:* Will shift own opinions to maintain team harmony.[21]

task specialist role

A role in which the individual devotes personal time and energy to helping the team accomplish its task.

socioemotional role

A role in which the individual provides support for team members' emotional needs and social unity.

Exhibit 17.3 illustrates task specialist and socioemotional roles in teams. When most individuals in a team play a social role, the team is socially oriented. Members do not criticize or disagree with one another and do not forcefully offer opinions or try to accomplish team tasks, because their primary interest is to keep the team happy. Teams with mostly socioemotional roles can be very satisfying, but they also can be unproductive. At the other extreme, a team made up primarily of task specialists will tend to have a singular concern for task accomplishment. This team will be effective for a short period of time but will not be satisfying for members over the long run. Task specialists convey little emotional concern for one another, are unsupportive, and ignore team members' social and emotional needs. The task-oriented team can be humorless and unsatisfying.

As Exhibit 17.3 illustrates, some team members may play a dual role. People with **dual roles** both contribute to the task and meet members' emotional needs. Such people may become team leaders because they satisfy both types of needs and are looked up to by other members. Exhibit 17.3 also shows the final type of role, called the *nonparticipator role*. People in the **nonparticipator role** contribute little to either the task or the social needs of team members. They typically are held in low esteem by the team.

The important thing for managers to remember is that <u>effective teams must have people in both task specialist and socioemotional roles</u>. Humor and social concern are as important to team effectiveness as are facts and problem solving. Managers also should remember that some people perform better in one type of role; some are inclined toward social

dual role

A role in which the individual both contributes to the team's task and supports members' emotional needs.

nonparticipator role

A role in which the individual contributes little to either the task or members' socioemotional needs.

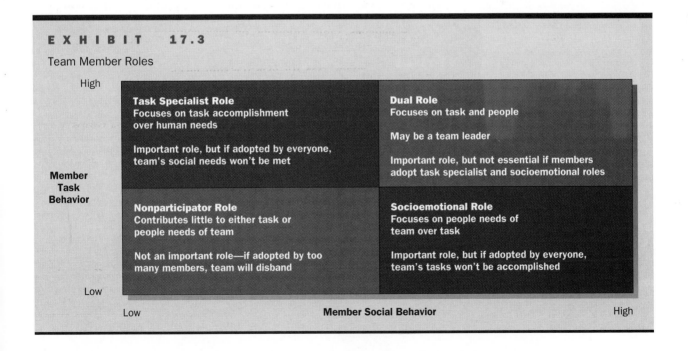

EXHIBIT   17.3

Team Member Roles

High		
	Task Specialist Role Focuses on task accomplishment over human needs Important role, but if adopted by everyone, team's social needs won't be met	**Dual Role** Focuses on task and people May be a team leader Important role, but not essential if members adopt task specialist and socioemotional roles
Member Task Behavior	**Nonparticipator Role** Contributes little to either task or people needs of team Not an important role—if adopted by too many members, team will disband	**Socioemotional Role** Focuses on people needs of team over task Important role, but if adopted by everyone, team's tasks won't be accomplished
Low		
	Low	**Member Social Behavior** High

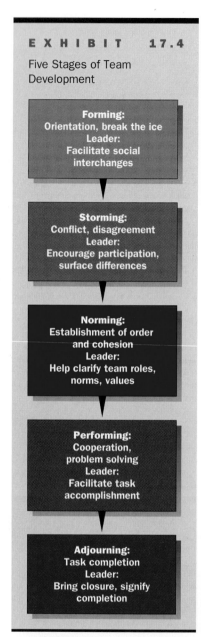

EXHIBIT   17.4

Five Stages of Team
Development

forming

The stage of team development characterized by orientation and acquaintance.

storming

The stage of team development in which individual personalities and roles, and resulting conflicts, emerge.

---

concerns and others toward task concerns. A well-balanced team will do best over the long term because it will be personally satisfying for team members and permit the accomplishment of team tasks.

● TEAM PROCESSES

Now we turn our attention to internal team processes. Team processes pertain to those dynamics that change over time and can be influenced by team leaders. In this section, we will discuss the team processes of stages of development, cohesiveness, and norms. The fourth type of team process, conflict, will be covered in the next section.

STAGES OF TEAM DEVELOPMENT

After a team has been created, there are distinct stages through which it develops.[22] New teams are different from mature teams. Recall a time when you were a member of a new team, such as a fraternity or sorority pledge class, a committee, or a small team formed to do a class assignment. Over time the team changed. In the beginning, team members had to get to know one another, establish roles and norms, divide the labor, and clarify the team's task. In this way, members became parts of a smoothly operating team. The challenge for leaders is to understand the stage of the team's development and take action that will help the group improve its functioning.

Research findings suggest that team development is not random but evolves over definitive stages. Several models describing these stages exist; one useful model is shown in Exhibit 17.4. The five stages typically occur in sequence. In teams that are under time pressure or that will exist for only a few days, the stages may occur rapidly. Each stage confronts team leaders and members with unique problems and challenges.[23]

FORMING.   The **forming** stage of development is a period of orientation and getting acquainted. Members break the ice and test one another for friendship possibilities and task orientation. Team members find which behaviors are acceptable to others. Uncertainty is high during this stage, and members usually accept whatever power or authority is offered by either formal or informal leaders. Members are dependent on the team until they find out what the ground rules are and what is expected of them. During this initial stage, members are concerned about such things as "What is expected of me?" "What is acceptable?" "Will I fit in?" During the forming stage, the team leader should provide time for members to get acquainted with one another and encourage them to engage in informal social discussions.

STORMING.   During the **storming** stage, individual personalities emerge. People become more assertive in clarifying their roles and what is expected of them. This stage is marked by conflict and disagreement. People may disagree over their perceptions of the team's mission. Members may jockey for positions, and coalitions or subgroups based on com-

Amgen, Inc., a California biotechnology firm, considers its teams to be "the family jewels." A product development team or a task force may range from 5 employees up to 80, with emphasis on *team member roles* and task accomplishment. Participation by all members is encouraged and department heads serve as facilitators to prevent a bureaucratic mind-set, as well as to remind all participants of the importance of working together. No one is "in charge," and cross-department discussion is important to team success. Bowling tournaments (shown here), chili cook-offs, and whale-watching trips all help build Amgen's team spirit.

mon interests may form. One subgroup may disagree with another over the total team's goals or how to achieve them. The team is not yet cohesive and may be characterized by a general lack of unity. Unless teams can successfully move beyond this stage, they may get bogged down and never achieve high performance. During the storming stage, the team leader should encourage participation by each team member. Members should propose ideas, disagree with one another, and work through the uncertainties and conflicting perceptions about team tasks and goals.

NORMING.   During the **norming** stage, conflict is resolved and team harmony and unity emerge. Consensus develops on who has the power, who is the leader, and members' roles. Members come to accept and understand one another. Differences are resolved, and members develop a sense of team cohesion. This stage typically is of short duration. During the norming stage, the team leader should emphasize oneness within the team and help clarify team norms and values.

norming

The stage of team development in which conflicts developed during the storming stage are resolved and team harmony and unity emerge.

PERFORMING.   During the **performing** stage, the major emphasis is on problem solving and accomplishing the assigned task. Members are committed to the team's mission. They are coordinated with one another and handle disagreements in a mature way. They confront and resolve problems in the interest of task accomplishment. They interact frequently and direct discussion and influence toward achieving team goals. During this stage, the leader should concentrate on managing high task performance. Both socioemotional and task specialists should contribute.

performing

The stage of team development in which members focus on problem solving and accomplishing the team's assigned task.

ADJOURNING.   The **adjourning** stage occurs in committees, task forces, and teams that have a limited task to perform and are disbanded afterward. During this stage, the emphasis is on wrapping up and gearing down. Task performance is no longer a top priority. Members may feel heightened emotionality, strong cohesiveness, and depression or

adjourning

The stage of team development in which members prepare for the team's disbandment.

even regret over the team's disbandment. They may feel happy about mission accomplishment and sad about the loss of friendship and associations. At this point, the leader may wish to signify the team's disbanding with a ritual or ceremony, perhaps giving out plaques and awards to signify closure and completeness.

TEAM COHESIVENESS

team cohesiveness

The extent to which team members are attracted to the team and motivated to remain in it.

Another important aspect of the team process is cohesiveness. **Team cohesiveness** is defined as the extent to which members are attracted to the team and motivated to remain in it.[24] Members of highly cohesive teams are committed to team activities, attend meetings, and are happy when the team succeeds. Members of less cohesive teams are less concerned about the team's welfare. High cohesiveness is normally considered an attractive feature of teams.

DETERMINANTS OF TEAM COHESIVENESS.   Characteristics of team structure and context influence cohesiveness. First is *team interaction*. The greater the amount of contact among team members and the more time spent together, the more cohesive the team. Through frequent interactions, members get to know one another and become more devoted to the team.[25] Second is the concept of *shared goals*. If team members agree on goals, they will be more cohesive. Agreeing on purpose and direction binds the team together. Third is *personal attraction to the team*, meaning that members have similar attitudes and values and enjoy being together.

Two factors in the team's context also influence group cohesiveness. The first is the presence of competition. When a team is in moderate competition with other teams, its cohesiveness increases as it strives to win. Whether competition is among sales teams to attain the top sales volume or among manufacturing departments to reduce rejects, competition increases team solidarity and cohesiveness.[26] Finally, team success and the favorable evaluation of the team by outsiders add to cohesiveness. When a team succeeds in its task and others in the organization recognize the success, members feel good, and their commitment to the team will be high.

Chaparral Steel, an amazingly successful steel company in Midlothian, Texas, encourages team cohesiveness through promotion of the "Chaparral Process." The steel maker strives to create super teams in which each member sees his or her job in relation to the entire organization and its goals. Commitment to cohesiveness and efficiency enables Chaparral teams to perform amazing tasks. The purchase and installation of new mill equipment is a highly complicated task for any steel company, and calibrating and fine-tuning the steel-making process can take years. However, a Chaparral team of four completed the worldwide search, purchase negotiations, shipment, and installation in one year.[27]

CONSEQUENCES OF TEAM COHESIVENESS.   The outcome of team cohesiveness can fall into two categories—morale and productivity. As a general rule, morale is higher in cohesive teams because of increased communication among members, a friendly team climate, maintenance

Team cohesiveness is the result of active participation and commitment by all members. These employees at Levi Strauss & Co.'s Harlingen, Texas, plant celebrate the success of their team effort in reducing lead time for moving garments through production to customer service centers. The self-managed team accepted responsibility for better scheduling and development of flexible, responsive operations all along the production process. Their dedicated team spirit resulted in significantly reduced lead times—from 43 days to 12.8 days.

of membership because of commitment to the team, loyalty, and member participation in team decisions and activities. High cohesiveness has almost uniformly good effects on the satisfaction and morale of team members.[28]

With respect to team performance, research findings are mixed,[29] but cohesiveness may have several effects. First, in a cohesive team, members' productivity tends to be more uniform. Productivity differences among members is small because the team exerts pressure toward conformity. Noncohesive teams do not have this control over member behavior and therefore tend to have wider variation in member productivity.

With respect to the productivity of the team as a whole, research findings suggest that cohesive teams have the potential to be productive, but the degree of productivity depends on the relationship between management and the working team. Thus, team cohesiveness does not necessarily lead to higher team productivity. One study surveyed over 200 work teams and correlated job performance with their cohesiveness.[30] Highly cohesive teams were more productive when team members felt management support and less productive when they sensed management hostility and negativism. Management hostility led to team norms and goals of low performance, and the highly cohesive teams performed poorly, in accordance with their norms and goals.

The relationship between performance outcomes and cohesiveness is illustrated in Exhibit 17.5. The highest productivity occurs when the team is cohesive and also has a high performance norm, which is a result of its positive relationship with management. Moderate productivity occurs when cohesiveness is low, because team members are less committed to performance norms. The lowest productivity occurs when cohesiveness is high and the team's performance norm is low. Thus, cohesive teams are able to attain their goals and enforce their norms, which can lead to either very high or very low productivity.

TEAM NORMS

norm

A standard of conduct that is shared by team members and guides their behavior.

A team **norm** is a standard of conduct that is shared by team members and guides their behavior.[31] Norms are informal. They are not written down as are rules and procedures. Norms are valuable because they define boundaries of acceptable behavior. They make life easier for team members by providing a frame of reference for what is right and wrong. Norms identify key values, clarify role expectations, and facilitate team survival. For example, union members may develop a norm of not cooperating with management because they do not trust management's motives. In this way, norms protect the group and express key values.

Norms begin to develop in the first interactions among members of a new team.[32] Norms that apply to both day-to-day behavior and employee output and performance gradually evolve. Norms thus tell members what is acceptable and direct members' actions toward acceptable productivity or performance. Four common ways in which norms develop for controlling and directing behavior are illustrated in Exhibit 17.6.[33]

CRITICAL EVENTS.   Often *critical events* in a team's history establish an important precedent. One example occurred when Arthur Schlesinger, despite his serious reservations about the Bay of Pigs invasion, was pressured by Attorney General Robert Kennedy not to raise his objections to President Kennedy. This critical incident helped create a norm in which team members refrained from expressing disagreement with the president.

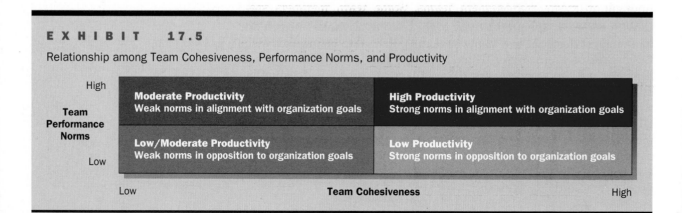

EXHIBIT   17.5

Relationship among Team Cohesiveness, Performance Norms, and Productivity

	Low Team Cohesiveness	High Team Cohesiveness
Team Performance Norms — High	**Moderate Productivity** — Weak norms in alignment with organization goals	**High Productivity** — Strong norms in alignment with organization goals
Team Performance Norms — Low	**Low/Moderate Productivity** — Weak norms in opposition to organization goals	**Low Productivity** — Strong norms in opposition to organization goals

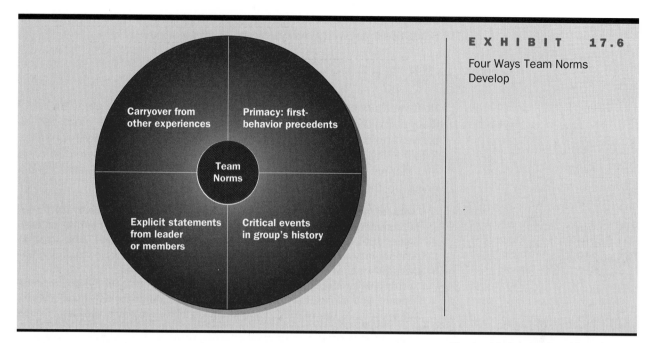

EXHIBIT 17.6

Four Ways Team Norms
Develop

Carryover from other experiences

Primacy: first-behavior precedents

Team Norms

Explicit statements from leader or members

Critical events in group's history

The trust being developed here in a team-building session is an example of the *primacy* cause of group norms. Such team building and project partnering is a major component in Gilbane Building Company's culture, and Gilbane is now extending the team concept to include clients, customers, and subcontractors.

Any critical event can lead to the creation of a norm. In one organization, a department head invited the entire staff to his house for dinner. The next day people discovered that no one had attended, and this resulted in a norm prohibiting outside entertaining.[34]

PRIMACY. *Primacy* means that the first behaviors that occur in a team often set a precedent for later team expectations. For example, when the president of Sun Company set up teams in the Dallas-based exploration division, top managers made sure the initial meetings involved solving genuine company problems. The initial success created a norm that team members carried into other work. "Suddenly we had two hundred evangelists," said Sun President McCormick.[35]

CARRYOVER BEHAVIORS. *Carryover behaviors* bring norms into the team from outside. One current example is the strong norm against smoking in many management teams. Some team members sneak around, gargling with mouthwash, and fear expulsion because the team culture believes everyone should kick the habit. At such companies as Johnson & Johnson, Dow Chemical, and Aetna Life & Casualty, the norm is, "If you want to advance, don't smoke."[36] Carryover behavior also influences small teams of college students assigned by instructors to do class work. Norms brought into the team from outside suggest that students should participate equally and help members get a reasonable grade.

EXPLICIT STATEMENTS. With *explicit statements*, leaders or team members can initiate norms by articulating them to the team. Explicit statements symbolize what counts and thus have considerable impact. Making explicit statements is probably the most effective way for

managers to change norms in an established team. For example, Richard Boyle of Honeywell wrote a memo to create a new norm.

HONEYWELL

Honeywell undertook a major change program to relax the company's traditional militaristic style of management and substitute a more participative approach. One norm of the company was excessive formality. Richard Boyle, vice-president and group executive for Honeywell Defense and Marine Systems Group in Minneapolis, wrote a memo called "Loosening Up the Tie." The memo said in part:

> I wish to announce a relaxed wearing apparel policy, and loosen my tie for the summer. Let's try it starting on May 15th and tentatively ending on September 15th. Since departments vary in customer contact and, depending on location, may even vary slightly in temperature, Department Heads are hereby given authority to allow variations. . . .
>   This change requires each of us to use good judgment. On the one extreme it means you do not have to wear a tie; on the other tennis shoes, shorts, and a t-shirt is too relaxed. Have a comfortable, enjoyable summer. I hope to.

The tie memo helped demonstrate management's interest in developing a relaxed, more casual atmosphere at Honeywell. Employee response suggested that the freedom to exercise common sense over arbitrary rules was healthy for the organization. When Mr. Boyle showed up at the office without a tie, people really began to believe that the new dress code was okay.[37] ■

MANAGING TEAM CONFLICT

The final characteristic of team process is conflict. Of all the skills required for effective team management, none is more important than handling the conflicts that inevitably arise among members. Whenever people work together in teams, some conflict is inevitable. Conflict can arise among members within a team or between one team and another. **Conflict** refers to antagonistic interaction in which one party attempts to block the intentions or goals of another.[38] Competition, which is rivalry between individuals or teams, can have a healthy impact because it energizes people toward higher performance.[39] However, too much conflict can be destructive, tear relationships apart, and interfere with the healthy exchange of ideas and information.[40]

conflict

Antagonistic interaction in which one party attempts to thwart the intentions or goals of another.

CAUSES OF CONFLICT

Several factors can cause people to engage in conflict:[41]

SCARCE RESOURCES.   Resources include money, information, and supplies. In their desire to achieve goals, individuals may wish to increase their resources, which throws them into conflict. Whenever individuals or teams must compete for scarce or declining resources, conflict is almost inevitable.

JURISDICTIONAL AMBIGUITIES.   Conflicts also emerge when job boundaries and responsibilities are unclear. When task responsibilities are well defined and predictable, people know where they stand. When they are unclear, people may disagree about who has responsibility for specific tasks or who has a claim on resources. The conflict between owners' and players' associations in both professional football and baseball is often a struggle to see which organization has jurisdiction over such things as drug testing.[42]

COMMUNICATION BREAKDOWN.   Communication, as described in Chapter 16, is sometimes faulty. Poor communications result in misperceptions and misunderstandings of other people and teams. In some cases, information may be intentionally withheld, which can jeopardize trust among teams and lead to long-lasting conflict.

PERSONALITY CLASHES.   A personality clash occurs when people simply do not get along with one another and do not see eye to eye on any issue. Personality clashes are caused by basic differences in personality, values, and attitudes. Often it's a good idea to simply separate the parties so that they need not interact with one another.

POWER AND STATUS DIFFERENCES.   Power and status differences occur when one party has disputable influence over another. Low-prestige individuals or departments may resist their low status. People may engage in conflict to increase their power and influence in the team or organization.

GOAL DIFFERENCES.   Conflict often occurs simply because people are pursuing conflicting goals. Goal differences are natural in organizations. Individual salespeople's targets may put them in conflict with one another or with the sales manager. Moreover, the sales department may have goals that conflict with those of manufacturing. One conflict emerged within the United Auto Workers (UAW) because one subgroup is against teamwork, believing that it exploits workers and does nothing but make them work harder. Other factions in the UAW believe it is beneficial for both workers and the organization. These opposing goals are causing major clashes between these UAW subgroups.[43]

An interesting example of conflict occurred within a product marketing team at Salvo, a designer of computer software programs.

 SALVO, INC.

Product marketing teams at Salvo develop demonstration tapes of its new games and programs for use in dealer stores. The tapes are filled with sound, color, and clever graphics that are successful sales tools. The marketing person on the team works up an outline for a tape based on product content. The outline is then submitted to the team member from the information systems department to work out the displays and graphics.

Larry from marketing is energetic, has a good sense of humor, and has a high standard for excellence. He knows what a computer can do, but he is not a programmer. Larry submitted an outline of a new videotape to Eric in information systems for development. Eric, a new member of the team, is serious and somewhat introverted. He sent a highly technical memo to Larry explaining why the project wouldn't work as requested. Larry was upset, because he didn't understand the memo or why Eric had written a memo instead of talking to him face-to-face.

Larry and Eric had a blowup at their first meeting because of their different goals and personalities. Miscommunication further aggravated the situation. Also, it was unclear who was responsible for each task in the development of the demonstration tapes, because Eric was new and unaccustomed to taking orders from another team member. Although both Eric and Larry supposedly had the same team goal, the problems with personality, communication, jurisdictional ambiguity, and individual goals caused an almost explosive conflict between them.[44] ■

STYLES TO HANDLE CONFLICT

Teams as well as individuals develop specific styles for dealing with conflict, based on the desire to satisfy their own concern versus the other party's concern. A model that describes five styles of handling conflict is in Exhibit 17.7. The two major dimensions are the extent to which an individual is assertive versus cooperative in his or her approach to conflict.

Effective team members vary their style of handling conflict to fit a specific situation. Each style is appropriate in certain cases.

1 The *competing style*, which reflects assertiveness to get one's own way, should be used when quick, decisive action is vital on important issues or unpopular actions, such as during emergencies or urgent cost cutting.

2 The *avoiding style*, which reflects neither assertiveness nor cooperativeness, is appropriate when an issue is trivial, when there is no chance of winning, when a delay to gather more information is needed, or when a disruption would be very costly.

3 The *compromising style* reflects a moderate amount of both assertiveness and cooperativeness. It is appropriate when the goals on both sides are equally important, when opponents have equal power and both sides want to split the difference, or when people need to arrive at temporary or expedient solutions under time pressure.

4 The *accommodating style* reflects a high degree of cooperativeness, which works best when people realize that they are wrong, when an issue is more important to others than to oneself, when building social credits for use in later discussions, and when maintaining harmony is especially important.

5 The *collaborating style* reflects both a high degree of assertiveness and cooperativeness. The collaborating style enables both parties to win, although it may require substantial bargaining and negotiation. The collaborating style is important when both sets of concerns are too important to be compromised, when insights from different

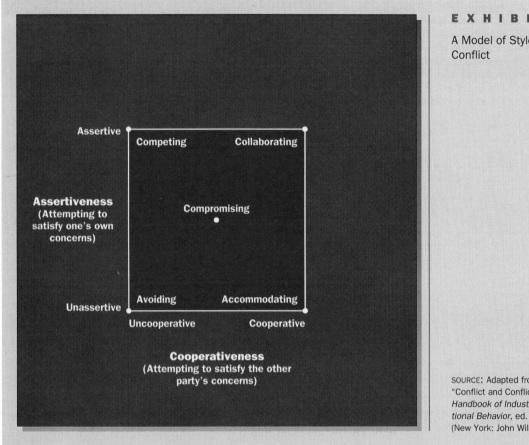

EXHIBIT   17.7

A Model of Styles to Handle
Conflict

SOURCE: Adapted from Kenneth Thomas,
"Conflict and Conflict Management," in
*Handbook of Industrial and Organiza-
tional Behavior*, ed. M. D. Dunnette
(New York: John Wiley, 1976), 900.

people need to be merged into an overall solution, and when the commitment of both sides is needed for a consensus.[45]

The various styles of handling conflict can be used when an individual disagrees with others. But what does a manager or team member do when a conflict erupts among others within a team or among teams for which the manager is responsible? Research suggests that several techniques can be used as strategies for resolving conflicts among people or departments. These techniques might also be used when conflict is formalized, such as between a union and management.

SUPERORDINATE GOALS.   The larger mission that cannot be attained by a single party is identified as a **superordinate goal**.[46] A superordinate goal requires the cooperation of the conflicting parties for achievement. People must pull together. To the extent that employees can be focused on team or organization goals, the conflict will decrease because they see the big picture and realize they must work together to achieve it.

BARGAINING/NEGOTIATION.   Bargaining and negotiation mean that the parties engage one another in an attempt to systematically reach a solution. They attempt logical problem solving to identify and correct

superordinate goal

A goal that cannot be reached by a
single party.

Like a football team trying to move the ball down the field to score, Marshall Industries' *superordinate goals* are based on shared principles, including quality and customer service. This electronics distributor uses superordinate goals to work toward alignment of all departments and reduction of conflict and competition. Employee energies are allocated to building an overall team rather than competing with one another. Successful execution of this game plan benefits Marshall, its clients, and suppliers.

Alignment:
Our Goal
In 1992

mediation

The process of using a third party to settle a dispute.

the conflict. This approach works well if the individuals can set aside personal animosities and deal with the conflict in a businesslike way.

MEDIATION. Using a third party to settle a dispute involves **mediation.** A mediator could be a supervisor, higher-level manager, or someone from the human resource department. The mediator can discuss the conflict with each party and work toward a solution. If a solution satisfactory to both sides cannot be reached, the parties may be willing to turn the conflict over to the mediator and abide by his or her solution.

PROVIDING WELL-DEFINED TASKS. When conflict is a result of ambiguity, managers can reduce it by clarifying responsibilities and tasks. In this way, all parties will know the tasks for which they are responsible and the limits of their authority.

FACILITATING COMMUNICATION. Managers can facilitate communication to ensure that conflicting parties hold accurate perceptions. Providing opportunities for the disputants to get together and exchange information reduces conflict. As they learn more about one another, suspicions diminish and improved teamwork becomes possible.

For example, the conflict between Larry and Eric at Salvo, Inc., over the demonstration tape was eventually resolved by improved communication, clear definition of their respective tasks, and stronger commitment to the superordinate goal of finishing the tape. Part of the problem was that Larry was using a competing style and Eric an avoiding style in dealing with this issue. Larry went to see Eric and discussed the problem with him. The discussion revealed that they were pursuing different goals because Larry wanted the tape right away and Eric wanted to keep it until he could perfect it. Discussing each point of view was a collaborative style that was a key to their solution. Debbie, another team member, agreed to help them so that the tape could be of high quality and still be finished in two weeks. Larry and Eric also worked out a clear schedule that specified their respective responsibilities and tasks.

● BENEFITS AND COSTS OF TEAMS

In deciding whether to use teams to perform specific tasks, managers must consider both benefits and costs. Teams may have positive impact on both the output productivity and satisfaction of members. On the other hand, teams may also create a situation in which motivation and performance are actually decreased.

POTENTIAL BENEFITS OF TEAMS

Teams come closest to achieving their full potential when they enhance individual productivity through increased member effort, members' personal satisfaction, integration of diverse abilities and skills, and increased organizational flexibility.

Anthony Industries, a manufacturer of thermoplastic monofilaments, has first-hand knowledge of the *benefits of teams*. A computerized material control system implemented by Shakespeare Monofilament's "Donut Winding Team" improved on-time deliveries by 50 percent and helped lower the "cost of quality" by $750,000. Today, Anthony Industries enjoys the benefits of employee knowledge and training through more than 80 improvement teams, making improvement "a way of doing business."

LEVEL OF EFFORT.   Employee teams often unleash enormous energy and creativity from workers who like the idea of using their brains as well as their bodies on the job. Companies such as Kimberly-Clark have noticed this change in effort among employees as they switched to team approaches.[47] One explanation for this motivation is the research finding that working in a team increases an individual's motivation and performance. **Social facilitation** refers to the tendency for the presence of others to enhance an individual's motivation and performance. Simply being in the presence of other people has an energizing effect.[48]

SATISFACTION OF MEMBERS.   As described in Chapter 15, employees have needs for belongingness and affiliation. Working in teams can help meet these needs. Participative teams reduce boredom and often increase employees' feeling of dignity and self-worth because the whole person is employed. People who have a satisfying team environment cope better with stress and enjoy their jobs.

EXPANDED JOB KNOWLEDGE AND SKILLS.   The third major benefit of using teams is that employees bring greater knowledge and ability to the task. For one thing, multiskilled employees learn all of the jobs that the team performs. Teams also have the intellectual resources of several members who can suggest shortcuts and offer alternative points of view for team decisions.

ORGANIZATIONAL FLEXIBILITY.   Traditional organizations are structured so that each worker does only one specific job. But when employee teams are used, from 5 to 15 people work next to one another and are able to exchange jobs. Work can be reorganized and workers reallocated as needed to produce products and services with great flexibility. The organization is able to be responsive to rapidly changing customer needs.

POTENTIAL COSTS OF TEAMS

When managers decide whether to use teams, they must assess certain costs or liabilities associated with teamwork. When teams do not work very well, the major reasons usually are power realignment, free riding, coordination costs, or legal hassles.

POWER REALIGNMENT.   When companies form shop workers into teams, the major losers are lower- and middle-level managers. These managers are reluctant to give up power. Indeed, when teams are successful, fewer supervisors are needed. This is especially true for self-managing teams, because workers take over supervisory responsibility. The adjustment is difficult for managers who fear the loss of status or even their job and who have to learn new, people-oriented skills to survive.[49]

FREE RIDING.   The term **free rider** refers to a team member who attains benefit from team membership but does not do a proportionate share of the work.[50] Free riding is sometimes called *social loafing*, because members do not exert equal effort. In large teams, some people are likely to work less. For example, research found that the pull exerted on a rope was greater by individuals working alone than by individuals in a group. Similarly, people who were asked to clap and make noise made more noise on a per person basis when working alone or in small groups than they did in a large group.[51] The problem of free riding has been experienced by people who have participated in student project groups. Some students put more effort into the group project than others, and often it seems that no members work as hard for the group as they do for their individual grades.

COORDINATION COSTS.   The time and energy required to coordinate the activities of a group to enable it to perform its task are called **coordination costs.** Groups must spend time getting ready to do work and lose productive time in deciding who is to do what and when.[52] Once again, student project groups illustrate coordination costs. Members must meet after class just to decide when they can meet to perform the task. Schedules must be checked, telephone calls made, and meeting times arranged in order to get down to business. Hours may be devoted to the administration and coordination of the group. Students often feel they could do the same project by themselves in less time.

LEGAL HASSLES.   As more companies utilize teams, new questions of legality surface. A 1990 National Labor Relations Board judgment against management's use of union-member teams at Electromation, Inc., has set a confusing precedent. The Wagner Act of 1935 was enacted to prevent companies from forming organizations or employee committees to undercut legitimate unions. Union leaders today support the formation of problem-solving teams but may balk when management takes an active role in the formation and direction of such teams. As union membership and power decline, increasingly vocal critics charge that the team concept is a management ploy to kill unions. Auto workers especially are challenging team approaches because union jobs continue to disappear despite repeated concessions. Although few experts expect the courts to halt teams altogether, most believe that strict new guidelines will be implemented to control the formation and use of teams.[53]

coordination costs

The time and energy needed to coordinate the activities of a team to enable it to perform its task.

SUMMARY AND MANAGEMENT SOLUTION

Several important concepts about teams were described in this chapter. Organizations use teams both to achieve coordination as part of the formal structure and to encourage employee involvement. Formal teams include vertical teams along the chain of command and horizontal teams such as cross-functional task forces and committees. Special-purpose teams are used for special, large-scale, creative organization projects. Employee involvement via teams is designed to bring lower-level employees into decision processes to improve quality, efficiency, and satisfaction. Companies typically start with problem-solving teams, which may evolve into self-managing teams that take on responsibility for management activities.

For example, Hearing Technology, Inc., described at the beginning of this chapter, grew rapidly to 80 employees and became sluggish in its response to hearing-aid dealers. President Tom Huber was frustrated because the three-day response time increased to eight days, provoking complaints from dealers. Huber's attempt to reenergize the company failed, and he tried a drastic restructuring into employee teams. Huber implemented three things that made the team approach work: Regular meetings of employee teams were held, usually every week; departments were encouraged to talk with one another and work together through cross-functional teams; and power was shared with employees. Four longtime employees supervised manufacturing as a team, reinforcing the team approach. With teams, the response time for custom orders was halved to four days, and dealers were happy again. Employees began enjoying themselves, too.[54]

Most teams go through systematic stages of development: forming, storming, norming, performing, and adjourning. Team characteristics that can influence organizational effectiveness are size, cohesiveness, norms, and members' roles. All teams experience some conflict because of scarce resources, ambiguous responsibility, communication breakdown, personality clashes, power and status differences, and goal conflicts. Techniques for resolving these conflicts include superordinate goals, bargaining, clear definition of task responsibilities, mediation, and communication. Advantages of using teams include increased motivation, diverse knowledge and skills, satisfaction of team members, and organizational flexibility. Potential costs of using teams are power realignment, free riding, coordination costs, and legal hassles.

DISCUSSION QUESTIONS

1. Volvo went to self-managed teams to assemble cars because of the need to attract and keep workers in Sweden, where pay raises are not a motivator (high taxes) and many other jobs are available. Is this a good reason for using a team approach? Discuss.

2. During your own work experience, have you been part of a formal vertical team? A task force? A committee? An employee involvement team? How did your work experience differ in each type of team?

3. What are the five stages of team development? What happens during each stage?

4. How would you explain the emergence of problem-solving and self-managing teams in companies throughout North America? Do you think implementation of the team concept is difficult in these companies? Discuss.

5. Assume that you are part of a student project team and one member is not doing his or her share. Which conflict resolution strategy would you use? Why?

6. Do you think a moderate level of conflict might be healthy for an organization? Discuss.

7. When you are a member of a team, do you adopt a task specialist or socioemotional role? Which role is more important for a team's effectiveness? Discuss.

8. What is the relationship between team cohesiveness and team performance?

9. Describe the advantages and disadvantages of teams. In what situations might the disadvantages outweigh the advantages?

10. What is a team norm? What norms have developed in teams to which you have belonged?

MANAGEMENT IN PRACTICE: ETHICAL DILEMMA

Nancy was part of a pharmaceutical team developing a product called loperamide, a liquid treatment for diarrhea for people unable to take solid medicine, namely infants, children, and the elderly. Loperamide contained 44 times the amount of saccharin allowed by the FDA in a 12-ounce soft drink, but there were no regulations governing saccharin content in medication.

Nancy was the only medical member of the seven-person project team. The team made a unanimous decision to reduce the saccharin content before marketing loperamide, so the team initiated a three-month effort for reformulation. In the meantime, management was pressuring the team to allow human testing with the original formula until the new formula became available. After a heated team debate, all the team members except Nancy voted to begin testing with the current formula.

Nancy believed it was unethical to test a drug she considered potentially dangerous on old people and children. As the only medical member of the team, she had to sign the forms allowing testing. She refused and was told that unless she signed, she would be removed from the project, demoted, and seen as a poor team player, nonpromotable, lacking in judgment, and unable to work with marketing people. Nancy was aware that no proof existed that high saccharin would be directly harmful to potential users of loperamide.

● WHAT DO YOU DO?

1. Refuse to sign. As a medical doctor, Nancy must stand up for what she believes is right.

2. Resign. There is no reason to stay in this company and be punished for ethically correct behavior. Testing the drug will become someone else's responsibility.

3. Sign the form. The judgment of other team members cannot be all wrong. The loperamide testing is not illegal and will move ahead anyway, so it would preserve team unity and company effectiveness to sign.

SOURCE: Based on Tom L. Beauchamp, *Ethical Theory and Business*, 2d ed. (Englewood Cliffs, N.J.: Prentice-Hall, 1983).

CASES FOR ANALYSIS

A. O. SMITH CORPORATION

A. O. Smith Corporation's Milwaukee plant had bored workers repeating the same robotlike task every 20 seconds, welding and riveting car and truck frames for supply to General Motors. Beginning in the early 1980s, General Motors shifted some of its business elsewhere. Later, GM and other automakers forced Smith and other suppliers to cut prices.

With resources getting tight, Smith tried a quality circle program as a way to introduce teamwork. Quality improved, but the union refused to be involved. As external threats became greater, union president Blackman began to support widespread application of the teamwork concept.

The union pressed for five- to seven-member teams, letting workers rotate jobs and elect team leaders. Smith's management went along, turning the control of the shops over to employees. The ratio of supervisors to workers was reduced from 1 supervisor to 10 workers to 1 supervisor to 34 workers.

Smith's executives moved slowly because a consultant argued that self-managed teams would not work until workers wanted them to happen; teams must evolve from their own experience. With the support of the union, Smith undertook the rare transformation from a traditional manufacturing plant with rigid work rules and labor-management warfare to a new culture with participation and equality. All the problems are not yet resolved, because the plant still has not reached its potential. However, observers believe an obsolete production system has been transformed into a competitive one.

● **QUESTIONS**

1. What types of teams discussed in the chapter are represented in this case?

2. Do you agree that workers must want the teamwork concept before it can be imposed by management? Explain.

3. What might be a next step to further improve the employee involvement climate at A. O. Smith?

SOURCE: Based on John Hoerr, "The Cultural Revolution at A. O. Smith," *Business Week*, May 29, 1989, 66–68.

SPECIAL TASK FORCE

Phil Douglas, supervisor of the Special Task Force, was proud of the amount and quality of work that the members of the force had done in the few weeks they had been working together. He remembered the time one of the task force members had an idea about one problem that was costing the company a lot of money. It was close to lunchtime, so the group decided to discuss the idea over lunch. They were so excited and optimistic over the chance of success that they had spent two-and-a-half hours at the restaurant discussing possible results, problems, and implementation. The idea was a success, and no one on the task force complained about all the nights spent working on the project.

However, Ted Young, Phil's boss, told Phil that some of the engineers in Fred Jacobi's department were griping about unfair treatment. "I'm sorry that some of our brainstorming and other creative techniques are being misunderstood, Ted," Phil replied, "but look at what we've been able to accomplish—we've improved the production methods and quality of our products, bringing in many more orders." Phil started to suggest, "Perhaps if Fred tried some of our methods, his engineers would be more content. . . ."

"Try to see this from another point of view, Phil," Ted interrupted. "You and I know that your people are actually working when they take a two-and-a-half-hour lunch to discuss some new idea, but it doesn't look that way. Fred's engineers see them laughing and talking in a restaurant at 12 and then see them coming back to the office at 2:30. How do you think that looks to them?"

"In their department, keeping regular hours is crucial. I think the only fair solution is to insist that the Special Task

Force people keep the same hours, lunch hours, and coffee breaks as everyone else," Ted concluded.

"But Ted, no one's here to see them when they work on past 5:00. It's their freedom from a rigid schedule that has brought such good results."

"I'm sorry to interrupt, Phil, but I have to make a management meeting at two."

Phil left Ted's office and stepped into an elevator with several workers from Fred Jacobi's department. "Must be nice to get back from coffee break in time to go home," one engineer commented. Phil laughed and replied, "It's none of your business, but I'm going to the library."

"Yeh. He's going to check out the new librarian," another man rejoined. The group laughed, and Phil left the elevator more troubled than before. He hadn't realized how much the other departments resented his group.

● **QUESTIONS**

1. What accounts for the high level of motivation on the Special Task Force? Evaluate other benefits and costs of using the task force.

2. What norms seem to have evolved on this task force? Is the group cohesive? If so, does this help or hurt productivity?

3. If you were Ted, what conflict-handling approach would you use to deal with Fred Jacobi's complaint?

SOURCE: Adapted by permission of the publisher, from " 'Special' Task Force," *Supervisory Management*, August 1983, 44–45, © 1983 American Management Association, New York. All rights reserved.

REFERENCES

1. Bruce G. Posner, "Divided We Fall," *INC.*, July 1989, 105–106.

2. "Training in the 1990s," *The Wall Street Journal*, March 1, 1990, B1.

3. Robert B. Reich, "Entrepreneurship Reconsidered: The Team as Hero," *Harvard Business Review* (May–June 1987), 77–83.

4. Frank V. Cespedes, Stephen X. Dole, and Robert J. Freedman, "Teamwork for Today's Selling," *Harvard Business Review* (March–April 1989), 44–55; Victoria J. Marsick, Ernie Turner, and Lars Cederholm, "International Managers as Team Leaders," *Management Review* (March 1989), 46–49; and "Team Goal-Setting," *Small Business Report* (January 1988), 76–77.

5. Carl E. Larson and Frank M. J. LaFasto, *TeamWork* (Newbury Park, Calif.: Sage, 1989).

6. Eric Sundstrom, Kenneth P. De Meuse, and David Futrell, "Work Teams," *American Psychologist* 45 (February 1990), 120–133.

7. Deborah L. Gladstein, "Groups in Context: A Model of Task Group Effectiveness," *Administrative Science Quarterly* 29 (1984), 499–517.

8. Thomas Owens, "Business Teams," *Small Business Report* (January 1989), 50–58.

9. "Participation Teams," *Small Business Report* (September 1987), 38–41.

10. Larson and LaFasto, *TeamWork*.

11. James H. Shonk, *Team-Based Organizations* (Homewood, Ill.: Business One Irwin, 1992), and John Hoerr, "The Payoff from Teamwork," *Business Week*, July 10, 1989, 56–62.

12. Gregory L. Miles, "Suddenly, USX Is Playing Mr. Nice Guy," *Business Week*, June 26, 1989, 151–152.

13. Thomas Owens, "The Self-Managing Work Team," *Small Business Reports*, February 1991, 53–65.

14. Brian Dumaine, "Who Needs a Boss?" *Fortune*, May 7, 1990, 52–60.

15. John Hoerr, "Benefits for the Back Office, Too," *Business Week*, July 10, 1989, 59.

16. John Hoerr, "Is Teamwork a Management Plot? Mostly Not," *Business Week*, February 20, 1989, 70.

17. David Woodruff, James B. Treece, Sunita Wadekar Bhargava, and Karen Lowery, "Saturn," *Business Week*, August 17, 1992, 87–91.

18. For research findings on group size, see M. E. Shaw, *Group Dynamics*, 3d ed. (New York: McGraw-Hill, 1981), and G. Manners, "Another Look at Group Size, Group Problem-Solving and Member Consensus," *Academy of Management Journal* 18 (1975), 715–724.

19. George Prince, "Recognizing Genuine Teamwork," *Supervisory Management* (April 1989), 25–36; K. D. Benne and P. Sheats, "Functional Roles of Group Members," *Journal of Social Issues* 4 (1948), 41–49; and R. F. Bales, *SYMOLOG Case Study Kit* (New York: Free Press, 1980).

20. Robert A. Baron, *Behavior in Organizations*, 2d ed. (Boston: Allyn & Bacon, 1986).

21. Ibid.

22. Kenneth G. Koehler, "Effective Team Management," *Small Business Report*, July 19, 1989, 14–16, and Connie J. G. Gersick, "Time and Transition in Work Teams: Toward a New Model of Group Development," *Academy of Management Journal* 31 (1988), 9–41.

23. Bruce W. Tuckman and Mary Ann C. Jensen, "Stages of Small-Group Development Revisited," *Group and Organizational Studies* 2 (1977), 419–427, and Bruce W. Tuckman, "Developmental Sequences in Small Groups," *Psychological Bulletin* 63 (1965), 384–399. See also Linda N. Jewell and H. Joseph Reitz, *Group Effectiveness in Organizations* (Glenview, Ill.: Scott, Foresman, 1981).

24. Shaw, *Group Dynamics*.

25. Daniel C. Feldman and Hugh J. Arnold, *Managing Individual and Group Behavior in Organizations* (New York: McGraw-Hill, 1983).

26. Ricky W. Griffin, *Management* (Boston: Houghton Mifflin, 1990).

27. Dumaine, "Who Needs a Boss?"

28. Dorwin Cartwright and Alvin Zander, *Group Dynamics: Research and Theory,* 3d ed. (New York: Harper & Row, 1968), and Elliot Aronson, *The Social Animal* (San Francisco: W. H. Freeman, 1976).

29. Peter E. Mudrack, "Group Cohesiveness and Productivity: A Closer Look," *Human Relations* 42 (1989), 771–785.

30. Stanley E. Seashore, *Group Cohesiveness in the Industrial Work Group* (Ann Arbor, Mich.: Institute for Social Research, 1954).

31. J. Richard Hackman, "Group Influences on Individuals," in *Handbook of Industrial and Organizational Psychology,* ed. M. Dunnette (Chicago: Rand McNally, 1976).

32. Kenneth Bettenhausen and J. Keith Murnighan, "The Emergence of Norms in Competitive Decision-Making Groups," *Administrative Science Quarterly* 30 (1985), 350–372.

33. The following discussion is based on Daniel C. Feldman, "The Development and Enforcement of Group Norms," *Academy of Management Review* 9 (1984), 47–53.

34. Hugh J. Arnold and Daniel C. Feldman, *Organizational Behavior* (New York: McGraw-Hill, 1986).

35. Kenneth Libich, "Making over Middle Managers," *Fortune,* May 8, 1989, 58–64.

36. Alix M. Freedman, "Cigarette Smoking Is Growing Hazardous to Career in Business," *The Wall Street Journal,* April 23, 1987, 1, 14.

37. Reprinted by permission of the *Harvard Business Review.* Excerpts from "Wrestling with Jellyfish" by Richard J. Boyle (January–February 1984). Copyright © 1984 by the President and Fellows of Harvard College; all rights reserved.

38. Stephen P. Robbins, *Managing Organizational Conflict: A Nontraditional Approach* (Englewood Cliffs, N.J.: Prentice-Hall, 1974).

39. Daniel Robey, Dana L. Farrow, and Charles R. Franz, "Group Process and Conflict in System Development," *Management Science* 35 (1989), 1172–1191.

40. Koehler, "Effective Team Management"; and Dean Tjosvold, "Making Conflict Productive," *Personnel Administrator* 29 (June 1984), 121.

41. This discussion is based in part on Richard L. Daft, *Organization Theory and Design* (St. Paul, Minn.: West, 1992), Chapter 13.

42. Brian Bremner, "That Head-Banging You Hear Is the NFL Owners," *Business Week,* September 4, 1989, 36.

43. Wendy Zeller, "The UAW Rebels Teaming Up against Teamwork," *Business Week,* March 27, 1989, 110–114, and Wendy Zeller, "Suddenly, the UAW Is Raising Its Voice at GM," *Business Week,* November 6, 1989, 96–100.

44. Based on Mary Jean Parson, "The Peer Conflict," *Supervisory Management* (May 1986), 25–31.

45. This discussion was based on K. W. Thomas, "Towards Multidimensional Values in Teaching: The Example of Conflict Behaviors," *Academy of Management Review* 2 (1977), 487.

46. Robbins, *Managing Organizational Conflict.*

47. Gary Jacobson, "A Teamwork Ultimatum Puts Kimberly-Clark's Mill Back on the Map," *Management Review* (July 1989), 28–31.

48. R. B. Zajonc, "Social Facilitation," *Science* 149 (1965), 269–274.

49. Aaron Bernstein, "Detroit vs. the UAW: At Odds over Teamwork," *Business Week,* August 24, 1987, 54–55.

50. Robert Albanese and David D. Van Fleet, "Rational Behavior in Groups: The Free-Riding Tendency," *Academy of Management Review* 10 (1985), 244–255.

51. Baron, *Behavior in Organizations.*

52. Harvey J. Brightman, *Group Problem Solving: An Improved Managerial Approach* (Atlanta: Georgia State University, 1988).

53. Aaron Bernstein, "Putting a Damper on That Old Team Spirit," *Business Week,* May 4, 1992, 60, and Hoerr, "Is Teamwork a Management Plot? Mostly Not," 70.

54. Posner, "Divided We Fall."

SATURN

Mel Prevost shoulders a heavy load of responsibility in his job at the Saturn Corporation. He makes hiring and budgeting decisions, wheels and deals with outside suppliers, and is constantly on the lookout for more efficient ways to get things done. His work week averages 50 hours, and sometimes stretches even longer.

Sound like the work of a top-level corporate executive? Guess again. Prevost is one of 14 members of a machine maintenance team, and like the other 6,000 employees at GM's revolutionary Saturn plant, he has the authority to make decisions that traditionally have been a manager's prerogative. Instead of taking orders from higher-ups, employees work in teams and have the authority to make key decisions.

To prepare new hires for such a radically different work environment, the company puts each worker through 300 to 700 hours of classes on everything from conflict management to problem solving. Arrangements also are made for them to spend at least 5 percent of their work time—or 92 hours a year—in follow-up training.

Once production is under way, the atmosphere is one of consensus. Even though each team is assigned two advisors, the employees take their responsibilities seriously, knowing that the ultimate decisions are theirs to make. "We are running our own bit of the business," says one worker whose team came up with a way to save the company $750,000 a year by eliminating an unnecessary component on car doors. Because of the plant's no-layoff policy, employees have an incentive to find ways to cut costs.

The plant's emphasis on quality is another area that received rave reviews from workers, many of whom had been hired from factories that GM had closed. The Saturn's high quality was not overlooked by buyers either. The car has already won a reputation for having as few defects as Hondas and Nissans, and customer satisfaction among owners ranks only behind Lexus and Infiniti.

Sales figures are even more telling. The subcompacts that roll off the assembly line at the Spring Hill, Tennessee, factory are selling as fast as they arrive on dealers' lots. In fact, demand is far outpacing supply, leaving some buyers waiting up to six weeks for delivery.

But despite all the good news at Saturn, there is some cause for concern. For starters, the subsidiary is losing money, and lots of it: Analysts estimate the 1992 loss at about $700 million. And workers, who just a couple of years ago were held up as an example to the rest of the auto industry, are becoming increasingly disgruntled.

Some problems stem from the very strategies that were supposed to make Saturn better than other GM plants. Take worker empowerment. Some employees have left their jobs because they could not get used to the new system. Others gripe that the union has gotten too cozy with managers. A recent survey of employees found that 29 percent wanted to see a change toward more traditional labor relations.

GM is making sure that those who are unhappy leave instead of infecting other workers with their bad attitude. The latest labor agreement offers severance pay ranging from $15,000 to $50,000 to anyone who wants out.

One reason for the discontent may be that new arrivals are not getting as much training as in the plant's early days. Employees now sit through only about 175 hours of classroom time, with much of the training focusing on technical issues, like power-tool operation, instead of on cooperative work methods. They are then jettisoned to the assembly line to relieve workers who have been averaging 50 hours or more a week for over a year.

Some workers also are upset over Saturn's efforts to raise productivity from about 240,000 cars a year to 310,000. Employees are even being offered a bonus of $3,000 if the company can boost productivity enough to get in the black and stay there. Still, some are warning that Saturn may be trying to do too much too fast. "We were not going to sacrifice quality to get productivity," says Michael Bennett, president of UAW Local 1853. Meanwhile, Saturn and other GM divisions have to compete for the limited money available to come up with new models.

No one disputes that GM finally has a winner in Saturn. But as the subsidiary enters its second decade, it will have to learn how to manage its growth and turn a profit at the same time. If it should fail, it would be a blow to the industry as a whole. No one knows that better than those who have been part of the great Saturn experiment. Says one worker: "We are the future of the American car industry, if it has a future."

● QUESTIONS

1. Discuss the advantages and disadvantages of the team approach at Saturn.

2. Can GM afford to continue its pioneering strategies at Saturn considering the company's overall contraction and retrenchment? Discuss.

3. Assuming that each employee could be adequately trained, do you think it would be better to implement a team approach with brand new employees or with experienced autoworkers relocated from other parts of the country? Why?

■ BEHAVIORAL STYLES

One key theme discussed throughout the chapters in Part IV was that leaders cannot expect one approach to work with all people in all situations. The best leaders analyze the personal characteristics of the members of their group and then adopt the best approaches for directing, motivating, and communicating with them. In this section, you'll have the opportunity to complete a behavioral styles questionnaire about yourself and a different questionnaire for assessing another person's profile of behavior.

THIS EXERCISE WILL HELP YOU

● Become more sensitive to the need to modify your leadership style with different people.

● Develop a specific plan for leading, motivating and communicating with someone based on his or her behavioral style.

● Discover your own behavioral style and its implications for the jobs and careers which may best suit you.

HOW TO LOCATE THE EXERCISE

When you see the main menu for Career Design, select "Leading," followed by "Behavioral Styles." Then, select "Overview" for advice on which options to select on the "Behavioral Styles" menu.

(More software exercises on leadership style may be found on page A-19, following Appendix A, "Insights on Individual Behavior.")

■ WHAT EMPLOYEES WANT MOST

Although a variety of motivational theories were discussed in Chapter 15, "Motivations in Organizations," all of them emphasized the pivotal role of rewards. Surveys of both managers and employees reveal a gap between what employees actually want most from their jobs and what their managers think they want. In this exercise, you'll have the opportunity to list your own priorities about what you want most from your work and then compare the results with other employees' responses and their superiors'.

THIS EXERCISE WILL HELP YOU

● Motivate others better by first determining what rewards they seek in their work.

● Develop a more flexible approach to motivating others.

● Clarify your own preferences for what you want most from your job.

HOW TO LOCATE THE EXERCISE

When you see the main menu for Career Design, select "Leading." Then select "What Employees Want Most."

PART **V**

CONTROL

IDS ensures control in a number of ways. Team-based control is maintained by promoting corporate values and goals through programs such as this summer workshop where regional office administrators (OAs) share ideas and receive instruction in areas such as team building. In this problem-solving exercise, OAs collaborate over a budget systems crossword puzzle. Quality control is maintained by providing efficient, state-of-the-art methods and information systems for meeting the financial needs of 1.7 million families and institutions. Knowledgeable, well-trained financial planners are backed by systems such as IDS TowerNet, a satellite broadcasting service.

QUALITY CONTROL AND PRODUCTIVITY 18

Charles Stott was installed as president and Richard Packer as vice-president for manufacturing at Whistler, one of the biggest U.S. sellers of radar detectors. Why? To take control of quality. Demand for radar detectors grew so fast that two plants went out of control—25 percent of the detectors failed inspection. Of Whistler's 250 production workers, more than 100 spent all their time fixing defective units. Against one plant wall stood $2 mil- lion of defective parts and

other stocks. Production costs were far higher than for a sis- ter plant in South Korea. Stott and Packer were told by Dynat- ech, the parent company, to get costs down and quality up or the U.S. plants would be closed.[1] ■ If you were a consul- tant to Stott and Packer, what would you recommend they do? How can they best go about improving quality control at Whistler's manufacturing plants?

At Abbott Laboratories' hospital products plant, quality control data on this video screen monitor the automated manufacture of I.V. infusion sets as part of Abbott's *organizational control system*. Optical scanners measure each infusion set for exact specifications, improving productivity and enabling Abbott to meet plans and standards of performance for its worldwide market.

organizational control

The systematic process through which managers regulate organizational activities to make them consistent with expectations established in plans, targets, and standards of performance.

Whistler had the luxury of a large demand for a great product, but poor quality was killing the company. In this typically well-run company, rejection rates went out of control. Whistler shows how vital quality control is to organizational success and how difficult it can be to achieve effective control.

Control, especially quality control, is an issue facing every manager in every organization today. Newspaper articles about the savings and loan scandal and about the enormous overdrafts by members of Congress at the House of Representatives Bank are about control. The time needed to resupply merchandise in stores, the length of time that customers must wait in check-out lines, and the number of steps to process and package a roll of film are all control concerns. Merrill Lynch's huge losses from loosely supervised traders, its 9,000 employee work force reduction, and its strategic refocus on customer service and profits are also about control. Control, including quality control, also involves office productivity, such as improved customer service, elimination of bottlenecks, and reduction in paperwork mistakes.[2]

● THE IMPORTANCE OF CONTROL

Here is a true story: Ken Jones, president of the Ontario Centre for Advanced Manufacturing, said that a few years ago IBM Canada Ltd. ordered some parts from a new supplier in Japan. The company stated in its order that acceptable quality allowed for 1.5 percent defects—a high standard in North America at that time. The Japanese sent the order, with a few parts packaged separately in plastic. Their letter said: "We don't know why you want 1.5 percent defective parts, but for your convenience we have packaged them separately."[3]

This story crystalizes the problems with control in North America. First is complacency, the assumption that our management techniques are the best in the world. Second is a top-down, pyramidal control style that is almost feudal in nature. Top management expects to control everything, making all decisions, while middle and lower managers implement decisions, and production workers do only as they are told.

This philosophy is now being stood on its head as a new control philosophy emerges. As we saw in the chapters on leadership, structure, motivation, and teams, low-level employees are being included in management and control decisions. Top management no longer decides the "right" way to do something. More and more, the people who are in control of a particular work setting are those who work within 50 feet of it. Thus at IBM Canada Ltd., *all* 11,000 employees have now been organized into participation groups. A 1.5 percent defect standard is no longer tolerable.[4]

Organizational control is defined as the systematic process through which managers regulate organizational activities to make them consistent with the expectations established in plans, targets, and standards of performance.[5] To effectively control an organization, managers (or workers) must plan and set performance standards, implement an information system that will provide knowledge of actual performance, and take action to correct deviations from the standard. For example, Whistler's managers understood the standard of performance and had information that rejection rates were too high. They did not, however, have a way to implement corrections that would change behavior to meet the standard.

(handwritten: ① PLANT SET STANDARDS ② information system ③ TAKE CORRECTIVE ACTION)

STEPS IN THE TRADITIONAL CONTROL PROCESS

Based on our definition of organizational control, a well-designed control system consists of four key steps, which are illustrated in Exhibit 18.1.

ESTABLISH STANDARDS OF PERFORMANCE.   Within the organization's overall strategic plan, managers define goals for organizational departments in specific, operational terms that include a *standard of performance* against which to compare organizational activities. A standard of performance could include "reducing the reject rate from 15 to 3 percent," "increasing the corporation's return on investment to 7 percent," or "reducing the number of accidents to 1 per each 100,000 hours of labor." American Airlines sets standards for such activities as acquiring additional aircraft for its fleet, designing discount fares to attract price-conscious travelers, improving passenger load factors, and increasing freight business. Standards must be defined in a precise way so that managers and workers can determine whether activities are on target. Standards can then be understood by the people in the organization responsible for achieving them.

(handwritten: ESTABLISH STANDARDS MEASURE PERFORMANCE Compare to standard TAKE CORRECTIVE ACTION)

MEASURE ACTUAL PERFORMANCE.   Many organizations develop quantitative measurements of performance that can be reviewed on a daily, weekly, or monthly basis. For example, Robert McDermott, CEO of USAA (an insurance and investment group), blamed his company's

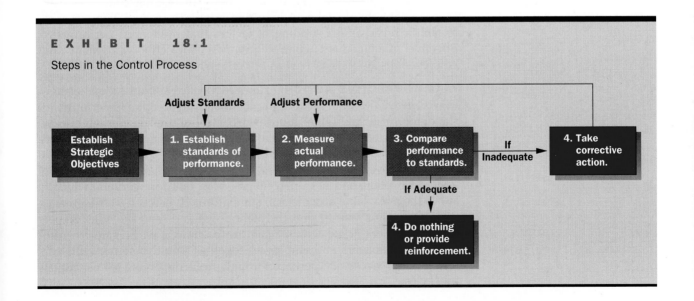

E X H I B I T   18.1

Steps in the Control Process

Establish Strategic Objectives → 1. Establish standards of performance. → 2. Measure actual performance. → 3. Compare performance to standards. → If Inadequate → 4. Take corrective action.

Adjust Standards   Adjust Performance

If Adequate → 4. Do nothing or provide reinforcement.

system of measurement, rather than employee ability, for a drop in productivity growth. A complete overhaul of USAA's measurement system resulted in creation of the family of measures (FOM), which charts and evaluates employees in four target areas: quality, quantity, timeliness, and customer service. Evaluations under the FOM system determine promotions and bonuses. USAA productivity was soon back on track and growing.[6] In most companies, however, managers do not rely exclusively on quantitative measures. They get out into the organization to see how things are going, especially for such goals as increasing employee participation and personal growth. Managers have to observe for themselves whether employees are participating in decision making and are being offered challenging opportunities for personal growth.

COMPARE PERFORMANCE TO STANDARDS.   The third step is the explicit comparison of actual activities to performance standards. Managers take time to read computer reports or walk through the plant and thereby compare actual performance to standards. In many companies, targeted performance standards are right on the computer printout along with the actual performance for the previous week and year. This makes the comparison easy for managers. A. O. Smith, manufacturer of heavy metal frames for automobiles, used comparison to determine whether it was meeting its plans to diversify products as a result of the changes in the design of automobiles. Smith's managers obtained data revealing that 20 percent of sales were from products not made five years earlier, indicating they were on target for diversification.

However, when performance falls below standard, remember that interpreting the comparison between standards and actual performance is not always easy. Managers are expected to dig beneath the surface and find the cause of the problem. If the sales goal is to increase the number of sales calls by 10 percent and a salesperson achieved an increase of 8 percent, where did she fail to achieve her goal? Perhaps several businesses on her route closed, additional salespeople were assigned to her area by competitors, or she needs training in making cold sales calls. Management should take an inquiring approach to deviations in order to gain a broad understanding of factors that influenced performance. Effective management control involves subjective judgment and employee discussions as well as objective analysis of performance data.

TAKE CORRECTIVE ACTION.   *Corrective action* should follow changes in work activities in order to bring them back to acceptable performance standards. In a traditional top-down control approach, managers exercise their formal authority to make necessary changes. Managers may encourage employees to work harder, redesign the production process, or fire employees. One Friday night, the night shift at the Toledo, Ohio, AMC Jeep plant had a 15 percent no-show rate for workers, which is above the acceptable absenteeism standard of 10 percent. Management's corrective action was to shut the plant down and send the other 85 percent of workers home without pay. In the newer, participative control approach, managers and employees together would determine the corrective action necessary, perhaps through problem-solving teams or quality circles.

In some cases, managers may take corrective action to change performance standards. They may realize that standards are too high or too low if departments continuously fail to meet or exceed standards. If contingency factors that influence organizational performance change, performance standards may need to be altered to be more realistic and provide positive motivation for employees.

Managers may wish to provide positive reinforcement when performance meets or exceeds targets. They may reward a department that has exceeded its planned goals or congratulate employees for a job well done. Managers should not ignore high-performing departments in favor of taking corrective actions elsewhere.

● CONTROL APPROACHES TO QUALITY

An organization's approaches to quality are based on its basic philosophy of control. With many organizations moving toward participation and employee empowerment, a choice must be made between the traditional bureaucratic and contemporary clan control approaches.

These two control approaches represent different philosophies of corporate culture, which was discussed in Chapter 4. Most organizations display some aspects of both bureaucratic and clan control, but many managers emphasize one or the other, depending on the culture within their organization and their own beliefs about control.

TRADITIONAL BUREAUCRATIC CONTROL

Bureaucratic control is the use of rules, policies, hierarchy of authority, written documentation, reward systems, and other formal mechanisms to influence employee behavior and assess performance.[7] Bureaucratic control relies on the cultural value of traditional top-down control and is implemented through the organization's administrative system. It assumes that quality targets can be defined and that employees' work behavior will conform to those targets if formal rules and regulations are provided. The following control elements are typically associated with bureaucratic control.

RULES AND PROCEDURES.   Rules and procedures include the standard operating procedures and policies that prescribe correct employee behavior. Rules are based on organizational experience and indicate acceptable behaviors and quality standards for employee performance, such as a 0.5 percent defect rate.

MANAGEMENT CONTROL SYSTEMS.   Management control systems include those internal organization systems, such as budgeting, financial reporting, reward systems, operations management, and management by objectives, that monitor and evaluate performance. These systems are normally quantitative in nature and sometimes measure performance on a daily or even hourly basis. Control systems will be discussed in detail in Chapters 19 through 21.

bureaucratic control

The use of rules, policies, hierarchy of authority, reward systems, and other formal devices to influence employee behavior and assess performance.

A member of Wendy's quality assurance team travels the country to see that Wendy's quality remains number one with customers. The *bureaucratic control* system measures and evaluates everything from restrooms and food storage facilities to signs of shelf corrosion and food temperature (pictured here). The goal is greater employee awareness about sanitation and food safety. These controls help to prevent the potential for foodborne illness and death that has hit other fast-food chains in the 1990s.

HIERARCHY OF AUTHORITY.   Hierarchy of authority relies on central authority and personal supervision for control. Managers are responsible for the control of subordinates through direct surveillance. The supervisor has formal authority for control purposes. Lower-level employees are not expected to participate in the control process.

QUALITY CONTROL DEPARTMENT.   In conjunction with the hierarchy of authority, a quality control department is assigned responsibility for monitoring performance of areas such as manufacturing. Quality control inspectors make periodic checks to ensure that employees are working according to minimum standards for quality performance. Responsibility for quality rests with the quality control department rather than with employees throughout the organization.

SELECTION AND TRAINING.   Under bureaucratic control methods, selection and training are highly formalized. Objective written tests are administered to see if employees meet hiring criteria. Demographic characteristics, such as education and work experience, are quantified to see whether applicants qualify. Formalized selection procedures are intended to allow broad opportunities for employment, but they are associated with extensive paperwork.

TECHNOLOGY.   Technology extends bureaucratic control in two ways. First, it can control the flow and pace of work. In an assembly line manufacturing plant, for example, the technology defines the speed and standards at which workers must perform. Second, computer-based technology can be used to monitor employees. This occurs frequently in service firms. AT&T has a monitoring system that counts the number of seconds that elapse before operators answer each call and the number of seconds spent on each call. American Express uses electronic techniques to monitor data entry personnel who record account payments as well as operators who answer phone queries from credit cardholders. The system reports daily productivity data for each operator and each department. New systems available to organizations enable supervisors to eavesdrop on employees and count the times they call home.[8] The ethics of using electronic control devices is discussed in the Focus on Ethics box, "Is Your Boss 'Bugging' You?"

Although many managers effectively use bureaucratic control, too much control can backfire. Employees resent being watched too closely, and they may try to sabotage the control system. However, too little bureaucratic control also can backfire. Finding the right level is the challenge.

CONTEMPORARY CLAN CONTROL

clan control

The use of social values, traditions, common beliefs, and trust to generate compliance with organizational goals.

Clan control represents cultural values that are almost the opposite of bureaucratic control. **Clan control** relies on social values, traditions, shared beliefs, and trust to foster compliance with organizational goals. Employees are trusted, and managers believe that employees are willing to perform correctly without extensive rules or supervision. Given minimal direction and standards, employees are assumed to perform well—indeed, they participate in setting standards and designing the control system. Clan control is usually implemented in the following areas.

focus on ETHICS

IS YOUR BOSS "BUGGING" YOU?

Suspecting theft of narcotics by staff members, Holy Cross Hospital installed television cameras in the nurses' locker room. Nurses were outraged upon discovery of the monitoring equipment because, among other reasons, the only employee with access to the broadcast was the hospital's male security chief. GE's Answer Center monitors and records agents' conversations with customers. GE insists that this quality control system provides feedback and continuous improvement, pointing with pride to a 96 percent customer satisfaction rate. Safeway Stores uses dashboard computers to monitor everything from driving speed and oil pressure to idling time on each of its 782 trucks.

Because of intense competition in today's global environment, employers have stepped up efforts to control their organizations, especially in such volatile areas as inventory control, health care costs, worker negligence or crime, and customer relations. Various measures are in place from the silent monitoring of phone calls to hidden cameras, bugging devices, tailing employees, to the use of high-tech snooping through computers.

Although there is universal agreement concerning the right of employers to protect their businesses, concern is growing about the extent of surveillance and the need to control the controller. Technology enables companies to extend bureaucratic control to the extreme. Is this any way to improve quality? Critics claim that these techniques are an invasion of privacy, and unions point to increases in stress-related complaints from employees who feel the pressure of constant surveillance.

Employers are protecting themselves from lawsuits by advising new employees of the possibility of monitoring, by having employees sign waivers to allow monitoring, and by providing written policies to employees. Employee dissatisfaction is reflected in increasing complaints, mounting lawsuits, and increased pressure for action in Congress. Observers foresee restrictions which may nudge companies to encourage employee participation rather than monitoring them. ∎

SOURCE: Jeffrey Rothfeder, Michele Galen, and Lisa Driscoll, "Is Your Boss Spying on You?" *Business Week,* January 15, 1990, 74–75, and Gene Bylinsky, "How Companies Spy on Employees," *Fortune,* November 4, 1991, 131–140.

CORPORATE CULTURE.   Corporate culture was described in Chapter 4 as the norms and values shared by organization members. If the organization has a strong corporate culture and the established values are consistent with its goals, corporate culture will be a powerful control device. The organization is like a large family, and each employee is committed to activities that will best serve it. Corporate traditions such as IBM's 100% Club and Mary Kay's pink Cadillac awards instill values in employees that are consistent with the goals and behaviors needed for corporate success.

PEER GROUP.   In Chapter 17, we saw that norms evolve in working teams and that cohesive teams influence employee behavior. If peer control is established, less top-down bureaucratic control is needed. Employees are likely to pressure coworkers into adhering to team norms and achieving departmental goals.

SELF-CONTROL.   No organization can control employees 100 percent of the time. Self-discipline and self-control are what keep employees

Cost reduction, a 15 percent rise in productivity, and on-time delivery helped these Campbell Soup Company employees at Maxton, N.C., win their second company-sponsored "World Class Manufacturing Award." Campbell values *clan control* in its manufacturing facilities. Through team empowerment and encouragement of innovation, Campbell is reaping rewards in areas such as continuous-flow manufacturing, continuous product replenishment, and just-in-time delivery—all of which improve productivity and keep Campbell competitive worldwide.

performing their tasks up to standard. Most employees bring to the job a belief in doing high-quality work and a desire to contribute to the organization's success in return for rewards and fair treatment. To the extent that managers can take greater advantage of employee self-control, bureaucratic controls can be reduced. Employees high in self-control often are those who have had several years of experience and training and hence have internal standards of performance. The experience, training, and socialization of professionals provide internal standards of performance that allow for self-control.[9]

EMPLOYEE SELECTION AND SOCIALIZATION. Clan methods of selection use personal evaluations rather than formal testing procedures. For example, companies that use clan control methods often subject employment candidates to a rigorous selection process. Tandem Computer subjects managers to 20 grueling hours of interviews. For an entry-level position at Procter & Gamble, the person is interviewed at length by line managers who have been trained to probe deeply into the applicant's qualities. Then there is a full day of one-on-one interviews at corporate headquarters and a group interview over lunch. After candidates are hired, they are subjected to intensive training in company values, standards, and traditions. Rigorous selection and socialization activities are an effective way to ensure that candidates buy into the company's values, goals, and quality traditions and hence need few rules and little supervision for control.

In summary, clan control utilizes methods different from those of bureaucratic control. The important point is that both methods provide organizational control. It is a mistake to assume that clan control is weak or represents the absence of control simply because visible rules, procedures, and supervision are absent. Indeed, some people believe that clan control is the stronger form of control because it engages employees' commitment and involvement. Clan control is the wave of the future, with more companies adopting it as part of a strong corporate culture that encourages employee involvement.

Exhibit 18.2 compares bureaucratic and clan control methods. Bureaucratic control is concerned with compliance and clan control with employee commitment.[10] Bureaucratic methods define explicit standards that translate into minimum performance and use top-down control. Compensation is based on individual performance. Employees rarely participate in the control process. With clan methods, employees strive to achieve standards beyond explicitly stated objectives. Influence is mutual, with employees having a say in how tasks are performed and even in determining standards of performance and design of control systems. Shared goals and values replace rules and procedures. Compensation is based on group, departmental, and organizational success rather than on individual performance. This induces individuals to help each other improve quality rather than compete against one another. Employees participate in a wide range of areas, including quality governance, objective setting, and performance standards.

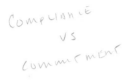

Compliance vs Commitment

An example of how far clan control can go is Marquette Electronics.

MARQUETTE ELECTRONICS

Marquette Electronics makes sophisticated medical devices that doctors use to make life-or-death decisions. Considering the seriousness of its task, it is surprising to see the company characterized by disorder. Some employees wear Hawaiian shirts and have a boom box playing in the

---

EXHIBIT 18.2

Bureaucratic and Clan Methods of Control

	Bureaucratic	**Clan**
Purpose	Employee compliance with rules	Employee commitment to quality
Techniques	Rules, formal control systems, hierarchy, QC inspectors, selection and training, technology	Corporate culture, peer group, self-control, selection, and socialization
Performance expectations	Measurable standards define minimum performance; fixed indicators	Emphasis on higher performance and oriented toward dynamic marketplace
Organization structure	Tall structure, top-down controls	Flat structure, mutual influence
	Rules and procedures for coordination and control	Shared goals, values, traditions for coordination and control
	Authority of position, QC department monitors quality	Authority of knowledge and expertise, everyone monitors quality
Rewards	Based on employee's achievement in own job	Based on group achievements and equity across employees
Participation	Formalized and narrow (e.g., grievance procedures)	Informal and broad, including quality control, system design, and organizational governance

SOURCE: Based on Richard E. Walton, "From Control to Commitment in the Workplace," *Harvard Business Review* (March–April 1985), 76–84.

background. In the company cafeteria, employees may enjoy a beer. The day care center takes care of employees' children, and employees can take time off to play with them. Managers at Marquette Electronics do not overcontrol. "The truth is, we're all quite bad managers," says the engineering vice-president. "Maybe we're not managers at all."

The company is well managed, but management consciously delegates important responsibilities to employees. Marquette's approach scorns policies and procedures and eschews memos and directives. The guiding philosophy, as expressed by President Mike Cudahy, follows: "People want to love their job, their boss, and their company. They want to perform. You've got to give people a voice in their jobs. You've got to give them a piece of the action and a chance to excel."

The Marquette culture is fluid and informal, but that does not mean a lack of control. People are not bound by traditional rules, but the group norms and the company culture encourage a high standard of quality. Everyone shares a simple but strong expectation: Make quality products, give good customer service, and do it all fast. This may seem an unusual approach to management, but as one former employee said, "Boy, does it work."[11] ■

● TOTAL QUALITY MANAGEMENT

About ten years ago, a *Wall Street Journal* survey confirmed the fears of U.S. managers by revealing that three-fourths of all Americans consider foreign-made products equal or superior in quality to products made in the United States. An NBC documentary entitled, "If Japan Can . . . Why Can't We?" also challenged U.S. quality standards. Executives saw the task of improving service and product quality as the most critical challenge facing their companies. Throughout the 1980s and into the 1990s, the quality revolution spread as U.S. executives saw quality improvement as the route to restoring global competitiveness, and many companies recommitted themselves to quality.[12]

The term used to describe this approach is *total quality management (TQM)*, which infuses quality throughout every activity in a company. This approach was successfully implemented by Japanese companies that earned an international reputation for high quality. As we saw in Chapter 2, much of the foundation for the Japanese system was laid by U.S. educators and consultants following World War II. The Japanese eagerly adopted the quality ideas of Americans such as Deming, Juran, and Feigenbaum.[13] The sounding of the quality alarm in North America and the publication of books such as *Quality Is Free: The Art of Making Quality Certain* by Philip Crosby and *The Deming Management Method* by Mary Walton helped reawaken managers to the need for quality throughout U.S. companies.[14]

The theme of **total quality management** is simple: "The burden of quality proof rests . . . with the makers of the part."[15] In other words, workers, not managers, are responsible for achieving standards of quality. This is a revolution in management thinking, because quality control

total quality management (TQM)

A control concept that gives workers rather than managers the responsibility for achieving standards of quality.

departments and formal control systems no longer have primary control responsibility. Companies that really want to improve quality are urged to stop inspecting every part and to get rid of their quality control departments. These companies are then told to train the workers and trust them to take care of quality.

This approach can give traditional executives several sleepless nights as their traditional means of control vanish. Total quality control means a shift from a bureaucratic to a clan method of control. Total quality uses clan methods to gain employees' commitment.

American Airlines is cited frequently by customers for the high quality of its service. Chairman Robert L. Crandall explains how it goes back to a policy decision to improve the traditionally adversarial relationship between labor and management.

> The airline business has historically had a strong military bent and developed as a rather rigid, procedures-based and confrontational workplace. On top of that, the industry became heavily unionized. Very early in the deregulation process, we made the decision to make a sustained, long-term effort to change the confrontational, non-cooperative, non-participative environment into an environment based on trust and mutual respect.[16]

Companywide participation in quality control requires quite a change in corporate culture values as described in Chapter 11. The mindset of both managers and employees must shift. Companies traditionally have practiced the Western notion of achieving an "acceptable quality level." This allows a certain percentage of defects and engenders a mentality

As part of its commitment to *total quality management (TQM)*, Goulds Pumps, Inc., invests in a unique program, Goulds Pumps Institute. Here, Jeryl Mitchell, the institute's director, discusses with her staff the curriculum focusing on the continuous improvement of employee skills, motivation, and expertise so important to total quality. The classes include total quality management, project management, time management, pump fundamentals, supervisory skills, and negotiating skills. In 1990, Goulds invested $2 million and over 56,000 hours in formal training programs.

that imperfections are okay. Only defects caught by a quality control department need be corrected. Total quality control not only engages the participation of all employees but has a target of zero defects. Everyone strives for perfection. A rejection rate of 2 percent will lead to a new quality target of 1 percent. This approach instills a habit of continuous improvement rather than the traditional Western approach of attempting to meet the minimum acceptable standard of performance.

Recent books and articles advocating a systematic quality effort suggest that to be successful, companywide quality control program:

1 Reflect total *commitment* to quality by management.

2 Be devoted to *prevention* rather than appraisal and correction.

3 Focus on quality *measurement* (using feedback).

4 *Reward* quality (employing incentives and penalties).

5 Focus on quality *training* at all levels.

6 Stress problem identification and *solution* (using teams).

7 Promote *innovation* and continuous *improvement*.

8 Promote total *participation*.

9 Stress high performance *standards* with zero defects.

10 Provide *calculations* and *reports* of cost savings.[17]

Quality control thus becomes part of the day-to-day business of every employee. Management needs to evaluate quality in terms of lost sales and total company performance rather than as some percentage indicator from a management control system. Each employee must internalize the value of preventing defects. When handled properly, the total quality approach really works. Standout companies using these techniques are Eastman Kodak, Ford Motor Company, Motorola, Westinghouse, CIGNA, Federal Express, and Florida Power & Light.[18]

The implementation of total quality control is similar to that of other control methods. Targets must be set for employee involvement and for new quality standards. Employees must be trained to think in terms of prevention, not detection, and they must be given the responsibility of correcting their own errors and exposing any quality problems they discover.

Renewed U.S. commitment to quality is exemplified by the Malcolm Baldrige National Quality Award, which is discussed in the Manager's Shoptalk box.

QUALITY CIRCLES

quality circle (QC)

A group of 6 to 12 volunteer employees who meet regularly to discuss and solve problems that affect their common work activities.

One approach to implementing a total quality philosophy and engaging the work force in a clan approach is that of quality circles (QCs). A **quality circle** is a group of from 6 to 12 volunteer employees who meet regularly to discuss and solve problems affecting their common work activities.[19] Time is set aside during the workweek for these groups to meet, identify problems, and try to find solutions. The key idea is that people who do the job know it better than anyone else and can make recommendations for improved performance. QCs also push control decision

THE MALCOLM BALDRIGE NATIONAL QUALITY AWARD

The motion picture industry has the Oscar, and the scientific, economic, and diplomatic communities have the Nobel Prize. In corporate America, the Malcolm Baldrige National Quality Award recognizes the standard of excellence. Established in 1987, and named for the former Secretary of Commerce, the Baldrige Award measures *management systems* for quality improvement programs. Awards are presented in three categories: manufacturing, service, and small business.

The application process for the Baldrige begins with completion of a lengthy application form answering 133 questions. Some participants such as Xerox (1989 winner) and Corning (1989 finalist) estimate thousands of labor hours were used in application and site-visit preparation processes. Each year thousands of companies make inquiries about the award, but only a handful complete the formidable application process. Competition is stiff among those who stay the course.

The National Institute of Standards and Technology (NIST) established the criteria for the Baldrige. Judges and senior examiners representing a cross-section of corporate America, consulting firms, and academia oversee the competition. The applications are evaluated and points awarded in a number of categories (see 1991 scoring listed here).

	Points
Leadership	100
Information and analysis	70
Strategic quality planning	60
Human resource utilization	150
Quality assurance of products and services	140
Quality results	180
Customer satisfaction	300
Total	1000

Only companies topping 600 points (on the 1,000 point scale) move to the next step—the on-site visit. During this critical step inspection teams probe all areas of the company for compliance with Baldrige quality standards.

The Baldrige Award has helped transform American business, encouraging executives to be aware of quality and to enjoy its rewards. Award winners gain enormous prestige and often include reference to the award in their advertising claim to high quality.

Some winners, such as Milliken and Globe Metallurgical are financial successes in their industries. However, critics point out that some award winners later have poor performance records. The most famous example is Wallace Co., a pipe-and-valve distributor and one of four 1990 Baldrige winners. By October 1991, Wallace was in the red and hounded by creditors as talk spread of possible bankruptcy. Proponents of the Baldrige counter that quality "systems," not financial performance, are the focus of evaluation for the award.

Is the Baldrige Award the answer to how to stimulate higher quality standards in the United States? The jury is still out. However, the award has certainly focused attention on the importance of quality in industry and business. ∎

SOURCE: Jeremy Main, "How to Win the Baldrige Award," *Fortune*, April 23, 1990, 101—116; "Debate: Does the Baldrige Award Really Work?" *Harvard Business Review*. (January–February 1992), 126–148; Jennifer E. Beaver, "How the Best Was Won," *Benchmark*, Spring 1990, 2–6; David A. Garvin, "How the Baldrige Award Really Works," *Harvard Business Review* (November–December 1991), 80–93; and Mark Ivey and John Carey, "The Ecstasy and the Agony," *Business Week*, October 21, 1991, 40.

making to a lower organizational level. Circle members are free to collect data and take surveys. In many companies, team members are given training in team building, problem solving, and statistical quality control to enable them to confront problems and solutions more readily. The groups do not focus on personal gripes and problems. Often a facilitator is present to help guide the discussion. Quality circles use many of the teamwork concepts described in Chapter 17. The quality circle process as used in most U.S. companies is illustrated in Exhibit 18.3, which begins with a selected problem and ends with a decision given back to the team.

The quality circle concept spread to the U.S. and Canada from Japan. It had been developed by Japanese companies as a method of gaining employee commitment to high standards. The success of quality circles impressed executives visiting Japan from Lockheed, the first company to adopt this practice. Many other North American companies, including Westinghouse, Digital Equipment, Martin Marietta Corporation, and Baltimore Gas & Electric Company, have since adopted quality circles. In several of these companies, managers attest to the improved performance and cost savings. Westinghouse has over 100 quality circles; a single innovation proposed by one group saved the company $2.4 million. To build on these successes, Westinghouse created the Productivity and Quality Center that assists departments throughout the company. It acts

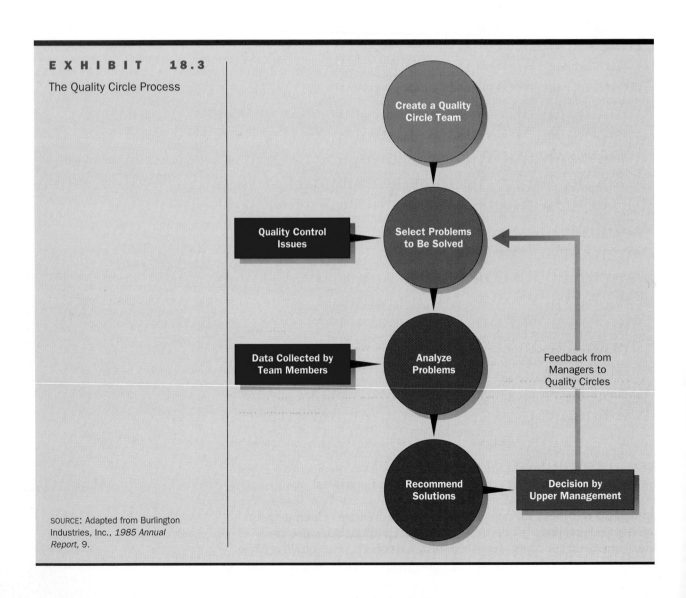

EXHIBIT   18.3

The Quality Circle Process

Create a Quality Circle Team

Quality Control Issues

Select Problems to Be Solved

Data Collected by Team Members

Analyze Problems

Feedback from Managers to Quality Circles

Recommend Solutions

Decision by Upper Management

SOURCE: Adapted from Burlington Industries, Inc., *1985 Annual Report*, 9.

Vishay Intertechnology is the largest producer in the United States and Europe of fixed resistors and resistor-based sensors. Quality is the key to Vishay's product reliability and service. *Quality circles*, such as the one pictured here, meet regularly to address manufacturing or product improvements. The success of quality circles enables many customer companies to move Vishay's resistor products directly to their electronic circuit assembly lines without additional cost or inspection steps.

as a SWAT team of sorts to help divisions do the same work in half the time with better quality results.[20]

TQM TECHNIQUES

The implementation of total quality management involves the use of many techniques. Most companies that have adopted TQM have incorporated benchmarking, outsourcing, reduced cycle time, and continuous improvement.

BENCHMARKING.   Introduced by Xerox in 1979, benchmarking is now a major TQM component. **Benchmarking** is defined by Xerox as "the continuous process of measuring products, services, and practices against the toughest competitors or those companies recognized as industry leaders."[21] The key to successful benchmarking lies in analysis. Starting with its own mission statement, a company must honestly analyze its current procedures and determine areas for improvement. As a second step, a company must *carefully* select competitors worthy of copying. For example, Xerox studied the order fulfillment techniques of L. L. Bean and learned ways to reduce warehouse costs by 10 percent. Companies can emulate internal processes and procedures of competitors, but with caution. For example, a small company may court failure by copying the "big boys" such as Ford or Xerox whose methods are incompatible with a small-company situation. Once a strong, compatible program is found and analyzed, the benchmarking company can then devise a strategy for implementing a new program.[22]

benchmarking

The continuous process of measuring products, services, and practices against the toughest competitors or those companies recognized as industry leaders.

OUTSOURCING.   One of the fastest-growing trends in U.S. business is **outsourcing**, the farming out of a company's in-house operation to a preferred vendor with a high quality level in the particular task area. A variety of companies, such as B. F. Goodrich, Glacxo Pharmaceuticals,

outsourcing

The farming out of a company's in-house operation to a preferred vendor.

Unisys, and NCNB Bank have latched on to outsourcing as a route to almost immediate savings and quality improvement. Traditional in-house operations can be farmed out to save costs on employee benefits, to reduce personnel, and to free existing personnel for other duties. For example, banks have outsourced the processing of credit cards to companies that can do it more cheaply. Large oil companies have outsourced the cleaning and maintenance of refineries. Eastman Kodak outsourced its computer operations to IBM. Manufacturing companies have outsourced the designing of new plants, and service organizations have outsourced mailrooms, warehousing, and delivery services. As with other quality systems, outsourcing is successful when care is taken in selecting the operations that can be accomplished with greater quality elsewhere and in finding the best outsourcing partner.[23]

REDUCED CYCLE TIME.   In the book *Quality Alone Is Not Enough*, the authors refer to cycle time as the "drivers of improvement." **Cycle time** refers to the steps taken to complete a company process, such as teaching a class, publishing a textbook, or designing a new car. The simplification of work cycles, including the dropping of barriers between work steps and between departments, and the removal of worthless steps in the process, is what enables a TQM program to succeed. Even if an organization decides not to use quality circles, substantial improvement is possible by focusing on improved responsiveness and acceleration of activities into a shorter time. Reduction in cycle time improves overall company performance as well as quality.[24]

For example, L. L. Bean, Inc., the Freeport, Maine, mail-order firm, is a recognized leader in cycle time control. Workers have used flowcharts to track their movements and pinpoint wasted motions, shifting high-volume merchandise closer to the packing station. Improvements such as these have enabled L. L. Bean to respond with a correct shipment rate of 99.9 percent within only a few hours after the order is received.[25]

CONTINUOUS IMPROVEMENT.   In North America, crash programs and grand designs have been the preferred method of innovation. Yet the finding from Japanese success is that continuous improvement produces an even more effective result. **Continuous improvement** is the implementation of a large number of small, incremental improvements in all areas of the organization on an on-going basis. In a successful TQM program, all employees learn that they are expected to contribute by initiating changes in their own job activities. The basic philosophy is that improving things a little bit at a time, all the time, has the highest probability of success. Find one small way to improve the job today and act on it. That improvement will suggest another useful piece tomorrow. No improvement is too small to implement—activities are fine-tuned all the time. In this way, innovations can start simple, and employees can run with their ideas. There is no end to the process. Improvements occur all the time, and the resulting changes give a company a significant competitive advantage.[26]

The continuous improvement concept applies to all departments, products, services, and activities throughout an organization. At South Carolina Baptist Hospital in Columbia, South Carolina, 2,500 employees

cycle time

The steps taken to complete a company process.

continuous improvement

The implementation of a large number of small, incremental improvements in all areas of the organization on an on-going basis.

At Armstrong's Thomasville Furniture plants, cycle time is determined by order-to-shipment time. *Reduced cycle time* is one thrust of Armstrong's "Eighty in Five" quality program. The goal is an "80 percent reduction in nonconformances that inhibit customer satisfaction," and the target date is 1995. Employees throughout the company are pitching in to achieve these ambitious goals. This process improvement team used innovations such as improved work-flow diagrams to reduce cycle time for chair production from 48 hours to less than 7. Photo courtesy of Armstrong World Industries, Inc.

have been trained in continuous improvement techniques. Managers learn a coaching role, empowering employees to recognize and act on their contributions. Baptist has learned that countless improvements require a long-term approach to building quality into the very fiber of the organization. Over time, project by project, human activity by human activity, quality through continuous improvement has become the way the hospital's employees do their work.[27]

TQM SUCCESS FACTORS

Despite its promise, total quality management does not always work. A few firms have had disappointing results. A recent survey of 500 executives showed that only about one-third of the respondents believed that quality programs truly improved their competitiveness. In another survey of 300 companies, two-thirds reported that a quality program had not reduced defects by more than 10 percent.

Many organizational contingency factors can influence the success of a quality circle or TQM program (see Exhibit 18.4).[28] For example, one positive contingency factor is the task skill demands on employees in the QC. When skill demands are great, the quality circle can further enhance productivity. When tasks are simple and require low skills, improved skills from TQM training will have little impact on output. TQM or QC success also increases when the program serves to enrich jobs and improve employee motivation. In addition, when the quality program improves workers' problem-solving skills, productivity is likely to increase. When the participation and teamwork aspects of TQM are used

EXHIBIT 18.4	Positive Factors	Negative Factors
Quality Program Success Factors	■ Tasks make high skill demands on employees.	■ Management expectations are unrealistically high.
	■ TQM serves to enrich jobs and motivate employees.	■ Middle managers are dissatisfied about loss of authority.
	■ Problem-solving skills are improved for all employees.	■ Workers are dissatisfied with other aspects of organizational life.
	■ Participation and teamwork are used to tackle significant problems.	■ Union leaders are left out of QC discussions.
	■ Continuous improvement is a way of life.	■ Managers wait for big, dramatic innovations.

to tackle significant problems, such as how to keep metal parts free of oil film, the outcome is better. TQM or quality circles should not be used to tackle simple, routine problems, such as where to locate the water cooler. Finally, a quality program has the greatest chance of success in a corporate culture that stresses continuous improvement as a way of life.

Quality programs often have trouble when senior management's expectations are too high. Managers quickly become disaffected if they are expecting immediate jumps in quality. Quality success comes through a series of small, incremental gains. Moreover, middle- and upper-level managers sometimes are dissatisfied because problem-solving opportunities are taken from them and given to employees on the shop floor. Also, when workers are dissatisfied with their organizational lives, quality programs have a smaller chance of success. Union leaders can also upset the quality program if they feel left out of the discussions between workers and management. Finally, if the corporate culture stresses big, dramatic innovations rather than continuous improvement, the quality program has less chance of adding significant improvements to productivity and output.

When correctly applied, quality programs generate enormous savings. At Lockheed, savings of $3 million were documented. At the Norfolk Naval Shipyard, savings of $3.41 for every dollar invested in a QC program were reported over an 18-month period. Another company that succeeded with a total quality control program is Florida Power & Light Company, the first company outside Japan to win a Deming Prize—Japan's prestigious award for quality.

FLORIDA POWER & LIGHT

Who would believe that a regulated monopoly with little pressure to excel would become a benchmark of business excellence? The judges for the Deming Prize believed it after spending 18 months scrutinizing Florida Power & Light's management techniques and delivery of services.

How does FPL do it? This is a story of quality management beginning with quality circles. Thousands of employees serve on about 1,900 volunteer teams. It is not unusual for a team of meter readers or lineworkers to pause from their daily work to diagram and analyze a particular service problem. But employees love the challenge, and they have produced startling results. A power-line team devised a plastic pipe to make line installation faster and easier. Meter readers were the most injury-prone employees because of dog bites, so a team devised a way to program hand-held computers to beep a warning at residences with a dog on the premises. One team even devised a way to reduce power outages caused by lightning strikes.

What does all this employee involvement mean? The hundreds of team suggestions have produced dramatic payoffs. The best quality indicator is customer satisfaction. Customers are delighted because FPL has not sought a rate increase in five years. The number of complaints to the Public Service Commission dropped 75 percent and is the best record of any utility in Florida. Another measure is service outages, which used to average 100 minutes per customer per year, similar to the national average—not a bad record. The average of outages has been reduced to 43 minutes, and it keeps declining.

Today, FPL is a laboratory. Nearly 1,000 companies have made pilgrimages to FPL, which had to develop a how-we-do-it seminar to spread the word that total quality management works.[29] ∎

● STRATEGIC PLANNING AND QUALITY CONTROL

To exert effective control for the organization, management must integrate quality control with the strategic planning ideas described in Part 2. If control simply monitors internal activities, it may not help the organization achieve its strategic objectives. The linkage of strategy to control is important because strategy reflects changes in the problems and opportunities that appear in the external environment.

ENVIRONMENTAL CHANGE

Environments create uncertainty for organizations because of change. As we discussed in Chapter 4, social, economic, technological, and political forces all influence an organization.[30] Sometimes environmental change is gradual, permitting organizations to shift internal controls in an incremental fashion. At other times, changes are **environmental discontinuities,** which are large changes over a short time period. Organizations may need to respond almost overnight. The banking business, for example, used to be straightforward. Interest rates and the number of banks were determined by the government. Suddenly—within a few months—the financial services industry spewed forth new organizations. Banks now compete with insurance companies and stockbrokers.

What do environmental discontinuities mean for organizational control? The firm adapts to these events through strategic planning. As described in the chapters on planning, the organization scans the environment and develops strategic plans that reflect opportunities and

environmental discontinuity

A large change in the organization's environment over a short period.

potential threats. Internal control systems must change to reflect new strategic objectives and new standards of performance. The internal control system should be flexible to accommodate factors considered uncontrollable.[31]

As illustrated in Exhibit 18.5, uncontrollable events lead to the creation of new strategic plans, which in turn lead to new standards of performance, activities, and feedback systems. Control flexibility usually requires employee involvement. Thus, the control cycle, which establishes standards, measures performance, and takes corrective action, is continuously changing. If managers do not carefully link control to strategy, the organization may exert tight control over current tasks—which are the wrong tasks for successful performance.

The Frito-Lay division of PepsiCo recently shortened its cycle time to meet strategic changes.

 FRITO-LAY

In the past, highly centralized Frito-Lay had the leverage of massive purchasing power and efficient, large-scale production. But it was slow to react to market changes. If sales dropped in Cleveland or Dallas, it would take four or five months to find out why.

To maintain a quality response, the cycle time had to be shortened, and the key was to obtain quick data on actual sales performance. With competition so intense in the snack-food industry, market share could be lost quickly to new products or price competition. The answer was 10,000 hand-held computers used by salespeople to report the day's sales to headquarters. The data on sales in every store in the country are ready to analyze within 24 hours. Salespeople no longer spend long hours filling out forms that languish in the pipeline for months. Instead, computers do the donkey work, with salespeople having more time to spend on promotions and exhortations. A minor decline in salty snacks is discovered immediately, and new promotions or price cuts are put in place. The flexible control response enables Frito-Lay to respond to sudden environmental changes.[32] ■

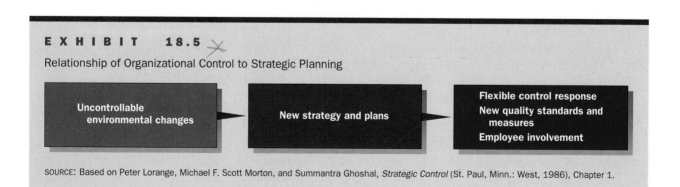

EXHIBIT   18.5

Relationship of Organizational Control to Strategic Planning

| Uncontrollable environmental changes | New strategy and plans | Flexible control response
New quality standards and measures
Employee involvement |

SOURCE: Based on Peter Lorange, Michael F. Scott Morton, and Summantra Ghoshal, *Strategic Control* (St. Paul, Minn.: West, 1986), Chapter 1.

⬤ ORGANIZATIONAL CONTROL FOCUS

When managers design and implement the four steps of control described above, on which part of the organization should they focus? The organization exists around a production process, and control can focus on events before, during, or after this process.[33] For example, a local automobile dealer can focus control on activities before, during, or after sales of new cars. Careful inspection of new cars and cautious selection of sales employees are examples of control that occur before sales take place. Monitoring how salespeople act with customers and providing rules and procedures for guiding the sales process would be considered control during the sales task. Counting the number of new cars sold during the month or telephoning buyers about their satisfaction with sales transactions would constitute control after sales have taken place. These three types of control are formally called *feedforward*, *concurrent*, and *feedback* and are illustrated in Exhibit 18.6.

FEEDFORWARD CONTROL

Feedforward control focuses on human, material, and financial resources that flow into the organization. Sometimes called *preliminary* or *preventive quality control*, its purpose is to ensure that input quality is sufficiently high to prevent problems when the organization performs its tasks.[34] Feedforward control is anticipatory and attempts to identify and prevent deviations before they occur.

Feedforward controls are evident in the selection and hiring of new employees. Westinghouse selects only 5 percent of job applicants for its College Station plant, because only a certain type of person fits the plant's culture. We mentioned earlier that Tandem Computer subjects potential middle managers to 20 grueling hours of interviews with both top-level managers and prospective peers to ensure that no problems will occur after hiring.[35] Before McDonald's could open its restaurant in Moscow, experts had to spend time in Russia helping farmers learn to grow high-quality potatoes and bakers to bake high-quality bread. These preventive control techniques enabled the Moscow restaurant to achieve world-class quality. The requirement that professional football, basketball, and baseball players pass a physical exam before their contracts are validated is still another form of feedforward control.

CONCURRENT CONTROL

Concurrent control monitors ongoing employee activities to ensure that they are consistent with quality standards. Concurrent control is a common form of control because it assesses current work activities. It relies on performance standards and includes rules and regulations for guiding employee tasks and behaviors. Concurrent control is designed to ensure that employee work activities produce the correct results.

At a construction company, the construction superintendent may hire laborers with little screening. Employees are given a chance to perform, and the superintendent monitors their behavior. If employees obey the rules and work effectively, they are allowed to stay; if they do not, they

feedforward control

Control that focuses on human, material, and financial resources flowing into the organization; also called *preliminary* or *preventive control*.

concurrent control

Control that consists of monitoring ongoing employee activities to ensure their consistency with established standards.

EXHIBIT 18.6

Organizational Control Focus

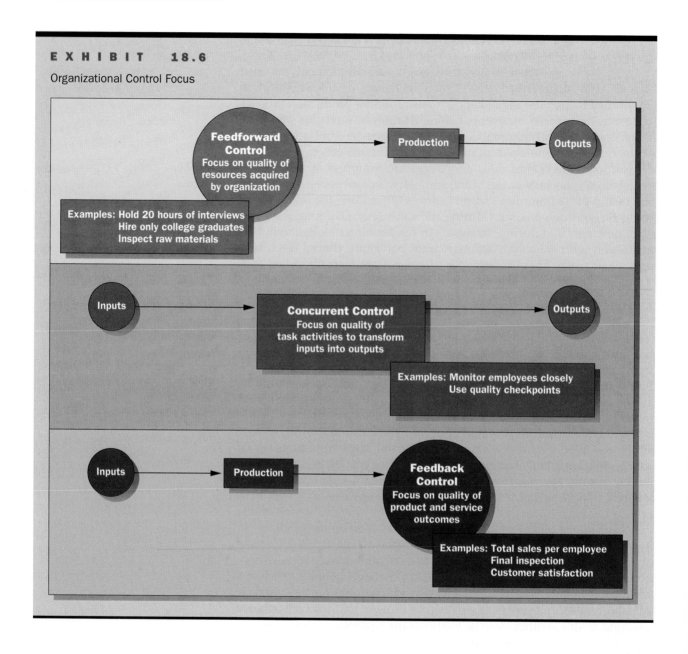

are let go. In a manufacturing firm, it is not unusual for production managers to have a series of quality checkpoints to see whether the production steps have been completed satisfactorily. Frito-Lay's use of hand-held computers to monitor daily sales activities is an example of concurrent control.

FEEDBACK CONTROL

feedback control

Control that focuses on the organization's outputs; also called *post-action* or *output control*.

Feedback control focuses on the organization's outputs. Sometimes called *post-action* or *output control*, it focuses on the quality of the end product or service after the organization's task is completed. An inten-

The Larsen Company, a subsidiary of Dean Foods Company, produces canned and frozen vegetables. These employees at Larsen's research lab in Green Bay, Wisconsin, use *feedback control* to test the company's output of canned vegetables during the weekly comparative product test. Inspections that surpass regulatory requirements are also performed on raw materials (*feedforward control*) and during food processing (*concurrent control*).

sive final inspection of a refrigerator at a General Electric assembly plant is an example of feedback control in the manufacturing department. Caterpillar Tractor Company uses feedback control when it surveys customers after 300 and 500 hours of product use. In the National Basketball Association, feedback control is used when team managers focus on games won or lost. If a basketball team wins the targeted number of games for the season, the organization is considered to have met quality standards.

● ELEMENTS OF EFFECTIVE ORGANIZATIONAL CONTROL

Whether organizational control focuses on feedforward or feedback activities, or emphasizes the bureaucratic or clan approach to quality control, certain characteristics should be present. For organizational controls to be effective, they should be tailored to the organization's needs and facilitate the accomplishment of its task. Effective controls share the following traits:[36]

1 **Are linked to strategy.** The control system should not simply measure what was important in the past or be tailored to current operations. It should reflect where the organization is going and adapt to new strategies. Moreover, the organization should focus on quality activities that are relevant for strategic objectives. If the dominant competitive issue facing a company is to reduce cycle time, the control system should not emphasize raw materials cost, which is unrelated to cycle time.

2 Use all control steps. The control steps consist of setting standards of performance, gathering information about actual performance, comparing standards to real performance, and taking corrective action. The control system will not be effective unless it involves each step. Assuming that people know what standard is expected, for example, is a mistake. Managers should make standards explicit and then identify and obtain relevant information on performance. With valid information on performance, managers or workers can take action to redirect activities to correct deficiencies.

3 Are accepted by members. The total quality management approach is effective because managers concentrate first on involving the entire organization membership in the control process. The more committed employees are to control standards, the more successful the control system will be. The control system should motivate rather than demotivate. It should set standards and provide information feedback that is meaningful to employees.

4 Balance objective and subjective data. Managers can be misled when control system data are either completely numeric or based

Through its commitment to quality, Bethlehem Steel's Burns Harbor plant received one of Ford Motor Company's 1991 Q-1 Awards, reserved for the most quality-conscious suppliers, as well as awards from GM (1990), Nissan (1991), and Mazda (1991). Why all the success? Burns Harbor and Bethlehem Steel have become recognized leaders in total quality by combining the *elements of effective quality control*, including continuous improvement and flexibility, total employee involvement and acceptance, linkage to company strategy, and statistical process data.

solely on subjective opinion. Control should be perceived as objective, but quantitative information tells only part of the story. Easily measured activities will receive more weight unless managers balance quantitative and qualitative performance indicators. Good control systems are unbiased and incorporate both hard and soft data to provide a well-rounded picture of performance.

5 Are accurate. Upward communication, especially about performance, often is influenced by what employees believe management wants to hear. Subordinates may distort communications to present a positive image of themselves. Junior managers tend to filter upward communications to highlight positive messages and downplay negative ones.[37] The control system must encourage accurate information in order to detect deviations. The senior management of the Boy Scouts of America learned that membership figures had been exaggerated in response to the pressures of a national membership drive. This campaign led people to feed inaccurate data into the system, and top managers mistakenly believed that the drive had been successful.

6 Are flexible. Organizations exist in changing environments. Internal goals and strategies change over time in response to the environment. The control system must be flexible enough to make adaptations from one year to the next. Managers who rely too heavily on existing controls will find themselves out of synchronization with changing events. The control system should allow for changing objectives and standards.

7 Are timely. The control system should provide information soon enough to permit a management response. Corrective action is of no value if performed too late. A study of air conditioner manufacturers in Japan and the United States found that control data were received twice as fast in Japanese companies and management's responses were quicker.[38] Organizations such as Campbell Taggart in the United States use computer-based control systems to get performance reports to managers on the same day the information is obtained.

SUMMARY AND MANAGEMENT SOLUTION

This chapter introduced a number of important concepts about organizational control. Organizational control is the systematic process through which managers regulate organizational activities to meet planned standards of performance. The implementation of control includes four steps: establishing standards of performance, measuring actual performance, comparing performance to standards, and taking corrective action. Control should be linked to strategic planning. Changes in the environment require that internal control systems adapt to strategic changes; control systems must not continue measuring what was important in the past.

A new approach to control being widely adopted in Canada and the United States is total quality management, which reflects clan control ideas rather than traditional bureaucratic control. TQM involves everyone in the organization who is committed to the control function. Four major techniques of TQM are benchmarking, reduced cycle time, outsourcing, and continuous improvement. Quality circles, which are teams of 6 to 12 employees who identify quality problems and discuss solutions, are one means of implementing a quality control philosophy in an organization.

Recall from the management problem at the beginning of the chapter that Whistler, the maker of radar detectors, had two plants out of control with 25 percent of detectors failing inspection. Charles Stott and Richard Packer were challenged to turn things around. "We were fat, dumb, and happy," said one manager. Now Whistler is lean and smart, because it created a new control structure. A consulting firm specializing in quality control was asked to help. Then a team of 25 employees from planning, testing, manufacturing, and engineering joined forces with the consultants to design a new production line. Employees, not managers, started making decisions. Circuit boards costing $5 previously were piled up carelessly but now were stored as if they cost $100. The quality team redefined every job and helped train workers in quality techniques. The most controversial move was to eliminate the quality control department, but the team believed this was necessary to make quality everyone's responsibility.

The results? The defect rate dropped to 1 percent, and that was expected to be cut in half. The production work force was reduced from 250 to 120 without lowering output or quality. Most of that savings was the 100 workers who previously spent all their time fixing defective units. Manufacturing costs became almost as low as those of its sister plant in Korea.[39]

The focus of organizational control can be on resource input, the production process, or product and service outputs. These forms of control are called, respectively, *feedforward, concurrent,* and *feedback.* Most organizations use all three types simultaneously but emphasize the form that most closely corresponds to their strategic objectives.

Finally, effective organizational control consists of several characteristics, including a link to strategy, use of all four control steps, acceptance by members, a balanced use of objective and subjective data, and the qualities of accuracy, flexibility, and timeliness.

DISCUSSION QUESTIONS

1. Federal policy is to take blood tests of operators after a train crash. Would it be more effective to take regular tests of operators on a random basis? What types of control do these different tests represent?

2. Why is control an important management function? How does it relate to the other management functions of planning, organizing, and leading?

3. Briefly describe the four steps of control. Give an example of each step from your own organizational work experience.

4. What does it mean to say that organizational control should be linked to strategic planning?

5. How might organizations use reduced cycle time, benchmarking, or outsourcing to improve the quality of products and services?

6. What is the difference between bureaucratic and clan control? Which do you think is the stronger form?

7. Which three concepts associated with successful total quality programs do you consider most essential? Explain.

8. The theme of total quality control is "The burden of quality proof rests . . . with the makers of the part." How does this differ from traditional North American approaches to quality?

9. What is a quality circle? How can it be used to improve organizational quality control?

MANAGEMENT IN PRACTICE: EXPERIENTIAL EXERCISE

● QUALITY IMPROVEMENT QUESTIONNAIRE

For each item circle the number that best describes your attitude or behavior on the job or at school.

	Disagree			Agree	
1. I recognize the practical constraints of existing conditions when someone proposes an improvement idea.	5	4	3	2	1
2. I like to support change efforts, even when the idea may not work	5	4	3	2	1
3. I believe that many small improvements are usually better than a few big improvements.	5	4	3	2	1
4. I encourage other people to express improvement ideas, even if they differ from mine.	5	4	3	2	1
5. There is truth to the statement, "If it isn't broke, don't fix it."	5	4	3	2	1
6. I work at the politics of change to build agreement for my improvement ideas.	5	4	3	2	1
7. I study suggestions carefully to avoid change just for the sake of change.	5	4	3	2	1

8. I like to have clear objectives that support improvement, even if changes upset my efficiency	5	4	3	2	1
9. I constantly talk about ways to improve what I'm doing.	5	4	3	2	1
10. I am able to get higher-ups to support my ideas for improvement.	5	4	3	2	1

Total Score _____

Your score indicates the extent to which you are a positive force for quality improvement. The questions represent behaviors associated with the Japanese approach to companywide continuous improvement of quality.

- 40–50: Great. A dynamo for quality improvement.
- 30–40: Good. A positive force.
- 20–30: Adequate. You have a typical North American attitude.
- 10–20: Poor. You may be dragging down quality efforts.

Go back over the questions on which you scored lowest and develop a plan to improve your approach toward quality. Discuss your ideas with other students.

CASES FOR ANALYSIS

LIGHTHOUSE ELECTRIC COMPANY

Jerry Dean was recently hired as director of Lighthouse Electric's quality control department. Lighthouse had once been a top-ranked manufacturer of electrical heaters and small electric motors, but its reputation had fallen in recent years along with market share. Jerry was expected to turn things around with an improved quality control program.

This morning Jerry went to see his boss, Andy Whitmore, vice-president of manufacturing, about a problem on the shop floor. Several fan blades on a shipment of 1021 electric heaters were too tight, and one of Jerry's inspectors red tagged them. Sheila Jackson, manufacturing director, felt it would take too long to fix the fans, so she turned all the electric heaters on high speed, burning the washers down to the right clearance. Marketing shipped the fans that afternoon. Andy listened to the story and Jerry's frustrations about not having the last word on whether items were shipped. Andy said, "We are all under pressure to make a good product, but we don't want to lose money doing it. There's no time to rework all these heaters."

Jerry investigated further, learning that Sheila was always under pressure from sales to deliver products immediately. One reason the fan blades were too tight was the poor training of new employees. People barely learned where to hang their coats before they started on the assembly line. No trainers were available from personnel. Moreover, Sheila reported wide variation in washers. Putting five washers on a fan shaft could leave a clearance of between five-thousandths and twenty-five-thousandths of an inch.

Jerry recommended that assemblers adjust for the variation when they assemble the electric heater. Sheila would have none of that, saying, "They can't use a micrometer every time they put a few washers on a shaft." However, she implied that if Jerry had enough people, his inspectors could measure those washers. "Besides," Sheila said, "95 percent of our orders are shipped on time, which is a great record. It's our delivery performance that gets us business. I'm not going to change that."

● QUESTIONS

1. What is the problem here? Is there a problem here?
2. What steps should Jerry Dean take to improve quality?
3. Is Lighthouse Electric likely to succeed in its desire to improve quality? Explain.

SOURCE: Based on Frank S. Leonard, "The Case of the Quality Crusader," *Harvard Business Review* (May–June 1988), 12–20.

UNIVERSITY MICROFILMS, INC.

The situation at University Microfilms, Inc. (UMI), was desperate. Because of a worsening economy and job market for several years, many college graduates had decided to postpone the job hunt and pursue master's and Ph.D. degrees, and a requirement of these degree programs is a dissertation. As the nation's top publisher of dissertations, UMI saw its business booming, and booming, and BOOMING. With increased volume came the nightmare of increased backlog. Despite the use of the newest technology, UMI was drowning under a sea of dissertations, with backlogs running in the thousands each year, and irate customers screaming over delays. By 1988, UMI backlogs had reached a whopping 8,000 dissertations, and the customer complaint rate hit 20 percent.

UMI set up quality teams to investigate the problem. The teams discovered that only two of the 150 days needed for publication of the average thesis were used working on the manuscript. Managers were shocked. What was going on during the other 148 days? The teams also discovered that although technology had changed, the publication process itself remained stagnant, stuck in the same sequence of steps that had always been followed. Workers in each department believed that each step in the process must be completed before moving on to the next stage. So the work on copyrights, indexing, and so on was postponed until after lengthy correspondence with the author had worked out some minor detail. After analyzing the process, the quality team recommended more flexible editing standards that reduced the 150-day holding time to half.

● QUESTIONS

1. Which TQM concepts best describe the improvements made at UMI?
2. If you were a consultant to UMI's senior management, what advice would you give them about launching a total quality management effort?

3. In a typical company, do you think more quality gains can be achieved in administrative functions or in the technical functions such as manufacturing?

SOURCE: Aaron Bernstein, "Quality Is Becoming Job One in the Office, Too," *Business Week,* April 29, 1991, 52–56.

REFERENCES

1. Joel Dreyfuss, "Victories in the Quality Crusade," *Fortune,* October 10, 1988, 80–88, and Herbert M. Baum, "White-Collar Quality Comes of Age," *Journal of Business Strategy,* (March–April 1990), 34–37.

2. Richard J. Schonberger, "Total Quality Management Cuts a Broad Swath—Through Manufacturing and Beyond," *Organizational Dynamics* (Spring 1992), 16–28; Leah Nathans Spiro, "Raging Bull," *Business Week,* November 25, 1991, 218–221; and Ronald Henkoff, "Make Your Office More Productive," *Fortune,* February 25, 1991, 72–84.

3. "Quality: The Soul of Productivity, the Key to Future Business Growth," *Interview,* Inter-City Gas Corporation, vol. 3 (Autumn 1988), 3–5. The story was originally related by Patrick Lush in *The Globe & Mail,* Toronto, June 15, 1988.

4. Ibid., and T. K. Das, "Organizational Control: An Evolutionary Perspective," *Journal of Management Studies* 26 (1989), 459–475.

5. Stephen G. Green and M. Ann Welsh, "Cybernetics and Dependence: Reframing the Control Concept," *Academy of Management Review* 13 (1988), 287–301, and Kenneth A. Merchant, *Control in Business Organizations* (Marshfield, Mass.: Pitman, 1985).

6. Henkoff, "Make Your Office More Productive."

7. William G. Ouchi, "Markets, Bureaucracies, and Clans," *Administrative Science Quarterly* 25 (1980), 129–141, and B. R. Baligia and Alfred M. Jaeger, "Multinational Corporations: Control Systems and Delegation Issues," *Journal of International Business Studies* (Fall 1984), 25–40.

8. Jeffrey Rothfeder and Michele Galen, "Is Your Boss Spying on You?" *Business Week,* January 15, 1990, 74–75, and Marlene C. Piturro, "Employee Performance Monitoring . . . or Meddling?" *Management Review,* May 19, 1989, 31–33.

9. Beverly H. Burris, "Technocratic Organization and Control," *Organization Studies* 10 (1989), 1–22.

10. Richard E. Walton, "From Control to Commitment in the Workplace," *Harvard Business Review* (March–April 1985), 76–84.

11. Ellen Wojahn, "Will the Company Please Come to Order," *INC.,* March 1986, 78–86, "Honor Roll of U.S. Exporters," *Business America,* March 12, 1990, 20.

12. John Loring, "Dr. Deming's Traveling Quality Show," *Canadian Business,* September 1990, 38–42; Nancy K. Austin, "Dr. Deming and the 'Q' Factor," *Working Woman,* September 1991, 31–34; and Ross Johnson and William O. Winchell, "Management and Quality," American Society for Quality Control, 1989.

13. A. V. Feigenbaum, *Total Quality Control: Engineering and Management* (New York: McGraw-Hill, 1961).

14. Philip B. Crosby, *Quality Is Free: The Art of Making Quality Certain* (New York: McGraw-Hill, 1979), and Mary Walton, *The Deming Management Method* (New York: Dodd-Meade & Co., 1986).

15. Richard J. Schonberger, "Production Workers Bear Major Quality Responsibility in Japanese Industry," *Industrial Engineering* (December 1982), 34–40.

16. Jerry G. Bowles, "Beyond Customer Satisfaction through Quality Improvement," *Fortune*, September 26, 1988, special insert.

17. Donna Brown, "Ten Ways to Boost Quality," *Management Review*, January 1991, 5; Schonberger, "Total Quality Management Cuts a Broad Swath—Through Manufacturing and Beyond"; and Michael Barrier, "Small Firms Put Quality First," *Nation's Business*, May 1992, 22–32.

18. Schonberger, "Production Workers."

19. Johnson and Winchell, "Management and Quality," and Edward E. Lawler III and Susan A. Mohrman, "Quality Circles after the Fad," *Harvard Business Review* (January–February 1985), 65–71.

20. Thomas A. Stewart, "Westinghouse Gets Respect at Last," *Fortune*, July 3, 1989, 92–98.

21. Howard Rothman, "You Need Not Be Big to Benchmark," *Nation's Business*, December 1992, 64–65.

22. Otis Port and Geoffrey Smith, "Beg, Borrow and Benchmark," *Business Week*, November 30, 1992, 74–75.

23. Donna Brown, "Outsourcing: How Companies Take Their Business Elsewhere," *Management Review*, February 1992, 16–18, and David Kirkpatrick, "Why Not Farm Out Your Computing?" *Fortune*, September 23, 1991, 103–112.

24. Philip R. Thomas, Larry J. Gallace, and Kenneth R. Martin, "Quality Alone Is Not Enough," *AMA Management Briefing* (New York: American Management Association, 1992).

25. Otis Port, John Carey, Kevin Kelly, and Stephanie Anderson Forest, "Quality: Small and Midsize Companies Seize the Challenge Not a Moment Too Soon," *Business Week*, November 30, 1992, 68–72.

26. "Beyond Total Quality," *Success*, October 1990, 48–49.

27. Robert W. Haney and Charles D. Beaman, Jr., "Management Leadership Critical to CQI Success," *Hospitals*, July 20, 1992, 64.

28. Rick Tetzeli, "News/Trends: Making Quality More Than a Fad," *Fortune*, May 18, 1992, 12–13; Thomas et al., "Quality Alone Is Not Enough"; David E. Bowen and Edward E. Lawler III, "Total Quality-Oriented Human Resources Management," *Organizational Dynamics* (Spring 1992), 29–41; Robert Wood, Frank Hull, and Koya Azumi, "Evaluating Quality Circles: The American Application," *California Management Review* 26 (Fall 1983), 37–53; and Gregory P. Shea, "Quality Circles: The Danger of Bottled Change," *Sloan Management Review* 27 (Spring 1986), 33–46.

29. Jeremy Main, "Quality Fever at Florida Power," *Fortune*, July 1, 1991, 65, and Donald C. Bacon, "A Pursuit of Excellence," *Nation's Business*, January 1990, 27–28.

30. Peter Lorange, Michael F. Scott Morton, and Sumantra Ghoshal, *Strategic Control* (St. Paul, Minn.: West, 1986), Chapter 1.

31. Scott S. Cowen and J. Kendall Middaugh II, "Matching an Organization's Planning and Control System to Its Environment," *Journal of General Management* 16 (Autumn 1990), 69–84.

32. "Frito-Lay Shortens Its Business Cycle," *Fortune*, January 19, 1990, 11.

33. William H. Newman, *Constructive Control* (Englewood Cliffs, N.J.: Prentice-Hall, 1975).

34. Edward P. Gardner, "A Systems Approach to Bank Credential Management and Supervision: The Utilization of Feed Forward Control," *Journal of Management Studies* 22 (1985), 1–24.

35. Myron Magnet, "Managing by Mystique at Tandem Computers," *Fortune*, June 28, 1982, 84–91.

36. James A. F. Stoner and R. Edward Freeman, *Management* (Englewood Cliffs, N.J.: Prentice-Hall, 1992), and Peter Lorange and Declan Murphy, "Considerations in Implementing Strategic Control," *Journal of Business Strategy* 4 (Spring 1984), 27–35.

37. W. H. Read, "Upward Communication in Industrial Hierarchies," *Human Relations* 15 (February 1962), 3–15, and Michelle J. Glauser, "Factors Which Facilitate or Impede Upward Communication in Organizations" (Paper presented at the Academy of Management meeting, New York, August 1982).

38. David A. Garbin, "Quality on the Line," *Harvard Business Review* 61 (September–October 1983), 65–75.

39. Herbert M. Baum, "White-Collar Quality Comes of Age," *Journal of Business Strategy* (March–April 1990), 34–37; and Dreyfuss, "Victories in the Quality Crusade."

MOTOROLA

When Robert Galvin accepted the 1988 Malcolm Baldrige Award for quality, the company's executive committee chairman summed up Motorola's total quality philosophy, saying "it will never cost money to have a quality program" because companies will always "have lower costs and better products when [they] have a quality program."

In the past, the company that attained economies of scale making the greatest number of products usually came out on top. In a globally competitive marketplace, that is no longer true. Now customers demand durable products that feature the latest technology. In short, customers want each and every product to be the best.

The pursuit of customer satisfaction and total quality management has become the Holy Grail at Motorola. The company began an internal Total Customer Satisfaction competition in the 1980s that today also extends to suppliers. Like Motorola's own in-house total customer satisfaction teams, suppliers now come to Schaumburg, Illinois, for the annual competition. They use audio/visual presentations, as well as some showmanship, to illustrate innovations that improve product quality and production time. Judges include Galvin, company chairman and Chief Executive George Fisher, as well as a host of other executives.

Participation is not mandatory. "This is voluntary, by invitation. By competing they will not only get recognition from Motorola, but because our demands are so rigid, if a company can become a preferred supplier to Motorola, it can supply to anybody," said Ron Vocalino, regional manager for Motorola's land mobile products division.

Motorola categorizes suppliers into one of two tiers. Companies in the preferred tier make up around 30 percent of the total suppliers and receive 85 percent of Motorola's yearly purchase volume. The remaining 70 percent have yet to embrace the Total Customer Satisfaction credo.

Some suppliers have adopted the new philosophy with enthusiasm. Since accepting the Baldrige award, Motorola estimates it has saved as much as $2.2 billion in manufacturing costs. As an end user, the company considers it imperative that each and every supplier produces components worthy of the prestigious award. Targ-it-tronics Corporation, which supplies Motorola with flexible circuit boards for pagers and hand-held radios, is an example of a supplier that has instituted sweeping changes. Its companywide competition included 12 teams vying for total quality management and customer satisfaction awards.

The total quality approach has led to the implementation of new styles of in-house management at Motorola as well. The traditional hierarchical style has given way to individual worker empowerment and cross-corporate teams.

Motorola employees now also receive at least 40 hours of mandatory training every year. The training arm of the corporation, called Motorola University, offers specialized classes in accounting and finance, short-cycle manufacturing, computer operation, software engineering, time management, statistical process control, and even telephone courtesy skills. Courses are selected by the employee and supervisor during performance reviews and goal planning meetings. Employees can elect to pursue higher education through other colleges on their own time and are eligible for tuition reimbursement. Suppliers can also enroll at Motorola University.

The object of all the intensive training is to create a work force capable of implementing Motorola's "Six Sigma" program. The goal of this program is the attainment of quality standards that allow only 3.4 defects per million parts, or practically speaking, defect-free manufacturing.

Along with "Six Sigma" defect-free production, Robert Galvin believes he has envisioned the next challenge. "In my estimation," he said, "the real test of quality in the early part of the next century is going to be what I call the quality of leadership." As he sees it, it will be necessary for leaders to foresee technological applications for products and processes, as well as evaluating whether they took advantage of opportunities better than the competition.

Motorola's high standards for suppliers, employees, and company executives resulted in the Malcolm Baldrige Quality Award, but the motivation came from customers who demanded the finest. The company continues to search quietly for strategies that assist suppliers in becoming better. An impressive list of major corporations, including IBM, have taken note of the changes at Motorola and raced to emulate them. Ron Vocalino synopsized the new world order, at least at Motorola: "The total customer satisfaction philosophy has changed the way we do business."

● QUESTIONS

1. Do you think in the past companies intentionally built obsolescence into products? Will speed of innovation in this day and age constitute the same thing?

2. Might worker empowerment and ongoing education of employees lead to "too many chiefs and not enough Indians"? How can the manufacturing process be structured so that all input is tabulated in a timely manner while still maintaining production schedules?

3. Will product quality improvements all be for naught if free access to worldwide markets is denied?

4. Name the ways emphasis on product quality could be counterproductive.

MANAGEMENT CONTROL SYSTEMS **19**

LEARNING OBJECTIVES

After studying this chapter, you should be able to

- Identify the components of the core management control system.

- Describe financial statements, financial analysis, and financial audits used for top management controls.

- Explain the concept of responsibility centers and their relationship to operating and financial budgets.

- Explain the advantages of top-down versus bottom-up budgeting

- Describe zero-based budgeting and how it applies to organizations.

- Describe organizational indicators of inadequate control systems.

R. S. Bacon Veneer Company, an entrepreneurial company, was doing nicely selling about $4 million worth of wood veneer products to furniture manufacturers. The confusion began when its Big Six accounting firm designed an elaborate financial report for control that contained about 100 pages of items such as "operating income theoreticals" and "yield variances." Then sales stagnated just after Bacon invested in a new production facility. President Jim McCracken and Chief Executive George Wilhelm could not get a handle on cash flow or appropriate inventory levels. The crisis exploded when the accounting firm warned that the company needed an infusion of capital, and a few months later it urged Bacon to liquidate because bankruptcy was imminent.[1] ■ Do you think the problem here is with the report or with management's inability to understand financial numbers? What would you recommend McCracken and Wilhelm do?

The crisis at R. S. Bacon Veneer illustrates a problem of control—the managers are unsure of where they are going and do not have the numbers to tell whether they are on target. The Bacon example also suggests that numbers can be a problem as well as a solution. Financial management techniques have been criticized as inadequate and out of date in this era of rapid change and global competition. Concepts such as discounted cash flow analysis for plant and equipment purchases, for example, are abstract and theoretical. Rather than rely on such an abstract concept, many managers are learning that they are better off asking workers which piece of equipment they need to be more efficient.[2] And cost accounting systems, which are supposed to tell managers the cost and profitability of each product line, were designed 70 years ago to evaluate inventory. Today inventories are minimized, and the cost system assigns numbers that price some products too high and some too low, thereby weakening strategic competitiveness.[3] Knowing accurate costs would let managers know which product lines to expand and where to reduce prices.

Despite these weaknesses, managers need management control systems, including financial analyses, budgets, management by objectives, and other statistical reports. These control systems provide formal data and reports for management problem identification and corrective action. Control systems can be used with the clan approach to control described in Chapter 18. The Japanese pioneered quality circles and other clan approaches, and one study showed that managers in Japanese firms also had more quantitative information available from formal control systems than did managers in U.S. firms.[4]

Every organization needs basic systems for allocating financial resources, approving and developing human resources, analyzing financial performance, and evaluating operational productivity. In long-established organizations such as Cummins Engine, Lever Brothers, and Mack Trucks, the challenge for managers is to know how to use these control systems and improve them. In new, entrepreneurial firms—especially those that have grown rapidly—managers must design and implement new control systems.

We will begin by explaining how multiple control systems fit together to provide overall control for top managers and then examine control systems used by middle managers.

● CORE MANAGEMENT CONTROL SYSTEM

core control system

The strategic plans, financial forecasts, budgets, management by objectives, operations management techniques, and MIS reports that form an integrated system for directing and monitoring organizational activities.

       Research into the design of control systems across organizations has revealed the existence of a core management control system. The **core control system** consists of the strategic plans, financial forecasts, budgets, management by objectives, operations management techniques, and MIS reports that together provide an integrated system for directing and monitoring organizational activities.[5] The elements of the core control system and their relationship to one another are illustrated in Exhibit 19.1. The strategic plan and financial forecast provide guidance for the budget, management by objectives (MBO), and operations management systems used at middle management levels. The definition of each element in the core control system is as follows:[6]

1 *Strategic plan.* The strategic plan consists of the organization's strategic objectives, as discussed in Chapters 6 and 7. It is based on in-depth analysis of the organization's industry position, internal strengths and weaknesses, and environmental opportunities and threats. The written plan typically discusses company products, competition, economic trends, and new business opportunities.

2 *Financial forecast.* The financial forecast is based on a one- to five-year projection of company sales and revenues. This forecast is used to project income statements, balance sheets, and departmental expenditures. This is the company's financial projection based on the overall strategic plan. Companies such as W. R. Grace, Teledyne, and Union Carbide use projected financial statements to estimate their future financial positions.

3 *Operating budget.* The operating budget is an annual projection of estimated expenses, revenues, assets, and related financial figures for each operating department for the coming year. Budget reports typically are issued monthly and include comparisons of expenditures with budget targets. Budget reports are developed for all divisions and departments.

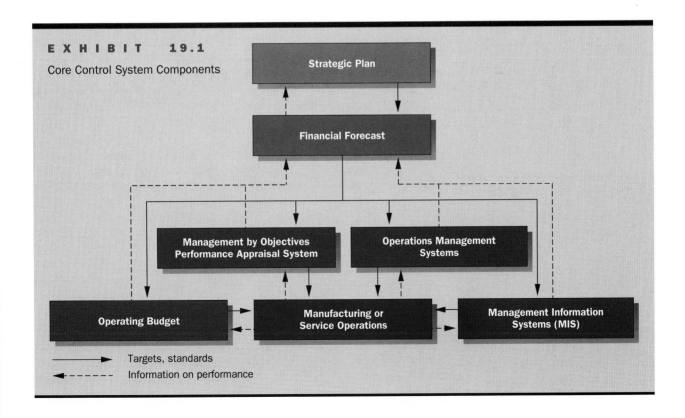

EXHIBIT   19.1

Core Control System Components

General Public Utilities Corporation (GPU) is reducing costs and improving efficiency, thanks to *core management control systems* that provide system-wide analysis of expenses, consolidation of functions, and elimination of unnecessary operations. For example, these Automated Cartridge System robots, installed at GPU's data center in Reading, Pennsylvania, retrieve and mount tapes with more accuracy and speed than humans, giving improved data reliability and accuracy as well as operational savings. The result of such innovations was a 6 percent reduction in administrative staff while maintaining or improving control system effectiveness.

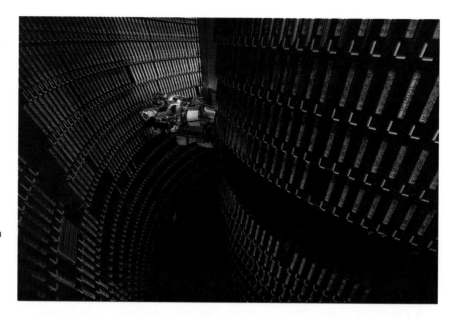

4 *Management by objectives.* Recall from Chapter 12 that performance appraisal is the formal method of evaluating and recording the performances of managers and employees. It typically includes standard forms and rating scales that evaluate employee skills and abilities. Many companies also use management by objectives, described in Chapter 6, to direct employee activities toward corporate objectives. MBO is integrated into the performance appraisal system and enhances management control.

5 *Operations management systems and reports.* Operations management systems pertain to inventory (economic order quantity, just-in-time), purchasing and distribution systems, and project management (PERT charts). Using operations management systems for control is the topic of Chapter 21.

6 *Management information system (MIS) reports.* MIS reports are composed of statistical data, such as personnel complements, volume of orders received, delinquent account ratios, percentage sales returns, and other statistical data relevant to the performance of a department or division. MIS reports typically contain nonfinancial data, whereas operating budgets contain financial data. MIS reports are issued weekly and monthly, and their exact content depends on the nature of tasks and available measures. A sales department MIS report may describe the number of new sales, whereas an assembly department report may record the number of parts assembled per hour. Management information systems will be discussed in Chapter 20.

Each control system component is separate and distinct from the others. The overall strategic plan is top management's responsibility and the financial forecast the controller's. The budget is concerned with the financial figures and is also the controller's responsibility. The management by objectives system is usually the responsibility of the human resource department. Operations management techniques are the responsibility of the production department. MIS reports are produced and distributed by the information system department. Although each control system element is distinct, a successful core control system combines them into an integrated package of controls.

In this chapter, we discuss control systems as they are used by top and middle management levels, as illustrated in Exhibit 19.2. Top management control systems concern financial performance for the organization as a whole and include financial statements, financial analyses, and audits. Middle managers are responsible for departments and rely heavily on budgets and MBO systems (described in Chapter 6) for control. The other components of the core control system—MIS reports and operations management techniques—will be discussed in Chapters 20 and 21, respectively.

Control systems are vital, regardless of the company size. One small company that focuses on strong core management control systems is Granite Rock Company of Watsonville, California.

 ## GRANITE ROCK COMPANY

Granite Rock is a family-owned company that quarries granite, produces and delivers concrete and asphalt, and sells building materials such as brick and cinder block. In an increasingly non-union industry where competitors are free of union regulations, Granite's twelve unionized plants employ 400 workers. Union wages, customer demands for quality and service, the enforcement of strict state regulations for air and water quality, computerized technology, and increased competition necessitate a strong core management control system in order to maintain growth. In Granite's $90 million operation, everyone watches numbers.

Brothers Bruce and Steve Woolpert, joint CEOs, implemented forecasting and strategic land acquisition systems, and long-range resource planning to maintain Granite's competitive edge. Granite's refined information gathering techniques such as the Granite Express computerized

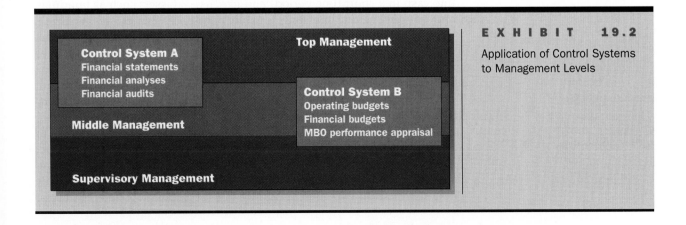

Top Management

Control System A
Financial statements
Financial analyses
Financial audits

Control System B
Operating budgets
Financial budgets
MBO performance appraisal

Middle Management

Supervisory Management

E X H I B I T   19.2

Application of Control Systems to Management Levels

loading system and statistical-process-control charts enable management and employees at all levels to measure performance in key areas such as resource allocation, customer service, and delivery. In-house training for all managers and hourly workers at Granite Rock University enables employees to keep abreast of new technology and control methods and to analyze the information they receive. Granite's feedback system is second to none. In addition to the famous "report cards" through which customers grade company performance in a number of categories, Granite follows up problems and complaints through detailed product-service discrepancy reports that contribute to evaluation of performance by analyzing the root cause of specific problems. Such control systems enable Granite to maintain top quality in its products and a healthy share of the market despite slightly higher prices than its competitors.[7] ■

● TOP MANAGEMENT FINANCIAL CONTROL

Based on the overall strategic plan, top management must define a financial forecast for the organization, perform financial analyses of selected ratios to reveal business performance, and use financial audits to evaluate internal operations. Each of these controls is based on financial statements—the building blocks of financial control.

FINANCIAL STATEMENTS: THE BASIC NUMBERS

Financial statements provide the basic information used for financial control of a company. Two major financial statements—the balance sheet and the income statement—are the starting points for financial control.

The **balance sheet** shows the firm's financial position with respect to assets and liabilities at a specific point in time. An example of a balance sheet is presented in Exhibit 19.3. The balance sheet provides three types of information: assets, liabilities, and owners' equity. *Assets* are what the company owns and include *current assets* (assets that can be converted into cash in a short time period) and *fixed assets* (assets such as buildings and equipment that are long term in nature). *Liabilities* are the firm's debts and include both *current debt* (obligations that will be paid by the company in the near future) and *long-term debt* (obligations payable over a long period). *Owners' equity* is the difference between assets and liabilities and is the company's net worth in stock and retained earnings.

The **income statement,** sometimes called a *profit-and-loss statement,* summarizes the firm's financial performance for a given time interval, usually one year. A sample income statement is given in Exhibit 19.4. Some firms calculate the income statement at three-month intervals during the year to see if they are on target for sales and profits. The income statement shows revenues coming into the organization from all sources and subtracts all expenses, including cost of goods sold, interest, taxes,

balance sheet

A financial statement showing the firm's financial position with respect to assets and liabilities at a specific point in time.

income statement

A financial statement that summarizes a company's financial performance over a given time interval.

E X H I B I T   19.3

Balance Sheet

Lester's Clothiers
Consolidated Balance Sheet
December 31, 1993

Assets			Liabilities and Owners' Equity		
Current assets:			Current liabilities:		
Cash	$ 25,000		Accounts payable	$200,000	
Accounts receivable	75,000		Accrued expenses	20,000	
Inventory	500,000		Income taxes payable	30,000	
Total current assets		$ 600,000	Total current liabilities		$ 250,000
Fixed assets:			Long-term liabilities:		
Land	250,000		Mortgages payable	350,000	
Buildings and fixtures	1,000,000		Bonds outstanding	250,000	
Less depreciation	200,000		Total long-term liabilities		$ 600,000
Total fixed assets		1,050,000	Owners' equity:		
			Common stock	540,000	
			Retained earnings	260,000	
			Total owners' equity		800,000
Total assets		$1,650,000	Total liabilities and net worth		$1,650,000

E X H I B I T   19.4

Income Statement

Lester's Clothiers
Statement of Income
For the Year Ended December 31, 1993

Gross sales	$3,100,000	
Less sales returns	200,000	
Net sales		$2,900,000
Less expenses and cost of goods sold:		
Cost of goods sold	2,110,000	
Depreciation	60,000	
Sales expenses	200,000	
Administrative expenses	90,000	2,460,000
Operating profit		440,000
Other income		20,000
Gross income		460,000
Less interest expense	80,000	
Income before taxes		380,000
Less taxes	165,000	
Net income		$ 215,000

Clothes with a little character.

"He's helping!" The continued popularity of Oshkosh B'Gosh children's wear provides solid financial strength for the Wisconsin-based apparel company by providing 95 percent of total sales. Oshkosh's *current ratio* in 1991 was 4.1, indicating solid financial strength to pay off current debts. Current assets include cash and accounts receivable, which are 4.1 times greater than current liabilities such as the short-term borrowings supported by $45 million in bank lines of credit to fund seasonal working capital needs.

liquidity ratio

A financial ratio that indicates the company's ability to meet its current debt obligations.

activity ratio

A ratio that measures the firm's internal performance with respect to key activities defined by management.

and depreciation. The bottom line indicates the net income—profit or loss—for the given time period.

For example, Jim Greenwood, founder of Aahs!, a specialty retailing chain in California, used the income statement to detect that sales and profits were dropping during the summer months. He immediately evaluated company activities and closed two money-losing stores. He also began a new education program to teach employees how to increase sales and decrease costs to improve net income. As a result, the Aahs! gross profit margin was 3 percent ahead of target.[8] This use of the income statement follows the control cycle described in Chapter 18, beginning with the measurement of actual performance and then taking corrective action to improve performance to meet targets.

FINANCIAL ANALYSIS: INTERPRETING THE NUMBERS

The most important numbers typically are not actual dollars spent or earned, but ratios. Any business is a set of hundreds of relationships among people, things, and events.[9] Key relationships are typically revealed in ratios that provide insight into some aspect of company behavior. These insights make manager decision making possible.

A *financial ratio* is the comparison of two financial numbers. To understand their business, managers have to understand financial ratios. For example, a small corner grocery store had plenty of customers but was losing money. The store's financial numbers looked okay, so the owners sought help. The consultant said the books looked good, except for the labor cost ratio, indicating labor costs were 18 percent of revenues. The owners did not know that a specialty food retailer typically cannot make a profit if labor exceeds 10 percent of sales. They cut labor and the store has been profitable ever since. When Paul Hawken started Smith & Hawken, he learned an absolutely vital ratio. In the catalog business, the cost of goods, the catalog, and any advertising must not exceed 70 percent of revenue. Monitoring this single ratio tells him how things are going on a weekly basis and whether to add or reduce labor.[10]

Several financial ratios can be studied to interpret company performance. Managers must decide which ratios reveal the most important relationships for their business. Frequently calculated ratios typically pertain to liquidity, activity, and profitability. Many companies compare their performance with those of other firms in the same industry as well as with their own budget targets.

LIQUIDITY RATIO.   A **liquidity ratio** indicates the organization's ability to meet its current debt obligations. For example, the *current ratio* tells whether there are sufficient assets to convert into cash to pay off debts if needed. If a hypothetical company, Oceanographics, Inc., had current assets of $600,000 and current liabilities of $250,000, the current ratio is 2.4, meaning it has sufficient funds to pay off immediate debts 2.4 times. This is normally considered a satisfactory margin of safety.

ACTIVITY RATIO.   An **activity ratio** measures internal performance with respect to key activities defined by management. For example, *inventory turnover* is calculated by dividing total sales by average inventory. This ratio tells how many times the inventory is turned over to meet the total sales figure. If inventory sits too long, money is wasted. For Oceanographics, Inc., inventory turnover is 10, which compares favorably to industry standards. The *conversion ratio* is purchase orders divided by customer inquiries, which measures company effectiveness in converting inquiries into sales. For Oceanographics, Inc., this ratio is 50 percent, which is low compared with 60 percent for the industry. A sharp manager will infer that the number of inquiries is low or the sales force is doing a poor job closing sales. After investigation, improvements will be made either in promotional advertising or sales force training.

PROFITABILITY RATIO.   **Profitability ratios** describe the organization's profits. One important profitability ratio is the *profit margin on sales,* which is calculated as net income divided by sales. For Oceanographics, Inc., the profit margin on sales is 8 percent. Another profitability measure is *return on total assets (ROA),* which is the percentage return to investors on assets. It is a valuable yardstick of the return on investment compared with other investment opportunities. Return on total assets for Oceanographics is 13 percent, which means senior managers are making good use of assets to earn profits; thus, the owners are unlikely to sell the company and invest their money elsewhere.

Analyzing these various financial ratios can help managers of U.S. companies understand their business more clearly, especially with the increase in global competition.

profitability ratio

A financial ratio that describes the firm's profits.

FINANCIAL AUDITS: VERIFYING THE NUMBERS

Financial audits are independent appraisals of the organization's financial records. Audits are of two types—external and internal.[11] An *external audit* is conducted by experts from outside the organization, typically certified public accountants (CPAs) or CPA firms. An *internal audit* is handled by experts within the organization. Large companies such as Allis-Chalmers, American Can, Boise Cascade, and Boeing have an accounting staff assigned to the internal audit function. The internal auditors evaluate departments and divisions throughout the corporation to ensure that operations are efficient and conducted according to prescribed company practices.

financial audit

An independent appraisal of the organization's financial records, conducted by external or internal experts.

Both external and internal audits should be thorough. Their purpose is to examine every nook and cranny to verify that the financial statement represents actual company operations. The following are some of the areas examined by auditors:

- *Cash:* Go to banks and confirm bank balances; review cash management procedures.
- *Receivables:* Obtain guarantees from customers concerning amounts owed and anticipated payments; confirm balances.
- *Inventory:* Conduct physical count of inventory and compare with financial statement; review for obsolescence.

- *Fixed assets:* Make physical observation, evaluate depreciation; determine whether insurance is adequate.
- *Loans:* Review loan agreements; summarize obligations.
- *Revenues and expenses:* Evaluate timing, propriety, and amount.[12]

USING FINANCIAL CONTROLS

Remember that the point of financial numbers is to gain insight into company relationships to identify areas out of control and take corrective action. Managers must use numbers wisely and see beneath the surface to decide exactly what is causing the problem and devise a solution. A financial performance shortfall often has several causes, and managers must be familiar with company operations and activities in order to make an accurate diagnosis. Managers can use numbers creatively and dig beneath the figures to find the causes of problems. After defining the causes, they can initiate programs that will rectify the problem and bring the financial figures back into line.

One superb example of using financial controls to bring a small company back into line occurred at Incomnet, Inc. Sam Schwartz, a major investor, took over the company after the financial statements suggested impending disaster.

 INCOMNET

Incomnet is a technology company in California that recently had annual sales of $1.2 million for its computer network that tracks used car parts for auto repair shops. Incomnet experienced extraordinary demand and overextended, growing far beyond its financial resources. Just five years old, the company had eaten up $13 million in investments without anything resembling a profit. When Schwartz took over, he interviewed everyone about problems, and he examined every line in Incomnet's woeful financial statements.

A close examination of the balance sheet showed that the current assets figure of $1.3 million was bloated because of obsolete and unsellable inventory. Moreover, accounts receivable were in disarray, with payments averaging 110 days. Further analysis and writeoffs dropped current assets to a small $180,000, but this was a number Schwartz could trust. Revamping accounts receivable led to customer payments for monthly services in advance, allowing cash flow to shift from a negative $60,000 monthly to a positive $50,000. Schwartz also found expenses too high, with "administrative expenses" out of control. Corporate overhead was $900,000 on sales of just $1.2 million. Schwartz moved to combine all corporate operations under one roof, pulled the plug on health club fees and luxury cars, and shrank the overhead figure to an acceptable $400,000 a year.

These changes were dramatic, and they changed the financial performance sharply. In two years, Incomnet saw its first profit—about $250,000 on sales of $2.7 million. Financial controls made the difference.[13] ■

● MIDDLE MANAGEMENT BUDGET CONTROL

Budgets are a primary control device for middle management. Of course, top managers too are involved with budgets for the company as a whole, but middle managers are responsible for the budget performance of their departments or divisions. Budgets identify both planned and actual expenditures for cash, assets, raw materials, salaries, and other resources departments need. Budgets are the most widely used control system, because they plan and control resources and revenues essential to the firm's health and survival.[14]

A budget is created for every division or department within the organization, no matter how small, so long as it performs a distinct project, program, or function. In order for budgets to be used, the organization must define each department as a responsibility center.

RESPONSIBILITY CENTERS

A responsibility center is the fundamental unit of analysis of a budget control system. A **responsibility center** is defined as any organizational department under the supervision of a single person who is responsible for its activity.[15] A three-person appliance sales office in Watertown, New York, is a responsibility center, as is General Electric's entire refrigerator manufacturing plant. The manager of each unit has budget "responsibility."

There are four major types of responsibility centers—cost centers, revenue centers, profit centers, and investment centers. The budget focus for each type of cost center is illustrated in Exhibit 19.5 on page 667.

COST CENTER. A *cost center* is a responsibility center in which the manager is held responsible for controlling cost inputs. The manager is responsible for salaries, supplies, and other costs relevant to the department's operation. Staff departments such as personnel, legal, and research typically are organized as cost centers, and budgets reflect the cost to run the department.

REVENUE CENTER. In a *revenue center,* the budget is based on generated revenues or income. Sales and marketing departments frequently are revenue centers. The department has a revenue goal, such as $3,500,000. Assuming that each salesperson can generate $250,000 of revenue per year, the department can be allocated 14 salespeople. Revenue budgets can also be calculated as the number of items to be sold rather than as total revenues. For example, the revenue budget for an appliance shop might include 50 refrigerators, 75 washers, 60 dryers, and 40 microwaves to be sold for 1994.

PROFIT CENTER. In a *profit center,* the budget measures the difference between revenues and costs. For budget purposes, the profit center is defined as a self-contained unit to enable a profit to be calculated. In Kollmorgen Corporation, each division is a profit center. Control is based on profit targets rather than on cost or revenue targets.

■

responsibility center

Any organizational department under the supervision of a single individual who is responsible for its activity.

Ohio Edison managed record sales during a weak economic period, in part by using *financial controls.* In 1991, Ohio Edison's strict cost-control systems reduced capital expenses by $35 million, employees by over 300, and streamlined operations by closing older facilities needing costly environmental controls to achieve compliance with the Clean Air Act. Here, a helicopter caps the stacks on one plant closed as part of Ohio Edison's financial control approach.

INVESTMENT CENTER.   An *investment center* is based on the value of assets employed to produce a given level of profit. Profits are calculated in the same way as in a profit center, but for control purposes, managers are concerned with return on the investment in assets for the division. For example, Exxon may acquire a gasoline refinery for a price of $40 million. If Exxon managers target a 10 percent return on investment, the gasoline refinery will be expected to generate profits of $4 million a year. Exxon managers are not concerned with the absolute dollar value of costs, revenues, or profits so long as the budgeted return on assets reaches 10 percent.

President Bush's signing of the Inter-modal Surface Transportation Efficiency Act of 1991 encouraged civil contractors to nab highway projects such as this one near San Jose, directed by Granite Construction Co. Unlike many competitors, Granite's strategy focuses on selective bidding centered on projects that meet strict profitability guidelines established by *profit center* managers. Granite's salaries for officers and profit center managers are lower than the industry norm, but with additional incentive pay linked to profit center results. At Granite, profitability takes precedence over volume as the company helps to rebuild the nation's aging infrastructure.

RELATIONSHIP TO STRUCTURE.   Responsibility centers are closely related to the types of organization structure described in Chapter 9. Cost centers and revenue centers typically exist in a functional structure. The production, assembly, finance, accounting, and human resource departments control expenditures through cost budgets. Marketing or sales departments, however, often are controlled as revenue centers. Profit centers typically exist in a divisional structure. Each self-contained division can be evaluated on the basis of total revenues minus total costs, which equals profits. Finally, very large companies in which each division is an autonomous business use investment centers. Frito-Lay and Taco Bell are investment centers for PepsiCo. PepsiCo managers are concerned with the return on investment from these companies, and each business is left alone so long as investment goals are met.

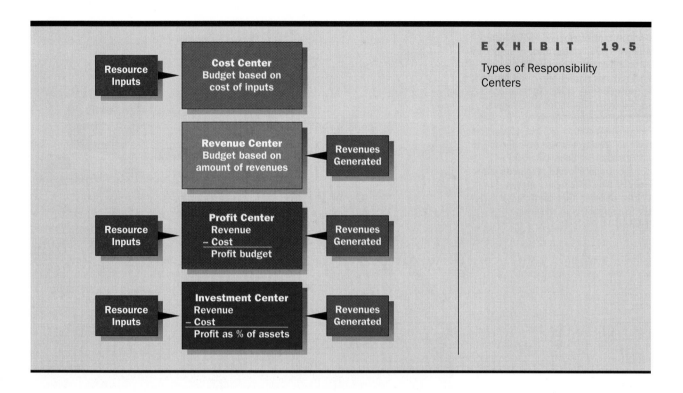

E X H I B I T 19.5

Types of Responsibility Centers

OPERATING BUDGETS

An **operating budget** is the financial plan for each organizational responsibility center for the budget period. The operating budget outlines the financial resources allocated to each responsibility center in dollar terms, typically calculated for a year in advance. The most common types of operating budgets are expense, revenue, and profit budgets.

EXPENSE BUDGET. An **expense budget** outlines the anticipated expenses for each responsibility center and for the total organization. Expense budgets apply to cost centers, as described above. The department of management at the University of Illinois may have a travel budget of $24,000; thus, the department head knows that the expense budget can be spent at approximately $2,000 per month. Three different kinds of expenses normally are evaluated in the expense budget—fixed, variable, and discretionary.

Fixed costs are based on a commitment from a prior budget period and cannot be changed. The price of expensive machinery purchased three years ago that is paid over a period of 10 years is a fixed cost. The same is true for the annual mortgage payments on a building amortized over 15 years.

Variable costs, often called *engineered costs,* are based on an explicit physical relationship with the volume of departmental activity. Variable costs are calculated in manufacturing departments when a separate cost

operating budget

The plan for the allocation of financial resources to each organizational responsibility center for the budget period under consideration.

expense budget

An operating budget that outlines the anticipated expenses for each responsibility center and for the organization as a whole.

fixed costs

Costs that are based on a commitment from a previous budget period and cannot be altered.

variable costs

Costs that are based on an explicit physical relationship with the volume of departmental activity; also called *engineered costs.*

Alaska Airlines watches its operating expense budget closely, and reported a profit in 1991, unlike most of its industry counterparts. *Fixed costs* are for airplanes, as shown here, and for new or expanded terminals. *Variable costs* are for expenditures for fuel, wages, and crew training. *Discretionary costs* include the addition of new routes, such as Alaska Airlines' new service to the Russian Far East, because managers can allocate resources elsewhere if they so choose. Alaska Airlines believes that cost control is a key to profitability in the airline business.

can be assigned for each product produced. A variable cost budget might allocate two hours of machine time for each turbine blade or $3 in supplies for each integrated circuit board. The greater the volume of production, the greater the expense budget the department will have.

Discretionary costs are based on management decisions. They are not based on a fixed, long-term commitment or on volume of items produced, because discretionary costs cannot be calculated with precision. In the judgment of top management, an expense budget of $120,000 might be assigned to the inspection department to pay the salaries of four inspectors, one assistant, and one secretary. This budget could be increased or decreased the following year, depending on whether management feels more inspectors are needed.

REVENUE BUDGET.   A **revenue budget** identifies the revenues required by the organization. The revenue budget is the responsibility of a revenue center, such as marketing or sales. The revenue budget for a small manufacturing firm could be $3 million, based on sales of 600,000 items at $5 each. The revenue budget of $6 million for a local school district would be calculated not on sales to customers but on the community's current tax rate and property values.

PROFIT BUDGET.   A **profit budget** combines both expense and revenue budgets into one statement to show gross and net profits. Profit budgets apply to profit and investment centers. If a bank has budgeted income of $2 million and budgeted expenses of $1,800,000, the estimated

---

discretionary costs

Costs based on management decisions and not on fixed commitments or volume of output.

revenue budget

An operating budget that identifies the revenues required by the organization.

profit budget

An operating budget that combines both expense and revenue budgets into one statement showing gross and net profits.

profit will be $200,000. If the budget profit is unacceptable, managers must develop a plan for increasing revenues or decreasing costs to achieve an acceptable profit return.

FINANCIAL BUDGETS

Financial budgets define where the organization will receive its cash and how it intends to spend it. Three important financial budgets are the cash, capital expenditure, and balance sheet budgets.

CASH BUDGET. The **cash budget** estimates cash flows on a daily or weekly basis to ensure that the organization has sufficient cash to meet its obligations. The cash budget shows the level of funds flowing through the organization and the nature of cash disbursements. If the cash budget shows that the firm has more cash than necessary, the company can arrange to invest the excess cash in Treasury bills to earn interest income. If the cash budget shows a payroll expenditure of $20,000 coming at the end of the week but only $10,000 in the bank, the controller must borrow cash to meet the payroll.

CAPITAL EXPENDITURE BUDGET. The **capital expenditure budget** plans future investments in major assets such as buildings, trucks, and heavy machinery. *Capital expenditures* are major purchases that are paid for over several years. Capital expenditures must be budgeted to determine their impact on cash flow and whether revenues are sufficient to cover capital expenditures and annual operating expenditures. Large corporations such as Navistar, Scott Paper, and Joseph E. Seagram & Sons assign financial analysts to work exclusively on the development of a capital expenditure budget. The analysts also monitor whether actual capital expenditures are being made according to plan.

financial budget

A budget that defines where the organization will receive its cash and how it will spend it.

cash budget

A financial budget that estimates cash flows on a daily or weekly basis to ensure that the company has sufficient cash to meet its obligations.

capital expenditure budget

A financial budget that plans future investments in major assets to be paid for over several years.

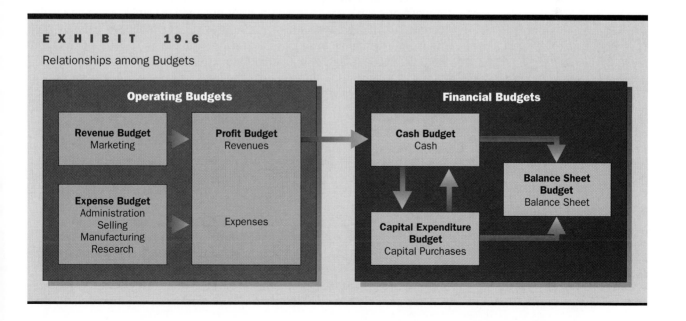

E X H I B I T   19.6

Relationships among Budgets

balance sheet budget

A financial budget that plans the amount of assets and liabilities for the end of the time period under consideration.

BALANCE SHEET BUDGET. The **balance sheet budget** plans the amount of assets and liabilities for the end of the time period under consideration. It indicates whether the capital expenditures and cash management, revenues, and operating expenses will mesh into the financial results desired by senior management. The balance sheet budget shows where future financial problems may exist. Financial ratio analysis can be performed on the balance sheet and profit budgets to see whether important ratio targets, such as debt to total assets or ROA, will be met.

The relationships among the operating and financial budgets are illustrated in Exhibit 19.6. All company budgets are interconnected. The revenue budget combined with the cost budget leads to the profit budget. The profit budget influences the amount of cash available, which in turn determines the amount of capital purchases the company can afford. The data from these budgets enable calculation of the balance sheet budget.

Rapid change and fluctuation in some industries makes budgeting, especially cash budgeting, extremely difficult. Trinity Computing Systems discovered how to manage its cash budget despite industry fluctuations.

 TRINITY COMPUTING SYSTEMS

Jim Pritchett and Dana Sellers, owners of Trinity Computing Systems, face many challenges. Their company's computers are installed in hospitals, but the average $200,000 price tag means slow payments over several months while the computer is installed and hospital personnel are fully trained. Unpredictable payments from clients, rapidly growing sales, and demands for payment from vendors created a wildly fluctuating cash flow that was handled by day-to-day crisis management. To solve the problem, Trinity went to a weekly financial cash budget, accompanied by a weekly forecast of cash coming in and flowing out, and a weekly meeting to discuss the cash situation with department heads. By collecting information on inventory, shipping dates, installation schedules, and collection dates every week, department heads could coordinate available resources and keep abreast of potential cash problems. The detailed cash budget enabled Trinity to reduce collections from 120 days to 80 days. Precise forecasting also strengthened Trinity's ability to borrow money and to buy goods on credit because the tight schedules testified to Trinity's sound management practices. Adopting a weekly cash budget literally saved Trinity from bankruptcy. As one manager said, "Without the cash-flow forecast, I doubt we would have had a product line worth selling."[16] ∎

THE BUDGETING PROCESS

The budgeting process is concerned with how budgets are actually formulated and implemented in an organization. In this section, we will briefly describe the procedure many companies use to develop the budget for the coming year.

TOP-DOWN OR BOTTOM-UP BUDGETING

Many traditional companies use **top-down budgeting,** which is consistent with the bureaucratic control approach discussed in Chapter 18. The budgeted amounts for the coming year are literally imposed on middle- and lower-level managers.[17] The top-down process has certain advantages: Top managers have information on overall economic projections; they know the financial goals and forecasts; and they have reliable information about the amount of resources available in the coming year. Thus, the top-down process enables managers to set budget targets for each department to meet the needs of overall company revenues and expenditures.

The problem with the top-down budgeting process is that lower managers often are not committed to achieving budget targets. They are excluded from the budgeting process and resent their lack of involvement in deciding the resources available to their departments in the coming year.[18]

In response to these negative outcomes, many organizations adopt **bottom-up budgeting,** which is in line with the clan approach to control. Lower managers anticipate their departments' resource needs, which are passed up the hierarchy and approved by top management. The advantage of the bottom-up process is that lower managers are able to identify resource requirements about which top managers are uninformed, have information on efficiencies and opportunities in their specialized areas, and are motivated to meet the budget because the budget plan is their responsibility.[19]

However, the bottom-up approach also has problems. Managers' estimates of future expenditures may be inconsistent with realistic economic projections for the industry or with company financial forecasts and objectives. A university accounting department may plan to increase the number of professors by 20 percent, which is too much if the university plans to increase accounting student enrollment by only 10 percent.

The result of these advantages and disadvantages is that many companies use a joint process. Top managers and the controller define economic projections and financial goals and forecasts and then inform lower managers of the anticipated resources available to them. Once these overall targets (for example, a resource increase of 4 to 7 percent) are made available, department managers can develop their budgets within them. Each department can take advantage of special information, resource requirements, and opportunities. The budget is then passed up to the next management level, where inconsistencies across departments can be removed.

The combined top-down and bottom-up process is illustrated in Exhibit 19.7. Top managers begin the cycle. They also end it by giving final approval to all departmental budgets. Departmental budgets fall within the guidelines provided by top management, and the overall company budget reflects the specific knowledge, needs, and opportunities within each department.

Quaker Oats Company employs a *top-down, bottom-up approach* to planning and budgeting. Its overall financial objectives, including earnings, dividends, growth rates, and profits, are established at the top and passed down to divisions. Specific budget plans and operating strategies within divisions, such as Quaker-Canada, are defined bottom-up. The two sets of plans are reviewed by senior management and integrated to meet the needs of divisions and the overall corporation.

top-down budgeting

A budgeting process in which middle- and lower-level managers set departmental budget targets in accordance with overall company revenues and expenditures specified by top management.

bottom-up budgeting

A budgeting process in which lower-level managers budget their departments' resource needs and pass them up to top management for approval.

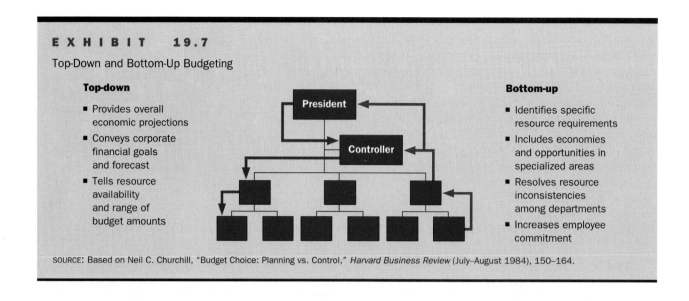

E X H I B I T   19.7

Top-Down and Bottom-Up Budgeting

Top-down

- Provides overall economic projections
- Conveys corporate financial goals and forecast
- Tells resource availability and range of budget amounts

President

Controller

Bottom-up

- Identifies specific resource requirements
- Includes economies and opportunities in specialized areas
- Resolves resource inconsistencies among departments
- Increases employee commitment

SOURCE: Based on Neil C. Churchill, "Budget Choice: Planning vs. Control," *Harvard Business Review* (July–August 1984), 150–164.

ZERO-BASED BUDGETING

In most organizations, the budgeting process begins with the previous year's expenditures; that is, managers plan future expenditures as an increase or decrease over the previous year. This procedure tends to lock departments into a stable spending pattern that lacks flexibility to meet environmental changes. **Zero-based budgeting (ZBB)** was designed to overcome this rigidity by having each department start from zero in calculating resource needs for the new budget period.[20] ZBB assumes that the previous year's budget is not a valid base from which to work. Rather, based on next year's strategic plans, each responsibility center justifies its work activities and needed personnel, supplies, and facilities for the next budget period. Responsibility centers that cannot justify expenditures for the coming year will receive fewer resources or be disbanded altogether. In zero-based budgeting, each year is viewed as bringing a new set of goals. It forces department managers to thoroughly examine their operations and justify their departments' activities based on their direct contribution to the achievement of organizational goals.[21]

The zero-based budgeting technique was originally developed for use in government organizations as a way to justify cost requests for the succeeding year. The U.S. Department of Agriculture was the first to use zero-based budgeting in the 1960s. ZBB was adopted by Texas Instruments in 1970 and by many government and business organizations during the 1970s and 1980s. Companies such as Ford, Westinghouse, Owens-Illinois, and New York Telephone, as well as government agencies at both the federal and state levels, use zero-based budgeting.

The specific steps used in zero-based budgeting are as follows:

1 Managers develop a *decision package* for their responsibility centers. The decision package includes written statements of the department's objectives, activities, costs, and benefits; alternative ways of achieving objectives; consequences of not performing each activity;

---

zero-based budgeting (ZBB)

A budgeting process in which each responsibility center calculates its resource needs based on the coming year's priorities rather than on the previous year's budget.

and personnel, equipment, and resources required during the coming year. Managers then assign a rank order to the activities in their department for the coming year.

2 The decision package is then forwarded to top management for review. Senior managers rank the decision packages from the responsibility centers according to their degree of benefit to the organization. These rankings involve widespread management discussions and may culminate in a voting process in which managers rate activities from "essential" to "would be nice to have" to "not needed."

3 Top management allocates organizational resources based on activity rankings. Budget resources are distributed according to the activities rated as essential to meeting organizational goals. Some departments may receive large budgets and others nothing at all.

Zero-based budgeting demands more time and energy than conventional budgeting. Because it forces management to abandon traditional budget practices, top management should develop a consensus among participants that ZBB will have a positive influence on both the company and its employees.

ADVANTAGES AND DISADVANTAGES OF BUDGET CONTROL

Budgeting is the most widely used control system in North American organizations. It offers several advantages to managers but can also create problems. The advantages and disadvantages of budgets are summarized in Exhibit 19.8.

The first major strength of budgeting is that it coordinates activities across departments. The budget ties together resource requirements from each responsibility center into a financial blueprint for the entire firm. Second, budgets translate strategic plans into action. They specify the resources, revenues, and activities required to carry out the strategic plan for the coming year. Third, budgets provide an excellent record of organizational activities. Fourth, budgets improve communication, because they provide information to employees. Budgets let people see where the

---

E X H I B I T   19.8
Advantages and Disadvantages of Budgets

Advantages

- Facilitate coordination across departments
- Translate strategic plans into departmental actions
- Record organizational activities
- Improve communication with employees
- Improve resource allocation
- Provide a tool for corrective action through reallocations

Disadvantages

- Can be used mechanically
- Can demotivate employees because of lack of participation
- Can cause perceptions of unfairness
- Can create competition for resources and politics
- Can limit opportunities for innovation and adaptation

NO TASTE FOR WASTE

Ken Hendricks touts his ABC roofing supply company in Beloit, Wisconsin, as "the biggest small company in America." Repeatedly listed as one of the fastest-growing companies in the United States, with sales of $350 million and an annual growth rate of 35 percent, ABC is a stickler for details. Cost control, budget control, and waste control are not simply axioms but are values central to ABC's corporate culture. Hendricks does not believe in wasting *anything*—money, time, buildings, or people. He claims that companies lose 30 percent productivity by people wasting time and calls this waste the "biggest factor in today's business."

ABC Supply proves that waste can be controlled through proper budgeting, especially when incorporated with strategic goals. ABC's rent is 1.8 percent of sales compared to an industry average of 3.9 percent. Truck expenses are 2 percent of sales, compared to an industry average 5 percent. ABC achieves an astonishing $450,000 in sales per employee, compared to a competitor average of about $200,000 per employee. The secret? A company-wide commitment to waste control.

ABC recycles everything. Stores are located in older, used buildings near the center of cities. Why? Because many potential customers are located in older sections of the city, not in the suburbs. Besides, real estate is cheaper in the city center. Hendricks scours the area for old equipment, old trucks, and so on that can be repaired for a fraction of the cost of new equipment. Moreover, Hendricks does not fire people. His policy is to utilize people, insisting it is far easier to retrain a "failed" manager than to locate and train a new manager.

The secret to waste reduction, according to Hendricks, is to study where waste is occurring and to set up strict budget standards. He advises looking at the company profit and loss statement to determine where money is being spent and to establish tough standards in those areas. At ABC Supply, every employee sees the financial numbers. Every employee understands what it costs to do business and how his or her performance fits into the overall picture. By providing monthly budget and profit figures compared to the previous year, employees can join management in finding ways to make their jobs quicker and easier. Making the money, Hendricks insists, is the *result* of good business practice, not the *goal*. ∎

SOURCE: Interview with Ken Hendricks, "Waste Not, Want Not," *INC.*, March 1991, 33–42.

organization is going and their role in that mission. Fifth, budgets improve prudent resource allocation, because all requests are clarified and justified. Senior managers get a chance to compare budget requests across departments and set priorities for resource allocation. Finally, budgets provide a way of implementing corrective action. For example, when personal computer sales declined in 1989, the PC managers at IBM used a budget to reduce expenditures for PC manufacturing and increase budgeted resources for other computer lines. The Winning Moves box describes how one company uses budgets effectively to squeeze waste out, enabling both rapid growth and solid profits.

Budgets can also cause headaches for managers when improperly used. The major problem occurs when budgets are applied mechanically and rigidly. The budgeting process is then only an exercise in filling out paperwork, with each department getting the same percentage increase or decrease as the others. Second, when managers and employees are not allowed to participate in the budget-setting process, budgeting is

This is Brunswick Corporation's MerCruiser, the largest selling brand of marine stern drives in the world. Despite a domestic marine recession, Brunswick has used the *advantages of budgets* to translate company strategy into departmental actions. Rightsizing was achieved by closing plants and a foundry, dealer inventories were reduced 17 percent, debt was lowered, and a significant number of new marine and recreational products was introduced to expand business in key areas. Budget and financial controls make a difference at Brunswick.

demotivating. If budgets are arbitrarily imposed top down, employees will not understand the reason for budgeted expenditures and will not be committed to them. A third weakness occurs when budget perceptions differ across hierarchical levels. Supervisors also may feel they did not receive a fair share of resources if top managers do not explain corporate priorities and budget decisions. Fourth, budgets may pit departments against one another. Managers may feel their own activities are essential and even resort to politics to get more resources. Finally, a rigid budget structure reduces initiative and innovation at lower levels, making it impossible to obtain money for new ideas. Some companies, such as 3M, set aside discretionary resources to prevent this problem.

Skilled managers who understand budgets and how to use them have a powerful control tool with which to attain departmental and organizational goals. One manager who knows how to use budgets to achieve goals is the CEO of a grocery store chain in Orlando, Florida.

 ## THRIFTY SCOTT WAREHOUSE FOOD

Bob Popaditch, CEO of Thrifty Scott Warehouse Food, likes to talk about cost control and profit margins. He understands budget matters and has learned how to use them to motivate managers.

In a talk to several of his store managers, he reviewed budget performance. "Let's talk about the last 36 weeks," he began. "You could say that things looked pretty good. Sales were just 2.9 percent off budget. Not bad. Payroll was over budget a bit, but only by 0.24 percent. Pretty close."

Popaditch knows that overall budget figures are abstract and boring for his managers. He has learned that budgets motivate people when "spoken" in their language. Thus, the 2 percent shortfall in sales amounts to $244,000 for the 36 weeks. Popaditch went on breaking down the sales shortfall. That comes down to $26.85 in sales per hour. The average number of customers per hour is 87, which is just $0.31 more sales per customer. Store managers understand this. They simply need to get each customer to buy $0.31 more while in the store.

What about payroll? Over budget by 0.24 percent is pretty close, but it amounts to $9,163 per store, or $254 per week for each store. That's about 52 hours of labor. Since each store has about 50 employees, that's one hour per employee per week.

So that's how Bob Popaditch gets his managers to look at the problem: "$0.30 per customer, 60 minutes per employee." A small increase in income and an easily manageable decrease in costs will lead to 100 percent attainment of budget targets and a tidy increase of $65,804 in net profit. Budget figures are not abstract numbers drawn out of the air. When used by effective managers, they translate into action that produces better performance.[22] ■

● SIGNS OF INADEQUATE CONTROL SYSTEMS

Financial statements, financial analysis, and budgets are designed to provide adequate control for the organization. Often, however, management control systems are not working properly. Then they must be examined for possible clarification, revision, or overhaul. Indicators of the need for a more effective control approach or revised management control systems are as follows:[23]

- Deadlines missed frequently.
- Poor quality of goods and services.
- Declining or stagnant sales or profits.
- Loss of leadership position or market share within the industry.
- Inability to obtain data necessary to evaluate employee or departmental performance.
- Low employee morale and high absenteeism.
- Insufficient employee involvement and management-employee communications.
- Excessive company debts, uncertain cash flow, or unpredictable borrowing requirements.
- Inefficient use of human and material resources, equipment, and facilities.

Management control systems help achieve overall company objectives. They help ensure that operations progress satisfactorily by identifying deviations and correcting problems. Properly used, controls help management respond to unforeseen developments and achieve strategic plans. Improperly designed and used, management control systems can lead a company into bankruptcy.

SUMMARY AND MANAGEMENT SOLUTION

This chapter introduced a number of important concepts about management control systems and techniques. Organizations have a core management control system consisting of the strategic plan, financial forecast, operating budget, management by objectives, operations management system, and management information system. Top management financial control uses the balance sheet, income statement, and financial analyses of these documents.

At the middle levels of the organization, budgets are an important control system. Departments are responsibility centers, each with a specific type of operating budget—expense, revenue, or profit. Financial budgets are also used for organizational control and include the cash, capital expenditure, and balance sheet budgets. The budget process can be either top down or bottom up, but a budget system that incorporates both seems most effective. Zero-based budgeting is a variation of the budget process and requires that managers start from zero to justify budget needs for the coming year. Finally, indicators of inadequate control systems were discussed.

The importance of the budget and financial control systems was illustrated in the management problem at the beginning of this chapter. R. S. Bacon Veneer Company was about to go bankrupt, despite 100 pages of accounting information. President McCracken and Chief Executive Wilhelm sought another opinion, throwing the Big Six accounting firm out the door. The new accountant from a Chicago firm began by quizzing Wilhelm and McCracken about the numbers they felt they could best benefit from knowing. Would it be helpful to know inventory levels to manage the company effectively? Did they want to know the profit margin of each veneer line? The goal was to find key financial items for control that would make up one monthly report of no more than ten pages. The new financial reports worked like a shot of penicillin to revive the company. Knowing the cost of each product spurred Wilhelm and McCracken to diversify to high-profit items. Low-margin lines were eventually dropped. Today, business is better than ever. Sales have increased 300 percent, and the new reports still give McCracken and Wilhelm superb control.[24]

DISCUSSION QUESTIONS

1. What is the core control system? How do its components relate to one another for control of the organization?
2. What are the four types of responsibility centers, and how do they relate to organization structure?
3. What types of analyses can be performed on financial statements to help managers diagnose a company's financial condition?

4. Which do you think is a more important use of financial analyses: diagnosing organizational problems or taking corrective action to solve them? Discuss.

5. Explain the difference among fixed costs, variable costs, and discretionary costs. In which situation would each be used?

6. What are the advantages of top-down versus bottom-up budgeting? Why is it better to combine the two approaches?

7. According to zero-based budgeting, a department that cannot justify a budget will cease to exist. Do you think this actually happens under zero-based budgeting? Discuss.

8. Why might low employee morale or insufficient employee involvement be indicators of inadequate controls in an organization?

MANAGEMENT IN PRACTICE: ETHICAL DILEMMA

● COMPUTER SCREWUP

Ken and Barbara are coworkers in the telecommunications department of a large firm. One weekend, Ken asked Barbara and several other coworkers to help him move to a new apartment. While placing Ken's computer into its original packing, Barbara noticed that the address on the box was for their telecom office. When Barbara questioned Ken about it, he replied, "Oh, yeah, we ordered ten terminals from the manufacturer a year ago, but they accidentally shipped eleven. We didn't get charged for it." When Barbara expressed disapproval, Ken became defensive and said the boss, Dave, knew about it. "Besides, I was the one who pushed that we buy from that manufacturer, and I do a lot of work on my home computer, so our company owes me something anyway."

● WHAT DO YOU DO?

1. Nothing. This is not your responsibility. The fault is with the two companies' control systems that let the computer slip through.

2. Try to persuade Ken to offer to pay for it. This would be the right thing for him to do even if his offer is refused.

3. Bring it up with your boss, Dave. If it's okay for your company to accept the extra computer, it should be shared with coworkers.

CASES FOR ANALYSIS

BATTERY & TIRE WAREHOUSE, INC.

When Charles Bodenstab took over Battery & Tire Warehouse in St. Paul, Minnesota, it was doing $7 million in sales but was losing money fast. Bodenstab gradually discovered inadequate financial controls in several areas.

One problem area was accounts receivable, about which Bodenstab knew nothing. In his experience in large companies, other managers handled the credit details. As manager of an entrepreneurial company, he needed to be involved in everything.

When Bodenstab asked his credit manager basic questions such as why the percentage of past due accounts was up, he heard a different answer each month. Yet the negative trends continued. Bodenstab had to act, and his first move was to replace the credit manager.

Next, he looked into the reports and was dissatisfied with the aggregate data. Some 3,000 accounts were listed on 120 pages. The report disguised problems rather than identified them.

After careful thought, Bodenstab decided he had to know two things each month. First, which accounts were deteriorating? Second, which customers were chronic deadbeats? Bodenstab decided to create two monthly reports—one on adverse change, the other on chronic problems. The adverse-change report would list all accounts that exhibited a pattern of deterioration, such as an increase in an overdue account. The chronic-problem report would include accounts that were consistently past due. He hired a local software firm to program his computer to provide this data.

Suddenly, the problem is under control. A recent adverse-change report listed 77 accounts that had deteriorated for one reason or another. Bodenstab could skim the report in 30 minutes. The new credit manager then takes necessary action. The chronic-problems report lists over 100 companies, and he and the credit manager developed a system for motivating them to pay. Moreover, new credit is not extended when customers are not paying. Compared with the previous aggregate credit report, the new system is a dream. The trick, says Bodenstab, is to choose the criteria. The management skill is knowing which data to identify and solve the problems. Then management's responsibility is to design control systems to provide those answers.

● QUESTIONS

1. Which signs of inadequate controls described in the text alerted Bodenstab to the credit control problem?
2. Would an MBO system apply here? Discuss.
3. Was it proper for Bodenstab to become personally involved in the credit reporting systems? Should he delegate more responsibility to the credit manager?

SOURCE: Based on Bruce C. Posner, "Hitting Your Numbers," *INC.,* April 1987, 106–108.

METALLIC FINISHES, INC.

Metallic Finishes, Inc., is a producer of chrome finishes and specialty metals. In 1990 the new executive vice-president, Stuart Galante, was committed to using the latest management techniques. His first step was to install a new management by objectives system for middle and senior managers. The plan was to apprise managers on goal achievement rather than on general activities. Each manager met with his or her superior to set objectives through mutual discussion.

One day Galante had lunch with Dr. Hank Gilman, vice-president for research and development. One of the topics discussed was whether the MBO system was working in the R&D department. Galante was concerned that Metallic Finishes would fail to achieve its long-term goal of having 25 percent of all sales come from new products by 1990.

Gilman reassured Galante that there was no problem. He explained that it took several years to produce a new product and top management should have confidence in the research team. To illustrate, Gilman said he had data showing an increase in the number of technical papers written and conferences attended and that equipment purchases were down 5 percent. Moreover, the waste rate on experimental materials had dropped 12 percent. The R&D

department also was employing one less researcher and one less lab technician than in the previous year. "All in all," said Gilman, "we are running a very efficient operation, and I don't see how we can do much more under this new MBO system of yours."

● QUESTIONS

1. Do you agree with Gilman's conclusions about the successful performance of the research and development department?
2. How does this MBO system fit the MBO model as summarized in Exhibit 18.9? What improvements would you make? Which aspects seem satisfactory?
3. Do you think the executive vice-president, Stuart Galante, did a good job of implementing the MBO system? Explain.

SOURCE: Based on "Metallic Finishes, Inc.," in Richard L. Daft, *Organization Theory and Design* (St. Paul, Minn.: West, 1986), 320–321, and "Goals and Gripes," in Richard N. Farmer, Barry M. Richman, and William G. Ryan, *Incidents for Studying Management and Organization* (Belmont, Calif.: Wadsworth, 1970), 83.

REFERENCES

1. Jill Andresky Fraser, "Straight Talk," *INC.,* March 19, 1990, 97–98.
2. Kate Ballen, "The New Look of Capital Spending," *Fortune,* March 13, 1989, 115–120.
3. Ford S. Worthy, "Accounting Bores You? Wake Up," *Fortune,* October 12, 1987, 43–52.
4. David A. Garvin, "Quality on the Line," *Harvard Business Review* (September–October 1983), 65–75.
5. Robert Simons, "Strategic Orientation and Top Management Attention to Control Systems," *Strategic Management Journal* 12 (1991), 49–62, and E. G. Flamholtz, "Accounting, Budgeting and Control Systems in Their

Organizational Context: Theoretical and Empirical Perspectives," *Accounting, Organizations and Society* 8 (1983), 153–169.

6. Richard L. Daft and Norman B. Macintosh, "The Nature and Use of Formal Control Systems for Management Control and Strategy Implementation," *Journal of Management* 10 (1984), 43–66.

7. Company Profile: "The Change," *INC.,* March 1992, 58–70, and Edward O. Welles, "How're We Doing?" *INC.,* May 1991, 80–83.

8. Bruce G. Posner, "How to Stop Worrying and Love the Next Recession," *INC.,* April 1986, 89–95.

9. Tom Richman, "The Language of Business," *INC.,* February 1990, 41–50, and Paul Hawken, "Mastering the Numbers," *INC.,* October 1987, 19–20.

10. Hawken, "Mastering the Numbers."

11. Arthur W. Holmes and Wayne S. Overmeyer, *Basic Auditing,* 5th ed. (Homewood, Ill.: Irwin, 1976).

12. John J. Welsh, "Pre-Acquisition Audit: Verifying the Bottom Line," *Management Accounting* (January 1983), 32–37.

13. Jill Andresky Fraser, "Honey, I Shrunk the Company," *INC.,* June 1990, 115–116.

14. Daft and Macintosh, "Formal Control Systems," and Robert N. Anthony, John Dearden, and Norton M. Bedford, *Management Control Systems,* 5th ed. (Homewood, Ill.: Irwin, 1984).

15. This discussion is based on Peter Lorange, Michael F. Scott Morton, and Sumantra Ghoshal, *Strategic Control* (St. Paul, Minn.: West, 1986), Chapter 4; Anthony, Dearden, and Bedford, *Management Control Systems,* and Richard F. Vancil, "What Kind of Management Control Do You Need?" *Harvard Business Review* (March–April 1973), 75–85.

16. Teri Lammers, "The Weekly Cash-Flow Planner," *INC.,* June 1992, 99–103.

17. Anthony, Dearden, and Bedford, *Management Control Systems.*

18. Participation in budget setting has been described in a number of studies, including Peter Brownell, "Leadership Style, Budgetary Participation and Managerial Behavior," *Accounting Organizations and Society* 8 (1983), 307–321, and Paul J. Carruth and Thurrell O. McClandon, "How Supervisors React to 'Meeting the Budget' Pressure," *Management Accounting* 66 (November 1984), 50–54.

19. Neil C. Churchill, "Budget Choice: Planning vs. Control," *Harvard Business Review* (July–August 1984), 150–164.

20. "Zero-based Budgeting," *Small Business Report* (April 1988), 52–57, and Peter A. Pyhrr, *Zero-Based Budgeting: A Practical Management Tool for Evaluating Expense* (New York: Wiley, 1973).

21. "Zero-Based Budgeting: Justifying All Business Activity from the Ground Up," *Small Business Report* (November 1983), 20–25, and M. Dirsmith and S. Jablonsky, "Zero-Based Budgeting as a Management Technique and Political Strategy," *Academy of Management Review* 4 (1979), 555–565.

22. Based on Tom Richman, "Talking Cost," *INC.,* February 1986, 105–108.

23. Based on "Controlling with Standards," *Small Business Report* (August 1987), 62–65.

24. Fraser, "Straight Talk."

OIL INDUSTRY

An oilfield wildcatter's biggest gamble used to be whether or not a strike would be made. These days that's only the first roll of the dice. The cost to drill, produce, and transport the product can all be reasonably forecasted and budgeted in advance. But what that product will then bring is out in the ether, and can be affected by everything from winter weather to war.

Similar uncertainties face the biggest oil companies and major producer countries around the world, except that the risks for them are exponentially higher. The commitment to develop a new field or increase refinery capacity is a multi-billion dollar proposition. Rolling snake eyes for those kinds of dollars can send oil executives into early retirement, and turn sheik oil ministers back into nomadic herdsmen.

Oil prices more than doubled to a record $41 a barrel when Iraq invaded Kuwait in August 1990. The day after the allied air sorties began, January 16, 1991, the price plunged $10 a barrel, another record. By the end of the month the price settled at $18.76 a barrel.

The volatility of world oil prices will likely never abate, but analysts predict the 1990s may be a period of greater stability than the past. The new approach to doing business will have countries with oil reserves entering into mutually beneficial working relationships with those in possession of the necessary technologies to maximize production of those resources.

Ironically, it is squabbling among OPEC countries and their inability to come to agreement that is driving them individually toward Western oil companies for the sole purpose of maintaining their respective market shares. World demand for oil is about 66 million barrels a day and is growing by 1.5 percent a year. As the decade progresses a producer's share will depend on output capabilities. A failure to invest, or enter into cooperative deals with Western companies, could leave a producing nation behind.

Countries like Argentina, Venezuela, and Libya, who have traditionally been open and cooperative with Western oil companies, are becoming even more so. Hard-line nations like Mexico and Iran, which in the past have strictly adhered to statutory restrictions prohibiting joint-venture-type agreements, are becoming more receptive to concessionary deals.

An example is Iran, whose decade-long shunning of all things Western nearly pushed the country off the technological curve. In a radical departure from the past, Iran entered an agreement with France's Total to develop an offshore field with the potential for 100,000 barrels-a-day production. The somewhat shocking aspect of the deal was that it had all the earmarks of an old-style concession, with the French company financing, developing, and marketing the field and its oil. This startling turnaround has other Western companies eager to begin doing business in Iran.

The picture for U.S. producers is muddled as well. Bill Clinton's environmental stance and his pledge to reduce the federal deficit may translate into some form of energy tax on both domestically produced and imported oil.

If Clinton can push such a measure through Congress, U.S. oil companies are hoping they have an ace up their sleeve in the form of recovering natural gas prices. Anemic gas prices have perplexed industry experts for years, but the price surge in the first quarter of 1993 was viewed by many as a significant turnaround rather than a technical aberration. Factors leading to this conclusion include demand for natural gas in excess of forecasts, as well as good acceptance of gas-fueled vehicles and a greater than expected shift by electric generating companies to gas.

An indication that at least one industry major is optimistic is the move by Exxon to go forward with the long-delayed Mobile Bay gas field project. Other companies agree that the time to move has arrived, but have also sounded cautionary notes about the long-term forecast. "What we don't want is for prices to go too high so that natural gas loses its attractiveness as an alternative to oil, said Gary Junco, president and chief operating officer of Enserch Corporation's oil and gas exploration company."

The venue of factors that contribute to the instability of pricing and production of oil and natural gas are limitless. The writing on the wall now is that everyone's best interests will be served through a spirit of cooperation that ushers in long-term price stability. The oil industry might then begin to resemble a business again, instead of a big casino.

● QUESTIONS

1. As an oil company executive, how would you design a core management control system to cope with the uncertainties of the industry? How would you classify the elements of the core management control system in order of importance for this particular industry?

2. How can an oil executive cope with and minimize the effects of worldwide events that exert critical influence on operations?

3. In view of the reality that oil companies must continually replace reserves that are produced and marketed, how dangerous is a wait-and-see approach in an unreasonable market of overproduction and uncertain product price?

4. What are the pitfalls of deals in countries such as Iran, and in the event of catastrophe, revolution, or war, what role should the U.S. government play?

INFORMATION SYSTEMS FOR MANAGEMENT

20 CHAPTER

At R. H. Macy & Co., the "more is always better than less" belief permeated corporate culture. This philosophy was visible in everything Macy did—from its extravagant annual Thanksgiving Day Parade to its bulging warehouse approach to inventory management; certainly, Macy's stores fairly bulged with merchandise. But by the end of 1991, the company was weighed down by $1.25 billion in losses. Creditors were howling, and the once-proud corporate star of the film classic *Miracle on 34th Street* scrambled to find a miracle of its own. By the fall of 1992, Macy filed for bankruptcy, appointed a new CEO, and began a major reorganization strategy. Central to

Macy's plans were computerized management information systems for efficient inventory control and accounting. But skeptics wondered if Macy's old "more is better" culture was too deeply entrenched to adapt to new information systems that might save the ailing company.[1] ■ What suggestions would you make to Macy's new chairman about where and how management information systems could be used? Can information systems really assist high-profile merchandising in a store like Macy?

MANAGEMENT PROBLEM

The problem confronting R. H. Macy & Co. is to develop internal data bases and information systems to help salespeople and store managers keep track of inventory, customers, and the profitable merchandise lines and departments.

Two issues face all managers, whether running an entrepreneurial business or a large corporation: getting access to disorganized data and turning the data into useful information.[2] Useful information can have remarkable benefits, in both improved control and improved competitiveness.

These two benefits—information for improved control and information as a competitive weapon—are the themes in this chapter. As described in Chapters 18 and 19, information systems provide a management control system in organizations. Yet the introduction of computers does not necessarily mean centralized, top-down control. Information can be shared widely and can be a tool for decentralizing decision making to employees at lower levels. Information systems can also serve as a competitive weapon by shortening the control cycle and response time of the organization.

The proliferation of new information technology can be overwhelming, causing managers to lose sight of the control and competitive purposes of information. Had the automobile industry experienced a similar rate of development, you could buy a Rolls Royce for $280 and drive it 1 million miles on a gallon of gas. Managers must try to understand the technology of the Information Age and how it can be used. Management of information is even more important with the increase of competition in the global marketplace and new alternatives for making employees more productive. As the New Horizons . . . Diversity box shows, management information systems such as telecommuting provide options that meet the changing needs of today's work force.

● INFORMATION AND MANAGEMENT

In a very realistic sense, information is the lifeblood of organizations. To appreciate how managers use information in control and decision making, let us first distinguish data from information and then look at the characteristics of useful information.

DATA VERSUS INFORMATION

data

Raw, unsummarized, and unanalyzed facts.

information

Data that are meaningful and alter the receiver's understanding.

The terms *data* and *information* often are used interchangeably. Yet there is an important difference. **Data** are raw, unsummarized, and unanalyzed facts. **Information** refers to data that are meaningful and alter the receiver's understanding.[3] Information is the data that managers actually use to interpret and understand events in the organization and the environment. For example, Hardee's Restaurants' information systems monitor thousands of data transactions, including food sales, sales tax, water and electricity use, and movement of inventory. However, the raw data are worthless. Data require proper organization to produce meaningful information, such as total sales for all Hardee's Restaurants, sales

TELECOMMUTING AND THE FAMILY

Newlywed Donna Cunningham, a media relations manager for AT&T Bell Laboratories in New Jersey, dreaded telling her supervisor of her plan to quit her job and move to Vermont with her new husband. She was both shocked and thrilled when her supervisor suggested that she continue her present job through a program called *telecommuting*.

Telecommuting addresses the needs of a diverse work force trying to balance business and family lives. Rapid improvements in PCs, fax machines, and voice mail enable an increasing number of employees to work at home while maintaining their salary and benefits.

From her home office in Vermont, Cunningham easily confers with staff in the New Jersey office. While she admits missing the comradery of the office, her productivity has remained high and she rates telecommuting as a "wonderful" experience. Workers such as Cunningham can set their own hours and work at their own pace and employers report that although schedules appear strange, with early mornings, late hours, and split work shifts, employees participating in telecommuting generally devote more hours to work than the traditional 9-to-5 workers and productivity improves.

So far, the majority of telecommuters are mid-level women employed in information industries who perform tasks such as programming, writing, or research. Most telecommuters are part-time employees, but they tend to be more productive and more prone to put in additional work time than their office counterparts. Some 500 companies have telecommuting programs in place, but they have not become more widespread because many managers are reluctant to give up close supervision of their employees.

Boston's U.S.TeleCenters is one company that actively promotes the telecommuting process. Approximately 100 employees participate in weekly meetings conducted by voice mail, and their project goals and completions are usually monitored by computer. "I think that a business that wants to be competitive in the 1990s will have to have an environment that supports family values," says U.S.TeleCenters president Franklin Reese III.

Companies stand to gain other benefits as society and business grow more complex. Telecommuting offers an employer alternatives to increased traffic congestion, downtown parking hassles, and skyrocketing real estate costs.

Telecommuting offers a significant work alternative for an increasingly diverse work force on the eve of the 21st century. ■

SOURCE: Michael Alexander, "Travel-Free Commuting," *Nation's Business*, December 1990, 33–37.

by store and region, and key efficiency and profitability ratios. By analyzing the data and making comparisons with past performance, planners can both measure results and project future activity. Hardee's successful use of this information system contributed significantly to its rise to number three in the fast-food industry.[4]

CHARACTERISTICS OF USEFUL INFORMATION

What makes information valuable? Information has many attributes, such as verifiability, accessibility, clarity, precision, and cost. Four factors that are especially important for management information are quality, timeliness, completeness, and relevance, as illustrated in Exhibit 20.1.[5]

QUALITY.   Information that accurately portrays reality is said to have **quality.** The data are accurate and reliable. If the data say that a valve

quality
The degree to which information accurately portrays reality.

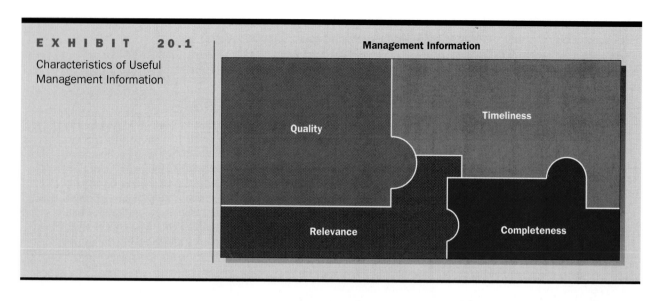

Management Information

Quality

Timeliness

Relevance

Completeness

---

in a nuclear power plant is open, such quality is important to management decision making. A police officer in San Jose, California, runs a license plate check by tapping into the state license plate records system. If the data were inaccurate, an innocent person could be stopped or a guilty one let go.[6] Quality is what makes any information system work. Once a system is known to have errors, managers will no longer use it, and its value for decision making will disappear.

TIMELINESS.   Information that is available soon after events occur has **timeliness.** Managers work at a fast pace, and things change quickly. The most immediate benefit of computerized management is quick response time. Companies can shorten new-product development time, respond immediately to competitive changes, and shrink the control and feedback cycle within organizations. At Oxford Industries, an Atlanta clothing company, workers' activities are clocked to a thousandth of a minute. Oxford has figured, for instance, that a stitcher should spend 3.4 seconds on each front pocket and may work on 5,000 pockets a day. The information system gives running updates throughout the day of each worker's pace so that problems can be solved immediately.[7]

COMPLETENESS.   Information **completeness** refers to the proper quantity of data. Too much data lead to information overload; too little fail to tell the complete story. As described in Chapters 18 and 19, managers exercise control by recognizing deviations from targets and instituting necessary changes. Managers often devise *exception reports* that contain only a few pages of deviations from target rather than hundreds of pages of raw data. These reports are complete because they contain key information, but in an amount managers can digest.

RELEVANCE.   Information **relevance** means that the information must pertain to the problems, decisions, and tasks for which a manager is responsible. Information relevance is a difficult problem for an information system to solve, because every manager's situation is unique. Pro-

timeliness

The degree to which information is available soon after events occur.

completeness

The extent to which information contains the appropriate amount of data.

relevance

The degree to which information pertains to the problems, decisions, and tasks for which a manager is responsible.

duction managers need data on scrap rates, production volume, and employee productivity. Human resource managers need data on employee background, work experience, insurance programs, employee demographics, and position descriptions. Marketing managers need data on customer accounts, sales forecasts, sales activity, and individual salespeople's commissions.

INFORMATION SYSTEMS

Now that we understand the characteristics of useful information, we will discuss systems for providing information to managers. An **information system** is a mechanism that collects, organizes, and distributes data to organizational personnel. Most information systems are manual, which means that people perform the information activities by hand. For example, Northrop Corporation's manual system generated 400,000 pieces of paper when building each fuselage for the F/A-18 jet fighter. A **computer-based information system (CBIS)** is a system that uses electronic computing technology to create the information system. A

information system

A mechanism for collecting, organizing, and distributing data to organizational employees.

computer-based information system (CBIS)

An information system that uses electronic computing technology to create the information system.

Computer-based information systems (CBIS) form the nerve center of corporations such as Deere & Company. The John Deere Information System (JDIS) pictured here assists John Deere dealers by linking them with Deere & Company for split-second information access. Software is available to provide up-to-the-minute information about customer sales profiles, sales-force effectiveness, financial management, parts management, and service management.

CBIS differs from a manual system only in the physical components that perform the functions. Input into a CBIS may be done through a terminal or automatic scanning systems. The computer manipulates data according to defined procedures. Data storage is electronic in the form of magnetic tapes and disks that can store huge volumes of data. Control over the system is provided by a software program that contains specific instructions for organizing data needed by users. Outputs are computer reports of data provided on a terminal screen.

Northrop converted to a computerized information system for building jet fighters. The 10-foot pile of paper (400,000 pieces) for each fuselage was put on one laser disk. Employees now consult a computer for instructions. Supervisors can make instant changes in procedures across the factory, avoiding the inconvenience and confusion of paper changes. Computerizing the information provided a remarkable improvement in timeliness, while maintaining high quality, completeness, and relevance. The new system helped Northrop save $20 million on the fuselage project.[8]

Connecticut Mutual Life Insurance Company cut average customer query response time from five days to a few hours and increased productivity over 35 percent by phasing out its "paper monster." Information on its 1.2 million policyholders, once housed in football field–size warehouses and requiring fleets of shuttle vans, is now stored on optical disks readily accessed by employees with IBM PCs.[9]

HARDWARE AND SOFTWARE

Hardware is the name given to the physical equipment used in a computer-based information system. The increase in computer use by business has emphasized different hardware. In the early 1970s, most businesses used mainframe computers, which are large machines that centralized all business computing in one location. Minicomputers became the rage by the late 1970s. These smaller, yet powerful, computers allowed data processing to be decentralized to departments and divisions. The next hardware wave was personal computers in the mid-1980s. These small computers decentralized computing even further, allowing individuals to achieve high efficiency. Right now network computers are popular. New hardware links PC workstations into networks by groups of scientists, engineers, or business and finance professionals. The network allows information sharing and coordination.[10]

Software is the set of instructions that control and direct computer processing. It is the primary device used for controlling an information system. Software transforms raw data into usable information. New software had to be developed for each wave of computer hardware. Software for linking computers into networks is especially complex. Some of the popular software programs managers use for minicomputer and PC applications include *VisiCalc* and *Lotus 1-2-3* (electronic spreadsheets) and *dBASE IV* (data base management system). As the Manager's Shoptalk box shows, innovations in both hardware and software are transforming information systems, creating an information revolution.

AN INFORMATION REVOLUTION

It seems that the days of "telling the boss to his or her face" are over. Today's employee is more likely to "tell the boss to his or her computer." One innovative empowerment technique is the *electronic meeting*, in which up to 50 employees and managers sit side by side and hammer out an entire meeting on PCs. Not a word is spoken. Companies using the electronic meeting find that shy employees are more open to blunt, honest exchanges through the anonymity of computers.

Electronic meetings are just one of many exciting trends in the information revolution that recently produced the lap-top, notebook, and hand-held computers. Companies such as United Parcel Service quickly latched onto the new technologies. Says UPS chairman Kent Nelson, "We realize that the leader in information management will be the leader in international package distribution—period."

Other recent information innovations include the following:
• *Pen computers*. Devised for employees with little or no access to office or lap-top systems, the pen computer allows limited data entry with workers using a pen to select menu items and record data.
• *PalmPAD*. Introduced by GRiD Systems, Inc., the PalmPAD straps to the user's wrist and allows improved field data collection.
• *Telform for Windows*. Devised by Cardiff Software, this software innovation combines the fax and computer to allow transmission of visual forms for improved data entry.
• Voice Control. Verbex Voice Systems combined add-in boards and software, allowing both commands and data entry with human speech.

Other innovations are on the horizon, and passage of the Americans with Disabilities Act ensures that more attention will be placed on devising computer systems that allow greater accessibility for disabled employees. ∎

SOURCE: Jim Bartimo, "At These Shouting Matches, No One Says a Word," *Business Week*, June 11, 1990, 78; Ripley Hotch, "Computers Find Their Voice," *Nation's Business*, May 1992, 49–54; and "Helping the Disabled Use Computers," *Nation's Business*, May 1992, 54; and Peter Coy, "The New Realism in Office Systems," *Business Week*, June 15, 1992, 128–133.

● INFORMATION SYSTEMS AND THE MANAGEMENT HIERARCHY

Recall from Chapter 1 that management activities differ according to top, middle, and first-line management levels in the hierarchy as illustrated in Exhibit 20.2. Hierarchical differences mean that managers need different kinds of information. For example, strategic planning is a primary responsibility at the top level, whereas operational control is a primary responsibility of first-line supervisors. Top managers work on nonprogrammable problems, such as new-product development, marketing plans, and acquisition of other companies. First-line managers, in contrast, deal with programmable decisions arising from well-defined problems, such as inventory control, production scheduling, and sales analysis.

The information top managers use pertains mostly to the external environment. It is broad in scope to cover unanticipated problems that

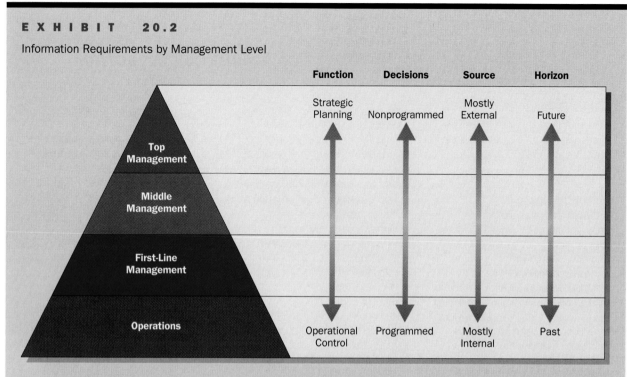

EXHIBIT 20.2

Information Requirements by Management Level

SOURCE: Adapted from Rolland Hurtubise, *Managing Information Systems: Concept and Tools* (West Hartford, Conn.: Kumarian Press, 1984), 57, and G. Anthony Gorry and Michael Scott Morton, "A Framework for Management Information Systems," *Sloan Management Review* 13 (1971), 55–70.

may arise and is oriented toward the future, including trends and forecasts. First-line managers need information on internal operations that is narrowly focused on specific activities and deals with past performance.

To meet the different information needs along the hierarchy, three types of computer-based information systems have evolved. At the lower organization level, transaction processing systems (TPSs) assist first-line supervisors with recordkeeping, routine calculations, and data sorting. Middle managers use management information systems (MISs). Top managers use executive information systems (EISs) to provide information for strategic and nonprogrammable decisions.

TRANSACTION PROCESSING SYSTEMS

transaction processing system (TPS)

A type of CBIS that performs the organization's routinely occurring transactions.

The initial purpose of business computing in the 1960s was to reduce clerical costs by speeding day-to-day business transactions. The **transaction processing system (TPS)** performs the organization's routine, recurring transactions. Examples of transactions include sending bills to customers, depositing checks in the bank, placing orders, recording receipts and payments, and paying invoices. Large companies such as American Airlines, AT&T, and American Express could not account for their operations, control their assets, or manage projects without huge transaction processing systems. American Express has 16 major information-

A unique *transactions processing system* provides the parents of these boys at a nursery school in Toyama, Japan, with a report on their activities, including how much they ate for lunch and when they were picked up at the end of the day. The system enables the school to keep detailed records on its 100 youngsters, handles accounting functions and salary records for the staff, and tracks nutritional content of school meals. Developed by IBM, the software can also provide *management information system* (*MIS*) data to nursery school managers for making decisions about school activities.

processing centers, 10 worldwide data networks, 90 mainframe computer systems, 400 minicomputer systems, and 30,000 individual workstations to support its transaction processing requirements. The TPS typically is not the concern of general managers, because specialists in information technology manage these systems.

MANAGEMENT INFORMATION SYSTEMS

A **management information system (MIS)** is a mechanism that collects, organizes, and distributes data used by managers in performing their management functions. As information systems evolved, management information systems were the next stage of evolution beyond transaction processing systems. As data bases accumulated, managers began visualizing ways in which the computer could help them make important decisions. Managers needed information in summary form that pertained to specific management problems. The lists of thousands of daily organizational transactions were useless for planning, controlling, or decision making.

MISs provide information reports designed to help managers make decisions. For example, when a production manager needs to make decisions about production scheduling, he or she may need data on the anticipated number of orders in the coming month based on trends, current inventory levels, and availability of equipment and personnel. The MIS can provide these data. At Visible Changes hair salons, for example, managers use the MIS to learn about customer age and sex, repeat business, and productivity by salon and hair stylist."[11]

The MIS requires more complex software that instructs computers to translate data into useful reports. Computer hardware also has become more complex and sophisticated because it needs greater capacity and the ability to integrate diverse data bases. For example, thousands of transactions take place daily in supermarkets. One leader in developing management information systems is Gromer Supermarket, Inc.

management information system (MIS)

A form of CBIS that collects, organizes, and distributes the data managers use in performing their management functions.

GROMER SUPERMARKET, INC.

Gromer is a huge superstore in Elgin, Illinois. The laser scanners at Gromer's ten checkout counters speed shoppers through the checkout lines, but more important, they provide a great deal of information. Millions of transactions are recorded, and a quarter of a million dollars' worth of computer hardware and software are used to provide management reports on everything from checker efficiency to bagging speed and food turnover. Take cereal, for example. The MIS data showed that Rice Krispies had six size categories, but two were slow movers and thus were eliminated.

In the meat department, MIS reports tell the meat manager how much gross margin a side of beef will produce. The system also describes the cuts from a pork loin that will maximize gross profits. Labor cost decisions are made efficiently because the number of baggers scheduled to work is chosen to fit the number of customers coming through the store and the known rate at which a bagger can bag. The millions of numbers crunched through the MIS system help managers decide how to display products, which products to stock, and how to make storage and delivery more efficient.[12] ■

EXECUTIVE INFORMATION SYSTEMS

Until recently, information systems have not possessed the sophistication and simplicity that senior executives needed. Executive information systems were developed because managers needed help with unanticipated and unstructured problems that MISs were not flexible enough to provide.

An **executive information system (EIS)** is the use of computer technology to support the information needs of senior managers.[13] EISs were formed from powerful PCs that could shape masses of numbers into simple, colorful charts and from networks that can weave together a company's different hardware and data bases.[14] EISs are also called *decision support systems,* because they allow an executive to interact with the information system to retrieve, manipulate, and display data needed to make specific decisions. For example, the CEO of Duracell asked for data comparing the performance of hourly and salaried work forces in the United States and overseas. Within seconds, he received a table showing that U.S. workers produced more sales. Asking for more data, he discovered that too many overseas salespeople were wasting time calling on small stores. As a result, executives made the decision to sign up distributors to cover small stores, improving foreign profits.[15] EISs give managers access to multiple data bases, depending on their immediate information needs, as illustrated in Exhibit 20.3.

Executive information systems deal with nonprogrammed decisions such as strategic planning. Consequently, the hardware and software technologies are very sophisticated. Indeed, to be accessible to top man-

executive information system (EIS)

An interactive CBIS that retrieves, manipulates, and displays information serving the needs of top managers; also called *decision support system.*

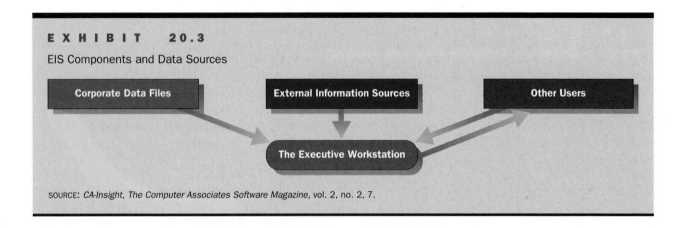

EXHIBIT 20.3

EIS Components and Data Sources

Corporate Data Files   External Information Sources   Other Users

The Executive Workstation

SOURCE: *CA-Insight, The Computer Associates Software Magazine*, vol. 2, no. 2, 7.

agers who are not computer experts, up to 75 percent of the computer system's capacity may be used for software that permits managers to "talk" to the system in everyday English. This frees the remaining 25 percent to handle multiple data bases, translate inquiries into simple graphs and charts, and provide an instant answer to almost any question. Initial research indicates that EISs help people make faster and more effective decisions, an important consideration in today's global marketplace.[16]

EISs are being adopted widely. The following are some examples:[17]

- At California Federal, an EIS is used to track CD maturity projections and both consumer and mortgage loan growth to develop a strategy to ensure that managers are on top of opportunities and problems.

- The president of Pratt & Whitney uses an EIS nearly every day to monitor and act on new engine development and manufacturing status information.

- The treasurer of General Motors uses an EIS to get immediate access to international currency information so he can direct currency moves and get instant answers when other GM executives call.

Exhibit 20.4 summarizes the evolution of computer-based information systems used in organizations. Transaction processing came first; it used simple hardware and software to reduce costs and improve efficiency at lower organization levels. Management information systems represented a higher level of complexity and allowed managers to make decisions to improve the performance of departments and divisions. Executive information systems represent the latest and most complex technology that is applicable to top management's nonprogrammed decisions. EISs can address broad strategic issues, help managers formulate strategic plans, and respond to rapid external changes.[18]

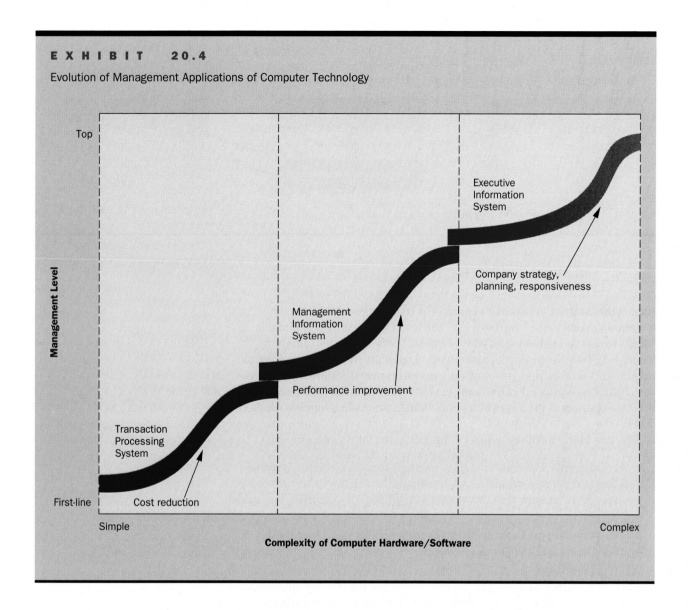

EXHIBIT 20.4

Evolution of Management Applications of Computer Technology

EMERGING INFORMATION TECHNOLOGIES

Developments in MISs and EISs have paralleled advances in other computer-based information technologies. The computerization of organizations has enabled the widespread use of electronic mail, computer conferencing, and electronic bulletin boards.[19] More recent advances are group decision support systems, artificial intelligence, and interorganizational networks. Each harnesses computer power to facilitate organizational work.

GROUP DECISION SUPPORT SYSTEMS

A **group decision support system (GDSS)** is an interactive computer-based system that facilitates group decision making.[20] Also called *collaborative work systems,* GDSSs are designed to allow team members to interact and at the same time take advantage of computer-based support data. Participating managers sit around a conference table equipped with a computer terminal at each position. Each participant can create displays on his or her own screen, and a large public display screen is also available.[21] More sophisticated versions of GDSS allow for team conferences of spatially separated participants. Members can use a live television hookup to see one another during their conference, and computer screens in each location allow participants to share data displays. Collaborative systems are especially helpful for contributing diverse data bases to team decision making and removing interpersonal communication barriers. These systems also facilitate brainstorming during problem solving by the team.

group decision support system (GDSS)

An interactive CBIS that facilitates group communication and decision making; also called *collaborative work system.*

ARTIFICIAL INTELLIGENCE

Artificial intelligence (AI) is information technology whose ultimate goal is to make computers think, see, talk, and listen like humans. Concepts from psychology, linguistics, and computer science have been combined to create programs that can perform tasks never before done by machines. For example, Hal, the supercomputer in the movies *2001* and *2010,* was the ideal result of AI technology; it could think, talk, and make decisions like a human being.

The area of AI that has had the greatest impact on organizations is called the *expert system.* An **expert system** attempts to duplicate the thinking process that professionals and managers use when making decisions. An expert system is developed by codifying a specialist's knowledge into decision rules that are written into a computer program to mimic the expert's problem-solving strategy.[22] For example, Campbell Soups was about to experience a serious loss when Aldo Cimino retired. He knew more than anyone about maintaining the seven-story soup sterilizers and kettles used in Campbell's kitchens. Campbell's solution was to develop an expert system that could duplicate Cimino's thought processes. Developing the expert system was painstaking and difficult. A programmer from Texas Instruments interviewed Cimino day after day to obtain the minutest details on what he thought and why he took every step. It took seven months to boil Cimino's experience down to 151 "if-then" rules that a computer could understand. Now whenever a problem comes up with a huge kettle, the expert system tells managers how Cimino would have responded.[23]

Companies such as Shearson Lehman, Spiegel, and Texaco have developed artificial intelligence to assist in predicting stock and performance, determining likely customers for specific products, and pinpointing subterranean oil and gas deposits. Meanwhile, a whole range of AI experimental programs are under way. Researchers at Carnegie Mellon are experimenting with Alvin, a land vehicle capable of

artificial intelligence (AI)

Information technology that attempts to make computers think, talk, see, and listen like people.

expert system

An area of AI that attempts to program a computer to duplicate an expert's decision-making and problem-solving strategies.

recognizing shapes and colors and then processing the video information to make decisions and apply the correct response, such as turning, accelerating, or braking.[24]

NETWORKING

networking

The linking together of people and departments within or among organizations for the purpose of sharing information resources.

Networking is the linking together of people and departments within or among organizations to share information resources such as data bases. Linking together stand-alone computers has the same potential for coordination that the telephone has for individuals. The problem is that computers in each part of the organization must use the same programs, formats, and computer languages. Once compatibility is achieved, managers across the network have access to the data bases and resources of all participants. For example, a credit union in Richmond, British Columbia, was drowning in bad loans. Top managers attacked the problem by trying to increase business through discounts to high-volume customers. A personal computer network was acquired that connected 250 tellers in six offices. New pricing information was shared immediately throughout the network, and revenues increased by $429,000 annually. Networks are powerful because they make it easier for employees to communicate by computer, cut down on meeting time, handle large amounts of information, and eliminate duplicate software purchases.[25]

electronic data interchange (EDI)

An interorganizational computer network used by trading partners to exchange business data.

Interorganizational networks are now being created to link the information systems of two or more organizations. The technology for this is called **electronic data interchange (EDI),** the computer-to-computer exchange of business data between trading partners.[26] EDI eliminates paperwork and dramatically speeds purchases, reordering, and invoicing. For example, J. C. Penney linked up with suppliers such as Levi

Electronic data interchange (*EDI*) provides an electronic link between Ryder System, Inc., and many of its customers, including automobile industry giants GM, Ford, Chrysler, Toyota, Honda, Nissan, and Volkswagen Audi. Today, Ryder is the largest highway transporter of cars and trucks in North America. Ryder's EDI system instantly links customers with Ryder's computers for information regarding geographic location, production schedules, delivery requirements, and status of delivery, thus lending support to Ryder's excellent on-time, 99 percent damage-free delivery record.

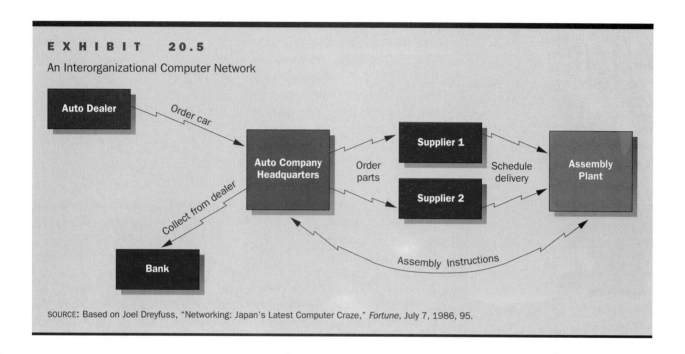

EXHIBIT   20.5

An Interorganizational Computer Network

SOURCE: Based on Joel Dreyfuss, "Networking: Japan's Latest Computer Craze," *Fortune*, July 7, 1986, 95.

Strauss and Vanity Fair via electronic information systems. With direct access to inventory and sales information, these suppliers can accurately estimate demand, sending merchandise as needed, so excess inventory does not languish in Penney's stockrooms. Penney cut inventory 20 percent with EDI.[27]

An example of a more complex EDI network is illustrated in Exhibit 20.5. This network is similar to those used by Japanese automakers.[28] The computer at the auto company headquarters electronically receives a car order specifying model, color, and options. It automatically orders the required parts from suppliers. The computer issues instructions for building a car at the assembly plant. The computer at company headquarters can electronically invoice the dealer and pay suppliers through the network linkage to the bank.

● STRATEGIC USE OF INFORMATION TECHNOLOGY

The adoption of MISs, EISs, GDSSs, or artificial intelligence has strategic consequences for organizations. One desired consequence is improved operational efficiency, especially in the management functions of decision making and controlling. Operational efficiency enables a company to lower costs, making it more competitive. Another desired consequence is to present new strategic options to senior managers. Information technology enables the organization to lock in customers and broaden market reach. These options differentiate the firm strategically, giving it advantage in the marketplace.

"Your package is waiting for you now at package pickup." Circuit City salespeople know the computer-based point-of-sales system has already speeded the transaction through store inventory, provided check and credit approval, and notified the warehouse to prepare for package pickup. The system allows greater management efficiency through *operational efficiency and control*.

cluster organization

An organizational form in which team members from different company locations use electronic mail and GDSSs to solve problems.

OPERATIONAL EFFICIENCY AND CONTROL

MANAGEMENT EFFICIENCY.   The impact of information technology on management falls primarily on the functions of decision making and control. Information technology is easily adapted to first-line management activities such as production, scheduling, inventory management, and office procedures. At middle management levels, desktop terminals give managers access to more information than ever before, and electronic mail and computer conferencing enable coordination and rapid communication. With electronic mail, managers can avoid telephone tag. Just the reduction in paperwork can improve management efficiency at all levels. Recall how Northrop saved 400,000 pieces of paper on each fuselage it built and how Connecticut Mutual Life Insurance Co. puts its documents on optical disks, giving employees immediate access to documents and saving tons of paperwork.[29]

The efficiency of information technology is realized in many companies by the appointment of a *chief information officer* (CIO) who is responsible for managing organizational data bases and implementing new information technology. Technology can be selected and implemented to fit the strategic needs of the organization. For example, at Primerica, a vice-president of information services spent 75 percent of his time using information technology to cut costs, the key need for Primerica to stay competitive.

A recent phenomenon is the new breed of "wired executives" who can increasingly abandon the confines of corporate offices while staying on top of business through technology. Portable computers, E-mail, cellular phones, voice mail, and faxes have freed executives and allowed them greater productivity. Manville Corp. CEO W. Thomas Stephens sees the computer as mind extension. "It gives you an opportunity to be a lot more powerful and to focus on being creative, rather than spending your time making charts and that sort of thing."[30]

IMPROVED COORDINATION, FLEXIBILITY.   Another efficiency of information technology is to break down barriers among departments and across hierarchical levels. Managers who are wired into a computer system communicate with anyone who can help solve a problem. Citicorp managers around the globe seek advice from one another thanks to a computer conferencing system.

A new organizational form is developing called the *cluster organization*. In a **cluster organization,** groups of people work together to solve business problems and then disband when the job is done.[31] At Digital Equipment Corporation, new teams are brought together face-to-face for a week or more to develop closeness and friendship. Then managers return to their regular locations around the world and communicate by electronic mail and group decision support systems. Teams can be clustered together in infinite combinations to solve problems that arise. When a problem is solved, the team disbands and individuals are reformed into new teams.

SMALLER MANAGEMENT STRUCTURE.   The general outcome of information technology has been to reverse the trend of hiring new managers. By speeding up information routing, the number of managers in many organizations has been reduced. This reduction has resulted in an increased span of control and a decrease in the number of levels in the management hierarchy.[32] Technology allows managers to increase their spans of control.

One organization that relies heavily on information technology is cookie retailer Mrs. Fields, Inc. Chairman Randy Fields firmly believes in technology as an important management tool to cut paper work, streamline decision making, and provide employees direct access to top managers. Technology has empowered employees at Mrs. Fields and shaved layers of management from the organization chart, creating a flat organization. Fields' commitment to technology is reflected in his day-to-day actions. "If someone comes into my office without their lap-top computer, I tell them, I don't think I can talk to you now. Get your lap-top."[33]

COMPETITIVE STRATEGY

LOCK IN CUSTOMERS.   One of the strengths of computer-based information technology is the competitive advantage with customers. Consider American Hospital Supply Corporation, a health goods manufacturer.

 ### AMERICAN HOSPITAL SUPPLY CORPORATION

In a smart strategic move, senior executives at American Hospital Supply Corp. decided to give computer terminals free to hospitals around the country. These terminals linked hospital purchasers with American Hospital Supply and enabled them to directly place orders for any of more than 100,000 products. This corporate strategy linked the company directly to its customers, and it was a strategic breakthrough. AHS gained sales and market share at competitors' expense. Hospitals had the advantage of lowered inventory carrying costs, because they were confident that orders with AHS would be processed quickly. AHS was one of the first companies to use information technology in corporate strategy. Customers were locked in because they could not switch to another supplier without losing efficiency and convenience.[34] Interorganizational linkage can link a company with suppliers and bankers as well as customers to gain speedy transactions, providing further competitive advantage. ■

BROADEN MARKET REACH.   Information technology can be used to tap into market intelligence data bases on competitors, demographics, customers, and census factors to spot unused niches and needs for new products. By having salespeople use lap-top computers in the field, a quick call can confirm inventory availability and instantly close a deal. Speed and timely service give an advantage over competitors. For example, Red Lion Inns uses a computer network to target messages to customer groups, give salespeople methods for entering orders directly through portable computers, and stimulate new product features.

Fingerhut Companies, Inc., one of the largest catalog marketing companies, has become a leader in information-based marketing through its *competitive strategy* of locking in customers and broadening corporate reach. Pictured here are some of the 300 customers who were brought together in Minnetonka, Minnesota, as part of a program to build relationships with customers, which includes personalized mailings, targeted surveys, focus groups, and innovative programs such as Adopt-A-Customer. Fingerhut's information systems provide up to 1400 data elements on each customer covering product preferences to payment habits. Fingerhut's customers feel that they are dealing with a company that knows them personally.

● IMPLEMENTATION OF INFORMATION TECHNOLOGY

Although information technology has undergone a revolution and can enhance corporate strategy as well as improve manager efficiency and control, it still suffers barriers to implementation. Some of these barriers pertain to the technology and others pertain to its lack of acceptance and use within organizations.

BARRIERS TO UTILIZATION

UNSUITABLE FOR MANY TASKS. CBISs have not yet become the primary source of management information. Recall from Chapter 1 that a manager's job is characterized by variety and fragmentation. Managers do not spend time analyzing data. Managers—especially top managers—work in an informal, reactive manner that is unsuited to the design of MISs or even of EISs. Moreover, as described in Chapter 16, managers need rich, face-to-face communications in order to interpret ambiguous events, establish personal relationships, and build coalitions for important decisions, none of which can be accomplished through a computer-based information system.

UNREALISTIC EXPECTATIONS.   Most organizations adopt new information technology with high expectations. Yet new information systems merely work within the organization's current information structure. If an information system suddenly provides data ten times as fast or provides ten times the volume of data, the improvement in manager performance may be only modest—say, 10 percent—because all that additional data and speed are unnecessary. Further, if the previous manual system did not provide useful data, the same worthless data will come through the computer system.

UNDERUSED OR SABOTAGED SYSTEMS.   The implementation of a new, computer-based information system has consequences for power and control—indeed, one motivation for adopting a new system is to increase management's control over the organization. The new system has the potential to provide data that will measure and monitor the performances of both individuals and departments. In response, operating personnel in some organizations have deliberately distorted or destroyed input data such as time cards and production control information. In one case, corporate accountants took the initiative of introducing the new system as a way of tightening control over organizational divisions. Division managers fought cooperation with the new system, attacking it for design, technical, and feasibility limitations. The most frequent problem is not sabotage but employees who avoid or bypass the new system.

IMPLEMENTATION TECHNIQUES

The implementation of information technology has generated many horror stories. For instance, Allstate Insurance Company designed a computer system to run its office operations and shorten the period needed to introduce new policies. The target cost was $8 million. One year after the expected date of completion, the project had already cost $15 million, and the revised cost estimate for completing the project was $100 million.[35]

As discussed in Chapter 11 on change, any new technology must be implemented properly in order for it to be successful. An effective strategy for developing and implementing a CBIS is called the **systems development life cycle,** which is the sequence of events that system designers should use to bring a new system to reality.[36] The life cycle starts with a feasibility study that ascertains user needs. Then the technology requirements are determined, followed by the system's design and physical construction. Physical construction consists of the design of appropriate software and acquisition of hardware. Next, the system is implemented. Implementation requires user participation, education, and communication. The more users are involved in the system's design, the more they will understand, accept, and use it.

systems development life cycle
The sequence of events that CBIS designers follow in developing and implementing a new system.

Barnett Banks, Inc., is a leader in the use of information technology. Barnett studies information technology in other industries and adapts that knowledge to banking. *Implementation* of new technology includes user participation, education, and communication. Here, a head teller receives training on the latest in paperless teller automation that speeds tasks such as locating customer account numbers or redeeming U.S. Savings Bonds. Barnett's focus on technology enables employees to spend more time with customers.

prototype

A working model of an information system developed to test the system's features.

Another variation for implementation used by some system designers is prototyping. A **prototype** is a working version of an information system developed to test the system's features.[37] The prototype provides samples of output to users and gives managers a chance to work with the output. A good implementation strategy is to ensure that management users are involved throughout all stages of development.[38]

TAILOR INFORMATION TO USER NEEDS. One of the biggest problems for both new and ongoing computer-based information systems is that information may not precisely fit what managers need to make decisions or control a large corporation. This is a continuing dilemma because as management problems change, the data provided by information systems also must change. Too often data end up being designed to satisfy machine requirements or design specialists rather than the managers who will use it. Specialists may be enamored with the volume of data a system can produce and overlook the need to provide small amounts of data in a timely and useful format for decision making.

Three techniques that help bridge the gap between information system specialists and managers' needs have been identified:

key indicator system

A technique for determining managers' information needs based on key business indicators, exception reporting, and the use of graphics packages.

1 *Key indicator system.* A **key indicator system** is based on the selection of key business indicators, exception reporting, and the use of graphics packages. The key indicator system emphasizes managers' control needs and provides specific data rapidly and selectively.

2 *Total study.* The **total study** is a process of assessing information needs at all levels of the management hierarchy. Managers are interviewed about their information requirements. Interview results are compared with available data bases, and priorities for information reports are set. The difficulty with this system is that it is time-consuming and tries to meet all managers' needs from the same information system, which may mean that no information needs are fully satisfied.

total study

A process that attempts to assess information requirements at all management levels.

3 *Critical success factors.* **Critical success factors (CSFs)** are the "limited number of areas in which results, if they are satisfactory, will ensure successful and competitive performance for the organization."[39] CSFs are obtained through lengthy interviews with individual managers, which define the managers' goals and methods for assessing goal attainment. Then the interviews are used to define which information will keep the managers apprised of key performance areas. CSFs differ from company to company and among managers within a firm. They force managers to consider only important information needs, thus eliminating useless data.

critical success factors (CSFs)

The particular areas in which satisfactory results will enhance the organization's overall performance.

ADDITIONAL IMPLEMENTATION TECHNIQUES. The first technique found to work in business organizations is to make technology believers of top management. This engages their support for the new technology and persuades employees to go along. Second, identifying technology champions also helps. Champions believe in the technology and persuade peers to try it. Third, a prototype can also be used in the sense that the first encounter with the new technology must be successful for employees. If they try the new technology in a way that is enjoyable and challenging, they will embrace the technology as part of their work.[40] Finally, measure the benefits. When technology alters behavior in a positive way or shows other tangible payoffs, report it widely to gain support. Using these techniques, along with the implementation techniques described in Chapter 11, can make new information technology a success.[41]

SUMMARY AND MANAGEMENT SOLUTION

This chapter discussed several important points about management information systems. Nontechnical managers need not understand hardware and software, but they should be aware of how information technology can enhance organizational efficiency and effectiveness. We are becoming an information society, and computer-based information systems are an important part of most organizations today.

Information systems process huge amounts of data and transform them into useful information for managers. Useful management information has the characteristics of quality, timeliness, completeness, and relevance. Computer-based information systems include three types: transaction processing, management information systems, and executive information systems. Transaction processing is used at lower organizational levels; MISs provide information for middle managers; and EISs help senior managers answer strategic questions. Other new technologies being adopted by organizations include group decision support systems, artificial intelligence, and networking.

Information technology has an impact on operational efficiency and business strategy. Information systems should be adopted and implemented in congruence with the organization's strategic objectives. Finally, computer-based information systems have some barriers to utilization, including unsuitability for many tasks, unrealistic expectations, and underused or sabotaged output. Implementation can be enhanced by tailoring systems to managers' specific needs.

Recall from the management problem at the beginning of this chapter that R. H. Macy & Co.'s "more is better" culture led to financial difficulty, because it was difficult to control inventories and maintain accurate accounting records. After declaring bankruptcy in 1992, R. H. Macy began reorganization plans, including improved information management systems. New CEO Myron Ullman III was appointed, because he is a no-nonsense numbers person who knows how to use information technology. Central to Macy's lower cost strategy is a computer system capable of inventory control that manages allocation of goods and helps Macy buy less while selling more. The computers will track customer preferences in sizes, colors and styles. Ullman sees the implementation of the new system as critical to productivity and cost reduction. Macy is also using the new information systems to make decisions about which stores to close and where and when to open new ones. Information systems are instrumental in the historic comeback of a company that wrote off over $300 million in worthless inventory in 1991.[42]

DISCUSSION QUESTIONS

1. Randy Fields of Mrs. Fields Cookies argues that managers must have a vision of what they want to accomplish with information technology. They must imagine which data they need and which functions they want to control, and not be constrained by the technology. Does this philosophy make sense to you? Explain.
2. What are four characteristics of useful information? How can information systems be designed to include these characteristics?
3. How do information needs for control and decision making differ by hierarchical level?
4. What are barriers to the use of computer-based information systems? Are they due to characteristics of technology or human behavior?
5. If you were asked to help design and implement an information system for a department at your university, how would you proceed? How would you overcome possible resistance?
6. What is an executive information system? How does an EIS differ from an MIS?

7. Describe artificial intelligence and expert systems. How do these systems differ from other computer-based information systems?
8. What are the possible effects of information technologies on organization structure? Discuss.
9. Recent thinking suggests that CBISs should be adopted to further competitive strategy. How might information systems be used in this way?

MANAGEMENT IN PRACTICE: ETHICAL DILEMMA

● BUYING A NETWORK

Purchasing agent Mike Stevens sat down with chief information officer George Sterns armed with supplier bids for 30 PC workstations that would be linked into a network. The system also would require cables and software that would interconnect with the current computer system.

Mike reported, "The companies are close with respect to quality and reputation. The only difference is price, with Kentucky Electronics on the low end and Quanton, Inc., on the high end. I think we should go with Kentucky."

Sterns responded, "Are you sure that's the best choice? After all, the plant is over 300 miles away, which could mean problems with delivery and service. I'd prefer Quanton, which we've used once before. It provided good service. Besides Frank Johns (one of their top people) and I go way back; we were fraternity brothers in college. I can count on him to smooth out any rough spots."

"But the extra 4 percent would put us over budget," said Mike. "The president won't like that."

"Don't worry. It's not such a big overrun. I'll explain the situation."

"But the purchasing regulations require us to accept the lowest bidder, unless there is a difference in quality or some other factor. I've also heard that Kentucky is hungry and has a staff of good programmers."

"A few extra pennies won't kill the budget. Hey, Johns is giving a barbecue next weekend. I'll give him a call and squeeze you in. He's a great guy, and you'll enjoy meeting him."

● WHAT DO YOU DO?

1. Select Quantron, Inc. Personal contacts are better for the company than formal bids and company regulations. Enjoy the party.
2. Pass the bids to the head of purchasing. Selecting Quantron, Inc., violates regulations, and Kentucky Electronics should be given a chance to compete.
3. Try to persuade the CIO to change his mind. Point out that he is using personal favoritism as his decision criterion. It's your responsibility to do the right thing, because you are the purchasing agent responsible for this project.

CASES FOR ANALYSIS

MEMORIAL COUNTY HOSPITAL

In 1989, Memorial County Hospital was hit by the same changes in Medicare reimbursement as all other hospitals. For years, the longer patients were hospitalized, the more Memorial County got paid. Now the government uses a fixed-fee system, under which hospitals are paid a specific amount for each disease. If the hospital's cost is less than the amount paid, the hospital keeps the profit; if too high, it takes the loss.

Memorial County is scrambling to implement a series of new information systems. An information systems department has been created, and an MIS expert, Jack Grant, has been hired to run it. The challenge facing Grant is awesome:

Memorial County must be able to track costs patient by patient, doctor by doctor, and disease by disease. Memorial County never needed this information before because it simply did a rough approximation of overhead costs for each patient before billing Medicare.

The system Grant wants to design will have several characteristics. When a pharmacist fills a prescription, the data will also go into the patient's computer file so that the hospital will know the cost immediately. Similarly, doctors will be expected to file information on patient treatments directly into the computer through terminals in their offices. The hospital has a strong incentive to treat patients as quickly and inexpensively as possible and expects doctors to help in the process. Grant also envisions a cost-tracking system that will follow each doctor's use of the X-ray department, laboratory tests, and other hospital resources. The information system also will report the consumption of all hospital resources per each patient and each disease. Weekly and monthly reports will reveal the different patterns among attending physicians and give Memorial County's senior managers a chance to buttonhole doctors to be aware of costs.

Another change Grant envisions is to integrate financial and medical records. These records were always kept separately, but now the medical record has financial implications, and both medical and financial data will be accessible from a patient's file.

The new technologies will cost Memorial County Hospital several hundred thousand dollars over the next three years. Administrators hope the new computer-based infor-mation systems will make the hospital more efficient. Managers will be able to determine, for example, that a cataract treatment costs $2,356 when reimbursement is only $2,128. With such information, administrators can concentrate on shortening hospital stays, reducing the number of tests, or treating some cases as outpatient.

● QUESTIONS

1. Has the change in Medicare reimbursement altered Memorial County Hospital's competitive strategy? Will information systems help implement that strategy?
2. What impact do you think the increase in information systems will have on structure, social relationships, and operational efficiency within Memorial County Hospital? Discuss.
3. Would you characterize the new information systems as transaction processing, MIS, or EIS? Explain.

UNITED WAY

In the summer of 1992, Jeremy Ramsey, director of a university computer center, was working at his desk when the phone rang. On the line was Susan Williams, an executive in charge of evaluation at the local United Way. She wondered if Ramsey would help design a consolidated information system that would help center directors cut paperwork and give more objective performance data for agency evaluation and control. Williams explained that in light of the recent controversy involving the national United Way organization, local agencies faced critical donation shortfalls. "It's more important than ever," she explained, "for local agencies to save money. We must find new cost-cutting methods to ensure the best value for the donations we receive."

Ramsey indicated that he was interested in helping. A week later he had his first meeting with the directors of eight neighborhood centers and executives from three funding agencies. The directors all faced similar problems. Most of the centers had evolved from local settlement houses to neighborhood centers that provided a number of services to local residents. Services varied widely but usually included housing, employment, recreation, food, clothing, child care, health services, and referrals and transportation to other agencies. Each had its own unique variety of funding sources, and each was inundated with paperwork.

During the discussion of a potential information system, Ramsey explained what might be done to reduce the paperwork. He pointed out that the current narrative reports written by the caseworkers and the wide variety of forms could be reduced to several standardized forms. From the information on the standardized forms, the computer could produce summaries that would eliminate 80 percent of the paperwork that the directors were doing. The presentation generated considerable enthusiasm, and it was agreed that Ramsey's staff would begin to wade through the numerous forms used in each of the agencies.

After three months, the computer staff had conducted over 100 interviews with people from all levels of the eight agencies and had gathered 190 forms that were currently in use. At a follow-up meeting with the eight center directors, however, it was clear that completion of the project would be impossible until the directors understood the system and how computerization could benefit them. Agency directors voiced the usual concerns about staff training on the new machines and the potential for "losing" information. In addition, they were uncertain about their own needs—which information should be transferred to the computer, and whether they could continue to use the paperwork as backup to the computer. Ramsey and his staff saw the need to work with agency directors and computer staff to design the system to fit the agency.

● QUESTIONS

1. What type of information system—transaction processing, MIS, or EIS—will be most appropriate for the United Way agency?
2. Do the United Way agencies truly need a computer-based information system? What limitations do you see in the ability of a CBIS to meet their information needs?

3. How would you characterize the procedure being used to design and implement the information system? What techniques should Ramsey's staff use to help managers define their information needs and overcome their resistance?

SOURCE: Robert E. Quinn, "Computers, People, and the Delivery of Services: How to Manage the Management Information System," in John E. Diettrich and Robert A. Zawacki, *People & Organizations*, 2d ed. (Plano, Tex.: Business Publications, 1985), 226–232, and Ron Stodgill II, "United They Stand?" *Business Week,* October 19, 1992, 40.

REFERENCES

1. Stephanie Strom, "A Key for a Macy Comeback," *The New York Times,* November 1, 1992, F4, and Laura Zinn, "Macy's Is Counting on a Number-Cruncher," *Business Week,* June 22, 1992, 72–73.

2. Joel Dreyfuss, "Catching the Computer Wave," *Fortune,* September 26, 1988, 78–82.

3. Steven L. Mandell, *Computers and Data Processing* (St. Paul, Minn.: West, 1985), and Richard L. Daft and Norman B. Macintosh, "A Tentative Exploration into the Amount and Equivocality of Information Processing in Organizational Work Units," *Administrative Science Quarterly* 26 (1981), 207–224.

4. Jeffrey P. Stamen, "Decision Support Systems Help Planners Hit Their Targets," *Journal of Business Strategy* (March/April 1990), 30–33, and Craig R. Waters, "Franchise Capital of America," *INC.,* September 1984, 99–108.

5. Charles A. O'Reilly III, "Variations in Decision Makers' Use of Information Sources: The Impact of Quality and Accessibility of Information," *Academy of Management Journal* 25 (1982), 756–771, and Niv Ahituv and Seev Neumann, *Principles of Information Systems for Management,* 2d ed. (Dubuque, Iowa: Wm. C. Brown, 1986).

6. Bob Davis, "As Government Keeps More Tabs on People, False Accusations Arise," *The Wall Street Journal,* August 20, 1987, 1, 10.

7. Michael W. Miller, "Computers Keep Eye on Workers and See If They Perform Well," *The Wall Street Journal,* June 3, 1985, 1, 12.

8. Frances Seghres, "A Search and Destroy Mission—Against Paper," *Business Week,* February 6, 1989, 91–95.

9. William C. Symonds, "Getting Rid of Paper Is Just the Beginning," *Business Week,* December 21, 1992, 88–89.

10. Stuart Gannes, "IBM and DEC Take on the Little Guys," *Fortune,* October 10, 1988, 108–114.

11. Bruce G. Posner and Bo Burlingham, "The Hottest Entrepreneur in America," *INC.,* January 1988, 44–58.

12. Gary Geipel, "At Today's Supermarket, the Computer Is Doing It All," *Business Week,* August 11, 1986, 64–65, and Tom Richman, "Supermarket," *INC.,* October 1985, 115–120.

13. Alan Paller, "A Guide to EIS for MIS Directors," *CA-Insight: The Computer Associates Software Magazine* 2 (1989), 5–9.

14. Jeremy Main, "At Last, Software CEOs Can Use," *Fortune,* March 13, 1989, 77–81.

15. Ibid.

16. Ramesh Sharda, Steve H. Barr, and James C. McDonald, "Decision Support System Effectiveness: A Review and an Empirical Test," *Management Science* 34 (1988), 139–159.

17. Paller, "A Guide to EIS for MIS Directors."

18. David Churbuck, "Next Time, Think Big," *Forbes*, June 12, 1989, 155–156.

19. Robert Reark, "Electronic Mail Speeds Business Communication," *Small Business Reports* (February 1989), 73–77, and David Churbuck, "Prepare for E-Mail Attack," *Forbes*, January 23, 1989, 82–87.

20. Richard C. Huseman and Edward W. Miles, "Organizational Communication in the Information Age: Implications of Computer-Based Systems," *Journal of Management* 14 (1988), 181–204.

21. George P. Huber, "Issues in the Design of Group Decision Support Systems," *MIS Quarterly* 8 (1984), 195–204.

22. G. Michael Ashmore, "Applying Expert Systems to Business Strategy," *The Journal of Business Strategy* (September–October 1989), 46–49.

23. Emily T. Smith, "Turning an Expert's Skills into Computer Software," *Business Week*, October 7, 1985, 104–108; David E. Whiteside, "Artificial Intelligence Finally Hits the Desktop," *Business Week*, June 9, 1986, 68–70; and Mary A. C. Fallon, "Losing an Expert? Hire an Expert System," Bryan-College Station *Eagle*, September 7, 1986, E1.

24. Evan I. Schwartz and James B. Treece, "Smart Programs Go to Work," *Business Week*, March 22, 1992, 97–105, and Otis Port, "Sure It Can Drive, but How Is It at Changing Tires?" *Business Week*, March 2, 1992, 98–99.

25. Richard Brandt and Deidre A. Depke, "The Personal Computer Finds Its Missing Link," *Business Week*, June 5, 1989, 120–128.

26. Anne E. Skagen, "Nurturing Relationships, Enhancing Quality with Electronic Data Interchange," *Management Review* (February 1989), 28–32.

27. Miron Magnet, "Who's Winning the Information Revolution?" *Fortune*, November 30, 1992, 110–117.

28. Joel Dreyfuss, "Networking: Japan's Latest Computer Craze," *Fortune*, July 7, 1986, 94–96.

29. Pam Carroll, "The Paperless Office Comes True," *Working Woman*, October 1989, 73–76.

30. Gene Bylinsky, "Saving Time with New Technology," *Fortune*, December 30, 1991, 98–104.

31. Lynda M. Applegate, James I. Cash, Jr., and D. Quinn Mills, "Information Technology and Tomorrow's Management," *Harvard Business Review* (November–December 1988), 128–136.

32. E. B. Swanson, "Information in Organization Theory: A Review" (Information Systems working paper, UCLA, 1986); John F. Magee, "What Information Technology Has in Store for Managers," *Sloan Management Review* (Winter 1985), 45–49; and John Child, "New Technology and Developments in Management Organization," *OMEGA* 12 (1984), 211–223.

33. Bylinsky, "Saving Time with New Technology."

34. Rudy Hirschatim and Dennis Adams, "Organizational Connectivity," *Journal of General Management* 17 (Winter 1990), 65–76; Laton McCartney, "Companies Get a Competitive Edge Using Strategic Computer Systems," *Dun's Business Month*, December 1985, 13–14, and Robert I. Benjamin, John F. Rockart, Michael S. Scott Morton, and John Wyman, "Information Technology: A Strategic Opportunity," *Sloan Management Review* 25 (Spring 1984), 3–10.

35. Tim R. V. Davis, "Information Technology and White Collar Productivity," *Academy of Management Executive* 5, no. 1 (1991), 55–67, and Jeffrey Rothfeder,

"It's Late, Costly, Incompetent—But Try Firing a Computer System," *Business Week*, November 7, 1988, 164–165.

36. David R. Hampton, *Management*, 3d ed. (New York: McGraw Hill, 1986), 723–725.

37. Ibid. 725.

38. John F. Rockart and Adam D. Crescenzi, "Engaging Top Management in Information Technology," *Sloan Management Review* 25 (Summer 1984), 3–16.

39. Andrew C. Boynton and Robert W. Zmud, "An Assessment of Critical Success Factors," *Sloan Management Review* 25 (Summer 1984), 17–27, and John F. Rockart, "Chief Executives Define Their Own Data Needs," *Harvard Business Review* 57 (March-April 1979), 81–93.

40. Tom Richman, "Break It to Me Gently," *INC.*, July 1989, 108–110.

41. Catherine L. Harris, "Office Automation: Making It Pay Off," *Business Week*, October 12, 1987, 134–146.

42. Strom, "A Key for a Macy Comeback," F4; Zinn, "Macy's Is Counting on a Number-Cruncher," 72–73; and Laura Zinn, "Prudence on 34th Street," *Business Week*, November 16, 1992, 44.

PROGRAM TRADING

An idealistic young doctor using the latest technology tried to create the perfect being. But instead of perfection, Frankenstein created a monster. Analogously, widespread use of computer-generated program trading, along with the advent of a vast array of so-called derivative securities, turned a monster loose on Wall Street in the 1980s.

These derivatives—options, futures, and stock index options—give the owner the right to buy or sell stocks or groups of stocks at fixed prices by certain dates. Programmed trading involves using computers to detect disparities between actual stock prices and these derivatives and then simultaneously executing several millions of dollars' worth of trades. The tremendous volume of equities bought or sold can generate catastrophic momentum, particularly to the downside. For a time this form of arbitrage was a relatively risk-free profit generator, but as larger trading houses joined in, the intermarket plays became a source of high anxiety that threatened investor confidence.

The first portent of trouble came in mid-September 1986. In two days, the Dow Jones average plunged 120.78 points, with futures-related trading making up an estimated 40 percent of that day's turnover. Prior to that year, the Dow had only twice moved more than 38 points in a day: during the crash of 1929 and when the bull market began in August 1982. The market for derivatives was dwarfing the stocks themselves. The NYSE's average daily cash turnover of stocks was $3.5 billion; the average value of the underlying securities of stock options was almost three times that, or $11 billion . On the day of the 120-point drop the $36 billion worth of stock futures contracts were traded, leading critics to charge that program trading had evolved from hedging or portfolio insurance to outright speculation.

The bloodbath the following year made the first computer-induced market slide look like minor profit taking. On October 19, 1987, the Dow lost 508 points, and in an unprecedented step, the New York Stock Exchange limited member use of program trading, saying it believed the move would minimize volatility.

While many laid the blame on computer trading, some feared that limitations or a wholesale ban could lead to more serious regulations of other securities practices that eventually would inhibit industry growth. Many also detected a hint of a sour-grapes double standard at play.

The results of the crash of 1987 were widespread. Investor caution dampened business for securities companies, and in an effort to cut costs, huge numbers of brokers and support personnel were laid off. By 1992, industry-wide employee cuts had reached 17 percent, but operating costs, in real terms, were three times as high as in 1980. Intractable costs forced brokerage companies to rethink how they did business. The key component of the organizational makeover was to streamline information systems to cope with an increasing number of new products and markets.

Merrill Lynch has led the way. Its Advanced Order Entry system went into operation in late 1991. The firm's 10,000-plus brokers are now able to enter orders from their desks instead of passing tickets to wire operators, who then must relay them to the exchange floor. An operation that took ten minutes, enough time for a precipitous price change, was cut down to one. The system not only saves time, but money as well. Merrill eliminated 500 wire-room clerks, and utilizes software that checks for entry mistakes, runs compliance checks, and does risk-management analysis. These functions screen out illegal or unduly risky trades, and provide protection for investors. Similar time- and cost-saving software is used to open new accounts; a process that used to take a week can now be accomplished by the following morning.

Rival firms have little choice but to board the technological bandwagon Merrill Lynch is driving. Firms are integrating research and sales offices in order to reduce processing costs through the elimination of paper-related tasks.

Right or wrong, computer-launched program trades were largely blamed for the stock market crash of 1987. A different sort of computer technology is bringing about cost savings in the securities business. Applying the proper operating system can return an industry to profitability, and even with the best intentions in mind, applying the wrong one can create a monster.

● QUESTIONS

1. Given that program trading contributed to the bull market of the 1980s, do you think that form of trading was unfairly singled out as a scapegoat when precipitous declines occurred?

2. Is it possible for large brokerage houses to ignore technology that generates huge profits? Do you think such firms would voluntarily cease and desist from such practices for the overall good of the market?

3. What rules could feasibly be adopted in the regulation of program trading?

4. Since nothing tangible—that is, a better mousetrap or the next generation of PCs—is created through program trading, debate the ethics of such practices as a contributor to the bottom line.

5. In retrospect, were brokerage houses, in general, overstaffed and inefficient before the crash of 1987? Would streamlining have occurred eventually?

OPERATIONS AND SERVICE MANAGEMENT

21 CHAPTER

Tom Blount, head of advanced manufacturing for refrigerators of GE's Major Appliance Business Group (MABG), had to do something about Building 4. That's where compressors for GE's refrigerators were made, a loud, dirty operation built with 1950s technology. It cost MABG over $48 to make a compressor. Japanese and Italian manufacturers were producing quality compressors for under $30, and a Singapore plant was aiming at $24. GE took 65 minutes of labor to make a compressor, compared with 25 minutes in Japan and Italy. Blount was  faced with two options. One was to buy quality compressors from foreign manufacturers at a cheap price to keep the cost of GE refrigerators down. The other option was to invest in a new, more effective manufacturing facility.[1] ■ Should Tom Blount buy inexpensive, high-quality compressors from overseas or take the risk of investing in a new plant? If you were an adviser, would you give MABG any chance of competing with foreign companies?

The *technical core* of H&R Block provides tax return preparation services for the taxpaying public. Tax preparation is the heart of Block's production process, which has expanded to include electronic filing, as shown here. Block's service operation is huge, involving over 16,000,000 returns prepared in more than 9,000 offices worldwide. *Operations management* develops special tools to manage services of this type.

The choice facing GE's refrigerator division is not unusual. Many companies have discovered that strategic success is contingent on efficient manufacturing operations. In the 1990s, the manufacturing function is held in high esteem in the corporate world and is considered a key to corporate success.

- The Timken Company gambled $500 million on an ultramodern steel plant when the roller bearing industry was in decline. In the face of withering foreign competition, it invested in new technology and won changes from the steel union on staffing and work rules.[2]

- Fireplace Manufacturers, Inc. (FMI), an entrepreneurial company, hired a Japanese manufacturing expert to redesign its factory, adopting just-in-time production techniques. Hardworking immigrants were hired and given substantial say over their jobs. As a result, scrap from the manufacturing process fell nearly 60 percent, inventory costs dropped, and overall productivity jumped more than 30 percent. The average price of FMI's stoves was cut 25 percent.[3]

- In a service industry, K mart's efforts to catch discount chain front-runner Wal-Mart include renovation and enlargement of facilities, upgrading merchandise lines, and installation of a high-tech inventory control system. In addition, K mart is experimenting with a superstore concept—combining discount retailing and supermarkets for true "one-stop shopping."[4]

Manufacturing and service operations such as these are important because they represent the company's basic purpose—indeed, its reason for existence. Without the ability to produce products and services that are competitive in the global marketplace, companies cannot expect to succeed.[5]

This chapter describes techniques for the planning and control of manufacturing and service operations. The three preceding chapters described overall control concepts, including management information systems. In this chapter, we will consider the management and control of production operations. First we define operations management. Then we look at how some companies bring operations into strategic decision making. Finally, we consider specific operational design issues such as plant layout, location planning, inventory management, manufacturing productivity, and structure of the operations management function.

● ORGANIZATIONS AS PRODUCTION SYSTEMS

In Chapter 1, the organization was described as a system used for transforming inputs into outputs. At the center of this transformation process is the **technical core,** which is the heart of the organization's production of its product or service.[6] In an automobile company, the technical core includes the plants that manufacture auto-

technical core

The heart of the organization's production of its product or service.

mobiles. In a university, the technical core includes the academic activities of teaching and research. Inputs into the technical core include human resources, land, equipment, buildings, and technology. Outputs from the technical core include the goods and services that are provided for customers and clients. Operations strategy and control feedback shape the quality of outputs and the efficiency of operations within the technical core.

The topic of operations management pertains to the day-to-day management of the technical core, as illustrated in Exhibit 21.1. **Operations management** is formally defined as the field of management that specializes in the production of goods and services and uses special tools and techniques for solving manufacturing problems. In essence, operating managers are concerned with all production activities within the organization.

operations management

The field of management that specializes in the physical production of goods or services and uses quantitative techniques for solving manufacturing problems.

MANUFACTURING AND SERVICE OPERATIONS

Although terms such as *production* and *operations* seem to imply manufacturing organizations, operations management applies to all organizations. The service sector has increased three times as fast as the manufacturing sector in the North American economy. Today more than one-half of all businesses are service organizations. Operations management tools and techniques apply to services as well as manufacturing.

Manufacturing organizations are those that produce physical goods. Ford Motor Company, which produces automobiles, and Levi Strauss, which makes clothing, are both manufacturing companies. In contrast, **service organizations** produce nonphysical outputs, such as medical,

manufacturing organization

An organization that produces physical goods.

service organization

An organization that produces nonphysical goods that require customer involvement and cannot be stored in inventory.

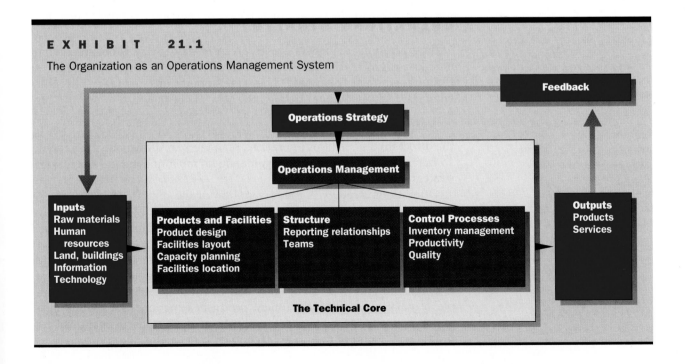

EXHIBIT   21.1

The Organization as an Operations Management System

Feedback

Operations Strategy

Operations Management

Inputs
Raw materials
Human
  resources
Land, buildings
Information
Technology

Products and Facilities
Product design
Facilities layout
Capacity planning
Facilities location

Structure
Reporting relationships
Teams

Control Processes
Inventory management
Productivity
Quality

Outputs
Products
Services

The Technical Core

educational, or transportation services provided for customers. Airlines, doctors, lawyers, and the local barber all provide services. Services also include the sale of merchandise. Although merchandise is a physical good, the service company does not manufacture it but merely sells it as a service to the customer. Retail stores such as Sears and McDonald's are service organizations.

Services differ from manufactured products in two ways. First, the service customer is involved in the actual production process.[7] The patient actually visits the doctor to receive the service, and it's difficult to imagine a barber or a hair stylist providing services without direct customer contact. The same is true for hospitals, restaurants, and banks. Second, manufactured goods can be placed in inventory whereas service outputs, being intangible, cannot be stored. Manufactured products such as clothes, food, cars, and VCRs can all be put in warehouses and sold at a later date. However, a hair stylist cannot wash, cut, and set hair in advance and leave it on the shelf for the customer's arrival, nor can a doctor place examinations in inventory. The service must be created and provided for the customer exactly when he or she wants it.

Despite the differences between manufacturing and service firms, they face similar operational problems. First, each kind of organization needs to be concerned with scheduling. A medical clinic must schedule appointments so that doctors' and patients' times will be used efficiently. Second, both manufacturing and service organizations must obtain materials and supplies. Third, both types of organizations should be concerned with quality and productivity. Because many operational problems are similar, operations management tools and techniques can and should be applied to service organizations as readily as they are to manufacturing.

OPERATIONS STRATEGY

Many operations managers are involved in day-to-day problem solving and lose sight of the fact that the best way to control operations is through strategic planning. The more operations managers become enmeshed in operational details, the less likely they are to see the big picture with respect to inventory buildups, parts shortages, and seasonal fluctuations.[8] Indeed, one reason suggested for the Japanese success is the direct involvement of operations managers in strategic management. To manage operations effectively, managers must understand operations strategy.

operations strategy

The recognition of the importance of operations to the firm's success and the involvement of operations managers in the organization's strategic planning.

Operations strategy is the recognition of the important role of operations in organizational success and the involvement of operations managers in the organization's strategic planning.[9] Exhibit 21.2 illustrates four stages in the evolution of operations strategy.

Many companies are at stage 1, where business strategy is set without considering the capability of operations. The operations department is concerned only with labor costs and operational efficiency. For example, a major electronics instrument producer experienced a serious mismatch between strategy and the ability of operations to manufacture products. Because of fast-paced technological changes, the company was

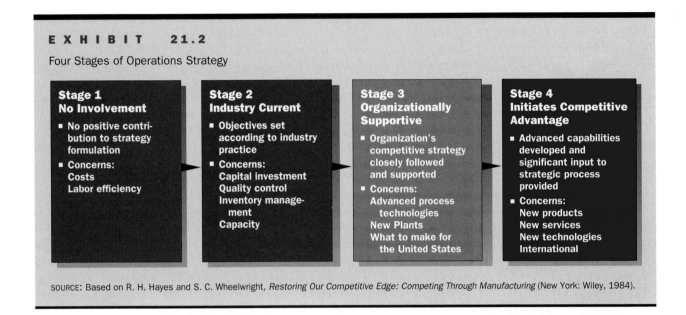

EXHIBIT 21.2

Four Stages of Operations Strategy

Stage 1
No Involvement

- No positive contribution to strategy formulation
- Concerns:
  Costs
  Labor efficiency

Stage 2
Industry Current

- Objectives set according to industry practice
- Concerns:
  Capital investment
  Quality control
  Inventory management
  Capacity

Stage 3
Organizationally Supportive

- Organization's competitive strategy closely followed and supported
- Concerns:
  Advanced process technologies
  New Plants
  What to make for the United States

Stage 4
Initiates Competitive Advantage

- Advanced capabilities developed and significant input to strategic process provided
- Concerns:
  New products
  New services
  New technologies
  International

SOURCE: Based on R. H. Hayes and S. C. Wheelwright, *Restoring Our Competitive Edge: Competing Through Manufacturing* (New York: Wiley, 1984).

changing its products and developing new ones. However, the manufacturer had installed a materials-handling system in the operations department that was efficient but could not handle diversity and change of this magnitude. Operations managers were blamed for the company's failure to achieve strategic objectives even though the operations department's capacity had never been considered during strategy formulation.

At stage 2, the operations department sets objectives according to industry practice.[10] The organization tries to be current with respect to operations management techniques and views capital investment in plant and equipment, quality control, or inventory management as ways to be competitive.

At stage 3, operations managers are more strategically active. Operations strategy is in concert with company strategy, and the operations department will seek new operational techniques and technologies to enhance strategy.

At the highest level of operations strategy, stage 4, operations managers may pursue new technologies on their own in order to do the best possible job of delivering the product or service. At stage 4, operations can be a genuine competitive weapon.[11] Operations departments develop new strategic concepts themselves. With the use of new technologies, operations management becomes a major force in overall company strategic planning. Operations can originate new products and processes that will add to or change company strategy.

Why will a company that operates at stage 3 or 4 be more competitive than those that rely on marketing and financial strategies? The reason is that customer orders are won through better price, quality, performance, delivery, or responsiveness to customer demand. These factors are affected by operations, which help the company win orders in the marketplace.[12]

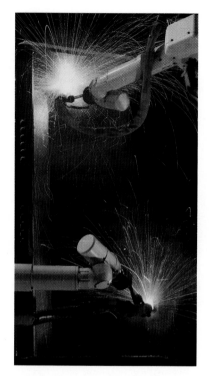

Clark Equipment Company has a *stage 4 operations strategy*. These robots in the Melroe division lead the industry, with one robot for every 45 employees. Grouped into cells, a welding robot and other machines require only three employees to produce axles for the popular Bobcat loaders, saving 50 percent of *manufacturing costs* compared to earlier manufacturing methods. Clark's worldwide redesign of manufacturing simultaneously increased sales and reduced costs, improving profits by $62.7 million.

One example of operations strategy is the shift at General Electric's headquarters from profit growth through massive acquisitions to squeezing more profits from existing businesses. The operations strategy is to increase manufacturing productivity, which is aligned with overall corporate strategy. General Electric created the post of productivity czar to help implement the strategy change. For example, in the electrical distribution business, new products are developed with the operational goals of reducing number of parts, assembly time, and total cost of materials, thereby producing new circuit breakers that are cheaper and more profitable. Production was consolidated from six plants into one, and the number of parts needed to produce various circuit breaker models plunged from 280,000 to fewer than 100. Structure was also changed, with shop floor teams given responsibility for scheduling inventory and production rates. This strategic approach to operations management has provided the big productivity gains General Electric desired.[13]

● DESIGNING OPERATIONS MANAGEMENT SYSTEMS

Every organization must design its production system. This starts with the design of the product or service to be produced. A restaurant designs the food items on the menu. An automobile manufacturer designs the cars it produces. Once products and services have been designed, the organization turns to other design considerations, including structural reengineering, facilities layout, production technology, facilities location, and capacity planning.

PRODUCT AND SERVICE DESIGN

A big trend in the business world is toward what is called *design for manufacturability and assembly* (DFMA).[14] Engineering designers have long fashioned products with disdain for how they would be produced. Elegant designs nearly always had too many parts. One study showed that simply eliminating screws and other fasteners from products saves up to 75 percent of assembly costs. Thus the watchword is *simplicity*, making the product easy and inexpensive to manufacture.[15]

Using DFMA is ridiculously inexpensive. IBM cut assembly time for a printer from 30 minutes to only 3 minutes, achieving efficiency better than the Japanese. DFMA often requires restructuring operations, creating teams of designers, manufacturers, and assemblers to work together. For example, Hewlett-Packard got designers to work with manufacturing to develop a new low-cost computer terminal. It uses 40 percent fewer parts and can be assembled in hours versus three days previously. The new model saves 55 percent on materials and 75 percent on labor. Breakthroughs in design simplicity are making U.S. manufacturers competitive again.[16]

The notions of simplicity and DFMA translate into four concerns for product design: producibility, cost, quality, and reliability. *Producibility* is the degree to which a product or service can actually be produced for the customer within the firm's existing operational capacity.

The issue of *cost* simply means the sum of the materials, labor, design, transportation, and overhead expense associated with a product or service. Striving for simplicity and few parts keeps product and service designs within reasonable costs.

The third issue is *quality*, which is the excellence of the product or service. Quality represents the serviceability and value that customers gain by purchasing the product.

Reliability, the fourth issue, is the degree to which the customer can count on the product or service to fulfill its intended function. The product should function as designed for a reasonable length of time. Highly complex products often have lower reliability because more things can go wrong.

IBM achieves these design attributes on its typewriters by putting as many of the same parts as possible in different products. Sharing parts allows IBM to maximize quality, reliability, and producibility by focusing on keeping parts count to a minimum. Its current typewriters have only one-fifth as many parts as the old Selectrics did. Screws and bolts are not allowed.[17]

In recent years, product design has also moved toward consumer-friendly products, resulting from a growing consumer alienation toward complex products. These trends are discussed in the Manager's Shoptalk box.

The design of services also should reflect producibility, cost, quality, and reliability. However, services have one additional design requirement: timing. *Timing* is the degree to which the provision of a service meets the customer's delivery requirements. Recall that a service cannot be stored in inventory and must be provided when the customer is present. If you take your friend or spouse to a restaurant for dinner, you expect the meal to be served in a timely manner. The powerful push for self-service reflects the need to provide service when the customer wants and needs it. Banking by machine, pumping your own gas, and trying on your own shoes are all ways that organizations provide timely service, which is important in today's time-pressure world.[18]

For example, when Pizza Hut announced a special lunch menu that could be served in five minutes or less, the timing required that operations—the kitchen—develop a small list of special items that could consistently be made in five minutes or less. Indeed, pizzas had to be redesigned to accommodate the five-minute requirement. Each step in the delivery of pizza items to customers had to be streamlined to ensure that the timing promise was kept.

PROCESS REENGINEERING

One new approach in operations management is called **reengineering,** defined as the reconsideration and redesign of business systems that bring together all elements of a single business process, enabling managers to eliminate waste and delays. Reengineering goes beyond mere speeding up or computerization of old processes. When a company reengineers a process, management systems, job design, and work flow are reevaluated and changed. Computers often play a major role in reengineering, and major computer companies such as IBM and the

reengineering

The reconsideration and redesign of business systems that bring together all elements of a single business process to eliminate waste and delays.

SIMPLIFY, STUPID!

I hate consulting a manual every time I use the machine.

There are so many colored lights flashing on my car dashboard, I wouldn't *know* if there was a problem.

I'm not a rocket scientist. I just want to be able to turn on the ?#!!*% thing.

The American consumer is frustrated by high-tech gizmos. Worse, consumers hate feeling like "technological illiterates" every time they purchase a new electronic product. Everything from blenders and microwaves to computers and stereos is a nightmare of buttons and dials and flashing lights. It seems that no one is spared. Tipper Gore, wife of Vice-President Al Gore, admitted placing black masking tape over her flashing VCR clock. American product designers are finally getting the message—*simplify*,

stupid! Suddenly, managers and designers in all industries are racing to find ways to simplify our lives and reduce stress. The results can be seen in a wide range of product innovations in the "Why didn't someone think of that before?" category. Many are winners of the Industrial Design Excellence Award (IDEA), sponsored by *Business Week* and conducted by the Industrial Designers Society of America.

For example, 1992 gold-medal winner, Texas Instruments, Inc., designed a hand-held Audit Trading Computer for use on the hectic floor of the Chicago Board of Trade. However, not all product innovations are high tech. OXO International's Good Grips kitchen utensils by New York's Smart Design, Inc., utilize a universal big handle for such items as kitchen knives, potato peelers, and pizza cutters. The enlarged handles (which prevent cramps) and rubbery, nonslip material can be easily used by anyone from 5 to 105.

Refinement of design is often undertaken through a new approach called *product mapping*, which

focuses on user needs. Careful analysis of *how* the consumer interacts with the product (hand movements, degree of difficulty in operation—pushing buttons, reading machine instructions) results in a refinement or design editing process. The result is a user-friendly product.

The future competitive success of American products depends on design innovation. Consumers in the United States and around the world will use products that offer the highest quality with the least hassle, and U.S. companies must be innovative in new product design and in refinement of old products.

Perhaps, someday, Tipper Gore and the rest of us will actually be able to set our VCR clocks! ∎

SOURCE: Zachary Schiller, "Winners: The Best Product Designs of the Year," *Business Week*, June 8, 1992, 52–57; Bruce Nussbaum, "What Works for One Works for All," *Business Week*, April 20, 1992, 112–113; and Bruce Nussbaum and Robert Neff, "I Can't Work This Thing!" *Business Week*, April 29, 1991, 58–66.

struggling Wang Laboratories recognize the new market potential in providing products for reengineering systems.[19] Reengineering can be applied to improve a single department, such as when Ford Motor Company applied reengineering to its accounts payable.

 ## FORD MOTOR COMPANY

The American automobile giant had a huge problem. Four hundred employees in Ford's accounts payable system were deluged in a sea of paperwork. Before the accounting department could pay vendors, a total of 14 items from a variety of sources—receipt records, purchase orders, and invoices—had to match precisely. The slightest delay in receipt of a form meant countless hours in tracking down the correct information, long payment delays, and angry vendors.

Ford considered installing more computers to speed the process but discovered that rival Mazda employed only five workers in its accounts payable division. Ford decided to radically reengineer the process. Now Ford's work redesign matches only three items in the purchase order and receipt records. Matching and check preparation are performed automatically by computer. The redesign reduced employees by 300, and Ford now pays vendors immediately upon receipt of the goods.[20] ■

FACILITIES LAYOUT

Once a product or service has been designed or reengineered, the organization must plan for the actual production. The four most common types of layout are process, product, cellular, and fixed position.[21] Exhibit 21.3 illustrates these four layouts.

At Beckman Instruments, Inc., managers realize the importance of product *design for manufacturability*. Manufacturing staff members, such as the production supervisor pictured here, work hand-in-hand with engineering design teams, advising them on ways to simplify product assembly through reduction of parts and assembly time. This employee is reviewing assembly techniques for the DU®7000 Diode Array Spectrophotometer, which requires minimal parts, a small manufacturing staff, and only a few hours for assembly. By designing products with improved manufacturability and through productivity improvement programs, Beckman's sales generated per employee rose 40 percent from 1986 to 1990.

E X H I B I T   2 1 . 3

Basic Production Layouts

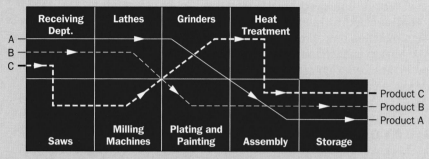

(a) Process Layout

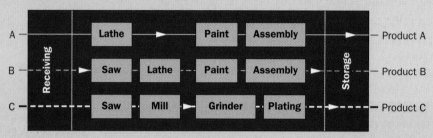

(b) Product Layout

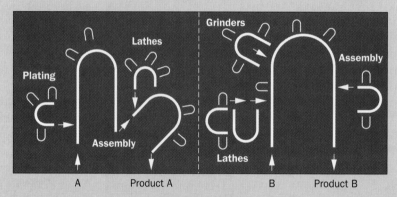

(c) Cellular Layout

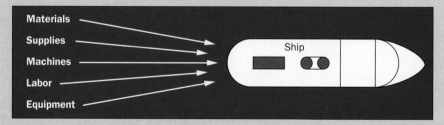

(d) Fixed-Position Layout

SOURCE: Based on J. T. Black, "Cellular Manufacturing Systems Reduce Setup Time, Make Small Lot Production Economical," *Industrial Engineering* (November 1983), 36–48, and Richard J. Schonberger, "Plant Layout Becomes Product-Oriented with Cellular, Just-in-Time Production Concepts," *Industrial Engineering* (November 1983), 66–77.

PROCESS LAYOUT. As illustrated in panel (a) of Exhibit 21.3, a **process layout** is one in which all machines that perform a similar function or task are grouped together. In a machine shop, the lathes perform a similar function and are located together in one section. The grinders are in another section of the shop. Equipment that performs a similar "process" is grouped together. Service organizations also use process layouts. In a bank, the loan officers are in one area, the tellers in another, and managers in a third.

The advantage of the process layout is that it has the potential for economies of scale and reduced costs. For example, having all painting done in one spray-painting area means that fewer machines and people are required to paint all products for the organization. In a bank, having all tellers located together in one controlled area provides increased security. Placing all operating rooms together in a hospital makes it possible to control the environment for all rooms simultaneously.

The drawback to the process layout, as illustrated in Exhibit 21.3(a), is that the actual path a product or service takes can be long and complicated. A product may need several different processes performed on it and thus must travel through many different areas before production is complete.

PRODUCT LAYOUT. Panel (b) of Exhibit 21.3 illustrates a **product layout**—one in which machines and tasks are arranged according to the progressive steps in producing a single product. The automobile assembly line is a classic example, because it produces a single product starting from the raw materials to the finished output. The product layout at Ford is so carefully tailored to each product line that Ford can make Mustangs only on the Mustang assembly line but cannot use it to make Thunderbirds. Many fast-food restaurants also use the product layout, with activities arranged in sequence to produce hamburgers or chicken, depending on the products available.

The product layout is efficient when the organization produces huge volumes of identical products. Note in Exhibit 21.3(b) that two lines have paint areas. This duplication of functions can be economical only if the volume is high enough to keep each paint area busy working on specialized products.

CELLULAR LAYOUT. Illustrated in panel (c) of Exhibit 21.3 is an innovative layout, called **cellular layout,** based on group-technology principles in which machines dedicated to sequences of operations are grouped into cells. Grouping technology into cells provides some of the efficiencies of both process and product layouts. Even more important, the U-shaped cells in Exhibit 21.3(c) provide efficiencies in material and tool handling and inventory movement. One advantage is that the workers work in clusters that facilitate teamwork and joint problem solving. Staffing flexibility is enhanced because one person can operate all the machines in the cell and walking distance is small.

FIXED-POSITION LAYOUT. As shown in panel (d) of Exhibit 21.3, the **fixed-position layout** is one in which the product remains in one location, and tasks and equipment are brought to it. The fixed-position

process layout

A facilities layout in which machines that perform the same function are grouped together in one location.

product layout

A facilities layout in which machines and tasks are arranged according to the sequence of steps in the production of a single product.

cellular layout

A facilities layout in which machines dedicated to sequences of production are grouped into cells in accordance with group-technology principles.

fixed-position layout

A facilities layout in which the product remains in one location and the required tasks and equipment are brought to it.

layout is used to create a product or service that is either very large or one of a kind, such as aircraft, ships, and buildings. The product cannot be moved from function to function or along an assembly line; rather, the people, materials, and machines all come to the fixed-position site for assembly and processing. This layout is not good for high volume but it is necessary for large, bulky products and custom orders.

PRODUCTION TECHNOLOGY

One goal of many operations management departments is to move toward more sophisticated technologies for producing products and services. New technology is sometimes called the "factory of the future." Extremely sophisticated systems that can work almost unaided by employees are being designed. For example, General Motors invested $52 million in the Vanguard plant in Saginaw, Michigan, to produce front-wheel-drive axles. Only 42 hourly workers are needed, because the work is done by robots. The product was designed to be made with supersophisticated technology. GM wants to learn whether robot technology is the most efficient way to proceed with its manufacturing operations.[22]

Two other types of production technologies that are becoming widely used in operations management are flexible manufacturing systems and CAD/CAM.

FLEXIBLE MANUFACTURING SYSTEMS. A small or medium-size automated production line that can be adapted to produce more than one line is called a **flexible manufacturing system**.[23] The machinery uses computers to coordinate and integrate the automated machines. Functions such as loading, unloading, storing parts, changing tools, and machining are done automatically. Moreover, the computer can instruct the machines to change parts, machining, and tools when a new product must be produced. This is a breakthrough compared with the product layout, in which a single line is restricted to a single product. With a flexible manufacturing system, a single line can be readily readapted to small batches of different products based on computer instructions. Cummins Engine, Chrysler, Caterpillar, and Rockwell have acquired FMSs.

CAD/CAM. CAD (computer-aided design) and CAM (computer-aided manufacturing) represent new uses of computers in operations management.

CAD enables engineers to develop new-product designs in about half the time required with traditional methods. Computers provide a visual display for the engineer and illustrate the implications of any design change. For example, CAD systems have helped a sportswear manufacturer adjust to rapidly changing product lines. Products change five times a year, and each new season's line requires new production standards, new bills of material for use on the shop floor, and new cutting patterns. Engineers can use the CAD system to design the pattern layouts and then determine the manufacturing changes needed to produce new sizes and styles, expected labor standards, and bills of material.[24]

---

flexible manufacturing system (FMS)

A small or medium-size automated production line that can be adapted to produce more than one product line.

CAD

A production technology in which computers perform new-product design.

CAM is similar to the use of computers in flexible manufacturing systems. The computer is harnessed to help guide and control the manufacturing system. For example, for the sportswear manufacturer, the entire sequence of manufacturing operations—pattern scaling, layout, and printing—has now been mechanized through the use of computers. Computer-controlled cutting tables have been installed. Once the computer has mathematically defined the geometry, it guides the cutting blade, eliminating the need for paper patterns. Fabric requisitions, production orders for cutting and sewing operations, and sewing line work can also be directed by computer programs.

FACILITY LOCATION

At some point, almost every organization must make a decision concerning the location of facilities. A bank needs to open a new branch office, Wendy's needs to find locations for some of the 100 or so new stores opened each year, or a manufacturer needs to build a warehouse. When these decisions are made unwisely, they are expensive and troublesome for the organization. For example, Modulate Corporation moved its head office six times in seven years because it had incorrectly anticipated its building requirements.

CAM

A production technology in which computers help guide and control the manufacturing system.

Mine Safety Appliances Company (MSA) produces protective equipment for a variety of hazardous industries, including fire fighting, asbestos abatement, hazardous materials cleanup, nuclear power generation, construction, and the military. New product design demands attention to minute details, so MSA utilizes high-powered *computer-aided design (CAD)* terminals to create and perfect equipment for these high-risk industries. *Computer-aided manufacturing (CAM)* systems speed production and guide products through the intricate production process. This technology protects those people who protect us.

The most common approach to selecting a site for a new location is to do a cost-benefit analysis.[25] For example, managers at bank headquarters may identify four possible locations. The costs associated with each location are the land (purchase or lease), moving from the current facility, and construction, including zoning laws, building codes, land features, and size of the parking lot. Taxes, utilities, rents, and maintenance are other cost factors to be considered in advance. Each possible bank location also will have certain benefits. Benefits to be evaluated are accessibility of customers, location of major competitors, general quality of working conditions, and nearness to restaurants and shops, which would be desirable for both employees and customers.

Once the bank managers have evaluated the worth of each benefit, total benefits can be divided by total costs for each location, and managers can select the location with the highest ratio.

Although local facilities may have some maneuverability regarding expansion and facility location, often these strategic decisions are made by the parent company with little local input. Sophisticated techniques that can aid in location decisions are described in Appendix B. These include linear programming, the payoff matrix, and decision tree analysis, each of which provides a useful framework for making a location decision.

CAPACITY PLANNING

capacity planning

The determination and adjustment of the organization's ability to produce products and services to match customer demand.

Capacity planning is the determination and adjustment of the organization's ability to produce products or services to match demand. For example, if a bank anticipates a customer increase of 20 percent over the next year, capacity planning is the procedure whereby it will ensure that it has sufficient capacity to service that demand.

Organizations can do several things to increase capacity. One is to create additional shifts and hire people to work on them. A second is to ask existing people to work overtime to add to capacity. A third is to outsource or subcontract extra work to other firms as described in Chapter 18. A fourth is to expand a plant and add more equipment. Each of these techniques will increase the organization's ability to meet demand without risk of major excess capacity.

For example, Cooper Tire & Rubber Company produces 531,000 tires a day. When expansion is necessary, Cooper refits existing plants instead of building new ones, allowing for gradual growth to fit capacity requirements. Gradual growth has increased production 40 percent over five years. Building new plants is undertaken only with major study and certainty of the demand for its products. Normally, adding people to a second shift or for overtime work increases capacity without long-term risk. Plant expansions are riskier but solve long-term capacity requirements. Such planning keeps Cooper's profitability high and adds tremendously to its corporate reputation. In rubber and plastics, Cooper ranked second only to Rubbermaid on *Fortune*'s annual ranking of America's most admired corporations.[26]

The biggest problem for most organizations, however, is excess capacity. When misjudgments occur, transportation companies have oil tankers sitting empty in the harbor, oil companies have refineries sitting

idle, semiconductor companies have plants shuttered, developers have office buildings half full, and the service industry may have hotels or amusement parks operating at partial capacity.[27] The challenge is for managers to add capacity as needed without excess.

● INVENTORY MANAGEMENT

A large portion of the operations manager's job consists of inventory management. **Inventory** is the goods the organization keeps on hand for use in the production process. Most organizations have three types of inventory—finished goods prior to shipment, work in process, and raw materials.

Finished-goods inventory includes items that have passed through the entire production process but have not been sold. This is highly visible inventory. The new cars sitting in the storage lot of an automobile factory are finished-goods inventory, as are the hamburgers and french fries waiting under the lamps at a McDonald's restaurant. Finished-goods inventory is expensive, because the organization has invested labor and other costs to make the finished product.

Work-in-process inventory includes the materials moving through the stages of the production process that are not completed products.

Borden, Inc., looks to *capacity planning* to secure continued leadership in pasta and widen its low-cost position in the industry. Recognizing that pasta represents its greatest growth opportunity in the 1990s, the company added 17 new production lines, increasing its North American capacity by 25 percent to nearly 1.5 billion pounds per year. The program's cornerstone is a new pasta hyperplant at St. Louis, Missouri—the largest pasta plant in North America and the most advanced in the world. With an annual capacity of 250-million pounds, the plant can be doubled in size to meet future demand for Borden pasta.

inventory

The goods that the organization keeps on hand for use in the production process up to the point of selling the final products to customers.

finished-goods inventory

Inventory consisting of items that have passed through the complete production process but have yet to be sold.

work-in-process inventory

Inventory composed of the materials that are still moving through the stages of the production process.

raw materials inventory

Inventory consisting of the basic inputs to the organization's production process.

Work-in-process inventory in an automobile plant includes engines, wheel and tire assemblies, and dashboards waiting to be installed. In a fast-food restaurant, the french fries in the fryer and hamburgers on the grill are work-in-process inventory.

Raw materials inventory includes the basic inputs to the organization's production process. This inventory is cheapest, because the organization has not yet invested labor in it. Steel, wire, glass, and paint are raw materials inventory for an auto plant. Meat patties, buns, and raw potatoes are the raw materials inventory in a fast-food restaurant.

THE IMPORTANCE OF INVENTORY

Inventory management is vitally important to organizations, because inventory sitting idly on the shop floor or in the warehouse costs money. Many years ago, a firm's wealth was measured by its inventory. Today inventory is recognized as an unproductive asset in cost conscious firms. Dollars not tied up in inventory can be used in other productive ventures. For example, "power retailers" such as Wal-Mart, Toys 'R' Us, Home Depot, or Circuit City understand the relationship between inventory and competitive pricing. State-of-the-art information systems allow tight inventory control with the capacity to meet customer needs "on demand." No excess inventory is needed. Suppliers such as Whirlpool have refined their delivery systems so that retail giants receive only the products needed to meet customer purchases.[28]

The Japanese analogy of rocks and water describes the current management attitude toward the importance of inventory.[29] As illustrated in Exhibit 21.4, the water in the stream is the inventory in the organization. The higher the water, the less managers have to worry about the rocks, which represent problems. In operations management, these problems apply to scheduling, plant layout, product design, and quality. When the water level goes down, managers see the rocks and must deal with them. When inventories are reduced, the problems of a poorly designed and managed production process also are revealed. The problems then must be solved. When inventory can be kept at an absolute minimum, operations management is considered excellent.

Ed Heard, a consultant who specializes in inventory management, has the following message:

> The best criterion for gauging the effectiveness of a manufacturing operation is inventory. If you have a lot of it sitting on the floor, you are probably not doing as good a job as you could be. Inventory is simply the best indicator of manufacturing performance that we have. There is no problem, no screw-up, that doesn't show up in the inventory number. Both raw materials and work-in-process are supposed to be where they are needed in the right quantity at the right time. Too much too soon and money invested in inventory is wasted. Too little too late and the production process is held up waiting for more inventory.[30]

We now consider specific techniques for inventory management. Four important ones are economic order quantity, materials requirement planning, manufacturing resource planning, and just-in-time inventory systems.

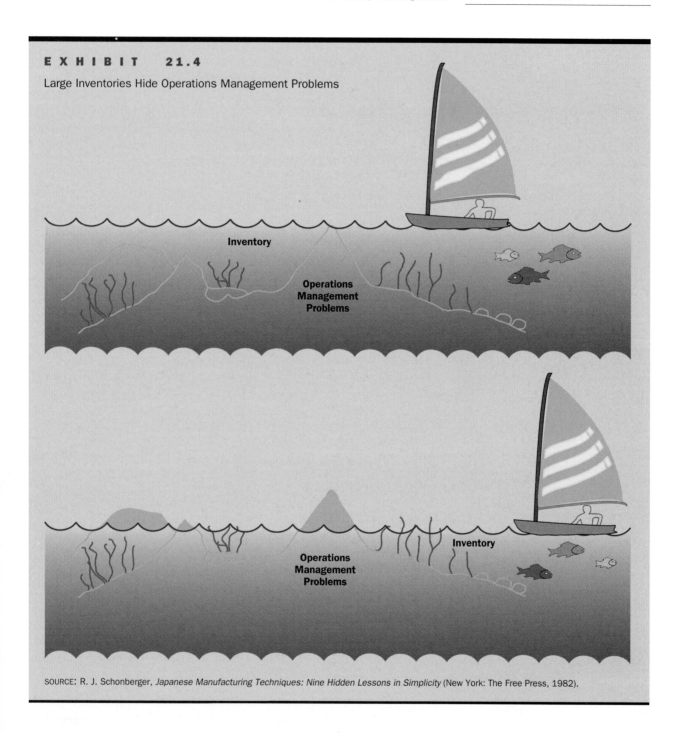

EXHIBIT   21.4

Large Inventories Hide Operations Management Problems

Inventory

Operations
Management
Problems

Operations
Management
Problems

Inventory

SOURCE: R. J. Schonberger, *Japanese Manufacturing Techniques: Nine Hidden Lessons in Simplicity* (New York: The Free Press, 1982).

ECONOMIC ORDER QUANTITY

Two basic decisions that can help minimize inventory are how much raw material to order and when to order from outside suppliers.[31] Ordering the minimum amounts at the right time keeps the raw materials, work-in-process, and finished-goods inventories at low levels. One popular

economic order quantity (EOQ)

An inventory management technique designed to minimize the total of ordering and holding costs for inventory items.

technique is **economic order quantity (EOQ),** which is designed to minimize the total of ordering costs and holding costs for inventory items. *Ordering costs* are the costs associated with actually placing the order, such as postage, receiving, and inspection. *Holding costs* are costs associated with keeping the item on hand, such as storage space charges, finance charges, and materials-handling expenses.

The EOQ calculation indicates the order quantity size that will minimize holding and ordering costs based on the organization's use of inventory. The EOQ formula includes ordering costs (C), holding costs (H), and annual demand (D). For example, consider a hospital's need to order surgical dressings. Based on hospital records, the ordering costs for surgical dressings are $15, the annual holding cost is $6, and the annual demand for dressings is 605. The following is the formula for the economic order quantity:

$$EOQ = \sqrt{\frac{2DC}{H}} = \sqrt{\frac{2(605)(15)}{6}} = 55.$$

The EOQ formula tells us that the best quantity to order is 55.

The next questions is when to make the order. For this decision, a different formula, called **reorder point (ROP),** is used. ROP is calculated by the following formula, which assumes that it takes three days to receive the order after the hospital has placed it:

$$ROP = \frac{D}{Time} \text{ (Lead time)} = \frac{605}{365}(3) = 4.97, \text{ or } 5.$$

reorder point (ROP)

The most economical level at which an inventory item should be reordered.

The reorder point tells us that because it takes three days to receive the order, at least five dressings should be on hand when the order is placed. As nurses use surgical dressings, operations managers will know that when the level reaches the point of 5, the new order should be placed for a quantity of 55.

This relationship is illustrated in Exhibit 21.5. Whenever the reorder point of 5 dressings is reached, the new order is initiated, and the 55 arrive just as the inventory is depleted. In a typical hospital, however, some variability in lead time and use of surgical dressings will occur. Thus, a few extra items of inventory, called *safety stock,* are used to ensure that the hospital does not run out of surgical dressings.

MATERIALS REQUIREMENT PLANNING

The EOQ formula works well when inventory items are not dependent on one another. For example, in a restaurant, the demand for hamburgers is independent of the demand for milkshakes; thus, an economic order quantity is calculated for each item. A more complicated inventory problem occurs with **dependent demand inventory,** meaning that item demand is related to the demand for other inventory items. For example, if Ford Motor Company decides to make 100,000 cars, it will also need 400,000 tires, 400,000 rims, and 400,000 hubcaps. The demand for tires is dependent on the demand for cars.

The most common inventory control system used for handling dependent demand inventory is **materials requirement planning (MRP).** MRP is a dependent demand inventory planning and control system that

dependent demand inventory

Inventory in which item demand is related to the demand for other inventory items.

materials requirement planning (MRP)

A dependent demand inventory planning and control system that schedules the precise amount of all materials required to support the production of desired end products.

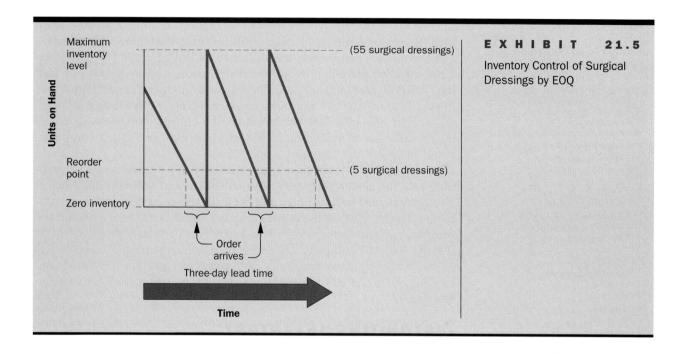

schedules the exact amount of all materials required to support the
desired end product. MRP is computer based and requires sophisticated
calculations to coordinate information on inventory location, bill of materials, purchasing, production planning, invoicing, and order entry.
Unlike with EOQ, inventory levels are not based on past consumption;
rather, they are based on precise estimates of future orders. With MRP,
inventory costs can be cut dramatically.[32]

For example, consider the hospital described earlier. Using an MRP
approach, the hospital would set up the surgical schedule for the coming week—the equivalent of a master production schedule. For each
scheduled surgery, a bill of materials would be issued listing the dressings and other needed items. The inventory status file would show how
many surgical dressings the hospital has on hand. Now assume that the
master production schedule shows that 20 surgeries will be performed
next week and the inventory status file shows 5 surgical dressings on
hand. MRP would then calculate that the hospital needs 20 surgical
dressings, less the 5 on hand; thus, 15 would be ordered. They arrive,
are used in the 20 operations, and the entire inventory is used up. There
are no extra inventory carrying costs and no risk of needing to scrap
excess or obsolete inventory. In the meantime, the schedule of surgeries
for the following week has been fed into the MRP system, the need for
surgical dressings identified, and the inventory ordered. Inventory flows
into the hospital as it is needed, thereby minimizing inventory storage
and handling costs.

MANUFACTURING RESOURCE PLANNING

Manufacturing resource planning, called **MRP II,** represents a major
development beyond MRP. MRP is a technique for managing inventory;

**manufacturing resource planning
(MRP II)**

An extension of MRP to include the
control of resources pertaining to all
operations of the organization.

MRP II reaches into every company operation to control all resources. MRP II creates a model of the overall business that allows senior managers to control production scheduling, cash flow, human resource planning, capacity planning, inventory, distribution, and materials purchasing. MRP II also supports marketing and engineering and provides financial information. It unites business functions by translating all operations into financial data and provides the entire company with access to the same set of numbers. In the ideal application, it is a computer-based model of the company's operations.

Although MRP II evolved from MRP, it plays a more strategic planning role for senior managers. The hardware and software for MRP II are sophisticated and complex and typically are used only in larger companies. Under MRP II, the entire company's efforts are analyzed and the computer produces corporate plans and solves corporate problems. MRP II starts with the company's business plan, which is translated into sales objectives by product line. Sales objectives, in turn, are translated into forecasts of materials requirements, inventory needs, and production schedules.[33]

JUST-IN-TIME INVENTORY

just-in-time (JIT) inventory systems

An inventory control system that schedules materials to arrive precisely when they are needed on a production line.

Just-in-time (JIT) inventory systems are designed to reduce the level of an organization's inventory to zero. Sometimes these systems are referred to as *stockless systems, zero inventory systems,* or *Kanban systems.* Each system centers on the concept that suppliers deliver materials only at the exact moment needed, thereby reducing raw material inventories to zero. Moreover, work-in-process inventories are kept to a minimum because goods are produced only as needed to service the next stage of production. Finished-goods inventories are minimized by matching them exactly to sales demand.

Just-in-time inventory requires that the production system be simple and well coordinated, as illustrated in Exhibit 21.6.[34] Each part of the production process produces and moves goods forward only when the next stage requires them. JIT is called a *demand-pull* system because each work station produces its product only when the next work station says it is ready to receive more input. This is in contrast to the traditional *batch-push system,* in which parts are made in large, supposedly efficient batches and pushed to the next operation on a fixed schedule, where they sit until used. In a push system, each work station produces at a constant rate regardless of the actual requirement of the next work station. The demand-pull system can result in reduced inventories, improved quality, and better responsiveness, but it requires excellent coordination among all parts of the production sequence.

Recall the Japanese analogy of the rocks and the water. To reduce inventory levels to zero means that all management and coordination problems will surface and must be resolved. Scheduling must be scrupulously precise. For example, Woodbridge Foam Corporation's plant in Saint-Jerome, Quebec, makes automobile seats just hours before they are installed in automobiles at GM's nearby Saint-Therese plant. GM electronically relays seat requirements based on the assembly line's car sequence. The Woodbridge plant uses the car sequence to quickly load

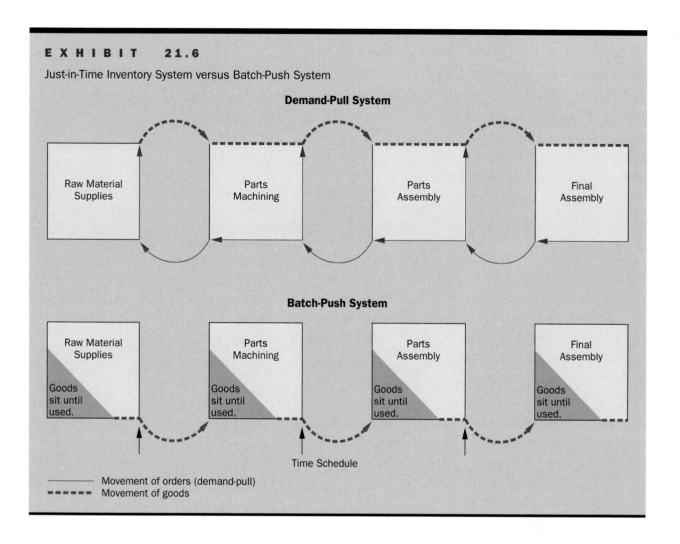

EXHIBIT   21.6

Just-in-Time Inventory System versus Batch-Push System

Demand-Pull System

Raw Material Supplies

Parts Machining

Parts Assembly

Final Assembly

Batch-Push System

Raw Material Supplies
Goods sit until used.

Parts Machining
Goods sit until used.

Parts Assembly
Goods sit until used.

Final Assembly
Goods sit until used.

Time Schedule

———— Movement of orders (demand-pull)
- - - - - Movement of goods

the trucks for the 20 kilometer drive. As seats are unloaded in the proper order, assembly is completed without missing a beat.[35]

Just-in-time inventory systems also require excellent employee motivation and cooperation. Workers are expected to perform at their best because they are entrusted with the responsibility and authority to make the zero inventory system work. Employees must help one another when they fall behind and must be capable of doing different jobs. Workers experience the satisfaction of being in charge of the system and making useful improvements in the company's operations.[36]

Just-in-time systems have tremendous advantages. The reduced inventory level frees productive capital for other company uses. For example, Omark Industries, a $300 million corporation in Oregon, saved an estimated $7 million in inventory carrying costs. It calls its version of just-in-time inventory the Zero Inventory Production System (ZIPS). General Motors has used a just-in-time inventory system since 1980, slashing inventory-related costs from $8 billion to $2 billion dollars. In a dramatic case, Polycom Huntsman, Inc., built its newest plant just 1,500 feet from General Motors' Harrison Radiator Division in Lockport, New York, and then connected the two factories by a pneumatic conveying system. Now when the GM plant starts to run low on plastic compounds, a computer-controlled system automatically begins shipping material from Polycom. "It's probably the best just-in-time system you've ever seen," said a GM purchasing manager.[37]

Another illustration of cost savings from inventory flexibility is the Coleman Company.

 COLEMAN COMPANY

When Coleman Co. of Wichita, Kansas, was taken over in 1989, the legendary maker of camp stoves and lanterns had fallen into a rut. Productivity was low, scrap was high, and the company stockpiled two months' worth of inventory in stoves and lanterns to meet the needs of giant retailers such as Wal-Mart.

New owner Ronald Perelman quickly restructured Coleman and brought in a consulting firm to improve speed, efficiency, and inventory management. Thousands of parts awaiting assembly bulged from ceiling racks suspended across the entire length of the 350,000-square-foot factory. The huge inventory had long covered up serious assembly and management problems at tremendous cost to company performance.

By adopting a just-in-time inventory strategy and training employees to implement the program successfully, Coleman lowered its inventory stockpiles. Parts and materials were assembled immediately on arrival from vendors, and the repair shop was relocated to the factory floor to reduce downtime resulting from machine breakdowns. Workers were encouraged to increase their speed on assembly and shipment. Within two years, Coleman's inventory costs were down $10 million with a 10 percent reduction in scrap and a 35 percent rise in productivity.[38] ∎

⬤ MANAGING PRODUCTIVITY

During the 1980s, globalization and increased competition from Japan and Europe created a sense of urgency among Americans regarding U.S. growth and productivity. Productivity is significant because it influences the well-being of the entire society as well as of individual companies. The only way to increase the output of goods and services to society is to increase organizational productivity.

MEASURING PRODUCTIVITY

productivity

The organization's output of products and services divided by its inputs.

What is productivity, and how is it measured? In simple terms, **productivity** is the organization's output of goods and services divided by its inputs. This means that productivity can be improved by either increasing the amount of output using the same level of inputs or reducing the number of inputs required to produce the output. For example, May Department Stores gauged productivity as sales per square foot. Sales was the measure of output, and floor space was a summary measure of

inputs. During one year, sales per square foot were $123, up 35 percent in three years, which meant that productivity was improving. May executives then designed new stores to have twice the productivity of old stores.

Typically, the accurate measure of productivity is more complex than dividing sales by square feet, which is a single measure of outputs and inputs. Two approaches for measuring productivity are total factor productivity and partial productivity.[39] **Total factor productivity** is the ratio of total outputs to the inputs from labor, capital, materials, and energy:

$$Total\ factor\ productivity = \frac{Output}{Labor + Capital + Materials + Energy}$$

Total factor productivity represents the best measure of how the organization is doing. Often, however, managers need to know about productivity with respect to certain inputs. **Partial productivity** is the ratio of total outputs to a major category of inputs. For example, many organizations are interested in labor productivity, which would be measured as follows:

$$Productivity = \frac{Output}{Labor\ dollars}$$

Calculating this formula for labor, capital, or materials provides information on whether improvements in each element are occurring. However, managers are often criticized for relying too heavily on partial

In an AT&T factory several football fields long, the speediest way to get parts to the assembly line is on wheels. AT&T has increased productivity in its factories with a *just-in-time inventory system* that delivers parts to the production line as they are needed. Working closely with suppliers, stocks are replenished just before they run out, and parts are pulled from stockrooms only when needed. The Denver factory has saved $150 million with better methods for carrying, storing, and managing inventory.

total factor productivity

The ratio of total outputs to the inputs from labor, capital, materials, and energy.

partial productivity

The ratio of total outputs to the inputs from a single major input category.

productivity measures, especially direct labor.[40] Measuring direct labor misses the valuable improvements in materials, manufacturing processes, and work quality. Labor productivity is easily measured but may show an increase as a result of capital improvements. Thus managers will misinterpret the reason for productivity increases.

TOTAL QUALITY MANAGEMENT

Recall from Chapter 18 that total quality management (TQM) improves quality and productivity by striving to perfect the entire manufacturing process. Under TQM, employees are encouraged to participate in the improvement of quality. Quality and productivity teams are created. Training budgets are increased. Statistical techniques are used to assist in spotting defects and correcting them. Moreover, TQM stresses coordination with other departments, especially product design, purchasing, sales, and service, so that all groups are working together to enhance manufacturing quality and productivity.

In the United States, operations managers traditionally have resisted spending money to improve quality, believing that productivity would suffer. In the new way of thinking, also discussed in the Manager's Shoptalk box, improvements in quality have a positive impact on productivity. One reason is that dollars spent on improved quality dramatically reduce waste. Poor quality causes huge delayed costs, such as the cost to rework defective products, the cost of maintenance, the cost of dissatisfied customers who do not buy additional products, and the time involved in dealing with dissatisfied customers and returned products.[41] One operations management technique for improving quality and productivity is statistical process control.

STATISTICAL QUALITY CONTROL

Quality is not just an abstract concept. It must be measured if a TQM system is to be successful. But measurement is by workers, not top managers or formal control systems. Workers must be given the training and tools to use statistical techniques to evaluate their tasks and make improvements as needed. The use of statistical measurements is a powerful weapon in the drive to improved quality.

statistical quality control

The application of statistical techniques to the control of quality.

statistical process control (SPC)

A type of managerial control that employs carefully gathered data and statistical analysis to evaluate the quality and productivity of employee activities.

Statistical quality control refers to the application of statistical techniques to the control of quality. The best known is called **statistical process control (SPC),** the application of statistical techniques to the control of work processes to detect production of defective items.[42] In addition, workers are often trained in traditional statistical concepts such as frequency distributions, regression and correlation, acceptance sampling, and tests of significance. These techniques are widely used in manufacturing departments, because production activities can be measured and analyzed.

For example, employees can be trained to use charts as graphic representations of work processes. A statistical process control chart measures a specific characteristic, as illustrated in Exhibit 21.7. In this particular chart, workers take a sample of five parts each hour, where the production rate is approximately 100 per hour. The diameters of the five

MANAGER'S
shop
talk

PRODUCTIVITY OR CUSTOMER SERVICE?

William H. Davidow and Bro Uttal, coauthors of *Total Customer Service: The Ultimate Weapon,* classify firms into two groups. The first group includes firms that promote quality and customer service regardless of the cost, such as IBM. Big Blue's machines are designed so they are easy for hardware and software designers to work with, and the company has invested in a reputation for service.

The second group includes firms that cut costs in an effort to maximize profits. For example, past chairman Ray McDonald of the now defunct Burroughs Corporation considered customer service "a skirmish between Burroughs and its customers." Cost-cutting efforts saved Burroughs money, but savings from omitting special hardware to diagnose machine failures were offset by lost sales, hundreds of lawsuits, and a damaged reputation.

Davidow and Uttal suggest that firms can increase productivity, quality, and customer service at the same time by looking hard at six components.

1. Develop a strategy for customer service. Determine customer expectations, and develop a plan to provide products and services they desire.

2. Communicate the importance of the service strategy and have leaders make personal visits to customers. Executive leadership is essential to provide an example of service.

3. Push authority and responsibility down to those employees so they can respond to customer demands quickly. Real customer service occurs when customers interact with frontline employees.

4. Design products and services with customer service in mind.

Poor service often can be traced back to an engineer who failed to listen to customer demands or field technicians when designing the product.

5. Restructure to create special teams devoted to a product or service for the sole purpose of looking after customer needs and wants.

6. Measure company performance on customer service. Involve employees in developing goals for customer service and analyze customer service records for feedback.

In an environment of complex manufacturing technology, investing in quality enhances both productivity and customer service. Investing wisely in operations management is the key to company survival. ■

SOURCE: Based on Christopher Elias, "Putting the Customer First Again," *Insight,* October 16, 1989, 40–41.

parts are measured, and the sample mean is calculated and plotted on the chart. If the upper control limit or lower control limit is exceeded, the variation is too great and is not due to chance alone. If either limit is exceeded, the operation is stopped and the cause determined. In the case illustrated in Exhibit 21.7, the tool had become loose, and so it was reset.

Procedures have been developed for implementing statistical quality control, which include the following steps.

1 *Define the characteristics of a high-quality output.* The output can be a hamburger produced by a Wendy's restaurant, a job description written by an employee in the human resource department, or a radial tire produced at a Firestone plant. The supervisor must provide an exact definition of a high-quality output or service.

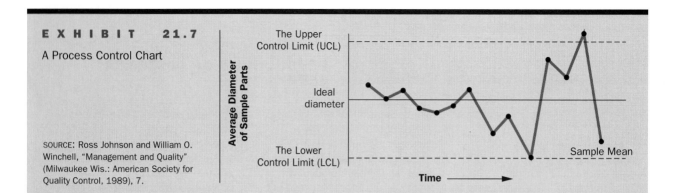

SOURCE: Ross Johnson and William O. Winchell, "Management and Quality" (Milwaukee Wis.: American Society for Quality Control, 1989), 7.

EXHIBIT   21.7

A Process Control Chart

2 *Decompose the work activities into the discrete elements required for producing a high-quality output.* For making a hamburger, one discrete element is forming the raw hamburger patty, a second is cooking it, and a third is garnishing it. The quality associated with each discrete element must be defined.

3 *Have a standard for each work element that is current and reasonable.* If standards for work elements are not already available, they must be developed. The standard is the basis for comparison of worker performance.

4 *Discuss specific performance expectations for every job with workers.* Each worker must understand what is expected with respect to his or her work elements and quality outputs. Workers should participate in decisions about how their performances will be measured.

5 *Make checksheets and collect data for each task element.* Written documents must be developed that reflect performance, and machine operators must be taught to collect data and assess whether their performances are up to standard. Likewise, supervisors can monitor departmental performance by gathering data on team outputs.

6 *Evaluate employee progress against standards at frequent intervals.* In some manufacturing situations, the output records should be checked for every worker several times during the day. If employees are involved in running several different batches of material, different standards will apply. If planned quality standards are not met, adjustments can be made before the end of the work period.

For example, Tridon Ltd., an Oakville, Ontario, manufacturer of windshield wiper blades, implemented an SPC program when it discovered that 25 percent of the output from the rubber extrusion line was defective. The rubber could not be reworked and thus was lost. To set up its program, Tridon conducted a feasibility study to identify the dimensions of high-quality parts. After defining standards for performance, it taught operators how the production line functioned and how to collect data that would indicate whether quality standards were being met. Setting up the SPC program cost almost $30,000 for studies, analysis, and training. Since implementing the SPC program, Tridon's scrap rate has decreased 10 percent. Now each part is higher quality but actually costs less to produce. Customers are happy and owners are, too.[43]

IMPROVING PRODUCTIVITY

Quality problems plague many firms. One Ford engine plant had so much variation in pistons for the same engine that they were classified into 13 sizes. Quality improvements over five years reduced the sizes to three and then to one. Now any piston fits any engine block, as do those made in Japan.[44]

When an organization decides that improving productivity is important, there are three places to look: technological productivity, worker productivity, and managerial productivity.

Increased *technological productivity* refers to the use of more efficient machines, robots, computers, and other technologies to increase outputs. The flexible manufacturing and CAD/CAM systems described earlier in this chapter are technological improvements that enhance productivity. Robots are another example.[45]

Increased *worker productivity* means having workers produce more output in the same time period. Improving worker productivity is a real challenge for American companies, because too often workers have an antagonistic relationship with management. At Corning Glass, workers

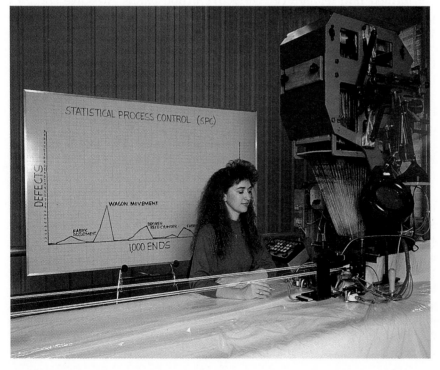

Albany International is a world leader and supplier of paper machine clothing, a fabric vital to the paper-making process. Albany has undertaken a comprehensive *total quality management* program that includes *statistical process control* (chart in background) methods. These methods are especially important during the automated joining process, pictured here. By identifying and reducing sources of variation in the process, automated joining of formed fabric produces uniform seams with a significant reduction in errors and production time.

EXHIBIT   21.8

Deming's 14 Points for
Management Productivity

SOURCE: Deming's 14 Points (January
1990 revision) reprinted from *Out of the
Crisis* by W. Edwards Deming by
permission of MIT and W. Edwards
Deming. Published by MIT, Center for
Advanced Engineering Study, Cambridge,
MA 02139. Copyright 1986 by
W. Edwards Deming.

1. Create and publish to all employees a statement of the aims and purposes of the company or other organization. The management must demonstrate constantly its commitment to this statement.
2. Learn the new philosophy, top management and everybody.
3. Understand the purpose of inspection, for improvement of processes and reduction of cost.
4. End the practice of awarding business on the basis of price tag alone.
5. Improve constantly and forever the system of production and service.
6. Institute training.
7. Teach and institute leadership.
8. Drive out fear. Create trust. Create a climate for innovation.
9. Optimize toward the aims and purposes of the company the efforts of teams, groups, staff areas.
10. Eliminate exhortations for the work force.
11. a. Eliminate numerical quotas for production. Instead, learn and institute methods for improvement
    b. Eliminate MBO. Instead, learn the capabilities of processes, and how to improve them.
12. Remove barriers that rob people of pride of workmanship.
13. Encourage education and self-improvement for everyone.
14. Take action to accomplish the transformation.

are formed into temporary "corrective action teams" to solve specific problems. Employees also fill out "method improvement requests," which are promptly reviewed. Zebco, a manufacturer of fishing reels, got its workers involved by taking them to a trade show to see how good the Japanese reels were. With workers' efforts, Zebco's productivity doubled in four years.[46]

Increased *managerial productivity* simply means that managers do a better job of running the business. Leading experts in productivity and quality have often stated that the real reason for productivity problems in the United States is poor management.[47] One of these authorities, W. Edwards Deming, proposed specific points for telling management how to improve productivity. These points are listed in Exhibit 21.8.

Management productivity improves when managers emphasize quality over quantity, break down barriers and empower their employees, and do not overmanage using numbers. Managers must learn to use reward systems, management by objectives, employee involvement, teamwork, and other management techniques that have been described throughout this book. For example, in the mid-1980s, a comparison between Honda and Jeep automobile assembly plants in Ohio revealed a dramatic difference in quality and productivity. The Honda plant produced 870 cars a day with 2,423 workers, and the Jeep plant produced 750 cars with 5,400 workers. The greater productivity in the Honda plant was attributed to better management.[48]

SUMMARY AND MANAGEMENT SOLUTION

This chapter described several points about operations management. Operations management pertains to the tools and techniques used to manage the organization's core production process. These techniques apply to both manufacturing and service organizations. Operations management has a great impact when it influences competitive strategy. Areas of operations management described in the chapter include product and service design, structural reengineering, location of facilities, facilities layout, capacity planning, and the use of new technologies.

The chapter also discussed inventory management. Three types of inventory are raw materials, work in process, and finished goods. Economic order quantity, materials requirement planning, and just-in-time inventory are techniques for minimizing inventory levels.

Another important concept is that operations management can enhance organizational productivity. Total factor productivity is the best measurement of organizational productivity. Total quality management is an approach to improving quality and productivity of operations. Managers can improve both quality and productivity through statistical process control, technology, management, and work-force improvements.

As described in the management problem at the beginning of this chapter, Tom Blount had to decide whether GE's Major Appliance Business Group (MABG) should buy inexpensive, high-quality refrigerator compressors from overseas or invest in a new plant to manufacture its own. After extensive study, the decision was made to introduce a new product design in the form of a rotary compressor that was simpler and more effective than the reciprocating unit. The new design reduced the number of parts from 51 to 29. The decision was made to invest $120 million in a new plant to compete head-to-head with already efficient plants in Japan and Italy. The decision seemed crazy, but Blount and his team pulled it off. GE's compressors are 20 percent cheaper than those of its competitors from overseas that pay dollar-an-hour wages. One reason for the plant's productivity is worker involvement. Some contributed 400 hours for their training without receiving a paycheck. The plant has achieved a level of precision that the suppliers of the automated technology did not believe possible. Miracles can happen with good product design and committed employees.[49]

DISCUSSION QUESTIONS

1. What is the difference between manufacturing and service organizations? Which has the greater need for operations management techniques?
2. Briefly explain the difference between process and product layout. What do you see as the advantages and disadvantages of each?

3. If you were asked by a local video store owner to help identify a location for a second video store, how would you proceed? How might you help the owner plan for the new store's capacity?

4. What are the three types of inventory? Which of these is most likely to be affected by the just-in-time inventory system? Explain.

5. What is materials requirement planning? How does it differ from using economic order quantity to reduce inventory?

6. Many managers believe that improvements in product quality reduce plant productivity. Why do you think managers feel this way? Are they correct?

7. Assume that a local manufacturing manager asks you about ways to improve productivity. What would you advise the manager?

8. What is the appropriate strategic role for operations management? Should operations management take the initiative in influencing competitive strategy?

9. What are the structural issues relevant to process reengineering? How might reengineering influence operations strategy?

MANAGEMENT IN PRACTICE: ETHICAL DILEMMA

● A STINKY SITUATION

At 3:30 A.M., Jacob Schilden, industrial relations manager, walked into the fuel tank assembly plant four hours earlier than usual. Jacob was called in because Sam Harding, a skilled welder, was threatening to walk off the job. Schilden was responsible for resolving conflicts between the managers, workers, and union representatives.

The problem involved a new process of dipping two metal halves of fuel tanks into an anticorrosion agent before welding them together. The design engineers said the agent was known to be highly toxic as a liquid but was safe after drying on the metal. Unfortunately, it created horrible fumes during welding, which was Sam's job.

The ventilation system installed by the engineers did not decrease the smell. Sam threatened to walk off the job unless the fumes were eliminated. Union representatives questioned whether safety standards were in jeopardy, saying perhaps the agent was toxic in gaseous form.

Management was trying to maintain high quality, which Schilden supports. Employee involvement teams had made a real difference, and Schilden did not want to alienate them. However, manufacturing management refused to stop the line to deal with this problem, because the gas tanks went to a car assembly plant ten miles away. The auto plant had no tanks in inventory, depending on just-in-time delivery from this assembly plant. Shutting down the tank assembly line would also shut down the car assembly plant. As of this moment, union representatives and management are in a heated argument about whether Sam should continue working.

● WHAT DO YOU DO?

1. Support Sam Harding and ask that the line be stopped. It is unethical to endanger Sam's health, and supporting the workers will enhance quality over the long term.

2. Support management's position of keeping the line going. Explain to Sam and the union representatives that the engineers studied the anticorrosion agent carefully. Management will work on improving ventilation first thing in the morning.

3. Propose an intermediate solution. Perhaps give Sam longer breaks than usual, set up fans in the area, or encourage worker rotation until the fumes can be removed.

CASES FOR ANALYSIS

XALOY, INC.

Xaloy, Inc., located in the Blue Ridge Mountains of Southwest Virginia, manufactures steel and alloy cylinders used to extrude plastics and other materials. The cylinders begin as logs of steel that are bored out, filled with a special metal alloy, and then heated to 2,000 °F. After cooling, the cylinders are straightened, ground smooth, and machined so that they can be connected to an extrusion machine. The cylinders are used to produce food products such as puffed rice and puffed wheat.

Plant manager Kelley Nunley and materials manager Danny Porter were concerned about a number of problems on the shop floor that indicate materials management inefficiencies. There were huge piles of cylinders stacked among the boring machines and latches; other giant cylinders hung from cranes above the shop floor. In all, some 2,000 cylinders were waiting to be worked on. One reason was that the bandsaw that cut the cylinders was the fastest machine in the place, so cylinders were stacked everywhere waiting to go on to other production stages.

A related problem was that workers liked to have lots of inventory sitting around. They associated accumulated cylinders with good times and no awaiting stacks of work with bad times. Workers thus had achieved comfort with high work-in-process inventory.

Another problem was plant layout. Xaloy made several cylinder sizes, each of which had to travel around the 96,000-square-foot plant because the machines that performed similar operations were located together. This created the potential for accidents and damage. Sometimes a cylinder would go back and forth in the plant several times in one week.

Still another problem was purchasing. A salesperson had offered a quantity discount, at which one of the senior managers jumped. Nearly 400,000 pounds of steel—a five- or six-month supply—arrived at the back door, overwhelming the raw materials inventory storage area. The manager believed that buying material cheaply in huge amounts was a smart way to save money.

The final problem that concerned Nunley and Porter was the cylinder-straightening process. They could not understand why the steel came into the plant straight and was precisely machined, yet was getting bent, necessitating later straightening. Something must have been happening to the steel during the production process.

● QUESTIONS

1. To what extent can the problems faced by Nunley and Porter be solved with operations management techniques?
2. Which operations management ideas described in this chapter are most appropriate to the Xaloy situation?
3. What suggestions would you make to help Xaloy improve productivity and quality?

SOURCE: Craig R. Waters, "Profit and Loss," *INC.*, April 1985, 103–112.

7-ELEVEN

7-Eleven CEO Clark J. Matthew II relays the new order in a heavy West Texas drawl, but the message is coming through loud and clear. The 6,300 convenience stores in 7-Eleven's U.S. chain will keep precise, up-to-date weekly inventories on everything from Big Gulp cups to milk and toothpaste—over 2,400 items.

It is all part of a complete overhaul at 7-Eleven and its parent, Southland Corp., since Japan's Ito-Yokado took control in 1990 just as Southland filed for Chapter 11 bankruptcy. At Ito-Yokado's insistence, 7-Eleven, the granddaddy of convenience stores, is revamping—trimming its labor force, introducing new product lines such as fresh fruits and vegetables, and experimenting with new store layouts and atmosphere. Brighter lighting and wider aisles have increased sales in experimental stores in Texas.

The centerpiece of the makeover is a new inventory control system called accelerated inventory management (AIM). Successfully used by Japan's 7-Eleven chain, AIM's computerized system cuts inventory guesswork and weeds out slow-moving product lines by providing managers with up-to-the-minute inventory data. It helps to know that Comet sells fast, but Ajax does not. Automatic reordering of store merchandise will not be far behind the inventory control system.

Although the AIM system will not be fully installed before 1996, Matthew insists franchisees hand post their weekly inventory totals now, and Southland offers incentives as encouragement. Still, some franchisees balk at the time needed away from customers to perform the weekly count. Many managers fear that their own costs will increase substantially under the new system while "headquarters" looks good.

● QUESTIONS

1. At what stage is 7-Eleven in its operations strategy? At what stage is it striving to be?

2. To what extent does the AIM system resemble an MRP inventory system? A just-in-time system?
3. What might be done to convince franchise owners to cooperate with the hand posting system until their stores are on-line?

SOURCE: Wendy Zellner and Karen Lowry Miller, "A New Roll of the Dice at 7-Eleven," *Business Week,* October 26, 1992, 100–101.

REFERENCES

1. Ira C. Magaziner and Mark Patinkin, "Cold Competition: GE Wages the Refrigerator War," *Harvard Business Review* (March–April 1989), 114–124.

2. John Holusha, "Beating Japan at Its Own Game," *The New York Times,* July 16, 1989, sec. 3, 1, 7.

3. Joel Kotkin, "The Great American Revival," *INC.,* February 1988, 52–63.

4. David Woodruff, "Attention K mart Shop . . . Hey, Where Is Everybody?" *Business Week,* January 18, 1993, 38.

5. Everett E. Adam, "Towards a Typology of Production and Operations Management Systems," *Academy of Management Review* 8 (1983), 365–375.

6. James D. Thompson, *Organizations in Action* (New York: McGraw-Hill, 1967).

7. Gregory B. Northcraft and Richard B. Chase, "Managing Service Demand at the Point of Delivery," *Academy of Management Review* 10 (1985), 66–75, and Richard B. Chase and David A. Tansik, "The Customer Contact Model for Organization Design," *Management Science* 29 (1983), 1037–1050.

8. Harlan C. Meal, "Putting Production Decisions Where They Belong," *Harvard Business Review* (March–April 1984), 102–111.

9. Everett E. Adam, Jr., and Paul M. Swamidass, "Assessing Operations Management from a Strategic Perspective," *Journal of Management* 15 (1989), 181–203.

10. W. Skinner, "Manufacturing: The Missing Link in Corporate Strategy," *Harvard Business Review* (May–June 1969), 136–145.

11. R. H. Hayes and S. C. Wheelwright, *Restoring Our Competitive Edge: Competing through Manufacturing* (New York: Wiley, 1984).

12. T. Hill, *Manufacturing Strategy: The Strategic Management of the Manufacturing Function* (London: Macmillan, 1985).

13. Todd Vogel, "Big Changes Are Galvanizing General Electric," *Business Week,* December 18, 1989, 100–102.

14. Otis Port, "Pssst! Want a Secret for Making Superproducts?" *Business Week,* October 2, 1989, 106–110.

15. Otis Port, "The Best-Engineered Part Is No Part At All," *Business Week,* May 8, 1989, 150.

16. Jonathan B. Levine, "How HP Built a Better Terminal," *Business Week,* March 7, 1988, 114, and Bruce Nussbaum, "Smart Design," *Business Week,* April 11, 1988, 102–108.

17. Zachary Schiller, "Big Blue's Overhaul," *Business Week,* Special Issue on Innovation, 1989, 147.

18. Claudia H. Deutsch, "The Powerful Push for Self-Service," *The New York Times,* April 9, 1989, sec. 3, 1, 15.

19. John A. Byrne, "Management's New Gurus," *Business Week,* August 31, 1992, 44–52, and John W. Verity and Gary McWilliams, "Is It Time to Junk the Way You Use Computers?" *Business Week,* July 21, 1991, 66–69.

20. Michael Hammer, "Reengineering Work: Don't Automate, Obliterate," *Harvard Business Review* (July–August 1990), 104–112.

21. Barbara B. Flynn and F. Robert Jacobs, "An Experimental Comparison of Cellular (Group Technology) Layout with Process Layout," *Decision Sciences* 18 (1987), 562–581; Richard J. Schonberger, "Plant Layout Becomes Product-Oriented with Cellular, Just-in-Time Production Concepts," *Industrial Engineering,* November 1983, 66–77; and Jack R. Meredith and Marianne M. Hill, "Justifying New Manufacturing Systems: A Managerial Approach," *Sloan Management Review* (Summer 1987), 49–61.

22. William J. Hampton, "GM Bets an Arm and a Leg on a People-Free Plant," *Business Week,* September 12, 1988, 72–73.

23. Sumer C. Aggarwal, "MRP, JIT, OPT, FMS?" *Harvard Business Review* 63 (September–October 1985), 8–16, and Paul Ranky, *The Design and Operation of Flexible Manufacturing Systems* (New York: Elsevier, 1983).

24. Kurt H. Schaffir, "Information Technology for the Manufacturer," *Management Review* (November 1985), 61–62.

25. Suren S. Singhvi, "A Quantitative Approach to Site Selection," *Management Review* (April 1987), 47–52.

26. Jennifer Reese, "America's Most Admired Corporations," *Fortune,* February 8, 1993, 44–72.

27. Marvin B. Lieberman, "Strategies for Capacity Expansion," *Sloan Management Review* (Summer 1987), 19–27.

28. Zachery Schiller, Wendy Zellner, Ron Stodghill II, and Mark Marmont, "Clout! More and More, Retail Giants Rule the Marketplace," *Business Week,* December 21, 1992, 67–73.

29. R. J. Schonberger, *Japanese Manufacturing Techniques: Nine Hidden Lessons in Simplicity* (New York: Free Press, 1982).

30. Craig R. Waters, "Profit and Loss," *INC.,* April 1985, 103–112.

31. Henry C. Ekstein, "Better Materials Control with Inventory Cardiograms," *Small Business Report* (March 1989), 76–79.

32. "Inventory Management: Controlling Costs to Maximize Profits," *Small Business Report* (August 1987), 50–53.

33. Joel C. Polakoff, "Inventory Accuracy: Getting Back to Basics," *Management Review* (November 1987), 44–46.

34. R. W. Hall, *Zero Inventories* (Homewood, Ill.: Dow Jones-Irwin, 1983).

35. John Lorinc, "Inventory: Taking Stock," *Canadian Business,* April 1991, 46–52.

36. "Kanban: The Just-in-Time Japanese Inventory System," *Small Business Report* (February 1984), 69–71, and Richard C. Walleigh, "What's Your Excuse for Not Using JIT?" *Harvard Business Review* 64 (March–April 1986), 38–54.

37. Martha E. Mangelsdorf, "Beyond Just-in-Time," *INC.,* February 1989, 21.

38. Brian Dumaine, "Earning More by Moving Faster," *Fortune,* October 7, 1991, 89–91.

39. E. E. Adam, Jr., J. C. Hershauer, and W. A. Ruch, *Productivity and Quality: Measurement as a Basis for Improvement,* 2d ed. (Columbia, Mo.: Research

Center, College of Business and Public Administration, University of Missouri–Columbia, 1986).

40. W. Bouce Chew, "No-Nonsense Guide to Measuring Productivity," *Harvard Business Review* (January–February 1988), 110–118.

41. Hank Johansson and Dan McArther, "Rediscovering the Fundamentals of Quality," *Management Review* (January 1988), 34–37.

42. Ross Johnson and William O. Winchell, "Management and Quality" (Milwaukee, Wis.: American Society for Quality Control, 1989).

43. Sherrie Posesorski, "Here's How to Put Statistical Process Control to Work for You," *Canadian Business,* December 1985, 163.

44. Jeremy Main, "Detroit's Cars Really Are Getting Better," *Fortune,* February 2, 1987, 90–98.

45. Kimberly J. Studer and Mark D. Dibner, "Robots Invade Small Businesses," *Management Review* (November 1988), 26–31.

46. Maggie McComas, "Cutting Costs without Killing the Business," *Fortune,* October 13, 1986, 70–78.

47. W. E. Deming, *Quality, Productivity, and Competitive Position* (Cambridge, Mass.: Center for Advanced Engineering Study, MIT, 1982), and P. B. Crosby, *Quality Is Free* (New York: McGraw-Hill, 1979).

48. J. Merwin, "A Tale of Two Worlds," *Forbes,* June 16, 1986.

49. Magaziner and Patinkin, "Cold Competition."

U.S. HEALTH-CARE SYSTEM

Nearly everyone concedes that the U.S. health-care system is sick, but few can seem to agree on how to cure it. Prescriptions for change range from managed care, where health insurance providers would negotiate with doctors and hospitals to get the best possible price, to so-called pay-or-play systems, which would require businesses to either cover their employees or pay into a state health care system. While debate over which treatment is best rages on, the symptoms keep getting worse.

By far the biggest problem facing the U.S. health-care system is high cost. Americans spent more than $800 billion on medical expenses in 1992 and will dish out about $900 billion in 1993. To put the numbers in perspective, consider that the U.S. medical bill is as high as the gross domestic products of Canada, Norway, and Sweden combined.

The reasons for higher costs include longer life spans and unnecessary treatment or expenditures. Surgeries such as caesarean operations, overprescribed diagnostic tests and physical therapy, the fear of malpractice suits, and fraud are among the culprits behind the high costs.

Lack of affordable insurance also ranks high on the list of health-care problems. Some 35 million Americans do not have health insurance because they do not have the money to pay for it, but are not poor enough or old enough to qualify for government aid.

Many of those without insurance are unemployed. But not everyone with a job has health benefits, especially those who work for a small company. According to the Employee Benefits Research Institute, nearly half of all uninsured workers are employed by businesses with less than 25 people.

The high cost of health insurance is also a burden for large U.S. corporations. At Ford Motor Company, the cost of providing health coverage for workers averages about $800 per car, nearly double the per-car cost of buying steel. The expense is not limited to employees on the payroll. In many cases, retirees also are entitled to health-care benefits, at ever increasing costs.

As the search goes on for solutions to the nation's health care problems, battle lines are being drawn between those who want to see more regulation to contain costs and those who prefer to let market forces rule. Among the former are those who advocate a national network of managed care. Under that type of system, doctors and hospitals are organized into networks to give people access to more cost-effective health care. With health maintenance organizations (HMOs), the earliest form of managed care, members can receive a range of services in return for a fixed monthly premium. With managed care, insurance providers seek to negotiate better deals with doctors and hospitals.

A variation of managed care is managed competition, which would allow Americans to enroll in an HMO or similar plan, but still leave them free to go outside the network as long as they paid extra for the privilege.

Managed competition would give small businesses the same kind of clout as large companies by grouping them together in "health insurance purchasing cooperatives." With doctor and hospital networks competing to win the business of these groups, it should lead to lower prices and improved service.

Doctors, who are often blamed for the U.S. health-care mess, have made some reform suggestions of their own. Surprisingly, the nation's largest group of medical specialists has proposed limiting doctors and hospital fees as a way of putting a national cap on health care spending. It also advocates limiting malpractice suits and cutting government paperwork.

A hodgepodge of other suggestions have been made that stop short of a complete overhaul of the system. Some Democrats in Congress have suggested a play-or-pay plan that would require businesses to either cover workers or make contributions to a state health insurance fund. Others have recommended an increase in Medicare premiums paid by the elderly who have a substantial amount of money.

The basic outline of the Clinton plan is to contain health costs and then use the savings to subsidize coverage for the uninsured. Whatever form the final version takes, it is clear the voters are ready for change. Businesses are ready, too. On the average, U.S. employers spend 45 percent of their after-tax profits on medical bills. But since few can agree on what action the government should take, the solution to the nation's health-care problems may be some years away.

● QUESTIONS

1. Which of the four aspects of product design, as described in Chapter 21, do you think are lacking in the American health care system?

2. If you were Hillary Rodham Clinton, what suggestions would you suggest reengineering the U.S. health care system?

3. Discuss some of the pros and cons of forming an organizational team, headed by the First Lady, to come up with solutions.

4. How could the U.S. government use management control systems to rein in the high costs of health care?

5. How has the health care system in the United States changed since this video case was aired?

■ SELF-CONTROL

Chapter 18, "Quality Control and Productivity," discussed an important method more and more companies are using to improve the quality of their products and services: Total Quality Management (TQM). This approach gives workers rather than managers the responsibility for achieving standards of quality as well as the responsibility of correcting their own errors and exposing any quality problems they discover. Are you prepared to assume this kind of responsibility?

THIS EXERCISE WILL HELP YOU

- Rate your level of diligence in ensuring that tasks are completed correctly and to the best of your ability.
- Learn some ways to improve your self-control on the job.

HOW TO LOCATE THE EXERCISE

When you see the main menu for Career Design, select "Controlling." Then select "Self-Control."

■ PERSONAL FINANCES

As you learned in Chapter 19, "Management Control Systems," companies create operational and financial budgets to determine what they require now and in the future to conduct their business successfully. You experience some of these same responsibilities on a much smaller scale with your own personal finances. It's important to determine your postgraduate expectations and what is required, both financially and professionally, to meet them.

THIS EXERCISE WILL HELP YOU

- Gain firsthand experience in the challenges of preparing and modifying a budget.
- Determine what level of compensation you will need upon graduation to meet your basic expenses for the life-style you want.
- Learn how to determine if a career direction you might pursue will meet those financial expectations.

HOW TO LOCATE THE EXERCISE

When you see the main menu for Career Design, select "Controlling." Then select "Personal Finances."

EMERGING

MANAGEMENT

ISSUES

During a Playing to Win seminar at an IDS National
Conference, financial planners
work in groups of two on a
"creating your future" exercise. To maintain its
competitive edge, IDS promotes employee career
development to
realize the poten-
tial within each
individual. As a
follow-up to its
basic leadership
course, IDS initiated
Management Development
Steps (MDS). The course prepares participants for leading
IDS into the next century.
Topics range from understanding the business to diversity
and team management.
Working together, participants
achieve both vision and autonomy in their IDS careers.

ENTREPRENEURSHIP AND SMALL BUSINESS MANAGEMENT

22 CHAPTER

Melinda and Robert Blanchard were unhappy with their jobs and wanted to start a business. They started one business, which they sold after it became moderately successful. Then they tried a second business, which failed. With a $2,000 tax refund from the failed business, they purchased jars for salad dressings, dessert toppings, and mustards Melinda had concocted.

The products went over great with neighbors, so they set up a display at a gourmet products show in San Francisco. Thrilled, the Blanchards returned with 75 orders averaging $300 apiece. Then reality sank in. How were they going to fill all those orders? How were they going to generate additional business? What did they do next? Their nine-year-old son and six neighbors volunteered to help.[1] ■ If you were a neighbor, what advice would you give the Blanchards? Have they started correctly in order to have a successful business?

The Blanchards represent a significant fact in American life. Most people dream of having their own business. In the local bookstore, titles such as *How to Run a Small Business, Entrepreneurial Life: How to Go for It and Get It,* and *Keeping the Family Business Healthy* outnumber books on how to get rich in stocks or real estate. Americans embrace entrepreneurship. Seventy-five percent of second-year MBA students at Harvard and Stanford signed up for courses on entrepreneurship. The enormous growth of franchising gives beginners an escorted route into a new business. Some 500 incubators for new companies have sprung up. So have self-help clubs through which entrepreneurs aid one another. Computers have given big-business power to little companies. The environment in the United States is favorable for entrepreneurs because of a market economy and the hero status of successful entrepreneurs such as Steven Jobs and Ross Perot.[2]

● WHAT IS ENTREPRENEURSHIP?

entrepreneurship

The process of initiating a business venture, organizing the necessary resources, and assuming the associated risks and rewards.

entrepreneur

Someone who recognizes a viable idea for a business product or service and carries it out.

Entrepreneurship is the process of initiating a business venture, organizing the necessary resources, and assuming the associated risks and rewards.[3] An entrepreneur is someone who engages in entrepreneurship. An **entrepreneur** recognizes a viable idea for a business product or service and carries it out. This means finding and assembling necessary resources—money, people, machinery, location—to undertake the business venture. The entrepreneur also assumes the risks and reaps the rewards of the business. He or she assumes the financial and legal risks of ownership and receives the business's profits.

For example, Marc Friedland creates artistic, handmade invitations and stationery for such celebrities as Ivana Trump, Melanie Griffith, and

Mike Sinyard (center) is living the dream of every bicycle-loving kid. Sinyard, a true *entrepreneur*, recognized the market for a variety of bicycle styles and parts. Sinyard set up his own business, Specialized Bicycle Components, featuring his own designs in components and bicycles, including all-terrain bicycles (ATBs). Among Sinyard's innovations are the Turbo, a durable, high-performance tire, and the Stumpjumper, the world's first mass-produced ATB. Sinyard was on the right track. Today, 1,200 dealers stock his bikes, while over 4,000 carry Specialized's bicycle equipment.

Pee Wee Herman. He stumbled upon a market of clients who need extravagant invitations to attract attention and get important people to attend their parties. He took the risk and is now reaping rewards.[4] Practically everyone has heard of Frederick Smith, who started Federal Express after he got a C on a term paper spelling out the idea for a nationwide overnight parcel delivery service. He borrowed money, acquired an initial fleet of 14 French-built Falcon jets, and on the first night delivered 16 packages. After two years of losses, the company took off like a rocket and spawned a new industry.[5]

● ENTREPRENEURSHIP AND THE ECONOMY

DEFINITION OF SMALL BUSINESS

Entrepreneurial businesses typically start small and hence fall within the definition of "small business" used by the Small Business Administration (SBA). The full definition of small business is detailed and complex, taking up 37 pages of SBA regulations. Most people think of a business as small if it has fewer than 500 employees. This general definition works fine, but the SBA further defines it by industry. Exhibit 22.1 gives a few examples of how the SBA defines small business for a sample of industries. It also illustrates the types of businesses most entrepreneurs start— retail, manufacturing, and service. Additional types of new small businesses are construction, agriculture, and wholesaling.

Industry	A Business Is Defined as Small If:
Manufacturing	
Meat packing	Its number of employees does not exceed 500.
Household laundry equipment	Its number of employees does not exceed 1,000.
Retail	
Hardware store	Average annual receipts for its preceding 3 fiscal years do not exceed $3.5 million.
Variety store	Average annual receipts for its preceding 3 fiscal years do not exceed $5.5 million.
Grocery store	Average annual receipts for its preceding 3 fiscal years do not exceed $13.5 million.
Service	
Carpet and upholstery cleaners	Average annual receipts for its preceding 3 fiscal years do not exceed $2.5 million.
Computer programmers	Average annual receipts for its preceding 3 fiscal years do not exceed $7.0 million.
Motion picture theaters	Average annual receipts for its preceding 3 fiscal years do not exceed $14.5 million.
Miscellaneous	
Banks	It has no more than $100 million in assets.

EXHIBIT 22.1

Examples of SBA Definitions of a Small Business

IMPACT OF ENTREPRENEURIAL COMPANIES

The U.S. economy is fertile soil for entrepreneurs. The economy changes constantly, providing opportunities for new businesses. For example, the demand for service is booming, and 97 percent of service firms are small, with fewer than 100 employees. Since government deregulation in 1980 removed restrictions that inhibited small-business formation, more than 13,000 trucking companies have been started. Technological change often helps small businesses. Using new technology in the steel industry, mini-mills with fewer than 100 workers can underprice giant steel manufacturers. Intense global competition and rapid environmental change also give competitive advantage to flexibility and fast response rather than to huge companies with economies of scale. Large, inflexible businesses often subcontract portions of their work to entrepreneurial companies. Another source of opportunity is the "Green" movement among businesses concerned about the environment, which is spawning many opportunities, as discussed in the Focus on Natural Environment box.

Understanding these environmental forces helps entrepreneurs identify the types of businesses that will survive. The impact of entrepreneurial companies on our economy is underscored by the latest figures: approximately 700,000 businesses are incorporated in the United States each year, along with another 600,000 unincorporated start-ups—about 1.3 million new enterprises in 1991, compared to 1.2 million in 1980 and only 90,000 in 1950. The risk that goes hand in hand with start-up is reflected in failure for two of every three new businesses within the first five years. Despite the failure rate, 1991 statistics revealed that more than a third of all retail sales in the United States were generated by franchises, and the appeal of entrepreneurship remains high. Many recent converts to entrepreneurship are corporate refugees (often middle management victims of corporate layoffs and downsizing) and corporate dropouts (those who prefer the uncertainty of self-employment to the corporate bureaucracy). New entrepreneurs most frequently start businesses in the areas of business services and restaurants. Demographic and life-style trends have created new opportunities in areas such as environmental services, children's markets, fitness, and child care.[6] The entrepreneurship miracle in the United States is an engine for job creation, innovation, and diversity.

JOB CREATION.   Although estimates vary, small entrepreneurial companies are responsible for the creation each year of from 40 percent to 80 percent of all new jobs in the United States.[7] Over 65 percent of all initial jobs for Americans are in a small business. Some 5 million jobs a year are created just from start-ups of new establishments.[8] The jobs created by new businesses give the United States an economic vitality that no other country can claim.

INNOVATION.   Entrepreneurial companies create a disproportionate number of new products and services. Of the notable products for which small businesses can be credited are cellophane, the jet engine, and the ball-point pen. Virtually every new business represents an innovation of some sort, whether a new product or service, how the product is deliv-

OPPORTUNITIES FOR ENTREPRENEURS

In the environmental market, "the real vitality," according to at least one market analyst, "is at the entrepreneur level." Indeed, small environmental companies are benefiting from the growing global concern for a cleaner natural environment. Events such as the 1992 Rio summit focused world attention on the mounting global environment problems. Consumer demands, increased environmental regulation, and increased litigation against the world's polluters have sent industries clamoring for environmental expertise and advice and the latest in environmental technology.

Many small companies, such as Seattle's Environmental Toxicology, Inc., or the California-based Brice Enviro Ventures, provide consulting services for companies. These and other small firms assist in a variety of areas ranging from growth management and assessment of environmental risks to research and education. Experts predict an 11 to 12 percent annual growth rate for firms in this hot market, as corporations scramble for cost-effective solutions to problems such as pollution control, recycling, and hazardous waste cleanup. Environmental concerns are expected to increase rapidly into the 21st century.

An example of growth potential is the success of Environmental Toxicology International, Inc. ETI analyzes data collected at potentially hazardous sites, determines the public health risk, and informs members of the community. Revenues climbed from $34,000 to $314,000 from the first to the second year of operation because of the demand for its services.

Entrepreneurs should not assume, however, that *any* environmental business is a guaranteed success. Securing capital has been a major roadblock for new environmental businesses, and venture capital groups have been one source of investment for such firms. Locating "environmentally literate" *and* "market-wise" managers is another tough hurdle in this new industry. Keeping up with constantly changing government regulations (including international regulations), developing knowledgeable project bidding practices in this new field, and building a top-notch team are some of the problems faced by entrepreneurs. However, environmental issues are here to stay, and sharp entrepreneurs can carve out a successful niche for themselves and "clean up" in more ways than one. ■

SOURCE: Bradford McKee, "From the Ground Up," *Nation's Business*, January 1991, 39–41, and Janet Beales, "How an Environmental Scientist's Business Grew from Contaminated Soil," *Nation's Business*, July 1991, 13.

---

ered, or how it is made.[9] Entrepreneurial innovation often spurs larger companies to try new things. Lamaur, Inc., created a new shampoo for permanent-waved hair. Soon three giant competitors launched similar products. Small-business innovation keeps U.S. companies competitive, which is especially important in today's global marketplace.

DIVERSITY.   Entrepreneurship offers opportunities for individuals who may feel blocked in established corporations. Large firms such as McDonald's and Wendy's make special efforts to recruit and provide financing for minorities. Derrick and Dorian Malloy, twin brothers, believed that being poor, black, and from a housing project would not be barriers to entrepreneurship. They acquired experience working at McDonald's and now they own two Wendy's restaurants.[10] Women-owned and minority-owned businesses have tremendous potential as the

In today's changing workplace, women-owned and minority-owned businesses are among the emerging growth companies, illustrating both *job creation* and *diversity*. An example is Shingobee Builders, a $7.4 million construction company in Loretto, Minnesota. Gae Veit (left), a Sioux and a company CEO, provides employment opportunities for native Americans, a group that ranks high in the state's unemployment. Investment in minority-owned companies benefits not only the company and its employees, but society as well through new jobs, reduced welfare, and improved living standards.

"emerging growth companies of this decade."[11] There are nearly 6 million women-owned businesses in the United States, and the growth is spectacular. One projection is that by the year 2000, half of all business owners will be women. Statistics for minorities are also impressive. Between 1982 and 1987, the number of black-owned businesses rose 37.6 percent, Hispanic-owned businesses rose over 80 percent, and Asian/Pacific Islander–owned businesses rose almost 90 percent.[12]

● WHO ARE ENTREPRENEURS?

The heroes of American business—Ray Kroc, Spike Lee, Henry Ford, Sam Walton, Mary Kay Ash, Steve Jobs, Ross Perot—are almost always entrepreneurs. Entrepreneurs start with a vision. Often they are unhappy with their present job and see an opportunity to bring together the resources needed for a new venture. However, the image of entrepreneurs as bold pioneers is probably overly romantic. A survey of the CEOs of the nation's fastest-growing small firms found that these entrepreneurs could be best characterized as hardworking and practical, with great familiarity with their market and industry.[13] For example, Bobby Frost worked 22 years in the mirror-manufacturing industry before leaving his employer. He started a mirror and glass fabrication business to use technology that his former employer refused to try and that Frost believed would work. It did. Eight years after its founding, Consolidated Glass & Mirror Corp. had 600 employees and $36 million in sales. Tom Scholl left Young & Rubicam ad agency after 13 years to set up his own agency serving clients he believed Y&R overlooked.

A number of studies have investigated the personality characteristics of entrepreneurs and how they differ from successful managers in established organizations. Some 40 traits have been identified as associated with entrepreneurship, but six have special importance.[14] These characteristics are illustrated in Exhibit 22.2.

LOCUS OF CONTROL. The task of starting and running a new business requires the belief that you can make things come out the way you want. The entrepreneur not only has a vision but also must be able to plan to achieve that vision and believe it will happen. An **internal locus of control** is the belief by individuals that their future is within their control and that other external forces will have little influence. For entrepreneurs, reaching the future is seen as being in the hands of the individual. Many people, however, feel that the world is highly uncertain and that they are unable to make things come out the way they want. An **external locus of control** is the belief by individuals that their future is not within their control but rather is influenced by external forces. Entrepreneurs are individuals who are convinced they can make the difference between success and failure; hence they are motivated to take the steps needed to achieve the goal of setting up and running a new business.

ENERGY LEVEL. A business start-up requires great effort. Most entrepreneurs report struggle and hardship. They persist and work incredibly hard despite traumas and obstacles.[15] A survey of business owners reported that half worked 60 hours or more per week. Another reported that entrepreneurs worked long hours, but that beyond 70 hours little benefit was gained. The data in Exhibit 22.3 show findings from a survey conducted by the National Confederation of Independent Business. New business owners work long hours, with only 23 percent working fewer than 50 hours, which is close to a normal work-week for managers in established businesses. For example, Bobby Frost, cofounder of Consolidated Glass & Mirror, recalls the long hours he and other company officials put in during the early years and provides a shot of small business work reality: "We'd all be president or whatever during the day and work in the plant at night."[16]

NEED TO ACHIEVE. Another human quality closely linked to entrepreneurship is the **need to achieve,** which means that people are motivated to excel and pick situations in which success is likely.[17] People who have high achievement needs like to set their own goals, which are

internal locus of control

The belief by individuals that their future is within their control and that external forces will have little influence.

external locus of control

The belief by individuals that their future is not within their control but rather is influenced by external forces.

need to achieve

A human quality linked to entrepreneurship in which people are motivated to excel and pick situations in which success is likely.

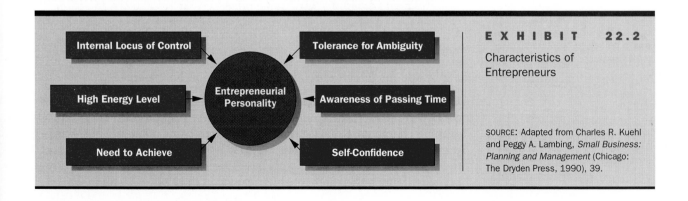

E X H I B I T 2 2 . 2

Characteristics of Entrepreneurs

SOURCE: Adapted from Charles R. Kuehl and Peggy A. Lambing, *Small Business: Planning and Management* (Chicago: The Dryden Press, 1990), 39.

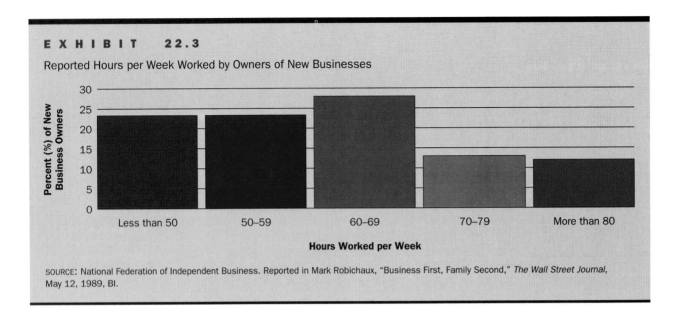

EXHIBIT 22.3

Reported Hours per Week Worked by Owners of New Businesses

SOURCE: National Federation of Independent Business. Reported in Mark Robichaux, "Business First, Family Second," *The Wall Street Journal*, May 12, 1989, B1.

moderately difficult. Easy goals present no challenge; unrealistically difficult goals cannot be achieved. Intermediate goals are challenging and provide great satisfaction when achieved. High achievers also like to pursue goals for which they can obtain feedback about their success.

SELF-CONFIDENCE. People who start and run a business must act decisively. They need confidence about their ability to master the day-to-day tasks of the business. They must feel sure about their ability to win customers, handle the technical details, and keep the business moving. Entrepreneurs also have a general feeling of confidence that they can deal with anything in the future; complex, unanticipated problems can be handled as they arise.

AWARENESS OF PASSING TIME. Entrepreneurs tend to be impatient; they feel a sense of urgency. They want things to progress as if there is no tomorrow. They want things moving immediately and seldom procrastinate. Entrepreneurs "seize the moment."

TOLERANCE FOR AMBIGUITY. Many people need work situations characterized by clear structure, specific instructions, and complete information. **Tolerance for ambiguity** is the psychological characteristic that allows a person to be untroubled by disorder and uncertainty. This is an important trait, because few situations present more uncertainty than starting a new business. Decisions are made without clear understanding of options or certainty about which option will succeed.

tolerance for ambiguity

The psychological characteristic that allows a person to be untroubled by disorder and uncertainty.

DEMOGRAPHIC FACTORS. In addition to the six personality traits described above, entrepreneurs often have background and demographic characteristics that distinguish them from other people. Entrepreneurs are more likely to be the first born within their families, and their parents are more likely to have been entrepreneurs. Most entrepreneurs launch their new business between the ages of 25 and 40. Children of immigrants also are more likely to be entrepreneurs, as are children for whom the father was absent for at least part of the childhood.[18]

A successful entrepreneur may have any combination of traits, and no one should be discouraged from starting a business because personality traits do not fit a specific profile. Sometimes entrepreneurial traits do not emerge until a person is in the right situation. Consider Kavelle Bajaj.

I-NET, INC.

When Kavelle Bajaj moved to the United States from India as a starry-eyed bride, her dreams were limited to setting up a home for her husband and starting a family. Later, with two growing sons, the desire for something more led the university-educated Bajaj to seek a career outlet for her talents, energy, and intellect. Bajaj challenged her mind with computer science courses while briefly pursuing careers in design (jewelry and handbags) and sales (Avon). The computer courses and the excitement and opportunities Bajaj saw in telecommunications captured her interest. With a $5,000 loan from her husband, Bajaj launched I-Net, Inc., a communication-information services company.

The recession helped Bajaj's new venture. Large companies were adjusting to lean times while I-NET offered top-quality services in matching telecommunications equipment, phone companies and customers at competitive prices. She won a government contract for minority firms. Rapid growth followed. No longer dependent on government contracts alone, Bajaj heads a $40 million company whose 450 employees include her husband. Her next goal? Making the Fortune 500. Bajaj says, "Most of us have a lot of talents which we don't really recognize or are afraid to open our eyes to because we're afraid of what we might find: the tiger in us!"[19] ■

● STARTING AN ENTREPRENEURIAL FIRM

For people who decide that the benefits of entrepreneurship are worth pursuing, the first step is to start with a viable idea for the new venture. With the new idea in mind, a business plan must be drawn and decisions made about legal structure, financing, and basic tactics, such as whether to start the business from scratch and whether to pursue international opportunities from the start.

NEW-BUSINESS IDEA

To some people, the idea for a new business is the easy part. They do not even consider entrepreneurship until they are inspired by an exciting idea. Other people decide they want to run their own business and set about looking for an idea or opportunity. Exhibit 22.4 shows the source of ideas based on a survey of 500 fast-growing firms in the United States. Note that 43 percent of business founders got the idea from work

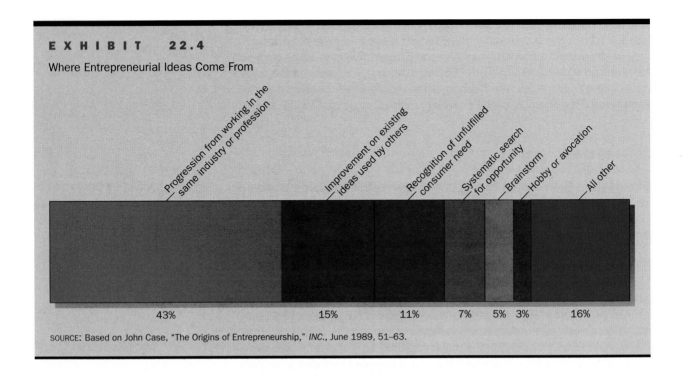

E X H I B I T   2 2 . 4

Where Entrepreneurial Ideas Come From

Progression from working in the same industry or profession — 43%

Improvement on existing ideas used by others — 15%

Recognition of unfulfilled consumer need — 11%

Systematic search for opportunity — 7%

Brainstorm — 5%

Hobby or avocation — 3%

All other — 16%

SOURCE: Based on John Case, "The Origins of Entrepreneurship," *INC.*, June 1989, 51–63.

experience in the industry or profession. A few entrepreneurs believed they could do something better, and 11 percent saw an unfilled niche in the marketplace.[20]

The trick for entrepreneurs is to blend their own skills and experience with a need in the marketplace. Acting strictly on one's own skills may produce something no one wants to buy. On the other hand, finding a market niche that you do not have the ability to fill does not work either. Both personal skill and market need typically must be present. For example, single-parent and two-earner households have led some entrepreneurs to use their skills to provide services that meet a need for people short of time. Reunion Time, Inc., arranges high-school reunions, contracting to track down alumni. Moment's Notice Cuisine delivers meals to the homes of its customers who are willing to pay 20 percent over the restaurant price.[21] Jean Griswold, a minister's wife, tried to find volunteers to help elderly parishioners. She had little luck until she realized the old folks would pay for help. She created Special Care, Inc., to hire students to do the work. It is now a $10 million business. She saw the need and had the skill to fill it.[22] The Winning Moves box describes how entrepreneur Frieda Caplan pioneered the U.S. market for exotic produce.

business plan

A document specifying the business details prepared by an entrepreneur in preparation for opening a new business.

THE BUSINESS PLAN

Once an entrepreneur is inspired by a new-business idea, careful planning is crucial. A **business plan** is a document specifying the business details prepared by an entrepreneur in preparation for opening a new

WINNING moves

FRIEDA'S FINEST BRINGS EXOTIC FARE TO U.S. GROCERIES

You may never have heard of the Chinese gooseberry, but thanks to California produce entrepreneur Frieda Caplan, many Americans have tasted a kiwifruit. The transformation of the unknown Chinese gooseberry into the trendy kiwifruit is just one of specialty produce wholesaler Caplan's many successes. What began as a new mother's part-time career has grown into a $20 million business. Frieda Caplan's story is similar to that of many entrepreneurs. She saw an opportunity in an unfilled market niche and pursued it despite standard industry practices that contradicted her plans.

Caplan launched Frieda's Finest/Produce Specialties in 1962 with a $10,000 loan from her father. In a field that was dominated by men, this native Californian broke all the rules. Traditionally, grocers have told the produce wholesalers what varieties they should carry. Caplan preferred to discover unusual produce that she thought should sell and then push it to the retailers until it did. "Our advantage has always been that we recognized that consumers were interested in what's new and unusual . . . right from the start we've never had a problem marketing an unusual produce item if we had a receptive retailer."

She began with fresh mushrooms. Now a common sight on the produce shelves, they were not readily available when Caplan set up her first stall in Los Angeles' Seventh Street Market. But Caplan's idea that cooks might prefer fresh mushrooms to canned proved to be correct. Soon her company was selling over $10,000 in fresh mushrooms each week. Caplan acquired a reputation as a wholesaler who was interested in unusual items.

In the mid-1960s Caplan's interest in the unusual brought a produce broker from New Zealand to her office. He was offering something called a Chinese gooseberry. Although Caplan had never seen the fruit, she recalled that six months before a produce buyer from a major grocery chain had asked her if she knew anything about it. Caplan purchased 2,400 pounds of the hairy brown gooseberries, but sales lagged and she had to warehouse them. When she realized that the name might be hindering sales, she convinced New Zealand growers to try "kiwifruit" instead. With the name change, sales soared. By 1967, Caplan had encouraged enough California growers to plant the fruit to establish a strong domestic industry as well.

Caplan took another risk when she began labeling her produce. Today the purple "Frieda" sticker is a symbol of quality. But in 1964, when she first proposed bagging and labeling some produce, she was told that it wouldn't work. When a major Chicago retail grocery chain agreed to carry packaged Sunchokes (Jerusalem artichokes), sales of the item rose 600 percent in two months. Now Frieda uses labels as a method of conveying information about her unusual fruits and vegetables. The labels on squash have proven most useful. They contain descriptions and cooking instructions that have helped to popularize many new varieties.

Frieda Caplan continues to explore new items. In 1990 she introduced the habanero chile, the hottest chile in the world, cactus pears, coquito nuts from Chile, and jackfruit from Thailand. She is also working with Noel Vietmeyer of the National Academy of Sciences to develop Philippine winged beans for the U.S. and Canadian markets. Vietmeyer calls Caplan the entrepreneur's entrepreneur. "By breaking open markets for exotic or unusual crops she provides an important impetus for scientists and growers to explore and develop fruits and vegetables that were previously unexplored." Frieda's Finest/Produce Specialties is now an 85-person operation, but it hasn't lost its entrepreneurial spirit. ∎

SOURCE: Based on Dennis Rodkin, "Produce Pro," *Entrepreneur*, May 1990, 138–144.

business. Planning forces the entrepreneur to carefully think through all of the issues and problems associated with starting and developing the business. Most entrepreneurs have to borrow money, and a business plan is absolutely critical to persuading lenders and investors to participate in the business.

The details of business plans may vary, but a typical business plan contains much of the following.

- Mission or vision of the company.
- Information about the industry and market.
- Information about suppliers.
- Information about the number and types of personnel needed.
- Financial information spelling out the sources and uses of start-up funds and operating funds.
- Plans for production of the product or service, including layout of the physical plant and production schedules.
- The business's policy for extending credit to customers.
- Legal considerations, such as information about licenses, patents, taxes, and compliance with government regulations.
- Critical risks that may threaten business success.

The business plan should indicate where the product or service fits into the overall industry and should draw on concepts described in other parts of this book. For example, Chapter 7 described Porter's competitive strategies that entrepreneurs can use. Other concepts, such as the breakeven point (Appendix B), income statements, and balance sheets (Chapter 19), are also helpful in developing the business plan. Detailed suggestions for writing a business plan are provided in the Manager's Shoptalk box.

LEGAL FORM

Before entrepreneurs have founded a business, and perhaps again as it expands, they must choose an appropriate legal structure for the company. The three basic choices are proprietorship, partnership, or corporation. A discussion of each type follows.

proprietorship

An unincorporated business owned by an individual for profit.

PROPRIETORSHIP.   A **proprietorship** is defined as an unincorporated business owned by an individual for profit. Proprietorships make up 70 percent of the 16 million businesses in the United States. The popularity of this form is that it is easy to start and has few legal requirements. A proprietor has total ownership and control of the company and can make all decisions without consulting anyone. However, this type of organization also has drawbacks. The owner has unlimited liability for the business, meaning that if someone sues, the owner's personal as well as business assets are at risk. Also, financing can be harder to obtain because business success rests on one person's shoulders.

partnership

An unincorporated business owned by two or more people.

PARTNERSHIP.   A **partnership** is an unincorporated business owned by two or more people. Partnerships, like proprietorships, are relatively

MANAGER'S shop talk

HINTS FOR WRITING THE BUSINESS PLAN

THE SUMMARY

■ Should have no more than three pages.
■ Is the most crucial part of your plan because it must capture the reader's interest.
■ Summarize what, how, why, where, etc.
■ Complete this part *after* the finished business plan has been written.

THE BUSINESS DESCRIPTION SEGMENT

■ The name of the business is stated.
■ A background of the industry with history of the company (if any) should be covered here.
■ The potential of the new venture should be described clearly.
■ Any unique or distinctive features of the venture should be spelled out.

THE MARKETING SEGMENT

■ Convince investors that sales projections and competition can be met.
■ Use and disclose market studies.
■ Identify target market, market position, and market share.
■ Evaluate *all* competition and specifically cover "why" and "how" you will be better than the competitors.
■ Identify all market sources and assistance used for this segment.
■ Demonstrate pricing strategy since your price must penetrate and maintain a market share to *produce profits*. Thus "lowest" price is *not* necessarily the "best" price.
■ Identify your advertising plans with cost estimates to validate the proposed strategy.

THE RESEARCH, DESIGN, AND DEVELOPMENT SEGMENT

■ Cover the *extent* and *costs* involved in needed research, testing, or development.
■ Explain carefully what has been accomplished *already* (prototype, lab testing, early development).
■ Mention any research or technical assistance that has been provided for you.

THE MANUFACTURING SEGMENT

■ Provide the advantages of your location (zoning, tax laws, wage rates).
■ List the production needs in terms of facilities (plant, storage, office space) and equipment (machinery, furnishings, supplies).
■ Describe the access to transportation (for shipping and receiving).
■ Explain proximity to your suppliers.
■ Mention the availability of labor in your location.
■ Provide estimates of manufacturing cost—be careful, too many entrepreneurs "underestimate" their costs.

THE MANAGEMENT SEGMENT

■ Provide resumes of all key people in the management of the venture.
■ Carefully describe the legal structure of the venture (sole proprietorship, partnership, or corporation).
■ Cover the added assistance (if any) of advisers, consultants, and directors.
■ Provide information on how everyone is to be compensated. (How much, also.)

THE CRITICAL RISKS SEGMENT

Point out potential risks *before* investors do:
■ Price cutting by competitors.
■ Potentially unfavorable industrywide trends.
■ Design or manufacturing costs in excess of estimates.
■ Sales projections not achieved.
■ Product development schedule not met.
■ Difficulties or long lead times encountered in the procurement of parts or raw materials.
■ Larger than expected innovation and development costs to stay competitive.
■ Alternative courses of action.

THE FINANCIAL SEGMENT

■ Provide statements.
■ Describe the needed sources for your funds and the uses you intend for the money.
■ Provide a budget.
■ Create stages of financing for purposes of allowing evaluation by investors at various points.

THE MILESTONE SCHEDULE SEGMENT

■ Provide a timetable to show when each phase of the venture is to be completed. This shows the relationship of events and provides a deadline for accomplishment. ■

SOURCE: Donald F. Kuratko and Ray V. Montagno, *The Entrepreneur's Guide to Venture Formation* (Center for Entrepreneurial Resources, Ball State University, 1986), 33–34. Reprinted with permission.

easy to start. Two friends may reach an agreement to start a pet store. To avoid misunderstandings and to make sure the business is well planned, it is wise to draw up and sign a formal partnership agreement with the help of an attorney. The agreement specifies how partners are to share responsibility and resources and how they will contribute their expertise. The disadvantages of partnerships are the unlimited liability of the partners and the disagreements that almost always occur between strong-minded people. A recent poll by *INC.* magazine illustrated the volatility of partnerships. Fifty-nine percent of respondents considered partnerships a bad business move, citing reasons such as partner problems and conflicts. Partnerships often dissolve within five years. Respondents who liked partnerships point to the equality of partners (sharing of workload and emotional and financial burdens) as the key to a successful partnership.[23]

corporation

An artificial entity created by the state and existing apart from its owners.

CORPORATION.   A **corporation** is an artificial entity created by the state and existing apart from its owners. As a separate legal entity, the corporation is liable for its actions and must pay taxes on its income. Unlike other forms of ownership, the corporation has a legal life of its own; it continues to exist regardless of whether the owners live or die. And the corporation, not the owners, is sued in the case of liability. Thus continuity and limits on owners' liability are two principal advantages of forming a corporation. For example, a physician can form a corporation so that liability for malpractice will not affect his or her personal assets. The major disadvantage of the corporation is that it is expensive and complex to do the paperwork required to incorporate the business and to keep the records required by law. When proprietorships and partnerships are successful and grow large, they often incorporate to limit liability and to raise funds through the sale of stock to investors.

FINANCIAL RESOURCES

A crucial concern for entrepreneurs is the financing of the business. An investment is usually required to acquire labor and raw materials and perhaps a building and equipment. The financing decision initially involves two options—whether to obtain loans that must be repaid (debt financing) or whether to share ownership (equity financing). A survey of successful growth businesses asked "How much money was needed to launch the company?" Approximately one-third were started on less than $10,000, one-third needed from $10,000 to $50,000, and one-third needed more than $50,000. The primary source of this money was the entrepreneurs' own resources, but they often had to mortgage their home, borrow money from the bank, or give part of the business to a venture capitalist.[24]

debt financing

Borrowing money that has to be repaid in order to start a business.

DEBT FINANCING.   Borrowing money that has to be repaid to start a business is **debt financing.** One common source of debt financing for a start-up is to borrow from family and friends. Another common source is a bank loan. Banks provide some 25 percent of all financing for small business. Sometimes entrepreneurs can obtain money from a finance company, wealthy individuals, or potential customers.

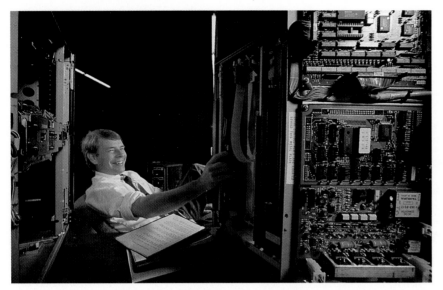

Alphatronix is a successful company that provides high-tech systems that integrate erasable optical disks with other computer hardware. The innovative company was founded through *debt financing*. CEO Robert Freese, pictured here, was a pioneer in erasable optical disk technology and was able to acquire loans from the future customers who would benefit from the success of the new technology. The reputation and skill of Alphatronix founders was instrumental in obtaining the funding to make the dream a reality.

Another form of loan financing is provided by the Small Business Administration (SBA). The SBA supplies direct loans to some entrepreneurs who are unable to get bank financing because they are considered high risk. The SBA's guaranteed loan program promises to repay the bank loan if the entrepreneur defaults. Bruce Burdick owns six Computer Land franchises in Kansas City and would not have gotten started without the guaranteed loan program. The SBA is especially helpful for people without substantial assets, providing an opportunity for single parents, minority group members, and others with a good idea.

EQUITY FINANCING. Any money invested by owners or by those who purchase stock in a corporation is considered equity funds. **Equity financing** consists of funds that are invested in exchange for ownership in the company. When a corporation's stock is sold only to friends and relatives, this is called a *private stock sale.* When the stock is available for sale to the general public, it is known as a *public sale.* For new businesses, a public sale is not a viable option because the company is not yet profitable. Once the business prospers, the company can sell stock publicly, providing a large financial windfall for the owner.

A **venture capital firm** is a group of companies or individuals that invests money in new or expanding businesses for ownership and potential profits. This is a potential form of capital for businesses with high earning and growth possibilities. Venture capital firms want new businesses with an extremely high rate of return, but in return the venture capitalist will provide assistance, advice, and information to help the entrepreneur prosper. A venture capital firm often has tens or hundreds of millions of dollars available for investment. Venture capitalists learn to spot promising businesses. A survey of venture capital firms indicated the criteria they use to evaluate entrepreneurial firms, which are listed in Exhibit 22.5. Of the top five items ranked, four pertain to characteristics of the entrepreneur. Venture capitalists bet on the person as well as the business.

equity financing

Financing that consists of funds that are invested in exchange for ownership in the company.

venture capital firm

A group of companies or individuals that invests money in new or expanding businesses for ownership and potential profits.

EXHIBIT 22.5	Criteria	Percent Rated Essential
New Business Criteria Rated Essential by Venture Capitalists	Capable of sustained intense effort	64
	Thoroughly familiar with market	62
	At least ten times return in 5–10 years	50
	Demonstrated leadership in the past	50
	Evaluates and reacts to risk well	48
SOURCE: From the Center for Entrepreneurial Studies, NYU Graduate School of Business, as reported in "Venture Capitalists' Criteria," *Management Review* (November 1985), 7–8.	Investment can be made liquid	44
	Significant market growth	43
	Track record relevant to venture	37
	Articulates venture well	31
	Proprietary protection	29

TACTICS

There are several ways an aspiring entrepreneur can become a business owner. These include starting a new business from scratch, buying an existing business, or starting a franchise. Other entrepreneurial tactics include participation in a business incubator, being a spin-off of a large corporation, or pursuing international markets from the beginning.

START A NEW BUSINESS.   One of the most common ways to become an entrepreneur is to start a new business from scratch. This is exciting because the entrepreneur sees a need for a product or service that has not been filled before and then sees the idea or dream become a reality. The advantage of this approach is the ability to develop and design the business in the entrepreneur's own way. The entrepreneur is solely responsible for its success. A potential disadvantage is the long time it can take to get the business off the ground and make it profitable. The uphill battle is caused by the lack of established clientele and the many mistakes made by someone new to the business. Moreover, no matter how much planning is done, a start-up is risky; there is no guarantee that the new idea will work.

BUY AN EXISTING BUSINESS.   Because of the long start-up time and the inevitable mistakes, some entrepreneurs prefer to reduce risk by purchasing an existing business. This offers the advantage of a shorter time to get started and an existing track record. The entrepreneur may get a bargain price if the owner wishes to retire or has other family considerations. Moreover, a new business may overwhelm an entrepreneur with the amount of work to be done and procedures to be established. An established business already has filing systems, a payroll tax system, and other operating procedures. Potential disadvantages are the need to pay for goodwill that the owner believes exists and the possible existence of ill will toward the business. In addition, the company may have bad habits and procedures or outdated technology, which may be why the business is for sale.

franchising

An arrangement by which the owner of a product or service allows others to purchase the right to distribute the product or service with help from the owner.

BUY A FRANCHISE.   Franchising is perhaps the most rapidly growing path to entrepreneurship. Over 500,000 franchisees operate businesses in the United States. **Franchising** is an arrangement by which the owner of a product or service allows others to purchase the right to distribute the product or service with help from the owner. The franchisee invests his or her money and owns the business but does not have to develop a new product, create a new company, or test the market. The franchisee typically pays a flat fee plus a percentage of gross sales. Franchises exist for weight-loss clinics, beauty salons, computer stores, real estate offices, rental cars, and auto tune-up shops.[25] The powerful advantage of a franchise is that management help is provided by the owner. For example, Burger King does not want a franchisee to fail and will provide the studies necessary to find a good location. The franchisor also provides an established name and national advertising to stimulate demand for the product or service. Potential disadvantages are the lack of control that occurs when franchisors want every business managed in exactly the same way. In addition, franchises can be very expensive, running as high as several hundred thousand dollars for a McDonald's restaurant. High costs are followed with monthly payments to the franchisor that can run from 2 percent to 12 percent of sales.

Entrepreneurs who are considering a franchise should investigate the company thoroughly. The entrepreneur is legally entitled to a copy of franchisor disclosure statements, which cover 20 areas, including lawsuits. The entrepreneur should also request information regarding franchisor assistance in selection of location, set-up costs, and securing credit. Entrepreneurs should understand under what circumstances a contract can be terminated and should obtain detailed information in areas such as the management and staff training programs provided (e.g., whether "training" is limited to the distribution of manuals).[26] Answers to such questions improve the chances for choosing a successful franchise.

PARTICIPATE IN A BUSINESS INCUBATOR.   An attractive innovation for entrepreneurs who want to start a business from scratch is to join a business incubator. Most incubators are sponsored by government

Mini Maid Services, Inc., is a *franchise* that operates in 24 states. A team can clean a house in only 55 minutes. Buying this franchise requires a cash investment of $12,500 and working capital from $18,000 to $20,000. Franchisees receive three weeks of intensive training, management assistance, advertising support, and continuous follow-up. CEO Leone Ackerly reports annual growth of 20 percent and extremely favorable customer response.

business incubator

An innovation that provides shared office space, management support services, and management advice to entrepreneurs.

spin-off

An independent company producing a product or service similar to that produced by the entrepreneur's former employer.

organizations to spark job creation and business development. The **business incubator** provides shared office space, management support services, and management advice to entrepreneurs. By sharing office space with other entrepreneurs, managers share information about local business, financial aid, and market opportunities. Although this innovation has been in existence only a few years, the number of business incubators nationwide jumped from 385 in 1990 to approximately 500 by January 1993.[27] What gives incubators an edge is the expertise of the in-house mentor, who serves as adviser, role model, and cheerleader for entrepreneurs. SORRA, Inc., a drug-trial company in Birmingham, Alabama, benefited from the incubation experience. While holding down start-up costs, incubation assisted owner Vally Nance in locating capital as well as a lawyer and an accountant. Nance credits incubation for helping her company to make a "transition of competence and confidence" as it moved from her home basement to the seventh floor offices of a clinic.[28]

BE A SPIN-OFF.   Spin-offs, a unique form of entrepreneurial company, were previously associated with and owe their start-up to another organization. A **spin-off** is an independent company producing a product or service similar to that produced by the entrepreneur's former employer.[29] Spin-offs occur when entrepreneurs quit their employers with a desire to produce a similar product, or in some cases produce a related product that is purchased by the former employer. The former employer may recognize that it can profit from the idea by selling patents to the spin-off and by investing in it. Employer approval is often the basis for a spin-off, although in some cases entrepreneurs start a new business because they disagree with former employers. Disagreement usually revolves around the failure of the employer to try a new idea that the entrepreneur believes in. A frustrated employee should discuss the possibility of starting a spin-off company with the support of his or her current employer. In this way, the spin-off reduces risk and has a source of management advice. The entrepreneur may also have a guaranteed customer for the spin-off's initial output.

CONSIDER GLOBALIZATION.   In today's global marketplace, many new firms start out with the idea of going international immediately. Other countries often provide the best market for American-made products and services. In fact, many businesses fail because the entrepreneur thinks provincially, being unaware of overseas markets. But if the entrepreneur has patience and commitment and is willing to do simple things such as write brochures in the local language, there is an excellent chance for success.

The ability to develop an international business is enhanced by new technology that bypasses former obstacles such as language. AT&T offers a 24-hour phone line with interpreters. Phone hook-ups offered by AT&T, MCI, and Sprint allow direct transmission of electronic mail to distributors' computers worldwide. PC software kits, export computer services, and translation devices such as Seiko's multilanguage translator assist small companies in achieving their export goals. Half of Life Corporation's emergency oxygen kits are shipped overseas. Vita-Mix

Corporation, a third generation family-owned business, exports blenders to 20 nations. At the height of the recent recession, Vita-Mix doubled its work force to keep up with orders pouring in to its 800 number. The owner of regional car washes in Portland, Oregon, launched his car wash system as an international business and is now selling in 71 countries and earning $100 million a year.[30]

The United States offers assistance to small companies wishing to enter the global arena. The Trade Information Center offers information on U.S. government export assistance programs and services. Many U.S. government departments offer counseling; research; assistance in finding overseas agents and sales leads; and help with export licensing, loans, export credit insurance, and other services. For example, Fred Schweser, president of Bird Corporation, received advice on test marketing his popular go-carts overseas. Today, exports account for 10 to 15 percent of Bird's go-cart sales.[31] With the rapid globalization of the U.S. economy, it makes sense for new companies to target foreign markets.

GETTING HELP

The advice given to most entrepreneurs is to find a good accountant and attorney. They can help with the financial and legal aspects of the business. For a business that is incorporated, another great source of help is a board of directors. The entrepreneur can bring together for several meetings a year people who have needed expertise. These people may be recruited from local businesses and universities or be retired executives. Major problems can be discussed with the board. The board receives a small monthly stipend, gets a chance to help a business grow, and in some cases is given part ownership.[32]

Other sources of help are available for new entrepreneurs. For example, the Small Business Administration provides a loan program, described earlier. The government also provides financial assistance for specialized needs:[33]

- Loans for disadvantaged small businesses.
- Loans for physical disasters, such as loss of property due to floods.
- Small-business energy loans for implementing specific energy measures.
- Small-business pollution-control loans to meet pollution-control requirements.

The federal government also provides assistance in exporting. The U.S. Department of Commerce publishes *A Basic Guide to Exporting,* which provides specific information on trade opportunities abroad, foreign markets, financial aid to exporters, tax advantages of exporting, and international trade exhibitions.

In addition, four major management-assistance programs are sponsored by the SBA. The *Service Corps of Retired Executives* (SCORE) provides retired experts to help new businesses. The *Active Corps of Executives* (ACE) is a program in which active executives volunteer service to small business. *Small Business Development Centers* (SBDCs) are typically

Tapping U.S. government information sources is one way small companies, such as Bird Corporation, a manufacturer of go-carts, are able to achieve *globalization.* Adhering to advice from the U.S. Commerce Department, Bird president Fred Schweser, shown here, placed an ad in the department's *Commercial News USA* monthly magazine. The ad elicited over 1,000 responses from around the world and resulted in establishment of a dozen go-cart distributorships from Japan to the United Kingdom.

located on college campuses and keep consulting staff available to provide assistance and research services. The *Small Business Institutes* (SBI) are also operated in conjunction with university business schools and provide student teams to work on planning and analysis with entrepreneurs under a professor's guidance.

● MANAGING A GROWING BUSINESS

Once an entrepreneurial business is up and running, how does the owner manage it? Often the traits of self-confidence, creativity, and internal locus of control lead to financial and personal grief as the enterprise grows. A hands-on entrepreneur who gave birth to the organization loves perfecting every detail. But after the start-up, continued growth requires a shift in management style. Those who fail to adjust to a growing business can be the cause of the problems rather than the solution.[34] In this section, we will look at the stages through which entrepreneurial companies move and then consider how managers should carry out their planning, organizing, leading, and controlling.

STAGES OF GROWTH

Entrepreneurial businesses go through distinct stages of growth. Recall from Chapter 10 that organizations go through a life cycle. During the early part of that life cycle, specific growth stages require different management skills. The five stages are illustrated in Exhibit 22.6.

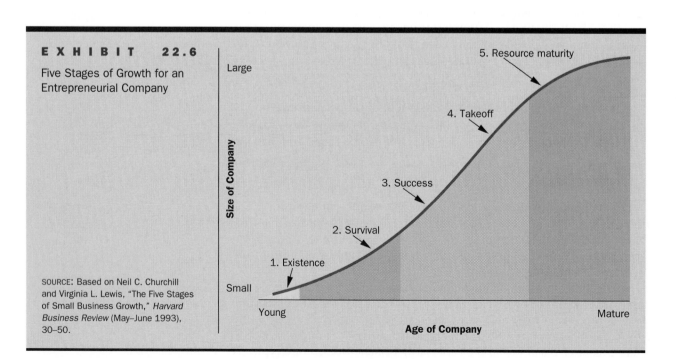

E X H I B I T   22.6

Five Stages of Growth for an Entrepreneurial Company

SOURCE: Based on Neil C. Churchill and Virginia L. Lewis, "The Five Stages of Small Business Growth," *Harvard Business Review* (May–June 1993), 30–50.

1 *Existence.* In this stage, the main problems are producing the product or service and obtaining customers. Key issues facing managers are: Can we get enough customers? Will we survive? Do we have enough money?

2 *Survival.* At this stage, the business has demonstrated that it is a workable business entity. It is producing a product or service and has sufficient customers. Concerns here have to do with finances— generating sufficient cash flow to run the business and making sure revenues exceed expenses. The organization will grow in size and profitability during this period.

3 *Success.* At this point, the company is solidly based and profitable. Systems and procedures are in place to allow the owner to slow down if desired. The owner can stay involved or consider turning the business over to professional managers.

4 *Takeoff.* Here the key problem is how to grow rapidly and finance that growth. The owner must learn to delegate, and the company must find sufficient capital to invest in major growth. This is a pivotal period in an entrepreneurial company's life. Properly managed, the company can become a big business.

5 *Resource maturity.* At this stage, the company has made substantial financial gains, but it may start to lose the advantages of small size, including flexibility and the entrepreneurial spirit. A company in this stage has the staff and financial resources to begin acting like a mature company with detailed planning and control systems.

PLANNING

In the early stage of existence, formal planning tends to be nonexistent except for the business plan described earlier in this chapter. The primary goal is simply to remain alive. As the organization grows, formal planning usually is not instituted until around the success stage. The firm may adopt a strategic plan similar to those described in Chapter 7.

Recall that Porter proposed three types of strategy that can be used by entrepreneurial businesses.[35] The *differentiation strategy* means the firm competes on the basis of its ability to do things differently than other firms. For example, the Sock Shop invaded New York from Britain and was instantly successful because of its convenience and colorful products.[36] An entrepreneurial firm that uses a *low-cost strategy* builds competitive advantage by producing goods or services at the lowest possible cost. For example, a small advertising agency in Philadelphia called Harris Edward Communications received a lot of attention when it standardized prices for more than 100 different types of advertising projects. These prices were below the competition, and the one-woman firm was so successful that it rapidly grew to a 35-person agency with $18 million in billings.[37] An entrepreneurial firm using a *focus strategy* is a specialist that serves a narrow market segment. For example, Richard Melman created the restaurant called Café Ba-Ba-Reeba! in Chicago. The restaurant gained favor for its unique menu and outstanding service. Melman has created several restaurants, each with a distinctive niche.[38]

Church's Chicken franchisee T. Scott Gross saw little progress in managing his restaurant "by the book," so he opted for a *differentiation strategy*. The result is "positively outrageous service" (POS). POS marketing uses the random and unexpected, and is an open invitation to customers to play along. The immediate response is "WOW!" and the borderline bizarre activity also results in customer loyalty and positive word-of-mouth promotions. POS strategy is working. Church's Chicken of Center Point, Texas, has enjoyed an average sales increase of 34.3 percent for two years in a row.

ORGANIZING

In the first two stages of growth, the organization's structure is very informal with all employees reporting to the owner. At about stage 3—success—functional managers are hired to take over duties performed by the owner. A functional organization structure will begin to evolve with managers in charge of finance, manufacturing, and marketing. During the latter stages of entrepreneurial growth, the manager must learn to delegate and decentralize authority. If the business has multiple product lines, the owner may consider creating teams or divisions responsible for each line. The organization must hire competent managers and have sufficient management talent to handle fast growth and eliminate problems caused by increasing size. The latter growth stages are also characterized by greater use of rules, procedures, and written job descriptions.

LEADING

The driving force in the early stages of development is the leader's vision. This vision combined with the leader's personality shapes corporate culture. The leader can signal cultural values of service, efficiency, quality, or ethics. Often entrepreneurs do not have good people skills but do have excellent task skills in either manufacturing or marketing. By the success stage of growth, the owner must either learn to motivate employees or bring in managers who can. Rapid takeoff is not likely to happen without employee cooperation.

For example, the president of Foreign Candy Company of Hull, Iowa, saw his company increase rapidly when he concentrated more on employee needs and less on financial growth. He made an effort to communicate with employees, conducted surveys to learn how they were feeling about the company, and found ways to involve them in decision making. His leadership style allowed the company to enter the takeoff stage with the right corporate culture and employee attitudes to sustain rapid growth.

Another reason leadership is important is that many small firms are having a hard time hiring qualified employees. Labor shortages often hurt small firms that grow rapidly. A healthy corporate culture can help attract and retain good people.[39]

CONTROLLING

Financial control is important in each stage of the entrepreneurial firm's growth. In the initial stages, control is exercised by simple accounting records and by personal supervision. By stage 3—success—operational budgets are in place and the owner should start implementing management by objectives or a similar goal-setting system. During the takeoff stage, the company will need to make greater use of budgets, standard cost systems, and perhaps acquire computers to provide statistical reports. These control techniques will become more sophisticated during the resource maturity stage. However, managers should not rely exclusively on bureaucratic control as described in Chapter 18. A strong corporate culture is a form of clan control in entrepreneurial firms.

The Sock Shop, which made such a hit in New York City with its differentiated product, eventually failed due to lack of control. Although sales progressed nicely, costs zoomed out of sight. Lack of control encouraged theft and poor decision making such as putting stores in the wrong locations. Indeed, the chain expanded so fast that the debt-to-equity ratio shot up to three to one. With poor financial control systems, losses led to abrupt store closings and the loss of the retailer's good name.

Caroline Jones, one of the nation's best-known black entrepreneurs and founder of the successful Caroline Jones advertising agency, believed in *financial control* during the initial stages of her new business. Jones advises, "Start a business with a business." Knowing a lack of cash plagues many new businesses, Jones sought and got a client base of $4 million in billings before setting up her own agency. This base saw Jones and her two employees through the initial start-up. Today, five years after start-up, the agency has 25 employees and bills $20 million annually.

● INTRAPRENEURSHIP IN A GROWING BUSINESS

intrapreneurship

The process of recognizing the need for innovation and promoting it within an organization.

intrapreneur

Someone who sees the need for innovation and promotes it within an existing organization.

As the entrepreneurial firm grows large, it has a tendency to lose its innovative spirit with the implementation of formal control systems and bureaucratic procedures. Established firms often lose innovative ideas to entrepreneurial spin-offs from frustrated employees. The way to keep innovation within the organization is to create conditions in which intrapreneurs can flourish. **Intrapreneurship** is the process whereby an individual sees the need for innovation and promotes it within an organization. An **intrapreneur** is similar to the idea champion described in Chapter 11. The goal for managers, who at one time were innovators themselves, is to create a climate that encourages intrapreneurs. Companies such as 3M are known for intrapreneurship. 3M intrapreneur Art Frey invented the Post-It Note as the result of personal frustration when his page markers repeatedly fell out of his church hymnal. Even the best ideas need nurturing, support, and financing in a large corporation. As you may recall from Chapter 11, some organizations have developed *skunkworks*, undercover areas of intrapreneur activity inside the organization, in which intrapreneurs receive management support and are allowed to deviate from company review and reporting policies.

The following rules provide an approach for developing the necessary atmosphere:

1 Encourage action.

2 Use informal meetings whenever possible.

3 Tolerate failure and use it as a learning experience.

4 Be persistent in getting an idea to market.

5 Reward innovation for innovation's sake.

6 Plan the physical layout of the firm to encourage informal communication.

7 Encourage clever bootlegging of ideas.

8 Organize people into small teams for future-oriented projects.

9 Strip away rigid procedures and encourage personnel to go around red tape when they find it.

10 Reward and/or promote innovative personnel.[40]

One company that maintains the innovative spirit is Hewlett-Packard.

 HEWLETT-PACKARD

Charles House is an intrapreneur in Hewlett-Packard's innovative culture. He was assigned to develop a Federal Aviation Agency monitor similar to a television picture tube but with greatly enhanced capacity. It failed to meet government specifications, but House was more interested in other applications. He took a prototype to customers to learn whether it would solve their problems—in violation of HP's rules. He fought for money to support the technology despite its lack of a proven market. Finally, the project was ordered killed by Dave Packard himself. House's immediate superiors still supported him, however, and gave him one more year. House and his team succeeded, generating $10 million in annual sales simply because House persisted and would not give up. House was awarded the Medal of Defiance, shown in Exhibit 22.7. This reward signals Hewlett-Packard's fundamental values in favor of innovation.[41]

In his book *Entrepreneuring*, Gifford Pinchot argues that people like Charles House are needed in organizations. When spotted, intrapreneurs should be encouraged. Characteristics of intrapreneurs include willingness to circumvent orders aimed at stopping their dream; willingness to do any job needed to make the project work; willingness to work underground as long as they can; willingness to be true to their goals; and willingness to remember it is easier to ask for forgiveness than for permission.[42] ■

Intrapreneurship is not always successful, however. Many companies, such as Control Data Corporation and Kodak, failed to generate profits from intrapreneur programs and dropped them. A good idea does not guarantee success. Intrapreneurs may be ill-prepared to follow through on their ideas and to make the sacrifice necessary to see the idea reach fruition. Managers may balk at the necessary capital investment or resist making exceptions to corporate policies.[43] As with any strategy, intrapreneurship is only as successful as the planning and support it receives throughout a company.

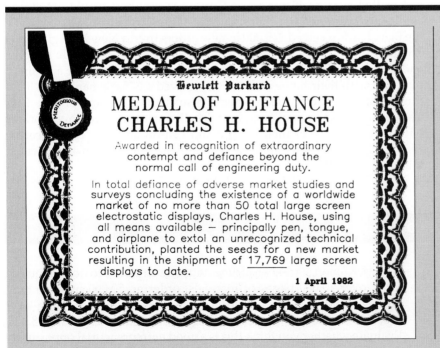

Hewlett Packard

MEDAL OF DEFIANCE
CHARLES H. HOUSE

Awarded in recognition of extraordinary contempt and defiance beyond the normal call of engineering duty.

In total defiance of adverse market studies and surveys concluding the existence of a worldwide market of no more than 50 total large screen electrostatic displays, Charles H. House, using all means available — principally pen, tongue, and airplane to extol an unrecognized technical contribution, planted the seeds for a new market resulting in the shipment of 17,769 large screen displays to date.

1 April 1982

EXHIBIT   22.7

Reward for Intrapreneurship at Hewlett-Packard

SOURCE: Courtesy of Hewlett-Packard Company.

SUMMARY AND MANAGEMENT SOLUTION

This chapter explored entrepreneurship and small-business management. Entrepreneurs start new businesses, and entrepreneurship plays an important role in the economy by stimulating job creation, innovation, and opportunities for minorities and women. An entrepreneurial personality includes the traits of internal locus of control, high energy level, need to achieve, tolerance for ambiguity, awareness of passing time, and self-confidence.

Starting an entrepreneurial firm requires a new-business idea. At that point a comprehensive business plan should be developed and decisions made about legal structure and financing. Tactical decisions for the new venture include whether to start, buy, or franchise, whether to participate in a business incubator, whether to be a company spin-off, and whether to go global. After the business is started, it will typically proceed through five stages of growth—existence, survival, success, takeoff, and resource maturity. The management functions of planning, organizing, leading, and controlling should be tailored to each stage of growth. Finally, intrapreneurship, a variation of entrepreneurship, is a mechanism for encouraging innovation within a larger firm.

Referring to the management problem described at the beginning of this chapter, Robert and Melinda Blanchard had 75 orders for Melinda's salad dressing, dessert toppings, and mustards, but they had no way to fill the orders. Six neighbors pitched in to help fill and label jars and pack them for shipping. Other neighbors offered working cash, leaving two $5,000 checks. Son Jesse, 9, became the premier jar labeler. With the first order filled, new problems arose. Corporate suppliers would not extend credit. Neither would the banks. Luckily, product quality was superb, and the Blanchards received $45,000 in new orders from a New York gift show. The president of a local family-owned firm decided to provide supplies and help get the business going. The Blanchards put together a business plan and with their home as security, received a $75,000 bank loan. They purchased a computer to keep track of inventory, cost, and profits. They also concentrated on quality and service. Department stores love working with them because of their energy and can-do attitude. They received $500,000 from a venture capitalist, and the company has grown to over $10 million in sales.[44]

DISCUSSION QUESTIONS

1. Dan McKinnon started an airline with one airplane. To do so required filing over 10,000 pages of manuals, ordering 50,000 luggage tags, buying more than $500 million in insurance, and spending over $300,000 to train employees. A single inspection test cost $18,000. Evaluate whether you think this is a good entrepreneurial opportunity and discuss why you think Dan McKinnon undertook it.

2. What do you think are the most important contributions of small business to our economy?
3. Why would small-business ownership have great appeal to immigrants, women, and minorities?
4. Consider the six personality characteristics of entrepreneurs. Which two traits do you think are most like managers in large companies? Which two are least like managers in large companies?
5. Why is purchasing an existing business or franchise less risky than starting a new business?
6. If you were to start a new business, would you have to search for an idea or do you already have an idea to try? Explain.
7. Many entrepreneurs say they did little planning, perhaps scratching notes on a legal pad. How is it possible for them to succeed?
8. What is the difference between debt financing and equity financing? What are common sources of each type?
9. How does an entrepreneurial firm in the existence stage differ from one in the success stage?
10. How do the management functions of organizing and controlling differ for the existence and success stages?
11. Explain the difference between entrepreneurship and intrapreneurship. Why would entrepreneurs want intrapreneurship within their companies? Would an entrepreneur's personality tend to inhibit intrapreneurship? Discuss.

MANAGEMENT IN PRACTICE: EXPERIENTIAL EXERCISE

● WHAT IS YOUR ENTREPRENEURIAL QUOTIENT?

The following questions are from a test developed by John R. Braun, psychology professor at the University of Bridgeport in Connecticut, and the Northwestern Mutual Life Insurance Company, based in Milwaukee. Simply answer yes or no to each question.

1. Are you a first-generation American?
2. Were you an honor student?
3. Did you enjoy group functions in school—clubs, team sports, even double dates?
4. As a youngster, did you prefer to be alone frequently?
5. As a child, did you have a paper route, a lemonade stand, or some other small enterprise?
6. Were you a stubborn child?
7. Were you a cautious youngster, the last in the neighborhood to try diving off the highboard?
8. Do you worry about what others think of you?
9. Are you in a rut, tired of the same routine day in and day out?
10. Would you be willing to dip deeply into your "nest egg"—and possibly lose all you invested—to go it alone?

11. If your new business should fail, would you get to work immediately on another?
12. Are you an optimist?

Answers:

1. Yes = 1, No = minus 1.
2. Yes = minus 4, No = 4.
3. Yes = minus 1, No = 1.
4. Yes = 1, No = minus 1.
5. Yes = 2, No = minus 2.
6. Yes = 1, No = minus 1.
7. Yes = minus 4, No = 4. If you were a particularly daring child, add another 4 points.
8. Yes = minus 1, No = 1.
9. Yes = 2, No = minus 2.
10. Yes = 2, No = minus 2.
11. Yes = 4, No = minus 4.
12. Yes = 2, No = minus 2.

Now calculate your total score. If you tallied 20 or more points, you have a strong entrepreneurial quotient. The score of 0 to 19 suggests that you have entrepreneurial possibilities. If you scored between 0 and minus 10, your chance of successfully starting an entrepreneurial business is marginal. A score below minus 11 suggests you are not the entrepreneurial type.

Go back over each question, thinking about changes you might make to become more or less entrepreneurial, depending on your career interests.

SOURCE: Peter Lohr, "Should You Be in Business for Yourself?" *Readers Digest*, July 1989, 49–52.

CASES FOR ANALYSIS

T. J. CINNAMONS

Ted and Joyce Rice started their business as a sideline. During a long vacation, they decided they would like to start a part-time business that would supplement their income. They were more interested in early retirement than a new career. They weighed many possibilities, finally deciding to sell cinnamon rolls. They believed that with showmanship they could make a go of it.

Joyce experimented at home until she developed a tasty recipe. They bought a custom-made trailer fitted as a mobile bakery and were soon selling rolls at cattle shows and state fairs. The response was incredibly positive.

They opened a permanent bakery in a Kansas City mall between two escalators. Ted wanted to catch shoppers coming and going. They put a glass roof on the bakery so shoppers could see the rolls being made.

They also noticed their T. J. Cinnamons bakery being observed by "a lot of people with yellow pads and stop-watches." They believed their idea was going to be copied quickly. They decided to team up with two businessmen and sell franchises for the bakery. To keep sales increasing in each store, a bakery menu of 50 items was developed.

At this point, their part-time business has grown into 200 gourmet bakeries with total sales of $56 million.

● QUESTIONS

1. To what extent was this start-up typical of entrepreneurial companies?
2. Evaluate the Rices' decision to franchise their business concept.
3. In what stage of growth is T. J. Cinnamons now? Explain.

SOURCE: Based on Michael Barrier, "Rolling in Dough," *Nation's Business*, February 1990, 15–17.

F.R.O.Y.D.

In a world of huggable toys, Carolyn Greene's creation, F.R.O.Y.D. (For Reality of Your Dreams) is a bright yellow, chubby fellow with a big nose and a lovable smile. He easily captured the hearts of toy makers but not their pocketbooks. F.R.O.Y.D. failed to gain the support of a manufacturer such as Kenner, Hasbro, Fisher-Price, Coleco, or Tyco Toys.

First sketched in 1979, the F.R.O.Y.D. character seemed a surefire toy line, complete with television show and licensing agreements. But Carolyn and Jeffery Greene discovered the difficulty involved in launching a new business in the rough and tumble world of toys. Although retailers scream for new products, manufacturers approach new ideas with extreme caution.

Throughout the 1980s, the Greenes doggedly pursued their dream. Research visits within the ranks of both manufacturers and retailers provided valuable information and new friends. Simultaneously, the Greenes pared down their own financial needs. Market research conducted by the same company that tested Cabbage Patch Kids proved the appeal of F.R.O.Y.D. to potential customers. But in 1989, with no manufacturer on the horizon, the Greenes concluded they had to manufacture the doll themselves.

Once again the Greenes encountered rejection as they searched the ranks of venture capitalists for financial backing, and they stepped back and revamped their strategy a second time. They estimated that $450,000 to $600,000 would finance a three-city live test of F.R.O.Y.D.'s sales potential, including advertising and production. Their plan was to seek investment from individuals they had met who seemed enthusiastic about the doll. This first-stage financing was successful, and they even received some commitments for further financing. Although F.R.O.Y.D. has many additional hurdles to cross, the tenacity of his creators thus far proves that hard work can lead to success.

● Q U E S T I O N S

1. Of the six personality traits of typical entrepreneurs, which seem most present in the Greenes?

2. Do you think you would have persisted this long for a product you believed in?

3. Do you think the Greenes will eventually succeed with F.R.O.Y.D.? Why?

SOURCE: Ellyn E. Spragins, "Intelligent Money," *INC.*, June 1990, 106–107.

REFERENCES

1. Stanley W. Angrist, "Family Affair," *Forbes*, October 5, 1987, 184–187.

2. Glenn Rifkin, "Inventing Heroes for the 21st Century," *The New York Times*, February 14, 1993, F10; Jeremy Main, "A Golden Age for Entrepreneurs," *Fortune*, February 12, 1990, 120–125; and Keith H. Hammonds, "What B-School Doesn't Teach You about Startups," *Business Week*, July 24, 1989, 40–41.

3. Donald F. Kuratko and Richard M. Hodgetts, *Entrepreneurship: A Contemporary Approach* (Chicago: The Dryden Press, 1989).

4. David J. Jefferson, "Creativity Isn't All That's Needed by a Creative Business," *The Wall Street Journal*, March 19, 1990, B2.

5. Eugene Carlson, "Federal Express Wasn't an Overnight Success," *The Wall Street Journal*, June 6, 1989, B2.

6. Thomas McCarroll, "Entrepreneurs: Starting Over," *Time*, January 6, 1992, 62–63; Susan Caminitti, "Look Who Likes Franchising Now," *Fortune*, September 23, 1991, 125–130; David L. Birch, "The Truth about Start-Ups," *INC.*, January 1988, 14–15; and Carl H. Vesper, *Entrepreneurship and National Policy* (Chicago: Heller Institute, 1983).

7. John Case, "The Disciples of David Birch," *INC.*, January 1989, 39–45.

8. Charles R. Kuehl and Peggy A. Lambing, *Small Business: Planning and Management*, 3d ed. (Chicago: The Dryden Press, 1994).

9. "100 Ideas for New Businesses," *Venture*, November 1988, 35–74.

10. Leon E. Wynter, "How Two Black Franchisees Owe Success to McDonald's," *The Wall Street Journal*, July 25, 1989, B1–B2.

11. Bradford McKee and Sharon Nelton, "Building Bridges to Minority Firms," *Nation's Business*, December 1992, 29–33.

12. Bureau of Census Statistics as reported in "Black Entrepreneurship: By the Numbers," *The Wall Street Journal*, April 3, 1992, R4.

13. John Case, "The Origins of Entrepreneurship," *INC.*, June 1989, 51–63.

14. This discussion is based on Kuehl and Lambing, *Small Business*.

15. Roger Ricklefs and Udayan Gupta, "Traumas of a New Entrepreneur," *The Wall Street Journal*, May 10, 1989, B1.

16. Case, "The Origins of Entrepreneurship."

17. David C. McClelland, *The Achieving Society*, (New York: Van Nostrand, 1961).

18. Robert D. Hisrich, "Entrepreneurship-Intrapreneurship," *American Psychologist*, February 1990, 209–222.

19. Sharon Nelton, "Making It," *Nation's Business*, June 1991, 10–11.

20. Case, "The Origins of Entrepreneurship."

21. Roger Ricklefs, "Pros Dare to Go Where Amateurs No Longer Bother," *The Wall Street Journal*, March 31, 1989, B2.

22. Case, "The Origins of Entrepreneurship."

23. The INC. FAXPOLL, *INC.,* February 1992, 24.

24. "Venture Capitalists' Criteria," *Management Review* (November 1985), 7–8.

25. Meg Whittemore, "Four Paths to Franchising," *Nation's Business,* October 1989, 75–85, and Nancy Croft Baker, "Franchising into the 90s," *Nation's Business,* March 1990, 61–68.

26. Kuehl and Lambing, *Small Business Planning and Management,* Chapter 5.

27. Alessandra Bianchi, "New Businesses: Incubator Update," *INC.,* January 1993, 49.

28. Bradford McKee, "Managing Your Small Business: Using Incubators as Steppingstones to Growth," *Nation's Business,* October 1991, 8.

29. Thomas S. Bateman and Carl P. Zeithaml, *Management Function and Strategy* (Homewood, Ill.: Irwin, 1990).

30. William J. Holstein and Kevin Kelly, "Little Companies, Big Exports," *Business Week,* April 13, 1992, 70–72, and Albert G. Holzinger, "Reach New Markets," *Nation's Business,* December 1990, 18–35.

31. Albert G. Holzinger, "Paving the Way for Small Exporters," *Nation's Business,* June 1992, 42–43.

32. Elizabeth Conlin, "Unlimited Partners," *INC.,* April 1990, 71–79.

33. Kuehl and Lambing, *Small Business.*

34. Carrie Dolan, "Entrepreneurs Often Fail as Managers," *The Wall Street Journal,* May 15, 1989, B1.

35. Michael Porter, *Competitive Strategies* (New York: Free Press, 1980).

36. Mark Maremont, "Did Sock Shop Get Too Big for Its Britches?" *Business Week,* January 15, 1990, 39–40.

37. "Revolution for the HEC of It," *INC.,* September 1988, 22.

38. Erik Larson, "The Man with the Golden Touch," *INC.,* October 1988, 67–77.

39. Udayan Gupta and Jeffrey A. Tannenbaum, "Labor Shortages Force Changes at Small Firms," *The Wall Street Journal,* May 22, 1989, B1, B2, and "Harnessing Employee Productivity," *Small Business Report* (November 1987), 46–49.

40. Kuratko and Hodgetts, *Entrepreneurship.*

41. Gifford Pinchot III, *Entrepreneurship* (New York: Harper & Row, 1985).

42. Ibid.

43. James S. Hirsch, "Kodak Effort at 'Intrapreneurship' Fails," *The Wall Street Journal,* August 17, 1990, B1.

44. Angrist, "Family Affair."

BARNEY

An entrepreneur's dilemma: What do you do with a 6-foot purple dinosaur with a weight distribution problem and very uneven musical talents? Put him on PBS crooning little ditties about sharing and caring with a gang of pint-sized pals. Call him Barney, and then sit back and wait for the chips to roll in.

Barney was created 5 years ago by Sheryl Leach and Kathy Parker, two schoolteachers from Allen, Texas, who were home on maternity leave. They were motivated by a dearth of quality video entertainment for preschoolers. Leach's first instincts were to create something on the order of the teddy-bear character, but she was overruled by her son Patrick. Bears are out, Mom, he informed her. Dinosaurs are in. It was a nice call for a four-year-old, or anybody else.

Leach and her partners formed the Lyons Group to market Barney. The pudgy dinosaur existed for several years as a character in a series of home videos before CPTV broached the idea of co-producing a PBS show. The deal called for the Lyons Group to retain merchandising rights while CPTV got a sales percentage of certain Barney items. Barney paraphernalia brought in $100 million in 1992, much of it through J. C. Penney stores where the selection at special Barney Boutiques includes pajamas T-shirts, coloring books, and party supplies. A talking Barney toy is expected out soon, along with more home videos and 13 new books. J. C. Penney sold 3 million Barney products last Christmas. The Lyons Group itself has sold 4 million Barney products since 1988. Hasbro, Inc., the world's largest toy company is launching a line of Barney products in its preschool division called Playskool. "My guess is this could conceivably be a $25–30 million piece of business, maybe more, for Hasbro," said John Taylor, an analyst with the L. H. Alton investment company.

Barney's television debut came in 1992 and the initial response was lukewarm. But when PBS threatened extinction for "Barney and Friends" after 30 episodes, his little fans raised such a fuss that funding was found to continue the program. The PBS broadcast, which is taped in Allen, became their top-rated kids show with 1.5 million tiny watchers on more than 200 public stations. Two networks are vying for the rights to produce a prime-time special, and the Lyons Group is meeting with several movie studios to develop a motion picture.

The half-hour television show consists of Barney telling a multicultural cast of scrubbed sidekicks how to handle daily setbacks, assuring them all the while that he loves them and they love him and everyone is stupendous. Beth Ryan, the spokeswoman of the Lyons Group said everything that goes into the show, the music, color, dancing and dialogue are all very specifically put in to connect with chil-

dren. Episodes are carefully reviewed and things that are likely to appeal to adults are taken out. "It is much more difficult to absolutely gear a show to appeal to a preschool child than it is to appeal to an adult," Ryan said. "We make sure everything about Barney appeals to young children."

Before television, Barney was already a busy leading man, starring in eight videos. The videos won a Parents' Choice Award in 1989 and were among TV Guide's list of top 10 children's videos in 1990 and 1991. Sales have topped 4 million. *People Magazine* named Barney one of the "25 Most Intriguing People of 1992." The "Barney and Friends" show received a Daytime Emmy Award nomination for outstanding children's series.

Not all adults are enthralled by Barney's spell. Some disparagements include smarmy, simplistic, too sweet and too repetitive. A *Washington Post* writer compared Barney to "Chinese water torture" that can make you "want to put your head under a bus."

"We don't feel insulted at all when parents don't like Barney. If they say, 'my children love him,' that's the ultimate compliment," Ryan said.

What is the future for the pop-star dino? The general consensus in children's programming is that Barney will likely be around for a while, if he's properly managed.

Sheryl Leach said the goal is to make Barney into a multigenerational international children's star, in the mold of Mickey Mouse or Big Bird. "We're on a very ambitious quest," she said. "We want Barney to be around for 50 years, teaching our children's children the same simple values we had when we grew up."

● QUESTIONS

1. Do you think it's possible to evaluate an entrepreneurial product or endeavor in advance of actually marketing it, or are consumer whims just too obscure?

2. Does an entrepreneur fill a need that already exists, or does he or she inspire the need through innovation?

3. How can an enterprise seeking to launch a unique innovation go about doing a realistic cost/income analysis in light of the huge uncertainty relating to future market acceptance?

4. If you've had the opportunity in 1988, would you have invested in Barney?

CAREER MANAGEMENT 23 CHAPTER

Kim Jackson had a lifelong love of politics. As a child, she handed out campaign literature for Chuck Percy and Richard Ogilvie in her hometown of Schaumburg, Illinois. While majoring in political science at Georgetown University, Jackson interned on Capitol Hill. After graduation, she accepted a staff position with a U.S. representative. Jackson eventually landed a job as Capitol Hill reporter for a Washington newspaper and was now on a career track to become a political correspondent. But now, in her mid-30s, her interest in politics is wan-

ing, and she wonders if a career change would be a wise move. Jackson has been asking herself questions such as these: Would a career change mean taking a giant step backward? What if the next job is no more satisfying than this one? Is this just a phase, or is it genuine career burnout?[1]

■ What advice would you give Kim Jackson about her career situation? Would she be better advised to explore new options within the field of politics rather than start a new career?

M A N A G E M E N T   P R O B L E M

Like Kim Jackson, everyone who works must make decisions about jobs and careers. These decisions determine whether one's work life will be satisfying, rewarding, and productive. Roger Smith, who started as an accounting clerk for GM, making $3,540 a year, became chairman of General Motors. Hamish Maxwell started as a $2,000-a-year travel agent for Thomas Cook in Paris, but eventually became president of Phillip Morris. Michael Dickens started out as a $2.30-an-hour lifeguard for a Guest Quarters hotel; he progressed through nine jobs over 16 years, including maintenance man and hotel general manager, to become president of Guest Quarters.[2]

The topic of careers is important to both individuals striving to succeed in organizations and organizations that want to assist the careers of their employees. The right fit between person and career makes a difference. For example, a survey of vice-presidents found that the most important criterion for career success is love of work: "People don't get to the top unless they really love what they are doing and are willing to work very, very hard."[3] Sometimes a career causes problems. Suzanne P. is so obsessed with career success that she blocks out all aspects of her life other than work. She is cool, impersonal, aloof, attractive, and has easily reached the upper middle management of a major corporation, but she is really not happy. Media coverage of such career problems highlights career burnout and mid-career crisis.

This chapter explores the topic of career management in organizations. First we examine the scope of career issues in today's organizations. Then we discuss individuals' career planning, including steps for self-analysis and career selection, stages in a successful career, and how to cope with stress. We also examine career management strategies from the organization's perspective, including career development systems, job matching, career paths, and succession planning. Finally, we will examine the special career problems of women, minorities, dual-career couples, and plateaued employees.

● CHANGING SCOPE OF CAREERS

CAREER VERSUS JOB

What does it mean to have a career? Most people do not want to just "go to work"; they want to "pursue a career." To some people, having a career requires successful movement up the corporate ladder, marked by boosts in salary and status. To others, a career means having a profession—doctors and professors have careers, whereas secretaries and blue-collar workers have jobs. Still others will tell you that no matter what the occupation, the difference between a career and a job is about 20 hours a week—that is, people who have careers are so involved in their work that they extend beyond its requirements. For these people, it is psychological involvement in their work that defines a career.

A **job** is a specific task performed for an organization. A **career** is the sequence of jobs a person holds over a life span and the person's attitudes toward involvement in those job experiences.[4] A career has a long-

job

A unit of work that a single employee is responsible for performing.

career

A sequence of work-related activities and behaviors over a person's life span viewed as movement through various job experiences and the individual's attitudes toward involvement in those experiences.

term perspective and includes a series of jobs. Moreover, to understand careers, we must look not only at people's work histories or résumés but also at their attitudes toward their work. People may have more or less money or power, be professional or blue collar, and vary in the importance they place on the work in relation to the rest of their lives—yet all may have careers.

A CAREER DEVELOPMENT PERSPECTIVE

Career development refers to employee progress or growth over time as a career unfolds. Career development is the result of two important activities: career planning and career management. *Career planning* emphasizes individual activities helpful in making career-related decisions. *Career management* focuses on organizational activities that foster employees' career growth.[5]

A career management perspective means adopting a "big picture" of work in the total context of people's lives and recognizing that each person's work experiences add up to a career. More importantly, as long as people are employed with an organization, they have an *organizational career,* which is the sequence of work-related activities and experiences they accumulate during their time with the organization.

A CAREER IN MANAGEMENT

Managers are responsible for developing people and helping manage their careers. But what about a career in management? What steps can a person take to become a manager? Recall from Chapter 1 that employees typically start out in organizations with a *technical skill* in an area such as finance, accounting, advertising, human resources, or computers. Most people get promoted into management positions after they become proficient in a technical skill area.

At some point, individuals will face the choice of whether to remain a technical specialist or take on supervisory and management responsibility. Examples of people who may choose to remain technical specialists are securities traders, lawyers, teachers, and investment bankers. More typically, at a company such as K mart or Sears, recent college graduates start out without management responsibilities. The first jobs provide basic training in store sales or merchandising. Successful employees then are given the opportunity to move into first-level management positions such as sales supervisor, visual sales manager, convenience center manager, or sales support supervisor. From there, a person's career may lead to higher-level positions such as regional merchandise manager, store operating manager, store manager, general merchandise manager, or operating manager for geographical area. The Manager's Shoptalk box describes the latest ideas about the skills needed for middle managers today and tomorrow.

Those people who choose to move into management must be willing to shift away from reliance on technical skills toward reliance on *human skills.* As described in Chapter 1, human skill is the person's ability to work with and through other people and to participate effectively as a team member. This skill is demonstrated by the ability to motivate,

career development

Employee progress or growth over time as a career unfolds.

In 1990, Avco Financial Services demonstrated its commitment to employee training and *careers in management* with the opening of Avco University in Nashville, Tennessee. By bringing together in one location Avco's management-track employees, Connie Moore, manager of Avco University, assures consistency in management training and skill development in areas such as performance management and problem solving.

MANAGEMENT CAREERS IN A NEW AGE

Is the sun rising or setting on management in corporate America? Many wax nostalgic for corporate America's "good old days" with its clearly defined leadership roles and managers who could tell employees what to do and when to do it. Today, old-style corporate leaders, like old-style political leaders, are being pushed aside by baby-boomers and sweeping changes in global competition. "It's not age, it's a mind-set," explained one management professor. America's golden years occurred while Japanese and European industries and economies were being reconstructed after World War II. Now, with those countries having caught up, the United States cannot maintain a management approach from the past.

Management positions, once a safe haven for men who worked their way up the corporate ladder, reveal the shift in corporate power. For example, the day of the imperial

CEO is over. A sample list of top corporate casualties reads like a corporate Who's Who: Robert Stempel of General Motors, Kenneth Olsen of Digital Equipment, Joseph "Rod" Canion of Compaq Computer, James Robinson of American Express, and John Akers of IBM. Middle managers, too, are feeling the heat. A survey by the American Management Association found that middle management composed 5 percent of the work force but suffered 22 percent of corporate layoffs in 1992. The new world order is here, and it includes stiff competition, demanding and informed customers and shareholders, and boards of directors willing to shed the chief and entire layers of managers in order to stay competitive and profitable.

As a result of these shake-ups, managers are taking a long, hard look at themselves. Self-managing teams and computers are making obsolete traditional managerial duties such as supervising tasks, scheduling, and handling information. Managers are even adopting new titles, such as

facilitator or sponsor. They are now determining how they can fit into the corporate picture of the future. Managers are beginning to understand that mastering skills as team builders and intrapreneurs enhances their value. New middle managers need a breadth of knowledge within their field, the ability to respond quickly to market changes, the ability to share information widely, resourcefulness in bringing together necessary people and tools, and the ability to motivate a diversified work force and satisfy growing demands to balance life and work.

For those people committed to the future and who are challenged by the opportunities of being new-style, nonmanager managers in the 21st century, the sun is indeed rising on corporate America. ■

SOURCE: Brian Dumaine, "The New Non-Managers," *Fortune*, February 22, 1993, 80–84; John A. Byrne, "Requiem for Yesterday's CEO," *Business Week*, February 15, 1993, 32–33; and Thomas A. Stewart, "The King Is Dead," *Fortune*, January 11, 1993, 34–40.

facilitate, coordinate, lead, communicate, get along with others, and resolve conflicts. Human skills can be developed through practice, by taking courses and seminars, and by entering jobs that require superb human skills. For example, product manager or brand manager jobs at a consumer products company require excellent human skills.

Brand managers were called *integrating managers* in Chapter 10. Recall that an integrating manager has the responsibility to coordinate across several functions, but without formal authority. A brand manager for Fritos, Tide, or M&Ms coordinates all functions necessary to produce the product, which is a lot like running his or her own small company. The brand manager uses human skills to persuade people to perform activities necessary for product success. The brand manager also practices *conceptual skills* such as planning the advertising, retail, and trade promotions; developing a new product or packaging; and developing ways to increase sales. Companies such as Procter & Gamble, General Mills, General Foods, Ralston Purina, and M&M-Mars use brand management systems. Some 18 percent to 20 percent of graduating classes from some universities go into brand management to acquire experience useful to management careers.[6]

● INDIVIDUAL CAREER PLANNING

"Work hard and you will be rewarded." When it comes to your career, the advice to work hard makes sense, but it is not enough. Although many organizations take great interest in the management of their employees' careers, you cannot expect to work hard and let the organization take care of your career. The responsibility for your career is yours alone. People who plan their careers improve their chance of having successful ones. Perhaps the title of a recent book by General Electric Chief Executive Jack Welch says it best: *Control Your Destiny or Someone Else Will.*

Career planning is the self-assessment, exploration of opportunities, goal setting, and other activities necessary for making informed career-related choices. It is a crucial step in linking your personal needs and capabilities with career opportunities. Career planning involves systematic thinking and attention to short-term and long-term career goals. It is an ongoing activity, not something limited to high school and college graduates making an initial job choice. Because the world and organizations change, a periodic review of your career plans and progress is a must.[7]

career planning
The self-assessment, exploration of opportunities, goal setting, and other activities necessary to make informed career-related decisions.

STEPS IN CAREER PLANNING

There are five steps involved in career planning.

1 Self-Assessment. The first step is gathering data on yourself—your values, interests, skills, abilities, and preferred activities. You must learn to see yourself clearly and objectively. Consider what makes you happy in work, how closely your self-image is tied to your occupation, and rewards that are important to you. Self-assessment exercises designed to clarify abilities and interests are provided in Exhibit 23.1. The questionnaire inventories for values and interests can be compared to those of people with similar interests who have successful careers. Richard K. Bernstein, a corporate vice-president for a housewares company, answered the following question as part of a self-assessment: "If you had two million dollars, how would you spend it?" Bernstein immediately pictured himself in medical school. Despite being 45 years old, he knew what he wanted and went on to study medicine and specialize in research and teaching on diabetes.[8]

EXHIBIT 23.1

Self-Assessment Exercises

SOURCE: Adapted from M. London and S. A. Stumpf, *Managing Careers* (Reading, Mass.: Addison-Wesley, 1982); J. G. Clawson, J. P. Kotter, V. A. Faux, and C. C. McArthur, *Self-Assessment and Career Development* (Englewood Cliffs, N.J.: Prentice-Hall, 1985); R. M. Bolles, *What Color Is Your Parachute?* (Berkeley, Cal.: Ten Speed Press, 1993).

1. Write an autobiographical summary including a general scenario of your life, the people in your life, your feelings about the future, the major changes that have occurred, the turning points, and the pros and cons of various career-related decisions and different jobs you have held.

2. Develop an inventory of your functional/transferable skills along such dimensions as machine or manual, athletic/outdoor/traveling, detail/follow-through, numerical/financial/accounting, influencing/persuading, leadership, developing/planning, language/reading, instructing/interpreting, serving/helping, intuitional and innovating, artistic, and so forth. Use data from your autobiographical summary.

3. Complete the Allport, Vernon, and Lindsey (AVL) *Study of Values*. The values indexed are theoretical, economic, aesthetic, social, political, and religious.[a]

4. Maintain a 24-hour diary of what you do over one (or more) 24-hour periods.

5. Complete the *Strong-Cambell Interest Inventory* or the *Self-Directed Search*.

6. Develop a representation of your life-style (i.e., a pictorial, graphic, or written representation of your current life-style).

7. Write down your memories about the past and your feelings about the present. Stimulate visions about the future. Review themes and images in your writing for clues to your true interests and abilities.

8. Examine your life space concerns—activities, thoughts, and feelings that shape how you are relating to work, family, community, outside activities, and self.

[a] See M. London and S. A. Stumpf, *Managing Careers* (Reading, Mass.: Addison-Wesley, 1982) or your college counseling office for information on obtaining these instruments.

2 Explore Opportunities. Step 2 involves gathering data on your opportunities and potential choices both within and outside your organization. Evaluate the job market and economic conditions. Also, find out about training and development opportunities offered by your organization, including chances to move into different jobs and departments. For example, when Sharon Burklund wanted to move from communications research into sales, her superiors were not interested. So, she used an industry directory and called possible employers directly. Through direct contact, she discovered some opportunities. Sharon got her big break when she talked to the head of a trade paper who was about to launch a new publication and needed help in sales.

3 Make Decisions and Set Goals. Once you have evaluated yourself and available opportunities, you must make decisions about short-term and long-term goals. What do you want to accomplish in the next year? To which areas of the organization do you desire exposure? What skills do you want to acquire? Decide which target jobs or departments will help you get the necessary exposure and accomplish your goals. Define projects and work assignments that will provide growth opportunities.

4 Action Planning. This is the "how-do-I-get-there" part of career planning. It involves setting deadline dates, defining needed resources, and making plans to get around barriers. For example, when Sharon Burklund could not get the sales job in her own organization, she made action plans to find out about opportunities in other companies.

5 Follow Up. Once your plan is in place, periodic review and updating are needed. Take it out every six months and ask yourself, "How am I doing? Am I growing? Did I accomplish what I wanted? Are there new target jobs or work assignments that would be better for me?"

For example, Cindy Johnson, general manager of the Hotel Sofitel in Chicago, credits planning with helping her career. After deciding on the hotel business, she worked part-time in every department of the Holiday Inn while attending the University of Minnesota. She gained technical skills in everything from housekeeping and reservations to banquets and catering. After rising through the ranks of the Holiday Inn after graduation, she reassessed herself and adopted new action plans. Her plan was to move to a larger hotel and broaden her experience even more. After two years, she became director of catering for Jumer's Castle Lodge in Davenport, Iowa. At that point, she had the human, technical, and conceptual skills to become a general manager and began looking for openings in other hotels. Hotel Sofitel recognized her years of experience and appointed her general manager of the Hotel Sofitel in Houston. From there she moved on to become general manager of the new hotel in Chicago, where she is responsible for the entire operation and a staff of 300. Understanding her own strengths and weaknesses, seeking opportunities, making decisions, and adopting action plans provided a valuable assist to Cindy Johnson's career.[9]

AVOIDING OVERPLANNING

Career planning should not be rigid, narrow one's options, or chart a single course at the expense of unexpected opportunities. No one can see 10 to 15 years into the future. The point of the plan is to assess yourself and chart a course consistent with your strengths.

Walter B. Wriston, who served 14 years as CEO of CitiBank, calls life a series of accidents. People must be prepared for opportunities. A big part of having a successful career is the corner you are standing on when the bus comes. If an organization is so static and employees so rigid that they know where they will be in five years, their jobs are not worth much. Every job Wriston had at the bank before becoming CEO did not exist when he joined it.[10] Likewise, the student newspaper of a large midwestern university ran the headline "Students Shouldn't Plan Their Careers" based on an interview with the university president. The president cautioned students against deciding too early on just one interest area and closing off other options.

The policy of paying careful attention to career planning is intended to do just the opposite. Career planning enables you to consider a broad range of options, identify several that will be satisfying, and choose the path that seems best at the time. Career planning provides you with self-insight to help you adjust your plans as you go along. Career planning gives you a criterion against which to evaluate unplanned opportunities so that you will know which ones to accept.

STAGES OF CAREER DEVELOPMENT

As their careers unfold, people pass through stages that signify the course of career development over time. Most careers go through four distinct stages, each associated with different issues and tasks. Dealing successfully with these stages leads to career satisfaction and growth. The four stages are illustrated in Exhibit 23.2.[11]

STAGE 1: EXPLORATION AND TRIAL.   The **exploration and trial stage** usually occurs between the ages of 15 and 25. A person accepts his or her first job and may try several jobs, some part-time. People must decide whether to stay with an organization or try a job with another company. Job training, developing an image of a preferred occupation, job interviews, and early job challenges and feedback are all part of the learning process associated with this stage.

STAGE 2: ESTABLISHMENT AND ADVANCEMENT.   During the **establishment and advancement stage**—typically from age 25 to 45—people experience progress within the organization. They are transferred and promoted, establish their worth to the organization, and become visible to those at higher levels. Many people form a specific career strategy, decide on a field of specialization, and find a mentor to support them. A person may receive offers from other organizations.

exploration and trial stage

The stage of career development during which a person accepts his or her first job and perhaps tries several jobs.

establishment and advancement stage

The stage of career development during which the individual experiences progress with the organization in the form of transfers, promotions, and/or high visibility.

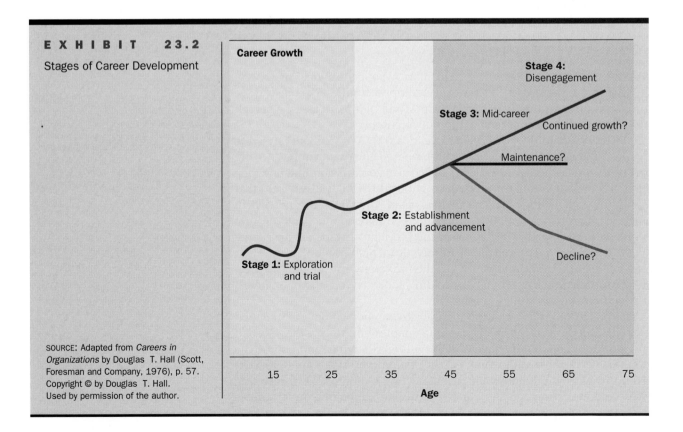

E X H I B I T   2 3 . 2

Stages of Career Development

SOURCE: Adapted from *Careers in Organizations* by Douglas T. Hall (Scott, Foresman and Company, 1976), p. 57. Copyright © by Douglas T. Hall. Used by permission of the author.

STAGE 3: MID-CAREER.   The **mid-career stage** often occurs from ages 45 to 65. Mid-career may move in three directions. If characterized by *growth*, the individual continues to progress, receiving promotions and increasing responsibility. The person may have a feeling of "making it" but fear stagnation and thus seek new challenges. If mid-career is characterized by *maintenance*, the person tends to remain in the same job or be transferred at the same level. The individual has job security and is loyal to the organization but stops progressing up the hierarchy. He or she enjoys professional accomplishments and may become a mentor. The person may also consider a second career. If the mid-career stage is characterized by *decline*, the individual is not valued by the organization. As a "surplus" employee, demotion is possible. Decline is characterized by insecurity, crisis, a feeling of failure, and possible early retirement.

mid-career stage

The stage of career development characterized by growth, maintenance, or decline.

STAGE 4: DISENGAGEMENT.   The **disengagement stage** comes toward the end of every career. The person prepares for retirement and begins to disengage from both the organization and the occupation. In today's uncertain economic environment, many older workers believe that their job security and futures are threatened as companies scale back employees and retirement benefits. During the disengagement stage, a person may polish job skills through refresher courses, establish networks inside and outside the company, and develop interests and a "nest egg" for life after work. Older employees may also prove their value to the company by offering their skills as mentor to younger employees or by offering their services as a half-time worker or as a consultant.[12]

disengagement stage

The stage of career development during which the person prepares for retirement and begins to disengage from both the organization and the occupation.

MENTOR RELATIONSHIPS

A **mentor** is a senior employee who acts as a sponsor and teacher to a newer, less experienced protégé.[13] The concept of mentor is derived from Greek mythology. Odysseus trusted the education of his son Telemachus to Mentor, a trusted counselor and friend. In today's organizations, mentors are senior, experienced employees who help newer ones navigate the organization. A mentor relationship typically lasts from two to five years and goes through periods of initiation, cultivation, and separation.[14] The *initiation stage* is a period of six months or so during which mentor and protégé get to know each other. *Cultivation* is the major period, during which the mentor "supports, guides, and counsels the new employee." During this period, the mentor-protégé relationship can be described by terms such as "master-apprentice" and "teacher-student." During the *separation* period, which lasts six months or so, the protégé may no longer want guidance, and the mentor is likely to move on to other junior employees.

Mentoring has career and social implications. Some of the characteristics of a mentor relationship are listed in Exhibit 23.3. The relationship often goes beyond coaching and training to become a close, personal friendship that includes mutual respect and affection, helping the protégé understand organizational norms, using power on the protégé's behalf, and taking the protégé along when the mentor moves to a new position. The mentor is a friend, counselor, and source of support.

mentor

A senior employee who acts as a sponsor and teacher to a newer, less experienced employee.

EXHIBIT 23.3	■ Trusted counselor, guide, role model, and teacher
Characteristics of a Mentor Role	■ Press agent/parent
	■ Respect with affection/caring
	■ Use of power on protégé's behalf
	■ Taking protégé along when moving to new position
	■ Sharing of value system, personal feelings, and political strategies
	■ Enduring relationship

A survey of top executives found that nearly two-thirds had a mentor at some point in their careers. The benefits of a mentoring relationship to an aspiring manager are substantial. Executives who had mentors received higher total compensation than did those who had not.[15] Mentors can be an important source of career development because they help new managers learn the ropes and benefit from the mentor's experience.[16]

Although mentoring relationships are valuable, they are not without problems. A study in Canada revealed a number of differences in the approach to mentoring by women and men. Among the findings: Men view having a mentor as a way of learning how to perform their jobs more effectively; women tend to use the mentor relationship to gain knowledge about corporate culture and thus bypass traditional barriers to their advancement. The study also revealed potential complications, especially those found in mixed (male/female) mentoring relationships, including gossip about them and charges of favoritism. Perhaps the most difficult and painful aspect is the ending of a mentoring relationship when the junior person is ready to progress on his or her own. The most successful mentoring efforts are usually found within companies that establish a voluntary mentoring program with trained mentors and the full support of the company.[17]

Senior managers generally initiate mentoring relationships, but there are steps that young managers can take to develop a mentoring relationship with experienced managers:

1 Determine who is successful and well thought of, and get to know him or her professionally and socially.

2 Seek out opportunities for exposure and visibility—committees and special projects—that will provide opportunities to work with experienced, successful people.

3 Inform experienced colleagues of your interests and goals; let your activities and successes be known to these people; seek specific feedback on your performance from experienced colleagues other than your boss.

4 Keep in mind that it may not be necessary to find a single, powerful senior manager to fulfill the mentor role. You may be able to develop mentoring relationships with a variety of experienced managers, including peers, during your career.[18]

Acquiring a mentor has made a difference in many careers. For example, Nancy Lane, executive producer at CNN News, was fortunate to have Mary Alice Williams, now NBC news anchor, as her mentor. Senator Bill Bradley saw special ability and skills in Betty Sapoch and took the time to help her gain confidence and skills necessary to become executive director of his election campaigns.[19]

● MANAGING CAREER STRESS

Recall from Chapter 1 that managerial work is characterized by brevity, variety, and discontinuity. In other chapters, we have seen that managers are responsible for organizing, controlling, and leading the organization. Successful managers are action oriented and responsible for high performance. Considering the nature of managerial work, stress is part of the job—indeed, many people have a stereotype of executives as harried, stressed-out, coronary-prone individuals.

Stress is defined as the physiological and emotional response to demands, constraints, and opportunities that create uncertainty when important outcomes are at stake.[20] A key notion concerning stress is that people perceive the situation as taxing or as beyond their resources for responding appropriately.[21] Thus, you experience stress if your workload is too heavy for the available time, a deadline is rapidly approaching and you need more information to make a decision, or your boss is dragging his feet on approving a project important to your career. Many life events, such as a promotion, a death in the family, marriage, divorce, or a new baby, can induce stress because of the adjustments they require.[22]

stress

The physiological and emotional response to demands, constraints, and opportunities that create uncertainty when important outcomes are at stake.

SOURCES OF STRESS

There are many sources of stress for managers. Some common ones are listed in Exhibit 23.4. Factors such as work overload, erratic schedules, job instability, and cutthroat competition influence the level of stress.[23] Managers also feel stress in the transition from one career stage to the next. Turbulence and uncertainty associated with the establishment and mid-career stages can be great, especially if the career is perceived as not going well or if there is no mentor relationship.

In recent years, much has been published about the "Type-A" personality as a potential source of stress.[24] People with Type-A behavior patterns demonstrate many potential leadership qualities and are viewed as competitive, action-oriented individuals. However, they are also prime targets for stress and stress-related diseases, such as high blood pressure, heart disease, and ulcers. Typical Type-A characteristics include the following:

- Impatience when standing in a line at the bank, store, or a restaurant.

- Excess energy and a tendency to have many projects going at once.

- Burning the candle at both ends.

- Irritability and a "hair trigger."

- Excessive need to lead in any group or organization.

By pacing themselves and by learning control and intelligent use of their natural tendencies, Type-A men and women can become powerful forces for innovation and leadership within their companies without creating stress-related problems for themselves.

An emerging source of stress for middle managers has been turbulence in the external environment, such as the threat of termination brought about by downsizing, shifts in corporate strategy based on global competition, and mergers and acquisitions. The fear and uncer-

---

EXHIBIT 23.4

Sources of Management Stress

- Work overload, excessive time demands, and "rush" deadlines
- Erratic work schedules and take-home work
- Ambiguity regarding work tasks, territory, and role
- Constant change and daily variability
- Role conflict (e.g., with immediate supervisor)
- Job instability and fear of unemployment
- Negative competition (e.g., "cutthroat," "one-upmanship," "zero-sum game," and "hidden aggression")

- Type of vigilance required in work assignments
- Ongoing contact with "stress carriers" (e.g., workaholics, passive-aggressive subordinates, anxious and indecisive individuals)
- Sexual harassment
- Accelerated recognition for achievement (e.g., the Peter Principle)
- Detrimental environmental conditions of lighting, ventilation, noise, and personal privacy

SOURCE: Based on K. R. Pelletier, *Healthy People in Unhealthy Places: Stress and Fitness at Work* (New York: Dell, 1984).

tainty surrounding possible job loss often create stress as great as that from actual job loss. Job insecurity and job loss due to rapid environmental changes and global competition will continue as major sources of manager stress through the 1990s.

One example of externally caused stress occurred at Phillips Petroleum Company. Due to a takeover attempt and a decline in the oil industry, 6,800 employees were laid off over several years in Bartlesville, Oklahoma, the company headquarters. The stress from job loss produced negative family consequences. Requests for assistance from a local shelter and counseling center for abused families shot up 69 percent. Women attending support groups for battered wives increased 41 percent. The number of children in counseling groups rose 74 percent. Emotional consequences were also felt by Phillips employees who did not lose their jobs.[25]

However, despite the negative consequences of severe stress, not all stress is bad. Hans Selye, one of the originators of stress research, observed that the only people who have no stress are dead![26] As illustrated in Exhibit 23.5, a moderate amount of stress has a positive effect on performance, but extremely high stress contributes to performance decline. Extended periods of high stress can lead to **burnout,** which is the emotional exhaustion arising from overexposure to stress.[27] Moderate job stress is a natural part of managerial work. Although executives may complain of stress, few want lower-pressure jobs.

burnout
The emotional exhaustion resulting from extended periods of stress.

SYMPTOMS OF STRESS

How do managers manifest too much stress? Common stress symptoms are anxiety and tension, depression, and physical disorders such as headache, low back pain, hypertension, and gastrointestinal problems. Behavioral symptoms include difficulty sleeping, loss of creativity, compulsive eating, and alcohol or drug abuse.[28] For example, after General Motors took over Hughes Aircraft, Robert Hearsch experienced a stress situation. A successful manager at Hughes, he was put in charge of

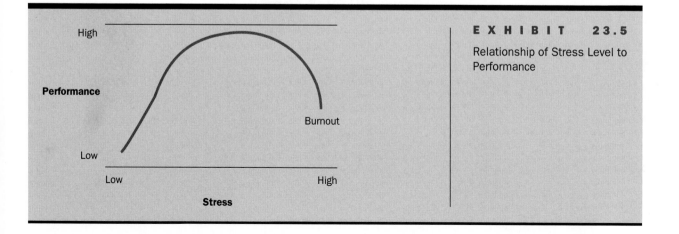

E X H I B I T   23.5

Relationship of Stress Level to Performance

In an effort to help employees *cope with stress*, National Medical Enterprises, Inc. (NME), provides a complete wellness program, staffed by fitness specialists, and housed in this modern, fully equipped wellness center. Employees in the company's headquarters are encouraged to participate in a regular exercise program and to stop smoking, lose weight, lower cholesterol and blood pressure levels, and monitor stress through biofeedback. In addition to the wellness program, NME aids stress reduction for working parents by providing on-site, high-quality child care.

buying pens and pencils. He worked hard but under the new system received constant criticism. He lost 20 pounds, his marriage hit the skids, and he suffered a minor nervous breakdown. A coworker handled his stress in another way, showing up at the office brandishing a handgun.[29]

COPING WITH STRESS

Research on effective ways of coping with managerial stress is just now emerging, but some trends have been identified. For example, ways to cope include learning to relax through meditation or regular exercise. Managers can learn to say no to unacceptable work overloads, stand up to the boss, and delegate responsibility to subordinates. Requesting resources needed to remove the cause of stress often helps.[30] Other effective behaviors are building resistance to stress through regular sleep, good eating and health habits, and discussing the stressful situation with coworkers, family, and friends.

Recent data indicate that factors under managerial control, such as performance feedback and clear job expectations, job decision latitude, and social support, are key factors in helping subordinates cope effectively with job stress.[31] In the end, however, each person must find his

focus on GLOBAL COMPETITION   **THE STRESS FACTOR IN JAPAN**

In Japan, *Karoshi* is defined as "sudden death by heart attack or stroke, triggered by overwork." It was so prevalent in Japan that an organization, the National Defense Council for Victims of Karoshi, was founded in 1988. Japanese workers are so committed to their organizations and to success that they work extraordinarily hard, experiencing high levels of stress. The founder of the organization estimates that 10,000 deaths result annually from *Karoshi*. Yet for years, stress-related death from overwork was seen by the Japanese as a blue-collar rather than a white-collar problem.

In 1992, the widow of one white-collar victim won a judgment from Tokyo's labor regulators recognizing that her husband had indeed died as a result of *Karoshi*. The ruling enabled her to collect annual worker's compensation and may result in similar judgments for survivors in other *Karoshi* cases.

Some companies, such as Mitsuy & Co., Matsushita Electric Industrial, and Nippon Telegraph & Telephone Corporation, are taking steps to improve the working conditions of office workers by extending vacation time, initiating programs in exercise and meditation, and assessing managers on how effectively they set overtime. Companies are also encouraging workers to maintain healthy life-styles and to actually use their vacation time.

In today's fast-paced global society, companies around the world are learning from one another about how to reduce stress and improve the physical and mental health of employees. ■

SOURCE: Karen Lowry Miller, "Now, Japan Is Admitting It: Work Kills Executives," *Business Week*, August 3, 1992, 35.

or her own strategies for coping with stress. For example, a survey of senior executives revealed a variety of techniques, including having other interests, maintaining a sense of humor, keeping in shape, keeping a balance in their lives, deciding not to let things bother them, and not taking matters too seriously.

At the company level, managers can ease employee stress by adopting sound corporate practices such as these:

- Implementing stress audits to determine factors that contribute to stress (including boredom as well as overwork, noise, danger, etc.).

- Utilizing employee assistance programs and wellness programs.

- Improved matching of employees with jobs and job rotation.

- Empowering employees, giving them a greater sense of control over their situation.

- Developing trauma contingency plans to assist employees in dealing with crises that may occur in the workplace.

- Improving educational, training, and information programs.[32]

Although North Americans tend to be individualistic and competitive, stress occurs in corporations around the world. The Focus on Global Competition box looks at stress in Japan.

● ORGANIZATIONAL POLICIES FOR CAREER MANAGEMENT

Up to this point, we have been dealing with career planning from the viewpoint of the individual employee. Now we turn to career management policies and strategies that organizations can use to promote effective employee career development.

Career management refers to organizational activities designed to promote employees' career development. These activities should function as a system designed to meet individual needs for job advancement, extension of skill, or the enhancement of human experience on the job and to relate these needs to the future requirements of the organization.[33] A career development system is created by coordinating various human resource functions, such as recruitment, performance appraisal, and staffing, while providing a variety of special policies and programs focusing specifically on employee career development.

Exhibit 23.6 illustrates the key components and functions of a career development system. The formal responsibility for career development is usually housed in the human resource management/personnel department. As with most human resource management programs, however, the success of career development depends on line managers' adoption of a career development perspective on a cooperative relationship with the human resource staff. The two dimensions in Exhibit 23.6 are career planning and career management. As described earlier, career planning emphasizes individual actions, whereas career management emphasizes organizational initiatives. Moreover, as the arrows in Exhibit 23.6 indicate, individual and organizational activities should jointly influence career development. Employees are more likely to do systematic career

career management

Organizational activities designed to promote employees' career development.

Liz Claiborne, Inc., is serious about *career management* to enhance its employees' career development. These new recruits are in Claiborne's Careers in Management program, an 18-month series of work assignments and seminars. Claiborne recruits the best and brightest for the program, and managers are proud of the diverse talents being developed to lead Claiborne's future.

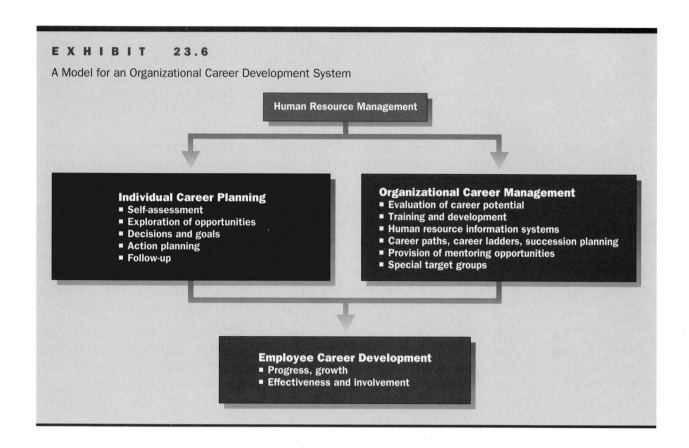

EXHIBIT 23.6

A Model for an Organizational Career Development System

Human Resource Management

Individual Career Planning
- Self-assessment
- Exploration of opportunities
- Decisions and goals
- Action planning
- Follow-up

Organizational Career Management
- Evaluation of career potential
- Training and development
- Human resource information systems
- Career paths, career ladders, succession planning
- Provision of mentoring opportunities
- Special target groups

Employee Career Development
- Progress, growth
- Effectiveness and involvement

planning if the organization provides opportunities and structure for this purpose. Organizationally prescribed performance feedback and discussion of career potential are an important impetus to individual efforts. Organizations can provide career planning programs such as workshops and counseling, but individuals must choose to invest energy and time in action planning and follow-up if career development is to take place.

The major components of the organization's career management system are an evaluation of potential, training and development, human resource information systems, career paths, career planning programs, and provision of mentoring opportunities.

EVALUATION OF CAREER POTENTIAL

A critical input into career development is the performance appraisal process described in Chapter 12. Feedback on job performance is important in all aspects of individual career planning, providing valuable data on skills and strengths and assisting employees in identifying realistic future goals.

The appraisal process also helps the organization assess future potential—the individual's probability of moving upward in the organization. Organizations may use a variety of tools to assess potential, such as com-

These young employees are part of a 21-member team established by Chugai Pharmaceutical Co., Ltd., to create a new company vision and strategy as part of training and *management development*. Through participation in Chugai's 21st Century Study Group, these younger employees, usually outside the decision-making loop, gain the experience and skills necessary to become resourceful managers of the future. The study group report included an outlook for the pharmaceutical industry worldwide and proposed a Chugai strategy of global leadership in comprehensive health-care operations.

mercially prepared tests and inventories, internally developed questionnaires, succession planning, or an assessment center. Often, however, it is the manager's role to determine future career potential using personal judgment. A section of the formal performance appraisal rating form can ask the manager to rate the employee's "future potential" or "promotability."

TRAINING AND MANAGEMENT DEVELOPMENT

The backbone of a career management program is organizational commitment to training and employee development. *Training* programs focus on the immediately applicable, technically oriented skills required for the next level of job. *Management development* suggests a longer-term view of expanding a person's confidence and growth. Many organizations have a wide range of training and development programs that employees can attend. Some new managers attend management training programs sponsored by universities and the American Management Association to develop their human and conceptual skills.

Another important aspect of training and development involves internal job moves. The most frequently used job moves for broadening and increasing an employee's potential for advancement are vertical and horizontal:

- *Vertical:* Moving up and down the organizational pyramid; job moves in this category involve changes in rank or organizational level.

- *Horizontal:* Lateral movement to a different function, division, or product line in the organization, such as from sales to marketing or from human resources to public relations.

HUMAN RESOURCE INFORMATION SYSTEMS

Effective career development systems depend on information. Data on organizational human resource planning and individual career planning must be available to managers and employees. These data usually come from job analysis and job matching systems.

JOB ANALYSIS.   *Job analysis* was referred to in Chapter 12 as the systematic collection of information about the purpose, responsibilities, tasks, knowledge, and abilities needed for a job. Data are collected by the personnel staff through interviews with job incumbents and supervisors.

human resource inventory

A data base that summarizes individuals' skills, abilities, work experiences, and career interests.

HUMAN RESOURCE INVENTORY.   The **human resource inventory** is a data base that summarizes individuals' skills, abilities, work experiences, and career interests. These data are made available to both managers and personnel specialists.

job matching system

A method that links qualified individuals with career opportunities within the organization.

JOB MATCHING SYSTEMS.   The component for bringing together both job data and human resource interests is a **job matching system,** which links individuals with career opportunities within the organization. The job matching system brings together the human resources inventory as well as the job characteristics, descriptions, and profiles derived from the job analysis. The job matching system searches through all potentially qualified or interested employees and matches them with present or future openings.

One type of matching system developed by Gannett Company, Inc., is the Talent Tracking System. The system is a computerized job matching network managed by the corporate news staff in Arlington, Virginia, for all of the company's newspapers. Over 1,500 names have been logged into the system, and top editors from around the country use a computer to review the credentials of job prospects. The system works like a giant cookie jar, with top managers able to select and recruit employees from around the Gannett system.[34]

CAREER PATHS, CAREER LADDERS, AND SUCCESSION PLANNING

Career paths are job progression routes along which employees can advance through the organization. Career paths typically are developed for specific employees, or they may be drawn up by the organization as general routes for employee advancement. They consist of a series of target jobs or functional areas that indicate future job moves appropriate for the individual's career. Career paths may include horizontal moves and an occasional downward move in order to obtain the needed experience.

Career ladders are formalized job progression routes based on jobs that are logically connected. Career ladders tend to be more precisely and objectively determined than career paths. Career ladders are based on data collected through job analysis and examination of personnel records showing historical patterns of employee job moves. An example of a career ladder for Link Flight Simulator Division of the Singer Company is illustrated in Exhibit 23.7. This career ladder charts the normal progression for engineers. After an engineer advances through the first four stages, a decision must be made. The person can concentrate on technical challenges and remain in the staff engineering track, or he or she may decide to pursue a management track.

There are two ladders associated with management—functional management within the engineering department and program management that involves the coordination of entire projects. The decision to pursue a specific track will be based on the individual's self-assessment and interest in becoming either a staff scientist or a manager.

Succession planning is the process used to create a plan for moving people into the higher levels of the organization. Succession planning applies to a specific group of employees who have the development potential to become top-level managers. "Top level" usually is defined as two to four levels below the CEO. Organizations with progressive career development systems have extended succession planning for all professional and managerial positions.

Succession planning defines both present and future job requirements and determines the availability of candidates and their readiness to move

career path

A job progression route along which an employee can advance through the organization.

career ladder

A formalized job progression route based on logically connected jobs.

succession planning

The process of creating a plan for moving people into higher organizational levels.

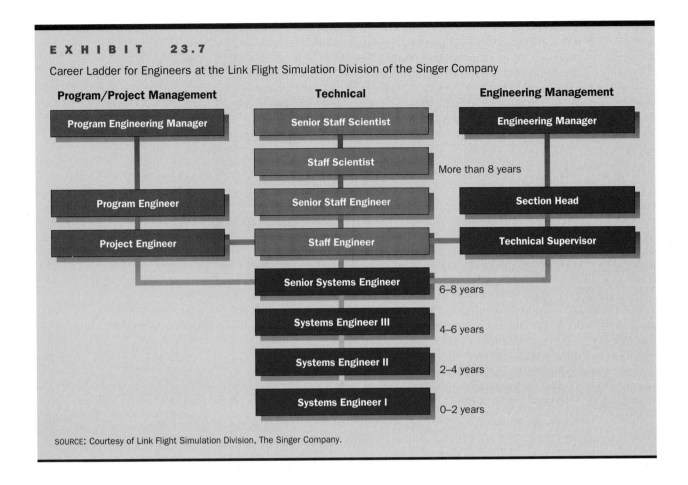

EXHIBIT   23.7

Career Ladder for Engineers at the Link Flight Simulation Division of the Singer Company

SOURCE: Courtesy of Link Flight Simulation Division, The Singer Company.

into top jobs.[35] It also uses *employee resource charts* discussed in Chapter 12 to identify likely successors for each management position. This system suggests possible career paths and career ladders for a set of managers and managerial jobs. The succession planning time horizon is usually 12 to 36 months and is periodically updated. The appropriate emphasis in succession planning is on developing a pool of talent rather than selecting a "crown prince" to assume a top position.

CAREER PLANNING PROGRAMS

Career planning programs offered by the organization can take the form of career planning workshops and individual career counseling sessions. Group workshops can be conducted by personnel department staff or outside consultants. The workshops take employees through the systematic steps of individual career planning by using individual assessment exercises, holding small-group discussions, and providing information on organizational opportunities.

Individual career counseling may be provided by the personnel department, but a major part takes place during career planning discussions with supervisors. Supervisors must be trained and knowledgeable about career planning and opportunities. Career counseling requires that a manager assume the role of coach and counselor. Sometimes it is difficult to do career planning during a performance appraisal session because employees become defensive. Some organizations resolve this problem by asking supervisors to hold separate sessions—the first for performance evaluation and the second for creating a career plan.[36]

MENTORING OPPORTUNITIES

As we discussed earlier, mentoring provides many advantages to the career development of junior managers. Although mentoring is something that junior managers can undertake on their own, mentor relationships can be an important organizational tool for employee career development.

One approach organizations can use to encourage and facilitate mentoring is education.[37] Educational programs help senior managers understand mentoring and its importance in career management and help establish norms and cultural values in support of mentoring. Other changes that facilitate mentoring include adjusting the reward system to place greater emphasis on mentoring, modifying the work design, adapting performance management systems, and even introducing a formal mentoring program. In this way, senior managers can be encouraged and rewarded for mentoring and may even be assigned junior managers to support and assist. Organizational efforts to facilitate mentoring are important because informally developed, one-to-one relationships may not be available to all promising junior managers. One outcome of mentoring programs is to foster multiple developmental relationships between junior managers and more experienced senior people. Companies that have formal mentor systems include Ortho Pharmaceutical Corporation, Eastman Kodak Company, Pacific Bell, and Clairol.

Small entrepreneurial companies often have a difficult time developing managers because they cannot afford formal training programs. General Alum & Chemical Corporation invented its own in-house mentoring system to solve this problem. To socialize new managers and train them into the corporate culture, senior executives were assigned to a handful of developing managers. The junior managers had great potential but lacked experience. The mentor relationship enabled these young men and women to learn about subtle aspects of management, including human and conceptual skills. Formally assigning mentors made sure that all potential managers had this positive experience.[38]

● SPECIAL CAREER MANAGEMENT PROBLEMS

Because of current social, economic, and legal pressures, organizational career management strategies may be focused on the unique needs of special target groups. Concerns about career development for women and minorities is a direct outgrowth of equal employment opportunity legislation. Although women and minorities are advancing within corporations, they are still underrepresented in middle- and top-level management.[39] The increasing number of dual-career couples has pressured organizations to solve the problems unique to this group of employees. Further, as organizations face increasing competition and are forced to streamline management structures, many management employees find they have plateaued because there are fewer opportunities to move up the hierarchy.

EMPLOYEE DIVERSITY

Because of common issues faced by women and minorities, recommended career development management strategies often consider these two target groups together. Organizations must confront issues related to assimilating and developing these two groups. For example, because minorities and women have only recently entered management ranks, they may have difficulty developing the social networking and mentoring helpful to career development. Recall from Chapter 1 that work-force diversity is a major issue facing organizations in the 1990s. White males will make up a smaller proportion of the management work force in future years.

WOMEN.   Issues that women face include balancing multiple roles of career and family and dealing with sexual harassment.[40] A recent survey found that nearly one out of three women who received MBAs from the nation's top business schools ten years ago have left the managerial work force.[41] Because many of these women left to devote more time to their families, some companies are experimenting with innovative programs that respond to family pressures and offer more flexibility for both men and women.

The pressures are so great that some women must make difficult choices. Phyllis Swersky, executive vice-president at AlCorp admits, "I don't cook. I don't take my children to malls and museums. And I don't have any close friends." She credits a live-in nanny and a supportive husband for creating a solid home structure that keeps her life on track. Many professional women make the choice between career and family. Author and Harvard economics professor Claudia Goldin enjoys life at the top of her profession, adding, "I don't know if I could have made it if I were married and had kids." Whether making a deliberate choice between family and career or trying to balance the two, women face difficult choices regarding time, priorities, and quality of life.[42]

Because only women have babies and often are responsible for child care, some female managers and professionals are leaving the fast track for what has been called the *mommy track*. These women devote time to raising a young family rather than devoting all their energies to career advancement. Some women dislike the notion of a mommy track, believing it identifies female employees as separate and unequal and may permanently derail women's careers, making them second-class citizens. Taking time to raise a family as well as work may confirm prejudices of male executives and contribute to perception of the glass ceiling. So-called mommy trackers are less likely to be considered for promotion to highly responsible positions.[43]

Many companies encourage women to take time for their children because it allows the company to retain valued employees. These employees may be given extended leave, flexible scheduling, or opportunities for job sharing and telecommuting that enable them to raise a family. These managers come back to regular work when the children are older. For example, Mellon Bank allows women to work flexible hours, work at home, and engage in job sharing. At KMPG Peat Marwick, women can opt for a lighter client load and a less than 40-hour workweek for two to three years. Procter & Gamble gives women eight weeks' paid maternity leave and six months' unpaid child care leave to either parent.[44]

MINORITIES. Despite a large and growing black middle class, the progress of blacks in U.S. corporations has been disappointing to blacks and whites alike. According to statistics from the Equal Employment Opportunity Commission, only 9.5 percent of all managers were minorities. One discouraged manager said, "The U.S. is in a global trade war and we're trying to fight without all our troops."[45]

The biggest barrier facing minorities, especially black managers, is advancement into upper management. Minorities must learn the "difficult, lonely and threatening way to navigate in a basically white environment." This environment is characterized by white executives' discomfort with nonwhites as well as the tendency to promote managers with backgrounds similar to their own. A recent survey of black managers revealed that many of them perceived the organizational climate for black managers in their organization as indifferent, patronizing, and reluctant to accept blacks. On the positive side, some organizational climates were seen as encouraging, supportive, and trusting.[46] Although the percentage is small, an increasing number of blacks have triumphed in corporate careers, becoming successful managers in major companies.

Recommendations for addressing the unique needs of women and minorities include providing them with access to information, allowing nontraditional career moves, enforcing affirmative action, and providing better assessment and coaching skills for potential managers. Organizations should pay particular attention to assisting women and minorities in identifying and examining career paths and the requirements for advancement. Training programs should emphasize the job skills that women and minorities need as well as the unique problems they face when advancing within the corporation.

DUAL-CAREER COUPLES

The growing number of dual-career couples has prompted organizational career management programs to focus on the corporate problems posed by this expanding group of employees.[47] Traditionally, it was assumed that if a wife worked, her own career took second place to her husband's. Today women are increasingly likely to place equal importance on their career involvement and are no longer expected to fit their careers to their husbands' career needs. As a result, more couples face the issue of having both a committed personal relationship and careers that are central to each spouse.

Company understanding and support from Price Waterhouse enables *dual-career couples* such as David and Kelly Sach, pictured here, to balance career and family demands. In addition to a generous benefits package, Price Water-house has assisted this globe-trotting management couple in a variety of ways—from ensuring jobs are available so the couple can be transferred to-gether, to pre-maternity leave, part-time work for Karen, who is expecting their second child, and setting up clients for her return to full-time work.

Dual-career relationships involve trade-offs, and both employees and managers are realizing that most people cannot "have it all"—happy marriage, children, charming home, many friends, and intense commit-ment to a career. Organizations are concerned because the pressures experienced by dual-career couples may harm productivity or morale and can pose difficulties when recruiting new employees or transferring current employees to new locations.[48]

There is a strong link between the career problems facing women and the problems of dual-career couples. Women MBAs who left the work force did so because of work-family conflicts. In the final analysis, in most families the responsibility for balancing work and family respon-sibilities falls disproportionately on the woman.[49]

These issues are difficult to resolve. Suppose, for example, that you have just been promoted to manager of market development for a fast-growing computer software firm in Chicago. Your spouse is offered a big promotion that requires a move to Dallas. What criteria would you use to decide whether to give up your new position or make your spouse pass up the promotion? Will you consider a commuting relationship? If so, for how long?

Ted Koppel resolved a dual-career dilemma by taking ten months off from his newscasting at ABC to be at home with the children so that his wife, Grace Anne, could start law school at Georgetown University. Many lesser-known couples make similar compromises. Others take turns promoting each other's careers. For example, Peter Briggs left a challenging job as data-processing manager with a Minneapolis bank to move with his family to Burlington, Vermont, so that his wife, Barbara Grant, could become an assistant professor of medicine at the University of Vermont. Following his spouse to a new city was an excruciating experience, because he had no job to look forward to. He found a new job at a bank in Burlington, but at a lower level.[50] Some couples end up taking jobs in separate locations and having a "commuter marriage." Robert and Marina Whitman live in Princeton, New Jersey. He commutes to Pittsburgh three days a week, where he teaches English at the University of Pittsburgh, and she commutes to New York and Detroit, where she is chief economist and vice-president for General Motors. Whenever they are in the same city, they always have dinner together.[51]

Corporations are finding ways to help dual-career couples eliminate stress and to help the company retain competent people. One change is dropping antiquated "antinepotism" rules that prevented husbands and wives from working together. Universities, law firms, publishing houses, newspapers, and corporate offices are just a few of the organizations to have realized that top men and women in the field meet and marry. Recruiting high-quality people increasingly means hiring both spouses in the same discipline or department.[52]

Other career management programs directed at dual-career couples include flexible work schedules, transfer policies, career planning assistance, and local support services such as day care for children. For example, at General Motors, when one spouse is hired by the company and relocated, the other gets counseling and referral help in finding a new job. Sometimes the spouse is hired too. At Lotus Development, more than 70 percent of the married people are part of two-career families; thus, generous parental leave benefits are available.[53]

PLATEAUED EMPLOYEES

A **career plateau** is "a point in a career from which the likelihood of additional hierarchical promotion, in the judgment of the organization, is very low."[54] Due to the high value most people place on upward mobility, plateauing has come to be viewed by organizations as a problem and may lead to the employee being written off or ignored with respect to career development opportunities. As a practical matter, there is nothing inherently negative about reaching a career plateau. It is a natural consequence of the narrowing pyramid shape of organizations, and many employees experience a career plateau somewhere during mid-career.

Plateaued employees can fall into one of two categories. "Solid citizens" are plateaued employees rated as performing satisfactorily. "Deadwood" are plateaued employees whose performance has fallen below the satisfactory level.[55] Many plateaued employees are effective performers, and they should not be stereotyped as unmotivated or performing inadequately. Indeed, many companies want to keep plateaued employees and their accumulated knowledge. Many people have spent their entire careers in excellent organizations such as IBM, GE, Eastman Kodak, Westinghouse, and Hewlett-Packard, even after they had no prospect of further advancement.[56]

Many organizations anticipate a larger number of plateaued employees in the future. Fewer promotional opportunities will be available because of leaner management staffs. This may also mean that

career plateau

A point in a career from which the opportunities for further promotion are scarce.

EXHIBIT   23.8

Techniques for Renewing
Plateaued Managers

SOURCE: Based on J. M. Bardwick,
"Plateauing and Productivity," *Sloan
Management Review* (Spring 1983),
67–73.

- Rotate people laterally among existing jobs.
- Use lateral or downward transfers to other departments.
- Increase job scope to require new knowledge and skills.
- Create temporary work units to solve specific problems.
- Provide training in current technical or administrative skills.
- Encourage development of mentoring, counseling, and advisory skills.
- Reward supplemental contributions such as mentoring and community or
  government relations.
- Use individuals as internal consultants in different parts of the organization.

plateauing will occur earlier than mid-career for some employees. Most managers will have plateaued employees and will need to devote attention to developing and maintaining these people's competence.

One study found that plateaued managers performed better when they and their bosses agreed on clear performance objectives and when the managers received feedback on specific tasks and overall performance. Other factors that helped plateaued employees' performances were whether they knew the basis on which their performances were being evaluated and whether they had challenging, satisfying, and clearly defined jobs that were important to the company.[57]

A number of career management techniques that organizations can use to help plateaued employees are listed in Exhibit 23.8. One is to enhance job challenge and task accomplishment opportunities. This can be done through transfers or by changing the scope of the present job. Other techniques include job changes, training programs that provide mentoring and career counseling, and managerial and technical updating.[58]

● CAREER DEVELOPMENT IN FOUR STAGES

To make career development more effective, the organization can focus on employee career stages. Rather than provide one program for all employees, the firm can offer several programs, each of which can match the needs of specific employee groups. Examples of career management strategies associated with each of the four career stages described earlier are illustrated in Exhibit 23.9.

In the exploration/trial stage, one concern is how to deal with *reality shock,* which is the upsetting experience and stress brought about by unmet expectations of organizational newcomers.[59] Reality shock can lead to early career dissatisfaction and high turnover. Thus, one career management strategy is to give new recruits *realistic job previews* that present job interviewees with the full picture of the organization without selling or "sugar coating" job opportunities. Other strategies during the early career stage are to provide varied job activities, opportunities for self-exploration, and opportunities to gain organizational knowledge.

For employees in the establishment/advancement stage, career management should focus on helping them gain competence in a specialty and develop personal creativity and innovation skills. People at this level should be encouraged to gain familiarity with different organizational areas, possibly through horizontal transfers. They should also be given an opportunity to develop and display their skills and expertise for potential mentor relationships and promotability.

For employees in mid-career, the organization should provide **mid-career renewal strategies,** which are designed to provide upward mobility for those who merit it while maximizing the contributions of plateaued employees who continue to perform satisfactorily. For employees who experience mid-career crises, planning workshops and support groups can help redirect career goals. The organization also can help managers combat obsolescence by providing technical and managerial skill training programs.

For employees in the disengagement stage of their careers, an increasingly popular career management strategy is to provide preretirement programs. **Preretirement programs** assist employees in managing the stress of transition from work to retirement. Some educational areas that facilitate the transition are financial planning, leisure activities, work/career alternatives, and health.[60] Other ways to keep disengaging managers contributing to the organization are to help them shift from a role of power and decision making to one of consultation, guidance, and development of key subordinates. The organization can also help disengaging people find meaningful activities outside the organization.

mid-career renewal strategies

A strategy designed to provide advancement opportunities for deserving mid-career employees while maximizing the contributions of plateaued employees who continue to perform satisfactorily.

preretirement program

A strategy designed to assist employees in coping with the stress of the transition from work to retirement.

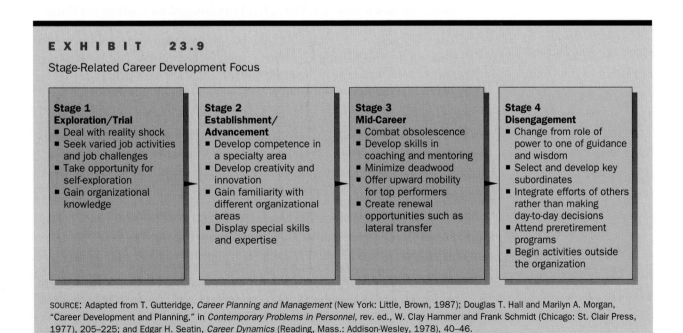

EXHIBIT   23.9

Stage-Related Career Development Focus

Stage 1
Exploration/Trial
- Deal with reality shock
- Seek varied job activities and job challenges
- Take opportunity for self-exploration
- Gain organizational knowledge

Stage 2
Establishment/Advancement
- Develop competence in a specialty area
- Develop creativity and innovation
- Gain familiarity with different organizational areas
- Display special skills and expertise

Stage 3
Mid-Career
- Combat obsolescence
- Develop skills in coaching and mentoring
- Minimize deadwood
- Offer upward mobility for top performers
- Create renewal opportunities such as lateral transfer

Stage 4
Disengagement
- Change from role of power to one of guidance and wisdom
- Select and develop key subordinates
- Integrate efforts of others rather than making day-to-day decisions
- Attend preretirement programs
- Begin activities outside the organization

SOURCE: Adapted from T. Gutteridge, *Career Planning and Management* (New York: Little, Brown, 1987); Douglas T. Hall and Marilyn A. Morgan, "Career Development and Planning," in *Contemporary Problems in Personnel*, rev. ed., W. Clay Hammer and Frank Schmidt (Chicago: St. Clair Press, 1977), 205–225; and Edgar H. Seatin, *Career Dynamics* (Reading, Mass.: Addison-Wesley, 1978), 40–46.

Focusing on employees' needs relative to their career stages coordinates the organization's career management strategies with the varied needs of all personnel. The potential bottom-line payoffs to the organization for effective career management are substantial. Productivity, satisfaction, retention, and commitment of valued employees, stress reduction, and a flexible work force will help the organization remain competitive in our global economy.

SUMMARY AND MANAGEMENT SOLUTION

This chapter covered several important issues about the management of careers. Career management was discussed from two perspectives: the individual who wants to have a successful career and the organization that wishes to provide career opportunities for its employees.

Individual career planning normally entails five steps—self-assessment, exploring opportunities, making decisions and setting goals, action planning, and follow-up. Individual careers follow predictable stages that include exploration and trial, establishment and advancement, midcareer, and disengagement. Other issues of concern to individual career planning are mentors and coping with stress.

Recall from the management problem at the beginning of this chapter that Kim Jackson's love of politics, hard work, and excellent research and writing skills placed her on a career track to becoming a political correspondent on Capitol Hill. When her interests and enthusiasm for the job waned, Jackson wondered if she should make a career change. Before making a major move, she discussed her concerns with her editor and a member of the human resource management office. The newspaper, which was reluctant to lose a reporter of Jackson's talents and background, provided an opportunity for her to undergo testing and experimentation in other potential areas of career interest. Eventually, a simple solution emerged: Jackson was moved to the international desk. Covering international political events renewed her enthusiasm and her years on Capitol Hill gave her special insight into U.S. reaction to global events.

As in Jackson's case, organizational policies can help with individual career planning. Organizational career management involves several systems and techniques.

These include evaluation of career potential, training and development programs, human resource information systems, career paths and succession planning, career planning programs, and facilitation of mentoring. Other organizational concerns pertain to women and minorities, dual-career couples, and plateaued employees. Dealing effectively with these target groups can enhance the organization's human resource base. Finally, effective career management programs target individuals' needs at each stage in their career.

DISCUSSION QUESTIONS

1. What is the difference between a career and a job? What satisfaction might come with having a job rather than a career?
2. What is job stress? What are the symptoms of high stress? Of moderate stress?
3. Think of someone you know, such as a parent or relative, who has been in a career for several years. In which career stage is this person? Have there been any problems with the transition from one stage to another?
4. What is the organization's responsibility toward a plateaued employee who has become deadwood? Was the individual or the organization the likely cause of this problem?
5. Many people go through a mid-life crisis between the ages of 40 and 50. What career factors might be associated with this crisis?
6. What career planning steps have you taken? What additional steps will you take as you get closer to graduation?
7. Some managers claim, "Individuals should not plan careers. They should remain open to opportunities." How do you respond to this statement?
8. Discuss some of the special problems of women, minorities, and dual-career couples. Is it fair for the organization to offer special programs or make exceptions for people in these groups?
9. Is it imperative to have a mentor for career success? Should you find a mentor or let a mentor find you?
10. Is career-management an individual or organizational concern? What types of systems can organizations adopt to facilitate employees' career development?

MANAGEMENT IN PRACTICE: ETHICAL DILEMMA

● DREADED DECLINE

You manage a 12-member product design department in a mid-size company. Your department has an excellent reputation as a top place to work, both within the company and throughout the industry. Over the years, the mentoring program you developed and nurtured has been especially successful in developing new talent. A special "family" relationship has emerged, and many designers have gone on to careers in middle management throughout the company.

Now a general downturn within the industry is forcing major cutbacks in your company. You recently received word to cut three employees. One member of the department is nearing retirement, so that will count as one reduction. But two more jobs must be cut, and seniority does not have to be the deciding factor. Suddenly mentors and protégés are competitors for the remaining positions, and you foresee terrible consequences for the department—not only for the people who will lose their jobs but also for the mentoring program and "family" relationship.

● WHAT DO YOU DO?

1. Pick the two people who have least seniority. Although this is not required, it provides an objective criterion and will cause the least damage to the department.
2. Pick the two people you consider the poorest performers and would like to replace. This will enable you to replace them and improve the department when it grows back to normal size.

3. Try to get around the rule. Discuss the situation with departmental employees and see if they are willing to take pay reductions so that no one has to lose his or her job.

4. Turn the decision over to employees. This will maintain a family atmosphere, and employees who might have been planning to leave anyway will be identified.

CASES FOR ANALYSIS

AMERICAN STEEL COMPANY

When Jeff Orr began job hunting during his senior year at a state university, he received four job offers. He accepted the offer from American Steel Company to be an assistant to the plant manager. He believed that this would give him an opportunity to learn all phases of the plant while utilizing the financial and accounting expertise he had acquired in college.

Three years later—when Orr was only 25—the plant controller died and Greg McDonald, plant manager, offered him the controller's job. It was a big responsibility, but the plant manager believed that Orr could handle it. Orr accepted and worked many 12-hour days. But it was challenging and exciting. He loved the responsibility and believed that he was making a difference in plant decisions.

After only two years as plant controller, Orr was called into Greg McDonald's office. "Headquarters in Philadelphia needs another person in the financial planning group. They've looked throughout the company and believe that you have the right combination of training and experience. Headquarters wants you to take a position with the headquarters' financial planning group. Although I hate to lose you, I recommended you highly and do not want to stand in your way."

Orr took the job and initially loved it. It utilized his ability to explain complex financial data to unsophisticated listeners. He could organize data logically, and he spoke well. His presentations at headquarters were always well received.

Orr was disappointed when his new boss, Gilbert Clark, said that Orr would not make the annual capital budget presentation to the board of directors. Clark told him, "It's

customary for the financial planning department head to appear before the board. You'll have to brief me thoroughly before I present next week." The briefing did not go well, because Clark was ignorant of many details and could not answer some questions. One proposal for remodernizing plants was shot down, which angered Greg McDonald and other plant managers, who had hoped Orr would help them get the equipment needed to improve productivity.

Orr suddenly found himself agonizing over his career. "What should I do about Mr. Clark?" he mused. "He's a real roadblock. He doesn't understand capital budgeting or financial planning or what I'm trying to do. He's still wearing a green eyeshade so far as new financial planning techniques are concerned. Should I sit tight until he retires in seven years? Or would it be better to transfer back to plant management? Maybe I should try to sneak around him in the hierarchy." Orr believed that he had made excellent progress in his career up to this point but now felt blocked and frustrated.

● QUESTIONS

1. In what career stages are Jeff Orr and Gilbert Clark? Do you see any special problems associated with either career from the organization's perspective?
2. How well has Orr planned his career? Do you think he should do more systematic planning? Explain.
3. What would you do in this situation?

SOURCE: Inspired by John L. Snook, Jr., "Sanford Jarvis Case" UVA-H-75 (Colgate Darden Graduate School of Business Administration, University of Virginia, 1976).

MICRONET HEALTH CARE, INC.

Robert Woodmont was pleased as he read over the speech he would be delivering at the stockholders meeting the next day. It would be a huge meeting, since most employees were stockholders and those who were not were also invited. As CEO and majority shareholder, Woodmont was

pleased with another year of increased growth and profits and enthusiastic about the announcement of the plan he had worked out with the human resources department.

Woodmont had changed a lot since he started the company 20 years ago, at 32 years of age. He believed that computers could be used to make paperwork and administrative processing in hospitals and doctors' offices much more efficient. Little did he realize that extraordinary improvements in computing technology combined with the escalating cost of health care would cause the demand for Micronet's services to skyrocket. The company's sales reached nearly $400 million, and Micronet now had more than 3,000 employees.

Wealthy beyond his dreams, Woodmont had created a foundation to which he contributed a substantial portion of his Micronet stock. A second marriage three years ago to a career woman in the banking industry enriched his life and also sensitized him to the career dilemmas of women, minorities, and single parents. He wanted Micronet to become a place where everyone could succeed, regardless of gender or race. The corporate culture was dominated by white male thinking, and he had been working with the head of human resource management to develop a program to increase opportunities for everyone. The elements of the new program that he would highlight in tomorrow's speech were as follows:

1. A career development program that would allow each employee to work through the steps of self-analysis, setting career goals, and contingency planning. All managers would be asked to hold an annual career discussion with each subordinate. Managers would be trained to provide effective career counseling, and all employees would be invited to attend career planning workshops.

Even more exciting to Woodmont were the special efforts to be made on behalf of women and minorities. Career planning for these people included several parts.

2. An outreach program would be started that would recruit women and minorities in percentages equal to their availability. Thus if women composed 50 percent of marketing graduates from business schools where Micronet recruited, then 50 percent of the new hires should be women. If 20 percent were blacks, the same percentage of new hires should be black.

3. Micronet would provide fast tracks for women and minorities currently employed and would target them for promotion opportunities. Company goals for the first two years would be for women to receive 35 percent of promotions and minorities to receive 20 percent, thereby increasing their percentages in management ranks.

4. Senior executives would be asked to invite women and minority managers to attend golfing or similar outings with clients.

5. Company social activities such as golf matches or poker games would be replaced with more univer-

sal activities such as picnics and bicycle rides, and lessons in tennis, swimming, and dancing would be provided by the health and recreation department.

6. The company would try to cut back travel, relocation, and long hours that would exclude people with pressing family responsibilities.

7. Male managers and employees would be asked to participate in awareness training to make them more sensitive to the problems experienced by minorities and women. This training would involve face-to-face discussions to give white male managers feedback that would identify and overcome the subconscious ways they unfairly treated women and minorities. Many male managers admitted being uncomfortable working with people different from themselves, and this training would help them stop "looking past" people and become more sensitive to racial and gender bias.

8. The HR department would start teaming groups of promising women and minorities with more experienced male executives. These "coaches" could give advice on corporate values, politics, and career strategies. One-on-one mixed mentoring would also be encouraged.

9. A "take a friend to lunch," program would be started in which the company each week would pay for employee lunches that involved mixed race or gender.

10. Strong family benefit policies would be implemented by the HR department to hold on to talented employees with family responsibilities. These benefits would include excellent maternity and child care benefits.

Woodmont believed that his program was daring, but he had never been afraid to take risks. He was looking forward to feedback from white males and other employees. He wondered how they would feel about working in a truly equal opportunity company.

● QUESTIONS

1. How do you feel about Micronet's career management program? How do you expect various employee groups to respond?

2. If you were in the human resource department, what problems would you expect in the implementation of this program?

3. How would you personally respond to this initiative if you worked for Micronet right now?

SOURCE: This case was based in part on Walecia Konrad, "Welcome to the Woman-Friendly Company," *Business Week*, August 6, 1990, 48–55.

REFERENCES

1. This case is based on the author's personal knowledge; names have been changed.

2. Janet Bamford, "Everyone Has to Start Somewhere," *Forbes*, July 14, 1986, 98–100.

3. R. Ricklafs, "Many Executives Complain of Stress, but Few Want Less-Pressure Jobs," *The Wall Street Journal*, September 29, 1982, 1.

4. Daniel C. Feldman, "Careers in Organizations: Recent Trends and Future Directions," *Journal of Management* 15 (1989), 135–156.

5. T. Gutteridge, *Career Planning and Management* (Boston: Little, Brown, 1987).

6. Janet Bamford, "Climb Quickly or Get Out Fast," *Forbes*, November 3, 1986, 224–226.

7. Mona Melanson, "Career Self-Assessment," *National Business Employment Weekly*, June 25, 1989, 9.

8. Scott Bronestein, "Past Forty and Back to Square One," *The New York Times*, October 20, 1985, 6F.

9. Edie Gibson, "Fast Track Often Starts at Bottom," *Chicago Tribune*, December 15, 1986, sec. 4, 15.

10. "Expert View," *Working Woman*, October 1985, 154.

11. The discussion of career stages is based on M. London and S. A. Stumpf, "Individual and Organizational Development in Changing Times," in *Career Development in Organizations*, ed. Douglas T. Hall and associates (San Francisco: Jossey-Bass, 1986).

12. Kenneth Labich, "Take Control of Your Career," *Fortune*, November 18, 1991, 1991, 87–96.

13. Kathy E. Kram, *Mentoring at Work: Developmental Relationships in Organizational Life* (Glenview, Ill.: Scott, Foresman, 1985).

14. Kathy E. Kram, "Phases of the Mentor Relationship," *Academy of Management Journal* 26 (1983), 608–625.

15. William Whitely, Thomas W. Dougherty, and George F. Dreher, "Relationships of Career Mentoring and Social Economic Origin to Managers' and Professionals' Early Career Progress," *Academy of Management Journal* 34 (1991), 331–351, and G. R. Roche, "Much Ado about Mentors," *Harvard Business Review* (January–February 1979), 14–28.

16. Kathy E. Kram and L. Isabella, "Mentoring Alternatives: The Role of Peer Relationships in Career Development," *Academy of Management Journal* 28 (1985), 110–132.

17. John Lorinc, "The Mentor Gap, Older Men Guiding Younger Women: The Perils and Payoffs," *Canadian Business*, September 1990, 93–94.

18. Rosabeth Moss Kanter, *Men and Women of the Corporation* (New York: Basic Books, 1977).

19. Aimee Lee Ball, "Mentors & Protégés," *Working Woman*, October 1989, 134–142.

20. T. A. Beehr and R. S. Bhagat, *Human Stress and Cognition in Organizations: An Integrated Perspective* (New York: Wiley, 1985).

21. R. S. Lazarus and S. Folkman, *Stress, Appraisal and Coping* (New York: Springer, 1984).

22. T. Homes and R. Rahe, "The Social Readjustment Rating Scale," *Journal of Psychosomatic Research* 11 (1967), 213–218.

23. K. R. Pelletier, *Healthy People in Unhealthy Places: Stress and Fitness at Work* (New York: Dell, 1984).

24. Daniel C. Ganster and John Schaubroeck, "Work Stress and Employee Health," *Journal of Management* 17 (1991), 235–271.

25. Emily T. Smith, "Stress: The Test Americans Are Failing," *Business Week*, April 18, 1988, 74–76.

26. Hans Selye, *The Stress of Life* (New York: McGraw-Hill, 1956).

27. Brian Dumaine, "Cool Cures for Burnout," *Fortune*, June 20, 1988, 78–84, and Jeannie Gaines and John M. Jermier, "Emotional Exhaustion in a High Stress Organization," *Academy of Management Journal* 26 (1983), 567–586.

28. Sana Siwolop, "The Crippling Ills That Stress Can Trigger," *Business Week*, April 18, 1988, 77–78.

29. Annetta Miller, "Stress on the Job," *Newsweek*, April 25, 1988, 40–45.

30. Ibid.

31. J. C. Latack, R. J. Aldag, and B. Joseph, "Job Stress: Determinants and Consequences of Coping Behaviors" (Working paper, Ohio State University, 1986), and R. A. Karasek, Jr., "Job Demands, Job Decision Latitude, and Mental Strain: Implications for Job Redesign," *Administrative Science Quarterly* 24 (1979), 285–308.

32. Alan Farnham, "Who Beats Stress Best—And How," *Fortune*, October 7, 1991, 71–86.

33. Jeffrey A. Sonnenfeld and Maury A. Peiperl, "Staffing Policy as a Strategic Response: A Topology of Career Systems," *Academy of Management Review* 13 (1988) 588–600; "Career Development Programs," *Small Business Report* (November 1987), 30–35; and E. H. Burack, *Career Planning and Management: A Managerial Summary* (Lake Forest, Ill.: Brace-Park Press, 1983).

34. Molly Badgett, "Computerized Talent Files Broaden Editors' Reach for New Employees," *Gannetteer*, published by Gannett Company, Inc. (June 1989), 4–5.

35. M. London, *Developing Managers* (San Francisco: Jossey-Bass, 1985).

36. D. T. Wight, "The Split Role in Performance Appraisal," *Personnel Administrator* (May 1985), 83–87, and A. H. Soerwine, "The Manager as Career Counselor: Some Issues and Approaches," in *Career Development in the 1980s*, ed. D. H. Montross and C. J. Shinkman (Springfield, Ill.: Charles C. Thomas, 1981).

37. Kram, *Mentoring at Work*.

38. Lisa R. Sheeran and Donna Fenn, "The Mentor System," *INC.*, June 1987, 136–142.

39. Anne B. Fisher, "Where Women Are Succeeding," *Fortune*, August 3, 1987, 78–86.

40. Felice N. Schwartz, "Management Women and the New Facts of Life," *Harvard Business Review* (January–February 1989), 65–76.

41. A. Taylor, "Why Women Managers Are Bailing Out," *Fortune*, August 18, 1986, 16–23.

42. Jaclyn Fierman, "Why Women Still Don't Hit the Top," *Fortune,* July 30, 1990, 40–62.

43. Elizabeth Ehrlich, "The Mommy Track," *Business Week,* March 20, 1989, 126–134.

44. Taylor, "Women Managers."

45. Colin Lolinster, "Black Executives: How They're Doing," *Fortune,* January 18, 1988, 109–120, and Joel Dreyfuss, "Get Ready for the New Work Force," *Fortune,* April 23, 1990, 165–181.

46. L. Riebstein, "Many Hurdles, Old and New, Keep Black Managers Out of Top Jobs," *The Wall Street Journal,* July 10, 1986, 1.

47. U. Sekaran, *Dual Career Families: Implications for Organizations and Counselors* (San Francisco: Jossey-Bass, 1986).

48. Colin Lolinster, "The Young Exec as Superdad," *Fortune,* April 25, 1988, 233–242.

49. D. T. Hall, "Career Development in Organizations: Where Do We Go from Here?" in *Career Development in Organizations,* ed. Douglas T. Hall and associates (San Francisco: Jossey-Bass, 1986).

50. Denise Weil, "Husbands Who Star in Supporting Roles," *Working Woman,* June 1986, 114–116.

51. "The Uneasy Life of the Corporate Spouse," *Fortune,* August 20, 1984, 26–32.

52. Fran Schumer, "The New Nepotism: Married Couples Are Working Together All Over," *New York,* November 19, 1990, 46–50.

53. Taylor, "Why Women Managers Are Bailing Out."

54. J. A. F. Stoner, T. P. Ference, E. K. Warren, and H. K. Christensen, *Managerial Career Plateaus: An Exploratory Study* (New York: Center for Research and Career Development, Columbia University, 1980).

55. Ibid.

56. Judith M. Bardwick, "How Executives Can Help Plateaued Employees," *Management Review* (January 1987), 40–46.

57. J. P. Carnazza, A. K. Korman, T. P. Ference, and J. A. F. Stoner, "Plateaued and Non-Plateaued Managers: Factors in Job Performance," *Journal of Management* 7 (1981), 7–25.

58. J. M. Bardwick, "Plateauing and Productivity," *Sloan Management Review* (Spring 1983), 67–73.

59. J. P. Wanous, *Organizational Entry: Recruitment, Selection, and Socialization of Newcomers* (Reading, Mass.: Addison-Wesley, 1980).

60. W. Arnone, "Preretirement Planning: An Employee Benefit That Has Come of Age," *Personnel* 61 (1982), 760–763.

Flexibility is the name of the game for the growing number of American couples who are trying to juggle a marriage, two jobs, and children. Families have learned that flexibility is the only way to pack fast-paced careers and quality home time into tight schedules. Employers have realized they also have to be flexible, if they want to avoid losing valued workers to burnout and stress. The result is some rather novel approaches to work and play in the 1990s.

Chip and Beth Davis are one of the decade's new breeds of dual-career couples. Chip gets up early every morning to go to work as a dayshift supervisor at a canning plant. His wife Beth stays home with the children. But at 3:00 every afternoon, their roles reverse. Chip gets home in time to pick up the older kids from school, while Beth packs her things and goes off to work as an evening reservations clerk at a hotel. And so it goes day in and day out. "It's the only way for us to get ahead," says Beth. "Child care is so expensive. It would hardly be worth my working if we used it."

Margie and William Freivogel also avoid using day care, but their arrangement gives them quite a bit more free time. The Freivogels have been sharing a single job for the last eight years. He works Mondays and Tuesdays as the assistant chief of the Washington bureau of the St. Louis *Post-Dispatch*. She works Wednesday and Thursdays in the same position. They split Fridays and the care of their four children, who range in age from 5 to 13. "The paper can have one of us at any time, but never both of us at the same time," says Margie.

Scores of other couples across the Unites States have more traditional setups, but learn to be flexible nonetheless. John and Sue Jones get up every morning and go off to work at separate jobs, but take turns shuttling their children to day care or doing the grocery shopping. Racine and Philip Hood say they have managed to keep their marriage solid, while raising two kids and getting ahead in their jobs, by setting priorities. "The earth is not going to come to an end because that table is not dusted. And before you know it, 25 years have passed around here, so where in the world has the time gone," says Philip.

Life is getting a little easier for couples like the Joneses and the Hoods because employers are starting to see it is worthwhile to do what they can to ease the burden for their workers. In a survey of 4,000 employees, aimed at assessing their social needs, the DuPont Company found that ignoring family issues could lead to the loss of good employees. "The fact that 25 percent of the men and about 50 percent of the women have considered seeking another employer who might offer more work or family flexibility shows how seriously these issues can affect the company," says Benjamin Wilkinson, personnel manager for DuPont.

Faith Wohl, co-chair of DuPont's 16-member Work and Family Committee, explains the results this way in a company publication: "In our survey, employees told us—loud and clear—that what they needed from DuPont to help them balance their work and family responsibilities is flexibility in our programs, and importantly, understanding when they have special problems."

Those employers who do go the extra mile often find it is well worth the effort. Maryles Casto, owner of Casto Travel, Inc., decided to take a new approach after repeatedly seeing valued employees quit because they could not find adequate day care. Since the $70-million-a-year business relies heavily on computers, Casto found she could put terminals in the homes of workers and still keep them on the job. They work full-time at home and are paid at the same rate as other employees. Since Casto extends the work-at-home privilege to employees who follow a spouse to a job in another city, she can expand her business.

Even high-profile employees have found that working at home can be the ideal way to balance career and family life. Deborah Norville decided not to return to her co-anchor job at NBC's "Today" show after her son was born in 1991. But ABC Radio later made her an offer she could not refuse. They asked her to host a nightly radio show from her home. "I thought they were pulling my leg," says Norville. "But the next thing I knew, these men with wires and headsets and microphones were scurrying through my house putting wires in walls."

A growing number of women are choosing to leave the corporate world altogether to start their own businesses and do things their own way. They can work long hours when they need to, but take days off if necessary. It's the output, not the work schedule that takes priority

Dana Friedman, co-president of the New York-based Families and Work Institute, says younger workers, especially, care more about quality of life than getting ahead in their jobs. "This runs counter to the career ethic, which implies that the employees will strive for promotions and perform even when their work is not particularly interesting or satisfying," she says. "Careerists are willing to sacrifice family and personal interest to succeed, but not so those subscribing to the self-development ethic."

A growing number of men also are expressing a desire to put family before career. In a 1989 survey commissioned by the executive recruiting firm Robert Half International, 74 percent of men said they would rather have a "daddy track" job than a "fast-track" job. Nearly half of the men surveyed said they were willing to forsake promotions in order to spend more time with their children. James Levine, director of the New York-based Fatherhood Project says many of the men who put family before careers are most likely baby-boomers who did not get to spend quality time with their own fathers.

The U.S. Supreme Court gave its support to family issues when it ruled on the legality of California legislation that bans pregnancy discrimination. The court said that female employees must have "the basic right to participate fully and equally in the work force, without denying them the fundamental right to full participation in family life."

Congress may have had similar issues in mind when it passed the Family and Medical Leave Bill, mandating that companies with 50 or more employees must provide up to 12 weeks unpaid leave every year for reasons ranging from physical or mental illness of a family member to spending time with a newly adopted child. The bill's broad language will allow dual-career couples greater flexibility in scheduling work around family needs without running the risk of being terminated.

Many employers are worried about the potential cost of the legislation. The law says the company can only deny family leave to top executives who are within the 10 percent most highly compensated, and only if it would cause "serious and grievous injury" to the business. "Most small businesses are hanging on by their fingernails. If you want successful businesses, you don't keep adding to their burden," says Harvey Goldstein, a managing partner of a mid-sized Los Angeles accounting firm.

But a study by the Family and Work Institute found that many employers fears may be unfounded. The study of four states that enacted family leave laws before the federal legislation went into effect concluded that "it is far less expensive to support a parental leave than to replace the employee permanently." The study also found that 94 percent of the leave-takers returned to their jobs after taking time off. "The economic realities are that most employees can't afford to be off without pay," says research associate Laurie Kane.

Companies that have been providing unpaid leave of their own accord support that view. Since AT&T began offering up to 12 months of unpaid leave with benefits and a job guarantee, less than 1 percent of its 300,000 employees have taken the company up on its offer every year. About 150 use it to care for a sick family member and 2,500 take the time to be with their children.

Companies of all sizes are learning to make concessions to keep their employees happy. Barrios Technology, Inc., which employs 300 people at its Houston headquarters, introduced flextime, allowing workers to arrive as early as 7 A.M. or leave as late as 6 P.M. as long as they keep a regular daily schedule. New mothers who live nearby are allowed to go home to nurse their infants and employees can use their own sick leave when they have to stay home to look after a sick child.

Barrios, which specializes in engineering and computer-related services, also gives its employees so-called flexible benefits. Parents can get up to $1,020 annually for child care. Childless employees can choose to apply that money to extra life insurance or a health club instead.

In some cases, employees find that flextime is theirs for the asking. That's how the Freivogels were able to get the green light to share their job at the newspaper. While their bosses were skeptical at first, neither side has regrets. Says *Post-Dispatch* managing editor David Lipman: "The quality of the work and the results have been good for the paper, and it's enabled us to keep in the workplace some very talented individuals who might otherwise have had to opt for something else." That's a lesson more employers may be learning in the future.

● QUESTIONS

1. Discuss both job and family priorities for working couples and individually list each in order of importance. Compare the two lists and reduce priorities further based on daily time constraints.

2. Is it feasible for major corporations with thousands of employees to attempt to accommodate worker needs on a case-by-case basis? Can flexible shifts be reconciled with production quotas, quality standards, meeting schedules, and other work-related contingencies?

3. Does increased worker independence threaten the traditional manager/employee relationship? What is the downside risk? Upside potential?

4. Given recent federal legislation, how should an employer cope with highly skilled employees taking leaves of absence?

■ ENTREPRENEURIAL QUOTIENT

In Chapter 22, "Entrepreneurship and Small Business Management," you learned that over one million businesses are started each year. In turn, these new enterprises generate over five million jobs annually. However, two out of three businesses fail in the first five years, even though the average entrepreneur works 60 or more hours per week.

Despite the hard work and risks, you may still have the desire at some point to start your own business. It would be helpful to know whether you are personally suited to this kind of venture.

THIS EXERCISE WILL HELP YOU

- Develop a realistic picture of what it takes to become an entrepreneur.
- Gain some personal insights into your inclination toward starting your own business.

HOW TO LOCATE THE EXERCISE:

When you see the main menu for Career Design, select "Other Management Issues." Then select "Entrepreneurship Quotient."

■ INTERESTS AND FASCINATIONS

In Chapter 23, "Career Management," you learned that the first step in planning your career is self-assessment. An important part of self-assessment is identifying your interests. It is one of the most important exercises in the career planning section of Career Design, although it may not seem that way now. As you progress through college and into your career, you will discover that anything which interests you is an important clue about your career direction. Most successful people are truly fascinated with their work.

When you are asked to list your interests, take the program's advice and type in as many of your interests as you can, regardless of whether or not you think they are job related.

THIS EXERCISE WILL HELP YOU

- Discover and keep track of your interests.
- Learn that choosing a career which interests you can result in better pay and job satisfaction.

HOW TO LOCATE THE EXERCISE:

When you see the main menu for Career Design, select "Other Management Topics," followed by "Career Planning." Then, select "Interests."

■ LISTING YOUR SKILLS

Another important part of self-assessment is identifying your skills and talents. You'll be surprised at the number of skills you possess. In fact, it's not unusual for students to uncover 50 or more of their skills in this exercise.

By the way, this is not a time to be modest. If you think you have a skill, type it in!

THIS EXERCISE WILL HELP YOU

● Identify many of your skills and talents.
● Discover you possess far more skills than you realized.
● Communicate your value to potential employers.

HOW TO LOCATE THE EXERCISE:

When you see the main menu for Career Design, select "Other Management Topics," followed by "Career Planning." Then, select "Listing Your Skills."

■ PEOPLE PREFERENCES

Here's an exercise about which you'll probably have some strong feelings. Have you ever thought about how you enjoyed a certain job—or hated one—because of the people at work? In this exercise, you will gather all the things you like and dislike about people you have encountered. You will even decide which of those items are so important that the next job you take has to fit that list.

People preferences are yet another part of the self-assessment step of career planning.

THIS EXERCISE WILL HELP YOU

● Develop a clear picture of exactly what kinds of people you prefer to encounter in your work setting.
● Learn that the people with whom you work can have a significant impact on job satisfaction.

HOW TO LOCATE THE EXERCISE:

When you see the main menu for Career Design, select "Other Management Topics," followed by "Career Planning." Then select "People Preferences."

■ WORK PREFERENCES

Have you ever thought about what makes a job appealing or unappealing? Obviously, the actual work you do plays a big part, but there are many other things. In fact, you may have talked to someone who said, "I don't really like what I'm doing, but this is such a great place to work that I don't want to quit." In this next Career Design Exercise, you'll find out what kind of working conditions you want on the job.

Listing your work preferences completes the group of self-assessment exercises which began with "Interests and Fascinations."

THIS EXERCISE WILL HELP YOU

● Develop a clear picture of exactly what working conditions are important to you.
● Learn that your work environment can be just as important to job satisfaction as the work itself.

HOW TO LOCATE THE EXERCISE:

When you see the main menu for Career Design, select "Other Management Topics," followed by "Career Planning." Then select "Work Preferences."

■ DATA GATHERING

The second step of career planning described in Chapter 23 involves gathering data on your opportunities and potential choices in the job market. If you're currently employed, it may also mean identifying your options within your own organization.

Before making any decisions about something important—such as choosing a major or deciding on a career or employer—you first need to gather information. That way, you can make an informed decision. It is valuable to not only read about your topic of interest, but to talk with people who are personally involved. For example, you could uncover many facts about a career interest in the *Occupational Outlook Handbook*. However, to get a "sense" for what it's really like on the job, you would need to visit with people who actually do the work.

In gathering your data about an important topic, you'll complete three sections: "Preparing a Plan," "Conducting a Survey," and "Evaluating Results."

THIS SET OF EXERCISES WILL HELP YOU

● Get the exact information you need to make good decisions.
● Learn how to research any topic of interest.

- Discover a method for making valuable contacts, such as potential employers.
- Verify that you have enough information before you make decisions.

HOW TO LOCATE THE EXERCISE:

When you see the main menu for Career Design, select "Other Management Topics," followed by "Career Planning." Then select "Data Gathering."

■INTERVIEW QUESTIONS

The third step of career planning is to make decisions and set goals. What do you want to accomplish in the next few years? What skills and experience do you want to acquire? In fact, many employers are likely to ask these kinds of questions in your job interviews.

The fourth step of career planning is determining how you can pursue your goals, including getting the job you want. Many job opportunities are lost instantly during the job interview, even though the person is qualified for the job because his or her interview skills are weak. The best way to ensure that your interviews result in a favorable impression is to prepare. That means learning how to best answer the questions you're likely to face.

THIS SET OF EXERCISES WILL HELP YOU

- Understand the reasons why interviewers ask certain questions.
- Prepare effective answers to tough interview questions.
- Convince the interviewer that you are ideally suited for the job.

HOW TO LOCATE THE EXERCISE:

When you see the main menu for Career Design, select "Other Management Topics," followed by "Career Planning." Then, select "Interview Questions" followed by "Overview." After reading the overview on the interviewing section, choose from the "Interview Questions" menu the category of questions for which you want to prepare, such as "Goals," "Education" or "Compatibility with Employer."

INSIGHTS INTO
INDIVIDUAL BEHAVIOR **A** A P P E N D I X

Do you ever "see" an assignment differently than others at work or at school? When discussing a movie? Have you ever felt that your work associates or your classmates just can't seem to get their message across to you? Or that they don't fully understand your point of view? Have you ever wondered why some people around you want to be told what to do, while others bristle at authority? If you answered "yes" to any of these questions, you have already experienced what practicing managers describe as their most time consuming task: *people problems*. People problems are based on the complex and unique qualities people bring to the workplace.

Leading is defined in the text as the management function that involves using influence to motivate employees to achieve organizational goals. Three basic skills associated with *leading* are at the core of dealing with people problems: (1) *diagnosing*, or gaining insight in the situation you as a manager are trying to influence; (2) *adapting* your behavior and other resources at your disposal to meet the needs of the situation; and (3) *communicating* in a way that others can understand and accept. Skill at dealing with people problems begins with *diagnosing* the situation. You have to have insight about individual differences to understand what a behavioral situation is now and be able to understand what it will be in the future. The discrepancy between the situation now and the desired future behavior is the problem to be solved.[1]

Note: Contributed by Susan Halfhill.

This appendix has been written with two purposes. One is to help you understand what makes you "you." With an awareness of what influences your behavior, you will gain insight both into yourself and into the behavior of others. The second purpose is to help you improve your management skill of *diagnosing*. By increasing your knowledge of individual differences in the areas of personality, problem-solving styles, perception, and learning styles, you will be able to understand and manage the behaviors of your associates in various workplace situations.

● PERSONALITY

When we talk about an individual's personality as pleasant, or bubbly, or stubborn, we are describing specific traits. When researchers talk about an individual's *personality,* they are referring to a set of characteristics that underlie a relatively stable pattern of behavior in response to ideas, objects, or people in the environment. Understanding an individual's personality can be useful in predicting how he or she will react in a particular situation.

Let's take a look at three specific work-related personality dimensions: locus of control, authoritarianism/dogmatism, and Machiavellianism.

LOCUS OF CONTROL

Some people believe that their actions can strongly influence what happens to them. They feel in control of their own fate. These individuals have a high *internal locus of control* (internals). Other people believe that events in their lives occur because of chance, luck, or outside people and events. They feel more like pawns of their fate. These individuals have a high *external locus of control* (externals).

Research on locus of control has shown real differences in behavior between internals and externals across a wide range of settings. Internals are easier to motivate because they believe the rewards are the result of their behavior. Internals are better able to handle complex information and problem solving, are more achievement oriented, but are also more independent and therefore more difficult to lead. On the other hand, externals are harder to motivate, less involved in their jobs, more likely to blame others when faced with a poor performance evaluation, but are more compliant and conforming, therefore, easier to lead than internals.[2]

Do you believe luck plays an important role in your life, or do you feel you control your fate? To find out more about your locus of control, read the instructions and complete the questionnaire called Measuring Locus of Control that appears in Exhibit A.1.[3]

AUTHORITARIANISM AND DOGMATISM

Authoritarianism is the belief that power and status differences *should* exist within the organization. Individuals high in authoritarianism tend to be concerned with power and toughness, obey recognized authority

E X H I B I T　　A . 1

Measuring Locus of Control

The questionnaire below is designed to measure locus of control beliefs. Researchers using this questionnaire in a recent study of college students found a mean of 51.8 for men and 52.2 for women, with a standard deviation of 6 for each. The higher your score on this questionnaire, the more you tend to believe that you are generally responsible for what happens to you; in other words, higher scores are associated with internal locus of control. Low scores are associated with external locus of control. Scoring low indicates that you tend to believe that forces beyond your control, such as powerful other people, fate, or chance, are responsible for what happens to you.

For each of these ten questions, indicate the extent to which you agree or disagree using the following scale:

1 = strongly disagree	5 = slightly agree
2 = disagree	6 = agree
3 = slightly disagree	7 = strongly agree
4 = neither disagree nor agree	

_____ 1. When I get what I want, it's usually because I worked hard for it.
_____ 2. When I make plans, I am almost certain to make them work.
_____ 3. I prefer games involving some luck over games requiring pure skill.
_____ 4. I can learn almost anything if I set my mind to it.
_____ 5. My major accomplishments are entirely due to my hard work and ability.
_____ 6. I usually don't set goals, because I have a hard time following through on them.
_____ 7. Competition discourages excellence.
_____ 8. Often people get ahead just by being lucky.
_____ 9. On any sort of exam or competition, I like to know how well I do relative to everyone else.
_____ 10. It's pointless to keep working on something that's too difficult for me.

To determine your score, reverse the values you selected for questions 3, 6, 7, 8, and 10 (1 = 7, 2 = 6, 3 = 5, 4 = 4, 5 = 3, 6 = 2, 7 = 1). For example, if you strongly disagreed with the statement in question 3, you would have given it a value of "1." Change this value to a "7." Reverse the scores in a similar manner for questions 6, 7, 8, and 10. Now add the point values from all ten questions together.

Your score: _____

SOURCE: Adapted from J. M. Burger, *Personality: Theory and Research* (Belmont, Calif.: Wadsworth, 1986), 400–401, cited in D. Hellriegel, J. W. Slocum, Jr., and R. W. Woodman, *Organizational Behavior*, 6th ed. (St. Paul, Minn.: West Publishing, 1992), 97–100.

above them, stick to conventional values, critically judge others, and oppose the use of subjective feelings.[4] This has important implications for managers in their formal use of authority in organizations. Consider for a minute how authoritarianism relates to the Chapter 9 discussion of authority, and how authoritarianism would be related to organizational decentralization or empowerment.

Dogmatism is a closely related term that refers to an individual's receptiveness to new ideas and opinions. A highly dogmatic person is closedminded and not receptive to new ideas. Research shows that highly dogmatic individuals see the world as a threatening place, readily accept orders from superiors, and may even prefer superiors who are highly directive in their leadership styles. Dogmatic individuals tend to make decisions quickly based on a minimum of information, and they are unreceptive to information that conflicts with their decisions.[5] Imagine the impact this personality trait could have on the quality of decision making, especially under conditions of risk, uncertainty, or ambiguity as described in Chapter 8.

Think for a few moments about people you know—friends, family members, coworkers, instructors—and how they differ on the personality dimensions of authoritarianism and dogmatism. What type of person on these dimensions would you like to have working for you? What type would you like to have as your manager? Discuss your conclusions with other people and see whether they agree.

MACHIAVELLIANISM

Machiavellianism is a personality dimension characterized by acquisition of power and by manipulation of other people for purely personal gain. The dimension is named after Niccolo Machiavelli, a sixteenth century author who wrote *The Prince,* a book for noblemen of the day on how to acquire and use power.[6] Psychologists have developed instruments to measure a person's Machiavellianism orientation.[7] Research shows that high-Machs are predisposed to being pragmatic, are capable of lying to achieve personal goals, are more likely to win in win-lose situations, and are more likely to persuade than be persuaded. In loosely structured situations, high-Machs actively take control, while low-Machs accept the direction given by others. On the other hand, low-Machs thrive in highly structured situations, while high-Machs perform in a detached, disinterested way. High-Machs are particularly good in jobs that require bargaining skills or that involve substantial rewards for winning.[8]

Do you think you are closer to a high-Mach or a low-Mach? You can assess your score by completing the Mach Assessment Instrument that appears in Exhibit A.2.[9] Discuss your score with classmates.

● PROBLEM-SOLVING STYLES[10]

Individuals differ in the way they go about gathering and evaluating information for problem solving and decision making. Four psychological functions have been identified by Carl Jung as related to this process: sensation, intuition, thinking, and feeling.[11]

Before you read further, complete the Problem-Solving Diagnostic Questionnaire, then the scoring key which appears in Exhibit A.3.[12] There are no "right" or "wrong" answers; just read each item carefully, then respond with your answer.

According to Jung, gathering information and evaluating information are separate activities. People gather information either by *sensation* or *intuition,* but not by both simultaneously. *Sensation-type* people would rather work with known facts and hard data and prefer routine and order in gathering information. *Intuitive-type* people would rather look for possibilities than work with facts and prefer solving new problems and using abstract concepts.

Information evaluation involves making judgments about the information a person has gathered. People evaluate information by *thinking* or *feeling.* These represent the extremes in orientation. *Thinking-type* indi-

EXHIBIT A.2

Mach Assessment Instrument

For each of the following statements, circle the number that most closely resembles your attitude.

	Disagree			Agree	
Statement	A lot	A little	Neutral	A little	A lot
1. The best way to handle people is to tell them what they want to hear.	1	2	3	4	5
2. When you ask someone to do something for you, it is best to give the real reason for wanting it rather than reasons that might carry more weight.	1	2	3	4	5
3. Anyone who completely trusts someone else is asking for trouble.	1	2	3	4	5
4. It is hard to get ahead without cutting corners here and there.	1	2	3	4	5
5. It is safest to assume that all people have a vicious streak, and it will come out when they are given a chance.	1	2	3	4	5
6. One should take action only when it is morally right.	1	2	3	4	5
7. Most people are basically good and kind.	1	2	3	4	5
8. There is no excuse for lying to someone else.	1	2	3	4	5
9. Most people forget more easily the death of their father than the loss of their property.	1	2	3	4	5
10. Generally speaking, people won't work hard unless forced to do so.	1	2	3	4	5

Scoring Key and Interpretation

This assessment is designed to compute your Machiavellianism (Mach) score. Mach is a personality characteristic that taps people's power orientation. The high-Mach personality is pragmatic, maintains emotional distance from others, and believes that ends can justify means. To obtain your Mach score, add up the numbers you checked for questions 1, 3, 4, 5, 9, and 10. For the other four questions, reverse the numbers you have checked so that 5 becomes 1, 4 is 2, and 1 is 5. Then total both sets of numbers to find your score. A random sample of adults found the national average to be 25. Students in business and management typically score higher.

The results of research using the Mach test have found: (1) men are generally more Machiavellian than women; (2) older adults tend to have lower Mach scores than younger adults; (3) there is no significant difference between high Machs and low Machs on measures of intelligence or ability; (4) Machiavellianism is not significantly related to demographic characteristics such as educational level or marital status; and (5) high Machs tend to be in professions that empasize the control and manipulation of people—for example, managers, lawyers, psychiatrists, and behavioral scientists.

SOURCE: Adapted from R. Christie and F. Geis, *Studies in Machiavellianism* (New York: Academic Press, 1970), cited in J. R. Schermerhorn, J. G. Hunt, and R. N. Osborn, *Managing Organizational Behavior*, 4th ed. (New York: John Wiley, 1991), 453–455.

viduals base their judgments on impersonal analysis, using reason and logic rather than personal values or emotional aspects of the situation. *Feeling-type* individuals base their judgments more on personal feelings such as harmony and tend to make decisions that result in approval from others.

According to Jung, only one of the four functions—sensation, intuition, thinking, or feeling—is dominant in an individual. However, the dominant function is usually backed up by one of the functions from

EXHIBIT A . 3

Problem-Solving Diagnostic
Questionnaire

Indicate your responses to the following questionnaire on a separate sheet of paper. There are no right or wrong responses to any of these items.

Part I. Circle the response that comes closest to how you usually feel or act.

1. I am more careful about
   A. People's feelings.
   B. Their rights.

2. I usually get on better with
   A. Imaginative people.
   B. Realistic people.

3. It is a higher compliment to be called
   A. A person of real feeling.
   B. A consistently reasonable person.

4. In doing something with many people, it appeals more to me
   A. To do it in the accepted way.
   B. To invent a way of my own.

5. I get more annoyed at
   A. Fancy theories.
   B. People who do not like theories.

6. It is higher praise to call someone
   A. A person of vision.
   B. A person of common sense.

7. I more often let
   A. My heart rule my head.
   B. My head rule my heart.

8. I think it is a worse fault
   A. To show too much warmth.
   B. To be unsympathetic.

9. If I were a teacher, I would rather teach
   A. Courses involving theory.
   B. Fact courses.

Part II. Which word in the following pair appeals to you more? Circle a. or b.

10. a. compassion	b. foresight
11. a. justice	b. mercy
12. a. production	b. design
13. a. gentle	b. firm
14. a. uncritical	b. critical
15. a. literal	b. figurative
16. a. imaginative	b. matter-of-fact

the other set of paired opposites. Exhibit A.4 shows the four problem-solving styles that result from these match-ups.[13]

Look back at your scores. What is your personal problem-solving style? Read the action tendencies. Do they fit? Studies show that the sensation-thinking combination characterizes many managers in western industrialized societies. Do you think the ST style is the best fit for most jobs in today's society? Exhibit A.4 also matches the four problem-solving styles with their occupational preferences. Is there a good fit between your individual style and your desired occupation?

Scoring Key to the Problem-Solving Questionnaire

EXHIBIT A.3

Continued

Mark each of your responses on the following scales. Then use the point value column to arrive at your score. For example, if you answered *a* to the first question, you would check *1a* in the feeling column. This response receives zero points when you add up the point value column. Instructions for classifying your scores are indicated below the scales.

Sensation	Point Value	Intuition	Point Value	Thinking	Point Value	Feeling	Point Value
2 b ___	1	2 a ___	2	1 b ___	1	1 a ___	0
4 a ___	1	4 b ___	1	3 b ___	2	3 a ___	1
5 a ___	1	5 b ___	1	7 b ___	1	7 a ___	1
6 b ___	1	6 a ___	0	8 a ___	0	8 b ___	1
9 b ___	2	9 a ___	2	10 b ___	2	10 a ___	1
12 a ___	1	12 b ___	0	11 a ___	2	11 b ___	1
15 a ___	1	15 b ___	1	13 b ___	1	13 a ___	1
16 b ___	2	16 a ___	0	14 b ___	0	14 a ___	1
Maximum Point Value: (10)		(7)		(9)		(7)	

Classifying Total Scores

- Write *intuition* if your intuition score is equal to or greater than your sensation score.
- Write *sensation* if your sensation score is greater than your intuition score.
- Write *feeling* if your feeling score is greater than your thinking score.
- Write *thinking* if your thinking score is greater than your feeling score.

SOURCE: Adapted from the Myers-Briggs Type Indicator, I. Myers, The *Myers-Briggs Type Indicator* (Princeton, N. J.: Educational Testing Service, 1962), cited in D. Hellriegel, J. W. Slocum, Jr., and R. W. Woodman, *Organizational Behavior*, 3rd ed. (St. Paul, Minn.: West Publishing, 1983), 128–143.

● PERCEPTION[14]

Remember the opening question about whether you ever "see" assignments differently from others at work or at school? Most people answer "yes" to that question because "seeing" things differently is the essence of perception. *Perception* is the process we use to make sense out of our environment by selecting, organizing, and interpreting information from the environment.

We are all aware of our environment, but not everything in it is equally important to our perception of it. We tune in to some data (e.g., a familiar voice off in the distance) and tune out other data (e.g., footsteps and paper shuffling next to us). Individual perceptual awareness varies widely. Recognizing the difference between what is "perceived" and what is "real" is a key element in *diagnosing* a situation.

We can think of perception as a step-by-step process. First, we observe information (sensory data) from the environment through our senses: taste, smell, hearing, sight, and touch. Next, our mind screens the data and will select only the items we will process further. Third, we *organize* the selected data into meaningful patterns for interpretation and response. Most differences in perception among people at work are related to how they select (perceptual selectivity) and organize (perceptual organization) sensory data.

EXHIBIT   A.4

Four Problem-Solving Styles

Personal Style	Action Tendencies	Likely Occupations
Sensation-thinking	■ Emphasizes details, facts, certainty ■ Is decisive, applied thinker ■ Focuses on short-term, realistic goals ■ Develops rules and regulations for judging performance	■ Accounting ■ Production ■ Computer programming ■ Market research ■ Engineering
Intuitive-thinking	■ Shows concern for current, real-life human problems ■ Is creative, progressive, perceptive thinker ■ Emphasizes detailed facts about people rather than tasks ■ Focuses on structuring organizations for the benefit of people	■ Systems design ■ Systems analysis ■ Law ■ Middle/Top management ■ Teaching business, economics
Sensation-feeling	■ Prefers dealing with theoretical or technical problems ■ Is pragmatic, analytical, methodical, and conscientious ■ Focuses on possibilities using interpersonal analysis ■ Is able to consider a number of options and problems simultaneously	■ Directing supervisor ■ Counseling ■ Negotiating ■ Selling ■ Interviewing
Intuitive-feeling	■ Avoids specifics ■ Is charismatic, participative, people oriented, and helpful ■ Focuses on general views, broad themes and feelings ■ Decentralizes decision making, develops few rules and regulations	■ Public relations ■ Advertising ■ Personnel ■ Politics ■ Customer services

PERCEPTUAL SELECTIVITY

Imagine standing on a busy street corner with cars honking, signs flashing, traffic lights changing, and a bus whizzing by just as a dog bites the cuff of your pants. Is it any wonder you never noticed the person tugging on your sleeve asking for directions? We are bombarded by so much sensory data that we cannot process it all. Our solution is to run the data through a perceptual filter that retains some parts (selective attention) and eliminates other parts.

Perceptual selectivity is defined as the screening and selecting of sensory data (objects and stimuli) that compete for one's attention. Exactly what we screen and select depends on a number of factors, some of which relate to the sensory data being perceived and some of which relate to the perceiver. Certain characteristics of the sensory data or of the object being perceived can enhance the chance it will be selected. Relevant characteristics of the object being perceived include *contrast, novelty, familiarity, intensity, motion, repetition,* and *size.* Descriptions of these characteristics are summarized in Exhibit A.5.

An organizational example of the influence of data characteristics on the perceptual process comes from an employment interview. Interviewers often compare a job applicant to other applicants interviewed for the same job instead of against a predetermined standard. Based on the characteristic of *contrast,* an applicant might be scored too low if preceded by an outstanding applicant, or too high if preceded by a poor

Contrast	The extent to which an object stands out against other objects in the background	**E X H I B I T A . 5**
Novelty	The extent to which an object is new or different from objects perceived previously	Perceptual Selectivity: Characteristics of the Perceived Object that Enhance Selection
Familiarity	The extent to which an object is known or familiar to the perceiver	
Intensity	The extent to which an object is more intense (e.g., brighter, louder) than objects surrounding it	
Motion	The extent of movement of the object	
Repetition	The number of times an object is repeated	
Size	The larger the size of the object	

applicant. This is also an example of a perceptual error that can occur without awareness by the perceiver.

Several characteristics of the perceiver can also influence the selection of sensory data. These include *needs* and *motivation, values* and *beliefs, personality, learning,* and *primacy* and *recency.* Descriptions of the perceiver's characteristics are contained in Exhibit A.6.

One example of the influence a perceiver's characteristics can have on perception relates to "first impressions." Most of us try to look our best when we are meeting someone for the first time, whether in an interview, at a meeting or on a blind date. We have been told repeatedly (often by our parents) that first impressions really count. In fact, studies support that conclusion. The *primacy* characteristic can cause us to form impressions quickly that are rather hard to change. Unfortunately, this could lead to a perceptual error. We also tend to be more attentive at the beginning and at the end of an activity, a tendency that is a common problem during job interviews. What you say to an interviewer during the middle of the interview may not be retained as well or carry as much weight as what you say at the beginning or the end.

From these examples, we should recognize that *perceptual selectivity* is not a simple process of reducing data down to an amount that is easy to perceive. It is a complex filtering process that determines which sensory data will receive our attention. Characteristics of the object and of ourselves are clues about why we "see" things differently from those around us.

Needs and motivation	People notice sensory data that will potentially satisfy their important needs.	**E X H I B I T A . 6**
Values and beliefs	People filter out sensory data that are inconsistent with their values and beliefs.	Perceptual Selectivity: Characteristics of the Perceiver that Influence Selection
Personality	Personality traits (e.g., Machiavellianism or Locus of Control) cause people to filter out or actively select sensory data based on their orientation.	
Learning	People notice sensory data based on their past experience with the same or similar data.	
Primacy and recency	People notice sensory data that occur toward the beginning of an event and toward the end of the event.	

PERCEPTUAL ORGANIZATION

Once people have selected the sensory data to be perceived, they begin grouping the data into recognizable patterns. *Perceptual organization* is the categorization of sensory data (stimuli or objects) according to our personal frame of reference. We have learned to simplify and make sense out of our perceptions through a gradual process of organizing sensory data as we experience life.

> For example, all of us have a mental picture of an object with the following properties: wood, four legs, a seat, a back, and an arm rest. This is our image of a chair. When we see an object that has all these properties, we recognize it as a chair. We have organized the incoming formation into a meaningful whole.[15]

Several factors in perceptual organization contribute to individual differences among people in the work setting.

Perceptual grouping is the organizing of sensory data into patterns by using mechanisms such as closure, continuity, proximity, and similarity.

Closure is the tendency to perceive incomplete data in its whole, complete form. What do you see in part (a) of Exhibit A.7? Most people see this series of spots as a dog, but others see 20 unrelated ink blobs.

Continuity is the tendency to perceive sensory data in continuous patterns, even if they are not. Read aloud the message in part (b) of Exhibit A.7. Do you see any discontinuity in the sentence? Read it again carefully. *The* appears at the end of the first line and is repeated at the beginning of the second line. Many people read this as a continuous sentence with only one *the*.

Proximity is the tendency to perceive sensory data as related because of close physical location. For example, people working on the same floor of a large office building may be perceived as a unit even though they represent portions of several departments of the company.

Similarity is the tendency to perceive sensory data as a common group because they are alike in some way. Similarity is valued at some private schools; thus, all students wear uniforms. The similarity provided by uniforms also diminishes attention to other differences among students. As another example, read the sentence below carefully.

> Finished files are the re-
> sult of years of scientif-
> ic study combined with the
> experience of many years.

Read the sentence several times *before reading any farther.*

Now, go back and count the number of times the letter *F* appears in the sentence.

How many did you count? Three? Six? Most people count only three the first time. If you counted three, go back and try again. The correct answer is six. The most common error is to overlook the word *of* because it has a *v* sound, not a *f* sound. Only the *f* sounds fall into a similar group for most people, hence a perceptual mistake is made because the *F*s with a *v* sound are not recognized.

(a)

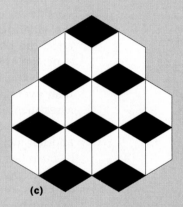

(c)

(b)
Read this sentence out loud.

A BIRD IN THE
THE HAND IS WORTHLESS.

Figure-ground is a second factor in perceptual organization. *Figure-ground* is the tendency to perceive the sensory data you are most attentive to as standing out against the background of sensory data to which you are less attentive. Look at part (c) of Exhibit A.7. How many blocks do you see, six or seven? Some people have to turn the figure upside down before they can see seven blocks. Although this is just a reversible figure-ground pattern, it shows us that once we have "seen" something one way, it is difficult for us to "see" it differently. Exhibit 16.2 in the text (page 554) shows another figure-ground pattern. What do you see first, a young girl or an old hag? What does that tell you about the sensory data you are most attentive to?

Perceptual distortions are errors in our perceptual judgment. Errors can arise from inaccuracies in any part of the perception process. Some types of errors are so common that managers should become familiar with them.

Stereotyping is the tendency to assign an individual to a group or broad category (e.g., female, black, elderly or male, white, disabled) and then to attribute widely held generalizations about the group to the individual (e.g., "females are emotional" or "males are stubborn"). Stereotyping clouds individual differences, and inappropriate stereotyping based on race, ethnicity, gender, and age contributes to hidden barriers limiting the advancement of individuals who are members of those categories.

Halo effect occurs when the perceiver develops an overall impression of a person or situation based on one attribute, either favorable or unfavorable. In other words, a halo blinds the perceiver to other attributes that should be used in generating a more complete assessment. The halo effect can play a significant role in performance appraisal. For example, a person with an outstanding attendance record may be assessed as responsible, industrious, and highly productive; another person with less than average attendance may be assessed as a poor performer. Either assessment may be true, but it is the manager's job to be sure the assessment is based on complete information about all job-related attributes and not just his or her preferences for good attendance.

Projection is the tendency of perceivers to see their own personal traits in other people; that is, they project their own needs, feelings, values, attitudes into their judgment of others. For example, a manager who is achievement oriented may assume that her subordinates are as well. This may cause her to restructure jobs in her department to be less routine and more challenging. However, subordinates might have been quite satisfied with the jobs that the manager saw as routine. Self-awareness and empathy are the best guards against errors based on projection.

Perceptual defense is the tendency of perceivers to protect themselves against ideas, objects, or people that are threatening. People perceive things that are satisfying and pleasant but tend to disregard things that are disturbing and unpleasant. In essence, people develop blind spots in the perceptual process so that negative sensory data do not hurt them. For example, a manager who suppressed the memory of his own sexual abuse as a child may avoid listening to and may not be sympathetic to a story of abuse to others. Recognizing these perceptual blind spots will help people develop a clearer picture of reality.

The point was made at the start of this section on perception that effective *diagnosing* in a situation was predicated on recognizing the difference between what is "perceived" and what is "real." If you have increased your knowledge and understanding of the perceptual process, you will have improved your ability to recognize reality.

● LEARNING[16]

Years of schooling have conditioned many students to think that learning is rather passive. Good teachers tell us what we need to know. Learning is the process of acquiring and remembering abstract ideas and concepts. Textbooks are important. And learning is an activity separate from the real world—after all, it takes place in a classroom. With this view, in the managerial world of time deadlines and concrete action, learning seems remote, even irrelevant. However, today's successful managers need specific knowledge and skills as well as the ability to adapt to changes in the world around them. Managers have to learn.

Learning is a change in behavior or performance that occurs as the result of one's experience. Learning is a person's way of adapting to events in the outside world. It is also linked to perception because learning depends on the ability to perceive sensory data. Think about what you read in the previous section concerning perception. If two individuals experience the same action, for example, they are transferred to a department in a foreign country, are they likely to adapt their behaviors (that is, learn) to the experience in the same way? Probably not. Let's take a closer look at the learning process and how individuals differ in this activity.

One model of the learning process is shown in Exhibit A.8.[17] In this model learning is conceived as a four-stage cycle. A concrete experience we encounter is followed by thinking and reflective observation, which lead to abstract conceptualizations, and in turn to active experimentation, which in turn leads to new experiences as the cycle repeats.

The arrows in this model are meant to imply that the learning cycle is continuously recurring. We continuously test our conceptualizations and adapt them as a result of our personal reflections and observations about the experience.

For example, while working on a term paper you might see (concrete experience) the need for a textbook used two years ago that provides a conceptual definition you cannot recall. After thinking (reflective observation) for a moment, you remember putting it on your bedroom shelf (abstract conceptualization), and you go there to find it (active experimentation). It is not there (concrete experience). You start the process

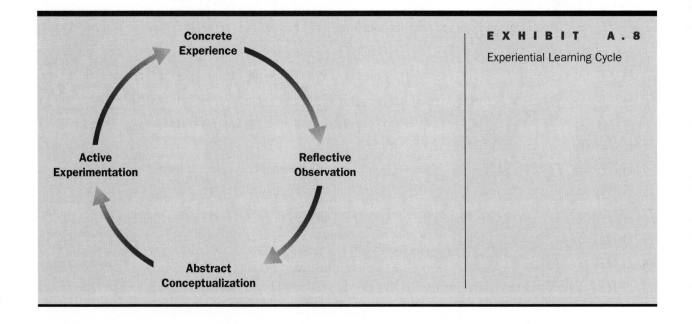

EXHIBIT A.8

Experiential Learning Cycle

again, this time looking in the garage. Success. You learned where the book was and found the definition.

Although this example is simple, the learning model in Exhibit A.8 is important because each of us develops a personal learning style that may place much more emphasis on one or two of the stages, while skipping the other stages in the cycle. These differences occur because the learning process is directed by our individual needs and goals. For example, an engineer may place greater emphasis on abstract concepts while a salesperson may place greater emphasis on concrete experiences. Per-

---

EXHIBIT   A.9

Learning Style Inventory (LSI)

Instructions

There are nine sets of four words listed below. Rank-order the words in each set by assigning a *4* to the word that best characterizes your learning style, a *3* to the word that next best characterizes your learning style, a *2* to the next most characteristic word, and a *1* to the word that is least characteristic of you as a learner.

You may find it hard to choose the words that best characterize your learning style. Nevertheless, keep in mind that there are no right or wrong answers—all the choices are equally acceptable. The aim of the inventory is to describe how you learn, not to evaluate your learning ability.

Be sure to assign a different rank number to each of the four words in each set; do not make ties.

1.	____discriminating	____tentative	____involved	____practical
2.	____receptive	____relevant	____analytical	____impartial
3.	____feeling	____watching	____thinking	____doing
4.	____accepting	____risk-taker	____evaluative	____aware
5.	____intuitive	____productive	____logical	____questioning
6.	____abstract	____observing	____concrete	____active
7.	____present-oriented	____reflecting	____future-oriented	____pragmatic
8.	____experience	____observation	____conceptualization	____experimentation
9.	____intense	____reserved	____rational	____responsible

Scoring

The four columns of words above correspond to the four learning style scales: CE, RO, AC, and AE. To compute your scale scores, write your rank numbers in the boxes below only for the designated items. For example, in the third column (AC), you would fill in the rank numbers you have assigned to items 2, 3, 4, 5, 8, and 9. Compute your scale scores by adding the rank numbers for each set of boxes.

Score items:	Score items:	Score items:	Score items:
2 3 4 5 7 8	1 3 6 7 8 9	2 3 4 5 8 9	1 3 6 7 8 9
☐☐☐☐☐☐	☐☐☐☐☐☐	☐☐☐☐☐☐	☐☐☐☐☐☐
CE = _____	RO = _____	AC = _____	AE = _____

To compute the two combination scores, subtract CE from AC and subtract RO from AE. Preserve negative signs if they appear.

$$\begin{array}{cc} \text{AC} & \text{CE} \\ \text{AC–CE:}\ \square - \square = \end{array} \qquad \begin{array}{cc} \text{AE} & \text{RO} \\ \text{AE–RO:}\ \square - \square = \end{array}$$

SOURCE: D. A. Kolb, I. M. Rubin, and J. M. McIntyre, *Organizational Psychology: An Experiential Approach*, 3rd ed. (Englewood Cliffs, N. J.: Prentice-Hall), 1984.

sonal learning styles typically have strong and weak points because of these preferences.

The Learning Style Inventory (LSI) is a self-description test based on the learning model in Exhibit A.8. It is designed to assess a person's strong and weak points as a learner in the learning cycle by measuring the relative emphasis on each of the four learning stages. In the LSI the learning stages are called "learning modes." The four modes are concrete experience (CE), reflective observation (RO), abstract conceptualization (AC), and active experimentation (AE).

Before you read further, complete the Learning Style Inventory in Exhibit A.9. There are no "right" and "wrong" answers; just follow the instructions and think about the way you learn or the way you deal with day-to-day situations in your life as you read the four word sets in the questionnaire.

You can get an indication of the learning modes you tend to emphasize by plotting your scores on the "target" graph in Exhibit A.9. This graph gives norms on CE, RO, AC, and AE for approximately 2,000 adults ranging from 18 to 60 years of age. The raw scores for each of the

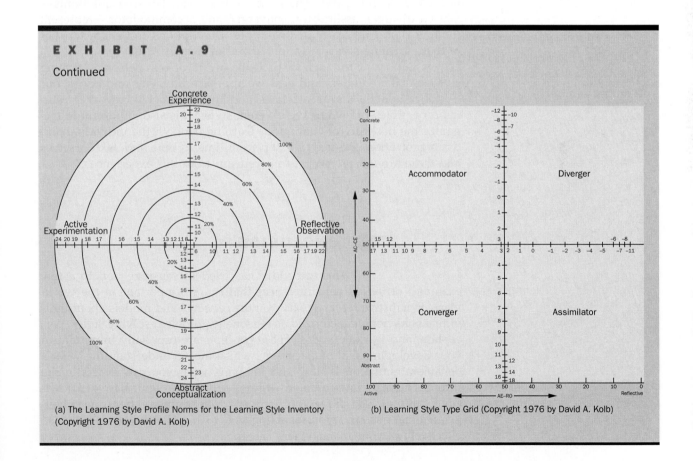

EXHIBIT A.9

Continued

(a) The Learning Style Profile Norms for the Learning Style Inventory (Copyright 1976 by David A. Kolb)

(b) Learning Style Type Grid (Copyright 1976 by David A. Kolb) four scales are listed on the crossed lines of the target. Circle your raw score for each scale and connect the points with straight lines to create a graphic representation of your learning style profile. Percentile scores for the population of respondents are represented by the concentric circles on the target graph.

Which learning modes do you tend to emphasize? Are you surprised? Few of us take the time to think about how we actually prefer to learn. How balanced is your learning style profile? Of concern is a very high score on one mode because that may indicate a tendency to overemphasize that stage of the learning process, or a very low score on one mode because that may indicate a tendency to avoid that aspect of learning. Not many people have totally balanced profiles, which is fine. The key to effective learning is being competent in each of the four modes when it is needed.

Because each person's learning style is a combination of the four learning modes, it is useful to describe your style by a single concept that combines the scores of all four modes. You can determine your learning style type by plotting the two combination scores, AC–CE and AE–RO on the Learning Style Type Grid in Exhibit A.9. By marking your raw scores on the two lines (AC–CE on the vertical and AE–RO on the horizontal) and plotting their points of intersection, you can see which of the four learning style quadrants you fall into. The four quadrants— labeled diverger, assimilator, converger, and accommodator—represent the four dominant learning style types. Descriptions and characteristics of these learning styles are summarized in Exhibit A.10.

It is important for each of us to be aware of our personal learning style so that we understand how we approach problems and issues, our learning strengths and weaknesses, and how we react to coworkers, students or professors who have different styles. It is also important to recognize the necessity of continuous learning for both the individual and the organization. We need to stop from time to time and ask ourselves and those around us, "What can we learn from this experience?"

● CONCLUSION

This appendix has tried to sensitize you to a few examples of individual differences that can be important in the workplace. Exhaustive research exists on the concepts and models about individual behavior characterized as personality, problem-solving styles, perception, and learning styles. These concepts are especially important to your developing skill of *diagnosing,* which means understanding what a behavioral situation is now and knowing what you can expect in the future. The material presented will not only add to your base of knowledge, but may also pique your curiosity to learn more about the behavior of others around you, enabling you to handle "people problems" effectively in your management career.

E X H I B I T   A . 1 0

Learning Style Types

Learning Style Type	Dominant Learning Abilities	Learning Characteristics	Likely Occupations
Converger	■ Abstract conceptualization ■ Active experimentation	■ Is good at decisiveness, practical application of ideas, and hypothetical deductive reasoning ■ Prefers dealing with technical tasks rather than interpersonal issues	■ Engineering ■ Production
Diverger	■ Concrete experience ■ Reflective observation	■ Is good at generating ideas, seeing a situation from multiple perspectives, and being aware of meaning and value ■ Tends to be interested in people, culture, and the arts	■ Human resource management ■ Counseling ■ Organization development specialists
Assimilator	■ Abstract conceptualization ■ Reflective observation	■ Is good at inductive reasoning, creating theoretical models, and combining disparate observations into an integrated explanation ■ Tends to be less concerned with people than ideas and abstract concepts	■ Research ■ Strategic planning
Accommodator	■ Concrete experience ■ Active experimentation	■ Is good at implementing decisions, carrying out plans, and getting involved in new experiences ■ Tends to be at ease with people but may be seen as impatient or pushy	■ Marketing ■ Sales

REFERENCES

1. Paul Hersey and Kenneth Blanchard, *Management of Organizational Behavior: Utilizing Human Resources*, 6th ed., (Engelwood Cliffs, N.J.: Prentice-Hall, 1993), 5–6.

2. See P. E. Spector, "Behavior in Organizations as a Function of Employee's Locus of Control," *Psychological Bulletin* (May 1982), 482–97.

3. Adapted from J. M. Burger, *Personality: Theory and Research* (Belmont, Calif.: Wadsworth, 1986), 400–401, cited in D. Hellriegel, J. W. Slocum, and R. W. Woodman, *Organizational Behavior*, 6th ed. (St. Paul, Minn.: West Publishing, 1992), 97–100.

4. This section is based on a discussion by Hellriegel et al., *Organizational Behavior*, 84.

5. Ibid.

6. Niccolo Machiavelli, *The Prince,* trans. George Bull (Middlesex: Penguin, 1961).

7. Richard Christie and Florence Geis, *Studies in Machiavellianism* (New York: Academic Press, 1970).

8. Ibid., and J. R. Schermerhorn, J. G. Hunt, and R. N. Osborn, *Managing Organizational Behavior*, 4th ed. (New York: John Wiley, 1991), 123.

9. Adapted from Christie and Geis, *Studies in Machiavellianism* cited in Schermerhorn et al., *Managing Organizational Behavior* 453–455.

10. This section is based on discussions by J. R. Schermerhorn, J. G. Hunt, and R. N. Osborn, *Managing Organizational Behavior*, 2nd ed. (New York: John Wiley, 1982), and Hellriegel et al., *Organizational Behavior*, 140–163.

11. Carl Jung, *Psychological Types* (London: Routledge and Kegan Paul, 1923).

12. Adapted from the Myers-Briggs Type Indicator, I. Myers, *The Myers-Briggs Type Indicator* (Princeton, N.J.: Educational Testing Service, 1962), cited in D. Hellriegel, J. W. Slocum and R. W. Woodman, *Organizational Behavior*, 3rd ed. (St. Paul, Minn.: West Publishing, 1983), 128, 143.

13. Adapted from Schermerhorn et al., *Managing Organizational Behavior*, 1982 and 1991.

14. This section is based on discussions by Mel Schnake, *Organizational Behavior Supplement* (Chicago: Dryden Press, 1991), and Hellriegel et al., *Organizational Behavior*, 1992.

15. Hellriegel et al., *Organizational Behavior*, 1992, 110.

16. This section is based on a discussion and exercise by D. A. Kolb, I. M. Rubin, and J. M. McIntyre, *Organizational Psychology: An Experiential Approach*, 3rd ed., (Englewood Cliffs, N.J.: Prentice-Hall, 1984), 27–54.

17. David A. Kolb, "Management and the Learning Process," *California Management Review* 18, no. 3 (Spring 1976), 21–31.

■ LEADERSHIP POTENTIAL

One section of Chapter 14, "Leadership in Organizations," explored the concept of autocratic versus democratic styles of leadership. Autocratic leaders tend to centralize authority, using their legitimate, reward, and coercive power to manage subordinates. Democratic leaders delegate authority to others and encourage participation. They rely on their expertise and the respect and admiration of their subordinates to gain cooperation.

The "Leadership Potential" exercise asks you questions that help you learn whether you gravitate toward an autocratic or democratic style.

THIS EXERCISE WILL HELP YOU

- Become more aware of your biases in leading others.
- Explore alternative ways of leading others.

HOW TO LOCATE THE EXERCISE:

When you see the main menu for Career Design, select "Leading." Then select "Leadership Potential."

■ LEADERSHIP STYLE

In Chapter 14, "Leadership in Organizations," you learned in the sections on the Ohio State studies and the Leadership Grid that leadership style may be measured according to two factors: concern for people and concern for production. Some studies have shown that the best leaders display both a high concern for people and a high concern for production. Other studies indicate that the best leadership style is more situational. It's helpful to know your leadership tendencies in order to determine whether a given situation already matches your "natural" leadership style or requires you to change it.

THIS EXERCISE WILL HELP YOU

- Identify situations where your favored leadership style works best.
- Improve your versatility as a leader by exploring ways to change your current leadership style in different situations.

HOW TO LOCATE THE EXERCISE:

When you see the main menu for Career Design, select "Leading." Then select "Leadership Style."

MANAGEMENT SCIENCE AIDS FOR PLANNING AND DECISION MAKING

B A P P E N D I X

In Chapters 6, 7, and 8 we saw how good managers are distinguished from poor ones by how effectively they set goals, develop plans with which to meet those goals, and make the necessary decisions. This appendix introduces quantitative techniques that can serve as valuable decision aids and planning tools. Management science techniques are especially effective when many factors affect a problem, when problems can be quantified, when relationships among factors can be defined, and when the decision maker can control the key factors affecting performance outcomes.[1] For example, management science techniques are invaluable to American Airlines. Its Decision Technologies unit develops quantitative models to enhance efficiency of the reservations division. The results: $1.4 billion in savings over three years.[2] American likewise schedules more than 8,300 pilots for 16,200 flights through development of TRIP (Trip Re-evaluation and Improvement Program), which is now considered a standard for the industry and is being implemented by other transportation companies.[3]

This appendix describes some of the more common management science techniques that are applicable to managerial planning and decision making. It discusses quantitative approaches to forecasting, breakeven analysis, linear programming, PERT charting, and the decision aids of payoff matrix and decision tree. These techniques are not covered in depth; managers need to understand only the basic approach and be able to communicate with management science experts.

● THE NATURE AND ROLE OF MANAGEMENT SCIENCE

Management science techniques are designed to supplement managerial planning and decision making. For many decisions, management science leads to better answers. For example, in today's organizations, it is not uncommon to find experts who use mathematical and statistical analyses to help managers make capital budgeting decisions; decide whether to open a new factory; predict economic trends or customer demands; determine whether to rent or buy a new computer system; schedule trucks, ships, or aircraft; decide among several proposals for research and development projects; and assess whether a new-product introduction is likely to be profitable.

Management science is defined as a set of quantitatively based decision models used to assist management decision makers. There are three key components in this definition.

First, *management science is a set of quantitative tools.* Mathematically based procedures impart a systematic rigor to the decision process. Certain types of data must be gathered, put into a specific format, and analyzed according to stringent mathematical rules.

Second, *management science uses decision models.* A *model* is a simplified representation of a real-life situation. For example, small-scale physical models were constructed for every set in the movie *Raiders of the Lost Ark* to diagnose filming problems before constructing the real sets. In a mathematical model, key elements are represented by numbers. Mathematical models are difficult for many students and managers because they use a language that is abstract and unfamiliar. However, outcomes from mathematical models can still aid in decision making.

Third, *quantitative models assist decision makers; they cannot substitute for or replace a manager.*[4] Management science models are simply one of many tools in a manager's tool kit. The manager's role is to provide information for use in the models, interpret the information they provide, and carry out the final plan of action.

Sometimes proponents of management science techniques oversell their value for managerial decision making. Conversely, managers who are unfamiliar with mathematics may resist the use of management science techniques and hence fail to take advantage of a powerful tool. The best management approach is to attempt to understand the types of problems to which management science aids apply and then work with specialists to formulate the necessary data and analytical procedures. For example, using models, a severity index was developed to enable physicians to predict survival time for persons diagnosed with AIDS. The index enables hospital administrators to anticipate necessary resources for patients, including beds, and to assess the effectiveness of the care program.[5]

Exhibit B.1 lists some of the more common management problems and applicable management science techniques. These techniques apply to problems in production, product distribution, new-product decisions, and sales force assignment. Scores of management science techniques are available. The remainder of this chapter will describe some of the most

management science

A set of quantitatively based decision models used to assist management decision makers.

Management Problem	Applicable Management Science Tool	EXHIBIT B.1
Production mix	Linear programming	Management Problems and Applicable Management Science Tools
Scheduling and sequencing	PERT network	
Distribution	Simulation	
New-product decisions	Payoff matrix Decision tree	
Pricing decisions	Payoff matrix Decision tree	
Sales force assignment	Assignment models	
Forecasting	Time series Regression analysis Econometric models	

important management science tools and illustrate their use in managerial planning and decision making.

● FORECASTING

Managers look into the future through forecasts. *Forecasts* are predictions about future organizational and environmental circumstances that will influence plans, decisions, and goal attainment. Forecasts are a basic part of the SWOT analysis described in Chapter 7. Virtually every planning decision depends on assumptions about future conditions.

Four types of forecasts are frequently used by managers.

1 **Sales forecasts** predict future company sales. Sales forecasting is critical, because it defines customers' demands for products or services. Sales forecasts determine production levels for three months, six months, or one year into the future. Managers use them to hire necessary personnel, buy needed raw materials, make plans to finance an expansion, and arrange needed transportation services. Medium- and large-size companies such as Sound Warehouse, Paychex, Wallace Computer Services, and Monsanto use sales forecasts to plan production activities.

2 **Technological forecasts** attempt to predict the advent of technological changes, especially major technological breakthroughs that could alter an organization's way of doing business. Companies forecast technological changes to avoid building plants or acquiring equipment that is out of date and noncompetitive. General Motors has been forecasting the use of robotics in automobile manufacturing so as to remain competitive with other American and Japanese automobile producers. Watch manufacturers tracked developments from a company called AT&E Corporation that found a high-tech way to transform a standard wristwatch into a paging device.

sales forecast

A forecast of future company sales based on projected customer demand for products or services.

technological forecast

A forecast of the occurrence of technological changes that could affect an organization's way of doing business.

demographic forecast

A forecast of societal characteristics such as birthrates, educational levels, marriage rates, and diseases.

human resources forecast

A forecast of the organization's future personnel needs.

3 Demographic forecasts pertain to the characteristics of society, including birthrates, educational levels, marriage rates, and diseases. For example, the baby boomlet of the 1980s will permit managers in schools and companies that make children's clothing and toys to plan for increased product demand in the near future.

4 Human resources forecasts predict the organization's future personnel needs.[6] When AT&T predicted a decrease of several thousand employees during the late 1980s, its human resources department arranged for early retirements and helped displaced employees find jobs elsewhere. Likewise, companies in rapidly growing industries must initiate employee recruitment programs and urge the location of new plants in areas where employees are available.

Forecasts provide information that reduces uncertainty in decision making. Several specific techniques, both quantitative and qualitative, help managers derive forecasts for use in their planning and decision making. Exhibit B.2 illustrates some of the forecasting techniques, their possible applications, and their degree of accuracy.

Let us now examine both the quantitative and qualitative techniques more closely.

QUANTITATIVE FORECASTING TECHNIQUES

quantitative forecast

A forecast that begins with a series of past data values and then applies a set of mathematical rules with which to predict future values.

Quantitative forecasts start with a series of past data values and then use a set of mathematical rules with which to predict future values.[7] Quantitative techniques have become widely used by managers for two reasons. First, the techniques have repeatedly demonstrated accuracy, especially in the short and intermediate term, thus earning managers' confidence as a planning aid. Second, improvements in computer hard-

---

EXHIBIT B.2

Forecasting Techniques Used by Organizations

Quantitative Techniques	Sample Application	Accuracy		
		Short Term	**Intermediate Term**	**Long Term**
Time series analysis	Sales, earnings, inventory control	Excellent	Good	Good
Regression analysis	Sales, earnings	Excellent	Excellent	Fair
Econometric models	GNP, sales, demographics, economic shifts	Excellent	Good	Fair
Qualitative Techniques				
Delphi	Product development, technological predictions	Good	Good	Good
Sales force composite	Sales projections, future customer demand	Fair	Fair	Poor
Jury of opinion	Sales, new-product development, earnings	Good	Fair	Poor

SOURCE: Adapted from J. Chambers, S. Mullick, and D. Smith, "How to Choose the Right Forecasting Technique," *Harvard Business Review* (July–August 1971), 55–64.

ware and software have increased the efficiency and decreased the expense of using quantitative techniques. A large number of variables can be incorporated into the analysis, and statistical refinements have improved the techniques' ability to meet the forecasting needs of company managers.

Quantitative forecasting techniques can be subdivided into two categories: time series analysis and causal models. Time series analysis projects past behavior into the future. Causal modeling attempts to unearth past causes of behavior as a way of projecting into the future.[8]

TIME SERIES ANALYSIS. The forecasting technique called **time series analysis** examines the patterns of movement in historical data. It defines patterns in terms of one of four categories.

1 Secular trends   **3** Seasonal variation

2 Cyclic patterns   **4** Random variation

A *secular trend* is the general behavior of a variable over a long period of time. Panel (a) of Exhibit B.3 shows a set of data with an upward trend in unit sales each year. The demand for this company's sales is growing regularly, and managers project sales for 1993 based on this growth.

time series analysis
A forecasting technique that examines the patterns of movement in historical data.

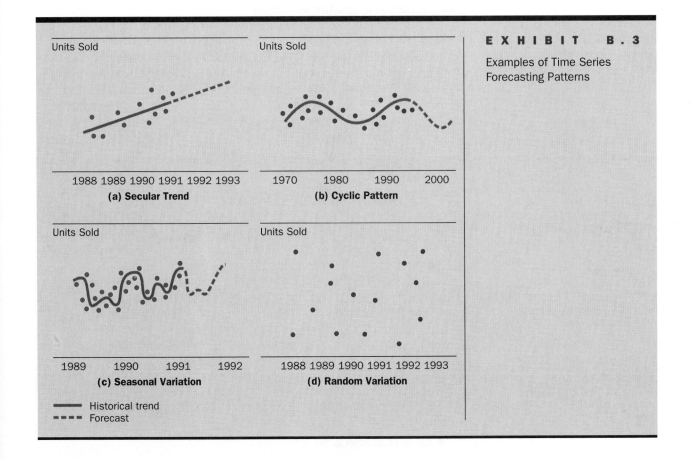

Units Sold

1988 1989 1990 1991 1992 1993
(a) Secular Trend

Units Sold

1970   1980   1990   2000
(b) Cyclic Pattern

Units Sold

1989   1990   1991   1992
(c) Seasonal Variation

Units Sold

1988 1989 1990 1991 1992 1993
(d) Random Variation

─────── Historical trend
- - - - Forecast

E X H I B I T   B . 3

Examples of Time Series
Forecasting Patterns

A *cyclic pattern* involves a recurring up-and-down movement that is periodic in nature. The pattern extends over several years and cannot always be counted on to repeat with precise regularity. Cyclic patterns are related to general business cycles of growth and recession, which managers find extremely valuable to predict. Panel (b) of Exhibit B.3 shows units sold over a typical business cycle of several years.

Seasonal variation is a regular variation in behavior that recurs within a period of one year or less. Climatic changes and social and religious customs can cause seasonal variation. For example, the coordinator for Montreal ambulances found seasonal variance in ambulance use, with higher winter demand for increased emergency use and hospital transfers, but a substantial decrease in the summer.[9]

In another example, bicycle sales normally peak in November and December—prior to Christmas—decline in the winter months, rise in the spring and summer, and decline again in the fall. Panel (c) of Exhibit B.3 shows a seasonal pattern of units sold that would help a manager predict future sales.

Random variation is not a pattern at all. *Random variation* means that there are changes in units sold, but they are unpredictable. These movements might be caused by random factors such as a strike, natural disaster, or changes in government regulations. Panel (d) of Exhibit B.3 shows data that have random variation. Managers are unable to use random variation to predict the future.

Time series analysis is used to predict both short-term and intermediate-term behavior. Its power is its ability to account for seasonal changes as well as long-run trends. Time series analysis works best when the business environment is relatively stable, that is, when the past is a good indicator of the future. In environments in which consumer tastes change radically or random occurrences have a great impact on sales, time series models tend to be inaccurate and of little value.

One company that was able to take advantage of time series forecasting is Huffy Corporation.

 HUFFY CORPORATION

Huffy Corporation is the largest U.S. producer of bicycles. In the early 1980s, Huffy's plants were producing at maximum capacity in several of its product lines. Huffy executives were concerned about whether they should undertake plans to increase future capacity. Because a major corporate goal was 100 percent customer satisfaction, managers realized that an accurate sales forecasting system was important.

The internal accounting and financial group was commissioned to develop a forecasting system with the following characteristics:

1 Be usable by managers responsible for all product lines and divisions.

2 Use data from the current management information system data base.

3 Be cost efficient.

4 Be easily maintained and readily understood by nontechnical managers.

5 Base forecasts on available sales data.

6 Produce forecasts accurate within ±5 percent for divisions, ±10 percent for each product, and ±10 percent for each brand.

After studying many forecasting techniques, Huffy's managers selected a time series model. They found it easy to use because it avoided complex statistics. The final model predicted future sales based on both cyclical and seasonal variation projected from six months of sales history. The time series model was easy to understand and accurate, meeting Huffy's forecasting objective.[10] ■

CAUSAL FORECASTING MODELS.   The forecasting technique called **causal modeling** attempts to predict behavior, called the *dependent variable,* by analyzing its causes, called *independent variables.* Thus, causal modeling may attempt to predict sales (the dependent variable) by examining those factors that cause sales to increase or decrease including amount of advertising expenditure, unit price, competitors' prices, and the overall inflation rate (independent variables). This technique differs from that of simply projecting future sales based on past sales.[11]

When choosing between time series predictions and causal modeling, managers should realize that time series predictions are better at describing seasonal sales variations and predicting changes in sales direction, and causal models provide better information on how to influence a dependent variable such as units sold. Both time series and causal forecasting approaches can produce reliable forecasts if they start with proper data and assumptions. Managers using causal or time series models may wish to work closely with management science experts for maximum benefit.

causal modeling

A forecasting technique that attempts to predict behavior (the dependent variable) by analyzing its causes (independent variables).

QUALITATIVE FORECASTING TECHNIQUES

Qualitative techniques are used when quantitative historical data are unavailable. **Qualitative forecasts** rely on experts' judgment. Three useful forms of qualitative forecasting are the Delphi technique, sales force composite, and jury of opinion.

DELPHI TECHNIQUE.   A process whereby experts come to a consensus about future events without face-to-face discussion is called the **Delphi technique.**[12] The Delphi procedure was described in Chapter 8 as a means of group decision making. It is especially effective for technological forecasts, because precise data for predicting technological breakthroughs are not available. Technological experts fill out a questionnaire about future events, and the responses are summarized and returned to participants. They then complete a new questionnaire based on their own previous responses and the estimates of other experts. The process continues until a consensus is reached. The Delphi technique promotes independent thought and precludes direct confrontations and participants' defensiveness about their ideas. Its biggest advantage is that

qualitative forecast

A forecast based on the opinions of experts in the absence of precise historical data.

Delphi technique

A qualitative forecasting method in which experts reach consensus about future events through a series of continuously refined questionnaires rather than through face-to-face discussion.

sales force composite

A type of qualitative forecasting that relies on the combined expert opinions of field sales personnel.

jury of opinion

A method of qualitative forecasting based on the average opinions of managers from various company divisions and departments.

experts with widely different opinions can share information with one another and reach agreement about future predictions.[13]

SALES FORCE COMPOSITE. Another technique, called the **sales force composite,** relies on the combined expert judgments of field sales personnel. Experienced salespeople know their customers and generally sense fluctuations in customers' needs and buying patterns before these changes are reflected in quantitative data. Salespeople are polled about their customers' expected purchases in the coming time period. Each estimate is reviewed by a district or regional sales manager, who combines these estimates and makes adjustments for expected changes in economic conditions. Findings by Dun and Bradstreet suggest that businesspeople are good forecasters except in times of unexpected or deep recession. During especially bad periods, both managers and salespeople tend to be overly optimistic about the future.[14]

JURY OF OPINION. A third technique is the **jury of opinion,** sometimes called the *jury of executive opinion,* which averages the opinions of managers from various company divisions and departments. It is similar to a Delphi procedure in that jury members need not meet face to face. Because opinions come from several people, the forecast is less risky than it would be if conducted by a single individual. The method is quick and inexpensive and does not require elaborate statistical analysis. It takes advantage of management's knowledge of the environment based on past experience and good judgment. Jury of opinion was used to forecast the 1990s glut of new automobiles. Experts saw that new plants built in the United States by Japanese and American carmakers would lead to overcapacity by 6 million units. Based on this forecast, some companies curtailed expansion plans.[15]

All forecasting is based on historical patterns, and qualitative techniques are used when precise, historical data are unavailable. If managers feel that experts' biases are affecting forecast accuracy, they can correct future forecasts through instructional feedback. As managers or other experts see that their forecasts are too high or too low, they learn to forecast more accurately in future periods.[16]

● QUANTITATIVE APPROACHES TO PLANNING

Once a sales forecast is developed, managers incorporate that information into their planning for the firm's future actions. Many quantitative techniques are available to help managers plan. Three of these techniques tell managers how many units must be sold before a product is profitable (breakeven analysis), which combination of products can minimize costs (linear programming), and how to schedule complex projects to be completed in the shortest amount of time (PERT). The following discussion illustrates how these techniques assist planning in some situations.

BREAKEVEN ANALYSIS

Breakeven analysis is a quantitative technique that helps managers determine the levels of sales at which total revenues equal total costs and, hence, the firm breaks even.[17] Breakeven analysis portrays the relationships among units of output, sales revenue, and costs, as illustrated in Exhibit B.4. This analysis is an important tool for small business and can answer such questions as: What would happen to sales volume and profits if fixed costs rise 10 percent and prices are held constant? What can we do if our competitor cuts prices 10 percent and our sales volume drops 5 percent? What increase in sales volume must be gained to justify a 15 percent increase in the advertising budget? At what point should company operations simply be shut down?[18] These questions can be answered using the following variables of breakeven analysis:

1 *Fixed costs:* Costs that remain the same regardless of the level of production, such as the payment on the building's mortgage. Fixed costs, represented by the horizontal line in Exhibit B.4, remain at $500 whether production is low or high.

2 *Variable costs:* Costs that vary with the number of units produced, such as the cost of raw material. These costs increase as production increases and are the difference between total costs and fixed costs in Exhibit B.4

3 *Total costs:* The sum of fixed and variable costs, illustrated by the diagonal line in Exhibit B.4.

breakeven analysis

A quantitative technique that helps managers determine the level of sales at which total revenues equal total costs.

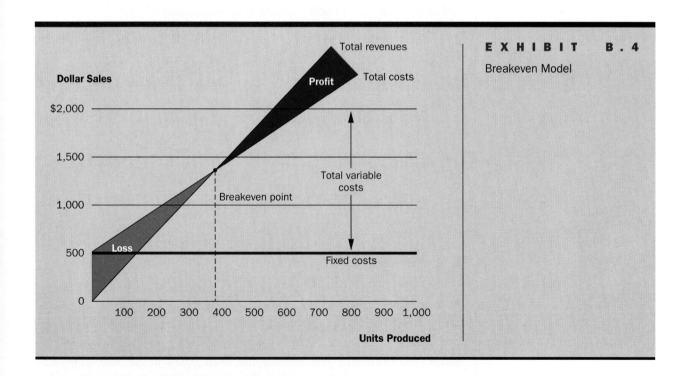

E X H I B I T   B . 4

Breakeven Model

4 *Total revenues:* Total revenue dollars for a given unit of production, as illustrated by the steep diagonal line in Exhibit B.4. Total revenues are calculated as units sold times unit price.

5 *Breakeven point:* The production volume at which total revenues equal total costs, illustrated by the crossover of the two diagonal lines in Exhibit B.4. As the dashed line indicates, the breakeven point in this particular case is about 380 units.

6 *Profit:* The amount by which total revenues exceed total costs. In Exhibit B.4, profit occurs at a production volume greater than the breakeven point.

7 *Loss:* The amount by which total costs exceed total revenues, which occurs at a production volume less than the breakeven point in Exhibit B.4.

The application of these concepts to an organizational situation can be illustrated by the computation of the breakeven point for CCC Bakeries, a small business in California.

 CCC BAKERIES

The cookie wars have gotten hot in Canada and the United States because profits are terrific. Cookie shops are small and normally have one of the highest sales per square foot of any kind of retail shop. Companies such as the Original Great American Chocolate Chip Cookie Company in Atlanta, Mrs. Field's Cookies, which originated in Park City, Utah, David's Cookies in New York City, and the Original Cookie Company in Cleveland are four rapidly expanding cookie chains.[19]

Jan Smith started the Chocolate Chip Cookies Bakeries in northern California. She has two shops and is considering a third in a San Francisco mall. Before opening the shop, she wants to calculate the cost of the operation and the sales volume required for profitability. She has contacted the owners of the San Francisco mall about the cost of rent and equipment rental, and she has a good idea from her other two shops about salary and raw material costs.

Following are her figures:

Fixed costs:	
Rent	$1,000
Salaries:	
Manager	1,000
Part-timers	500
Equipment rental	800
Total fixed costs	$2,300
Variable costs:	
Cookie mixture	$0.25/cookie
Paper bags and tissue	0.01/cookie
Total variable costs	$0.26/cookie
Estimated revenue	$0.53/cookie

Exhibit B.5 shows the breakeven analysis for the proposed cookie store. The horizontal line reflects the fixed costs of $2,300. The total cost line is computed by adding the variable costs to the fixed costs.

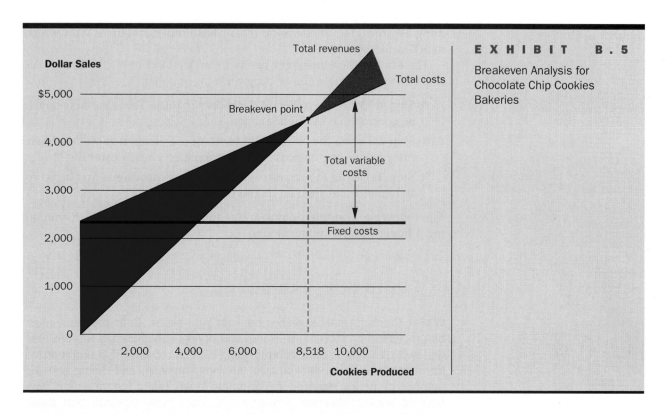

The total revenue line reflects the $0.53 income per cookie. The analysis shows that Jan must sell 8,518 cookies to break even. At this point, Jan's revenue and costs both will be approximately $4,515. If Jan can sell 10,000 cookies a month, she will make a profit of $400. The cookie business has high fixed costs relative to variable costs. Exhibit B.5 shows that once the breakeven point is reached, profits will increase rapidly. High profits can be earned as volume increases to a high level. ■

LINEAR PROGRAMMING

Linear programming applies to such planning problems as allocating resources across competing demands or mixing things together efficiently. Farmers want to blend the cheapest feeds to provide enough nutrition to fatten chickens. Oil companies must decide whether to make more jet fuel or heating oil at a refinery, depending on the costs of crude oil and market prices. Airlines must decide what mix of planes to put on routes, depending on fuel costs and passenger loads. Manufacturing managers must decide whether their profits can be maximized by producing more of product A and less of product B, or vice versa. Linear programming is a technique for solving these kinds of problems.[20] For example, linear programming was used to model the planning and management of New Zealand forest, including the amounts and types of trees to harvest, trees to replace, and estimated cash flow.[21]

Linear programming is a mathematical technique that allocates resources to optimize a predefined objective. Moreover, linear program-

linear programming

A quantitative technique that allocates resources to optimize a predefined organizational objective.

ming assumes that the decision maker has limited resources with which to attain the objective.

The nontechnical manager needs to understand only the three basic steps in formulating a linear programming problem:

- **Step 1:** Define the relevant decision variables. These variables must be controllable by the manager.
- **Step 2:** Define the objective in terms of the decision variables. There can be only one objective; thus, it must be chosen carefully.
- **Step 3:** Define the resource restrictions or constraints *first* as word statements and then as mathematical statements.

The following example demonstrates the three steps used in formulating a linear programming model.

 WICKER CLASSICS

Wicker Classics makes wicker baskets and seats. Both products must be processed by soaking, weaving, and drying. A basket has a profit margin of $3.25 and a seat a profit margin of $5. Exhibit B.6 summarizes the number of hours available for soaking, weaving, and drying and the number of hours required to complete each task. The question confronting Wicker Classics' managers is: How many baskets and seats should Wicker make per day to maximize profits?

Step 1 is to define the decision variables. What can Wicker managers control in the production process? Two readily controllable variables are the number of baskets and seats to be produced. Thus, we can let X_1 = Number of baskets to produce and X_2 = Number of seats to produce.

Step 2 is to define an objective function. The objective is clear: Maximize profits. This objective can be described mathematically by using the two decision variables. The profit for each basket is $3.25, or 3.25X_1$. Similarly, the profit for each seat produced is $5, or 5X_2$. Total profits for the firm will be the sum of these two components:

$$\text{Maximize profits} = \$3.25X_1 + \$5.00X_2.$$

Step 3 is to define resource constraints. This is the most difficult step in formulating a linear programming model. Wicker is constrained by three scarce resources, expressed in words as appears on the following page.

EXHIBIT B.6 Resource Requirements for Wicker Classics		Soaking Time (Hours)	Weaving Time (Hours)	Drying Time (Hours)	Profit
	Per basket	0.2	0.4	0.3	$3.25
	Per seat	0.4	0.4	0.8	5.00
	Available hours	60.0	90.0	108.0	

1 Soaking time cannot exceed 60 hours.

2 Weaving time cannot exceed 90 hours.

3 Drying time cannot exceed 108 hours.

These constraints enable us to state in mathematical terms that total soaking time must be less than or equal to 60 hours. Every basket takes 0.2 hours of soaking time and every seat 0.4 hours. The total production of baskets and seats cannot exceed 60 hours; therefore, our mathematical statement can be

$$0.2X_1 + 0.4X_2 \leq 60.$$

The remaining constraints can be described in similar fashion. Weaving time cannot exceed 90 hours, which is expressed as

$$0.4X_1 + 0.4X_2 \leq 90.$$

Drying time cannot exceed 108 hours, which is expressed mathematically as

$$0.3X_1 + 0.8X_2 \leq 108.$$

A final constraint for keeping the mathematical calculations in the correct range is that neither seats nor baskets can be produced in a volume of less than zero. This is expressed mathematically as

$$X_1 \geq 0$$
$$X_2 \geq 0.$$

The completed problem formulation looks like this:

- Maximize profits $= 3.25X_1 + 5X_2$
- Subject to
  Soaking time: $0.2X_1 + 0.4X_2 \leq 60$
  Weaving time: $0.4X_1 + 0.4X_2 \leq 90$
  Drying time: $0.3X_1 + 0.8X_2 \leq 108$
  Nonnegativity: $X_1 \geq 0, X_2 \geq 0$

Exhibit B.7 graphs the constraints for Wicker Classics. Each constraint defines a boundary called the *feasibility region,* which is that region bounded by a resource restriction. The optimal solution for maximizing profits is found at the intersection of two or more constraints at the edge of the feasibility region. Those intersections are at point A, B, C, or D.

Management science specialists use computers and sophisticated software to solve linear programming problems. For a simple problem such as Wicker Classics, the solution can be defined on the graph in Exhibit B.7. Profit maximization is formally defined as the point (A, B, C, or D) that lies farthest from the origin (O) and through which a line can be drawn that has only one point in common with the feasibility region. In Exhibit B.7 this is point C, because it is farthest from the origin and the green line drawn through point C touches the feasibility region at only one point. Thus, the production mix to maximize profits is 125 baskets and 85 seats.[22] ■

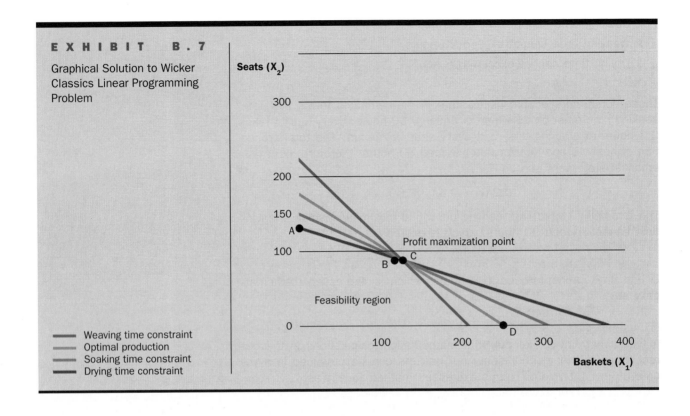

EXHIBIT   B.7

Graphical Solution to Wicker
Classics Linear Programming
Problem

Weaving time constraint
Optimal production
Soaking time constraint
Drying time constraint

PERSONAL COMPUTERS.   Linear programming may seem complicated, but it has many applications in small business. With the advent of personal computers and new software such as *"What's Best!"* small businesses can use this powerful tool for planning and decision making. A user simply sets up the information on costs and other constraints on the *Lotus 1-2-3* spreadsheet, and the computer will calculate what should be optimized. The cost for software is inexpensive, ranging from $200 to $1,000 depending on complexity. Hawley Fuel Corporation, for example, uses a personal computer to make the cheapest blend of coal that meets utility customers' demands for a particular sulfur content, ash content, and heating value. Even small-business managers who do not understand the underlying mathematics can use PCs and linear programming software for decision making.[23]

PERT

Organizations often confront a situation in which they have a large project to complete for which a complicated, single-use plan is developed. A large project may consist of many interrelated activities. In 1958, the U.S. Navy was confronted with the enormous task of coordinating thousands of contractors to build the Polaris nuclear submarine. The Program Evaluation and Review Technique (PERT) was developed to manage the building of submarines.

PERT allows managers to decompose a project into specific activities and to plan far in advance when it is to be completed. PERT can pinpoint bottlenecks and indicate whether resources should be reallocated. It also provides a map of the project and allows managers to control its execution by determining whether activities are completed on time and in the correct sequence.

There are four basic steps required in the use of PERT:

1 Identify all major activities (tasks) to be performed in the project.

2 Determine the sequence in which the tasks must be completed and whether tasks can be performed simultaneously.

3 Determine the amount of time required to complete each task.

4 Draw a PERT network for controlling the project.

A PERT network is a graphical representation of a large project. *Activities* are the tasks that must be completed in order to finish the project. Each activity must have a discrete beginning and ending. Activities are illustrated as solid lines on a PERT network. *Events* represent the beginning and ending of specific activities. Events are represented on the PERT network as circled numbers. *Paths* are strings of activities and events on a network diagram. Project managers determine the sequence of activities that must be performed in order to complete the entire project. A *critical activity* is one that if delayed will cause a slowdown in the entire project. The path with the longest total time is called the **critical path** and represents the total time required for the project.[24]

The application of PERT can best be seen through an illustration.

PERT

The Program Evaluation and Review Technique; consists of breaking down a project into a network of specific activities and mapping out their sequence and necessary completion dates.

critical path

The path with the longest total time; represents the total time required for the project.

 CAREER RESOURCES, INC.

Career Resources, Inc., is a consulting firm that provides training seminars for companies all around the country. Planning these seminars can be a difficult project, because each company's requirements are different and a number of factors must be brought together in a timely fashion. Doug Black is director of Executive Training Programs, and he decided to develop a PERT network for the next training seminar. He began by listing all activities to be completed and determined whether each had to be done before or after other activities, as illustrated in Exhibit B.8.

Doug's next step was to determine the length of time required for each activity. To do this, he and two other managers decided on an optimistic, most likely, and pessimistic estimate of how long each activity would take. The optimistic time indicates how quickly the activity will be completed if there are no problems or obstacles. The pessimistic time indicates the amount of time required if everything goes wrong. The most likely time is the estimate assuming that only a few routine problems will occur.

The expected time is a weighted average of the three estimates. The most likely time is weighted by four. The estimated time is calculated as shown in the formula on the following page.

$$\text{Estimated time} = \frac{\text{Optimistic} + (4)\text{ Most likely} + \text{Pessimistic}}{6}$$

The expected time for completing each activity is shown in the right-hand column of Exhibit B.8.

Based on the information listed in Exhibit B.8, Doug drew the PERT network illustrated in Exhibit B.9. This network shows when activities must be completed in order to move on to the next activity. The critical path is the longest path through the network, which for Doug's project is A-B-G-H-I-J. Thus, the project is expected to take 4 + 6 + 5 + 3 + 8 + 4 = 30 weeks to complete. ∎

PERSONAL COMPUTERS. Doug Black of Career Resources, Inc., drew the PERT chart by hand, but microcomputers have made PERT charting much easier. More than two dozen project-planning software packages are now on the market. These packages provide an easy method of charting and following any kind of task. For example, Rick Gehrig, production coordinator at Westuff Tool & Die, St. Louis, can coordinate 80 different projects at once, printing out charts and schedules for each one, on his IBM PC. He even links the projects together in one big schedule to show resource needs for the whole plant. Nuvatec, Inc., located in Downers Grove, Illinois, manages 50 consulting projects with a microcomputer. The tasks and times required for each step in a consulting project are plugged into the computer, which provides a nice method for reporting the status of consulting projects to customers as well as forestalling unpleasant surprises.[25]

EXHIBIT B.8

Activities Required for Designing a Training Program

Activity	Description	Immediate Predecessor(s)	Optimistic	Most Likely	Pessimistic	Expected
				Estimated Time (Weeks)		
A	Determine topic	—	3.0	4.0	5.0	4.0
B	Locate speakers	A	4.0	5.0	12.0	6.0
C	Find potential meeting sites	—	2.0	4.0	6.0	4.0
D	Select location	C	3.0	4.0	5.0	4.0
E	Arrange speaker travel plans	B, D	1.0	2.0	3.0	2.0
F	Finalize speaker plans	E	2.0	4.0	6.0	4.0
G	Prepare announcements	B, D	2.0	4.0	12.0	5.0
H	Distribute announcements	G	2.0	3.0	4.0	3.0
I	Take reservations	H	6.0	8.0	10.0	8.0
J	Attend to last-minute details	F, I	3.0	4.0	5.0	4.0

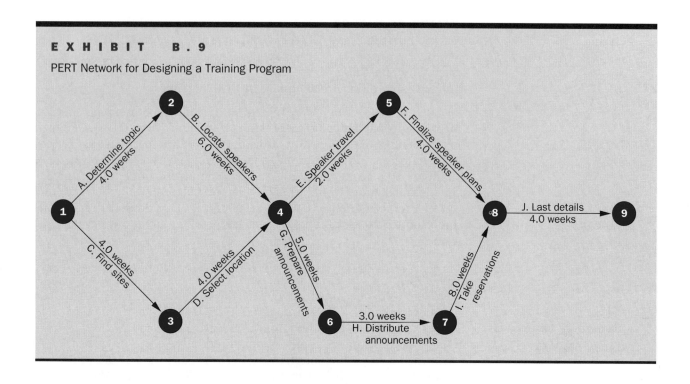

EXHIBIT B.9

PERT Network for Designing a Training Program

QUANTITATIVE APPROACHES TO DECISION MAKING

Now we turn to quantitative techniques that help managers make choices under conditions of risk and uncertainty. Recall from Chapter 8 that managerial decision making follows six steps: problem definition, diagnosis, development of alternatives, selection of an alternative, implementation, and evaluation/feedback. Decision aids focus on the fourth step—selecting an alternative. First we will examine two quantitative decision approaches: the payoff matrix and the decision tree. Then we will discuss simulation models, an extension of the two decision approaches.

PAYOFF MATRIX

To use the **payoff matrix** as an aid to decision making, a manager must be able to define four variables.

STRATEGIES. *Strategies* are the decision alternatives. There can be two strategies or ten, depending on the number of alternatives available. For example, a manager wanting to open a new store might consider four different locations, or a university considering an expansion of its football stadium might consider three expansion alternatives of 8,000, 15,000, and 20,000 seats.

payoff matrix

A decision-making aid comprising relevant strategies, states of nature, probability of occurrence of states of nature, and expected outcome(s).

state of nature

A future event or condition that is relevant to a decision outcome.

expected value

The weighted average of each possible outcome for a decision alternative.

STATES OF NATURE.   Future events or conditions that are relevant to decision outcomes are called **states of nature.** For example, the states of nature for a new store location could be the anticipated sales volume at each site, and those for expanding the football stadium could be the number of additional paying fans at football games.

PROBABILITY.   *Probability* represents the likelihood, expressed as a percentage, that a given state of nature will occur. Thus, the store owner may calculate the probability of making a profit in location 1 as 20 percent, in location 2 as 30 percent, and in location 3 as 50 percent. A probability of 50 percent would be listed in the payoff matrix as 0.5. University administrators would estimate the probability of filling the stadium under each condition of 8,000, 15,000, and 20,000 additional seats. The probabilities associated with the states of nature must add up to 100 percent.

OUTCOME.   The outcome is the payoff calculated for each strategy given the probabilities associated with each state of nature. The outcome is called the **expected value,** which is the weighted average of each possible outcome for a decision alternative. For example, the store owner could calculate the expected profit from each store location, and the university administrators could calculate the expected returns associated with each construction alternative of 8,000, 15,000, and 20,000 seats.

To illustrate the payoff matrix in action, let us consider the problem facing Sanders Industries' managers, who are trying to decide how to finance the construction of a new plant and its equipment.

 SANDERS INDUSTRIES

The senior managers at Sanders Industries wish to raise funds to finance the construction and new machinery for a new plant to be located in Alberta, Canada. They have determined that they have three alternative funding sources: to issue common stock, bonds, or preferred stock. The desired decision outcome is the net dollars that can be raised through each financing vehicle. The state of nature that affects the decision is the interest rate at the time the securities are issued, because interest rates influence the firm's ability to attract investment dollars. If interest rates are high, investors prefer bonds; if interest rates are low, they prefer stocks. Sanders' financial experts have advised that if interest rates are high, a common stock issue will bring $1 million, bonds $5 million, and preferred stock $3 million. If interest rates are moderate, common stocks will yield $3.5 million, bonds $3.5 million, preferred stock $3 million. If interest rates are low, common stock will return $7.5 million, bonds $2.5 million, and preferred stock $4 million. The financial experts also have estimated the likelihood of low interest rates at 10 percent, of moderate interest rates at 40 percent, and of high interest rates at 50 percent.

Sanders' senior managers want to use a logical structure to make this decision, and the payoff matrix is appropriate. The three decision alternatives of stock, bonds, and preferred stock are shown in Exhibit B.10.

Strategy (Decision Alternative)	Event (Interest Rate Level/ State of Nature)		
	Low (0.1)	Moderate (0.4)	High (0.5)
Common stock	$7,500,000	$3,500,000	$1,000,000
Bonds	2,500,000	3,500,000	5,000,000
Preferred Stock	4,000,000	3,000,000	3,000,000

EXHIBIT B.10

Payoff Matrix for Sanders Industries

The three states of nature—low, moderate, and high interest rates—are listed across the top of the exhibit. The listing of strategy on one side and of states of nature on the other side composes the payoff matrix. The probability associated with each interest rate is also included in the exhibit.

The decision outcome as defined by the managers is to gain the highest expected monetary value from issuing a security. Thus, the managers must calculate the expected monetary return associated with each decision alternative. The calculation of expected value for each decision alternative is performed by multiplying each dollar amount by the probability of occurrence. For the figures in Exhibit B.10, the expected value of each strategy is calculated as follows:

$$\text{Expected value of common stock} = (0.1)(7.5 \text{ million})$$
$$+ (0.4)(3.5 \text{ million})$$
$$+ (0.5)(1 \text{ million})$$
$$= \$2,650,000$$

$$\text{Expected value of bonds} = (0.1)(2.5 \text{ million})$$
$$+ (0.4)(3.5 \text{ million})$$
$$+ (0.5)(5 \text{ million})$$
$$\$4,150,000$$

$$\text{Expected value of preferred stock} = (0.1)(4 \text{ million})$$
$$+ (0.4)(3 \text{ million})$$
$$+ (0.5)(3 \text{ million})$$
$$= \$3,100,000$$

From this analysis, the best decision clearly is to issue bonds, which have an expected value of $4,150,000. Although managers cannot be certain about which state of nature will actually occur, the expected value calculation weights each possibility and indicates the choice with the highest likelihood of success. ■

DECISION TREE

Management problems often require that several decisions be made in sequence. As the outcome of one decision becomes obvious or as additional information becomes available, another decision is required to correct past mistakes or take advantage of new information. For instance, a production manager analyzing the company's product line may decide

decision tree

A decision-making aid used for decision situations that occur in sequence; consists of a pictorial representation of decision alternatives, states of nature, and outcomes of each course of action.

to add a new product on a trial basis. If customers buy the product, the manager must then decide how to increase production to meet demand. Conversely, if the new product fails to generate sufficient demand, the manager must then decide whether to drop the product.

This type of decision is difficult to structure into a payoff matrix because of the decision sequence. **Decision trees** are an alternative to payoff tables for decision situations that occur in sequence. The objective of decision tree analysis is the same as for payoff tables: to select the decision that will provide the greatest return to the company. The decision tree approach requires the following variables:

1 The decision tree, which is a pictorial representation of decision alternatives, states of nature, and the outcomes of each course of action.

2 The estimated probabilities of each outcome occurring.

3 The payoff (profit or loss) associated with each outcome.

4 The expected value, which is calculated based on the probabilities and conditional payoffs along each branch of the decision tree.

The decision tree consists of a series of nodes and connecting lines. A square node, called a *decision fork*, represents the alternative strategies available to the decision maker *at that time*. From a decision fork, the decision maker must choose one branch to follow. A round node, called a *chance fork*, represents states of nature over which the decision maker has no control. For branches emanating from a chance fork, the decision maker cannot choose which path to follow and must wait until after the decision has been made to see which state of nature occurred.

The use of a decision tree for decision making can be illustrated by the risks and uncertainties associated with the decision to use fire in contemporary forest management.

 NATIONAL FOREST SERVICE

Forest management personnel often use fires under controlled conditions to reduce natural fire hazards and enhance the wildlife habitat. However, decision uncertainties are inherent in the use of fire. For example, the decision to commit personnel and equipment to the burn site and to actually initiate the burn must be made before weather conditions and fire behavior can be determined with certainty.

A specific burn has two basic alternatives, as illustrated in Exhibit B.11. Decision fork 1 shows that forest managers can either (1) commit resources to the burn or (2) postpone the burn. Two uncertainties are central to this decision. The first is the actual weather conditions on the day of the burn, illustrated in chance fork A. There is a 50 percent likelihood that the weather will be poor, in which case the burn will have to be canceled. The second results from the decision to carry out the burn: Will the objectives be met, or will the burn be only marginally successful? This decision is illustrated by chance fork B in Exhibit B.11. The experts have estimated a 60 percent probability of a successful burn and a 40 percent probability of a marginal burn in that situation.

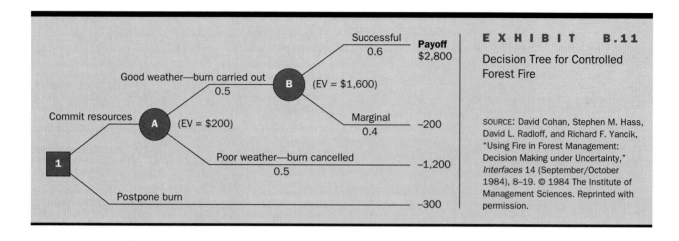

EXHIBIT B.11

Decision Tree for Controlled Forest Fire

SOURCE: David Cohan, Stephen M. Hass, David L. Radloff, and Richard F. Yancik, "Using Fire in Forest Management: Decision Making under Uncertainty," *Interfaces* 14 (September/October 1984), 8–19. © 1984 The Institute of Management Sciences. Reprinted with permission.

Given the uncertainties facing National Forest Service managers, should they decide to commit the resources or postpone the burn to await better information? The payoff value of each outcome is listed on the far right in Exhibit B.11. If everything is successful, the benefit to the forest service will be $2,800. If a marginal burn occurs, there will be a loss of $200. If the burn is canceled after resources have been committed, there will be a loss of $1,200. If the burn is postponed indefinitely, there will be a loss of $300 in management costs.

The way to choose the best decision is through a procedure known as *rollback*. The rollback procedure begins with the end branches and works backward through the tree by assigning a value to each decision fork and chance fork. A fork's value is the expected return from the branches emanating from the fork. Applying the rollback procedure to the data in Exhibit B.11 produces the following outcomes: The expected value (EV) of chance fork B is $(0.6)(2,800) + 0.4(-200) = \$1,600$; the expected value of chance fork A is $(0.5)(1,600) + 0.5(-1,200) = \$200$.

These figures provide the information needed for the decision. If the managers decide to commit resources, there is a positive expected value of $200. If they postpone the burn, there is a certain loss of $300. Thus, it is worthwhile to go ahead with the planned burn despite management's uncertainty about the weather and possible outcomes.[26] ∎

Decision tree analysis is one of the most widely used decision analysis techniques.[27] As with linear programming and PERT charting described earlier, excellent software programs are available. General managers and small-business managers can use decision tree analysis without hiring a staff specialist. This technique can be used for any decision situation in which probabilities can be estimated and decisions occur in sequence, such as those concerning new-product introduction, pricing, plant expansion, advertising campaigns, or even acquiring another firm.

SIMULATION MODELS

Another useful tool for management decision makers is a simulation model. **Simulation models** are mathematical representations of the

simulation model

A mathematical representation of the relationships among variables in real-world organizational situations.

relationships among variables in real-life organizational situations.[28] For example, simulations are popular for the risky business of new-product innovations. For, say, a new bar of soap, managers can feed data into a computer about where the soap will be introduced, how much money will be spent on advertising, and what kind of promotion will be done. Data from past new products are in the computer, providing comparisons. The simulation model can predict the new soap's yearly sales. Simulation would take no more than 90 days and cost around $50,000, compared with a minimum 9 months and $1 million dollars to test a real product. Simulations will not always be accurate, however, especially for highly innovative products that have no historical base, but simulations have become very accurate where firms have compiled new-product case histories.[29]

Simulations have many applications, and because they typically are done by computer, many options can be tried. For example, Monsanto Corporation has one ocean-going chemical tanker, and managers wished to have a model that would help them determine the number of trips per year that would provide the most income. A simulation model provided the answer. The model included nine ports, fuel prices, operating charges for the tanker, voyage time, amount of fuel used, time in port, time steaming, and voyage itinerary. The simulation model gave operating managers an ongoing decision tool. If vessel managers needed to evaluate the impact of taking on an additional load, they simply simulated the current trip using the model. By inserting the data for the additional load and expenses for the extra stop, they could also ask the model if the steaming speed for the voyage could be increased so that the additional stop would not increase total voyage time. They could also calculate the cost increase from making the additional stop and simply charge the additional cost plus a reasonable profit to the customer. Using the simulation model to assist management decisions on scheduling the tanker has saved Monsanto an estimated $20,000 per year.[30]

● STRENGTHS AND LIMITATIONS OF MANAGEMENT SCIENCE AIDS

When selectively applied, management science techniques provide information for improving both planning and decision making. Many businesses have operations research departments in which experts apply management science techniques to organizational problems. And with the use of microcomputers and the many available software programs, management science aids can also be used by small-business managers. Whether using these techniques in small businesses or large businesses, however, managers should be aware of their basic strengths and limitations, which are summarized in Exhibit B.12.

STRENGTHS

The primary strength of management science aids is their ability to enhance decision effectiveness in many situations. For example, time series forecasting helps predict seasonal sales variations. Causal models

Stengths	Limitations	E X H I B I T B.12
■ Enhance decision effectiveness in many situations ■ Provide a framework for handling complex problems ■ Promote rationality ■ Are inexpensive compared with alternatives	■ Do not fit many situations ■ May not reflect reality ■ Require overhead costs ■ Are given too much legitimacy	Strengths and Limitations of Management Science Techniques

help managers understand the reasons for future sales increases or decreases. Decision trees, payoff matrices, and PERT networks are valuable when data can be organized into the framework the model requires.

Another strength of management science techniques is that they provide a systematic way of thinking about and organizing complex problems. Managers may use these models intuitively, perhaps sketching things out to clarify their thinking. Moreover, new software packages ask all the right questions so managers will provide the correct data. The computer helps managers organize their thinking and reach the best decision.

Still another strength is that the models promote management rationality when fully applied. They help managers define a problem, select alternatives, gauge probabilities of alternatives' success, and understand the trade-offs and potential payoffs. Managers need not rely on hunch or intuition to make a complicated, multidimensional decision.

Finally, management science aids are inexpensive compared with alternatives such as organizational experiments. If an organization actually had to build a new plant to learn whether it would increase profits, a failure would be enormously expensive. Management science models provide a way to experiment with the decision without having to build the plant.

LIMITATIONS

The growth of management science has led to some problems. First—and perhaps most important—management science techniques do not yet fit many decision situations. Many management decisions are too ambiguous and subjective. For example, management science techniques have little impact on the poorly structured strategic problems at the top levels of corporations.

A second limitation is that they may not reflect the reality of the organizational situation. The management science model is a simplification, and the outcome can be no better than the numbers and assumptions fed into the model. If these numbers are not good or important variables are left out, the outcome will be unrealistic.

A third limitation is overhead costs. The organization may hire management science specialists and provide computer facilities. If these specialists are not frequently used to help solve real problems, they will add to the organization's overhead costs while providing little return.[31]

Finally, management science techniques can be given too much legitimacy. When managers are trying to make a decision under uncertainty, they may be desperate for a clear and precise answer. A management science model may produce an answer that is taken as fact even though the model is only a simplification of reality and the decision needs the interpretation and judgment of experienced managers.

SUMMARY

This chapter described several important points about management science aids for managerial planning and decision making. Forecasting is the attempt to predict behavior in the future. Forecasting techniques can be either quantitative or qualitative. Quantitative techniques include time series analysis and causal modeling. Qualitative techniques include the Delphi method, sales force composite, and jury of opinion.

Quantitative aids to management planning include breakeven analysis, linear programming, and PERT. Breakeven analysis indicates the volume at which a new product will earn enough revenues to cover costs. Linear programming helps managers decide which product mix will maximize profits or minimize costs. PERT helps managers plan, monitor, and control project progress.

Management science aids to decision choices also were described. The payoff matrix helps managers determine the expected value of various alternatives. The decision tree is a similar procedure that is used for decisions made in sequence. Simulation models use mathematics to evaluate the impact of management decisions. Microcomputers and new software make all of these techniques accessible to managers, but managers should remember that management science aids have limitations as well as strengths.

REFERENCES

1. David R. Anderson, Dennis J. Sweeney, and Thomas A. Williams, *Quantitative Methods for Business,* 4th ed. (St. Paul, Minn.: West, 1989), and H. Watson and P. Marett, "A Survey of Management Science Implementation Problems," *Interfaces* 9 (August 1979), 124–128.

2. Barry C. Smith, John F. Leimkuhler, and Ross M. Darrow, "Yield Management at American Airlines," *Interfaces* (January-February 1992), 8–31.

3. Ranga Anbil, Eric Gelman, Bruce Patty, and Rajan Tanga, "Recent Advances in Crew-Pairing Optimization at American Airlines," *Interfaces* 21 (January-February 1991), 62–74.

4. For further explanation of management science techniques, see B. Render and R. Stair, *Quantitative Analysis for Management,* 2d ed. (Boston: Allyn & Bacon, 1985), and S. Lee, L. Moore, and B. Taylor, *Management Science* (Dubuque, Iowa: W. C. Brown, 1981).

5. Farrokh Alemi, Barbara Turner, Leona Markson, Richard Szorady, and Tom McCarron, "Prognosis after AIDS: A Severity Index Based on Expert's Judgments," *Interfaces* 21 (May-June 1991), 109–116.

6. Thomas H. Stone and Jack Fiorito, "A Perceived Uncertainty Model of Human Resource Forecasting Technique Use," *Academy of Management Review* 11 (1986), 635–642.

7. S. C. Wheelwright and S. Makridakis, *Forecasting Methods for Management* (New York: Wiley, 1973).

8. Ibid.

9. Jean Aubin, "Scheduling Ambulances," *Interfaces* 22 (March-April, 1992), 1–10.

10. Robert F. Reilly, "Developing a Sales Forecasting System," *Managerial Planning* (July-August 1981), 24–30.

11. Dexter Hutchins, "And Now, the Home-Brewed Forecast," *Fortune,* January 20, 1986, 53–54.

12. N. Dalkey, *The Delphi Method: An Experimental Study of Group Opinion* (Santa Monica, Calif.: Rand Corporation, 1969).

13. Bruce Blaylock and L. Reese, "Cognitive Style and the Usefulness of Information," *Decision Sciences* 15 (Winter 1984), 74–91.

14. J. Duncan, "Businessmen Are Good Sales Forecasters," *Dun's Review* (July 1986).

15. Alex Taylor III, "Who's Afraid in the World Auto War," *Fortune,* November 9, 1987, 74–88.

16. M. Moriarty, "Design Features of Forecasting Systems Involving Management Judgments," *Journal of Marketing Research* 22 (November 1985), 353–364, and D. Kahneman, B. Slovic, and A. Tversky, eds., *Judgment under Uncertainty: Heuristics and Biases* (Cambridge, Mass.: Cambridge Press, 1982).

17. M. Anderson and R. Lievano, *Quantitative Management: An Introduction*, 2d ed. (Boston: Kent, 1986).

18. "Break-Even Analysis: Analyzing the Relationship between Costs and Revenues," *Small Business Report* (August 1986), 22–24.

19. Kevin McManus, "The Cookie Wars," *Forbes*, November 7, 1983, 150–152.

20. Anderson and Lievano, *Quantitative Management*; J. Byrd and L. Moore, "The Application of a Product Mix Linear Programming Model in Corporate Policy Making," *Management Science* 24 (September 1978), 1342–1350; and D. Darnell and C. Lofflin, "National Airlines Fuel Management and Allocation Model," *Interfaces* 7 (February 1977), 1–16.

21. Bruce R. Manley and John A. Threadgill, "LP Used for Valuation and Planning of New Zealand Plantation Forests," *Interfaces* 21 (November-December 1991), 66–79.

22. P. Williams, "A Linear Programming Approach to Production Scheduling," *Production and Inventory Management* 11 (3d Quarter 1970), 39–49.

23. William M. Bulkeley, "The Right Mix: New Software Makes the Choice Much Easier," *The Wall Street Journal*, March 27, 1987, 25.

24. W. J. Erikson and O. P. Hall, *Computer Models for Management Science* (Reading, Mass.: Addison-Wesley, 1986).

25. Nancy Madlin, "Streamlining the PERT Chart," *Management Review* (September 1986), 67–68.

26. David Cohan, Stephen M. Haas, David L. Radloff, and Richard F. Yancik, "Using Fire in Forest Management: Decision Making under Uncertainty," *Interfaces* 14 (September-October 1984), 8–19.

27. J. W. Ulvila and R. V. Brown, "Decision Analysis Comes of Age," *Harvard Business Review* (September-October 1982), 130–141.

28. Render and Stair, *Quantitative Analysis for Management*.

29. Toni Mack, "Let the Computer Do It," *Forbes*, August 10, 1987, 94.

30. Raymond F. Boykin and Reuven R. Levary, "An Interactive Decision Support System for Analyzing Ship Voyage Alternatives," *Interfaces* 15 (March-April 1985), 81–84.

31. T. Naylor and H. Schauland, "A Survey of Users of Corporate Planning Models," *Management Science* 22 (1976), 927–937.

accommodative response A response to social demands in which the organization accepts—often under pressure—social responsibility for its actions to comply with the public interest.

accountability The fact that the people with authority and responsibility are subject to reporting and justifying task outcomes to those about them in the chain of command.

activity ratio A ratio that measures the firm's internal performance with respect to key activities defined by management.

adjourning The stage of team development in which members prepare for the team's disbandment.

administrative model A decision-making model that describes how managers actually make decisions in situations characterized by nonprogrammed decisions, uncertainty, and ambiguity.

administrative overhead The resources allocated to administrative and support activities.

administrative principles A subfield of the classical management perspective that focused on the total organization rather than the individual worker, delineating the management functions of planning, organizing, commanding, coordinating, and controlling.

affirmative action A policy requiring employers to take positive steps to guarantee equal employment opportunities for people within protected groups.

application form A device for collecting information about an applicant's education, previous job experience, and other background characteristics.

artificial intelligence (AI) Information technology that attempts to make computers think, talk, see, and listen like people.

assessment center A technique for selecting individuals with high managerial potential based on their performance on a series of simulated managerial tasks.

authority The formal and legitimate right of a manager to make decisions, issue orders, and allocate resources to achieve organizationally desired outcomes.

autocratic leader A leader who tends to centralize authority and rely on legitimate, reward, and coercive power to manage subordinates.

balance sheet A financial statement showing the firm's financial position with respect to assets and liabilities at a specific point in time.

balance sheet budget A financial budget that plans the amount of assets and liabilities for the end of the time period under consideration.

BCG matrix A concept developed by the Boston Consulting Group that evaluates SBUs with respect to the dimensions of business growth rate and market share.

behaviorally anchored rating scale (BARS) A rating technique that relates an employee's performance to specific job-related incidents.

behavioral sciences approach A subfield of the human resource management perspective that applied social science in an organizational context, drawing from economics, psychology, sociology, and other disciplines.

behavior modification The set of techniques by which reinforcement theory is used to modify human behavior.

benchmarking The continuous process of measuring products, services, and practices against the toughest competitors or those companies recognized as industry leaders.

birth stage The phase of the organization life cycle in which the company is created.

bottom-up budgeting A budgeting process in which lower-level managers budget their departments' resource needs and pass them up to top management for approval.

boundary-spanning roles Roles assumed by people and/or departments that link and coordinate the organization with key elements in the external environment.

bounded rationality The concept that people have the time and cognitive ability to process only a limited amount of information on which to base decisions.

brainstorming A decision-making technique in which group members present spontaneous suggestions for problem solution, regardless of their likelihood of implementation, in order to promote freer, more creative thinking within the group.

breakeven analysis A quantitative technique that helps managers determine the level of sales at which total revenues equal total costs.

bureaucratic control The use of rules, policies, hierarchy of authority, reward systems, and other formal devices to influence employee behavior and assess performance.

bureaucratic organizations A subfield of the classical management perspective that emphasized management on an impersonal, rational basis through elements such as clearly defined authority and responsibility, formal record-keeping, and separation of management and ownership.

burnout The emotional exhaustion resulting from extended periods of stress.

business incubator An innovation that provides shared office space, management support services, and management advice to entrepreneurs.

business-level strategy The level of strategy concerned with the question: "How do we compete?" Pertains to each business unit or product line within the organization.

business plan A document specifying the business details prepared by an entrepreneur in preparation for opening a new business.

CAD A production technology in which computers perform new-product design.

CAM A production technology in which computers help guide and control the manufacturing system.

capacity planning The determination and adjustment of the organization's ability to produce products and services to match customer demand.

capital expenditure budget A financial budget that plans future investments in major assets to be paid for over several years.

career A sequence of work-related activities and behaviors over a person's life span viewed as movement through various job experiences and the individual's attitudes toward involvement in those experiences.

career development Employee progress or growth over time as a career unfolds.

career ladder A formalized job progression route based on logically connected jobs.

career management Organizational activities designed to promote employees' career development.

career path A job progression route along which an employee can advance through the organization.

career planning The self-assessment, exploration of opportunities, goal setting, and other activities necessary to make informed career-related decisions.

career plateau A point in a career from which the opportunities for further promotion are scarce.

cash budget A financial budget that estimates cash flows on a daily or weekly basis to ensure that the company has sufficient cash to meet its obligations.

causal modeling A forecasting technique that attempts to predict behavior (the dependent variable) by analyzing its causes (independent variables).

cellular layout A facilities layout in which machines dedicated to sequences of production are grouped into cells in accordance with group-technology principles.

centralization The location of decision authority near top organizational levels.

centralized network A team communication structure in which team members communicate through a single individual to solve problems or make decisions.

central planning department A group of planning specialists who develop plans for the organization as a whole and its major divisions and departments and typically report to the president or CEO.

ceremony A planned activity that makes up a special event and is conducted for the benefit of an audience.

chain of command An unbroken line of authority that links all individuals in the organization and specifies who reports to whom.

change agent An OD specialist who contracts with an organization to facilitate change.

changing A step in the intervention stage of organizational development in which individuals experiment with new workplace behavior.

channel The carrier of a communication.

channel richness The amount of information that can be transmitted during a communication episode.

charismatic leader A leader who has the ability to motivate subordinates to transcend their expected performance.

clan control The use of social values, traditions, common beliefs, and trust to generate compliance with organizational goals.

classical model A decision-making model based on the assumption that managers should make logical decisions that will be in the organization's best economic interests.

classical perspective A management perspective that emerged during the nineteenth and early twentieth centuries that emphasized a rational, scientific approach to the study of management and sought to make organizations efficient operating machines.

closed system A system that does not interact with the external environment.

cluster organization An organizational form in which team members from different company locations use electronic mail and GDSSs to solve problems.

coalition An informal alliance among managers who support a specific goal.

code of ethics A formal statement of the organization's values regarding ethics and social issues.

coercive power Power that stems from the leader's authority to punish or recommend punishment.

collectivism A preference for a tightly knit social framework in which individuals look after one another and organizations protect their members' interests.

committee A long-lasting, sometimes permanent team in the organization structure created to deal with tasks that recur regularly.

communication The process by which information is exchanged and understood by two or more people, usually with the intent to motivate or influence behavior.

compensation Monetary payments (wages, salaries) and nonmonetary goods/commodities (fringe benefits, vacations) used to reward employees.

compensatory justice The concept that individuals should be compensated for the cost of their injuries by the party responsible and also that individuals should not be held responsible for matters over which they have no control.

competitors Other organizations in the same industry or type of business that provide goods or services to the same set of customers.

completeness The extent to which information contains the appropriate amount of data.

computer-based information system (CBIS) An information system that uses electronic computing technology to create the information system.

conceptual skill The cognitive ability to see the organization as a whole and the relationship among its parts.

concurrent control Control that consists of monitoring ongoing employee activities to ensure their consistency with established standards.

conflict Antagonistic interaction in which one party attempts to thwart the intentions or goals of another.

consideration A type of leader behavior that describes the extent to which a leader is sensitive to subordinates, respects their ideas and feelings, and establishes mutual trust.

content theories A group of theories that emphasize the needs that motivate people.

contingency approach A model of leadership that describes the relationship between leadership styles and specific organizational situations.

contingency plans Plans that define company responses to specific situations such as emergencies or setbacks.

contingency view An extension of the human resource perspective in which the successful resolution of organizational problems is thought to depend on managers' identification of key variables in the situation at hand.

continuous improvement The implementation of a large number of small, incremental improvements in all areas of the organization on an ongoing basis.

continuous process production A type of technology involving mechanization of the entire work flow and nonstop production.

continuous reinforcement schedule A schedule in which every occurrence of the desired behavior is reinforced.

controlling The management function concerned with monitoring employees' activities, keeping the organization on track toward its goals, and making corrections as needed.

coordination The quality of collaboration across departments.

coordination costs The time and energy needed to coordinate the activities of a team to enable it to perform its task.

core control system The strategic plans, financial forecasts, budgets, management by objectives, operations management techniques, and MIS reports that form an integrated system for directing and monitoring organizational activities.

corporate-level strategy The level of strategy concerned with the question: "What business are we in?" Pertains to the organization as a whole and the combination of business units and product lines that make it up.

corporation An artificial entity created by the state and existing apart from its owners.

cost leadership A type of competitive strategy with which the organization aggressively seeks efficient facilities, cuts costs, and employs tight cost controls to be more efficient than competitors.

countertrade The barter of products for other products rather than their sale for currency.

creativity The development of novel solutions to perceived organizational problems.

critical path The path with the longest total time; represents the total time required for the project.

critical success factors (CSFs) The particular areas in which satisfactory results will enhance the organization's overall performance.

cross-functional team A group of employees assigned to a functional department that meets as a team to resolve mutual problems.

culture The set of key values, beliefs, understandings, and norms that members of an organization share; the shared knowledge, beliefs, values, behaviors, and ways of thinking among members of a society.

culture gap The difference between an organization's desired cultural norms and values and actual norms and values.

culture/people change A change in employees' values, norms, attitudes, beliefs, and behavior.

customers People and organizations in the environment who acquire goods or services from the organization.

cycle time The steps taken to complete a company process.

data Raw, unsummarized, and unanalyzed facts.

debt financing Borrowing money that has to be repaid in order to start a business.

decentralization The location of decision authority near lower organizational levels.

decentralized network A team communication structure in which team members freely communicate with one another and arrive at decisions together.

decentralized planning staff A group of planning specialists assigned to major departments and divisions to help managers develop their own strategic plans.

decision A choice made from available alternatives.

decision making The process of identifying problems and opportunities and then resolving them.

decision tree A decision-making aid used for decision situations that occur in sequence; consists of a pictorial representation of decision alternatives, states of nature, and outcomes of each course of action.

decode To translate the symbols used in a message for the purpose of interpreting its meaning.

defensive response A response to social demands in which the organization admits to some errors of commission or omission but does not act obtrusively.

delegation The process managers use to transfer authority and responsibility to positions below them in the hierarchy.

Delphi group A group decision-making format that involves the circulation among participants of questionnaires on the selected problem, sharing of answers, and continuous recirculation/refinement of questionnaires until a consensus has been obtained.

Delphi technique A qualitative forecasting method in which experts reach consensus about future events through a series of continuously refined questionnaires rather than through face-to-face discussion.

democratic leader A leader who delegates authority to others, encourages participation, and relies on expert and referent power to manage subordinates.

demographic forecast A forecast of societal characteristics such as birthrates, educational levels, marriage rates, and diseases.

departmentalization The basis on which individuals are grouped into departments and departments into total organizations.

dependent demand inventory Inventory in which item demand is related to the demand for other inventory items.

descriptive An approach that describes how managers actually make decisions rather than how they should.

devil's advocate A decision-making technique in which an individual is assigned the role of challenging the assumptions and assertions made by the group to prevent premature consensus.

diagnosis The step in the decision-making process in which managers analyze underlying causal factors associated with the decision situation.

differentiation A type of competitive strategy with which the organization seeks to distinguish its products or services from competitors'.

direct investment An entry strategy in which the organization is involved in managing its production facilities in a foreign country.

discretionary costs Costs based on management decisions and not on fixed commitments or volume of output.

discretionary responsibility Organizational responsibility that is voluntary and guided by the organization's desire to make social contributions not mandated by economics, law, or ethics.

discrimination The hiring or promoting of applicants based on criteria that are not job relevant.

disengagement state The stage of career development during which the person prepares for retirement and begins to disengage from both the organization and the occupation.

distributive justice The concept that differential treatment of people should not be based on arbitrary characteristics. In the case of substantive differences, people should be treated differently in proportion to the differences between them.

divisional structure An organizational structure in which departments are grouped based on similar organizational outputs.

downsizing The systematic reduction in the number of managers and employees to make a company more cost efficient and competitive.

downward communication Messages sent from top management down to subordinates.

dual role A role in which the individual both contributes to the team's task and supports members' emotional needs.

economic dimension The dimension of the general environment representing the overall economic health of the country or region in which the organization functions.

economic forces Forces that affect the availability, production, and distribution of a society's resources among competing users.

economic order quantity (EOQ) An inventory management technique designed to minimize the total of ordering and holding costs for inventory items.

effectiveness The degree to which the organization achieves a stated objective.

efficiency The use of minimal resources—raw materials, money, and people—to produce a desired volume of output.

electronic data interchange (EDI) All interorganizational computer network used by trading partners to exchange business data.

employee stock ownership plan (ESOP) A motivational compensation program that gives employees part ownership of the organization.

encode To select symbols with which to compose a message.

entrepreneur Someone who recognizes a viable idea for a business product or service and carries it out.

entrepreneurship The process of initiating a business venture, organizing the necessary resources, and assuming the associated risks and rewards.

entropy The tendency for a system to run down and die.

environmental discontinuity A large change in the organization's environment over a short period.

E → P expectancy Expectancy that putting effort into a given task will lead to high performance.

equity A situation that exists when the ratio of one person's outcomes to inputs equals that of another's.

equity financing Financing that consists of funds that are invested in exchange for ownership in the company.

equity theory A process theory that focuses on individuals' perceptions of how fairly they are treated relative to others.

ERG theory A modification of the needs hierarchy theory that proposes three categories of needs: existence, relatedness, and growth.

establishment and advancement stage The stage of career development during which the individual experiences progress with the organization in the form of transfers, promotions, and/or high visibility.

ethical dilemma A situation that arises when all alternative choices or behaviors have been deemed undesirable because of potentially negative ethical consequences, making it difficult to distinguish right from wrong.

ethical ombudsman An official given the responsibility of corporate conscience who hears and investigates ethical complaints and points out potential ethical failures to top management.

ethics The code of moral principles and values that govern the behaviors of a person or group with respect to what is right or wrong.

ethics committee A group of executives assigned to oversee the organization's ethics by ruling on questionable issues and disciplining violators.

ethnocentrism A cultural attitude marked by the tendency to regard one's own culture as superior to others.

ethnorelativism The belief that groups and subcultures are inherently equal.

excellence characteristics A group of eight features found to typify the highest-performing U.S. companies.

executive information system (EIS) An interactive CBIS that retrieves, manipulates, and displays information serving the needs of top managers; also called *decision support system.*

exit interview An interview conducted with departing employees to determine the reasons for their termination.

expatriates Employees who live and work in a country other than their own.

expectancy theory A process theory that proposes that motivation depends on individuals' expectations about their ability to perform tasks and receive desired rewards.

expected value The weighted average of each possible outcome for a decision alternative.

expense budget An operating budget that outlines the anticipated expenses for each responsibility center and for the organization as a whole.

expert power Power that stems from the leader's special knowledge of or skill in the tasks performed by subordinates.

expert system An area of AI that attempts to program a computer to duplicate an expert's decision-making and problem-solving strategies.

exploration and trial stage The stage of career development during which a person accepts his or her first job and perhaps tries several jobs.

exporting An entry strategy in which the organization maintains its production facilities within its home country and transfers its products for sale in foreign markets.

external locus of control The belief by individuals that their future is not within their control but rather is influenced by external forces.

extrinsic reward A reward given by another person.

feedback The degree to which doing the job provides information back to the employee regarding his or her performance; a response by the receiver to the sender's communication.

feedback control Control that focuses on the organization's output; also called *post-action* or *output control.*

feedforward control Control that focuses on human, material, and financial resources flowing into the organization; also called *preliminary* or *preventive control.*

femininity A cultural preference for modesty, tending to the weak, and quality of life.

financial audit An independent appraisal of the organization's financial records, conducted by external or internal experts.

financial budget A budget that defines where the organization will receive its cash and how it will spend it.

finished-goods inventory Inventory consisting of items that have passed through the complete production process but have yet to be sold.

first-line manager A manager who is at the first or second management level and directly responsible for the production of goods and services.

fixed costs Costs that are based on a commitment from a previous budget period and cannot be altered.

fixed-position layout A facilities layout in which the product remains in one location and the required tasks and equipment are brought to it.

flat structure A management structure characterized by an overall broad span of control and relatively few hierarchical levels.

flexible manufacturing A manufacturing technology using computers to automate and integrate manufacturing components such as robots, machines, product design, and engineering analysis.

flexible manufacturing system (FMS) A small- or medium-size automated production line that can be adapted to produce more than one product line.

focus A type of competitive strategy that emphasizes concentration on a specific regional market or buyer group.

force field analysis The process of determining which forces drive and which resist a proposed change.

formal communication channel A communication channel that flows within the chain of command or task responsibility defined by the organization.

formalization The written documentation used to direct and control employees.

formal team A team created by the organization as part of the formal organizational structure.

forming The stage of team development characterized by orientation and acquaintance.

franchising A form of licensing in which an organization provides its foreign franchisees with a complete assortment of materials and services; an arrangement by which the owner of a product or service allows others to purchase the right to distribute the product or service with help from the owner.

free rider A person who benefits from team membership but does not make a proportionate contribution to the team's work.

frustration-regression principle The idea that failure to meet a higher-order need may cause a regression to an already satisfied lower-order need.

functional-level strategy The level of strategy concerned with the question: "How do we support the business-level strategy?" Pertains to all of the organization's major departments.

functional manager A manager who is responsible for a department that performs a single functional task and has employees with similar training and skills.

functional structure An organizational structure in which positions are grouped into departments based on similar skills, expertise, and resource use.

gain sharing A motivational compensation program that rewards employees and managers when predetermined performance targets are met.

general environment The layer of the external environment that affects the organization indirectly.

general manager A manager who is responsible for several departments that perform different functions.

glass ceiling An invisible barrier that separates women and minorities from top management positions.

globalization The standardization of product design and advertising strategies throughout the world.

goal A desired future state that the organization attempts to realize.

grand strategy The general plan or major action by which an organization intends to achieve its long-term objectives.

grapevine An informal, person-to-person communication network of employees that is not officially sanctioned by the organization.

group decision support system (GDSS) An interactive CBIS that facilitates group decision making; also called *collaborative work system.*

groupthink A phenomenon in which group members are so committed to the group that they are reluctant to express contrary opinions.

halo error A type of rating error that occurs when an employee receives the same rating on all dimensions regardless of his or her performance on individual ones.

Hawthorne studies A series of experiments on worker productivity begun in 1924 at the Hawthorne plant of Western Electric Company in Illinois; attributed employees' increased output to managers' better treatment of them during the study.

hero A figure who exemplifies the deeds, character, and attributes of a corporate culture.

hierarchy of needs theory A content theory that proposes that people are motivated by five categories of needs—physiological, safety, belongingness, esteem, and self-actualization—that exist in a hierarchical order.

homogeneity A type of rating error that occurs when a rater gives all employees a similar rating regardless of their individual performances.

horizontal communication The lateral or diagonal exchange of messages among peers or coworkers.

horizontal linkage model An approach to product change that emphasizes shared development of innovations among several departments.

horizontal team A formal team composed of employees from about the same hierarchical level but from different areas of expertise.

human relations movement A movement in management thinking and practice that emphasized satisfaction of employees' basic needs as the key to increased worker productivity.

human resource inventory A data base that summarizes individuals' skills, abilities, work experiences, and career interests.

human resource management (HRM) Activities undertaken to attract, develop, and maintain an effective work force within an organization.

human resource perspective A management perspective that emerged during the late nineteenth century that emphasized enlightened treatment of workers and power sharing between managers and employees.

human resource planning The forecasting of human resource needs and the projected matching of individuals with expected job vacancies.

human resources forecast A forecast of the organization's future personnel needs.

human skill The ability to work with and through other people and to work effectively as a group member.

hygiene factors Factors that involve the presence or absence of job dissatisfiers, including working conditions, pay, company policies, and interpersonal relationships.

idea champion A person who sees the need for and champions productive change within the organization.

implementation The step in the decision-making process that involves the employment of managerial, administrative, and persuasive abilities to translate the chosen alternative into action.

income statement A financial statement that summarizes a company's financial performance over a given time interval.

individualism A preference for a loosely knit social framework in which individuals are expected to take care of themselves.

individualism approach The ethical concept that acts are moral when they promote the individual's best long-term interests, which ultimately leads to the greater good.

informal communication channel A communication channel that exists outside formally authorized channels without regard for the organization's hierarchy of authority.

information Data that are meaningful and alter the receiver's understanding.

information system A written or electronic internal system for processing data and information among employees; a mechanism for collecting, organizing, and distributing data to organizational employees.

infrastructure A country's physical facilities that support economic activities.

initiating structure A type of leader behavior that describes the extent to which a leader is task oriented and directs subordinates' work activities toward goal achievement.

integrating manager An individual responsible for coordinating the activities of several departments on a full-time basis to achieve specific project or product outcomes.

interactive leader A leader who is concerned with consensus building, is open and inclusive, and encourages participation.

interdependence The extent to which departments depend on each other for resources or materials to accomplish their tasks.

internal environment The environment within the organization's boundaries.

internal locus of control The belief by individuals that their future is within their control and that other external forces will have little influence.

international dimension The dimension of the general environment representing events that originate in foreign countries and opportunities for American firms abroad.

international management The management of business operations conducted in more than one country.

intrapreneur Someone who sees the need for innovation and promotes it within an existing organization.

intrapreneurship The process of recognizing the need for innovation and promoting it within an organization.

intrinsic reward A reward received as a direct consequence of a person's actions.

inventory The goods that the organization keeps on hand for use in the production process.

invisible minorities Individuals who share a social stigma that is not visibly recognizable.

job A unit of work that a single employee is responsible for performing.

job characteristics model A model of job design that comprises core job dimensions, critical psychological states, and employee growth-need strength.

job description A listing of duties as well as desirable qualifications for a particular job.

job design The application of motivational theories to the structure of work for improving productivity and satisfaction.

job enlargement A job design that combines a series of tasks into one new, broader job to give employees variety and challenge.

job enrichment A job design that incorporates achievement, recognition, and other high-level motivators into the work.

job evaluation The process of determining the values of jobs within an organization through an examination of job content.

job matching system A method that links qualified individuals with career opportunities within the organization.

job rotation A job design that systematically moves employees from one job to another to provide them with variety and stimulation.

job simplification A job design whose purpose is to improve task efficiency by reducing the number of tasks a single person must perform.

joint venture A strategic alliance or program by two or more organizations; a variation of direct investment in which an organization shares costs and risks with another firm to build a manufacturing facility, develop new products, or set up a sales and distribution network.

jury of opinion A method of qualitative forecasting based on the average opinions of managers from various company divisions and departments.

justice approach The ethical concept that moral decisions must be based on standards of equity, fairness, and impartiality.

just-in-time (JIT) inventory systems An inventory control system that schedules materials to arrive precisely when they are needed on a production line.

key indicator system A technique for determining managers' information needs based on key business indicators, exception reporting, and the use of graphics packages.

labor market The people available for hire by the organization.

law of effect The assumption that positively reinforced behavior tends to be repeated and unreinforced or negatively reinforced behavior tends to be inhibited.

leadership The ability to influence people toward the attainment of organizational goals.

leading The management function that involves the use of influence to motivate employees to achieve the organization's goals.

legal-political dimension The dimension of the general environment that includes federal, state, and local government regulations and political activities designed to control company behavior.

legitimate power Power that stems from a formal management position in an organization and the authority granted to it.

licensing An entry strategy in which an organization in one country makes certain resources available to companies in another in order to participate in the production and sale of its products abroad.

line authority A form of authority in which individuals in management positions have the formal power to direct and control immediate subordinates.

linear programming A quantitative technique that allocates resource so as to optimize a predefined organizational objective.

liquidity ratio A financial ratio that indicates the company's ability to meet its current debt obligations.

listening The skill of receiving messages to accurately grasp facts and feelings to interpret the genuine meaning.

LPC scale A questionnaire designed to measure relationship-oriented versus task-oriented leadership style according to the leader's choice of adjectives for describing the "least preferred coworker."

lump-sum bonus A motivational compensation program that rewards employees with a one-time cash payment based on performance.

management The attainment of organizational goals in an effective and efficient manner through planning, organizing, leading, and controlling organizational resources.

management by objectives (MBO) A method whereby managers and employees define objectives for each department, project, and employee and use them to control subsequent performance.

management by wandering around (MBWA) A communication technique in which managers interact directly with workers to exchange information.

management information system (MIS) A form of CBIS that collects, organizes, and distributes the data managers use in performing their management functions.

management science A set of quantitatively based decision models used to assist management decision makers.

management science perspective A management perspective that emerged after World War II and applied mathematics, statistics, and other quantitative techniques to managerial problems.

managerial grid A two-dimensional leadership theory that measures a leader's concern for people and concern for production.

manufacturing organization An organization that produces physical goods.

manufacturing resource planning (MRP II) An extension of MRP to include the

control of resources pertaining to all operations of the organization.

market entry strategy An organizational strategy for entering a foreign market.

masculinity A cultural preference for achievement, heroism, assertiveness, and material success.

mass production A type of technology characterized by the production of a large volume of products with the same specifications.

matching model An employee selection approach in which the organization and the applicant attempt to match each other's needs, interests, and values.

materials requirement planning (MRP) A dependent demand inventory planning and control system that schedules the precise amount of all materials required to support the production of desired end products.

matrix boss A product or functional boss, responsible for one side of the matrix.

matrix structure An organizational structure that utilizes functional and divisional chains of command simultaneously in the same part of the organization; a global organization structure that permits an MNC to achieve vertical control and horizontal coordination simultaneously.

maturity stage The phase of the organization life cycle in which the organization has become exceedingly large and mechanistic.

mechanistic structure An organizational structure characterized by rigidly defined tasks, many rules and regulations, little teamwork, and centralized decision making.

mediation The process of using a third party to settle a dispute.

mentor A senior employee who acts as a sponsor and teacher to a less experienced employee.

merger The combination of two or more organizations into one.

message The tangible formulation of an idea to be sent to a receiver.

mid-career renewal strategies A strategy designed to provide advancement opportunities for deserving mid-career employees while maximizing the contributions of plateaued employees who continue to perform satisfactorily.

mid-career stage The stage of career development characterized by growth, maintenance, or decline.

middle manager A manager who works at the middle levels of the organization and is responsible for major departments.

midlife stage The phase of the organization life cycle in which the firm has reached prosperity and grown substantially large.

mission The organization's reason for existence.

mission statement A broadly stated definition of the organization's basic business scope and operations that distinguish it from similar types of organizations.

monoculture A culture that accepts only one way of doing things and one set of values and beliefs.

moral-rights approach The ethical concept that moral decisions are those that best maintain the rights of those people affected by them.

motivation The arousal, direction, and persistence of behavior.

motivators Factors that influence job satisfaction based on fulfillment of higher-level needs such as achievement, recognition, responsibility, and opportunity for growth.

multidomestic strategy The modification of product design and advertising strategies to suit the specific needs of individual countries.

multinational corporation (MNC) An organization that receives more than 25 percent of its total sales revenues from operations outside the parent company's home country; also called *global corporation* or *transnational corporation.*

multiple advocacy A decision-making technique that involves several advocates and presentation of multiple points of view, including minority and unpopular opinions.

need to achieve A human quality linked to entrepreneurship in which people are motivated to excel and pick situations in which success is likely.

networking The linking together of people and departments within or among organizations for the purpose of sharing information resources.

network structure An organizational structure that disaggregates major functions into separate companies that are brokered by a small headquarters organization.

neutralizer A situational variable that counteracts a leadership style and prevents the leader from displaying certain behaviors.

new-venture fund A fund providing resources from which individuals and groups draw to develop new ideas, products, or businesses.

new-venture team A unit separate from the mainstream of the organization that is responsible for developing and initiating innovations.

nominal group A group decision-making format that emphasizes equal participation in the decision process by all group members.

nonparticipator role A role in which the individual contributes little to either the task or members' socioemotional needs.

nonprogrammed decision A decision made in response to a situation that is unique, is poorly defined and largely unstructured, and has important consequences for the organization.

nonroutine service technology Service technology in which there are no specific procedures for directing employees, problem situations are varied, and employees must rely on personal resources for problem solving.

nonverbal communication A communication transmitted through actions and behaviors rather than through words.

norm A standard of conduct that is shared by team members and guides their behavior.

normative An approach that defines how a decision maker should make decisions and provides guidelines for reaching an ideal outcome for the organization.

norming The stage of team development in which conflicts developed during the storming stage are resolved and team harmony and unity emerge.

obstructive response A response to social demands in which the organization denies responsibility, claims that evidence of misconduct is misleading or distorted, and attempts to obstruct investigation.

on-the-job training (OJT) A type of training in which an experienced employee "adopts" a new employee to teach him or her how to perform job duties.

open system A system that interacts with the external environment.

operating budget The plan for the allocation of financial resources to each organizational responsibility center for the budget period under consideration.

operational objectives Specific, measurable results expected from departments, work groups, and individuals within the organization.

operational plans Plans developed at the organization's lower levels that specify action steps toward achieving operational goals and support tactical planning activities.

operations management The field of management that specializes in the physical production of goods or services and uses quantitative techniques for solving manufacturing problems.

operations strategy The recognition of the importance of operations to the firm's success and the involvement of operations managers in the organization's strategic planning.

opportunity A situation in which managers see potential organizational accomplishments that exceed current objectives.

organic structure An organizational structure that is free flowing, has few rules and regulations, encourages employee teamwork, and decentralizes decision making to employees doing the job.

organization A social entity that is goal directed and deliberately structured.

organizational change The adoption of a new idea or behavior by an organization.

organizational control The systematic process through which managers regulate organizational activities to make them consistent with the expectations established in plans, targets, and performance standards.

organizational development (OD) The application of behavioral science techniques to improve an organization's health and effectiveness through its ability to cope with environmental changes, improve internal relationships, and increase problem-solving capabilities.

organizational environment All elements existing outside the organization's boundaries that have the potential to affect the organization.

organizational structure The framework in which the organization defines how tasks are divided, resources are deployed, and departments are coordinated.

organization chart The visual representation of an organization's structure.

organization life cycle The organization's evolution through major developmental stages.

organizing The management function concerned with assigning tasks, grouping tasks into departments, and allocating resources to departments; the deployment of organizational resources to achieve strategic objectives.

outsourcing Engaging in the international division of labor so as to obtain the cheapest sources of labor and supplies regardless of country; also called *global sourcing;* the farming out of a company's in-house operation to a preferred vendor.

paper-and-pencil test A written test designed to measure a particular attribute such as intelligence or aptitude.

partial productivity The ratio of total outputs to the inputs from a single major input category.

partial reinforcement schedule A schedule in which only some occurrences of the desired behavior are reinforced.

partnership An unincorporated business owned by two or more people.

path-goal theory A contingency approach to leadership specifying that the leader's responsibility is to increase subordinates' motivation by clarifying the behaviors necessary for task accomplishment and rewards.

pay for knowledge A motivational compensation program that links employee's salary with the number of tasks performed.

pay for performance A motivational compensation program that rewards employees in proportion to their performance contributions.

payoff matrix A decision-making aid comprised of relevant strategies, states of nature, probability of occurrence of states of nature, and expected outcome(s).

pay survey A study of what other companies pay employees in jobs that correspond to a sample of key positions selected by the organization.

pay-trend line A graph that shows the relationship between pay and total job point values for determining the worth of a given job.

perception The process of making sense out of one's environment.

perceptual organization The categorization of an object or stimulus according to one's frame of reference.

perceptual selectivity The screening and selection of objects and stimuli that compete for one's attention.

performance The organization's ability to attain its goals by using resources in an efficient and effective manner.

performance appraisal The process of observing and evaluating an employee's performance, recording the assessment, and providing feedback to the employee.

performance appraisal interview A formal review of an employee's performance conducted between the superior and the subordinate.

performance gap A disparity between existing and desired performance levels.

performing The stage of team development in which members focus on problem solving and accomplishing the team's assigned task.

permanent team A group of participants from several departments that meets regularly to solve ongoing problems of common interest.

PERT The Program Evaluation and Review Technique; consists of breaking down a project into a network of specific activities and mapping out their sequence and necessary completion dates.

plan A blueprint specifying the resource allocations, schedules, and other actions necessary for attaining goals.

planning The management function concerned with defining goals for future organizational performance and deciding on the tasks and resource use needed to attain them; the act of determining the organization's goals and the means for achieving them.

planning task force A temporary group consisting of line managers responsible for developing strategic plans.

pluralism The policy that an organization accommodates several subcultures.

P → O expectancy Expectancy that successful performance of a task will lead to the desired outcome.

point system A job evaluation system that assigns a predetermined point value to each compensable job factor in order to determine the worth of a given job.

policy A general statement based on the organization's overall goals and strategic plans that provides directions for individuals within the company.

political activity Organizational attempts, such as lobbying, to influence government legislation and regulation.

political forces The influence of political and legal institutions on people and organizations.

political risk A company's risk of loss of assets, earning power, or managerial control due to politically motivated events or actions by host governments.

portfolio strategy A type of corporate-level strategy that pertains to the organization's mix of SBUs and product lines that fit together in such a way as to provide the corporation with synergy and competitive advantage.

power The potential ability to influence others' behavior.

power distance The degree to which people accept inequality in power among institutions, organizations, and people.

preretirement program A strategy designed to assist employees in coping with the stress of the transition from work to retirement.

proactive response A response to social demands in which the organization seeks to learn what is in its constituencies' interest and to respond without pressure from them.

problem A situation in which organizational accomplishments have failed to meet established objectives.

problem-solving team Typically 5 to 12 hourly employees from the same department who meet to discuss ways of improv-

ing quality, efficiency, and the work environment.

procedural justice The concept that rules should be clearly stated and consistently and impartially enforced.

procedure A specific series of steps to be used in achieving certain objectives; usually applies to individual jobs.

process layout A facilities layout in which machines that perform the same function are grouped together in one location.

process theories A group of theories that explain how employees select behaviors with which to meet their needs and determine whether their choices were successful.

product change A change in the organization's product or service output.

productivity The organization's output of products and services divided by its inputs.

product layout A facilities layout in which machines and tasks are arranged according to the sequence of steps in the production of a single product.

product life cycle The stages through which a product or service goes: (1) development and introduction into the marketplace, (2) growth, (3) maturity, and (4) decline.

profitability ratio A financial ratio that describes the firm's profits.

profit budget An operating budget that combines both expense and revenue budgets into one statement showing gross and net profits.

program A complex set of objectives and plans for achieving an important, one-time organizational goal.

programmed decision A decision made in response to a situation that has occurred often enough to enable decision rules to be developed and applied in the future.

project A set of relatively short-term, narrow objectives and plans for achieving a major, one-time organizational goal.

project manager A manager who coordinates people across several departments to accomplish a specific project.

proprietorship An unincorporated business owned by an individual for profit.

prototype A working model of an information system developed to test the system's features.

qualitative forecast A forecast based on the opinions of experts in the absence of precise historical data.

quality The degree to which information accurately portrays reality.

quality circle A group of six to twelve volunteer employees who meet regularly to discuss and solve problems that affect their common work activities.

quantitative forecast A forecast that begins with a series of past data values and then applies a set of mathematical rules with which to predict future values.

raw materials inventory Inventory consisting of the basic inputs to the organization's production process.

realistic job preview (RJP) A recruiting approach that gives applicants all pertinent and realistic information about the job and the organization.

recruiting The activities or practices that define the desired characteristics of applicants for specific jobs.

referent power Power that results from leader characteristics that command subordinates' identification with, respect and admiration for, and desire to emulate the leader.

refreezing A step in the reinforcement stage of organizational development in which individuals acquire a desired new skill or attitude and are rewarded for it by the organization.

reinforcement Anything that causes a given behavior to be repeated or inhibited.

reinforcement theory A motivation theory based on the relationship between a given behavior and its consequences.

relevance The degree to which information pertains to the problems, decisions, and tasks for which a manager is responsible.

reorder point (ROP) The most economical level at which an inventory item should be reordered.

responsibility The duty to perform the task or activity an employee has been assigned.

responsibility center Any organizational department under the supervision of a single individual who is responsible for its activity.

revenue budget An operating budget that identifies the revenues required by the organization.

reward power Power that results from the leader's authority to reward others.

risk propensity The willingness to undertake risk with the opportunity of gaining an increased payoff.

role A set of expectations for one's behavior.

routine service technology Service technology in which work can be broken down into explicit steps and employees can follow objective procedures for serving customers and solving problems.

rule A statement describing how a specific action is to be performed.

sales force composite A type of qualitative forecasting that relies on the combined expert opinions of field sales personnel.

sales forecast A forecast of future company sales based on projected customer demand for products or services.

satisfice To choose the first solution alternative that satisfies minimal decision criteria regardless of whether better solutions are presumed to exist.

schedule of reinforcement The frequency with and intervals over which reinforcement occurs.

scientific management A subfield of the classical management perspective that emphasized scientifically determined changes in management practices as the solution to improving labor productivity.

search The process of learning about current developments inside or outside the organization that can be used to meet a perceived need for change.

selection The process of determining the skills, abilities, and other attributes needed to perform a particular job.

self-managing team A team consisting of 5 to 12 multiskilled workers who rotate jobs to produce an entire product or service and perform managerial duties, often supervised by an elected member.

semantics The meaning of words and the way they are used.

service organization An organization that produces nonphysical goods that require customer involvement and cannot be stored in inventory.

service technology Technology characterized by intangible outputs and direct contact between employees and customers.

simulation model A mathematical representation of the relationships among variables in real-world organizational situations.

single-use plans Plans that are developed to achieve a set of objectives that are unlikely to be repeated in the future.

situational theory A contingency approach to leadership that links the leader's two-dimensional style with the task maturity of subordinates.

situation analysis Analysis of the strengths, weaknesses, opportunities, and threats (SWOT) that affect organizational performance.

size The organization's scope or magnitude, typically measured by number of employees.

skunkworks Small, informal, and sometimes unauthorized groups that create innovations.

slogan A phrase or sentence that succinctly expresses a key corporate value.

small batch production A type of technology that involves the production of goods in batches of one or a few products designed to customer specifications.

social facilitation The tendency for the presence of others to influence an individual's motivation and performance.

social forces The aspects of a culture that guide and influence relationships among people—their values, needs, and standards of behavior.

social responsibility The obligation of organization management to make decisions and take actions that will enhance the welfare and interests of society as well as the organization's.

sociocultural dimension The dimension of the general environment representing the demographic characteristics, norms, customs, and values of the population within which the organization operates.

socioemotional role A role in which the individual provides support for team members' emotional needs and social unity.

span of management The number of employees who report to a supervisor; also called *span of control.*

special-purpose team A team created outside the formal organization to undertake a project of special importance or creativity.

spin-off An independent company producing a project or service similar to that produced by the entrepreneur's former employer.

staff authority A form of authority granted to staff specialists in their areas of expertise.

stakeholder Any group within or outside the organization that has a stake in the organization's performance.

standing plans Ongoing plans that are used as guidance for tasks performed repeatedly within the organization.

state of nature A future event or condition that is relevant to a decision outcome.

statistical process control (SPC) A type of managerial control that employs carefully gathered data and statistical analysis to evaluate the quality and productivity of employee activities.

statistical quality control The application of statistical techniques to the control of quality.

stereotype A widely held generalization about a group of people that assigns attributes to them solely on the basis of a limited number of categories.

storming The stage of team development in which individual personalities and roles, and resulting conflicts, emerge.

story A narrative based on true events that is repeated frequently and shared by organizational employees.

strategic business unit (SBU) A division of the organization that has a unique business mission, product line, competitors, and markets relative to other SBUs in the same corporation.

strategic goals Broad statements of where the organization wants to be in the future; pertain to the organization as a whole rather than to specific divisions or departments.

strategic management The set of decisions and actions used to formulate and implement strategies that will provide a competitively superior fit between the organization and its environment so as to achieve organizational objectives.

strategic plans The action steps by which an organization intends to attain its strategic goals.

strategy The plan of action that prescribes resource allocation and other activities for dealing with the environment and helping the organization attain its goals.

strategy formulation The stage of strategic management that involves the planning and decision making that lead to the establishment of the organization's goals and of a specific strategic plan.

strategy implementation The stage of strategic management that involves the use of managerial and organizational tools to direct resources toward achieving strategic outcomes.

stress The physiological and emotional response to demands, constraints, and opportunities that create uncertainty when important outcomes are at stake.

structural change Any change in the way in which the organization is designed and managed.

substitute A situational variable that makes a leadership style redundant or unnecessary.

subsystems Parts of a system that depend on one another for their functioning.

succession planning The process of creating a plan for moving people into higher organizational levels.

superordinate goal A goal that cannot be reached by a single party.

suppliers People and organizations who provide the raw materials the organization uses to produce its output.

survey feedback A type of OD intervention in which questionnaires on organizational climate and other factors are distributed among employees and the results reported back to them by a change agent.

symbol An object, act, or event that conveys meaning to others.

symbolic manager A manager who defines and uses signals and symbols to influence corporate culture.

synergy The concept that the whole is greater than the sum of its parts; the condition that exists when the organization's parts interact to produce a joint effect that is greater than the sum of the parts acting alone.

system A set of interrelated parts that function as a whole to achieve a common purpose.

systems development life cycle The sequence of events that CBIS designers follow in developing and implementing a new system.

systems theory An extension of the human resources perspective that describes organizations as open systems that are characterized by entropy, synergy, and subsystem interdependence.

tactical objectives Objectives that define the outcomes that major divisions and departments must achieve in order for the organization to reach its overall goals.

tall structure A management structure characterized by an overall narrow span of management and a relatively large number of hierarchical levels.

task environment The layer of the external environment that directly influences the organization's operations and performance.

task force A temporary team or committee formed to solve a specific short-run problem involving several departments.

task specialist role A role in which the individual devotes personal time and energy to helping the team accomplish its task.

team A group of participants from several departments who meet regularly to solve ongoing problems of common interest; a unit of two or more people who interact and coordinate their work to accomplish a specific objective.

team building A type of OD intervention that enhances the cohesiveness of departments by helping members to learn to function as a team.

team cohesiveness The extent to which team members are attracted to the team and motivated to remain in it.

technical complexity The degree to which machinery is involved in the production process to the exclusion of people.

technical core The heart of the organization's production of its product or service.

technical skill The understanding of and proficiency in the performance of specific tasks.

technological dimension The dimension of the general environment that in-

cludes scientific and technological advancements in the industry and society at large.

technological forecast A forecast of the occurrence of technological changes that could effect an organization's way of doing business.

technology The knowledge, tools techniques, and activities used to transform the organization's inputs into outputs.

technology change A change that pertains to the organization's production process.

Theory Z A management perspective that incorporates techniques from both Japanese and North American management practices.

time-based competition A strategy of competition based on the ability to deliver products and services faster than competitors.

timeliness The degree to which information is available soon after events occur.

time series analysis A forecasting technique that examines the patterns of movement in historical data.

tolerance for ambiguity The psychological characteristic that allows a person to be untroubled by disorder and uncertainty.

top-down budgeting A budgeting process in which middle- and lower-level managers set departmental budget targets in accordance with overall company revenues and expenditures specified by top management.

top leader The overseer of both the product and the functional chains of command, responsible for the entire matrix.

top manager A manager who is at the top of the organizational hierarchy and responsible for the entire organization.

total factor productivity The ratio of total outputs to the inputs from labor, capital, materials, and energy.

total quality management (TQM) Operations management that strives to perfect the entire manufacturing process through improvements in quality and productivity; a control concept that gives workers rather than managers the responsibility for achieving standards of quality.

total study A process that attempts to assess information requirements at all management levels.

trade association An association made up of organizations with similar interests for the purpose of influencing the environment.

traits The distinguishing personal characteristics of a leader, such as intelligence, values, and appearance.

transactional leader A leader who clarifies subordinates' role and task requirements, initiates structure, provides rewards, and displays consideration for subordinates.

transaction processing system (TPS) A type of CBIS that performs the organization's routinely occurring transactions.

transformational leader A leader distinguished by a special ability to bring about motivation and change.

two-boss employee An employee who reports to two supervisors simultaneously.

uncertainty avoidance A value characterized by people's intolerance for uncertainty and ambiguity and resulting support for beliefs that promise certainty and conformity.

unfreezing A step in the diagnosis stage of organizational development in which participants are made aware of problems in order to increase their willingness to change their behavior.

upward communication Messages transmitted from the lower to the higher level in the organization's hierarchy.

utilitarian approach The ethical concept that moral behaviors produce the greatest good for the greatest number.

valence The value of outcomes for the individual.

validity The relationship between an applicant's score on a selection device and his or her future job performance.

variable costs Costs that are based on an explicit physical relationship with the volume of department activity; also called *engineered costs*.

venture capital firm A group of companies or individuals that invest money in new or expanding businesses for ownership and potential profits.

vertical team A formal team composed of a manager and his or her subordinates in the organization's formal chain of command.

Vroom-Jago model A model designed to help managers gauge the amount of subordinate participation in decision making.

whistle-blowing The disclosure by an employee of illegal, immoral, or illegitimate practices by the organization.

wholly owned foreign affiliate A foreign subsidiary over which an organization has complete control.

work-force diversity The inclusion of people with different human qualities who belong to different cultural groups.

work-in-process inventory Inventory composed of the materials that are still moving through the stages of the production process.

work redesign The altering of jobs to increase both the quality of employees' work experience and their productivity.

work specialization The degree to which organizational tasks are subdivided into individual jobs; also called *division of labor*.

youth stage The phase of the organization life cycle in which the organization is growing rapidly and has a product enjoying some marketplace success.

zero-based budgeting (ZBB) A budgeting process in which each responsibility center calculates its resource needs based on the coming year's priorities rather than on the previous year's budget.

PHOTO CREDITS

CHAPTER 1

Page **6** © John Abbott. Page **11** Reprinted with permission of Compaq Computer Corporation. All Rights Reserved. Page **13** Reprinted with permission of Dole Food Company. Page **20** Copyright Jack Carroll Photography. Page **23** Copyright Eric Myer for Sizzler International. Page **25** Courtesy of Reynolds Metals Company. Page **27** Courtesy of Bank One Corporation. Page **29** Courtesy of The Dow Chemical Company.

CHAPTER 2

Page **42** Courtesy of Wells Fargo Bank. Photographer, Rob Gage. Page **42** From the collection of Walter and Naomi Rosenblum. Used with permission. Page **45** Frederick W. Taylor Collection, S. C. Williams Library. Stevens Institute of Technology. Page **46** Courtesy of Ford Motor Company. Page **46** Courtesy of Ronald G. Greenwood. Page **48** Courtesy of German Information Center. Page **49** Courtesy of Ronald G. Greenwood. Page **50** National Archives. Page **52** Western Electric Photographic Services. Page **58** General Host Corporation 1991 Annual Report. Photographer, Ted Kawalerski. Page **60** © The Walt Disney Company. Page **63** Courtesy of The Stanley Works. Al Ferreira, photographer. Page **66** Courtesy of Gerber Products Company.

CHAPTER 3

Page **79** Courtesy of NIKE, Inc. Page **84** Courtesy of Archer Daniels Midland and Jones+Thomas Advertising-Public Relations. Page **85** Copyright by P. LeSegretain—SYGMA. Page **89** Courtesy of J. B. Hunt Transport, Inc. Photo by Dan Bryant. Page **91** Courtesy of LSI Logic Corporation. Page **95** © 1992 James Schnepf. Page **98** Mark Tuschman/The Upjohn Company.

CHAPTER 4

Page **113** Courtesy of Ford Motor Company. Page **115** Courtesy of Morrison Knudsen Corporation. Page **116** © 1992 Randy Duchaine. All Rights Reserved. Page **120** Courtesy of The Stanley Works. Page **123** Courtesy of *Spirit* magazine, McDonnell Douglas Corporation. Page **126** Courtesy of First Security Corporation. Page **128** Courtesy of ITOCHU Corporation. Page **132** © 1991 Arthur Meyerson. All rights reserved.

CHAPTER 5

Page **150** Copyright Dave Morrison for Florida Progress Corporation. Page **154** Courtesy of Werner Enterprises, Inc. Page **156** © Copyright Will van Overbeek. Page **158** Courtesy of ServiceMaster. Page **166** Photograph by Steve Henry, Houston, TX. Page **168** Courtesy of The Stride Rite Corporation. Page **170** Courtesy of Rockwell International/David Perry. Page **172** Courtesy of Rohm and Haas Company.

CHAPTER 6

Page **186** Courtesy of Lennox Industries, Inc., worldwide manufacturer of comfort equipment. Page **189** Used with permission of The Toro Company. Page **194** Courtesy of Blockbuster Entertainment Corporation. Page **195** Courtesy of Tenneco Gas. Page **199** © Gregory Edwards. Page **201** © Copyright British Telecommunications plc. Page **202** Courtesy of Tomen Corporation (Annual Report 1992). Page **206** Courtesy of PSEG. Photo by T. J. Miller.

CHAPTER 7

Page **217** TM and cartoon © 1993 Hanna-Barbera Productions, Inc. All Rights Reserved. © 1993 Turner Broadcasting Systems, Inc. All Rights Reserved. Page **219** Courtesy of Colgate-Palmolive Company. Page **225** © Waterhouse Stock Photography. Courtesy of Mobil Corporation. Page **227** © Playskool Baby, Inc., a subsidiary of Hasbro, Inc. Page **232** © Tom Tracy for Dreyer's Grand Ice Cream. Page **235** Courtesy of Toys "R" Us. Page **239** Courtesy of Motors Insurance Corporation.

CHAPTER 8

Page **251** Courtesy of TOSHIBA. Page **256** © George Simian for Terra Industries, Inc. Used with permission. Page **258** Courtesy of Quad/Photo. Page **260** Reproduced with permission, © PepsiCo, Inc. 1990. Page **262** Chevron Corporation/photographer, Cameron Davidson, © 1992. Page **271** Courtesy of CSX Corporation. Page **273** Courtesy of Kimball International, Inc., Jasper, IN 47549.

CHAPTER 9

Page **290** Courtesy of Kellogg Company. Page **293** Courtesy of Sara Lee Corporation. Page **298** © Flip Chalfant, photographer/Will Sumpter & Associates. Page **307** Courtesy of Gaylord Entertainment Company. Photo by Donnie Beauchamp. Page **308** Courtesy of Airborne Express. Page **314** Courtesy of Chrysler Corporation. Page **317** Courtesy of Safeguard Scientifics, Inc.

CHAPTER 10

Page **332** Reprinted with permission of Compaq Computer Corporation. All Rights Reserved. Page **337** U.S. Marines. Page **344** Photo by Brownie Harris/Courtesy GE. Page **347** © Peter Sibbald 1992. Page **349** Courtesy of International Technology Corporation. Photographer: Tony Verebes.

CHAPTER 11

Page **363** Courtesy of James River Corporation. Page **367** TAKASHIMAYA Annual Report. Courtesy of TAKASHIMAYA Co., Ltd. Page **369** © John Abbott. Page **371** © Michael Melford 1992. Page **375** Courtesy of Consolidated

Rail Corporation. Jim Cunningham, photographer. Page **379** Courtesy of The Boeing Company. Page **380** Courtesy of Ocean Spray Cranberries, Inc., 1993. Page **382** Courtesy of Weirton Steel Corporation. Page **384** © Steven Rubin 1992/JB Pictures. Page **385** © Alen MacWeeney 1991.

CHAPTER 12

Page **398** Courtesy of MagneTek, Inc. Page **401** © Christina M. Freitag for Louisville Gas & Electric Company. Page **405** Photo by Lou Kulikauskas for Federal-Mogul Corporation. Page **407** Courtesy of Galen Health Care, Inc. (John F. Johnston). Page **409** Courtesy of Franklin Resources, Inc. Page **415** Paul E. Grosjean/Dow Corning Corporation. Page **419** Courtesy of Varian Associates, Incorporated. Page **420** Courtesy of MDU Resources Group, Inc. Page **423** Courtesy of NationsBank Corporation.

CHAPTER 13

Page **437** Courtesy of Consumers' Gas Company, Ltd., Toronto, Canada. Page **441** © Wayne Sorce. Page **444** © Charles Moore/Black Star. Page **446** Courtesy of The British Petroleum Company p.l.c. Page **449** Courtesy of *Spirit* magazine, McDonnell Douglas Corporation. Page **458** Courtesy of Safeway, Inc./Vince Finnigan, photographer. Page **460** Courtesy of Texas Instruments. Page **463** Courtesy of The Vons Companies, Inc.

CHAPTER 14

Page **478** Allan Birnbach, photographer and ASARCO Incorporated. Page **480** © 1993 Brian Smith. Page **484** 1992 Nation's Business/T. Michael Keza. Page **487** © Ed Kashi. All Rights Reserved. Page **492** © Pam Francis. Page **498** Courtesy of The Walt Disney Company.

CHAPTER 15

Page **514** Courtesy of GMAC Financial Services. Page **517** Jay Thompson, Bowden Productions. Page **520** Courtesy of *Frontline Magazine* published by Taco Bell Public Affairs Department. Page **521** Courtesy of The Lincoln Electric Company. Page **532** © 1993 Brian Smith. Page **534** Courtesy of Chaparral Steel Company. Page **537** © Science Applications International Corporation 1992. All rights reserved.

CHAPTER 16

Page **554** Courtesy of Securities Department, Ito-Yokado Co., Ltd. Page **560** Courtesy of Mobil. Page **562** John Nicksich, Northwest Pipeline Corporation, 1992. Page **563** Courtesy of Northrop Corporation. Page **565** Courtesy of Hewlett-Packard Company. Page **567** Courtesy of Flowers Industries, Inc. Photographer: Ovak Arslanian, New York. Page **572** Courtesy of Florida Power and Light Co.

CHAPTER 17

Page **582** © Michael O'Neill. Page **586** Courtesy of JWP, Inc. Page **587** Courtesy of *CrossTalk*, Carolina Telephone and Telegraph Company. Page **595** © Blake Little/ONYX. Page **597**

Courtesy of Levi-Strauss & Co. Page **600** Courtesy of Gilbane Building Company. Page **604** G. Robert Nease for Marshall Industries. Page **605** © 1993 Marc Carter for Anthony Industries, Inc.

CHAPTER 18

Page **622** © Mark Joseph, Chicago for Abbott Laboratories. Page **626** Courtesy of Wendy's International, Inc. Page **628** Courtesy of Campbell Soup Company. Page **631** Courtesy of Goulds Pumps, Inc. Page **635** Courtesy of Vishay Intertechnology, Inc. Page **637** Courtesy of Armstrong World Industries, Inc. Page **643** Courtesy of The Larson Company, a subsidiary of Dean Foods Company. Page **644** Courtesy of Bethlehem Steel Corporation.

CHAPTER 19

Page **658** © 1990 Gary Gladstone for General Public Utilities Corporation (GPU). Page **662** Courtesy of OshKosh B'Gosh, Inc. Page **665** © Rick Zaidan for Ohio Edison Co. Page **667** Courtesy of Granite Construction, Inc. Page **668** Courtesy of Alaska Air Group, Inc. David Watanobe, photographer. Page **671** Courtesy of The Quaker Oats Company. Page **675** Courtesy of Brunswick Corporation.

CHAPTER 20

Page **687** Courtesy *JD Journal*, Deere & Company's worldwide corporate magazine. Photographer, Larry Volbruck. Page **691** Courtesy of International Business Machines Corporation. Page **696** Courtesy of Ryder System, Inc. Page **698** © Jeffrey Zaruba. Page **700** Courtesy of Fingerhut Companies, Inc. Page **702** Courtesy of Barnett Banks, Inc.

CHAPTER 21

Page **714** Courtesy of H & R Block, Inc. Page **718** Courtesy of Clark Equipment Company. Page **721** Courtesy Beckman Instruments, Inc. Photograph by Ken Whitmore. Page **725** Courtesy of MSA (Mine Safety Appliances Co.). Page **727** Courtesy of Borden, Inc. Page **735** Courtesy of AT&T. Page **739** Courtesy of Albany International.

CHAPTER 22

Page **754** © Shmuel Thaler. Page **758** © 1992 Steve Woit. All Rights Reserved. Page **767** © Duane Hall 1992. Page **769** Courtesy of MiniMaid Services, Inc. Leone Ackerly, founder and CEO. Page **771** © 1992 Randy Hampton/Black Star. Page **774** © Dennis Dunleavy/Black Star. Page **775** © 1992 Wayne Sorce.

CHAPTER 23

Page **787** © Rich LaSalle for Avco Financial Services, Inc. Page **795** © Paul Fetters. Page **798** © Eric Myer. Page **800** © William Taufic 1992. All Rights Reserved. Page **802** Courtesy of Chugai Pharmaceutical Co., Ltd. Page **806** © 1991 Kelly/Mooney.

● NAME INDEX

COMPANY INDEX

● SUBJECT INDEX